MOSCOW

Scale.
1 Verst
0 1000 2000 3000 3500 FEET

LEGEND.

Stadt Berlin Hotel ....D 3	University ....C 3
Slavianski Bazaar Hotel ..C 3	Public Museum ....C 3
Dussaux Hotel ....C 4	Monument ....D 4
Billo Hotel ....C 4	Great Theatre ....C 3
Dresden Hotel ....C 3	Petrofski Palace .....A 1
Metropole Hotel ....C 4	Suharef Tower ....B 4
Continental Hotel .....C 3	Nobility Club

SERGEY PROKOFIEV
DIARIES 1915–1923

by the same author

Sergey Prokofiev Diaries 1907–1914
Prodigious Youth
Translated and Annotated by Anthony Phillips

Story of a Friendship
The letters of Dmitry Shostakovich to Isaak Glikman
with a commentary by Isaak Glikman
Translated by Anthony Phillips

Sergey Prokofiev Diaries

1915–1923
BEHIND THE MASK

TRANSLATED AND ANNOTATED BY
Anthony Phillips

faber and faber

First published in 2008
by Faber and Faber Limited
3 Queen Square London WC1N 3AU

Photoset by Agnesi Text, Hadleigh
Printed in England by T J International, Padstow, Cornwall

All rights reserved
© The Sergey Prokofiev Estate, 2002
This translation © Anthony Phillips, 2008

The right of Anthony Phillips to be identified as translator
of this work has been asserted in accordance with
Section 77 of the Copyright, Design and Patents Act 1988

A CIP record for this book
is available from the British Library

ISBN 978–0–571–22630–6
ISBN 0–571–22630–2

2 4 6 8 10 9 7 5 3 1

IN MEMORY OF MSTISLAV ROSTROPOVICH 1927–2007

Contents

List of Plates, ix

Introduction, xiii

Acknowledgements, xx

A Note on Text, Transliteration, Dates, Forms of Address
and Other Conventions, xxii

THE DIARIES

1915, 3

1916, 61

1917, 163

1918, 245

1919, 377

1920, 457

1921, 571

1922, 661

1923, 699

Appendix 1
Prokofiev's Notes on Characters in *The Gambler*, based on the
descriptions in Dostoyevsky's novella, 715

Appendix 2
Description of 'The Seven', 718

Appendix 3
'The Russian Composer Prokofiev in Japan'
by Eleonora Sablina, 720

CONTENTS

Appendix 4
Musical America, 28 September 1918
article by Frederick H. Martens, 732

Appendix 5
Interview in *Vechernye Birzhevye Novosti*, 12 May 1916, 734

Appendix 6
'Fantastic Lollypops'
by Ben Hecht, 735

Bibliography, 738

Index, 743

Plates

1. Nevsky Prospekt, Petrograd, 4 July 1912
   © *Proletarskiya revolyutsiya v obrazakh i kartinakh, Izdanie Muzei Revolyutsii SSSR, Moscow 1926*
2. Sergey Prokofiev at the piano, New York, 1918
   photograph 1918 by Underwood & Underwood, Fifth Avenue, New York, public domain
3. Ivan Yershov, Nina and Natalya Meshcherskaya at the Meshchersky dacha in Gurzuf, Crimea, summer 1913
   © *The Krivoshein-Yershov Family Archive*
4. Boris Demchinsky
   courtesy of The Serge Prokofiev Estate, Paris
5. The Meshchersky Family in Exile, 1924
   © *The Krivoshein-Yershov Family Archive*
6. Sergey Prokofiev at his desk, New York, 1918
   Unknown photographer. From the George Grantham Bain Collection of the Library of Congress, Washington DC, public domain. Courtesy of The Serge Prokofiev Estate
7. Sergey Prokofiev, Boris Anisfeld and Adolph Bolm, New York, 1919
   courtesy of The Serge Prokofiev Estate
8. International Company Pullman Car of the Trans-Siberian Railway, c. 1918
   courtesy of Vladimir Muratov, www.transsib.ru
9. Poster for Sergey Prokofiev's recital at the Aeolian Hall, New York, 30 March 1919
   courtesy of The Serge Prokofiev Estate
10. Giulio Gatti-Casazza, General Manager of the Metropolitan Opera, New York
    photograph by Herman Mishkin, © *The Metropolitan Opera Archives*
11. José Raúl Capablanca
    Topical Press Images, 1 January 1919 © *Getty Images*
12. Stella Adler, studio portrait
    Private collection
13. Serge Diaghilev, drawing by Christopher Wood
    courtesy of Bob Lockyer

PLATES

14 Prokofiev and Stravinsky in Paris, 1920
   Photograph by Adolph Bolm
15 Postcard of the steamer *Souirah* loading at Marseilles docks, c. 1920
   Private collection
16 Sketch by Mikhail Larionov of the front curtain for *Chout*, 1921
   reproduced from Anthony Parton, Mikhail Larionov and the Russian avant-garde, *Princeton University Press, 1993, © Princeton University Press*
17 Konstantin Balmont, 1921
   courtesy of The Serge Prokofiev Estate
18 Henri Matisse, portrait of Sergey Prokofiev, 1921, commissioned for the programme of the Ballets Russes (original drawing lost)
19 Carolina Codina wearing her grey fur coat
   © The Serge Prokofiev Estate
20 Dagmar Godowsky
   courtesy of Leopold Godowsky III
21 Mary Garden at her desk as 'Directa' of the Chicago Opera
   courtesy of Charles Mintzer
22 Caricature of Emerald, Lady Cunard by Anthony Wysard
   © reserved; collection National Portrait Gallery, London
23 Sergey Prokofiev in front of the Congress Hotel, Chicago, 1921
   Chicago Daily News Negatives Collection DN-00073666, courtesy of the Chicago Historical Society
24 Nina Koshetz, studio portrait
   courtesy of Charles Mintzer
25 MS of the first page of Sergey Prokofiev's short story 'Death of the Watchmaker' on Auditorium Hotel, Chicago notepaper, 1921
   © The Serge Prokofiev Estate
26 Auditorium Theatre, Chicago, Illinois, interior view c. 1890s; unknown photographer (possibly J. W. Taylor)
   © Historic Architecture and Landscape Image Collection (accession no. 49665), Ryerson and Burnham Archives, The Art Institute of Chicago
27 Sketch by Boris Anisfeld of his setting for Act III Scene II of *The Love for Three Oranges*, Chicago Opera, 1921
   Historical Scenic Collection, Northern Illinois University Library, DeKalb, with thanks to Alexander Adducci
28 The Villa Christophorus, Ettal, Bavaria, c. 1922
   © The Serge Prokofiev Estate
29 Carolina Codina
   © The Serge Prokofiev Estate
30 Sergey Prokofiev and Boris Bashkirov in the garden of the Villa Christophorus
   © The Serge Prokofiev Estate

page 658 Programme for the first performance of *The Love for Three Oranges*, Chicago Opera, 30 December 1921
Chicago Public Library, Special Collections and Preservation Division

The endpaper at the front of this book is a map of Moscow from *Handbook for Travellers in Russia, Poland and Finland*, published by John Murray, Paris, 1893. The back endpaper is from *Rider's Guide to New York City*, published by Henry Holt & Co., New York, 1916. Both maps are in the collection of the Perry-Castañeda Library of the University of Texas, whose courtesy is gratefully acknowledged.

Every effort has been made to contact copyright holders of images reproduced in this book. Apologies to any it has not been possible to trace.

Introduction

I do not know the wisdom others claim,
I capture fleeting visions in my verse, and that is all.
In every fleeting vision I see worlds
Filled with the fickle play of rainbows.

Spare me your curses, wise ones. What am I to you?
I'm nothing but a wisp of cloud, full of fire.
Naught but a wisp of cloud. See me drifting by,
Calling to those who dream . . . but not to you!
                                    KONSTANTIN BALMONT

Some idea of the importance Sergey Prokofiev attached to the Diary he kept between 1907 and 1933 may be gauged from his despairing reaction to the news that part of it had definitely been lost in the chaotic circumstances that followed his departure from the family apartment in Petrograd, armed with an exit visa signed by Lunacharsky allowing him to travel abroad, at the beginning of May 1918. Ninety years on, with hindsight's awareness of what lay in store for Russia and for Prokofiev personally, it is hard to reconstruct the confusion, the swirl of private thoughts, the utter impossibility of making reliable plans for the future. All we can be sure of is that it cannot have looked at the time remotely as it does to us today.

Not that his was a panic-induced flight. As the Diary makes plain, it was considered, planned and, considering the times, anything but precipitous. Prokofiev fully expected to return to Russia in the measurable future – when, to paraphrase Balmont, 'this idiocy will have ended' – and even if he had already decided to spend more time than hitherto in the warm and welcoming south instead of cold, grey Petrograd, he cannot have foreseen that he would never again enter the apartment at No. 1 Pervaya Rota Street. All the same, he was prudent enough to take certain precautions. The previous August he had packed a trunk of precious papers and manuscripts and deposited them in the secure vaults of Koussevitzky's publishing company in Moscow – to keep them safe not from Bolsheviks or looters but from an expected German invasion – and now various well-connected people were deputed to keep an eye on the property and its remaining contents. Suvchinsky installed his building supervisor in the empty flat to keep guard.

The composer asked Asafyev, a man already well in with the new regime, to take if need be at least the papers and manuscripts into safe keeping. Arthur Lourié would ensure the necessary authorisations – Lourié, as Lunacharsky's nominated Commissar for Music in Narkompros, the Commissariat for Enlightenment, was the most powerful single individual in music in the Bolshevik regime. But, as Prokofiev had already deduced from a letter sent by his Petrograd friend Vera Miller in August 1920, none of this happened. Suvchinsky's man disappeared, Asafyev failed to retrieve the papers, Lourié either from indifference or malice did nothing about it, the flat was ransacked and its contents looted or destroyed. Now, in December 1922, Eleonora Damskaya was writing to confirm that all hope was lost.

One and all those who have let him down (including Damskaya) are excoriated in the Diary by his infuriated pen. The score of the Second Piano Concerto, seventy-odd unpublished early piano pieces, other juvenile scores (let us remember that this is a composer whose early ideas continued to furnish material for later masterpieces, witness the first Piano Concerto and the Third and Fourth Piano Sonatas), meticulously preserved and catalogued correspondence with his father, precious photographs, detailed records of triumphant chess matches with Capablanca and Lasker – and the notebook in which the Diary from September 1916 to February 1917 was written. All gone up in smoke.

A catastrophe indeed. One thinks of Parts Two and Three of Gogol's *Dead Souls*, Mendelssohn's Cello Concerto, Byron's *Memoirs*, the destruction of the Library at Alexandria, Richard Burton's translation of *The Perfumed Garden* – a vast, ghostly storehouse of works lost to their creators and to us. But of this particular loss, what causes Prokofiev the greatest anguish? 'Most of all I mourn the loss of the Diary . . . All the music of the Second Piano Concerto still exists, the childhood compositions do not mean so much to me because I was not then the person I am now, and the main thematic material I remember and can note down "for my biography". But the loss of the Diary is a tragedy, as there was so much of interest in it . . .' and he goes on to rehearse in considerable detail all he can recall of what he clearly feels has been wrenched from his grasp, the wound still raw and open (Diary entry for 16 December 1922).

As it turns out, the pain and misery were misplaced because (as the reader of this volume will realise) the missing notebook was, after all, in the trunk deposited in Koussevitzky's Moscow vaults. But that is another story, and one of which Prokofiev himself would remain unaware until his first visit to the Soviet Union in 1927, when Myaskovsky surreptitiously restored to him the manuscripts and papers he had, at considerable and conscious personal risk, been safeguarding ever since Asafyev, to whom Koussevitzky had entrusted them when he himself left Russia, had in turn given them to him for safe-keeping. These were not matters to be discussed in letters to and from the Soviet Union. What the December 1922 Diary entry shows us is how much his Diary meant to Prokofiev and why, if we want to know more about him, we must take it seriously.

The present volume covers the years from January 1915 until December 1923, one of the most eventful periods of the composer's life, seen from both interior and exterior perspectives. As it opens, his passion for Nina Meshcherskaya, accompanied by emotional swings and soul-searchings laid bare with characteristic ingenousness, moves swiftly to its farcical and humiliating climax, thereafter to be as ruthlessly suppressed and discarded as firmly as an inferior melodic idea. We shall experience several more romantic excursions as the chronicle proceeds, some more significant than others, but the general line always tending away – however seductive the attractions – from the flamboyant and provocative (Dagmar Godowsky, Nina Koshetz) towards the more serious and reflective: Stella Adler, the former Meyerhold student Maria Baranovskaya, and at journey's end the woman who more than any other weathered the long-drawn-out reservations and vacillations to capture his heart, through sheer conviction and a loyalty that never seems to have wavered until the end of her days. Sergey Prokofiev and Carolina Codina were married in Ettal in the closing months of the last year of this volume and the hunger to find a true love, a thread that runs throughout the first two volumes of the Diary, was finally satisfied.

It is almost a commonplace to say that Prokofiev was a political *naïf*, concerned only for his career and his art, ignorant of and indifferent to the reality of the momentous events unfolding around him. A reading of this Diary shows this to be at best only partially fair.

> An American recently back from Russia gave a lecture to a large audience about the present situation in Russia. I listened to what he had to say and thought how strange it was that intuition had led me to flee from that milieu and had brought me to this place of honour [as a guest of the Chicago Chamber of Commerce] where, sitting in a comfortable armchair, I was hearing an account of the horrors now being visited on my homeland. 'You are running away from history,' Demchinsky had said to me when I left Petrograd, 'and history will not forgive you. When you return to Russia you will not be understood, because you will not have suffered what Russia has suffered, and the language you speak will not be Russia's language.' There is much wisdom in these words, and not a little envy of the man who has evaded misfortune. But the art I create is outside time and space.' [21 November/4 December 1918.]

Back in 1917 Prokofiev's apparent detachment, in common, one suspects, with the great majority of intellectuals, seems to have stemmed more from a conscious neutrality rather than indifference to or lack of appreciation of the significance of events: 'I am neither a counter-revolutionary nor a revolutionary. I am on neither side' was his comment on Kornilov's misguided attempt in August of that year to overthrow (or was it to defend? The true motive for this disastrous adventure remains mysterious to this day) the Provisional Government. Once out of 'what is in all but name the prison of Russia', influenced certainly by concern for his mother and the friends left behind, his reservations about the Bolshevik regime harden into outright detestation, to the extent that subsequent discovery of the Diary during his lifetime by the Soviets would have undoubtedly been very damaging to the composer and his family. As the news from Russia worsens and his mother's situation grows daily more hazardous, he is aware that his decision to go abroad and leave her behind might meet with less than universal approval: 'An as yet unpronounced verdict had been hanging over my head: was I a man who had rescued himself and his mother from the maelstrom of Russia, or was I someone who had looked after himself but abandoned his mother to the mercy of events?' Fortunately, in the event the judgement did not have to be called and his mother was among the thousands who successfully made their escape from their shattered homeland. But if it had been we may be sure that Prokofiev would have carried the burden for the remainder of his life.

In any event, it is hardly special pleading to see in this dilemma yet another instance of the author's instinct to put the demands of his art in front of any other considerations. It colours his often tangled love life, in which commitment appears all too often in its familiar guise as an Enemy of Promise. Allied to a display of naivety more convincing than the deficiency of his political judgements, or lack of them, it helped to put him on a collision course with the hard-nosed management of the Chicago Opera over the agreement to produce *The Love for Three Oranges* in 1919. Reading his own account of the circumstantial problems faced by the opera company, the delays, the provocations, the tactical *démarches*, one need hardly be a negotiating genius to spot the dangers a mile off. But Prokofiev and his well-meaning advisers so signally failed to take on board the difference between the autocratic regime of the Russian Imperial Theatres and the business environment of an American cultural institution that the debacle of November 1920, when the opera company abruptly cancelled the production altogether at the cost of writing off the huge sums already invested in it, was almost inevitable. The consequent pre-emption of the threatened lawsuit can only be a matter for relief. The irony is that the production was ultimately rescued by precisely that Tsarist-style *deus ex machina* Prokofiev had intuitively been looking for, but although he certainly appreciated no longer having to deal with 'low-grade accountants and salespeople: now, suddenly, I was talking to a real artist', he perhaps never realised how unusual and aberrant was the brief, maverick reign of 'Directa' Mary Garden. It was a lucky break for him, lucky for Chicago, and lucky for us.

This volume of the Diary embraces a kaleidoscope of experiences whose effect was, not surprisingly, to cause the callow, precociously gifted adolescent author of Volume One to grow up fast. Eyewitness experiences of the February Revolution in Petrograd; the journey across Russia on the last Trans-Siberian train to get through before the entire region dissolved into the chaos of revolutionary and counter-revolutionary armies, marauding warlords and militias; arrival in a new continent virtually penniless and the struggle to achieve recognition there; a serious, even life-threatening illness; time after time to be so near and yet so far from fulfilling his aspirations as a composer, especially of opera and ballet; the nagging worry over his mother's fate; the ever present shadows cast by his great compatriots Rachmaninoff in America and Stravinsky in Europe – all this and more could easily have crushed a lesser spirit. Yet it is remarkable how often in the Diary he seems to be saying, with Mary Coleridge: 'We were young, we were merry, we were very, very wise, And the door stood open to our feast.' Life was good, life was exciting, and he knew what he had to offer. If from time to time, as in Coleridge's poem, unwelcome visitors joined the feast, his determination and belief in himself were enough to show them the door.

The Diary reveals a composer, and a fervent if sporadic prose writer, engaged in unremitting pursuit of ever deeper and more original development of his material. From the experiments that had begun with *Maddalena* and *The Ugly Duckling*, through brief and improbable flirtations with notions of operetta and even musicals (what a pity no such seductive possibilities ever materialised!), Prokofiev's conviction that he was destined to stake out new, anti-conventional territory in opera grew strong enough to withstand the disparaging hostility of Diaghilev, aided and abetted by Stravinsky. It was essential, he declared, for the composer to be responsible for his own libretto: only the composer could successfully unite into a dramatic whole words, music and scenic action. The line continues through *The Gambler* and *The Love for Three Oranges* to reach its apogee in *The Fiery Angel*, that uniquely impractical excursion into sixteenth-century esoteric mysticism. Leaps into the future like the extraordinary *Seven, They Are Seven* (he describes Koussevitzky's reaction: 'the world has never seen such a score before') gestated in periods of solitude, such as the summer of 1917 which Prokofiev spent blissfully secluded in the village of Sablino, reading Schopenhauer and Kant, gazing at the stars through his beloved telescope, writing short stories and walking in the surrounding country while the world a few kilometres beyond his domain careered on its destructive path to war, famine, revolution and mayhem.

The brief but productive flowering of Prokofiev's literary ambitions that roughly coincided with the long terrestrial and psychological journey from Russia to the West, is seen with typically clear-eyed objectivity.

> What precisely is my attitude to my writing? The top and bottom of it is that I tremendously enjoy it. That is in itself enough of an answer. And should it turn out that it is, in addition, very good writing (the pity of it is that it would never be enough for me to be simply good), then am I not doubly justified?! As for the expenditure of time and energy that I might otherwise devote to composition, I can in all conscience say that up till now I have worked a great deal, and if there is a short intermission it may do me some good as a means of refreshment to work better in the future. I agree that the results may seem to be not very good, but at the present time I am unable to be precise about wherein lie their deficiencies. [Diary entry for 12/25 June 1918, in the midst of involuntary lotus-eating in Japan.]

We may regret that there is not more of a literary legacy, but what has survived is enough to demonstrate the work of an exceptional stylist with an idiosyncratic imagination and a keen awareness of the power of words to suggest tone and atmosphere. The honing of these skills was soon to leave its mark in the opera librettos, beginning with *Three Oranges*, not to mention the Diary itself (the idea of bringing over some of Russia's more obtuse critics for a session in one of Osaka's ear-cleaning parlours is worthy of H. L. Mencken) and the later Autobiographies. In literature as in music (and chess, and one may infer in life as a whole) the competitive element is ever present, as instanced by the unholy glee with which Prokofiev successfully routs the 'born and bred poet' in the extraordinary sonnet-translating competition, complete with rules and independent adjudication, he and Bashkirov devised in Ettal.

Not, as he concedes, a person who normally took criticism easily (except from himself), Prokofiev proved surprisingly ready to submit to Diaghilev's strictures – amounting to comprehensive rejection – on the score of the projected ballet *Ala and Lolli* that he brought to the impresario in the spring of 1915. Castigated as old-fashioned, the music 'international' rather than 'national', the libretto unconvincing and jejune, the project had to be torn up and a fresh start made. Nothing daunted, Prokofiev squirreled away for later recycling what he knew to be good music, even if the ballet itself was a mess, and set to work with enthusiasm on the Stravinsky-inspired choice of Afanasyev folk tales about a crafty practical joker that would become *Chout*. Despite the surge of creative energy that sparked off the initial creation of the score, it was to be hardly more plain sailing than *Ala and Lolli*: six years of war, revolution and the vicissitudes of the Ballets Russes would elapse before *Chout* could be seen on the stage of the Théâtre de la Gaîté in Paris.

Even then Diaghilev demanded radical changes for the immediately following London season: the elimination of part of the fifth scene, the introduction of orchestral interludes to cover scene changes, and the general recasting of the music away from mimetic illustration towards symphonic development. Once again Prokofiev was ready, indeed eager to comply. When a figure of Diaghilev's understanding and authority engaged critically with his work, Prokofiev would be responsive to suggestions.

> Diaghilev invariably spoke with great heat and conviction. Sometimes his statements would strike you as ridiculous, but it was impossible to object to them because as soon as you tried he would immediately support them with an avalanche of impeccably reasoned theses that would with irrefutable clarity demonstrate the justice of the propositions, however absurd.

But the world does not contain many Diaghilevs.

As we follow the trajectory of the Diary from the final months at the Conservatoire, through growing recognition of the composer–performer in Russia and abroad, the havoc of revolution and civil war, the flight from Russia, the continual travelling, the uncertainties of all aspects of life and work in the West, the steady accumulation of compositions owing little or nothing to other masters, we acquire a deepening sense of a restless, probing, reflecting mind ceaselessly at work, transforming through the alchemy of inspiration the fleeting visions of experience into the music of a composer approaching full maturity. The mask of the matchlessly gifted, invincibly self-confident iconoclast of legend is moved aside to show us the man within.

ANTHONY PHILLIPS
Argyll, November 2007

Acknowledgements

I begin by recording my gratitude to the people who collectively make up the Serge Prokofiev Foundation. Without this diffuse (to an outsider, at least) but wonderful organisation's great practical and moral support, as full of imagination as it is of information and resources, it would have impossible for this project of making Prokofiev's Diaries available to an English-speaking readership even to have started, let alone reached the two-thirds mark. In particular the composer's grandson Serge Prokofiev in the Paris wing of the Foundation, or sprkfv jr. as he is known to the world of Prokofiev scholars and adherents, is the port to which I have turned, always with advantage, in successive storms of confusion or worse. At Goldsmiths University of London, where the Prokofiev Archive is housed, Noëlle Mann, the Archive's founding Curator, and Fiona McKnight, its current Archivist, both possess a deep and wide store of knowledge that they have generously shared whenever I have appealed.

When I was about halfway through translating the text of this volume and writing my commentary, there occurred the death in Moscow of one of the author's most inspired and inspiring champions, Mstislav Rostropovich. Not only is it the case that without Rostropovich those masterworks the Symphony-Concerto and the Concertino would not have come into being, still less his emblematic performances of them and the Sonata, but his death has removed the last remaining creative link to Prokofiev the man and the composer. Young as Rostropovich was (twenty-six when Prokofiev died in 1953), the composer unhesitatingly regarded him as collaborator and friend, a judgement that was not misplaced. This book is dedicated to his memory.

In the world outside special Prokofiev affiliations I have had priceless linguistic and musical advice from the pianists and teachers Dina Parakhina in Manchester and (once again) Irina Anastasieva of the Gnessin Russian Academy of Music in Moscow, and from my wife Karine Georgian. In America, where so much of the action of the present volume takes place, Ellen Adler and Leopold Godowsky III readily provided or pointed me towards striking images of their forebears for inclusion in the book's plate section, as did from their own collections or archives Charles Mintzer, Norman Pellegrini and Alexander Adducci. My thanks also go to Stephen D. Press, whose recent book *Prokofiev's Ballets for Diaghilev* has become an indispensable source. The Russian musicologist Eleonora Sablina kindly allowed me to translate from the Russian and reproduce her version of Prokofiev's interview with a Japanese writer on music, uncovered by her researches in a Tokyo archive. Thanks to Lidia Ader of the St Petersburg Conservatoire for her detective work in pre-Revolutionary Petersburg newspapers on the obscure opera *Megae* by Adam Wieniawski, so curtly dismissed by Prokofiev as a musical zero.

The Faber and Faber editorial team led by Belinda Matthews, Lesley Felce and Katherine Armstrong, along with their colleague Jill Burrows, again consistently eased my path with their encouragement, forbearance and expertise. I am truly grateful to them.

It will be obvious from the foregoing that I have had a lot of help from a lot of people, many more indeed than those I have mentioned. I thank them all most sincerely. This is the place to assure them all, and the reader, that any errors of fact, omissions, inconsistencies and clumsy turns of phrase are not due to them, only to me.

A.P.

A Note on Text, Transliteration, Dates, Forms of Address and Other Conventions

The manuscript of Prokofiev's Diaries is contained in a series of notebooks, now preserved in the Russian State Archive of Literature and Art in Moscow (RGALI). They are not merely handwritten, but mostly composed in a vowel-less shorthand script of the author's own devising, a parallel version of the shorthand he developed for the laborious process of writing out orchestral scores. A sample of his handwriting may be seen in Plate 25. The Herculean task of deciphering, transcribing and editing more than three-quarters of a million words was carried out by the composer's son and grandson, and the text I have translated is that published by them under the sprkfv imprint.

Russian orthography can be transliterated into Latin script in a bewildering variety of ways (as the Prokofiev Archive recognises). My aim in rendering the hundreds of Russian names and proper nouns that appear in the text has been to make them as accessible and phonetically plausible as possible to the English-speaking reader, largely consistent with the system adopted by the *New Grove Dictionary of Music and Musicians* (London: Macmillan, 1980) but with modifications intended to make the results look less alarming than a strict adherence often makes them. Names of people and places already familiar to English readers have been kept in their commonly used forms when they depart from the system, hence Alexander, Tchaikovsky, Steinberg, Diaghilev, Koussevitzky, Schlüsselberg. (Strictly, Prokofiev's own name ought to be written Prokof'ev). Sergey Rachmaninoff specifically requested that his surname be written thus in English, rather than the 'correct' Rakhmaninov. In bibliographical references, however, I have adhered to the *Grove* system. Where I have included citations from other writers I have preserved their spellings.

In place of the standard Russian formal way of referring to a person – the first name followed by the patronymic (Alexander Konstantinovich), roughly corresponding to the English Mr, Mrs, Miss followed by the surname – I have generally resorted to the English custom of first name followed by surname (Alexander Glazunov) when the reference is simply to an individual appearing in the narrative, but I have preserved the Russian style when the author is either directly addressing an interlocutor or enjoys a long-running or close personal relationship with the person concerned. Where it seems appropriate, but not invariably, I have followed the Russian custom of attaching feminine endings to women's surnames. I have also preserved precisely as written the innumerable diminutives and affectionate nicknames to which Prokofiev, as Russians generally, was addicted.

On 18 January 1918 (OS) the Council of People's Commissars (Sovnarkom) issued a Decree whereby on the last day of the month, 31 January, Russia would formally change from the Julian to the Gregorian calendar. The following day would accordingly be 14 February. The fact that Prokofiev spent the year 1918 partly in Russia and partly travelling to the West via Japan only adds to the potential for confusion. I have given dates for the entries he made in his Diary throughout 1918 in both Old and New styles, the latter enclosed in square brackets. Where elsewhere there might be confusion I have noted whether the date in question is OS (Old Style, i.e. Russian Julian) or NS (New Style, Western Gregorian).

A. P.

1915

1 January

I spent the first day of the New Year in holiday mode: sleeping until half-past twelve, then going for a walk until half-past two. Until half-past five I paid some calls, then spent some time with Bashkirov[1] relaxing from these exertions until half-past eight, and finally went to play bridge at the Meshcherskys until eleven thirty. The most enjoyable time was, needless to say, the last. Nina, the darling, was loving but had evidently caught cold in Konkale and was suffering from a cough, a temperature and palpitations. According to her Zaitsev[2] visits more and more frequently – but whenever I put in an appearance he turns pale and falls silent.

2 January

I am on the point of a break-through with my Concerto.

Spoke on the telephone to Nina – a long and tender conversation. She is once again confined to the house and feeling wretched. We discussed what we could do to belong finally to one another. I said this could come about within two years because I could guarantee that by that time I would unquestionably have become a celebrity abroad. Then she would be able to shake off the dust of Petrograd and settle in Paris, where I would arrange a position for her and create an interesting social environment.

Bashkirov came to dine and afterwards we went together to the Conservatoire concert, which because of the war had replaced the traditional General Studies class ball. It is hilarious to see how heartily Bashkirov detests Zakharov.[3] Eleonora[4] feels the same, and neither of them likes his playing at

---

1   Boris Bashkirov (1891–?), close friend and confidant of Prokofiev who shared his interest in philosophy and literature. Bashkirov wrote poetry under the name of Boris Verin. See *Diaries*, vol. 1, p. 671 and *passim*.
2   Kirill Zaitsev, at one time Prokofiev's rival for the affections of Nina Meshcherskaya. See *Diaries*, vol. 1, pp. 407, 487 and *passim*.
3   Ibid., p. 4n and *passim*. Boris Zakharov (1867–1942), from a wealthy family, was a pianist, fellow student and (with interruptions) close friend of Prokofiev. Zakharov had some success as a pianist in Russia and later in Europe, but was overshadowed by the international fame of his future wife, the violinist Cecilia Hansen.
4   Ibid., p. 330 and *passim*. Eleonora Damskaya (1898–?) was a harp student at the Conservatoire with whom Prokofiev maintained a friendship and correspondence throughout his time in Petersburg, Petrograd, his years in the West and after his return to the Soviet Union. She had

all, although on this occasion my 'Gavotte', which he gave as an encore, was not half bad. Eleonora herself played very nicely and sent Bashkirov into raptures.

Read some short stories by Averchenko,[1] whom hitherto I had known only from his stories in *Satyricon*, which I like very much, but reading him now at full length I derive all the more pleasure from him.

Benois[2] has told Tcherepnin[3] that Diaghilev[4] is pinning great hopes on me and on my ballet. Tcherepnin's advice is to work more intensively on it but, idiot that I am, I have not lifted a finger for at least a month! . . .

---

influential connections with leading members of the Provisional Government after the February 1917 Revolution, notably Alexander Kerensky. Friendship and correspondence lapsed between 1927 and 1948, largely because of Damskaya's perceived unwillingness to help trace the Shreder grand piano with which Prokofiev had been presented as winner of the Conservatoire's Rubinstein Prize, and which he had left behind in Petrograd in 1918. Contact was later resumed, however, and continued until shortly before the composer's death. Several letters from the unpublished Russian correspondence have been translated by Harlow Robinson and included in his *Selected Letters of Sergei Prokofiev* (North Eastern University Press, Boston, 1998).

1 Arkady Averchenko (1881–1925), playwright, short-story writer and humorist, sometimes called 'the Russian Mark Twain'. He mainly published in Prokofiev's favourite Petersburg journal *Satyricon*, which he also edited (*Satyricon* was a later incarnation of *Strekoza* (*The Dragonfly*) for which Chekhov had written many of his early humorous stories). A strong supporter of the Constitutional Democrats, Averchenko was a committed anti-Bolshevik and from post-Revolution exile in Prague continued to turn out savagely satirical attacks on the Soviet regime.

2 Alexander Benois (1870–1960), painter, scenic designer, critic and founder member with, among others, Léon Bakst and Sergey Diaghilev of the *Mir Isskustva* (*World of Art*) aesthetic movement which brought together artists, designers, writers and musicians. Benois edited the movement's eponymous journal, and from his vantage point as scenic director of the Mariinsky Theatre virtually created the integrated aesthetic philosophy that was the impetus behind the first Ballets Russes seasons in Paris. See *Diaries*, vol. 1, p. 357n and *passim*.

3 Nikolay Tcherepnin (1873–1945), composer and conductor, among the first to recognise and promote Prokofiev's genius as a composer and, after initial doubts, support him as a conductor. Tcherepnin was unquestionably Prokofiev's most influential mentor at the Conservatoire. An outstandingly skilful and accomplished, if derivative, composer, he had been virtually an in-house provider of scores for the initial Paris seasons of Diaghilev's Ballets Russes (notably *Le Pavillon d'Armide, Narcisse, The Enchanted Kingdom*), and an essential component of the *Gesamtkunstwerk* ideal of the enterprise. Ibid., p. 10, and *passim*.

4 Sergey Diaghilev (1872–1929), the twentieth-century's most famous impresario, initially gained his reputation as an art critic, founding the *Mir Isskustva* journal in 1899 with Bakst and Benois, with financial backing (in the acquisition of which he necessarily spent much of his life becoming a master) from Savva Mamantov and the Princess Tenisheva, and mounting epoch-making exhibitions of Russian art. The foundation of the Ballets Russes, again with Bakst and Benois playing a leading role, followed with an inaugural season in Paris in 1909, preceded by two previous seasons of concerts and opera. Over the years Diaghilev's artistic collaborators embraced so astonishing a stable of the greatest and most innovative artists in different genres that this short note can mention only a handful: Stravinsky, Prokofiev, Ravel, Poulenc, Debussy, Richard Strauss, Nijinsky, Pavlova, Karsavina, Bolm, Markova, Dolin, Fokine, Massine, Balanchine, Benois, Bakst, Roerich, Rouault, Matisse, Picasso. It would be hard to overstate the influence exerted by Diaghilev on the young Prokofiev, who first encountered him in London in the summer of 1914. Ibid., p. 427, and *passim*.

3 January

Applied myself to the ballet and it went quite well; the whole of the end of the second scene took shape. The only thing is that I don't know how the setting of the sun should be; this is something Gorodetsky[1] and I did not manage to settle at the time (he wanted the sun to set just so, as a normal daily event, with which I did not agree), and now Gorodetsky and I have fallen out and both preserve a frosty silence.

Nina and I squabbled about nothing in particular on the telephone. Eleonora thinks we should avoid telephone conversations, since being on opposite ends of a telephone line inevitably seems to lead to quarrels.

In the evening I went to the fourth 'Contemporaries' evening. Zakharov played *The Tale of the Fisherman and the Fish* indifferently, and some pieces from the same composer's [Tcherepnin's] marvellous *Alphabet* very well indeed. There were a lot of musicians there I knew and it was generally a pleasant time.

4 January

Scene 1 of the ballet is inching forward, in between my learning the Second Concerto.

Vera Nikolayevna invited me to their box at the French Theatre today and to eat pancakes beforehand. Nina came up with a perceptive insight: it had been the wrong time in our paths through life to have met one another; three years earlier or three years later would have been better.

The Andreyevs[2] came, we had dinner, and then went to the French Theatre. The girls did not come with us, partly because of not feeling well and partly because of the inconsequentiality of the play, a lightweight, vapid affair.

---

1   Sergey Gorodetsky (1884–1967) had founded with Nikolay Gumilyov the poetry movement known as Acmeism, in reaction to the Symbolism espoused by Bryusov, Bely, Sologub, Balmont and Blok. The most brilliantly gifted of the Acmeists were Anna Akhmatova (for a time Gumilyov's wife) and Osip Mandelshtam. After the Revolution, Gorodetsky irreparably damaged his reputation by his slavish revision of the libretto of Glinka's *A Life for the Tsar* into the politically acceptable *Ivan Susanin*, and above all by his repudiation of any connection to the Acmeists and his posthumous denunciation of Gumilyov, who was arrested and executed in 1921. Diaghilev had proposed that Gorodetsky provide the libretto for the ballet he wanted to commission from Prokofiev, which began fitful and eventually extinguished life as *Ala and Lolli*, not before siring, however, the music for the *Scythian Suite*. *Diaries*, vol. 1, p. 707, and *passim*.
2   The husband and wife singers Nikolay Vasilievich Andreyev and Anna Grigorievna Zherebtsova-Andreyeva: Nikolay Andreyev (d. 1919), tenor soloist of the Mariinsky Theatre and a regular principal in Diahgilev's opera productions; Anna Grigorievna Zherebtsova-Andreyeva (1868–1944), mezzo-soprano, much favoured by Anton Rubinstein, with whom she often appeared in concert. Gave many first performances of works by Stravinsky and Prokofiev. See Ibid., p. 218, and *passim*.

13 January

I came to the conclusion this evening that my relations with Nina, which up until now I have been regarding as a delightful but not very important flirtation accompanied by vague fantasies of a far-off future, were beginning to assume very substantial proportions. I cannot settle to work, can see no women other than Nina – in a word, the situation is becoming inappropriate and undesirable, and I shall have to get out of it.

The solution is simple: break off relations. But to do so would lose me the best of what I now had. I resolved to promulgate a 'decree' whereby we would completely break off relations for two months.

14–31 January

The morning brought a wave of depression, but my resolve was firm. Before long, however, appeared a new concept; what occasioned it I cannot say. Mama was at the hospital; alone in the apartment, pacing up and down its length from end to end, I surprised myself at the direction my thoughts were taking when all of a sudden I found myself reversing the 'decree' to its exact opposite: we should marry. I was astonished at my own decision, inasmuch as hitherto my unshakeable conviction has been that I shall remain a bachelor until I am forty years old. The fuss of the wedding ceremony, the momentous preparations surrounding it, these have always put me off. I was also thinking of Mama and what would become of her.

At six o'clock I arrived at the Meshcherskys – today was Nina's name-day and she had asked me to be there at six. Here was revealed an amazing coincidence: over the past few days Nina had also been anguishing, her mind in turmoil, and she had come to the same conclusion: some way out must be found. She had also considered a break – but found the idea inconceivable. The next morning, the 16th, I got a wonderful letter from Nina, filled with love and expressions of tender feelings. That afternoon we had our first really serious telephone conversation, in the course of which we clarified our joint conclusion that the only imaginable outcome of our relationship must be to get married. Nina thought that so far as her father was concerned this would be quite straightforward, but we could expect opposition from her mother to be impassioned and obdurate.

The premiere of *Duckling*[1] took place on the 17th in the Small Hall of the Conservatoire. The singer was Anna Grigorievna, and I accompanied. Anna Grigorievna had prepared the work with a dedication born of love, and sang it very well. We had expected a huge success, but in fact it was rather modest,

---

1 *The Ugly Duckling*, Op. 18, fairy-tale for voice and piano after Hans Andersen. Nina Meshcherskaya had contributed the original draft of the libretto.

the audience not really understanding it even though many people said how delighted they were with it.

In the days that followed, telephone conversations with Nina were interspersed with rehearsals for my performance of the Second Piano Concerto for the IRMS.[1] I played well, and had an enormous success, the angry booing from some quarters only serving to enhance it. I gave four encores, the first of them Fyaka's 'Rigaudon'.[2] The same evening I got the news that I would be going to Rome, as Diaghilev announced that he was prepared not only to pay my fare and would arrange a concert for me in Rome, but had also found me a travelling companion: the Russian consul in Rome, currently back in Petersburg on a visit. He told me that the journey would be hazardous, but that he would soon be returning there himself. I was desperately anxious to go, not least because in terms of my relationship with Nina a two months' cooling-off period was the best thing that could possibly happen, and also I would be seeing the world.

Some people were appalled at the idea of my going abroad at such a dangerous time while others were envious. Nina felt as I did, that it would be a very good thing. The next day I went to see her, requesting that we avoid any serious discussions, and it was wonderful: I saw that Nina really loved me.

In the meantime I met Alexeyev, the Russian consul, a most attractive gentleman, and we arranged our departure for the end of the week. The intervening time was distinguished by a quarrel with Bashkirov, who ostentatiously made it known to anyone who would listen that he was going to accompany me to Italy – secure in the knowledge, as he thought, that I would not in the end make the trip. When it became clear that on the contrary I was firmly resolved to go, he wavered and eventually completely lost his head. I accused him of empty braggadoccio and being a Khlestyakov,[3] and told him I could not count such people among my friends. He responded by sending me his visiting card with the money he owed for his lessons,[4] and diplomatic relations between us were broken off.

Two hitches occurred the day before I left: 1) Diaghilev had not sent

1   The Imperial Russian Musical Society was in existence from 1859 until its dissolution in 1917. The classes in music instruction instigated by the Society in St Petersburg in 1859 had formed the basis for what was to become the St Petersburg Music Conservatoire. Somewhat to his surprise, in October 1914 Prokofiev had been invited by the notoriously conservative IRMS to perform his *First* Piano Concerto at one of its concerts. Presumably the programme was changed between October and January. The conductor at the concert on 24 January was Nikolay Malko. Prokofiev later performed the First Piano Concerto for the IRMS in January 1917. See *Diaries*, vol. 1, pp. 749–50, also below, p. 165.
2   'Fyaka' was Prokofiev's nickname for Nina Meshcherskaya. The 'Rigaudon', Op. 12 No. 3, was dedicated to her; ibid., pp. 473–4, 508.
3   The ridiculously vain and unscrupulous hero of Gogol's satirical masterpiece *The Inspector-General*.
4   Prokofiev had been giving Bashkirov piano lessons. See ibid., pp. 742, 744, and *passim*.

any money for the journey; 2) there was a rumour flying round that war was about to be declared either today or tomorrow between Bulgaria and Romania. The prospect of not being able to leave Petrograd was appalling to me, and what a happy moment it was when both obstacles disappeared of their own accord: the money turned up and the rumours proved unfounded. The journey itself was going to be fascinating, and a lot would be clarified, confirmed and settled by it!

The Journey to Italy

1 February

Had it not been for suffering from a cold, everything would have been fine, but bearing in mind that a cold is nothing to worry about anyhow, everything was indeed fine. Immaculate in my short-trousered Swiss suit, a grey scarf, green overcoat and English check cap, I awaited the arrival of the consul on Tsarskoselskoye station. He was transporting to Niš[1] two small cases, each with eight seals and so staggeringly heavy it was almost impossible to lift them. They contained gold bars that we were taking to the beleaguered Serbs, and we were duly conscious of the importance of our mission. The consul was under orders to lug these boxes about himself, and to sit on them all the time, like Fafner on his golden treasure.

Ever-faithful Eleonora came to see me off, and the train pulled out. It was cramped in our second class half-compartment, but Aleksey Ivanovich[2] is very good company and towards evening we transferred to an International Company[3] carriage, which afforded us both great satisfaction. Generally, the first day's travelling did not offer much variety, as might be expected. The train jogged easily along the uninteresting Vindavo–Rybinsk line while I, not to waste time, attempted to gain some acquaintance with the wisdom of Italy.

2 February

We slept not badly. In our carriage we discovered three other people going to Italy, not counting an important counsellor from the Russian Embassy in Rome who was also bound for that city. As the day wore on we realised to

---

1 Provincial administrative capital in South-East Serbia, one of the oldest cities in the Balkans.
2 Alexeyev, the consul.
3 This would have been a sleeping car belonging to and operated by the Compagnie Internationale des Wagon-Lits, established in 1883 to provide sleeping and restaurant cars on the growing network of main lines throughout Europe and Russia, including the Trans-Siberian Railway. The point is that these trains were independent of the Russian railway system and the service was European, although naturally they used the Russian permanent way.

our dismay that the train was falling more and more behind schedule, the delay amounting eventually to seven hours. At almost all the stations where we stopped we met military trains coming in the opposite direction, evidently bound for the area round Vilnius where there was fighting going on. I am learning Italian, my mood is excellent; in the evening, before getting to Kiev, we had a sleep.

3 February

We arrived in Kiev some time after three o'clock in the morning, instead of half-past eight in the evening. We clambered briskly out of our bunks and dragged the Serbian gold into the station. The train to Odessa was due to leave at nine o'clock. Had we arrived on time we could have spent the night in a hotel, instead of which, after gulping down a mug of tea, I left the consul guarding his gold and went to walk round the town. It reminded me of the time, two years ago, when Max[1] and I had walked round Alexandrovsk, also at four in the morning, also in February, also waiting for a train, and also in a dark, sleeping city.

Kiev was asleep, and fitfully illuminated only by occasional streetlamps. I sought out the Kreshchatik[2] and walked for about two hours, thinking of Nina. At six o'clock I returned and lay down to sleep on top of the gold, while Alexey Ivanovich went off to track down the Babastro family, who were to come with us to Italy. At nine o'clock we were sitting in the train where, thanks to the Serbian gold, we had been allocated a compartment to ourselves. Babastro proved to be a straightforward sort of fellow, cheerful, kind and foul-mouthed, a singer who was Russian by birth and Italian by nationality. He was accompanied by his wife and his daughter, Galya, aged nine.

The nearer we got to the battle zone the more the stations teemed with soldiers, and we saw several groups of Austrian prisoners-of-war in field-grey greatcoats, the look of happiness on their faces more often than not betraying their satisfaction at being out of the fighting. There was no buffet car on the train so we had recourse to hurriedly snatched lunches and dinners and cups of tea when we stopped at stations. Babastro spouted a stream of cheerful nonsense larded with smutty remarks. Outside the sun shone brightly, the snow was melting and in places had gone altogether. I was still plagued with my cold which seemed to oscillate between one nostril and the other, stopping me enjoying the weather and getting on with learning Italian.

1 Maximilian Schmidthof, Prokofiev's closest friend from the Conservatoire, who committed suicide on 27 April 1913. See *Diaries*, vol. 1, p. 92 and *passim*.
2 The principal street of Kiev.

4 February

We were woken at five o'clock, before dawn. This was Razdolnaya station, where we had to change trains for Kishinyov, near the border with Romania. In the grey pre-dawn mist we scrambled out on to the platform and at seven o'clock were already aboard the train to Kishinyov and Ungheni. All the talk was of the German attacks in East Prussia, but we were more concerned with our own imminent travel through the Balkans: would we be able to carry letters through the frontier, was there cholera in Romania, would we able to get a sleeping car in Bucharest? – and so on. The weather became very overcast, but at least my cold was better. Some time after three the train reached Ungheni, a wretched little station on the Romanian border.[1]

The addition of the Babastro family had now swelled our party to five, and the quantity of luggage had reached gargantuan proportions. However, Alexeyev's 'diplomatic passport' saved us from any formalities or inspection. We spent several tedious hours kicking our heels in a cramped, dark and boring waiting-room with hoar-frost outside the windows. Eventually we were herded into a filthy Romanian train with no separate carriages, more like a kind of tram, which took us over the frontier into Romania. Farewell, Russia! A slight rumble and we crossed the River Prut.[2]

Another Customs point, this time a sort of tumbledown shed, but outside it an elegantly turned-out Romanian officer. Everyone else had their bags inspected and thoroughly turned over, but once again our 'diplomatic passport' saved us and we found ourselves back on the tramcar. After interminable halts and delays we finally arrived in Iasi,[3] a largish town. Here all our efforts were concentrated on finding sleeping-car berths, a far from easy task: there was only one carriage with sleeping accommodation in it, and literally everybody wanted a berth. Frozen stiff, I drank some cognac, bought Romanian marks, conversed with the locals in German and French, and was mightily relieved at last to get into a bright, warm, soft sleeper.

I thought about Nina.

5 February

We woke at five a.m. to an announcement from the guard: 'The axle has overheated.' We had to get up, anathematising the smouldering axle, and move into an ordinary carriage, which was crowded and not at all comfortable. Outside it was still night, soon to be overtaken by a grey dawn, coffee

---

1 In what is now Moldova.
2 The Prut now forms the border between Moldova and Romania; it joins the Danube just before the latter flows into the Black Sea.
3 The principal city of North-East Romania.

at some unknown station, and a new day with glimpses through the window of unremarkable countryside, not unlike our Yekaterinoslav province, and eventually Bucharest.

Bucharest styles itself a mini-Paris, and while this is a gross exaggeration since most of the streets are quite unworthy of the name, some of them are quite picturesque with reasonable shops and tree-lined pavements *à la* Paris. We made for an extremely elegant hotel, the Athené Palace, but it was full up so we had to leave our bags there and wait for rooms to become free in the evening.

I suggested to Alexeyev that he stand guard over the Serbian gold, and to Babastro that he do the rounds of the consulates and extract the necessary visas from them, while I set off to look round the city. Whenever I arrive in a new foreign city I have a passion to go immediately out into the streets and criss-cross it from end to end. It was particularly interesting to see the Romanian capital, since while it would be not unusual to find oneself in France or Germany, it is not such a common occurrence to be in Romania. (At this point it crossed my mind how extremely tedious it would be to have a wife hanging on my arm, especially one who could not walk very fast.)

I went into a café and glanced at a local French-language newspaper, to find out the latest news about the war. It was intriguing to read the reports from our General Staff alongside those of the German High Command, but there was little cheer in any of them, since our forces had retreated from East Prussia, a development the Germans were making full use of to trumpet tremendous victories. I then walked about the town, lunched with our party in the luxurious hotel, had a row with Alexeyev over something he said, wrote postcards, sent a telegram to Mama, went out for another walk, this time deciding that the town was quite pleasant but still far from a 'mini-Paris', and then returned to the hotel, where I wrote up these notes in the comfortable salon.

A host of people, clearly from the upper social echelons, came through the splendid entrance foyer, the salon and the restaurant in the evening: tycoons, young people out for a good time, elaborately made-up women, even though the most striking of the Romanian women were not particularly good-looking, while the most dashing men fell a long way short of an English gentleman. Alexeyev, seeing that I had really been quite angry with him, was exceptionally nice to me; we were sharing a double room and soon made friends again.

6 February

At six o'clock in the morning while it was still dark outside, the telephone shrilled right above my head – time to hurry on some clothes and continue our journey. Our migrations were unwieldy affairs, due to the mountains of luggage the Babastros had with them. From one point of view this was rather tedious, but since Babastro took care of it all himself, and incidentally my trunk as well, and got all the tickets and reservations, my own travel was quite carefree. We had stocked up on things to eat, as the train had no restaurant car, and by noon were at the Danube. Alexeyev and Babastro were amused at the number of postcards I sent, but most of them were to Mama, quite a number to my friend Eleonora, and only a few to all the others. Before crossing the Danube – the border between Romania and Bulgaria – we had to pass through Romanian Customs, but Alexeyev's 'diplomatic passport' spared us from inspection and we were soon on board the steamer. I said facetiously that we ought to watch out for foreign mines in the Danube, left there by the Austrians for use against the Serbs in Belgrade, and indeed there had been some brief references to this in the newspapers. Everyone laughed, taking what I said as a joke, but it later transpired that on this very day and not far from this spot the Romanians did find two mines. Crossing the Danube, we had risked being blown sky high.

Undaunted, we docked safely on the Bulgarian bank of the river, where we saw our 'brother' soldiers wearing the same uniform as our own at home. Overall Bulgaria gave an impression of being a reflection of Russia: the locals understood Russian and when I bought a newspaper I found I could read Bulgarian quite easily. But the Petrograd press had recently been carrying so many stories about the Bulgarians' hostility to Russia that we were cautious. Once again Alexeyev saved us in Customs, after which we entrained from Rushchuk[1] for Sofia, or, as the Bulgarians call it, Sófya with the accent on the first syllable. In general the Bulgarian landscape was as lacking in interest as Romania, but was to some extent enlivened by trees spaced singly at intervals of a couple of hundred sazhens[2] throughout the whole country.

At the main stations we encountered the Bulgarian population. The people had a more colourful and 'southern' appearance, but there were no attractive faces to be seen. A restaurant car was attached to the train, which helped to pass the time. Babastro became more and more extravagant, delivering himself of a stream of witticisms and even more *risqué* remarks that eventually became so indelicate that I turned my back on him and left, declining to respond to his further overtures.

We passed through Plevna, providing the occasion for a Bulgarian gentleman to outline to me with a wealth of impassioned detail exactly how

---

1 Fortress town on the Bulgarian bank of the Danube. The fortress constructed by the Ottomans during the Russian–Turkish war of 1806 was encircled and successfully besieged by General Kutuzov, its fall proving to be the decisive victory of the war.
2 A sazhen was 2.13 metres, so the trees were approximately half a kilometre apart.

Skobolev had crushed Osman-pasha,[1] pointing out all the historic hills, graveyards and monuments. In the evening we came to a beautiful mountainous region, very sparsely populated, where we plunged into tunnels and wound our way along river banks, finally emerging onto a broad plateau edged with mountains in the midst of which sparkled the lights of Sofia. We took a group decision not to carry on with our journey on the morrow but to stay in Sofia for twenty-four hours.

Piling into a cab, we made our way through exceedingly humble streets, which for some reason reminded me of Simferopol. Our eyes were constantly assailed by signs saying 'Hotel This' or 'Hotel That' or 'Hotel The Other' but after a long drive during which we passed a drab-looking palace, we put up at the best hotel, the Hotel de Bulgarie. But it could not hold a candle to the hotel in Bucharest we had stayed in, and like the whole town it was hideous, although, as matter of fact, as a hotel it turned out to be not too awful. I wandered about the quiet streets for a while, but it was already midnight and I went to bed.

7 February

When next day I went up to Babastro to say good morning, he said: 'I don't understand; yesterday you would not speak to me, but today you come up all smiles . . .' and refused to return my salutation.

I turned my back ostentatiously and walked off, deeply hurt. After this incident we did not speak to one another all day and I took my meals at another table with Mr and Mrs Korevo (he an elderly nobleman, she a young and extremely *soignée* Frenchwoman who had married him three years ago; they were on their way to Paris) and Mme Subbotkina, a cultured woman going to Genoa (damn, Genoa is pronounced Genova in Italian and I'm always calling it Geneva).

In the afternoon I made a quick tour of Sofia. The cathedral is superb, the interior so light and joyful and every inch of it covered with paintings. Some of the streets had Russian names and there was a statue of Alexander III on the main square, but the newspapers are full of articles against Russia and spilling such filth that it is painful to read. The people on the streets have a coarse, plebeian air about them, and if you do happen on a member of the

---

1 In the Russian–Turkish war of 1878 Plevna, defended by the Ottomans under Osman-pasha, was successfully attacked by the Russian army under Skobolev. However, reinforcements were not forthcoming and he was forced to retreat, leading to a widespread belief that this was because his immense popularity would be dangerously enhanced by the victory, something that could not be tolerated. The bloody conflict continued with huge losses on the Russian side for another six months, until the fortress was eventually encircled and blockaded, and capitulated.

intelligentsia he or she will lack the slightest sign of dandyism. Things became more interesting towards evening, when the crowds started pouring out of their workplaces preparatory to their Sunday day off, adding a touch of south-eastern colour and gaiety to the prevailing grey.

The rumours circulating about Serbia are most dispiriting: spotted typhoid fever is said to be advancing by the day and there is also news of another, even more virulent form of typhoid abroad, spread by insects. We found this extremely disconcerting, but we had no choice but to go on and therefore undertook a thousand preventive measures: providing ourselves with food and drink so that we would not have to buy anything Serb; mercury chloride and eau-de-Cologne for hands and lips, insect powder and a kind of aromatic ointment which we smeared over ourselves and which, according to the chemist, would present an impregnable barrier to any louse for at least a week.

Alexeyev went out for a walk, keenly disappointed that he did not meet any girls.

I wrote a lot of postcards and enjoyed an evening at the ballet.

8 February

I was still in bed when Alexeyev came into my room and tried obliquely to find out what I thought of Babastro. Speaking of the latter, when I saw him he had decided to be conciliatory: 'Look, yesterday I was rude to you and the day before you were rude to me. So now we are quits; let's be friends again.' I agreed, and good relations were restored.

All our things were packed and we set off again on our travels. Around noon we were at Tsarigrad, on the border between Bulgaria and Serbia. There we had the usual story with passports and Customs, mercifully abbreviated by the Alexeyev passport. Straight into a Serb railway carriage and Serbia, which immediately brought about a distinct change for the better, the aspect of the people greatly more attractive than the Bulgarians: more cultivated, handsomer, manlier, and better disposed to Russians than to their brothers across the frontier. Oh, if only there were no typhoid!

Because of the gold we were bringing them they gave us a compartment all to ourselves, even providing a guard. This was welcome in so far as the rest of the train and the corridors were packed so full of people one could hardly get through or even breathe. But it did become rather tedious being forced to stay in the compartment until evening without being able to go out, under arrest by our own gaoler. Galya was close to tears, Babastro exhausted his entire stock of jokes, but the hours passed and at long last, more or less shattered, we arrived in Niš. In Petrograd I had joked that the first person we would see on the platform in Niš would be the King of

Serbia, but we were now all so terrified of typhoid that we hastened to get on to the train for Salonika. It was already in and waiting, and on the point of leaving.

We barely managed to heave all the Babastro luggage into the sleeping car we had previously reserved by telegram, whereupon we discovered, to our indescribable chagrin, that there were no berths for us. Before us lay a twenty-four hour journey to Salonika, and we were dog tired. Alexeyev took in with him the Counsellor from the Embassy, Babastro somehow found space for his wife and Galya in the next carriage, and Babastro and I stayed outside in the corridor to spend the night there. I made an attempt to squeeze myself into the adjoining carriage, but there were people both lying and standing and the stench was such that I retreated hastily, sure I must have caught typhoid. Our sleeping car was an aristocrat's drawing-room in comparison. Babastro and I moaned and groaned for a while, and he entertained me with crude stories, some of which in my naivety I could not understand, and then on the warm carpet covering the floor we made up beds by combining bolsters and cushions purloined from various compartments, and slept wonderfully well until morning. I was not worried about fleas, because having smeared the evil-smelling grease all over myself I put my faith in the assurances of the Sofia chemist that no biting insect would be capable of getting through it for at least three days. 'Mais vous embaumez, monsieur!'[1] declared the ladies.

9 February

Early in the morning we arrived at Üsküb, or as it is known locally Skopje, a town whose name had become familiar during the First Balkan War.[2] This was a particularly disgusting staging post, in which we had to wait about two hours while I tried to buy postcards and stamps, succeeding only with great difficulty, but there seemed to be no post office so the only thing I could do was deposit them in the post van of the train going in the opposite direction, back to Russia. My travelling companions were highly amused at the quantity of postcards I despatched. I walked round the place with great circumspection, mindful of typhoid even though the general consensus was that it could be spread only by insects. God alone knows whether this is true

---

1 'But you smell so delicious, monsieur!'
2 Üsküb was the Ottoman name for Skopje, now the capital of Macedonia. The First Balkan War (1812–13) saw the Balkan League (Serbia, Montenegro, Bulgaria and Greece) victorious in the struggle against Turkey and the Ottoman Empire. The war ended with the hopelessly flawed Treaty of London which so dissatisfied all the participants as to result almost immediately in the Second Balkan War, in which Bulgaria changed sides and took to the field against its former allies. Even the final armistice proved to be merely a prelude to the First World War.

or not. The walls and fences of the station were all covered with notices and disinfectant.

At last we moved off again. Up till now what we had seen through the window had been uniformly grey, and I smiled as I recalled Bashkirov and his plans to go to Constantinople by car once the war was over, and his enthusiastic description of the 'exotic' journey we would make through Romania and Bulgaria. Soon after leaving Üsküb we found ourselves following the bank of a great river that stayed with us until evening, almost as far as Salonika. By now we were over the spine of the Balkan mountains, and through the open window we began to smell the warm, fragrant air of the southern spring. This was such a treat that we were reluctant to go to bed, although sleeping berths had become available from Üsküb onwards.

In the afternoon we crossed the border with Greece, witnessing in the last town in Serbia – where we stayed without moving for a long time – the largest number of people we had seen suffering from the dreaded typhoid. By evening we were in Salonika; someone told us that Salonika was on a war footing by reason of Greek–Turkish complications, and this alarmed us a little, but it proved just wild talk. What was a real problem, however, was that shortly before our arrival a large steamer had come into port and filled up all the hotels, so that by the time we succeeded in finding some truly revolting accommodation we were completely exhausted. Alexeyev had caught cold and was feeling very ill. Still fearful of the epidemic and untreated water, I went to bed without washing and hardly undressed at all.

10 February

We were awoken by the sound of a cannonade. Was Salonika under bombardment?! Heaven knows, in these parts you cannot work out who is fighting whom. But all our speculations proved wrong: all that had happened was that an English cruiser had come into port and was exchanging salutes.

The weather was dim and overcast, but warm. We had prepared ourselves to have to wait several days in Salonika for a steamer, but it turned out there was quite a small one, around three thousand tons but perfectly decent, leaving today, and we decided to take it at least as far as Athens. The town of Salonika had a tinge of the East about it, and had the weather been at all sunny we would probably have been dazzled by the colourful costumes of the inhabitants. The streets were narrow and dirty, and in one lane Babastro and I saw an Asiatic individual who bore more of a resemblance to a cholera bacillus than to a person.

At three o'clock we loaded the mountain of Babastro impedimenta into a boat and from the boat into the steamer. There was enough of a wind to promise some pitching and tossing, and my companions apprehensively took proprietary powders to combat the expected seasickness. I refrained, preferring to rely on myself. This was the right course of action, for in the event the ship rolled hardly at all and caused me no discomfort.

We sailed south from the port of Salonika, keeping to the coast to both right and left, sometimes mainland and sometimes islands. I strolled about the ship savouring the sensation of being on southern seas that had looked so enticing on maps of Europe. Hitherto all my sea voyages had been in the north; this was the first time I had ventured so far south. Towards evening the wind freshened and it grew colder. Some people went below to turn in, but I stepped out briskly on the almost deserted deck and gazed with pleasure at the dark sea. I wished it had been rougher and the boat had tossed more.

11 February

Our voyage now took on a more agreeable aspect, even though the wind and the waves were stronger, but not overmuch so. I spent all my time on deck, learning Italian and looking at the shore. It was sunny and would have been warm had it not been for the wind. All in all I was enjoying being in the south. My greatest desire was to go to India, and I decided that, should it prove impossible to return the way we had come, I would try to take a boat to India and come back via Vladivostok. The prospect of a month on board did not frighten me, on the contrary it appealed.

Towards evening we approached Piraeus, the port for Athens about four versts[1] from the town, which could be seen rising up on the higher ground in the distance. The spectacle thus presented was of magical beauty: sea, city, the ancient buildings, the Acropolis with its broken columns, and behind it the intricately etched line of the mountains, the whole scene lit by the setting sun over the sea and touched with the most delicate colours: pale blue, pink, lilac. These colours altered every minute, as we shifted our position from moment to moment until we entered the port and exchanged the poetry of our vision for the prosaic business of getting into the tender, unloading the Babastro baggage, Customs and the electric railway into Athens.

Athens itself, however, was sheer delight, white, brightly lit and teeming with life, and our hotel had columns and marble – a veritable temple.

After dinner I abandoned my companions and followed my usual practice of walking round the streets. This was wonderful: the air was balmy, there were palm trees everywhere, enormous buildings studded here and there with columns, the white houses and, best of all, the pavements also white, constructed of marble or at least something very like it.

---

1 A verst is slighter more than a kilometre.

12–13 February

We took time off in Athens, waiting two days and three nights for the big steamer to Brindisi. Athens was a joy: summer weather, bright sunlight, the gleaming white exterior of the buildings, the antiquities, the colonnades, the shady alleyways. We visited the Acropolis; we walked everywhere and did not notice the time passing.

We rose early, loaded our stuff into the landau and went to take the ship from Piraeus. Part of our way took us through fields smelling deliciously of spring. As we climbed up from the tender to board the steamer, we spotted another of our travelling companions last seen in Sofia, whom we had dubbed 'ptichka', 'little bird': a young woman, almost a girl in the full bloom of youth with dazzling white teeth, a very nice, good natured person. Although we had exchanged only the odd word as far as Sofia, we now greeted one another as old friends and she immediately bore me off to explore the ship. We sat together at dinner, and although the maître d'hôtel insisted that all the places had been reserved in advance we pretended to be brother and sister, calling each other 'bro' and 'sis' for the rest of the voyage.

It was a large ship, and a good one, and the voyage to Italy was excellent. Luckily the Greeks had recently permitted passage through the Corinthian Canal, and not having to circumnavigate Greece made the trip a good deal shorter. The Corinthian Canal is a very curious structure. It is as straight as an arrow with high embankments, and so when one first enters it, one thinks it must be very short, but in fact we were sailing through it for an hour and a half, the rain drizzling down. Bro and Sis sat together, Sis asking Bro about the bracelet he wore on his wrist. Bro enquired of Sis how long she had been married, and if she was happy living with her husband.

In the evening we came to Patras, where our group thought to go ashore, but the rain came on so hard we had to forgo that pleasure. As a result of Alexeyev's and Babastro's insistence I had no choice but to play for them, on condition that it was kept a secret from the other passengers. I sensed that formerly they had not had an especially high opinion of me, but now they were extravagant in their astonishment and appreciation.

15 February

The day was marked by high wind and waves. The passengers began disappearing below, and by the time the ship's rolling reached such a pitch that the propeller jumped right out of the water and behaved in the oddest fashion, there were only ten people left on deck. I felt proud that my sea legs were strong enough not to make me feel in the slightest seasick, on the contrary the experience was very interesting. I thought I would go right up into the bow, where the rolling was at its height, but the wind there was diabolical, it snatched my cap from my head, the waves poured over the deck and made it impossibly slippery. I was hurled from one rail to the other but managed to grab some projecting piece of the ship or other to hang on to, tore my overcoat, all but got pitched into the sea and was much relieved to get back safely from my expedition. After that even I started to feel queasy. I was most discomfited by this, but ensconcing myself in a deckchair on the upper deck soon recovered my emotional composure, although I made no further efforts to leave the safety of the deckchair. There were not many people at dinner, although Alexeyev managed to crawl out for it. In honour of its being Sunday, champagne was served.

In the evening we arrived at Corfu, but we rode at anchor some way off shore. I should have liked to go ashore, as to judge from the postcards it was a beautiful place, but it was too far. Meanwhile we stayed put all night, as the continuing hostilities made it possible to sail only during the hours of daylight.

The outline of Corfu brought to mind Jules Verne's novel *Hector Servadac*.[1]

16 February

The sea was calmer today, and the sun baking hot. Little by little the passengers crawled back on deck. We had to write down our names and nationalities in case a French cruiser should intercept us, but rather to my disappointment this did not happen. At two o'clock there came into view a faint strip of land that was Italy, and the next thing we knew we were in Brindisi.

As always when arriving in a new country, I studied the Italian physiognomies with the greatest possible interest until we were allowed off the ship. At last we were on dry land (for some reason I experienced a tinge of regret), passed through the boring little town of Brindisi, reached the incredible chaos characteristic of the Italian railway station, boarded the train and sped through the attractively pastoral Italian landscape towards Bari, where we were to spend the night.

17 February

Bari is celebrated for the relics of the Orthodox St Nikolay, patron saint of sailors (bringing to mind thoughts of *Sadko*[2]). Next morning we continued

---

1 Jules Verne, *Hector Servadac, voyages et aventures à travers le monde solaire*, 1877.
2 Opera (1897) by Rimsky-Korsakov. The hero, Sadko, is a troubadour turned sea-faring adventurer.

towards Rome, but in Foggia Babastro and I suffered a humiliation: we were still having lunch when the train left without us. Relieved that at least we had our tickets with us, we had to send telegrams, wait around for four hours freezing to death because the weather had turned cold and we had nothing to put on over our jackets, and finally hurtle off in pursuit on the *diretissimo*.

At eleven o'clock at night we emerged on to the platform at Rome station, to be met by an ironically smiling Alexeyev. He took us to the 'Oriento' hotel, where he was staying. My first impression of Rome was to be amazed by the tunnel, but I had no chance to see anything else. The streets seemed very narrow.

18 February
Rome

And so, here I am in Rome! The trams start running at five in the morning, and altogether there is such a din from the streets that it was impossible to sleep. After a chat with Alexeyev I went out to accomplish some minor tasks: drink coffee, buy a hat, buy a map of the city, walk about the town with its narrow streets and exceptionally attractive appearance, glance at the magnificent 'washbasin',[1] the monument to Vittorio Emanuele,[2] the Colosseum, and make sure I was at the Grand Hôtel by eleven to meet Diaghilev.

Extending his hand in welcome, he told me that he had twice gone to meet me at the station yesterday, having discovered from the Embassy when Alexeyev was due to arrive. He showed me the room reserved for me, connecting to a drawing-room with a grand piano in it, as Diaghilev had taken an entire apartment in the hotel. He wanted to know whether I was planning to return home soon. I answered that such indeed had been my intention, since there had been so much talk about Bulgaria soon becoming impassable, leading to some urgency, but for the time being these fears appeared groundless. Diaghilev said that after my concert he would be going for four days to Naples, and then three days in Palermo. After that he planned to join Stravinsky in Montreux. He added that Stravinsky, who had recently had an enormous success appearing with the Augusteo Orchestra, was anxious to meet me, and would be very glad if I would come too. We could thus make the whole trip together and in two weeks' time I could give a concert in Geneva, which would be interesting since at the present time the city was full of people fleeing from the war.

He then told me about Molinari, the principal conductor of the Augusteo Orchestra, a competent and knowledgeable musician but a dangerously

---

1   Presumably the Trevi Fountain.
2   The enormous and grandiose Monumento Nazionale near the Piazza Venezia to King Vittorio Emanuele II.

Jesuitical enemy to any outsider who might be tempted to try to get a foot in the door of the Augusteo. The president of the society that ran the orchestra, however, the wealthy and influential Count San Martino, was the complete opposite: a charming and benign individual, although well known to be extremely parsimonious, so how much I would be paid and indeed whether I would be paid at all was far from certain.

At this point appeared the delightful youth Massine,[1] and we went to lunch. From this moment began the whirl of activity that continued throughout my stay in Rome from the 18th to the 24th of February.

Introducing my Concerto to Molinari,[2] three rehearsals, searching for and obtaining a decent concert piano (not an easy task in Rome) – such were the activities surrounding in particular the concert. We also attended several other concerts, at which Diaghilev never let an opportunity slip to introduce me to various critics and generally did a sterling publicity job. We lunched and dined in the company of Italian countesses and duchesses, as well as with the very agreeable Mme Khvoshchinskaya, the wife of the Secretary of our Embassy.[3] I did as much sightseeing in Rome as I could, but there was not much time.

Molinari at once showed himself to be an excellent conductor and I was delighted at the care he took over the accompaniment. Diaghilev continued to puff my reputation on all sides and rhapsodised passionately about the concert. I had a slight *contretemps* with Molinari at the general rehearsal: he did not want me to open the lid of the piano because it interfered with some players in the orchestra being able to see his baton (during the rehearsal the piano was not in its position on the forestage, but in among the orchestra). I protested, but he paid no attention and began conducting. In the third bar I did not come in, and refused to play. The piano lid had to be opened, Diaghilev was delighted by my refusal to compromise, and afterwards Molinari asked if he had offended me.

1   Léonide Massine [Leonid Myasin] (1896–1979), dancer and choreographer. Hand-picked by the jilted Diaghilev to replace Nijinsky, he became the leading male dancer and choreographer of the Ballets Russes, and after Diaghilev's death played a leading role in the Ballet Russe de Monte Carlo. Important creations of Massine both as dancer and choreographer include Falla's *The Three-Cornered Hat*, Rossini/Respighi's *La Boutique Fantasque*, Offenbach's *Gaité Parisienne* and Rimsky-Korsakov's *Capriccio Espagnol*.
2   Despite Prokofiev's admiration for him, Bernardino Molinari (1880–1952) was not considered in the front rank of Italian conductors, although he was responsible for the first performance of Respighi's *The Pines of Rome* and gave conducting lessons to Carlo Maria Giulini, who was at the time playing the viola in the Augusteo Orchestra (now the Santa Cecilia Orchestra). His reputation has not been enhanced by an unkind comment by Toscanini in a private letter: 'Our poor Bernardino, who is so proud of possessing two big, hard b[alls], is in truth the victim of the disproportionate weight of his accessories, because the blood, exiting from his brain and infiltrating down below, leaves his intelligence very anaemic.'
3   Vasily Khvoshchinsky and his wife Ruzhina were friends of both Stravinsky and Diaghilev. Mme Khvoshchinskaya was rumoured to have more than a passing interest in Massine.

There were several newspaper articles about me in advance of the concert, and red, ten-foot-high posters advertising the 'Pianisto e compositore russo Sergio Prokofiew'. The 'russo' tag did no harm at all as there was much popular feeling against Austria. For the concert the audience numbered about two thousand, but since it is such an enormous space it was not nearly full. At first I was not nervous at all, but there were places in the middle where I was. I did not tire in the Scherzo, but in the Finale I became so dreadfully exhausted I could scarcely carry on to the end. All in all it was not bad, but I did not play as well as I had done in Petrograd, and Molinari's accompaniment was less accomplished than it had been in the rehearsal. After the first movement there was applause mixed with booing, after the Scherzo undiluted applause, more restrained clapping after the third movement and at the end of the piece I was received quite warmly. The solo pieces I played in the second half of the concert were better liked than the Concerto.

As usual all those present were very complimentary, but the way the numerous reviews treated the event was mixed to say the least: almost all had praise for the pianist but only a few had anything good to say about the work. And even though there were several attempts at detailed critiques and lengthy dissertations, my opinion is that they simply did not understand the Concerto. All in all, although it was a very good success, after what had happened in Petrograd I had expected more.

Diaghilev was anxious to know what was the state of progress with the ballet. I outlined the subject to him, and then played through the music. This prokoved a monumental discussion along the following lines: 'What on earth are you, a Russian composer with a Russian theme, thinking of, writing international music?! This will not do.' In Diaghilev's view, there can be no place for international music. Naturally, the term 'national' should not be taken to mean simple folk melodies or a narrow interpretation, but it was a *sine qua non* that there should be a bedrock of the Russian spirit. Not that this was in any way alien to me, as could be seen in much of the Second Piano Concerto.

Diaghilev: 'After Stravinsky there is only one composer in Russia, and that is you. No one else is in the picture at all. How is it that a country that has produced so many national composers like Borodin, Musorgsky, Dargomyzhsky, has completely dried up? Your Petrograd has no concept of valuing anything truly Russian; it is a swamp from which you must extricate yourself, otherwise it will simply swallow you up. Now, you might think that we could leave your ballet as it is, and stick on to your non-Russian music a demonstrably Russian production, obviously Russian scenery and costumes – no, my dear sir, Paris is too sharp for that, Paris will see right through it, and the rest of the world will follow Paris. I don't want your ballet just to have three or four performances and then no more . . .'

I do not usually yield my position easily, but Diaghilev was so convincing that I immediately agreed to eliminate half the music from the ballet. Diaghilev added: 'And completely revise the subject.'

There was even more to it than that: writing music that was national in character rather than international was for me a completely new notion, and it immediately attracted me. We did not have any more discussion about the ballet, because I was fully occupied with the Concerto. Only once did Diaghilev become terribly excited and shout at me, and that was when he heard of my determination to compose an opera. Opera, in his opinion, was an outmoded art form, destined to become as extinct as the concerto. On this subject, while I wanted to concentrate on my performance, we went so far as to get somewhat at odds with one another, but afterwards Diaghilev very sweetly asked me not to pay any attention to him banging his fist on the table, as he said he did this only to clarify his meaning. He hoped we would have many more occasions to foam at the mouth when arguing, and this was a good sign.

The day after the concert we dined with Count San Martino, a merry old gent married to a delightful young woman. They live in a venerable palace, surrounded by the strictest etiquette. Although we spent a most pleasant evening with them, it struck me all the same that the pretty young Countess must find life boring in that palace.

Later another countess, Mme Antonelli, a simpler soul with a passing resemblance to Sonya Esche,[1] drove us round the picturesque country surrounding Rome. We went for a wonderful drive in her automobile along the Appian Way, and then on the evening of the 24th, Diaghilev, Massine and I left for Naples.

My visit was altogether beginning to assume the character of a remorseless steamroller: we were always pressing on, during my stay in Rome there was endless fussing over the rehearsals, invitations to dinners, from dinners to museums. Whenever I stopped to draw breath I got bored. For this reason, when Diaghilev suggested that I stay two months in Switzerland so that I could complete the whole ballet under his very eyes, far away from the pernicious influence of the Petrograd ballet scene, I did not have to think twice about declining the proposal, despite its obvious attractions. (On the other hand, I did dream up a new plan, a complete fantasy but a terribly attractive one: I would return to Petrograd, abduct Nina, marry her and bring her away with me to Switzerland, where I would finish the ballet in two months. This would be perfect in all respects. But to achieve it I would have to have from Diaghilev 2,000 francs for my return journey and a contract for the ballet, say 3,000 roubles with 1,000 in advance.)

---

1   Sofia Esche, a friend from the Conservatoire, the younger of two sisters to whom for a time Prokofiev was attracted. Ibid., pp. 8, 233 and *passim*.

25 February – 5 March
Naples

Diaghilev's reasons for going to Naples were partly to get to know the city and the artistic legacy buried in its museums, and partly to talk to Futurists there about a project to create a balleto-futurist theatre production on the theme of a Neapolitan national holiday. Strictly from the point of view of getting on with my own ballet this was a waste of time for me, except for my conversations with Diaghilev in which he teased out my musical physiognomy and I his novel ideas on ballet.

But it was very interesting to get to know Naples, and would have been even more so had my soul been at peace. This it was not, because by the latter part of my stay in Naples thoughts of Nina increased to such an intensity that I was overwhelmed by the dull, empty ache in my heart. Later on this subsided, perhaps because the time was approaching for our visit to Switzerland, after which I would be able to return to Russia. As for the rest I spent the time very pleasantly and with great interest, because never for a moment did we sit around doing nothing, and my spirits remained high. All the same, each morning my first conscious sensation would be one of anxiety (and longing) in my heart, which after ten minutes would disappear. Ultimately I put it down to nervous fatigue and ceased to pay it any attention.

Diaghilev and I had three or four passionate and lengthy conversations about the ballet. They were not necessarily confined to my ballet, they were more about current tendencies. Diaghilev invariably spoke with great heat and conviction. Sometimes his statements would strike you as ridiculous, but it was impossible to object to them because as soon as you tried he would immediately support them with an avalanche of impeccably reasoned theses that would with irrefutable clarity demonstrate the justice of the propositions, however absurd.

As for my ballet, the subject was obviously too old, too unoriginal, too stiff and too clumsy, and what I must do was create an intimate, playful, grotesque, fresh-minted work based on a Russian fable. We would probably find the right fable at Stravinsky's because he had a great predilection for such things, had a whole library full of them, and more than likely, as a ballet composer himself, already had his eye on one or two but, being the exceptionally generous person he was, would be more than ready to share them with us. As for me, my style should unequivocally be grotesque, grotesque and grotesque, with none of those pompous sagas about Wagnerian heroes, please. In sum, he utterly convinced me, we put a decisive line through my Ala, Lolli, and their like, and settled down to wait for Stravinsky, Switzerland and the land of fairy-tales.

Diaghilev put enormous pressure on me to stay the two months and work, but to his astonishment it was not something I could even contemplate. He absolutely could not understand my stubborn desire to return to Russia when I was being offered such ideal working conditions in Switzerland, far away from everyone but at the same time in close contact with Stravinsky and Diaghilev, not to mention the ballet company and its choreographers, who would be gathering there in about a month. The money question would be easily settled to my satisfaction. But I stayed immovable as a rock or, from his perspective, as stubborn as an ass, and produced a thousand reasons why I must go back to Russia: my mother, the Studio,[1] the concert with the Court Orchestra, and all manner of other obligations that Diaghilev obviously found anything but persuasive. No doubt he suspected an affair of the heart, but neither he nor I said a word about it.

'All the good being here has done you, even the short time you have spent in Italy, you now propose to throw it all away again back in your Petrograd swamp!'

I did not try to argue against this perceived danger because I had it in mind to come back for a second visit. I even casually mentioned this as one way out of the difficulty, but he exploded: 'What! Two weeks coming out here, two weeks going back, two weeks coming back a second time and two weeks on the way back: that's a total of two months on the road – you must be out of your mind!'

I replied that this was nothing: Tchaikovsky composed on board ship and Glinka in the coach, and the only real question was whether he grudged the money for the travel or not.

As for our aim of seeing all that Naples has to offer, Diaghilev, who has put on a lot of weight and now waddles rather than walks, tapped into surprising reserves of energy, and we were on our feet from morning till night. The noisy, vital city often made me think of Moscow, but its special charm was a labyrinth of narrow little lanes no more than ten feet wide or so and six storeys high, in which life seethed not so much in the houses as outside in the streets, the walls festooned from top to bottom with drying laundry. It was an extraordinary and curious sight. Vesuvius puffed out its cloud of white smoke. I was told that the last eruption had done serious damage to the former nobility of its conical form. A couple of times we lunched on the hills outside the city, from where we had staggeringly beautiful views over the town and the bay. Four mornings we spent examining the treasures of the National Museum, filled with antiquities from Pompeii; I found the passion and knowledge Diaghilev and Massine displayed for ancient sculpture inspiring, having previously been quite indifferent to its attractions.

One wonderful excursion we made was to Pompeii, walking through the

---

1   Prokofiev had been engaged to teach piano at the Music Studio in Petrograd. See *Diaries*, vol. 1, p. 667 and *passim*.

dead streets and hearing the expositions of the guide. (Very interesting, and wherever one turned one's attention, there would be a sign announcing to the world that such and such a house was a brothel.) Our stay in Naples concluded with a trip to the island of Capri, about which I had heard much and which I was most interested to see. My first thought was that once I had achieved all my plans and got back here in a couple of months' time to write my ballet, Capri could be where I would base myself. But, wonderful though it is, Capri turned out to be so mountainous, so overpopulated and crowded, that I abandoned the idea. We arrived on a balmy and moonlit evening and walked along the cliffs; Diaghilev and Massine were like a pair of love-birds. We spent a day and a half on the island and then came back to Naples via lovely Sorrento, and thence back to Rome.[1]

6–9 March

We returned to Rome 'just for a couple of days'. Diaghilev needed to collect some papers, and insure his life for a large sum: this was part of his contractual obligations with America. The two days stretched into four, the four into a week, and the week into two weeks. I was bored and angry, because the time was being wasted. We stayed in a hotel that was the last word in luxury, went to theatres, dined with the entrancing Ruzhina Khvoshchinskaya, toured the surrounding countryside by car, but all the time I was straining with every fibre of my being towards Switzerland so that I could meet the creator of *Petrushka* and get on with my ballet.

All the same, those two weeks did produce two important developments: (1) Diaghilev, realising that I could not be deflected from my determination to go to Petrograd, agreed that yes, I must certainly come back again even though I was manifestly a madman whose reason for going was 'no doubt some little Marusya or Katyusha or somebody'; (2) we acquired five volumes of Russian fairy-tales by Afanasiev,[2] which we spent three days reading and

---

1 'Diaghilev is nervous whenever he is on the water, and would not allow the rowers to sing. There was a light breeze, and although the boat rocked only slightly, it was enough to frighten Diaghilev. When the oarsmen started to sing softly, Diaghilev stopped them, saying that this was no time to sing, seeing that any moment we might be drowned.' (Later marginal note by Prokofiev.)

2 Alexander Afanasiev (1826–1871), ethnographer and folklorist, gathered from both oral and published sources a wonderful collection of more than six hundred folk tales which, following the example of the Brothers Grimm, he grouped according to subject matter and imagery and published in eight volumes of *Russkiye Narodnye Skazki* (*Russian Folk Tales*) between 1856 and 1863. Unlike the Grimms, however, he declined to sanitise or bowdlerise the tales, and many of them ran foul of the censor for blasphemy or obscenity, and had to be published abroad. Partly for this reason and partly for his affiliations with radical political writers such as Herzen he suffered persecution by the authorities and died in poverty from tuberculosis at the age of forty-five. Stravinsky drew on Afanasiev's nonsense poems or riddles for his *Pribaoutki*, while his 'The Deserter and the Devil' is the basis for Ramuz's libretto for *The Soldier's Tale*.

from which we selected a tale about a clown. Stravinsky had already mentioned it to Diaghilev as a suitable subject for a ballet. But the story itself, consisting of a whole series of adventures, did not immediately lend itself to scenic treatment. One day Massine thought of dividing one of the adventures into three, to which I added another adventure, and then linked the sequence chronologically. The two fitted together perfectly – and in all of five minutes the plot was ready, falling admirably into six scenes.

The next three or four days we devoted to developing and polishing these scenes, with Diaghilev excitedly adding valuable contributions, and Massine marvellously entertaining us as he improvised an opening dance of washing the floor. I was enraptured with this subject, and Diaghilev was overjoyed that it was absolutely right for me, moreover the principal role was perfect for Nijinsky, who would choreograph it.

20–22 March

At last the long-awaited day came when Diaghilev's business was concluded, the telegram sent to Stravinsky, and we left for Milan. There was now no point in going to Switzerland as Diaghilev would still have to come back to Rome, I was going away in any case, and Stravinsky wanted to come to Milan in order to hear for himself the new musical instruments being promoted by the Futurists. Accordingly a rendezvous was arranged in Milan (apropos, a most attractive city, somewhat after the style of Berlin). I met the leader of this most curious tendency, Marinetti,[1] with whose ideas I already had some familiarity through his audacious, crazy book and through Diaghilev's numerous mentions of him in Rome, since Diaghilev knew him well personally and had staged one ballet in collaboration with his group.[2]

1   Filippo Tommaso Marinetti (1876–1944), poet and founder of the Italian Futurist movement and the Partito Politico Futurista, later absorbed by Mussolini's Fascist Party. The book Prokofiev probably refers to is Marinetti's *The Founding and Manifesto of Futurism*, originally published in French in *Le Figaro* in 1909. Pivotal elements of the Manifesto included: '1.We desire to sing the love of danger, the habit of energy and of temerity; 2.The essential elements of our poetry will be courage, daring, and revolt; 3. Literature having hitherto glorified the immobility of reflection, ecstasy and sleep, we now desire to exalt the aggressive gesture, the fever of insomnia, the leap of the gymnast, the perilous leap, the box on the ear and the fisticuff; 4.We declare that the splendour of the world has been enriched by a new beauty: the beauty of speed. A racing car with its body adorned by great exhaust pipes like snakes with explosive breath . . . a roaring car seeming to hurtle under a volley of shrapnel, is more beautiful than the Winged Victory of Samothrace [the magnificent second-century BC statue of the goddess Nike from the island of Samothrace that stands at the head of the Daru staircase in the Louvre].'
2   Prokofiev must mean *Printing-Machine Ballet*, a Futurist ballet by Giacomo Balla in which twelve robot-like dancers impersonated the actions of a rotary printing press, some miming the in–out movement of a piston, others the rotation of the wheel being driven by the piston. The music consisted of 'rumorist onomatopeia' rhythmically declaimed by the dancers. The ballet was never in fact staged for the public, but Diaghilev was sufficiently interested for Balla to arrange a private performance for him in 1914. (Virgilio Marchi, an architect who was one

The Futurists clung to Diaghilev because he represented tremendous publicity for them, and Diaghilev clave to the Futurists because he found their ideas fresh and interesting and because they always succeeded in making a great deal of noise about their activities. Consequently their mutual partiality was extreme, and now in Milan they were keen to demonstrate their musical instruments,[1] seeking particularly the opinion of Stravinsky, whose music they passionately admired. Their leader was Marinetti, a fiery, stentorian orator, a chatterbox, and a person of incredible animation and energy. Among others I would single out the gifted artist Balla.[2]

I was keenly interested in getting to know Stravinsky, because I had begun to love his works more and more, works to which a couple of years ago I had been almost positively hostile. In addition Diaghilev everywhere sang his praises in extraordinarily ardent terms. I had a distant personal memory of him from about nine years ago, when he used to turn up with other Korsakovian students at Rimsky-Korsakov's rehearsals; this was about the time when I was myself starting at the Conservatoire. Then I remember meeting him in the spring of 1910 at an evening of contemporary music at *Apollon* magazine, at which I played my Sonata Op. 1 and Stravinsky excerpts from *The Firebird*, which I did not like at all.[3] We may have been introduced to one another that evening. Diaghilev even remembers that I was rude to Stravinsky, but I have absolutely no recollection of that. Whatever the facts of this, we now greeted each other as the greatest of friends.

Diaghilev, Massine and I went to meet him at the station, where we got lost and separated: Diaghilev and Massine met the wrong train, got flustered and went back to the hotel. I met the right train, but could not find the

---

of the participants, wrote of the occasion: 'Balla, needless to say, had reserved for himself the more delicate syllables, onomatopoetic sounds and verbalizations, which issued from his lips with his unforgettable Piedmontese 'neh', while the shameless, bearded Semyonov kept popping the corks of bottles of Frascati, turning the whole performance into a highly intelligent and most amusing grotesque.' But Diaghilev did later get Balla to design a light-show to provide the decor for a production of Stravinsky's *Fireworks* at the Teatro Constanzi in April 1917. See Lynn Garafola, *Diaghilev's Ballets Russes* (Oxford University Press, New York, 1989).

1   The instruments in question were Luigi Russolo's '*intonarumori*' ('noise machines'): 'buzzers, whistlers, rattlers, exploders, murmurers, cracklers, thunderers, gurglers and roarers'. (Programme details from the London Coliseum for 15 June 1914, quoted in Vera Stravinsky and Robert Craft, *Stravinsky in Pictures and Documents* (Simon & Schuster, New York, 1978). In his manifesto *L'arte dei rumori* (*The Art of Noises*), published in 1913, Russolo divided noises for compositional purposes into six categories as follows: (1) rumbles, roars, explosions, crashes, splashes, booms; (2) whistles, hisses, snorts; (3) whispers, murmurs, mumbles, grumbles, gurgles; (4) screeches, creaks, rustles, buzzes, crackles, scrapes; (5) percussive noises on metal, wood, skin, stone, terracotta, etc.; (6) animal and human voices: shouts, screams, groans, shrieks, howls, laughs, wheezes, sobs.
2   Giacomo Balla (1871–1958). His 1914 canvas *Velocità astratta + rumore* (*Abstract Speed + Sound*) and his sculpture *Boccioni's Fist* were two of the iconic artworks of the Italian Futurist movement.
3   See *Diaries*, vol. 1, p. 155.

composer, perhaps because I was insufficiently familiar with his physiognomy. Returning to the hotel I found the whole company talking happily at the top of their voices. Stravinsky and I had adjoining rooms, so we unlocked the communicating door and had long conversations in the mornings and evenings. When he heard my Second Piano Concerto, *Toccata* and the Second Sonata, Stravinsky was seized by the wildest enthusiasm, declaring that I was a real Russian composer, the only one to be found in Russia. For my part I was genuinely enthralled by his new *Pribaoutki*,[1] which he performed in a highly amusing style.

Then, in the presence of the Futurists, we played the piano-duet version of *The Rite of Spring*. At this point I had heard the work only once at Koussevitzky's concert, and had a less than clear understanding of it. Now, sitting down to play it with the composer in front of a large gathering, I was extremely nervous as I knew that it was incredibly difficult. Stravinsky, normally small and bloodless as he was, became engorged with blood while playing, sweated, sang or rather croaked, and laid down such a strong, good rhythm that we played *Le Sacre* to stunning effect. To my total and unexpected amazement I saw that *Le Sacre* is a magnificent work, with its incredible colours, its clarity and mastery. I sincerely congratulated the composer, and he in return praised my performance. He warmly approved my idea of composing *Chout*,[2] welcomed me into their circle,[3] invited me to visit him in Switzerland, passed on a mass of practical lore about publishers, and was generally as nice as could be. He had arrived on the 20th, and the 22nd was Easter Sunday, which the four of us celebrated with Mme Khvoshchinskaya and her sister-in-law. On Easter Saturday we dined without the ladies, stimulating Stravinsky to demonstrate a limitless capacity for Asti; he became in the process quite tipsy and insisted for some reason on relating the complicated plot of some film or other he had seen at the cinema.

On the first day of the holiday Stravinsky left to go home to Switzerland, that evening Diaghilev and Massine were returning to Rome, and I – well, I hesitated: on the one hand I wanted to go straight to Brindisi and take the little Greek boat back to Salonika, on the other, the boat was very small and very dirty and there was a larger one leaving in three days' time. I had not signed a contract with Diaghilev and I wanted the opportunity to have an

---

1 *Pribaoutki* (*Catchphrases, Riddles*) for male voice and eight instruments, 1914.
2 The Russian word 'shut' (as it would normally be transliterated) pronounced 'shoot', means fool, jester, clown, buffoon. The full title of Prokofiev's ballet, *Skazka pro shuta, semerikh shutov pereshutivshogo* (*The Tale of the Buffoon Who Out-buffooned Seven Other Buffoons*), is usually abbreviated by Russians to the single word of the protagonist, while English audiences likewise generally opt either for *The Buffoon* or *Chout*, in the latter case using the French transliteration to avoid confusion with 'shoot' or 'shut'. This English version of the *Diaries* will call the ballet *Chout*.
3 i.e. Diaghilev and the Ballets Russes.

important and conclusive discussion with him. In the end I put off my departure for three days and went with Diaghilev to Rome, because news was also emerging from the Balkans of furious fighting between the Serbs and Balkan saboteurs. This was beginning to smell like war between Serbia and Bulgaria, into which Russia might well be drawn on the opposite side from Bulgaria. In that event it would be pointless to leave, because I would not get through in any case. Suddenly, out of the blue there arose a potentially unsurmountable threat: there would be no way back to Russia! (What would become of Nina, and all my plans?)

Impatiently I awaited the evening papers, and there I read the following: Russia was calling the 1916 reserves to the colours. This was quite unexpected; everyone thought it would be later. Diaghilev and Co. jeered in chorus: 'Oh yes, there you are you see, of course now you'll have to go back for the 1916 year call-up and the Second Militia Reserve, go ahead, straight back to Russia where they'll put the screws on you and no mistake. You *could* stay abroad as long as you like, you don't have to read the papers, you don't have to know anything about anything, but as soon as you go back to Russia, no sir, away with you to the Carpathians!' In short, they so addled my brains that the instant I arrived in Rome I definitely decided to leave: things appeared to be quietening down on the Serb-Bulgarian border, while the threat of calling up the Second Reserve militiamen also seemed for the time being less likely.[1]

One result of my decision to leave was a fight with Diaghilev on a specific subject. I must explain that he had paid 1,000 roubles for *The Firebird*, 1,500 roubles apiece for *Petrushka* and *Narcisse*,[2] and to Strauss for that dreadful *Joseph*[3] a sum I cannot even persuade my tongue to utter. I decided to disregard all of these, but (because of Nina) I needed five thousand, a figure which only in extremis would I be prepared to drop to three thousand. However, even before I had opened my mouth, Diaghilev declared that he was ready to reach agreement with me on the same basis as *Narcisse*, but taking into consideration the expenses of the first trip, and the expenses of the

[1] The terms First Militia and Second Militia derive from the 'Time of Troubles' (1604–13) when civilian armies were raised to defend the Motherland and to counter the occupation of Moscow by Polish interventionists and their boyar allies. It was the Second Militia, raised in Nizhny Novgorod in 1612 by Kozma Minin and led by Prince Dmitry Pozharsky, that succeeded in ejecting the Poles from the Kremlin, thus coming to symbolise the unquenchable determination of the Russian people to fight to the death for their country, the obligation to answer the call, if needed, lying upon all Russian citizens. Prokofiev as the only son of a widow would normally be exempt from conventional military conscription, but could not guarantee to be relieved from a requirement to join the Second Militia should the Tsar, as was his prerogative, decide to raise this body.
[2] Ballet by Nikolay Tcherepnin for the Ballets Russes with choreography by Mikhail Fokine, sets and costumes by Léon Bakst, first produced Monte Carlo, 1911.
[3] *Josephslegende*, ballet by Richard Strauss, choreographed by Boris Romanov, first produced Paris, 1914.

second . . . I at once objected that while travel expenses had certainly been incurred, I still needed three thousand. Diaghilev, appalled, shouted: 'What! What about Stravinsky, what about Tcherepnin?! You're out of your mind! Not for the world!' After this he began to tot up the whole amount, convert it into francs, and came up with the result that Ravel and Debussy together had received less than I was asking just for myself. But my resolve stayed firm (the image of Nina fortifying me) and I said this would be my total earnings for a year, since the composition of the ballet would take a year. 'And Paris? What about Paris, where you will become famous all over the world?'

Finally I declared that the whole project was looking more and more like a charity concert organised by some great Princess, at which the artists are glad to perform in the presence of the high and the mighty for no reward except the unalloyed honour of having been invited to do so. Diaghilev was deeply offended, and saying that he was in no need whatsoever of any philanthropy, stormed out slamming the door. The next day, however, discussion was resumed, during which I tried to show that I did not especially care about Paris – whether they liked me there or not. In Petrograd I had no need of Paris to be loved. Diaghilev replied that it made no odds whether or not they loved me in Kharkov either, and personally he could not see much difference between Petrograd and Kharkov. This time the conversation ended by my saying that talking to him [Diaghilev] was no better than talking to Jurgenson or Bessel.[1] At the mention of the last-named, Diaghilev lost his composure even more than the previous day; bowing low from the waist, he said: 'Thank you very much . . . this conversation is terminated, sir . . . thank you . . .' and left the room with an air of finality.

For the next two days there was a complete breakdown in relations. I had made Diaghilev extremely angry, and also puzzled him. I calculated that in the end he would agree to my conditions. It seemed quite out of character for him to decline altogether to work with me on account of a thousand roubles here or there, but the possibility that stubbornness might lead him to postpone commissioning of the ballet for a year represented a threat to my entire plan of campaign. At ten o'clock on the evening before my departure (I was leaving at seven o'clock in the morning) I went to his room, thanked him for his consideration, and said that in comparing him to Bessel I had not meant in any way to offend him. I expressed my regret that the story of the ballet should end so unhappily. Diaghilev responded that he could not entertain any thought of allowing money to come between us, and the negotiations began once more. This time there was a positive outcome:

---

1   Jurgenson was Prokofiev's publisher in Moscow and regarded by him as unduly tight-fisted; Bessel was a St Petersburg publisher with whom the composer had had less than satisfactory dealings, also because of money.

the contract would be for 3,000 roubles but the return trip would be at my expense. The agreement was signed between two and three o'clock in the morning, a time which had me cursing and swearing, but Diaghilev was very happy that the business had been satisfactorily concluded. We kissed one another, and parted until the summer.

I had almost no sleep; they woke me at six, when I had to pack my things and dash for the train. The terms of the contract brought me little joy: they were not generous enough for me to be able to afford to come back. But then it occurred to me that I might just be able to make a separate arrangement with Jurgenson, and that consoled me so I journeyed back across Italy towards Brindisi in a good mood. All the way the Italians talked about the war, and on learning that I was Russian, were keen to express their support for my country. To my own surprise, I carried on the conversation in Italian. Among the passengers on the steamer were twenty-four Polish men and women and a dozen or so Russians, all homeward bound. I kept myself pretty much to myself, felt a little melancholy and tried to get a tan in the southern sunshine. The weather was superb and the sea calm for the whole voyage to Salonika. Here we spent a day, stocked up with food supplies and anti-typhoid remedies for the onward journey, Serbia still not being completely free of the disease. I bought some Egyptian presents for Mama, Nina, Eleonora and Katya Schmidthof.[1] I travelled through Serbia in the company of some French journalists, to whom a Serb officer was relaying the details of a Bulgarian guerrilla attack on Serb frontier guards. The train stopped and we walked over to see the site of the conflict and the graves of the murdered Serb officers and soldiers. We had been expecting to encounter some hostility when we reached Bulgaria, but in fact the opposite was true, the 'brothers' were friendly.

Profiting from my experience on the journey out, I now knew my way about: I got good rates when I changed money, always boarded the right train, got sleeping-car reservations and generally had an excellent journey. Three days and nights after leaving Salonika we arrived at Iasi where the early morning view through the windows of the train was of the Austrian Carpathians. Another two hours and we were in Ungheni, the Romanian side first and then over the border into Russia. Greetings, Mother Russia! I was very happy to be back.

(End of the journey to Italy)

---

1 The sister of Max Schmidthof, Prokofiev's closest Conservatoire friend who had committed suicide in April 1913. See *Diaries*, vol. 1, p. 251 and *passim*.

3–12 April

I made notes of my two-month-long foreign travels in a separate pocket book, which I took with me everywhere. I now continue my main Diary from the moment I set foot again on Russian soil, which occurred on 3 April at two o'clock in the afternoon, at Ungheni station.

During my absence I had apparently become quite famous. The reasons for this were: (1) my appearance at the Imperial Russian Musical Society on 24 January and the enthusiastic press reaction; (2) in part, my previous appearance at the 'Contemporaries' recital with my Sonata and some of the smaller pieces, and (3) most of all, my trip to Italy to see Diaghilev and the news that Diaghilev was commissioning a ballet from me.

As a result of this, my success when I returned to Russia was in danger of quite turning my head. I stopped off in Kiev, and spent a day with Glière,[1] who had convened all the professors at the Conservatoire to meet me. They all knew my music, had the scores, and were enthralled by my playing (apropos, I made the acquaintance there of the violinist Kokhánski[2] and the composer Szymanowski,[3] whose music I liked very much). As soon as I arrived in Moscow I made straight for Jurgenson. Since my epistolary tiff with his brother[4] in the autumn I had had no contact with either man.

---

1   Reinhold Glière (1874–1956), composer, and Prokofiev's first real teacher, who at the suggestion of Taneyev spent the summers of 1902 and 1903 with the Prokofiev family in Sontsovka. Between 1913 and 1920 Glière served as Director of the Kiev Conservatoire, and after the Second World War became Chairman of the Union of Soviet Composers. One of the most influential teachers of composition in Russia, he could number Prokofiev, Khachaturian and Myaskovsky among his students. Ibid., p 62 and *passim*.

2   Paweł Kokhánski (1887–1934), outstanding Polish violinist whose technical and interpretative gifts made many composers besides Prokofiev turn to him as a valued collaborator, notably Szymanowski (who dedicated his Violin Concerto No. 1 to him) and Stravinsky (who wrote for him the five-movement arrangement for violin and piano of the *Pulcinella* Suite). It was Kokhánski who, having being denied the opportunity to give the planned premiere of Prokofiev's First Violin Concerto in Petrograd because of the October Revolution, made his own edition of the solo violin part and brought it out with him when he left Russia in 1921 for the United States, where he became a professor at the Juilliard School of Music in New York.

3   Karol Szymanowski (1887–1932), composer and poet, was of Polish nationality by virtue of having been born in an area then part of Poland but subsequently in Ukraine, but received his musical training at Gustav (father of Heinrich) Neuhaus's Music Academy in Yelizavetgrad, in Southern Ukraine. Opportunities for a significant career in music in Poland were limited, so it was in Ukraine, and Kiev in particular, that he was primarily active at this time. There he associated especially with his compatriots Kokhánski and Artur Rubinstein. In 1919 Szymanowski fell briefly in love with the then fifteen-year-old Boris Kochno, to whom he wrote (in French) four touching love poems and dedicated his novel *Efebos*. Two years later Kochno, looking both for a job and a 'higher attachment', would replace the rejected Massine in the affections of Diaghilev, and remain a powerful figure in the Ballets Russes until the end of the impresario's life (at Diaghilev's suggestion he was to write the libretto for *The Prodigal Son*, although the extent of his collaboration was later disputed by Prokofiev).

4   See *Diaries*, vol. 1, pp. 767-8 and 772 for an account of the cause of this coolness in relations.

Now Boris Petrovich behaved in such a pleasant and friendly manner it was as if Jupiter had been transmogrified into Venus. I said I had come to offer him the rights to my still embryonic ballet. Jurgenson agreed readily. I then said that I wanted three thousand for the rights, to which Jurgenson apologetically demurred: 'That is rather a lot, Sergey Sergeyevich . . .' and asked for time to think it over and discuss the proposition with his brother.

However, the following day he agreed, on condition that my downpayment would be five hundred roubles, a further fifteen hundred to follow once sales reached five hundred, and the final thousand after another five hundred sales. I objected to the initial fee retention, explaining that I needed the money now whereas in a year or two's time my needs would be less urgent, and also that by that time today's thousand roubles would have been reduced in value to not much more than five hundred. Although we discussed the matter for a full five hours over these two days we did not succeed in reaching agreement and so left it, each side urging the other to think again and communicate by letter. Besides Jurgenson in Moscow I saw Goncharova and Larionov[1] in order to pass on Diaghilev's request that they should travel to Italy to create scenery and costumes[2] for his productions. How I love talented people! I then saw the Derzhanovskys[3] and Lyolya, who has grown even taller and is quite unable – perhaps she does not want to – to conceal her love for me.

By next day I was in Petrograd, where Mama was anxiously awaiting my arrival. The same day I looked in at a rehearsal in the Conservatoire of the student production of *Rusalka*.[4] People came rushing up to greet me, wrung my hand, envied me my time in Italy, exclaimed how tanned I was, and so on. Among them were Tcherepnin, Dranishnikov,[5] Kreisler,[6]

1   Natalia Goncharova (1881–1962), great-niece of her namesake, the wife of Alexander Pushkin, and her husband Mikhail Larionov (1881–1964) were the prime movers of the pre-Revolutionary Russian avant-garde in painting and sculpture, and also members of the *Blaue Reiter* group in Munich. They inaugurated the abstract school known as Rayonism, incorporating into their work elements of Cubism, Fauvism and Futurism, in the last of which they were associated with Mayakovsky and with the Italian Futurists. Both designed sets and costumes for Diaghilev's Ballets Russes.
2   The inference is for *Chout*, for which Larionov did design sets and costumes, although the first performance did not take place until 17 May 1921 in Paris.
3   Vladimir Derzhanovsky, Moscow impresario and publisher of the magazine *Muzyka*, also a prime mover in Mardzhanov's Moscow Free Theatre, and his wife, the singer Yekaterina Koposova-Derzhanovskaya. Lyolya was Yelena Zvyagintseva, Yekaterina's considerably younger half-sister. See *Diaries*, vol. 1, pp. 212, 522, 553–4, 587–90 and *passim*.
4   Opera (1856) by Dargomyzhsky.
5   Vladimir Dranishnikov (1893–1939) became a leading Soviet conductor of opera and ballet, holding music director posts at the Kirov Theatre (as the Mariinsky Theatre became under the Soviets) and the Shevchenko Theatre in Kiev. A friend and supporter of Prokofiev at the Conservatoire, he had accompanied the composer's Rubinstein Prize-winning graduation performance of his First Piano Concerto in April 1914. In Petrograd/Leningrad during the 1920s

Damskaya, Khantsin[1] (who has grown and blossomed), Dranishnikov's sister, even Struve[2] and Lipinskaya. Bashkirov came round in the evening; while I was in Italy he had sent me a telegram saying how much he was missing me. And thus we made peace, and I went round to see him.

The day after I got back, rehearsals for the Second Piano Concerto with the Court Orchestra[3] began. Wahrlich[4] was ecstatic over the Concerto, pumped my hand after each movement, and the orchestra gave me an ovation. (Zakharov teased me by saying that the orchestra had been ordered to do this to give encouragement to inexperienced artists.)[5]

As Stravinsky had suggested, I divided the first movement cadenza into two halves by giving an interjection to the horns, and this seemed to work quite well (I later eliminated this change).[6] On my own initiative I re-orchestrated the opening of the third movement. Malko[7] invited me to appear in Sestroretsk during the summer, Fitelberg[8] wanted to put on a whole concert of my works in Pavlovsk, Glière the same in Kiev in the autumn, Bryskin[9] proposed a tour of Russia – in a word, I hardly knew what to do about all these invitations. Ziloti[10] expressed regret that it would not be possible to

---

    Dranishnikov was responsible for many first performances in the Soviet Union, among them Prokofiev's *Love for Three Oranges* (1926), Berg's *Wozzeck* (1927), Strauss's *Rosenkavalier* (1982), as well as the first Soviet production of Musorgsky's *Boris Godunov* (1928). See ibid., p. 272 and *passim*.
6 Not the violinist, but a fellow conducting student. Ibid., p. 515 and *passim*.
1 Isabella Khantsin, Conservatoire student. *Diaries*, vol. 1, pp. 330, 347, 358.
2 Lidia Struve, a student of singing at the Conservatoire and a serious attachment of Prokofiev in 1914. Ibid., p. 593 and *passim*. Lipinskaya was Lidia Struve's friend.
3 The earliest State-run symphonic ensemble in Russia, established on the initiative of Rimsky-Korsakov in the late 1890s to form an orchestral component for the Glinka Capella, the Imperial musical training institution established by Peter the Great at the beginning of the eighteenth century. By the end of the nineteenth century the Capella and its Court Orchestra had grown to be among the most prominent music institutions in the capital, and the orchestra under conductors such as Glazunov, Nikisch and Mahler gave many important first performances, notably of Wagner, Strauss and Bruckner. The Court Orchestra was later reincarnated as the Leningrad Philharmonic Orchestra. See ibid., pp. 70, 81–5 and *passim*.
4 Hugo Wahrlich (1836–1922), German-born violinist and conductor of the Court Orchestra. Ibid., pp. 82–5 and *passim*.
5 Later marginal note by Prokofiev.
6 Later marginal note by Prokofiev.
7 Nikolay Malko (1883–1961), conductor with a distinguished international career. Until he left the Soviet Union in 1928 he conducted at the Mariinsky (later Kirov) Theatre and in 1926 in Leningrad undertook the sensational premiere of Shostakovich's Symphony No. 1. From 1956 to 1961 he was Chief Conductor of the Sydney Symphony in Australia. Ibid., p. 24 and *passim*.
8 Grzegorz Fitelberg (1879–1953), Polish conductor, prominent member of the Young Poland group of composers, which included Szymanowski, subsequently founder and Chief Conductor of the Polish Radio Symphony Orchestra, and from 1947 Chief Conductor of the Katowice Symphony Orchestra.
9 Arkady Bryskin, conductor. Ibid., p. 325.
10 Alexander Ziloti (1863–1945), pianist, conductor and concert organiser, cousin of Sergey Rachmaninoff. Ziloti had been one of Liszt's favourite pupils and co-founded with him the

stage my new ballet at the Mariinsky Theatre, but immediately invited me to perform it in a concert as part of his season in a year's time.

I went to call on the Meshcherskys. Talya and Vera Nikolayevna[1] were there, and were waiting for Nina to appear at any moment from Tsarskoye.[2] But Nina did not turn up, Vera Nikolayevna became angry and assumed a sour expression, while I related my news to her and to Talya. It was time for me to go; I was due to meet Khvoshchinsky[3] at the Astoria Hotel. Vera Nikolayevna said that she would drive me there, so we waited for the car bringing Nina back, which could then take us on. Eventually the car arrived, Nina appeared, looking terribly small, warmly pressed my hand, and turned to talk to the others. I followed suit, paying her no attention until I left, three or four minutes later. We only exchanged a few phrases, and when Nina said: 'You could at least stay and watch me drink tea . . .', I replied: 'I'd rather go to the Astoria, I can drink tea myself there.'

Talya asked for two tickets for my concert on Monday, for herself and a companion. When I asked Nina if she would be in Petrograd on Monday, she replied that on Monday she would be going to Tsarskoye. I swiftly turned back to Talya: 'So, just two tickets then.' Nina realised her mistake and said: 'Oh, if it's a concert, then I . . .'

But I was already outside, going down the stairs. I thought I had detected an artificial note in Nina's voice when she was speaking to me, a kind of constriction, as though she were trying unsuccessfully to control her nervousness. All the time I was abroad I had spent much of my time thinking about how I would behave when we met, and how she would respond, but now that the encounter had actually taken place I found my reaction had been extraordinarily flippant and superficial. I was not quite sure why this was: either all the musical praise Petrograd had showered on my triumphant return – all those compliments, adulatory handshakes, treatment of me as little short of a genius – had completely gone to my head, or else I had become too much a prisoner of my dreams and had lost touch with the real

---

Liszt Verein in Leipzig (Prokofiev states with relish in the *Autobiography* that Liszt used to call him 'Zilotissimo'). Ziloti was a truly remarkable musical figure; to quote Michael Steinberg: 'To most people who listen to and read about classical music, Ziloti is at best a name in a footnote to a programme note about his cousin Rachmaninoff. But an immense public force and presence in his great years, Ziloti was a remarkable musician – pianist, conductor, composer, teacher, editor, impresario – whose life-path intersected with those of a multitude of characters from Liszt to Eugene Istomin by way of Tchaikovsky, all three piano-playing Rubinsteins, Elgar, Scriabin, Schoenberg, Stravinsky, Prokofiev, Ysaÿe, and Casals, to list just a few of the most famous.' (From a review of *Lost in the Stars*, a biography of Ziloti by Charles Barber (Scarecrow Press, Lanham, 2003).) He conducted many Mariinsky Theatre performances, and in 1918 after the Revolution was appointed Intendant in succession to Telyakovsky, but left Russia in 1919, finally settling in New York where he lived until his death. See *Diaries*, vol. 1, p. 79 and *passim*.
1   Respectively, Nina Meshcherskaya's sister and mother. Ibid., pp. 279, 472 and *passim*.
2   Tsarskoye Selo, a dacha area outside Petrograd, where Nina Meshcherskaya's cousin had a dacha.
3   First Secretary at the Russian Embassy in Rome.

Nina; or then again, having made such firm and concrete plans while I was away about what I was going to do, perhaps I was once again wavering . . . But after two months of continuous, almost literally uninterrupted thoughts of Nina, for our meeting now to have such an inconsequential, offhand character! Strange, very strange.

The next day was my birthday, and in the evening the Andreyevs came, the Rayevskys,[1] and Zakharov. Mama was keen to invite the Meshcherskys, but I resisted on the grounds that they had not sent me birthday wishes. Mama, however, seeing that the evening was going very well and everyone was having a good time, rang them up without telling me, and a great noisy crowd of six of them, including male and female cousins, came piling in on us. I received them as best I could, Nina less effusively than the others, but she insisted that I translate my Italian reviews for her and during tea we found ourselves sitting beside one another. I chattered away in a lively fashion. There was no hint of our former relationship, and I was not very polite to Vera Nikolayevna. Nina announced that she was now as thin as it was possible to be, and let me know in passing that she was bored and lonely in Tsarskoye. When I showed her a piece of glass from a sign advertising Norddeutsche Lloyd[2] that had been smashed by the crowd in Rome and that I had picked up and brought back with me as a souvenir, she snatched it away from me, stowed it in her handbag, and refused to give it back.

The next evening I went to play bridge at their house, and as was by now traditional we played together as a single hand. I talked a lot about Italy, and addressed continual facetious comments to her as if to a distant acquaintance. I could see this was making Nina more and more morose and dispirited, and it gave me enormous satisfaction.

After bridge we sat down together at the piano with the piano score of *Saltan*.[3] Nina strummed for a bit, and then said: 'This music is enough to make one want to shoot oneself.' She then announced that she had found a revolver in one of the Kuchinskys'[4] drawers. When I asked how she was

1   Yekaterina Zhitkova, Prokofiev's mother's elder sister (Aunt Katya), was married to Alexander Rayevsky (Uncle Sasha), a prominent and well-connected civil servant in St Petersburg. Their children, the composer's cousins, were Andrey (Andryusha), Alexander (Shurik) and Yekaterina (Cousin Katya).
2   North German Lloyd was one of the most prominent European shipping lines, established in 1856 to carry passengers from Bremerhaven to New York. By the outbreak of the First World War its liners were carrying nearly a quarter of a million passengers a year across the Atlantic. After the war its fleet was requisitioned by the Allies as part of the Versailles Treaty reparations, but by 1922 the firm was again in business. The pattern of events having been repeated during and after the Second World War, the company subsequently merged with its nineteenth-century rival, the Hamburg-based transatlantic shipping line HAPAG, to become the present-day transportation, container ship and cruise line HAPAG–Lloyd.
3   *The Tale of Tsar Saltan*, opera (1900) by Rimsky-Korsakov.
4   Kuchinsky had married Nina Meshcherskaya's cousin; it was in their house in Tsarskoye Selo that Nina was staying.

getting on in Tsarskoye, she replied that she was working hard at her painting and making progress. She asked me to come out to the 'old green lady', as I used to call the dacha in Tsarskoye, and said that when I came she would tell me everything in detail. We talked for the rest of the evening, Nina alternating between fixing her whole attention on me and being completely distracted, I maintaining an aloof reserve. Just as I was leaving, I promised to come out to the 'old green lady' in two or three days' time, without letting any of the others know. At this there crept into Nina's voice a new and touching note, which I had heard at most only a couple of times before.

13 April

The performance with the Court Orchestra took place in the perfectly decent hall of the Pevchesky Chapel.[1] It was extremely well attended, many of the tickets having been booked in advance. I played the Second Concerto quite well, and as an encore the 'Fairy Tale'[2] so beloved of Anna Grigorievna.[3] But it was not much liked, and although I was called back for a second encore, the applause was somewhat limp. However, when I followed it with the Etude No. 4,[4] the hall came to life and applauded vociferously. Altogether the evening was a notable success; I was presented with a wreath with a red ribbon and a card inscribed 'to the creator of aural joys' – a phrase Bashkirov had taken from a recent article about me in *Muzyka*. A very touching moment occurred when I emerged on to the street and the students of the Pevchesky Chapel, who had been waiting for me to appear, accorded me a little ovation. It moved me as much as the occasion in Rome, when on the day after I had played my concert there, I went into a museum and was accosted by one of the guards, who exclaimed: 'Ah, signor pianista!' and complimented me on my performance.

14–25 April

I was very pleased to be back in Petrograd. I was having a lot of attention paid to me, and I was happy to be seeing all my friends and acquaintances.

1 The Pevcheskaya Kapella, or Choristers' Chapel, of the Imperial Court is one of the most ancient musical foundations in Russia. Originally established in 1476 by Tsar Ivan III to provide a trained body of singing monks for liturgical purposes, by the middle of the nineteenth century, although concentrating on choral music, it had grown to encompass all aspects of music-making and training, and occupied magnificent premises on the Moyka Canal. In 1837 Mikhail Glinka was appointed director, and after his death the building, and particularly the fine concert hall, became known as the Glinka Chapel (Capella). Since 1991 it has officially reverted to its former title, but it is as the Glinka Capella that most people still know it.
2 Op. 3 No. 1.
3 Zherebtsova-Andreyeva.
4 Op. 2 No. 4.

In the mornings I worked on completing the fifth movement of the *Sinfonietta*; when it was finished I could give the complete work to Ziloti's copyist to make the parts. I went to the Sokol,[1] and to Berlitz, where in preparation for my next trip I studied Italian; I played bridge with Zakharov, Andreyev and Serge Bazavov,[2] all four of us taking the greatest pleasure in the game. Now and again I went into the Conservatoire, where the public examinations were running their course. My close friendship with Damskaya continued as before.

Three days after my concert I went out to Tsarskoye. I told no one I was going and took great precautions not to be observed, even so the following day Damskaya told me I had been seen there. I could not decide how I should behave towards Nina. She was very tender with me, and I told her her bracelet had never once, day and night, even during my concert, even in the bath, been off my wrist during the whole two months I was away.

Three days later I was at Kirochnaya Street[3] for bridge, as on Sundays Nina came into town. We had no chance at all to speak that evening. I was very outgoing and told jokes; Nina was on edge. As I was leaving she told me she found my demeanour very strange: surely I could see what an emotionally vulnerable state she was in, so why was I acting so peculiarly and coldly?

I had in the meantime reached a final decision to carry out the plan I had formed in Italy, and made a second trip out to Tsarskoye to have it out conclusively with Nina. This visit was a legitimate one, because in theory a whole group of people had been invited, but in fact only Volodya Littauer[4] came, and we soon got rid of him. We were thus left alone together, and I told Nina that I would be returning to Italy no later than the middle of May, otherwise I might be prevented from leaving because I could be called up for military service; it would be August before I returned to Russia, and perhaps not even then if I went with Diaghilev's company to America...

'And what about me...?' Nina asked.

'Each of us will have complete freedom to do as we wish, but for now our

1 The gymnastics and fitness club Prokofiev set so much store by. The Sokol movement ('sokol' in Slav languages means 'falcon') was a gymnastics movement for young people founded in Prague in the 1860s by Miroslav Tyrš. Its *mens sana in corpore sano* ethos allied to growing anti-Habsburg sentiment caused it to spread rapidly throughout the entire Slav world, not unlike Baden-Powell's Scouting movement in the West. The Bolshevik Revolution effectively suppressed the many Sokol clubs in Russia, although elements of their ideals and spirit of volunteerism found their way into the Soviet Union's Pioneer movement. However, the movement continued to flourish elsewhere in the Slav world, membership rising to about three-quarters of a million during the inter-war years. It still exists today in much reduced numbers and influence.
2 Sergey (Serge) Bazavov, a cousin of Nina Meshcherskaya with whom Prokofiev had struck up a friendship when staying at the Meshcherskys' dacha in Gurzuf in the summer of 1913.
3 The street where the Meshcherskys had their apartment in Petrograd.
4 Vladimir Littauer, an army Lieutenant, son of a recently deceased family friend of the Meshsherskys.

relationship will cease. When I return in a year's time, if our feelings have not changed, then . . .'

Nina flushed deeply, her face grew sombre, her glance turned away and at dinner she drank a lot of red wine. When she had recovered her composure, she said: 'So, this is our last time.'

'No,' I replied, 'you're coming with me to Italy.'

'Serge, you know that what you are saying is impossible.'

I embarked on an attempt to persuade her that it was entirely possible, that this was precisely the plan I had been nurturing while I was in Italy, and it was the only way out of our present situation. The idea that in two or three weeks she might be *en route* with me to Italy quite overwhelmed Nina. I told her I had worked out the plan to the last detail: whatever happened I would be leaving for Italy in the middle of May and if Nina was not with me, then all would be over between us. Not only that, but because of the war it might be that I would stay in Italy not just for two months, but for a year, or two, until the end of the war. There was no point in going on with one of us pining for the other: we must either be together, or we must part now.

The following day Nina asked her father to come to Tsarskoye, which despite his burden of vitally important business affairs he did at once. But Nina herself had evidently not fully grasped the true position, and so when Alexey Pavlovich objected that it would be madness to travel to Italy at the present time, she gave in and agreed that it would, indeed, be better to wait until the autumn. A few days later – this was at the beginning of April – I came out once more to Tsarskoye. Nina had done her hair very simply with a single plait at the side, and looked enchanting, but what she told me did not please me at all, even though she was madly affectionate and obviously genuinely in love. I lost my temper with her, especially when I learned that in her discussion with her father she had not stuck to her guns, and I said firmly that there could be no question of the autumn, my decision about May was unalterable, I was not prepared to be miserable for two years, and if she truly loved me she would come with me, with or without her parents' consent. But if not – then there must be an immediate and final end to our relations. I meant it: such was genuinely my firm resolve.

Nina understood this. But there was no way her father would allow her to go to Italy, and to sever relations with him was too hard for her – she knew that for him she was the only person in the world. Once again I explained that to put off the decision until the autumn was impossible. Nina seemed at last to have grasped the iron logic of the position.

Her second attempt to persuade her father was rebuffed in a manner similar to the first: her father had no objection to any of her intentions except our immediate marriage and departure for Italy – that was out of the question. It was arranged that he and I should meet face to face to discuss the matter. Alexey Pavlovich was friendliness and courtesy itself, and we started with a long conversation about my recent trip before eventually he got round to broaching the main topic. He said that to take a delicately reared young girl, whose health was far from strong, out of the country on a difficult and dangerous journey to face unknown circumstances and conditions, and to keep her there perhaps for as much as a year or more, was beyond what he, as a father, could contemplate.

Altogether the whole business was seriously affecting my life: I could think of nothing else; I lost the ability to work at anything; I did nothing except play Rachmaninoff's Third Concerto, for which I had suddenly developed a great liking, and the late sonatas of Scriabin, in memory of that wonderful composer's untimely end.

May

On 2 May Nina and I met in the third-class waiting-room of the Nikolayevsky Station. Our meeting had important consequences, in that Nina made up her mind to take decisive action, to make one final attempt to persuade her father, and if that failed, to speak to her mother. The battle took place the next evening. Nina rang me afterwards and nervously, but not without a tinge of triumph, announced that she had just spoken with her mother. Vera Nikolayevna had reacted with indulgent condescension to the news that Nina loved me and wanted to marry me, but as for an immediate wedding and going abroad with me, this was categorically forbidden. For her part, Nina was in a state of extreme agitation and demanded that I forthwith set out the whole situation to my mother. We barely finished our telephone conversation. Mama was quite shocked by the revelation, but with her customary nobility of character did not protest.

That evening I played at Dobychina's[1] Contemporary Music evening. Eleonora and Bashkirov were both there, and could not help noticing my distracted air. Eleonora was aware of the reason, Bashkirov was not. I played some of my smaller pieces, not very well.

The next morning Nina was back on the telephone to say that there was no point whatsoever in her talking to her mother; she simply would not hear of it. Although Vera Nikolayevna was not keen on a face-to-face meeting, afraid that I might forget myself and be rude to her, Nina felt that it would still be better if I came myself and spoke to her. I went. While I was sitting

---

1 Nadezhda Dobychina (1884–1949) was a gallery owner, artist representative and organiser of exhibitions, musical and literary evenings. She was also an imaginative concert impresario and a force to be reckoned with in Petersburg artistic circles. The Dobychina agency existed from 1911 until 1929 as an influential and well-informed source of important pictures by artists such as Marc Chagall. See *Diaries*, vol. 1, p. 656.

with Nina in the billiard room, Vera Nikolayevna entered, sat down in a chair and informed me that the course of action I proposed was absurd. To begin with, Nina's health was too fragile; she might even be suffering from tuberculosis, and in any case she was too young to be married. Then, should something happen to her in Italy, who would look after her? The conversation, though lengthy, was in truth pointless, since neither side had any wish to understand the other. It was conducted in an unemotional, plain-speaking way, with a faint undertone of hostility. Nina said nothing.

'To think that all this farrago has been engineered merely because some Diaghilev fellow wants a ballet!' exclaimed Vera Nikolayevna, rising from her seat to conclude the discussion.

Nina promised to come to see me today, because she was worried about my mother's attitude to her. She arrived at four o'clock, small, quiet and ill at ease. Mama received her kindly, warmly even; nevertheless in her heart she too was sure we were making a huge mistake. Shortly before Nina arrived, she let fall the phrase: 'She is not the wife I had been hoping for', but left it at that. Afterwards, when I was taking Nina home, we congratulated ourselves on our courage, and walked arm in arm along the street. (I am tall, Nina is tiny. Seeing another couple, a father and his young daughter, I said how nice it was to see a big man walking with a small woman. Nina corrected me: 'Only if the woman is a ten-year-old girl.')[1]

The following day, the 6th, at five o'clock I again called on them. Alexey Pavlovich was drinking tea in his study and was rather at a loss to know what there was to talk about, seeing that everything had already been settled: the latest conversations Nina had had with him had merely gone over the same ground. Nevertheless we did talk, at some length, and it is true, repeated what had been said before. Nina did not say much, although whenever she did open her mouth she did her best to support me. It was very hard for the poor girl to wrench herself away from her father and her home. We decided that for the next day we would do nothing, but if tomorrow there was no movement towards compromise, then the day after Nina would elope with me. It would have to be done soon: Lent was due to begin on the 18th and after that it would not be possible to get married.

As I was leaving, the chambermaid came to Nina and said: 'The mistress and the master would like to see you in their bedroom.' Nina looked at me with a despairing expression on her face. I kissed her and even made the sign of the cross over her.

Later that evening she telephoned me and told me what had happened in the bedroom. Her mother had alternated between abusing the twin objects of her ire, Nina and me, while her father veered between implacable sternness

---

1 Later interpolation by Prokofiev.

and embraces, saying he hoped she would never be able to bring herself to leave them. But they both agreed there could be no question of permission for her to go abroad.

Next morning I waited for Nina while Bashkirov sat round the corner in his car, in case Nina should appear with a companion, in which case we would be able to put her in the car and drive straight off with her. But Nina did not appear, and at two o'clock Talya telephoned me to tell me the following: Nina, having obtained her father's permission in the morning, had set out to come to see me, but her mother, seeing her on the way out of the apartment, had countermanded her husband's permission and ordered the building commissionaire to bring Nina back.

After this unsuccessful attempt at flight, I was strung up to the highest pitch and started hatching plans to go and take Nina. But Vera Nikolayevna telephoned my mother to warn me against any attempt to abduct Nina by force, as the footmen and concierges had been forewarned and there would be serious repercussions.

Nina did not telephone, but the next day – the 9th – I received a written note from Vera Nikolayevna to the effect that in view of my attempt to take Nina away she had had no choice but to remove Nina from Petrograd. Nina had added a postscript: 'Life is very hard, I was powerless to prevent this, I hope this is not our final parting, *au revoir* until autumn.'

Events now moved into a new phase, starting with energetic attempts on my part to track down Nina. Their house was deserted, Talya had also gone away, Alexey Pavlovich was at work in the factory, none of the servants would tell me anything. The only thing I managed to discover was that Vera Nikolayevna was in Finland. I waited from moment to moment for some sort of communication from Nina which would at least let me know where she was, but nothing was forthcoming.

In the meantime rumours were flying round the town that the Second Reserve militia was about to be called up any day now, or possibly in a month's time. My state of mind was now execrable, mainly because this latest development had removed my last chance of achieving anything with regard to Nina. To abduct the girl, cause her to quarrel with her parents and then be taken into the army with no contract from Diaghilev and therefore with no money, would be the height of stupidity.

Understandably, I could not seriously settle to any real work, and all I achieved was in fits and starts to proof-read the *Ballade*,[1] and the score and the parts of the First Piano Concerto – the amount of mistakes in the latter parts surpassing, incidentally, anything I had ever seen before. Nevertheless I did manage to compose a little: fragments of theme, some passages and

---

1 *Ballade* for cello and piano, Op. 15.

hooks that might perhaps lead somewhere for *Chout*, not digging very deep into them but simply trying to get some ideas for the characters' personalities and the main events of the ballet's story. To my great surprise little melodic fragments began pouring out of me as if from a cornucopia. It was long since material had come into my head with such ease. Several times a day I went to the piano and sat down for five minutes, and almost every time a theme would appear that filled me with joy. Unexpectedly, these two or three weeks in May produced a very respectable crop of more than fifty fragments of material for the future ballet, a huge amount, all of it infused with a strong national flavour. All the time I was composing, I was conscious of being a Russian composer, my clowns were Russian clowns, and this feeling revealed a whole new, previously untapped, field of creativity. Perhaps this accounts for the ease with which the shapes and curls and whorls of these themes came to me.

Needless to say I was in a highly nervous state, a condition that manifested itself in symptoms similar to those I had experienced in Naples and in Rome, when I would awake early in the morning with my heart contracting from anxious longing. And at such times I could not bear to be alone, experiencing a desperate longing to be with people. I attended the Graduation Ceremony in the Conservatoire and several of the public examinations, I went to Pavlovsk for the opening orchestral concerts of the season there, I often visited Bashkirov and spent a great deal of time on the telephone to Eleonora.

Zakharov rang me up almost every day, inviting me to Terioki or to gossip inconsequentially. When he asked me to Terioki on the 21st I said yes with alacrity. But while I was there I was terribly distracted and found it impossible to make myself behave normally. Zakharov was intrigued and puzzled, and asked me all sorts of leading questions trying find out what might be amiss. I spent two nights and one day there, and by the end had become quite irritable. Back in Petrograd I saw very few people except Bashkirov, although I did go to a few musical gatherings *chez* Karatygin,[1] Gessen, Benois, Ruzsky and Ossovsky.[2] Everywhere people were playing my

[1] Vyacheslav Karatygin (1875–1925), composer, also one of the most knowledgeable and perceptive critics of new music, an admirer of Stravinsky, Schoenberg and Prokofiev. Karatygin's reviews of the notoriously scandalous premiere of Prokofiev's Second Piano Concerto at Pavlovsk are, for example, models of intelligent and far-sighted commentary. Karatygin's reviews appeared in *Teatr i Isskustvo* No. 35 (1913) and *Apollon* No. 7 (1913). They are included in *Sergey Prokofiev Stat'i i Materialy*, edited by I. Nest'ev and G. Edel'man (Muzyka, Moscow, 1965). See *Diaries*, vol. 1, p. 72n and *passim*.
[2] Alexander Ossovsky (1871–1957) was a prominent musicologist and critic, having studied composition with Rimsky-Korsakov. An early and perceptive champion of Prokofiev, Ossovsky was a survivor and in the 1930s after a distinguished teaching career in the Conservatoire became Artistic Director of the Leningrad Philharmonia. His wife Varvara was professor of piano at the Conservatoire. Ibid., pp. 122–3 and *passim*.

latest opus, the *Sarcasms*, invariably to stunning effect, but mostly from the outside; very few people appreciated their inner content. Nurok[1] and Nouvel[2] commented: 'After the *Sarcasms*, your next opus will have to be called *Five Charges of Assault and Battery*, and laughed immoderately at their witticism.[3]

Ziloti's attitude to me was the diametric opposite of what it had been previously: he was charming and paid me compliments, and wanted all my future orchestral works to have their premieres in his concert season. How firmly had his door been closed to me before!

At the beginning of May I cabled Diaghilev stating that I was ready to leave and for this purpose awaited his payment of 500 roubles. And indeed, I was quite certain that in a week or so I would be on my way back to Italy. Diaghilev's response was indeed to send the 500 roubles, but Italy's response was to declare war on Austria, the Adriatic was sown with mines, the port of Brindisi was closed and the southern route became impassable. Diaghilev cabled: 'Conseil beaucoup prendre voie du Nord, bon voyage.'[4] A kind thought, and a prompt piece of advice, but the 'northern route' – via Bergen, Newcastle and the English Channel, where to judge from the newspapers ships were being blown up by floating mines and submarines every day – did not greatly appeal.

Then I discovered an even more northerly route: via Arkhangelsk, which apparently had thriving communications with America, thence to Iceland, where ships *en route* from Arkhangelsk to America put in, and from Iceland to Bordeaux or whichever western European port (not England, however), one could get a passage. Safe, and rather dramatic – to Italy via Iceland! If only it had not been for Nina, and if only the Militia Reserve call-up did not come too soon, I would be free to go however and whenever I wished. And so I cabled Diaghilev: 'Voie Nord convient. Graves affaires retiendront quelque temps Petrograd. Argent touche pas. Compose beaucoup matériaux',[5] in order that he should not think I was trying to swindle him over the return journey he had paid for and was simply living off the money.

---

1 Alfred Nurok (1871–1919), critic and writer, close associate of Diaghilev and musical editor of *Mir Isskustva* journal, also music critic of *Apollon* magazine. Along with Vyacheslav Karatygin, Walter Nouvel, Alexander Benois and Dmitry Filosofov, Nurok was one of the original 'Nevsky Pickwickians', the group of aesthetes who formed the nucleus of the *World of Art* movement which needed only the arrival of Diaghilev to spur it into international life. Nurok was also a prime mover in the Evenings of Contemporary Music that enlivened Petersburg musical life in the early 1900s and provided Prokofiev with his first public platform. Ibid., p. 41 and *passim*.
2 Walter Nouvel (1871–1949), critic and writer, a close associate of Diaghilev and the *Mir Isskustva*, co-organiser with Nurok, Karatygin, Medem and Senilov of the Evenings of Contemporary Music. Ibid., p. 41 and *passim*.
3 There are five pieces in the collection of *Sarcasms*, Op. 17. The Pickwickians' ponderous pun depends on the literal meaning of the Russian legal term being 'active insult'.
4 'Strongly recommend you take northern route, *bon voyage*.'
5 'Northern route acceptable. Important business means some delay leaving Petrograd. Not touching money. Composing much material.'

But I was not too dejected in spirit. For one thing, there was better news about the Reserve. There might or might not be a call-up, but the talk was now about the years: 1913, 1914 and 1915, and I was 1912,[1] so that at least until the autumn I could rest easy. But Nina maintained her silence, which I found incredible: surely she could not be so closely watched for two whole weeks that she could not find a way to send me a postcard? But Eleonora had another, and simpler explanation: she had been persuaded to agree not to. In the grip of despair and longing, I made another visit to Terioki, where Zakharov welcomed me with joyous exclamations: 'Look who's turned up, the great idiot! I'm so happy to see you!' This would have been around 20 May.

At first I thought I would be bored there. The Karneyeva girls[2] had not yet moved out to their dacha, but Lyovka was there and I beat him easily at chess. Tanyusha Granat, from a neighbouring dacha, appeared, an interesting Jewish girl of about seventeen whom I had met on my last visit when we had gone together to the cinema. One afternoon she went with some friends over to Kellomyaki,[3] and I was delighted to attach myself to the group, since Katya Schmidthof spent her summers in Kellomyaki and I had long intended to pay her a visit. Tanyusha and I prided ourselves as walkers and decided we would beat the speed record for walking to Kellomyaki, so raced ahead to arrive half an hour before any of the others; a puffing and panting Tanyusha was full of admiration for me. I spent a very nice hour with Katya and then returned to Terioki with Tanya and Boris's sisters, this time walking at a more leisurely pace.

On my return to Petrograd I satisfied myself that there had been no further news of Nina, and concluding that nothing decisive was likely to occur during the following week, I agreed to Malko's invitation to perform the Second Piano Concerto in Sestroretsk on the 27th. Malko had gone so far as to postpone the planned performance of the Scriabin Concerto in order to open the season with me. Generally I spent the time correcting the proofs of the orchestra parts of the First Piano Concerto, continuing to compose material for *Chout* and even making a start on the first scene, spending most evenings with Bashkirov, whose apartment had a marvellous balcony overlooking the Neva and protected from the wind by awnings, with two comfortable armchairs and a low chess table, beside which stood a big tall bowl of strawberries. We would play chess, talk for a while, and then he would take me back to my apartment.

1   Referring to the year in which an individual attained the age of twenty-one.
2   Lidia and Zoya Karneyeva. See *Diaries*, vol. 1, pp. 170–71 and *passim*. Lev (Lyovka) was their younger brother.
3   Kellomyaki (now Komarovo), and Terioki (now Zelenogorsk) are both resort towns on the Gulf of Finland along the southern shore of the Karelian isthmus. Until the aftermath of the Russo-Finnish War of 1939–40, when Karelia was ceded to the Soviet Union, this was part of Finland, hence the change of names.

I practised the Concerto for Sestroretsk, and then on the 23rd Vera Nikolayevna telephoned to say that she had returned to Petersburg quite unwell, was confined to bed, and would very much like to see my mother – would Mama visit her? When Mama did so Vera Nikolayevna told her that Nina was in Finland. She further confirmed that no further discussion could be entertained before autumn; Nina had given her word not to write to me and not to let me know her whereabouts or anything about her.

Somehow I could not entirely believe the picture as presented by Vera Nikolayevna, nevertheless there was something about it I did not like at all. After the rehearsal, waiting for the train back, I walked in drizzling rain along the beach – and suddenly arrived at an important decision. For the first time I saw the whole picture clearly: suppose I were to break off everything with Nina . . . ? At once I felt all my chains slipping from me, chains of which I had not previously even been aware.

The restored sense of freedom, which I had lost without noticing, or more precisely to the loss of which I had been deliberately closing my eyes, was so seductive that everything else I had to do seemed delightfully easy to achieve. And so on 25 May I decided to finish the affair in the same summary fashion as on 14 January I had initiated it. I went home seeing the world through different eyes; it felt a little strange as I had not yet quite reached my final decision, but the back of my enslavement was broken and the spell Nina had cast on me was already losing its force in the joyous light of freedom.

The next day my resolve was unaltered, rather it had strengthened. I said nothing about it to anyone.

On the 27th I went to Sestroretsk for the general rehearsal. *Dreams*, which I was now hearing for the first time in the revised version I had made two years ago, had been played so appallingly at the previous rehearsal that when Malko afterwards asked me not to be too angry, I was able to tell him: 'Not the least bit: after all, there wasn't a single note of my music, so I heard it as if it was a work by someone else.'

But at the general rehearsal it was not too bad. The Concerto went well, and we even decided to position the piano so that I would be sitting with my back to Malko. During the rehearsal I introduced a flute into the second subject of the finale (where this theme, after having been stated by the piano, is given to the bassoons); previously this passage was orchestrated differently.

At that evening's concert the reception of *Dreams* was lukewarm, but the Concerto – which I played very well – was a huge success. I believe it was the first occasion on which there was no booing. I played three encores, Boris Nikolayevich[1] applauding frenziedly. I wondered whether Boris Zakharov would come over from Terioki, but he did not. Stravinsky's Symphony was

1 Bashkirov.

quite beautiful, and when I got back home I found a postcard from the composer, which pleased me very much.

June

My ballet was making excellent progress, rapid, fluent and extremely Russian. I had a mass of material, so much that I began to be afraid it might be over-rich. In the breaks from composition I played through the sonatas of Myaskovsky[1] and thoroughly enjoyed them, especially the Second, dedicated to Zakharov, which the ultra-conservative Boris did not appreciate at its true worth.

I went out to several of the Pavlovsk orchestral concerts. At one of them Zakharov was scheduled to play and we all went to hear him, but it coincided with the death of the Grand Duke[2] and the concert did not take place. Aslanov[3] was deeply put out that I was playing with Fitelberg and not with him. 'When you were a student at the Conservatoire I was the first person to conduct both of your concertos, and took the brunt of all the catcalling and imprecations, and by way of thanks, now you are famous, you turn your back on me and appear with Fitelberg.'

Although the tone in which he thus took me to task was light-hearted, I could see that he was genuinely offended that I would not be appearing under his baton, but the truth is that there was a serious and acrimonious rivalry between the two conductors. Fitelberg had offered me the engagement and I had accepted, not even knowing whether or not Aslanov wanted me to appear with him. Eventually, a solution was found which satisfied all

---

1 Nikolay Myaskovsky (1881–1950), composer, Prokofiev's staunchest and most trusted musical friend from early acquaintance at the Conservatoire. Despite their ten-year age difference and Myaskovsky's career as an army officer, the friendship lasted throughout Prokofiev's life. Acknowledged by Prokofiev as a consummate craftsman, Myaskovsky's output included 27 symphonies, concertos for violin and cello, 11 piano sonatas, 13 string quartets, and a quantity of smaller instrumental and vocal works. A man utterly dedicated to music, he was also a committed teacher, numbering among his students Khachaturian, Kabalevsky and Shebalin.
2 Zakharov was a family friend of the Grand Duke Konstantin Konstantinovich Romanov and his son. The Grand Duke Konstantin Konstantinovich (1858–1915), who wrote poetry and plays under the pen-name of K.R., was the grandson of Tsar Nicholas I. Although, as his remarkably candid and moving diaries posthumously revealed, his inclinations were homosexual, he dutifully married and fathered nine children, of which the fourth, born in 1881, was a son named Konstantin and was thus also Konstantin Konstantinovich. As well as being a gifted writer and translator, K.R. was a good musician, served as Chairman of the Russian Musical Society, and was a generous and effective champion of the arts generally. Dying in 1915 he was spared the terrible retribution visited on most of the Romanov family; not so his children, three of whom (including Konstantin) were murdered in 1918 by their Bolshevik captors in the Urals town of Alapeyevsk within twenty-four hours of the murder of the Tsar and his immediate family in Yekaterinburg. See *Diaries*, vol. 1, p. 441.
3 Alexander Aslanov, conductor and artistic director of summer seasons of concerts in Pavlovsk. Ibid., p. 234 and *passim*.

parties, including mine: I played one concerto with one of them and the other with the other. Fitelberg declared that I ought to get, not the usual fee of 50 roubles, but no less than 200. This was extremely flattering.

On the 6th I went out to Terioki once more. And although up until that moment I had been feeling very anxious and on edge, as soon as I sat in the train I put everything out of my mind and began to feel great contentment. This time Lida and Zoya[1] were in residence. As before, Lyovka invited us over, and in this way harmony was restored with both sisters, the affianced and unaffianced[2] (Lida had become officially engaged to Captain Barkov, chiefly noteworthy for being 'a very good chap', now in Japan). At the Karneyev dacha there was a great vogue for 'Stukolka',[3] everybody without exception playing the game for hours. I did not know how to play, but boldly made a start anyway, learning as I went along, having seen that each player put down a stake of 15 kopecks. But before long I had lost 10 roubles, after which I thought I had better learn it properly. Boris was utterly in thrall to the game, and we spent the whole evening at the card table; only once did I manage to drag everyone down to the sea.

Next day we again played Stukolka and walked to the sea with the Karneyeva sisters. In the evening, as we were coming out of the cinema to which I had gone with the Karneyeva girls and Zakharov, I ran into Tanyusha. We decided that early the next morning we would go on a long walk and try to set a new record. Then, after downing two glasses of Swedish rum, I was rushing back to the Karneyevs to play Stukolka again when I met the whole company coming back from the cinema, upon which I grabbed hold of Zoya and lifted her up in my arms. I won back all my losses and at one o'clock persuaded Boris it was time to go to bed.

In the morning I jumped out of bed and to my surprise Boris, whose bedroom I was sharing, yawned, stretched, looked out of the window, saw that the weather was good, and suggested going down to the lake. That evening I went back to Petrograd.

That dear, wonderful man Sergey Ivanovich Taneyev has died. Long ago we went for a walk together, each of us singing themes for the other to identify and say what work it came from. He stumped me with *Ruslan*, which I did not know well, and I him with Glazunov's symphonies. Sergey Ivanovich was the first person who inspired me to study music seriously, and encouraged me to take lessons first with Pomerantsev[3] and later with Glière. He

---

1 Karneyeva.
2 See *Diaries*, vol. 1, pp. 516, 535, 579.
3 Card game with elements of poker and bridge, incorporating trumps, bidding and the staking of money.
3 At the age of eleven, on a visit to Moscow with his parents in 1902, Prokofiev was taken to meet Yury Pomerantsev (1878–1933), then a composition and conducting student at the Moscow Conservatoire. Pomerantsev, duly impressed, recommended the boy to Taneyev, who in turn

always called me 'Seryozhenka'. One other detail intrigued me: he remained a virgin all his life.

On my return to Petrograd from Terioki I telephoned Boris Bashkirov, who told me he had received a letter from Nina Mescherskaya. She had not been able to bear my month-long silence, and although she had given her word to her parents that she would not contact me, had decided to get round it by asking Bashkirov why I had not gone abroad and why I was making no attempt to get in touch with her. The letter was long and passionate.

But my reply was a very different matter, one I dictated almost without a qualm. Until this moment my repudiation of Nina had been an entirely internal matter. I knew if I wished to return to Nina I could do so, because no one was aware of what had transpired within me. Up to this point our relationship could still exist as an ideal, but the time had now come to dismantle it completely. I scarcely wavered, and composed the letter with great care, Boris Nikolayevich typed it out without a word, and I took it with me to put in the post.

On 12 June, the letter typed but not yet sent, I met Nina in Pavlovsk. I was with Zorya,[1] and as we had not seen one another for two years, we were having an animated conversation. Talya, Nina, Kuchinsky and some others (not, however, her parents) were in a little group almost directly in front of us. I pretended that, deep in conversation, I did not notice anything going on around me. Nina then detached herself from her party and demonstratively came towards us. There was quite a crowd by us, and I made use of this to draw Zorya away from the Mescherskys. The encounter had a very strong effect on me. Nina's whole attitude as she came towards me, talking and laughing with her companions, was filled with life and energy. As I travelled home in the train I felt real regret for the past, but there was no turning back and the next day I posted the letter.

And so ended our romance.

The following day I received from Kuchinsky a package containing Max's ring, which Nina still had, and a few days later I entrusted to his care Nina's diamond brooch and bracelet, the one I had never removed during the two months I was in Italy. The brooch was pinned into some cardboard, and the bracelet attached to the brooch.

*

---

suggested some basic tuition from Pomerantsev prior to a more concentrated period of study with Reinhold Glière. Pomerantsev later conducted for the Zimin private opera company, and for the Bolshoy Theatre. After the Revolution he emigrated to Bulgaria, where he founded the country's first symphony orchestra, and ended up in Paris.

1 Zora Grevs. See *Diaries*, vol. 1, p. 277.

Diaghilev has been asking why I was not yet on my way. In reply I said that I was being held up by 'service' matters, meaning to suggest military service, and in truth some people did think we were going to be called up, although others thought it was unlikely. The most plausible theory was that if there was going to be a call-up, it would be for four of the eligible years. But here was the rub: would these four years go up to and include 1916 or not? If they did, then I would escape it,[1] but if they did not and embraced the earlier period then I would fall within the net. But whatever the case my real reason for not going back to Diaghilev was that I did not want to: life was better here, and there were mines in the English Channel and the North Sea. And there was yet another, even stronger reason: I felt sure that the war would not be over by the spring, and that meant that there would be no season in Paris, and consequently there was no rush to finish the ballet. It did not follow, however, that I was being lazy about it, on the contrary, I was pressing on in great earnest and on 15 June we were able to cable Diaghilev back: 'Ballet avance rapidement, deux tableaux finis, extrèmement national.'[2] It was no exaggeration: I was finding the nationalist idiom very near my heart, and even made Zakharov smile when I played him one or two excerpts.

Incidentally, this same Mr Zakharov suddenly announced that in a few days' time he would be going to Anapa,[3] and then for two more weeks to Kislovodsk, in other words he would be disappearing until the end of July. This was extremely disappointing news, as I had been counting on going often to Terioki, where life promised in every way to be so agreeable. On the 12th, Zakharov played in Pavlovsk with considerable success, and the 13th he left. Hansen[4] was in Anapa, a fact that Zakharov concealed almost up to the hour of his departure, in order to prevent gossip about their getting married.

Before Zakharov left, Bashkirov also departed for his country estate; he said he was going for five days but vanished for what seemed like an indefinite period. He wrote to me incessantly, a succession of uniquely inconsequential postcards, and some rather more acceptable letters.

I thus found myself without friends to hand, and felt somewhat disconsolate. I buried myself even more in work: the ballet forged ahead, and I also dug out *Autumnal*, a work I love very much and which last year I had made a start on revising. At that time I completed about half the job, but now I threw myself into it and it was soon finished. I have a great affection for *Autumnal*; in my opinion it is one of my subtlest pieces, but probably it is destined to make little impact on the public.

1 Because, as Prokofiev has told us, his 'year' was 1912, the year in which he had reached the age of twenty one, while the four call-up years would be 1913, 1914, 1915 and 1916.
2 'Ballet making rapid progress, two scenes finished, extremely national.'
3 Black Sea resort south-west of the Caucasus mountains, east of the Crimean peninsula.
4 Cecilia Hansen, the violinist, whom Zakharov later married. See *Diaries*, vol. 1, p. 157.

The only friend I had left in town was Eleonora. We went several times together to concerts in Pavlovsk, but although this year the park was seething with visitors, I did not seem to know many of them, except for musicians. The Andreyevs were there, but I was a little nervous of them – they might start asking me about the Meshcherskys!

Looking through my old ballet *Ala and Lolli*, I found there was much in it that was not at all bad, and began to think it would be no very difficult task to recast it as purely symphonic music, if it were made into the form of a suite. It would not be an easy piece to orchestrate, but to make a four-movement work of it would present an interesting challenge. I started thinking about instrumentation. Since four scenes of *Chout* were already done, and it was continuing to move forward more quickly than it really needed to (all six scenes by 1 August) I allowed myself to settle down to the score of *Ala* and put *Chout* aside for the time being.

I threw myself into the new suite with tremendous enthusiasm and sat over the huge score for days on end. It was indeed a dreadfully difficult thing to orchestrate, but more satisfying than I had anticipated, and that made the work go ahead at a rate of knots. In this way I worked intensively from 20 to 30 June and was pleased to note that I had orchestrated almost the whole work. Thrilled, I wrote to Ziloti and suggested substituting *Ala and Lolli* for the *Sinfonietta*. In an impressively generous gesture that clearly demonstrated his new-found inclination to regard me as the most important composer now writing, he responded by inviting me to conduct both works. At the back of my mind I had in fact envisaged this happening, and was very gratified that it did.

In view of the harmonious relations that had now been re-established with Lida and Zoya, I visited Lida at the Japanese hospital in which she now most industriously works as a nurse. She looks more beautiful than ever, and was very nice to me, as I was to her.

On the 21st I went to see them in Terioki and had a very enjoyable time, as the sun was shining, it was a holiday, there was a festive crowd at the station. I went to the Karneyevs making up my mind to be charming and to make frequent return visits. The girls and I concocted an amusing composite letter to send to Boris.

I sometimes thought of Nina. But, my God, what a wonderful thing is freedom! Just the feeling of not being tied to anyone!

On the 24th the building superintendent[1] came to me wanting to establish which category in the Militia Reserve I was, first or second. On learning

---

1 This functionary had, and still has, an official position in city administrations in both pre- and post-Revolutionary Russia, where the overwhelming majority of the population lives in very large buildings with a great many apartments in them. The position is an administrative as well as a janitorial one and is used to provide information on who lives where and does what.

that I was the second, he told me I would not be required; the authorities were interested only in the first. In general the news about this was becoming less worrying; at least I would not need to worry about it until the autumn.

Mama was beginning to get herself organised to go to the Caucasus. I told her I would not be coming to Yessentuki,[1] but would stay with friends in and around the capital. Zoya sometimes came into the city from Terioki, and would ring up and invite me there. 'Why can't you compose something for us? You really are such a swine, Sergusya!'

I sat down at the piano and decided to write some little squibs of pieces, 'doggies'[2] as I used to call them eight years or so ago. And the doggies started to grow incredibly easily, I liked them very much and they emerged with impeccable finish. Three of them were completed on the first day: for Zoya (No. 6), for Lida (No. 5) – with a peal of bells to celebrate her marriage – and for Katya Schmidthof (No. 16). I decided to dedicate all of these doggies to my friends. That'll teach you, Nina, to write such rubbish about me to Boryusya. Another two were quickly added (one of them for Tanyusha), and then the new-born opus (22 in prospect) temporarily lapsed into silence.[3]

On the 29th I travelled out along the Nikolayevsky line[4] as I needed to find a dacha to rent. My first idea was to look for somewhere near Lyuban, but then I decided to try Ushki. I enjoyed playing the part of a Petrograd 'dachnik' stalking a dacha. The weather was superb, and I had a keen sense of pleasure as I walked among the green fields of Ushki: its marvellous blend of meadows, fields, rivers, and groups of trees immediately predisposed me towards Ushki. Isolated, well-spaced-out dachas – perfect! But it proved almost impossible to find one. In the first place I did not know how to search: there were no 'To Let' signs or notices, and it seemed that every one was taken. The cottages were delightful, but there was no sign of any elegant population. I asked someone I met and it was clear that everywhere was, in fact, full, except for one empty upstairs apartment, so cheap that I mistook the rent for the whole summer for just a week, but it was not suitable.

I got on the train again and went back to Sablino, nearer to the city, exactly an hour from Petrograd. I liked it there also, because in the little shop at the station I immediately found my favourite chocolate. After wandering about for two hours I found a marvellous little dacha, quite new, painted yellow

---

1 Spa resort in the Caucasus. See *Diaries*, vol. 1, pp. 105–8 and *passim*.
2 Prokofiev's childhood friend from Sontsovka, the musical vet Vasily Morolyov (1880–1949), came up with this description of the piano pieces the young composer wrote in 1907, because of their 'painful bite'. See *Diaries*, vol. 1, pp. 6, 180–81, 235n and *passim*.
3 The numbers refer to these three pieces' placing in the eventually resulting opus, *Mimolyotnosti* (*Visions fugitives*), Op. 22, the collection of which they are the harbinger.
4 This is the main railway line from St Petersburg to Moscow and the south. After 1924 it was known as the Oktyabrsky line, and its terminus, the former Nikolayevsky Station at the end of Nevsky Prospect, became the Moskovsky Station.

and very attractive. It stood apart from all the others, beside a stream, with woods on two of its sides, a view of an old-fashioned church peeping through the trees on the third side; only from the fourth side could the house be seen at all, and that from some way off. In short, there were no people at all, which is how I wanted it, and it was simplicity itself, the owner a very nice old lady living upstairs, who for 45 roubles let me have the two downstairs rooms with a balcony, a kitchen, a hall, a store room and so on. Against it were: (1) there was no furniture, but bearing in mind how cheap the rent was, for the vast expense of 20 roubles I could buy a couple of beds, a table and chairs, and the landlady promised to provide an armchair; (2) the stream might make it so damp that I might get rheumatism or a fever, and there might be God alone knows what nasty bugs in the plaster. But for now it was so bright and warm and sunny that the damp did not seem to be a problem. I paid a deposit and returned to the city, happy to have more or less settled the business.

July

At the beginning of July Mama left for the Caucasus. I had not said anything to her about Nina. This was clearly worrying her, and she made several discreet attempts to find out how matters stood. Eventually, just before she left, I told her that everything between Nina and me was over. Mama went off in an excellent frame of mind, seen off at the station by me and Marfusha.[1] The next day Marfusha went to a monastery, the servant was let go, and I was alone in the apartment, although I had assured Mama before she left that I would be going straight away to Pavlovsk[2] or Terioki. At first I was afraid I would not like sleeping on my own in such a large, empty flat, but as it turned out, it was quite fine. I took my meals at the Tsarskoye Selo station, a short six-minute walk away where the food was very good, and at home there was plenty of boiled water with a selection of powders to make lemonade, kvass,[3] different kinds of chocolate, and so on, and the wherewithal to make pastry. I decided that as I was due to perform in Pavlovsk on the 7th,

---

1 Maria Grigorievna Prokofieva's housemaid.
2 Pavlovsk, about twenty miles from the centre of St Petersburg, is named after the Emperor Paul, son of Catherine The Great, who in 1780 commissioned the Scottish architect Charles Cameron to design for her son a Grand Palace and an enormous English park. In 1837 Pavlovsk became the destination of the first railway line to be built in Russia, dignified by a magnificent station modelled on the English Vauxhall pleasure garden. (This is why the Russian word for a railway station is Voksal.) In turn the Vauxhall Pavilion became known for its excellent properties as a concert hall, and regular seasons of concerts were given there, a further attraction for Petersburgers wanting a day out in a magnificent park. Johann Strauss II, Liszt and Schumann were among the many international celebrities who performed there.
3 A very low-alcohol drink made from mildly fermented bread, often flavoured with berries and soft fruits.

it was not worth before then removing to Zet (as I had referred to Sablino in conversation with Eleonora).

Jurgenson has printed the score and parts of the First Piano Concerto and sent me off-prints, which are very good. On the 7th I performed it with Fitelberg in Pavlovsk. I got to know Fitelberg during the winter; he is an excellent conductor from Warsaw who took up an appointment this year with the Musical Drama Theatre in Petrograd, and was invited jointly with Aslanov to conduct in Pavlovsk. Aslanov was indignant that I am now, traitorously in his opinion, playing with Fitelberg (there is no love lost between the two conductors) but all I had done was accept the first engagement offered, and do not consider myself in any way to blame.

Lida and Zoya came to the concert, both very pretty, we went out to the park and strolled and played around there for so long we were almost late for the concert. The first item on the programme was *Dreams*, which received a respectable but rather listless performance. I have never heard it played really well. Then I played the First Piano Concerto. Fitelberg loves the work and conducted it with stunning engagement and passion. I likewise felt the Concerto tremendously alive in my fingers, and took a tempo half as fast again as I had ever done before. The orchestral playing was not quite immaculate but executed with enormous enjoyment, and in the rehearsal the musicians accorded me so clamorous an ovation I was quite taken by surprise. Altogether, therefore, this was a most auspicious performance, crowned with a striking success. For an encore I bashed my way through the whole of the First Sonata and thought that would be plenty to satisfy the audience, but after it I had to come and take two more bows. The scene in the artists' room afterwards was a merry one, with great crowds of people: the Karneyeva sisters, the Damskaya sisters, the Andreyevs husband and wife, some critics, my chess-playing friend Tereshchenko,[1] the violinist Akhron[2] and many others. Zaitsev was full of effusive compliments, but what pleased me most was his judgement that, of course, I played the First Sonata much better than Romanovsky. The success Romanovsky has had with this Sonata has always disturbed my peace of mind.

After the concert I escorted Lida and Zoya to Tsarskoye, where they were spending the night with Zorya,[3] and then made my way back to Pavlovsk to stay with the Andreyevs. Next morning I set off back to where the Karneyeva sisters had spent the night, so that I could go for a walk with Zoya. Our plan was to walk back into town, and while I was waiting for her at the gates of the dacha, I fell to studying the list of residents, since there was not just one

---

1   N. S. Tereshchenko, a chess-playing acquaintance from a wealthy Petersburg family. See *Diaries*, vol. 1, pp. 345, 487, 582–4.
2   Ibid., vol. 1, p. 4n.
3   Grevs.

dacha there but six. What was my astonishment when I read the name of Meshchersky, and remembered that they had been planning to come and stay somewhere along this road. With an uncommon turn of speed I took myself out through the gates and waited for Zoya at a safe distance away. Not for nothing is it said that the murderer is always drawn back to the scene of his crime!

On the 19th, which was a Sunday, I went out to Terioki, where of course I had a very enjoyable time with the Karneyeva girls.

On the 21st I returned to Pavlovsk for another performance. What had happened was that because of the rivalry between the conductors it had been decided that I should divide my performances between the two of them: I should have played the Second Concerto with Aslanov a week after the First with Fitelberg, but since the original fee I had been promised of 100 roubles for each appearance was later reduced to 50, I derided them for being a bunch of miserable skinflints and said that was it, I was not going to play again. However, a week later Diederichs[1] asked me 'as a personal favour to him' to play my Second Sonata and said he would pay 150 roubles for both appearances. 'As a personal favour to him' I agreed, and so performed again on the 21st. Before the concert I went to offer my condolences to Anna Grigorievna,[2] whose eighteen-year-old son (from her first husband) had been killed in the war. As I came through the garden gate I saw Anna Grigorievna, her sister, Vera Nikolayevna and Talya, the two latter in the process of bidding farewell to the two former. I had no chance to withdraw, since Anna Grigorievna had already called out: 'Ah, Seryozhenka!' when she saw me, so I approached the group.

Anna Grigorievna was standing to one side, apart from the others, and this is what saved me. I greeted Anna Grigorievna and then her sister, who engaged me in conversation for ten seconds; these seconds were enough for Vera Nikolayevna, separated from me by the table, to make a move towards the gate still talking to Anna Grigorievna and not looking at me. Only Talya, who was timidly pressing up to her mother, glanced over at me. I bowed, and she responded. Vera Nikolayevna, standing with her back to me, ostentatiously went on talking to Anna Grigorievna for about a minute, and then went away. Anna Grigorievna asked no questions, and I decided she must already be apprised of the situation. Having expressed my sympathy in her loss, after five minutes I took myself off as I was in a hurry to get to the concert.

My performance of the Second Sonata followed a symphony by Kalinnikov. Playing a solo piece in the middle of an orchestral concert, with no

---

1 Andrey Diederichs and his brother Leonid were piano manufacturers and also promoted concerts. *Diaries*, vol. 1, p. 687.
2 Zherebtsova-Andreyeva. Ibid., p. 279n and *passim*; see also p. 5, n. 2.

orchestral backing, is a rather dispiriting thing to do. There is something rather lonely and ineffectual about it, all on one's own on a huge stage surrounded by empty music desks and abandoned instruments, nothing to inspire one. Also, today there was a lot of noise and coming and going in the hall. However, I decided to pull myself together and concentrate, for therein lies the key to a good performance. The Sonata was very well received, less tumultuously than on the previous occasion, but some parts of the audience, numbering perhaps a couple of hundred, applauded with amazing vigour and insistence, compelling me to play four encores, the stage management even having to douse and then again bring up the lights.

Fewer people came backstage to the artists' room today, but there were a few new faces – Marusya Pavlova,[1] tanned to the colour of parchment and with teeth like pearls, and then an apparition from the past in the shape of Sonya Esche with her *bien-aimé*, an elegant gent of some forty summers. Zaitsev was full of praise for my music. Eleonora was not present, probably as a protest against my not having come to see her at Sestroretsk and for concealing from her the whereabouts of Zet.

Svetlov,[2] the ballet critic and friend of Diaghilev, told me that he had received a cable from the impresario: what is happening with Prokofiev? It was perfectly true that 3 June was the latest date by which, to quote from my contract with him, I should have presented myself 'in whichever European city Diaghilev is at that time', in order to finish and polish the ballet in his presence. Ten days before this date I had myself received a telegram: 'Oubliez pas, que 3/7 devez être Lausanne.' And on the 2nd I cabled him back: '4 tableaux composés. Faut-il continuer ou vaut pas la peine?'[3]

My meaning was this: I was in breach of contract, so was the ballet to be scrapped or should it in any case be completed? It was important to have his confirmation that it should be completed so that he would still be obliged to pay the three thousand, and not reduce the sum due on the grounds that I had not fulfilled the terms of the contract. I am sure that when Diaghilev received my telegram he will have stamped his foot and cursed me in the most dreadful language, but he sent no reply and was now asking for news through Svetlov, not deigning to honour me with a personal communication. I asked Svetlov to cable back that because of military-service obligations

---

1   Maria (Marusya) Pavlova, a singing student from the Conservatoire. See *Diaries*, vol. 1, pp. 200–201, 377 and *passim*.
2   Valerian Svetlov, ballet critic and one of Diaghilev's original Ballets Russes support group in St Petersburg, especially in its early years. Svetlov's monograph on Anna Pavlova, written and published in emigration in Paris (M. de Brunoff, Paris, 1922), with its wealth of beautifully reproduced photographs and costume designs by Bakst and other artists, remains one of the most intelligent and passionate portrayals in print of a great artist of the dance.
3   'Don't forget that on 3/7 you should be in Lausanne.' 'Four scenes completed. Should I continue or is it not worth it?'

I was not able to travel at the present time, and in addition took advantage of the choreographer Sergey Grigoriev,[1] who was travelling out to meet Diaghilev, to hand-carry a letter. In this letter I explained that as it was now clear the war was not going to be over by the spring, it seemed unlikely there would be a season in Paris, therefore there was no urgency for me to complete the ballet. I had to write the letter in French, so that the international censor could understand its contents and pass it.

My friends Bashkirov and Zakharov failed to gladden my heart with any letters: Bashkirov sent a quantity of pointless postcards, saying no more than 'Sending you greetings', while Zakharov[2] stayed completely silent, evidently as a direct consequence of Nina's letter to him, which had embarrassed him.

And so, after my performance of the Sonata in Pavlovsk, I returned to Zet. I was very happy on the journey, it was so green and quiet there, and no one knew where I had hidden myself, but I was extremely disconcerted when I arrived to find that in my absence an upright piano had been brought in, and some of the neighbours had read a review in the newspapers about Prokofiev. Putting these two facts together they worked out that I must be this person, a famous artist, and needless to say the news generated great excitement in this remote backwater. I was furious, said there were a great many people with the same name as mine, and I had nothing whatsoever to do with this man, I was a normal, decent human being. I don't know whether they believed me, but seeing how angry I was, at least they pretended they did.

---

1 Sergey (Serge) Grigoriev (1883–1968) was the indispensable ballet-master for the Ballets Russes repertoire, having been recommended to Diaghilev by Mikhail Fokine. After Diaghilev's death he continued in this role for Col. De Basil's Ballet Russe de Monte Carlo, and well into the 1950s for the Royal Ballet in London. He was famous for his encyclopaedic knowledge of the detailed choreography of the entire Ballets Russes repertoire, which enabled him to rehearse any production that needed to be revised.
2 A slip of the pen? It was Boris Bashkirov, not Boris Zakharov, to whom Nina had written.

1916

1 January

Devil take it, my Diary lapsed into complete suspended animation for the year which has just come to an end! (By the way, must train myself to write the date with a 6 from now on). I promise to be more punctilious.

Slept until twelve. Composed some of my *Gamblerette*; I'm glad to have got past the boring part with Astley, although for Coates[1] I will have to make an effort with the languid Englishman, seeing that relative to the novel I have already cut his part severely. Am impatient for Babulenka's arrival – a little while yet to wait, though.[2] This is the plan: in January finish Act II (in spite of a two-week interruption around the performance of *Ala and Lolli*). In February, compose Act III – a short one, and attractive. And by the end of March be full steam ahead on Act IV. Then the opera will be 'in principle' ready and can be shown to any appropriate person.

I am not paying any more calls, but went in just to offer New Year greetings to Eleonora, where swilling three glasses of champagne served to addle my brains slightly. Tanya came while I was at the Ruzskys,[3] and we revived our old friendship. I was friendly, silver-tongued and generally rather controlled.

Returning home I found an incredible thing had happened – the flat had

1 Albert Coates (1882–1953), English conductor born in Russia, a committed and consistent supporter of Prokofiev. He conducted at the Mariinsky from 1910, becoming Principal Conductor from 1914 to 1919. Coates subsequently became well known in London (Covent Garden; Principal Conductor of the London Symphony Orchestra), America and South Africa. See *Diaries*, vol. 1, p. 655 and *passim*.

2 One consequence of the gap in diary-writing for which Prokofiev berates himself in the first entry of the New Year is that this is the first we have been told about the start of work on *The Gambler*. But in his *Short Autobiography*, written for *Sovetskaya Muzyka* in Moscow in 1941 to mark his fiftieth birthday, we learn that in the autumn of 1915, just after a galvanic conversation with Albert Coates at the Mariinsky Theatre in the course of which Coates airily said: 'Write your *Gambler*, and we'll stage it', he started work on it immediately. (*Sergey Prokof'iev, Kratkaya Avtobiografiya (Short Autobiography)* in *Materialy, Dokumenty, Vospominaniya*, edited by S. I. Shlifshteyn (Gosudarstvennoye Muzykal'noye Izdatel'stvo, Moscow 1956).) By the end of 1915 he was already well into Act II. Mr Astley and Babulenka ('Grandma') are two of the characters; the other principals unhappily swimming in the goldfish bowl of the Grand Hôtel-Casino in Roulettenberg are the General, the General's ward Polina, his demi-mondaine inamorata Blanche, the hero Alexey and the malignantly shady Marquis.

3 The Ruzsky family consisted of Nikolay, his wife Olga, his daughters Tatyana (Tanya) and Irina (Ira), with both of whom Prokofiev had a mostly but not invariably prickly relationship, and his son Nikolay (Kolya). Ruzsky, a wealthy music-lover and passable amateur cellist for whom Prokofiev wrote his *Ballade*, Op. 15, became a close friend and helpful supporter, and Prokofiev often enjoyed the lavish hospitality he dispensed. Ibid., p. 77, and *passim*.

been burgled while Mama and the servant were out. On the floor in front of every table and cupboard was a small mountain of upended contents. I suffered the loss of 200 roubles (alas for my First Concerto) and Mama all her jewellery and our silver. We then had to put up with policemen hanging about until four in the morning asking questions and writing in their notebooks, stolidly making a detailed inventory of what had been stolen. I gathered up my scattered letters and mentally composed a letter to Jurgenson requesting a fresh injection of funds, but I was not terribly upset. At least they had not touched *The Gambler*! Mama was distraught.

2 January

The aftermath of yesterday's disorder did not allow much time for composition. The Marquis is having it out with Alexey. What should be happening is that Alexey's material is derived from his previous conversation with the General, while the Marquis's should likewise derive from his rejoinder to the General, but for some reason I am writing new music for this scene.

Here is a remarkable fact: before Christmas Bashkirov took me to see Semyonov, a Privy Councillor,[1] where a clairvoyant was telling fortunes, a young girl between nine and twelve years old, staring into a glass of water with something in it. She trotted out a load of the usual bland, everyday nonsense ('Your bride will be smaller than you and dark-haired' – well, all women are smaller than me and most of them have dark hair!) but then she said: 'Has anyone stolen anything from you recently?' 'No.' 'Well, take care: they're going to.' Unquestionably shares in Semyonov, with his vulgar spiritualism and those 'spirits of the underworld' he is always talking about, have risen.

Today Mama continues to grieve over the injury she has suffered. I ostentatiously affect to despise this malign turn of fate and am in a cheerful mood.

The traditional Conservatoire party has been transmogrified into a concert with a long interval. I always used to go to these affairs and enjoyed them, but today I hardly knew anyone there and generally am finding I have outgrown the Conservatoire. But I was not too bored, since I found myself in the company of the prince[2] and Eleonora, who was performing. In the artists' room Ziloti invited Glazunov[3] to his house for the first time; Glazunov seemed very dubious and looked away.

---

1   Semyonov was a *Kamerger*, an Imperial Court appointment, the second-highest rank in the unwieldy table of ranks established by Peter the Great that survived until the Revolution. The equivalent in the Civil Service was a substantive privy councillor, and in the military, a general.
2   Boris Bashkirov's nickname.
3   Alexander Glazunov (1835–1936) composer and teacher, the first and, along with Rimsky-Korsakov, for many years most prominent and gifted of the composers of the Belyayev Circle (if one excepts Scriabin, always an odd one out in this company). Glazunov was appointed

I have decided, as Demchinsky[1] put it, to 'permit myself to risk descending to the level of a salon pianist' and learn some pieces by heart. This happened after Demchinsky had vainly asked me to play something, anything at all, and on receiving the answer that I could not remember anything by heart, he exclaimed: 'Well, when are you going to learn to play properly?' Over the holiday, therefore, I learned some pieces by Chopin and Grieg and feel pleased with myself.

3 January

The prince, enraged that I am not going to dine with him today, has launched an assault on the regularity of my working habits, saying it is not right to spend every day from ten until one on creative labours. This thrust is in response to my teasing him about his Mondays. Nevertheless I did not dine with him, but spent the evening with Demchinsky playing chess. I may say that I had already gained the upper hand in our series of games and ought to have won a straight flush of five–nil – a result that is hard to account for, since Demchinsky is an excellent player. But I lost a rook (something I have not done for a long time) and lost. The match overall now stands at 4–1. After chess we had a long, abstract conversation.

For my repertoire of salon pieces I have been learning two études of Chopin. It is clear that my organ studies (specifically, fingering), have strengthened my fourth and fifth fingers, so that the Etude No. 2 suddenly took off with unexpected velocity.

Director of the St Petersburg Conservatoire in the wake of the student and general political disturbances of 1905, and continued to serve in that capacity through the Revolution and until 1922, emigrating only in 1928. In his *Diaries* and autobiographical writings, and in his letters, Prokofiev makes no secret of his disdain for Glazunov both as a man and, latterly at least, as a composer, but this seems to have been more on account of Glazunov's undoubted streak of conservatism than any real malice on either side, and there are many accounts of his enlightened humanity and generosity to generations of students, notably the young Shostakovich – whose music cannot have been any more congenial to him than Prokofiev's – to counterbalance the unflattering portrait that emerges from the pages of volume 1 of the *Diaries*.

1 Boris Demchinsky (1877–1942), philologist and writer. Prokofiev was much attracted to his personality, wide-ranging literary interests and knowledge, and later enlisted his help in completing the librettos of *The Gambler* and *The Fiery Angel*. 'Still a young man of about thirty, he spoke in tones of great evenness, a slight smile playing about his lips. I thought to myself: what interesting things could be heard from such a man.' (*Kratkaya Avtobiografiya*, in Shlifstheyn, op. cit.) As the years went Prokofiev's respect for his friend's searching intellect, wit and forthright aesthetic judgment only increased. Demchinsky perished tragically of starvation during the 900 terrible days of the Leningrad blockade imposed by the Germans in 1941–44.

4 January

Bashkirov can say what he likes about my regular compositional activities, but today the scene with the Marquis and Alyosha raced ahead and I have almost arrived at the Babulenka. Isn't that marvellous!

At a loose end I telephoned Zakharov but he is not free to play bridge this evening. But then I received from Ziloti a pile of orchestral parts to proof-read. I am thrilled that I am at last going to hear *Ala*, really thrilled, but reading proofs is such a terrible trial.

I read in the newspapers that the Swiss firm of Hoppe & Co. is being taken to court. I was ecstatic at seeing this familiar name in the papers: after all this is the very firm Alexey describes as epitomising solidity in having existed for six generations.[1] And so, the solid firm still exists and is even now as I write being sued in court!

Yesterday I was consulting Demchinsky about the best title for the fourth part of *Ala and Lolli*, concerning Lolli and his pursuit of Ala. I thought of something along the lines of 'Wanderung'. Demchinsky's suggestion was 'Lolli's Pursuit'. Very good.

5 January

Alexey and the Marquis have been put to one side and proof-reading now rules the world. The audience for the Malozemova Competition (for female pianists who have graduated from the Petrograd Conservatoire),[2] which I attended once I had checked everything Ziloti sent me, proved rather more interesting than the contestants. Borovsky,[3] who was on the jury representing

---

1 In Dostoevsky's 'The Gambler', and as adapted in Prokofiev's libretto. Actually, five generations, as Alexey's magnificent invective against German mercantile caution and sanctimonious probity makes clear: 'In turn the eldest son becomes a virtuous "Vater", and the old story begins again. In fifty or sixty years' time the grandson of the original "Vater" will have amassed a considerable sum; and that sum he will hand over to his son, and the latter to *his* son, and so on for several generations; until at length there will issue a Baron Rothschild, or a 'Hoppe and Company', or the devil knows what! Is it not a beautiful spectacle – this spectacle of a century or two of inherited labour, patience, intellect, rectitude, character, perseverance, and calculation, with a stork sitting on the roof above it all? What is more; they think there can never be anything better than this; wherefore, from their point of view they begin to judge the rest of the world, and to censure all who are at fault – that is to say, who are not exactly like themselves. Yes, there you have it in a nutshell. As for me, I would rather grow fat after the Russian manner, or squander my whole substance at roulette. I have no wish to be "Hoppe and Company" at the end of five generations. I want the money for myself, for in no way do I look upon my personality as necessary to, or meet to be given over to, capital. I may be wrong, but there you have it. Those are my views.'
2 Sofia Malozemova (1846–1908) studied with Theodor Leschetitsky and was thus a fellow student, and from 1894 fellow professor at the St Petersburg Conservatoire, of Prokofiev's teacher Anna Yesipova. The piano competition in her memory was established in 1911.
3 Alexander Borovsky, pianist. See *Diaries*, vol. 1, p. 121n and *passim*.

the Moscow Conservatoire, says that thanks to me he is getting his just deserts in Moscow by making propaganda for me and getting plenty of opposition for it. His concert in Petrograd is on the 7th, and he will be playing the 'Scherzo' from Op. 12, the one I have never managed to play decently myself. He told me that that the first half of his programme will consist of new Russian classics: Glazunov, Medtner and myself. He introduced me to a professor of the Saratov Conservatoire, Sklyarevsky.[1] In two weeks' time he is due to give a recital of new compositions, including my 'Scherzo' and 'Gavotte'.[2] Bravo, I have arrived even in Saratov! Dzbanovsky,[3] that apology for a critic from the *Evening Times*, came for a walk with me, sedulously taking my arm; he insisted on giving me his telephone number so that I could pass on all kinds of information about myself for inclusion in the musical pages of his newspaper. All very nice, but the nicest of all was Umnenkaya, *die alte Liebe*.[4] I had not seen her for so long, and she was looking so pretty today that I was even late for my English lesson.

Tomorrow is the first rehearsal for *Ala*, just the strings. I am terribly happy about '*Alochka*'. After all, for two and a half years since the Second Piano Concerto I have not presented any novelties, and at that time it was still my most advanced piece. As a novelty, the *Sinfonietta* is a distinctly old-fashioned one.

6 January

The programme consists mainly of Tcherepnin's *Red Mask*[5] and *Ala*, the rest being trifles, consequently he and I are dividing the rehearsal time between us. According to Tcherepnin: 'If we were both hooligans each of us would be trying to grab extra time from the other. But as in fact what we shall both do is tiptoe delicately and modestly around each other, the outcome will be neither piece being properly rehearsed.' An elaborate thesis, but I soon worked it out: the tactic was to infuse me with feelings of delicacy, and then play on them. The result was that at the first rehearsal Tcherepnin had one hour and forty-five minutes whereas my work had half an hour. And even then he wore an injured expression, as if to say that he had not had time to get through everything he needed to. Because Ziloti had been late with his copyist, I had the parts of only the first two movements, although I must admit they had been excellently copied and checked.

1 Alexander Sklyarevsky, pianist, professor at the Saratov Conservatoire.
2 Op. 12, Nos. 10 and 2 respectively.
3 Alexander Dzbanovsky (1870–1938), composer and critic.
4 Lidia Umnova, a former romantic interest of the composer, nicknamed by him alternately 'Umnenkaya' ('the clever girl') and 'Glupenkaya' ('the stupid girl'). *Diaries*, vol. 1, p. 247 and *passim*.
5 The ballet score *La masque de la mort rouge*, based on Edgar Allan Poe's 'The Mask of the Red Death'. Ibid., p. 684n.

It was definitely a shrewd move on my part to start with the second movement, because the orchestra attacked it with enthusiasm, even seeming to enjoy learning the passage-work. Parts of it sound extremely interesting, and altogether it looks as though '*Alochka*' is going to take off like a rocket. The orchestra played the first movement very well indeed, and it was only in the harmonics that we came to grief. At that point we stopped, since the rehearsal time had run out.

Even though I had only rehearsed for half an hour I was so exhausted that when I got home I had to have a sleep. Afterwards I went back to the competition, but heard nothing interesting and the audience was less interesting today. It was nine o'clock in the evening before the prize was finally awarded to someone called Termen, a young lady unknown to all, so that there was general excited discussion along the lines of 'Can you point out this Termen to me? I'd like to know what she looks like.' Golubovskaya was quite properly awarded the second prize; she never wins but never comes in third either, this is the third time in a row.[1]

7 January

I was intending to proof-read the parts for the remaining two movements, but as I had only received some of the folders from Ziloti, I corrected the *Sarcasms* instead and sent them back to Moscow.[2] In the evening I attended a performance of works by Gnessin,[3] organised by the 'Contemporaries', with whom I have had a falling-out and therefore have not been going to their concerts. All Gnessin's music is cast in the same mould: a minor tonality that maintains an unvarying equilibrium, never deepening to tragedy nor rising to radiance, and is thus dreadfully fatiguing to listen to, not to mention the fact that it is all terribly turgid because there are never any quick tempos. But it is well-written music. What would one not give for just one song by Stravinsky with that spark of life in it! Alchevsky[4] sang wonderfully well. He would be the perfect Alexey: a fine voice and temperament to burn, and such an eager, upturned nose – but he is rather stout, our Alchevsky, could do with massaging away some of that stomach, perhaps?

---

1   Nadezhda Golubovskaya won second prize in the 1913 Rubinstein Competition, at which Prokofiev carried off the first prize and grand piano. See *Diaries*, vol. 1, pp. 658–64 and *passim*.
2   To the publisher, Jurgenson.
3   Mikhail Gnessin (1883–1957). Ibid., vol. 1, p. 498n.
4   Ivan Alchevsky (1878–1917), tenor, principal singer at the Mariinsky and Bolshoy Theatres, guest principal also at the Paris Grand Opéra.

8 January

At the general rehearsal for the IRMS concert (I forced myself to get up early and go and listen to it) I much enjoyed hearing Tchaikovsky's First Symphony, which I hardly know at all. What a delight the first movement is! Borovsky, a fine pianist and a fine musician, played the Korsakov Concerto. After the rehearsal we lunched together at the Astoria, and passed an hour and a half in lively conversation, because from the musical point of view we have the greatest mutual respect for one another.

Ziloti then unloaded on to me a crushing weight of folders bulging with orchestral parts to correct, on which I had to labour until nightfall, but even so managed less than a quarter of them before the throbbing of my temples forced me to desist.

9 January

Today I succeeded in arranging dual rehearsals: one with the strings and one with the wind, proceeding simultaneously in the hall and in the foyer. The string rehearsal was a very lively affair and I brought the violins out in a sweat learning the passage-work. The harmonics were less satisfactory, squealing and out of tune. A lot of the musicians laughed, but I paid no attention. And when some of them pulled indignant faces, seeing for example that they had to play a C while their neighbour in the next desk had a C sharp, I explained as follows: 'The note is written as a C sharp as a convenience to you, rather than D flat, because the voices are progressing in minor ninths with suspended thirds and a flattened fifth.' Not a syllable of this elucidation did they understand, but because I rapped it out in a confident fusillade of incontestable conviction, launching into it without a second's thought the instant the question was raised, they immediately lapsed into silence, unwilling to admit that they had no idea what I was talking about.

At eleven o'clock they had a break after which Tcherepnin and I changed over, he coming to the strings and I taking over the wind. Here things were not so good: an atmosphere of indolence, everything terribly loud, the music more complex than that for the strings, the dissonances sounding more strident and occasioning even angrier grimaces, while I, empathising with the bassoons and horns, could even admit to a certain embarrassment that I was obliging them to make such disagreeable sounds. In addition, from lack of practice, I got extremely tired.

Back at home I read *Satyricon*, ate some mint gingerbread and gradually relaxed until evening. Admittedly, my heart was tired, and the same thing happens with Coates, whom I met today after the rehearsal. Three weeks ago he suffered a heart attack brought on by exhaustion, but is better now. We kissed: he is altogether the most enchanting man.

In the evening the Ruzskys were celebrating their silver wedding. I put on my tails and went to them, looking in first on the IRMS concert, where Tcherepnin and I sat together like a pair of love-birds listening to Borovsky. Malko said to me: 'I'd like to become your impresario and arrange a concert for you. We have to give these "Contemporaries" a poke in the nose, and in any case you haven't played for a whole season!'

A nice idea, although I can't summon up much enthusiasm. I only wish Malko's idea had been a different one: his wife, Stepanova,[1] has indicated she would like to perform my songs. Now, if only she could be put together with Alchevsky, we might really have something to talk about.

At the Ruzskys all was full evening dress, *décolleté*, lavish hospitality for the world and his wife, and a grand musical entertainment with vocal and string quartets and Ziloti playing piano duets with Romanovsky. Both quartets badgered me with requests to write works appropriate to their ensembles. I purposely kept my distance from Mlle Kishinskaya,[2] knowing that her sister was a friend of Nina's, and fearing unwanted conversation. But knowing also that this same sister had recently run off with some man or other, towards the end of the evening I had quite a jolly talk with her, and to the inscription on her card penned by Kedrov,[3] a professor of singing at our Conservatoire, who was clearly besotted by her, I added a series of question marks in front of the admirable qualities he had listed as possessed by her, plus a postscript: 'Nevertheless, you are quite nice.' In response to which she shrugged her shoulders.

The dancers danced, a great quantity of wine was drunk, and a highly inebriated Romanovsky, who all through the autumn has been complaining about my criticisms of his Scriabin Fourth Sonata, drank to our intimate *tutoiement* when I clinked glasses with him. This amused me greatly, and created a sensation among Ziloti's children. And no doubt will do so in other quarters as well. Somewhat unsteadily, I went home on foot at seven o'clock in the morning, mildly entertained by my own lack of sobriety.

10 January

Woke sometime after noon with a splitting headache from my drunkenness. Feeling rotten I took some pyramidon[4] and went for an hour's walk, after

1 Yelena Stepanova (1891–1978), lyric/coloratura soprano, later a distinguished prima donna of the Bolshoy Theatre. In 1937 she was named People's Artist of the Soviet Union.
2 Varvara (Varya) Kishinskaya, the younger of two sisters. See *Diaries*, vol. 1, p. 375.
3 Nikolay Kedrov (1871–1940), baritone and founder of the Kedrov Vocal Quartet. This famous male group was toured by Diaghilev, gave concerts and recorded with Chaliapin.
4 Analgesic and anti-fever compound.

which I felt better. Today's rehearsal was a small one just with harps, piano and celesta, arranged by Tcherepnin, and I slept in. Yesterday I asked Ziloti if I could be excused from attending. 'No, better if you do come,' said Ziloti. 'But supposing I oversleep?' 'Well, if you oversleep, don't come.' A profound and perceptive observation.

I corrected some orchestral parts. The prince telephoned and when Mama answered, spoke to her. He asked if I was at home, and on receiving the answer in the affirmative, did not ask to speak to me but rang off after finishing his conversation with Mama. He's got completely out of hand, the little nincompoop. But I'll make him smart for it.

11 January

My absence yesterday has compromised my reputation for reliability in Ziloti's eyes, and at nine o'clock this morning he was on the telephone checking whether I was up and ready to come to the rehearsal. The whole complement was on hand today, with the exception of some percussion instruments, the piano and others of that sort. Once again I began with the second movement, and after several repetitions, not completely devoid of brilliant effects albeit a trifle rough here and there, the orchestra rewarded me with a brief ovation. I certainly was not expecting this, despite the fact that the second movement is the most accessible and orchestras always have a weakness for strongly rhythmically accented pieces that end with a bang. The first half of the opening movement also went surprisingly well, but the second half was lamentable, everything *mezzo-forte*, tentative and muddy. The third movement was likewise undiluted mud, the only convincing sonorities being the sinister bottom Bs near the beginning. But thereafter there was no poetry, no terror, merely an intermediate sort of noise – Chuzhhbog's nocturnal assault on the chained Ala made no effect at all, because the trombones did not play *forte*. 'Lolli's Pursuit' caused the orchestra to burst out laughing, and we did not succeed in getting through 'The Procession of the Sun' to the end. The outcome of the rehearsal was fatigue with no sense of the sonority achieved.

In the afternoon I proof-read the percussion parts, and in the evening played chess with Tyulin[1] – match drawn.

---

1 Yuri Tyulin (1893–1978), musicologist and composer, a distinguished writer on various aspects of music theory and biography, professor at the St Petersburg Conservatoire and later at the Moscow Conservatoire and Gnessin Institute. In 1976 Tyulin wrote an interesting personal memoir about his friendship with the young Prokofiev, 'On the Path to Recognition', for the publication *Sergey Prokof'ev Materialy, Stat'i, Interv'iu* (*Sergey Prokofiev, Materials, Articles, Interviews*), edited by V. Blok (Progress Publishers, Moscow 1976; English translation, 1978). See *Diaries*, vol. 1, p. 791n.

12 January

Today in the rehearsal I was on first. I so harried the orchestra and tortured their brains that by the time Tcherepnin arrived they were hardly in a condition to play at all. We had a full orchestra today. I began with 'The Procession of the Sun', and it seemed not bad, vividly coloured, although I did not completely hear all the sonorities I wanted. I think the flutes were a little too strident at the top of their register. The orchestra no longer laughs during 'Lolli's Pursuit'. I'm not happy with the conjunction of the xylophone and the trumpet. The third movement was very nearly right and I managed to squeeze out really raucous ejaculations from the trombones. The first movement is beginning to make complete sense, too. Much of the piece is turning out marvellously. In the second movement I demanded of the tam-tam and the timpani that they begin at maximum possible volume, and drove them to such a pitch of fury that the uproar they created caused their neighbour, the second trombone, to turn pale, leap up from his seat and cry out: 'I'm going! . . . I'm going! This banging and crashing is simply insupportable!' All in all, though, the second movement was not quite as good as yesterday. I was satisfied with the rehearsal: today for the first time some things began to work, and *Ala* has started to emerge from the shadows.

In the interval I was surrounded by players from the orchestra, and one of them said to me that the constant extreme dissonances had affected his nerves so badly that he was becoming quite ill. He enquired why I should want to write in this way, surely it could not be from the heart so much as the fruit of a distorted and perverse imagination? I replied that it was purely from the heart, otherwise it would have been impossible to engage the orchestra in the way that, for example, the second movement had done. Concerning dissonances, I said that I found them a necessary, stronger and newer means to express my musical thoughts; they were underpinned by a compelling logic and therefore I was confident that sooner or later they would be understood and appreciated. 'If I see people laughing or pulling faces, I don't react because they are not to blame; they have not yet grasped the logic, but when they do, perhaps after five rehearsals, or even after five performances, they will understand them and come to appreciate them.'

I said quite a bit more, citing history, the textbooks of music theory, Japanese music, and finally the fact that sitting in the midst of the orchestra it was hard to get a feeling for the general concept of the music, and that only added to the incomprehensibility. The musician heard me out with interest and from time to time responded to my arguments with expressions of approval. Chernyavsky,[1] a young cellist, gazed at me with adoration in his

---

1 Iosif Chernyavsky. Chernyavsky was also a member of the Jewish chamber group the Zimro Ensemble, for whom later in New York Prokofiev was to write the *Overture on Hebrew Themes*, Op. 34.

eyes and when someone remarked that he was acting like a man in love, he said: 'This is a historic conversation.'

In the afternoon I went to give my good wishes to Tanya Ruzskaya on her birthday and had such difficulty getting away that I missed my English lesson. The evening I spent at home with my Diary and making a few corrections to the orchestral parts.

Tcherepnin has been joking that the public is already gearing up for the 16th: special death-squads are already prowling the streets to catch cats and crush them to death in order to make them soft enough to throw at insolent composers at the concert on the 16th. The price of rotten eggs has gone up, and the only apples left in any quantity in the Sennaya[1] are bad ones ...

13 January

Ziloti did not come to the rehearsal today on the pretext of studying the Grieg Concerto. I was beside myself with rage because the piano was not there, likewise the attendant whose job it is to arrange the stands and seating. In a word, a shambles. As for the actual rehearsal, my reaction was mixed. In one sense it was beginning to come together, but it is still not there. My overriding feeling was one of tiredness, and I definitely put too much strain on my heart whenever I get carried away, I risk doing it real damage soon. Today I had real difficulty getting my breath. Overall, although the players have learned the notes, there is no piano, no nuancing, and all too often the subsidiary material gets in the way of the main subject. If yesterday Tcherepnin emerged discontented from the rehearsal, today it was my turn to be tired, dissatisfied and in a bad temper, even though Ziloti said it sounded splendid. But when a number of people in the orchestra privately expressed their indignation at the appalling music they were being forced to play, Ziloti said to them: 'Quite true, in your position I should not like to play it either, it sounds so awful when you are sitting in the orchestra. But I have been listening from the hall, and there it comes out magnificently.' I was told that Tcherepnin, on hearing these words, clutched his head and exclaimed: 'Have you taken leave of your senses? You're inciting the orchestra to mutiny!!'

In the evening we played bridge first, and then turned to Macao.[2] Boryusya,[3]

1 Sennaya ('Hay') Square, at the junction of Sadovaya Street and Moscow Prospect, had been the site of a horse, cattle and food market since the middle of the eighteenth century. The market was still there in 1916, but was transferred to the other end of Moscow Prospect in the 1930s. Sennaya Square itself was renamed Peace Square in Soviet times, but in 1991 reverted to the name it had borne for two centuries.
2 Card game originally played by colonial officers in the Portuguese colony of Macao, in which the object is to get rid of all the cards in the player's hand by matching them to the upturned card in the undealt deck.
3 Zakharov.

playing for the highest stakes, was completely taken apart and lost 40 roubles. I had some badly needed good fortune and won 25 roubles, very timely since I was poverty-stricken after the burglary and goodness knows when I shall ever get any money from that Judenson.[1] At one o'clock I turned everyone out, because of the rehearsal early tomorrow morning.

14 January

The object of today's rehearsal is to achieve a *piano* and a *forte*, since the music itself has been more or less sorted out. I played through the whole Suite almost without stopping, and everything now seems to be clear. True, there is still no *pianissimo*, only *piano*, and no *fortissimo*, we never get more than *forte*, moreover God only knows what is wrong with the trombones: instead of the 'raucousness' of which Rimsky-Korsakov writes in his orchestration manual, ours sounds more like the buzzing of mosquitoes. Tyulin came to listen, and was ecstatic. He is offering to make a four-hand version of the Suite. I knew him first as a Sokol member, then as a chess-player, and now it turns out that he graduated from the Conservatoire in theory of composition and knows all my music. For the time being we have decided that he should transcribe the *Sinfonietta*.

Tcherepnin said that it is hard to imagine the giant leap I have made in orchestration, especially in *piano* passages, the *fortes* being more conventional. As for the music, he finds that the new work is in many places less strongly individual than my earlier works; there is a good deal of 'Diaghilevshchina' and 'Stravinshchina' in it. Bearing in mind that Tcherepnin's relations with the group tend these days towards the frigid, one might think that in former, happier times this would have been seen as a matter for praise. The most piquant aspect of it is that when in Milan I played excerpts from 'Lolli's Pursuit' to Stravinsky, he and Diaghilev both said: 'You know, the Second Concerto is a better piece, in this one there is . . . how can I put it . . . a bit too much Tcherepnin . . .'

I love being at the Benois[2] 'Thursdays', and spent two happy hours there this evening, having to tear myself away at half-past eleven on account of tomorrow's rehearsal.

Today is the anniversary of my decision to marry Nina, and it is also her name-day. What are my feelings now about the year gone by? Something, in fact, like an interesting fairy-story. It must be conceded that I acted very

---

1 A not very complimentary reference to Prokofiev's publisher, Jurgenson.
2 See *Diaries*, vol. 1, p. 639 and *passim*. The note referring to Mme Benois on p. 267 of vol. 1 is incorrect: this was Alexander Benois's daughter Yelena, not his second wife. Benois was married only once, to the painter Anna Kind.

boldly. And Nina was magnetically attractive. Today I have reverted to my confirmed bachelor status, but if the whole affair had come off, it would of course have been very nice. Returning home from the Benois', I met Umnenkaya and walked her home.

15 January

General rehearsal. Benois, Coates, Malko, Steinberg,[1] Shteiman,[2] Walter,[3] Nurok, the Damskaya sisters, Mama, my aunts. I addressed the trombones, asking them to play at maximum volume. The work was played right through without stopping, and pretty well – the eighth rehearsal, after all. At the end, some of the orchestra applauded, fifteen or so booed, and the remainder indignantly reproached their colleagues: 'That's enough! Stop that, it's uncalled-for . . .' Ziloti was in total ecstasy, rushing round the hall shouting: 'A slap! A real slap!' meaning that in this piece I was giving the audience a good slap in the face. As soon as Tcherepnin ascended the podium and I went into the body of the hall, Ziloti and Coates came and sat either side of me and began:

Ziloti: 'Anything you compose I will at once perform . . .'
Coates: 'Whatever you compose we'll put on immediately . . .'
Ziloti: 'What have you ready for next season?'
Coates: 'What stage is the opera at?'
Ziloti: 'I wouldn't put this size of orchestra together for anyone else but you – if you need a hundred and fifty players, that will be fine, no problem.'

Malko was very happy, Nurok absolutely delighted, as was Benois, Steinberg was very critical, Walter benevolent but totally at sea, a bewildered expression on his face. I introduced Coates to Mama and also to Eleonora, who almost fainted with surprise and pleasure.

In the evening I visited Demchinsky. We played chess, and I was annihilated as never before. Demchinsky had yielded to persuasion and attended Bashkirov's latest 'Monday', which he categorised as a 'recasting of the Gospels for two balalaikas, one of which was Boris Verin[5] and the other Privy Councillor Semyonov'.

---

1 Maximilian Steinberg (1883–1946), composer and teacher. Much loved by his teacher (and eventual father-in-law) Rimsky-Korsakov, he never fulfilled his early promise as a composer but became a greatly respected teacher of composition in the Rimsky tradition, numbering Shostakovich among his pupils. See *Diaries*, vol. 1, p. 44 and *passim*.
2 Mikhail Shteiman (?–1949), conductor. He was later to become Principal Conductor of the Ukrainian National Opera. Ibid., pp. 128, 435–41 and *passim*.
3 Viktor Walter (1865–1935), who in addition to being a music critic was the leader of the Mariinsky Theatre Orchestra. Ibid., p. 674.
4 The pen name of Boris Bashkirov, under which he wrote poetry.

16 January

I have grown so used to going to rehearsal every morning that it seemed strange not to be doing so today.

Before the concert I dictated a review of my own concert for Dzbanovsky, the critic of the *Evening Times*, an utter peasant but a very nice fellow, who is ill and unable to attend the concert. He asked me to give him a report on the Suite and state frankly what in it is worthy of attention. Skinflint Jurgenson has sent a note, laconic to the point of discourtesy, to the effect that he will not make me an advance. This very day I intend to canvas with Ossovsky[1] the possibility of Russian Music Editions.

Arriving at the Mariinsky Theatre I felt on top form. I had a talk with the timpanist and the tam-tam player, asking them to begin the second movement with as much power as possible, and then with a sense of enjoyment took my place at the conductor's stand. There was applause in the hall, which I turned to acknowledge with a bow. The audience quickly settled in their seats; the hall was full. I saw the prince in the front row. Was Meshcherskaya there, I wondered. I knew they had subscription tickets in the fifth row on the left. Imagine, a year ago I had proposed to Nina! The Suite began in fine style, but when the first movement died away there was silence from the audience. The second movement begins with a wild explosion on the timpani, which although loud was sadly not ear-splitting enough, nor was it later on. Nevertheless, the skin of the timpani split, causing Ziloti to tell me later he wanted to donate it to me as a souvenir. There was quite lively applause after the 'Dance of the Spirits', which made me, and even the orchestra happy, and we took a short pause to get our breath back.

'Night' went well, although lacking the last ounce of refinement, and the reaction was muted. 'Lolli's Pursuit' was exuberant, and 'The Procession of the Sun' flooded the room with sound – I was thrilled. The audience booed and clapped, clapped and booed. I left the stage, but straight away returned, bowed once more and thanked the leader for the orchestra's performance. Someone on the back desk of the violins booed vigorously, at which Chernyavsky rushed across to try to quieten him down. I shook his hand and went out to Ziloti in the artists' room. Ziloti showed me two wreaths, from the Ruzskys and the Gessens[2] (I found the latter especially flattering) which for some unknown reason he had not arranged to be presented to me on

---

1   See *Diaries*, vol. 1, p. 153n.
2   Iosif Gessen (1886–1943), lawyer and journalist, editor of *Rech* (*Speech*). Gessen was a friend and political ally in the Second Duma of Pavel Milyukov, the Constitutional Democrat leader, and went with him into exile after the Revolution, basing himself in Berlin where he edited the émigré newspaper *Rul'* (*The Helm*), a sister publication to Milyukov's Paris paper *Poslednye Novosti* (*Latest News*).

stage (the swine!). I went out once more to take a bow on the forestage. The entire audience was on its feet by now, cheering, clapping and catcalling. I took several more bows.

Coates came backstage and congratulated me heartily. Then Aslanov informed me that Glazunov had ostentatiously walked out of the hall during the 'Procession of the Sun'. Ironically, that very afternoon I had gone into the Conservatoire to invite him to the concert. In our box, to which I made my way from the artists' room, were Mama, Eleonora, Asafyev,[1] Malko and Myaskovsky – who had that morning come from Revel especially for *Ala*, going back tomorrow morning.[2] He was a little bemused by the piece, but liked it all the same. Nurok and Nouvel confessed that when I had played them excerpts from the ballet the previous winter they had not understood anything of the music.[3] Now old Nurok was especially delighted with it. Demchinsky did not like it all, and his wife none of it.

After the concert I had supper with Ziloti, and spoke with Ossovsky about Russian Music Editions,[4] where they have a new system in operation: if a composer is invited to join the list, he is accepted lock, stock and barrel. 'And if you will give me authority to do so, I will put the question of your joining the roster on the agenda for our next Shrovetide meeting.' This is splendid, to hell with Jurgenson. Ziloti asked me about works for next season; so far there is only *Autumnal*. But I mentioned a whole series of piano, vocal and chamber works, which could make up an ensemble programme. Ziloti took warmly to the idea, but said there was no reason to wait until the autumn to arrange this, it should be done right away. We had a long discussion about which performers should take part; particularly desirable from my point of view would be Alchevsky, Popova,[5] and Beloúsov.[6]

---

1 Boris Asafyev (1884–1949), who as well as being a prolific composer wrote music criticism under the pseudonym Igor Glebov, became one of the earliest and staunchest propagandists for Prokofiev's music, earning the dedication of his First Symphony, the 'Classical'. Three of his own twenty-eight ballets (*The Fountains of Bakhchisaray*, *The Flames of Paris*, *The Stone Guest*) are still in the repertory, but after the Revolution as a composer he concentrated mainly on the relatively safe area of music for children. He never moved away from his native city and survived the 900 days of the Leningrad blockade from September 1941 to January 1944. See *Diaries*, vol. 1, p. 5 and *passim*.
2 Myaskovsky, who as a former engineer officer in the Russian Army had been called up for service in the First World War, first saw active service in Galicia, after which he had been seconded to the naval garrison in Revel (now Tallinn in Estonia).
3 Ibid., entry for 27 November 1914, p. 784.
4 The music publishing house established by Serge Koussevitzky and his wife Natalya to publish works by Russian composers. Like the Belyayev Editions, RME (aka Russische Musikverlag, Editions Russes de musique) was based for copyright reasons in Berlin.
5 Yelena Popova, soprano. Ibid., vol. 1, pp. 286, 318, 592.
6 Yevsey Beloúsov (1881–1945), cellist sonata partner of Alexander Borovsky, gave many first performances including Myaskovsky's First Cello Sonata. He left Russia in 1922 and settled in

17–24 January

Lots of reviews, praise from Gessen, endearments from the Ruzskys, peace overtures from Boris Nikolayevich,[1] and a general feeling of exhaustion after the intensive work of the past week. For about three mornings I worked on the Babulenka, the composition of whose music flowed with delicious ease. The aroma of Mother Russia must fill the stage from the moment she appears in her wheelchair. I called on the Zilotis, Madame having invited me to visit them without ceremony. They were all charming to me, and asked me to lunch, to dine, and so on and so forth.

I went to a 'Contemporaries' evening at which were performed works by Obukhov,[2] who is said 'to surpass even Prokofiev'. The effect in the hall was reminiscent of the first performance in Russia of music by Schoenberg, given by myself five years previously, in June 1911, at one of the Evenings of Contemporary Music: people laughed loudly, left the hall clicking their heels as they went, and so forth.[3] At the end of the concert I almost had my arm torn off by people hanging on to it asking: 'Well, what did you think of it?' My opinion was as follows: interesting harmonic invention, but thematically dull – routine even, fragmented, and sterile. All this I can forgive, but the last-named is particularly dispiriting.

25 January

In the evening I went to see Rausch von Traubenberg,[4] my old friend from the Chess Society. Since then he has fought a duel, married, left the capital to live in the country, but now he has now returned and extends the most pressing invitations. Today was the name-day of his wife, a singer and delightful, vivacious lady. There were a lot of attractive people there and I enjoyed myself.

New York, where he continued to perform, becoming professor at the Juilliard School of Music. He had partnered Prokofiev in the premiere of the *Ballade* in Moscow in January 1914. *Diaries*, vol. 1, pp. 470, 586–9 and *passim*.

1. Bashkirov.
2. Nikolay Obukhov (1892–1954). Obukhov was certainly not short of innovative ideas; influenced both by Scriabinesque mysticism and dodecaphonic techniques, his large-scale oratorios with titles such as *Nicolas l'illuminé* and *The Book of Life* employed *inter alia* electronic instruments of his own devising, notably a 'croix sonore' in the form of a cross. Obukhov left Russia in 1919 and lived in Paris for the remainder of his life.
3. Ibid., pp. 214–15.
4. Baron Konstantin Rausch von Traubenberg (1871–1935) was an artist, sculptor and chess-player. He had exhibited at the 6th Exhibition of the Society of Russian Artists and at the Paris Exhibition 'New Arts from Russia' in 1908. Ibid, p. 39 and *passim*.

26 January

I overslept and missed my lesson with Handschin.[1]

Mama's name-day, but she is not celebrating it on account of the war and the expense. Visits from relations, and then Boris Nikolayevich. He arrived fresh from his mentor Lotin, a preacher and mesmerist[2] who holds sessions on Tuesdays. Boris invited me to attend one of the sessions with him. I demurred: since Lotin is credited with having detected infernal elements in my *Ala*, would I not therefore be unwelcome in his house? Boris Nikolayevich countered that he had already asked for and obtained permission for me to attend, having recommended me as a person who, although not an adherent of mysticism, possessed a soul of crystalline purity. Thus am I recommended by my good friend Verin.

27 January

Babulenka, and then to the Mariinsky Theatre for the general rehearsal of *The Snowstorm*,[3] a deadly effusion of maudlin anguish by a composer of exalted rank, which induced a level of boredom so profound that it failed even to provoke indignation.

Suvchinsky,[4] with whom friendly relations have been restored, says to me:

---

1   Jacques Handschin, Swiss-born organ professor at the Petrograd Conservatoire. See *Diaries*, vol. 1, p. 784n. In order to stay registered as a student of the Conservatoire, Prokofiev was taking the organ course under Handschin.
2   The Russian word is *magnetizyor*. Towards the end of the eighteenth century, first in Vienna and later in Paris, the German scientist and healer Franz Mesmer had become successful and notorious in equal measure for his claimed identification and exploitation of a vital fluid in the bodies of breathing creatures, including human beings, which could be passed from one to the other by means of 'animal magnetism' (the animal here referring to the Latin word for breath, rather than to distinguish men from beasts). Despite the findings of the Royal Commission established by Louis XVI in 1784 (among whose members was Benjamin Franklin) that the existence of such a fluid was a myth, Mesmer's ideas persisted for many decades, as did lucrative treatment of the credulous according to his principles.
3   *Metel'* (*The Snowstorm*) was an opera by Alexander Taneyev (1850–1918), a distant relation of his better-known namesake. After studying composition with Rimsky-Korsakov, he managed to combine a prolific output as a composer (now almost entirely forgotten) with a senior position (*Oberhofmeister*, in overall charge of ceremonial occasions and Head of the Imperial Chancellery) at the Imperial Court. There was a particular reason for his being close to the imperial couple: he was the father of the notorious Anna Vyrubova, the Empress's closest confidante and go-between with Rasputin. Prokofiev was surely right to despise his opera, but as the *Diaries* later reveal he did turn out to be useful in the matter of securing exemption from the threat of military service.
4   Pierre (Pyotr) Suvchinsky (1892–1985), a wealthy and cosmopolitan man of impressively wide culture, wrote on musical and general cultural matters. In 1915 he founded with Andrey Rimsky-Korsakov, the son of the composer, the journal *Muzykal'ny Sovremennik* (*Musical Contemporary*) and as well as backing it financially was its editor for the two years it existed. After the 1917 February Revolution he subsidised and co-edited with Boris Asafyev another

'I do hope, Sergey Sergeyevich, that you will provide us with a song for our next season.'

A momentary pause ensued, after which I replied: 'But I doubt whether you will be interested in them once Ziloti has already given them a performance.'

A shadow crossed Suvchinsky's face. 'Is he putting on an evening just for you?' 'Yes, he is.'

However, Suvchinsky maintained a tone of friendliness, and said he had one piece of advice for me: not to have Zherebtsova-Andreyeva sing. Of course my first choices would be Alchevsky and Popova. Popova has already shown interest in my songs, but the key is Alchevsky, and he is in Moscow. We await his return and then will get going on the organisation of the concert.

28 January

Yesterday as a result of Zakharov's pleading I organised a bridge evening, which then progressed to a session of Macao, resulting in my being done out of 45 roubles. And this in my present state of penury! I cannot wait to get hold of some money, either from Ziloti for the concert, or if Ossovsky manages to arrange matters, from Russian Music Editions. Oh, what a phalanx of publications I shall have then: the Second Piano Concerto, the *Sinfonietta*, *Dreams*, *Autumnal*, the *Scythian Suite*, the *Ugly Duckling*, seven songs, and before long *The Gambler*, *Maddalena* and the ballet! Not a bad haul!

Finished Act II,[1] three days ahead of schedule. However, there are a few gaps that will need to be filled in.

29 January

Handschin advised me that I must sit my final examination in the spring. That's an interesting thought. He then gently chided me for missing lessons without a reasonable excuse.

Corrected the second proofs of *Sarcasms* and did not find many mistakes. Evidently my proof-reading is improving in accuracy and diligence.

Went to the Sokol, which on account of *Ala* I have not been to for a whole month. I then went on to Boris Nikolayevich, who was ill and feeling sorry

---

short-lived music journal entitled *Melos*. With Andrey Rimsky-Korsakov he had also revived the Evenings of Contemporary Music, which in their new incarnation took place in the Small Hall of the Conservatoire. After emigrating in 1920 Suvchinsky became one of Prokofiev's closest and most trusted friends.

1 Of *The Gambler*.

for himself, and had implored me to go to see him for a chat and to give him the benefit of my advice about something or other. Apparently the mere fact of my presence has a healing effect on him. The matter turned out to be this: his brother in Samara has sent him a present of 50,000 roubles (I held it in my hands, a small packet of rather unprepossessing-looking shares). The question was: to accept them or not to accept them? Was this an expression of brotherly love or rather a desire to show off his millions? The prince said that his first reaction had been to decline the gift, but his mother had expressed such horror at this that now he did not know what to do, and wanted to place himself entirely in my hands.

On reflection, I said I thought Boris Nikolayevich should take the money, in order to avoid unnecessary offence to geese that might in the future lay more golden eggs, but that he should include in his thank-you letter to his brother a request for more clarification of the spiritual motivations underlying the gift, rather than just the details of the shareholding.

30 January

There is something horribly wrong with the trams and the cabs today, it is impossible to get hold of a taxi, and the Bashkirov automobile has broken down, so I spent the night at the prince's. I did not sleep well, mainly because Boris Nikolayevich was declaiming poetry to his sister at the top of his voice until four in the morning, so that it was one o'clock in the afternoon by the time I got home. However, I did manage a few little snippets in the second act. Because of the tram situation my English teacher could not come today, which was a pity.

In the evening BNB was making his debut as a performer,[1] but I defected and went to Ziloti's concert, not only because of the interesting programme, but because I also simply wanted to see people and show myself after the *Ala* scandal.

Kal:[2] 'You're so diabolically talented, quite diabolically! But do tell me, just between ourselves naturally, is there not just a hint here, a tiny hint, of your pulling the audience's leg?' I replied that, greatly though I might enjoy that activity, the price I would have to pay subsequently would be too high. The probity of my honourable past should be all the proof needed that any such suggestion was mistaken.

During the interval, as I was walking through the hall, I caught sight of Nina. She was sitting provocatively on one of the seats, talking to a student.

---

1   As a poetry reciter.
2   Professor Alexey Kal (1878–?) critic and Professor of Music History at St Petersburg University. See *Diaries*, vol. 1, pp. 553, 624, 685 and below, p. 559 and *passim*.

As I passed, I naturally looked the other way. Whether she had also been at the *Ala* concert or whether her mother and sister had come without her, I do not know.

The programme included: a drab but not totally uninteresting piece by Gubenko, *Valisneria*, Steinberg's untalented *La Princesse Maleine*,[1] and Ravel's delicious *Rapsodie espagnole*. I am definitely beginning to like French composers, whereas as recently as last spring, even after Diaghilev's most importunate attempts to persuade me otherwise, I still could not accept what appeared to me their shallowness, their surface glitter without substance or refinement.

Coates was very nice and kissed me five times.

31 January

Filled in some gaps in *The Gambler*. Attended a student concert, at which Anna Grigorievna[2] caressed me with her sweetest smile, to which my response was a coldly formal bow. There was a meeting of the 'Bronze Horseman'[3] committee to which I have elected, at which it was resolved to set up an independent organisation and to commence operations with a concert at Shrovetide, involving member-composers.

Dined at Gessen's with the fashionable Lakiardopolous,[4] who had just returned from travelling through Germany and Austria, and whose newspaper reports had created a stir. A modest, dark-haired young man. In general I love being at the Gessens', where one always hears the latest news.

1 Overture by Maximilian Steinberg to a production of Maeterlinck's 1889 drama *La princesse Maleine*, probably originally intended for Konstantin Mardzhanov's Free Theatre in Moscow, which collapsed in 1913, one of the casualties being this production.
2 Zherebtsova-Andreyeva.
3 The 'Medny Vsadnik' ('Bronze Horseman') Club was one of dozens of literary and arts clubs that flourished in Silver Age St Petersburg; members would gather for discussions, lectures, readings and performances of contemporary literature and music.
4 Sic. Prokofiev is referring to the polyglot and polymath Michael Lykiardopoulos, journalist, critic, secretary of the Moscow Art Theatre and Russia correspondent of John Middleton Murry's modernist London art and literature quarterly *Rhythm*. According to R. H. Bruce Lockhart, who met him in Moscow when he (Lockhart) was serving as British Vice-Consul, and who employed Lykiardopoulos as propaganda agent for British interests in Russia during the First World War, sending him out disguised as a Greek tobacco merchant on the hazardous undercover mission referred to through Austria and Germany, '"Lyki" was a strange, lovable creature; one-third Greek, one-third Russian, and one-third English . . . He had real literary flair, an excellent Russian prose style, and a quite remarkable knowledge of eight or nine European languages. He knew most of the great writers of Europe and had translated their best works into Russian. It was through him that I first met H. G. Wells, Robert Ross, Lytton Strachey, Granville Barker, Gordon Craig, Aleister Crowley, not to mention numerous hangers-on of literature who came to worship at the shrine of Russian art. In his spare time he acted as ballet critic for one of the leading Moscow newspapers. He knew everyone in the literary, artistic, and dramatic world of Moscow, and, through him, many doors, which otherwise would have remained closed, were opened to me.' R. H. Bruce Lockhart, *Memoirs of a British Agent* (Putnam, London, 1932).

According to Gessen, Sazonov[1] has become interested enough in my music to listen to some of it (the *Sinfonietta*, apparently), but was not especially taken with it.

1 February

A year ago today I set off for Italy. Overall it seems that the year must have been a fairly exciting one, seeing how many anniversaries it produced.

Baron Driesen telephoned. Three years ago or so his group established the Antique Theatre.[2] Now he wants to get it going again and is inviting me to participate in the management committee, the other members being Gorodetsky, Benois, Roerich,[3] and Yakovlev.[4] Recently I seem to be spending my whole life in one committee after another.

In the evening I went to see Eleonora, who has begun taking English lessons from the same English teacher as mine. But this evening I started to teach her Italian, exactly a year after I first started on it myself. Interestingly, she is picking it up more quickly, but at the same time it helps me bring my own knowledge into order.

2 February

Made a start on Act III, which is pouring out of me in an unstoppable torrent. This is a short act, but a terribly interesting one, with what will be an especially marvellous passage with Babulenka following the loss of all her money at the tables. Although I do not start composing very early in the morning, not before eleven, today I worked until three so did not stop for lunch until then, and afterwards went for a walk.

---

1   Sergey Sazonov, Foreign Minister in the Tsarist Government. See *Diaries*, vol. 1, p. 718.
2   The Antique Theatre was the creation of the theatre historian and administrator Baron Nikolay Driesen von Osten, who persuaded many eminent actors, directors, academics, designers and musicians, including the opera and theatre director Alexander Sanin, the painter and designer Nicholas Roerich, Benois, the musicologist and historian Livery Sacchetti and Glazunov, to collaborate with him in his dream of re-creating authentic mediaeval mystery and miracle plays. The Antique Theatre opened for a single season in 1907 but then closed again until 1911–12, when it was revived for a season of Spanish plays by Cervantes, Lope de Vega and Calderón. As well as his enthusiasm for re-creating mediaeval and other early theatre, Baron Driesen von Osten was the literary censor to the Directorate of the Imperial Censors. He emigrated to Paris in 1919. See *Diaries*, vol. 1, pp. 514 and 571.
3   Nicholas Roerich (1874–1947), painter, scenic designer (of *inter alia* the Ballets Russes production of *The Rite of Spring*), and theosophist. Ibid., p. 514.
4   Alexander Yakovlev (1887–1938) ('Sasha Yasha'), painter, graphic artist (a regular contributor to Prokofiev's favourite magazine *Satyricon*) and scenic designer, known for incorporating neo-classical stylistic elements into his modernist canvases, and for his interest in African and Asiatic subjects. After the Revolution Yakovlev went first to China, then to Paris, where except for a two-year stint teaching at the School of Fine Arts in Boston, USA, he remained for the remainder of his life.

3 February

Today things did not go so well. I even played through the *Sarcasms* in the morning. Oh Lord, when is Alchevsky going to come back from Moscow – we simply must get on with arranging this concert.

Played the organ and dropped in on the rehearsal for *The Tsar's Bride*.[1] Yershov,[2] who has taken over from Palachek,[3] is working feverishly and not without scandalising a few people.

At five o'clock there was a meeting in my house of the 'Bronze Horseman' management committee to discuss the first literary–musical event. After that B.N. called for me to take me to his house for bliny, at my request. He told me that at his most recent session Lotin had mentioned *Ala and Lolli* by name and had accused the talented composer of aiming to depict devilry, thus sowing confusion among people instead of transporting them to higher planes by means of the divine language of music. I retorted that Lotin was too narrow in his censure. Which did he find the more convincing image: the simple commandment Do not Kill, or a prone human figure with his skull smashed in?

4 February

More on *The Gambler*, which compared to yesterday raced ahead. Organ practice in the afternoon, then I looked in at the *Tsar's Bride* rehearsal, and gave Eleonora an Italian lesson (!).

I don't know what to do about Tanya Ruzskaya. She has now written to me twice from Kiev, saying all kinds of nonsense.

5 February

In the evening I went to see Coates in his comfortable and handsome wooden house out on the No. 21 tram route. He had invited me so that I could hear his opera *Assurbanipal*.[4] The first half of this opera was too full of whole-tone harmonies and progressions, but the second half was extremely entertaining, although I cannot claim to have absorbed it very precisely since the six- and eight-part harmony he uses throughout does not help the ear to

---

1 Opera (1898) by Rimsky-Korsakov.
2 Ivan Yershov (1867–1943), dramatic tenor, leading soloist of the Mariinsky Theatre and after Chaliapin the most famous singer of his day, professor at the St Petersburg Conservatoire. See *Diaries*, vol. 1, p. 132 and *passim*.
3 Josef Palechek (1842–1915), Czech-born bass singer, soloist and producer at the Mariinsky Theatre, responsible for premiere productions there of Rimsky-Korsakov's *Mlada* and *Servilia*, professor of opera at the St Petersburg Conservatoire. Ibid., p. 46n and *passim*.
4 Opera (1915), one of nine by Albert Coates.

orientate itself instantaneously, especially in a performance on the piano that necessarily left out half of what was written. I drew attention to the whole-tone construction as a defect that could sink the whole opera. Coates agreed that he too found it oppressive; it was a tendency he would try to correct, and he asked me to come again later to hear what changes he had made.

I was introduced to Balmont,[1] who dropped by informally in a food-stained jacket. Coates quickly ushered him into the adjoining room because his talking was interrupting the playing of the opera. Balmont is translating the text of *Assurbanipal* into Russian, Coates having originally set it in German. At tea, which was served at a low table encircled by deep armchairs in a half-darkened room, Balmont expatiated seductively on his beloved Maoris and Samoans, on whose culture he is currently delivering a course of lectures, and as he went out asked me if I was really that 'hope of Russian music' he had been hearing about? I told him I had written two songs to his words, and launched into a panegyric about his visionary poem 'There Are Other Planets'. Balmont agreed that this was indeed one of his best poems, and asked me to play my song. Unfortunately my memory of it by heart was not perfect, and without the words it did not amount to much. As far as I could see Balmont understood very little of it, although of course he was polite. As for my two settings for female chorus, he liked the idea of the women's voices with orchestra, but was less interested in the verses I had set.[2]

6 February

For some reason my *Gambler* is not going so well. I had thought that the third act would get along in an even more lively way than the second had done, but clearly it is not going to be possible to canter through the whole work in one fell swoop.

Dined at Gessen's, after a telephone conversation today full of mutual endearments and compliments. Borovsky was also there, now a man of stature with a professorship at the Moscow Conservatoire. I always enjoy being at Gessen's, and one hears all the latest gossip. Later in the evening I went to Baron Driesen's for a meeting about the Antique Theatre. None of the appointed *grands maîtres* (Benois, Roerich, etc.) turned up, but it was still quite interesting although I was paralysed with boredom when we got bogged down in an interminable discussion about immemorial ages. But the

---

1 Konstantin Balmont (1867–1942), a leading Symbolist poet. Prokofiev had already set three of Balmont's poems by the time of their first meeting; he was to become an even more important source of literary inspiration as their friendship deepened, both in Russia and after Balmont's emigration in 1920, in France.
2 'The White Swan', Op. 7 No. 1, and 'The Wave', Op. 7 No. 2, for female chorus and orchestra.

scenery for one Italian play made me hug myself with delight: on stage right we had Jerusalem, and on stage left Lyon – in the middle of the sea. Not bad! What a subject for an opera!

7 February

I want to compose, and at the same time I don't want to. I think it's time for me to go away for a while.

In the afternoon a long, but very enjoyable meeting at the 'Bronze Horseman'. I was talked into writing an article about music for their almanac; they specifically want me to be critical and provocative, but there is nothing I particularly feel like savaging at the moment. I am so busy with my own work that I am simply not interested in immersing myself in the rest of the musical world! It passes before my eyes like an alluring picture, but I do not experience it with the same passion as do other musicians who are less in thrall to the exigencies of their inner creative urges. One can admire other women at the same time as being in love with one's wife, and in that case one appreciates the beauty of other women and views them with the eyes of a connoisseur without feeling the need to agonise over them. But the 'Horseman' wants me to agonise, and expose meretricious details of other musical activities.

In the evening I went to Borovsky's concert. Every year that goes by he plays better and better, and has now become an absolutely remarkable pianist. He played my 'Scherzo' from Op. 12, a piece I have never myself managed to bring off to perfection, at such a speed I was afraid he must stumble. But he sailed through one difficulty after another, and although he slightly muffed the ending, flew like the wind to the final note and elicited a storm of applause from the audience.

Whenever a piece of mine is played a shiver always goes through me, mainly because I know that at the end I'll be called out and everyone will turn to look at me in smiling approbation; I will have to make the long way up to the stage, and so on. It is stupid to worry about it, since it is actually a very pleasant experience. There were calls for the composer today, but I exploited the fact that they were drowned by the loud applause, to which Borovsky responded by taking several bows, so I stayed where I was.

A year ago I played this same 'Scherzo' at a 'Contemporaries' concert, and now as I accompanied Suvchinsky to his house (friendly relations have been re-established between us), I said: 'Well, Pyotr Petrovich, you must forgive me for not having played it as well as that in your concert.' Gessen was wildly enthusiastic, saying that my music had today entirely won over Milyukov,[1]

---

1 Pavel Milyukov (1859–1943), historian and politician. The founder of the Constitutional Democratic Party ('Kadets', from the acronym KD), Milyukov became Foreign Minister in the

who had hitherto not been an admirer of it. The Kadets are now unequivocally on my side.

After the concert, Borovsky's young sister came up to me and said that although she was not sure whether we had been introduced (I don't bow to her as I consider her a pushy little girl) she hoped I would not refuse an invitation to come to their house for tea after the concert. And although I was being heavily importuned by Boris Verin, who was expiring from ecstasy over the 'Scherzo', I did go to the Borovskys.

It was a piquant moment when, as I made my entrance and greeted the group of ladies assembled there, I also greeted Bushen,[1] who was standing to one side. At first she was covered in confusion, but then, seeing that it was all right to extend her hand, did so and pressed mine warmly. The two little Borovsky sisters overwhelmed me with their affection.

Borovsky played truly wonderfully today, especially Scriabin's Fourth Sonata. I am very glad that I had hissed Romanovsky when he played it in September: he bashed his way through it then without the slightest understanding.

8 February

I hardly did anything on *The Gambler*, and went to the general rehearsal of the student production of *The Tsar's Bride*. It was last done five years ago, in my time, and although I did not conduct any of the performances myself I was involved in the production. Dranishnikov has really come on, and conducted outstandingly well. Yershov goes to incredible lengths to curry popularity among the students, hurling imprecations at all the Conservatoire directorate. I felt sorry for Tcherepnin, but Glazunov and Lavrov and all the others – they deserve it. Eleonora, Shapiro[2] and I all sat together. I like Shapiro very much.

First Provisional Government following the February 1917 Revolution, and as such was the author of 'Milyukov's Note' to the Allied Governments that guaranteed Russia's continuing involvement in the First World War. Fleeing Russia for Paris after the Civil War, Milyukov published and edited there the émigré newspaper *Poslednye Novosti* (*Latest News*).

1 Alexandra Bushen (1891–1991) was a piano student at the Conservatoire who had become a passionate admirer of Prokofiev's music and an intimate friend because of her superior intellect and her all-important (for Prokofiev) prowess as a walking companion. After graduation Bushen began a career as a pianist but on the advice of Asafyev switched to writing on music, publishing translations of Verdi's correspondence and a novel *Molodoy Verdi* (*The Young Verdi*), translated into English as *The Path to Opera*. Her second husband was the pianist and teacher Alexander Kamensky, celebrated not only for his musicianship but for his heroic recitals and broadcasts during the siege of Leningrad in the Second World War, joining the poet Olga Berggolts in that select band of artists who by staying and suffering the terrible privations of their fellow citizens did much to raise their morale by their regular radio readings and performances.
2 Klara Shapiro, a Conservatoire student. See *Diaries*, vol. 1, p. 792.

Butomo-Nazvanova[1] is going to sing *Duckling* in Moscow, accompanied by Karatygin. She has transposed it a tone lower, and I heard this version today. The effect of the transposition is extraordinary, it sounds completely different and I found myself listening to some passages as if the music had been written by someone else. This experience may have given me an inkling of what my works must sound like to someone hearing them for the first time and being perplexed by the unfamiliar juxtapositions.

It was rather entertaining when I sat down to accompany Butomo in the *Duckling* and got terribly lost, reading the transposed key and then in the most delicious section absent-mindedly shifting to the proper key, prompting the singer to stop and exclaim in amazement: 'Why has it suddenly gone up so high?'

9 February

Handschin, and then lunch with Borovsky at the 'Astoria'. We have an arrangement to lunch there every time he comes to the city. It is such a rare occurrence for me to show my face in socially smart environments that I take the greatest pleasure in it. Also, there is always so much to talk to Borovsky about, and he pays close attention to my comments on his performance. Apropos, this time I criticised his inaccurate playing of the bass line in the Glazunov Sonata.

10 February

Great excitement and feverish chatter about the re-opening of the State Duma.

The Gambler is not making any progress at all, damn it. I took the plunge, put it to one side and settled down to making a piano reduction of the Second Piano Concerto, against the possibility that Russian Music Editions might become my publishers. My desire to move to them is now stronger and more definite than ever. It would be a huge satisfaction to see my whole phalanx of works in print.

Spent the evening at B.N.'s He says my presence relieves his facial neuralgia. X-rays, says the prince. By the way, at the Borovsky concert he gave me a hundred roubles, as a 'private loan', since I have no money at all at the moment and there is no prospect of any from Russian Music Editions – even if they take me on – or from Ziloti – if his concert takes place – for at

---

1 Olga Butomo-Nazvanova (1888–1960), celebrated mezzo-soprano specialising in the Russian chamber and symphonic repertoire, closely associated with the conductors Koussevitzky, Ziloti and Blumenfeld.

least a month. I have no wish whatever to be obliged to B.N., but when I glanced at the cash he was handing me and airily remarked: 'All right then, let me have a hundred roubles just for a little while, since you fleeced me at Macao', he seemed genuinely pleased.

11 February

At ten o'clock in the morning – a marvellous telegram. First things first – where was it from? Chicago. Then, listen to this: Diaghilev is sending me 1,500 roubles for my ballet. Thanks be to heaven above! I had forgotten all about Diaghilev, reckoning that at best I might get the money once the war was over. And now, all of a sudden, it never rains but it pours. Diaghilev must be seriously enamoured of my ballet to disgorge such a substantial pile of cash, in consequence of which, honoured sirs, I am a rich man, no whit poorer than that twenty-fold millionaire brother of Bashkirov's in Samara. Never have I had in my hands at any one time more than 500 roubles, and now suddenly I have three times that amount. Fantastic.

I could not restrain myself from boasting about the telegram at that evening's 'Contemporaries' concert. The event itself was as drab and boring as could be, inflicting on us pieces by Akimenko,[1] Yulia Weisberg[2] and other such prunes, while that alley-cat of a Zakharov had once again failed to learn Myaskovsky's Second Sonata. Ossovsky congratulated me on the telegram and concerning RME told me that he had been discussing me with Messrs Rachmaninoff and Koussevitzky. Koussevitzky had said, 'All right, let's talk about it', but what Rachmaninoff said Ossovsky did not relate. The omens do not appear particularly good to me. But these are the publishers I definitely want to be with.

17 February

You take your eye off the Diary for a moment, and before you know it a week has gone by.

The main impressions I have retained of the past days have been these: first, the pleasing sense of seeing the road clear ahead for my ballet and of being a man of substance, although only yesterday did I actually receive the money. I grandly gave Mama 200 roubles and gave the prince his hundred

---

1 Fyodor Akimenko (1876–1945). Akimenko, at that time a recent graduate of Rimsky's composition course at the Conservatoire, had been, for a brief and rather unsuccessful period in 1900, Stravinsky's first teacher in the theory of composition.
2 Yulia Weisberg (1878–1942), composer of conservative inclinations, member of the editorial board of journal *Muzykalny Sovremennik* edited by Andrey Rimsky-Korsakov (to whom she was married) and Suvchinsky. See *Diaries*, vol. 1, p. 362 and *passim*.

back – my fingers were generally itching to scatter money about. Secondly, I began a romance with Alya P., the most enchanting little thing; she says 'khoroshó'¹ just like Max used to, relishing it, slightly through her nose and rolling the 'r'.

The Gambler also got a new lease of life. I played through the first act; it is very different from the third, but so enticing, it's pure delight. I was wrong to think that the best thing was the Babulenka scene: the first act yields nothing to it.

What a marvellous opera could be made of Gogol's 'The Tale of How Ivan Ivanovich Quarrelled With Ivan Nikiforovich'.² The most strikingly poetical moments are when the descriptions wrench one away from everyday life – thus, among the banal bickering of these two gentlemen, what wondrous glimpses of Little Russian³ life could one depict!

18 February

Spent the evening with the prince, and won a chess game with Demchinsky that gave me the match (hurrah! 5–2, a splendid result), and because it was late stayed the night. This morning sat down to play chess again, after which he came back home with me and we played once more. So it turned into twenty-four hours of chess.

19 February

Slight headache.

A christening at Erasmus's.⁴ All very pleasant, but nothing special and I extricated myself from the dinner to go to the Sokol.

20 February

Headache again. Walked to the Islands, because of the dazzling sunshine that I love so much. It and the medicine cleared the headache.

Alchevsky has come back and Ziloti has talked to him. He expressed an interest in getting to know my songs, and will telephone me in a week's time. Ziloti recommends waiting until the autumn for the concert, to minimise the risks of undue haste. It is a little disappointing, but of course the autumn would be a better time; that had been my original suggestion to Ziloti, and it was he who wanted to bring it forward to the spring.

1   'Good', 'splendid'.
2   One of the short stories in Gogol's collection *Mirgorod* (1865).
3   Russians called the Ukraine 'Malorossiya', 'Little Russia', as in the nickname the critic Nikolay Kashkin gave to Tchaikovsky's Second Symphony because of its use of Ukrainian folk melodies.
4   Artur Erasmus, a friend of Prokofiev's second cousin Sergey Sebryakov.

I asked Ziloti what the prospects might be for *The Gambler*, as I had read in the newspapers that the Mariinsky Theatre management was going to be considering future repertoire during the first week of Lent. Ziloti wanted to know how much of the opera was ready, and when I told him that two and a half acts out of four were complete, said he would telephone Telyakovsky.[1] This is splendid: it would be quite something to be performed at the Mariinsky.

Dined at Sosnitsky's,[2] the vice-chairman of our Chess Society, now mothballed because of the war. In his tiny apartment we ate delicious bliny and drank masses of wine in inebriated company with chess-players and people who work at *New Times*. Velikhov, despite being a member of the State Duma, sang indecent songs, and I thrashed Levin, one of Petrograd's strongest chess-players. When some of those present asked me to play I sat down at the piano and played a few trifles. Sitting nearby was Yury Belyayev, author of *Psyche*,[3] who evidently knew nothing of my credentials and kept murmuring benevolently: 'You play nicely, very nicely, but for God's sake don't run away with the idea that you have any talent.' This last because of my having complained 'Oh, what a racket they're making in the dining room.'

21 February

A demonstration for Telyakovsky's benefit, so I must bring the first act into some sort of order. I have a short orchestral introduction, which I love, but the first scene itself does not yet exist at all, because I began writing the opera in the autumn with Alexey's diatribe against the good Vater. I am still not clear about the opening scene, because it does not square with my idea of starting the opera with the most gripping piece of action. All the same, even if it is not a complete knock-out it can still be lively and interesting, and I set to work with gusto today.

In the evening I went to Eleonora's concert. She had doubled the ticket prices and attracted a full house. Of course, she plays very well, but I think

---

1 Vladimir Telyakovsky, Director of the Imperial Theatres up to the time of the October Revolution. See *Diaries*, vol. 1, pp. 568–9.
2 Yuli Sosnitsky (1878–1919), antique bookseller and collector, and possessor of an unrivalled library of chess literature. In 1912 he took over from Alexander Alekhine as chess editor of *New Times*. Sosnitsky, along with Pyotr Saburov and Boris Malyutin, was one of the 'three pillars' of the St Petersburg Chess Club. Ibid., pp. 646, 675 and *passim*.
3 Yury Belyayev (1876–1917) as well as being a playwright and theatre critic was a regular columnist for *New Times*. His play *Psyche* had a great vogue in St Petersburg in 1911–12, partly on account of its flamboyant leading lady Olga Glebova-Sudeikina, inspiration of Anna Akhmatova's hymn to the St Petersburg of the 'Stray Dog' café 'Poem without a Hero'. (Olga was the first wife of the artist Sergey Sudeikin who, having lost her to the composer Arthur Lourié subsequently also lost his second wife Vera to an even more celebrated composer: Igor Stravinsky.)

the concert was a little premature. The programme included my 'Prelude' from Op. 12, which was very well played, and scored a great success with cries of 'composer!' but the composer did not make an appearance.

There was supper at Eleonora's afterwards, and I appear to have offended her greatly by leaving early to go to Gessen's. The Prokofiev household was, however, represented by Mama, who had been pressingly invited and who was there for the first time.

At Gessen's Karatygin exclaimed: 'At last we have someone to write a review of this evening's concert!' I was glad to agree to write one. If I were not a composer I'm sure I would have made a very trenchant critic.

Butomo related the success of the Moscow performance of the *Duckling*, and Koussevitzky's declaration that he had been 'stunned' by it. I laughed and replied that when I had played him my First Piano Concerto he was not merely stunned but in 'a state of e-e-c-s-t-a-s-y', although this had not prevented him from continuing to ignore my music (and indeed, from that day to this he has virtually disappeared from the face of the earth as far as any relationship with me is concerned). Alexander Benois was charming, but Polotskaya-Yemtsova[1] was rude.

22 February

In the evening I was at B.N.'s and finished our chess match with the final result of +10-1+2, which for him is deplorable. Demchinsky declared that since 'a quest without ambition, and creation without a quest' aroused his wrath, he would not visit the prince today, because were he to come he would be unable to restrain himself from telling him exactly what he thought of him.

23 February

Handshin, English lesson, Sokol.

24 February

Today at long last I made my visit to Terioki. There I found white snow and sweet-smelling air.

---

1 Sofia (Sara) Polotskaya-Yemtsova (1878–1957), pianist, was a favoured musical associate of the poet, critic and gallery-owner Konstantin Makovsky and of Karatygin, closely associated with the international musical, artistic and literary aspirations of *Apollon* magazine. See *Diaries*, vol. 1, p. 553.

25 February

We made an expedition to Tiurisyavi[1] and to Shchuchye Lake,[2] and then on to Beloóstrov for lunch. On the train back to Terioki I ran into Cecilia and Elfrieda Hansen[3] on their way to give a concert in Vyborg. I made a great show of greeting them, and then made myself scarce, accompanied by vocal protestations that I could at least take off my glove when shaking hands.

26 February

Rose at nine and in dazzling sunshine returned from Terioki to Petrograd, feeling pleased with life.

At home it took me no time to finish the section of the first act that was still not linked to Alexey's invective against the Vater. I had promised to play the first and second acts through to Coates today, but the meeting was postponed owing to Coates's need to conduct a 'new' opera – *Onegin* – on the morrow and pleading for time to study the score.

Mme Winkler, the same lady who got me the upright piano for Zet and has taken charge of selling my old grand, tells me that there is a buyer for it at 525 roubles. Splendid. Another pot of money I had completely forgotten about. This is very timely, since my calculations were that the fee from Diaghilev would last me only until 1 June.

27 February

The third act of *The Gambler* is moving along well, meaning that it has come back to life.

I was invited to dine today at the Tcherepnins, an invitation they have been extending to me for quite some time now, first Mama Tcherepnin and then repeated by their son. I was greatly embarrassed when I arrived on the doorstep in my dinner jacket at seven o'clock to find the family finishing their modest quotidian repast. I don't know whose mistake it was, theirs or mine, but may I lose my head if it was mine, because I distinctly remember the invitation. However, it turned out that this evening they were not having guests for dinner, but for later in the evening. I quickly recovered myself, saying I had just had dinner myself and had come early so that I could listen to their son's compositions. He protested at length, but was eventually

---

1 A wealthy holiday resort on the Gulf of Finland coast between Terioki and the Russia–Finland border at Beloóstrov, distinguished by particularly palatial dachas.
2 A beauty spot near Kellomyaki (now Komarovo).
3 Elfrieda Hansen, pianist, sister of the violinist Cecilia Hansen and former romantic interest of the composer, see *Diaries*, vol. 1, p. 147 and *passim*.

persuaded to play, and through a morass of blatantly modish padding and desultory fragments of melody could occasionally be glimpsed passages of real interest.[1] This Sasha and his friend, the son of Benois, also showed what amounted to a whole exhibition of their paintings, some of which were interesting and witty. It was all very enjoyable, much enlivened by Tcherepnin and Benois *pères*. The latter issued an invitation to drop in 'informally' to the French Ambassador, M. Paléologue.[2] So this is my second Excellency; in the summer the Karneveys had dragged me along to meet the Chinese Ambassador.

28 February

Nevertheless I remained discontented with yesterday evening, and this is the reason: the Ossovskys were present, and while neither of them had anything very significant to say to me, in conversation with Madame I learned that they had recently come back from Moscow. It follows that he must have been to a meeting at Russian Music Editions, and must have raised the question of my being published by them. The fact that he said nothing means the battle must have been lost. There's the 'falange' for you. The result is that once again I have no idea which of my works will be published, or when. I am very reluctant to sell myself again to Jurgenson, especially as relations between us are now frankly bad.

Today I finished the first half of Act Two of *The Gambler*: Alexey is left alone. Now comes his impassioned monologue, the scene with Polina, Babulenka – about which I am already salivating – and then the general finale of the act.

The Damskaya sisters paid us a visit in return for Mama's post-concert visit to them. I dined with Boris Nikolayevich, which was enjoyable, and accompanied him to Dr Izhevsky, who has been treating his facial neuralgia with an array of complicated electrical machines. He was put into a sort of cage through which an electrical charge was introduced. Dr Izhevsky claims that this works wonders, nourishing and restoring the nervous system.

---

1   The son was Alexander Tcherepnin (1899–1977), who became a prolific and well-established composer with an output including three operas, four symphonies, concertos for various instruments, operas, ballets, choral music and works for solo piano. With his family he emigrated after the Revolution first to Paris and later to the United States. His son Ivan (1943–1998), also a composer although of markedly more radical tendencies than his father, was thus the third representative of the Tcherepnin composing dynasty.
2   Maurice Georges Paléologue (1855–1944), son of an exiled Romanian revolutionary, was French Ambassador to the Imperial Court from 1914 to 1917. His colourful three-volume memoir of his experiences, with its insights into the Tsar's family life and the Court's involvement in the conduct of the war, was published in Paris in 1923 as *Le Crépuscule des Tsars* and appeared in an English translation by F. A. Holt as *An Ambassador's Memoirs* (George H. Doran, New York, 1924).

When we returned home, B.N. launched furiously into chess, but was smashed 'like the drum in *Ala and Lolli*'.

29 February

Spent the evening at Eleonora's: I need her absolutely to arrange a position of some kind for Katya Schmidthof[1] in Moscow, because Katya has quarrelled with her aunt and must now find some way of earning her bread. The prince sent his car over to collect me from Eleonora's with an urgent request for me to come and annihilate his cousin at chess, his cousin being a bungling chess psychopath rejoicing in the ridiculous nickname of Solnyshko.[2] As a matter of fact he is quite a strong player, but I succeeded in maintaining my reputation and won two good games, remarking as his collapse became increasingly imminent: 'relieves easily and painlessly', a reference to newspaper advertisements for 'Ara' laxative pills.[3] B.N. exclaimed that it gave him 'the keenest pleasure to watch Zhenechka being defeated', and told him: 'Not much of a Sun, are you – more of a smoky paraffin lamp, I'd say!'

Altogether the prince is feeling rotten, and at night his nerve was so painful that he went into hysterics.

1 March

After the previous evening's chess exertions a headache was threatening to come on. In the evening I was at Coates's with Mama, whom he had generously insisted on inviting. I brought along two acts of *The Gambler*, and started by reading through the libretto, which prompted Coates to say: 'A strange subject; I cannot conceive at all how one could write music to it.' But he became very interested, and some moments prompted a delighted reaction. I then played him the score. At the first words of Blanche Coates became very animated, he greatly approved of Astley's material and listened with the keenest attention to all the dialogue with Polina. He laughed like a maniac at the scandalous incident with the Baron. Act Two he listened to even more attentively than Act One; at the passage in which the Marquis promises to arrange everything he gripped my shoulder, appreciating in particular Astley's reserve, but the high point was undoubtedly Babulenka. She provoked a volley of exclamations, praise and delight from all those present:

---

1 Katya Schmidthof was the sister of Prokofiev's friend Max Schmidthof, who committed suicide in April 1913.
2 'Little Sunshine'.
3 'Ara laxative pills purify the blood and afford gentle, painless relief with successful results when taken in cases of disturbance to the digestive organs. 95 kopecks the box.'

Coates, his wife, my Mama and Dukes.[1] Coates declared that the opera must be staged without delay, that he had already spoken to Telyakovsky about it, and that it should be performed in January. I preferred December, against the possibility that I might have to go to America for the production of my ballet. Coates replied that this certainly should be possible, and outlined the following schedule: in October *The Nightingale*,[2] in December *The Gambler*, and in February his own opera *Assurbanipal*. We talked over casting for the roles, and scenery. He advises against Golovin,[3] since with him there would be no hope of an autumn production: he never delivers on time. He recommended Lambin,[4] but I have never heard anything about him.

In the score of his own opera he has removed many of the progressions in thirds and whole tones, and this has greatly sharpened up the piece. I am still not sure whether this is real music or *Kapellmeister* music. Much of it I truly like, but a score on fifty staves does have a somewhat overwhelming effect. Coates calls me his professor and acts on the slightest hint I let drop.

Mama was delighted with *The Gambler* and for the first time, to her surprise, began to feel that it will really happen and be a success.

2 March

In the evening I arranged a Blitz Chess tournament[5] with Demchinsky, the prince, Solnyshko, Tyulin and myself. Rausch was indisposed. It was an extremely lively occasion and ended with a victorious Demchinsky being crowned with a wreath. I was a little distracted by the organisational demands and played below my strength, but still managed 50 per cent. Little Sunshine behaved atrociously, complaining, quarrelling, picking fights, walking out on his game with me, so that I really got angry with him.

---

1 Paul Dukes (1899–1967), repetiteur at the Mariinsky Theatre. See Charles Barber's *Lost in the Stars* for a riveting account of the many extraordinary lives of this musician who doubled as a British Secret Service agent.
2 Opera (composed 1908 to 1914) by Stravinsky.
3 Alexander Golovin (1863–1930), painter and scenic designer who rose to prominence particularly with his designs, a mixture of Symbolism and Modernism, for Meyerhold's theatre productions. His sets and costumes played a large part in the sensational success of Diaghilev's Paris productions of *Boris Godunov* (1908) and *The Firebird* (1911), and although many precious Golovin sets and costumes were destroyed in the disastrous fire at the Mariinsky Theatre scenery store in November 2003, his magnificent house curtain in the auditorium is there to this day.
4 Pyotr Lambin (1962–1923), a house designer at the Mariinsky Theatre, best known for his settings for the 1900 production of Marius Petipa's *La Bayadère*.
5 A form of chess in which the game is strictly time-limited, necessitating a highly developed strategic approach. There are five generally accepted categories depending on the permitted duration of the game: Speed Chess (30 minutes); Rapid Chess (10 minutes); Classic Blitz (5 minutes); Modern Blitz (3 minutes); and Bullet Chess (1 minute).

I asked Demchinsky to give me his autograph, but the request embarrassed him greatly (yes, it really did) and he promised to give it to me next time. The story of the 'Wooden Book' is as follows: one day in the summer Eleonora and I were on the train going to Sestroretsk, and we came up with the idea that if I were to collect the autographs of important and interesting people I would be able to create a remarkable album. I decided that simply asking for the signature, accompanied perhaps by some kind of general *aperçu*, would merely cause the individual in question to rack his brains – 'Oh, for heaven's sake, what am I going to write for the fellow, damn it?' and would not be particularly interesting. But supposing everybody were invited to respond to the same question, that would be a different, and much more rewarding, matter. But what should the question be? Here imagination was silent, and for a while the project lapsed. Eventually, however, the question proposed itself to me: what are your thoughts on the sun? Splendid! Especially as I had recently been so powerfully drawn to it.[1] And as all the 'Cavaliers of the Wooden Book' would be taken completely unawares by the question, what a fertile field it would make for answers![2]

'C'est un peu du style de Boris Nikolaevitch,'[3] was Eleonora's reaction on the telephone, but later she warmed to the task of tracking down the right volume, since I told her under no circumstances must it be an ordinary school notebook, but one with a binding made of two plain pieces of wood edged with coarse black leather attached with ordinary nails, not fancy ones, and with a metal clasp such that hands coming into contact with it would immediately smell of metal. The size should be the same as a rouble banknote. The combination of the rough exterior and the rare preciousness of the autographs within would provide an element of piquancy. Those invited to contribute to the book would be notable figures or those who played a role in my life. Eleonora complained that she could not find a competent craftsman prepared to make an object of such crudity, particularly as the paper inside the book had to be of such exceptional quality, but at length the book was ready. It was not quite as I had envisaged, being rather too elegant, 'a peasant in silk stockings', but at least it was original and graceful, and the main thing was – it was made of wood. The person chosen to inaugurate it was Demchinsky, but because of his bashfulness this had to be postponed.

---

1 The sun and the sun-god are images that inform *Ala and Lolli* and the *Scythian Suite*.
2 See *Diaries*, vol. 1, p. 244n., where my footnote is, regrettably, mistaken. The 'Yellow Book' in which Prokofiev and Max Schmidthof amused themselves by writing down their adolescent romantic encounters and fantasies is a completely different tome. It seems to have been lost along with other papers when the composer's apartment was ransacked in the aftermath of the Revolution. (See below, p. 694. The 'Wooden Book' is preserved in RGALI, and contains 48 pages of autographed messages.
3 'Rather more Boris Nikolayevich's style.'

3 March

I awoke with a disgusting headache emanating somewhere from the back of the head that after climbing to the top of the crown turned down to my left temple and threatened to develop into my besetting neuralgia, of the eye, the teeth and so forth. It must have resulted from yesterday's chess tournament. Today I did no composing, no organ practice, but doggedly forced myself to walk for hours.

In the evening I went to the 'Contemporaries' concert at which Medtner was playing his own works. Suvchinsky, a broad smile on his face, put out feelers about my performing for them next season, even if the repertoire had to be confined to old works. I was evasive, stopping short of saying 'yes'. Medtner played his new Sonata, Op. 30, excessively Medtnerish with nothing particularly new in it, but good all the same and I would like to play it myself. But precisely that dangerous inclination to play it oneself is the point: Medtner's tragedy is that just as his music is so enjoyable to play for oneself, so it can be monotonous and boring to hear performed on the concert platform. This is exactly the experience I had when I was listening to his *Sonata-Ballade*. I am generally of the opinion that after his core work, his E minor Sonata, he, like Schumann in his later years, withdrew too deeply into the depths of his own psyche, a process accompanied by an impoverishment of his purely musical powers.[1] Some of his songs are extraordinarily beautiful, but he is not truly a lyric composer and texts do not inspire him.

I went backstage to see him in the artists' room and told him how Yesipova[2] in times gone by had virtually ejected me from her class after I insisted on playing one of his *Fairy Tales*. I complimented him on his E minor Sonata (which was not, however, in his programme today) and apparently perpetrated a gaffe by remarking that when he plays *forte* his right hand cannot be heard above his left. He has a ruddy, burly appearance, is amazingly bald and has small, deep-set eyes. His bow-tie was awry and the waistcoat under his tails crumpled. But I love his music. On the whole, I am reasonably certain it was he who put paid to my candidature to join the Russian Music Editions roster.

---

1 *Sonata-Ballade* in F sharp, Op. 27; Sonata in A minor, Op. 30; Sonata in E minor ('Night Wind'), Op. 25/2.
2 The second of Prokofiev's two piano teachers in the St Petersburg Conservatoire. Anna Yesipova (1851–1914), one of the most brilliant pianists of her generation. Like Prokofiev's other teacher, Alexander Winkler, she had studied with Theodor Leschetitzky in Vienna (but unlike Winkler then married her teacher), and enjoyed an acclaimed virtuoso career in Europe and America before returning to St Petersburg in 1893 to take up a professorship at the St Petersburg Conservatoire. See *Diaries*, vol. 1, pp. 112–20 and *passim*.

4 March

Today there was a grand dinner at the home of the French Ambassador. The modest-looking house proved to be a veritable palace inside with many rare works of art, an elegant suite of public rooms, liveried footmen standing at attention, and last but not least the effortlessly urbane host with his venomous eyes and nervous movements. About fifteen of us sat down to dinner, Benois and his wife among the company. The food we were served was delicious and refined, but there was not much of it. Afterwards I was asked to play, and not allowed to rise from the piano stool until I had given my listeners about eight pieces. The French did not grind my face in the mud; on the contrary, the music they most appreciated was the most 'left', the *Sarcasms*. Karatygin (also visiting for the first time) arrived about eleven o'clock. The very idea of Karatygin being *au fait* with the *soigné* French took some getting used to! But he had had a haircut, put on evening dress and conducted himself with an independent air.

At half-past eleven I thanked the Ambassador, who expressed the hope that we might soon arrange *une soirée plus intime*, and I then took myself off to the first closed-invitation 'Bronze Horseman' evening, which was taking place in Professor Svyatlovsky's apartment.[1] Here everything was in full swing, although there were not many musicians there. I played and was well received, although the Russian poets were some way behind the French aficionados: they were baffled by the *Sarcasms*, so much so that the host actually got angry and was heard to say in the next room: 'Yes, well, of course, Prokofiev has proved in his earlier works that he is talented, but that hardly gives him the right to make fun of the public as he does in his latest things!'

5 March

I'm getting later and later sitting down to work: eleven o'clock. And on a day like today, when I have an appointment at one o'clock, I don't manage to get much done. Today I went to the general rehearsal of *Megaye*[2] because Coates suggested that I have a look at Lambin's scenery. Well, I liked the Buddhist shrine very much, although everyone tells me that Lambin is an old-fashioned and routine artist who is currently, for some reason, trying to project himself into the contemporary world. The music of this opera is a zero, but what followed, Cui's *The Mandarin's Son*,[3] was not worth a tuppenny damn.

---

1 Professor V. V. Svyatlovsky was a celebrated anthropologist and ethnographer who had amassed a remarkable collection of Australian aborigine artefacts.
2 Opera (Warsaw, 1912), the first of five by Adam Tadeusz Wieniawski (1879–1950), nephew of the violinist and composer Henryk Wieniawski.
3 Comic opera in one act based on a fable by Ivan Krylov.

All the same, what fun it would be to write a comic opera! And again there came into my head an idea for an opera I had thought about one day in Italy: Jules Verne's *La fantaisie du docteur Ox*.[1] Yes indeed, none other than Jules Verne. I would make it full of ensembles, wailings and gnashings of teeth, and lots of rushing about on stage.

Alchevsky, who this season has transformed himself into 'le grand Altchevsky', informed me that on the basis of what Ziloti had told him, he would like to get to know my songs and hopes to come to see me within a week. He confessed that he had not at all liked *Dreams*, which he had heard in Moscow, but my 'Scherzo', as performed by Borovsky, he had found quite delightful. Beyond these works he knows nothing of my music. I think he will like the songs. Suvchinsky, who was standing beside us, said: 'Medtner heard *Dreams* as well, and took away a bad impression.' I don't remember when it was I said that some people adored my compositions but considered me personally offensive, while others found me a charming young man who wrote complete rubbish. Suvchinsky added that there was a third category: people who regard me as an excellent composer *and* a very nice person – but still think they ought to criticise me.

6 March

At eleven o'clock I went for a walk along the Okhta river, had lunch at the Finland Station, and returned home at two. Dined with B.N. (preparatory to visiting the Ambassador) and destroyed him at chess. Recently I have grown to like his company more and more.

7 March

The Gambler made great progress today. Alexey alone on stage. I got almost as far as Babulenka's second appearance. In the evening, bridge. I've almost forgotten how to play, and to tell the truth, have grown a little tired of it. The others were Zakharov, Danilov[2] and Subbotin.[3] Oleg Subbotin is now living out in the country and is hardly ever seen in town. Since the time last May when Nina asked him if he would be one of the Attendants[4] at her marriage

---

1 'Le docteur Ox' was the title story in a collection of short stories by Jules Verne published in 1874.
2 A. Danilov. See *Diaries*, vol. 1, pp. 224, 777.
3 Prokofiev had made friends with Oleg Subbotin when they were both house guests of the Meshcherskys at their dacha in Gurzuf in the summer of 1913. Ibid., p. 473 and *passim*.
4 Nina Meshcherskaya had obviously thought that the marriage to Prokofiev would in fact take place and was beginning to make the appropriate preparations. In the Russian Orthodox wedding ceremony bride and groom are both supported by a number of nominated attendants who have specific roles to play in the ceremony, analogous to bridesmaids, pages, best man, father of the bride, etc., in Roman Catholic and Protestant ceremonies.

we have not seen one another, and from time to time I caught a hint of curiosity in his glance. Zakharov and I were very affectionate (and indeed I do feel the strongest attachment to him), and on learning that I did not plan to move far away from Petrograd during the summer, invited me to Terioki.

The aftermath of the bridge was another hour of Macao, that is to say down 25 roubles. And no word from Mme Winkler about the sale of the piano.

8 March

Composed, thanks to Handschin having moved his lesson to the afternoon (he is allowing me for the first time on to the great organ in the Small Hall). As for *The Gambler*, I got as far as Babulenka's entrance. In the evening at the Sokol I got a touch of lumbago, either I must have pulled a muscle or been in a draught. Now I am in agony.

Today there is a dancer of some kind called Karina, who is apparently dancing her astronomical interpretation, 'The Girl from Mars', to my Sonata. Charming. I did not attend, on principle.

The piano has been sold for 525 roubles.

9 March

My back hurts, but I can hobble round the room. I didn't compose any of Babulenka's music; I'm in no state to approach my most cherished parts of the opera. In the evening I was visited by both Boris Nikolayeviches.[1] Demchinsky winced a bit when he knew the prince would be coming: he cannot forgive him for his addiction to Lotin, regarding the latter as a complete waste of space and time, 'Jesus Christ's lawyer', he calls him. 'I would much rather spend the evening just with you,' he said. I replied that this was extremely flattering. Today Demchinsky finally inaugurated the 'Wooden Book', and being Demchinsky, the message was naturally witty.[2]

---

1 Demchinsky and Bashkirov.
2 'Nothing induces fragrant flowers to bloom more than the sun; as nothing hastens more readily the decomposition of stinking corpses. To serve everyone and everything with equal readiness is the sole prerogative of gods and hetaerae. Boris Demchinsky, Petrograd, on the day of the sun's festival, 9 March 1916.' Note: Demchinsky seems to have been two days out, or one day, depending on how you look at it: the 1916 vernal equinox occurred at 10.29 p.m. on 7 March (Old Style).

10 March

In the evening I was at the Benois'. I had hoped to net the second autograph for the 'Wooden Book', but a lot of people were present, and there was too much coming and going.

11 March

Finally launched into Babulenka, and not without success.

Went to the concert given by Zakharov and Cecilia. So now they are a betrothed couple; the tarantass to which they are jointly yoked has set out upon the broad highway of art. And the best of luck to them! They played well, but it was a dull programme. Anna Grigorievna invited me for Wednesday, and included Mama in the invitation. Making use of this last, I said: 'Thank you, I'll pass it on to Mama.' The poor lady, suffering from the loss of her artistic bearings, has fallen in love, yes really, literally, not metaphorically, with our dear prince, and everyone is already gossiping about it. The prince is embarrassed.

12 March

Babulenka. 'The grandmother's tone of voice and demeanour both have undergone a sharp change',[1] but no, not entirely: her former cantankerous contrariness still shines through. I am writing with love.

Eleonora and I went together to a *'Mir Isskustva'* exhibition, including works by artists I know personally: Benois, the wonderful Yakovlev,[2] Vodkin,[3] and many others who are good.

In the evening I played the first two acts of *The Gambler* to Malko. I was not personally very keen on doing this, but Malko insisted: 'You've played it for one *Kapellmeister*, well, you can play to another one', so I had little choice in the matter. Also present were two of my most devoted and sincere admirers: Milyukov and Igor Glebov, that is to say Asafyev.[4] Malko was very enthusiastic about the word-setting.

---

1   Direct quotation from Dostoyevsky's novella. See Appendix 1 for Prokofiev's own encapsulation, printed in the vocal score he made in 1929 for Koussevitzky's Edition Russe de Musique, of Dostoyevsky's characterisations in *The Gambler*.
2   Alexander Yakovlev (Sasha-Yasha). See p. 81 n. 4 above.
3   Kuzma Petrov-Vodkin (1878–1939), one of the most original (and controversial) artists on the St Petersburg scene in the early years of the twentieth century. Championed especially by Benois, Petrov-Vodkin introduced a bewildering and apparently incompatible variety of influences into his art, ranging from Russian icons and nineteenth-century landscape painters to the artists of the Munich Secession, Gauguin and Matisse.
4   Boris Asafyev wrote his influential music criticism under the pen-name of Igor Glebov.

What a difference there is between Coates and Malko! Coates is a scion of a socially élite family, and on top of that a talented fellow and excellent company. Malko is a serious musician, much more so than Coates, but is somehow less polished in the way of the world.

13 March

Babulenka is finished, the old girl has left the stage, to be replaced by the General, who has lost his reason.

Asafyev rang up during the afternoon about *The Gambler*. He was full of praise for Babulenka and the General, but thinks that Polina should be less sharply characterised and more enigmatic, as she is in Dostoyevsky. When I asked him if my old woman is the genuine article, a real Russian babushka or only a pseudo-Russian one, he cheered me greatly by saying that she is 'a proper Russian babushka'. Dined with B.N.B. and exposed his rook in a game of our ongoing chess match.

14 March

An invitation from some sort of dining establishment to appear in an orchestral concert conducted by Coates. I discussed it with him, and he asked me to play my First Piano Concerto. The orchestra would be that of the Preobrazhensky Regiment,[1] but because it is currently full of excellent musicians doing their military service in it, it is very good, and I am in any case longing to play with Coates. Learning that Act Three is nearing completion, Coates said he would come on Wednesday afternoon to listen to it, so today I made haste to finish it, just managing to do so.

In the evening Alchevsky called on me to get to know my songs. He is inclined to be sceptical, even though the laudatory opinions of Suvchinsky and Ziloti have influenced him in my favour. He was clearly impressed and obviously liked the *Duckling*. He liked the songs as well, except for 'The Grey Dress' and 'Under the Roof'[2] ('I am not fond of socialist songs'), but was utterly and completely bowled over by *Sarcasms*, especially the last. Stunned, he wanted to know what could possibly be in my heart to call forth such unconfined pessimism? He stayed until half-past one in the morning and said he would sing any and all of my songs, even 'socialist' ones. I am delighted to have had such a success with a singer of his excellence.

---

1 One of the oldest and most distinguished of Russian regiments, famous above all for the heroic part it played in the war against the French culminating in the Battle of Borodino in 1812.
2 Five Poems for voice and piano, Op. 23, respectively Nos. 2 (words by Zinaida Gippius) and 1 (words by Vyacheslav Goryansky).

15 March

The prince has persuaded me to go to Lotin's so that I can see for myself what sort of a man he is and experience his preaching. So today I went to Boris Nikolayevich's for dinner and then we set off together. Lotin sat at a desk and, closing his eyes, launched into a methodical, coherent discourse. About twenty women and a few men listened attentively, some of them reverentially. Lotin has an unattractive face bearing the marks of a partiality to alcohol, and an unpleasant, clerkishly crabbed speaking voice. He spoke of loving one's neighbour and quoted a great many texts. In the first instance I found myself inclined to agree with Demchinsky, who considers Lotin an empty windbag, and his witticism about 'Jesus Christ's lawyer' kept coming into my mind; but I was also swayed by the prince, who never misses any of Lotin's Tuesdays; and thirdly, following the promptings of my own consciousness, I was led to acknowledge that Lotin undoubtedly does some good in that the women hanging so submissively on the words that fall from his lips would be impelled by them to good deeds, at least to the extent of not deceiving their husbands.

I resolved to base my conclusion about Lotin strictly objectively, that is to say scientifically, not allowing any of these three influences to dominate. To begin with it was not easy, but without quite realising I was doing so I gradually began to concentrate on what he was actually saying (and his delivery was impeccably smooth, albeit lacking any of Demchinsky's brilliance), with the result that when I eventually came back to my sceptical point of view my opinion had hardened into certainty. Yes! This was not the real thing, it was a simulacrum, everyday, humdrum stuff, God without beauty, faith without passion – and Lotin was nothing but a consummate talking machine. Having formed my conclusion I grew bored, and tried to indicate to Boris Nikolayevich that it was time to go home. He pleaded to stay a little longer, and so we did.

It was at this point that I myself came under attack. Lotin had finished his sermon, and without leaving his seat or changing his attitude initiated a discussion, responding to various questions of a religious nature put to him by those present. Someone asked why there is no mention of science in the Gospels. Lotin answered the question, but immediately took the opportunity to switch the subject from science to art and launched an attack on new music, which according to him is devoid of grace, is chaotic, gives utterance to the ravings of the dark forces of the Underworld, and prevents its listeners approaching the Gospels. This was a specific attack on me and on my *Ala*, the performance of which Lotin had come to hear. He even turned his gaze on me. I sat motionless, avoided returning his gaze, and promised myself I would say nothing whatever in response to him.

Eventually Lotin ran out of steam and lapsed into silence. The company began to disperse, and we were among the first to leave. B.N. showered me with questions: 'Well what did you think?' I answered that I was sorry Lotin had chosen to attack me, because it deprived me of the opportunity to counter his views, since everyone would write off my critique as mere retaliation. On the other hand, I was glad it had happened, because it had finally disabused me of any belief in Lotin. Because, what was the point of the onslaught? To persuade me? But that is hardly the way to do it. To produce an effect on the audience? But these nice, stupid women are so removed from current tendencies in art that it is as irrelevant to warn them against the evils of 'chaotic composition' as it would be against the danger of snakes in Jamaica. The only explanation is that he wanted to show off his oratory and be able to boast that he had given a dressing-down to none other than Prokofiev. To sum up, Lotin had, if nothing else, given a perfect demonstration of the real qualities of a man like Demchinsky, and what the prince had taken for genuine diamonds was nothing but a fake.

16 March

Settled down to Act Three and finished it, since I was expecting Coates to come in the afternoon and hear it. But he cried off, delayed by theatre management business. Alchevsky invited me to dine with him at the 'Donon' restaurant,[1] saying that Koussevitzky would also be there, also Suvchinsky and Obukhov. I said: 'Well, I expect Koussevitzky and I will fall out', having in mind what I was hearing on all sides: about Koussevitzky's extravagant praise for my *Duckling*. If he now said the same thing to my face I would tell him these were empty words, since three years ago he was saying exactly the same thing about my First Piano Concerto, but in those three years had made no attempt to familiarise himself with any of my works.

When, slightly late, I entered the private dining room at the 'Donon', Kousseviztky put out his hand to me in a broad gesture of welcome and said affectionately: 'I hear you have a bone to pick with me? Do please begin.' The expression on his face was one of such friendliness it was quite impossible to say anything impolite, so I contented myself with replying: 'Oh, I can do that any time.'

All present then drank a toast to *The Gambler*, and vied with one another to be nice to me. Koussevitzky said the *Duckling* in Moscow had been an enormous success; he was sorry that he had not heard *Ala and Lolli*. Had the work been promised to Jurgenson, or was it true that Jurgenson and I were in dispute? Apropos, I have still not heard what the situation is regarding my

---

1 See *Diaries*, vol. 1, p. 269, for a description of a previous evening at the Donon restaurant.

works being published by his (Koussevitzky's) company. It would be rather intriguing if, after my candidature had been rejected, he was so amiably discussing publishing matters with me. Or perhaps the possibility had not yet been discussed, after all? Dinner proceeded with the liveliest conversation.

At the 'Bronze Horseman', to the second gathering of which I repaired after the 'Donon', I played my Sonata No. 2. So far not many musicians turn up to these sessions, and Tcherepnin and Miklashevskaya,[1] who arrived at different times, were bored. From the 'Horseman' I went on around midnight to Suvchinsky's, where the same company who had been at dinner had repaired to round off the evening. Suvchinsky was terribly pleased that I came, and evidently the shadow cast by the incident in the autumn had passed. Obukhov was just coming to the end of playing some of his compositions. These certainly contained glimpses of extremely interesting ideas, although too often harmonies of genuine refinement were accompanied by truly crass melodies. I again played my Second Sonata and then the *Sarcasms*, the latter having to be repeated and, apparently, creating a very strong impression.

17 March

I tidied up the third act and changed a few things, because yesterday in expectation of Coates's attendance I had finished in a rush and not everything was as it should be. For some reason my spine is hurting again – how delightful! I shall have to keep away from the Sokol for a while. In the evening I went to an *Apollon* event,[2] where Koussevitzky played some early music pieces on the double-bass. It was touching to see the two concert managers, Ziloti and Koussevitzky, rivals and erstwhile enemies, warmly shaking each other by the hand and outdoing one another in courtesies.

Ziloti was uncommonly friendly to me and said that we would arrange not just a single concert, but would probably repeat it. He and I listened from an adjoining room, while the performance went on next door with the electric lights doused. When Koussevitzky had finished playing and given way to a singer, he came into the room where we were and caught sight of Ziloti. Not noticing that I was sitting beside him, he began amiably conversing. When they had both moved a few paces away, I overheard Koussevitzky talking about something or other in a very animated tone and then whispering: 'And he played *Sarcasms*. I must tell you, you know, it was terrific . . . terrific . . . absolutely terrific!'

1 Irina Miklashevskaya (aka Mikhelson) (1883–1956), pianist and teacher at the Conservatoire. See *Diaries*, vol. 1, p. 619 and *passim*.
2 The magazine also organized musical soirées, often of new music, see ibid., pp. 155–6 and 553 for accounts of previous appearances by Prokofiev at them.

The word 'terrific' is, of course, too general to have much precise meaning, but it was uttered with such dramatic feeling that it was easy to believe that the work had sincerely affected Koussevitzky. Ziloti hurriedly said: 'Let's move into the corridor, we're disturbing people listening to the singer here', and they both went out.

18 March

After my lesson with Handschin I worked on the libretto of the first scene of Act Four. I don't find this particularly difficult: what I do is think for a while, then eliminate everything superfluous. But how exactly I am going to treat the roulette scene I still don't know. I believe it is possible, and should even make a stunning effect, but how? How?

In the evening, a performance by students of Musina's[1] class, a whole phalanx of enchanting young ladies. When I saw Nikolay Vasilievich[2] we smiled broadly at one another, after which he said that we must put a stop to this business. I said, most willingly, and indeed I had never had a quarrel with him. But when, overjoyed, he got put through on the telephone to his home and suggested I speak myself to Anya, I declined. I'll telephone her myself with an olive branch at some point!

19 March

Today I walked for a long time up and down Sedmaya Rota Street and thought over the roulette scene. I came up with more or less what I was looking for, although I did not manage to settle all the details, which will come of their own accord. The main thing is to find a conceptual design for the scene such that everything will be clear, natural and alive with febrile passion. I think I have found the way.

Dined with the prince. The medical re-examination of white ticket-holders, which was supposed to have taken place today, has been postponed, the threat hanging over the prince has therefore receded and he is as happy as a child.[3] Today he was revoltingly full of himself over his new-found prowess at chess, at which he had won in quick succession games in both the

---

1 Musina-Ozorovskaya was a professor of harp at the Petrograd Conservatoire.
2 Nikolay Andreyev, tenor, with whom and with his wife the mezzo-soprano Anna Zherebtsova-Andreyeva (Anya) Prokofiev had formerly been on terms of close friendship. The cause of the rift is not known: it must have occurred between July 1915 and January 1916, a period when Prokofiev, as he ruefully admits, made no Diary entries. It may have had something to do with Andreyeva's friendship with Nina Meshcherskaya's mother Vera Nikolayevna, or Prokofiev's growing disenchantment with her voice and preference for other singers, or Andreyeva's partiality for the detested Lotin.
3 White ticket-holders (*belobiletniki*) are those who have been passed unfit for military service for medical or other reasons.

second and first categories. This stung me, and with tension at fever pitch we sat down to play a game under match conditions. I set out a classical queen's pawn opening, sacrificed one pawn and then another, then a knight, then the second knight, finally a rook, and in the 22nd move checkmated him with all of his pieces intact except one. It was one of my best-ever games.

After that the prince, somewhat discomfited by his defeat, dragged me off to meet his new friends, the Princes Golitsyn.[1] I did not want to go, but when the eldest Prince descanted a stream of the most obliging courtesies to me over the telephone, I decided I would. B.N. says it gives him the keenest pleasure to observe my behaviour when I appear in the *beau monde*.

20 March

Today I thought about and clarified in my mind the third and final scene of the Act. It went quickly and easily, with none of the difficulties I had been afraid of in a love scene. The ending of the opera I had worked out in my mind long ago, in September, and somewhere or other I even have a sketch of Alexey's valedictory phrase, which, however, I am not making use of.[2]

Did nothing special in the afternoon except look through some old geography books from school and contemplate interesting destinations to travel to – because that is what I am going to do, I am going to travel all over the world. As the day wore on I became more and more anxious that I was in for a bout of the neuralgia from which I often suffer. Spent the evening at Gessen's.

21 March

Got down to Act Four. The first theme depicts Alexey's mood after Babulenka has departed: a little distracted, a little dreamy, a little – if one may use the expression – domestic.

I was visited by a pianist, Vilkreiskaya, who wanted to play through to me my 'Scherzo' and 'Prelude' as she is performing them in her concert a week from now. I am becoming an established composer, one of whom audience is sought in order to bow the knee. She plays not badly, but of course is no Borovsky. She and her sister stayed long enough to generate a headache (mine, naturally).

---

1 The Golitsyn (or Galitzine) family was one of the most ancient, and prolific, noble families of Russia. It is impossible to say which particular princes these were (Russian nobility never followed the Western practice of primogeniture) but the elder may have been the physicist and seismologist Prince Boris Golitsyn (1862–1916), in which case this meeting would have occurred shortly before his death on 4 May 1916.
2 '"Who would have thought that red would come up twenty times in a row! Ha-ha!" As he plunges his hands into the pile of banknotes, his eyes fixed on an invisible roulette wheel, the curtain falls.' (Prokofiev's libretto and stage directions.)

In the evening I went to Koussevitzky's concert in the People's House[1] to hear Medtner's account of Beethoven's Fourth Piano Concerto. He plays wonderfully, and the first of the two cadenzas he composed is very successful, but the second is not good style and just too Medtnerish. The most interesting aspect of the concert was that I met Marinochka Pavlova again.[2] She is as pretty as ever, but things are not going well for her: her father suffered a financial crash and went to the Caucasus, where he has some kind of job, her sister is married, while Marinochka herself is in Petrograd on her own, in very straitened circumstances, receiving practically nothing from her father. After finishing her studies at the Narodnaya Conservatoire,[3] she directed all her efforts to joining the Musical Drama Theatre, but 'the cards were against her', because '... one has to push oneself relentlessly in order to get anywhere'. So now she is living in one tiny room. She told me all this with a simplicity and trustfulness most unlike her former self, said how glad she was to see me, a friend from her youth so to say, and how insensitive she found the attitude of Zakharov (who in his time had courted her assiduously, and not without reciprocal feelings) as soon as Cecilia appeared on the scene: he had dropped her completely and cut off all contact. I felt genuinely sorry for her, more importantly was truly glad to see her and even more to sense her interest in me, which had never formerly been very pronounced. I asked her if I could see her again in the near future; she was embarrassed about her cramped little room, but I said that I would be glad if she would do me the favour of paying me a call. She agreed readily, and this made me extraordinarily happy.

---

1   The idea of People's Houses or Palaces arrived from Britain and Continental Europe in St Petersburg in 1899 with the opening of the Narodny Dom in Alexandrovsky Park. January 1912 saw the addition of a magnificent and appropriately vast new opera house, with a stage and fly-tower bigger and higher than the Mariinsky's, designed to outdo anything in Europe. The architect G. A. Lyutseradsky exploited the latest ferro-concrete materials and construction techniques and boasted of the building's total impregnability to fire. A huge conflagration duly occurred (fortunately at night) two days after the grand opening, after which the building remained closed for many months. The theatre still exists and is known today as the Music Hall.
2   See *Diaries*, vol. 1, pp. 200–201 and *passim*. Maria Nikolayevna, 'Marusya' and 'Marinochka' Pavlova all seem to be the same Conservatoire singing student.
3   The first Narodnaya Konservatoriya (People's Conservatoire), an offshoot of the People's Universities movement, opened in Moscow in 1906, instigated by public-spirited musicians such as Sergey Taneyev and Boleslav Yavorsky. The concept soon spread to other major cities, having the aim of making available broadly based training in music to a much wider cross-section of the population than the specialised Conservatoires with their emphasis on high professional standards of execution, composition and theory in classical disciplines. Folk music, choral singing and traditional instruments, for example, figured prominently in the curriculum.

22 March

The concert with Coates has been abandoned, because the capricious gentleman has taken offence at someone or other over something or other.

I carried on composing Act Four, making good progress, but for fear of my neuralgia I did not want to work for long, so stopped after an hour and a half or so.

I am in a wonderful mood today, happy as a lark – and all because of Marinochka! In the evening I was at B.N.'s (with my usual victory in a chess match). He even failed to turn up at Lotin's, where his absence provoked a sensation, as we heard from a midnight telephone conversation with Anna Grigorievna during which she informed us that Lotin's homily had today been one of uncommon inspiration. There was general astonishment at how uninspired he had been when Prokofiev was present, and at how Prokofiev had left without bowing to Lotin, an event which would lose B.N. to the group. 'No, Seryozha, you're definitely a Satanist!' said the prince delightedly as we walked through the hall together.

23 March

The Marquis's reading of the letter moves forward. In the evening I again went to the Koussevitzky concert. Needless to say, the main point was to be with Marinochka, but also to hear Alchevsky, who sang the long part in Berlioz's *The Damnation of Faust*. The work itself is tedious in the extreme, neither moving the listener with real tragedy nor beguiling him with lyricism, but the orchestration is in places so amazing as to make one gasp – with coloration that although written seventy years ago makes one think of Strauss (Richard). Suvchinsky drove me home afterwards and urged me to call on him tomorrow afternoon.

24 March

I am already, of course, making plans: suppose I were to spend the summer somewhere in Norway? Would that not be delightful! Could I afford it? This question was today settled by my uncle from America, Diaghilev. By all appearances he must be rolling in money, as today I received a fresh notification from the bank that money is being sent from New York. An absolute torrent of gold, if I cast my mind back to January, when I was glad of every 5-kopeck piece.

How much money (the notice did not specify)? At most it could be a thousand, as I have already had two thousand. The minimum would be a hundred roubles, bearing in mind this is what he still owes me for the Italian trip. But this is not likely, more probably it will be for the score,[1] of which, be it said, I have not yet written a single note.

Suvchinsky held a grand reception: Alchevsky, Koussevitzky, Diederichs, Andrey Rimsky-Korsakov[2] with Yulia,[3] Blumenfeld,[4] Zakharov with Cecilia, Obukhov, Asafyev. We all listened to visitors from Kiev: the composer Szymanowski and the outstanding violinist Paweł Kochánski. I had already heard them a year ago in Kiev. Szymanowski writes wonderfully for the violin: 'Not just a violin, but a whole orchestra,' says Zakharov. His music is interesting, but somehow lacking in inner substance. 'An adjective rather than a noun,' says Yulia Weisberg. 'Or even an adverb,' adds A. Rimsky-Korsakov.

Suvchinsky never left my side for a moment. I kept my distance from Koussevitzky. Obukhov invited me to call on him. I asked him what impression my *Sarcasms* had made on him, and was told: 'A very strong one.' I was interested in his reaction to my harmonies, since he has his own clearly defined and, according to his own opinion purist, system of harmonic construction. 'Do they sound clean to you?' I probed. 'If not always absolutely clean,' he replied, 'extremely convincing.' At this point Koussevitzky came up and asked, in his slow voice: 'Now, who is going to conduct *Ala and Lolli* in my season next year – you or I?' In order to make a bit of a show of it I did not immediately bite his hand off, but turned the conversation to concert halls. When he repeated the question, however, I first thanked him for the invitation and then said that I honestly did not know which would be better: to conduct it myself or to ask him to do so so that I could hear the work. On that we parted.

In the evening I attended the general rehearsal of a concert for the benefit of war wounded, to which Coates had dragged me along. I assumed that he wanted to introduce me to Telyakovsky, otherwise why would I be interested in a concert for war wounded? Although the introduction did not take place, Malko told me that he had recently been to see 'Telyak', and Telyak had in his presence telephoned Glazunov, teasing him by saying: 'You know, we're thinking of putting on an opera by one of your favourites . . .' 'Who?' 'Prokofiev.'

---

1   That is, the full orchestral score of *Chout*.
2   Andrey Rimsky-Korsakov (1878–1940), critic, scholar and writer, son of Nikolay Rimsky-Korsakov. See *Diaries*, vol. 1, p. 773.
3   Weisberg.
4   Felix Blumenfeld (1863–1931), pianist, conductor and composer. As a conductor of the Mariinsky Theatre he had been responsible *inter alia* for the premiere of Rimsky-Korsakov's *Legend of the Invisible City of Kitezh*. Blumenfeld was a prominent ally of Rimsky-Korsakov, Glazunov, Lyadov and the student body against the Directorate in the events of 1905 that led to the temporary closure of the Conservatoire and its re-opening under a new autonomous statute. See ibid., p. 368 and *passim*.

Malko warned me that while the opera would definitely be accepted and a contract signed, even with a guarantee of ten performances, it was almost equally certain that there would be no production in the coming season. Well, we shall have to wait and see!

25 March

The opera is coming on apace.

In the afternoon, a visit to the Golitsyns, and my English lesson. In the evening, the 'Bronze Horseman'. I was very glad to see Demchinsky there, not having seen him for some time.

26 March

This afternoon I had a visit from Marinochka, ostensibly so that she could show me how much her singing had come on, and to hear the song I had suggested to her five years ago but which she had not yet performed. Her voice has grown in strength and volume since that time, but whether it is now big enough I am not sure. Her phrasing is delightful. She was not completely won over by the song I had originally suggested, preferring 'Trust Me'.[1] It was evident that she appreciates the distance I have travelled, musically speaking, since those days.

Went to the bank to collect the money from my American Uncle. They answered that some necessary document or other was not to hand, and would I come back the day after tomorrow? That's a turn-up! Suppose it is all a mistake?

27 March

Finished the first scene. Now comes Alexey's flight, dark as the night through which he flees, disturbed and fragmentary as his thoughts, and as the curtain rises, a dazzlingly brilliant chord as if coming into a brightly lit hall from the darkness outside.[2]

In the afternoon I went for a fast walk to dispel a headache which threatened to flare up so painfully it frightened me. But when I came back home I launched into the libretto of Scene Two, completing more than half of it in a single sitting. I believe it is good; although the words alone are not much,

---

1   See *Diaries*, vol. 1, p. 562. The first song referred to is 'The Boat Cast Off', Op. 9 No. 2, to words by Alexey Apukhtin; the later one is to words by Boris Verin (aka Bashkirov), Op. 23 No. 3.
2   Alexey's frantic dash to the casino is depicted by an orchestral entr'acte, and the chord as the curtain rises on the roulette tables for the second scene of Act Four is an overwhelming tutti A major triad *fff* over a D major bass.

when put together with the music they should be compelling. My headache became unbearably painful although – unusually – when I went to take part in a concert for the Studio,[1] it went away. Zakharov was also playing in this concert, and smudged some passages, which upset him greatly. I played a few *morceaux* from Op. 12 and had an extraordinary success. An entire menagerie of baying female faces pressed up to the stage, grievously putting me off as I played an encore. Later, when I descended the staircase to go out into the street, they gave me another ovation.

After leaving the Tenishev Hall,[2] where the concert took place, in company with Asafyev and the Kavos girls[3] I set off for the *Mir Isskustva* exhibition, which is closing today with a grand banquet with the artists, at which I had been asked to play a few pieces. I always like to play for artists. However, they did not seem to understand much about *Sarcasms*, although Op. 12 had a huge success. I knew a lot of people there and had a very nice time. Petrov-Vodkin came and very civilly introduced himself to me.

I left the exhibition with Tamara Glebova,[4] with whom I have long been on bad terms. She now has two babies, and is much nicer. At two o'clock in the morning she and I wandered up and down Kirochnaya Street talking our heads off.

28 March

The bank has now sorted out its documents and handed me the money: 1,500 roubles, that is to say more than what he owes me in total for the ballet. Perhaps he has forgotten that he already sent me one and a half thousand and is now sending it to me a second time? Whatever the reason, I am now a seriously rich man.

In the afternoon I once again tried to walk off my headache, in which I eventually succeeded. All the same, they are becoming unbearable.

In the evening I was with Coates, playing him and also singing the third act until all that was left of my voice was a croak. Coates was thrilled beyond measure at the General's sobbing, and himself sang after me: 'ee-ee-ee-ee-ya-

---

1   The Music Studio, in which for a time Prokofiev gave piano lessons. See *Diaries*, vol. 1, pp. 650, 667 and *passim*.
2   The Tenishev Institute was established by the ethnographer and archaeologist Vyacheslav Tenishev (1844–1903). He also founded the ethnographically influenced arts-and-crafts community and workshops on his estate at Talashkino where his daughter-in-law Princess Maria Klavdievna Tenisheva invited Nikolay Roerich and Igor Stravinsky to work on the concept that was to become *The Rite of Spring*, thus creating the touchstone of primitive, ritualistic, pagan Russian nationalist tendencies in art.
3   The two beautiful Kavos sisters were friends of Alexander Borovsky and Boris Zakharov. Ibid., pp. 311, 571.
4   Tamara (Tamochka) Glebova (1892–?), former harp student at the Conservatoire. Ibid., pp. 325, 498, 551.

a-a-a!' until he collapsed in giggles. He thinks the third act is more integrated and less cinematographic than the first, but pointed out a passage from Babulenka that he thinks resembles too closely one in Puccini's *Madama Butterfly*, a work I have never heard. I'll have to have a look at that and if necessary change it, because, after all, what an unflattering comparison.

Coates told me that I would be having a meeting with the Director within days. We then discussed how to proceed in order that the opera should be produced this season. The whole season is cram full of new productions, but Coates still hopes to be able to push it through, especially if the singers can get going on learning it right at the beginning of the autumn and if the scenery can be entrusted to Lambin who, of course, is no Golovin but on the other hand can be relied upon to deliver it on time. I said I would want to raise the question of a guaranteed run of ten performances during the 1916–17 season, to which Coates replied: 'But don't present it in any way as an ultimatum. He will understand in any case.'

We then planned who should sing the various roles. Coates definitely wants to give the role of Alexey to Piotrovsky,[1] but Piotrovsky is not only too young, his voice is not the most bewitching, and is probably not strong enough for such a demanding part. I held out for Alchevsky. Polina would be Popova,[2] and I am very happy about that. Babulenka – Nikolayeva[3] and [Polina] Cherkasskaya.[4] The Marquis naturally would be Andreyev.

29 March

Had a telephone conversation with Ziloti. He was incredibly friendly and said that whatever I offer him he would play in his concert season and that there was no time limit; even if I were to tell him about a new work two days before he published his programme for the entire season, that would not be too late. He said that Koussevitzky was seriously interested in publishing me, that discussion of the proposal Ossovsky had made at a jury meeting had been postponed because some members of the jury were not sufficiently familiar with my later compositions. But if the jury were to turn me down, Koussevitzky would still want to publish me with the Gutheil publishing house he had recently acquired, where the contractual conditions would be

---

1 Kipras Piotrovsky (Petrauskas) (1885–1968), Lithuanian-born lyric-dramatic tenor. Later in his career Petrauskas was one of the founders of the Lithuanian State Opera Theatre in Vilnius. He was made a People's Artist of the Soviet Union in 1950.
2 Yelena Popova, soprano, see *Diaries*, vol. 1, pp. 318, 592.
3 Lyubov Nikolayeva.
4 *Sic*. This is odd, since Babulenka is a contralto role and Marianna Cherkasskaya-Palechek (1875–1934), one of the original interpreters of Fevronia in Rimsky-Korsakov's opera *The Legend of the Invisible City of Kitezh*, was a soprano. The later entry for 22 April on p. 125 makes it clear that Cherkasskaya was being considered for the role of Polina.

the same as with the Russian Music Editions. The main reason *Ala and Lolli* had been scheduled for performance in Moscow was to enable jury members to acquaint themselves with my latest profile.

This information could not have pleased me more. My star is once again in the ascendant. Overall, what successes have come my way in the past few days! On top of it all I am on the way to becoming a genuinely wealthy man: if everything happens as planned, I could end up with as much as 15,000 roubles this year.

30 March

Went on composing Alexey's flight.

In the evening, Vilkreiskaya's concert. In the final analysis she is not a very good pianist. My 'Scherzo' was anything but clean, and as if that were not enough she inflicted it on me twice because she repeated it as an encore. After the 'Scherzo' I made a dash to go to see Eleonora.

31 March

Alexey has got to the end of his sprint and arrived in the brightly illuminated gaming house. Right on cue the croupier calls: 'Les jeux sont faits.' The gaming house must be a real gambling den not, as in *The Queen of Spades*, merely a gathering of all the guests. As far as the closing of the first table my libretto is ready, and I think the scene will make a brilliantly lively and dynamic spectacle even though the actual text and all the hectic activity are pretty vacuous. I have not yet worked out in my mind how the second half of the scene is to go, since there is not much interest in simply seeing Alexey put down one stake after another and hearing the croupier's announcements. On the other hand it is essential to keep up and even heighten a sense of the amounts of money being staked.

1 April

Eagerly embarked on the roulette scene.

In the evening was at the 'Horseman' where I tangled with a young poetess, Larissa Reisner.[1] My response to the stream of super-clever and

---

1 Larissa Reisner (1896–1926), poet and Revolutionary, was an outstandingly attractive, colourful and romantic figure among those writers who not only enthusiastically welcomed the Bolshevik Revolution but actively engaged in its political and military struggle during the Civil War. Following an affair with Nikolay Gumilyov, who had by then separated from his first wife Anna Akhmatova, she became a Commissar of the Baltic Fleet, took part in daring military actions, met and married the fleet's celebrated Commander, Fyodor Raskolnikov, personally negotiated

super-unintelligible effusions she trilled about my compositions was that composers, not necessarily expert at bandying sophistries, compose, while so-called clever people spend their time and energy discoursing learnedly and at length on the compositions. Any composer so unfortunate as to be exposed to disquisitions of this sort will probably lose all desire to compose for at least three weeks.

This week I have been in correspondence with Suvchinsky: he is asking me to appear in their concerts in Moscow,[1] naming my own terms and conditions. 'Name my own terms and conditions' – that's the way to get a man to jump through hoops! The generosity of the gesture impelled me to play the part of *noblesse oblige*, so I replied that I would accept whatever conditions they were disposed to offer. But the ploy misfired, because they came back with a proposal of 300 roubles. Not much, but what the hell. And so, peace has broken out with the *Musical Contemporary*.

2 April

I am composing the roulette scene quite effortlessly and it is turning out even better than I expected. In the afternoon I went looking for presents for Eleonora and the prince. What a chore! In the evening I was at Gessen's.

3 April

The roulette is going well, but I am not writing very much so as not to get a headache. Demchinsky recommends taking regular, but small, doses of quinine bromide.

Aslanov telephoned to invite me to play a concerto and conduct my *Sinfonietta* at Pavlovsk (in connection with which he had managed to fall out yet again with Fitelberg, although on this occasion Fitelberg was in the

---

his release from British custody in London after he was captured on a reconnaissance mission in 1918, and went with him to Afghanistan when he was appointed Soviet Ambassador. Tiring of the role of a senior diplomat's consort, she returned to the continuing struggle within Russia, where she fell deeply in love with Karl Radek. She contracted typhoid and died in 1926 at the age of thirty, to be commemorated in one of Radek's most moving and emotionally committed articles. Her biographer, Cathy Porter, defines her as 'fighter, writer, the first Bolshevik woman commissar . . . the "Revolutionary Pallas" . . . a larger-than-life figure [whose short life was so full] that it is often hard to see her clearly through the halo of legends and hyperboles surrounding her.' (Cathy Porter, *Larissa Reisner* (Virago Pioneers, 1988)). The British journalist Andrew Rothstein wrote of meeting her in terms similar to, if more starry-eyed than, Prokofiev's: 'On entering the compartment I was quite unprepared for Larissa Reisner's beauty, which was enough to take one's breath away, but even less prepared for the entrancing, cascading gaiety of her speech, the exaltation of her ideas, and the limpid delights of her literary style.'

1   Promoted by the *Muzykalny Sovremennik*, Suvchinsky's and Andrey Rimsky-Korsakov's quarterly journal, which appeared from September 1915 until May 1917, with associated concert series.

wrong), and then relayed to me a committee meeting of old stagers at the Mariinsky Theatre: Cui, Solovyov,[1] A. Taneyev[2] and Lyapunov.[3] They were looking at possibilities for new operatic repertoire, and approved the following: a Spanish opera by Albeniz[4] and *Sappho* by our own modest, in all senses of the word, Chesnokov.[5] Coates had planned to include my *Gambler* on the audition list, apparently in order to create a scandal with the committee, that is to say to make them gasp in horror, and as a matter of fact the opera did appear on the list. However, Malko and Aslanov persuaded Telyakovsky against such inflammatory experiments and *The Gambler* will be auditioned separately some time soon, after the committee has completed its work. Only conductors, producers and, perhaps, Ziloti will be in attendance then.

In the evening I was at Bashkirov's. We played chess. A wonderful poem by Balmont: 'Dimitry the Fair'.[6]

4 April

The roulette is going well. In the evening, bridge at Andreyev's, Nikolay Vasilievich exceptionally affectionate. Anna Grigorievna, to my great relief, was not there.

5 April

Today is the birthday of two of my friends, Eleonora (eighteen) and the prince (twenty-five). My present to the prince was a most elegant album in which to inscribe his latest poetic productions, with xxv in Roman numerals on the binding. Up till now the prince has always written his poems in a deplorably scruffy notebook. Eleonora has been making insistent demands that I compose something for her. I have been too lazy to do so, but could

---

1 Nikolay Feopemptovich Solovyov (1846–1916 (December)), composer and teacher.
2 Not the composer Sergey Taneyev, who had died the previous year, but Alexander Taneyev (1850–1918), a composer and high Imperial Court official.
3 Sergey Lyapunov (1859–1924) composer, pianist and professor at the St Petersburg Conservatoire. Lyapunov had been one of the jury members for the Rubinstein Prize Prokofiev most feared. A disciple of the 'Mighty Handful', he was particularly associated with Balakirev. An extant piano-roll recording he made of his *Elegy on the Death of Franz Liszt* (Etude No. 12) reveals him to have been a prodigious pianist. See *Diaries*, vol. 1, p. 343 and *passim*.
4 Presumably *Pepita Jimenez* (1896), one of the more successful fruits of Albéniz's 'Faustian Pact' with Francis Money-Coutts whereby in return for generous financial support the composer set the wealthy banker's librettos.
5 Pavel Chesnokov (1877–1944), choral conductor and composer.
6 'Smert' Dimitriya Krasnogo', poem written in 1899 by Balmont about the mysterious death and miraculous apparent resurrection of the 'unhappy prince' Dimitri, whose song on rising from the grave heralded the overthrow of the Mongol yoke and the coming of freedom for the Russian people.

not think of anything to give her. Eventually I found a puzzle in which one object had to be disentangled from another, and so on. She was quite horrified by its difficulty and said that if she were successful in solving the puzzle I would have to write her another prelude.

Mama and I dined at the Damskys, after which Eleonora and I went for the evening to B.N.'s. There took place an interesting verbal duel between on the one side Demchinsky, Stavrovich and myself, and on the other an Imperial Court official, one Hofmeister Zlobin.[1] Of late B.N. has been much taken with this official, considering him one of the cleverest men in the world, but this evening he was definitively dislodged from this elevated status and was reduced to uttering nonsensical statements. At dinner, in my and Demchinsky's honour, the prince made speeches, while Stavrovich uttered a series of paradoxes and, starting from the premise that 'distance lends enchantment', said something astonishingly true, namely that one should view people around one in their proper perspective, and that is the path to happiness, for distance conceals the defects of some while proximity enhances the merits of others.

Aslanov informed me that I am bidden to Telyakovsky the day after tomorrow at two o'clock, when all the conductors, Ziloti and the others, will assemble to hear *The Gambler*. Aslanov is being terribly solicitous and wants to understudy Coates as conductor of *The Gambler*.

6 April

Did not compose, but played through *The Gambler* for tomorrow's audition. I am not nervous about it, on the contrary am very pleased that it is finally taking place. When all's said and done it is splendid that I am being admitted into the Imperial Theatre. That has a great ring to it.

Was at Demchinsky's, who welcomed me joyfully. His prescription of quinine bromide has all but cured my neuralgia. The prince was there too.

---

1   Zlobin was a Court Hofmeister, that is to say on the third rung from the top of the ladder of fourteen ranks covering military, Civil Service and Court appointments laid down by Peter the Great. His rank was the equivalent of Privy Councillor in the Civil Service. Above Zlobin would be Oberhofmeister and in the stratosphere above him the highest Court official the Chief Chamberlain. Zlobin, whose appointment would be a personal matter for the Tsar, would properly be addressed as 'Your Excellency' (to distinguish him from his boss's 'Your High Excellency' and his junior's 'Your High Ancestry'). On a level with the Oberforschneider (Chief Portion Master), the Stahlmeister (Stable Master) and the Jägermeister (Hunt Master) the job entailed supervision of Court employees and ceremonial occasions. No wonder the February 1917 Revolution, at least, enjoyed widespread sympathy.

7 April

In the morning, played through some of *The Gambler*, although did not manage to play all of it. Aslanov suggested that I call on him first in the Mariinsky Theatre, so that we could go together to Telyakovsky. The arrangement was clearly made to suit him, but as it did me also, that is what I did. Precisely at two o'clock we arrived at Telyakovsky's apartment in the government building just behind the Alexandrinsky Theatre. Ziloti and Coates were already waiting in the entrance hall, and we were later joined by Malko, Pokhitonov[1] and Tartakov.[2]

I felt wonderful, on top form. The Director kept us waiting for five or ten minutes, after which the great door was flung open and we were invited to step inside. A small, unprepossessing individual. A couple of years ago I had been introduced to him at a Conservatoire opera performance, but needless to say he neither remembered an insignificant Conservatoire student, nor had I succeeded in retaining his Excellency's physiognomy in my memory.[3] Having exchanged greetings we all sat down: everyone around the circular table and I a few paces away on the sofa. I embarked on an outline of the subject of the opera, which most of those present naturally did not know, gave a historical sketch of Dostoyevsky's circumstances at the time he wrote the novella, of his trip abroad and his losses at the roulette table, and then read a few excerpts from the novella, pointing up details of the characters involved.[4] Finally I ran through the plot, not of the novel, but of the opera. I spoke fluently, inspired by Demchinsky and Bashkirov, and with considerable confidence. My account was quite exhaustive, but even so I prefaced my performance of each act with a reading of the libretto. While I was reading the description of the characters a footman entered and handed Telyakovsky a letter. He opened it and made as if to read it to the accompaniment of my peroration. I stopped. Telyakovsky raised his eyes to mine; I stayed silent. Telyakovsky began to read his letter but immediately again looked over in my direction. I waited. Telyakovsky then folded up the letter, at which I continued my recitation. When Telyakovsky was looking at me a shadow crossed his face. I found this unpleasant, but resolved to preserve my demeanour.

---

1 Daniil Pokhitonov (1878–1957), conductor and teacher, one of the regular conductors at the Maly Opera and the Mariinsky Theatre, where he was a favourite of Chaliapin.
2 Joachim Tartakov (1860–1923), former singer (baritone, a fine Figaro) now Director of Productions at the Mariinsky Theatre. Prokofiev had met him before, on holiday in Kislovodsk with the Meshcherskys in the summer of 1914, when they had both been involved in a comically chaotic charity concert. See *Diaries*, vol. 1, pp. 725, 727.
3 In December 1913, backstage at the Conservatoire's theatre when Prokofiev had been conducting a student production of *Aida*. Ibid., pp. 568–9.
4 See Appendix 1.

And so, having read through the libretto of Act One, I started to play it. Malko turned pages for me, Ziloti looked over my shoulder, and the others stayed where they were, at the table. I played pretty well, very well actually, but I have no sort of a voice and could do no more than declaim the text, and even sometimes tap out the vocal line on the piano, but my declaiming could hardly be heard above the music. On top of that I soon became hoarse, and Ziloti later said I used much too much pedal. After the first act I took a short break and then, already completely exhausted, read through the second act libretto, then did the same with the third. Tartakov was evidently very interested in Babulenka: several times coming up to look at the score.

Telyakovsky had understood nothing whatsoever. But of course he found it necessary to attribute any confusion to my performance: without hearing the work sung it was impossible to form an impression of the vocal parts and the overall melodic shape. For that reason, would it not be better . . . of course, it was rather late in the day now, perhaps in the autumn? . . . to have the singers study at least one act and then perform it with orchestra? Then the opera itself would become clear.

I found this delaying tactic, neither 'yes' nor 'no', but certainly 'no' as far as the coming season was concerned, intolerable, so I decided to go for the throat. I replied that, of course it was possible to proceed as was being suggested, but I felt it my duty to inform them that as recently as last week Diaghilev had sent me 1,500 roubles which, since I had already received payment for the ballet[1] in full, clearly must be understood as a down-payment on the opera. (This was very nearly a legitimate interpretation, since my agreement was to receive 1,000 roubles only after delivery of the full score. However to date only the piano score was ready, for which I had already received the 2,000 I was due.) It followed that putting off the audition of the opera until the autumn would mean that only at that point would there be either a positive or a negative response, and therefore, should Diaghilev wish to conclude a contract now or during the summer, I would sign it in order to avoid falling between two stools. And as was well known, even if Diaghilev was not presenting performances in Russia, he invariably extends his agreements to cover Russia.

Oh yes, this they knew all too well from previous experiences with Stravinsky and Tcherepnin, and they knew also that Diaghilev would be doing everything in his power to wrest the plums from the Mariinsky. For this reason my announcement had an immediate and powerful effect. Telyakovsky withdrew into a corner to consult with those present, and after a little while came back to address me. 'What conditions do you require?' he asked.

1 *Chout*.

Well, this was a completely different state of affairs. I replied that I knew the Imperial Theatres offered the same conditions to all composers, but I wanted a guarantee of ten performances in the coming season. They countered by objecting that there would be no time even for one performance, let alone ten, next season: there were so many new productions, and so many revivals of old ones. More consultation, and then Telyakovsky asked if we could meet again in a week's time – the Wednesday after Easter, and in the meantime he would establish with the relevant committee whether or not there would be funds for a new production. I had thought Telyakovsky was the ultimate overlord of the Imperial Theatres, but apparently even he is subject to superior control. Bidding me good day, Telyakovsky said: 'At least for the time being do not telegraph to Diaghilev.' Naturally, I undertook not to do so. Coates called after me: 'Wait for me, let's go and buy some crayons!'

This meant I had to wait another twenty minutes, as after I left the room there were further discussions. Emerging, Coates and Ziloti disclosed that there could be no question of as many as ten performances next season, and therefore I was likely to be offered ten spread over two seasons, and they were very insistent that I should agree to this. Ziloti got particularly agitated over this, saying it was thanks to the efforts of himself and Coates that the theatre was at long last beginning to take an interest in young composers, but if those young composers were to show themselves as difficult and capricious, all these promising beginnings could go to the devil.

Coates and I then bought some Koh-I-Noor crayons[1] and I returned home, tired out but almost happy about my meeting with the Director.

In the evening the prince came to show off a new electrical device he had acquired.

9 April

Kolechka Myaskovsky telephoned, which made me very glad; he is here for two days from his Revel posting.[2]

---

1 'In 1802 the founding family of Josef Hardtmuth patented his invention for manufacturing graphite leads. The Hardtmuth factory was then in Vienna, but in 1848 it moved outside Prague to Ceské Budejovice in what is now the Czech Republic, where the company spent its first century known as Hardtmuth. 'Koh-I-Noor' became part of its name in 1890. The story is told, however apocryphal, of the famous yellow Koh-I-Noor diamond of India. Meaning 'mountain of light', the 105-carat stone found its way to England and Queen Victoria in 1850, and today it still resides there as part of Britain's Crown Jewels. When Queen Victoria was presented with Hardtmuth's pencils, she is said to have pronounced them "the Koh-I-Noor of pencils". Thus did Hardtmuth become Koh-I-Noor, and yellow – the colour of the diamond – come to symbolize Hardtmuth's high quality.' (Contemporary advertisement for Koh-I-Noor pencils).
2 Revel was the Russian name for Tallinn, the capital of Estonia, part of the Russian Empire until the Treaty of Brest-Litovsk. Myaskovsky, as a serving Army Engineer Officer had been posted to Revel.

Today is Easter Saturday, and I went to the service of Prime[1] in the Conservatoire. Last year I had written to Eleonora from Italy regretting that I would be missing this event. Tartakov saw me and kissed me affectionately with the words: 'Talented, talented . . .'

I asked Popova if she would like to sing in my opera. Karakash[2] immediately jumped in with 'Of course she would!'

I said to Zakharov, who had taken Communion yesterday because of his forthcoming marriage, that it was ten years since I had last done so. He pushed me away from him with a comic-serious exclamation of 'Away from me, foul infidel!'

Glazunov kissed me ceremoniously.

10 April
Easter Day

Carried on composing the roulette scene. I decided not to pay calls except for the Ruzskys, whom I have not visited for three months. But there was no one at home today: the daughters are working in the hospital in Kiev, father and son were out paying calls. In the evening I went to see Myaskovsky. The fourth and fifth *Sarcasms* made a huge impression on him. He has bought the collected works of Lyadov, and was tearing them to shreds.

11 April

I am twenty five-years old today, and was in complete birthday mode. In the morning Myaskovsky and Aslanov came by in order that Myaskovsky and I could play him the four-hand version of N.M.'s Third Symphony as a preliminary to its forthcoming performance this summer. I love this symphony very much.

In the evening I had guests: Myaskovsky, Nikolay Vasilievich [Andreyev], Eleonora, the prince, Demchinsky with his wife, and Stavrovich. The prince made a grand entrance into the drawing-room, staggering under the weight of a basket so enormous he was hard put to it to lift it at all. This was my present. We put it in the middle of the drawing-room and undid the wrapping. It proved to be a complete herd of bronze goats, making up a highly original desk-set of beautifully made writing implements.

Stavrovich, in my house for the first time, which gave me great pleasure, was in excellent form and entertained the company throughout the evening.

---

1 See *Diaries*, vol. 1, pp. 637–8.
2 M. N. Karakash (1887–1937), baritone soloist at the Mariinsky and Bolshoy Theatres. He was another outstanding Figaro in the 1913 Bolshoy Theatre production of *The Barber of Seville*, along with Chaliapin (Don Basilio) and Nezhdanova as Rosina.

But the prince was at odds with Demchinsky (now there's a thing!) on account of some slight by Demchinsky, and left early on the pretext of having to hurry back to his 'Monday' soirée which, allegedly, he had left in order to come to me. This quarrel upset me greatly.

12 April

The day after tomorrow, to commemorate the anniversary of Scriabin's death, Borovsky is playing a whole programme of his works at the 'Contemporaries'. Borovsky arrived in Petrograd a few days ago, and in accordance with our normal practice, we lunched together.

13 April

Today was the day of my second appointment with the Director of the Imperial Theatres, and precisely at noon I was in His Excellency's office. Telyakovsky was exceptionally friendly, and enquired whether I still wanted the opera to be performed in the coming season. Learning that I most certainly did, he went on for some considerable time about how full the repertoire was. Alongside this he wanted to know my thoughts on singers and designers, and what sort of effect I thought the opera might have on the public. He preened himself on his lifelong commitment to presenting new works, sometimes even contrary to the wishes of the Tsar, who nevertheless held him in great favour. Winding up, he said that he would once again talk the matter through with Tartakov and Coates to see if they could see any way of including it next season, and if they could, he would invite me to sign a contract. I left well pleased with the interview.

14 April

Scriabin died a year ago today. Borovsky played a recital of his works with his customary excellence, the Sixth Sonata being particularly fine. I have not hitherto known this sonata very well, but this time it gave me tremendous pleasure. I sat next to Obukhov during the performance and had quite a long talk with him.

15 April

Telephoned Marinochka and learned that she has just returned from Helsingfors.[1] She was happy to accept my invitation to the matinee performance

---

1 The Russian name for Helsinki, which was then in the autonomous Russian province of Finland.

of *The Stone Guest*,[1] and we heard the opera. I liked it even more than before. Oh, how marvellous the way Dargomyzhsky sets words is! If only the music was more brilliant and more profound, and Pushkin's play more flexible and adapted to the stage, what an opera it would be, and what a leap into the future!

Marinochka was simply enchanting. She had been to visit relations in Helsingfors and had been able to equip herself with a summer wardrobe, since everything is better and cheaper there. She confessed to me that her dream was to travel, and listened enviously to the picturesque descriptions I gave of my journeys abroad.

In the evening I performed in the Tenishev Hall at an evening of 'Contemporary Poetry and Music' in aid of the wounded, and had quite a tumultuous success.[2] Two rather swarthy girls burst into the artists' room and presented me with a bunch of crimson roses. For some reason Marinochka had very much wanted to hear me play, so I gave her a ticket, and afterwards I took her to the 'Bronze Horseman', to which she came with some trepidation, although the only person there of whom she approved was Demchinsky. I presented her with my magnificent roses. There is in her face a kind of elusive quality which always somehow escapes the memory.

16 April

Today's papers reported variously on the fact that *The Gambler* had been accepted for production. Dvinsky, a journalist on the *Vechernye Birzhevye Novosti* (*Stock Exchange Evening News*), meeting me in the Conservatoire, confirmed that Tartakov had told him this very morning *The Gambler* was to be put on during the coming season. From this I deduce that Telyakovsky's negotiations with Tartakov had reached a positive conclusion.

In the evening I was at the Kavos's, and made a number of new acquaintances there. In general I am not fond of social evenings; I prefer activities like chess, bridge, concerts.

17 April

Today I invited Marinochka out to Pavlovsk to a farm where they serve you omelettes ('Nous boirons du lait sur l'herbe fraîche', to quote the

---

1 Opera (1872) by Dargomyzhsky.
2 This must have been a Silver Age evening to remember. With Prokofiev (who performed his First Piano Sonata) on the bill were Butomo-Nazvanova and Artyemeva-Leontevskaya in songs by Stravinsky and Yulia Weisberg, and the poets Anna Akhmatova, Fyodor Sologub, Alexander Blok, Osip Mandelshtam, Mikhail Kuzmin and the peasant poet Nikolay Klyuyev, all reading their own verses.

Marquis in *The Gambler*[1]), but she was not able to come. I went on my own.

In the evening I went to Demchinsky's, took a game of chess off him, and in answer to the question, how my work was going, told him that today I had finished the first half of the roulette scene and now found myself in some difficulty not being able for the life of me see how I was going to do the second half. To continue in the same style with more cries of 'les jeux sont faits' and 'rien ne va plus' from the croupier would be no good; it would become tedious. So Alexey must move to another table away from centre stage, whilst in the foreground the players comment excitedly on his unprecedented run of good fortune, only the occasional cry from Alexey's far-off table signalling that his success has not come to an end. It was the text for this scene I was finding hard to create. Because, apart from all other considerations, it was essential that the second half of the roulette scene be even more tense and fevered than the first half.

Demchinsky took the problem earnestly to heart and suggested the introduction of a new character: the Director of the casino, summoned in connection with the closing of the table.[2] He seemed to grasp what was required and promised to come to me tomorrow so that we could map out the scene together, and said he would look through Dostoyevsky's diaries and letters to check on his feelings about roulette, in order that the scene we were concocting should so far as possible be faithful to the spirit of Dostoyevsky.

18 April

Set to work on the final scene in order not to be held up waiting for the roulette scene libretto. The last scene is swinging along splendidly; Polina's 'the Marquis's mistress is not worth fifty thousand' has come out superbly.

I cannot understand why Telyakovsky has not telephoned me about the contract. After all, the piano score has to be written out and given to the singers in time for them to study it over the summer.

Demchinsky came to see me in the evening. I played him the roulette scene, and although I was worried about the thinness of the text, it earned his approval. 'You're right not to have anything more extended than disjointed phrases and random ejaculations,' he said. We then proceeded to sketch out the second half of the scene, which Demchinsky sees not merely in terms of

---

1 'We shall drink milk on the cool grass' – in Dostoyevsky, not in Prokofiev's libretto. The Marquis is sarcastically backing up the General's ludicrous attempts to head off his aunt, the Babulenka, from a potentially disastrous return visit to the Casino by suggesting a drive out into the country for tea. Babulenka puts him right in characteristically forthright terms: 'You and your milk! Go and guzzle it yourself, it gives me the bellyache.'
2 Alexey having broken the bank at the first table he played.

the physical narrative but – in the words of the Director when he predicts Alexey's downfall – as in the deepest sense the essence of *The Gambler*.

Demchinsky said he would work on and refine the sketches we had made.

19 April

After yesterday's labours with Demchinsky I awoke feeling lazy. But thoughts of Marinochka momentarily brightened my mood.

Went for my lesson with Handschin. I'll need to pull myself together and try to finish with at least a diploma next year, as they have already begun conscripting students, so they might nab me in the autumn.

Andreyev says that Telyakovsky has gone out of town to his estate for the rye sowing and will not return until the end of the week, and that is why I have not been invited to sign a contract. Nikolay Vasilievich was truly disappointed that all my songs had passed from his hands into those of Alchevsky, who would be singing them for Ziloti.

20 April

Polina's hysterical outburst and every other aspect of this scene raced forward – six horns wailing on a top E after the money is thrown down, and then the final bars of the opera – pleasant recollections of the roulette table.

In the afternoon I practised the organ. In the evening I went to Boris Verin's, where I have not been for two weeks (as a result of the abrupt manner in which he left my birthday party). But he still wants to settle how we are going to spend the summer together, and whether we should not rent a little cottage somewhere.

21 April

The final scene makes steady progress, although slightly less intensively than yesterday. Demchinsky telephoned to say that he had a concept for the end of the roulette scene – how wonderful!

Today we are to be invaded by a clutch of relations, some of them on leave from war service. We'll have to play vint.[1]

---

1   A popular card game, mixing elements of whist and preference and involving the classic procedures of trumps, bidding, tricks and the successful or unsuccessful gaining of a contract by the end of each hand. The name 'vint' (in Russian 'screw') derives from the clockwise bidding procedure and the technique of forcing one's opponents to increase ('screw up') their bids to the point at which they will fail to meet the contract. See *Diaries*, vol. 1, p. 112 and *passim*.

22 April

Tried to get away from Handshin as early as possible in order to go to Pavlovsk with Marinochka. At two o'clock we set off for Tsarskoye Selo in a first-class carriage, and then took a carriage on to Pavlovsk, walked for a long time in the park, ate omelettes at the farm, and came back to Petrograd at seven in the evening. Marinochka was delighted with her excursion. Another thing: Zakharov rang her up today, and she had long wanted to re-establish relations with him. She told me he had always been very jealous of me on her account. Interesting. Her future plans involve going down the Volga to the Caucasus to see her father. When she asked me what my plans are for the summer, I told her merely that I am going to spend a month touring Scandinavia.

When I got home I found a telegram from Tartakov inviting me to come to the Mariinsky that evening at Telyakovsky's request to discuss the cast for the opera and allocating the roles. I did so, and we spent quite a long time deciding on Alchevsky and Yershov for Alexey (about which I am thrilled), Popova and Cherkasskaya for Polina, Bossé[1] as the General, and Andreyev as the Marquis. Tartakov's recommendation for the Babulenka was Panina,[2] but as I did not know her he suggested I come on Monday to hear her in *Megaye*. He asked me to let the theatre office have the manuscript as soon as possible so that they could get on with copying the parts. 'You see, my dear, I must give the singers their parts by the 15th of May, otherwise we shall never be able to start rehearsals in September!' said he.

So all this is extremely satisfactory. Rehearsals in September! And this after being told so often that 'we won't have time to put on the opera . . .'

23 April

I cannot say that I composed a great deal, but all the same the final scene is moving forward and is turning out well. I got from Demchinsky the libretto for the last part of the roulette scene, and am absolutely thrilled with it. There are only a few places I have a question mark over it from the point of view of liveliness and dramatic interest, but everything he has done speaks of great knowledge of the stage. What a pity I did not 'discover' Demchinsky before! But he will stand me in excellent stead for the future, and the very near future at that: in the final scene not many words are needed for the love climax.

---

1   Gwalter Bossé (1877–1953), bass principal singer at the Mariinsky Theatre, possessor of a particularly resonant deep bass voice, and a noted Wotan. Other roles in which he excelled were Saint Bris in *Les Huguenots* and Khan Konchak in *Prince Igor*.
2   Antonida Panina (Panafutina), mezzo-soprano principal at the Mariinsky Theatre.

Dined at Gessen's, where a large company had gathered to hear *The Gambler*. Before starting I had to outline the subject, which I did in such a confusing way that no one understood a thing. In fact I can speak well when I need to persuade someone of something, but to have to give an account of something without being quite sure what – the novel itself, or my interpretation of it, the psychological nuances or the action, and doing so sitting in the middle of a drawing-room with people in front of me and behind me – well, this is a recipe for incoherence. Matters got worse: I cannot sing, and I could not be bothered to bawl out the words as I did at Telyakovsky's, so I mumbled them *sotto voce*, and the only people who could hear anything were Benois and Karatygin, sitting beside me. No one else understood anything. The strange thing was that inwardly I was laughing at them, thinking how marvellous it was going to be on stage. Karatygin did not take much of it in. Benois found the roulette scene convincing.

When Karatygin asked why I was going home so early, I replied: 'Because being made to play an opera and trying to make people understand it is a lot more tiring than listening to it without understanding it.'

24 April

Wrote very little today.

In the afternoon I went to listen to the piano competition at the Conservatoire, for which this year not one but two pianos were to be awarded as prizes. As usual the crowds were out in force and there was an atmosphere of great excitement. Zelensky played extremely well and with great *élan*, but the most interesting performance was by Zakharov and Eleonora, who stoked up great fires of passion behind a mask of each refusing to acknowledge the existence of the other.[1]

At seven o'clock, as I was on course up Nevsky to visit the prince, I was accosted by a nurse who then kept pace with me all the way, expostulating at her rapture in making my acquaintance, and apologising for having been, in default of other avenues, reduced to this most primitive device to achieve her objective. The prince, looking out of his window in expectation of my arrival and seeing me accompanied by a medical sister whose dress and demeanour was some way short of elegant, was consumed by curiosity to know in what latest romantic adventure I had got myself embroiled. At the entrance to his building I bade farewell to the energetic sister, resisting her importunate proposals for further assignations.

---

1   In the concerto section of the Rubinstein Prize Competition the orchestral part was played by a second piano. On this occasion Eleonora Damskaya was competing and Boris Zakharov (who had already graduated) was accompanying her.

25 April

Woke up first at six o'clock, then again at eight, got up and briskly dressed, for at nine I was due to go and collect Marinochka as today we were making an expedition to Schlüsselberg.[1] How utterly captivating was the single tender word 'Seryozhenka...' with which she greeted me as she came out into the entrance hall where I stood waiting for her! The car took us quickly through the town to the Voskresensky embankment, where we boarded the steamer. It was the first time Marinochka had been aboard a steamer, and at first she was frightened, but as soon as we were under way she realised there was nothing to be alarmed about. Although it was still April it was warm and we were in light summer clothes, the sun shone brightly and all cares were far away. The voyage took four hours, followed by Schlüsselberg itself with the restless dark, dark blue and chill breeze over the boundless expanse of Lake Ladoga, then a relaxing time on the grass below the ramparts, and finally the voyage home.

'Marinochka, will you come to Norway with me?'

'Is that somewhere near Petrograd?'

'A bit farther than that,' and I smilingly began to describe the sight-seeing trip we would make to Stockholm, Trolgot and Kristiania.[2] She listened, but I could see she was not taking it seriously.

After we said goodbye I went immediately to the Mariinsky Theatre as Tartakov had asked me to come and hear Panina in *Megaye*. Would she or would she not be right for Babulenka? I apologised for the inappropriateness of my casual dress for the theatre and explained that I had come straight from the trip to Schlüsselberg. I did not think much of Panina, the voice was too small.

26 April

The third anniversary of Max's death. How far I have moved away from the interests I once shared with him, how trivial and even comic they now seem to me, and yet how dear is the friend I have been without all this time. Ah, Max!

In the evening I was at Demchinsky's to talk over the roulette scene and the final love scene. He is a superb adviser.

---

1 Fortress town at the head of the Neva river on Lake Ladoga, 45 kilometres east of St Petersburg. The fortress had been captured from the Swedes by Peter the Great in 1702 and renamed Schlüsselburg ('Key Town' in German) to balance Peter's western companion fortress at the mouth of the Neva, which he had likewise captured and called Schlotburg ('Lock Town'). See *Diaries*, vol. 1, p. 222n.

2 The former name for Oslo.

27 April

Telephoned Marinochka to see if she was coming to see me today as planned. She said she could not after all, she was busy. However, she promised to come tomorrow.

I gave the Imperial Theatres library the score of two acts of *The Gambler*, to be copied. They groaned at how much work there was and the short time in which it had to be done. And what about Telyakovsky? Shouldn't we sign the contract, finally?

28 April

I ought to finish *The Gambler*, but something is holding me back. Nevertheless, the scene where Polina throws the money back at him just fits my mood. I composed it today, and it's good. And the wailing of the six horns on high E is absolutely thrilling.

All afternoon I waited for evening to come, Marinochka having confirmed her promise to visit at six o'clock, but at eight there was no sign of her, nor at nine, and at half-past nine she telephoned to say she was sorry, but she would not be coming. As it was a dismal prospect to sit at home on my own, I went to Eleonora's. She was pleased to see me, and told me all about Boryusya,[1] who is in hot pursuit of her. Eleonora was amused to see me looking so disgruntled. Who my own love is, she does not know.

29 April

Went to the public singing examination and met Marinochka there. 'How peeved you look after yesterday evening,' she laughed. But she promised to come today and bring with her *Butterfly*, remembering Coates's accusation that I, not knowing the opera, had lifted from it a phrase in Babulenka's part.

This evening Marinochka arrived even earlier than I was expecting her, and spent a while arranging on my desk the bronze goats Bashkirov had given me. I asked her why she was going down the Volga when I was inviting her to Norway? She said that had it been next year it would have been fine, but for the present she is too dependent on her father and the rest of her family to think of taking such liberties.

---

1 Boris Zakharov.

May

The 1st of May was a Sunday, a day of sunshine, just like my mood. I telephoned Telyakovsky's office and asked for him to be passed a message that I would soon be going away and would like to know before I did so what was the state of affairs with *The Gambler*. To my great satisfaction Telyakovsky made an appointment with me that very evening, and at five o'clock I was very graciously received. He even left before the end of *Boris Godunov*, in which Kurzner[1] was making his debut, so as not to keep me waiting. He said that in a few days' time Baron Kusov[2] would sign the agreement with me and that I could have an advance of two thousand. If the opera were a success they would present it the following season in Moscow. I decided not to hold out for a guarantee of ten performances in one season, and accepted their proposal of spreading them over two.

In the evening I played the roulette scene for Coates, and the final scene of the opera.

At Boris Verin's name-day party, an occasion of great pomp, I was in the foulest of moods; I chain-smoked and spent the whole evening at the chess board taking Little Sunshine apart. The cause of my mood was roughly this: I knew of course that everything was all right, the opera had been accepted, I had a mass of concert engagements and plenty of money, I was becoming better and better known, and I was not so desperately in love with Marinochka that a trip down the Volga to the Caucasus with Boris Verin – who was anxiously awaiting my agreement – was not a perfectly satisfactory alternative to my dreams of being with her. Of all this I was quite well aware, but there was a void in my heart, a reluctance to settle down to anything. I had been in love with my plan, had invested so much fantasy in it, had become so obsessed by it, that I was quite distraught at the prospect of having to live without it.

Meanwhile the prince, to whom I had signalled that I was at his disposal, invited me to spend some weeks at his mother's dacha in Kuokkale,[3] preparatory to taking a trip down the Volga starting about 10–15 June, and

---

1 Pavel Kurzner (1886–1949), bass principal at the Mariinsky Theatre.
2 Vice-director of the Imperial Theatres in Petrograd.
3 After the construction of the railway line from Petersburg to Vyborg in the 1860s, the whole 'kurortny rayon', 'resort area' along the southern shore of the Karelian isthmus became during the nineteenth and twentieth centuries a favoured dacha destination for the Petersburg middle classes, artists and intelligentsia. At the time Prokofiev was writing, the names of the settlements were all still Finnish; after the Russo-Finnish War of 1939–40, which resulted in Finland ceding Karelia to the Soviet Union, names were changed into Russian, including the much prized resorts of Terioki (to Zelenogorsk), Kuokkale (to Repino), Kellomyaki (to Komarovo). The two last-named became official artists' rest homes under the Soviets (Shostakovich holidayed and stayed in dachas in Repino, Sestroretsk and Komarovo).

then visiting his multi-millionaire relations in Samara. This was agreed upon.

On 10 May I had my organ exam, for which I diligently studied a four-part Bach fugue with the theme even appearing in the pedals. The exam took place in our organ classroom and was a closed, not a public, affair. The jury consisted of Glazunov, Wihtol[1] and my old enemy Petrov.[2] Handschin, who had attired himself in a long frock-coat for the occasion, assumed an energetic, business-like air. I played with considerable gusto, although my pedalling was not always immaculately precise; also I mixed up the manuals. Glazunov made notes about each student, and on mine wrote: 'Some inaccurate disposition' (or similar intellectual expression) 'of the feet, but the hands were good.'

On the 11th I was asked by a functionary called Tyuflev to come to the offices of the Imperial Theatres to sign the contract. For form's sake I conversed a while with Baron Kusov, the Vice-Director, after which I signed the typed contract, to which had been added a handwritten note that ten performances would be guaranteed in the course the next two seasons. I wrote a request for an advance of 2,000 roubles and then had a long wait while they went out for duty stamps (which I had to pay for). A fair-haired man, whom I took to be another official but was in fact a reporter, took advantage of the delay to take down in pencil on a scrap of paper a statement from me about *The Gambler*, and a couple of days later the fulsome story he wrote appeared in the Petrograd papers, accompanied by a photograph of the composer. All the newspapers carried the interview, and as a result there were many telephone calls and I was congratulated on all sides.[3]

Work on the opera proceeded more slowly during May than hitherto, and I found it difficult to make myself complete it. The roulette scene was finished on 16 May and I counted it a complete success, but the final scene dragged on until June. Sections of it were ready, but the whole thing was not stitched together. The first three acts were already in the hands of the Imperial Theatre being copied.

It was around this time that I got to know Chaliapin.[4] Our acquaintance

---

1 Joseph Wihtol (Jāzeps Vītols) (1863–1948), Latvian composer, teacher and critic, student of Rimsky-Korsakov, an influential member of the Belyayev circle and as critic of the German-language *Sankt Petersburger Zeitung* implacably hostile to progressive tendencies. His attitude to Prokofiev, however, softened considerably after he left Russia to return to his native Riga in the newly independent Latvia after the Revolution, where he conducted the National Opera and founded the Latvian Conservatory of Music. See *Diaries*, vol. 1, p. 61 and *passim*.
2 Alexey Petrov (1851–1818), professor of music theory at the Conservatoire and author of a well-known textbook of music analysis. Ibid., pp. 91, 374.
3 See Appendix 5 for a translation of part of this interview as published in the *Vechernye birzhevye novosti* (*Stock Exchange Evening News*) on 12 May 1916, outlining his approach to opera in general and the question of setting Dostoyevsky's prose in particular.
4 Fyodor Chaliapin (1873–1938), bass, the most celebrated Russian opera singer of the age, indeed perhaps of the century, and a performer of irresistible stage magnetism, as Prokofiev

dated from a most interesting dinner at the French Ambassador's attended by a whole series of celebrities: Chaliapin, Benois, Ziloti and others. It so happened that my interview about *The Gambler* had appeared in the press a few days prior to this, with much lofty speculation about the extent of my concern for the scenographic aspect of the opera. This had attracted Chaliapin's attention and caused him to become very interested in me; as a result he spent half the evening talking to me and even suggested I write an opera for him on the subject of Stenka Razin,[1] but I told him this subject was not one close to my heart. Not only that, but it was no longer possible to approach it in the manner of Rimsky-Korsakov, and I did not as yet know how to do so otherwise. Chaliapin expressed interest in *The Gambler* and said that he would come when it was being rehearsed in the autumn.

At the end of May I repaired with B.N. to Kuokkale, where his mother had rented a fine dacha right on the seashore with, most importantly, a tennis court. I just about knew the rules of this elegant sport, but was hopelessly bad at it because I never had any opportunity to practise, so now I was delighted at the chance of doing so whenever I fancied. And even my partners were just right: slightly better than me.

June

The Kuokkale dacha was not over-endowed with luxury but was very comfortable, the hosts charming, my time was my own, the fare excellent and sweetmeats in abundance.

I settled down to orchestrating *The Gambler*, completing about five pages a day, rising later to ten. In between I played tennis. Borya and I got on very well, although we squabbled whenever he tried to cheat, shouting 'right' instead of 'out'[2] or when I roused him from his bed at noon with the aid of cold water. I also made friends with his younger sister Tatyana Nikolayevna, a very nice woman of twenty-three, who was staying in the next-door dacha. I was not so close to his other sister, Varya, the Princess Magalova,[3] a

---

had discovered in June 1913 when he first heard him in Paris and London in Diaghilev's productions of *Khovanshchina* and *Boris Godunov*, the latter being the role in which he came to personify the art of Russian singing (see *Diaries*, vol. 1, pp. 429, 437). Largely self-taught, Chaliapin had started his career in Georgia and then as a member of Savva Mamontov's Private Opera in Moscow, where he formed a lifelong friendship with Rachmaninoff, a prelude to national and international stardom in the opera houses and concert platforms of the world.

1 Stenka (Stepan) Razin was a seventeenth-century Cossack warlord whose rebellion against the Tsar and nobility of Muscovy came not far off establishing a Cossack republic along the whole length of the Volga and threatening Moscow itself before he was eventually defeated, brought to Moscow, tortured and executed in 1671. Glazunov wrote a symphonic poem and Shostakovich a cantata (*The Execution of Stepan Razin*, to words by Yevgeny Yevtushenko) on the subject.
2 'Right' and 'out' are written in English.
3 Princess Varvara Magalova, sister of Boris Bashkirov and wife of Prince Magalov. The pianist

more unpredictable person, but she arrived later and I did not come across her much.

Until Mama left the city to go south I went into Petrograd quite often.

On 14 June I played my Second Piano Concerto in Pavlovsk, which although I had not practised it enough I performed with unusual brilliance. The audience applauded tumultuously and shouted bravo when I played the *Sarcasms* as an encore.

Several times I went over to Terioki, looked in on Karnovich,[1] on the Zakharovs (Boris and Cecilia were away in Zheleznovodsk[2]), and went to church in the secret hope of seeing there my Tanyusha from the year before. But this time I was out of luck: I met every one else – her father, her brother, her sister – but Tanyusha herself, like the golden fish, slipped through the net.

And so my time in Kuokkale passed between work on the score and the tennis court, a little uneventful but still very pleasant. Of course, Kuokkale did not have the same enchantment for me that Terioki held and still holds, but I was very happy with the month I spent there. And at the end of June Borenka and I set out for the Volga, *en route* to the Caucasus.

The opera as a whole was now composed and the score of Act One completed.

July

We kept travel notes, but they were interrupted halfway along because at that point Borenka and I went separate ways. This happened when we were staying with his brother in Samara, where Borenka fell head over heels in love with the seventeen-year-old Vera Suroshnikova (inevitably no ordinary love affair, this, but on the most elevated plane, a transcendental, 'once in a lifetime' experience). As a result he could not bring himself to leave, whereas I was bored and anxious to continue the journey. Vera was an enigmatic girl and not without a certain panache, but the rest of the company, with its tens of millions of roubles, was excruciatingly dull.

And so, following a heavy session explaining my reasons to Borenka, I left to go my way alone, but had got no further than Tsaritsyno when I received an urgent telegram asking me to wait, as the poet had also set out and would be there a day later. I replied in verse:

Nikita Magalov (1912–1882) was their son. Prokofiev had given the Princess some piano lessons in 1914. See *Diaries*, vol. 1, pp. 738–42 and *passim*.

1   Composition student at the Conservatoire whose *Variations for Orchestra* Prokofiev had conducted a the Graduation Concert in April 1913. Ibid., p. 362 and *passim*.
2   Spa town, along with Yessentuki, Pyatigorsk, Kislovodsk and Mineralnye Vody one of the Caucasus Mineral Waters complex of resorts.

> Received your news, deeply impressed,
> Congratulations on your plan.
> Tsaratsyno finds me depressed,
> So we'll meet up in Astrakhan.

And that is what we did.

On the steamer *en route* to Astrakhan I was for some unknown reason – I suppose my appearance – taken for a poet. That at least is what the group of young people on board decided. To begin with I assumed the persona of the poet believed me to be, then in turn a Futurist artist, then a composer, then a foreign composer, then a travelling salesman for a large American firm, then a representative of a Russian company interested in establishing a factory on the shore of the Caspian Sea, then a landowner who had from boredom taken up theology (I was as it happened reading Schuré's[1] *The Great Initiates* at the time), then a famous chess master (I easily defeated everyone on board). I enjoyed myself hugely pitching all these different tales and by dint of injecting streams of specialised terms and expressions into my fictitious accounts left my listeners utterly confused, so that when we eventually parted company, despite all pleas for clarification I left them no wiser than they were before.

The reunion in Astrakhan with Boris Verin (the pseudonym he had now adopted in honour of his beloved Vera) was joyous, and while waiting for the steamer to sail onwards to the Caspian Sea we stayed in our cabin guzzling caviare and happily pottering about in a motor boat upon the broad bosom of Mother Volga. And when our little boat came alongside the steamer on which Boris Verin had arrived in Astrakhan, and naturally knew everyone on board, the acknowledgement of our presence was truly imperial: as we kept to our course alongside there was much waving of hats and handkerchiefs, the passengers all crowded on to the deck, the hooter hooted, the engines

---

[1] Edouard Schuré (1841–1921), French poet, playwright and theosophist. Schuré lived a life of exhaustingly high-voltage intellectual, aesthetic, emotional and spiritual exaltation, passing through an early phase of adoring Wagner, with whom he made personal contact and who, following several meetings and correspondence, warmly approved his young French acolyte's *Histoire du drame musical*, a detailed analysis published in 1875 of all the Master's music-dramas. But Schuré was already drawn to study of the esoteric and the occult, and in 1899, under the influence of a rich and smoulderingly beautiful, sphinx-like Greek doyenne of a Paris literary salon called Marguérite Albana Mignaty, with whom he fell passionately in love and to whom he wrote over nine thousand letters, published the book for which among his voluminous output he became best known: *Les grands initiés*, a comprehensive survey of the 'secret history of religions', embracing Indian, Aryan, Brahmanic and Vedic mysteries, Judaism, Greek Delphic, Dionysian, Pythagorean and Platonic thought, Zoroastrian, Egyptian and Christian revelation. This is the book Prokofiev was reading as he sailed down the Volga amusing himself with a series of invented personae to bewilder his shipmates. Later, Schuré became imbued with the theosophical ideas of Rudolf Steiner, becoming closely associated with the educationalist and founder of the pan-Germanic branch of the Theosophical Society.

slowed, the ship lost way and the captain saluted us from the bridge, and so on.

However, in Astrakhan composer and poet parted once again: Boris Verin was constitutionally unable to get up at half-past eight in the morning, and when I poured cold water over him to wake him up, he lost his temper and out of spite overslept, missing the sailing of the steamer to the Caspian. So I went on alone.

The further away from Astrakhan we sailed the narrower the Volga became. Then the water suddenly widened out to extend to the horizon and became the [Caspian] sea. We put into a twelve-foot roads, and after transferring from our river steamer into a sea-going one continued out into the open sea. This was repellently calm and relentlessly grey, the weather neither warm nor cold, the ship a miserable craft loaded to the gunwales with people, but the worst thing of all was the midges. At least they did not bite, but the air was so thick with them that you could hang an axe on them, and they clustered mercilessly in your nose, your eyes, in the tea, in the caviare. I found a cosy little lifeboat where I attempted to get some sleep, but in the middle of the night was frightened of tipping into the sea and so went back into my cabin. The following day at noon we reached Petrovsk. By this time I was heartily sick of the Caspian, and abandoning my ticket to Baku made a dash for a train standing in the station there bound for Tiflis,[1] where I arrived the following evening.

First of all, it was delightful to be once again in the South. Then, Tiflis was a place I liked very much: an attractive, handsome and lively city. Going into a club to have something to eat that evening I heard a good symphony orchestra playing Liszt's *Tasso*. I visited and luxuriated blissfully in the Oriental Baths. The next day, in an open-sided railway carriage, I travelled along a beautiful line to Borzhom.[2] This is a town I was very interested to see, because I love the mineral water named after it. The spa nestles charmingly between dark, forest-clad mountains. Compared to Kislovodsk it is quiet, but not so much as to qualify as a 'quiet little corner'. I met Gutman, a student I knew from the Petrograd Conservatoire, and she and I went for a marvellous, sun-kissed walk to the top of a local hill, Bakuriani.[3] From Borzhom I returned to Tiflis, whence I took the post-chaise to Vladikavkaz along the Georgian Military Road.[4] Meeting Igor Subbotin, brother of Oleg,

---

1 Now Tbilisi.
2 In Georgia today this town is known as Borzhomi, where the water from the famous springs with its high concentration of mineral salts is still bottled.
3 Nowadays popular as a winter ski resort.
4 Completed by Russia at the very end of the eighteenth century, the Georgian Military Road runs between Tbilisi in Georgia and Vladikavkaz in Russia, and is still the only road by which wheeled traffic can cross the mountains of the High Caucasus that form the frontier between Georgia and Russia. Spectacularly beautiful and a magnificent example of civil engineering, it rises at times to a height of nearly 8,000 feet.

and his travelling companion, an engineer, I was regaled with wonderful stories about Transcaucasia, which in the course of their employment they criss-crossed repeatedly. Their dithyrambs on the subject of Georgian women, their beauty, femininity and prowess at making love, were breathtaking.

I had been greatly looking forward to the Georgian Military Road and it lived up to all my expectations. Sometimes bumping along in an enormous, antediluvian carriage, sometimes riding on a goat's back, hatless and with a kerchief knotted round my head against the sun, I travelled along it for two days. Of course I had to retrace my steps and come back in the opposite direction, but that was no less enjoyable. Particularly beautiful were the monastery at Mtskheta,[1] the valley of the Aragvi River, later on the precipitous heights above the meeting of the waters,[2] Mount Kazbek and, best of all, the Darial Gorge.[3] Among other things, rocking along on my goats, I suddenly discovered a rhythmic pattern and composed a few verses of a humorous nature.

Vladikavkaz proved to be, as I had suspected, a delightful town, but so cut off from the world that I could not find anyone who could tell me how to get back to Petrograd. I had expected to be able to collect my mail there, but there was none. I had sent a postcard to Marinochka Pavlova from Borzhom with the single word 'Greetings!' on it, but so muddled the address that not surprisingly the card never reached its destination.

Three days later, that is on 27 July, I was back in the Palmyra of the North.[4]

August

On my return to the north I planned to take up Zakharov's invitation to spend the month of August in Terioki, and therefore straight away went out to Terioki. I found the Zakharov dacha in a very different state from former days. Their elderly father was in residence, suffering from degenerative heart disease that made all around live in constant fear of a catastrophe. Everyone was cautious and on tiptoe, there was none of the noisy cheerfulness that

---

1 The Jvari Monastery is a Georgian Orthodox monastery dating from the sixth century. It is near the ancient town of Mtskheta, the capital of Georgia in the fourth century AD.
2 The Aragvi river meets the Mtkari river just below Mtskheta. The Aragvi is now dammed upstream of the meeting point, forming a reservoir and supplying a hydro-electric power station that supplies a large proportion of Georgia's electricity.
3 The Darial Gorge forms the easternmost flank of Mount Kazbek and has been sliced vertically through solid rock by the River Terek to a width of no more than eight metres. As it has been, since time immemorial, the only passage through the Caucasus, it has always been heavily fortified.
4 Petrograd. St Petersburg rejoiced in various poetic names, for instance 'Venice of the North' (because it was built on islands and is intersected by so many canals and waterways) and 'Palmyra of the North' (because of its classical architecture).

had distinguished previous times. Borya and his young wife greeted me with extreme affection and kindness, not least Cecilia, who had always hitherto approached me with some mistrust, one might even say with hostility. It was clear that Boris was now exerting considerable influence over her. But despite the friendliness of the morning welcome Boris said nothing about his invitation to stay with them, and so I hastened to announce that I was going on to Kuokkale, and a day later I was there.

Tatyana and Varvara Nikolayevna[1] euphorically opened their arms to me and insisted that I stay with them. The sun was shining and the tennis court was in fine shape, my room awaited me; I settled in at Kuokkale. The time passed very pleasantly. The Prince – Varvara's husband – Varvara herself, Tanechka and I played tennis with a will. I got on confidently and quickly with orchestrating Act Two. I had taken the second and third acts along with me down the Volga and had frequently sat down to think out the instrumentation and make pencilled notes. Thanks to this the work now went easily: and on some good days I managed as many as thirteen pages of score.

Time passed uneventfully, but agreeably. The Prince was a most attractive gentleman. His wife Varvara, however, was the opposite: often moody and unpredictable. Twice we quarrelled to the point of forgetting ourselves, but immediately made up again. Tatyana and I became real friends, especially when I accidentally penetrated her great secret, a deeply romantic one, and thus became quite indispensable to her.

Nikolay Andreyev visited, also the entertaining and boisterous Prince Andronnikov,[2] Alenitsyn the champion tennis-player,[3] and other guests.

---

1   Boris Bashkirov's sisters.
2   Assuming this is the same Prince Mikhail Andronnikov, which seems at least plausible from Prokofiev's description, the flamboyant, somewhat raffish charm which he deployed in *haute-bourgeoisie* circles masked a corrupt and degenerate figure leading a double, or even treble, life. Moving seamlessly from the murky world of pre-Revolutionary proto-fascism (he was a close associate of Alexander Dubrovin and the Black Hundreds), to Rasputin and the last tottering days of the Imperial Court. (He was 'the high-life crook who calls himself Prince Andronnikov and is the bosom friend of the *starets* [Rasputin], his usual broker and go-between,' according to Maurice Paléologue in *An Ambassador's Memoirs*, op. cit., vol. 2, January/February 1916). He provided his invaluable services to Alexander Parvus in acquiring (probably from the German High Command, although this has never been proved) and laundering the funds that enabled Lenin, Trotsky, Zinoviev and Dzerzhinsky to return to Russia and mastermind the October Revolution. (Andronnikov is said to have hidden Dzerzhinsky in his Petrograd flat prior to the Revolution.) After the Revolution a grateful regime transformed Andronnikov into the 'Prince-Chekist', appointing him Head of the Cheka in Kronstadt. With Lenin's approval he grafted his former social connections on to his new geographical and political power base in order to maintain the Party's coffers by extracting vast amounts of money from aristocrats, bankers, merchants, etc., desperate to flee across the Gulf into Finland with as many of their possessions as they could carry. In the process he diverted substantial sums into his own Swedish and Norwegian bank accounts before being found out and executed – not, indeed, for corruption, but as a German spy.
3   Alexander Alenitsyn was one of Russia's strongest tennis-players before the Revolution, winner

As well as tennis we played bridge for high stakes, a rouble a point, that is to say ten times the amount we used to play for in the winter. At first this made me very nervous, especially as both Princes were excellent players, but I was lucky and after losing on the first occasion won on the second, lost on the third and won again on the fourth, after which I won every time. As well as bridge, on rainy days we played 66,[1] and here I was unstoppable, finishing around 800 roubles up. This could not have come at a better time, because around the time when I finally got the 1,500-rouble advance for *The Gambler* in my hands I had taken it into my head to play the stock exchange and bought 'wagons',[2] but they fell by 500 roubles, leaving me in a state of anxious uncertainty.

I went over to Terioki a few times to spend time with Boris, and played chess with Lyovka,[3] who has improved so much that having lost a serious game against him, I proposed another under match conditions. I went looking for Tanyusha and eventually found her on 6 August at a dachniks' ball I went to with Lyovka's sisters. I was awfully glad to see her, and both of us ragged about and played the fool without stopping the whole evening. Her teeth still gleam as they did and her profile is as lovely as ever.

The beginning of the month saw an incident with Malko. Calling in at the Imperial Theatres music library, where *The Gambler* was being copied in special chemical ink so that it could be lithographed, I learned that not only had it not yet been distributed to the singers, it had not yet been lithographed and some of it had not even been copied. This made me very worried, and I rounded angrily on the librarian and the copyists, accusing them of slackness in their work. I went off to see the person in charge of the lithography, Madame Semechkina. I thought this would have helped the situation, but a few days later I received a quite sharply worded letter from Malko, in overall charge of the Mariinsky Theatre's copying department, asking me not to visit the library in future but to address all concerns personally to him. I answered this letter with one equally tartly expressed, but matters were later smoothed over with a friendly conversation.

On the 16th I conducted the *Sinfonietta* at Pavlovsk. The orchestra was

---

of both the St Petersburg and Moscow championships from 1909 to 1911. In 1913 the All-Russian Association of Lawn Tennis Clubs was formed and immediately began competing in international tournaments under the auspices of the equally newly formed International Lawn Tennis Federation (now the International Tennis Federation, the sport's governing body). Alenitsyn was a member of the Russian national team against Great Britain the same year. But the First World War dealt a death blow to the emerging international championship circuit.

1   A card game for two or three players of the 'Marriage' type, that is to say in which the object is to win tricks and earn bonus points by melding matched pairs of kings and queens. Also known as Mariage, Schnapsen and Gaigel. See *Diaries*, vol. 1, p. 441 and *passim*.
2   Railway stock.
3   Lev (Lyovka) Karneyev. See Ibid., p. 170 and *passim*.

well disposed to me and accommodating, and I felt free and confident in directing the performance I wanted to achieve. I was told that my gestures were too extravagant in the rehearsals, but other people said that in the performance I was very good. It was successful, but did not approach the triumph of my concerto appearances. Aslanov was exceptionally friendly and kept mentioning that he would like to be the second conductor for Coates in *The Gambler*. I originally had Malko in mind for this, but if we are going to have conflicts like the recent one . . .

I finished the score of the second act on 20 August, and to this period also belong some thoughts on, and some thematic material for, the Third Piano Concerto, which was to be in five short movements with a common *leitmotiv*. But I would not allow myself to be too distracted from *The Gambler*, and after three days continued scoring Act Three.

Mama returned from the south towards the end of August, to my chagrin showing little if any improvement in her health. Some of the time I stayed with her in Petrograd, some out in Kuokkale. Then Boris Verin reappeared, in high spirits because at the cost of a gruelling mud treatment in Yessentuki the accursed pain of his facial neuralgia had been cured. I was very glad of this. Within an hour of his arriving back in Petrograd he telephoned me, and needless to say of our difference of opinion in Astrakhan not a word was said. That same day we went to Kuokkale, where life became more lively as a result of our discussions on poetry and philosophy.

September

However, this was not to last long. In the first days of September the Prince[1] and I had a serious quarrel in consequence of which I left the house. The Prince had the habit of intervening in the games of 66 I played with Tatyana Nikolayevna, and every time the cards were dealt would explain to her where she was going wrong. Eventually I could take no more of this and announced that if he continued his interference I would play no longer. And certainly the stakes we were playing for were quite serious: 20 roubles a point (or 'mouse', as we called them.) The Prince was mortally offended, his eyes nearly popped out of his head, he began to shout, in short he was transformed from a metropolitan nobleman into an Ossetian warlord uttering bloodcurdling threats! At first I laughed, but then I also took offence and went into the next room. An embarrassed Tatyana (who, by the way, had just lost 300 roubles to me) followed. The next morning, in spite of the agitation caused to the ladies and B.N. and their efforts to effect a reconciliation between the Prince and me, I left the house.

---

1 This is, of course, the real Prince Magalov, not Boris Bashkirov, nicknamed by Prokofiev 'the prince'.

B. Verin, to my great surprise, himself protested to the Prince and left Kuokkale together with me. We rode over to Sestroretsk, bathed in the swimming pool there and arrived back that evening in Petrograd, B.N. asking me to keep quiet about the incident.

Back in Petrograd I continued working on Act Three. I had three telephone conversations with Malko, but God alone knew what was happening with the lithographing and Malko himself was not always fully abreast of the state of affairs. Finally I became so exasperated that I delivered myself of the opinion that we should stop addressing questions to the lithographer Semechkina and simply string her up instead. In reply, Malko instead of hanging Semechkina hung up the telephone receiver, and from that moment on our relations assumed a distinctly hostile character. I am waiting for Coates in the hope that his return will break the present log-jam, but Coates is sunning himself swimming down in Novorossiisk and will not be back until the 15th.

I called on Lambin, my scenic designer. At first he was frosty, not knowing who I was, but when he realised that I was the composer of *The Gambler* he changed to become very friendly. I explained the opera and my wishes for it in great detail. He is a red-faced old man of unremarkable appearance, not particularly clever, and certainly not 'artistic'. No doubt this is why he clings to his one great merit: that his designs are always ready in time.

And so, I carried on scoring the third act, which was ready by 16 September.

At this time also a series of major events occurred in the life of Eleonora. First, her beloved cousin Vovka was killed, as was a few days later the famous Sergey Vladimirovich.[1] On learning the news I was the first person she turned to, summoning me immediately to the entrance hall of her building. I spent a whole hour walking with her in Tarasov Lane consoling and soothing her. Of course she had not loved him, but it was still a great shock. She discovered that Sergey Vladimirovich had bequeathed to her all his worldly goods, his country estate, his villas, his town houses, reportedly eight millions or thereabouts. Her instinct was to refuse it, but I told her she should take it; if she did not, it would simply be stolen by others since there were no direct heirs.

Boris Verin, with whom I was spending a good deal of time, reproached me bitterly for burying my talent as a pianist, which he considers quite out of the ordinary, and says I should practise for at least one hour a day. Bowing to his judgement I went back to the keyboard and have all but learnt the

---

1 Two years before Eleonora Damskaya had had an on–off relationship with a suitor who very much wished to marry her, which was also the strongly expressed wish of her family. Prokofiev, as Eleonora's intimate confidant, had assisted her with correspondence and a general strategy of resistance to this outcome, treating it as a grand 'chess game'. See *Diaries*, vol. 1, p. 759 and *passim*.

Second Piano Concerto of Saint-Saëns. But I also had to do some organ playing, and that took time. I even had to hire a pedal keyboard and hook it up to my piano.

Boris Verin and I set about a joint reading of Schopenhauer's *Aphorisms on the Wisdom of Life*,[1] which at one time had once attracted me very much and which, because it is not a book one should skim through in the cursory manner I had done before, I had now decided to reread.

Starting on 17 September I orchestrated Act Four, although in these wartime days I did not find it easy to get hold of enough manuscript paper. The first scene went smoothly, but I got bogged down in the entr'acte, the sketches I had made being not as full and the instrumentation more complex than for the dialogue scenes. On the other hand progress on the roulette scene was exceptionally quick and enjoyable.

On the 23rd Eleonora, Boris Verin and I went to hear *Tsar Saltan*.[2] The conductor was Coates, who had just returned to the city. I went backstage to see him and we embraced jubilantly. He has completed his *Assurbanipal*. When someone asked him whether it would soon be produced, he replied: 'We'll give it a try-out, but what I am going to concentrate on is learning Serge's opera.'

I was amazed that the kick-start I had been hoping for with *The Gambler* was about to become a reality, and told Coates I was thrilled he had at last come back and would be able to put an end to the chaos surrounding the copying of the music. Coates replied: 'Malko is upset himself, but we'll get Act One finished next week.' I don't want to hear about him being upset! It was his indifference that had allowed the scribes to be so undisciplined in the first place.

A few days after that I played the entire opera through to Coates. A small group of people assembled to hear it: Irinochka Mikhelson,[3] two of the repetiteurs, Brewer and Dukes, and an American visiting Russia with his wife. He was here on business, partly in Siberia where he had been charged with checking on the conditions in which prisoners-of-war were being kept. Coates was in a state of wild excitement over *The Gambler*.

I celebrated my name-day on the 25th, inviting my friends: the Demchinskys, Stavrovich, Boris Verin, Boris Zakharov, the Damskaya sisters.

---

1 One of the essays in Schopenhauer's final work, *Parerga und Paralipomena* (1851), in which the philosopher makes a plea for will and reason to prevail over irrational impulses. Despite Schopenhauer's reputation for unrelieved pessimism, in this essay he advances the view that it is possible so to arrange life as to yield the optimal degree of pleasure and success, and offers prescriptions to this end. The literal meaning of *Parerga and Paralipomena*, from the Greek, is 'complementary works and matters omitted': it is a collection of essays both amplifying and digressing from his main philosophical propositions.
2 *The Tale of Tsar Saltan*, opera (1900) by Rimsky-Korsakov.
3 Aka Miklashevskaya. See above, p. 104 n. 1.

Aunt Katya and cousin Katechka, who were also invited to the party, found the company extraordinarily interesting and clever. And rightly so: Boris Demchinsky is unquestionably a star.

As the month drew to a close the lithographed parts for the opera were not ready, despite Coates's reassurances. I was furious with Malko and would not speak to him, barely greeting him when our paths crossed. I corrected the orchestral parts of *Autumnal* in preparation for the forthcoming performance in Ziloti's season, and carried on scoring the roulette scene.

2 October

Yesterday Mama came with me to Coates, where he had convened another group to listen to *The Gambler* – Popova, Karakash, Alchevsky, Meyerhold,[1] the American and his wife. I played the score right through from beginning to end to the loud approval of those listening. Popova was ecstatic over her part, Karakash begged to be given any part, however small, Meyerhold said: 'You cannot know yourself what you have created: it will overturn the entire art of opera.'

Alchevsky – actually the best musician of them all – was alternately perplexed and embarrassed by the demands of his part, and ventured that while the character of Babulenka and the General had clearly defined lineaments, that of Alexey was much harder for him to grasp. He was evidently also alarmed by the vocal difficulty of the role. Coates beamed triumphantly and was quite prepared for people to start studying their parts the very next day – except that the parts were not yet available. Damn that Malko, and the whole incompetent gang in the library, where after God knows how long they still have not managed to produce the vocal scores!

---

1   Vsevolod Meyerhold (1874–1940), outstanding actor and theatre director, who began his career under Nemirovich-Danchenko in the Moscow Art Theatre. By the time he met Prokofiev, Meyerhold had moved on from the Stanislavskian ideals of the Art Theatre and was developing experimental approaches to theatre owing allegiance to Symbolism and *commedia dell'arte*. An enthusiastic supporter of the October Revolution, Meyerhold became a member of the Bolshevik Party but his free-wheeling avant-gardism and ill-concealed contempt for the dead hand of Socialist Realism inevitably brought him into conflict with the regime during the 1930s. In the meantime, in 1918 he had virtually single-handedly set Soviet theatre on a radical new path with its first great theatre production, Mayakovsky's *Misteria-Bouffe*, to be followed by a string of seminal Constructivist productions for his own Meyerhold Theatre, and successfully infected Prokofiev with his enthusiasm for *commedia dell'arte* in the shape of his own treatment of Carlo Gozzi's *The Love for Three Oranges*. The Soviet authorities finally closed down Meyerhold's theatre in 1938; two years later he was arrested and executed and his wife, the actress Zinaida Raikh, brutally murdered in their Moscow apartment.

3 October

I attended one of Verin's 'Mondays', the first time I had done so. There I found my 'enemies' assembled: Hofmeister Zlobin and Anna Grigorievna. I landed a few telling blows on Anna Grigorievna, while Zlobin, for some unknown reason, was furious with me. B.N. read from Lewis on Pythagoras, but I did not think much of his exposition. Karatygin had some interesting things to say. It was his second time at B.N.'s, and he revealed a dazzlingly erudite knowledge of philosophy, so that it was pure pleasure to listen to him. As a convinced materialist, for him all paths lead to materialism. Demchinsky agrees that he is interesting, but complains that he is hopelessly deficient in the slightest vestige of poetry. He related some interesting examples of suggestion: remarkably, it seems that that the power of suggestion weakens with distance, but if the object in question and the person generating the suggestion are placed between two concave mirrors, the power of suggestion achieves maximum intensity.

4 October

The first rehearsal of *Autumnal*. As usual with such occasions I derived little pleasure from it.

Autumnal will not be a success with the public. It has too little surface appeal for that, and of course its depths will not be appreciated. Even so, for those who accuse me of grotesquery and a lack of lyricism and poetry, this piece will provide some evidence to the contrary.

Wrote some verses about Zlobin. He bored me yesterday evening, and also, so I heard, abused me after my departure. I hugely enjoyed writing the verses, which came to me very easily.

5 October

Lutherans do not have saints whose name-days they can celebrate, so Eleonora makes one up for herself exactly six months after her birthday, and today is that day for her. We marked it by going to the theatre. The play was extremely dull, and since during the afternoon I had written out eight pages of score, I sank into a comatose state. And yet, in summer, interspersed with tennis, I had sometimes managed as many as thirteen pages!

23 October

My attempt to write a diary entry every day has not met with much success. I shall catch up briefly.

The first rehearsal of *The Gambler* took place, eventually, on the 21st, in one of the inner rooms of the Mariinsky Theatre with a piano up on a platform. I sat at the piano and played, this time without singing a single word. The theatre's library had finally succeeded in producing lithographed vocal scores of the first and second acts, and the singers sat with them attempting (not always successfully) to sing along.

Coates was in ecstasy, Aslanov was very happy, Yershov pored over the vocal score and made helpful observations. The majestically imposing Slavina,[1] although comporting herself as if on a pedestal, made no bones about her wish to sing Babulenka. Popova and Karakash were also openly enthusiastic, and the whole rehearsal proceeded in an atmosphere of elevated ardour.

The performance of *Autumnal* was quite decent and was even well received, arousing great admiration from Coates and Koussevitzky, the latter being unexpectedly present. Both also praised my conducting, in a way that was not patronising but genuinely warm. Press reaction was either laudatory or cautiously critical, but no one divined the 'autumnal' significance, which is that the piece neither attempts to illustrate that season of the year nor represent nature, but bears the title purely by association: the world it described is interior, not exterior. Such an autumn could equally well be a spring. Only in the *Muzykalny Sovremennik* (one suspects the hand of Igor Glebov) did the writer get anywhere near the heart of it.

The following day Koussevitzky called on me and first of all told me he would not be able to perform *Ala* in Moscow because almost all his orchestral musicians had been called up to serve in the army and there was no chance whatever of getting hold of eight horns. Secondly, he proposed that my works should be published by Gutheil, the firm he had recently acquired. I had been expecting this proposal and welcomed it, indeed it could not very well have failed to come about. But although a sister company, it is not Russian Music Editions, my accession to which is still opposed by two members of the selection jury, Rachmaninoff and Medtner. In the case of Gutheil there is no jury; Koussevitzky is sole proprietor and authority. He hopes that in a year or two it will be possible for me to move over to RME.

Among other events in my musical life I should mention: on the 20th I completed the score of the roulette scene. My courage slightly failed at the orchestral interlude, the sketches for which were very far from advanced.

---

1 Maria Slavina (1858–1951) was indeed the grandest of operatic grandes dames. Having made her debut as Amneris in *Aida* in 1879 she went on to create many important roles, including the Countess in Tchaikovsky's *The Queen of Spades* and Princess Evpraxia in *The Enchantress*, Konchakovna in Borodin's *Prince Igor*, and she was Russia's first Carmen. In private life by marriage Baroness Medem, she emigrated to Paris in 1920, where she lived for another thirty-one years, dying at the age of ninety-six.

The nearer I get to the end of composing *The Gambler*, the stronger grows my desire to write a third piano concerto, although I am well aware that I shall come in for a lot of criticism for wanting to compose a work in concerto, rather than symphonic, form. In August, in Kuokkale, I had noted down a couple of themes for it.

I was asked to write music for a mime production on a subject by Remizov.[1] Although I was put under incredible pressure to comply, I declined. Nevertheless, Remizov read through to me *Alaley and Leila*, a ballet libretto he had written, over which Lyadov had been licking his lips five years ago, confining, however, any actual composition to ten bars (the note 'lya'[2] accompanies the shining of a star). After Lyadov died, Tcherepnin, Steinberg and others were all after Remizov to let them have the libretto, but Remizov was determined that the composer should be none other than myself.

A specialist in all kinds of Russian evil spirits, and himself resembling a sort of Kikimora[3] figure, Remizov had garlanded *Alaley* with such a gallery of fantastic forest denizens with amazingly outlandish names, cognomens, cries and utterances, all expressed in such delectably ornate, rococo language, that it was instantly clear to me its flavour would be lost in a ballet:

1   Alexey Remizov (1877–1957), Modernist writer with a taste for the fantastic and bizarre, especially in the context of the more luridly Gothic imaginings of Russian folk tales, and peasant culture. This interest brought him into contact with Nikolay Roerich and the arts and crafts community based in Princess Maria Tenisheva's estate at Talashkino. After the Revolution Remizov emigrated to Paris, where despite his extreme poverty, his demonically inspired fantasies made him something of a celebrity among writers like James Joyce. The original inspiration for the *Alaley* ballet, with its pre-Christian theme of pagan ritual had come from the surprising source of Mikhail Tereshchenko, a relation of Prokofiev's chess-playing friend. Tereshchenko was a fabulously wealthy businessman, publisher, deviser of special projects for the Imperial Theatres Directorate under Telyakovsky, and eventual Minister of Finance in the Provisional Government. The music was supposed to be by Lyadov and the resulting ballet one of a pair, the other being by Glazunov to a libretto by Alexander Blok (Remizov acting at Tereshchenko's request as go-between with the great poet). Neither project came to fruition as intended, but in the case of Blok the seed was sown first for an opera and ultimately, outgrowing even these enlarged dramatic possibilities, for one of the poet's greatest works, the verse drama *The Rose and the Cross*, based on medieval French troubadour legends and published by Tereshchenko's Petersburg publishing firm Sirin. Operatically, it had been 'a thwarted attempt to realise the enigmatic musical ideals of his time and place. It constitutes the most elaborate product of a short-lived endeavour among the "mystic" Symbolist poets to write opera libretti, song texts, and plays calling for incidental music.' (Simon Morrison, *Russian Opera and the Symbolist Movement* (University of California Press, Berkeley and Los Angeles, 2002).)
2   'A', 'la' in the sol-fa scale, is in Russian 'lya'.
3   The Kikimora is a house spirit in Russian mythology, a tiny ugly figure with chicken feet who lives behind the stove. Her fiefdom is the domestic running of the household and the small-holding (especially poultry), and until placated she will visit plagues and disasters on the children of badly run establishments. She also appears, spinning flax, at deathbeds. One of the three orchestral miniatures *chefs d'oeuvre* for which Lyadov is still remembered is *Kikimora*. Cf. also Musorgsky's *Pictures from an Exhibition*.

it had to be an opera. But it was too soon for me to be thinking of another opera – perhaps in a year's time. *Alaley and Leila* is a delight, but its wealth of material makes a new scenario imperative. I will compose this opera.

What else? I received an engagement for Kiev; this will be a very pleasant trip. I am to play my First Piano Concerto, which will be pure enjoyment, and the Second – which will be a burden.

Now for matters outside music. I have become deeply interested in the stars. I have always felt drawn to astronomy, and now that I have got hold of Ignatiev's little book[1] I have begun to study the stars in the night sky, committing their names to memory and tracing out the constellations on paper. But alas, every night last week was cloudy.

With Boris Verin there has occurred a rift: I imposed a month's moratorium on contact with him for having left before the end of the chess tournament I arranged at my home on 9 October claiming that he had a guest waiting for him at his house. The tournament was a very enjoyable occasion and resulted in a victory for Tyulin, followed (in that order) by Demchinsky, Rudin, myself, Lev Karenin and Boris Verin.

A wonderful article about me has appeared in the English press,[2] prompted by my *Scherzo for four bassoons* having been performed there somewhere. Zherebtsovna is green with envy! (Ahem!) A curious thing about the *Scherzo*, seemingly, was that this was its first performance in England although my works get played a lot in Russia!

All right, enough of self-congratulation. A twenty-five-year-old youth has a bit of success, is thrilled to bits and can't stop jabbering about how wonderful he is. Revolting! This week is a week of rehearsals: four *Gambler*s and three *Ala*s. Coates has a boil inside his nose and is confined to home, so the *Gambler* rehearsals were taken by Dranishnikov and me. We were competing with Aslanov simultaneously rehearsing *Le Prophète*,[3] which was drawing off all those involved in our opera, but such was the interest in *The Gambler* that, rather touchingly, they all came in every spare moment they had, so there was always someone to rehearse our piece. Yershov applied himself very seriously to the work and never missed a rehearsal. He was deeply absorbed, made mistakes, apologised, gestured expansively and generally displayed enormous talent for the stage whenever he was illustrating one or another passage. Popova knew her part and sang it accurately; Bossé as the General was excellent; the Babulenka did not put in an appearance at all. The General's role in the second act provoked much general hilarity.

---

1 *The World of the Heavens* [*Nebesny Mir*], *An Illustrated Astronomy for the General Reader* by E. I. Ignatiev, published in St Petersburg in 1916.
2 By M. Montagu-Nathan in the *Musical Times*, October 1916. Montagu-Nathan expressed surprise that such a considerable composer should be introduced to English by so trivial a work.
3 Opera (1849) by Meyerbeer.

28 October

I worked diligently through two of the *Ala* rehearsals, but at the third, the general rehearsal, there was an incident. We had always been short of percussionists, but three additional players had been engaged for the general rehearsal. However, the orchestra manager succeeded in finding only one, but did not inform me. As a result, we were short one tam-tam and two cymbals. At first I thought that there had simply not been room on the platform to set up the instruments, but when I realised they were not there at all and, had I not noticed this at the rehearsal we would have done the concert without the tam-tam (and what, pray would be the point of the *Procession of the Sun* without the tam-tam?), I became very agitated, stopped the orchestra and demanded an explanation from the orchestra manager. Why were the instruments not in place, and why I had not been told? He could not give me a satisfactory answer, so I let him know my opinion that this was no way to behave and called him an 'anti-artistic individual'. Offended, he muttered something in reply and left the scene. Ziloti, alarmed, came up to the orchestra and did his best to calm me down, saying: 'They will be there, Sergey Sergeyevich, they'll be there tomorrow, don't worry about it, just carry on . . .'

Extremely upset, and observing that even if they were there for the performance we would be playing the work without a proper rehearsal, the sort of situation one might expect to find in Kharkov, I continued the rehearsal.

I went to see Alchevsky and rehearsed the *Duckling* with him, meeting there the great Konstantin Balmont. Initially I thought that Balmont would not know anything at all about me, and behaved accordingly, that is to say I made small talk for the sake of saying something. But it turned out that he had read a number of laudatory press reports about me, and on hearing me play *Sarcasms* not only expressed the greatest enthusiasm but told me what images they suggested to him: frenzied passion and wonderful lyricism in the third, death in the fourth, and the insistent knocking of the devil in the fifth. I said that none of the pieces had a programme, and if any hints of one could be detected, it could only stem from our own inner spiritual world. I did not tell him anything of the programme of the fifth *Sarcasm*. It is something like this: there are occasions when the evil, coarse side of our nature leads us to poke callous fun at something or other, but closer inspection shows us that the object of our ridicule is so pitiful, so wretched in its utter insignificance, so touching, that we are frightened by our laughter, it rings louder and louder in our ears, and then we hear that our own laughter has turned itself on us.[1]

---

1 In his *Short Autobiography*, written in the Soviet Union in 1941, Prokofiev uses almost the same words: 'I have preserved the programme for one of the *Sarcasms* (No. 5); "Sometimes we callously laugh at someone or something, but when we look more closely we see how pathetic

Balmont read his newly composed Sonnets, offered them to me as song lyrics, invited me to visit him (which pleased me very much), and promised to come and hear *Ala* even though he had guests that evening.

Today Mama drily informed me: 'You had a telephone call from Pavlova.' Since the spring I have heard neither hide nor hair of her! I shall be awfully glad to see her!

3 November

On the 29th [October], the day of the *Ala* performance – for me a day of great significance – I was in the foulest mood imaginable, which lasted through the evening. The reason was the annoying misunderstandings of the previous day that spilled over into the day of the performance.

The performance of *Ala* had all the trappings of a great occasion – crowds of people wanting to hear it, all tickets sold out, and so forth. What was a great joy to me was to hear, from the very first bars, how much better the orchestra sounded on stage and with the iron curtain.[1] The orchestra played much better than it had done in January, but could have done with still more refinement. As it was, from a certain lack of confidence in the barbaric music, also occasionally from hostility, the orchestra neither could nor would play sensitively. All the same, the finale came off with blinding *éclat*, and the newly provided tam-tam player unleashed dazzlingly golden sound. Conducting the *Procession of the Sun* was a pleasure for me, since the orchestration proved to have been meticulously calculated. I set about wringing from the orchestra every last ounce they could possibly give, and still there was more to come until the very last bar.

The success exceeded my expectations: from the stage the catcalling could not be heard, only thunderous applause. When this started to die down there was one bellow of 'Get off!' (or according to some it was 'That's enough!') after which there erupted such a storm of applause as to eclipse completely the audience's darling Rachmaninoff, who had played his Second Piano Concerto immediately before *Ala*. No more than half of the orchestra was booing maliciously, while a group of musicians led by Chernyavsky wildly shouted 'bravo'. Popova and Karakash dashed into the artists' room in a frenzy of delight and said that they had not so much heard the *Procession of the Sun* as seen it.

Supper at Ziloti's was not a very interesting occasion, and Rachmaninoff and I were placed at opposite ends of the table, presumably so that we should

---

and wretched is the object of our ridicule; then we feel uneasy, we hear the laughter in our ears, but now it is laughing at us." The other *Sarcasms* had no programme.' (*Kratkaya Avtobiografiya*, in Shlifshteyn, op. cit.)

1   The orchestra was presumably placed on a platform built over the orchestra pit, and thus with the iron curtain forming an acoustic barrier between it and the vast stage and fly tower behind.

not have to talk to one another. Only three days later did Ziloti tell me that after I had left, he and Ossovsky had quizzed Rachmaninoff on his reaction to *Ala*, to which the latter had responded by saying that he found much to admire in the vivid scoring and in the way I had conducted the piece. There were even several passages in the Suite he had liked, along with others that he considered 'musical face-pulling' and that he could not bear to listen to, nevertheless it was a very talented work and Koussevitzky should publish it. It transpired that although Koussevitzky had already accepted me for the Gutheil wing of his organisation, Rachmaninoff was on the jury for this as well (Koussevitzky, Rachmaninoff and Struve[1]) and had initially been opposed, only now coming round to agreeing.

The next day I was very interested to hear some of his songs. The latest cycle, to words by new poets, is sheer delight.[2] Nina Koshetz,[3] who sang them, is an artist meriting the closest attention. But she was so unbearably full of herself at the Ziloti supper party afterwards that I could not avoid getting at loggerheads with her. We exchanged a few caustic remarks.

Now that I had heard a whole evening of songs I decided it was time I composed some new ones. Suvchinsky turned up with a volume of Anna Akhmatova,[3] in whom I had long been interested, and to whose poems indeed I had dreamed of making intimate, simple settings stripped of the six-storey-high superstructure of the Op. 23 songs. I spent the next few days, from 31 October to 3 November, in a rare degree of absorption, fluency and love composing Op. 27. The result of these four days was five songs that please me more and more as time goes on, so that now I am completely transported by what I have composed. I have even begun to think that they

---

1 Nikolay Struve (?–1920), Berlin director of Koussevitzky's publishing house Russische Musikverlag (Russian Music Editions). See *Diaries*, vol. 1, p. 333.
2 *Six Songs for Voice and Piano*, Op. 38. The verses had been suggested to Rachmaninoff by Marietta Shaginyan and initially his conservative literary tastes had been, as he wrote to Shaginyan, 'appalled' by the Modernist, Symbolist tone of the poets in question. But Rachmaninoff's reservations were soon allayed, not least by the romantic attachment he developed for the then twenty-two-year-old soprano Nina Koshetz, to whom the cycle is dedicated. The six songs are: 'In My Garden At Night', a translation by Alexander Blok from the Armenian of Avetik Isaakian), 'To Her' (Andrey Bely), 'Daisies' (Igor Severyanin), 'The Pied Piper' (Valery Bryusov), 'Dreams' (Fyodor Sologub), 'A-oo' (Konstantin Balmont).
3 Nina Koshetz (1894–1965) was an exceptionally cultivated musician, both her mother and father having enjoyed prominent careers as singers in the Imperial Opera, and having herself studied piano with Konstantin Igumnov, composition with Sergey Taneyev, and singing with Félia Litvinne. As beautiful as she was talented, her romance with Rachmaninoff became the talk of artistic Russia. Settling in America after the Revolution she enjoyed a glittering career there as well, singing the part of Fata Morgana in the Chicago Opera premiere production of Prokofiev's *Love for Three Oranges*, making a series of recordings for Victor (still available), and appearing in a number of Hollywood films.
4 Anna Akhmatova (Gorenko) (1889–1996), 'the soul of the Silver Age', one of the greatest of all Russian poets. The years in St Petersburg just before the Revolution were the happiest of her life, as retrospectively recalled in her 'Poem Without a Hero'.

represent a significant step in the evolution of my opuses: I am referring here to their intimate lyricism.

7 November

When I played my songs to Suvchinsky he threw his arms around my neck and kissed me in a paroxysm of rapture. He raved on about Koshetz (Koshketz,[1] as he calls her) and dreams about her performing the songs at a 'Contemporaries' evening.

Action on the *Gambler* front has gone quiet, as Coates is still suffering from his boil and is not to be seen in the theatre, which is otherwise occupied with *Le Prophète*. Yershov alone is prepared to give me time to see me to go through the opera meticulously. I am rehearsing for my chamber recital with Popova, Alchevsky and Wolf-Israel,[2] and writing out the *Gambler* libretto for Bogolyubov.[3]

I was at Balmont's, where there were several guests: the famously flinty Sologub,[4] a handful of pallid poetasters and a couple of pretty, decadent girls. Balmont was amiable, ginger-haired, a scarf belonging to one of the girls around his neck as he was freezing with cold. He showed great interest in my music (especially, to my great joy, the five *Sarcasms*) and presented me with one of his books inscribed to 'the Magician of sounds S. S. Prokofiev, of whose great gifts I am convinced'. This made me very proud, and in general I was extremely touched by the sincere marks of attention he paid me. After all, this is an Olympian. Boris Verin and I are continually engrossed in his poetry.

Coming away from Balmont's, I feasted my eyes on the stars. The layer of cloud had finally dispersed, and what joy it was to see the beauty of Orion, red Aldebaran[5] and Betelgeuse,[6] and the wonderful green and white diamond of Sirius. I gazed at them with newly opened eyes recognising them from the astronomical maps I had been studying – and felt as though invisible threads were connecting me to the heavens! It was four o'clock in the morning, I should have been asleep, but white Sirius stood directly in front of my window and I could not take my eyes away from him!

I took a copy of *Sarcasms* round to Balmont, with the inscription: 'To our Sun, a few fragments of darkness'.

---

1. 'Koshka' means a (female) cat, so 'pussy-cat'.
2. Yevgeny Wolf-Israel (1874–1956), principal cello of the Mariinsky Orchestra.
3. Nikolay Bogolyubov (1870–1951), opera producer, Director of Productions at the Mariinsky Theatre from 1911 to 1918.
4. Fyodor Sologub, pen-name of Fyodor Teternikov (1863–1929), Symbolist poet, playwright and novelist, the perverse violence and sensuality of whose 1907 novel *The Little Demon* had touched a particular nerve with its portrayal of the sadistically paranoid schoolmaster Peredonov.
5. The brightest star in the constellation Taurus, also known as the Bull's Eye.
6. The second brightest star in the Orion constellation, also reddish-orange to the eye.

15 November

Coates has developed a second boil, and then a third, so *The Gambler* has completely gone to sleep. To my ironic comments, Tartakov said: 'Don't worry. The opera has to be produced this season, and produced it will be.'

Borovsky's concert was on the 14th. Recalling his magnificent performance of my 'Scherzo' from Op. 12 last year, I was greatly looking forward to my Second Sonata, but was disappointed: the first movement was played without much warmth, the Scherzo too fast and consequently lacking clarity. The Andante was good, but the Finale went completely to pieces with an exaggerated tempo. Normally the Sonata is very successful, but on this occasion it was received coldly. The next day we lunched together at the 'Bear',[1] and I animadverted that Borovsky Musician was in danger of turning into Borovsky Narcissist, spellbinding the public with glittering passagework and pianistic effects while forgetting the heart of the music. He said that this was not yet the case, but he would take care not to allow it to become so. He had played the Sonata a week before in Moscow, and played it better there because neither the composer nor fans of the composer's own interpretation were present. He said that the Moscow attitude to my music was more hostile than friendly, although the Sonata was well received, and there are undoubtedly some there who truly love my music.

15–23 November

I was very happy when the day for my departure to Kiev finally came. Even though I had reserved my sleeping-car berth ten days before, they had still managed to sell it twice over, so I had to move into another compartment.

The next morning, bright sunshine, so conspicuously absent in Petrograd in November, testified to the fact that we were already far towards the south. We arrived in Kiev before sun-up, at six o'clock in the morning. But by the time I had made my way onto the platform, crowded with officers and soldiers on their way to Romania, day had dawned and at nine o'clock I went straight to the rehearsal. Well, they play quite well, although of course the orchestra is a little rocky and Glière is a pretty rotten conductor, but I was not in the mood to find fault. I am on the best of terms with Glière, who still calls me Seryozha and uses the intimate form as he did when I was a child, while I respectfully address him as Reinhold Moritsevich and use the formal style. After the rehearsal Glière took me to the Conservatoire and in company with the Head of Studies introduced me to it and it to me. I met the professors. This was very entertaining: the teachers all shook me by the

---

1   A well-known restaurant.

hand, some of them making compliments and others, not knowing what to say, staying silent. I tried to find something nice to say about Kiev and about the spaciousness of the classrooms. The female students jumped to their feet as we entered and stood respectfully at attention, scanning with curious eyes the visitor from Petrograd.

We dined with the French Consul, a wealthy local Jew named Bolakhovsky. Because there were no train tickets to Moscow available, he telephoned the Commandant and arranged a first-class reservation for me as an emissary of the French Consulate.

The next day, after the general rehearsal at four o'clock, I gave a recital for the staff and students of the Conservatoire, the Hall of the Conservatoire being filled to overflowing for the occasion. Reinhold Moritsevich had been nervous about asking me to do this just before my concert, but in fact I was delighted to agree. I remember, not so long ago, the excitement whenever a notice went up in our Conservatoire about some travelling eminence having 'kindly consented' to play for the students, what a commotion, furore indeed, this provoked, and how the hall would be besieged by all those wanting to hear. And now, as I entered the Kiev Conservatoire, I found it very satisfying to see how many of the young people had gathered to listen to me. The hall was packed to the rafters by the time we made our entrance: the Director, the Heads of Department, some professors and I. The audience rose to its feet as we approached, and I laughed as I said to Glière: 'All rise for His Honour the Judge'.

The Head of Studies announced that I would play my Sonata No. 1, *Toccata* and *Sarcasms*, and I sat down at the piano. I made a pause after each number, and came down from the stage to the first row of the auditorium to talk to the professors, who were unstinting in their praise, even the most conservative among them (not, though, for *Sarcasms*). The students went on clapping throughout the pauses, while I sat and conversed. When I had finished they called loudly for *Suggestion Diabolique* and there was such a storm of applause that I had to give three encores. In the Director's study, to which we retreated while the applause was still continuing, the professors were replaced by students clamouring to shake my hand and demanding my autograph on copies of my works, and so forth. The greatest success was obtained by the *Toccata*, while some preferred the fifth *Sarcasm*. When I left the precincts of the Conservatoire the students staged a series of supplementary ovations, and some of the girls and younger boys followed me down the street as I walked off with Glière. Happy with the turn of events, I went for a walk along the Dnieper, somewhat regretting that I had not invited any of my more demonstrative admirers of both sexes to keep me company.

Then came the concert, for which all tickets had been sold at least two days beforehand. This cannot, of course, be ascribed to either Stravinsky or to me, but to the comparative rarity of symphonic concerts in a deeply musical city. A slight hitch occurred just before the concert: I was a little late arriving, so someone was despatched to collect me. In the meantime I arrived, but the person sent for me had taken with him the key to unlock the piano. We waited, fretting over the delay, for him to come back.

The concert was not flawless from the point of view of the orchestra, and on one occasion it actually knocked me off course. I played well, and with incredible composure even when I played wrong notes, because the musicians of Kiev had already given me their seal of approval and for the rest there would be no one able to criticise details. It was a great success, although less vociferous than for *Ala* in Petrograd. I got seven curtain calls and gave three encores, among them the *Toccata* as a warm-up for Petrograd.[1] There appeared at the piano, I do not know where from, a basket of white chrysanthemums. At first I did not pay too much attention to them, imagining that they had come either from Eleonora (she had once said, for instance: 'I can be living in Petrograd and still send flowers by telegraph to Kiev') or from the French Consul, or perhaps from the directorate of the Conservatoire. But when I looked more closely at the accompanying card, I saw: 'Boryunechka, in sending these flowers, sends you greetings.'[2] At once the blooms expanded to the dimensions of a tropical forest, and I was indescribably pleased and touched. No! This was a truly elegant gesture: sending flowers from another city! Threading one of the chrysanthemums into Glière's buttonhole after the concert, I asked what time the train would leave for Kharkov. He was greatly astonished, and the company at supper even more so, when I put someone right who was asking when I proposed to leave for Moscow by saying: 'No, I'm going to Kharkov.' I had to decline the consul's good offices, but

1   Among the audience for this concert was Vladimir Dukelsky, later to become a close friend of Prokofiev in America and Europe. In his later Broadway incarnation as Vernon Duke, Dukelsky wrote a fascinating autobiography, *Passport to Paris*, which contained this iconic description of his first experience of Prokofiev's unorthodox approach to the keyboard: 'Prokofiev wore dazzlingly elegant tails, a beautifully cut waistcoat, and flashing black pumps. The strangely gauche manner in which he traversed the stage was no indication of what was to follow: after sitting down and adjusting the piano stool with an abrupt jerk, Prokofiev let go with an unrelenting muscular exhibition of a completely novel kind of piano-playing. This young man's music and his performance of it reminded me of the onrushing forwards in my one unfortunate soccer experience; there was no sentiment, no sweetness there – nothing but unrelenting energy and athletic joy of living. There was frenetic applause and no less than six flower horseshoes were handed to Prokofiev, who was now greeted with astonished laughter. He bowed clumsily, dropping his head almost to his knees and recovering with a yank.' V. Duke, *Passport to Paris* (Little, Brown, Boston, 1955).
2   The context makes it clear the flowers were sent by the seventeen-year-old Polina Podolskaya, (see below, p. 693) – why 'Boryunechka', which would normally be an affectionate name for a boy, is not clear. Polina was evidently a former romantic attachment, albeit as explained an extremely youthful one, from 1912, when she was thirteen and Prokofiev twenty-one. That we have not previously encountered her is presumably explained by the fact that no Diary entries have survived from between April and August of that year; those notebooks were probably among the papers lost or destroyed in the Petrograd flat after the Revolution.

I was lucky enough to obtain tickets to Kharkov, and the following evening found myself, in the sunniest of moods, on the train bound for there.

The reason for my smile was that I was on the way to see Polina, with whom my last encounter had taken place four and half years ago, and at that age four and a half years is an eternity. At that time she had been a mere thirteen years old; now she was seventeen. I sent her a telegram announcing my arrival, and was sure that she would clap her hands with glee on receiving it. Such indeed proved to be the case. Polina was there to meet me at the station, as young and graceful as ever, looking even younger than her years, with her enchanting smile, demure way of walking and unaffected joy at seeing me. Despite the intervening four and a half years neither of us had changed much, and mutual recognition was instant. Her hair, from being light-brown, had become more russet, an improvement, her eyes widely spaced, with a pretty little nose and sharply chiselled chin.

She had wanted to come to Kiev for my concert but had instead had to go to visit her father in Taganrog, so had not been able to. We spent the whole evening together, driving round the town, going for a walk, having dinner in a restaurant, and going to her house. In the restaurant she begged for a private room so that I could play to her on an upright piano there, and I delighted in doing so for her on this apology for an instrument. Her dream was to get back to Petrograd, and she implored me to arrange matters so that she could enrol in the Medical Institute. The problem is that she is Jewish, and there is a 3 per cent quota there.

Arriving in Moscow I plunged straight into a busy working atmosphere, hardly managing to get myself a hotel room to stay in. Only at the nineteenth attempt was I successful, so full up was the city. The first day, from eleven o'clock at night to one the next morning, I talked to Struve, the director of Koussevitzky's publishing house, a gentleman of imposing stature and impeccable manners, and then again the following day from three o'clock to ten o'clock in the evening. I twice got a severe headache, and once even had to get up, go out and walk about for twenty minutes. He showed me almost all the firm's latest publications and exhibited a genuine passion for his work. Finally, at dinner in the 'Prague' restaurant, we virtually reached agreement. The conditions were not bad, but the royalty percentages were not over-generous. In the end we did not reach a complete agreement, but I promised to think it over and write to him (songs and piano pieces 100–200; sonatas, trios and quartets 300–500; symphonic works 400–1,000; concertos 500–800, ballets and small-scale operas 2,000–3,000; grand operas 3,000–5,000. The first printing to be 300 copies with no royalties; second and succeeding editions 10 per cent of sale price.) As soon as the war was over he would hope to shift me to the Russian Music Edition roster, possibly including works already published under the Gutheil imprint.

23–30 November

In Petrograd I have so much to do: on the 27th Ziloti's chamber concert of my works will take place, and I have to rehearse with the cellist, the bassoonists, Popova and Alchevsky, especially the two last-named. I am not so worried about my own contributions, since I had been able to prepare the *Toccata* and *Sarcasms* when I was in Kiev. There was a disaster with the singers, because Karakash's father had died, and Popova had not only not learnt her songs but was only by the grace of God prevented from cancelling altogether.

Then Alchin[1] announced that he would not sing 'I do not know',[2] and added for good measure: 'If you are not happy about this, then I am prepared to withdraw altogether from the concert.' I replied: 'That is what, in my heart of hearts, I should prefer, but since your absence would wreck the concert, I must ask you to sing the remaining songs.'

On the 27th, the hall was full, all tickets having been sold almost two months ago, as, incidentally, is not unusual for Ziloti's concerts. Boris Verin, who has been granted an amnesty and is in consequence speechless with joy, sat in the front row wearing a dinner-jacket and applauding 'like a man berserk'. I began with the *Toccata*, received in a rather lukewarm manner. Then followed Alchevsky in the *Duckling*: some uncertainty at the beginning and some awful mistakes in the text – in a word, he had not learnt it properly. The appearance of the four bassoonists sheepishly making their way on to the stage, not in tails (none of them possessed them), one with his cheek all bandaged up, provoked amused laughter in the audience. The *Scherzo* was encored. Wolf-Israel's performance of the *Ballade* was almost very good. This was the work's fourth performance, but the first to be met with success. Popovochka chirruped away enchantingly in an incredible white gown, trying her hardest, but apart from 'The Boat Cast Off'[3] sang everything badly.

In the second interval Alchevsky – now feeling himself right in the firing line – was hideously nervous about singing 'In My Garden' and 'The Wizard'.[4] He still sang them well, even though there were mistakes in 'The Wizard'. The same thing: he had not learnt it properly. 'The Wizard' was encored. I went off to be by myself for a little while in order to concentrate before going on

---

1 Alchevsky.
2 The first line of 'Under the Roof', the first of the *Five Poems for Voice and Piano*, Op. 23, words by Vyacheslav Goryansky.
3 The second of *Two Poems for Voice and Piano*, Op. 9, words by Alexey Apukhtin.
4 Op. 23, Nos. 4 and 5, settings respectively of poems by Balmont and Nikolay Agnitsev. Shlifshteyn, in his comprehensive survey of Prokofiev's works and first performances, says that Alchevsky sang only 'The Wizard' ('Kudesnik') in this recital. (Shlifshteyn, *op. cit.*)

to play *Sarcasms*. In my perception I played them better than I had ever done before. The fifth *Sarcasm* ended the concert, I was presented with a wreath (from Gessen, which made me very proud), a huge laurel lyre on a stand, and a basket of flowers. Ivan from the Conservatoire, who had to lug the laurels on to the stage, whispered to me: 'S.S., you know this is a pretty rare event at any concert these days.'

The lyre had come from Boris Verin, with a quatrain attached to the ribbon:

> The sacred beacon of your lyre
> Burns ever fiercer, blazing bright.
> Singing its songs of the sun's fire,
> Shining its rays of the sun's light.

The crowd surged down to the rail at the front of the stage, applauding with all its might. I came out to bow several times, and eventually played the fifth *Sarcasm* again as an encore. I did not want to play anything else, wishing to maintain the seriousness of the concert, and not to make myself a cheap audience favourite. While I was playing, some of the audience who were pressing up to the rail were following the score and casually turning over the pages right by my feet, which I found very unsettling and liable to make me go wrong. I wanted to give them a kick. I played no more encores, and the audience, after shouting and clapping a bit more, dispersed. From Ziloti I received 420 roubles and a statement of account: the entire profit from the concert. God knows it wasn't much, but it was still unexpected since I had not discussed money with him at all and had anticipated him getting away scot-free.

After the concert I had fifteen friends round to my house: Myaskovsky, Zakharov and Cecilia, Boris Verin, Demchinsky, Stavrovich, Suvchinsky, Asafyev, Eleonora and her sister, Derzhanovsky (who was on a visit from Moscow and with whom I had made my peace), Aunt Katya and Katechka. Boris Verin was delighted with the company: 'Not a single outsider!'

All the works in the concert, except for the *Duckling* and 'There Are Other Planets'[1] were new to the Petrograd public (the *Ballade* had been previously performed in Moscow and the *Toccata* in Kiev as an encore).

1–10 December

Following the concert I spent my time in the following manner: I dined twice with Boris Verin, where his brother Vladimir favoured me with an unusual degree of attention, making me play Chopin's Funeral March for

---

1 Op. 9 No. 1, to words by Balmont.

him and proposing in all seriousness that I should become the husband of a rich lady's daughter from Samara who was worth no more and no less than 60 million. I visited Obukhov, who played his latest compositions to the consternation of Fitelberg and the audible guffaws of Suvchinsky. Koussevitzky pretended to understand something of the music and I made the observation that it was interesting vertically but not horizontally, by which I meant that the harmonies, or at least the chords, were interesting but that there was no connection between them, the melodic lines were naive and in places – oh horrors! – vulgar.

I was invited to give a concert in Saratov, which was very agreeable since it is always nice to take a trip or two during the winter. I am to play a whole solo evening, and I welcome this because it can be a kind of provincial try-out for a future *Klavierabend* in the capital.

From an admirer I don't know, called Wanda Ossolinskaya, I received a fervently couched missive about my concert, which concluded: 'Farewell, magician, beloved of the gods.' But naturally the most significant mark of attention came from Polina, who wrote that the only thing sustaining her in life was the hope of moving to Petrograd. I decided to appeal for help to Gessen, but held back out of reluctance to burden with trifles a man preoccupied with heaven knows what weighty affairs of state.

But then I suddenly began to run a high temperature, going up as far as 39°, and had to take to my bed. Fearing that I might be developing typhoid (Boris Verin was already suffering from paratyphoid), I hastened to telephone Gessen to try to do something about Polina before I succumbed to a full-blown sickness. I said I wanted to consult him about a Jewish matter, and when this somewhat surprised him, went on to explain about Polina's hoped-for move. When he enquired benevolently: 'Is this an affair of the heart?' I replied: 'No, more of an opera. It concerns a certain Polina, the namesake of my heroine, similarly russet-haired, gracefully slim and doe-eyed. How could I possibly not be concerned about her?'

Gessen generously undertook to take the matter up with Verkhovsky, the Director of the Institute, and a day later telephoned me to tell me the result: 'What year is your Polina in?' 'The first year.' 'Then I'm afraid there is no hope. Verkhovsky said that had she been in the third or fourth year he might have been able to so something, but the first two years are so oversubscribed that one cannot even think of it. Not because she is Jewish but because all the laboratories are completely overwhelmed with students.'

I thanked him and wrote to Polina with news of our first reverse.

18 December

Yesterday, to quote Boris Verin, I declared myself restored to health, and went out of doors for the first time. I felt entitled to do so because my temperature had been normal for two days. Boris was also better, but as his illness had been more serious than mine he was still staying in bed.

Yesterday rumours started flying round about the murder of Rasputin (the name will enter the history books, literature also and perhaps even music – a subject for an opera??!), the world and his wife are congratulating their neighbours and at Ziloti's concert that evening there were calls for the National Anthem to be played. The newspapers are silent on the subject, but the general belief is that the assassin was Count Sumarokov-Elston,[1] who among the Guards officers involved had drawn the fateful lot.

Things are moving with *The Gambler*, or rather there have been daily rehearsals and singing coaching sessions which I have not been able to attend because of illness, instead staying at home and orchestrating the entr'acte. I could not get it to come right, however I tried, until I hit on the idea of starting by making a sketch of the score, using eight staves. Into this I composed passages which I then worked on, altering, crossing out and then finally transcribing what emerged, leaving blank spaces wherever I ran into difficulties. Finally, in the space of about three days, the sketch of the whole score was ready, and in such detail that all that will be needed will be to transfer it to the full score. Today I embarked on the final scene. It will soon be finished, and then I look forward with joyful anticipation to the Piano Concerto No. 3, the Violin Concerto and the 'Classical' Symphony.

The despicable Theatre library has finally lithographed all the material. I have received the ten copies I ordered and already sent one on to Moscow with Derzhanovsky, whose *Muzyka* journal has been resurrected, in order (to use a vulgar expression) to start sniffing out some possibilities with Cooper[2] and

---

[1] The nomenclature and title of the Yusupov family around the turn of the twentieth century is complicated. Our man's mother was one of the wealthiest and most beautiful women in Russia, Princess Zinaida Yusupova, daughter and heiress of Prince Nikolay Yusupov II, who had died in 1891. By the time of Nikolay's death his daughter had married Count Felix Sumarokov-Elston, who was by special dispensation of Tsar Alexander III permitted to assume the title of 'Prince Yusupov and Count Sumarokov-Elston', and to pass it to his own heirs. Felix and Zinaida's first-born son and heir was killed in a duel in 1908, and this is how their second son, the Oxford-educated Felix Felixovich, the eventual killer of Rasputin, became the last Prince Yusupov. Placed under house arrest for his part in Rasputin's murder, he returned to Petrograd in 1917 but soon emigrated permanently via the traditional aristocratic flight route through the Crimea, ending up in Paris where he lived until his death in 1967. He published several accounts of his involvement in the plot to kill Rasputin, the most detailed of which is contained in his autobiography, *Lost Splendor* (G. P. Putman's Sons, New York, 1954).

[2] Emil Cooper (1877–1960), distinguished Russian symphonic and opera conductor. He rose to prominence in the West in 1909 with Diaghilev's Paris and London seasons, and later conducted

the Bolshoy Theatre. I shall be in Moscow myself on 5 February, and then we can have some formal discussions.

On the 13th, not yet fully recovered and with a handkerchief still wrapped round my mouth, I took a closed carriage and went to take part in a charity concert organised by Olga Borisovna, one of our Class Inspectors at the Conservatoire.[1] I had a great success, and three young girls, particularly one of them by the name of Elli, a student of Zherebtsova-Andreyeva, rushed up to me in the artists' room almost expiring with ecstasy. Red-haired Elli, a Georgian from the remote wildness of Svanetia,[2] now telephones me every other day and we have rather pleasant conversations.

24 December

I attended a rehearsal of the roulette scene. At first I was not very happy: much of the singing seemed tentative, without much understanding of why a given phrase should be as it was or the reasons for it sounding harmonically 'wrong'. The result was stupid. But then matters righted themselves, things began to go better, and the end of the scene was being sung with gusto, some characters singing by heart.

In the Conservatoire I played some Bach organ fugues really well for Handschin, which as a result of being ill at home I had studied reasonably diligently. Generally I have made some progress, but the Swiss stickler for form still says that I will not be ready to graduate in the spring, and therefore according to our agreement I shall have to leave the Conservatoire. This annoyed me, and so I went straight to Coates saying that I was about to become liable for conscription and I wanted Telyakovsky to extend to me the privilege of becoming a Mariinsky Theatre employee. That very evening, at a performance of A. S. Taneyev's excruciatingly tedious opera *The Snowstorm*, I went to see Coates in his dressing-room, when in bounced a rotund, beaming old gentleman in a dinner-jacket – the eminent personage of the composer himself. We were introduced, whereupon he showered me with compliments. Coates immediately buttonholed him, exclaiming in tones of horror that I was about to be taken as a soldier. Taneyev: 'But that's impossible, you must not on any account join the army! It is my duty to help you, as your colleague in the profession, although of course you may well not regard me

---

regular series of symphony concerts in Moscow. Cooper emigrated in 1923 and settled in America, conducting the Chicago Lyric Opera and becoming Music Director of the Montreal Opera Guild. See *Diaries*, vol. 1, p. 181 and *passim*.

1   Olga Borisovna had been unexpectedly supportive of Prokofiev's ambition to win the Rubinstein Prize at his graduation performance. Ibid., pp. 647–51.
2   Svanetia, a remote region on the southern slopes of the Central Caucasus mountains, is the highest inhabited region in Europe, famous for the richness of its flora.

as such . . .' As he left he said that if he could genuinely be of help to me I should telephone him and he would take the call. Obediently I followed his instructions, and the next day at five o'clock was given an appointment at the Mikhailovsky Palace.

25–31 December

In what has by now become a tradition (three years running) I spent Christmas Eve at Demchinsky's. This time Boris Verin was not present, he and Demchinsky having fallen out.

On the third day of the holiday I organised a big chess tournament *a tempo* – the Third Pervorotny Tournament.[1] I became obsessively absorbed in the arrangements, and for the most part the participants were also fired with enthusiasm for the contest. Demchinsky alone preserved an Olympian composure, saying that he had other matters on his mind besides chess. Among the new competitors were Baron Rausch von Traubenberg and Rostovsky, who was terribly pleased to have been invited. The tournament started at ten o'clock in the evening and finished at six o'clock the next morning, with a victory for Rausch. An atmosphere of high excitement and animation prevailed throughout.

On the 30th I called on Lidusya Karneyeva, now Barkova. She had recently reappeared from the Far East and had rung me up. We were very happy to see one another again. What a delightful person she is, and how affectionate!

As for orchestration, I spent the whole of Christmas struggling with Polina's hysterical scene. I had to learn about horn glissandos and generally create appropriate orchestral colours for this scene, which I believe I did achieve and it will sound extremely original.

There is a new development with *The Gambler*: after it had been written up in the press, suddenly everyone started talking about Dostoyevsky's widow (apparently there is such a person) who, so it was said, considered she had a claim on me for having made use of her novel without permission. 'Her' novel, because on Dostoyevsky's death all rights in his work had passed to her and the novel was therefore her property. Bogolyubov's opinion is that this is all nonsense, nevertheless it would be politic to seek a meeting with her. This is all very boring.

Mama and I saw the New Year in at Alexander Benois's. All the young people were making a racket, it was noisy and good fun. I very much liked Benois's daughter, whom when I had first met them I had mistaken for his wife. Something about her reminds me of Nina Meshcherskaya. I had to walk home because there were no cabs, and I hardly made it staggering

---

1   The Prokofievs' apartment was on Pervaya Rota Street.

under the weight of three volumes of *L'Illustration* from 1865 that Benois gave me to help with the production of *The Gambler*.[1] The Mariinsky Theatre people seem to have completely lost their heads and have no idea how or where to research the epoch with which the novel deals.

Nouvel's New Year toast wished for me the 'glories of Meyerbeer'. The swine! He also said that if I were to present the opera without Mme Dostoyevsky's permission I could face six months in prison.

1   From its inception in 1843 *L'Illustration* was one of the first and the best of the French weekly illustrated news magazines, with extremely high quality in its graphic reproductions, printed in large format on heavy art-quality paper. Until the end of the nineteenth century printing technology in this size was by and large restricted to woodcuts and metal engravings, but the copies Benois lent Prokofiev will still have provided an unrivalled picture of the architecture, interiors, fashions and general ambiance of a European spa town in 1865.

1917

January

On 1 January I paid no calls, except that on my way to Gessen's I took my card into my new lord protector Taneyev.

At Gessen's the Mme. Dostoyevsaya saga provoked much lively discussion: Gessen, Karatygin, Rodichev,[1] Kamenka all rooted about in legal and juridical textbooks, each coming up with contradictory opinions. The law on author's copyright is so unclear that some sources would award all rights to Dostoyevna, while according to others she had none at all. Gessen became very excited and said he would protect my interests in court.

The next day I telephoned Bogolyubov and sought his counsel on what to do about the whole business. His advice was to negotiate with the widow, and I accepted the suggestion of Tyufyayev, an official of the Imperial Theatres and a friend of the Dostoyevsky household, that I should meet with Dostoyevskaya and discuss the matter with her personally. She lives out in Sestroretsk, but came into Petrograd on the 6th, to her son's apartment. And there, at four o'clock, by arrangement, I went to see her.

Dostoyevskaya proved to be a small, nice-looking old lady – she is seventy-one years of age – with an alert, shrewd expression in her eyes. She was dressed in black, with a black head-dress fastened with pins, and she sat on a small sofa by the table. I began with polite expressions of my pleasure at meeting the wife of such a celebrated personage, of whom I stood in awe and admiration. I then apologised for not having approached her earlier, but explained that this was because I had been entirely ignorant of the existence of any law of copyright. Altogether, it did not take long to establish a very good relationship; the actual business we had to discuss took no more than five seconds. She indicated that she would like to have 25 per cent of anything I earned from *The Gambler*, and I said I would think about it. I outlined for her the way I was putting the novel on the stage, and did so with great emotion, spurred on by the keen attention with which she listened to me, catching her breath and flushing with excitement, her eyes alight for all the world like those of a young girl.

When I had finished, she said: 'I always thought it could be done successfully, but I never imagined it could be as good as this!'

---

1   Fyodor Rodichev (1853–1932), prominent member of the Octobrist wing of the Kadets (Constitutional Democrats) and member of the Duma. Later, for the Provisional Government, Rodichev was to become Governor-General of Finland.

The aspects I had been concerned about – the abbreviation of the novella's end, the introduction of the Casino Director, the phrase with which Alexey ends the opera – all these things she approved. She especially liked the character of the Director, and Alexey's final exclamation: 'Who would have thought that red would come up twenty times in a row!'

She told me that *The Gambler* held especially precious memories for her: when she arrived at Dostoyevsky's house as a young stenographer he explained to her that he had less than a month in which to write a novella of this length, otherwise he would be in breach of contract and would be ruined.[1] He had already worked out the novel in his mind, but was in dread of not being able to write it in time.

The young stenographer sat down nervously at the great writer's desk while he paced about the room, crossing from corner to stove and back again, and every time he reached the stove he would knock on it twice. Dostoyevsky began dictating: 'At last I have returned from my two weeks' absence. Our group has already been in Roulettenburg for three days.' And so on. This was *The Gambler*. At the end of the first page of dictation, he stopped and asked her to read it.

'Why Roulettenburg?' he interrupted sharply as she read.

'That is what you said.'

'I did not.'

But the young woman insisted, objecting: 'But this name must have come from your imagination. How else could I possibly have known about it?'

'True,' agreed Dostoyevsky. 'All right, leave it as it is.'

Dictation continued, for half an hour or an hour each day, sometimes straight from Dostoyevsky's head, sometimes from drafts he had made during the previous night, often quite detailed ones. By the end of the month *The Gambler* was finished and despatched to Russia. Four months later they were married. This was the old lady's story.

---

[1] The stakes Dostoyevsky was playing for when writing *The Gambler* might have made even Babulenka blench. In an effort to alleviate his acute financial problems he had signed a highly risky contract with a dubious bookseller and 'literary speculator' called Stellovsky, according to which he would receive a desperately needed 3,000 roubles for the rights to a new three-volume edition of his works to date, plus a new novella of a stipulated length to be delivered by 1 November 1866. Failure to deliver the new work on time would cede to Stellovsky the rights to everything Dostoyevsky would write during the next nine years. Preoccupied by *Crime and Punishment*, already promised to another publisher, by the end of September Dostoyevsky had not even started *The Gambler*, and in desperation agreed to a friend's suggestion that he engage the star graduate of the recently established school of stenography in St Petersburg, Anna Snitkina. The last page of the novella was dictated on 29 October, Anna made Dostoyevsky's final corrections the following day, and on 1 November the completed manuscript was left at a nearby police station for collection by Stellovsky (who was, possibly by design, out at the time) with a dated receipt. Bearing in mind the fraught financial and emotional background to the creation of the novella, it is perhaps understandable that even fifty years later Mme Dostoyevskaya *née* Snitkina would be concerned to extract as much money as possible from any residual rights.

We parted with many expressions of mutual regard. She asked me to present her with an inscribed copy of the lithographed vocal score for the Dostoyevsky Museum in Moscow, a request with which I was very happy to comply. In return I got her autograph for the 'Wooden Book'. The old lady did not look as though she was accustomed to people paying much attention to her or paying her compliments, and reacted shyly when I did so.

I was very happy with the outcome of our meeting, although somewhat surprised by her appetite for money, which I resolved to dampen as much as I could.

On 14 January I performed my First Piano Concerto at a concert of the Imperial Russian Musical Society.[1] These days IRMS concerts are extremely grand affairs, with packed audiences, thanks to an injection of funds from Koussevitzky, who has no concerts of his own this season. On the 13th I appeared for the public dress rehearsal, not exchanging a single word with Malko, who was conducting. I was sure he would be able to conduct the Concerto without any prior discussion, and after the trouble we had had with the copyists during the autumn I found it most distasteful to have to talk to him. I was not mistaken: the Concerto went well at rehearsal, and extremely so at the concert. It was a success, and two unknown admirers, who never let any of my appearances pass without giving me flowers, this time presented a wreath with the inscription: 'To the young genius'. I was immensely proud of it, but Boris Verin shrugged his shoulders and said: '"Young" is rather a utilitarian epithet to attach to "genius", don't you think?!'

I have decided that, generally speaking, encores should be eliminated, as being essentially not serious. Only, therefore, after prolonged calls back to the platform did I play two little pieces from Op. 22,[2] and then only in order to give something to those few genuine musicians expecting to hear something new from me. The general public did not understand them and the applause soon died down. Malko, attempting to re-establish confidential relations with me, said: 'You can't imagine how comfortable I am conducting you, you are so rhythmic!' But I was cold and unfriendly with him.

After the concert I went to Boris Nikolayevich's, and as we drove along Nevsky I saw the windows of the Meshchersky home brilliantly illuminated: they were celebrating Nina's name-day. Among the guests at the Bashkirovs' were the Kurlina sisters, the same whose mother has a fortune of 60 million, probably by now 80 million, and for both of whom Vladimir envisages marriage: for Lyudmila a poet, for Zhenechka a composer. Each would have a dowry of 5 million. The sisters were very alike, Zhenechka the better of the two. To my surprise they were both very nice, even elegant, with well-defined

---

1 See above, p. 7 n. 1.
2 *Mimolyotnosti* (*Visions Fugitives*).

features, black eyes and hair, white teeth, beautifully manicured nails and tiny feet, very quiet and affectionate, a little too reticent although able to chatter away in a variety of languages. In fact B.N. had at one time had something going with Lyudmila, prior to Vera Suroshnikova, while Zhenechka gained some notoriety three years ago for marrying against her parents' wishes and living in poverty as a result, but after a month her husband was killed in the war and she had returned to the bosom of her family.

Needless to say I found the notion of marrying Zhenechka absurd. But B.N., spluttering as is his wont when excited, implored me to 'dazzle Zhenechka, to whom the whole of Moscow is paying court, and win her heart'. Once in a while, for the sake of amusement, I did pay her a few compliments, but in general more or less ignored her. All the same, it seems I had a tremendous success with her: she found my eyes brilliant and, moreover, had been completely conquered by my playing.

The chess tournament at my house on the 15th was a choice occasion. I had come up with a new idea: everyone must play simultaneous matches against everyone else. For six people this meant fifteen boards, and as each match would consist of three games, the total number of games would be forty-five. A hundred and fifty roubles was requisitioned from Boris Verin, who had recently won money off me at cards, and deployed to buy up all the chess sets in Petrograd (they had become a scarce commodity because of the war). On the day of the tournament all the boards were set out in a line of tables extending for 24 arshins[1] (there were not enough tables so they had to be connected by means of ironing boards), and the complete installation ran in a crooked line through the drawing-room into the dining-room. The tournament began at ten o'clock, the competitors being Boris Verin, Tyulin, Karenin, Rudin, Rostovsky and myself, and finished at six the next morning with victory going to me. Everyone walked between the boards, not sitting down, silently making his move. Occasionally there would be a cry that such and such a move was not permissible, and I would have to calm matters down. Demchinsky, foreseeing that the proceedings would probably go on until morning, declined to take part, and solemnly pronounced his opinion that 'the tournament was one for sufferers from haemorrhoids' (because no one would be sitting down).

After the IRMS concert and the chess tournament (after all, it was a major event), I buckled down to finishing Act Four. The last hurdle I had to overcome was the scoring of the lovers' embrace, and that caused me some difficulty, but after that all went smoothly and quickly, so that on 22 January the orchestration of *The Gambler* was completed. Oof! What a weight from my shoulders! The whole scoring business has taken an unconscionable amount

---

1 About 17 metres.

of time – after all, Act Three had been finished in September. But Act Four will be interesting, and it contains some quite new sounds.

I thought that now I would have more free time and could unearth my sketches for the Violin Concerto. But it was not to be: a hideous farrago of botheration and nuisance took up all my time before leaving to go to Saratov for my first ever solo piano recital. The causes of the various imbroglios were the following: first of all the business with Dostoyevsky's widow, in connection with which I had to carry out a number of researches into the nature of her rights. It transpired that she did indeed have some, but not to the extent she was demanding, i.e. 25 per cent, because while a librettist enjoys rights up to 33 per cent, in this case the librettist was myself and she was merely the owner of the subject. Coates and I went to see the Director: he advised that negotiations with the widow should be remitted to Tyufyayev, since he was so proud of his friendship with her. This was decided upon. I instructed him to offer 1,000 roubles as a single payment, in order not to spend the whole of my life worrying my head with financial calculations.

Coates and I also went to see Benois to consult him about the scenery, since our Lambin was not inspiring much confidence. Not only that, but in these wartime conditions the directorate of the theatre had begun to grouse about the cost and was making noises about a combination of stock scenery from the store, commissioning new designs only where nothing suitable was available, for example the roulette scene. Benois has an ancient feud with the Mariinsky, but is extremely fond of me personally and was most willing to talk about *The Gambler*. The advice he came up with was unexpected: to stage the opera in soft hangings rather than scenery flats, as had been successfully done with *The Brothers Karamazov* at the Arts Theatre. Armed with this notion we went to the Director who, to our surprise, was more than willing to agree to the idea of soft hangings and even suggested that the best person to take on the work would be Golovin, a pre-eminently talented scenic artist employed by the Imperial Theatres. And so, quite unexpectedly, a quite new version of the project had emerged: from a Lambin–Bogolyubov production to one designed by Golovin and produced by Meyerhold, a gifted director with enormous powers of imagination that sometimes work to his disadvantage. With Golovin he had recently staged *The Stone Guest*[1] with an intelligence and refinement that caused me to offer him my warm congratulations, to which I received this response: 'It is a particular pleasure to hear this praise from you. I hope that we shall have the opportunity to work together.'

Now I said to the Director: 'From my short acquaintance with Bogolyubov I have formed the conviction that he is absolutely hopeless, and if he

---

1 Opera (1872) by Dargomyzhsky.

were to be the producer of the opera then the reality would be that the producer would be myself. I doubt whether you would in practice wish to entrust the production to someone of my inexperience, and therefore I consider it essential that the producer should be Meyerhold.'

The Director agreed and undertook to speak to Golovin and Meyerhold. I went to Saratov on 30 January; the first orchestral rehearsal took place two days before, on the 28th. This was, I think, for me the most interesting moment of the opera's production. I sat with Aslanov and followed the music with passionate attention from the second copy of the score. Everything had come off! This was wonderful! It meant that I had developed real skill at orchestrating, and the next step on the ladder would be the achievement of total mastery. It was no longer enough to see that something had 'come off', I wanted to single out those moments that were particularly vivid or appetising. Some of the 'grotesque' sound-images were very good, especially in the second act, which was as far as the rehearsal got. The orchestra's reaction was somewhat mistrustful, and they did not seem to understand what the music was about. Coates conducted with total commitment.

I went to Medtner's concert, at which several of his songs were sung by Koshetz, a young singer with a flaming temperament and a striking ability to vary gradations of tenderness in her interpretation, who earned great praise for her appearance in Petrograd today. I love playing Medtner's sonatas on the piano, and generally have great affection for his music, reserving a corner for him – perhaps not a very big one – in the pantheon of Russian music. But his songs are not good because he does not understand the texts, or, if I may put it like this, he lacks a sense of the individual words in the text. His songs are constructed in such a way that the piece reflects the poem as a whole, and the composer is not concerned how particular moments may be expressed by particular phrases. As a result his vocal parts lack lustre and expressivity. I went backstage to see Medtner in the interval. He was more communicative this time, even friendly, and said he was looking forward to my concert in Moscow. I repeated to him my regret that he was not playing his great E minor Sonata. 'Because pieces like these', I added, 'one can play at home with one's own domestic resources, but the E minor Sonata is so demanding that one really needs to hear it in the composer's own performance.'

Medtner for some reason took offence and asked: 'What makes you think a concert should consist only of works that cannot be played at home?'

And a whole saga developed from this exchange: when Medtner returned to Moscow he reported to Rachmaninoff that I had said his sonatas were only for domestic consumption. So now, when Rachmaninoff produces a new work, he apparently asks jestingly: 'Well, now, I wonder: is this for a concert or for domestic use?'

But to revert to that evening, after the concert, at Suvchinsky's – who has plainly taken charge of my welfare – there was supper. Medtner was tired and did not attend, but Koshetz did, the object of adulation both by Suvchinsky and by Igor Glebov. I rate her very highly as a singer, and I must admit as a woman – it is no wonder she captivated Rachmaninoff – but last autumn at Ziloti's she had been so full of herself, drivelling on about how wonderful she was, that I have still not overcome my resistance and ostentatiously paid her no attention. This evidently disconcerted her, and so this evening she made a great attempt to work on me. And did so to some effect, because by the end of the evening, when everyone had left except Suvchinsky, Glebov, Koshetz and me, we were conversing without constraint, and at five o'clock in the morning we all piled into Suvchinsky's car and went to the Islands. It was about 30° below freezing, the moonlight dazzling on the snow and casting black shadows from the trunks of the trees. Koshetz leaned out of the car window and said: 'Oh, how good it is to be alive!'

February

I played a concert in Saratov on 2 February (for the Conservatoire[1]) and then in Moscow on the 5th (for the *Musical Contemporary* journal). I barely managed to get away at all: the whole of central Russia was engulfed in snowstorms with monstrous drifts and trains were delayed for up to twenty-four hours, and to make matters worse trains had been requisitioned to transport foodstuffs to the capital for 'Market Week' (or even fortnight) which disrupted the whole timetable. Elli Kornelievna[2] managed to get me a ticket in second class, and so I left on 30 January.

Instead of the thirty-six hours it should have taken, my journey to Saratov lasted forty-eight, most of which I spent asleep and enjoying the rest from the hectic bustle of Petrograd. My tourist passport did not entitle me to a hotel room, and so I stayed with Skvortsov, a leading figure in the Saratov Conservatoire. Skvortsov was a young man, a talented lawyer of uncommon energy, a gymnast and athlete, fashionable man-about-town, and a delightful companion. I went for a walk along the frozen Volga, practised what I had not fully prepared before arriving in Saratov, and played through Rachmaninoff's new songs, very wonderful. At nine o'clock in the evening I gave my combined first-ever solo-piano recital and provincial debut, not counting the concert appearance in Kiev (for which, by the way, Glière had got

---

1 The Saratov Conservatoire, founded in 1912, was at the time the third-biggest music-training institution in Russia, considering Russia proper that is, not the Ukraine or Finland or Poland or other major cities of the Empire.
2 Akhvlediani, the singing student of Anna Zherebtsova Andreyeva Prokofiev had met backstage at a charity concert in St Petersburg two months before.

into hot water from Rachmaninoff and Glazunov: how dared he corrupt the students of the Conservatoire by making them listen to my works?).

Most of my attention was focused on my imminent recital in Moscow, while Saratov I regarded as being in the nature of a diversion. I opened the programme with my First Sonata, playing with unusual brio and brilliance, but began to tire towards the end and suddenly realised that a full and demanding programme still lay before me. I therefore decided to observe a more moderate approach in tempo, expression and effort. Next was Op. 2. I had been reasonably relaxed about the Sonata No. 1, but Opp. 2 and 3[1] were another matter: however one looks at them, they are 'modernist'. But Op. 3 went down well, and the Etudes were a sensational success. Following my new practice I did not come out to take a bow. In Op. 4[2] *Suggestion Diabolique* caused a furore, the audience shouted for it to be encored, but once again I did not return to the stage. Because of its difficulty I don't very often play this piece, but just now it was in my fingers. Op. 12,[3] which followed, was also a great success, but the Second Sonata less so. During *Sarcasms* there were mild rustling, shuffling noises and whispers of incomprehension to be heard in the hall, but afterwards there were cries of 'encore' for, once again, *Suggestion Diabolique*.

Eventually, I yielded to the entreaties and appeared once more on stage, provoking a veritable uproar in the balcony where people were screaming for *Suggestion Diabolique* and pounding their chairs on the floor, a success outdoing even the one I had had in Petersburg. I encored *Suggestion Diabolique*, also the 'Gavotte' and the 'Prelude' from Op. 12. There was a scrum of people in the artists' room at the end of the recital, demanding autographs on programmes and albums of my compositions. I was quite surprised by the enthusiasm some people displayed for 'Legenda'[4] and *Sarcasms*.[5]

Early the next morning Skvortsov and I left for Moscow. From somewhere he had got hold of a military priority certificate for our train, and we therefore took possession of a magnificent first-class carriage, with wine, fruit, savoury appetisers and sweets, altogether the perfect way to travel, even though the journey took thirty-six hours instead of the sixteen it should have done.

On arrival in Moscow I made my way to Tatyana Nikolayevna's, Boris Verin's sister, where I had said I would stay. She has an exceedingly comfortable apartment, and she and I are on the friendliest imaginable terms.

1 *Four études for piano (Winkler études), Op. 2; Four pieces for piano, Op. 3.*
2 *Four pieces for piano, Op. 4.*
3 *Ten pieces for piano, Op. 12.*
4 Op. 12 No. 6.
5 An almost inconceivably long and demanding programme: a total of thirty-two separate pieces (including the four movements of the Second Sonata), some of extreme difficulty. Prokofiev must have been relieved he had not included the Op. 11 *Toccata*.

The whole world without exception had elected to come to my concert: Rachmaninoff, Medtner, Koussevitzky, Cooper, Balmont, Mayakovsky,[1] Borovsky, Igumnov,[2] Koshetz – in a word *le tout Moscou*, musically speaking. I was told it was a long time since such an audience had been seen. Exaggerated rumours subsequently circulated to the effect that some frightfully important person or other had not been able to find a seat. The fact remained that my singers – Butomo and Artemyeva[3] – had such stage-fright that they messed up all my songs, or at least failed to shine in them. All the same, the *Duckling* and the especially lovely Op. 27[4] – receiving its first performance – had a success. In general my compositions were well received, even very well, but the enthusiastic response of Saratov was not repeated. As before I did not come out to take a bow, which made someone comment that while Saratov might be educable, Moscow was not. Nevertheless I stuck to my guns and did not come out, only encoring *Suggestion Diabolique* at the very end.

After the concert some of my associates – Suvchinsky, Igor Glebov, Balmont and his wife – gathered at Tatyana Nikolayevna's. I, and particularly Tatyana Nikolayevna, were very proud that Balmont came. I promised to compose music to his incantation *Seven, They Are Seven*, for male voice, chorus and orchestra. This incantation had produced on me the strongest impression.[5] It was reported that my compositions had sent Medtner into a paroxysm of abhorrence. 'Either this is not music,' he declared, 'or I am not a musician!'

1 Vladimir Mayakovsky (1893–1930), Futurist and Agitprop poet whose work originally appeared in the Futurist publication *A Slap in the Face of Public Taste* in 1912. By the time of this meeting he had already produced his first major poem, *A Cloud in Trousers*, and had become a celebrity, as much for his passionate love affair with Lilia Brik (wife of his publisher Osip Brik) as for the ferocious power of his verse's demotic language.
2 Konstantin Igumnov (1873–1948), pianist. Igumnov was one of the greatest Russian pianists and teachers in the direct Liszt tradition, having been taught (alongside Rachmaninoff and Scriabin) by Nikolay Zverev, followed by training at the Moscow Conservatoire under Alexander Ziloti and Pavel Pabst. In 1939 Igumnov gave the first performance in the Soviet Union of Rachmaninoff's *Rhapsody on a Theme of Paganini*, five years after the work's composition. Among his own pupils were Lev Oborin and Yakov Flier.
3 Zinaida Artemyeva-Leontevskaya (1888–1963), singer. She and Butomo had appeared with Prokofiev in the recital given in the Tenishev Hall on 15 April the previous year.
4 *Five Poems of Anna Akhmatova*, Op. 27.
5 The inscription translated by Balmont was originally written in Old Akkadian, a pre-Babylonian language in the cuneiform script written and spoken throughout Mesopotamia in the third millennium BC. The most ancient of the Semitic languages, it is the language of the *Epic of Gilgamesh*, the world's oldest known literary work (the most complete version of which was preserved on clay tablets in the library of the Assyrian King Assurbanipal, the subject of Albert Coates's opera). Many years later, in his 1941 'Short' Autobiography, written for Soviet consumption, Prokofiev would somewhat disingenuously claim that 'The revolutionary events that had rocked Russia went deep into my subconscious and demanded expression. I did not know how to achieve this, and my ambitions took the unlikely direction of turning to themes of antiquity. The fact that thoughts and feelings of that time had survived many millennia had

Rachmaninoff sat near the gangway in the second row, next to Koussevitzky, immobile as a statue of the Buddha. I was told that after some of the pieces the audience started to applaud, but on looking to see the reaction of their idol and seeing him apparently turned to stone, lapsed into embarrassed silence. I was most interested to know his impression, and later learned that he had left displeased with the concert, but was still heard to say: 'All the same, he is talented.'

Also present was Sabaneyev, who had so comprehensively disgraced himself on my account. Many people amused themselves – in dreadfully poor taste, of course – at the fact of his presence, suggesting that he would have to preface his review by some such phrase as: 'Having obtained the composer's written confirmation that I did actually attend the concert . . .', etc.[1] But in the event he settled for merely castigating me as usual in an unsigned review.

The next day I had to chase about to get a train ticket to return to Petrograd. I gave Struve the *Duckling* and Op. 9.[2] I saw Lyolya;[3] she has grown a little prettier, and in the evening jumped up to accompany me out to the entrance hall. Before leaving I called on Cooper, who was also entertaining Shkafer,[4] the Chief Producer of the Bolshoy Theatre, and Olenin,[5] another producer. I played them *The Gambler*. They found my preliminary recitation of the opera's plot very entertaining, but *messieurs* the producers were baffled by the music. When I asked Cooper what he thought, he said

---

a powerful effect on my imagination. Such was the Chaldean incantation inscribed in cuneiform script on the walls of an Accadian temple and deciphered by Winkler and translated into poetry by Balmont.' (*Kratkaya Avtobiografiya*, in Shlifshteyn, *op. cit.*)

1 Leonid Sabaneyev, critic and composer, diehard opponent of Modernist tendencies in Stravinsky and Prokofiev and passionate admirer of Scriabin. The day after the scheduled performance of the *Scythian Suite* at Koussevitzky's concert in Moscow the previous December that did not take place because too many of the musicians had been called up for military service (see p. 143 above) *Novosti Sezona* (*Seasonal News*) printed a venomous review of the work by Sabaneyev. In his 1941 'Short' Autobiography, Prokofiev tells us: 'He had written the review in advance, had not bothered to go to the concert and was therefore ignorant of the changed programme . . . Now the enemy had dug his own grave! The odd thing is that although Sabaneyev had not heard the *Suite* or even seen the score, he would have had at his disposal plenty of detailed information about it and probably would not have altered a single word in his article if in fact he had heard the music. The fiasco resulted in his having to resign from several newspapers and the damage to his reputation as a critic lasted a long time.' (*Kratkaya Avtobiografiya*, in Shlifshteyn, *op. cit.*). See also *Diaries*, vol. 1, p. 234 and *passim*.

2 *Two poems for voice and piano*, Op. 9.

3 Zvyagintseva, Derzhanovsky's young sister-in-law, an infatuated admirer of Prokofiev.

4 Vasily Shkafer (1867–1937), singer and opera producer. A fine tenor, Shkafer had produced the premiere productions of Rimsky-Korsakov's *The Tsar's Bride* and Rachmaninoff's *The Miserly Knight* and *Francesca da Rimini*. From 1911 until 1917 he was Chief Producer at the Bolshoy Theatre.

5 Pyotr Olenin (1874–1922), singer and opera producer. Also a fine singer (baritone), specialising in character roles, Olenin was responsible for the premiere production of Rimsky's *The Golden Cockerel* and the Moscow premiere of *Mlada*.

proudly: 'Nothing frightens me.' As far as he was concerned he would be happy to include *The Gambler* in the Bolshoy Theatre's repertoire next season, but the final decision would lie with Telyakovsky[1] and I must speak to him about him directly I returned to Petrograd. Delighted with this, I left Moscow, this time in third class, since first and second were full up with members of the State Duma and high-ranking officers. But at least I had a reserved berth, my companions were educated people, and Tatyana Nikolayevna had thoughtfully provided me with a mattress, sheet, blanket and a pillow encased in a lacy pillowslip.

Pleasant news awaited me in Petrograd: the transfer of responsibility for the production of *The Gambler* to Meyerhold and Golovin had been accomplished, and notices to this effect had even appeared in the press. The Director received me extremely graciously and said that he had no objection to the opera being staged in Moscow. The situation with *The Gambler* is thus in fine shape, the only remaining problem being la Dostoyevna.

I arrived back in Petrograd on the 7th, and on the 9th Polina was due to arrive; I had placed my room at her disposal. I got up at seven o'clock to meet her at the station, but the train was late and it was ten o'clock by the time she arrived.

Polina was lovely and lost no time in getting on the right side of Mama, who secretly harbours hostility towards any female who appears in my life. However, I could not help noticing that the expression on Polina's face throughout her stay in the capital was a little sadder than was necessary. We spent the whole of her visit – five days – in each other's company, hardly ever being apart, going to all the theatres and to St Isaac's Cathedral, out to the Islands, and to the 'Bear'. On the eve of her departure I played at the Dobychina art gallery, where Gorky was also reading from his works. We had a very nice time there: Polina, I, Mama and Skvortsov, who had also come up to Petrograd. Polina feasted her eyes on the celebrated Maxim, while Maxim himself was so voluble in praise of *Sarcasms* that I had seldom heard anything to equal his eulogy. 'You must write, and go on writing, as much as you possibly can,' he said, pumping my hand. On the subject of the *Scherzo for four bassoons* he said it reminded him of four retired colonels laughing and joking as they gathered for a reunion.

After I had seen Polina off on the 13th, I decided in the first instance to take some time off as I needed a break. I did not want composition to turn me into nothing but the servant of my own music. In any case I was exhausted. I resolved to be a free man for a time – not to compose, not to study, not to

---

1   Telyakovsky was the overall Director of the Imperial Theatres and therefore in charge of the Bolshoy Theatre in Moscow as well as the Mariinsky in Petrograd.

worry about any mortal thing. As it happened, Coates had gone to Finland to conduct and Meyerhold was still immersed in *Masquerade*,[1] so for the time being *The Gambler* had of its own accord receded into the background.

I frequented Boris Nikolayevich, read a book about astronomy (I am deeply interested in this subject), caught up on my Diary, went to art exhibitions, slept, and went for walks. Of course I could not do entirely without music, and soon began gently, but very successfully, to make progress on the Violin Concerto, sketching out the scherzo (which I plan to make the scherzo of all scherzos) from previously conceived fragments, and a few phrases of the finale. The first-movement exposition had already been completed last year. Alongside this I rooted out some 'doggies' destined for Op. 22,[2] and also did some work on revising my old A minor Sonata, which I still do not know what to call, whether Sonata No. 3 or Sonata-Fantasia, Op. 1-bis.[3] In this way, despite my principled intention to be idle, I did unexpectedly compose quite a bit. I also spent some time with Suvchinsky. He and Igor Glebov have had a rift with Andrey Rimsky-Korsakov over their differing attitudes to new composers, notably myself, Stravinsky and Rachmaninoff. Rimsky-Korsakov at first wanted to resign from his position as editor,[4] but his Jewish colleagues, headed by Weisberg and Steinberg, jumped all over him. After that Suvchinsky, Glebov and Belyayev[5] themselves decided to pull out and publish their own journal. Weisberg nastily observed: 'I suppose you'll be calling your new magazine "*Prkfv*".'[6]

However this may be, when Karatygin, who was close to Rimsky-

1 Lermontov's early play in verse, directed by Meyerhold with incidental music by Glazunov and designs by Golovin, had its opening night in the Alexandrinsky Theatre on 25 February 1917. One of the most famous of all Russian theatrical productions, it ran for a total of nearly five hundred performances.
2 *Mimolyotnosti* (*Visions Fugitives*), twenty pieces for piano, Op. 22.
3 This was to be Sonata No. 3 in A minor in one movement, 'From Old Notebooks', Op. 28.
4 From the *Muzykalnyi Sovremennik* (*Musical Contemporary*). See *Diaries*, vol. 1, p. 773n. The trigger for the rift had been a review Asafyev had written for the journal of the IRMS concert conducted by Malko on 14 January, at which Prokofiev had been the soloist in his First Piano Concerto, flanked by *Petrushka* and Myaskovsky's Second Symphony. Asafyev insisted that, whether or not one liked the three composers, 'fail to reckon with them one cannot. To do the last would be to turn away from contemporary life, from the forms in which it manifests itself.' Rimsky-Korsakov refused to publish the review, upon which Asafyev and Suvchinsky resigned their positions. (Asafyev quotation from R. Taruskin, Stravinsky and the Russian Traditions, vol. II, p. 1122 (Oxford University Press, 1966).
5 Viktor Belyayev (1888–1934), critic and musicologist, a pupil of Wihtol. Later he played a prominent role in the Association of Contemporary Musicians (ACM), the relatively liberal and cultivated organisation that in 1931 ominously lost out to the more militant Russian Association of Proletarian Musicians (RAPM), heralding an era of ideological conformism, artistic repression and the strait-jacket of Socialist Realism. See *Diaries*, vol. 1, p. 607.
6 The new magazine was in fact called *Melos*. Having the bad luck, or bad timing, to launch in September 1917, it managed only two issues before becoming a casualty of the post-October Revolution chaos.

Korsakov, proposed on behalf of the older magazine that I should appear in their next concert with the *Akhmatova Songs*, I declined, giving the most spurious of excuses. Next season Ziloti will have a new chamber music evening in his series, and on that occasion again all the works will be first performances. This is a great thing for a composer: to have a chamber concert every season consisting of new works! And so everything proceeded quietly and peacefully, Boris Verin and I read and enjoyed Schopenhauer, and only muffled rumours of strikes and movements among the workers in the Petrograd factories reached our ears. Our servant would rush in and, goggle-eyed, relate appalling gossip, and Mme Yablonskaya, whom I nicknamed the Wolff Agency[1] on account of the sensational but inaccurate information she was fond of purveying, was always ringing up breathless with excitement at the latest revelations. Mysterious faces would appear out of nowhere and whisper into one's ear, which I found truly exasperating.

On Friday, 24 February, emerging from the International Bank at around noon, I saw an agitated lady in the vestibule, to whom the Commissionaire was saying: 'There is nothing, don't worry, there is nothing left.' Supposing that the lady could have suffered a loss on the stock exchange I paid no attention and went towards the exit door which, however, proved to be locked. The Commissionaire rushed up to open it and let me out on to the street. It was a bright, sunny day and there were crowds on Nevsky Prospect. Some of them were walking along as usual, but some were keeping close to the walls and creeping up the steps into the entrances of the buildings, while other faces peered out from shop windows. A detachment of Cossacks came riding fast along Nevsky going towards the Anichkov Bridge; obviously there must be demonstrations taking place in that area. Of course, the normal thing to do would have been to go home, but Nevsky had such a lively, sunny aspect, and the crowds seemed to be going quite merrily in the same direction as the Cossacks, so without stopping to think I went along with them. I could see quite a concentration of people on the Anichkov Bridge, mainly working men in short blouses and high boots. Cavalcades of Cossacks passed through the crowd in detachments of ten, armed with lances. It looked as though there might be some shooting, but the mass of people including women and children and elderly generals appeared quite unconcerned and stared open-mouthed at such unfamiliar sights on the Nevsky.

I crossed over the Anichkov Bridge and set off towards Liteiny, where I found the nub of the activity: a vast crowd of workers completely blocking the street. The Cossacks attempted to push them back, but the crowd simply

---

1 The Continental Telegraphen Compagnie of Berlin, otherwise known as the Wolff Agency, established in 1849, was one of the first international news agencies (the others being Havas in France, and Reuters), and during the First World War functioned more or less as an unofficial mouthpiece of the German Government.

broke through and moved in the direction of Gostiny Dvor, evidently heading for the Winter Palace. From time to time a cry erupted from hundreds of pairs of lungs, but somehow this was not at all frightening. Whenever a cavalcade of Cossacks drew near there would be shouts of 'Bravo, Cossacks!' At first I thought that elements such as janitors and police spies must have been ordered to cheer on the Cossacks in this way, but the cheers turned out to have come from the workers themselves, reluctant to confront the troops of their own country at a time when it was at war with Germany. For their part the mounted Cossacks handled the crowd as gently as they could, occasionally riding up on to the pavement to disperse idle spectators gathering in too great numbers. When this happened the crowd would flee shrieking with terror and try to take refuge behind gates or in shops, and I followed suit. As soon as the Cossacks moved on, out would come the people again.

At one point the crowd broke through the chain of Cossacks and flowed in a solid black mass of people along Nevsky. Some of the Cossacks, led by a strikingly impressive ensign, rushed forward to head off the crowd and bar the way again. I went back to the Anichkov Bridge, where Cossacks had just succeeded in driving some of the crowd on to the Fontanka. An officer was screaming at the top of his voice that they should hurry and disperse while they still had time. This was greeted with cries of: 'Shame on you, Cossacks!' and a young girl squealed: 'Yes, yes, shame on you all!' At this some Cossacks turned their horses in her direction and she promptly scampered back into the safety of the crowd, ending up on the far side of the bridge. An old woman with a stupid face, utterly misunderstanding the meaning of what was happening, called for 'the yids to be beaten up'. One of the working men patiently explained to her that this movement had nothing to do with the Jews, it was about something completely different, but his eloquence was wasted on the imbecile old crone.

I walked along the whole of Nevsky as far as Morskaya Street, everywhere awash with crowds and Cossacks trying to contain them. Sometimes one could walk quite freely, at others the way would be blocked with people or Cossacks. From time to time the Cossacks would charge at the crowd, and when this happened the crowd would scatter and dive for the safety of entrances and gates in front of buildings. I turned into a side street, hailed a cab and went home. My overall impression was that I had witnessed a gigantic demonstration, but a peaceful one.

The next day, a Saturday, I went to Ziloti's concert, but the Mariinsky Theatre was two-thirds empty. Apparently there were bullets flying on Nevsky, so music-lovers living on the far side of the thoroughfare were wary of crossing over it to come to the concert.

On Sunday there was talk of serious disorders and gun battles, but the newspapers were silent on the subject. I sat and worked on the Violin

Concerto, only going out for a while in the afternoon to walk around our local streets. Here everything was quiet, so much so that I was inclined to write off the rumours of shooting on the streets as just that, pure rumour. However, I did notice that the trams were not running. In the evening I went to Zakharov's to play bridge and Ninth Wave.[1] By this time the amount of activity on the streets was indescribable, the crowds resembling those before the Easter midnight service. The cabs had vanished, so people were all over the pavement and the roadway. At Zakharov's we went on playing until five in the morning, and when I walked home the streets were empty and everything was quiet.

On Monday the 27th I attended the general rehearsal of the student production of *Yevgeny Onegin* at the Conservatoire, to which I had been invited by my Georgian friend Elli Kornelievna. I was delighted to go, as I always love the lively atmosphere at these rehearsals. The library porter told me that there was a full-blown battle going on at Liteiny Prospect near the Arsenal and the shooting there was terrible, because some soldiers had gone over to the side of the workers. There was also shooting on many of the city's main streets. But inside the Conservatoire all attention was focused on the rehearsal, and the events in the town were soon forgotten.

As the rehearsal threatened to go on interminably, I decided to leave at half-past five. In the foyer I heard more about the serious gun battle on Liteiny. I said to our Librarian, Friebus:[2] 'Why don't we go and have a look, Alexander Ivanovich?' but he categorically declined. I then said, jokingly: 'Well, I'm going. Goodbye, Alexander Ivanovich, we may never meet again!'

I went out on to Morskaya Street and set off towards Nevsky. There were not very many people about, nevertheless some officials had left their desks, and there were women and even children as well. There seemed no reason why I should not go further, seeing that all was quiet, the crowds were not too oppressive and there was no shooting to be heard. I decided I would proceed, but keeping a good lookout for any unexpected riots or armed confrontations, and I would also take careful note of conveniently situated gates or corners of buildings that might offer some protection from bullets. Emerging on to Nevsky, I was met by complete silence. There was no traffic at all on the road, and although some people were afoot even here, there were not many of them. A few groups stood around at street corners, but they looked more like curious onlookers than workers.

1   Card game of skill and chance in which the banker plays against the other players who stake on the cards they draw against the bank's selected nine cards, the last one, if successful, paying out the stake ninefold. Seafaring lore has it that the ninth wave will the biggest and most powerful. See *Diaries*, vol. 1, p. 172 and *passim*.
2   Alexander Friebus, head librarian of the St Petersburg Conservatoire and subsequently at the Mariinsky Theatre. A small, hunchbacked man, his nickname among the students was 'Diminished Fifth'. See Ibid., p. 339 and *passim*.

I dropped into Peretz's restaurant[1] and had some eel. Then I continued along Nevsky to the Admiralty. Here the mounted Cossacks were much in evidence, and infantry detachments as well, otherwise all was quiet. But when I emerged into Palace Square a very different picture met my eyes. In front of the Palace stood an enormously long column of soldiers with rifles, confronting a huge crowd of people actually on the square being harangued by someone. It seemed that members of the State Duma were speaking to the people. I wanted to get closer, and decided the way to do so would be to go round the Palace by the embankment and then back into Palace Square from the other side via Millionaya Street. My manoeuvre was successful, although it was on the embankment that I heard shots for the first time, some way off, either from the Vyborg side or from Liteiny Prospect, but shots none the less.

When I emerged from Millionaya Street into Palace Square I saw the vast column of soldiers being ordered to turn about and go back into the garden of the Palace. Left behind on the square was a much smaller crowd of perhaps three hundred people listening to someone speaking. I attached myself to this group and saw a captain stalwartly proclaiming his devotion to his men, ensuring they got enough to eat. This did not strike me as particularly interesting, so I began to retrace my steps back to Millionaya. Just as I was nearing the street, shots rang out, one after the other, several cartridge clips. The crowd bolted towards Millionaya Street, and I with them without, however, experiencing any great sensation of terror. I had earlier marked out the first gates along the street as offering cover in the event of shooting, so I quickly made a dive to get through them. The moment I had done so the watchman locked the gates, and through the wrought iron I watched the people running down Millionaya. Some of them fell down, but from panic, not from the bullets, as they immediately picked themselves up again and went on running.

Before long everything was quiet again, no more shots were heard, some of the people came back and cautiously made their way back into the square. I asked the watchman to let me out, and also returned to Palace Square. There were no corpses lying on the ground, and I heard later that the shots had come from policemen on the Arch, from Morskaya Street, and that they were only blank cartridges.

I went along Millionaya Street to the Field of Mars, where matters had clearly taken a turn for the worse. From the direction of Liteiny Prospect there were distinct sounds of gunfire and over on the far side of the Summer Garden a thick column of smoke rose into the air. Apparently the District Court had been set on fire. From somewhere over by the Troitsky Bridge there were distant cries of 'Hurrah!' Behind me, near the Palace, more

---

1 See *Diaries*, vol. 1, p. 276 and *passim*.

shooting started up, much more than there had been when I was there. It was also getting dark and no street lights were coming on. I began to feel uneasy and decided to go home. My plan was to go along Sadovaya Street and from there make my way to Gostiny Dvor, but no sooner had I turned into Sadovaya than it dawned on me that I was the only person going in my direction, everyone else was coming towards me with panic written all over their faces. So I turned and went the other way past the Summer Garden towards the Fontanka, thinking I would be able to get round that way.

On the bridge over the Fontanka I halted because I could hear the lively rattle of small-arms fire coming from Liteiny Prospect. I asked a worker standing next to me if it was possible to get across the Fontanka. His reply was encouraging: 'Yes, you can. On you go. It's our people holding the line here.' 'What do you mean, "our" people?' 'I mean the armed workers and the soldiers who have come over to our side.'

This was news to me. 'Armed workers' – thank you very much. It looks as though we have a real fight on our hands now. I asked: 'What about getting through along Liteiny?' In the same calm and reassuring tone the worker explained: 'That wouldn't be so good. "They" are well dug in there.'

At this point I was hailed by someone I knew from the Conservatoire, together with his wife. 'I wouldn't go along Liteiny,' he said in a frightened voice. 'We've just come from Mokhovaya Street; they've set up a command post in our house, and the shooting is so bad we've decided to go to our parents.'

It turned out this was in the same direction as mine, so we went together. After some debate we worked out a route along the Fontanka, not on the side where 'our boys' were holding the line, but the other side, the one with the gardens, the Engineer's Palace[1] and the Circus. Here it was pretty quiet and comfortingly dark. I asked a few people we met whether it was possible to get across Nevsky. One said he didn't know; another said: 'Don't even think of it. There's shooting all the time there.'

I approached a little knot of people at a corner. A student was telling of his experiences: '... so they thrust a rifle into my hands. I haven't a clue what to do with it, I'm scared stiff it might go off. But you have no choice, you can't not take it, because if you don't they'll beat you up. So, anyhow, I took it, went off round the corner and dumped it there.'

I asked him if he thought I would be able to get across Nevsky. He replied: 'On the corner of Sadovaya and Engineer Street they're destroying an army

---

1 The magnificent Mikhailovsky Palace was dedicated on the feast day of the Archangel Michael in 1800 as the official residence of Tsar Paul I. Paul's guardian angel did not, however, protect him from being murdered in his own bedroom soon after taking up residence. In 1823 the building was taken over by the School of Military Engineering, hence the name it is still known by today. It is now a museum.

command post. They've lit fires and are burning whatever they can get hold of. It's not safe there at all, that's where I've just come from.'

My Conservatoire acquaintance and his wife said they did not want to come any further and thought they could now go back to their apartment on Mokhovaya Street. It certainly was beginning to look as if there were no way out. Nevsky was like a canal, a conduit for bullets. How and where could I get across it to the other side? I decided I would go back to the Palace, even though some of the shooting that could be heard seemed to be coming from there, and try to get past it along the Palace Embankment, in the hope that there would not be any shooting on that side. In that way Nevsky would be some way to one side. I walked past the Engineer's Palace and on to Sadovaya Street. Out of the half-darkness a heavy lorry thundered past, with twenty or so workers armed with rifles on board, a large red flag waving above them. I thought to myself: they're mad! I had not realised the Revolution had taken such a decisive step towards its goal.

Once again I found myself back on the Field of Mars, only by now it had grown much darker. On the far side of the field I could hear the crowds shouting 'hurrah!' by the Troitsky Bridge, and some shots could be heard. At a half-run I edged along the side of the square, but I had no galoshes and my feet slid on the frozen pavements. At one point I slipped so badly I could hardly stay upright, and grabbed at the arm of a passing colonel. He swivelled round to look at me, and I said: 'Excuse me, I think I must have frightened you.' 'On the contrary,' replied the colonel, 'I was afraid you might fall.' And then added: 'Why are you running? The bullets will catch you up in any case. As you see, I'm not running, I'm walking.'

I could have objected that if one takes one minute to cross an open space rather than three, one has three times less chance of being shot while doing so. But I was not in the mood for rational discourse, so I contented myself with saying: 'Yes, but I am in a hurry', bowed and carried on.

When I found myself near the '*Mir Isskustva*' exhibition it occurred to me that it might be easier to go to Dobychina's and ask if I could spend the night there, since there was such a volley of shooting near the Palace it seemed pointless to carry on in that direction. To start with I thought I would try to cut through along the Yekaterinsky Canal: all seemed quiet there and there was no reason to expect any unrest on that street. But hardly had I turned into the Yekaterinsky Canal when on the other side of the water appeared a crowd of soldiers surrounded by workers, singing noisily as they approached the Field of Mars, obviously soldiers who had gone over to join the Revolutionaries. Taking advantage of the fact that there was water between us, I quickly got as far as the Church of the Saviour of the Blood, calculating that if an exchange of fire were to break out I would be able to take cover behind its walls. I kept asking people I met if it was possible to get across Nevsky, and got varying replies: some said it was possible if one ran quickly, others said it was too terrifying to contemplate. One woman said: 'Don't try it. There are people with revolvers up on the roofs shooting at anything that moves.'

However, I did not give this much credence, and pressed on. People loomed briefly out of the gloom like grey shadows, and it occurred to me that I was myself such a shadow, and I did not see how every such shadow could be shot at.

Finally I reached Nevsky Prospect. To my astonishment not a single shot was to be heard. Little groups of people stood at the street corners, and one or two were walking along the pavements. Some crossed the road. The street-lamps, normally so bright, now shone with a dim reddish glow, presumably because of reduced electrical current, and this lent the street an eerie, sinister appearance.

Actually, it was not a particularly frightening matter to cross the street, and I did so without difficulty. How relieved I was to have it behind me at last! Now I could more or less count on getting home, and much encouraged I stepped out briskly along the half-darkened streets. Sennaya Square was packed with people shouting 'hurrah!', and generally the streets were noisy, dark and restless. There was a good deal of shooting coming from Izmailovsky Prospect, where the Izmailovsky Regiment had its barracks. It was nine o'clock in the evening, and I was terribly hungry. Mama had been desperately worried at my absence.

All evening there was to-ing and fro-ing along our Pervaya Rota Street: hurrah-shouting crowds surged, automobiles drove up and down, shots were fired. At length soldiers bearing a red flag marched past, on their way to the Izmailovsky Barracks to persuade the men of the regiment to join the Revolutionaries. At first there were some exchanges of gunfire, then some of the Izmailovskies agreed to come over while others retreated into the barracks and continued the fight until the next morning, causing a desperate cannonade that went on all night. Suvchinsky telephoned to celebrate the advent of the new government, meaning the Temporary Committee formed from the most popular members of the State Duma.[1]

During the night I was woken up by deafening gunfire, seeming to come from right by my ear: someone was firing in our courtyard. Things eventually quietened down, but next morning our servant roused me saying that a

---

1 The 'Temporary Committee of Duma Members for the Restoration of Order in the Capital and the Establishment of Relations with Individuals and Institutions', to give it its somewhat decorous full title, had been formed by members of the Progressive Bloc of the Duma along with Kerensky and Chkheidze, on the afternoon of 27 February 1917, largely to foil the more naked ambitions of the Executive Committee of the Petrograd Soviet of Workers' Deputies, set up earlier in the day.

police machine-gun had been spotted either on our roof or on the roof next door, and as a result all attics were being searched, and the apartments would be next. For some reason, however, they missed out our apartment, and no one was discovered in any of the attics. All that happened was that one soldier, in the process of ransacking an attic, contrived to shoot off his finger.

I went outside. The sun was shining brightly, just as it had done on the day war was declared with Germany. The streets were overflowing with people, and because there were no trams or cabs they filled the streets from side to side as well as the pavements. Colourful red banners met the eye at every turn. All military units had now joined the Revolutionaries, so no more fighting was to be expected.

On the Fontanka I saw a huge bonfire, at least two sazhens[1] across, the flames from which reached up two storeys high. From a flat in the next-door house the window-frames were being torn out and hurled with a wrenching crash to the ground, followed by all manner of household utensils and furniture. The home of a local divisional police chief was in the process of being systematically wrecked. Out of the third-floor windows flew green sofas, tablecloths, whole cupboards full of papers. The cupboards were a particularly impressive sight as they slowly toppled over the window-sills then hurtled down to crash with a kind of wheezing groan on to the pavement, right into the blaze. There they disintegrated, the glass doors shattered, the papers fanned out to be borne aloft by the smoke and the wind high above even the roofs of the buildings. The crowd bayed with unholy glee: 'Bloodsucker! That's our blood he's been drinking!'

I could not share the feelings of the mob, and was sickened by the violence. I wondered if the policeman's family had managed to flee the pogrom.

That afternoon Mama and I went out to look at Revolutionary Petrograd, which had a distinctly holiday air about it. At Gostiny Dvor there was another incident with a policeman: I saw two students dragging off a stout, grey-haired man in civilian clothes pursued by a furious mob screaming: 'A plain-clothes copper!' People came running up from all directions, and I could see that it was a poor lookout for him. But then someone shouted: 'No lynch-law!'[2] and I immediately chimed in with 'No lynch-law!' Some people supported me, calling for the same thing, but others cried: 'Kill him!' and thrust their fists right in his face. He tried to say something, but seemed to

---

1 About two and a half metres.
2 The word used is 'samosud', literally 'do-it-yourself justice'. Gorky, in particular, was appalled by the scale and ferocity with which such summary justice continued to be meted out by the mob on the streets of Petrograd and other cities, and in the country where the collapse of the regime gave the peasants the chance to vent their fury on their hated feudal masters. In Gorky's view, and that of like-minded members of the intelligentsia who supported the ideals of the Revolution, such barbarism symbolised the fundamental betrayal of the political and social principles for which opponents of Tsarist autocracy and corruption had fought for so long.

be unable to see anything in front of him. One of the '*no samosud*' faction raised a cry for the soldiers to surround him, but none of them could break through the furious crowd to get to him. The policeman was on quite a high section of pavement a few paces from me; I pressed backwards as hard as I could and forced a few people back off the pavement, while some of the soldiers rushed into the space thus created and succeeded in isolating the policeman from the crowd, rendering him more or less safe.

I found Mama and we went on our way. We ran into Gessen, and this was the best person we could possibly have met at this particular moment, because of all people he was most able to tell us what was happening in the political sphere. We accompanied Gessen to the *Rech* newspaper offices, and then went on with him to take tea at his house. On the streets there was a lively resumption of shooting; a machine-gun had been set up on top of their house. I asked Gessen how he saw the future, where the Revolution was heading, what kind of administration did he see coming into being, but he obstinately kept silent and changed the subject. When the shooting died down, Mama and I made our way home. The date was 28 February.

March

The days just past – the first days of March – were marked by the ceaseless movement of the crowds: thousands, tens of thousands of people filled the streets with red ribbons pinned to their chests. A mass of vehicles – all automobiles had been requisitioned for the purpose – roared about in all directions, filled to overflowing with workers and soldiers, bristling at every conceivable point with bayonets and red flags. I was more interested in the people who were distributing leaflets, newspapers and proclamations, throwing them into the crowd. Like everyone else I rushed to pick them up. Once I went right up to the car and asked for a leaflet. I was handed one, but the wind caught it and whirled it away down the street, with me running after it, but it was picked up by one of the soldiers. I told him the leaflet had been given to me and asked him to hand it back, but although he could not read he refused. Even though by now the city was completely in the hands of the soldiers, I stood my ground until another soldier came to my aid. At this point it was discovered that there were actually two copies of the leaflet, so both sides could part satisfied. This was the so-called Order No. 1, which when I read it troubled me very much.[1]

---

1 And no wonder. Order No. 1, the first, and one of the most crucial, proclamations of the Petrograd Soviet, was a reaction to the unsuccessful attempts of the rival power-base – the Temporary Committee of the Duma – through its Military Commission to persuade the mutinous soldiers to return to barracks and accept some kind of command structure. The Soviet's Order No. 1, in effect drafted at the behest of the soldiers in the Soviet, abolished all

Somewhere in the bowels of the Duma an immense work was in progress that would determine the fate of Russia. High up on the roofs of the city the old regime had its police snipers firing on its opponents in the crowds, while below on the streets people continued to mill about in such a monotonously aimless manner that very soon it began to irritate me. With relief I sat at home and took up my work again. I finished the Sonata No. 3, sketched out some pieces for Op. 22 (including the penultimate one, which reflected my mood brought on by the events of the time).[1] And I settled down to further work on the Violin Concerto.

Of my remaining impressions of the Revolution two moments especially stay in the memory. The first is when I was standing on the street and heard a gentleman in spectacles reading a leaflet aloud to the crowd. The subject was the form of government that we should have, and it was at this point that I first found myself to be in clear and convinced agreement that Russia should be a republic, and it made me feel very glad. The second was reading a poster on the wall announcing the establishment of the Provisional Government. I was enthusiastically in favour of the content of this announcement and concluded that if it were to be solidly established then the whole transformation would proceed with exemplary simplicity and smoothness.

And thus, in tune with the cheerfully optimistic nature of my character, I formed the conclusion that the Revolution was succeeding brilliantly. I was even not too upset that *The Gambler* would not now be produced until the autumn – now was certainly not the right time, bearing in mind that someone like Chkheidze[2] (or, as Boris Verin miscalled him, Chekhidze) might suddenly appear without warning on the stage and start haranguing the audience on the merits of a single- or dual-chamber republic, an intrusion

---

traditional marks of authority and respect between officers and the ranks, and, significantly, recognised only the authority of the Soviet as the supreme commander of the army. At a stroke it destroyed the basic disciplinary structure that underpins any dependable military force and replaced it with a spurious, pseudo-democratic collectivist consensus.

[1] In the 1941 *Short Autobiography*, written in wartime Soviet Moscow, Prokofiev understandably puts a slightly (but only very slightly) more politically defensible gloss on his artistic reaction to the February Revolution: 'The February Revolution found me in Petrograd. I, and the circles in which I moved, welcomed it with joy. While the actual Revolution was taking place I was out on the streets of Petrograd, hiding behind projections jutting out from walls whenever the shooting was intense. The 19th *Vision Fugitive*, written around this time, in part reflects impressions – more the agitation of the crowd than the inner essence of the Revolution.' (*Kratkaya Avtobiografiya*, in Shlifshteyn, *op. cit.*)

[2] Nikolay Chkheidze (1864–1926), one of the founders of the Georgian Social Democratic Party and a leader of the Menshevik wing of the Russian Social Democratic Labour Party. Chkheidze became the first Chairman of the Petrograd Soviet but although he opposed the Bolshevism of his more radical colleagues in the RSDLP he declined to join the Provisional Government. Providentially in Georgia at the time of the Bolshevik coup in October, he became Chairman of the Georgian Constituent Assembly and wrote the Republic's first Constitution, but fled to France when the Bolsheviks took power in 1921. He took his own life five years later.

that would certainly put paid to any chance of the audience enjoying the performance. Meyerhold and Golovin – a most charming and handsome man with greying hair who when we finally met showered me with compliments – could not have been more positive about *The Gambler*, and were also loud in their praise of Remizov's *Leila*,[1] telling me how delighted they were that I planned to write an opera on the subject.

About *Leila* I consulted Demchinsky, and his reaction to Remizov's draft was that it represented a fabulous thesaurus of language but hardly a subject for an opera. A subject to be so magnificently apparelled, a libretto for a work of substance – assuming that is what I was in search of – must itself consist of a profoundly resonant legend or symbolic theme, rather than the suggested ephemeral, fairy-tale type of entertainment that upon leaving the theatre would leave no trace on the memory. I took Demchinsky along to a small meeting in Golovin's studio in the Mariinsky Theatre to talk about *Leila*. He spoke about Altaic legends[2] while the remainder of those present listened in silence. Remizov agreed with Demchinsky's assessment and took back *Leila* to subject it to root-and-branch revision.

At the end of March Suvchinsky went off to his estate near Kiev and invited me to go with him. I was very tempted to do so, wanting to see the first burgeonings of spring, and thinking that on the way back I could spend a day in Kharkov and see Polina. But fate was against my making the journey, as chaos and random timetabling reigned supreme over the railways, all classes of which were in any case full to the gunwales with soldiers. Each spring it seems to be my lot to make plans for a fantastic trip and each time to see them crumble to dust.

In musical circle there was much talk of the national anthem 'God Save the Tsar' having outlived its usefulness and the need for a new one. To my mind there could be no better national anthem than Glinka's 'All Hail!',[3] except that it would need new words. What could be more radiant or uplifting? But the worm of ambition gnaws at all composers' vitals: hold on a minute – composer of the National Anthem, think what a celebrity that would make you!

I confess there were moments when the worm gnawed at mine too, but almost immediately I would be terribly ashamed of myself. In the meantime Glazunov was hard at work writing, Grechaninov had already published one, and in no time at all there would be fifteen more, each one worse than the other. And when I thought of all the pathetic junk that would be

---

1 *Alaley and Leila*. See above, p. 144.
2 The peoples of the Altay Mountains in Mongolia were the inheritors of a rich and ancient store of mythology, legends and stories, mostly in the Turkic tongue, many of them concerning the creation of the world.
3 The final chorus, 'Hail to the Tsar!' from Glinka's opera *A Life for the Tsar* (1836).

served up, all the mean-spirited poverty of invention, all those unimaginative hack musicians scribbling down their feeble little ideas worrying lest their grand vision be not understood and all the time being quite unable to grasp themselves what kind of music was needed – at moments like this I too wanted to compose an anthem. Once I even rang up Dobychina, just to talk about it. She seized on the thought, raised the matter with Gorky and Benois, but by then I had already lost interest. A couple of weeks later she telephoned me again. The same evening I wrote two anthems and took them over to play to her. She liked them tremendously, but once again I could not rid myself of the notion that this was no more and no less than an attempt to win cheap popularity, and abandoned them.

At the beginning of March there took place in the Mikhailovsky Theatre a grand gathering of everyone having any sort of connection with a branch of the arts. I did not attend, but was told that when there had been elections for representatives from the world of music, and Tcherepnin and Ziloti were appointed, with myself and Glazunov also nominated as candidates, Glazunov, sitting on the platform, rose to his feet to announce morosely: 'If Prokofiev gets in, I wish to withdraw my candidature.' This drew applause from the body of the hall, but frenzied boos and catcalls from the box full of my supporters.

April

On 1 April I went to the Conservatoire for the midnight Prime service. I love this event that marks the beginning of Easter, and always attend. This year, however, it seemed a little less glamorous than before, although the Procession of the Cross had its usual effect of putting me in a wonderful frame of mind.

On the second day of the holiday there took place the grand opening of the Finnish Exhibition, which assumed the character of a political celebration occasioned by the granting of freedom to Finland.[1] Milyukov, Rodichev

---

1 In April 1917 this freedom was only partial. The abdication of the Tsar, who had ruled Finland as Grand Duke, and the refusal of his brother, the Grand Duke Mikhail, to take his crown, left the Grand Duchy of Finland without a monarch but still, according to the Russian Provisional Government, owing sovereignty to Russia as the inheritor of the Tsar's authority. The Finns did not see it the same way and pressed for independence. At the time of the Finnish Exhibition the situation was a compromise, Finland had its constitution restored and was therefore no longer subject to direct rule, but was still in theory ultimately answerable to the Russian Governor-General (Rodichev) rather than to the Finnish Parliament. The hopeful fiction that this would eventually be resolved by the much heralded Constituent Assembly could not last, and by late June the Finns had declared UDI, precipitating yet another crisis the beleaguered Provisional Government could well do without. The ancient and deep-rooted Russian insistence that Finland owed sovereignty to Russia was also at the root of the White General Yudenich's North West Army failure to capture Petrograd in May 1919: had he been prepared

and Gorky all made speeches. I was on the Committee of Honour, and was proud to be so, for it was a glittering assembly of the greatest names in the arts and politics. The exhibition itself was monochrome and uninteresting; there was not a single exciting subject, no bright canvases, everything seemed to have been painted on a grey day. To see so much as a splash of red in a picture was a joyful event.

At the 'Donon' restaurant, where a dinner was held after the opening of the exhibition, we were subjected to a series of interminable speeches in several languages. One Finnish sculptor invited Russian artists to join hands with their Finnish brothers and then, hand in hand, 'nous épaterons le monde'.[1]

I made the acquaintance of the Futurist Mayakovsky, the violent impetuosity of whose manner I found at first rather alarming, but later on he expressed his strong partiality for me and said he would come to see me for a serious talk, seeing that I was writing such marvellous music to all kinds of worthless texts, like those of Balmont and others. He felt it his duty to acquaint me with 'real modern poetry'. Furthermore, I was the first, in fact the only, composer of today, and since Russian music was in the vanguard of the whole world, he and I must join forces, he from literature, I from music and Burlyuk[2] from sculpture, and together we would conquer the world.

'Certainly,' I replied. 'Delighted.'

On the 5th Boris Verin celebrated his twenty-sixth birthday with a banquet attended by numerous guests, among them Tcherepnin. I had been hoping to watch Kozlovskaya, an extremely glamorous but far from innocent red-haired thirty-year-old, a great friend of Boris Verin, flirt with Tcherepnin, but instead of that she turned the full force of her artillery on me. Tcherepnin, meanwhile, elected to bestow his company on Demchinsky, with whom he has positively fallen in love; I am very glad of this.

On the 8th I arranged one of my regular Pervaya Rota chess tournaments, which as usual occupied me to the exclusion of pretty much everything else. This time there were new faces: Orlov and Anichkov, friends of Tyulin. Anichkov it was who took first prize, and then astonished me by sitting down at the piano and dashing off at a furious tempo the finale of

---

to agree the granting of subsequent independence to Finland he would have had the crack Finnish Army at his disposal, and the outcome would very likely have been different. But to a Russian patriot the idea was unthinkable.
1   'We shall astonish the world.'
2   David Burlyuk (1882–1967), Futurist painter, illustrator and poet, one of the founders of the 'Hylaea' Futuro-Cubist group emanating from the Ukraine, along with his brothers Vladimir and Nikolay, Velimir Khlebnikov and Alexey Kruchonykh the 'nonsense' ('*zaumny*') invented-language poets, Kamensky and Mayakovsky. It was Hylaea that had issued the seminal Russian Futurist manifesto *A Slap in the Face of Public Taste* in 1912. After the Revolution Burlyuk emigrated to Japan and America, and the group disintegrated.

Beethoven's 'Appassionata' Sonata. The competition absorbed so much of our attention that it quite took our minds off the deeply unsettling rumours about the Germans taking advantage of the disorganised state of our armies, and the weaknesses that had appeared in the defences of the Gulf of Finland, to launch an assault on Petrograd. They had even, so we heard, occupied Esel Island.[1] I tried to hurry up Mama to get her away to Yessentuki, where she already had a room booked. It would make life much easier for me: if she were not around I could stay in the capital until the very eve of the anticipated German invasion of Petrograd, and then, briefcase full of manuscripts in hand, I could escape on foot along the Neva to the east. Boris Verin had actually planned to buy a small motorboat and keep it locked up in his garage, making use of the fact that his house was on the banks of the Neva. At the last moment we could take it out and navigate into Lake Ladoga, and thence to the Volga.

I tried to sound out the possibility of getting hold of a passport to travel abroad. It seemed that via Gessen there might be some hope of this, but it was not clear what authority had the power to issue such a document.

On the 9th Meyerhold telephoned to inform me that as a member of the Society of Workers in the Arts – a broadly based union aimed at bringing together artists of all kinds throughout Russia – I had been chosen by an extremely left-leaning group of artists to join a deputation to one Golovin, Commissar of the Imperial Theatres – not my designer, but a namesake.[2] This was as a result of the election, my candidature for which had caused Glazunov to utter his protest. The aim of the deputation was to protest against the soon-to-be-established Ministry of Culture in which, so it was believed, the likes of Benois and Gorky had already been manoeuvring in a bid to seize power. I had no inclination whatever to ally myself with any committees or deputations, being unshakeably convinced that the job of a composer is to sit and compose music, but Meyerhold was vocal in his insistence that I had been elected by an overwhelming majority of votes (which I found very flattering) and that after seeing Golovin we must report to the Soviet of Workers' and Soldiers' Deputies, which would also be very interesting. I agreed to go to the Academy of Arts. As a precaution I rang up Benois to ask him, since I was joining an organisation dedicated to seeing him ejected from the future Ministry of Culture, if he would be kind enough to supply me with some rationale for this course of action. Benois roared with laughter and said: 'You must convince them none of us has the slightest interest in taking power.'

---

1   Now known by its Estonian name of Saaremaa, a large island effectively controlling the entrance to the Gulf of Riga in the Baltic Sea.
2   Fyodor Golovin (1867–1929?), a Deputy in the Second State Duma.

The next day our delegation, with Sologub at its head, went to the Winter Palace, where we were received by Golovin. I did not consider our representations well founded, and made it clear the only reason I was going was to see how Golovin, a first-class orator and President of the Second State Duma, would demolish our arguments. However, Sologub proved to be an effective debater and produced detailed counter-arguments, notably that in times like these, words like 'organisation', 'constitution', 'society' – even when applied to more or less fictitious entities like ours – carried exceptional weight, and as a result our declaration was taken into account. Personally, I was much more interested in the palace and the manner in which it had been transferred from the monarch to the cause of art.

On 11 April I achieved twenty-six years of age. My twenty-seventh year – quite a serious matter. Serious enough for Onegin to cry out in despair:

> I've lived until I'm twenty-six,
> No goals, no love, no occupation,
> And now I don't know what to do ...[1]

Not that this really applies to me, although I do love these lines. For my birthday I gathered together my friends at home: Boris Verin, Demchinsky, Boris Borisovich Gershun,[2] a young cousin of Eleonora and someone who impresses me very much by his erudition and refined approach, Tcherepnin, Suvchinsky, Dobychina, Eleonora herself, and finally the 'old guard' of Nurok and Nouvel. I played them my most recent compositions: the Third Sonata and *Visions Fugitives*. The Sonata made a great impression on the 'old guard' because it was so well crafted, but of course the real centre of gravity was *Visions Fugitives*. This piece produced a very strong reaction from Demchinsky, who said it represented a gigantic, unprecedented step forward. 'Hitherto your music has been that of a pagan apostrophising the sun. But now music has appeared that leaves me nothing to do other than to congratulate you.'

On the 14th I attended a recital of works by Scriabin marking the second

---

1 Somewhat inaccurately misremembered from the eighth and final chapter of Pushkin's *Yevgeny Onegin*. Pushkin's original has:

> Onegin ... having lived without a goal
> Or occupation, till the age of twenty six,
> Oppressed by inactivity's endless void,
> No job, no wife, no business to attend,
> Had no employment for his mind.

2 Boris Gershun (1898–1969) was born Boris Bozhnev and is better known by this name, Gershun being the name of his adoptive father after his own father had died young. An uncommonly gifted poet, artist and musician, he became one of the most promising poets of the first wave of Russian intelligensia emigrating to Paris, where he was initially sent to study at the University in 1919. His circle of friends included Paul Claudel, Chaim Soutine and Fernand Léger.

anniversary of his death. And it was a strange experience: I came to it from the second act of *Kitezh*,[1] and after the terrors of the Tartar flight Scriabin's Preludes seemed to me so neutral, so tame and irrelevant, that I suffered intolerable pangs of boredom and only woke up towards the end of the concert with the Seventh and Ninth Sonatas. I did not much care for Borovsky's interpretation either: it was cold and superficial.

On the 16th I finally made my promised trip to Kharkov, having luckily managed to get hold of a first-class ticket to Kiev, which would take me as far as Kursk. Elli Kornelievna had been instrumental in getting me my ticket, as we were going the same way, but such was the mayhem at the station that we got on different trains. I slept wonderfully in my upper berth, while a dozen or so, not more, soldiers crowded into the corridor. They behaved impeccably, but from Moscow onwards the entire carriage including our compartment was invaded by such a crush of not just soldiers but public generally, that there seemed no hope of ever getting out of the carriage at all. Salvation lay in my staying on my upper shelf for the whole thirty-six hours the journey lasted.

Arriving in Kharkov I took my little suitcase and bounded on to the platform, falling almost straight into the arms of Polina. But this was sheer coincidence: she had not received any of my telegrams and was seeing off one of her friends, whom she squeezed into the carriage I had just left. After an exchange of surprised exclamations we set off round the streets of the town. It was 18 April, and that meant that according to the new calendar it would be 1 May,[2] so this was cause enough for the celebration, no one was at work, there were no cabs, the trams were not running, the streets, bathed in bright sunlight, were alive with people. There were processions with red flags, and dotted among them the pale blue flags of the Jews and the black flags of the Anarchists. We walked on out of the town, where it was green and warm, and it was six o'clock before we found a restaurant where we could have dinner. The purpose of our meeting that day was to decide whether or not we were going to go to the Sandwich Islands.[3] Or more accurately, was Polina going to go? Polina declined to give a straight answer.

Returning to the capital I had expected to be able to hear orchestral rehearsals of the third and fourth acts of *The Gambler*, but Coates informed me that it was out of the question to think of the orchestra starting to

1   *The Legend of the Invisible City of Kitezh*, opera (1904) by Rimsky-Korsakov.
2   The Russian Empire did not in fact officially change from the Julian to the Gregorian calendar until 1 February 1918 (by order of the Council of People's Commissars on 18 January 1918) so this celebration was premature, but it was presumably in the wind long beforehand and after all, why should one not take an extra day's holiday in anticipation?
3   Sandwich Islands was the name given to the Hawaiian Islands (after his patron John Montague, 4th Earl of Sandwich) by Captain Cook on his third voyage of discovery in 1778, the year before he unwisely returned there to be killed by disaffected Hawaiians.

rehearse anything beyond the immediate schedule of opera performance, such was the state of confusion in the theatre with no one knowing who was supposed to be in charge of what. The orchestra was in any case spending the majority of its time in meetings aimed at reconstituting itself. I was very disappointed by the news, since I had derived so much pleasure from hearing how the scoring of the first and second acts sounded, but the effects that I hoped would manifest themselves in the third and fourth acts were potentially much more interesting. And it was really important for me to hear them now, since during the summer I definitely planned to compose the Chaldean incantation *Seven, They Are Seven* with a large chorus, and I wanted its sound-world to be far in advance even of *Ala*. The instrumentation of *The Gambler* would be a step along this path.

On the 22nd, I went to Boris Verin's to carry on our tradition of reading Schopenhauer with him. To be precise, he would read (and very well) while I sat either in the deep armchair next to the fireplace, or lay on the sofa. On this occasion Tatyana Nikolayevna was sitting in the drawing-room, with Lyunechka[1] and the young Princes Golitsyn. I was happy to play them the Third Sonata and a couple of the *Visions Fugitives*. After that Boris Verin and I, to the displeasure of those assembled, withdrew to his study, preferring the company of Schopenhauer to idle chatter. After a chapter of Schopenhauer we moved on to Nietzche's *Zarathustra*, which I had discovered before Boris did, and which had bowled me over with the extreme refinement of its strange thought.

On 23 April Mama left for Yessentuki. In spite of the disorder on the railways she got away in reasonable comfort, and since no one was in any position to guarantee a peaceful future for Petrograd, either from the point of view of its internal upheavals or of irruptions from outside, I was relieved to be sending her to the Northern Caucasus, one of the quietest places in all Russia from every perspective.

Left alone in Petrograd, to begin with I did very little. Above all my thoughts centred around the long-awaited decision from Polina. True, I did get on with, and enjoyed, transforming an old suite for strings into my Fourth Piano Sonata, but with less single-minded attention than usual. I needed a new Andante for it, and I knew I had one somewhere among exercises I had done for my [Conservatoire] classes in Form, but nowhere could I find the lost manuscript, even though I turned out every single cupboard, shelf and drawer. I was delighted when I remembered the Andante from my E minor Symphony, which would go perfectly for piano, while I saw little prospect of ever resurrecting the symphony itself from its long-buried obscurity.[2]

1   Lyudmila Kurlina.
2   The sonata was published as Sonata No. 4, Op. 29. The theme of the Andante had originally been used for the slow movement of the E minor Symphony given an airing by Hugo

On the 25th a telegram from Polina was delivered. The odd thing was, I was rather nervous about reading it: what if the answer was 'yes' and I did not have time to arrange permission to leave the country? That could be amusing! But my alarm was, alas, unfounded. The telegram explained that by reason of her being a minor she could not be given a passport to travel abroad. This made me angry, because I suspected that rather than giving me an outright refusal Polina was resorting to evasion.

As a result, I felt I was standing on the shore while the great Transpacific liner left without me. As a substitute I now had to think about a river steamer: I decided that in May I would go down the Volga, as I still had the happiest memories of last year's trip. Boris Nikolayevich and Alekhine[1] said they would come with me. Alekhine had turned up again in Petrograd from somewhere or other, and I was always glad to see him because of the faintly exotic air that hung about him; as Boris Verin was fond of saying: 'Alexander Alexandrovich, you are such an exotic creature, aren't you?'

As the month drew to a close I did not do much work, but I was in good spirits despite a certain sense of being rudderless. I therefore entertained myself by organising a grand session of *chemin-de-fer*.[2] Taking part were Zakharov, Verin, Alekhine (who arrived at half-past one at night), and a few others making nine in all, putting the total stakes at more than 1,500 roubles. Although I limited myself to 150, being short of money, I still lost 700 to Boris Verin. However, the next day I received 4,000 from Gutheil for a whole series of songs and for *Visions Fugitives*, which made me regret that now I was in the money I was not going to the Sandwich Islands!

The Red Cross[3] was very understanding. My section head asked me to go and see him and said that although times had changed he wanted the relations between us to stay as they were, meaning that I did not need to burden myself with duties for them but should leave myself free to concentrate on my creative work. But as it was still necessary to demonstrate my affiliation to the Red Cross, perhaps I could do so in my own field, that is to say by giving concerts in aid of it, or something of the sort. Thanking the directorate for its kind understanding I said that the present time was not

---

Warhlich's Court Orchestra in 1909, and was eventually to re-emerge once again in orchestral dress in the composer's 1934 transcription for orchestra of the Fourth Sonata's slow movement, Op. 29A. See *Diaries*, vol. 1, p. 280.

1 The chess grandmaster Alexander Alekhine. See *Diaries*, vol. 1, pp. 584, 640–42 and *passim*.
2 One of the forms of the baccarat card game, in which players bet against the bank (who is himself one of the players) on the values of the cards they have been dealt.
3 We have not been told how or in what capacity Prokofiev was accredited to the Red Cross, but no doubt the fact that his friend Nikolay Ruzsky was a high-up official in the organisation (see ibid., p. 759) had something to do with it, likewise the intervention of Alexander Taneyev. (See above, pp. 158–9.)

conducive to this kind of special concert, which would be unlikely to make any money, on the other hand I had plans to appear in a series of other concerts and the proceeds of those I would donate to the Red Cross.

May

Relinquishing the notion of the Sandwich Islands (of course I will return to them another time) I applied myself to thinking about what I was going to do during the summer, and came up with a rough plan. The confused situation in Russia generally and particularly the collapse of the railway system meant that travelling would be difficult, and whatever I chose to do would necessarily be modest in scope and cautious in implementation. Thus, at the end of May I would take a trip down the Volga, which had so enchanted me the previous year and which would now be even more in spate, and the countryside even more ravishingly in bloom than last July. Then in July I would go for a month to Yessentuki, where Mama would be waiting for me and for which I had an affection going back many years. Early May, June and August I would stay in the north, obviously not in Petrograd itself. I would have to find some green spot where I could both work and walk. With this in mind my thoughts turned to my 'Zet' of two years ago, i.e. Sablino, not to the cramped little dacha I had rented then but to a wonderful farm two versts[1] from the station, well away from the main dacha district where during my previous sojourn I had sometimes walked to drink milk and have lunch. Attached to the farm was a kind of small guest house. On 30 April I went out to have a look.

It was a glorious, smiling, sunny day, the trees were clad in green and the countryside smelled of spring and the joy of nature, a far cry from the grime of the city out of which, due to the Revolution, I had scarcely poked my nose for so long. The farm stood where it always had, in its smiling verdant comfort. But the hotel had ceased to take visitors and the ground floor was now occupied by the family of a merchant. The upper floor, however, was to let. Needless to say I did not exactly need six rooms with four beds and two divans, the more so as the rent was all of 500 roubles. But for a dacha the rooms were impeccably furnished, everything was new, clean and although on the primitive side, well thought out and comfortable. The main advantage was that the farm would provide delicious and wholesome food, whereas most dacha-dwellers from Petrograd were finding it literally hard to get anything at all to eat. I considered, and came to the somewhat unexpected conclusion that this upper floor was just the place I should rent. I did so, and it was an excellent decision.

---

1   A little over two kilometres.

I returned to Petrograd, intending to come out after four days to my country estate, as I now thought of my farm. I told not a living soul about the dacha, because I took particular pleasure in being able to vanish into the void, with nobody able to disturb tranquillity. Least of all did I want Eleonora to know where I was – her aptitude for detective work knows no limits – nor B. Verin, whose garrulity makes him equivalent to placing an advertisement in the newspapers. At this time, sociable creature though I am, I found Schopenhauer's recommendation of solitude surprisingly to my taste. Of course, I would not have been able to bear complete isolation, but even Schopenhauer did not advocate it for someone of my age. Nevertheless, to be able to work at composing, to read, to study astronomy, to go for walks through the spring countryside, to go into Petrograd once a week – and to know that nobody in this dacha community of petty officials and shopkeepers has the slightest inkling of my identity, nor do any of my friends know where I am – is that not pure joy?

Musically I also took an important decision: to do without a piano. For some time I had contemplated composing my 'Classical' Symphony away from the piano, and all the work I had so far done on it I had done in my head. Now I resolved to finish it. It seemed to me that composing with or without a piano was purely a matter of habit, and it would be good to gain more experience with a work as uncomplicated as this symphony. I would not need a piano for the orchestration of the Violin Concerto either. This would be the work I would concentrate on while at my estate.

As spring continued my astronomical interest deepened. Naturally, in the perpetually cloudy skies over Petrograd it was a rare gift to be able to see the stars, even so by the time I moved out to my dacha I knew the main stars well enough to distinguish them not merely by their relationship to other heavenly bodies but in their own right, so to say, each one face to face. I decided to buy a telescope and set it up on the balcony of the dacha so that I could look at the stars by night. Wartime conditions in Petrograd meant that the choice was down to two, one of which was a splendid three-inch Fraunhofer (i.e. one of the best makes)[1] refractor, which I bought for 200

---

[1] Joseph von Fraunhofer (1787–1826), founder of the Munich optical instrument-making firm whose development of the achromatic refractor accompanied by the best German precision mounting and tracking engineering represented state-of-the-art astronomical apparatus until the end of the nineteenth century, when visual observation began to be replaced by photography. Fraunhofer was the first to measure the spectrum of sunlight and characterize the dark absorption strips it contains: the 'Fraunhofer lines'. In partnership with the businessman Joseph Utzschneider he set up in business making both domestic and observatory telescopes (the latter including in 1824 the great 9-inch refractor at the observatory in Tartu, at that time the largest refracting telescope in the world). The oldest still-functioning telescope in the USA, a Fraunhofer-designed instrument manufactured by the firm's successor Merz & Mahler in 1842, is still in use by astronomers in Cincinnati. Presumably Prokofiev's Fraunhofer was looted or destroyed in the Petrograd flat after his departure in 1918. It would be worth a fortune today.

roubles. It is quite portable, about two arshins[1] in length mounted on a high tripod base and a lens giving a magnification to the power of seventy. I was incredibly pleased with my purchase and awaited with the greatest impatience a chance to point it at the heavens.

On 3 May I went to a reading by Mayakovsky, and on the 5th by Igor Severyanin, both of whom I was hearing for the first time.[2] Although I already knew many (almost all) of Severyanin's works, and liked a lot of them very much, I did not know much, if anything, of Mayakovsky's, and what I knew I did not like; however, hearing him read in person I had quite the contrary impression. Igor's miaouing delivery and the sickly way he played to the gallery somehow vulgarised and diminished the effect of the brilliant flashes with which he peppers his verse; Mayakovsky on the other hand compressed into a single powerful whole the gamut of his scattershot, apparently incoherent phrases. He read with the high-voltage energy characteristic of the Futurists, a little coarse but extremely convincing.

A few words about Larissa Reisner, with whom I had got into a sharp-tongued debate about my music some time ago at the 'Bronze Horseman'. This young woman is obsessed with her own cleverness, and indeed she is far from stupid and knows about absolutely everything, that is to say literature, art, politics, philosophy, all of which she talks about with an attractive irony. She is always busy with something and edits some kind of journal. Our mutual relations were also marked by just this insouciant brand of irony, but as recently we have always seemed to run into one another wherever I am – at exhibitions, at Mayakovsky's evening or Igor's – this flippant tone has changed into one of friendship, and we have spent many happy hours in each other's company.

On the 6th I gathered up my telescope, my suitcase and all my things and departed for my country estate. The weather was marvellous, everything was green, but no sooner had I arrived, installed myself, pleasurably inspected my six rooms, corridor, balcony and attic than the thermometer started falling rapidly and it came on to snow, at first mixed with rain and then in earnest, so that the following morning everything around me was as white as if it were January, and not a green leaf anywhere was to be seen poking through the blanket of snow.

My desire to pursue my astronomical activities was so great that when, that first evening, the great clouds scudding across the sky parted just enough to reveal a patch through which stars sparkled, I rushed to mark the place and

---

1 Roughly one and a half metres.
2 Igor Severyanin was the pen-name of the poet Igor Lotarev (1887–1941), whose aping of the Italian Futurists' celebration of technology and the speed of city life, allied to a sensuous command of rhythm and language, made him extremely popular, especially with young people. It was not quite the first time Prokofiev had heard him read, as he had done so at the Bestuzhev Insitute in November 1913. See *Diaries*, vol. 1, p. 549.

set up the telescope, huddled in overcoat and scarf and freezing with cold, so that should that part of the sky clear again I would be able to capture the star in my 3-inch refractor. After several unsuccessful attempts I dismantled the telescope and went to bed. My 'first telescope night' had not been very successful! After two more days the weather reverted to spring and on the 9th I went into Petrograd to attend the Graduation Concert at the Conservatoire.

As usual the Graduation Concert was a grand occasion, full of life and interest, but this year's crop of graduates did not exhibit any special talents. Entering the hall, I soon encountered Marinochka, and since I was unaffectedly glad to see her, we had a very nice conversation. One of her first questions was: 'Why haven't you been called up into the army? Is it because of your talent?' To which I replied: 'Yes, of course. How did you guess?'

I enjoyed myself very much at the concert and even felt a reluctance to return to my 'estate' in the evening! I went to Andreyev's to play bridge, but this was basically an error of judgement because the sky cleared and became very 'telescopic'. The planets Mars, Venus and Jupiter were all in conjunction with the Taurus constellation, and I should not have put off viewing them because later on in May Taurus would be in the sky during the day and would not be visible at night.

I returned to my dacha on the 10th to warm weather and the unequivocal arrival of spring. Boris Verin once said that the modest, almost imperceptible onset of our northern spring brings a more subtle pleasure than the heady extravagance of the south. I liked this idea in principle, but putting it to the test just now I could not but regret the absence of that interplay of colours, that ecstatic chirping, those rays of light and fragrances that make the southern burgeoning such a gift to the senses.

I settled down to work: thinking out every last detail of the orchestration of the Violin Concerto, which was an easy and pleasant task, and also, as I walked through the fields, composing the 'Classical' Symphony. I wrote down what I had already composed, but not yet in the form of a score. When our classically inclined musicians and professors (to my mind *faux*-classical) hear this symphony, they will be bound to scream in protest at this new example of Prokofiev's insolence, look how he will not let even Mozart lie quiet in his grave but must come prodding at him with his grubby hands, contaminating the pure classical pearls with horrible Prokofievish dissonances. But my true friends will see that the style of my symphony is precisely Mozartian classicism and will value it accordingly, while the public will no doubt just be content to hear happy and uncomplicated music which it will, of course, applaud. After the symphony I have another project: a similarly small-scale 'Russian' symphony in a pure Russian style. I shall dedicate it to Diaghilev, in memory of his fervent appeals to me, a Russian, to write unabashedly Russian music.

My firm intention to write an opera on *Leila* had been weakened in the first place by Demchinsky's judgement, and in the second by the categorical opposition to the idea voiced by Suvchinsky and Igor Glebov. They convinced me that this whole fantastic world of the forest would, when translated to the stage, turn into a feeble sham. Since Remizov had not come up with any new invention to replace the version rejected by Demchinsky (probably he was not able to think of anything) and on top of this Golovin and Meyerhold were keeping a post-Revolution low profile in the Mariinsky Theatre, the project gradually faded away to a vague blur in my imagination. In its place came a new idea of utter genius for an opera, one which no one had ever thought of before! The stage would represent a cross-section of a multi-storey house, most likely a two-storey one with two rooms upstairs and two down. The action would proceed sometimes simultaneously in all four spaces, sometimes in two, sometimes moving from one room to another. The subject – well, so far I have not thought of it, but the idea offers the most fantastic possibilities with incredible ensembles and contrasted moods: laughter in one room, grief in another. Probably, however, it lends itself more to comedy than to drama.

After a couple of days I went back to Petrograd, where I learned that Ziloti had been appointed Director of the Mariinsky Theatre. This is marvellous news, but what followed was less good: the government was not providing any money for new productions, and so impoverished an institution as the Mariinsky would be unlikely to have the wherewithal to stage *The Gambler* next year. I take a fairly resigned attitude to this circumstance: it is actually less the production that interests me than hearing what the orchestra sounds like in the fourth act. And that I believe I shall somehow manage to achieve. As for the production, everyone is so caught up in the Revolution at the moment that nobody is going to pay much attention to a new opera.

Apropos scenes of the Revolution, here is an illustrative one. I needed some new shoes. A large consignment arrived at an American shop called 'Walk Over', but in order to get a voucher entitling me to buy a pair I had to join a queue at six o'clock in the morning, where I found I was about four thousandth in line, being in the hundred and twenty-eighth group of thirty people in each, and there were at least as many again behind me. It took until four o'clock in the afternoon for me (or rather the messenger I hired to stand in line for me) to be given a voucher to get a pair of shoes in a month's time. In order to take my place in the queue at six I decided not to go to bed the night before, and therefore organised a grand *chemin-de-fer*. I started off by winning 500 roubles but subsequently lost the lot, except for 80 roubles that would pay for my shoes. Zakharov and Boris Verin won on this occasion, and departed wreathed in smiles after I had left to join the shoe queue.

On the 14th I came back to the dacha and again immersed myself in musical activities, walks through the green countryside and reading Schopenhauer. I am reading his *Aphorisms on the Wisdom of Life in Parerga and Paralipomena*[1] for the second time, making marginal notes in pencil, and cannot tear myself away from it. The White Nights[2] are hopeless for the telescope: only the brightest stars (Vega and Arcturus) are visible. I trained the telescope on them but did not derive any great satisfaction; they are simple, uninteresting stars. But I did observe the moon in her first quarter, studying her empty seas and the craters with which her surface is pitted as though with smallpox. In the intervals of music, reading, astronomy and walking I rested, smoked English and Egyptian cigarettes, ate chocolate and generally gave myself up to blissful indolence, feeling wonderful.

On the 16th I went into town to buy more cigarettes and have dinner with Marinochka. She has finally secured an engagement at the Musical Drama Theatre, not a particularly illustrious position but one of which she is inordinately proud. Probably for that reason she was wearing rather a lot of make-up. I told her how glad I was to see her, and took her to the 'Kontan' which Marinochka, not an habituée of fashionable restaurants, liked enormously.[3] Having in this way spent a very pleasant evening, I returned to our flat, where I discovered that Boris Verin had several times spent the night there, so exhausted was he by the attentions of his fiancée. A few days later he consented to be married, in order to be left in peace, but not before taking the precaution of securing from his bride an agreement to divorce and declaring that there could be no possibility of any relations between them, whether intimate or distant. To me this seemed an odd way to be left in peace.

---

1   See p. 140 n. 1.
2   The White Nights in St Petersburg are normally regarded as lasting from 11 June to 2 July. During this period the sun does not descend far enough below the horizon for the sky to become dark.
3   Lieutenant Yury Makarov of the Semyonovsky Life Guards Regiment, reminiscing far away from and long after the time he is describing, writes: 'One could only go to first-class restaurants, and into this category fell the "Cuba" on Morskaya, the "Ernest" on Kamennoóstrovsky, the "Bear" on Konyushennaya, the two "Donons", one on the Moyka, the other on the Nikolayevsky Bridge, and the "Kontan" on the Moyka. It was also permissible to go to the French hotel, to the "Pivato" on Morskaya and the "Vienna" on Gogol Street, but only to eat, not for prestige. In the first six of these restaurants everything was truly first class, and so were the prices. Dinner for two, with house wine, cost at least 10–15 roubles, and if one arrived late in the evening, after the normal hour for dining, champagne was obligatory. At one time our gilded youth made a point of going to the "Kontan", which was not far away from the Regiment, at this after-dinner hour. The "Kontan" was a small but extremely cosy restaurant, which one entered down a long corridor with a carpet so deep one's feet sank into it, the predominant colours dark red and gold. The windows overlooked a garden. As we entered, the celebrated Romanian maestro Jean Gulescu would stop whatever the orchestra was playing and launch into the Semyonovsky regimental march, for which he would be rewarded with a goblet of champagne served on a plate with a gold 5-rouble piece.' (Yu. V. Makarov, *Moya sluzhba v staroy gvardii 1905–1917, mirnoye vremya i voyna* (*My Service in the Old Guard 1905–1917 in Peacetime and War*) (Buenos Aires, 1951).)

I returned to my 'Zet' and also on the 19th played my First Piano Concerto for the opening of Pavlovsk (my fee donated to the Red Cross in accordance with my promise to Kurlyandsky). After that I set off down the Volga. I have played this concerto often enough by now not to be nervous or to treat it as an event. It was a success crowned with a bouquet of flowers, and two *Visions Fugitives* as encores, which despite their transparency of design left the audience bemused, and the somewhat embarrassed applause quickly died away.

On the 21st, paying no heed to oohs and aahs and dire predictions of gangs of marauding soldiers and deserters terrorising the Volga, I took my small suitcase and went away for a two-week trip. I proceeded on the assumption that the danger area where people were knifing each other would be where it was said to be, to the south of Nizhni Novgorod, in which case I would be able to sail down the northern stretch, that is to say between Tver and Nizhni. And I so wanted to make this trip! The main thing was to gulp down great draughts of fresh, sweet air from the wide open spaces of the Volga. But one way or another I had heard so much nonsense about the dangers, especially from that disgusting coward Verin (who is now presumably in his new marital status Boris Lyudmilin[1]), that even at the railway station I was still wondering whether I should abandon the whole idea.

But I did not abandon it, and the moment I entered the carriage matters improved. I was hailed by a cry of 'Prokofiev!': this was Aslanov, who turned out also to be going down the Volga, along with his wife and several tons of luggage. He fixed me up with a place in his compartment, exhibited a refreshingly cavalier attitude to the atrocity rumours, and we went merrily on our way. On the jetty at Rybinsk I was told that the rumours of marauding soldiers were grossly inflated, there had been some excesses at the beginning of the navigable period, but everything was now peaceful. I rejoiced at this and as the ship pulled away from the shore down Mother Volga mentally consigned to perdition the pusillanimous poet and all his alarmist *confrères*. I loved the voyage, drinking in the views of the river banks and gulping down the fresh Volga air. I have a passion for air; among my most treasured memories of Kislovodsk are those of the glorious morning air there. The Aslanovs proved to be ideal companions, he a vastly more attractive personality than he ever is on the conductor's podium, while the only intimations of Revolutionary disturbance came from the third-class passengers on the upper deck spitting out sunflower-seed shells, but even this was done in an atmosphere of placid decorum.

After three days' voyage, just before we arrived at Kazan where the

---

1 Boris Bashkirov, as a result of falling in love with the seventeen-year-old Vera Suroshnikova, had assumed the *nom de plume* of Boris Verin. His new, evidently not especially beloved, bride was Lyudmila Kurlina.

Aslanovs disembarked, I debated with myself in which direction to continue my journey: on the one hand I was drawn to the sun, that is to say to the south, to Astrakhan.[1] But I had already been down this stretch, and it was also a very long way. Not only that but the 'Bolsheviks' (a new word in the vocabulary) were said to be causing a lot of trouble in Astrakhan. The alternative was to do what I had long dreamed of doing: to head north-east along the Kama,[2] whose beauties were said to eclipse even those of the Volga. In the end curiosity prevailed, aided by the fact that a very good steamer was just leaving to sail up the Kama. I transferred to it and left the Volga behind.

The voyage from Kazan to Perm takes three days. Ours was a most elegant ship, and I had a cabin to myself. The passengers were mostly Tatar businessmen and officials,[3] because there are no railways at all in the rural area we traversed during these three days.

The Kama indeed proved to be more beautiful than the Volga, and the higher up we went, the more beautiful it became. Here and there the high banks, covered with fresh green grass, descended abruptly into the water in bright red precipices, as if the earth's crust had been sliced through to expose all its geological strata, while up above, beyond the grass, were pine forests whose dark, thickly clustered tops surmounted tall, straight, naked trunks through which could be glimpsed an entrancingly blue sky. Sometimes the banks were low and the eye could see right to the horizon across three bands of fabulous colours: first the dark yellow sand of the shore, then the luminous green of the grass, and finally the far-off forest, which was quite blue, a true dark blue. At other times the banks were mountainous, grey and rocky: this was already a northern landscape. Up above was the dark forest of Siberian pine, almost black against the setting sun, while the calm reflection of the rocks and the dark green trees graced the astounding clarity of the water near the banks.[4]

One evening I had my first sight of the most beautiful and most ancient star Antares.[5] This star is in the southern hemisphere and from our northern lands can be seen only in early summer, appearing so low above the horizon that it is invisible through the roofs and buildings of Petrograd. For

---

1 I.e. to the mouth of the Volga Delta, whence it flows into the Caspian Sea.
2 The longest of the innumerable tributaries of the Volga. It rises to the west of the Ural mountains before sweeping round in a great arc to flow south-west through Perm to join the mother-river at Kazan.
3 The Kama flows through the Republic of Tatarstan.
4 Today (2007) it is estimated that only 3 per cent of the water in the Volga basin (which extends over nearly 1.4 million square kilometres, 10 per cent of the entire Russian Federation) is considered safe to drink. Each year 42 million tons of toxic waste are discharged into it. (Source: Global Resource Information Database [GRID] Europe, United Nations Environment Programme, 2007.)
5 The brightest star in the Scorpio constellation.

several evenings I watched for it on the Kama, and at last it appeared through the clouds precisely in the spot where I was looking for it. This was a great joy to me.

When I arrived in Perm the purser, a man born and bred on the banks of the Kama and a passionate lover of his homeland, recommended me to continue up the river and then branch along the Vishera, where he said the surrounding countryside is even more beautiful, and to go on as far as the little town of Cherdynya, remarkable only for the fact that its inhabitants are known as 'Cherdaks',[1] and then to retrace my steps to Perm.

I was much taken by a legend about the town of Okhansk: when the devil was tempting Jesus Christ he showed him all the beauties of the earth, but covered Okhansk with the tip of his tail so that Christ should be spared the sight of such ugliness.[2]

Since parting from the Aslanovs at Kazan I had hardly got to know any of my fellow passengers, spending my time in solitary contemplation of the countryside, or thinking out the instrumentation of the Violin Concerto, or reading. I read a book in Italian to refresh my memory of the language, and then read a couple of novels of the sort one reads on journeys, but my primary reading consisted of Schopenhauer's *Parerga and Paralipomena*. This had a profound effect on me, especially the chapters on fame and physiognomy. I found the chapter on women less convincing, and not universal enough in scope. Women who read Schopenhauer usually begin with this chapter, turn up their noses at it, are led to write Schopenhauer off as nothing out of the ordinary (in this instance they are right), and discard all of his writing. But what a loss to them! Schopenhauer, however, was not much exercised whether or not he was read by women.

This reading of Schopenhauer was a revelation to me, and may be described as an important stage in my life. For now I could stand firmly and consciously on my own two feet, finding an amazing and comprehensive balance that had so far eluded me, although I had not been aware of lacking it. How many times, four or five years ago, had Max Schmidthof urged me to read him, but I, having picked up from somewhere or other that Schopenhauer was a hopeless pessimist, hesitated to plunge into them. Now, however, although I had still not properly read his most important works, the effect on me was precisely the opposite: I began in some sense to see everything that happened with greater clarity, to appreciate and enjoy all that was laid before me. I also absorbed and accepted for myself a principle of the ancients Schopenhauer develops at length: not to demand an extra ration of

---

1 *Cherdak* is the Russian word for an attic.
2 Even so, Okhansk is the world's only known source of Volkonskoite Green, a natural earth pigment much prized by artists.

happiness but to regard happiness as the absence of pain, anything more than this being an unanticipated blessing (and how many of these the future will then bring!), with the result that one immediately becomes twice as happy as before!

Thanks to Schopenhauer I reacted philosophically to alarming reports in the newspapers that Kerensky, now Minister for War, had ordered all medical orderly personnel below the age of forty to be sent to the front. This could apply to me, even though just before I left I had been told that the Headquarters Administration of the Red Cross, to which I was attached, was exempt. I did not doubt that, even were I to be mobilised, I would still somehow or other be released, but it would certainly mean a lot of unpleasantness and fuss, and uncertainty as to whether life subsequently would be as agreeable as it presently was. In these circumstances Schopenhauer had a vital role to play: I resolved to continue my journey not worrying about what the future might bring, as the deadline for responding to the call-up had in any case been set for three weeks hence, so there was still plenty of time and no reason to abandon my journey. If I were to agonise and worry about it, and on my return find that the order did not apply to me, how stupid I would think myself! And if they did take me, I should have lost the opportunity to enjoy my last trip as a free man! Thus I reasoned: in either case it was better to carry on with my trip and forget about the order. This suited me down to the ground.

One of my few shipboard acquaintances was a young girl from Sarapul in the depths of the country.[1] She was in second class but came into our deck saloon and cheerfully started to strum on the piano there. I went over and at the appropriate moment turned the pages of the score she was playing from, an ability she evidently found quite amazing. Having more or less got to the end of the piece, she jumped up and dashed out of the saloon. A little while later, meeting her on deck, I asked her if she would play some more. At first she declined, but when I said that I was not a player at all, later admitting that, perhaps, just a little, not as good as she was, she consented, but only on condition that I play for her as well. We agreed to draw lots for which of us should begin and tossed down a 3-kopeck piece. 'Heads!' I cried, but it was tails. I assumed that meant I would have to play, having lost the toss, but she exclaimed sulkily: 'Oh, it's tails. So it's my turn.'

And proceeded to play a Beethoven sonata. I was impressed by her confident and intelligent, nuanced playing and praised it, not omitting, however, to make a few suggestions for improvement. But the girl proved to be have an exceptionally high opinion of her own abilities, no doubt being a star in her local Sarapul music institute, so chewing her lip she said: 'All right, then, now you play something.'

---

1   In Udmurtia, near the source of the Kama.

I had no inclination whatsoever to play in a saloon full of Tatars yelling at the top of their voices and diners rattling knives and plates and glasses, and in any case on board ship is one place I never play. But I had given my word, and therefore chose the Allegro from the 'Pathétique' Sonata, which I played very fast and *pianissimo* throughout, as if with the mute on. When I had finished, my rival addressed me with the words: 'Well, you're pretty good at criticising others, but look at how you yourself play!' and read me a long lecture on what I should pay attention to in order to develop further in the future.

This was marvellous! But even better was that for the remainder of the voyage she showed her contempt by hardly addressing another word to me.

And so, having come back to Perm, I took a train and after three miserable days arrived back in Petrograd. Hardly had I managed to install myself in a carriage full to bursting of civilian and military passengers than an axle broke and we had to squash in to whatever alternative place we could find. I tried to get into a carriage of recently released political prisoners who were on their way from Siberia back to Petrograd. There was in fact quite a lot of room in their compartment, but to my great surprise these hardened and embittered people had not the slightest intention of letting me in, saying that they had suffered quite enough privations and disturbance in their time.

Nettled, I said that in this company I would have expected to meet with humanity, whereas instead I was encountering nothing but resentment and ruthless selfishness. Clambering over piles of luggage and collapsed people in the corridor I eventually made my way to the last compartment in the train, which was occupied by a dozen soldiers. These were Bolsheviks who in the first days of the Revolution had knifed and murdered their officers in Helsingfors, but now they accommodated me quite civilly into their space, and I even slept comfortably sharing the top bunk with one of the non-commissioned officers. When the talk turned to politics, they complimented me on my knowledge and intelligence. I was greatly flattered by this observation.

I got back to Petrograd after a delay of thirty-three hours, on 4 June at two o'clock in the morning.

June

Back in Petrograd the first thing I did was to go to the Red Cross to ascertain my fate. Although I was told that the order did apply to our noble Headquarters Administration, I was not too worried and while waiting for Kurlyandsky to receive me worked out in my head the first movement development of the Violin Concerto, which I succeeded in doing in spite of the inappropriateness for composition both of the surroundings and of the time. Kurlyandsky was friendly, as usual, but confirmed that Headquarters not only was subject in principle to the terms of the order but had specifically been placed on a par with other departments. Once the Minister had issued the order he, Kurlyandsky, was powerless to do anything about it. Still, I still had time on my side, and his advice was to take what steps I could to resolve my fate without delay.

I decided to start by approaching Benois, who was in Petrograd and warmly invited me to come and see him. Benois erupted violently at my news and immediately telephoned Gorky. Ever since Gorky and I had appeared together at Dobychina's at Shrovetide and he had heard me play my *Sarcasms*, he had come to recognise me as an excellent composer and held me personally in great esteem. At heart a pacifist, he suffered particularly at the prospect of artists being sent to the front and was at the time engaged in applications for the release of a great number of artists. In answer to Benois's telephone call he asked me to call on him tomorrow, when he would give me a letter for Kerensky containing a request that I should be left in peace.

Handing me the typed letter, Gorky advised me to seek out Kerensky as soon as I could and put the letter personally into his hands. I found the prospect of making a personal appeal for my release distasteful, but Gorky insisted that I must discuss the matter personally with Kerensky, that he was a cultivated individual and was probably in any case aware of my existence.

None the less, getting hold of Kerensky was a far from easy matter: he would either be away at the front, or if he was in Petrograd would be at the Army or the Navy Ministry, or at a meeting of the Government, or some other unknown destination. At this point Eleonora rode to the rescue, and incidentally I may say that recently she has been behaving very well, not wearing me out with her usual excesses. The amazing creature turned out to know Kerensky, because she had donated for the use of war-wounded one of the large number of estates left to her by the deceased Sergey Vladimirovich, and had received a personal telephone call of thanks from Kerensky. Thanks to this she quickly established that I would be able to catch Kerensky at nine in the morning in the Admiralty, where he now has a flat and spends the night. I went there, handed the letter to an aide and said that Gorky had requested a personal reply. At the name of Gorky the aide bowed and scraped, and after an hour had elapsed informed me that the letter had been delivered to the Minister and there would be a reply shortly.

While waiting for it I sat for quite a long time in the spacious foyer of the Admiralty decorated with images of the gunnery and profiles of warships. I was apprehensive about meeting Kerensky, mainly because I could not rid myself of the unpleasant thought that I was appearing in the guise of a supplicant begging to be excused military duty. But the spirit of Schopenhauer manifested itself and put me to shame: this was not a plea I was making, but a demand on behalf of Sergey Prokofiev, occupant of a distinguished and important position in Russian art. Furthermore I knew who I was, but Kerensky was still an unknown quantity: perhaps indeed the saviour of Russia, but also perhaps no more than a chance figure adroitly riding the crest of the political moment. I had no reason to fear an encounter with him. And having thus settled the matter to my own satisfaction I proceeded to wait calmly and confidently, resolving to answer along these lines any questions that might be put to me.

Just after noon the foyer took on an air of excitement and bustle: people ran hither and thither, someone shouted for a car to be brought, down the staircase came a group of people including both the aides I had seen, and a few paces from me appeared an individual dressed in khaki with features not unlike Rachmaninoff's. He looked intently at me (I sat and stared back), then with a word to the doorman and to his own entourage disappeared. After he had gone I realised this was Kerensky, and seeing that no more was to be achieved by staying where I was, went home. An aide wrote down my telephone number and that of Gorky, and promised to ring.

A day or two later Eleonora established that Kerensky had gone to the front and had taken Gorky's letter in his pocket. At the same time it emerged that the timetable for calling up medical personnel had been extended until 1 July, and so the immediate necessity for action was postponed. Joyfully I shook off the dust of Petrograd, never a very agreeable place to be in the summer, and took myself off back to my 'country estate'.

It was already 10 June, in the country everything was in full bloom. The fields were full of flowers, the sun was warm; my attentive landlady had flung wide open all the windows of my dacha. At noon there were such swarms of bumble-bees and honey-bees round the flowers that it was impossible to walk through the fields. With a feeling of rare content I settled back into my spacious domain.

I decided I would tackle Schopenhauer's most important work *The World as Will*, but the very first pages laid bare the depth of my ignorance and prevented me from reading any further until I had familiarised myself with Kant,[1] and *The Fourfold Root*.[2] I decided to put off *The World as Will* (seeing

---

1 'Why should we believe in radical idealism? Why should we believe the extraordinary thesis that, in the final analysis, material objects do not really exist? Mostly, Schopenhauer's answer is simply: "Read Kant!" Read, in particular, the Aesthetic, the first major section of the *Critique of Pure Reason*. "This", says Schopenhauer, "is a work of such merit that it alone would be sufficient to immortalise the name of Kant. Its proofs have such a complete power of conviction that I number its propositions among the incontestable truths."' (Julian Young, *Schopenhauer* (Routledge, London & New York, 2005).)
2 *The Fourfold Root of the Principle of Sufficient Reason*, Schopenhauer's 1813 Ph.D. dissertation, which sets out to examine and, if possible, simplify Kant's thesis that the world as experienced by us is no more than representation, the appearance of reality rather than reality itself.

that the author himself forbids reading it) and took up *The Fourfold Root of the Principle of Sufficient Reason* as a preliminary study for it.

I became absorbed in orchestrating the scherzo of the Violin Concerto, which is turning out stunningly transparent and should sound lustrous. Alongside the Concerto I was composing the Symphony, all of whose four movements were progressing at once, while the third movement (the Gavotte) had been completed some time before. This Gavotte had been phenomenally well received by Benois, even threatening to put into the shade my old G minor piece,[1] about which I would be very glad, so heartily have I now come to dislike it.

On the 14th I came into Petrograd and rang up Gorky, from whom I learnt that a Kerensky aide had informed him that 'all would be done'. Accordingly, although I did not have an actual piece of paper in my hands, the word of the Minister of War was enough to allow me to celebrate my release. I was very proud of this and wrote to Mama that it demonstrated 'the Government's clear acknowledgement of my services to Russian art'.

On my visits to Petrograd I spent the evenings with B. Verin, who was being very nice at the time. Together we went several times to the Islands and then dined at his club, No. 16 Nevsky Prospect. In general the cost of living in Petrograd, especially food, indeed everything in the shops, has risen impossibly high: I have 1,000 roubles a month, and it is now absolutely obvious to me that this will not be enough.

I was invited on to the Committee for the Arts in the Commissariat of the former Imperial Court Ministry. This committee was charged with responsibility for all arts activities and institutions formerly controlled by the Court Ministry. Its sessions were held in the Winter Palace, which so far as I was concerned was its most desirable feature. The meetings themselves were not every interesting, and it was not long before I began to drop out of them. After a couple of days in Petrograd I returned to my Zet.

An idea: since *The Gambler* had now become available once again, why not try to get it produced at the Musical Drama Theatre? I consulted Asafyev, who approved and said he would speak to the appropriate people.

On 20 June there was great excitement on the streets of Petrograd, crowds out in force waving flags at the news that our Russian troops had launched an offensive. I was overjoyed at the news: perhaps they would succeed in meeting up with our English and French allies and see them face to face![2]

1   Op. 12 No. 2, which itself had a long pre-history before appearing in this guise. See *Diaries*, vol. 1, pp. 241, 279 and *passim*.
2   The June Offensive, 'the dying gasp of the old Russian army' as the historian Richard Pipes describes it, began on 16 June on the Southern Front, the Eighth Army under General Kornilov having some initial success against the Austrians in Galicia. But the advance very soon petered out, turning into a catastrophic rout in the face of the German counter-attack, and signalled the end of Kerensky's chances both of keeping Russia in the war and of uniting the country into anything resembling a stable, constitutional democracy.

At one of the meetings of the Arts Committee in the Palace I was approached by McCormick,[1] a member of a special American delegation visiting Russia in the wake of the Revolution,[2] who had managed by virtue of his position to get himself billeted in the Palace. He wanted my recommendations of Russian musical compositions generally, and mine in particular, to send to America. To this end a copy was made of the *Scythian Suite*, and all of my works in print purchased, as well as a series of works by Myaskovsky. In addition to the works recommended by me, they also paid 700 roubles for an enormous chest of scores, two-thirds of which were second rate: Kastalsky,[3] Kalinnikov,[4] Glière. This made me angry and I said to McCormick: 'Vous avez emporté toute la mauvaise musique qu'il y a en Russie!'[5]

McCormick looked at me and gave a laugh that could be heard all over the Winter Palace. When he asked me if I had any special wishes about America I gave him the piano score of *The Gambler*, saying that I would be very happy if it were to be produced, told him that I was a free man as far as military or now civilian service was concerned, and if there were to be any interest in America I could go there to give concerts. McCormick took on board what I told him and promised to telegraph me.

I spent the last days of the month on my estate, in thrall to the most wonderful sunny days. The meadows, which were everywhere about because of the Tosna river flowing through the area, were a riot of different colours, lilac, violet, yellow, white – a veritable carpet of flowers. I recalled what I knew of botany, a subject in which my father had done his best to enlighten me, and regretted no longer having to hand Mayevsky's little book,[6] which would have enabled me to name all the flowers.

I scrapped the finale of my Symphony, which now seemed to me too ponderous and not characterful enough for a classical symphony. Asafyev put into my mind an idea he was developing, that there is no true joyfulness to be found in Russian music. Thinking about this, I composed a new finale, lively and blithe enough for there to be a complete absence of minor triads in the whole movement, only major ones. From my original finale I salvaged

---

1 Cyrus McCormick Jr, grandson of the original inventor and son of the developer of the eponymous combine harvester that played a significant part in transforming agriculture in the nineteenth century: 'Westward the Course of Empire Takes Its Way with McCormick Reapers in the Van' as the company's advertisements proudly boasted.
2 The main purpose of the delegation was as part of a broadly based attempt to ensure Russia's continued involvement in the First World War as a member of the Allies.
3 Alexander Kastalsky (1856–1926), composer and choral conductor, a leading figure in the 'new direction' of Russian liturgical music at the end of the nineteenth century.
4 Vasily Kalinnikov (1866–1900), mainly remembered for his two tuneful symphonies, owing much to Russian folk music.
5 'You are taking away with you all the bad music there is in Russia.'
6 Pyotr Mayevsky (1851–1892), botanist. Prokofiev is probably referring to his *Flora Sredney Rossii* (*The Flora of Central Russia*) first published in 1892.

only the second subject. I found the movement extraordinarily easy to write, and the only thing I was concerned with was that its gaiety might border on the indecently irresponsible. But in the first place it never actually crosses this line, and in the second, this kind of finale is quite appropriate to Mozartian style. I was hugging myself with delight all the time I was composing it!

Not long afterwards there appeared in *New Life*[1] an article by Asafyev on the subject of joy in Russian music. To my astonishment, having dissected the whole corpus of Russian music and rejected any evidence of true joyfulness therein, he suddenly singled out the 'Procession of the Sun' from the *Scythian Suite* as an example of unbridled exultation. I was overwhelmed and overjoyed in the highest degree by this, not least because he had said nothing to me about it beforehand and had thus steered me towards writing my carefree finale which, while the ultimate in blitheness, exhibits a different strain of joy from that in the *Scythian Suite*.

My readings in philosophy, however much pleasure they afforded me, proceeded at a slow pace because they demanded so much intellectual effort and concentration, whereas I was devoting the best hours of the day, the mornings, to composing the Symphony and orchestrating the finale of the Concerto, restricting my reading to the later part of the day by which time my brain was getting tired from the work I had done. I plunged with great enthusiasm into *The Fourfold Root*, but at first found it quite difficult to read, and I could not fully assimilate the thrust of the argument. However, after a few dozen pages I got into the groove and accommodated myself to the style, after which it started to become comprehensible. *The Fourfold Root* is one the earliest works of Schopenhauer, but in old age he published a second edition with voluminous addenda, of little interest to anyone except Schopenhauer himself, since in them he indulges in polemics with German professors and mocks those less intellectually able than himself, sometimes at such length that by the end of the polemic he has forgotten the main thrust of his argument. I would recommend reading *The Fourfold Root* in the first edition of his youth: it is less prolix and stays closer to the essence.

As soon as I had read *The Fourfold Root* right through I read it again, making notes in the margin, and thoroughly absorbed it. It is not a universal book so much as one dedicated to a particular theme, and is somewhat dry, but very interesting.

On the 27th, as I lay awake in bed, it occurred to me that when I am dead

---

1 *Novaya Zhizn'*, the magazine founded by Gorky originally in 1905 and after the February Revolution edited by him, an often despairing voice for sanity (notably in Gorky's own column 'Nevovremennye Mysli' ('Untimely Thoughts')) against the ungovernable excesses of prejudice, malice, cruelty and stupidity that he saw threatening the ideals, indeed the very basis, of the Revolution. The magazine was closed down by Lenin in July 1918.

it will be very unpleasant to be nailed down into a coffin and buried underground. But neither is the prospect of being burnt very attractive, and there is something stupid about sitting in a jar as a heap of ashes. I decided I would donate my skeleton to a museum where I could be put under glass. At my feet would be a notice: 'My friends, I am glad that you are here.'[1]

July

On 1 July I went out to Terioki to Boris Zakharov, who with his wife and new-born daughter had ensconced himself there for the whole summer without moving from the place, surrounded by sisters, sisters-in-law and a vast number of very young children. Boris, so recently having fought his way to the top, had now clearly descended from the heights to drown in this swampy routine of bourgeois domesticity. The nursery! The nappies! The semolina kasha! The conversations about cows and cucumbers! The price of buttons and the expense of getting a cook! How appalling it all was! For an artist to be living like this . . . one could see a tide of inert water swirling about the whole huge dacha. As soon as I arrived they all leapt at me to spend all day playing cards, this being the only pulse of life discernible in the household. And when I eventually won a hundred roubles (the results of our games invariably fell somewhere between fifty and a hundred and fifty roubles) his sister cried: 'Boris! Boris! He'll keep coming back here and winning!'

It was slightly better at the Karneyevs, where a series of extremely handsome young people are growing up. Unexpectedly I ran into Tanyusha, who I thought had gone to Siberia. She not only had a pulse but positively seethed with life. She took me off into the forest and regaled me with an account of her romantic adventures, which these days did appear to be crossing the threshold of maidenly purity. Here there was life and *joie de vivre*. Tanyusha's eyes and teeth gleamed, and she was just as pretty as she had ever been.

Returning to Petrograd on the 3rd, I dined with Boris Verin at the 'Kontan', where all was elegance and animation, and where despite the general food crisis one could eat extremely well. True, the prices were insanely high, but since every day that goes by the value of money is falling, what is the point of hanging on to it?

As we walked about the streets in the evening we witnessed an unusual occurrence: there was a lot of noise, soldiers were marching with rifles and there were crowds bearing placards saying: 'Down with the capitalist ministers'.

---

1 The Polish pianist and composer André Tchaikowsky, himself a luminous interpreter of Prokofiev's music, bequeathed his skull to the Royal Shakespeare Company at his death in 1982 at the age of forty-seven, to be used as a prop for performances of *Hamlet*.

Before our eyes private cars were being stopped, the owners invited to step out to be replaced by machine-guns. As if someone had waved a magic wand, the streets at once assumed the aspect recalled from the first days of the Revolution. Bolsheviks and Kronstadters,[1] workers and soldiers harangued the crowds about the failings of the Provisional Government.

Hardly had Boris Verin and I reached the safety of his club when shooting broke out on Nevsky Prospect. The outer doors of the club were fastened shut, and thick shutters placed over the windows. Only a few inveterate card-players remained at their tables feverishly continuing to stake their thousands.

As soon as the shooting died down – there was not much of it and it was later said to be mainly provocation – I decided to take advantage of the lull and the darkness to go home. As a matter of fact, the only place one was liable to get caught in the firing line was on Nevsky, and even then only in the vicinity of the government buildings; on the side streets everything was quiet, there was nothing to provoke any skirmishes, and the moment I turned off the Nevsky thoroughfare I felt quite easy. Only on Sadovaya did I run into a dense black crowd: this was the Putilov workers coming to the aid of the Bolsheviks. On our Pervaya Rota Street peace and calm reigned.

The next morning I learned from a telephone call that Nevsky was also calm: the Bolsheviks, having demonstrated until late at night, were now having a rest. I decided to exploit this to go out into the Prospect. Some of the shops were open, so I bought English cigarettes, lobsters, and Kuno Fischer's book on Kant,[2] and made my way to the Nikolayevsky station. I left the city at one o'clock, and later learned that half an hour later the Bolsheviks woke up and there were lively gun battles all the way along Nevsky.

But in the meantime I had safely arrived at my Sablino, thoroughly delighted by my haven of perfect peace, silence, sunshine, blue skies and flowers. I buried myself with relish in the scoring of the Concerto's finale and composing my Symphony. In between I walked through the picturesque scenery with which my dacha was surrounded, smoked my cigarettes and dissected my lobsters. I cut the pages of Kuno Fischer and immersed myself in the wisdom of Kant.

1 On 3 July the Bolshevik Military Organisation, which had been agitating since the middle of June for an armed uprising to overthrow the Provisional Government and force the Bolshevik Party to seize power on behalf of the recalcitrant Petrograd Soviet, mobilized the anti-government elements of the Petrograd garrison, the militant workers from the factories in the Vyborg district, and above all the sailors of the Kronstadt Naval Base, to flood into the centre of Petrograd. Come they did, in overwhelming numbers, but with no clear plan and no direction or endorsement from the Party leadership, the uprising disintegrated into disorderly looting and random acts of violence.
2 Kuno Fischer, *Kant's Leben und die Grundlagen seiner Lehre* (*Kant's Life and the Basis of his Teaching*) (Carl Winter's Universitätsbuchhandlung, Heidelberg, 1860).)

Thus I lived my tranquil life thirty versts from the violent destruction and shooting in Petrograd as the fate of Russia unfolded. The only time I stirred from it was an expedition every other day to the station three versts away to get the newspapers, which were full of sensational but confusing reports. After five days or so the tone of the reports became more cheerful: Petrograd was reverting to calm, and I could go there.

My intention in July was to go to Mama in Yessentuki, which happened to be where Boris Verin also wanted me to go as he was taking a cure for his neuralgia and had rented a dacha with a spare room. I dislike the idea of a whole summer without spending any time in the real south, and gladly fell in with the plan of going for three weeks to Yessentuki. Moreover the black southern sky with its brilliant stars, so unlike those in the pale north, was a seductive prospect for my astronomical passion! In order to be able to leave Petrograd and its immediate surroundings, however, I had to settle my military obligations, and that was the main reason I needed to go into Petrograd. Even though I felt drawn to Yessentuki, I had grown so attached to my country estate that I felt sad at the prospect of leaving it.

And so, entering the now quiet city and taking steps to obtain the promised paper from Kerensky, I was immediately confronted by the realisation that my situation had taken a distinct turn for the worse. The matter was this: Gorky's *New Life* newspaper had come out strongly in support of the Bolshevik cause, and now that this cause had effectively been suppressed in Petrograd but was still fatally influential among our troops at the front, Gorky himself had become the target of mud-slinging to the extent that he was accused of virtually betraying his country to the Germans. It was of course crystal clear that Gorky was doing nothing of the sort, and that if he was now entering the lists for peace on the side of the Bolsheviks it was because he was an idealist. But others were of a different opinion, and a furious Kerensky was now an opponent. It was in these circumstances that I now had to try to get Kerensky to honour his promise to Gorky. In addition, Kerensky was shuttling between brief stays in Petrograd, a day or two at a time, and the front, where collapse was imminent and where the enemy was delivering blow after blow to our forces. In Petrograd he was faced with the task of forming a new Government, as half of the former Government had resigned and the same level of disorganisation reigned as at the front. It was invidious even to think of pestering a person with such responsibilities with personal trifles. But there was Mama in Yessentuki writing frantically that July was half over, Petrograd was in turmoil and I was not yet on my way. Finally, it was still the fact that Kerensky had already given his promise and all he had to do was scribble his signature on a wretched little piece of paper . . .

At this point Eleonora came to the rescue, and when I said that I was about to give up and disappear back to my 'estate', she took matters into her own hands. Since coming into her vast inheritance, her dream had been to secure my freedom by donating a million roubles to some cause of State or public benefit. She had dropped hints of such a plan to me on several occasions. And just at this point appeared a convenient opportunity: in the first place she had already been in discussion with Kerensky about making over one of the large estates she now owned for the benefit of war wounded, and on the other my business was already in train and it was only a question of how to nudge it to a successful conclusion. Eleonora set to work. I must say that she did so most energetically and effectively, considering that Kerensky was besieged by a hundred demands more pressing than mine, and was often overwhelmed to the point of complete breakdown. But as well as being very fond of Eleonora he desperately wanted to get his hands on her estate for the war wounded, the more so as such a gift would be 'a positive initiative and an example to others'.

In all probability Eleonora's strategy would have led to a positive outcome, but she herself hesitated, at war with her own conscience. Her dilemma was that what I wanted was a document freeing me 'to work as an artist' on a similar basis to the manner in which participants in scientific projects or expeditions are given licence to carry on their work in the interests of science. But then I would be completely free to live wherever I wanted in Russia and even to travel, if I wished, to America. Eleonora, however, wanted to bind me to Petrograd, in pursuit of which she couched her request in terms of maintaining my secondment to the Red Cross. I suspect that Kerensky was not very keen to grant this request, correctly seeing that it would be perceived as an arbitrary exemption, but Eleonora then played another card, offering a second, smaller estate for the war wounded in addition to the first one. In the end the Red Cross assignment was agreed, but the General Staff refused to approve it, on the grounds that no doubt the Minister had forgotten that he was the very authority who had decreed that no supernumeraries should be left with the Red Cross.

At this point I had to take some action myself: Ziloti – now Director of the Mariinsky Theatre – wrote an application for me to be given deferment as a musician. Eleonora presented this petition to Kerensky, who wrote on it: 'Deferment to be granted with immediate effect.' While the Red Cross ploy had taken exactly twelve days, the alternative approach produced results with magical rapidity: Ziloti gave me his letter at ten o'clock in the morning, I handed it to Eleonora at eleven, Kerensky signed it at one o'clock and at three o'clock I submitted it to the General Staff. This was on 21 July. The following day at 2 p.m. the General Staff issued me with a certificate of deferment 'until further specific notice'; an hour later I obtained from military headquarters a document entitling me to reside at will anywhere in Russia, and at half-past nine in the evening I left for the Caucasus, seen off at the station by Eleonora and by Boris Verin, who had so far not succeeded in getting a permit to travel for his neuralgia treatment.

Those two weeks I had spent in Petrograd, devoting myself exclusively to the obtaining of my deferment, had exhausted me terribly. It was stuffy and dusty in the city, I was living in a completely empty flat thick with dust, and eating poor but expensive food in restaurants (a dinner that used to cost four roubles now cost eighteen). The deferment business was dragging on and running into the sand. In the later of the two weeks I had a valid train ticket each day, and each day I had to postpone it for the next. I could not drive myself to do any work, and if while I was at Zet Yessentuki had been a benign prospect, it now loomed perpetually in my thoughts as an unattainable paradise.

In the evenings B. Verin dragged me to the 'Ernest' club, where *chemin-de-fer* was played. I probably would not have gone if I had not been so dispirited by the downward spiral of the general situation. However, gambling clubs represent no particular danger to me, since I am not prone to lose money in them. This is because I so much hate the thought of losing money at cards, and consider it a stupid activity. For this reason, whenever I go to a club, I decide in advance how much I am prepared to lose, and make sure not to exceed that amount. If I win, I get up and leave. Not only that, but I regard playing cards as a complete and tiring waste of time.[1] The result of my five visits to the card tables was: +300, -300, +50, -250, +1,000. The last one crowned my efforts: I won the bank with seven cards. This happened on the eve of my departure to Yessentuki and was extremely timely for my journey.

On 10 June I performed my First Piano Concerto with Fitelberg in the summer concert season at the Musical Drama Theatre. Although this was on a day when there had been gloomy news from the front and this was reflected in the depressed mood of the audience, my concert had the effect of stimulating the audience. Myself I did not feel much like playing, but decided that I must take myself in hand and compel the audience to come to life. If there is power in my music, it is bound to overcome feelings of anxiety. So it proved: there was warm applause and I played *Visions Fugitives* as an encore.

Fitelberg and some of the directors of the Musical Drama Theatre asked about *The Gambler*, but not fervently enough for my liking. Fitelberg asked me if I would work on it with a singer so that it could be rehearsed with orchestra. I declined, saying that it would take too much time and effort.

And so the long-desired day finally came, and on the 22nd I was sitting in a comfortable first-class compartment with my suitcase and my telescope speeding to the south. The edge was slightly taken off the journey by

---

1 Obviously, Prokofiev is here referring to playing cards as a purely gambling activity, rather than card games of skill such as bridge, which he enjoyed playing very much and in which he was proud of his prowess.

toothache, which bothered me the whole way and had to be treated when I got to Yessentuki. Sitting in the station buffet in Taganrog wolfing down a cutlet because the train only waited there for ten minutes, I heard my name suddenly called. I looked up and saw Polina sitting opposite and looking at me. It was quite a surprise. I knew she lived in Taganrog, but what had prompted her to come especially to the station? After all, the last letter I had written to her, after she revealed she was not going to be my travelling companion, had been expressed in such viciously insultingly terms I had imagined it would constitute a final break in our relations.[1] And now here she was talking to me quite unconcernedly, as though nothing had occurred. I was rather taken aback by the unexpectedness of the encounter, and at first behaved as if the person in front of me was only half there. But Polina was friendly and straightforward, and seemed to be expecting something from me. I did not hold back, and boasted about the freedom conferred on me by order of the head of the Russian Government. Polina said: 'I meant to reply to your last letter, but as I saw it had been stamped at the Nikolayevsky Station, I thought you must have posted it as you were leaving to go abroad.'

This conversation all took place very quickly, as the train was about to depart. As I left I said to her that all in all it had been very nice to see her. As the train was already moving forwards and I was walking along the carriage in the opposite direction, Polina and I found ourselves aligned. 'Will you write to me?' she asked. Some of the passengers standing in the corridor knew who I was, and were looking at us with some curiosity. There was nothing left for me to do except to say: 'All right', although I did not really want to.

In Yessentuki I installed myself in a marvellous four-roomed dacha that Boris Verin had rented. In the south again, and full of joy to be there. Sunshine, and at night the southern stars. I can only imagine how bright they must be at the Equator! The park full of people, but not many people I knew, not that this worried me much. Nevertheless somewhere in Yessentuki and Kislovodsk I knew there were Koshetz, Balmont and Chaliapin, and all of them I very much wanted to see.

I took my meals in the sanatorium[2] where Mama was staying, as a result of which three times a day I took quite a long walk from my dacha to the main park where the sanatorium was. Not that I had anything against these

---

1   See pp. 693–4 below.
2   In Russian, indeed in Europe generally, the word has somewhat different connotations from its usual English usage. Although Yessentuki and Kislovodsk were spa towns and therefore their institutions and accommodation designed for visitors usually bore some relationship to 'taking the waters' or other aspects of a health-giving regimen, they were primarily holiday resorts and a 'sanatorium' would not necessarily have an especially medical atmosphere, nor would most of the people staying there be ill or convalescent.

walks. In the morning I worked, but not at music, rather at literature – first of all bringing my neglected Diary up to date, but also at literature in the true sense. It happened like this: on one of those tedious days in Petrograd, when I was so frustrated at not getting anywhere with obtaining my deferment I could do no work, I began looking through a drawer containing all kinds of papers and manuscripts from my childhood. Among them were six chapters of an unfinished novel, which I read through with much enjoyment and even read over the telephone to Eleonora. I found it unbearably prolix, but on the other hand thought that I could probably write rather good short stories, provided I could find ideas.

I was not sure about my style: did it have character or was it merely truculent? It must be one or the other, not something else. If the former then I could definitely write, if the latter then I would merely be making a fool of myself. The shade of Dostoeyevsky came to my aid here: his style certainly has plenty of character but it borders on the truculent. It was of course absurd to be drawing analogies with Dostoyevsky when I had not written so much as a line, but the important point to grasp was: if there is an idea, then the idea will dictate the style. I have an idea, *ergo* I can write.

Having come to this conclusion I was thrilled at thus giving myself licence to write a short story, and started to conceive it in my mind. When I had done so down to the level of individual scenes and expressions, I sat down to write. This was 'Poodle'.[1] Even here Schopenhauer gave me no peace.[2] A second story, 'An Incident with a Leg'[3] was thought up in the train and both stories were completed in Yessentuki.

In the afternoons I read Kuno Fischer, and in the evenings I either went to bed early or looked at the stars. I went sometimes to Kislovodsk, where Bogolyubov and the local conductor, Berdyayev,[4] were busying themselves with the organisation of a concert devoted to my works. Aunt Katya and my cousin Katya[5] were staying at the sanatorium with my mother.

---

1   As completed by Prokofiev and eventually published (S.S. Prokof'ev, *Rasskazy*, ed. A. Bretanitskaya (Izdatel'stvo 'Kompozitor', Moscow, 2003) the title is 'Merzkaya sobaka' ('A Bad Dog'), and this is also the title of David McDuff's translation in *Sergei Prokofiev: Soviet Diary 1927 and Other Writings*, ed. O. Prokofiev and C. Palmer (Faber and Faber, London, 1991).
2   At the end of the story the identity of the dog's owner is revealed: 'Maria's arms tenderly entwined my neck. "Arthur Schopenhauer," she said. "Some foreigner." I really do not know how that barbarous name has remained in my memory. At that moment I felt only her arm gently, tenderly entwining my neck, all I could see were her black eyes gazing ardently at me . . .'
3   This story does not seem to have survived.
4   Presumably Valerian Berdyayev (1885–1956), Polish-born conductor then at the Mariinsky Theatre and therefore a colleague of Bogolyubov. He later returned to Poland, where he became Director and Chief Conductor of the Krakow Philharmonia.
5   The composer's mother's sister Yekaterina Rayevskaya, *née* Snitkova, and her daughter, also Yekaterina.

August

I did not find Koshetz right away: she did not appear in the park, and even when I found out her address failed to track her down at home. Our meeting, when it did take place late one evening, turned out to be quite dramatic. I was coming out of the park when a cab hurtled past me containing three ladies dressed in white. I was not close enough to see who they were when all three began shouting and waving and trying to get their evil-looking driver to stop. I hastened to run after them, but was stopped at the exit from the park where some sort of document was demanded of me. Thinking the official must want to see my season ticket, I angrily retorted that season tickets had to be shown at the entrance to the park, not at the exit. But they would not let me pass, insisting on seeing my passport. I sent them to the devil, saying that within the confines of the resort nobody was obliged to carry a passport. My interlocutor objected that I had no right to address the police in an insulting manner, and in no time a whole farrago ensued. At this point Koshetz ran up, took hold of the policeman's arm and pleaded with him in heartfelt tones: 'I swear to you, he's not a deserter! You must believe me, I wouldn't lie to you!'

Oh, feminine logic! Why on earth should he believe her? But the best thing about it was that he immediately let me go. Koshetz then explained to me what it was all about: today the police had been rounding up deserters, in which context they were checking the documents of all young people. The ladies – the two others were Koshetz's sister and a young Armenian, Sonya Avanova, an ardent admirer of Koshetz – then took me into their carriage and we went to Koshetz's house. Koshetz and I expressed our great mutual pleasure at seeing one another again, and she said she had been waiting impatiently for my arrival in Yessentuki. She then said a few words about Rachmaninoff, who had recently left having been there for some time, and who had said of me that of course I was very talented but had not yet reached my full potential as a composer. By this last I was given to understand that I had not attained that sphere to which he, Rachmaninoff, had, compositionally speaking, access. If some day I should chance to reach it, then Rachmaninoff would be able to say that in those works I had fulfilled my potential.

On the way back from Koshetz's I again went through the park and was again stopped at the exit gate, but this time at the other end of the park. I now knew the reason, and had no objection to accompanying the gendarmes to the military commissariat. I did not even bridle too much when one of the soldiers who met us there asked: 'Catch one, then?' and my escort proudly responded: 'Yes, got one here.'

In the Commissariat were sitting a few depressed-looking gentlemen who had been so unfortunate as to have been apprehended without their papers, but I was so adamant in my insistence that my deferment was by specific order of none other than the War Minister that my interrogators' determination wavered and eventually they let me go on condition that I brought in my papers the next day.

All next morning (31 July) I spent with Koshetz in the park. When she remarked that of late she felt she had completely lost her way in life, I gave her a philosophical explanation of why this might be. Koshetz came to my dacha to write postcards to Asafyev and Suvchinsky, and wrote in my 'Wooden Book' that of the two suns that bestowed their rays upon her she wished to be warmed not by the old, long-standing one, but the young one. As decoded: Rachmaninoff and Prokofiev.

In the evening we went together to Kislovodsk, where Koshetz was appearing in Halévy's *La Juive*.[1] Koshetz's generous description of this opera, which I did not know at all, was that it was a pseudo-classical opera. In fact it turned out to be technically speaking such a hopelessly inept piece of work, so dramatically clumsy, so wooden in its character development, that when to these defects were added a bad production and a feeble cast of principals (except Koshetz), it was all I could do not to rush from the theatre. I was restrained only by Sonya Avanova whispering in my ear every minute: 'Isn't Nina Palna[2] gorgeous? Look, do look!' I did look, but only because I was being badgered into doing so.

Still and all, the return train journey to Yessentuki was a triumphant procession. Koshetz travelled with a whole entourage, and the bouquets she had been presented with turned our carriage into something like the garden from *Kitezh*. I did not go to supper with her, as I was terribly tired.

The next day I called on her intending to go riding as she said she was an excellent horsewoman. To my astonishment I discovered Nina Pavlovna in considerable *déshabille*. She was sitting surrounded by the seven trunks into which she was packing her forty or so dresses, having this very morning taken even herself by surprise by conceiving the notion of going to Moscow. I sincerely regretted this precipitate move, and spent a couple of hours sitting on her balcony while she continued packing. I read verses by some of the poets she was proposing to me as song lyrics. Koshetz ran in and out, presented me with photographs, showed off her hats to me, threw a few words over her shoulder and buried herself anew in her cases.

As I left to go home, promising to appear at the station, Koshetz took me

---

1   Opera (1835) by Fromental Halévy (1799–1862). Prokofiev calls the work *Zhidovka*, which to today's politically correct ears may sound more offensive that it was meant to be. In Russia the work was variously known as *Zhidovka*, *Yevreika* (*The Jewess*) and *The Daughter of the Cardinal*.
2   Nina Pavlovna.

by the arm and accompanied me to the door. She wanted to say something to me that would imprint itself on my heart, and murmured many endearments, asking me to pay no attention to her 'frightful whirligig gyrations', and as we parted, after a little hesitation, suddenly gave me a kiss.

At the station, where a great crowd of people had assembled to see her off, Koshetz asked me in a whisper to be a dear and accompany her as far as Mineralnye Vody. This coincided with my own wishes, and I got on the train to go with her, but in such a way that nobody in fact noticed that I was there or where I was going. At Mineralnye Vody she exclaimed: 'Ah, Mineralnye Vody! Not long ago I was myself seeing someone off here!' and wrote on the photograph of herself she had presented to me: 'Tout passe, tout casse, tout lasse.'[1] When I observed that this was a strange sentiment to inscribe on her portrait, she replied that I had not understood: a month ago this was where she had said goodbye to Rachmaninoff, but . . . everything passes . . .

She wanted me to dedicate the *Akhmatova Songs* to her, to which I responded that in a sense she already had a certain right to them, since they had been composed the day after her concert, but 'I had not wanted to create an unfavourable comparison with another set of songs dedicated to her.' I was hinting at the very good songs Rachmaninoff had dedicated to her. Koshetz said: 'You're so cheeky, but I like that!' It was indeed a piece of cheek to compare them to the best songs of the ineffably divine Rachmaninoff! I love his songs very much, but as a matter of fact mine are better, they are among my most successful opuses.

Koshetz invited me to tour with her next winter. A final parting kiss, and the train began to move. Koshetz stood on the train's outside platform as I walked alongside. As the train began to pick up speed and move away I stopped and threw on to the platform of the train the flower I had been holding in my hand. She cried out with surprise and quickly bent down to pick it up, and with that the train disappeared from view. I took my seat in the local train and went back. Looking through the window at the stars, I saw for the first time my beloved Fomalhaut,[2] a southern-hemisphere star visible to us in the north only in early autumn, and very seldom indeed from the latitude of Petrograd. I have long admired it on the map, where it appears quite on its own, far away from other stars.

For a few days after the departure of the fantastic, volcanic Koshetz I did little but rest; the two days I had spent in her company had completely worn me out. Once I had fully thought through the sketches of the Symphony from the orchestration point of view I finally embarked on the score, which

---

1 'Everything passes, everything breaks, one tires of everything.'
2 The brightest star in the Pisces constellation, visible from Earth with the naked eye. The name derives from Arabic 'Fum al Hut' – 'Fish's Mouth'.

went easily, pleasantly and classically, if a little slowly at first owing to the need to become accustomed to the style.

I had given up hope of Boris Verin ever coming, but one day a telegram arrived and on the 7th the poet himself appeared. I went to the station to meet him, and he was very elegant and charming as he leapt down from the sleeping car with his natty little suitcase. I refrained, however, from complimenting him on his appearance, confining myself to remarking that he looked just like an American travelling salesman. We were very glad to see one another and even managed not to quarrel, although he regularly stayed in bed until half-past twelve.

On the 8th I went to Kislovodsk with the intention of visiting Chaliapin. We had met a few days earlier in the Kursaal (oh! how magnificent his gesture when he took his chair and placed it at the table!) and I thought he would not recognise me after the year and a half that had elapsed since our last acquaintance, but to my surprise Chaliapin began immediately: 'All the same, I don't believe you are right in what you say about the chorus on stage . . .', thus continuing a conversation we had begun at Paléologue's eighteen months previously, during which I had been advancing my view that the conventional way composers treat the chorus should be abandoned as being undramatic, and another way should be found.

And so on the 8th I was going over to see him, to find out his views on the stage and on opera, but in the park I ran across Balmont and so never got to Chaliapin. Balmont was with his diminutive wife and ten-year-old daughter Mirra, a proper little devil of a girl.[1] I rushed to embrace him, and Balmont seemed equally glad to see me. We sat at a table and ordered chocolate. I asked him all sorts of questions about 'Seven, They Are Seven' and outlined my plan for the work I was planning to write for dramatic tenor (the Priest), chorus and orchestra, while he repeated what he had said in Petrograd last winter, that I was a brave man to undertake such a thing. I asked him if he thought it would be a permissible device for the chorus's exclamations after the Priest's incantation simply to repeat the last words of each phrase, for example: 'In the depths of the ocean they are seven!' – chorus: 'They are seven!'; or the Priest's 'On the thrones of Heaven and Earth they sit!' – chorus: 'Earth they sit!' Although as it stands 'Earth they sit!' makes no sense, in view of the fact that the chorus's interjections follow directly after each phrase Balmont found it to be perfectly apposite and saw nothing wrong with it.

The talk then turned to the new, allegedly simplified orthography recently

---

1   Balmont had earlier had an impassioned and widely known affair with a poet called Mirra Lokhvitskaya (1869–1905). His daughter, born two years after Lokhvitskaya's death, must have been named in memory of this former love.

introduced by the Ministry of Public Education, and I took Balmont to task for not defending tradition (I had already written an impassioned newspaper article protesting against this stupid innovation). Balmont said he also was indignant about it, was speaking and writing on the subject, and would be raising the question again as soon as he returned to Moscow. 'We poets are the lords of the word,' he said. 'Scholars are no more than guardians and should never be allowed to distort their heritage.'[1]

Balmont then announced that he was off to visit an enchanting woman laid up with a broken leg, and asked me to go for a walk with his wife and Mirra, and to join him after an hour, when we would all be together. I really wanted to go and see Chaliapin, but since Balmont had made such a specific request I could not refuse. His wife made a *moue* of discontent that he was going off on his own to visit an enchanting woman, but did not go so far as to protest, and so he left us. We walked in the park for about an hour, with Mirra behaving quite insupportably all the time, and from hints dropped by Balmont's wife I learned that the woman in question, Kira Nikolayevna, was hopelessly in love with Balmont and the reason she had broken her leg in three places was that she had thrown herself from the cliff known locally as the 'Rock of Perfidy and Love'[2] – 'trying to fly', as the wife put it. Balmont, who was (as I was later told) terribly drunk at the time, carried her back into Kislovodsk in his arms and has since visited her every day, despite the fact that he himself is staying in Pyatigorsk, having been unable to find anywhere in overcrowded Kislovodsk.

Our hour being up, we turned off Poplar Avenue and after crossing three bridges over the Olkhovka river approached a poetically situated cottage beside a watermill, with a tiny front garden. Downstairs there was just one room, with a door opening directly on to the street! On the bed lay the enchanting Kira, a gloriously beautiful woman of about twenty-three with

---

[1] The way in which the Cyrillic alphabet was written and printed had, after many ad hoc and only partially accepted modifications during the eighteenth and nineteenth centuries, been finally standardised by the philologist Yakov Grot in 1885. This 'old orthography' remained hallowed by universal usage until the Provisional Government (as if they had nothing else to worry about) issued the decree in the summer of 1917 to which Prokofiev and Balmont were at this time objecting. The simplification consisted of eliminating three letters altogether and the silent hard sign ъ after final consonants. Because the Bolsheviks later made adoption of the reforms a point of principle, one of the eliminated letters, the yat (ѣ), became something of a political football, for some years émigré writers ostentatiously continuing to use it as a symbol of their adherence to the *ancien régime*.

[2] A famous and dramatic beauty spot near Kislovodsk. The legend tells of Dauta, only daughter of a ruthless warlord, who loves the son of a humble shepherd and is loved in return. The flinty-hearted prince, having destined his beloved daughter to a rich neighbour, refuses to let her wed the shepherd boy, whereupon the unhappy couple resolve to die in each other's arms by leaping together from the cliff. The young man, crying out that to die for love holds no terrors for him, plunges to his death in the abyss (love), but Dauta takes fright, returns home and marries the rich neighbour (perfidy).

superb eyelashes, wearing a white bonnet with a blue bow. Balmont sat at her feet, obviously besotted with her, and they were billing and cooing in Spanish, as both of them were linguists and able to converse in all manner of languages. His wife meekly poured out tea while Mirra ran about the garden. Kira was extremely nice, gentle, affectionate, cultivated, a music-lover, knew many marvellous legends and stories and was good at telling them. In the corner stood an ancient piano, a sort of hybrid piano-harpsichord. Both my Gavottes sounded rather good on it, but the *Sarcasms*, much loved by Balmont, came out as pure caricatures. Balmont, by the way, revealed that the stress in his name should fall on the last syllable, not on the first, as many people (including me up to that point) pronounce it.

Kira Nikolayevna invited me to visit her whenever I liked, and having obtained her permission to come tomorrow with a friend, I left the party. When he heard how I had been spending my time in Kislovodsk, Boris Verin was beside himself with agitation.

The next day I invited him to come with me to Kira's, anticipating that we would find Balmont there. Verin was very nervous and spent time titivating himself, but I admonished him that he should try and behave himself in a restrained manner and not embarrassingly throw himself at Balmont's feet, nor should he pay exaggerated attentions to Kira.

The picture that met our eyes as we entered was identical to yesterday's: the long eyelashes, the white bonnet – adorned this time with a lilac bow, Balmont sitting beside the bed holding Kira's hand while his wife busied herself with the samovar; Mirra running about the garden. Balmont wore white trousers, a beige-coloured Indian silk jacket, and with his long hair, rosy-fresh complexion and pointed beard he looked fifteen years younger than the fifty he in fact is. Boris Verin behaved himself well. I played quite a lot on the harpsichord-type instrument, and while I was playing my First Sonata, Balmont composed for my 'Wooden Book' a sonnet, a magnificent improvisation which he dedicated to me and of which I am immensely proud, considering it an adornment to the 'Wooden Book'. I played the *Mimolyotnosti*,[1] and given that my title had been taken from Balmont's verses:

> In every fleeting vision [*mimolyotnosti*] I see worlds
> Filled with the fickle play of rainbows

I asked if he found it appropriate to the music. Balmont liked both the piece and the title very much, and Kira, who spoke excellent French, came up with a French translation for the term: 'Visions fugitives'. Up till that moment I had not been able to find it.

That evening in the Kursaal B. Verin arranged a dinner for Balmont with

---

[1] The Russian title of Op. 22, literally 'transiences' or 'ephemeralities'.

caviare, savouries and champagne, at a table set with flowers. Balmont seemed pleased to be honoured in this way. As for B. Verin, he was in the seventh heaven of rapture on account of both 'Kostya'[1] and Kira.

The following day Balmont lunched with us at the dacha. We told the owner of the house, as a joke, that we were going to affix a big sign to the front of the balcony saying 'Balmont had lunch here' and next year he would be able to add 200 roubles to the price of the dacha.

Mama was also there, and liked Balmont very much, although she was rather shocked by his answer when she asked him, was he not disgusted by Grigory Rasputin? 'Not at all, this was a man who very much loved women.'

After lunch Balmont yielded to my request to read *Seven, They Are Seven*. His reading was designed to emphasise and heighten the horror of the poem's content, but although he read magnificently, the effect was not as stunning as I had imagined. Nevertheless, I did my best to fix in my memory certain characteristics of his reading in order to reproduce them later musically. Among them were the manner in which he began, in a terrifying whisper, and also the rhythm and intonation of the words 'seven, they are seven', 'seven', 'earth they sit'. After *Seven, They Are Seven*, Balmont read a Malay incantation, also marvellous, but not nearly as overwhelming as the Chaldean. In my opinion this is one of the most fearsome things ever written. Not for nothing have its enigmatic cuneiform hieroglyphs been brought out into the light after being buried in the ground for a thousand years, to resound once again, perhaps more apocalyptically even than before! Balmont has reproduced it in different forms in no fewer than three of his books, and suggested that I take any of the three texts and even, if I wished, combine them.[2]

Next day Balmont left Pyatigorsk for Moscow, and Boris Verin took him to the station. I went to Kislovodsk to perform the First Piano Concerto in an orchestral concert. Berdyayev was the conductor, quite good. The audience was small (it can hear a symphony orchestra every day for nothing in the open air so is hardly motivated to come indoors and pay in the evening). I had a success, though. B.N. rushed in towards the end of the evening, having just decanted Balmont into his train at Pyatigorsk. The poet had got very hot under the collar at another passenger who was getting in the way of his hoisting in through the carriage window the suitcase Verin was lifting up to him, calling him a 'stomach on two legs'. 'You're nothing but a stomach on legs!' screeched Balmont, and then, bidding farewell to Boris Verin (and

1 Konstantin (Balmont).
2 The text of the incantation, as found in Akkadian and Sumerian script on the sixteenth tablet of a series known as the Evil Demon series, was translated into English by R. C. Thompson in 1903 (R. C. Thompson, *The Devils and Evil Spirits of Bablyonia*, vols 1 and 2, (Luzac & Co., London, 1903).) For this version, see Appendix 2.

kissing him tenderly, it's a real love affair), mused: 'Yes, you have quite a lot of walking stomachs down here in Pyatigorsk!' We very much liked this expression.

From Pyatigorsk B. Verin dashed to Yessentuki, where Balmont had been supposed to read at a charity event but was not able to owing to his departure. Boris made an announcement from the stage: 'My friend Balmont has asked me to tell you that owing to his departure he is not able to read himself, but if you so desire, I can in his stead read you some of his poems.' The audience did so desire, and Verin commenced his reading. It turned out that B. Verin knows more of Balmont's poems by heart than the author does, even though the author constantly appears in public reading his poetry. Balmont knows some fifty or so, Verin more than a hundred.

When I came back from Kislovodsk to Yessentuki, B. Verin and I trained my telescope, the one I had brought from Petrograd, on Jupiter and found all six of its satellites.[1] As I had just come from my concert I was still in my tails, and so this is how we observed Jupiter – ceremonial dress to honour the splendour of the planet. Also, this evening I learned the disposition of the Hercules constellation, to which our own sun belongs. It is not a simple constellation to master, as its form is complex, the stars are not easily visible, and it is very spread out across the heavens. But Balmont knows it.

Little by little over the course of these days, the notion took hold of me that I might spend the winter in Kislovodsk, and more importantly, that Mama could do so. Petrograd was under threat from the Germans, there were disorders caused by the opening of the Constituent Assembly, while in Kislovodsk all was peaceful, there was plenty of food in reserve and the climate was wonderful. I did not mean to spend the whole winter there, but as she had said that being there on her own would be too depressing, I promised Mama that I would spend half the time there. My plan was to take turn and turn about, a month here followed by a month in Petrograd.

Accordingly, on the 14th I got ready to travel north. The main motive for the journey was that here I had spent so much time endlessly chasing about after Balmont, or Koshetz, or B. Verin, I now wanted to live quietly in my beautiful 'estate', to get on with my work and have time to concentrate. So on the 14th, seen off by my mother and my friend, I boarded the train and sped northwards. When B.N. asked me what message I had for Kira Nikolayevna, I replied: 'Tell her that, objectively, I like her very much.'

Apparently when this was transmitted to her she took great offence.

At Rostov a carriage from Novorossisk was hooked up to our train, and

---

1   Galileo had discovered four of Jupiter's moons in 1610, the first time moons other than the Earth's were identified. A fifth moon was discovered in 1892, and several more in the early years of the twentieth century. At the latest count there were sixty-three.

in it was Balmont, who had gone to Yekaterinodar to give a lecture and was now going on to Moscow. On the way we ate melon and talked. He said people were wrong to think that North America was a country exclusively devoted to money and to the rush and urgency of industrial life; it was a country of fabulous natural beauty, California was especially lovely as were Californian women! But best of all was Mexico. When I asked if he had ever been to South America, Balmont replied: 'Thank God, I have not been there yet. One of the most wonderful corners of the globe still awaits me.' The other corners he has succeeded in getting to.

My train, late of course, brought me into Petrograd during the night of the 18th. Well, it was quite nice to be there really, even if damp and dirty. The first person I saw was Eleonora, who told me (with what degree of accuracy I do not know) that the General Staff had queried my release, finding it a very strange notion that a person should be exempted from military service simply because he was a composer. They wanted to evict me from my sanctuary, but according to Eleonora, Kerensky had gone himself to the General Staff and ordered them once and for all to leave me alone so long as he remained at the head of the War Ministry and the Government.

And so, everything was in order. While in the city I lunched regularly at the 'Bear' with Diederichs where we discussed future autumn concerts, and with Koussevitzky, who had been appointed Director of the former Court Orchestra.[1] Ziloti was proposing that I appear three times: with the 'Classical' Symphony, the Violin Concerto, and *Seven, They Are Seven*, which I promised to have finished by the autumn. In addition there would be a chamber evening with all new compositions: the Third and Fourth Sonatas, *Visions Fugitives* and the *Akhmatova Songs*. In the absence of any grants becoming available for new stage works there was no prospect of *The Gambler*, or indeed any new opera productions, this winter, and the theatre office clearly wanted to skate over this question. But seeing that nothing was going to come of it in any case, I declared categorically that since the theatre was not in a position to carry out its undertaking to present the opera over two seasons, I considered it was in breach of contract with me, accordingly that I was released from its terms and should be paid the fee due for the ten guaranteed performances. I did this because I thought it preferable to take the initiative in terminating the agreement rather than waiting until it was announced that *The Gambler* was being removed from the repertoire and would not be produced, even if the only reason for this was the lack of funds for its production.

On the 22nd alarming news broke: Riga had been captured by the Germans.

---

1 The Court Orchestra was formally reconstituted as the Philharmonic, later the Leningrad Philharmonic Orchestra, in 1920.

The armoured fist was now raised over Petrograd itself. And although the blow would not fall immediately, it was not certain how strong the Revolutionary troops were, nor was there any way of knowing what the situation might be when 3 million Petrograders were fleeing helter-skelter for their lives out of the city. And any day now the dear little Zeppelinchiki could come dropping by. I was relieved that Mama was safely out of the way in the Caucasus; it made me feel much more secure myself, since getting her away in the midst of panic and disorder would be tremendously difficult. I still had in my hands my manuscripts, my diaries and letters, which I had no intention of allowing to fall into German hands, so I packed them all up into a trunk, but when it was done I found the trunk was as heavy as lead, weighing a couple of poods.[1] Not exactly the ideal piece of luggage to flee with.

I decided to take advantage of Koussevitzky leaving for Moscow, having by some miracle procured a separate International Company compartment, to entrust to him the precious trunk for safe-keeping in Moscow in the vaults of the Russian Music Editions. There was a tremendous crowd at the station, with terrified residents of the city cramming into overcrowded trains to get away to the south. But my trunk was safely in its own compartment, and so now I was on my own, a free man relieved of all cares. I felt especially tender towards the bulky package containing my diaries.

Next I packed a very small suitcase with necessities for Zet, and on the 24th settled back into my estate conscious of a deep feeling of satisfaction. Although the weather was awful my heart was full of joy, I suppose because I had regained the peace of my private sanctum after the disorderliness of Petrograd and the threat of German incursion. Outside the wind blew and the rain drizzled, but inside it was roomy and warm, and there was a sufficiency of good things – hard to come by at times like these! A whole collection of differently coloured boxes containing various kinds of English and Egyptian cigarettes (as many as fifteen different brands) filled one of the drawers in my commode. Then there were chocolate and sweets, halva, honey, dried apricots and delicious compotes. Eleonora presented me with two pounds of real white flour (a real rarity!), so for lunch there would be bliny, caviare and superb, one could almost say phemonenal, smoked eel.

My working activities concentrated on orchestrating the Symphony, while in the evenings I thought about more short stories. I made plans for quite a collection of them, but without working out the details. My two first stories I read down the telephone to Eleonora (she was the only person to know about my debut in this genre), and they were a tremendous success with her, 'The Poodle' in particular, with its 'succulent apricot tart'.

---

1   A pood was just over 16 kilograms, so the trunk would have weighed about 32 kilos, or a little more than 70 pounds.

On the 28th, when I went out to the station for the newspapers and returned home, I disposed myself comfortably on the sofa to read them only to be stunned by the news that the Commander-in-Chief General Kornilov was moving up on Petrograd from the south to overthrow Kerensky, while troops loyal to Kerensky had left Petrograd to meet and crush Kornilov. Internecine war, and fate had plunged me into the epicentre of the action. What would happen next?

The next day I went into Petrograd. There were not many people on the train, but I could detect a note of alarm in what they said. Soldiers boarded the train checking papers for some reason. I arrived in Petrograd in an anxious frame of mind, fearful that the city might become a field of slaughter or that the attacking forces might cut the railway lines, precipitating a true state of siege. Eleonora, who had been in touch with Kerensky, telephoned to say that it was not so bad, Kerensky's confidence was high and although, of course, the situation was serious, he was acting decisively and was sure of victory over Kornilov. I decided that my best course of action was to return immediately to my estate and there await developments. Ignoring Eleonora's protests I declined her invitation to dinner and hurried back to the station.

Sitting in the carriage I looked over to the west, to the darkening skies beyond Tsarskoye over by Pavlovsk, where it was expected that the opposing forces would come face to face, and the prospect was distinctly ominous. But Sablino was its old peaceful and reassuring self, even though detachments of soldiers with machine-guns were drawn up at some of the stations through which we passed.

At home, in the dacha, I spread out a map of the Petrograd region and with the help of the newspaper set out flags representing the Kerensky and Kornilov forces. The nodal point of the conflict appeared likely to be Pavlovsk and Tsarskoye. Kornilov's right flank had advanced as far as the Tosna,[1] while Kerensky's left flank had reached Kolpino. Sablino lay directly between them. My dacha, standing on its own on high ground, could well be a good observation point. This is a position known as falling flat on one's face into the soup. I did no work on scoring that day, and all night kept waking up expecting to hear the sound of gunfire. But the next morning the newspapers confirmed that there had been no fighting, that when the troops met they exchanged not shells but words, and that Kornilov's troops had surrendered, not knowing where they had been brought to or for what reason. And in this way the 'Ka–Ka' incident had been brought to a conclusion.

I am neither a counter-revolutionary nor a revolutionary. I am on neither

---

1 The Tosna river flows no more than two miles from Sablino, while the town of Kolpino is five miles or so to the north-west of the village.

side. But I could not help regretting that Kornilov's enterprise had faded away to nothing: it had about it a whiff of romanticism.[1]

September

Apart from Riga and Kornilov there was nothing to disturb the peace of Sablino. August imperceptibly merged into September, and it was so comfortable there that I had no desire to leave my Zet. At night it rained, but the days were sunny. From the first of the month the leaves gradually began turning yellow, then red and russet, while others side by side with them stayed fresh and green, so that the combination of bright red leaves and the vivid yellows with which the maples were clad from top to bottom formed a magnificent, richly hued tapestry of glowing colours. It was amazing that the unprepossessing hamlet of Sablino could conceal a landscape of such beauty: ravines, dachas, the river. Walking through the countryside, I thought how beautiful was the northern autumn, and how at its heart every autumn harbours a gentle melancholy, because it is, withal, a dying. I, however, at the end of the month would be going south again, to Kislovodsk and the sun, where the loveliness of autumn would not lead inexorably to the rains of November with its long, gloomy nights, and so with a light heart I savoured all the beauty around me. Every five days or so I journeyed into the city to sort out my affairs, and also to buy sweetmeats and English cigarettes (but oh, how hard and expensive it had become these days to find any of them!), returning each time with gladness in my heart.

The score of the Symphony proceeded apace and was finished around the 10th. But a much more significant event of this September was the composition of *Seven, They Are Seven*. It was a work I had been pondering for some time, circling round it in my mind, and when I eventually set to work on it I already felt it would be something remarkable. I had some thoughts and ideas, I knew what I wanted to achieve, I could somehow feel it, but as

---

[1] In fact, as later became clear, Kornilov had ordered his troops to Petrograd under the impression that he was *supporting* Kerensky and the Provisional Government in their escalating conflict with the Bolshevik faction, not in order to overthrow them. The Kerensky–Kornilov stand-off was the result of a series of possibly engineered misunderstandings between two intransigent and egoistic individuals, whose respective armies (the Committee for Struggle Against the Counter-Revolution on the one hand and General Krymov's Cossacks on the other) realised much more quickly than their leaders that there was in fact nothing to fight about, which was why there was no battle. But the consequences were almost apocalyptic not just for Ka–Ka but for the fate of Russia: Kerensky had signed the death warrant of his leadership, and Kornilov was driven into the leadership of the White counter-revolution. The possibility of Russia's becoming a constitutional democracy of any hue had suffered its severest reverse. See O. Figes, *A People's Tragedy, The Russian Revolution 1891–1924* (Pimlico, London, 1996) for an admirably clear account of this episode.

yet there was nothing concrete to show for it. At last on 4 September I started work. Never before had I approached the composition of a work in this way. Now I was setting down not music onto the page but contours, sometimes a single vocal line, or instead of notes I would be writing a graphic representation, a kind of general shape with an outline of orchestration.

I became engrossed in the work to the point of obsession. Sometimes my absorption would rise to such a pitch that I would have to stop and go for a walk in order to calm the pounding of my heart. I did not work on *Seven, They Are Seven* for long at a time, not more than half an hour or an hour a day, and not every day. But I spent a great deal of time thinking. The sketches were finished on 15 September, that is to say within the space of twelve days, of which seven were spent working, and no writing on the other five.

> 4 September – from the beginning to Fig. 7, to the Priests' exclamations of 'Telal! Telal!'[1]
>
> 7 September – two of the texts, up to the orchestral *fortissimo*.
>
> 8 September – up to and including 'They are evil!' (between Figs. 11 and 12).
>
> 9 September – up to the women's unison chorus: 'Spirit of the Heavens!'
>
> 13 September – 'Spirit of the Heavens!' and 'Spirit of the Earth!', the women's and men's episode, as far as Fig. 18.
>
> 14 September – to the fourfold repetition of 'They Are Seven!' (after Fig. 28, although at this time the plan was to have only two repetitions).
>
> 15 September – addition of two more 'They Are Seven!' and the final bars, although the finale had already been planned beforehand, five days ago.

However, these sketches were no more than the barest outline and quite superficial. Most detailed were the vocal parts, the chorus and the main points of the scoring. The counterpoint was barely indicated, while harmonies existed for only a few of the pages. For the rest they were scattered about more or less at random, not thought out, because to allow myself to be distracted by them would have meant being deflected from the overall conception of the piece. The general framework was, nevertheless, composed all at once, and once and for all, and was not subjected to any later alteration. As for the harmonies, the following passages were composed at the time and subsequently remained unaltered: the opening chord, as far as 'They Are Seven!' and forming the basis for the following incantation, and the final fifth on F and C. In the episodes for the women 'Spirit of the Heavens!', and for the men 'Spirit of the Earth!', the melodic lines survived

---

1 In the Sumerian language, a wicked demon, or warrior.

unaltered, but in the women's section the accompaniment was not notated but simply indicated by rising and falling lines, while the harmonies of the men's section were later revised. Later, beginning at 'Evil winds! Evil storms!' all the harmony was random and underwent several changes at later stages until assuming its final form.

Such was the nature of the original sketch-plan of the work. Satisfied, I laid it aside. Although I knew that an immense amount of work remained to be done, this would be a matter of technique and of invention; the skeleton of the basic conception with its terrible intensity had been created. No one but myself would be able to make head or tail of the score, but for me the main work was already complete.

My other occupation was reading Kant (courtesy of Kuno Fischer). I did so with great interest, although making slow progress because of the inordinate complexity of the construction. Some chapters I read twice in order to achieve a better grasp of them. As for my new stories, on the 17th I started one about an 'Inedible Mushroom'. It is in a somewhat different style from its predecessors, as it no doubt will be from its successors, and was the result of my solitary wanderings through the forests and valleys where I would stop before the most beautiful mukhomors,[1] touch them and examine them closely.

My long-standing essays at gymnastics had led me this time to the decision to exercise regularly according to the Miller system, which I began to study and put into practice. I also meticulously took cold-water showers with the window open, in spite of the hellish cold, even to the extent of ground frosts in the mornings. The occasional passer-by, had he raised his eyes to the second floor, might have observed bare feet flashing round in a circular motion: this would have been me, lying athwart the bed vigorously aerial bicycling with my legs as prescribed by Miller.[2]

On the 20th the time came for me finally to part with my dear Zet. The weather had grown cold, damp and dark. I carried away with me the most affectionate memories of a place where amazingly enough in the midst of war, revolution, civil strife and famine it was possible for a young, far from

1 The mukhomor ('fly-killer', more properly fly-agaric) mushroom, found all over Russia, is the classic fairy-tale round-domed mushroom, red with white spots. Broken-off parts of the cap in a saucer of milk will stupefy flies, hence the name. The mukhomor is a strong hallucinogen and intoxicant, especially when dried, but care is needed as ingesting the magic mushroom in the wrong way or at the wrong time can have fatal consequences. The title of Prokofiev's story is 'Skazka po grib-poganku' ('The Tale of the Poisonous Mushroom', ed. Bretanitskaya, *op. cit.*) and a fragment appears translated by Oleg Prokofiev and Christopher Palmer with the title 'Tanya and the Mushroom Kingdom' in *Soviet Diary 1927 and Other Writings, op. cit.*
2 William Miller (1846–1838) was an outstanding Australian athlete, gymnast, boxer and wrestler, the only athlete to have held the Australian championships in boxing, fencing, wrestling and weight-lifting. In 1895 in Melbourne he published his exercise system under the title *Health, Exercise and Amusement*. From 1903 Miller lived in America, where among his other activities he served as athletics instructor to the New York Police Department.

rich young man of conscriptable age to live as well, as easily and carefree as I had done. My sense of inner peace and happiness had come from Schopenhauer and the truth of his insight: do not pursue happiness but strive to be free of pain. What a wealth of possibilities are contained in this truth! And for the person who accepts it and incarnates it in his own being, what rapture-inducing revelations does life have to offer!

And so I found myself back in sodden Petrograd, only to leave again on the 21st for the Caucasus. However, the intervening twenty-four hours I spent in an unremitting scramble to get everything ready for my departure. I gave the Symphony to Ziloti for copying, while the parts for the Violin Concerto had already been made and had been scrutinised with the utmost care and understanding by Kokhánski, an outstanding violinist and musician. Both works were scheduled for performance in November, although Ziloti, made nervous by the uncertainty of the times, had not yet announced the concerts. With Diederichs we pencilled in two piano recitals in Petrograd and one in Moscow, also in November. The month of October I would spend in Kislovodsk.

Boris Verin returned to Petrograd on the 20th. His neuralgia was better, and he looked fresh and tanned. He had visited Kira, whom he described as an exceptionally interesting and cultivated woman, every day: in the mornings he slept, in the afternoons had treatment for his nerves, and in the evenings flew to her side in Kislovodsk, where he had entirely captured her heart. I mockingly took him to task for his 'impropriety' in worshipping Balmont while at the same time stealing his woman. Mama rented our Petrograd apartment to him so that it should not remain empty and become a target for vandals and thieves. B. Verin jumped at the idea, because one result of his ill-starred marriage was a complete rift with his family and he had therefore decided to live independently. This he could do 'at Serge's'.

All day on the 21st I rushed back and forth with all the things I had to do. Mama sent me a list of tasks – such-and-such had to be brought, such-and-such had to be done – with no fewer than fifty items on it. I had to rummage through a thousand drawers, trunks and cardboard boxes, and by the time I had found everything no amount of cases, boxes and baskets would suffice to transport it all. There was no servant, the concierge was grumpy, so there was nothing for it but to handle everything myself. At long last fourteen pieces of luggage had been packed and B.N. by some miracle succeeded in taking me to dinner at the 'Kontan' (where for the first time we were given the new-style money in 20- and 40-rouble notes – it is appalling to contemplate how the value of money has fallen!). At half-past nine that evening, with my traditional escort to the station of Eleonora and B. Verin, and after entirely filling a compartment of the International Company's train from floor to ceiling, I left Petrograd. For a month, I thought. I had no thought of a longer absence.

On the 23rd in the evening I unshipped my load of boxes on to the platform at Yessentuki and was met by Mama, who was extravagantly glad to see me as she had grown very miserable thinking herself an abandoned refugee. My arrival restored her energy and good spirits. I had a large room reserved for me at the Kislovodsk Sanatorium, with a view looking straight at Beshtau.[1] What a beauty Beshtau is – my favourite, even in Switzerland, surrounded by mountains of all shapes and features, I had never forgotten its noble form. Now I spent long hours gazing at it from my balcony, seeing it covered by clouds or aglow with the tints of the setting sun. It was delightfully warm in Yessentuki, but the trees were clothed less magnificently than they had been in the north. Down here the leaves simply withered and most of them fell.

Life fell into the following pattern: I rose at half-past seven, because at that time the children next door started making a noise. Not that I had any objection to getting up at this early hour. I did my Miller exercises, accompanied by all the appropriate ablutions, until I found these latter beginning to interfere with my sleep, after which I took to doing the exercises every day and the ablutions every other day. This was followed by a walk, then coffee and the morning's work.

I took out my sketches for *Seven, They Are Seven*, and sitting in an armchair studied and thought about them. Little by little the empty spaces began to fill up with textures and figures: the skeleton acquired muscles. Parallel with this I eliminated the random harmonies and replaced them with the real ones. To this activity I devoted an hour. Then I sat on the balcony and read Kant, but sometimes, for a change, wrote 'The Poisonous Mushroom', which I finished by 1 October, or caught up on my Diary. I dined at one, and from two until four went to the cinema: an enormous, empty space with a beat-up upright piano in it on which I practised, partly exercises to bring my technique back into working order but also learning the Third Sonata. Since I was planning a series of concert appearances in the autumn after an entire summer without a piano it was very useful to be able to concentrate on my technique. From five until six I was back on my balcony, continuing my morning activities, then a walk, supper and for relaxation an evening chapter of aesthetics. By half-past ten I was in bed.

In this way a week passed, my name-day unnoticed during it. The peace of disengagement from the world reigned throughout September.

---

1 A five-peak mountain near Pyatigorsk. The name comes from the Turkmen language and, as does the Russian Pyatigorsk, means Five Mountains. See *Diaries*, vol. 1, pp. 105–6.

October

On 1 October I unexpectedly made a trip to Teberda. This is a fascinating part of the country, lying high up in the mountains on the Sukhum Military Road, which runs from the station at Nevinnomyssky (two hours by train from Mineralnye Vody), crossing the tremendous barrier of the Caucasus mountain range to descend sharply into Sukhum. Teberda is twenty versts distant from the pass through the mountains, and is famous for its clear, cloudless skies and its wonderful air 4,750 feet above sea level. It has every prospect of becoming a noted resort town.

We were a party of four: an Englishman, Ruffman, the one who had talked me into coming with him, myself, and the two Dzhunkovsky brothers whom I, in turn, had persuaded to join us. Towards the evening of the 1st we set off by train to Nevinnomyssky station, accompanied by an Italian woman, Mme Collini, regarded by most people as a charming lady, but not, at least yet, by me. More of this anon.

Arriving at 'Nevinka' (as it is known hereabouts) after midnight, we spent the night (not much of a night, from two o'clock until six) in our carriage in a siding, and at dawn climbed into two carriages to go to Batalpashinsk, a large Cossack *stanitsa*[1] fifty versts away. There we spent our second night in a quite decent hotel (ceilings about twenty arshins[2] high) and, come the dawn, set off for Teberda in the car we had procured. At first the road took us across the steppe and was rather monotonous, but as it penetrated deeper into the mountains it grew more attractive, and by evening, as we neared Teberda (a hundred and fifty versts from Nevinnomyssky) it was truly beautiful. The Englishman was especially enthusiastic, never having seen a proper mountain among the shallow contours of his homeland. I found the process of travelling in the car through the open countryside very enjoyable in itself, because hitherto I had usually had to confine this pleasure to the narrow streets of the city.

Teberda proved to be genuinely a glorious place, hemmed in by mountains, with a view of the graceful Amanaus glacier and pure, extremely rarefied air that caused one to stop and catch one's breath when incautiously ascending a steep slope at too rapid a pace. Next morning, the Englishman stayed behind to look into possibilities for developing a sanatorium while the remainder of the party set off riding in single file along the Sukhum Military Road as far as the pass, and there came upon a prospect of the most ravishing beauty. It is truly claimed that the Sukhum Military Road is

---

1 A *stanitsa* is a Cossack village. Originally it was a purely military grouping, the main unit of a Cossack host.
2 *Sic.* An arshin being 0.71 metres, the ceilings must have been over forty feet high.

lovelier than the Ossetian Military Road, the Ossetian Military Road is lovelier than the Georgian Military Road – and the beauties of the Georgian Military Road are known to all.[1]

We emerged into a landscape of incredible wildness, terrifying precipices suddenly dropping away for hundreds of metres below our feet, while above our heads the mountain-tops reared up to the sky. Torrents raged in the abysses, while in other directions could be seen the deep black of the virgin forests and yet more mountains, even more lofty, luminous with a range of fantastic colours. I thought myself in the magical kingdom of a fairy-tale. Eventually we arrived at the sentry post at the foot of the pass; from there on there was a path traversable only on foot. We left the horses at the sentry post along with our rations and an Austrian prisoner-of-war, equipped ourselves with walking sticks and started off on the climb up to the Klukhor Pass, a further two thousand feet above us.[2]

At this point it became apparent that the citizen of the north is not a natural mountain-dweller. As the Dzhunkovsky brothers, natives of Transcaucasia, bounded goat-like from rock to rock, I was soon out of breath from the thinness of the air and the steepness of the climb, and began to fall behind. However, our aim was to reach the pass before nightfall, cast our eyes over the immense slope extending down from it to the shores of the Black Sea, and return to the sentry post. I told the Dzhunkovskys to go on and pay no attention to me, saying that if I felt better I would catch them up, but if I did not then I would go back down to the post. The Dzhunkovskys soon disappeared from view in the heights, and I, after resting for a while in the baking hot sun, continued my ascent until I reached the permanent snow line, and then returned to the sentry post. Not long afterwards the Dzhunkovskys reappeared, having almost but not quite reached the difficult highest point of the pass. After a furious argument (I said we should spend the night in the post while they insisted on riding back to Teberda) we set off through the impenetrable blackness of the night, picking our way among the rocks and precipices. Around midnight we somehow managed to get back to Teberda, and the next day, towards evening, took the car right back to Yessentuki, where we arrived contented, tired and sunburnt.

The day after, the 6th, I went to Kislovodsk, to see whether I could move there from Yessentuki, where the town had emptied of people and the weather had grown cold and windy. In Kislovodsk the sun was shining and the town was full of people. The war, and more than the war the Revolution, had chased so many people south for the winter that everywhere to stay was

---

1   The three main military roads through the Caucasus Crest were constructed at the very end of the eighteenth century, after the Russo-Turkish War of 1877–78, with the dual aim of opening up Georgia and of binding it more firmly to the Russian Empire.
2   The highest point of the Klukhor Pass is 2,781 metres.

crammed full at fabulous prices. But I had set my sights on no less than the Grand Hotel. While others drove themselves to a state of nervous collapse scouring Kislovodsk for somewhere to lay their heads, I sauntered round the park where I ran into Reznikov, the proprietor of the Grand Hotel and brother of the well-known entrepreneur, and asked him for a room. One soon became available, and the following day I left Yessentuki and moved to Kislovodsk. My arrival provoked an amusing incident, because Mme Collini, the alluring Italian (who by now I did like a little better) had by mistake been allocated the same room, so that we both entered it with all our luggage at one and the same time. Investigations revealed that hers was in fact a different room, but I laughed that I had not only got a charming room but as a bonus a charming woman in it. The room itself was wonderful: it had two balconies so caught the sun twice a day, first when it was in the south and then later in the west, and the room was flooded with its rays. After a few days Mama came to keep me company.

Early in my stay I spent time with Diederichs, who had also come to the resort and was extraordinarily friendly to me. We drank to our *Bruderschaft*.[1] I went to see Kira Nikolayevna, but somehow for me her charms had faded. I also went to see the Safonov family, the old maestro[2] excessively Olympian and Zeus-like in his demeanour but patricianly indulgent towards me. Referring to modern music, he said that he 'tolerated it'. One event that held particular fascination for me was the walk I took with the utterly entrancing General Ruzsky,[3] a man to whom I bow the knee not merely as the most remarkable Russian commander of this war, but as the leader who saved Russia from defeat. And this was the elderly gentleman, in civilian clothes,

---

1   The ritual in which Russians pledge close and enduring friendship to one another (symbolised by the use of the intimate 'family' second person singular, rather than the formal second person plural form of address).
2   Vasily Safonov (1852–1918) pianist, conductor and Rector of the Moscow Conservatoire between 1889 and 1905, during which time he quarrelled spectacularly with Ziloti, following which he moved to New York for a spell as Chief Conductor of the New York Philharmonic. See *Diaries*, vol. 1, p. 725 and *passim*.
3   General Nikolay Vladimirovovich Ruzsky (1854–1918), the cousin of Prokofiev's cello-playing friend from Petrograd Nikolay Ruzsky, had formerly been in command of the North Western Front, at the time in retreat from East Prussia. He had earned this promotion from the success – which made him a household name – of his previous command, of the Third Army, in recapturing the city of Lvov from the Austro-Hungarian army in August. Ruzsky ultimately assumed command of the entire Northern Front, including Petrograd, and became the prime mover of the military commanders' determination to achieve the abdication of the Tsar as representing the only hope for future successful prosecution of the war. It was Rusky who received from the Tsar's hands the signed abdication document in the Imperial train on 2 March 1917 (old style). His patriotically inspired actions earned him no favour with the Bolsheviks: in October 1918 in Pyatigorsk General Ruzsky was taken hostage and summarily executed with characteristically callous brutality by the Cheka, along with fifty-eight other distinguished military and aristocratic leaders of the *ancien régime*. See also ibid., p. 743.

with a soft collar and grey hat, now strolling leisurely by my side. In answer to my cautiously phrased questions he willingly gave an account of strategic plans, his views on the general conduct of the war, its mistakes and opportunities. I was amazed by the simplicity and openness with which this hero, the central figure of so many illustrious events, told me all these things. And how irresistible was the gentleness of this great man!

Once acclimatised to Kislovodsk I began to prepare for the concert arranged for me by the Director of the Kursaal. In between I worked on the second movement of the new Sonata[1] (recomposed from the Adagio of my old symphony) and on *Seven, They Are Seven*.

Thoughts at this time also turned to Nina Mescherskaya, and for this reason: while I was with Ruzsky, someone mentioned that such-and-such a dacha had been taken by some people called Meshchersky. This is not such an uncommon name, but naturally it set off a train of thought. Then at Safonov's, in an album in which the young members of the family were collecting autographs of writers, I saw the name of Vera Nikolayevna Meshcherskaya. And indeed, not long afterwards I saw Talya, the very same Talya Meshcherskaya, dressed incidentally very simply and not very presentably. Eventually, in the Narzan Galleries, I met Talya and Nina. Whether it actually was Nina or not I could not be sure: I was walking fast and only happened to glance up and see them by accident. She was carrying a tennis racquet and looking at me. Nina, if it was indeed she, was still wearing her hair short. While I was in love with her I was always asking her to cut her hair, and she did so the moment we parted.

The 14th was the day of my concert in the Kursaal, at which I performed for the first time my Third Sonata and the *Visions Fugitives*. Of course, these premieres should have taken place in Petrograd, not in Kislovodsk, but I looked on this recital as a rehearsal for a later performance in the capital. I expected the hall to be full: Kislovodsk was awash with Petrograders and Muscovites, who would know who I was, but in the event there were not many people in the hall. Through a hole in the curtain at the back I could see Talya and Vera Nikolayevna; in spite of prolonged searching I could not see Nina and she did not seem to have come. The concert had a more than average success: the audience may not have particularly enjoyed what I played, but it did enjoy the way I played it.

Afterwards Mama told me that Vera Nikolayevna had come up to her to say that there had never been any quarrel between them, as mothers, and therefore she, Vera Nikolayevna, was very glad to see Mama and talk with her. Mama was very touched by this gesture, although she refrained from any overt display, not being able to predict my reaction. 'Seryozha has been

---

[1] Sonata No. 4, Op. 29.

getting on very well.' 'Talya is married to an army officer now at the Front.' I listened to Mama's account in silence. She continued: 'And the other one . . . what was her name . . . Nina, wasn't it? . . . also got married this autumn, to a student.' I said nothing, and leaving Mama went into my room. I was in the grip of strong emotions, but after all, what could be more likely? Two and a half years had passed, Nina was twenty-one, of course she would be married. I have no idea who the student could be, probably a new face.[1] I did not see them again in Kislovodsk. My attention was taken by a note I was handed after my concert, from an unknown Asya Lesnaya, enraptured by my playing and wanting to meet me. The language and handwriting suggested a gymnasium student. I smiled, and went to bed.

Four days later I gave the second of my recitals. The audience was even smaller, so much so that it was positively disagreeable to have to play, but I took myself in hand: after all, this was not really a recital but a rehearsal for Moscow – specifically Moscow, not Petrograd, because in Petrograd I am known and loved, while Moscow I have still to conquer. The praise heaped there on Orlov,[2] the darling of the Moscow public, a young and stylish but essentially hollow pianist, gives me no peace. And when Orlov has been dealt with, there will still be Rachmaninoff.

In this recital I played very well indeed, and with great subtlety. Mama, who is always severely critical, was in raptures. Old man Safonov also praised it highly, having discerned through all the unfamiliar modernism the tenderness and delicacy of my nuancing. Asya Lesnaya sat in the front row and came into the artists' room at the end of the recital. She was, it turned out, no gymnasium schoolgirl but a twenty-year-old drama student of Meyerhold, with a Polish-Jewish cast of features more unusual than obviously attractive although in her own way she was attractive, tall, supple, dressed with more than a hint of contemporary originality and wearing a red hat (she was known around Kislovodsk as 'Krasnaya Shapochka', 'Little Red Riding-Hood'). Lesnaya was a stage name; her real name was Khmelnitskaya. As we left the artists' room and went into the street I received an ovation, but we immediately turned and crossed a little bridge into the Hill of the Cross, where we went for a walk.[3]

---

1 In her autobiography Nina Mescherskaya Krivosheina, writing of the little group with which she fled from Russia through Finland in 1919, has this to say of her first marriage: 'And there was myself and my first husband, Nikolay Ivanovich Levitsky. I do not propose to say much about him . . . Our life together was short (about four years), a disaster in every respect, and there seemed never to be so much as a ray of hope of its improving. Therefore it is better to forget it, to put a line through this unnecessary marriage, to obliterate with ashes everything that took place between us in life.' (N. A. Krivosheina, *Chetyre treti nashei zhizni* (*Four Thirds of our Life*) (Russkii Put', Moscow, 1999) See below, p. 265.
2 Nikolay Orlov (1892–1964), pianist, pupil of Konstantin Igumnov. Orlov left the Soviet Union in 1922 and had a successful career in the West as a Chopin specialist. See *Diaries*, vol. 1, p. 325.
3 The Kislovodsk valley is intersected at various points by spurs of the Dzhinal Ridge that watches

Alongside Little Red Riding-Hood other characters appeared, the most curious of whom was an Anarchist called Zmiyev. He came up to me in the foyer of the Grand Hotel and asked for a light for his cigarette. We fell to talking and he told me he had recently arrived from London. He was a young man, lively, with a sharp wit and a view of the world quite unlike any I had come across before. He described himself as an Anarchist Party member of the Petrograd Soviet of Workers, and this was of course a very piquant circumstance, although I am not now certain it was true. Many people simply regarded him as a charlatan, but I do not agree with this assessment. An opportunist, unquestionably. Anarchist, possibly so, at the very least he knew many astonishing things in this sphere. He became very attached to me, and for my part I was happy to spend time with him, as I was intrigued by his anarchist viewpoint – broadly speaking, that everything should be turned upside-down. Also, as I have said, he possessed a lively and trenchant wit.

In this way I passed much of my time in the company of Asya and Zmiyev and emerged somewhat from my previously somewhat isolated way of life. Now Asya would ask me to go for a walk with her, now the Anarchist would enliven me with details from the life of Kropotkin.[1] The weather and the air in Kislovodsk were so seductive that one was permanently drawn to be out of doors. Nevertheless, I spent two hours or so each day on the Andante of the Fourth Sonata, and devoted another hour and a half to Kant, absorbing the mind-bending complexities of his transcendental analysis. In the evening I often went to the Operetta in the Kursaal, where I had a seat reserved in the front row of the stalls. I had hardly ever been to the operetta before, having a thoroughgoing disdain for it, but now I became very interested and viewed the whole repertory with a critical eye less, needless to say, on account of the music than from the point of view of action and stagecraft.

And what was my verdict? That operetta composers don't really know how to write music. For the most part the drama is confined to those scenes where the dialogue is spoken, without music: the composers simply lack both the technique and the dramatic imagination to write music for them. There are places where the action does come alive and the drama takes wing, and sometimes there is a certain refinement (not of a very high order, be it said), but it could all be done a thousand times better. I even conceived the desire myself to write – not an operetta, I would not have the cheek to do

---

over the town to the east, forming a series of eminences in the town and its outskirts. One of these is known as the Hill of the Cross, because of the stone cross placed on its summit at the end of the eighteenth century to commemorate the first Russian visitors to the town.

1 Prince Pyotr Kropotkin (1842–1921), the leading advocate of Anarchist Communism, a commune-based model of society based on local associations independent of central control by the state or the monarch. Universally regarded (even by Lenin) as a saintly character, he was offered but declined the post of Minister of Education in the Provisional Government, and after the October Revolution spoke out cogently against the authoritarian excesses of the Bolshevik regime.

that – but a lively, gay opera with a light touch. For the time being I have laid this idea aside, but I will return to it. And along with this project, another: an opera on the life of anarchists: *The Anarchist*.

I talked a lot about this to Zmiyev, but we never reached a conclusion for the following reason: news was coming in from Petrograd of a Bolshevik uprising. The Government had barricaded itself inside the Winter Palace and was defending itself with cannon against the attacks of the Red Guards. Kerensky had cleverly contrived to slip away from Petrograd and was said to be on his way back at the head of his loyal troops, riding to the rescue. Later, the news was that the Bolsheviks were surrendering and the revolt had been put down. At this point things began to look not very good for anarchist Zmiyev, and losing no time he decamped to Rostov, where there were factories with anarchist cells. With him vanished not only our discussions about the opera but a hundred roubles that he had borrowed from me in dribs and drabs, and some of my linen which I had lent him while his was being laundered.

On the 26th I finished the Andante. Now I did not know whether to go to Petrograd or not. The premieres of the 'Classical' Symphony and the Violin Concerto were scheduled for a Ziloti concert on 4 November, and I would have to be in the capital for a week beforehand, but so far Ziloti had not said whether or not the concerts would take place. Eventually, on the 25th, a telegram arrived saying that the concert was postponed until December. That meant that my next engagement would be the piano recital in Moscow on 9 November.

On the 31st, therefore, I packed my case, bade farewell to sunshine and the glorious Kislovodsk climate (never again will I spend the autumn in Petrograd) and departed for Moscow. It was a little premature to leave on the 31st for an engagement on the 9th, but all direct trains were being taken off from the 1st of the month. The papers were full of disquieting news, there were Bolshevik uprisings everywhere, there was shooting in Moscow and Petrograd, but my hope was that everything would have settled down by the 9th.

My departure was quite a triumphant affair: no fewer than eleven people came to see me off, although admittedly several of them did so in order to give me letters to hand-carry, since the postal service was now completely unreliable. Mme Collini brought a bunch of white flowers. At Mineralnye Vody we immediately descended into the terrible grip of autumn: freezing fog, damp, and a species of mucous slime all over the platform. The train was supposed to wait two hours there. The news in the papers was astounding: events were rapidly developing in a quite different direction from anything that had gone before. The Bolsheviks were gaining the ascendancy everywhere, there was no word of Kerensky, and Moscow was under siege with crossfire from guns and rifles. I was in several minds whether or not to go:

whatever else it hardly seemed a propitious time for concerts. There was no doubt that the soldiers at the front would decide to come back to support the Bolsheviks, but this could be countered by strikes on all the railway lines, as had already been threatened, and should that happen I would find myself stuck for no purpose in a cold and dangerous Moscow. Would it not be better to turn back, while it was still not too late?

The matter was decided by the arrival of a train from Moscow, the guard full of alarming stories of fighting there and terrible disruptions all along the line. Even so, militating against a return to Kislovodsk was first of all my financial situation: as it was I had borrowed two and a half thousand from Mama, and if I cancelled my concerts I would have to extend the credit and go still further into her debt. Secondly, it was very awkward to have been seen off amid pomp, flowers and well-wishers, and to reappear the very next day in Kislovodsk. But on the other hand I was faced with the likelihood of not actually being able to give the concerts, which meant that any point there had been in going had now evaporated. And Kislovodsk beckoned so temptingly with its comfortable way of life, its peace and quiet and sunshine, all of which I particularly craved at this moment: hardly had I settled into my seat in the carriage when I was plunged into a morass of soldiers fighting with one another and smashing windows, political rallies in Mineralnye Vody, and the horrible autumn slush.

I decided to go back. And despite the contradictory nature of the factors contributing to the decision, it proved to have been the right course of action because, as very soon became apparent, turmoil and carnage erupted all over Russia, and it would have been idiotic for me to turn up in Moscow with my untimely concert. I got a porter to carry my bags over to a local train and bought a ticket back to Kislovodsk, where I arrived at four in the morning. I fell into the Grand Hotel, to find that my lovely room had already been taken, and I was given another one, not quite so good, next door. Mama was deliriously happy that I had returned, but I did not have much money and, as I did not wish to borrow any more, was forced to economise.

November

Mama gives me 200 roubles every ten days, which is just about enough, bearing in mind that, for instance, chocolate, which used to cost 1 rouble 20 kopecks a pound, is today 32 roubles. My return coincided with the end of the summer weather in Kislovodsk, light frosts began to appear with some snow, sometimes thawing only to appear again. But when the weather was clear, the air was clean and smelled amazingly delicious, and the sun poured down. God, how much sun I have lost in my life, living in Petrograd! How is it possible to live in such a dim, slush-bound city? Henceforth I shall go there only for concerts, and the rest of the time I shall take my freedom where there is sun and space!

News of the Bolsheviks: their victories and vandalism are spreading all over Russia. Slaughter on the streets of Moscow. A shell has fallen in the apartment I would have been staying in. This happened on the evening of the 3rd, the day I was due to have arrived in the morning, but of course I might never have got there. How clever of me not to have gone at all!

My state of mind. A strange serenity. Somehow I looked on it all as something inevitable, through which I must struggle and suffer and survive, and there seemed to be no single person whose fate would cause me grief. I did sometimes think of Nina Meshcherskaya, but she was now the wife of another. The disturbances, thank God, have not reached our doors, the Caucasus in general seems immune from them. How prudent had been my idea of settling in Kislovodsk! Here I stayed in spiritual equilibrium between the sun, the air, the Fourth Sonata – which I finished – Kant – which I also finished in November – Asya, walks, and games of chess with old Prince Urusov.

I succeeded in assimilating the general outline of Kant's thought, but the demands involved in understanding his concepts, the unfamiliar terminology he uses, and the extreme complexity of his constructions were all very great. In contrast, with what joy and reverence did I embark on my beloved Schopenhauer's *The World as Will and Representation*! In parallel with this, as soon as I finished the Fourth Sonata, I started work on 10 November making detailed sketches for *Seven, They Are Seven*. The shadowy sketches I had made in September, whose bones nonetheless survived intact down to the last note, now started to be filled out with harmonies, and the complete body of the work gradually came to life in all its texture and instrumentation. I had to work slowly, as there were tremendous difficulties to overcome which tested to the limit all my powers, but the work moved steadily forward.

In the meantime the unrest all over the country caused the cancellation of one concert after another, and by the end of the month I was firmly embedded in Kislovodsk.

There was a fleeting reappearance by the Anarchist, who had already succeeded in getting to Petrograd and slipping out again through the cordons thrown up all over Russia. He enfolded me in an embrace: I still did not know whether he was a real anarchist or a fraud, but I did take pleasure in his attitude to me. He said he would give me back my money, but disappeared again without giving me back anything.

On the 24th I was able to move back into my large sunny room in the hotel. The dawn chorus in the rays of the rising sun.

Elections to the Constituent Assembly. (Venus–Jupiter–Sirius–The Moon).

At the end of the month the atmosphere in Kislovodsk grew tense: the Bolsheviks were engaged in a fight to the death with the Cossacks on the

Don, their implacable and resourceful enemies. It was said that the armies of the Red Guard were converging on them from all sides with heavy artillery, and were this dam to be breached, our Kislovodsk home would be engulfed in the benighted tide.

December

Finished the sketches of *Seven, They Are Seven*.

Preliminary work on the new Concerto. The Glazunov Concerto and my Third Concerto.

My stories – all in all they are turning out not badly. I must finish writing them.

The middle of month was a bad patch: I was discontented and achieved little. A sketch of the Third Concerto, plan for the finale (*movimento*) and another plan (a dance).

Visit of Hartmann,[1] bringing manuscript paper. At last! Started to make a fair copy of the score, enormous work but enjoyable and not demanding.

Christmas. Cold and clear.

The month's end passed in transcribing *Seven, They Are Seven* and contemplation of an engrossing new idea: Lina Collini mentioned in passing one day that she was planning to leave Russia for America – and it suddenly struck me that there was no need for me to stay in Russia either. In the flow of idle chatter this tiny spark was seemingly extinguished almost at once, but in fact what appeared at the time to be no more than a passing remark proved to be explosive material that in an instant flared up into a conflagration.

To go to America! Of course! Here was wretchedness; there life brimming over. Here, slaughter and barbaric rhetoric; there, cultivated life. Here, shabby concerts in Kislovodsk; there, New York, Chicago! No time for hesitation. In the spring I will go. If only America does not turn against a Russia that has now abandoned the war! Such was the flag under which I greeted the New Year. Surely it will not disappoint my hopes?

---

1 Foma (Thomas de) Hartmann (1885–1956), composer, pianist and conductor. A student of Yesipova, Taneyev and Arensky, his compositions in Russia tended towards the Nationalist style and were much influenced by Musorgsky, but he seems to have privately harboured more radical ambitions, because in 1919 he emigrated, first to Paris and then to New York, where he fundamentally changed his style to embrace polytonal and polyrhythmic techniques. Hartmann had issued the invitation from the Petrograd branch of the IRMS to perform the First Piano Concerto in January 1916. Not to be confused with the German composer Karl Amadeus Hartmann. See *Diaries*, vol. 1, p. 749.

1918

Beginning of January

Saw in the New Year at Lina's (before that with Mama). Interesting company, fireworks,[1] very jolly.

Project to go to America growing in potency and resolve – maybe I won't wait for the spring but will go as soon as possible, the sooner the better. Problem is the fighting on the Don (Bolsheviks against Cossacks), which one has to cross at some point, and the strife in Petrograd (because of the Constituent Assembly).[2] I cannot leave the country without making a trip to Petrograd first.

At the beginning of January, I worked on *Seven, They Are Seven*. Corrections.

---

1   Or possibly crackers – Russians use the same word, 'strelba' ('shooting'), for both these New Year entertainments.
2   At the beginning of January 1918 a democratically elected Constituent Assembly for Russia was still the rallying dream of every element except one in the great but fragmented liberal–intellectual–revolutionary nexus that had united to topple the autocracy almost a year earlier. Belief in and support for the Assembly extended from the Constitutional Democrats (Kadets) on the right through the Mensheviks and Social Revolutionaries (SRs) to the moderate Bolsheviks on the left. Only the extreme Bolshevik faction (led by Lenin) was not in favour of it, regarding it as the redundant halfway house of bourgeois parliamentary democracy. But since the ostensible justification for the Bolshevik seizure of power had been the ensuring of elections to a Constituent Assembly that they had manoeuvred the Provisional Government into appearing to oppose, Lenin's party dictatorship could not actually cancel the elections, which duly took place in the weeks after 12 November and resulted in the Bolshevik Party gaining just 24 per cent of the votes cast, the largest party being the SRs with 38 per cent of the vote. Lenin's solution was twofold: first to harry, intimidate and stall the process of convening the first meeting of the Assembly, scheduled for 28 November, and second to allow it to meet once and then close it down by force. This is indeed what happened: the first and only meeting of the Assembly took place on 5 January, by which time the Bolshevik Government had placed Petrograd under martial law and banned public demonstrations. A large demonstration organised by the Union for the Defence of the Constituent Assembly nevertheless marched to the Tauride Palace, being fired on by Government snipers from the roofs of buildings along the way, provoking one of Gorky's bitterest and most outspoken editorials in *Novaya Zhizn* in which he drew an overt parallel between the Tsarist massacre of innocent and unarmed demonstrators on Bloody Sunday 1905 and the Bolshevik massacre almost to the day thirteen years later. The Assembly met at 4 p.m. on 5 January, threw out by 237 votes to 146 a Bolshevik motion to approve the Lenin-drafted Declaration of the Rights of the Working Man, adjourned at 4.40 a.m. on the morning of the 6th, after which on Lenin's orders the Red Guards locked and bolted the Tauride Palace. By the time the Deputies returned the following day to continue the session the Government had issued a decree dissolving the Assembly. (Grateful acknowledgement to Orlando Figes's *A People's Tragedy: The Russian Revolution 1891–1924* (Jonathan Cape, London, 1996), for the background information used in writing this note.)

10 [23] January[1]

Today I bought this notebook.[2]

11 [24] January

Baltimore – centre of culinary art.
   Boston – intellectual centre.
   Philadelphia – old culture; Chicago – new culture.
   San Francisco – cosmopolitan.

12 [25] January

Finished the corrections.

13 [26] January

Finished the score of *Seven, They Are Seven*.
   Read through 'The Poodle'. Liked it very much, improved a few phrases here and there.

14 [27] January

Memories of Nina a little dimmed, but fond (today is her name-day).
   Thoughts of a new story, but as yet with no details; too soon to start writing, although the desire to do so is keen.
   Read a book on chiromancy.[3] It was interesting, but still more interesting were the attempts to base it on serious historical foundations.

15 [28] January

Began going to Tsints[4] to play the piano there (an hour a day from half-past eleven to half-past twelve).

---

1 On 18 January 1918 the Council of People's Commissars (Sovnarkom) issued a decree that Russia would, with effect from the last day of the month, adopt the Gregorian calendar. The next day after Thursday 31 January would therefore be Thursday 14 February. Entries for the year 1918 in this translation of Prokofiev's *Diaries* are dated in both old and new style, the latter in square brackets.
2 The notebook in which this part of the *Diaries* is written.
3 Foretelling a person's future by interpreting the lines on the hand.
4 Tsintsinator, a chemist's shop in Kislovodsk with an upstairs room containing an upright piano, where in the summer of 1912 Prokofiev had composed much of the Second Piano Sonata, Op. 14. See *Diaries*, vol. 1, p. 234.

'The dreaded Empress, called the Plague, Advances to our very door.'[1] The first sign of it is in Pyatigorsk, but so far seems less dramatic than its appearance in Trapezund.[2]

16 [29] January

1915: first performance of *The Ugly Duckling*.
   1916: first performance of *Ala and Lolli*.
   Began catching up on my Diary (to August)
   Practised at Lina's, where the atmosphere is more congenial than at the chemist's.
   Made some refinements to the theme of the second movement of the Concerto, and finished it.

17 [30] January

Flute register – an octave higher than the female voice.
   Carried on with the Concerto.[3]

18 [31] January

'American impresarios include a slew of penalties in their contracts and there will inevitably be one of them that will trip you up.'
   Podpevsky.
   When the flute is accompanying, make scale flourishes for one or two octaves.
   Lively (rhythmic) music as a background for action on stage, almost to make an ensemble of the two.

19 January [1 February]

A theme: a gentleman, recognising his double in a dog. A priest tries to grab the dog but gets caught. A bad lookout. How to finish it?[4]

---

1 Quotation from Pushkin's *A Feast in Time of Plague*, his 'Little Tragedy' consisting of a free translation of a long 1816 verse play, *City of the Plague* by the Edinburgh writer John Wilson (1785–1854). Pushkin was inspired by the psychological power of Wilson's portrayal of a group of desperate revellers careless of the danger and misery all around them in seventeenth-century plague-devastated London; seventy-three years later the images resonated again in the mind of the twelve-year-old Prokofiev, who composed an opera based on Pushkin's poem. Only a fragment of the overture survives.
2 Trabzond (or Trebizond), city on the Black Sea coast of north-eastern Turkey.
3 The Piano Concerto No. 3.
4 The story appears to have remained embryonic.

Instead of working at the piano, thought about the first movement of the Concerto away from the piano. Extraordinary how much clearer everything is without it. The detailed plan and general shape of the music of the first movement are almost complete.

20 January [2 February]

(Serbian passport.) This makes the journey to America more of a real possibility.

21 January [3 February]

(Headache, slept badly at night, Pyramidon no help.)
For ten days now no news has come from Petrograd except that Lenin has been killed. Can only assume that something momentous is happening there, perhaps the fall of the Bolshevik Government.

22 January [4 February]

Changed 4,000 roubles of Mama's into 1,065 gold francs. I am glad to have done it: the value of paper money will fall still further. Even so the price is (exactly) double what it was before the war.

23 January [5 February]

Got a superb atlas from Khodzhayev,[1] and studied the street plan of New York. Why are there two Fifth Avenues?

24 January [6 February]

Since the Bolsheviks apparently believe everyone in Kislovodsk to be a millionaire, their supporters are today calling for all millionaires and bourgeoisie to be eliminated. This *Kinderfest* is supposed to happen tomorrow. No one believes it; everyone finds these constant rumours simply boring.
Went to Pyatigorsk.
Apparently one can get to America via Persia.

---

1 Prokofiev became friendly with the Khodzhayev family in Kislovodsk.

25 January [7 February]

Astounding news: Constantinople has fallen to the English. The English are at the Black Sea. Shattering effect. Impossible to absorb all these events. It could affect the way I travel to America.

26 January [8 February]

Rumours that the English have landed in Batum.
   A good composition session on the Concerto.
   Sarovich is definitely going to America. He is a Romanian, thirty to thirty-five years old, and quite an interesting person. He owns a casino in a Romanian resort called Sinaia[1] (but is not at all like the Casino Director from my *Gambler*, much gentler and more elegant, no hint of the catastrophic about him). Up till now I have been the one urging on Lina and Sarovich, but now that Constantinople has fallen my resolve has faltered, while they have taken over the leadership and insist that we must leave at the earliest possible opportunity.
   Apparently the English venture is a myth, but it is true that the Bolsheviks are advancing on Pyatigorsk.
   A headache, but not a terribly bad one; I don't know what brought it on, but I don't have any Pyramidon.

27 January [9 February]

At half-past four this morning the Grand Hotel was searched, because of an officers' organisation in Pyatigorsk. It was not a frightening procedure.
   Four soldiers. Correct behaviour. Cigar case. About the pistol.
   Sarovich re travelling via Constantinople. His proposal that I should give concerts on the Riviera. I give it serious consideration, but is he in any position to make guarantees? I tell him I believe the attitude of the French is hostile.

28 January [10 February]

Composed the first variation in the second movement of the Concerto.
   The news about Constantinople is confirmed, or at least repeated. Kolchak?[2]

---

1   A fashionable resort in the Carpathian mountains, much favoured by the Bucharest social élite. The Romanian royal family used to spend its summers there in the Summer Palace built by King Charles in 1880.
2   Admiral Alexander Kolchak (1874–1920) was one of the most distinguished Russian naval officers during the First World War. Initially in command of the Baltic Fleet, in 1916 he was

Reading geography – a gymnasium textbook. An excellent edition with illustrations, a great pleasure to read.

29 January [11 February]

To Pyatigorsk to see about a Serbian passport, second time. The whole day. Mama has started learning English.

30 January [12 February]

Second variation.

In the evening, a long and earnest conversation with Lina: via Constantinople or Vladivostok? And which would be better for me: to start with the Riviera, where Sarovich has said he will organise concerts, or go straight to New York?

31 January [13 February]

Finished the second variation (only the orchestra; the solo part is merely conceived).

Started 'Beethoven'.[1]

The news about Constantinople is turning out to be a bluff.

Sarovich is turning up the pressure to go to America and is making valiant attempts to persuade me of my guarantee of success there. All that would be needed is a little money, enough to live on independently for the first month there.

I am now making plans to leave on the 15th, old style.

1 [14] February

Did no work today.

News about the fate of Kaledin's[2] rebellion. But my thoughts are fixed on America.

---

appointed Commander-in-Chief of the Black Sea Fleet, from which position in February 1917 he declared in support of Kerensky and the Provisional Government. Sent to America to plan a joint Allied operation aimed at taking control of the Bosphorus, he was in Japan on his way home at the time of the October Revolution, and foreseeing Russia's departure from the war offered his services to the British Navy. Later he would join the anti-Bolshevik Socialist Government established in Omsk, where he seized power in a coup d'état to become Supreme Ruler. Eventually yielding power to the Siberian warlord Semyonov, in 1920 he was betrayed to the Bolsheviks in Irkutsk by the Czech Legion and executed.

1   Presumably another short story that seems not to have survived.
2   General Alexey Kaledin, a distinguished cavalry officer, had been named Ataman of the anti-revolutionary Don Cossack forces opposing the Red Army on the Don. After a bitter struggle

2 [15] February

Beginnings of a headache (stayed up late playing chess) but it did not develop.

Am learning the Fourth Sonata and practising the Third. Playing through some Chopin pieces.

3 [16] February

Worked a little on the first-movement development.

4 [17] February

Wrote 'Beethoven'.

Was challenged to play the Chopin F sharp Nocturne at Safonov's. Some bafflement, as it bore no relation to the way they were accustomed to hearing the piece. Guarded approval. The old man accompanied me out to the hall and invited me to stop by before my departure for a 'talk about America'.

(An idea for an autograph book of everyone I meet: a book of complaints.)

Two hundred and fifty criminals have escaped from the Pyatigorsk gaol. With a mob like that on the loose, especially after the disarmament of the intelligentsia, our very existence is threatened.[1]

5 [18] February

A hundred and fifty of them have already been recaptured.

Having played some Chopin and realised that I can do so successfully, I decided to learn some repertoire for America: four Waltzes, two Nocturnes, two Mazurkas, two Etudes and a Ballade. It's a pity I cannot find the B flat minor Sonata.[2]

Safonov has had a stroke.

---

the Cossacks were overwhelmed by a combination of superior forces and the hostility of most of the local population. On 29 January [11 February] Kaledin as Ataman convened the Military Government of the Don and made the following announcement: 'Our position is hopeless. The population not only does not support us, it is actively hostile. I do not desire further needless sacrifices, nor the purposeless shedding of blood, and therefore propose to resign my command ... In my heart I must obey the inviolable rule of the officer's code of honour: if one is not able to cleanse the stain of offence with the blood of the offender, one must atone for it with one's own life.' General Kaledin then left the room and shot himself.

[1] By the end of December 1917, as Orlando Figes (*op. cit.*) points out, the new Government had gaoled so many of its erstwhile comrades as political prisoners – 'enemies of the people' – that they were obliged to release common criminals in order to make room.

[2] Prokofiev had studied this Sonata intensively with his teacher Anna Yesipova at the Conservatoire. See *Diaries*, vol. 1, pp. 292, 308, 315 and *passim*.

6 [19] February

Some friends of the Tolstoys have arrived from Moscow, the journey took them five days, and one woman spent thirteen days *en route*. Question: how many days will it take me? At present there is no way to get a ticket from here either to Rostov or to Tsaritsyn.[1]

I am greatly enjoying playing Chopin.

Have put Piano Concerto No. 3 aside for the time being.

PRINCIPLES GOVERNING MENTAL STATE WHEN TRAVELLING

How great is the difference between a long journey filled with anxiety, frustration and resentment, and one undertaken in an all-encompassing spirit of contentment! The latter state may not be easy to achieve at first, but as time goes on all one's efforts must be directed to keeping up spirits, working towards this end as to a difficult, but rewarding task, looking on it ultimately as a kind of game. To maintain good spirits throughout the entire journey – that is the goal! The heart must be firmly under lock and key, and all external circumstances regarded with impassivity. This will help enormously in avoiding fruitless anxiety: it is not in one's power to do anything to help the situation in any case.

It is the contemplation of a joyful future that brings consolation: time will inevitably pass and the moment will come when one can look back on it all as having happened in the past. Fix this moment in the imagination.

Long delays and interruptions which seem intolerable because they prolong the journey time are in fact indispensable components of the traveller's lot. The fact is, the journey consists mainly of them; if it were not so, 1,200 versts[2] in eight days (200 hours) amounts to 6 versts an hour, which is impossible.

7 [20] February

Difficulty of making concrete plans for America. The Caucasus is an island surrounded by the raging sea which is Russia, a tangle of impenetrable layers. Somewhere in the far beyond there are foreign countries, from which no word now reaches us, only distant memories. (Develop this concept as a point of departure to understand the difficulty of my plans.)

Prince Urusov is eighty-two years old. +4° is the optimum temperature for preserving meat, therefore he sleeps in a room kept at +4° and advises me not to complain about my room being cold.

---

1   The important railheads on respectively the Don and the Volga. One cannot go north from the Caucasus by rail without passing through one or the other. Tsaritsyn became Stalingrad in 1925, and Volgograd in 1961.
2   The verst = 1.06 kilometres.

8 [21] February

Mama's room has been searched.

When Lina was talking about how important success in America would be for me, I replied that the only reason success there was important to me was the external, specifically financial, perspective. Internally it would be of minimal value, since the musical perceptions of the Americans are not sufficiently refined to cause me to pay much attention to them.

9 [22] February

In proportion as my plans for America, departure for which is now fixed for the 15th, become increasingly elaborate, my interest declines in all activities not directly connected thereto: the Third Piano Concerto, Schopenhauer, writing my stories. However, I assiduously play Chopin for two or three hours a day, this being one half of my American programme – which is working out well, as well as the Fourth Sonata, which I plan to leave in Moscow with the publishers and therefore must by then know firmly by heart.

10 [23] February

Examined with interest a hundred-dollar bill, a currency with which I shall in future have much to do. We have grown so used to the fragile value of our currency that it is strange to see money whose value is practically absolute.

11 [24] February

I am concerned for Mama, who will be left alone until the autumn. But she can stay with the Nikolskys in Yessentuki, where she will be in a nice house with a family in the middle of a Cossack *stanitsa*, safe from attacks from the 'Maximalists', as the foreign newspapers describe our Bolsheviks.[1]

Lina has been asking why I have changed. I replied that 'tout m'embête',[2]

---

1 Strictly speaking, the Bolsheviki ('Maximalists', from 'bolshinstvo', 'majority') were one faction of the Russian Social Democratic Labour Party, which split in two at its second Party Congress in 1903, when Lenin's 'hard' faction, based on exclusive professional revolutionary membership and strict centralised control, gained a slight but inconclusive majority over Julius Martov's 'soft', 'menshinstvo' ('minority') faction, which wanted membership of the party to remain open to non-professional sympathisers. Unfortunately for historians there was also a 'Maximalist' faction within the rural/peasant-orientated Social Revolutionary Party, ideologically significantly at variance with the urban/proletariat orientation of both wings of the RSDLP. This confusing fact, along with the nihilistic whiff of totalitarian implacability still inseparably associated with the Russian word, led to the gradual abandonment of the otherwise accurate English version by foreign commentators.
2 'Everything annoys me'.

and indeed, I am wholly focused on leaving. Everyone here in Kislovodsk bores me, even Lina.

12 [25] February

Obtained, finally, the necessary stamp. Had to spend the whole day going to Pyatigorsk and back. Lina said she was going to travel in a sleeping-car together with the Kokovtsovs[1] and some other super-bourgeois high-ups, and was planning to take her furs with her. I said that 'chacun s'arrange comme il peut'[2] and the very last thing I would do would be to travel in this carriage, which was almost bound to be attacked and robbed.

13 [26] February

Lina is highly indignant at my announcement ('chacun s'arrange', etc.). We ended up by quarrelling and I said *au revoir* until New York.

14 [27] February

Safonov has died.

Preparations for leaving. I am told that the best way to start the journey is by ordinary local train, as not all of these are *teplushki*,[3] some of them have proper railway carriages with compartments, but not nearly as many people try to travel in them. I have decided to travel via Tsaritsyn.

15 [28] February

At three o'clock in the middle of the night there was an earthquake. I was woken by a powerful and frightening sensation of shaking, glasses rattling, and at first I did not know what was happening. Then I thought it must be an explosion on a floor below. At once, hearing the alarm being raised all over the hotel, I hurried on some clothes. All the residents poured out into the corridors, where it soon became clear that there had been some powerful underground shocks. A lot of people stayed outside the building, fearing stronger ones to come. After half an hour I went back to bed.

My departure has been postponed, as I have been offered a sleeping-car berth, not in a bourgeois train but in a semi-Soviet one, and cheaper than the 1,500-rouble cost of the former. I have not seen Lina at all.

---

1   Count Vladimir Kokovtsov had been the Prime Minister of the Tsarist Government from 1911 until 1914. See *Diaries*, vol. 1, p. 318.
2   'Every man for himself.'
3   A *teplushka* was a minimally equipped heated goods van, more like a cattle truck in which people could travel.

16 February [1 March]

Safonov's funeral.

Obtained a document from the Soviet of Workers' Deputies qualifying me for assisted passage.

Spent the day with Khodzhayev, practised the piano for my appearance the following day.

Sarovich asked if I would travel with him and Lina if there were to be a free berth in their carriage. I said no.

Krasilnikov has proposed arranging a concert in the Grand Hotel before I leave. 'Why not earn a bit of money for the journey, and at the same time give us the pleasure of hearing you?' I consented. I'll play on Sunday evening, as it probably will not be possible to arrange it before then.

17 February [2 March]

Terrible amount of rushing about: leaving, the sleeping-car, the concert.

Lina and Sarovich due to leave at eight o'clock.

Headache, not a particularly severe one though, from all the pressure.

In the evening, my appearance in a charity concert in the Kursaal, playing Chopin (my first time in public not playing my own compositions). Played quite well. Supper afterwards.

Very jolly time with Lucy and Liza Khodzhaeva, and got quite drunk, a rare event. Principle of maintaining a refined demeanour.

18 February [3 March]

Sarovich and Lina, who should have left yesterday, did not do so: their carriage did not arrive because of the fighting in Armavir.[1]

Rumours that the Germans have occupied Petrograd.

At half-past five I played my concert in the Grand Hotel. There were not many people present, about a hundred, but the room would not have accommodated more than a hundred and fifty in any case. It was a great success, and receipts amounted to 500 roubles.

19 February [4 March]

Lina's departure. I decided to go to see her off (a formal courtesy) and found her in her compartment five minutes before departure. Our farewells were

---

1 A city near Krasnodar, on the left bank of the Kuban river. The name comes from the original settlement by Armenians. The town was the scene of particularly brutal fighting that continued until the Red Army's defeat of General Denikin's White Army in 1920 brought an effective end to the Civil War.

brief but affectionate, on the surface not very meaningful, but I could not help noticing the joy in her voice as she thanked me for coming. After she had gone I felt sad. I don't know her address in Moscow, and she doesn't know mine.

There are rumours that a decree has been issued calling for universal military conscription, more evidence of the escalating war against the invading Germans.

20 February [5 March]

Felt down and did no work. Waited for a postcard from Lina, but none came. I am longing to get away.

The Germans have occupied Pskov and Revel.[1] Also, so one hears, Petrograd. But at least I will get as far as Moscow, and from there I can go to Vladivostok. If I could just get 5,000 from the publishers, and a few letters of recommendation, for example from Chaliapin, Balmont and Koussevitzky.

Spent the day with the Khodzhayevs.

21 February [6 March]

Everywhere there are announcements about the new-style calendar.

No, I have got to get away. I should have left when Lina did. Surely to goodness a single man, not affiliated to any political party or caste, can manage to get himself to Moscow and from there to the border, especially if he has a passport. There is an International Company car leaving tomorrow; there's no hope of getting a berth, but I am definitely going, even if I have to stand in the corridor.

I have one more paper from the Soviet of Soldiers' Deputies confirming that I have the right to travel unimpeded to Moscow, even in the event of general mobilisation.

22 February [7 March]

Quite by chance I came into possession of a ticket for a berth. Mama gave me 500 roubles, as a result of which I have a total of 600 in my pocket. Even if I do not manage to get as far as Moscow, I shall turn off and go straight to Vladivostok and thereafter support myself with concerts.

Spent a somewhat anxious night but in the morning was cheerful and full of energy. I was sorry to leave Mama.

At eight o'clock in the evening I set out on my long and far-flung travels.

---

1 The Russian name for Tallinn, capital of Estonia, at the time still a part of the Russian empire.

But I could have no certainty that circumstances (such as mobilisation, failure to acquire funds) might not conspire to force me back again. My suit.

23 February [8 March]

The train left at two in the morning and waited twenty-four hours at Mineralnye Vody, on account of the fighting at Tikhoretsk.[1] Apparently the train in which Lina was travelling had come under fire, but managed to continue on its way, the passengers taking cover by lying on the floor. At 2 a.m. on the second day we were told we would be waiting in Mineralnye Vody for another two days, but an hour later, unexpectedly, we began to move. The fighting had ceased. Not only that, but we would be going via Rostov, which would save two whole days over the Tsaritsyn route. Ours would be the first train to get through Rostov in a month.

Headache from travelling, but it passed off.

24 February [9 March]

Astonishingly, we are moving at a cracking rate, just like the good old days, even though we have twice the normal complement of passengers and have to sleep head to toe, two in a bed. Apparently there is no direct threat to Moscow at the present time, nor has Petrograd yet fallen to the Germans. I begin to think that I shall soon be in America. We had our papers checked seven times, but as soon as I showed my document from the Soviet of Workers' Deputies I was not troubled.

In the evening, Rostov, where I learned that all the passengers on Lina's train had been thrown off it at Tikhoretsk, but then had somehow managed to get themselves to Rostov and a lot of them were still staying in a hotel there. Just in case, I went to the hotel, and the first person I saw was Lina. The decision she has now come to is to abandon the difficult and complicated journey to America in favour of an easier alternative that has only just emerged as a possibility: Romania. Romania has concluded a separate peace with Germany and she would soon be able to go there directly. I went back to the station, and half an hour later my train left. Lina was lost to me.

25 February [10 March]

Thanks to a bribe of a thousand roubles our carriage avoided being requisitioned in Rostov and was coupled to a goods train designated as a 'Deputies'

---

1 Another city in the Krasnodar Region.

train. As a result we are rolling along in great comfort, with nobody trying to force their way in, but at a speed of no more than 200 versts a day.

26 February [11 March]

Wrote to Lina (dating it the previous day).

Daylight and sunshine chased away my gloomy thoughts. Once again America drew me powerfully to her. Before me lay such a range of possibilities, dependent on events, the presence of the Germans, what might happen in the capital cities I had not seen for so long, that nothing concrete could be hoped for, nor indeed regretted: 'rien n'est certain'.

27 February [12 March]

I have worked out Lina's psychology and come to terms with it. She had found the idea of coming with me to America attractive, but when she reached Rostov she had access to all the foreign consulates and began to realise that she might contrive to end up in her native Romania. At that point the whole question resolved itself into a clear and simple choice. On the one hand, a difficult and dangerous journey with a man who might well love her but might equally well vanish at any moment, on top of which there would be continual problems with money running out, and things would have to be sold. On the other, a trouble-free return to her native Romania, the source of all her wealth, not to mention a little gentle flattery from the snake in the grass.[1] It was a clear and simple decision that she had to take, and my probing questioning of her was simply mistimed and misplaced: I was debating abstractions, of the depth of our feelings for one another, while she was confronting the reality of things.

28 February [13 March]

We are moving more slowly now, and stopping at nights. My mood has regained its equilibrium, my thoughts are bent towards America.

A letter to Polina Podolskaya in Taganrog: 'Dear friend, I am writing to you from an International carriage, strange as this may seem, on the way from Kislovodsk to Moscow. Since getting a letter from you several months ago that began with the words "I am writing to give you my address" but ended without giving any address, I have not had any news of you. Do drop me a line to Moscow, Kudrinskaya Square 1, Apartment 38. If your letter does not reach me there, they will forward it to wherever I am. Keep well and happy, and accept my cordial best wishes. S. P.'

---

[1] The 'snake in the grass' is, we must assume, Lina Collini's compatriot Sarovich.

1 [14] March

Slowly crawling towards Moscow. Headache from being on the train.

2 [15] March

We arrived at seven in the morning. Impressions of Moscow. The tram, and reactions to my suit. The Metropole Hotel and the Bolshoy Theatre. General feeling of depression, arising from a number of things besides the music situation: people sent into exile, the anarchists. Koshetz, and immediately a completely different atmosphere. She had a concert today including the *Akhmatova Songs*, in which I accompanied her. She suggested I move to her apartment. Her husband. His piano. I had not expected him to be so young or so insignificant. I have fallen right into the nexus. The concert, and Koshetz's joy. Although essentially I had written the songs for her, I could not just suddenly, off the cuff, get right to the heart of them. We hardly rehearsed at all. The performance was not completely together (the first song), but as it was Koshetz, of course it was good. Amazed by my sudden *entrée* into the feverish epicentre of artistic life.

3 [16] March

Spent the night at Koshetz's. *Bliny*[1] in Zamoskvorechye.[2] On the way there Koshetz's husband was anxious to draw our attention to the brains, spattered all over a fence, of a robber who had been shot the previous night. In the evening Koshetz would have dragged me out to a theatre, but I enjoyed lolling about on her divinely luxurious low, soft, pale-grey sofa with a mass of cushions and a conveniently placed electric lamp, reading Asafyev and a fabulous book about South America, smoking good Egyptian cigarettes and talking to her husband about the Postnikovs' American plans.[3]

4 [17] March

Again spent the night at Koshetz's. Koshetz in *Yevgeny Onegin*. The Letter Scene. Girlish naivety and maidenly blushes in place of drama. Very good,

---

1   The small, round pancakes with a variety of fillings such as meat, caviare, fish, originally eaten during Maslenitsa, 'butter days', the feast days that traditionally precede the dietary rigours of Lent.
2   The historic part of the centre of Moscow just the other side of the Moscow river from the southern walls of the Kremlin.
3   Probably Alexander Postnikov (1865–1940), a wealthy (his money came from cattle-breeding) connoisseur and collector who had established a well-known Moscow antique shop called 'Byloye' ('The Past').

except for the heaviness of her figure which, however, in the Letter Scene she managed to conceal.

Rumours circulate about Japan becoming an ally of Germany and America coming to the aid of Russia against Japan. Such a development would close off that exit route, whatever might be worked out with the Postnikovs.

5 [18] March

Went to Russian Musical Editions. Op. 27[1] is published. Met an American there, but his principal consultant is a conservatively inclined critic called Kurov,[2] so quite hopeless, no prospect of anything there. In any case, his project would only start in the summer, and I need something now, and above all without tying myself down in a contract. For all that there is no real business to be done with him, it still might be possible to get advice and general orientation.

Resolved to develop my power of memory.

6 [19] March

Bought a book of mnemonics and will learn a little poem each day, repeating its predecessors.

Received 500 for the Piano Sonata No. 4.

The sun is shining in Moscow and there are crowds of people out walking, some of them even fashionably dressed. Discovered an excellent and inexpensive vegetarian restaurant, as I don't wish to dine at Koshetz's.

The Futurists have all but come to blows with the Anarchists. I should much like to see Mayakovsky. Of course, I am not a Futurist, but I enjoy associating with them, and they would very much like to consider me one of them.

7 [20] March

At eight o'clock in the morning I telephoned to Petrograd and spoke to Eleonora. She was thrilled. Begged me to come to Petrograd, promised exit permission for me any day I wanted through Lunacharsky[3] (because of the

---

1 *Five Poems of Anna Akhmatova.*
2 Nikolay Kurov (1882–?).
3 Anatoly Lunacharsky (1875–1933) had joined the Russian Social Democratic Labour Party while still a student at Zurich University, and sided with Lenin's Bolshevik faction in the knife-edge vote against Martov's Mensheviks at the Second Party Congress of the RSDLP. After spending time with Gorky in the latter's School for Socialist Workers in Capri, he returned to

evacuation it is impossible to leave the city even in a desperately overcrowded *teplushka*). There seems to be no sign of the Germans, and no scarcity of sugar and flour. Perhaps I really should go there next week. There are many possibilities for America I could explore.

Lunch with Koussevitzky, a good spread in spite of the famine. *Seven, They Are Seven*. His impression: the world has never seen such a score before, but amazingly he believes everything in it will sound right. As for America, he does not recommend any association with Postnikov. Evidently I will get paid for *The Gambler*, and possibly very well paid. Went for a walk with Koshetz. Her relationship with me. Rachmaninoff has been dragged off to live in Switzerland.[1] The narrow-minded bourgeois attitudes of her family, his family, the man himself,[2] compared with my lack of such attitudes. She expects something more from our relationship.

8 [21] March

Proofs of the Piano Sonata No. 3 and *Visions Fugitives*.

Spoke slightingly of Kurov to Postnikov. He thinks the total cost of getting to America and setting myself up there will be 6,000 roubles. Equipping myself: concert tails, visiting cards and two jackets $100, $85, $60 and $45, linen and shoes $110: total $400. Living expenses (modest) $200 a month. I think as long as I have $1,000 I can go.

9 [22] March

Met Sabaneyev (at Koshetz's). Her husband, relishing the encounter, deliberately introduced us to one another while we were in the act of shaking hands. I immediately turned and left the room. But Sabaneyev stayed to dinner. Despite all his efforts to engage me in conversation I refused to utter a word, and when he came up to say goodbye I proffered my hand bound in a handkerchief.

A celebration (unexpected) in my honour by the Futurists at the Poets

---

Russia in 1917 and was appointed by Lenin Commissar of Enlightenment (Narodny Kommissar Prosveshcheniya, Narkompros) in the first Soviet Government, a post he held until 1929. He was extremely influential, having responsibility for education, a portfolio in which he achieved great success, notably in a huge increase in literacy. Lunacharsky was an example, so rare as to be almost unique, of an educated and civilised senior Bolshevik politician with a genuine appreciation of, and desire to support, the living traditions of Russian art.

1   This seems to be a misunderstanding, perhaps a slip of the pen for Scandinavia. Rachmaninoff and his immediate family had left Petrograd for Stockholm on 23 December (Old Style) 1917, taking advantage of an unexpected invitation for a concert tour in neutral Scandinavia, and from Stockholm went on to Copenhagen, which remained his base until he booked (with borrowed money) a steamer passage from Oslo to New York in November 1918. See below, pp. 351–2.
2   Referring to Rachmaninoff and his wife, his first cousin, the former Natalya Satina.

Café. Mayakovsky, Kamensky,[1] Burlyuk. The President of Planet Earth.[2] Their connection with anarchists and general behaviour in Moscow has been very apparent recently, and has upset most, practically all, people. My own opinion is that they are people of fresh and interesting ideas, even if there is often an element of coarseness and fraudulence about them.[3]

10 [23] March

Many lunches, dinners and suppers in private houses. These are parts the famine has not yet reached. Moscow has taken me joyously to its heart.
The three paths of my creativity.

11 [24] March

Lunch with Koussevitzky. Talk of Rachmaninoff in Denmark, the lack of success he is having with his concerts because of the war with Germany. His straitened circumstances.
Played *Seven, They Are Seven* for Balmont and Koussevitzky. Walking through the side streets arm in arm with Balmont, I passionately explaining

---

1 Vasily Kamensky (1884–1961), Futurist poet, close associate of Khlebnikov and Burlyuk, and one of the founders of the Hylaea Cubo-futurist group of poets. He was also one of the first aviators in Russia, having acquired a Blériot monoplane as early as 1911, which he enthusiastically piloted far and wide across the country promoting the Futurist message of speed and the aesthetics of machinery.
2 This was Velimir (Viktor) Khlebnikov (1885–1922), to whom his colleagues attached the sobriquet (and indeed emblazoned it on his coffin), 'President of Planet Earth and King of Time Velimir I', when he died of famine near Astrakhan in 1922, having refused any kind of collaboration with the new government authorities. The Presidential appellation was due not so much to megalomania as to Khlebnikov's dream of an anarchic society where everyone would be president, a world government of artists, scientists and intellectuals devoted to counteracting the evils fostered by political states. He was of the most extreme and (with Mayakovsky) most considerable of the Russian avant-garde writers of the early twentieth century; Khlebnikov's interests extended beyond the literary experiments for which he is most remembered, to futurologically prescient essays in the manner of H. G. Wells or Arthur C. Clarke about imagined developments in transport, communication, architecture, society, etc. Together with Alexey Kruchonykh he invented a pure, aurally conceived 'zaumny' 'beyond-sense' Cyrillic language which is, naturally, virtually untranslatable. Attempts have, however, been made, and as Paul Schmidt has explained: 'The capacity of language to affect the world was one of his passions. For him the shift in sound that produces a shift in meaning was a shift in the structure of the universe.' There would seem to be here an effect comparable to that of enharmonic modulations in music. (*The King of Time, poems, fictions, visions of the future by Velimir Khlebnikov*, trans. Paul Schmidt, ed. Charlotte Douglas (Harvard University Press, 1985)).
3 This was the occasion that called forth Kamensky's much quoted description of Prokofiev's piano-playing: 'It seemed as though the café itself was all on fire, beams and door-jambs collapsing in flames like those of the composer's hair, while we stood ready to be consumed alive by the furnace of his unheard-of music, the young maestro incandescent on the shattered piano, himself under the spell of his elemental music.' (V. Kamenskii, *Zhizn's Mayakovskim*, Moscow, 1940.)

and declaiming *Seven*. Later, Balmont comically imagined being met by horrified friends moved by pity and fear at the spectacle of him escorting this gibbering, gesticulating individual to a lunatic asylum.[1]

12 [25] March

On the face of it there seems no reason why I should not stay in Moscow, nobody wants to get rid of me, there are proposals to arrange concerts, but I must hold to the line and keep America in my sights.

Koussevitzky and the 6,000: ' . . . and for the future, the more time goes on, the more you will receive.' He advises asking for a fee of $300 a concert, but only for a short series, after which everything will become clear.

13 [26] March

Long late-night talks with Koshetz. I got very tired.

Bliny at Koshetz's. Balmont. An ebullient dinner in honour of Balmont, I very much in the forefront. When asked why he was not planning to leave Russia, Balmont answered: 'I shall stay here and wait for this idiocy to end.'

An evening with the Futurists. Impressions on the second hearing of 'Man'[2] (the first having been on Kuznetsky Bridge).[3] I played the Sonata No. 1, by way of a subtle challenge to them;[4] their delighted approval. Underneath all the provocation, garish licence and chaos there is much that genuinely sparkles.

14 [27] March

Balmont dedicates some passionate verses to Koshetz. ' . . . Nina Pavlovna is so cold. And I was ready to dedicate not just three poems to her, but a whole book . . .'

Visited Vyacheslav Ivanov[5] with Balmont. Although I know little of his

1   Balmont later recalled, in an unpublished memoir, Koussevitzky's reaction when Prokofiev had played through the score and left: 'As soon as he has gone, Koussevitzky leafs through the score, stands up, strides up and down the room, sighs and, flushing with emotion, says: "You know, in richness and originality of orchestration there's nothing in the world that can match this for such outstanding musical imagination."' (Unpublished article, February 1927, in the Serge Prokofiev Archive, Goldsmiths College, London).
2   Poem by Mayakovsky written in 1916–17 and dealing with the poet's frustrations arising from his passion for Lilya Brik, translated, typically, into the cosmic sphere.
3   A Moscow street running from the side of the Bolshoy Theatre up the hill to the Lubyanka, originally with a bridge over the Neglinnaya river which is now underground.
4   Because of the First Sonata's unmistakably conservative idiom.
5   Vyacheslav Ivanov (1866–1949), Symbolist poet. Before he moved to Moscow from St Petersburg in 1913 he was regarded as the most significant of the Petersburg Symbolists, and his apart-

work I have great respect for him. On the subject of my own versifying he had various abstruse observations to make, of which I understood not a word.

15 [28] March

American consulates have been instructed by Washington not to issue visas to any Russians. Individual exceptions, if any, may be made only on receipt of preliminary approval telegraphed from Washington, which takes up to six weeks. This is serious, but I have to continue my efforts.

Koussevitzky: 'Why not stay?' This is an important question to answer, as I would feel embarrassed at having taken money from him for America on false pretences, subsequently using them to live on here. In any event, I am going to America.

16 [29] March

Left Moscow at three o'clock. Thanks to the papers from the Soviet of Workers' Deputies I got a ticket easily and without having to queue. But there were plenty of obstacles getting into Petrograd at the other end. Mine was a second-class carriage of the local type. It was very crowded at first, but mainly with people going to their dachas.

Nina came to see me off. The book and what she wrote in it. Her affection and agitation really surprised me. The farewell kiss. A completely new Nina has been revealed to me.

17 [30] March

I still had to sleep sitting up, but at least it only took eighteen hours to arrive in Petrograd at nine o'clock the next morning instead of the thirty-two we had been promised. Petrograd was quiet as usual, even sunny and welcoming. The cab driver asked for 20 roubles, so I hoisted my bags on to a tram and went that way. Our flat was in good shape, as the concierge's family had been put into it in order to avoid it being requisitioned. The joy of going into my room and finding my things there. For these days there are many luxuries: plenty of English cigarettes, perfume and so on.

---

ment (known as 'The Tower') had been effectively the crucible of the movement. Ivanov's poetry is elaborately declamatory, erudite and full of classical allusions, although the later *Winter Sonnets*, written in 1920 and describing the hardships suffered by the poet during the Civil War, are touching in their direct humanity. In 1924 Ivanov defected from the USSR on a cultural visit to Italy, where he remained until his death, mainly teaching classics at universities.

Eleonora asked me to lunch and dinner with her every day 'for a year if you like'. After such a long absence she was lovely to be with and very nice to me, feeding me all kinds of delicacies despite the famine. She has managed to get her diamonds out of the country into Switzerland. I always knew she would find a way to fix herself up.

B. Verin. Much mutual joy and kisses at our reunion. I am genuinely terribly glad to see him, and he calls me his absolutely first and best friend. He has made great progress with his poetry: he is on the way to becoming a good poet. Evidence of self-criticism. At long last!

18 [31] March

Matinee concert conducted by Coates. Extravagantly loving reunion with him and an invitation to perform. It looks as though I shall not be able to get away from Petrograd for at least two weeks.

Nina Meshcherskaya has married Levitsky, described by Eleonora as a young, not particularly good-looking boy, who was (so B. Verin informed me) after her money. But now the Meshcherskys themselves have lost all their money. I did not see her myself, but passing her house one day said to Verin: 'All the same people here, the same faces!' B. Verin says I should have seen the looks that were directed at me.

19 March [1 April]

Suvchinsky, Asafyev. 'Your appearance is the brightest event of the season.' Suvchinsky has lost his mansion, but has nevertheless contrived to set himself up very well. Lots of stories about Koshetz. I contributed some of my own in an affectionately ironic tone. Suvchinsky recounted a visit Rachmaninoff had paid him just before leaving for Denmark. He had referred to me as possessing enormous talent, but often writing strange music that was incomprehensible to him. When he heard that my attitude to his music was the opposite of hostile, that I liked it very much, he brightened and asked for his greetings to be conveyed to me. Suvchinsky had written to me, but the letter had gone astray.

One of B. Verin's 'Monday Evenings'; they are still taking place, and this time there was a discussion of ancient cults. Stavrovich is suffering from the famine and is emaciated, but spoke much and with great spirituality. After the discussion we all fell on the supper.

20 March [2 April]

During the winter B. Verin had read some of my poems to Igor Severyanin, who had said that the writer possesses real talent and a remarkable sense of rhythm. I enquired whether this had been simply for the sake of saying something, or whether it was a serious judgement. B. Verin replied that it was absolutely serious, as the verses had really pleased Severyanin, especially 'You, with DM . . .'. This was very nice to hear, as I have always regarded my attempts at poetry as worthless. However, I am not going to devote much time to poetry, as I want to concentrate on prose.

21st March (3rd April)

Dinner at Suvchinsky's. Benois. A telegram from Diaghilev, about the possibility of a season. Could this really be a possibility?[1] Promised to mention it to Lunacharsky, but Lunacharsky is away for a few days in Moscow. According to Suvchinsky, Benois is now installed in the Winter Palace engaged in 'interceding on behalf of decent people'. I had a very great success with *Visions Fugitives*, the Third and Fourth Sonatas, especially the Andante of the last.

22 March [4 April]

Decided to announce two concerts on the 2nd and 4th of the month (old style).

Talked to Vecherin at the suggestion of Postnikov. A nice man, and may come with me to America. He says my plan of becoming established in America is a glimpse into the future. From a practical point of view he is right.

B. Verin dreams of coming with me. I would be delighted, but do not have a lot of faith in his dreams.

23 March [5 April]

Started to prepare seriously for my concert.

Opinions about America vary to an extraordinary degree, mainly on the subject of American attitudes to Russian people. I still believe this does not matter too much, although it is as well to be forewarned, and if nothing comes of the United States, then what about South America?

---

1 Presumably a Diaghilev season in Moscow or Petrograd. An extraordinary thought.

24 March [6 April]

Myaskovsky suffered what seems to be a nervous breakdown that caused him to lose the use of his arm and his leg, but has now recovered and is applying himself once again with great energy to composition, two symphonies in the space of two months. He played them to us at Suvchinsky's. In my opinion they are a great advance on his Third, possessing unity, brilliance and an absence of tendentious moralising. The Fourth is stronger and more brilliant, but the Fifth more arresting, with its change of direction towards major key modes and a pastoral atmosphere.

25 March [7 April]

Spending time very enjoyably with Suvchinsky, Eleonora and B. Asafyev. Preparing for my concert and awaiting the return of Lunacharsky in order to obtain, through Boris Nikolayevich[1] a passport to travel abroad (and possibly some foreign currency?).

27 March [9 April]

Very glad to learn that the Trans-Siberian Express leaves every Tuesday. True, at present it goes only as far as Irkutsk, beyond which are all kinds of dreadful things. But I plan to get as far as Irkutsk, things will be clearer on the spot and less problematical than they appear from here. After all, to get to Petrograd and Moscow from Kislovodsk seemed at the time an impossibly difficult enterprise!

28 March [10 April]

Decided to travel either through China or Japan, with my destination either the United States or, if that proves to be a less than welcoming environment for Russians, then to Argentina. In either case the route lies through my beloved Sandwich Islands. Once I get there it will be clear what I should do.

29th March (11th April)

Boris Nikolayevich says he wants to come with me, but I am planning to leave on the 23rd and it will be at least two weeks after that before he is ready

---

[1] Whether Demchinsky or Bashkirov is not clear, but the former seems more likely to have had connections with Lunacharsky's office. The entries for 29 and 30 March refer to Bashkirov, however.

to leave. Well, I'm not going to wait for him, but he might be able to catch up with me in Japan.

Through Mme Koussevitzkaya in Moscow I can get dollars at a rate of seven and a half roubles to the dollar, whereas I am told here they have already gone up to twelve.

30 March [12 April]

Finished 'the Mirror of the Soul'. Boris Nikolayevich says that on judging by my letters I must possess a splendid prose style. This pleased me very much, although I am not yet telling him anything about my stories.

I am worried that there will not be much publicity about my concerts and people will not know they are happening. I am ready to perform now and believe I will play pretty well.

2 [15] April

My concert. The first public performance of the Third Sonata and *Visions Fugitives*.

Because of badly distributed publicity, also the ignorance of the public, the hall was no more than half full, and to begin with almost empty, as it had been in Kislovodsk. The success was very great, especially for the Third Sonata, which was encored. The artists' room was full of ecstatic members of the audience, notable among them Lida and Zoya,[1] Benois, Mr *Seven* himself,[2] B.N.,[3] and shyly off in a corner Miller and Jung,[4] who had sent wonderful red roses. 'Oh, how many friends you have!' said Miller, with touching simplicity. Eleonora was put in the shade and very put out. Benois asked about Miller: 'Who is she? She's not bad-looking at all.' I passed this on to her later; she was immensely flattered at this praise from such a great artist.

Another of B.N.'s Monday Evenings. An idea for a story about 'Rameses-Yankee.'[5]

---

1 Karneyeva.
2 Balmont.
3 Bashkirov.
4 Vera Miller and Adelina Jung, friends of Eleonora Damskaya and admirers of Prokofiev from Conservatoire days. The latter was the daughter of the principal viola-player in the Mariinsky Theatre orchestra.
5 This story was eventually called 'Ultra-violet Freedom' and tells of a somewhat unlikely encounter between an American businessman and a Pharoah.

3 [16] April

Meyerhold told me that *The Gambler* has been included in next year's repertoire. I am sceptical, but he insists that it is settled. Recently I played through *The Gambler* and was filled with regret that so much good music is still hidden under a bushel.

The second of my concerts. First performance of the Fourth Sonata. Quite a large audience, but not completely full. A very warm reception; colossal enthusiasm for *Suggestion Diabolique*. I had not predicted a great success for the Fourth Sonata, but I was quite wrong: the serious elements of the audience all immediately appreciated the second movement, while the others liked the finale, which I played for the first time as it should be played, taking the crescendo leading up to the final statement of the main theme to the very top. Hitherto I had been afraid that I had produced a finale with too abruptly docked a tail, but now it became clear to me that it is good, and that if the final climax is done correctly it represents precisely that culminating point of the sonata after which it must come swiftly to a conclusion. Demchinsky said of the finale that one 'would have to be an octopus to be able to play it!'

Tamara Glebova – the spluttering incoherence of her excited reaction. I told her: 'You leave out all the commas when you speak', but her exaltation was very gratifying to me. Asafyev, Suvchinsky and Myaskovsky were especially taken with the *Visions Fugitives*. Even the normally restrained Myaskovsky said that they were – perfection. By popular demand, I encored *Suggestion Diabolique* and the Third Sonata. Afterwards I was very tired.

5 [18] April

Rehearsal of the 'Classical' Symphony with the State Orchestra.[1] I conducted it myself, completely improvising, having forgotten the score and never indeed having studied it from a conducting perspective. I thought it might be a complete debacle, but nothing happened and in any case the parts had so many mistakes in them that the session turned mainly into one for making corrections. It sounds delightful, and exactly what I had in mind. In Kislovodsk I had worried that there would be some antagonism from a 'Revolutionary orchestra' playing my new works, but the opposite was the case: the State Orchestra, infused with much new young blood, was flexible and attentive, and played the Symphony with evident enjoyment.

Benois, who is now working in the Winter Palace, brought me together

---

1 The former Court Orchestra had been renamed State Orchestra, later to become the Leningrad Philharmonic.

with Sternberg, a small, exceedingly polite and unusual Jew, a cartoonist.[1] He is Lunacharsky's right-hand man and promised to do everything in his power to help me get my passport to travel abroad.

6 [19] April

Second rehearsal. Went quite well. The orchestra gave me an ovation.

7 [20] April

When I came to the Winter Palace to see Sternberg, it turned out that Lunacharsky himself wanted to see me. He spoke about Mayakovsky and gave me an exceptionally friendly welcome. 'You ought to stay here, what do you want to go to America for?' 'I've worked for a year and now want to get some fresh air.' 'We have all the fresh air you could want in Russia.' 'But that is in the moral sense, and my present need for air is a purely physical one. Just think of it, to be cutting diagonally right across the great Pacific ocean!' 'All right, just fill in this form and we'll give you the necessary papers.'

While I was waiting for the documents I sat in Lunacharsky's office as he continued receiving people. There was a writers' delegation headed by Sologub, a delegation of young poets, and another from working-class professionals wanting free travel vouchers. Lunacharsky directed the flow of petitioners with great good humour, laughing and joking, but wasted a lot of time on trivialities. His features are not attractive, and he speaks with a slight burr, as children do.

At half-past two I jumped to my feet, saying I had to go. Lunacharsky thought that I had taken offence at having to wait so long and said: right away, right away, they'll give it to you right now. I explained that the public dress rehearsal of my new symphony would be starting in half an hour's time; he was very interested and said what a pity it was that he had a meeting scheduled, as he would very much have liked to come and listen to it. I replied: 'But you can be a little late for your meeting; the symphony only lasts fifteen minutes. Please come!' He said: 'Really. Then I'll come.' When I entered the chapel, there was his official car standing in front of the entrance. I conducted well and the orchestra, while not flawless, played with sprightly precision. As I stepped on to the podium my head was bathed in light from the rays of the sun streaming in from the window above. I could see purple circles in front of my eyes, but as I made my bow to the audience

---

1   Pavel Sternberg (1865–1920), a distinguished physicist and astronomer, formerly Director of the Moscow Observatory and holder of the medal of the Russian Geographical Society, whom Lunacharsky had made his deputy with special responsibility for higher education. He does not, however, seem to have entered the history books as a cartoonist.

I seemed to be expressing my feeling that the sun was sending its greeting to my heliophilous symphony and to me. This at least was how Tcherepnin wrote about it when he signed my 'Wooden Book'. Dinner at Suvchinsky's, very good company honouring me for my symphony. Diederichs has connections all over South America; perhaps I really should go straight to Buenos Aires?

8 [21] April?

A nine o'clock meeting with Meyerhold and Golovin about *The Gambler*. I said I needed a new contract, but should receive money according to the old one. Meyerhold agreed. My departure is now fixed for next Tuesday. I have stayed here too long, but everything now seems to have been settled. When I told Meyerhold of my desire to find an effervescent subject for an opera, he gave me *The Love for Three Oranges* to read.[1]

The concert with the 'Classical' Symphony was at two o'clock, so I had to leave. Again the same rays from the sun. This was amazing! Fantastic! The Symphony went marvellously and was a huge success. The circumstances under which the Symphony's first themes were composed.

9 [22] April

Went with Benois to see Sternberg. I asked Benois to drop a few hints about my getting a more substantial allocation of dollars via the state coffers. To my astonishment, Sternberg told me to come back tomorrow at twelve, and everything would be done according to my wishes. Could it be that the Symphony had produced an effect?

That evening, in the café, there was a cry of 'Hands up, nobody move!' It was not terribly frightening, as there were so many people there. I remembered that I had only 65 roubles on me. It was a search for weapons, carried out quite courteously, even pleasantly, by the police, not the political section,[2] three detectives. A sombre little cortège: three detectives and three soldiers – detective–soldier, detective–soldier, detective–soldier. Steely, penetrating gaze. I laughed in his face, at which he dropped his gaze.

---

1 It was Guillaume Apollinaire who had first interested Meyerhold in the plays of Carlo Gozzi, and what Meyerhold gave to Prokofiev was a copy of the first issue of the magazine he founded and called *Lyubov k tryom apelsinam* (*The Love For Three Oranges*), published in 1914, which contained his scenario based on Carlo Gozzi's version of the story.

2 The Military Revolutionary Committee, the organisation that had fanned the spark that grew into the flames of the October Revolution, had been abolished by Lenin in December 1917, and its counter-revolutionary security functions transferred immediately to the new Cheka (CHrEzvychainaya KommissiyA, 'Extraordinary Commission for Struggle Against Counter-Revolution and Sabotage') headed by Dzerzhinsky. But it was not until later that summer that it developed its fearsome reputation as the spearpoint of centrally organised political terror.

10 [23] April

Second visit to Lunacharsky. I was a little embarrassed about the dollars, but he said he would support the request with all the means at his disposal.

When I asked Lunacharsky how he had liked the Symphony, he said he had liked it very much. 'What I recognise in you, at a time when everyone else is concerned with destruction, is that you are building.'

Went to watch the departure of the Trans-Siberian Express, consumed with envy that I have to wait another week before I can be on it. It is a splendid train, a truly European enterprise, not one of your 'democratic' apologies that set your teeth on edge.[1]

11 [24] April

Went to the Smolny[2] for my passport. Yet another reverse: the official responsible for issuing passports is in Moscow and will not be back for three days. Surely I am not going to miss next Tuesday's departure as well? If so, I'm going to hang myself!

To the Mariinsky to see Meyerhold. Nowadays I appear there as an Important Person, since word is out that *The Gambler* has been confirmed for next season. It had not been a very nice feeling to be seen as the author of a production that had been cancelled.

I made a formal request that, in view of my imminent departure, a new contract for *The Gambler* should be prepared, and that the financial obligations according to the old one should be honoured in addition to advance on the new one.

Yesterday was my twenty-seventh birthday. Twenty-seven is a fateful number for me, bringing both happiness and unhappiness. The first time I became aware of its significance (despite my rational rejection of superstition) was when I told Mama of Max's death.[3] She said: 'Today is the 27th.' It has stayed in my memory as a moment of great nervous shock. I did not celebrate yesterday, but got on with what I had to do. However, in the evening I went to see B.N. (much to Eleonora's dismay), as he had arranged a birthday roulette session, which ended the following day at eleven in the morning (I left at five). I played according to my system and won three hundred.

---

1   See above, pp. 8–9.
2   Built at the beginning of the nineteenth century as the Institute for the Education of Noble Maidens, the elegant Palladian building was requisitioned as the headquarters of the new Bolshevik Government (and the temporary residence of its leader) after the October Revolution, and remained so until about this time, when the national government moved to the Kremlin in Moscow. The Smolny remained as the Petrograd Communist Party headquarters.
3   See *Diaries*, vol. 1, pp. 382–6.

12 [25] April

God knows what chaos is afflicting the currency exchange market – the Russian state has been reduced to beggary and has not so much as a *sou* in the till to give me, even if it wished to do so. Countess N. has kindly agreed to get me a more or less tolerable rate from the English Embassy.

13 [26] April

Read T*he Love for Three Oranges*. It is wonderful! Something could really be done with it, except that the plot would need to be completely rewritten. The music should be clear, lively, and as simple as it can be made.

As Meyerhold and I were walking along Morskaya Street discussing *Three Oranges*, shots rang out from the side of St Isaac's Square. We ran in the opposite direction, afraid of getting caught up in a political mêlée. Meyerhold, who was ahead of me, shouted: 'Get down! Get down!' We ran to the shelter of the corner of a building, and stopped there. Later it transpired that the shots were the innocent backfiring of an automobile.

14 [27] April

Finally I can get my passport. I shall go on Tuesday even if I only have a hundred pounds, but if the theatre can give me an advance, then I'll have two hundred. That will be all right.

Benois made a pencil sketch of me sitting on a sofa at Asafyev's. I was very flattered that he did so, but I am not particularly happy with the result.

15 [28] April

Those scoundrels in the theatre administration say they cannot sign the contract earlier than in three weeks' time; it has to go through all kinds of time-consuming bureaucratic hoops. They suggest that I give someone authority to conclude the agreement on my behalf. I was angry, and said all kinds of silly things.

Dined with Chaliapin. My attitude to this great artist, whose merest gesture on stage I regard as law, is one of near-reverence and great love. Chaliapin was charming, suggested some subjects for opera (none of which I liked) and showed great interest in *The Gambler*. On the same occasion I met Ekskuzovich,[1] with whom I had tangled acrimoniously earlier in the

---

1 Ivan Ekskuzovich (1883–1942), theatre administrator, Telyakovsky's replacement after the Revolution as head of the former Imperial Theatres in Petrograd. From 1923 to 1928 he was even more important as overall head of all the flagship State Theatres of the Russian Federation.

day about the contract. We agreed that Suvchinsky would have power of attorney to agree the contract. It still means that I shall be leaving without my much-needed six thousand.

16 [29] April

Today, all but packed and ready to go, I went to the Wagons-Lits office to get my ticket for tomorrow's express, only to be informed that the train was cancelled and would be leaving from Moscow, since as from today the capital of Russia was Moscow! Calamity! I was bitterly upset, but will go immediately to Moscow since now I have to the best of my ability settled all my business affairs I cannot endure the thought of staying a moment longer. As it is I will not get to Buenos Aires much before the end of the season and I simply cannot afford to waste any more time.

Ionin promised to get me a letter of credit from the English Military Mission stating that I was travelling on their business. This would be very helpful.

Eleonora's behaviour during my visit was for the most part exemplary: she provided delicacies such as chocolate, pineapple jam and caramelised condensed milk made into a kind of toffee. But just before my departure the barometer fell through the floor and she announced that she would be following in my footsteps.

17 [30] April

Today should by rights have been my departure day and the hours between three and six should have been occupied by final packing. For this reason all my friends came to see me, and since the departure was not now happening we had a relaxed 'five o'clock'. Suvchinsky was there, Asafyev, Eleonora, Boris Nikolayevich, Benois and Miller. The last-named brought German translations she made of the texts of my songs: as far as I could see from my memories of this all-but forgotten language she had done them very well and even poetically. After all, in the past she had written some delightful verses in German for me. Now this brave girl is undertaking to translate the libretto of *The Gambler* into French and German during the summer.

18 April [1 May]

Today is 1 May, a revolutionary holiday, and the streets are decorated with Futurist placards and images. I suppose I should be glad, but as a matter of fact I found them distasteful to look at. They were evidently the work of bad Futurists. The festivities lacked any genuinely popular feel about them, and seemed more like an official expression of state-sponsored euphoria.

19 April [2 May]

I finally left for Moscow at eight o'clock to take the Trans-Siberian Express from there. Eleonora came to my house just before I left, ill, distraught and heavily made up. I told her that if she was going to cry or make a scene like the disgraceful way she had carried on yesterday, I would not speak to her.

B.N. got a cab and accompanied me to the station. He said that my journey would be a difficult one and in the end he was relieved not to be coming with me, a remark that very nearly succeeded in spoiling my mood.

20 April [3 May]

At the last moment, Ionin turned up with a ticket[1] costing a mere 400 roubles – almost free.

The journey to Moscow was splendid. The whole train seethed with people except for our International Company carriage, which was airy and spacious. My companion treated me to wine and grouse – not exactly starving Petrograd.

At twelve o'clock I appeared at Koshetz's door – and my God, what an explosion of joy: Seryozha's come to spend Easter with me! As indeed I had, for the train was not leaving until Tuesday.

21 April [4 May]

After Prime, which we attended in a nearby church, we broke the fast in Koshetz's flat chock-a-block with gaudy throws and cushions – a simple supper, very gay and with plenty to drink. Nina and I drank to our *Bruderschaft*.

22 April [5 May]

This afternoon a mass of visitors came to Koshetz's, including my dear Balmont. Taking advantage of Easter, everyone kissed everyone else on both cheeks, but not serious kissing, Nina with all her friends, I with Sonya Avanova, a pretty Armenian woman.

In the evening Nina, deeply moved, sang a song someone had fashioned from Chopin's Third Etude. She sang it divinely: at first I was appalled at the desecration wrought by the lyrics, but then melted completely under the spell of her singing.[2]

---

1 For the Trans-Siberian Express to Vladivostok.
2 Nina Koshetz sang a version of the famous 'Tristesse' tune of Chopin's Etude, Op. 10 No. 3, made by her teacher Félia Litvinne. 'Summer has fled, the light fades o'er the fields/Already dusk casts shadows on the lea;/Long since the birds have ceased/Their song in fields and woods;/Cold winds have come to stop their lovely song/No longer can I hear their dear

23 April [6 May]

What a delicious piece is S. Taneyev's Minuet. It is never off my piano desk; I play and sing it every day.

24 April [7 May]

At eight o'clock this evening I found myself aboard the Express, in a roomy first-class half-compartment, simply staggered by the level of comfort afforded by this train. We have completely forgotten what it is like to have the luxury of a restaurant car, with a piano in it to boot, and with polite, attentive waiters.

Every minute the train gathered speed and was soon moving at a lively speed, like a real express.

26 April [8 May]

The first day of my journey. My mood is buoyant, if my feelings a little mixed. I am reading Winckler's *Babylonian Culture*[1] and writing postcards sitting in the restaurant car, a pleasure I have not enjoyed for three years. All thoughts are focused on Buenos.

I am prey to the most enchanting memories of Nina Koshetz.

Winter is still all around us, there are hardly any signs of spring: green pine-trees, snow and puddles. Not very May-like!

To Nina Koshetz in Moscow: 'My dearest (I'm not sure if I may call you that) Ninochka. So far my train is living up to its honourable name: it speeds boldly along and is very comfortable inside. It has a restaurant car with maître d'hôtel, extravagantly overtipped waiters, a piano, wines, table linen and no sign of any soldiers. I am reading *Babylonian Culture*, smoking, thinking of the ocean and remembering Moscow. The perfume you let fall on my handkerchief is, sad to say, fading, but my memories of you are as fragrant as ever. I kiss you, my dearest, and send my warmest greetings to all. Seryozha. Tell A. A.[2] that he has messed up all my ties. I am in despair.'

---

refrain./And yet in spring their myriad flocks/Sang through the cool shadows of the days.' Koshetz's 1928 Victor recording can still be heard (Nimbus NI 7935/6) and can still melt the listener as it did Prokofiev and, no doubt, Rachmaninoff.

1 *Die babylonische Geisteskultur in ihren Beziehungen zur Kulturentwicklung der Menschheit*, Quelle & Meyer, Leipzig, 1907. The German archaeologist Hugo Winckler had excavated the ancient Hittite capital city of Hattusha-Boghazköy in Anatolia between 1906 and 1912. There he had unearthed an enormous archive of tablets, thus contributing substantially to the authentification of relevant parts of the Old Testament.

2 Nina Koshetz's husband was the artist Alexander von Schubert.

26 April [9 May]

By morning we were in Vyatka,[1] where it is still fully winter. But by the afternoon it was warming up and getting greener. I am greatly enjoying the journey.

Have started studying Spanish, partly learning the rules of grammar and partly vocabulary. I must learn twenty words a day and meticulously repeat those I have learned previously.

Am thinking of more stories. I am anxious to write 'The White Friend', but it is hard to concentrate.

27 April [10 May]

Rose at six to see the Urals, but there are no peaks in these parts, more like rolling uplands, lovely but not remarkable.

Sat in the restaurant car and thought of 'The Friend' and 'The Tower' and wrote a little of 'MacCook'.[2] The rocking of the train makes it difficult to write.

Learning Spanish. I cannot always work out where the accent should fall and whether the 'i' should be pronounced short or long.

To V. Miller, to be delivered personally: 'Dear friend, after celebrating Easter in Moscow I am at last on the splendid Express today speeding eastwards. Good luck with *The Gambler*. If for any reason you cannot get hold of a copy from Karatygin, please telephone P. P. Suvchinsky, whom you know (plump, rubicund man sitting opposite you), 4.41.80 - he will get one for you. My very warmest wishes to you, also to your friend. Your S.P.'

28 April [11 May]

Next leg of the journey between Tyumen and Omsk. Fewer forests and more open fields. And winter, white winter. Just the occasional glimpse here and there of green grass.

Learning Spanish and can already conjugate three auxiliary verbs.

This evening there erupted a blizzard of such ferocity that the carriage shook while it was standing in the station and one could distinctly feel it rocking. There was a fear that snowdrifts might block the line, but thank God, the wind was blowing from behind us.

To Asafyev in Petersburg: 'Dearest Borenka, I celebrated Easter in Moscow,

---

1 City, railhead and port just west of the Ural mountains on the Vyatka river, now called Kirov.
2 'The Wandering Tower'. MacCook might be an earlier name for Charles H. MacIntosh, the American businessman in 'Ultra-violet Freedom'. 'The White Friend' does not seem to have been realised.

a very enjoyable and lively time, and am now heading east on the Express, a magnificent European-class train; today we passed through Omsk. Here it is winter, with snowstorms, masses of good country food, I'm feeling fine, putting on weight and learning Spanish. How is *The Gambler*? I heard that because I was going away there was talk of shelving it. Do ask Pyotr Petrovich[1] to keep telling everyone loud and clear that I shall be back in October. In the meantime I embrace you, my dear. Best regards to your wife and to Pyotr Petrovich. If Ninochka plans to come to Petrograd, kiss her for me (literally). S.'

29 April [12 May]

We are running twenty-four hours late. But what difference does it make, whether we travel for six days or seven? As long as it's not twelve, or if at least we make it to Vladivostok at all.

Started writing 'The Wandering Tower', and it is good. But 'The White Friend' is very slow. I feel it should be good, but am finding it hard to find the right tone.

30 April [13 May]

The snow has gone, and green has started to appear, but only here and there. Around Krasnoyarsk the countryside is very interesting and beautiful.

Apparently Semyonov all but reached Chita[2] and succeeded in his aim of cutting the way to Vladivostok, but has now been chased away.

Am studying Spanish and pleased with my progress. Also writing 'Tower', with enjoyment, but a little at a time.

To Boris Nikolayevich Bashkirov, Petrograd: 'Dear Borenka, I embrace you and send you my best wishes for your imminent name-day, hoping that you will spend it very agreeably; meanwhile hauled by our sturdy American

---

1 Suvchinsky.
2 Grigory Semyonov (1890–1946), Cossack warlord who led an anti-Bolshevik rebellion in the Baikal region after having been the local Commissar of the Provisional Government until the October Revolution. From the safety of Manchuria he worked to restore his power-base in Baikal with the support of the Czechoslovak Legions, but succeeded in this endeavour only in August 1918, consequently at the time Prokofiev wrote this diary entry he could not have been more than a peripatetic threat. Ultimately Semyonov did establish in the region a regime of unparalleled brutality and was (somewhat reluctantly) appointed by Admiral Kolchak's Omsk Government as Commander-in-Chief of the White Armies of the Chita Military District. In the end Kolchak was forced to hand over all military power to Semyonov, but with the final defeat of the last remnants of White resistance in 1921, Semyonov fled back to Manchuria and to the USA, where he continued in every way open to him to combat Soviet interests. Retribution finally came when the Red Army captured him in China at the end of the Second World War; he was executed in 1945.

locomotive we are speeding towards Irkutsk, a journey which should take altogether seven days. I am not finding the journey tiring; on the contrary my mind is full of thoughts, all the more so as my neighbour is agreeably taciturn. I am also keeping my Spanish up to the mark: two hundred words have already lodged themselves in my head, and I can conjugate four auxiliary verbs with ease. I kiss you. The line to Harbin is closed, so we are going to Vladivostok via Blagoveshchensk.¹ S.'

To Polina, near Taganrog: 'Dear Polina, my wish is at last coming true: I am sitting in a small compartment of the Siberian Express with a passport to travel abroad in one pocket and an authority from the British Military Mission in the other, making my way to the open expanse of the Pacific Ocean. I send you my greetings and remember you fondly. S.P.'

1 [14] May

Through the window, beautiful birch forests with white trunks. The line to Vladivostok, apparently, is open and there are even direct trains from Irkutsk. The only problem is the mass of passengers on board the train.

There have been several searches, looking for weapons, alcohol and cocaine. They were conducted courteously.

The first swallows heralding abroad have been seen: hawkers with foreign cigarettes on their trays at half the price they are in Petrograd.

2 [15] May

Irkutsk early in the morning, when we had to change from the Express into an ordinary first-class carriage. However, it is relatively cheap and I am in a large compartment with the Danish mission. The line runs along the picturesque banks of the Angara river with its clear, cold waters apparently unruffled by the corpses of the many foolhardy souls who have drowned in it. But the wonderful view of Lake Baikal itself was an unexpected revelation, suddenly opening up before our eyes as the Angara flows into it. Flooded with sunshine, pale blue and inconceivably vast, with still snow-capped mountains, it was an utterly enthralling sight.

---

1 At the end of the nineteenth century Russia extended the Trans-Siberian Railway to cut through the north-eastern corner of China, thus shortening considerably the distance to Vladivostok on the Pacific coast. In so doing it established a strong Russian presence in Harbin, the main town on the route, and the Tsarist government deliberately fostered this presence by means of extending special privileges to Russians prepared to settle there. Blagoveshchensk is a border town to the north-west, on the original pre-Harbin route of the railway line.

3 [16] May

My mood is somewhat mixed, even anxious, as I contemplated how far I have still to go and for how long I shall be away. But the mood soon passed as I argued with myself successfully how stupid I was being to think like that.

Chita 1, then Chita 2. At the first I enquired whether there was a telegram from Koshetz, but there was none, and at the second I was daydreaming, and am sorry to say forgot to ask. But this was because I was sure there would not be any telegram. I have left, Nina has stayed. It is better this way: she would have made too many demands.

To B.N. in Petrograd: 'Dear Amoeba, am approaching Chita still under the tremendous impression created by Baikal. The best part was when we were rushing towards it along the banks of the Angara, and seeing it light blue, serene, sunlit, encircled by snow-capped mountains. I feel no fatigue from the nine days travelling, my ambiance is in good order, and although the Express only went as far as Irkutsk we transferred there to a perfectly acceptable first-class carriage. Because of the activities of the Manchurian Yesaul[1] we are having to make a detour round Sretensk and Khabarovsk, which will add a couple of days to our journey. Embraces, S.'

4 [17] May

Today we came on to a circuitous American[2] part of the line and are trundling slowly through lovely, hilly country.

Good news: the yen in Vladivostok is trading at 2 roubles 70 kopecks, which means I shall have 2,000 yen – 1,000 dollars – a sum I never dreamed of. I am a rich man and shall be able to go to Buenos Aires with no hold-ups anywhere.

My travelling companion sings the praises of Japanese geishas in Vladivostok. 'They are so polite,' he says.

---

1 A reference to Grigory Semyonov. A yesaul is an officer in a Cossack unit.
2 The original route of the Trans-Siberian Railway made a steep curve up to the north before coming south again to pass through Blagoveshchensk and Khabarovsk on its way to the final destination of Vladivostok. By 1897 the final part of the track from Vladivostok to Khabarovsk was in place, but because of unwelcome American, English and Japanese ambitions to extend their sphere of influence in the Far East of Russia the Government decided to abandon the idea of connecting it with the western section of the line, cutting instead through Manchuria via Harbin. Taking the longer, northerly route, which as Prokofiev explains had to be done on this occasion because of the danger from Semyonov, involved using an American-built section of the original route.

5 [18] May

Our slow meandering is getting tiresome, especially as in the fourth compartment there is continual conversation that stops me concentrating on my Spanish and on 'The Wandering Tower', and drives me to distraction.

Today we completed the last and most significant curve to the north, bringing us almost to the same latitude as Ryazan. From now on I shall no longer be heading north but south – all the way to Buenos Aires.[1]

6 [19] May

It smells of spring, the late, northern spring. I love these smells. The line runs through bright-green wooded hills, sometimes a vivid white from the trunks of all the silver birches. I am glad to have caught a snatch of spring, even through the window of a train, as all the worries and tribulations of embarking on my American adventure have cost me the time of year I love most. The consolation is that I shall meet it again in September in Argentina, in the flowers of the Pampas.

7 [20] May

The day drags by in sluggish idleness. The thirteenth day of travelling has taken its toll, and although I am not physically tired, a certain inertia grips me.

We have passed Blagoveshchensk. The views are steppe-like, monotonous.

To Nikolay Yakovlevich Myaskovsky, Petrograd: 'Dearest Nyamchik,[2] I am writing to you from Arkhara,[3] notable mainly for being the birthplace of all known Arkharovites (the places one gets to, on the way to America!). Tomorrow we shall get to Khabarovsk, and thirty hours after that to Vladivostok. I embrace you tenderly and send you my best congratulations on your name-day, and best wishes for your instrumentation of an orchestral *morceau*. Your S.P.'

8 [21] May

In a dream I saw Max Schmidthof with startling clarity. We spent quite a long time together. I was so glad to see him, and my only worry was that he

---

1 The actual town of Blagoveshchensk, on the Chinese border, is on the 50th parallel, but the most northerly point of the wide detour this particular train had to take is around latitude 55, as are Ryazan, Moscow, Copenhagen and Glasgow.
2 A frequent Prokofiev nickname for Myaskovsky: N̲. Y̲a̲. M̲yaskovsky.
3 A small town in Amur Oblast with a station on the Trans-Siberian Railway.

might disappear. But then I woke up and indeed Max did disappear. It is now five years since he shot himself dead, and although it is only a short while since I dedicated to him the Fourth Sonata (as the dedication on the first edition states), the image of him in my mind's eye has begun to fade and recede into the distant background. But at this moment his loss stings sharply.

The green of the land and the blue of the hills are very striking. They say such colours can be seen only on virgin soil.

9 [22] May

Had I ever imagined that one day I would be in Khabarovsk? As a matter of fact, Khabarovsk turned out to be a most attractive place with fine houses and poetic-looking squares, high up on the bank of the Amur, an enticing backdrop to adolescent romance. The way of life is patriarchal, and the social culture definitely counter-Revolutionary.

At two o'clock we left for Vladivostok, heading due south. It is strange to think of, but Vladivostok is on the same latitude as Kislovodsk. Thanks to my English Mission authority, I got a compartment to myself.

10 [23] May

The sixteenth and final day of my railway journey passed idly. We arrived in Vladivostok at eight o'clock in the evening and immediately debouched in a noisy, eight-storey-high station built on American lines. Although the city was bursting with people, my companion – a Moscow journalist – and I managed to get quite a decent hotel room. I started to put my letters of introduction to work and got on the telephone. Dukelsky[1] was in Japan, but the editor of the main local newspaper was charming and I spent that first evening at his house.

There is apparently a boat leaving for Japan the day after tomorrow; the formalities for leaving the country are trivial (and we had been so frightened by them in Russia!), but alas the yen, the yen, which so recently stood at 2.70, now costs 4 roubles. Once again I am a poor man.

---

1 Vladimir Dukelsky, aka Vernon Duke (1903–1969), composer with a true double life. The classical Dukelsky enjoyed respect and considerable success in the field of serious music with, *inter alia* Diaghilev, alongside the extremely successful Broadway and popular songwriter Vernon Duke – 'April in Paris', 'Autumn in New York', 'Walk a Little Faster' – until 1955, after which his compositions in all genres were credited to Vernon Duke. He was also a gifted writer in both Russian and English, and his autobiography *Passport to Paris*, published in 1955, well merits republishing, having been long out of print. A fellow student with Prokofiev of Reinhold Glière, although not at the same time, the two were later to become close friends in France and America when both were living in the West. See above, pp. 150–53.

11 [24] May

My first call was on the Japanese Consul for a visa. This unconscionable pedant requires five days to visa a passport. The Japanese are very fearful of Russian Bolsheviks and German spies. 'You understand', said the Consul, 'that if we were simply to issue you with a visa without further ado, it would not have much validity?' And when I started to insist, basing my case on my documented credentials, etc., he replied that my visa would be more expeditiously obtained if I were to go and get the necessary photograph of myself than if I detained him in further conversation. I was most displeased with this observation and went to the bazaar to an instant photographer. So here I am, stuck in Vladivostok for five days until Wednesday. The only thing that allows me to keep my temper is that before leaving Kislovodsk, I foresaw that there would be many delays during my travels, and made a resolution there and then that I must keep cool when they occurred and not let them to spoil my disposition.

Vladivostok is quite a lively town with many cafés that serve delicacies Petrograders have long forgotten ever existed: *pâtisserie*, chocolate, sweet rolls and any amount of sugar, the proper white sugar that sifts like diamonds.

12 [25] May

My mood is up and down, but generally not very sunny – would it perhaps have been better to stay in Russia where all my friends are, and the music? But all such thoughts are weakness and the result of enforced idleness and inactivity in Vladivostok.

Am carrying on with learning Spanish, and now have a reliable vocabulary of about six hundred words.

13 [26] May

Resumed writing my stories today. The 'dream' story is forging ahead rapidly, and that has greatly improved my mood.

In the afternoon I went to the races, where the horses of Mme Yankovskaya, Balmont's friend, were running and winning. It is exciting when they come up to the finishing line, but the rest of it palls after an hour or two.

Spent the evening with the local Futurists. They try to be as provocative as the real ones, but their efforts are fairly innocent. As a President of Planet Earth, that is to say a representative of their governing body, I was tempted to take them in hand (because the genuine, Italian, Futurists are very disciplined), but questioned if it would really be worth the effort.

14 [27] May

On this day thirteen years ago the Battle of Tsushima took place.[1] It was a strange moment seeing side by side in Vladivostok harbour the *Asahi* and her prize the *Oryol*, whom she had captured, both ships now serving as Japanese station ships (and possibly future occupiers of Vladivostok?).[2]

I wrote some of the 'dream' story, to which I gave the title 'Misunderstandings Sometimes Occur', with enormous pleasure. The reason it had taken me so long to get going on it was that my original idea had been to write it in a serious style: 'In Norway, a respectable engineer . . .', but as soon as I injected a more ironic, humorous tone it immediately began to flow easily in its groove.

15 [18] May

I have my visa. The newspaper editor promised to get me a ticket for tomorrow's steamer and to exchange my roubles for yen, but they are going up in price and are already at 5 roubles. I decided to divide my money in half: half to buy yen and half to risk taking with me concealed in the lining of my hat, since apparently there will not be any serious searches.

The story is racing ahead. I thought I might finish it today, but a headache began to threaten so I stopped at the last chapter.

To near Taganrog: 'Dear Borenka,[3] I now have everything, visa and Japanese yen. Tomorrow at twelve noon I shall board the *Hosan-Maru* and

---

1 The Battle of the Tsushima Straits was the decisive battle of the disastrous (for Russia) Russo-Japanese War of 1904-5, on 14 and 15 May 1905, in the course of which Admiral Togo's fleet destroyed two-thirds of Admiral Rozhdestvensky's Baltic Fleet, which had sailed all of 30,000 kilometres from the North Sea right round Africa and Indochina in a futile effort to relieve the blockade of the Russian settlement at Port Arthur. By the time they got there, the Japanese had already destroyed the Russian Pacific Fleet. As soon as Rozhdestvensky realised that the settlement had already capitulated he made a run for home (Vladivostok) by the shortest route through the Tsushima Straits between Japan and Korea, but Togo had anticipated this and cut him off at the pass. The Russians lost their entire fleet and 10,000 men killed or captured; the Japanese lost three torpedo boats. The war had swiftly to be brought to an end on crushingly unfavourable terms to Russia, and the resulting military and political ignominy materially hastened the end of the Romanov dynasty. As a young boy Prokofiev was deeply interested in naval matters and compiled lists of battleships. In a touching moment, related in his Autobiography, his father sympathised with him over the loss of his beloved ships. (S. Prokof'ev *Avtobiografiya*, ed. M. Kozlova, Sovietsky Kompozitor, Moscow 1973). See also pp. 691-2 below.
2 In contrast to the other Allied countries with their murky cocktail of interventionist strategies following the formal end to Russia's state of war with the Central Powers brought about by the Brest-Litovsk Treaty in March 1918, few people doubted that Japan's objectives were strictly territorial: to take control, if possible, of Russia's Far East.
3 Neither Asafyev nor Bashkirov would have travelled to Taganrog in the Ukraine from Petrograd at such a time. 'Borenka' and 'Boryunechka' (see p. 152), although derived from a boy's name, must have been nicknames for Polina Podolskaya.

two days later shall be in Yokohama. Farewell Russia, farewell my old dreams, hail new shores! S. P.'

16 [29] May

Although the steamer was completely booked out, my connections secured me a second-class berth, which I was glad of as I had prepared to go third class if necessary. But the rate of exchange for yen I had to settle for at the last moment was terrible: 5.60, meaning 11.20 roubles to the dollar, which is catastrophic. I bought just 2,500 roubles' worth and put the remainder in my hat. Although I was afraid I might be searched on board and arrested, nothing in fact happened – my suitcase was not even opened and I was asked no questions. All the same, I was not certain I had successfully passed through the eyes of all the needles until we finally cast off from the shore. Conversation with one of the ship's officers: three miles.

And so, farewell Bolsheviks! Farewell 'comrades'! From today it will no longer be a badge of infamy to wear a tie and no one will tread on my toes.

17 [30] May

Slept badly on account of the cramped cabin with four people and two children in it. The steamer *Hosan-Maru* displaces 2,340 tons and can reach 12 knots.[1] The sea was calm but there was a thick fog, caused by evaporation from the cold current from the Sea of Okhotsk meeting the warm water of an offshoot of the Kouro-Sivo current.[2] In consequence during the day the temperature rose quickly, and by the evening was delightfully warm and the weather clear: we were in warm waters.

I was in good spirits, relaxed and dreamy. That evening I thought out the end of my story and looked at the stars.

18 [31] May

When I went on deck next morning we were already approaching Tsurugi,[3] and on either side could see high, sharply etched mountains. It was a pity that on this day in the Land of the Rising Sun its ascent was masked by clouds. The mountains were steep and splendid, their features unlike what we were used to, with tiny, toy villages grouped around their base. In Tsurugi

---

1 Records of the Naval Historical Centre of the US Navy Department in Washington show that the transport ship *Hosan-Maru* was torpedoed and sent to the bottom by the US submarine *Redfish* when in convoy through the Formosa Straits on 23 November 1944.
2 The Kouro-Sivo current flows roughly from the island of Taiwan to Japan.
3 Port on the narrow Noto Peninsula, now merged into the larger municipality of Hakusan.

we were pestered by interminable police examinations: where were we going, for what purpose, who am I, who was my father, who are my friends, how much money do I have, etc. . . . It was, as well, a demonstration of monarchical principles: first class first, followed by second class (at home we would have started with third), and as a result only a few of the first-class passengers were able to catch the Tokyo Express. I had to wait until the ordinary local stopping train at one o'clock.

Stepping on to Japanese soil I experienced that rush of pleasure I invariably have when arriving in foreign parts with their promise of so much that is new. And especially now, after what is in all but name the prison of Russia, to touch down in a prosperous country that does not know war and revolution – does not that in itself give rise to a holiday feeling?

I strolled round the hills surrounding Tsurugi, luxuriant with flowers and bushes in bloom, and gave myself up to meditation. Then I took a rickshaw, a two-wheeled carriage hauled by a Japanese, and went to the station. It felt shameful to be thus transported by a human being, but he was so anxious that I should engage him and so pleased when I sat in his carriage, that I could think of no reason why I should not give 40 yen to pay him for running for twenty minutes. On the train, masses of Russians piled on board, but an hour later, when I changed to another one bound directly for Tokyo, our luxurious first-class compartment was comfortable and roomy, and sometimes the little toy train galloped along like a real English express. I had by no means prepared myself to be impressed by Japan, and was even aware of some feelings of hostility towards the Japanese at their ambitions to annex eastern Siberia, but I had to admit that I had never seen such a delightful country. Enchanting green, steep-sided mountains alternated with fields immaculately parcelled into tiny squares, and so lovingly and carefully tended that those of our comrades who are preoccupied with land reform could certainly do much worse than come and look at how this country does things!

19 May [1 June]

Arrived in Tokyo at five o'clock in the morning. I found a fine room right on the spot, at the Station Hotel, an excellent, stylish even, hotel built above the train station itself. But the first thing that struck my eyes was a notice from the Tokyo Kisen Kaisha Steamship Company regarding boats to Valparaiso. The last boat had left three days ago and there would not be another for two months! Catastrophe! True, the voyage of the recently departed steamer was scheduled to last 69 days via San Francisco and all ports along the west coast of America, but even so by 2 August I would have been where I wanted to be, and it was cheap, only 500 yen. It would have suited me down to the ground, and the only consolation was that a week before sailing there would probably not have been a single berth left! One has to make one's dispositions a month in advance here. With these thoughts I strolled around the far-flung environs of Tokyo and then took a bath (but could not do my Miller exercises as the warm, damp climate would have brought me out in a sweat immediately). After that I took the electric train to Yokohama.

Oh, what an effect my first glimpse of the bright, calm expanse of the Pacific Ocean at Yokohama had on me! I was acutely conscious that this was no ordinary sea but the great, majestic ocean itself.

In Russia we have quite forgotten what it is like to be waited on by polite and ingratiating servants. At breakfast a Japanese bowed low and showered me with a thousand small attentions as he apologised for the bad weather and thanked me for the honour I did him by accepting his service, and placed a cushion under each arm in the smoking-room. Very kind, and to each country its customs, but I did find this a little excessive.

In Yokohama the first thing I did, to my great satisfaction, was buy a pair of yellow shoes, after which I made the rounds of the steamship companies and visited the Argentinian Consulate to find out what ships bound for South America would be sailing, and when. Everywhere I got the same discouraging answer: the voyage would be long, and no sailings were envisaged for the near future.

Today was Saturday, and at one o'clock everywhere closed until Monday. With no good news to console me, I had no option but to hang up my boots for two days.

About this time I caught sight of a poster for a 'Concert by Meyerovich and Piastro,[1] presented by Strock.' Thus does the prey rush towards the hunter!

Strock is the most active and effective impresario in the Far East and exotic territories such as Java and Siam. His base is in Shanghai, and it was partly on account of him that I had thought of going there. But now, all of a sudden, he is here and so am I.

It was not long before I ran into Meyerovich[2] in the Grand Hotel. He had won the Rubinstein Prize graduating from Yesipova's class in the same year as I entered it. Although he hardly knew me at all, after six years in the East he had heard something – not very much – of me. But as it happened his brother had asked me to pass on a letter to him if I ever got to Shanghai, so that Meyerovich was delighted to see me and to get the letter. He and my old classmate Piastro (from the General Studies class at the Conservatoire) have

---

1 Mikhail (Misha) Piastro, violinist, see *Diaries*, vol. 1, p. 8 and *passim*. 'A stout, round-headed youth whose silhouette reminded me of a pawn.' (*Avtobiografiya*, op. cit.)
2 Alfred Meyerovich (1884–1959), pianist. See ibid., pp. 77, 87, 95.

built a huge career and status in the Far East and now live like millionaires. Strock, according to Meyerovich, is now totally beholden to them rather than the other way round. Meyerovich suggested that I should do a series of concerts in their footsteps around the region for Strock, to whom, of course, he would be delighted to introduce me, as the duo was going to take two months off before going to Java. In Asia they had just played eighteen concerts in Shanghai, sixty in Java, and so on. I began to think: might it not be better to take the Asian bird in the hand than the two in the American bush? Perhaps to travel around these tropical centres is no less an attractive proposition than America? In any case, when I left Russia I had had some such ideas in mind, and since there is no early prospect of a passage to South America I must think seriously about what could be a potential enterprise here and now. I am so tired of having to spend every waking moment calculating whether I have enough money and economising on everything.

20 May [2 June]

Tea at four o'clock with Meyerovich, Piastro and Strock. To begin with I felt a little uncomfortable having to depend on two minor-league artists to be promoted on the local concert stage, being obliged to pay attention to their advice and proposals. But they conducted themselves with considerable tact and modesty, great good humour and every sign of acting in my best interests. In this way the atmosphere got off to a friendly and cheerful start, while Strock himself bowed and scraped and announced that in a week's time, as soon as his present involvement with Meyerovich and Piastro came to an end, he was at my disposal to arrange concerts for me in Tokyo and Yokohama. It was a pity the season was now over in Shanghai, otherwise it would have been possible to give a whole series there.

In the evening I accompanied Meyerovich, an admirer of his and her friend – both completely wild girls – to the Café Lion, where we had a private room in which the four of us behaved disgracefully.

To B.N. Verin in Petrograd, from Yokohama: 'Dear Borenka, I am sitting in the Grand Hotel in Yokohama, fifty minutes from Tokyo by electric train, on the veranda washed by the pure, calm expanse of the Pacific Ocean. Several huge ships of twenty, thirty thousand tons are gracing the harbour. Inside the café Japanese waiters, bowing three-quarters of the way to the floor, render me thanks for the honour my presence accords them. From the neighbouring tables I hear the calls of 'double' emanating from Russian émigrés playing bridge. My ship left three days ago for Valparaiso, so I shall be here for a while. I'm going to play some concerts. I kiss you. S.'

21 May [3 June]

Lunched with Vysotsky (to whom I had a letter of recommendation from Meyerhold) in Yokohama. It is confirmed that there are no steamers at all, and if I decide to go via North America then I shall need a transit visa for the United States, which is a near impossibility for a Russian.

Strock and Meyerovich are advising me to go to New York in August. They say it is not true that Russian artists are not welcome there: Zimbalist, Elman, Auer[1] are stars who make a great deal of money there. So should I not strengthen my position here with concerts meanwhile, and then go later to New York, as indeed I had planned to do before the notion of going to Argentina took hold?

In the evening I walked in the Ginza,[2] in the centre of the city, a lively and attractive area hung with little lanterns. It was a gay and animated scene. I should like to meet a pretty Japanese girl.

22 May [4 June]

Dined with Strock, who was terribly reverential. This impresario, a Polish Jew, sets great store by associating only with serious artists. He would very much like to do business with me, but says that to have a real success as a concert artist in the countries of this region it is essential to be a duo. If I could only tour with a good singer (Koshetz?) he would be able to organise more than sixty concerts in Japan, China and even India (!).

America or India? And, would I be able to persuade Koshetz? In the evening I went to the recital by Meyerovich and Piastro, and took away a very favourable impression. The audience was European, well turned out, and the programme consisted of serious music pretty well played. Meyerovich is not bad, although I would not call him a truly outstanding pianist. Piastro, though, is an excellent violinist. An idea: I should compose a violin sonata! In the evening, Meyerovich, Strock and I went to visit Number Nine. On the

---

1   Three famous Russian violinists, the first two students of the third. Efrem Zimbalist (1889–1985) settled in America where from 1941 to 1968 he was Director of the Curtis Institute in Philadelphia and produced further generations of distinguished violinists. Mischa Elman (1891–1967) also lived in America, where he left a very large recorded legacy for HMV and RCA Victor. Leopold Auer (1845–1930) is most famous for the number of spectacularly gifted violinists who passed through his hands at the St Petersburg Conservatoire between 1868 and 1917 (Jascha Heifetz but one name to add to those of Elman and Zimbalist), and later at the Curtis Institute, and also for not giving the premiere of Tchaikovsky's Violin Concerto, written for him but considered by him to be unplayable. (But he did relent and play it later.) See *Diaries*, vol. 1, pp. 132, 134 and *passim*.
2   A fashionable district in the centre of Tokyo, famous for dining, entertainment, art galleries and shopping.

way Meyerovich dropped out, so it was just Strock and I who went into what is, to put it plainly, a brothel, with rooms for Japanese and for Europeans. We were welcomed by the elderly madam, who looked to me like a Hottentot. Four Japanese girls then appeared, two of whom were extremely attractive. These four young, admirably trained slaves entered decorously, bowed low to us and arranged themselves along the wall. Ten minutes later, having bought for each of them a glass of a syrupy species of liquid which they raised to their lips, took one sip to drink our health, and then replaced on the table, we left. Our visit had had no ulterior motive, it had been undertaken purely from curiosity.

To A. N. Benois, Petrograd: 'Very dear A. N., I faithfully swear to you on the Water Shrine depicted overleaf[1] that I had a perfectly ideal journey, that it is beautiful here, and that I send my most loving greetings to you and your family. I am playing some concerts and shall be immured here for several weeks. Your letter to Sasha-Yasha, if I don't have an opportunity to go to Pekin in the near future, I will drop in the post. With sincere affection, S. P.'

23 May [5 June]

Strock came to lunch. He wants to send a telegram to Koshetz, but as I told him, if she were to agree to come it would be at my behest, not his. And if I ask her she will misunderstand the motive. Also, I have not completely given up the idea of going to North America.

Began to compose a violin sonata, and pulled out my stories to look at them. In the evening went for a stroll through the bright lights of the Ginza. Had supper in the 'Shimbashi' café.

Strock asked me if I considered Meyerovich and Piastro truly great artists. I replied that they were good, but not first class. What else could I say? He asked me if they would be successful in Moscow and Petrograd. I said 'no'. Surely I don't have to lie and say 'yes'? After all, they have already made their name here.

24 May [6 June]

In the morning went on composing the sonata. In the afternoon visited the Vysotskys in Tokyo, where I found the people very stylishly dressed. Strock has gone to Kobe to arrange Meyerovich's concert there. There are long articles about me in the Tokyo newspapers. In the evening had a Japanese girl, but caution rather inhibited my pleasure.

1   The Shinto water deity Suiten, or Suijin, is widely worshipped at 'Suiten-gu' shrines throughout Japan, the most famous being the one at Kurume in Fukuoka.

25 May [7 June]

Began 'Guilty Passion'.[1] Violin Sonata. Is it possible that the scherzo is shallow and stupid? One must compose well, otherwise there is no point in writing at all. In the afternoon I called on Aiko Ose, for whom I had a letter to pass on from Balmont. He speaks Russian and publishes a newspaper about Russia in both the Russian and Japanese languages. He adores Balmont. Was not all that interesting.

Ariadna Nikolayevna, whose married name is Rumanova,[2] has recently passed through Japan and, true to her old self, turned every head. Would it ever have occurred to Max Schmidthof, when we were writing to her all those years ago, that in five years' time, walking down the main street of Tokyo with two Japanese journalists, I would be speaking of Ariadna, who has now just crossed the Pacific on her way to America? 'Terribly chic!' Max would have said. She apparently gave a concert somewhere hereabouts but, according to my Japanese informant, played with her face rather than with her fingers.

This morning a policeman came to see me and, in the same way as when we disembarked from the steamer, asked me a whole series of questions about who, why, where from, who my father was, and so on. But one should not be upset by this as it happens to everyone. He showed me a list of about twenty people, Americans and Russians, who were all staying in the hotel.

26 May [8 June]

Telegraphic communication with Russia has been interrupted for the past ten days because of the Bolsheviks' struggle with the Czech echelons in Irkutsk.[3]

---

1 The sadly unfinished short story 'Prestupnaya strast' ('Guilty Passion').
2 Née Nikolskaya, piano student at St Petersburg Conservatoire. See *Diaries*, vol. 1, pp. 251–2, 353–4 and *passim*.
3 The Czech Legion, by this time 35,000-strong and highly trained by comparison with the fragmented, poorly supplied and disaffected Russian Army (whichever side its various components eventually took in the Civil War), was in contrast bound together by its members' common ambition to defeat the Central Powers and free themselves from the yoke of the Austro-Hungarian Empire. After Brest-Litovsk they decided this would best be achieved by quitting Russia and continuing the war in Western Europe, but instead of taking the direct route back through Eastern Europe (and the hazards of crossing enemy territory) the plan was to return through Siberia and America. Although initially there was co-operation from the new Government, local Soviet forces along the way acted with increasing hostility, reflecting the Russian population's generally confused ambivalence towards Germany and the necessity or otherwise of continuing the war, until by the middle of May 1918 open conflict between the Czechs and their persecutors was the norm all along the Trans-Siberian railway line. Once the gloves were off the Czechs had little difficulty in taking control of one town after another all the way until their final seizure of Vladivostok on 29 June. Prokofiev's train had been the last to get through.

My plans are gradually clarifying themselves. Strock has secured the Imperial Theatre for 6 and 7 July, and envisages a further series of concerts after that. Then, assuming I have as much as 1,700 yen (and a visa), I shall go to New York and spend a month there. If it turns out that I can give concerts there, I shall stay, and if not I shall come back to Shanghai in October and give concerts with orchestra.

If only I could be sure that Koshetz or Kokhánski would come, it would make sense to cross out America, stay here and give more concerts in the Far East, but since in the present state of communications with Russia nothing can be relied upon, America is at present the horse I have to put my shirt on, particularly so as there is more point in performing to audiences who understand something (although actually I do not have all that much faith in the understanding of the American public) than to Asians and semi-Europeans.

27 May [9 June]

A certain Obolsky, to whom someone introduced me, has kindly offered his services in connection with my American visa. The day after tomorrow he is leaving for New York, and will visit the Embassy there as well as a number of influential Russians. I seized on his offer with alacrity and asked him to bend all his efforts towards getting me a visa.

Am writing 'Guilty Passion'.

The Violin Sonata has got stuck.

28 May [10 June]

My second visit to the Russian Embassy. They have now got wind of the fact that I am a composer of some sort, have become extraordinarily friendly, and gave me a letter for the Russian Embassy in Washington, which I passed to Obolsky along with McCormick's letter and 20 yen to spend on cabling to let me know the results of his efforts. He promised to do all he could to ensure that a month from now I would be in possession of a visa.

In the Russian Embassy they also know about Ariadna Rumanova. Baron Behr, the Embassy Secretary, explained with a hint of venom that in America they were counting on the similarity of 'Rumanov' to 'Romanov' to create an opportunity for her to pass as a scion, perhaps even an illegitimate one, of the imperial family.

29 May [11 June]

Meyerovich, Piastro and Strock are leaving for concerts in Kyoto and Osaka. Meyerovich invited me to come along and see what ancient, authentic

Japanese towns are like. It would be very interesting, and I have nothing to do in Tokyo; generally I have a whole month with nothing to do if Strock really cannot arrange anything before 6 July. But Strock's explanation is that in Japan it is essential to begin with the Imperial Theatre in Tokyo, and the first date on which it is available is 6 July. Nor is there any point in getting to America before the end of August, so in the meantime I should simply get on with my work and enjoy Japan.

To P. P. Suvchinsky: 'Dear friend, for two weeks now I have been enjoying life in the capital of the Japanese Empire. I am planning to visit some of the beautiful places in Japan, then to play some concerts, and then – onwards, ever onwards! Greetings, S.P.'

30 May [12 June]

At half-past eight in the morning Meyerovich and I left on the express train to Kyoto, an eleven-hour journey. The express has a small but very elegant saloon, and an impressive turn of speed. I was extraordinarily impressed with our trip through beautiful, smiling and very well-ordered Japan. Meyerovich is a splendid chap. Seated on armchairs in the saloon carriage we laughed about what we would have thought in Yesipova's class had we known one day we were going to be speeding in an express train through the heart of Japan chatting about Debussy's *Feux d'artifice*.

My store of yen is appreciably diminishing, and it is only my faith in Strock that prevents my situation becoming parlous.

31 May [13 June]

We went by electric tram into Osaka, a lively and completely Japanese town where we did not encounter a single European. One especially fantastic sight was the theatre, not so much the stage, but the auditorium, in which the whole audience was sitting in what resembled little square boxes gobbling rice and fluttering their fans with incredible rapidity. The streets at evening presented a curious spectacle, with thousands of lanterns large and small, and huge crowds promenading. At home our hairdressers have special manicure sections, but here there are whole departments for cleaning ears. It might not be a bad idea to send some of our cloth-eared musicians here.

1 [14 June]

I have done no work for five days, and am experiencing such cravings that I am glad I do not have to go anywhere today. Wandered round the environs of Kyoto with Meyerovich among thousands of Buddhist shrines and amazing water-engineering projects (canals carried through tunnels) in a delightful landscape. This is the real Japan. Meyerovich suggested giving a concert in Honolulu on my way to America, and this is a most seductive idea; after all, I have long dreamed of going to Honolulu. My room is lovely, half European-style and half Japanese, with movable walls of carved screens and mats on the floor. The only problem is that it is terribly expensive, my yen are evaporating fast and the rouble has fallen still further. I'm not sure how much I will get when I change my remaining 'fivers',[1] and it pains me to think how much they used to be worth!

2 [15] June

I spent the whole day on my own today, wrote 'Guilty Passion' (with enormous enjoyment), learned some Chopin by reading the score, and thought. In the evening Meyerovich and I went to a tea-house. There are hundreds of these places with geishas dancing. Four girls danced a 'naked dance' for us, that is to say a dance of the naked girls. As far as I could see all they did was leap about a bit for the benefit of gullible Europeans, but at least they did genuinely remove all their clothes and even suggested 'short sleep'.[2] Eventually one of them, the prettiest, while sitting on my lap removed my jewelled brooch. A good thing I realised in time, when I found my brooch which she had managed, don't you know, to attach to her hair while laying her head on my chest.

3 [16] June

Wrote 'Guilty Passion'. I also read through *The Love for Three Oranges*. I am very attracted by the idea of writing an opera on this subject, and I think I probably will do so, but I do not like the way the story has been developed. Benois gave me the Italian original,[3] and I must read it in that language. Then I have to distinguish the parallel events of the 'underground forces' and integrate them with the goings-on above ground.

4 [17] June

With Piastro and the very pretty girlfriend he picked up in Shanghai I went on a trip along the canal system, remarkable for the fact that they go through a series of long tunnels.

---

1 Five-rouble notes.
2 Prokofiev wrote 'naked dance' and 'short sleep' in English.
3 Carlo Gozzi produced his *commedia dell'arte L'amore della tre melarance* in 1761. Gozzi himself had taken it from an ancient Neapolitan fairy-tale included by Giambattista Basile in his *Pentamerone* collection, published (posthumously) in 1636.

5 [18] June

Tuesday. Finished 'Misunderstandings Sometimes Occur'. That is six,[1] and concepts for another four. Altogether ten, and that will be enough for now.

Piastro has gone to the seaside with his elegant girlfriend. Meyerovich has moved out to Nara, two hours' journey from here, and rang up to persuade me to go there too. He says there is a wonderful hotel in the middle of a park. I might just do that.

6 [19] June

An idea for the Andante of the Violin Sonata. At four o'clock I moved to Nara, where there is a marvellous hotel situated right on the shore of a lake in the middle of a huge sacred park with a mass of shrines and memorials. Sacred deer wander about the park; they are quite tame and will come right up to you if you offer them bread. In the pond there are goldfish an arshin long,[2] plump and repellent, also sacred. It is quiet and relaxed here. There is a wonderful bell shaped like a mitre, but the sound it makes is like an enormous, noble gong.

7 [20] June

'The White Friend' began to emerge from the mists. Sometimes I think it is going to be the most successful of all the stories, at others that it is a ludicrous attempt to write a seriously poetic piece.

This is a good environment to work in, but I cannot get down to it. Last summer, which is such a golden memory for me, generated its own momentum for using the time, so that without feeling subject to continual pressure I could take pleasure in my work and way of life in my lovely dacha. But here I feel in flux (all this year I have lived under the shadow of relentless striving) and cannot concentrate or bury myself in my work as I did before. In

---

[1] Three of these six stories are: 'A Bad Dog', 'The Tale of the Poisonous Mushroom' and 'Misunderstandings Sometimes Occur'. 'An Incident with a Leg' and 'Mirror of the Soul', both of which Prokofiev states he finished, appear to have disappeared. Six more stories: 'Ultraviolet Freedom', 'The Smoking Room', 'The Wandering Tower', 'The Toads', 'The Two Marquises' and 'Death of the Watchmaker' were all completed later. 'Guilty Passion' and a fragment beginning 'Do you know when the boat for Africa sails?' survived but were not finished. All the extant short stories and fragments were collected and published by Alla Bretanitskaya in an edition to mark the fiftieth anniversary of the composer's death: *S. S. Prokof'ev, Rasskazy*, Kompozitor, Moscow, 2003. 'A Bad Dog', 'The Wandering Tower', parts of 'Misunderstandings Sometimes Occur', 'The Tale of the Poisonous Mushroom' and 'The Two Marquises' were translated by David McDuff, Oleg Prokofiev and Christopher Palmer, and are included in the collection *Sergei Prokofiev Soviet Diary 1927 and Other Writings*, edited by Oleg Prokofiev (Faber and Faber, London, 1991).

[2] 1.7 metres.

general I am coming to the conclusion (oh, shame!) that I like having money and perhaps, after this trip, I will have some.

8 [21] June

'The White Friend' is getting on well, but I have got bogged down with Forccio[1] in the third chapter of his story, one I am most attached to.

Telegrams arrive from Russia saying that the Czechs have captured the Siberian railway line from Tomsk to Samara and are fighting the Bolsheviks. I slipped through on the last train; a good thing I have not been counting on Koshetz! And although trains previous to mine did get through, they were subjected to all kinds of dreadful searches and other forms of harassment. My trip was a magical fairy-tale.

An idea has come to me for a 'white quartet'. I jotted down a couple of thoughts and recalled an old theme (for the main subject).[2]

9 [22] June

Went back to Kyoto. Strock has written to an impresario in Honolulu, about which I am delighted.

Tickets are cheap for Meyerovich's and Piastro's concerts (5 yen).[3] The concerts are mainly interesting in that they represent attempts to play serious compositions to an alien population which is nevertheless starting to take an interest in European music. On the one hand, the attitude of the Japanese is extremely attentive, on the other it is obvious that with all their studious attention they do not understand anything and would not be able to tell whether what you were playing them was a Beethoven sonata or something improvised out of your own head. The things that engender enthusiasm are superficial effects like *pizzicato*, pearly runs on the piano, that kind of thing. It is interesting to play once or twice for such an audience, but thereafter it would lack all stimulus.

10 [23] June

It is pleasant being in Nara but rather boring. I am surprised at myself for finding it boring to be on my own, but the reason lies in the fact that I am neither writing nor composing (I am taking a short break from both activities) and the only reading matter I have with me is Schopenhauer. I am rereading *The World As Will* and derive a great deal of pleasure from it, but

---

1   Forccio della Furccia is a character in the story 'Guilty Passion'.
2   This was not first time the idea had come to Prokofiev: he had conceived a similar notion in October 1914. Possibly the theme he mentions comes from that time? See *Diaries*, vol. 1, p. 751.
3   In fact, as Prokofiev later discovered (see p. 301 below), this was quite an expensive ticket price.

it is not a book one can read much of at a time: an hour or two a day. In consequence I have many hours a day to fill.

11 [24] June

Piastro and his Marusya have reappeared, and I am glad to see them. We have been for walks, drunk cocktails and played billiards. Piastro had amazing stories to tell of Java, Siam and India, where he has been on many concert tours.

An extraordinary thing: all the walls of the hotel here are hung with pictures, landscapes and so on, but when I wanted a map of Europe to find the Princes' Islands[1] for my story, such a thing was not to be found anywhere. Europe may think it is the centre of the world, but the world hereabouts gets on quite well without it.

12 [25] June

What precisely is my attitude to my writing? The top and bottom of it is that I tremendously enjoy it. That is in itself enough of an answer. And should it turn out that, in addition, it is very good writing (the pity of it is that it would never be enough for me to be simply good), then am I not doubly justified?! As for the expenditure of time and energy that I might otherwise devote to composition, I can in all conscience say that up till now I have worked a great deal, and if there is a short intermission it may do me some good as a means of refreshment to work better in the future.

I agree that the results may seem to be not very good, but at the present time I am unable to be precise about what it is that makes them not good.

13 [26] June

There was a domestic spat today between Piastro and his pretty friend – and indeed I am glad that there is no Lina nor Koshetz nor Eleonora here. Eventually the two of them calmed down.

14 [27] June

Life is stagnating at the moment, and the rain is pouring down. I read Schopenhauer with great pleasure, the last book of *Will*, but I cannot accommodate myself to his pessimism.

My thoughts turn with great affection to my friends, B. Verin, Asafyev, and also Suvchinsky.

---

1   A chain of nine small islands off Istanbul in the Sea of Marmara, the largest of which is Büyükada (Greek Prinkipo, meaning 'Prince').

15 [28] June

Went over to Kyoto with the aim of returning tomorrow to Tokyo. I ought to refresh my memory of the repertoire before the concerts, although to play for such an audience hardly merits great efforts. Nevertheless, it is two and a half months since I touched a piano.

Thought of a story about a man with no bones.[1]

16 [29] June

In the morning boarded the Limited Express for Tokyo and sat in the observation car. Once again I had the pleasure of travelling by day through beautiful and well-groomed Japan. Every square inch of ground amenable to cultivation, and even much that is not very amenable is tilled with a love and a care unheard-of in Europe. I caught only the odd glimpse of Fujiyama appearing through the clouds, conical and severe, as we rounded a curve. I put up at the Station Hotel, in the same room as I had stayed in before. There were no letters for me from Russia, and indeed I had hardly expected any in view of the Czechoslovak blockade of the Siberian railway.

17 [30] June

In Tokyo it was hot, dusty and unpleasant. I went to Yokohama and decided I would like to move out there. The Grand Hotel is expensive, but it has a marvellous terrace overlooking the Pacific, and that alone makes it worth while being there.

The first announcements of my concert have appeared.

I long to be off to the Sandwich Islands and New York.

18 June [1 July]

Moved to the Grand Hotel in Yokohama. I need to put on a bit of style before my concerts. Also, it is cooler here and there are more Europeans. When it is sultry I love the way the horizon appears as a vague line imperceptibly shading into the sky. At night there is a wonderful view of Scorpio and its red Antares. In this region the whole constellation glitters in impressive visibility and does genuinely look like a terrifying mystical beast.

---

[1] This became 'The Toads' ('Zhaby').

19 June [2 July]

Strock is proposing to sell for 850 yen both Tokyo concerts to a promoter (500 to me and 350 to him). I was appalled at such a pittance, but he says we will certainly not get any more for afternoon concerts out of season. Accordingly we decided to prostitute ourselves and sell them for this amount.

This is bad news indeed: I need 1,700 to 2,000 yen to go to America and if all I can get is a handful of kopecks like this I am in danger of failing to scrape up enough. I shall have to pin my hopes on Honolulu. But to appear in public for 250 roubles – what on earth was the point of becoming famous?

I dined in a Japanese restaurant with a Japanese journalist, a meeting set up by the Director of the Imperial Theatre with the object of generating some publicity. Otaguro's book about music contains several references to me. When the book appeared it created a great impression in the press; Otaguro himself, who is also the director of the publishing house, is extremely well informed about Russian music and we spent the whole dinner, served Japanese-style with us squatting on our haunches, talking (in English). It was a place where geishas danced, so each diner had two young, attractively dressed Japanese girls sitting opposite him. Very nice.[1]

20 June [3 July]

In the mornings I play the piano at the Vysotskys and in the afternoons go with them to the beach. It is very hot. The hotel is comfortable and good quality. At breakfast there are sixty-two separate dishes on offer. That would be something to show the poor hungry people of Petrograd!

In Vladivostok the Czechs have routed the Bolsheviks. There is fighting all over Siberia. It is clear that there is a second revolution going on in Russia. But will it bring order and stability?

---

1   Motoo Otaguro (1893–?) was the son of one of the founders of what became the Toshiba industrial empire. A music-lover of unusual cultivation and breadth of knowledge, he had studied in London before returning to Japan on the outbreak of war. His house and garden in Suginami became a centre for Japan's growing lovers of Western music to hear performances of composers such as Debussy; in his will he bequeathed the estate to the city and it is now – because Otaguro was also a well-known practitioner of the tea-ceremony – a celebrated garden and traditional tea-house. In 2004 the Russian musicologist Eleonora Sablina discovered in Tokyo's Archives of Modern Japanese Music – a building just across the street from the Russian Embassy – vol. 3 no. 8 of the magazine founded by Otaguro, *Ongaku to bungaku*, containing his article based on this interview with Prokofiev. Transcribed by Otaguro evidently more or less verbatim, it gives so revealing an insight into Prokofiev's view on music, his life and prospects and other matters of interest at the time that, with Eleonora Sablina's generous permission, I have retranslated into English and included as Appendix 3 her Russian translation of Otaguro's Japanese version of what, as the composer tells us, was a conversation conducted in uncertain English by a Japanese and a Russian. I hope the circuitous transition from English via Japanese and Russian back to English manages to preserve something of what was obviously an unusually lively and candid exchange.

Gessen has brought out *Rech* in Berlin. I am very pleased that he has sprung to life again.¹

21 June [4 July]

Today is American Independence Day, and therefore the cause of a magnificent celebration in the Grand Hotel, gawked at by crowds tramping up and down outside the hotel. Seeing them, the Americans persuaded themselves that they too must be celebrating their democratic festival.

As for me I donned a frock-coat and strolled through the elegant terraces and salons, relishing the sight of the fashionable gowns and handsome faces. Whichever way one looks at it, nowhere in Russia had I seen such a gathering since the beginning of the war, still less since the Revolution. There were quite a number of people I knew, and I enjoyed myself very much. I took a terrific fancy to one dusky-skinned Filipino woman of about seventeen, the wife of some diplomat or other, but although I managed to strike up an acquaintance with her I had, sadly, no success.

22 June [5 July]

Began to draft out 'The Toads', my first static story.² The idea for the beginning came from yesterday's festivities.

In the evening I had an upset stomach, probably from something I ate, and on the way to the lavatory I fainted. Strock was very alarmed that tomorrow's concert might have to be cancelled, and took extra solicitous care of me. The doctor came (an Englishman in a dinner-jacket) and said that it was nothing to worry about, it happens to everyone here, and I would be fine to play the next day.

23 June [6 July]

Next morning I felt quite well and set off for the concert, albeit a little warily. I played without much emotional engagement, looking on it as a job that had to be done. There were very few people there (it was a Saturday, at 1.15 p.m. on a hot day) so it was a good thing we had sold the concert. The audience

---

1 As a prominent Kadet, Iosif Gessen declared his opposition to the Bolshevik Party immediately after the October Revolution and first joined the general staff of General Nikolay Yudenich's somewhat equivocally Allied-supported North-Western Army. Gessen may have visited Berlin in 1918, but it was not until the following year that he finally left Russia for Finland, and a year after that that he founded with his close friend and collaborator Vladimir Dmitrievich Nabokov, father of the novelist, another Social-Democratic newspaper in Berlin, and then it was not called *Rech* ('Speech') but *Rul'* ('The Helm').

2 With no action, purely dialogue.

was almost exclusively Japanese, and they listened very attentively. They did not applaud much, and when they did it was in response to technically arresting things. They were not at all disconcerted by dissonances, because for a Japanese, accustomed to a completely different kind of music, there is hardly any difference between what our ears hear as consonances and dissonances.

24 June [7 July]

The second concert. There was a bigger audience, because the director of the hall had distributed a hundred complimentary tickets, so that at least it looked respectable. Respectable was also the word for how they listened. At the request of some local musicians I had included *Suggestion Diabolique* in the programme for this concert, and as before the greatest success was reserved for the technically demanding numbers. Again we were the gainers for having the sold the concert: if we had promoted it ourselves Strock and I would have earned 300 between us.

In the evening I wrote more of 'The Toads'.

25 June [8 July]

In the evening read through 'The Toads' and came to the conclusion that I had misjudged the tone. What emerged was a kind of Gorkyesque mish-mash, in a word God only knows what it was. I crossed it out and threw it away.

26 June [9 July]

In the evening, my concert in Yokohama, in the new hall of the Grand Hotel, with the same programme as the first of the Tokyo recitals. Tickets cost 5 yen, but this proved to be so expensive that a lot of people left without buying a ticket. The audience was tiny (forty to fifty people) but listened with great seriousness. My net receipts amounted to 41 yen. Not only this, but Strock received a letter telling him that the concerts in Kobe and Osaka, and a third one planned for Tokyo, could not take place.

So that put paid to the 2,000 yen I needed for America. Instead I had in my pocket 850 yen, and no more in prospect. But I did not want to wait for another round of autumn concerts with Strock, this would be tedious and moreover would probably not produce much money either. It was urgent to get to New York, but the money I had at my disposal would not suffice to get me there even in second class. I therefore decided to go to Honolulu, where I would play a couple of concerts and accumulate some more dollars, and then – New York.

At the concert today four Russian musicians, members of the hotel's salon orchestra, came up to me and after many respectful compliments told me that they had been in Honolulu and there was a great demand for serious concerts there.

27 June [10 July]

Strock has departed. When he wished me 'all the best', I replied, 'And the best thing of all – would be a better impresario.' He placed the blame on the heat and the fact that it was not the season, and generally said how distressed he was that our concerts had proceeded so ingloriously, because he never undertook anything 'that was not first class'. I said: 'Just once in a blue moon God sent you a truly first-class artist, but you did not know how to make anything of him.'

I visited my old acquaintances the Konshins,[1] who are living an hour's journey from Yokohama with their extensive family. I thoroughly enjoyed the day; the company included many fashionable girls and ladies.

28 June [11 July]

I rewrote everything I had eliminated from 'The Toads', and this time it turned out well. I have to be circumspect in the dialogue: of course this type of person is not going to speak like a member of the intelligentsia, but God preserve me from too many genuinely coarse expressions. I need to find more of a 'psychological coarseness', not simply one of style.

When am I going to get a telegram from New York? Every day that passes more of my money dribbles away, and the only thing keeping me here is that telegram.

I very much like Japanese geishas.

29 June [12 July]

An Englishman has offered me the use of a Bechstein in an empty apartment, and I have begun going there in the mornings to work and practise. I looked through the material I had sketched out for the Violin Sonata, but I have got out of the way of composing at the piano and did not achieve much. However, the Sonata has the potential to turn out well. I comprehensively tore up the first movement from top to tail.

---

1 See *Diaries*, vol. 1, p. 199 and *passim*. Alexey Konshin had been Director of the Russian State Bank and since the outbreak of war until he emigrated President of the Russian Commercial-Industrial Bank.

I went into Tokyo to dine with the Marquis Tokugawa, a young and uncommonly engaging Japanese who is deeply interested in European music. I was interested in having the chance to observe from close up the attitudes and demeanour of a scion of the Japanese aristocracy, but the Marquis proved to be completely Europeanised and an extremely charming and straightforward gentleman, so I was not rewarded with any glimpses of the East.[1]

30 June [13 July]

The Englishman has an excellent library of modern music. I did not compose today, but played Reger, Roger,[2] Ravel, Medtner, which gave me great pleasure. Despite the noisy *réclame* of modernism, all this music is harmonious, admirably done and pleasant to the ear. But it is not profound. My music is better.

1 [14] July

My life has turned into a mere waiting-room where I pass the time until I can move to the next stage. This is the cause of my anxiety, which prevents me wanting to do anything, and the result of this is boredom and depression. I force myself to look at the matter philosophically, and this has a great effect on my mood. After all, no amount of whining will make the telegram come any sooner.

Finished reading *The World As Will*. Schopenhauer has of course, been a great event in my life, but I still cannot accept *The World As Will*. I do not dispute his ideas, on the contrary I embrace them with enthusiasm, nevertheless for myself I am not able to see the world as suffering, rather as cause for rejoicing.

---

1 The Marquis Yoshichika Tokugawa, nineteenth head of the once all-powerful *daimyo* (feudal lord) Owari Tokugawa family and a relation of Emperor Hirohito, was one of Japan's greatest cultural philanthropists between the two world wars. An early supporter of Dr Suzuki and his universal violin-teaching method, he was acutely conscious of the dichotomy between his hereditary status as a prominent member of the old aristocracy and the need for social reform. In 1935 he donated to the nation what became the Tokugawa Art Museum in Nagoya, a priceless repository of art treasures and memorabilia that had been in the possession of his family for many centuries, notably those from the Edo period dating from the start of the seventeenth century. During the Second World War Marquis Tokugawa was sent to occupied Singapore as Director of the Raffles Library and Museum, where he made himself responsible for an unprecedented (at the time) collaboration between British and Japanese scholars passionately determined to preserve the library's unique heritage from the looting and destruction that would otherwise certainly have destroyed it.
2 Jean Roger-Ducasse (1873–1954), French composer and teacher, who succeeded Gabriel Fauré (with whom he had studied) as professor of composition at the Paris Conservatoire.

2 [15] July

Decided to pursue a parallel course over my visa through the American Consul, because I may have to wait until the autumn for a telegram to come from Obolsky. I was reluctant to appeal to the Consul, having pictured him as some kind of wild beast (so many Russians have had terrible experiences getting this visa) but the old gentleman proved to be very pleasant, and after making me fill out a questionnaire sent me on to the American Embassy in Tokyo. They were nice there as well, considered McCormick an excellent referee, and said that I would undoubtedly be given a visa. The problem was that one of the two existing telegraphic cable connections was broken at present, and the remaining one was so overloaded with telegrams that no answer could be expected before three weeks. They took 72 yen from me for the telegram, but this was better than the 200 I had been expecting. It was therefore a present, and a much needed one for someone as impoverished as I.

3 [16] July

The Spaniards Albeniz and Granados are attractive, but shallow and occasionally primitive in their technique. Debussy's refinement, in the introductory passage of his *Faun*, is full of enchantment and poetry, despite the way he mutates interminably from the aimless to the vacuous. His early works are just plain bad.

In the evening a game of bridge left me 31 yen poorer, a most inopportune outcome.

4 [17] July

The hotel department of greatest interest to me is pigeon-hole No. 23 in the office, where messages for me are deposited. In particular I am waiting for Obolsky's telegram, and for a letter from Tokugawa who, Baron Behr says, wants to commission a work from me. (And this means yen, damn it.)

5 [18] July

In light of the proposed intervention in Siberia, the value of the rouble has risen, so at the moment I ought to be able to sell my three remaining 500-rouble notes for 375 yen. If so, my total assets would amount to 600 yen. This will be enough to live on until I get my visa, to pay for the voyage to Honolulu in second class, and still leave about 200 yen over. Up to a point, therefore, I can stop being so worried about money.

6 [19] July

At the invitation of my English friend, at whose place I continue to spend the mornings playing modern music, I accompanied him to a place called Karuizawa, six hours' journey away through smoke soot and heat, right in the middle of Nippon, three thousand feet above sea-level. Because of the elevation it is much cooler than in the frying-pan of Yokohama, and thus more pleasant to be in. The Englishman (in fact he is an Australian) has rented a simple Japanese house with movable walls there, lived in by the wife of a musician.

7 [20] July

I have done a lot of walking. Karuizawa is not distinguished for its beauty, but there is a certain charm attached to spending time in the real Japanese countryside. Our hosts are kind people and very interested in new music, but the children cry and scream like wild animals and drive one to distraction. It is amazing how Japanese children never seem to cry at all. Basically, the Japanese are a contented people who are always smiling, are never quarrelsome, and would be very attractive were it not for their tendency to be sly and secretive.

9 [22] July

Returned to Yokohama and, although I was not anticipating any good news from the post, found a letter from Baron Behr (the Secretary of the Russian Embassy) containing a request passed on from Tokugawa to compose a work for him, also a card from Minster, a delightful young man, telling me that if I liked the idea there was an exceptionally cheap room going in a good (so he says) hotel in the town of Omori, between Tokyo and Yokohama, where he lives with his utterly delightful wife.

I am happy to leave Yokohama with its heat, dust and expense.

10 [23] July

The hotel in Omori is quiet, although not particularly luxuriously appointed. The Minsters have a nice circle of French friends, also staying in the hotel. Mme Minster herself is an attractive young woman and from what I can tell seems a most charming personality.

I wrote letters and some more of 'Guilty Passion', and strolled among the fabulously cultivated and cared-for Japanese fields.

Am more relaxed about having to wait for my visa.

11 [24] July

Ariadna the Magnificent has left her mark in this little corner as well: walking in the garden I came across a taciturn Italian whistling themes from *Boris Godunov*. This he was doing in memory of a Russian lady with whom he had fallen in love. Apparently she had played him *Boris Godunov* and then left for America. The lady's name was Rumanova.

12 [25] July

Svirsky, one of the people staying in the hotel, is an outstanding pianist (I would place him among the genuinely first class), but suffers spasms while playing and has therefore abandoned his musical career in favour of tennis.

People here went into ecstasies when I played them my music, although I preferred to play Medtner. Of the Gavottes, thank God, they liked the D major.[1] I have now transcribed it for piano, having previously always played it without notating any transcription.

Svirsky: 'Debussy is a complete fraud.'(!) Well, not complete, but often enough.

13 [26] July

I am delighted with my stay in Omori. And the main thing is, I have started work again: I am writing 'The Tower' and 'Passion'.

I wrote for Otaguro an article about Myaskovsky for his Japanese journal. Am reading a Spanish novel. Even though the immediate necessity of knowing this language has passed, it has long been part of my general plan to master six languages (should the seventh be Esperanto?), so having nothing more urgent to do I shall do some reading in Spanish. It is a pity that I cannot find a dictionary here anywhere.

It seems as though my financial situation will also become easier, as the correspondence with Tokugawa via Baron Behr is moving towards a conclusion. I have asked 500 yen for the work. I think this is quite high for a Japanese, no matter how rich.

14 [27] July

Whenever I think of Mama and imagine how she must be fretting with no news of me, I become very distressed. But what with the conflict with the

---

1 The third movement of the 'Classical' Symphony, not the piano piece from Op. 12, which is in G minor.

Czechoslovaks, I don't suppose she has heard anything from or about me, and it will be some time before she does. But I had to leave, because had I stayed I would have effectively been buried alive, moreover what would we have had to live on by the autumn? The only consolation is that if the Caucasus really is occupied by the Germans, or indeed is directly threatened by such an eventuality, Mama will be relieved that I am not there.

15 [28] July

Went to Miyanoshita: first, because it is a very beautiful place in the mountains, second, it is only two hours away; and third, I promised Tokugawa I would visit him and in any case we have to settle the commission. Even though I don't expect to come back with any of the money, I am sure my turning up there will have an effect.

Miyanoshito is a beautiful spot with a fine hotel, where I met a group of Russians with whom we all went on a bus to look at the surrounding countryside. I did not find Togugawa at home, but saw him for five minutes while I was sitting in the bus waiting for the return journey. He promised to come to see me in Omori, but did not mention the commission. However, after all the negotiations that have gone through the Embassy, I think it would be difficult for him altogether to withdraw the offer on the grounds of the fee being asked.

16 [29] July

Went to the American Embassy in Tokyo. They were very nice, but there is still no visa, even though the second cable has been repaired.

I have now sufficient facility in the language to start the Spanish novel again from the beginning. I'm also returning to the book about Babylon. It is incredibly interesting.[1]

17 [30] July

I wrote some more of 'The Wandering Tower', and think I will finish it in a few days. I had rather cooled towards it, but the Babylon book rekindled my interest.

In the evening I talked long with the astoundingly nice Mme Minster (Froska-san, as her friends call her), who is interested in everything. I have the warmest impression of her, while I imagine she thinks of me as a clever and deeply unpleasant man.

---

1   See p. 276 n. 1 above.

18 [31] July

A telephone call from the American Embassy to inform me that they have received authorisation to grant me a visa. In a state of wild excitement I rushed upstairs to pass on the good news to the Minsters and to Svirsky, and immediately set off for the Embassy back in Tokyo. There they took an additional 28 yen off me (because the telegram had come via Europe, no less), and despatched me with a missive in a superb envelope to the Consul in Yokohama, who within five minutes gave me the precious visa. While I was in his office I met a Cook's representative, who told me that he could let me have a ticket to Honolulu for a sailing the day after tomorrow. I paid a deposit, and in two days' time I shall be out of Japan.

But Tokugawa? And what about the money? Might it not be better to wait for the commission and go straight to America without calling in at Honolulu? But then again, what if the commission was not forthcoming? No, the sooner I go, the better. Accordingly I set about paying my farewell calls and went to see Kosato.[1]

19 July [1 August]

Made my farewell call at the Russian Embassy. Baron Behr advised me to send Tokugawa a telegram telling him I was leaving the country. I said that I had no wish to impose myself on him, but Baron Behr explained that it was simply a matter of courtesy, since there was no question that Tokugawa really did want me to write a piece of music for him. I sent the telegram.

That afternoon in Omori we played bridge. Everyone envied me my imminent departure, and it was a holiday atmosphere.

In the evening I packed my things. Frosya-san kept coming into my room, lavishing attention on me and being as nice as can be.

20 July [2 August]

There was a slight earthquake at four o'clock in the morning, but it was not a very frightening one and, if one may put it so, a rather more refined one than in Kislovodsk. The pleasant shaking sensation lasted about five seconds.

I spoke to Tokugawa on the telephone. He is extremely distressed that he has not got a work from me, and wants to stay in correspondence. But to hell with him, I should have realised that actually nothing would come of it. On top of that, I exchanged my last 1,500 roubles not for 375 yen, as I had expected, but for 300. The result is that, once I have bought my ticket, I shall

---

1   An acquaintance in Yokohama.

have 73 dollars for Honolulu. I was most annoyed. The Minsters came to Yokohama to see me off, and when I laughingly told them that I was leaving the country with 73 dollars and a diamond brooch, Minster insisted on lending me 100 dollars, and five large gold pieces for which he had no use at the moment. I did not want to take any of it, especially the gold pieces which are unobtainable at the moment. But he was so nice, and so insistent that I was making unnecessary difficulties from misplaced delicacy and I might really need the funds in Honolulu, that I took them, promising to return them in gold in due course. And I must admit that, once on board, I was extremely glad to have the gold pieces with me.

I was allocated a state room on my own, even though I only had a second-class ticket. Lying on my chaise-longue I hardly noticed us slipping imperceptibly away from the shore. The steamship *Grotius* is a fairly large Dutch boat, 8,000 tons, *en route* from Java to San Francisco. All evening we stayed in sight of the shore.

That night I slept well, and coming on deck at four o'clock just before dawn, saw the most wonderful sight: in the lightening sky, from which the stars were already disappearing, hung the waning moon and alongside her Jupiter and bright, bright Venus.

21 July [3 August]

And so, my first day on the ocean. The water is dark blue, like ultramarine. The ship has a slight roll, and this is very noticeable at meals in the second-class dining-room. Feeling somewhat seasick, I decided to miss breakfast, and took lunch out on deck in my chaise-longue. After lunch I walked round the deck, felt wretched and ended up 'feeding the caviare'. After that I went to sleep on my chaise and when I woke up felt better, although I decided I would not be stirring much from my chaise.

Today they have carried out a repair of some kind on the ship's engines and our speed has increased from twelve and half knots to fourteen and a half.

22 July [4 August]

Slept well, rocked by the rolling of the ship. At four o'clock went on deck to see if I could see Venus, but the night was too cloudy. Next morning the sea was steel-grey under the clouds. The ship was rolling more now, but in long, lazy motions. However, I felt better than I did the day before, and took a few turns round the deck although preferring out of caution to stay mainly in my chaise-longue. It is extremely nasty in my state room, especially when I hear the noise of caviare-feeding proceeding from the adjacent cabins. I decided I would go down to the restaurant for lunch, but thought better of it and had it out on deck.

Read *Tristan et Iseut*, a very poetic account of the legend in French, given to me by Frosya-san in return for the promise she extracted from me that I would read it during the first days of the voyage.

23 July [5 August]

The night being terribly stuffy, at four o'clock I went on deck. Venus had hidden herself behind clouds, but the dawn was magnificent. I then slept outside in my chaise-longue.

Today the sea is calm and the sun is shining. I am used to the motion of the ship now, and feel fine.

Finished (in my head) 'The Wandering Tower', of which I already had the beginning and the end, but had not worked the details of the middle.

Read *Tristan* and started on Taine,[1] also a present from Frosya-san.

24 July [6 August]

Overslept and missed not only the dawn but also, very nearly, breakfast. The rolling of the ship has almost completely ceased. The ocean is a bright, deep blue, with thousands of sparkling highlights on the waves at play in the sunshine. I feel wonderful.

Am reading Taine, a stimulating and brilliantly written book on art. I must, as a priority, master the history of art. My knowledge of this subject is far too skimpy, and it is an inexcusable lacuna.

25 July [7 August]

The rolling was bad again today, the sky grey and overcast. By now I am hardly aware of the rolling, but still do not feel as well as when it is calm. Up till now the ship has been sailing east, but now at last she has turned towards the south. It's about time: the weather has grown grey and windy, and my arm has been in a draught.

All evening I had a horrible headache, and took an aspirin at night.

---

[1] Hippolyte Taine (1828–1893), French critic and historian, one of the most prominent intellectual forces of his period. Taine's deterministic ideas, his belief that man and the development of human society are the product of heredity, historical conditioning and environment, had a deep and widespread effect on European philosophy, aesthetics, literary criticism and the social sciences.

26 July [8 August]

My arm is better, and the weather has improved. It is warm, the sea blue and calm.

Annihilated two friendly Dutchmen at chess. They play seriously, slowly and cautiously, but in the end badly.

Finished 'The Wandering Tower'. I had actually written the end in Omori, but many places in the middle I had not put together. It means that I have seven stories to show for a year's 'literary' activity, plus two half-finished fragments ('The Toads' and 'Guilty Passion'), thus a total of eight. Were I to carry on in the same way for forty years, I would have a corpus of three hundred and twenty stories. A substantial writer.

27 July [9 August]

The ocean is calm. The voyage is becoming monotonous. I read Taine, and lack all inclination to compose anything: I cannot concentrate, because round every corner I hear the sound of a Dutchman whistling. I look at the stars and find them absorbing. Mars is in conjunction with Antares: the reddest planet with the reddest star. Which is the brighter and more beautiful I cannot decide, but the light from Antares is alive, while that from Mars is merely a reflection.

27 July [9 August] bis

A remarkable event today: the second Friday in a single week. As we move eastwards, the time moves forward by half an hour in each day, so there are actually only twenty-three-and-a-half hours in every twenty-four. In this way a complete extra day eventually accumulates, which is accounted for when one crosses the 180-degree meridian.[1]

A sheaf of telegrams from Honolulu by wireless telegraph, among them one stating that Russia has declared war on England. This news produced a sensation among the passengers. The friendly Dutch crowded round me and a couple of other Russian passengers, anxious to know what effect this war would have, and did we not think we would be arrested the moment we disembarked on American soil? We explained that war of this nature would be simply an aspect of the class struggle, and not a conventional war between nations. Later it transpired that the news had emanated from dispatches from Berlin, and was therefore in all probability a piece of provocation.[2]

---

1 180°, exactly halfway round the circumference of the globe from the Greenwich, or Prime, Meridian.
2 See pp. 175–6 above.

28 July [10 August]

Another wireless telegraph communication arrived today, with the news that the Soviet Government had declared a state of war against all the Allies, but qualifying it by saying that the war was purely a matter of defence. This, being interpreted, amounted to a simple matter of preparations to combat the growing possibility of Western intervention. But it is still a most unwelcome development, even if the Americans make a clear distinction between Russians generally and Bolsheviks in particular.[1] However this may be, it may give rise to all kinds of unpleasantnesses in America. Suppose they do not let us land in Honolulu? I don't think this will happen, but it might.

Red Mars changes its position every day, and I observe its progress. Scorpio is already high in the sky, promising many new southern stars, but the lower part of the sky is always obscured by storm clouds.

29 July [11 August]

The voyage is assuming a rather monotonous character, although I am not yet experiencing actual boredom. I am saved from this by Taine and Babylon, and the occasional game of chess with the Dutchmen (result: +13 out of thirteen).

My state of mind is not completely calm, however, because I cannot be sure what little surprises America may be preparing for me in the light of the Soviet Government's declaration of war, and also because I have heard that America proposes to institute general military conscription, including that of foreign nationals.

I have been reading through my diary entries from the Caucasus. How inconceivable it would have seemed at the time that I should now be sailing on the blue waters off the coast of the Sandwich Islands!

30 July [12 August]

An air of excitement is creeping into the voyage: tomorrow at dawn we shall be in Honolulu. At eleven o'clock in the morning we sailed over the Tropic

---

1 There seems no more historical evidence of this diplomatic event than of the declaration of war against England. Nevertheless, the confused and often contradictory motives of the Allies to intervene in Russia's Civil War, exacerbated by the Czech Legion uprising in Siberia, did result in the unsuccessful North Russian Campaign, a mainly British and French force which landed in Arkhangelsk on 2 August 1918, to be joined a month later by the so-called Polar Bear American Expeditionary Force. These developments, mainly aimed at protecting the large amount of war *matériel* stockpiled in Arkhangelsk as well as supporting the Czechs thousands of miles away in Siberia, so enraged Trotsky that the various Allied missions in Petrograd, Moscow and Vologda were closed. See George F. Kennan, *The Decision To Intervene*, vol. 2 of *Soviet–American Relations 1917–20*, Princeton Univerity Press, 1989.

of Cancer, not that there was any evidence of our being in the tropics, for there was a strong northerly wind and an overcast sky. At two o'clock the vague outlines of the first two small islands on the horizon, followed at five o'clock by a large island irradiated by tones of red and green from the rays of the dying sun. Clouds cast shadows over the island, spotting it with beautiful stains. All evening we skirted this island, which lies a hundred miles from Honolulu.

Another wireless telegraph informed us that Lenin and Trotsky had fled the counter-Revolutionary forces and taken sanctuary in Kronstadt. The passengers indulged in witticisms to the effect that the Bolsheviks must have got so exhausted by their efforts fighting the Allies that they had taken time off to go for a swim.

31 July [13 August]

At six o'clock in the morning we docked in a Honolulu blanketed by early-morning mist. Brisk little motor boats with American flags surrounded our steamer, bringing on board a doctor to examine the passengers, officials to question them, and so on. By eight o'clock the formalities were completed and I took my suitcases down to Customs. After a superficial inspection, in which by the way they paid practically no notice to my letters of recommendation, one of the officials, who looked like a Russian Jew, once he had satisfied himself why I was there and how long I proposed to stay, said: 'My advice to you is to get straight back on board this ship and continue your voyage, otherwise you will not get away until November. There are hundreds of well-off people here waiting their turn for a berth on a ship, any ship, and there is nothing they can do about it. All passenger liners have been requisitioned for the war.'

This sent shivers of alarm through me. It was no part of my plans to stay until November. I went into Cook's and discovered that what I had been told was quite true: there were a hundred and twenty claimants for a passage for the next ship (in twelve days' time, from Yokohama *en route* to San Francisco), on which there might be space for no more than five or six more passengers. I returned to the ship and begged the Captain to take me to San Francisco. My stateroom had already been allocated, but the Captain was a kind man and found a narrow little cot for me in some corner or other. The boat would sail in seven hours' time. A great pity.

Adams,[1] whom I went to see to ask about the proposed concerts, said he would have been able to organise two, from which I might receive in the region of four hundred dollars. Not really a great sum, but it would have

---

1   The Honolulu impresario who had undertaken to arrange concerts for Prokofiev.

been a colossal improvement to my present circumstances. As things stood, after the additional cost of my passage to San Francisco, I would have in my pocket 100 dollars (Minster's gold pieces). Would this be enough to get me to New York? And, in reserve, Eleonora's brooch.

In a very bad mood I set off to walk round Honolulu, thinking of Polina and my plans last year to spend the summer here with her. It was raining and I was soon soaked through to my bones, but this did not stop me seeing the amazing enchantment of this island. When the sun came out and I found myself on Waikiki Beach, Honolulu's favourite bathing spot, I stood completely bewitched: here was light, a range of colours, a joyous nature unlike anything I had ever even imagined when dreaming of coming to Honolulu. Entire trees were covered in red, pink, lilac and yellow flowers. Until the last moment before the steamer sailed I wandered and drove amongst the palm trees, the flowering trees in bloom, and the lovely villas hidden amongst them. I forgot about my lack of money and could only regret that in a few hours I would have to leave this paradise. Yes, my memories of Polina might have faded almost away, but to spend the summer in a little house among these flowers and these sunbeams would be sheer intoxication. Clutching a bundle of tropical fruits I made my way back on board, to the puzzled cries of the other passengers who had earlier seen me disembarking. As the boat cast off I felt a mixture of joy at having encountered such incredible beauty with the sadness of parting. It was like leaving a beloved woman. But we shall see one another again, dear Honolulu!

1 [14] August

And so, under way once again. I am still under the spell of Honolulu and now I am back on board feel a being from another race. The plan had been so admirably conceived, and was working out so well: two concerts, some dollars, and two weeks in the most beautiful corner of the whole world – and suddenly this hiccup, that there were no ships going between Honolulu and the mainland. Who could have imagined this?

I hear that the railway tariff in America has risen by 30 per cent and a ticket to New York now costs considerably more than a hundred dollars. But that is all I have. I am quite ready to put up with third class, but there is apparently no such thing. Surely Eleonora's brooch cannot be under threat?

2 [15] August

For some unknown reason my spirits are reasonably high. Honolulu recedes into the past, a vision of enchantment, but I am re-entering shipboard life. I am reading the *Comparative Study of Paintings* by Foll.[1] Themes for the Violin Sonata keep coming into my head. The ocean is calm, sunny and blue. But alas, we are heading north. Farewell, the tropics, farewell the southern stars.

It has been announced that in San Francisco we shall have to present all letters and manuscripts in our possession for scrutiny by the censor. Surely my stories are not going to be censored as well?! If so, their first readers will be the American censors.

3 [16] August

The tempers of everyone on board are beginning to fray from the long voyage. Only the cursed Filipinos remain irritatingly cheerful and whistle like little devils in every nook and cranny. This stops me composing when, as quite often happens, themes come into my head. Today it was a second subject for the 'white' quartet.

A wireless cable today says that the English have taken Baku from the Persians.

4 [17] August

A final shipboard anecdote: while in Honolulu a dark-skinned twelve-year-old girl from first class was taken to see the Aquarium there – it is truly a remarkable institution with fish of all extraordinary shapes and sizes and colours, among them several octopi. When she came back on board, the little girl announced to all within earshot: 'When Mummy and Daddy are playing octopuses you can never get them apart.' The mother blushed crimson and hastily disappeared into her stateroom. An unintended consequence of a visit to the Aquarium.

In the evening there was a ball, but I did not attend.

5 [18] August

Kucheryavy, an engineer and a very nice man, who is arranging for Sklyarevsky[2] to tour America, gave me a piece of advice: to translate some of the articles that have been written about me into English. I took out Karatygin's article and, arming myself with a dictionary, patience and motivation,

---

1 The translation from the German by V. Favorsky and B. Rosenfeld of the cultural historian Karl Foll's *Experiences in the Comparative Study of Paintings* was published in Petrograd in 1916.
2 Alexander Sklyarevsky, pianist, professor at the Saratov Conservatoire. Prokofiev had met him with Alexander Borovsky in Petrograd in January 1916. See p. 65 above.

settled down to make a translation of it. After several weeks of idleness I found the work very enjoyable.[1]

6 [19] August

The article is enormously long and written in such a florid and ornate style that I wouldn't know how to translate it even with a dictionary. But the challenge of overcoming such difficulties spurs me on and I have been sitting over it all day.

The weather has turned quite cold, and we have been issued with warm blankets. The reason is the cold-water current coming down from the Bering Straits as far as San Francisco. Traces of it turn towards the south and reach as far as the Sandwich Islands, and it is their effect that moderates what would otherwise be the intense heat there and assures the mild climate of the islands.

7 [20] August

Woke up with a headache. I must have been in a draught yesterday. The combination with a heavy swell was not very pleasant. I took phenacetin and lay down.

This being the last day of the voyage, I did no work and did not finish the third section of the Karatygin article either. But I have done enough for now.

8 [21] August

At six o'clock I went on deck because the steamer was already at anchor. A thick fog shrouded us, but I was told that a short while earlier I would have been able to see the mountains all around, as we were in the Gulf of San Francisco. Small boats flying the American flag were already approaching, and the medical inspection and police investigation of passengers soon began. As the mist began to dissipate, the beautiful outlines of the bay began to show themselves. From somewhere came the sound of a bell, not from a church but from foghorns. I did not, of course, expect this to be a place to look for picturesque landscapes, or castles, or legends. This was a country of miraculous comfort, of gold dollars and irreproachable 'all right'.

The police questioning delayed the passengers for hours, and resulted in twenty people not being allowed to go ashore, among them all those who had come from Russia (except people who were not arriving in America for the first time), including me. Our group was obliged to undergo yet another interrogation, to show our letters, papers and so forth. There was a great fear of German spies and Bolsheviks coming from Russia.

---

1 Karatygin wroe several laudatory and perceptive articles about Prokofiev; a likely candidate for this calling card to his new circle of potential supporters is that published in *Isskustvo*, 1917, vol. 1, entitled 'The Art of Prokofiev'.

'What is this?'
'Music.'
'Did you write it yourself?'
'I did, on board ship.'
'Can you play it?'
'I can.'
'Play it, then.'

On the piano in the ship's saloon, I played the main theme of the Violin Sonata on its own, without accompaniment. It was not appreciated.

'Can you play Chopin?'
'What would you like me to play?'
'The Funeral March.'

I played four bars. The official evidently enjoyed it.

'Very good,' he said, with feeling.
'Do you know for whose death it was composed?'
'No.'
'His dog's.'

The man shook his head disapprovingly.

Rifling through all my compositions but not finding any letters, the official announced that although we would all have to be taken to the island, we would probably be released with an hour. 'The island' – this sounded ominous, as we had seen it on entering the bay: small, rocky and rather beautiful, but entirely built over with prisons.[1] Eventually they told us that as it was now four o'clock the reception facility on the island was closing, and we would be taken there tomorrow morning. In the meantime we would have to spend the night on board the ship. We mooched gloomily around the deserted deck complaining to one another what a boring city San Francisco was.

That evening the passengers asked me to play to them, and although I usually refuse, on this occasion I said I would, got very absorbed and played for over two hours. Among the passengers were some connoisseurs of music, and they went wild with enthusiasm, toasted me with champagne, so that altogether we had a very jolly evening of it. 'We're so glad they kept us on board,' they kept saying. One rich Jew confided to me that, should I have any difficulties or need for money, I could appeal directly to him.

9 [22] August

In the morning they put us in a cutter and the whole 'picnic' was shipped over to the island. Happily, it turned out to be not the prison island we had seen, but the adjacent one called Angel Island, where the 'Emigration Station' was situated. I was of course extremely irritated by the whole

---

1 Presumably Alcatraz.

situation, but I recalled the rule I had imposed on myself, not to allow myself to be upset by anything at all in the way of travel inconveniences, and did my best to observe it. When we unloaded ourselves and our luggage on to the island, I facetiously enquired why we were not being escorted by a guard with machine-guns, but the only response was to take us into a building and put us into a room with bars. Although in a show of delicacy the door on the other side of the bars was left half-open, it still left an extraordinarily unpleasant impression. Particularly disagreeable was the camera, evidently put there to record the features of everyone brought in. I openly surmised that before long they would be taking prints of our fingers, and possibly toes. The affair was taking a distinctly disagreeable turn.

There were twenty of us 'convicts', three Dutch, suspected of involvement with German firms; four wealthy Jews; a poor Jewish family from Romania who did not have enough money with them to be permitted to enter the United States; a Czech with an Austrian passport; a Greek; an Italian couple named Vernetta, returning from Odessa to Italy; I, and five Chinese. The interrogation process did not begin until eleven, and at noon the investigators broke for lunch until one. First in line were the rich Jews, who were tormented for three hours and then released. Next, the poor Jewish family was released after being interrogated, but the Dutch couple was detained and interned on the island pending further clarification.

At four o'clock they announced that the reception process was finished for the day, and that we would be spending the night in the hospital on the island for the interrogation to proceed on the following day. At this I really lost my temper: these devils were working a mere four hours a day, and we were having to wait three whole days for them! Going out into the vestibule, I shouted after them in English that such behaviour was a disgrace to America! But the only reaction was an impassive 'all right', after which they left to go into the city, as they were not themselves staying on the island. We were allowed to go out and walk about in front of the building, and heard from one of the Czechs who had been detained there that as a result of losing his papers he had been interned for three months, but was expecting at last to be released tomorrow. All kinds of people had been interned there: an English colonel, a French Consul from a South American country with six children. They had all been very angry, the men cursed and swore, the women wept, but the only answer they ever got was the same 'all right' and after three days or so they were set free. It was a relaxed, unhurried sort of institution, established principally to control Chinese and Japanese immigrants and quite unused to Europeans, who had begun to enter the United States by this route only since the outbreak of war. There was no point in taking offence, the only choice was to sit out the time patiently, especially as the people were polite, the meals provided were acceptable, there was clean linen in which to sleep, and in the evening one was permitted to stroll about the square planted with flowers and palm trees. What the Czech had to tell us was reassuring. Mr Vernetta and I slept well in the hospital, which was entirely devoid of patients. During the evening an elephant appeared in front of the window, and at night it bellowed.

10 [23] August

They woke us at six. What on earth for? We would spend all day drifting about from pillar to post, and the officials would not be there to begin their interrogation before eleven.

Yesterday's elephant turned out to be washing drying on the line, and its bellowing the sound of the foghorns. There was a breath of autumn about the cool morning air, and a faint sense of regret that winter was on its way. The officials arrived at half-past nine and started the interrogation at ten, an hour earlier than yesterday. They began by questioning the third of the Dutch trio, then the Greek and then the Czech. The first two were released, but the Czech was interned for further investigation. The Chinese had already been removed yesterday to a special department for coloured people where, so we heard, up to forty different Asian and native Australian nationalities were incarcerated.

There remained only the Vernettas and I. I prepared to send a telegram to McCormick, informing him that I had been arrested for no reason and asking for his help. Tomorrow was Saturday: the officials would be there for two hours and would leave again at noon until Monday. This was becoming intolerable. What was more, the newspapers were writing that the Bolsheviks, having declared war on the Allies, had arrested a great number of Americans in Moscow and Petrograd, and it was to be expected that in reprisal the authorities here would hold as many Russians as they pleased. It was at this point that I got an explanation which was at least a starting point: the reason the interrogation here was proceeding so slowly was that no report had been received from the counter-espionage questioning carried out on the ship. Without this they were unable to start their own investigations. The report on me had at last been received today, they would interrogate me tomorrow, and provided I could satisfy them on all points I would then be released. I decided that the reason my report had been held up was because it was taking them so long to go through all the numerous documents, letters and manuscripts they had taken from me on the ship. I composed myself to wait for tomorrow. The Vernettas for their part were highly indignant. 'What sort of allies are they, to go around arresting us!' they cried. I did my best to pacify them.

11 [24] August

Next morning we were apprehensive: if we were not interrogated during the two hours the officials would be present, the island would go into suspended animation for the next two days and we would be detained for an unspecified duration, and while the island was a beautiful place, it was hardly a comfortable environment to be cooped up in with a lot of interned Germans and Hungarians whose behaviour left much to be desired. My only consolation was the number of ideas for the 'white' quartet that kept coming into my mind. At ten o'clock, however, I was called in and subjected to an hour-long interrogation, during which I was asked a lot of questions both sensible and stupid, but some of them were *chefs d'oeuvre*:

'Are you in sympathy with the declaration of war on the Allies?'
'I am.'
'Are you in sympathy with the Bolsheviks?'
'I am not.'
'Why not?'
'Because they took my money away.'
'Have you ever attended their meetings?'
'I have.'
'Do they speak well?'
'They speak well, but illogically.'
'Where is your father?'
'In his grave.'
'Did he take part in the war?'
'No.'
'Why not?'
'Because he was dead.'
'Are you a member of any society?'
'The Petrograd Chess Society.'
'Of a political party?'
'No.'
'Why not?'
'Because I consider that an artist must be detached from politics.'
'Do you believe in polygamy?'
'I do not have even one wife.'
'Have you ever been in prison?'
'Yours.'
Etcetera.

Of course, these questions were interspersed with a mass of others in the course of a whole hour. Much time was spent on their concern that I had only 100 dollars with me, but eventually they let me go.

After I had been finished with the Vernettas were questioned, and at noon we went together into San Francisco on the same boat as the officials who half an hour before had been interrogating me. Now they were all smiles and offered cigarettes, but I found their ugly mugs so repellent that I went up on deck. Oof! How wonderful it was to have one's freedom restored to one, to climb into a soft-sprung automobile and to be taken to the Plaza Hotel. At the entrance we were met by Nikolay Titovich Kucheryavy, who had been interceding on our behalf with the Russian Consul and the Italian Consul, and who had been told that we were to be released at noon that day. It appeared that the Russian Consul knew my name and had gone to considerable lengths to ensure my deliverance.

Now it was time to have a shave, to change our clothes and, with much cheerful conversation about our recent experiences, to go to dinner. Although San Francisco is not New York or Chicago, it is still a very impressive place in its energy, fine civic appointments and above all, wealth. The shops were groaning with all manner of splendid goods, and it was obvious that dollars here flowed like water. When we had supper that evening in a café, people were dancing the one-step right there in the restaurant: masses of elegant young ladies and well-turned-out gentlemen – and these were shopgirls, salesmen, factory hands. Over here the middle classes live in ease and prosperity.

12 [25] August

Accompanied the Vernettas to a Catholic church. I very much liked the Catholic service, which I was hearing for the first time. The quiet introductory playing of the organ was very nice, and so was the priest intoning against this background.

In the afternoon we took a limousine and toured the suburbs of San Francisco. They are very beautiful, and the amenities, prosperity and wealth (of all classes of society) smiled on us from every side.

The little group formed of the Vernettas, Kucheryavy and myself spent all our time together. It must be admitted that all of us (myself included) were great gourmets, and relished putting away great quantities of crab, steak, strawberries and other toothsome comestibles.

13 [26] August

We booked tickets for New York for the whole group, taking Kucheryavy's advice to go via Vancouver, Canada and Chicago – the long way round, but costing no more. We would see California and rocky Canada. I was delighted with the prospect of seeing something of Canada as well as famous

California, although its most scenic parts lay to the south of San Francisco and would not be on our route.

I sought out Zelikman,[1] my erstwhile rival for the Rubinstein Prize. Before I left Petrograd his teacher, Nikolayev,[2] had told me proudly that Zelikman was in San Francisco with his own school, and at the time I even felt a twinge of envy that while we were expiring from the blows of internecine warfare, there were some who really knew how to get themselves well set up! Now, when I visited him I found not exactly a school, but a small room in which he gave lessons. He greeted me joyfully and within ten minutes was pumping my hand and calling me Seryozhenka. In truth I could well have expected him to give me rather a sour welcome. Evidently he is managing to live well here, but does not seem to have made much of an impact. He played a couple of concerts 'with brilliant success' two years ago, but somehow I failed to rise to his obvious conversational lead. Life has wrought changes in him. He is less arrogant than he was, behaved modestly and predicted a brilliant success for me in New York, where he has himself been planning to go for the past two years. From talking to him I learned some useful and interesting things: first, that Russian musicians are in demand and the rise of Bolshevism has in no way cast a shadow over the enthusiasm for Russian art; second, Russians who do not have 'first papers', that is the initial documents on the road to acquiring American citizenship, will not be called to the colours; and thirdly, Altschuler,[3] Johns[4] and Steinway,[5] to all of whom I have letters of introduction, are genuinely influential people in the musical world.

Ariadna is here, as I had already heard when on Angel Island. As soon as she arrived she gave an interview in which she made it clear she was not a Romanov daughter. She is soon to appear at one of the big theatres, in a variety show. A somewhat unexpected, and not particularly glorious, conclusion to her triumphal procession.

1 A. V. Zelikman, pianist. See *Diaries*, vol. 1, pp. 251, 659–63 and *passim*.
2 Leonid Nikolayev (1878–1942), influential pianist and teacher at the St Petersburg Conservatoire. He was later to be Shostakovich's much loved piano teacher. See ibid., pp. 129–30 and *passim*.
3 Modest Altschuler (1873–1963), cellist and conductor who had been living in the United States since 1895, where he founded the Russian Symphony Orchestra Society of New York, a prominent showcase for contemporary Russian music.
4 Herbert Johnson, at this time business comptroller of the Chicago Opera. For some reason in the *Diaries* Prokofiev refers to him variously as Johns and Johnson.
5 The first Steinway of Steinway & Sons was Heinrich Steinweg, who immigrated from Germany in 1850, and the Sons were Carl (Charles), Wilhelm (William), Heinrich Jr (Henry Jr) and the youngest, Theodore. In 1918 the head of the firm was Charles Steinway Jr, the grandson of the founder. He died the following year, to be succeeded by the Steinway most probably referred to here, his brother Frederick T. Steinway, who until his death in 1927 presided over one of the company's most successful periods, from both artistic and commercial standpoints.

14 [27] August

A trip in a superbly comfortable automobile round the widely spread-out environs of San Francisco and its famous hills. Engineer Kucheryavy, who has developed not only the most powerful attachment to me but an unshakeable conviction of my success in America, has taken me in hand and told me that his business affairs, which had brought him to America in the first place, are prospering to the extent that the moment he arrives in New York he will be able to lay his hands on $15,000 and will be glad to share his good fortune with me, so I should not worry about lack of funds to establish myself in New York. Moreover I should not rush to sign the first contract I am offered. This is very kind: I had certainly hoped for help to cover the journey to New York, but not generosity on this scale.

15 [28] August

I have finally recovered my letters and papers from Customs, to whom I had conscientiously submitted my entire portfolio on the ship. Now in order to recover them I had to go nine different offices, sent from one to another. When, at the ninth, I was told to go back to the first one I had been to, I lost my temper, so instead of me they sent one of their officials, who returned bearing the complete portfolio with a meticulous report on and analysis of my letters and stories (!). They had obviously read everything. But the only document they kept was a postcard with a view of Honolulu. Very clever people!

I went to the cinema to see a film, a superb production of a feeble story overlaid with an intolerably naive flavour of moralising edification, and a clumsily tacked-on 'patriotic' ending.

16 [29] August

At ten o'clock in the morning we embarked on our lengthy roundabout route to New York. For the first two and half days we were going north, to Vancouver. American railway carriages are built on completely different lines from those of other countries, incredibly spacious and with greater comfort than any others with the possible exception of Russia – when, that is, Russia makes an effort. But they do have one accursed drawback in that they are constructed of iron, and as the temperature today rose without warning to 40° Réamur,[1] they turned into an oven. This was the dominant impression of our day. The countryside through which we passed was flat and uninteresting, and the speed of the train, although creditable, was hardly startling.

---

1   50° Celsius.

17 [30] August

Unfortunately it was night-time while we were travelling through the best part of Northern California. Mme Vernetta, waking up in the night and looking out of the window, said that it looked remarkably beautiful by moonlight. But I slept on in my spacious compartment, snug behind green curtains. American women behave more freely than we are used to; they strike up conversations with men. Some smiled at me and asked me if I would sharpen their pencils. I was polite but aloof, and preserved my composure. The State of Oregon, which we traversed during the day, is beautiful; from the observation car we could see forests, rivers and mountains. It looked rather like the landscape you see as you approach Novorossiisk.

18 [31] August

We were exactly eleven hours late, because of an overheated shaft that had to be repaired. We spent the evening in Seattle, a young, fast-growing city and the principal Pacific port in the north of the United States. Its expansion had been inhibited by a mountain – so the American city fathers simply levelled it to the ground. When, at midnight, we boarded a ship to take us past a series of islands into Canada (a ten-hour voyage), we had to endure another Customs inspection and interrogation. This could have lasted a long time, except that the ship's Captain announced that he was not going to wait for us any longer. The Customs men accordingly said 'all right' and let us go on with our journey. Dragging our mound of luggage (not mine – the Vernettas' and Kucheryavy's) at a fast run, we barely made it back on board in time. Kucheryavy and I were not disconcerted by the inspection, in fact we rather approved of it, but the Vernettas were incensed and Madame cried.

19 August [1 September]

Our pleasant and comfortable steamer brought us next morning to the Canadian port of Vancouver. All night we had sailed between the islands, all of which seemed to have the same name, and the mainland, passing attractive shorelines. It was a pity we were not doing this in the daytime. Vancouver in its outward appearance and its way of life reminded me of England; I had not realised that the English possessions in America would be so very different from the United States. This was particularly apparent because it was a Sunday, a day on which life in an English town simply comes to a standstill. Here they drive on the left side of the road, there is a greater sense of decorum and an air of patriarchy, there are fewer skyscrapers and shops.

We tracked down Sklyarevsky, who had been brought over from Russia by Kucheryavy but who had not succeeded in obtaining a visa for the USA and was therefore in Canada, where he had already been booked for a tour of thirty concerts. This is an encouraging sign, although of course I would not myself particularly want to trawl round small Canadian townships. In the afternoon we followed our usual practice of taking a drive round the city and looking at its beautiful environs.

At eight o'clock we set off on our journey to New York aboard the famous Canadian Pacific Express, whose fame and popularity has reached as far as Russia. I was extraordinarily happy to be travelling on such a magnificent train.

To Morolyov in Nikopol: 'Are you aware, Sir, of the location of the island of Vancouver? Oh no, Sir, you are not. You do not know where it is situated. And therefore from the green ferns of the aforesaid island I address to you my most humble and profound greetings. S. P.'

20 August [2 September]

Today was the most picturesque day of our travels across America: from morning until evening we climbed up high through the Rocky Mountains. There was an observation car attached to the rear of the train: a simple but very clever idea, consisting of an enclosed platform with bench seats on it. From here one had an ideal view in all directions, and when the train rounded a curve, there was the whole train in front of one. On every side there were high, rocky mountains thickly covered in pines. We passed along river banks, crossing from side to side of the water and sometimes plunging into tunnels. Eventually I got a piece of soot in my eye and had to retreat inside.

The newspapers are reporting the death of Lenin. This is a man who has played a significant role in world history. He brought much evil upon Russia, but then one must consider that from the point of view of true socialism there is no Russia and no Germany, there is only the Internationale. Even though I believe the ultimate aims of socialism are misconceived, bearing in mind that nature herself eschews the concept of equality, I have nevertheless always had a high regard for the nobility of its ideas. Lenin has done great harm to socialism and in the eyes of many has compromised its ideals. But should it ever come to pass that socialism rules on earth, at that time Lenin will be seen as a man surpassing other men, and statues will be erected to him.

21 August [3 September]

Waking up next morning in the wide, comfortable bed of my American sleeping-car and looking out of the window, I saw a wide, flat expanse of steppe like that in Yekaterinoslav guberniya. All day the train ran through the landscape at a steady 60 versts an hour. Towards midnight we came to the Canada/USA border. I was a little apprehensive, the Vernettas even more so, that we would once again find obstacles put in our way, especially as I no longer had an American visa having had it taken from me in San Francisco as no longer needed. But in fact we had merely been in transit through Canada coming from the USA back into the USA, and the official did no more than ask me a few innocent questions, spoke to me in Russian, because he was himself Russian, and we entered the USA.

Lenin, according to the newspaper, is alive.

22 August [4 September]

Now we were in the USA the train picked up speed. We were further east, and the countryside grew more beautiful, with groups of trees and, by evening, whole forests.

I occupied myself with translating articles about me into English.

I was in good spirits. I had accomplished the plan I had conceived in Kislovodsk and had arrived in America. It had not been easy, but for eight months I had not deviated from my aim, and now, here I was! It was time for Stage Two: to conquer this America I had come to. I have a good feeling about it.

23 August [5 September]

Chicago – for so long a city of mythical status for me. 'Just wait until you're conducting in Chicago . . .' had been Tcherepnin's ironic refrain in his conducting class. I anticipated being bowled over by Chicago's overwhelming energy and mobility, and I did feel something of this, but the city itself seemed somehow cramped and unattractive, with large tracts of soot-stained houses. I walked past the glittering displays in shop windows, but my store of dollars was at an end and shops were dangerous places for a man who had no more than twenty cents in his pocket, not counting the hundred dollars I owed Minster and another hundred to Kucheryavy.

Our little group took a three-hour omnibus tour round Chicago and the parks that encircle it in a long chain. The parks are good examples of their kind, but I had had my fill of seeing American parks. They are nice enough, but by now no longer electrifying. I wanted to see our Auer,[1] who has been tempted to the local Conservatoire with a tremendous fanfare of publicity, and I went in to try to find him there, but he has not yet arrived. The Conservatoire building is very elegant, but very small compared to ours. With Kucheryavy's help I telephoned McCormick, but his secretary apologised on his behalf, saying that he was about to leave for New York and was up to his neck with work. He would see me in New York in a few days' time.

At eight o'clock that evening we left on the train to New York, averaging over 80 versts an hour. But the track and the rolling stock are so good that one is scarcely aware of the speed at which one is travelling. True, in France they go at 100 versts an hour, but they also throw you about so much your head can hit the ceiling.

24 August [6 September]

I almost missed Niagara next morning. There was a glimpse of it through a cutting in the forest and then it disappeared again. But I did get a chance to see, from behind so to speak, the well-known precipitous contours of the falls, as the cutting emerged a little above the falls themselves. Then, a little further on, the train curved sharply round and crossed a high bridge, with the river far below confined in its post-falls course between high banks. In the distance could be seen another bridge, behind which a white cloud hid the waterfall itself, the smoky morning mist hovering above it. So we were not able to get a proper view of wonderful Niagara, nevertheless, we did get an eyeful of the horrible factories that have been thrown up everywhere round about. Yes! The Americans, despite their flamboyance and their sense of scale, are still not sophisticated enough to cherish the luxury of a treasure such as Niagara. O aesthetes! And these are the people to whom I am proposing to play my music!

The day passed in rapid progress towards New York, the train, despite its 100 versts an hour, being so steady as to make it appear that we were going at no more than 50. Our way lay along the banks of the Hudson River, which grew ever wider as we neared New York, and graced with beautiful buildings and palaces adding interest to the view. At length we began to see grid-style numbered streets, then we descended into the earth and without surfacing again arrived at the station. Immediately almost asphyxiated by the petrol fumes of the automobiles that are permitted to come right into the entrance of the station, we emerged and drove through the streets of New York. 'Where are Wilson[2] and the welcome deputation from the city?' I said. All the

---

1 The violinist Leopold Auer. See above, p. 289 n. 1.
2 President Woodrow Wilson.

same New York, while stopping short of overwhelming, made an excellent impression.

Nodding off to sleep, I thought to myself: 'Can I really be in New York? I've thought about it so much, and it seems such an impossible feat to have got here in the present circumstances! And our cities at home are in the grip of fighting and slaughter...'

25 August [7 September]

New York is a very good city and I am glad to be here. The only thing that worries me is the thought that Mama must be missing me and worrying that she has no news of me.

We moved from our hotel, which was too expensive and neither Kucheryavy nor I have a cent to our name, to 109th Street, where we rented what are known here as 'apartments', that is to say furnished flats. I really had not expected Kucheryavy to be completely out of funds. It really was a most odd situation: he had assigned to an American firm of glue manufacturers the secrets of an idea they had not thought of themselves, upon which they immediately clutched him to their bosom and offered him a position at a salary of $12,000. However, so far there was no contract, nor was there any money. He had two additional inventions concerned with lubricants and grease, which he expected would eventually bring him in many tens of thousands of dollars, but at the present time, he had not a cent to his name. Convinced of my future success, he professed a paternally protective affection for me, being perfectly ready to offer me money when he had none himself.

'Nikolay Titovich, could you spare me a quarter...?'

N. T. would look in his purse, which contained a dollar and fifty cents. 'Here's half a dollar,' he said with an expansive gesture, offering me the fifty cents.

My apartment had two rooms and a bathroom. It was not impressive in appearance, but this did not worry me in the slightest. All I needed was quiet, a comfortable armchair and a table on which to write that did not rock. I even liked the fact that the floor below housed a gloomy-looking Negro. The only thing that did worry me was that Americans are snobs, and would consider the place a hovel not fit for a famous musician to be living in. But in the first place there was nothing to be done about it, and in the second, it would be only until I secured my first advance, and in the third, I would not be inviting anybody to visit me here.

1 Petrograd street, 4 July 1917. Troops loyal to the Provisional Government have just fired on crowds demonstrating in support of the Constituent Assembly.   2 The composer at the piano, New York, 1918.   3 (From left) Ivan Yershov, Nina and Natalya Meshcherskaya, Gurzuf, 1913.   4 Boris Demchinsky.   5 The Meshchersky family in exile. Front row: (from left) Nina and Natalya; (second from right) Vera Nikolayevna. Alexey Meshchersky, having separated from his wife, is not present

6 The composer at his desk, New York, 1918

7 (From left) Prokofiev, Boris Anisfeld and Adolph Bolm, New York, 1918

8 International Company Pullman car of the Trans-Siberian Railway, *c.*1918

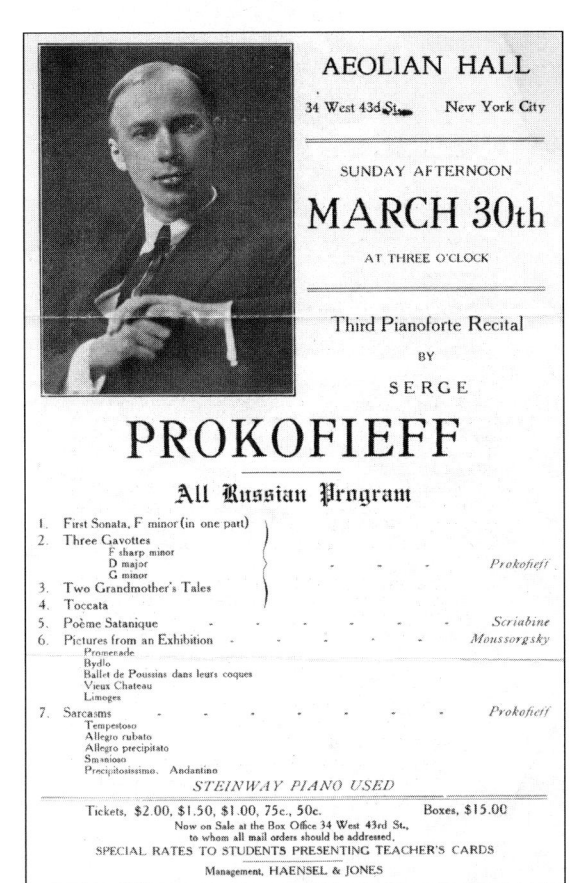

9 Aeolian Hall recital poster, New York, 30 March 1919.   10 Giulio Gatti-Casazza, General Manager of the Metropolitan Opera, New York.   11 José Raúl Capablanca.   12 Stella Adler: a studio portrait

13 Serge Diaghilev: drawing by Christopher Wood

14 Prokofiev and Stravinsky on a Paris street, 1920

15 The *Souirah*, on which Maria Grigorievna Prokofieva sailed from Constantinople to Marseilles in June 1920

16 Mikhail Larionov's cubist-inspired front curtain for *Chout*, May 1921

17 Konstantin Balmont

18 Matisse portrait of Prokofiev for the programme of the Ballets Russes season, Paris, May 1921

19 Lina Codina, in her grey fur coat

20 Dagmar Godowsky

21 Mary Garden as 'Directa' (her own job description) of the Chicago Opera, 1921

22 Caricature of Emerald, Lady Cunard, by Anthony Wysard

23 Prokofiev outside the Congress Hotel, Chicago, December 1921

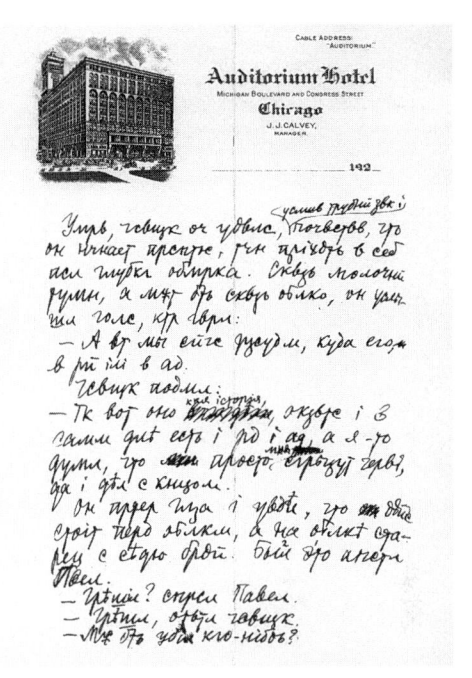

24 Nina Koshetz. The photograph is inscribed to 'her dear colleague Sergey Vasilievich Popov'.
25 MS of the first page of the short story 'Death of the Watchmaker', written on notepaper from the Auditorium Hotel, Chicago.   26 The cavernous interior of the Auditorium Theater, Chicago

27 Boris Anisfeld's sketch for the set of *Love for Three Oranges*, Act III Scene II

28 The Villa Christophorus, Ettal, Bavaria

29 Prokofiev's bride, Lina Codina

30 Prokofiev and Boris Bashkirov in the garden of the Villa Christophorus, 1922

26 August [8 September]

McCormick has asked to see me tomorrow. As today is Sunday, I would have paid some calls on people to whom I have letters of recommendation, but my luggage has not arrived yet and all the letters are in it.

Walked in Central Park and round the city. Despite our poverty, Kucheryavy and I eat famously: oysters, lobsters, all kinds of fish, peaches and cream. Kucheryavy has pawned his gold watch.

27 August [9 September]

McCormick was extraordinarily welcoming, and said that he would do everything in his power to introduce me to the musical world, and when I thanked him for my visa said that he was very interested that I had come to America. But he was so insanely busy in the political sphere (in the United States he occupies a truly commanding position) that he is almost being torn into pieces. 'Two people are supposed to be dining with me at this moment, and two more are already sitting and waiting upstairs.' Tomorrow evening he is going to Washington, but will have dinner with me before he goes.

28 August [10 September]

Today I commenced offensive manoeuvres on the citadel of New York. One person who was particularly pleased that I had arrived was Schindler,[1] who four years ago had been in my house in Petrograd. He immediately dragged me off to see Schirmer,[2] one of the most prominent music publishers, for whom he, Schindler, works as an adviser on scores that have been submitted. Schirmer offered to publish my works, but there is a question mark hanging over this: apparently American law does not support my musical property rights as no copyright convention currently exists between Russia and America.

At dinner McCormick asked me many questions about Russia, and provided me with many personal recommendations. He will return in a week and promises further co-operation then. With some circumspection I gave him a critical account of my treatment on Angel Island and expressed my regret that Japan was spearheading the military intervention in Siberia rather than America: the Americans are trusted by Russia, the Japanese are not.

---

1   Kurt Schindler (1882–1935), composer, conductor, writer on music and publisher's reader for G. Schirmer. See *Diaries*, vol. 1, pp. 685–7.
2   Ernst Charles Schirmer, the current head of the G. Schirmer music-publishing firm, founded in 1861 and until 1961 still a family-owned business. As well as music by contemporary composers, the firm also published the enormously popular 'Library of Musical Classics', and the journal the *Musical Quarterly*.

Went to see Stahl, whom I had met in Yokohama and seen on two occasions for five minutes, long enough to have taken a great liking to him. Stahl is a brilliant lawyer, and during the time when Kerensky was in power had served as Public Prosecutor for political cases. When the Bolsheviks came to power he shaved off his beard and escaped to America. Today our meeting was joyous; he has already been spreading the word about me. He gave me valuable advice about publishers, and altogether this is a person I am very pleased indeed to have met again.[1]

29 August [11 September]

Schirmer rang, to direct me towards Adams, a manager, namesake of my impresario in Honolulu and described by Schirmer as a leading impresario and an honest man.[2] Adams's advice was to start with orchestral appearances, and thanks to the McCormick connection gave me Damrosch's card and suggested I get in touch with him.[3] Damrosch is a conductor presently very much *à la mode* – *à la mode patriotique*, I should say, having recently returned from France where he has been giving concerts for the troops.

Bolm,[4] one of the most famous *danseurs* of Diaghilev's troupe, now producing Russian opera at the Metropolitan Opera to counter-balance the

1 Alexey Stahl, lawyer, formerly Public Prosecutor of the Provisional Government. Prokofiev's admiration and affection were not shared by all. When Arthur Rubinstein first met the composer in New York early in 1919, he had this to say of his new friend's friends: 'We were often together, sometimes just the two of us, sometimes with a Greco-Brazilian singer, Vera Janacopoulos, who sang Prokofiev's songs to his liking (she had a dreadful husband, however, a bearded Russian who drank vodka in great quantities). A. Rubinstein, *My Many Years*, Jonathan Cape, London, 1980.
2 Adams was at the time head of the Wolfsohn Musical Bureau, the longest-established artists' agency in America. In 1930 Wolfsohn was one of seven agencies (including Prokofiev's subsequent New York managers Haensel and Jones) who merged under the aegis of Columbia Broadcasting Systems and Concert Management Arthur Judson to form Columbia Artists Management Inc. (CAMI).
3 Walter Damrosch (1862–1950), German-born composer and conductor. The Damrosch dynasty was by this time an important one in New York, Walter's father Leopold having been closely associated with Liszt before emigrating to the USA in 1871, where he founded the New York Symphony Orchestra (one half of the ensemble that, after a merger in 1928, was eventually to become the New York Philharmonic). Walter Damrosch had taken over the orchestra on his father's death in 1885. Later he was hired by David Sarnoff to become Music Director of the National Broadcasting Corporation, and as well as presiding over the glory days of Toscanini's NBC Symphony Orchestra in the 1930s, became a national figure through hosting the network's weekly *Music Appreciation Hour*.
4 Adolph Bolm (1884–1951), ballet dancer and choreographer, had been one of the leading dancers in Diaghilev's inaugural Paris season in 1909, along with such other Mariinsky luminaries as Mathilde Kshessinska, Anna Pavlova, Tamara Karsavina, Ida Rubinstein, Mikhail Fokine, Bronislava and Vaclav Nijinsky. When Diaghilev's Ballets Russes toured America in 1916, Bolm had assumed the main responsibility for forming the company and directing it. After the tour Bolm stayed behind in New York and was at this time directing opera and ballet productions at the Metropolitan Opera (*The Golden Cockerel*, *Petrushka*).

prevailing Italianery there, was terribly pleased to learn that I was here. He gave me a wealth of valuable advice on how to find my way about life in New York. 'The main thing', he said, 'is not to be in too much of a hurry, do everything deliberately, and make your own decisions. Whatever happens remember the season does not start until October, or even November.'

I learned sad things about the justly celebrated Diaghilev company: it had virtually disintegrated as a result of the war. Although they had recently toured successfully to Spain, and now Diaghilev had obtained permission to come to London (which was not at all easy to achieve), the company was small and according to press reports the scenery had not yet arrived. Stravinsky was very ill, having almost died from an infection of the lungs, and was in dire need of money. The patriotic French, having carried him shoulder high before the war, following the Brest armistice now did not want to hear any of his music. Just recently his prospects and his health had improved, and he was working once more.[1] Diaghilev had received my ballet *Chout* (Lord, I had forgotten all about it) in America two years previously. He had walked up and down with it in his hands, asked pianists to play it to him, and exclaimed: 'God only knows what this is all about! I don't understand a thing!' Yet it is such good music, and so transparent!

I spent the evening with Stahl and enjoyed myself so much I hardly noticed the time passing as I listened to his wonderful stories about the Bolsheviks' siege of the Kremlin which – as a member of the Provisional Government – he had experienced. He lives with a French singer, an enchanting young woman, somewhat reminiscent of Nina Meshcherskaya.[2] She possesses more gentleness, kindness and beauty than Nina, and a less venomous tongue. Yet how constant remains my attraction to that type!

V. N. Bashkirov,[3] who was in New York having fled the Bolsheviks and come to America in November, had telephoned to Stahl's, overjoyed at the news that I was here. Stahl said: 'I was amazed at the passion that the news of your arrival evoked in this normally so self-controlled person.' Bashkirov cried out that I must move to his house and at once asked for my address. I

---

1 This seems a little overstated, at least from the health perspective: Stravinsky had indeed suffered from pleurisy at the beginning of the year, while the combination of Diaghilev's financial difficulties and the loss to war and revolution of the Stravinsky family estate in the Ukraine meant constant money worries. The following year, 1919, a committee of philanthropic ladies, Mrs Otto Kahn prominent among them, was set up in New York to provide financial assistance to the struggling genius. But the autumn of 1918 was also the period of Stravinsky's intensive collaboration with C. F. Ramuz on *The Soldier's Tale*, whose first, self-mounted tour was soon to take place. (This, though, resulted in anything but financial salvation, as the Spanish influenza pandemic that killed nearly 100 million people in eighteen months erupted just in time to wreck every planned engagement on the tour except the first night in Lausanne on 28 September.) See S. Walsh, *Igor Stravinsky, A Creative Spring, Russia and France 1882–1934* (Jonathan Cape, London, 2000).
2 *Sic*. Vera Janacopulos was in fact Brazilian, but spoke excellent French.
3 Vladimir Nikolayevich Bashkirov, Boris Bashkirov's millionaire brother.

asked Bolm to reply that, having been so upset by his behaviour towards me in Petrograd, I did not want him to have my address. This was in connection with the crudeness of his attitude to Borenka's wedding. Stahl reported that on hearing this, Bashkirov's voice fell and he said: 'Surely he's not still remembering that old history?' and put down the telephone. This was unkind of me since, as well as everything else, he would have the chance to hear from me the latest news of his family, but his behaviour over the wedding business was truly disgraceful.

30 August [12 September]

The Bolsheviks have shot dead the Tsar's daughters. What a disgusting thing to do!

Petrograd is on fire (not literally, I believe) but in the sense that it has been occupied by hordes of peasants forming a White Guard. Or perhaps this is an invention of the Americans! In any case, I left just in time.

Today a universal population census took place, but it does not mean that everyone will necessarily be conscripted. It was simply a matter of taking down details, enumerating people and placing them into one or another category. Foreigners are in category 5, as befits our white-ticket status.[1] I attended, was given a questionnaire to fill out, and am now answering the questions.

Composed a little of the Violin Sonata. I desperately miss not having a piano.

Damrosch and I exchanged civilities and tomorrow he will receive me to hear a play-through of the 'Classical' Symphony and the First Piano Concerto.

Spent the evening with Schindler. He and Bolm discussed with tremendous excitement and sympathetic understanding the best way of presenting me to New York and New York to me. 'You have chosen the best possible time to come here: America has been starved of new music for two years. The fact is, there isn't any, in France the composers are all fighting in the war, Germany is our enemy, and nothing has been coming out of Russia. All the conductors will be falling over themselves to get your scores. But unfortunately you really should not make your debut any earlier than November. (Not fashionable.)

31 August [13 September]

An interview with a 'thick' journal reporter in Bolm's flat. The 'interrogation' lasted for three hours and covered myself, my compositions, my travels, my impressions of America, musical life in Russia, the effects on it of Bolshevism and the war, the activities of other composers, the general political situation in Russia, and other matters.

1   See above, pp. 105–6.

The journalist, Martens,[1] said that many of the important publishers (like Fischer, and others) would be happy to publish my works. I said that if they were interested they ought to get a move on, because at the present time I had no manuscripts ready although I had a quantity of material I had composed on board ship that was now ready to be worked up. Therefore, if someone wished to give me a commission now, I could compose a series of piano pieces, but then I would be occupied with giving concerts.

The essence of this is that I need to earn dollars as quickly as possible! It would be very unpleasant to have to live on short commons and wait until November to play concerts!

1 [14] September

Altschuler, a Russian conductor and fervent propagandist for Russian music, to whom Koussevitzky had given me an introduction, rang me up himself without any preliminary correspondence, and expressed his great pleasure at my arrival. Eighteen months ago he had written to Ziloti asking for scores of my compositions, but Ziloti had not mentioned it to me, probably from fear that I might immediately decamp to America in pursuit of the requested compositions. The swine. What a difference it would have made to my appearance here now if my scores had already been heard.

Spent the evening with Stahl, as I like both him and her (she is from Brazil) very much indeed. Bashkirov has given Stahl his own side of the story as to why we are at odds with one another, but at least admitted that he had behaved discourteously and promised, if I so wished, to make a public apology.

2 [15] September

Altschuler is in a state of ecstasy over my compositions. He finds both my music and my notions of orchestration unique, and has proposed to devote the first concert of his season exclusively to me.

There are two 'buts'. The first is that this concert cannot take place until 10 December. The second is that Altschuler's concerts are not at the pinnacle of the fashionable register (although he earned himself $75,000 this year and is riding very high in consequence). If the 'Friends of Music' concert does not come off, it is excellent to have Altschuler in reserve.

In the evening I went with Bolm to some sort of American artistic society, where 'clever' ladies harangued me with complicated homilies about the

---

1 Frederick H. Martens, composer and music critic. The long interview appeared in *Musical America*, New York, on 28 September 1918, and is reproduced as Appendix 4. Another article by Martens was published in the *Musical Observer* for November 1918.

stars under whose protection I currently was. But I went on to the attack and proved to them that they lacked even the most elementary knowledge of astronomy. The organisation had tenuous links with Postnikov and his enterprise, and along the way I had come into possession of certain plausible information suggesting that Postnikov was a cheat and a swindler. The ladies were much astonished.

3 [16] September

I have already been a week without a piano, and am going out of my mind with kind but vague promises. Schirmer should either do what he promises, or not make the promise in the first place.

Today is the Jewish Day of Judgment. I went to the synagogue, hoping to hear an aspect of singing new to me, some Jewish mumbling that would make an interesting impression. But there were only some clean-shaven bankers there in gleaming top hats listening to the monotonous reading of the rabbi. I grew bored and left, being reprimanded as I went out for having got up at the wrong moment.

In the evening I put on tails, chapeau-claque (just as in the good old days in London) and went with Bolm to the opening night of a frivolous variety show. But what passes for the most daring American dancing turned out to be irreproachably sedate, the ballerinas elegant, attractive and entirely wholesome. The overall impression was pleasant, colourful and very enjoyable, the audience in evening dress, the women *décolletées*. Very nice – a long time since I have seen anything like it.

4 [17] September

I played Damrosch the 'Classical' Symphony and the First Piano Concerto. He mortally offended me by turning over the pages while I was playing the reprise (to save time) and by comparing the symphony with Kalinnikov's. I launched a full frontal counter-attack, but it appears that coming from him this was a great compliment, since he adores Kalinnikov's symphony. When I played the Concerto he had some difficulty in following the score and often turned over four bars before or after the turn. In general this great American luminary hardly impressed with his musicality. On parting, he uttered a stream of compliments, but said nothing about a performance. I left in a bad temper.

Spent the evening with Obolsky, the same friendly, good-looking but essentially dull-witted young man who in June had brought my request for a visa with him to America. He has installed himself here in a small place for $130 a month, and has already had two short-lived affairs with American women (women fall for this handsome twenty-two-year-old, who is not too particular about their qualities). It was very pleasant to wander with him about the streets of New York talking about nothing in particular and getting first-hand information about the strict laws governing illicit cohabitation (you must either marry, or pay up, or be deported, or be sent to gaol). All the same, Americans have a gift for managing their affairs to the best advantage. Money, money – that is what you need, and until you have it, keep your head down and stay out of trouble.

5 [18] September

According to Martens, the critic who is writing the article about me, there are no publishers in America working in the interest of good music, only of commercial profit, and the result is that for one worthwhile work that comes out there are a hundred pieces of rubbish. I goaded him with the examples of Belyayev and Koussevitzky,[1] and suggested founding a millionaires' academy to teach them how to spend their money usefully! Mme Bolm counsels me to keep my sword sheathed a little more often – I won't win every battle and will only damage myself. She believes that I am misjudging America in thinking it anti-artistic. Even if true art has not yet been born here, there is no question that a tremendously strong interest in it has developed.

At five o'clock the Bolms held a 'punch' party for me, to which they had invited a raft of critics and musicians. I told them what was happening in Russia just now, and played the First Piano Sonata and some of the *Visions Fugitives*. I was told that the Sonata had not been a particularly good choice, better would have been the Third, since these gentlemen have a weakness for the modern.

Altschuler, who is being extremely kind and attentive to me, showed me an interesting collection of letters written by Rachmaninoff, Scriabin and Glazunov. All of them write very smoothly, with all the commas in the right places. Scriabin has a refined, sweeping hand, Rachmaninoff's is small and spidery, and he writes with a dry sense of humour: 'I shall need a nanny for America; I've grown old and mischievous.' What about Ninochka Koshetz, then? Anyhow, in the end he rejected America.[2]

Altschuler is orchestrating Scriabin's Ninth Sonata and *Poème Satanique*. I am not very impressed by Altschuler's ideas, but they did inspire me to one

---

1 Mitrofan Belyayev, among whose philanthropic activities on behalf of Russian music was the foundation of a publishing house, M. P. Beliaeff based in Leipzig, and Serge Koussevitzky, who used his money to found the Editions Russes de Musique/Russische Musikverlag, to which he later added the Gutheil publishing house.
2 The decision not to come to America, if Rachmaninoff had ever in fact made it, was soon reversed: he arrived with his family in New York on 29 October/10 November.

of my own: to orchestrate the Fifth Sonata! It could be sensational. Scriabin never succeeded in fully realising his visionary flights: he was held back either by the limitations of the piano or by his inability to master the orchestra. I believe I could make something wonderful out of the Fifth Sonata.

6 [19] September

There are articles about me in all the papers – the result of yesterday's punch.[1] Meanwhile the famous composer sits with three dollars (other people's) in his pocket, without the means to take out a single girl he might fancy. (I am in debt to Nikolay Titovich; N. T., who has not yet signed his contract, is in debt to the Vernettas, and the Vernettas, whose cheque has still for some reason not been cashed, are in debt to the Italian Consul. This little piggy goes to market, this little piggy stays home . . . etc.)

7 [20] September

Today brought my first significant victory: I played to the Chicago conductor Stock,[2] and Schirmer happened to be there at the same time. Stock went into ecstasies, and Schirmer was deeply impressed. The result was an invitation to perform and conduct in Chicago in November, and I have the impression that a few more tasty morsels will come my way, details to be clarified in the next few days.

Schirmer, at whom I grumbled about the absence of a piano (and it truly is a dirty trick!) said that tomorrow he would send over his own grand. Something also appears to be cooking in the publishing sphere. When I get the piano I shall compose a few trifles and cobble them together, because I have had quite enough of beggary!

8 [21] September

Sat at home and fretted at the lack of a piano. But today is Saturday, and if they do not manage to get it here by noon, it means goodbye until Monday. I composed without the piano.

I need some little pieces for a publisher, something not too demanding, a sonatina or some 'Fairy Tales'. My inclination is for some 'Tales of an Old Grandmother', whose senile rambling through the mists of her decrepitude yields glimpses of far-off memories.

---

1 At least one entertaining account of the party appeared in *The World* magazine on 27 October 1918.
2 Frederick Stock (1872–1942), Music Director of the Chicago Symphony from 1911 until his death, a tenure at a major American orchestra surpassed in length only by Eugene Ormandy's at Philadelphia. Under Stock the Chicago Symphony made the first recordings by an American orchestra under its music director, in 1916 for Columbia.

Went to see my compatriot, the artist Anisfeld,[1] who telephoned without knowing me personally, something I found very flattering. He is a pleasant individual, but rather strange, and does not at first meeting make a very strong impression. Naturally, he had a thousand questions about Russia.

9 [22] September

Went with Kucheryavy to Coney Island, where there is a Luna Park[2] and all kinds of entertainments. I loved my ride on the American Mountains (here they are called the Russian Mountains) down which the Americans launch themselves at an inconceivable velocity. Here I encountered for the first time a new friend: the Atlantic Ocean. When I was travelling to London I had not really seen it, only the English Channel.

Spent the evening at Stahl's. He had as usual interesting things to say about the political events he had lived through in Russia. The American press is energetically unmasking the Bolsheviks as German spies and collaborators. Stahl says this is irrefutable.

What is going on in Petrograd is sheer horror. It is best not to think about it – there is nothing one can do.

10 [23] September

Stokowski,[3] the conductor from Philadelphia and a good musician, is inviting me to give a concert. This is the second very promising development. It

---

1   Boris Anisfeld (1878–1973), painter and theatre designer, had been a member of the *Mir Isskustva* group and had designed several productions for Diaghilev's Ballets Russes seasons, both on his own account and in collaboration with Bakst. The reason he and his family were in America was because the Brooklyn Museum had invited him to mount a large exhibition of his paintings. Later he created productions for the Metropolitan Opera and for the Chicago Opera, notably the latter's December 1921 production of *The Love for Three Oranges*.
2   In the early years of the twentieth century, Coney Island was the largest amusement facility in America, with three separate parks each with their own rides and attractions: Dreamland, Steeplechase Park and Luna Park. In 1913 Prokofiev had enjoyed a visit to the St Petersburg version of Luna Park; see *Diaries*, vol. 1, p. 419. Russians call the roller-coaster 'American Mountains': these 'Russian Mountains' are probably the Luna Park's Cyclone Roller-Coaster.
3   Leopold Stokowski (1882–1977) was appointed Music Director of the Philadelphia Orchestra in the summer of 1912 and remained in sole artistic charge until 1936, after which he worked until 1940 in tandem with his then Associate Conductor Eugene Ormandy, subsequently absenting himself from the orchestra for twenty years before making a triumphant come-back in the 1960s. The 'Philadelphia Sound', a particularly rich sonority from strings and brass, was Stokowski's legacy, and can largely be traced to his introduction of free (i.e. unsynchronised) bowing by the strings and parallel free breathing by the brass and woodwind. Once he had full charge of the artistic reins, Ormandy discontinued the free-bowing principle, still contriving, however, to maintain the essence of the 'Philadelphia Sound', perhaps in a more controlled manner. (Ormandy himself attributed the difference to the fact that as a violinist he, like his mentor Toscanini (cello) and Koussevitzky (double-bass) was a string-player, while Stokowski's instrument was the organ.)

appears that he has been searching for my compositions for two years, but has not been able to find them anywhere.

Schirmer asked me to call on him at his office. I thought this would be to discuss publication, but it was all about the ill-fated piano. Schirmer was affability itself, although suffering from a bad attack of asthma, and told me that Steinway had become aware of my presence in the city and himself wanted to provide me with a piano, which I would receive in about three days. I left in a fury and rang up Schindler from the first public telephone I came to, to berate Schirmer's attitude. Schindler assumed that he was the object of my ire, and was offended.

11 [24] September

Mischa Elman, one of my new New York acquaintances, whose violin has turned him into a millionaire, is still 'Mischa' despite his thirty years and his bald head. He babbles on in a disagreeably high-pitched soprano and continually waves both his arms about, but among the musical fraternity he is the champion chess-player, and so I was particularly pleased to beat him in our first encounter.[1]

12 [25] September

Schindler, to whom it has been explained that I was not shouting at him but at Schirmer, entertained me to lunch and said that if I was short of money he could put at my disposal the amount of $160 which had been deposited with him for the benefit of 'politicals'. No beneficiary has at present been identified for this money, while I as a non-Bolshevik can legally be classified as a 'political', and so he can let me have it for a month, to be returned when after that time I have become a rich man.

13 [26] September

At long last an upright piano has been delivered, sent by Steinway. I accordingly spent the entire day at home composing a 'Fairy Tale'. After being so long deprived of an instrument and the opportunity to compose at it, I at first found it hard to concentrate.

The old grandmother tells her story, coughing and mumbling, muddling

---

1 Elman was the butt of several of the amiable Leopold Godowsky's happiest one-liners. In her autobiography Godowsky's daughter Dagmar tells of Elman calling round after an exceptionally successful tour of Japan and boasting interminably of his success. 'And how much money do you think I made, Popsy?' 'Half,' conjectured Father. 'Half.' (D. Godowsky, *First Person Plural, the Lives of Dagmar Godowsky by Herself* (Viking Press, New York, 1958)).

up much of how things really were, but with occasional flashes of clarity that bring back precious moments as if they had happened yesterday. From time to time the tale she tells is veiled by a profound serenity or wisdom.

Two more games with Elman, both of which I won.

14 [27] September

Although I roughed out a second piece, and as a matter of fact it is better then the first, it took up the whole day and put me in a bad temper.

A great victory: when Bolm and I were in the office of the director of the manufacturers of a mechanical reproducing piano (who, incidentally, treats me as the acknowledged leader of Russian music today) we were joined by Campanini,[1] the conductor of the opera in Chicago, who proceeded to ask me questions about *The Gambler*. He then said: 'I want you to give me your word that before you come to see me in Chicago you will not sign a contract with anyone else for this opera.'

'And what will I have in return for giving you my word of honour?'

'My word of honour that *The Gambler* will be presented in Chicago,' said Campanini, adding: 'Campanini does not give his word of honour lightly.'

How about that! I have never known an unknown opera to be accepted in the space of five minutes!

15 [28] September

Sorted out the second 'Fairy Tale' and sketched a third. Then I practised, as I have to get my piano-playing up to its most brilliant level.

Am learning Scriabin's *Poème Satanique*.

16 [20] September

Now I have three 'Tales' and the general outlines of a fourth. Stahl tells me the Russian Embassy in New York is the most musically orientated of all and is very interested in me. He thinks they will feel under obligation to grant me a subsidy (in the form of a loan) of a thousand dollars in order that I may

---

1   Cleofonte Campanini (1860–1919) had come to the United States in 1906 from La Scala at the invitation of Oscar Hammerstein I to take charge of his newly formed Manhattan Opera Company. For a time the company was a serious rival to the Met, but in 1910 it folded, apparently as a result of an unrefusable proposal made in secret by the Met to Hammerstein, who owned both the Opera Company and the theatre, not to present any opera in New York for ten years. Campanini, who was married to Eva Tetrazzini, sister of the celebrated Luisa, then moved to Chicago to the post he held until his death. The four-week touring season he was now presenting at the Lexington Opera House included the New York debut of Galli-Curci, whom Campanini had talent-spotted and engaged in 1916.

function as a representative of Russian music, because it is important that its head should be held high.

17 [30] September

Lunch with the director of the mechanical-piano company, whose instruments perfectly reproduce the slightest nuances and all the character of the player. What impressed me most were some pieces of Granados, performed by him a month before his death.[1]

It appears that the wheels of war have turned sharply in an unexpected direction: the fall of Bulgaria has prefigured the fate of Germany. There is no one for whom I feel less sympathy than for the Bulgarians: first they betrayed Russia, calling her 'a corpse, for whom any happiness would be a joke', and as soon as Germany stumbled, betrayed her also. No doubt, this is an example of what is known as 'statesmanlike politics'.

18 September [1 October]

Today we continued the negotiations with the mechanical-piano company, Duo-Art. I played some of my things so that they could see whether they could satisfactorily reproduce them. As an experiment I played the Gavotte from the 'Classical' Symphony, and three minutes later they played back to me my performance, of course without any refinements and rather characterless, but all my accents, ritardandi and wrong notes were there. I was afraid they might exploit the Gavotte and therefore played the middle section in the wrong key in case I needed some evidence to establish their guilt. But when the director suggested I play him four pieces for a fee of $50 each, I replied with great good humour that since my concept of a fee differed so radically from theirs, I would naturally not play for that money. However, if they agreed to pay me properly, I would be pleased to play for nothing. They did not immediately understand my little joke, and for a moment thought they were going to walk off with a good profit scot-free. The American soul is dollar-shaped; here even honour comes wrapped in a dollar bill.

---

1   Enrique Granados y Campiña (1867–1916) drowned on 24 March 1916 when crossing the English Channel. Douglas Riva, writing in the *Pianola Journal*, says of the piano-roll recordings Granados made: 'The importance of any composer's recordings is unquestionable. However, in the case of Spanish composer and pianist Enrique Granados, his piano roll and acoustic recordings of his performances of his own compositions have a particular and unusual significance. Undoubtedly Granados's recordings preserve some of his artistry at the keyboard. However, in addition, Granados's recordings document the very notes that he intended for his finished compositions – intentions which were not reflected in scores of Granados's compositions as published during his lifetime.' (*Pianola Journal*, vol. 15, 2003.)

19 September [2 October]

Kucheryavy has moved with all his family to Indianapolis. We took tender farewells of one another and promised to write. I owe him $254.

Amidst all the excitements of today I had a desperate struggle to compose the fourth 'Fairy Tale' (in F sharp minor), but I think it is the best of the set.

Evening at Stahl's, where our Ambassador Bakhmetiev[1] and [Vladimir] Bashkirov were also present. The meeting with Bashkirov was affectionate, he was obviously very pleased to see me, wanted to hear everything that had been going on in Russia, and was genuinely interested in my doings in New York. The Ambassador was friendly and good company. He was extravagantly complimentary about my music.

20 September [3 October]

I am gripped by complete panic about Spanish influenza. Hitherto, although I first heard about it in Japan, it has touched me only anecdotally, with strange accounts of the prostration it is said to induce, but today the newspapers are reporting thousands of cases a day just in New York, with a 5 per cent mortality rate. New York, though, is relatively in a state of grace, as in other cities there is a true pandemic. To flee from Bolshevism and succumb to Spanish 'flu in New York – what a morbid joke! People say that if you immediately take to your bed at the first symptoms and lie there for a week you will be all right, and the most important thing is to avoid getting pneumonia, which is the main cause of death.

21 September [4 October]

Having no money at all I sustained myself yesterday evening by eating some biscuits I happened to have. Today I went to see Schindler and got a cheque from him for $160 'contraband' money, which he was more than ready to give me. Oof! For over a month the largest sum of money I have had in my pocket is three dollars, and what a marvellous feeling it is to have a hundred. I gave $50 to my tailor as a deposit on some suits, and ordered a complete wardrobe for $500. I trust that by the time it is all ready in two weeks' time I shall have some funds.

---

1 Boris Bakhmetiev (1880–1954) was, like his consular colleagues in San Francisco and Chicago, the representative of the now overthrown Provisional Government of Russia (which the United States had been the first Western government to recognize in March 1917), not the Bolshevik regime. America did not formally recognize the Soviet Union until 1933. Bakhmetiev himself was a dedicated anti-Bolshevik and a vocal supporter of Admiral Kolchak.

22 September [5 October]

An operetta tenor introduced himself to me with the libretto of an American musical and proposed that I write the music. If it was a hit the receipts would be fantastic. I said 'all right', but with the proviso that I would cede to him the credit for composing it, as I did not wish to sully my good name with a musical, while by separate agreement he would give me author's copyright, allegedly 'for notating the score'. The tenor accepted the deal, but agreement foundered on my demand that on receipt of the music he would pay me an immediate advance of $1,000. This he did not wish to do, but from my point of view it was important to have my work protected independently of the production. I said I would be able to compose four acts in four days, and generally took a rather supercilious attitude. It may be all to the good that we did not reach an eventual agreement, since for me it would, of course, be an act of musical prostitution.

23 September [6 October]

I am practising diligently every day. Lunched with V. N. Bashkirov, very kind and affectionate. He is making strenuous efforts to promote my success.

Germany is suing for peace. I must think carefully about the implications while everything is still up in the air. Perhaps I could return to Russia across the Atlantic?

24 September [7 October]

My encounter with the musical has reawakened my thoughts about a light-hearted opera, and to the *Three Oranges*. I did not care for the final scene in the kitchen, but today I have thought up a new ending to the whole fable. I like it, and am now confident that while I am in America I shall be able to finish not only the libretto but some of the music. The music will be transparent in texture, and integrated throughout with the action on stage.

Dined with Fischer,[1] a leading publisher, who professed delight at my pieces (even, to my astonishment, the *Grandmother's Tales*). He wants to publish me, but will he still want to when I ask him for $500 for each *Tale*?

---

1 Walter Fischer, whose German-born father Carl had established in 1872 the musical-instrument shop that by this time had grown into the substantial music-publishing house.

25 September [8 October]

Schindler set up a 'smotriny'[1] of Prokofiev by the local ichthyosauri: Bauer,[2] Stokowski, Mme Lanier[3] (founder of the Society of Friends of Music, a very influential and respected organisation). The result: they were all conquered by my music. Stokowski, a very nice fellow and by all accounts one of the best conductors here, invited me to conduct the *Scythian Suite* in Philadelphia (when, is not known), and Mme Lanier insisted that my debut recital must be under their auspices. The question is, will the Society be able to afford me?

In the evening I went to relax at V. N. Bashkirov's. He is truly being extraordinarily kind.

26 September [9 October]

What with the new-style dates and all the fuss and pother of New York, I forgot that yesterday was my name-day, and remembered it only today.

Because Fischer had indicated that to ensure wider distribution of my music (and more profits for his firm) they would like to publish a few more pieces in addition to the *Tales*, perhaps more accessible, like for example the 'Gavotte', today I jotted down some ideas for a set of dances to keep the rogues quiet.

27 September [10 October]

Composed a Minuet. But I would much prefer to be working on an opera or finishing my dear 'white' quartet.

Stahl absolutely adored the *Tales*.

28 September [11 October]

Dictated to Martens an article about Russian sonatas. Sketched a Waltz. In the end the music will be quite good, but the Waltz is sugary-sweet and boring. If I did not need the money I would not be writing any of this rubbish.

---

1   Literally, a 'looking over', the Russian folk tradition of inspecting prospective brides.
2   Harold Bauer (1873–1951), London-born son of a German violinist, whose first instrument was the violin. Having been introduced to Paderewski, however, he switched to the piano and became a front-rank interpreter both of the staple German masterworks but also of new French music – he was the first to play Ravel's G major Concerto in the United States. He moved to America during the First World War and took American citizenship in 1917, heading the piano department at the Manhattan School of Music.
3   Harriet Bishop Lanier (d. 1931), wife of the banker James Lanier, who over a period of nineteen years is credited with supporting the 'Society of Friends of Music of New York' to the tune of $1 million.

Austria and Turkey are negotiating peace terms. How quickly this has all happened.

29 September [12 October]

Continued with the Valse. There's nothing good in any of these dances. But I want to get this opus finished whatever happens.

The influenza rate has risen to four and a half thousand a day. I am becoming quite frightened. I bought an atomiser for my nose and some pine oil.

30 September [13 October]

Spent the whole day writing out the *Tales*.

My hundred and sixty 'contraband' dollars are running out. If I don't succeed in making a sale to Fischer tomorrow, I shall have to make use of Stahl's good offices to gain access to the Ambassador. I am at the end of my tether sitting around with no money, unable to afford anything, skimping and saving, counting every cent – it's enough to make a cat sick. And it's not helped by hearing on every side how famous I am, reading about myself every other day in the newspapers, waiting three months to get, if not tens of thousands, at least a thousand dollars. So just give them to me now, you fools!

1 [14] October

Fischer invited me to come and discuss terms for the *Tales*. I gave him a figure of $1,000. He did not blink, but said he would consider and give me an answer. The answer came that evening: he cannot pay so much.

Was at Stahl's. He is coughing like a lunatic, but says that his temperature is normal and the doctor has told him it is not the 'flu. I inhaled camphor to disinfect my nose. In the morning he had been to see his tailor – he had died during the night. He went to another – the same story.

2 [15] October

Stahl is in bed, with influenza. I am very afraid he may have infected me.

Vladimir Nikolayevich is very concerned that all I have to live on is $15 and handed me $150, saying that I should not hesitate to count on him at any time. An extraordinarily kind gesture. America has changed him.

In the evening I went to the Metropolitan Opera for the first orchestral concert of the season (a French orchestra with a French programme: they did not play as well as ours). More and more I long to appear myself as soon as possible. But alas, December! December!

3 [16] October

It seems to be happening: my temperature is 98.6° Fahrenheit (that is 37° in our Celsius scale), just slightly above normal. I am coughing and my legs hurt. I stayed at home. If it is influenza, there's nothing to be done about it; I just have to suffer it patiently until it goes away. I therefore approach it philosophically.

Finished the 'Gavotte'.

By evening my temperature was normal.

4 [17] October

Next morning I felt fine. I have not got influenza.

Telephoned V.N. He told me people been been asking him questions about B.N.[1] Can B.N. really be coming to America? That would be fantastic! I was in a state of wild excitement, such as I had not been since the time in Japan when I got my American visa. I realised that at heart I have been starved of contact with real people, especially my friends. But alas! it was nothing to do with B.N., just a telegram for V.N. from Omsk.

5 [18] October

Finished the *Dances*.[2] They are a little boring; I have no particular preference for one over another.

Telephoned Obolsky, suggesting a joint escapade of some sort together.

Stahl is at crisis point: 104° Fahrenheit. The numbers on the Fahrenheit scale certainly are impressive. The influenza epidemic in the city is on the wane.

Mme Bolm and Mme Schindler called on me.

6 [19] October

I have been weeping all day: my cold has gone into my eyes. I cannot even read. But by evening I was better, my temperature is normal and I went to Carnegie Hall to take part in a Russian concert in aid of the American Loan.

The point of this loan is quite incomprehensible to me; they have been shouting about it for two weeks now. But it is no easy matter to screw six-and-half billion dollars out of The Public! A lot of people said to me that I was making a great mistake in agreeing to make my first appearance in this

---

1 Vladimir Bashkirov's brother Boris, Prokofiev's poet friend from Petrograd.
2 *Four Pieces for Piano*, Op. 32: 1 Dance; 2 Minuet; 3 Gavotte; 4 Waltz. Op. 31 is *Tales of an Old Grandmother*, four pieces for piano.

concert, and thus risk spoiling my official debut. But it was really not an option for me to refuse to play for this cause. My attitude to my actual performance was one of complete indifference, and it was my good fortune that the concert was so delayed by the lengthy procedure of collecting money for the loan that the last part of the programme, in which I was to appear, was cancelled. For me it was the best of all worlds: I had been announced, but did not appear.

Nevertheless, the Russians excelled themselves and raised $23 million this evening. Caruso, McCormick and Elman between them collected $4 million.

7 [20] October

I forced myself to go out less and spent the whole day writing 'The Two Marquises', the idea for which came into my head yesterday. I wrote the whole thing in a day. A bit of a rush job. But afterwards I was tired to the point of stupefaction.

8 [21] October

I said goodbye to my 109th Street and moved to the Hotel Wellington, which is quite centrally located. It is a quiet hotel, guests stay there on a monthly basis, they do not mind you playing the piano and quite a lot of artists live there. I have two nice rooms with a bathroom and two walk-in closets, ideal for concealing other people's wives if furious husbands force their way in through the door. But alas, for the time being the romantic side of my life is limping badly.

I have recovered from my head cold and my fear of catching influenza.

9 [22] October

It is essential that I organise a solo recital, because it would be downright intolerable to have to wait until my December appearances. All I need is $500, and that should not be too difficult to get hold of. I raised the matter with Adams. He is polite, but has no interest in the recital. 'If you raise the money, by all means let us organise it,' he said, without much enthusiasm.

I dined with Obolsky, and commissioned him to find out what adventures of a romantic nature could be engaged in. There seems to be a drastic dearth of such possibilities in this America of theirs!

10 [23] October

The 'flu is not dying down after all: infections have now risen to four or five thousand a day, with eight hundred deaths. In some cases the disease runs its course with extreme rapidity: within twelve hours all is over. The last rites. Apparently it is a variety of pulmonary plague. What more can one say – an attractive prospect, indeed! However, I feel it is not impossible that by falling slightly ill a few days ago I might have had a touch of para-influenza, and therefore may now be to a certain extent inoculated against the real thing.

11 [24] October

It is absolutely essential to organise a recital. I have starting focusing all my attention on this. I have been practising a lot and have the fingers now, also a number of pieces in good playing order.

12 [25] October

I have taken to going to the library (American libraries are famous) where I am reading a biography of Schopenhauer. In Russia neither B.N. nor I could find any biographical information about him.

13 [26] October

Danilov, a nice man, a school friend of Zakharov's and my constant bridge partner in Petrograd,[1] has recently managed to get himself over here from London. We had dinner and spent the evening together. He says that America is better disposed towards Russians than England is, although in England they draw a clear distinction between Russians and Bolsheviks. But Russian art continues to exert its charm in England. Thank God for that; I had begun to fear that the English were too concerned with politics and had forgotten the value of art.

14 [27] October

An idea for a concerto for two pianos and orchestra (could be beautiful).

15 [28] October

In what a strange and unexpected way the war is ending! Who would have thought that invincible Germany, having fought with such menace and

---

1 A. Danilov, a bridge-playing friend from St Petersburg. See *Diaries*, vol. 1, pp. 226, 777.

bellicosity for four years, would all of a sudden come apart at the seams so meekly and prosaically!

16 [29] October

To coincide with the private view of Anisfeld's exhibition in the Brooklyn Museum there was a small concert of Russian music. I played the *Toccata*, the *Prelude*, the D major *Gavotte* and the Scherzo from the Second Sonata, and then Bolm danced to the *Visions Fugitives*, the first of them very attractively. In a way this was my New York debut, but not really, as the audience was all invited and there were not many of them, about two hundred. It was quite a select gathering, and it was enjoyable to play for them. The reception was cordial, even warm.

After the concert the audience came into the exhibition hall, a gay and rowdy scene where, as usual with a private view, the last thing anyone thought of doing was look at the pictures. I was introduced to a mass of ladies and gentlemen, not one of whom I remember. I was the centre of attention, though, and while at first I found it embarrassing eventually I liked it.

17 [30] October

When Schindler and Bolm, from excessive partiality towards me, set about raising money for my recital from various sources, $200 from one, as much as $500 from another, I flew into a rage and said I had no intention of going round begging like a church mouse. Anisfeld was also upset by the tactic and appealed to Vyshnegradsky,[1] who willingly agreed to put up $450 for the concert. This was a much simpler, and better, solution.

18 [31] October

News has come in of the opening of the Dardanelles, which was achieved at six o'clock this morning! Now at last I shall be able to send a telegram to Mama and before long establish communication with her. The lack of it has been a torment to me.

Plans for the concert are now proceeding on rails. The Aeolian Hall[2] has

---

1 Alexander Vyshnegradsky (1867–1925), formerly head of the Petrograd International Bank, who had been imprisoned in the Peter and Paul Fortress in December 1917. Vyshnegradsky was also a composer, and during his incarceration completed a fourth symphony. On his release he emigrated.
2 At the time, a major recital venue on 42nd Street near Times Square, built in 1912 for the Aeolian Piano Company, and a favoured location for leading performers. It was in the Aeolian

been booked for the afternoon of the 20th. It will be better to have the small Aeolian full (even so, 1,300 seats) than a half-empty Carnegie Hall. Adams pessimistically opines that I am not yet well enough known in America to be able to count on a sell-out. We must send out more invitations. Adams advises including in the programme not just my works but also those of others. The public is more inclined to flock to concerts of Russian music than to an unknown composer. I bought some Rachmaninoff and also found some Scriabin pieces.

19 October [1 November]

Am absorbed in learning three Rachmaninoff Preludes and something by Scriabin, not too daunting in order not to frighten the Americans. The frightening stuff can wait until later concerts.

Dined with Vyshnegradsky, who as usual was a charming host plying me with wines, asked me how I proposed to publicise my music, and when I replied that I was planning an orchestral concert, said that if need be he would be happy to underwrite it financially. Generally he acted like a perfect gentleman.

20 October [2 November]

Learning my pieces, practising three times a day with tremendous application. In the evening Obolsky and I had dinner in the Baltimore Hotel, where the atmosphere was one of fun and fashion and colour, and many of the guests were dancing.

21 October [3 November]

Austria has concluded peace. V.N. and I (we are now great friends) are hatching a plan to return to Russia via Nice and Vienna, on the Nice Express. But this is not immediately a serious proposition; the political horizon is still far too cloudy, with the threat of revolutions everywhere. I do not fear even a worldwide revolution, but will art survive as a living force? Although, perhaps, it might open up wider horizons for art in the future.

Hall in February 1924 that Paul Whiteman's Orchestra gave the first performance of Gershwin's *Rhapsody in Blue*, with the composer playing the solo piano part – a defining moment in American music. Soon after this, however, the building was sold and the Hall ceased to be a venue for music.

22 October [4 November]

Received $450 from Vyshnedgradsky and passed it to Adams. The concert will soon be announced. I am preparing intensively for it. Vyshnedgradsky did not even want a receipt for the money, but I insisted.

The influenza, thank God, is passing away from New York.

23 October [5 November]

The main way I spend my time at the moment is preparing for the concert, not so much my things as the pieces by Scriabin and especially Rachmaninoff. It was quicker and easier for me to get on top of mine, as the burden of responsibility with them is less: if people don't like the pianist at least they will like the composer. But with other people's music I have to take particular care, because that is where I shall be compared and judged. All the same, my fingers are fleeter than they have ever been. And so they should be, with three hours gymnastics a day!

Adams is not expecting a sell-out, but the Bolm faction has already sold twelve boxes. The word is that the hall should be full. One thing everyone agrees on is that the critics and musicians will be present *in corpore*.

24 October [6 November]

I must admit that my spiritual life has gone into hibernation compared to its former vitality. This does not greatly worry me: it is not a catastrophe for concentration to give way to a period of distraction. If only B.N. could appear – that would be a great joy for me.

25 October

When I went out into the streets today I was met by the hooting of horns everywhere I turned. A passing American gave me a smile and said 'over'.[1] I took this to mean that Germany had responded positively to peace overtures and that the war was over. I went on to Fifth Avenue, where there was a flood of people and the cars were stationary six abreast, with no possibility of moving either forward or back. Old and young ran up and down waving flags, parping on toy trumpets, honking car horns, banging on tin plates. Scraps of torn-up paper were being thrown from the windows of skyscrapers, spiralling down through the air like snow. A young girl first honked in my air then took hold of my hand and dragged me onwards. I smiled, remembering Obolsky, who would certainly have whipped out his notebook

---

1 Written in English.

and asked for her address. The girl soon desisted, the cars were diverted into the cross streets and an avalanche of clerks and office workers poured down into the street. Fifth Avenue was entirely filled for several miles with people shouting for joy, grabbing one another, dancing, bearing aloft a coffin for the Kaiser. I rejoiced that the war was over, but in my ears resounded the words of Demchinsky, uttered at the beginning of the war: 'An inglorious war, seven against one!' Yes! Germany had been buffeted right and left before being broken. I went into a beautiful white cathedral. There were quite a number of people inside, mostly women, and the atmosphere was better, although spoilt by the tasteless and triumphalist improvising of an organ. Oh! to have been at home in Moscow, where instead of these stupid hooters we would have had the pealing of forty bells!

No, the Americans have no conception of poetry! But in Moscow they will not know about the war, they have their own war to be getting on with! However, the day ended amusingly here: the newspapers came out with a retraction of the earlier stories, announcing that not only was the war not ended, the German delegates had not yet arrived. The crowd read the retraction, the mood changed to anger, the newspapers were torn up and the jollifications continued until morning.

In the evening I went to Monteux's concert at Carnegie Hall. The very first person to conduct in this hall had been Tchaikovsky. Today was the twenty-fifth anniversary of his death, but neither the indifferent Frenchman nor the amnesic Americans could be bothered to remember him.

26 October [8 November]

Lunch with Mrs Flannery, a rich American lady who keeps open house frequented by a lot of young people. It is some time since I was in society, and I enjoyed the lunch party.

28 October [10 November]

A pointless day paying social calls, so I hardly practised at all. Nevertheless the programme is shaping up well and is almost ready. Ten days before the concert this is good.

29 October [11 November]

At nine o'clock in the morning Mme Schindler telephoned with two pieces of news: first, that peace has been declared, this time unambiguously, and therefore there will be more public rejoicing, and second, that quite unexpectedly and unheralded, Rachmaninoff has arrived.

This is a truly remarkable turn of events. Before I left Japan I heard that he did have plans to come here, and was receiving all kinds of glittering proposals, but he had turned them all down. 'I've grown old and mischievous.' And now suddenly, without saying a word to anyone, he has appeared. I was thrilled at his arrival and immediately went to the Hotel Netherland, where I found him already closeted with Adams. I was not sure what Rachmaninoff's attitude to me would be: some time ago he had been irritated by my criticisms of his performance of Scriabin's works; later he had endorsed me as exceptionally talented but producing unintelligible music; then, before his departure for Denmark, Suvchinsky and Asafyev had gone to great lengths to pacify him on my behalf; and finally there was the whole story with Koshetz. But I felt sure that if I went to see him with an open heart everything would resolve itself. And so it proved.

Rachmaninoff was in absolutely splendid form, grumbling amusingly about the Americans and about his journey, and asked me to come and dine with him. Since he was obviously in the middle of a business discussion I did not stay long, but when I came back for dinner, although it was the hour he had expected to be back and his wife and two daughters (one of whom is already quite grown-up and a rather pleasant girl)[1] were waiting hungrily, the composer had vanished somewhere and did not reappear. I politely waited for half an hour and then went away. Later he apologised profusely and said that he had been detained somewhere.

In the evening I went to the Metropolitan Opera for the opening night of the season. Huge crowds were out on the streets celebrating the victory, dancing and jigging with tipsy sailors whom the girls kissed with deep and voluptuous abandon. In the crush someone threw confetti in my eyes and a drunk soldier knocked off my top hat, never to be seen again. I went in to Bolm's apartment and borrowed another one.

The Metropolitan was all evening dress and *décolleté*, not a seat but was occupied by persons in possession of millions. The singers were famous[2] and the opera, *Samson et Dalila*, tedious with uninspired settings. I did not stay long.

30 October [12 November]

Spent the evening with Danilov, who poured a variety of cocktails down my throat and made me thoroughly drunk, although I bore up bravely and refrained from saying anything too idiotic. I stepped out briskly on the way home and behaved with propriety (a point of honour when I drink), but as soon as I lay down the bed started to rock as though in a rough sea.

---

1 Rachmaninoff had two daughters, Irina (born May 1903, so a fifteen-year-old at this time) and Tatyana, born July 1907.
2 Caruso as Samson and Louise Homer as Dalila. The conductor was Monteux.

31 October [13 November]

Went to see Rachmaninoff, who was painstakingly revising his First Piano Concerto for a new edition which has not yet been performed. We had an hour's most cordial conversation, and Rachmasha is truly a marvellous person. He is full of complaints about getting old, his health is not good, he has lost all his money to the Bolsheviks. He is not going to rush into giving concerts here; he wants to have a quiet life for a while. The telephone rang incessantly, at which he would sigh and curse at the intrusive caller, and send me off to talk to someone else. He gave me some excellent advice about how to bandage my finger, where the skin has broken and the flesh of the tip is raw. You must first apply collodion, then cover it with a thin layer of cotto-wool, then more collodion, more cotton-wool and so on four times. I did this and the result was a most effective bandage, through which I could still feel the keys, but without any pain.

1 [14] November

Today I am feeling a little disgruntled, annoyed that I shall be playing to an empty hall because Adams has been slack about managing the concert. In the final analysis, while it is not very pleasant if the hall is not full, it does not really matter because the concert will be a success in any case and the critics will be there, and then we shall see what we shall see.

I played a bit with my bandaged finger, but it does get in the way.

3 [16] November

At Mme Lanier's (the same who could not find the money to put on my concert through the 'Friends of Music' and who is now telling me how much she regrets that I am making my debut not under their auspices) I met the gifted composer Bloch,[1] who had a great success here last year. A benign, round-faced Jew he is now, despite his kudos, starving (because he is not a pianist) and is making strenuous efforts to get back to his native Switzerland.

---

1 Ernest Bloch (1880–1959), Swiss-born composer who took American citizenship in 1924. His music is strongly influenced by Jewish liturgical and folk music, notably *Schelomo* for cello and orchestra, and the *Israel Symphony*, both from 1916. He did indeed return to Switzerland for a time, but not until the 1930s, having in the meantime been rescued from penury by his appointment as Music Director of the Cleveland Institute of Music in 1920.

4 [17] November

My funds are exhausted, and V.N. has gone away to Washington. I had to be very creative with my last remaining dollar. Instead of dinner I drank coffee.

Wrote some of the story about the American and the Egyptian.[1]

The programme is ready now, and the Rachmaninoff pieces are the best prepared of all. That's what happens when you apply yourself seriously.

6 [19] November

Today I have in my pocket precisely 30 cents. For lunch I had coffee and a sandwich, and the Bolms had me to dinner. No one knows of my financial crisis, and Bashkirov comes back tomorrow.

In the evening, feeling sorry for myself because it is such a disagreeable prospect to be performing before an empty hall (which I had no doubt would be the case), I received a telephone call from a lady who complained that she had not been able to get a ticket because they had all been sold two days ago. I only half believed her, but went to sleep in a wonderful mood and slept the sleep of the dead, visited by the sweetest of dreams. (It later transpired that her imperfect grasp of English had completely misled her: there were plenty of tickets, but quite by accident her prophesy turned out to be correct.)

7 [20] November

When Mme Bolm telephoned me in the morning and asked how I was feeling, I replied that I was 'thirsting for blood'). And indeed, I was in the mood to go out and do battle. For some reason my fingers had come back to life and the only depressing prospect was an unresponsive piano. All the same I was nervous, and was afraid that I would be nervous when playing, and this is something one must at all costs avoid because it does nothing whatsoever to help, it only makes matters worse. I had to draw on all my reserves to generate confidence. I tried convincing myself 'from Schopenhauer' that I was a musician of genius and the public no more than a 'mass-produced product from nature's factory', and I would only be making myself ridiculous in my own eyes if I yielded to anxiety before them. But there was a counter-argument: this audience would be a select one, and there would be people among them sufficiently educated to have a nice discrimination between what aspects of my playing were good and what were not.

I then took another tack: looking at my musical life as a whole, my American debut was a barely detectable event, and whether or not I was a

---

[1] 'Ultra-violet Freedom'.

success in New York would have no effect whatever on my ultimate career in music. But to this I had a riposte as well: there was a vast difference between leaving America loaded with triumph and the dollars I needed to be able to live freely as I wished – or slinking away a failure, obliged to borrow money so that I could buy a ticket, weighed down by dissatisfaction even though I knew that all the Americans were interested in was ragtime and my lack of success could not deflect me from my path. But finally I had a third line of reasoning up my sleeve: in my life I have often been faced with important and responsible moments such as not everyone is fated to undergo but many would give much to experience. If to such moments I react with anxiousness and hysteria, how will I be able to make use of them? How much better to accept them with gladness and a clear understanding! This approach seemed to me the most intelligent and persuasive: I could find no legitimate objection to it, but took hold of it and resolved to put it into action today.

When I arrived at the Aeolian Hall it seemed to be full. This was a pleasant start. I went straight out to play, to be greeted by an ovation, but – that damned heavy piano! – in the technically demanding section of the first Etude, before I had settled down enough to play with complete control, my fingers simply refused to make some of the notes sound. This threw me off course, I went wrong and had to jump to the calmer passage in C major. True, I succeeded immediately in taking myself in hand and from then on paid more attention to producing the sound I wanted, but it was an unpleasant shock because if the same thing were to happen in other pieces, God knows what a dog's breakfast I would come up with. Happily this did not happen, and although that damned Steinway forced me to simplify one or two passages, and on occasion to force the sound, there were no more actual incidents. The Allegro of the Second Sonata was received less enthusiastically (not as showy, you see) but the Scherzo and Finale brought the audience to its feet.[1]

The Rachmaninoff I played very well, there is simply no other word for it, but the Scriabin was less scrupulous in terms of accuracy, although the Etude No. 12 came off effectively. The last sequence (Prokofiev, Scriabin, the 'Gavotte' from Op. 12 and *Suggestion Diabolique*) went very well. Adams came round to the Green Room and showed me when to take a bow and when to play an encore. The audience pressed up to the platform, applauding as they came, but less full-bloodedly than in Petrograd. I took altogether ten

1   The complete programme of Prokofiev's formal debut recital at 3 p.m. on Wednesday, 20 November 1918 in Aeolian Hall, New York, billed as an All-Russian programme, was: Prokofiev: *Four études for piano*, Op. 2; Sonata No. 2, Op. 14; interval; Rachmaninoff: Three Preludes; Scriabin: *Feuillet d'albom*, Op. 45 No. 1; Deux Etudes; interval; Prokofiev: 'Prelude', 'Scherzo', 'Gavotte', Op. 12 Nos. 7, 10, 3; *Suggestion Diabolique*, Op. 4 No. 4. Tickets were priced at 0.75 cents, $1.00, $1.50, with boxes at $12.

bows during the pauses in the programme (4 + 4 + 3) and eight at the end, including three encores. I was then brought round to the artists' foyer in the hall, where the musical world had gathered in force to award me its fervent congratulations. At least fifty people must have shaken my hand. All in all, the success exceeded expectations. I spent the evening quietly at home with the Bolms.

8 [21] November

Press reviews day (eleven of them). The general impression is as follows: all the critics had been nonplussed by the short notice of the unexpected concert, but wanted to show themselves knowledgeable and accordingly wrote a great deal of nonsense. What mattered was that they wrote at length, and contrived to interpolate a reference to Caruso in their reviews. And Caruso is the champion tenor and (for New York) an untouchable maestro.

Adams congratulated me on my success and said that he had personally enjoyed the recital very much, but had no suggestions to make for the future.

I lunched at Steinway's in the company of Rachmaninoff, who observed with a benevolent smile: 'I should have liked to come to your concert, but you did not send me an invitation, so I concluded you did not want me to come.'

'Sergey Vasilievich, I would have been so nervous at playing your Prelude in your presence that I am glad you were not there to hear it. And my own compositions do not, of course, interest you.'

Rachmaninoff laughed and said: 'That all depends, depends on which compositions!'

9 [22] November

Lunched with Coppicus, the Metropolitan Manager.[1] He very much wants to do business with me, but wants to have me also next season, which for him is the current centre of gravity. If that is possible he will immediately start spraying money and publicity about. But I want to return to Russia, and am interested only in the current season. However, if, say, it could be two months next season, for instance January and February (1920), and then if there is a possibility in the meantime for me to make the journey back to Russia, I cannot see why it would be too difficult to come back once again to New York.

---

1 F. C. Coppicus was also an artist manager, head of the Metropolitan Musical Bureau (not the Opera), another of the agencies eventually forming part of CAMI, of which he later became a Vice-President. Among the artists Coppicus represented was Vladimir de Pachmann, which must have prevented his life from becoming too dull.

10 [23] November

Capablanca,[1] who was at my concert and has developed a tremendous partiality for me, let me know that he would be free this afternoon and would like to spend some time with me. We went to the National Museum,[2] which has some superb Rembrandts and a number of splendid Goyas. After that we took tea at the Ritz-Carlton, where there were a bevy of attractive women to look at, and chatted idly. In the evening a Cuban friend of Capablanca took him out boozing, and I went soberly home.

Rachmaninoff had been against my appearing in recital in advance of making my debut with orchestra because he thought it quite likely nobody would come. From having been quite clear that the right context for his own launch would be an orchestral concert, he has now changed his mind because of the success of my recital and decided to begin with a recital himself.

11 [24] November

Capablanca is turning out to be a boon companion, and today we went out into the town together, to Bronx Park.

American women are much better than I thought. Japanese women are less good. This evening I did not stay quietly at home.

The Negro liftman smiled at me and, pointing to my arm up near the shoulder, said: 'You have good muscles.' This must be because he had read the review that talked about me having muscles of steel;[3] presumably he sees me as some kind of ferocious boxer, and thus to be treated with respect.

12 [25] November

Am learning the Concerto for Chicago. But as it was learnt once and for all time it needed only a couple of hours to bring it back.

With Capablanca to see Miss Eleanor Young, the lady he lived with for six years. She is a most refined young woman, slender, pale, very charming and very American. Colossal success (mine with her). Capablanca, who is on the point of marrying someone else, counsels me to exploit this success.

---

1 José Raul Capablanca, world chess champion. See *Diaries*, vol. 1, pp. 582, 669–79 and *passim*.
2 Presumably the Metropolitan Museum of Art on Fifth Avenue.
3 Richard Aldrich, in the *New York Times* of 21 November 1918, wrote: 'His fingers are steel, his wrists steel, his biceps and triceps steel, his scapula steel.'

13 [26] November

Learning the Concerto, and also learned the *Tales of an Old Grandmother* by heart. I am pleased to have written them.

Capablanca and his friend dragged me to some cocottes who live in grand style. Just to have a look and drink tea. These ladies were unspeakably awful in every way.

In the evening at Schindler's I met Lebedev, who had been Kerensky's Navy Minister.[1] He was an exceptionally highly strung individual of about thirty-five, and a passionate music-lover. He had been responsible for recapturing Kazan from the Bolsheviks and had carried away from that city about 500 millions in Russian gold for the Omsk Government. I asked him if in the course of the fighting to raise the siege of Kazan he had ever hanged anyone. He replied: 'I had about two hundred shot.' And when I exclaimed: 'Two hundred?!' he added: 'Scoundrels!' and went off to ask Schindler to play something by Kalinnikov. He loves the gentle side of things. Anisfeld cried out: 'To hell with him!' and went into another room.

14 [27] November

Adams discussed the coming season with me. He has in mind January–February, and if I would like, March. If so, now would be the time to start the publicity. We would start serious negotiations after my symphonic appearance in two weeks' time, but what I really need to know is how much I can expect to earn this season.

I spent the evening in someone's home where the atmosphere was conducive to talking about art and philosophy. I have long been deprived of that pleasure.

15 [28] November

Called on Ochs, a Russian-American married to one of our graduates from the Petersburg Conservatoire. He has a villa near New York and sent his car to collect and take me there. It was a delight to drive in the open air outside the city.

---

1 At the time of the February Revolution V. I. Lebedev was serving as a Volunteer in the French Army. As an SR (Social Revolutionary) party member, and still wearing the uniform of a French Army Lieutenant, he hastened back to Petrograd where he rapidly came to the attention of party leaders and was given the portfolio of naval affairs in the Petrograd Soviet. Kerensky as War Minister subsequently appointed him his deputy for naval matters, in which capacity he chaired, disastrously, the first Congress of Baltic Seamen in Helsingfors, where he was almost lynched for attempting to push through Kerensky's reforms in the teeth of an increasingly Bolshevised Baltic Fleet.

16 [29] November

Had a great many things to do before going to Chicago. I lunched with Vyshnegradsky, who was uncommonly friendly, and particularly appreciates the fact that I treat him as a composer and not as a banker. The moment communications open up between Odessa and Italy he wants to send for his two-year-old daughter and his wife's relations from Kiev. He suggests Mama join this group, and thinks I should sign a contract for next season.

Vyshhnegradsky gave me a lot of wine to drink, and I drank yesterday, and the day before as well. It's so disgusting and I am repelled by myself.

17 [30] November

At six o'clock I left for Chicago, having played through *The Gambler* before I did so (after all I shall have to play it for Campanini and I want to sign a contract), but in the first place the piano score is in a terrible state (lithographed with a thousand errors) and in the second I can already see that some things in the music and the vocal parts will have to be changed. And that is not all: I have no idea how I am going to get the score out of Russia, or get the libretto translated into French or English. If I do stay here for next season (can I really be thinking of doing that?), would it not be simpler to create a new opera – perhaps *Three Oranges*? It probably would be simpler, and cleaner, and would go better in America. For this reason I took *Oranges* along with me on the train and did quite a lot of work on the libretto. The main problem is the beginning (I have already written a new ending); it is amusing in Gozzi but somehow too esoteric.[1] I thought a lot about how people like Demchinsky will attack me for contemplating writing an opera like *The Love for Three Oranges*: this is not the time, they will say, when the world is groaning under the yoke (but the art I create is outside time and locality). On the other hand it has been the assaults of those who want from me lyricism and sensuousness that gave me idea for the Prologue, which I started sketching out on the train.

18 November [1 December]

Arrived in Chicago at 3 p.m. Although I enjoyed the train journey I suffered from an accursed headache that spoilt my pleasure at arriving in Chicago. I put up at one of the best hotels (The Congress) because this time I have

---

1 Having an overtly polemical cast to his satire, Gozzi spends much of the opening scenes in parodies and attacks on the fashionable Venetian theatre of his day as exemplified by the realistic comedies of Goldoni, which a hundred and fifty years later in a different environment had rather lost their sting.

come as a *barin*,[1] an agreeably different sensation from the last time I was here when I had all of twenty cents in my pocket. The windows of my room look out over Lake Michigan, but the lake is always shrouded either by mist or by fog. Mist and fog seem to be emblematic of this city. The Avenue that goes along the shore of the lake is very fine, with luxurious shops but the town itself seems cramped and sooty.

The hotel has a cavernous, dimly lit entrance hall decorated in lugubrious-romantic style, with deep armchairs and dark-shaded lamps. A perfect setting for an assignation with a dreamy-eyed girl or for plotting a dastardly murder. What on earth can have prompted the Americans to come up with a hall like this!

19 November [2 December]

Rehearsal at ten o'clock. We went straight into *Ala and Lolli*. I was a little uneasy, because I was not sure how I was going to be able to explain what I wanted to the orchestra in English. But most of the terminology is Italian, the international *lingua franca*, and in any case by now I am able to speak English reasonably freely and without embarrassment. There were just a few basic words I did not know, like 'bar',[2] 'woodwind', and so on, but a Russian violinist sitting in the first desk put me right in a whisper. I started with the second movement, as I had done in Petrograd, and this straight away produces a good impression on the orchestra because it contains difficult passages that do not immediately work naturally, so the musicians, not wishing to disgrace themselves, get annoyed with themselves, and so our collaborative work starts to cook nicely. After an hour and a half I was dog-tired and handed over the remainder of the rehearsal to De Lamarter, who soothed the players with a Haydn symphony.

20 November [3 December]

The second rehearsal. I took the strings alone, and must say that they have made huge strides in their interpretation and played with spectacular precision and velocity. I am delighted.

I lunched with the Russian Consul, Volkov, a charming man who told me many things that I found most interesting about South America and Persia, both places in which he had served. McCormick also dropped in briefly for lunch and was, as usual, very friendly, a passionate Russia-lover, and up to his ears in work.

In the evening I went with Volkov to the Opera. I liked the theatre very

---

[1] A landowning nobleman, a gentleman of standing.
[2] In America this would be 'measure'.

much, and was impressed by its size and the originality of its construction.[1] The orchestra and the singers were good, the scenery less so. I went backstage to see Campanini, who asked me to come to see him tomorrow bringing *The Gambler*, and referred to the promise he had given me in New York. I did not altogether believe in this promise at the time, but now, seeing this excellent theatre packed to the roof with people, it seemed to me a very interesting prospect to stage the opera here.

21 November [4 December]

The orchestra played *Scythian Suite* very well, but the Concerto was not good at all. De Lamarter, who is here only temporarily and somewhat accidentally,[2] is to put it plainly no sort of a conductor, and to add to it did not know the score, so his ineffectual arm-waving produced a travesty of the piece. Although it is not done to discredit a conductor by making suggestions to him in front of the orchestra, De Lamarter can never have had any credit to lose anyhow, so I took charge of the rehearsal myself leaving De Lamarter off to one side. I concentrated on getting the musicians to repeat unsatisfactory passages, giving them instructions and demonstrations on the piano of what was required, and after an hour things began to move forward. Today my arms are less painful from the conducting, and it begins to seem as though the combination of pianistic and conducting performance will work well.

McCormick took me to a big lunch at the Chamber of Commerce, where one American recently back from Russia gave a lecture to a large audience

---

1   The building was the massive and magnificent Chicago Auditorium, designed by Dankmar Adler and Louis Sullivan to the commission of a consortium of Chicago businessmen, headed by Ferdinand Peck, determined to provide the city with an opera house larger and more opulent than any in the world – especially New York. The building opened in December 1889. In an attempt to make the 4,300-seat theatre both affordable to the public and financially self-sufficient, it was enclosed within a complex of revenue-producing offices and a hotel; although this aim was not fully realised the principle has since been emulated in new cultural buildings in almost every major city in the world. The construction innovations Prokofiev mentions refer to the foundations of the huge building, which the chosen site's deep layer of soft clay made unsuitable for current conventional foundation techniques. The solution was a vast floating mat of criss-crossed railway sleepers below a double layer of steel rails embedded in concrete. As originally conceived the outer walls of the building were to have been faced not with stone but with the much lighter terra cotta; civic pride, however, demanded stone, the use of which caused considerable subsidence round the edge of the building, still to be seen today. Initially the Auditorium was the home of the Chicago Opera and the Chicago Symphony, but the orchestra moved to Orchestra Hall in 1904 and the opera company to the Civic Opera House in 1929. The theatre closed during the Depression and in 1946 the entire building became the home of Roosevelt University. After a major renovation in 2001 the theatre is once again a venue for large-scale touring attractions and popular concerts.
2   Neither charge seems to be the case. Eric De Lamarter (1888–1953) was Associate Conductor of the Chicago Symphony Orchestra under Frederick Stock; a music critic for a number of Chicago newspapers; a respected organist and choirmaster; and a composer of symphonic, chamber, vocal, and liturgical music.

about the present situation in Russia. I listened to what he had to say and thought how strange it was that intuition had led me to flee from that milieu and had brought me to this place of honour where, sitting in a comfortable armchair, I was hearing an account of the horrors now being visited on my homeland. 'You are running away from history,' Demchinsky had said to me when I left Petrograd, 'and history will not forgive you. When you return to Russia you will not be understood because you will not have suffered what Russia has suffered, and the language you speak will not be Russia's language.' There is much wisdom in these words, and not a little envy of the man who has evaded misfortune. But the art I create is outside time and space.

My meeting with Campanini took place at five o'clock. Beforehand I played through some passages from *The Gambler* and tried to look at it through the eyes of an Italian. I did not much like what I saw, but its success or otherwise with Campanini did not concern me. In fact I immediately turned the conversation to *Three Oranges*, laying stress on the Italian source of the subject, but the effect was the opposite of what I expected. An Italian subject appealed to Campanini much less than a purely Russian one, and he absolutely loved the scene with Babulenka. He beamed a wide smile, and exclaimed: 'Bravo, bravo, maestro!'

Campanini said that he very much wanted to stage my opera, but then a whole series of technical problems came up: would I be able to get hold of the score, what about the translation of the libretto, what to do about the vocal scores? Perhaps, after all, it might be better to think about *Three Oranges*? I did not insist on a decision being made there and then, preferring to wait until after the orchestral concert had taken place, when, once it had been a success, there would be a different song to be sung. Nevertheless, the discussion with Campanini gave me great encouragement; returning home I leafed through *Three Oranges* with mounting pleasure and excitement and decided that I would compose it quickly and easily. It is almost a year since I have composed a large-scale work, and after this fallow period I could well scale the heights.

That evening, sitting in the hotel lobby and looking at the well-dressed American ladies, I had an idea for a story about a beautiful woman and her homely cavalier.

22 November [5 December]

We played the *Suite* straight through from start to finish without stopping. The orchestra was splendid. De Lamarter stumbles, but is at least making an effort.

23 November [6 December]

The first concert took place at two o'clock this afternoon – what would in the past have been the public dress rehearsal. For some reason I was greeted by an ovation from the absolutely full hall when I stepped on the platform. I suppose Stokowski had been right when he said that my appearance in concert had been eagerly awaited. If I had a few tremors I calmed myself by repeating under my breath: tomorrow you have another concert, in three days' time you play again in New York – it's not worth worrying about. This time the Steinway was a good one, light and responsive, but with dirty keys. Lamarter dragged, but avoided gross disasters. The success was great, also for *Scythian Suite*, but still not as great as it had been at its last performance in the Mariinsky Theatre. This can be explained by the fact that it was a weekday afternoon and so 90 per cent of the audience consisted of women whose gloved hands inhibited the making of a great noise. I took seven curtain calls (I am compiling statistics of these during my American sojourn, it is very much in the American spirit). My detailed biography was printed in the programme as well as a learned background note, evidently taken from the encyclopaedia, on the Scythians, which descended into such details as the information that they suffered from dysentery. What a swine (the programme-note writer)!

Campanini came into the Green Room and kissed me. He said he had never heard anything to equal it.

24 November [7 December]

At eleven o'clock I was summoned to Campanini's office for talks. He had come down in favour of *Three Oranges* (because *The Gambler* would certainly require Russian singers, and this was something Campanini did not think would be feasible in the present political circumstances, although his dream was at some future time to mount a season of Russian opera with a company ascending as far as Chaliapin). This decision pleased me. Campanini asked me what terms I required, and I said that I would like what I had previously agreed with the Mariinsky, that is 10 per cent of the gross receipts and a guarantee of ten performances. Campanini replied that such an arrangement was not the local practice, and suggested instead agreeing a fixed fee. Having been shown figures that indicated box-office receipts varying between $3,000 and $9,000, I proposed $6,000. Campanini countered with $4,000, and then upped that to $5,000. I said I could agree $5,000 provided that the fee could be paid as follows: $1,000 on signature of the agreement, $2,000 on provision of the piano-vocal scores, and $2,000 on provision of the full score.

After demurring on a few points, Campanini agreed in principle, but explained that he would have to present the proposal to the financial and administrative directors of the company for their final confirmation. And so, without any particular sensation that I had done so, I have taken on my shoulders an enormous work. But I think I will be able to do it without great strain. The main thing is that it is exactly the kind of work I should be doing: my task is to compose, not to distract myself with playing concerts. It is more of a worry that I have a deadline (1 October), but I shall approach it with optimism and high hopes and finish it before time!

The concert today, an evening one, was greeted with more vociferous success than yesterday's. There were twelve or ten curtain calls (7 + 5 or 5 + 5). I was terribly tired afterwards, but had to accompany the Russian Consul, the Japanese Consul and McCormick to some victory ball or other, from which I made my escape as soon as I could.

25 November [8 December]

The press reaction last night and today is very good, often enthusiastic, but superficial. It was a great joy to see N. T. Kucheryavy again, and we spent a happy morning in conversation. He persuaded me that it would be better to base myself in America for the coming season, to earn a lot of money and set myself up at the age of twenty-nine to be a free man. It is likely to be some time before Europe recovers its equilibrium.

At 12.40 a.m. I left for New York on the 'Twentieth Century Limited', the fastest express train in the world.[1] But I have already sated my taste for American expresses: they no longer thrill me as they once did. The track is so good and the carriages so well built that 100 versts an hour seem like 50 on our railways at home.

Wrote the libretto of the first act, which flowed rapidly forwards. It is so important to write one's own libretto: when you write the words of a phrase the idea of the music appears in the mind at the same time (the idea, of course, not the actual music).

26 November [9 December]

Into New York at nine in the morning, and straight to a rehearsal with Altschuler. It felt strange to be rehearsing the 'Classical' Symphony after the *Scythian Suite*: quite different gestures are needed, and different demands on the orchestra. Altschuler has already played it somewhere in the provinces on

---

1 The fastest, and probably most famous, train in the world at the time. It covered the 966 miles between Chicago and New York in 20 hours.

one of his tours and therefore the orchestra played it quite fluently, only here and there with dubious intonation. There was another rehearsal in the afternoon. After the week in Chicago I feel utterly exhausted.

I am being plagued with a sort of swelling or tumour. I thought it might be cancer, but the doctor diagnosed it as a deep-seated boil. It is rare to get cancer before the age of forty. I am such a terrible hypochondriac.

27 November [10 December]

Two more rehearsals today and then the evening concert in Carnegie. The hall was full, which is unusual for an Altschuler concert. The first item on the programme was Rachmaninoff's E minor Symphony,[1] which I heard with great enjoyment. At the end of the performance the composer, trying to hide behind his wife, was identified and made to stand up and acknowledge an ovation. There followed a series of small orchestral pieces including my *Scherzo for Four Bassoons*.[2] It was played with great gusto and at a faster tempo than I had expected. Altschuler had inserted it into the programme before the Piano Concerto 'to establish good relations between the audience and me'. The audience certainly did seem to like the piece, and demanded an encore. The Concerto also went well and I was called back to the platform seven times. Adams once again demonstrated the effectiveness of his services to me by coming backstage and directing my responses to the calls for my appearance. After the performance I received many congratulations on my success. The Schindlers and the Bolms (who are touchingly solicitous of my welfare) took me to a restaurant where we ate cheese and drank beer.

28 November [11 December]

The second of the two Altschuler concerts. I am growing tired, both physically and metaphorically, of concerts, even though they are all premieres. There were fewer people than yesterday. The Third Sonata was well received, the smaller pieces less so, which rather lowered my spirits for the next work, which was my conducting of the 'Classical' Symphony. Although this lacked some of the transparency it needs, it was still quite well played, and despite being the last item of the programme had a good success. Altogether I was called back to the platform seven times (3 + 2 + 2). At the end I was extremely tired and on edge, and sent to the devil a female correspondent who wanted to interview me which, evidently, displeased Adams.

Rachmaninoff did not attend, as he was not well. He asked Schindler

---

1 Symphony No. 2 in E minor, Op. 27 (1906–7).
2 Humoresque Scherzo, Op. 12a (1912).

why I had forgotten him and asked for my telephone number. Schindler explained that I had been away in Chicago. Coming from Rachmaninoff, I am very touched by this.

29 November [12 December]

There is a great deal of press coverage yesterday and today (twenty-five reviews), most of it negative, not sparing even the Symphony. The level of understanding revealed is positively asinine. Even the Symphony is found to be lacking in grace and melody. About a quarter of the press is favourable, but less so than in Chicago. All in all both Altschuler concerts have been less successful for me than either the Chicago appearances or the solo recital, which is not what I expected.

30 November [13 December]

At five o'clock I left for Ann Arbor, a small town six hours away from Chicago on the way from New York. I was to play the New York recital programme for the university there.[1] Five hundred dollars is not an insignificant fee, but I do not wish it to become the established rate for my concert appearances, therefore I agreed to accept the engagement only because it was on my way to Chicago.

In the train I became absorbed in writing the libretto, which is racing ahead and assuming a dazzling aspect. Gozzi is very theatrical and witty, but there are weaknesses in his dramaturgy, which I am recasting in my own way. Generally, the libretto is going to be unique; nothing quite like it will have been done before. When it is finished, Gozzi will have provided a trunk on to which completely different foliage will have been grafted.

1 [14] December

Ann Arbor is a small place with wonderfully fresh air after New York. The day was taken up by four interviews and a look round the collection of instruments, and lunch with the directors. The hall is huge, seating five thousand, and it was almost full for the evening concert. I suffered some internal resentment relating the size of the box-office receipts this must have generated to the fee of $500 I am being paid, but it was later explained to me that they run a subscription series lasting the whole winter and therefore the admission prices are low. The audience was unlike one from the metropolis; there was a good deal of coughing and restless shifting about in

---

1   The University of Michigan at Ann Arbor, which continues to present a prominent concert series.

the seats. I did not have very high hopes of being understood, and even though I played reasonably well I did so without much temperament. It could in general terms be counted a success, but not an outstanding one. My pianism was enjoyed but there was little appreciation of the music. My curtain calls were 2 + 2 + 4 + 0 + 3 = 11. A group of eight Russian students from the university surrounded me after the concert and escorted me to where I was staying.

2 [15] December

At eight o'clock the next morning I was on the train to Chicago, six hours' journey away. If I do not have any concert engagements in the immediate future I shall take my $1,000 from Campanini and go to Florida to compose *Oranges* in the sunshine. Would that not be a fine thing to do in the middle of winter?!

I arrived in Chicago already as an old hand in the city. Saw Kahn, Campanini's Russian secretary. Stokowski was extraordinarily nice to me and spoke glowingly of the success I had enjoyed here in Chicago. He suggested that I arrange a recital. After having suffered at the hands of the New York critics, I begin to have a warm appreciation of friendly Chicago.

3 [16] December

The discussion with Campanini began in a most disagreeable manner: he announced that when in the heat of the moment he had agreed to pay me $5,000, he had done so without the necessary authority. For other world premieres they had paid $3,000. I told him this was not just a world premiere but a commission of a new work from scratch, and in order for me to have the peace and security to compose it well, I had to be financially provided for during the eight months it would take me to compose it. Three thousand dollars was not enough for this. Further discussion on this was adjourned until the morrow. I telephoned McCormick, who is one of the financial sponsors of the Chicago Opera, but he as usual was frantically busy and was leaving that evening for Washington.

That evening I was in a very bad temper, because I now desperately wanted to compose *Three Oranges*. I resolved to do battle with Campanini, but if he is immovable then I will have to give way.

4 [17] December

Campanini proposed $4,000 as his last and final offer. I said I would agree, but only for one season (five performances). To this I would add permission to revive the production for the following season for a further five performances at $200 a performance. Since a fee of $200 a performance is terribly low, Campanini asked me to repeat what I had just said and then immediately agreed, not having made the calculation that for the first season he would be paying $800 a performance, which is rather high. In the end I thus got my $5,000, albeit with $1,000 retained for a year. The contract was immediately drawn up and I signed it. My copy, signed by Campanini together with the cheque for the advance payment of $1,000, would be sent to me within a few days. At five o'clock I left Chicago for New York and spent the time until the evening avidly writing the libretto.

5 [18] December

The libretto is making good progress. I studied the map of Florida. It is warm there and one can go swimming. If the lymphatic Adams does not arrange anything for me, I shall definitely go to Florida.

Arrived in New York at 5 p.m. and spent the evening with Bolms, where I feel very much at home.

6 [19] December

Instead of any new concert engagements Adams has sent me a bill for 10 per cent of the old ones, including Altschuler's, with which he had nothing whatever to do. As for a recital in Chicago, he told me it would cost $700 to put on. If I were to make such a sum available to him, he would do the work. No, to hell with a manager who works like this! I must find another.

I wanted to continue writing the libretto, but could not restrain myself from starting on the music. I could not tear myself away from it for the whole day, and completed almost half the Prologue.

7 [20] December

Absorbed, I carried on composing the Prologue and all but finished it. While I am actually in the process of composing I am also thinking so deeply about the staging and the transformation of the action into music that there is sometimes simply not a moment to stop and choose one or another harmony, one or another theme. If I stop to work on the detail of the music and laboriously choose material, it feels as though I shall lose the whirlwind momentum of the drama. When I play through what I have written, sometimes it strikes me as hugely interesting and effective, and sometimes as aimless note-spinning. I believe that in the last analysis both impressions are just: in among the happy inspirations there will be many places that are below my level. Nevertheless, the general tone will be as captivating as anything has ever been.

8 [24] December

I did not compose today, as I had business matters to attend to this morning and in the afternoon went to Rachmaninoff's concert. Carnegie Hall was packed to the rafters and many people were turned away, unable to get tickets.

His programme . . . No, Rachmaninoff has sold his soul to the devil for American dollars! Chopin Waltzes, Liszt Rhapsodies, Mozart Variations, his own Polka – dreadful! He should instead have devoted at least three-quarters of the programme to his own compositions. Nevertheless, he achieved a success and a notable quantity of dollars. I am glad that our beloved compatriot has been successful, and glad also that a man the Bolsheviks ruined is regaining in America what he has lost, but I regret the waste of his talents on such a 'public' programme. Probably, at the root of it lies less a practical calculation than a profound contempt for Americans. In Russia he would never have done such a thing. He played well, but in an aggressive, Rachmaninovian way that subjectively I do not like although objectively I know it is estimable.

After the concert I went to greet him in the Green Room, which was crammed as full as a church for the Easter Prime Service. Rachmaninoff, to my surprise, would for a long time not let me go, chided me affectionately for not visiting him, and said: 'I've been expecting you . . .' I replied, with mock astonishment: 'Surely you weren't really expecting me?!' 'Indeed I was indeed expecting you,' he repeated emphatically.

I was tremendously pleased by his attention.

9 [22] December

I worked hard again today. I successfully completed the Prologue and made a start on the first scene. It is a long time since I worked at this pace.

Gozzi in his original play has too much that is personal and of purely topical interest, with his campaign against Goldoni and other theatrical tendencies of the time. Many of the attacks on his contemporaries are incomprehensible and irrelevant today, but some of them are not, such as the fight against bombast, triviality, and so on. I am removing local and topical elements and replacing them, at least that is my intention, with the universal and timeless.

I know that when my opera is performed in Petrograd I shall be attacked by some who say that at a time of worldwide conflict and social convulsion one must be an insensible block of wood to alight on such a heedless, shallow subject (but might it not be that one is a person too much dedicated to pure art?! What say you, Gentlemen Tragicals?). Others will see it as yet another example of my propensity for restless overactivity, rather than lyricism. It is for this reason that I have so thoroughly enjoyed composing the Prologue with its Tragicals, Lyricals and other assorted spectators who will assault with their umbrellas.

10 [23] December

The pace of composition continues without slackening. I have reached the Eccentrics: 'He is forgetting his greatness!' And the music, I think, is pretty good. I am making a supreme effort for clarity.

Spent the evening with Rachmaninoff, who was amiable and, if I may put it this way, passive. His advice is not to bother with concerts, but to get on with composing the opera. He liked the subject and said that to be commissioned to write an opera is the most enviable position in which to find oneself, in America.

Bashkirov had been to see him over some business matter or other, and they had taken to each other most warmly. 'And such an intelligent phizzog he has on him,' said Rachmaninoff of Bashkirov.

11 [24] December

Somehow things did not go so well today, although I did manage three pages. When the desire to compose is on you but the work refuses to flow and you pace up and down unable to do or think about anything else, it is very dispiriting and upsetting to the nerves. This is why I am apprehensive about taking off to California or Florida to compose. I might hit a writer's block and be unable to produce anything. If that happened I would lose my mind. It is one thing to go somewhere to live quietly and get on with some composing at the same time, as I did in Sablino, but quite another to go for the express purpose of composing.

I spent Christmas Eve at Schindler's with the Bolms. It was very nice. I recalled being at Demchinsky's three years in a row.

12 [25] December

Christmas. Although I do not even know whether Christmas still exists in Russia, or whether it is still celebrated in the old way, even when people are living in a new way.

I did not compose much today: only the King's appeal to Truffaldino. But the music is good. However, I am not completely happy with Truffaldino's entrance.

In the afternoon I was at Bashkirov's, and in the evening at the Bolms, a quiet and domestic family time. This was very pleasant.

13 [26] December

Leander – and the first scene is finished a day earlier than I envisaged. I played through the whole thing, and oh horror! the first scene is nine minutes plus three for the Prologue, making twelve minutes in all. After twelve minutes, nothing of the actual plot has yet happened at all! I must prune it, and then prune it again, because in this opera so much happens that my famous succinctness threatens to turn into an interminable prolixity.

I am leaving no stone unturned to find a way of sending Mama a telegram. The thought that since March she has probably had no news of me give me no peace.

14 [27] December

Although I did not pass a very peaceful night, the next day is quite often a very good one for composition. So it was today. The second scene did not so much progress as race off into the distance. There was no libretto as such, but it did not need it: instead of words we have a series of howls and exclamations, a continual whirlwind of diabolical commotion. The scene is halfway done.

In the evening I was so tired I went to the cinema, something I very rarely do.

15 [28] December

Slept long and late today, but then the work went well and the second scene is finished. It has turned out well, although there is a lot more work to be done on the orchestration. The duration is three minutes, which is actually shorter than I expected. Consequently, the length of the opera is within the parameters I set: there are no *longueurs*.

16 [29] December

I did not compose in the morning as I went to Altschuler's rehearsal, where Stahl's Verochka[1] was singing Rimsky-Korsakov's song 'The Rose and the

---

1   Vera Janacopulos (1892–1955), the Brazilian-born soprano married to Alexey Stahl.

Nightingale' in my orchestration. I had made this version at her request a month or two ago, and the accompaniment was so simple that practically nothing had to be done. But when I heard it today it sounded so good it was pure delight. I am happy that I have made such a successful orchestral version of the song.

For a long time the opening of the third scene refused to come together, and this quite spoilt my mood, but it suddenly passed and with it the blockage, so that it is now good. Had it not been that the hour was late and I was tired I would have gone on until the entrance of the Tragicals.

17 [30] December

Managed a good chunk today, finishing the Tragicals leaving the stage.

In the afternoon I went shopping and bought myself a top hat to replace the one knocked from my head during the peaceful demonstration. Spent the evening at Bashkirov's. It looks as though the Allies will soon take Petrograd. I can just imagine the joy of the starving, terrified, half-condemned intelligentsia! Could it really be that come summer it will be possible to get on a train and pass through Europe to Petrograd?

18 [31] December

Composition has come to a halt because the departure of the Tragicals has brought me to the end of the libretto. I wrote more, and finished the act, but not a note of music.

I saw in the New Year at Mme Lewisohn's, an exceptionally interesting and cultivated woman living in splendour on Fifth Avenue.[1] She said to me: 'Do not stay too long in America, you will be crushed by the environment. You need the greater refinement of European society.' For an American to utter such an opinion is testament to her being anything but a stupid woman. It was the first time I had been to their house, and I had not particularly wanted to celebrate New Year in a new place amid unfamiliar people. But it is not the custom here to greet the New Year with solemn ritual, the clocks

---

1 Mrs Lewisohn was the wife of the fabulously wealthy mining tycoon and philanthropist Adolph Lewisohn, who had come to America from Germany in 1865 at the age of sixteen. Among his gifts to the City of New York was the huge Lewisohn Stadium for City College in Upper Manhattan, with 6,000 seats and room for mny more standing. Lewisohn Stadium opened in May 1915 and immediately became a staple of the city's cultural as well as sporting life, hosting a great variety of symphony concerts, and summer seasons of outdoor performances by the New York Philharmonic (when this orchestra recorded for labels other than its contractual partner CBS it used the name Stadium Symphony Orchestra of New York). The Lewisohn home at 881 Fifth Avenue, with its magnificent ballroom, was a magnet for musicians and artists.

do not strike their twelve slow chimes while everyone stands, gripped by the solemnity of the hour and reflecting on hopes, wishes and memories until the moment when the host, with raised glass, pronounces the first toast of the year. There is not the tradition here, nor the dear, humble superstitions. When I took out my watch at a quarter to twelve, the hostess, sitting next to me, asked: 'Surely you are not rushing off?' 'No,' I replied, 'but I should like to know how near we are to the New Year.' She smiled: 'Don't worry, when it comes there will be such a racket.'

And indeed, a racket there was. People whirled rattles, tinkled little bells, blew toy trumpets. In front of every place at the table was some kind of object to make a noise with. The racket went on for five minutes, after which we all stood up and drank champagne – which, as a matter of fact, we had been already drinking for some time – and clinked glasses with our neighbours. Yes, the way the New Year is welcomed in here is juvenile, silly, gay and trivial. The childishness may well mask a deeper, unconscious wisdom. But it has no poetry.

And so to 1919. Nineteen eighteen was thirteen days shorter than the normal year, as I had welcomed its inception according to the old calendar, now passed into oblivion. The whole year had passed under the aegis of America: January and February in making plans; from March to August on the journey; and from September to December in America herself. I had been prepared for either of two eventualities: fabulous success, or poverty-driven shoe-shining. The actual line had fallen between the two – nearer to fabulous success, apart for the incomprehension with which my music has been greeted. But I have got away from Russia, and that is a great deal. If only I could bring Mama out as well! The telegraph cable through Constantinople, though, is still closed.

In contrast to mine, the fantastic success enjoyed by Rachmaninoff, materialising gloomily and impassively from his Copenhagen retreat, is a curious phenomenon. But the popularity his two Preludes[1] have maintained over the eight years since his first visit here, dinning in the ears of every young girl who takes music lessons, have invested him with a stardom he can never have dreamed of, still less expected. And now his concerts sell out and the tens of thousands of dollars flow in. I am glad for him and for Russian music, and am even ready to take an indulgent view of his protesting, despite his great fondness for me, against Altschuler's proposal to include the *Scythian Suite* in the concert in which he, Rachmaninoff, was appearing. Oh, you older generation! The thoughts of the young do not interest you, but we understand this and do not blame you. And our only revenge will be

---

1 Prelude in C sharp minor, Op. 3 No. 2; Prelude in G minor, Op. 23 No. 5.

to recall that once upon a time the *Scythian Suite* could cast a shadow over your success!

And so farewell, my dear notebook, in which I have faithfully written every day. It is time to begin another, American, book.

1919

1 January

Nothing particularly noteworthy happened on New Year's Day. I was at Bolm's and Vladimir Nikolayevich's; dropped off a few cards to American acquaintances, less to pay New Year calls, that is not the custom here, than of simply having somewhere to go. In the evening I played bridge with my dear Samoilenko,[1] from which I derived great pleasure.

In the morning I did more work on the opera, and not badly either, but something peculiar is going on. It is now two weeks since I left Chicago and there is no sign of any contract or a cheque, or even a response to the telegram I sent with my queries. It may be pure negligence, or it may be that Kahn (Campanini's Russian secretary) is doing me down on purpose (as Bolm puts it, 'it stinks') because I didn't pay him any commission for his so-called efforts. That's the way it is here, you see.

2 January

Oranges are rushing towards the end of Act One. Strange how the heat of composition jostles in my mind against the thought that I've been duped.

I finished the libretto of the first act. In Gozzi the end is rather clumsy, and I had to think up something else. My ending is terribly abrupt, but I think I am not wrong in my calculations that when put together with the music and the staging it will come off very well.

3 January

Finished the act. Oh, what a marvellous final chord!

It took altogether sixteen days. If it goes on like this, the opera will be all done by 20 February. But until there is a contract I shall shut up shop and not write any more.

---

1 Boris Nikolayevich Samoilenko and his Azerbaijani wife Fatma Hanum were acquaintances in New York and later in Paris, where Fatma Hanum had a successful business as a fashionable milliner. Samoilenko had been an officer in the White Army in Russia.

4 January

Bashkirov and Altschuler are very critical of me for being so irresponsible as to leave Chicago without a written agreement from Campanini. But what could I do? If Campanini really did not want to give me an agreement he would have found a reason for not doing so, claiming for example that he needed more time to clarify some point or other. But if it is negligence, then I will get the contract in a few days. In any case I cannot see why there should be any deception: after all the commission was entirely Campanini's idea. So what would be the point? What hook could he be trying to put me on?

Bashkirov sent a telegram to the Russian Consul in Chicago, Volkov, asking him to intervene energetically on behalf of *Oranges*. As a last resort there is always McCormick, who subsidises the enterprise.[1]

5 January

Reviewing the results of my four months' activity in America, with its concerts, successes and lengthy reviews, I was rather disconcerted to discover a big, fat zero: the opera is hanging in the air, Adams has nothing to say and there are no concert engagements. Well worth coming here!

In fact, of course, it was worth while. For in Russia there is complete lawlessness, there is famine in Petrograd, the mood of the mob is ugly and embittered, and there are no prospects at all for a composer and pianist – altogether a thousand times worse than the minor setbacks here. What I must do is settle the questions over the opera, find a new manager and get some money together to do my own publicity. This is the immediate plan.

A grand dinner was held today, a much more interesting occasion than I expected, given by the Bohemian Club in honour of Rachmaninoff. The dinner was in the big hall of the Biltmore Hotel, large enough for three, or perhaps even six, hundred people. I was at the 'invited guests' table, but this was so enormous that I managed to go up and speak to Rachmaninoff only at the end of the dinner. Rachmaninoff was, as usual, very nice although a touch patronising, and asked me: 'Well, how are things with you?'

Being patronised like this by someone for whom everything is turning out so splendidly needled me a little, and I replied: 'Well, thank you, I've been sitting down and composing for the past two weeks, and one act is already finished.'

Rachmaninoff, who has not sat down to compose anything for two years, was astonished: 'Is it not a bit soon to be composing, Sergey Sergeyevich?'

---

[1] The McCormick family, notably Cyrus's brother Harold and Harold's wife Edith, *née* Rockefeller, were the most important financial backers of the Chicago Opera.

I replied: 'You see, Sergey Vasiliyevich, when the urge to compose comes upon me, I try not to restrain myself.'

'Yes, yes, of course,' said Rachmaninoff. 'Some time you must play me what you have written.'

'All right, but I'm sure you won't like it,' said I good-naturedly.

'Well, we don't know that yet,' responded Rachmaninoff with equal good humour. 'I have not completely lost my powers of understanding.'

With that we parted, and I promised to telephone him.

Rachmaninoff has conducted himself with great outward civility towards the American public, and this is the very quality that has prevented them from seeing through his mildly insulting arrogance. When after a thunderous ovation they begged him to play some more, he said that he thought an appropriate work to play on an occasion such as this was an Italian polka he had noted down from a mechanical organ. And play it he did, to give him credit, brilliantly.[1] When the audience, not perceiving that the occasion really demanded something rather more substantial, burst into a renewed frenzy of applause, Rachmaninoff got up and said, in English, 'That's all,' at which everyone sat down again.

7 January

Today there was an evening of my compositions at the Modern Music Society, a small group akin to our late 'Evenings of Contemporary Music'. Because I had asked for it to be a very private[2] affair they had rather overdone this aspect and arranged the event in someone's very cramped apartment with a room seating about eighty people, so many people could not get in.

At all events I enjoyed playing my Second and Fourth Sonatas and, for the first time, *Tales of a Grandmother*, because it recalled to me the pleasant objectives of the 'Evenings of Contemporary Music'. It was incidentally, the tenth anniversary of my debut as a concert performer. My first appearance at the 'Evenings' was on 28 December 1908 old style, that is 10 January 1909

1 Rachmaninoff's cousin, Anna Trubnikova, writing in 1954 of a holiday she spent with the composer and his wife in Florence: 'A tiny donkey with very long ears pulled an upright mechanical piano on wheels and a cot with a baby in it was attached to the piano. The young man sang popular ballads and the woman wound up the piano. Our favourite number in their repertoire was a simple but quite melodious polka.' (A. A. Trubnikova, 'Sergey Rakhmaninov' in *Vospominaniya o Rakhmaninove*, 2 vols, edited by Z. A. Apetyan, 'Muzyka', Moscow, 1988) In the published score, and as recorded by the composer and his wife in 1938 (at a private party), it is an attractive 1'19" piece for piano four hands, but contemporary accounts say that Rachmaninoff often played it as an encore in a greatly embellished, probably partly improvised solo piano version.

2 Written in English.

new style.)¹ But no one was aware of this. The Society made me an honorary member.

9 January

Finally a telegram from Volkov: with some difficulty he had got Campanini to give him his word he would send me a contract within a few days. The sly old devil is probably thinking up some way to get out of it. But why? After all it was he who stirred the pot to begin with. Bashkirov, however, is congratulating me on having the contract already in my pocket.

10 January

In the evening I had an American girl, typical of Americans in being beautiful, flat-chested and unresponsive.

11 January

Adams greeted me with an affectionate smile, the more so because I presented him with a cheque in payment of his bill (10 per cent of my earnings). I asked for his advice (!) on whether I ought not to find another manager who would be more energetic in helping me settle my debts. Adams benignly said he would think about it, and asked me to come back on Monday morning for a final discussion.

The point is that I need one and a half thousand for publicity. Even with generous instalments I can't spend that. That is why I need a manager who can get me that sort of money.

I studied Tchaikovsky's Sonata and two pieces of Scriabin – *Prélude* and *Désir*.² I know both of them by heart.

12 January

The whole day went on visitors and going to receptions, although I did play for a while.

I heard Rachmaninoff, his Second Concerto, which he played magnificently. The success was overwhelming, which pleased me greatly, and I joined heartily in the applause. I went backstage to see him but there was such a savage expression on his face that I immediately went away again.

At home in the evening the urge came upon me to write an orchestral

---

1   Prokofiev's first appearance at the Evenings of Contemporary Music in St Petersburg was in fact on 18 December old style 1908, which would have been 31 December new style. See *Diaries*, vol. 1, p. 72.
2   Op. 59 No. 2 and Op. 57 No. 1 respectively.

piece, not too complicated – a 'Fairy Tale' perhaps? The plan was soon clear in my mind: a serene, lyrical, narrative theme which would come back unaltered several times to enclose a series of episodes, one stormy, another joyful, a third lyrical. There is (for the information of future critics) no programme but in exchange for a specific subject the listener will have a clear field in which his imagination can range.

13 January

I went to see Adams – and we are divorcing by consent. The parting was amicable and Adams asked me to get in touch whenever I needed him. I went straight from him to Meyer, who wants very much to become my manager. He will start talking talks with piano companies – on his own account, naturally, not mine.

I finally got a letter from Campanini with an unsigned contract that had had some small changes made to it. This will take up yet more time and several hundred dollars for having another copy made of the score. But at least I have some documents in my hand, and that is important.

I did no piano practice nor did I compose any of the opera, but much enjoyed writing the 'Fairy Tale' for orchestra.[1] Why am I suddenly so taken with this? Probably the reason is the pleasure I experienced when I heard the orchestra perform my scoring of the Rimsky-Korsakov song, and this moved me to write an orchestral piece of my own.

14 January

Bashkirov advised me not to worry about the changes in the contract so I signed it and sent it to Volkov (not to Campanini).

'Fairy Tale' is progressing. I really should not have got involved with it. Of course it is very enjoyable, but now that *Oranges* is back on track I should not be distracted from it.

15 January

I decided to carry on with the 'Fairy Tale' until I get the contract, at which point I will put it to one side and throw myself into Act Two, setting it down in one gulp.

I have had discussions with two managers, both of whom are now out trying to find me some money. My second recital will probably take place at the beginning of February.

---

1 This ultimately became the theme for the variations in the Second Symphony. [Author's subsequent note]

16 January

The 'Fairy Tale' is good, as much as I have written that is, but made no further progress today. So I am learning the Tchaikovsky Sonata.

I had an idea for a story about an idealist indirectly bribed by a rich man. I started to write it.

17 January

Had toothache. Did not do much.

18 January

Practised a lot. Made a start on the libretto for the first scene of the second act. Composed a bit of the 'Fairy Tale'.

19 January

Finished the libretto for the whole of the second scene of the second act today. It is astonishing how little time it took (one hour), but the scenario and even some phrases had been done earlier. As well as that, I really enjoyed the writing, and that is always important for getting things done quickly.

20 January

Played the piano. Since the 'Fairy Tale' seems not to be going anywhere and I'm not writing the opera, I had better concentrate on getting things together for the recital. But neither Meyer nor Haensel has so far managed to come up with any money, and I need $2,000 for general publicity; that is the point of departure for all my future concert activity.

This evening Mme Lewisohn gave me two seats for the Metropolitan Opera in the front row, so having abducted Mme Samoilenko I went with her to this season's premiere of *The Golden Cockerel*. I had a wonderful time.

21 January

I finally managed to send a letter to Mama via the person who is going out to Tiflis as American Consul. The letter won't reach her for a month and a half, but thanks be for small mercies; the problem with Mama is the most painful aspect of my life.

22 January

My patience ran out today, and although I still have no contract, I started on Act Two. However, it took a long time for the opening bars to come right (I'm out of practice at composing), but then the music began to flow.

A really gorgeous American girl. At last.

23 January

The opera is going splendidly: quickly, easily and pleasantly.

As Campanini's company will shortly be coming on tour to New York, and as I still have not received the contract, I decided to seek him out. I found his office, and the maestro himself inside it. I had been afraid that I would end up having harsh words with him and with Kahn, and generally creating a scene. But Campanini was affability itself and exclaimed: 'Ah, maestro!' He had signed the contract on Monday and ordered his manager to forward it to me with the cheque; I should receive it in a day or two. Campanini asked me if I had started writing; I told him: 'I've made a few sketches . . .', wished him success and left, thinking to myself what confirmed scoundrels he and Kahn are.

24 January

The March – and the scene was quickly finished. I could not have imagined that I would finish it today. I don't think I have ever written anything with such speed and fluency. To begin with I had doubts about whether the music I was writing was good or just so-so. But now all qualms are cast aside and I am simply composing.

I went to the concert of Yamada,[1] the Japanese composer. He has no talent for symphonic music, but I liked one song on a Japanese subject (or rather the theme was Japanese).

In the evening I went to see Bashkirov. He was in a rather minor key and talked a lot of sophisms. The reason for this was the wretched political situation: what made the Allies invite both Bolsheviks and anti-Bolsheviks from

---

1 Kosaku Yamada (1886–1965) had studied in Western conservatoires, and back in his native Japan brought together the group of instrumentalists that grew into the Tokyo Philharmonic Orchestra, of which he became the founder and first Principal Conductor. By the time of this New York concert he had already composed three operas on Japanese subjects, and a large corpus of other symphonic and piano music. The *Vanity Fair* reviewer of the concert in the February 1919 issue found that: 'The composer arranged a series of Japanese melodies paraphrased in Western musical idiom: they are models of arrangement and development. The harmony is rich and appropriate, and the whole effect is to bring out a charming and particularly unique vein of beauty – all that haunting miniature mood that we find in Japanese poetry.'

Russia to their conference? And why to the Princes Islands, of all places?[1] I try my best to keep up with the political situation, although I often lose the thread of what it is all leading to. When the entire globe has been dislodged from its normal axis it is hard to foresee all the phenomena that may ensue.

25 January

I'm getting on with the entr'acte. I must do a lively march to prepare for the festivities.

Haensel said that he could arrange for newspaper advertising on credit, with payment delayed until the autumn. It is clear that he seriously wants to work with me, and so I decided to stay with him and we settled on 17 February for the concert. It is rather late, but any earlier would coincide with 'dangerous' concerts at Carnegie Hall.

27 January

I got as far as the Monsters' fight, but got stuck there.

28 January

Rachmaninoff gave the first performance today of his new version of the First Concerto. I love the first movement very much, it is naive and poetical, if a little long. Now everything has been skilfully smoothed out, but when Rachmaninoff decides to insert a touch of modernism in the shape of consecutive triads with parallel fifths, it jars unpleasantly on the ear; it's not at all stylish. Nor is the new final section very successful; after the dreamy subsidiary episodes its bluster is repellent. It used to be commonly agreed that the second and third movements are plain bad, but in the new version the second movement is very beautiful and it is only the finale, alas, that remains as bad as ever. The performance was a great success with the public.

The influenza shows no signs of abating, there are three hundred new cases every day. Today poor Mme Schindler was carried off by a dreadful pneumonia within twenty-four hours, a charming, healthy, beautiful woman.

---

1 On 18 January 1919 the delegates to the Paris Peace Conference, to which no Russian (or German) participants were invited, instituted a Council of Five: United States, Great Britain, France, Italy, and Japan, which was to take part in all meetings, hear all commissions, and execute all decisions. Other Powers would take part in questions which concern them, the neutrals appearing only by invitation. On 22 January the Council approved President Wilson's proposal to invite representatives of all the belligerent Russian groups (i.e. Whites, Reds and all shades in between) to meet representatives of the Council at Princes' Island (Prinkipo), in the sea of Marmara. The meeting never took place.

Schindler is destroyed, the Bolms are in tears. I am very sorry for them, but I shall not visit them for fear of infection.

29 January

Today I had to have three teeth extracted, in pursuit of an extensive programme of repairs to my mouth drawn up by Dr Hussa, a famous dentist in these parts. The procedure for extractions here is to use gas, and I was very interested to find out how this is done, how one moment I can lose consciousness and enter a state of non-being such that I am unaware of my teeth being pulled out, and a moment later come to having spent the intervening time no one knows where. A rubber hose with a wide rubber bell opening was inserted into my mouth completely filling it, and I was told to breathe normally. I felt the gas beginning to come in, but it did not make any particular impression and actually tasted quite pleasant. This lasted for ten seconds or so, long enough for me to decide that my organism was such that the gas would have no effect on me. Then I suddenly started to catch my breath and felt as if I were suffocating; this was painful. I wanted to grab the bell and wrench it out of my mouth. But although a pale mist was already swirling about me I still had enough presence of mind to realise that I must co-operate with the doctor and not interrupt his work. So I clenched my fingers firmly and kept still.

After that I did lose consciousness and my sensations were, if I may so describe them, geometrical, by which I mean that I felt rather than saw geometrical shapes, which I suppose were the forms of the teeth that were being extracted from me. One especially vivid impression must have been the point where a tooth would not come out all at once but had to be waggled about in the recently formed wound. I think this would have been the second of the three teeth. But after that my memory entirely disappeared, even though by the third extraction the power of the gas was beginning to weaken. The extraction of this tooth was distinctly painful, but it felt more like a huge millstone that was being pulled out, not a tooth. After that I began to come to (a most enjoyable sensation) and noticed a spittoon before my mouth. The doctor said: 'Spit it out', word for word as Truffaldino encourages the Prince.

My first reaction was that this was quite a powerful experience to have gone through, but as I thought they had succeeded in taking out only one tooth, I would have to put off the others until tomorrow. My tongue still tied in knots, I asked, in English: 'One or three?' The doctor answered, 'All three, and you did splendidly.' Afterwards I could make the sensations of my semi-conscious state account for three teeth, but at the time everything seemed to have happened so quickly there could only have been time to take out one tooth. My subsequent return to full consciousness was quick and pleasant. The girl put a paper cup of cold water into my mouth and I was able to rinse out. I got up from the chair in great good humour and set off for home. The bleeding went on for three hours.

30 January

Mme Schindler's funeral, American style: The cars took us at high speed right through the city to the crematorium. I have always been upset whenever I have seen this mad dash to the grave, but today I wondered: might it not be better like this – quicker, and less punishing on the nerves? And yet, in our solemn processions there is a certain significance, an attitude befitting the occasion, whereas here it just seems to be business, getting it over and done with in the shortest possible time. To which an American would respond: 'The very procession you cherish is a visible symbol of your lack of sincerity.'

31 January

At last, the contract and the cheque. Several items of business in consequence: arrangements for the concert, settling the hotel bill, and so on. All the same, I got a bit further with *Oranges*. I've moved on from the Monsters' fight.

1 February

I have moved out of the Wellington, which is like a conservatoire – every room has someone practising in it, which interferes terribly with my composing – and moved into private accommodation, very comfortable, and right on Fifth Avenue. I have two large, carpeted rooms. And complete quiet.

4 February

I made the acquaintance of the pianist Arthur Rubinstein,[1] who has just come from South America. I have heard about him, but not the man himself. He proved to be a most interesting person and likes my music very much.

This evening, when I was at Samoilenko's, Fatma Hanum received a letter from Baku written pretty recently, on 12 December. It had been brought over

---

1 Artur Rubinstein (1887–1982), Polish pianist. Rubinstein was a man of extraordinarily wide culture (he read and communicated fluently in eight languages) and was an enthusiastic proponent of new music, especially of French, Spanish and South American composers, as well as by his compatriot Szymanowski. His two books of memoirs (*My Young Years*, published in 1973, and *My Many Years*, published in 1980), are irresistible accounts of his life, times and encounters.

by an English officer serving in the forces now occupying Baku. There was both sad and joyful news in the letter, but what was distressing for me was that there was no mention of Mama, and on top of everything else she has no idea whether I am in Buenos Aires or New York. Baku has been a place of dreadful carnage, perpetrated more between nationalities than between classes. The city has been dominated in turn by Tatars, then Bolsheviks, then Turks, and now the English. Many of Fatma's Muslim relations and friends perished in the butchery, and the revelations caused her to burst into tears, although on the whole she controlled herself admirably. In Kislovodsk there has also been a purge of generals and wealthy people; one who died was that nice General Ruzsky.[1] I had already read of his death in the newspapers here, but thought that it was not true, as had turned out to be the case with others. I am sure none of these events will have affected Mama, since she is well out of it, in a quiet, modest little country house. Yes, Stahl was right when he said: 'Who knows what black deeds we shall yet have to read about!'

5 February

I saw for the first time *Pelléas et Mélisande* in the production by 'our' Chicago Opera, currently on tour here at the Lexington Theatre.[2] *Pelléas* absolutely enchanted me with the magical power of its poetic dream world. One is caught in its meshes as in a web, and transported who knows where. Is it good music? Perhaps. It has all the charm of understatement; an understatement at times so pronounced that to go beyond it would result in nothing at all. It opens up amazing possibilities for operatic exposition, but it seems to me one could explore them still further. When I immerse myself again in my *Oranges* I shall be returning to dream-world subjects.

The opera was performed very acceptably and the theatre was full. I begin to think that they really will produce *Oranges*. Kahn and Campanini both came up to me graciously and shook my hand, but I can hardly bear to look at them.

10 February

Rubinstein visited me and praised the Fourth Sonata extravagantly when I played it to him. He is a lively, interesting person. He speaks eight languages excellently. He and I immediately became friends.

---

1 See above, p. 234 n. 3, and *Diaries*, vol. 1, p. 743.
2 With Mary Garden as Mélisande.

11 February

Although I had promised myself not to do any composition before the 17th, that is to say until the concert, but to concentrate seriously on practising, I got bored and composed a little today.

12 February

Did not practise the piano much.
   Finished the Drunkards and the Gluttons.[1]
   The 'Ultraviolet Story' unexpectedly brought itself to completion. I have recently become interested in archaeology and ancient history either because of the story, or ancient history has made me interested in the story. Whichever way round it was, I was looking at books in English about Egypt and Babylon, and started jotting down a story. Today it suddenly all came together and I finished it. (I had already written the ending.) I'm very pleased.

14 February

Stahl and Mlle Janacopulos said they would like to undertake the translation of *Oranges* into French. Things are not going too well for Stahl, it seems, and he is not averse to earning $300 on the side. This is an unexpected and very convenient combination for me, and I think they will do it well.

15 February

Today the Prince's laughter came out well, I think. This was a difficult passage.
   Korzukhin, a very intelligent man who arrived in New York on the same liner as Rachmaninoff, and who is a great admirer of mine, told me a story about Rachmaninoff. Rachmaninoff had been talking to Glazunov after a performance of the *Scythian Suite*. It seems Glazunov had been very dismissive of it, but Rachmaninoff found there was 'something in it', whereupon Glazunov lost his temper (as much as such a thing is possible for someone so equable). This is a fascinating vignette from the life of two conservative maestros, but I find it hard to believe that Rachmaninoff would have made a very vigorous defence of the *Suite*.

---

1   Non-singing characters in *The Love for Three Oranges*.

16 February

Godowsky's daughter is very pretty, but a terrible flirt. People say: 'Poor Godowsky,[1] to have such a wild daughter.' (However this opinion is mainly voiced by the most solid citizenesses.) At tea today chez Liebman,[2] she made a bee-line for me, and after five minutes' conversation announced: 'I liked you as soon as you came in.'

I replied: 'I like you now, but I did not like you at first.'

She: 'Oh, now I hate you. But why do you like me now when you didn't at first?'

'Because I don't like you when you're jumping about, but I do when you sit quietly as you are doing now.'

17 February

My attitude to today's concert has been calm throughout, detached even, although I was aware that it was important for my prospects in the coming concert season. Yesterday evening I played bridge with Samoilenko until one in the morning (eight rubbers) and only just before the concert itself did I begin to experience any disagreeable nerves. However I was relaxed about the programme because I knew every piece through and through. Even when I tried to turn my mind to reflecting philosophically on my last recital, I

---

1 Leopold Godowsky (1870–1938), the Polish pianist who for many remains still the touchstone of the virtuoso pianist. Almost completely self-taught, he was the first great pianist to adopt and teach the principle of weight release, rather than muscular impetus, as the most efficient method of playing. His transcriptions and arrangements of other composers' works, both for piano and for voice and other instruments, have long been valued by pianists, and his own compositions are today slowly beginning to be recognised as original contributions to the repertoire. Godowsky's daughter Dagmar, at this time a sensationally beautiful twenty-one-year-old, was already well into the lurid but fascinating cultivation of celebrities that makes her freewheeling, breathlessly related autobiography (*First Person Plural*, op. cit.) an unputdownable read. The limitlessly hospitable Godowsky household in New York was memorably captured in Abram Chasins's book *Speaking of Pianists*: 'Once anyone entered Godowsky's door, he became a disciple . . . Everyone and anyone was welcome. There seemed to be a perpetual party going on. The table was always set and loaded with food and drink. Godowsky was a born host. His sons and daughters came naturally by their linguistic virtuosity and easy sociability. Popsy [Godowsky's nickname] loved people and loved to be surrounded by them. If he invited you to come over 'just for a little quiet talk and music', you might arrive to find twenty people who had just dropped in, among them not only musicians but also, likely as not, Popsy's music-loving tailor or butcher, a man he had met the day before who said he liked music. Everyone was treated with equal informality and graciousness. Popsy's old-world courtesy and sparkling humor pervaded every word and action as he waddled between the living-room and adjacent dining-room filling plates and glasses, emptying ashtrays, scattering remarks and vicious jibes.' (A. Chasins, *Speaking of Pianists* (Alfred Knopf, New York, 1957).)
2 Henry and Zelda Liebman were wealthy and cultivated New York supporters of music and the arts. Prokofiev's hostess was probably their daughter.

found I had no need of this. Quite a lot of people came, the hall was about three-quarters full, although many of them were guests and had not bought their tickets.

This time the piano was an excellent one and I played the Fourth Sonata well. In fact I relaxed and played the whole concert without problems, better than I had expected, due to the fine piano.

The first movement of the Sonata was not particularly warmly received, but it was better after the second and best of all after the finale – just as it should be. I played Scriabin's *Prélude* and *Désir* very softly and the Etude No. 12 (which I had already played at my first recital) tempestuously. A selection of ten *Visions Fugitives* had a greater success that I had expected. There was some laughter during the humorous numbers, and exclamations of 'Ah!' after the unexpectedly short ones. The concert ended with Tchaikovsky's Sonata, the best thing about which is its scale, so I tried to play it with real sweep. It is the first time that I have performed such a large piece by another composer, too large if I may be permitted to say so, and I made a series of cuts in order to render the form more elegant. I made my own arrangement of the penultimate page of the finale, and it sounded spectacular.

The success was very great, and the audience stormed the stage. Three encores. In all, I had 18 curtain calls: $3 + 3 + 4 + 8 = 18$.

In the Green Room I was surrounded by a good crowd, among whom were many beautiful girls and women. Young Gertrude shrank modestly to one side, but Dagmar Godowsky boldly hung on my arm. Her addresses and those of her friend Liebman are nothing if not energetic. Afterwards I drank tea with Samoilenko at Cherri's, and later in the evening played bridge.

18 February

Today was the day for reviews, which proved to be worse than I had played and than the success the concert had enjoyed. All the same, some were not bad, drawing attention to the sensitivity of my performance.

Gertrude, who had sent me a bunch of roses yesterday, came to see me and acted like a true American girl: she came right out with it and said simply: 'I love you.' Then she admitted that she was jealous of Dagmar because of the way she had clung on to my arm yesterday.

I said, in English: 'It is because Dagmar has more passion than you.'

Gertrude: 'I am also passioned but I control myself.'[1]

---

1   This exchange is recounted in English.

19 February

Result of the concert: invitations from Ampico and Duo-Art, two mechanical-piano firms, to make piano rolls for them. It seems I can now earn $250 a piece (the same fee as I had unsuccessfully demanded in the autumn) or even more. The two offers are mutually exclusive, so I shall have to decide with which of them I want to conclude an agreement.

20 February

In *Oranges* the Prince has run off and been caught. But the work is proceeding slowly, in fits and starts, because I keep getting distracted from it.

In the afternoon I went to Rubinstein's concert, his first appearance in New York. He plays well, in places astonishingly so, but sometimes rather uninterestingly. He is at his best in modern music: Albéniz and Debussy. Tea with Liebman after the concert, and again Dagmar was there. In the evening Liebman and Dagmar dragged me to some little theatre or other, after which we went to their friend's studio, where there was a real fireplace with logs, not the gas kind you usually find in America.

21 February

What has been stopping me composing is the negotiations with the mechanical-piano firms. I have to go and listen to their rolls to determine which are better, and make shrewd decisions about the conditions I must have. Even so I did compose a little.

In the evening I went to the Metropolitan to hear a boring *Prophète*. Rubinstein extricated me and took me into his box with Besanzoni, his girlfriend and New York's newest star mezzo-soprano.[1] After the performance we dined in the elegant Crystal Room. Rubinstein advised me to go to South America, where there is plenty of money to be made.

Incidentally, the loss on the recital was $230. Not good. I had hoped I would at least break even.

---

1   Gabriella Besanzoni (1888–1962), mezzo-soprano with a distinctively velvet tone that can still be heard on historic recordings (she made several for RCA Victor in 1920–21), and having a superb Carmen among her many roles. She made her Metropolitan Opera debut as Amneris in November 1919, and subsequently sang Dalila to Caruso's Samson as well as Marina Mnishek in the Rimsky version of *Boris Godunov*, but somehow failed to capture the enthusiasm of New Yorkers and was not invited back at the end of the season. However, in her native Italy and in South America she continued to have a distinguished career until her retirement on the eve of the Second World War.

22 February

For the past three weeks Bashkirov and I have been having a slight cooling of relations (he did not come to see me when I was feeling unwell), but today he took the initiative and called me. This was generous on his part, and I immediately went over to see him.

I got through more work today, since there were fewer distractions.

In the evening I went to Rubinstein's second performance, a Brahms concerto. Good, but boring, music, excellently played on this occasion. It was a great success, followed by supper with Rubinstein at his hotel, which I went to mainly on account of Dagmar. But there were too many people of all different kinds there, jabbering away in different languages.

23 February

In the afternoon a concert by Rachmaninoff with, at last, a Russian programme, a modern one, no less: Rachmaninoff, Scriabin, Medtner. It was magnificently played, but badly chosen. When I went into the green room, which was full of people, Rachmaninoff received me very oddly: he graciously extended his large, soft hand but did not interrupt the conversation he was having with some gentleman or other. I could have been offended by this, but later I thought: three years ago I had been tactless, even if legitimate, in criticising his approach to Scriabin. Now he is afraid I might make further inappropriate strictures.

24 February

Because the man who comes to clean my apartment has fallen ill with Spanish 'flu, the landlady did the cleaning today. She picked up the hairpins Dagmar had scattered about the place (seven in all) and in icy reproof laid them out in a row on the marble mantelpiece, each one like a dagger reproaching me for my scandalous behaviour. At first this made me feel acutely uncomfortable, but then very cheerful.

25 February

I signed a five-year contract with Duo-Art, for five pieces a year at $250 a piece. Five years is a long time, but they are not willing to incur their substantial publicity costs – an important consideration – for a shorter period than this. Not only that, but I can immediately record two years' worth, i.e. ten pieces, for which I shall receive $2,500. If I add to that the $1,500 I am going to get for the piano score of *Oranges*, then out of the blue my summer seems secure. I really had been expecting grave difficulties in getting myself out of the financial mess I am in. I had been thinking I shall have to borrow money again.

Dagmar did not telephone today, but she has still set me on fire. This evening, lying on the divan, I cried out in satisfaction: 'what a hell of a girl!' and laughed out loud remembering the aphorism 'Poor Godowsky, to have a daughter like her!'

26 February

Capablanca telephoned on his return from Chicago, where out of three hundred matches he had lost three, and we lunched together. Then I hurried home, because Gertrude was due to come by. As always she appeared punctually and unaccompanied, and said she knew an extremely attractive girl who had been sent into raptures by my concert and who wanted to come and greet me. She would soon be passing by outside on the street, and if I was agreeable to her coming in, Gertrude would give her a sign. I was not very keen at first, but since Gertrude insisted that she was really very good-looking, I said all right and the exchange of signals took place as planned.

When she appeared her loveliness exceeded all expectations. She was a delicate American beauty, slender and supple. A most lovely face surrounded by thick dark-blond tresses, peeped out from below an enormous hat. She asked forgiveness for arriving without leave, but she had been so transported by my music and by my person! In the end they both stayed for over three hours (I would not let them go) and all the while Stella Adler (such was her name) was so delightful, so dreamily gentle and tender, that Gertrude was quite put in the shade, which caused something of a drama.[1]

---

1   Stella Adler (1901–1992) was to become one of the most celebrated American actresses, directors and teachers of her generation. Daughter of Jacob and Sara Adler and thus (from the age of four) a member of America's most famous Yiddish theatre troupe, she was later to add to this heritage the ideas and teaching of Stanislavsky's Moscow Art Theatre, with whom she studied and spent some time in 1934, and became the first actor to introduce his system into American theatre since when it has hardly ever, if at all, lost its seminal importance. With her second husband, Harold Clurman, and Lee Strasberg, she was a founder member of the New York Group Theatre collective. Becoming uncomfortable with the political stance of some of her colleagues and also, based on her own first-hand rather than vicariously derived experience, with Strasberg's interpretation of the Stanislavsky system, she made a complete career change and went to Hollywood (reportedly with a nose job to improve her chances) in 1937, but returned dissatisfied to New York and the stage in 1940, where she was teaching in Erwin Piscator's Dramatic Workshop at the New School for Social Research at the time the young Marlon Brando happened to wander in and come into her orbit. Her favourite, and perhaps the most gifted of all her students, Brando may be said to have inaugurated modern American acting with his incarnation of the Adler philosophy of the theatre at the opening night of his performance in *A Streetcar Named Desire* in the Ethel Barrymore Theatre on 3 December 1949. Among other graduates of what became the Stella Adler Studio of Acting, to this day a prominent acting school in New York, are Robert de Niro, Warren Beatty, Elaine Stritch, Harvey Keitel and Candice Bergen.

27 February

Act Two is rapidly nearing its conclusion.

In the evening I went to *Pelléas*. The original plan had been to go with Dagmar, but as she did not telephone I went on my own. In the end we ended up in the same box, having both obtained passes from the management. I wanted very much to immerse myself in the opera, which moves me deeply, but I found my equilibrium disturbed by Dagmar's proximity so that Dagmar spoilt *Pelléas* for me and *Pelléas* spoilt Dagmar. I parted coldly from her and returned home upset. Sitting by the fire with my pipe, some philosophical reflections restored my equanimity.

28 February

I cut my first two piano rolls for Duo-Art: the Prelude from my op. 12 and two Scriabin pieces.[1] I was a little nervous, aware of my responsibilities especially in my own works. In fifty years' time people will listen critically and say: 'Ah, so that's how he played.' So one cannot be too wilful, on the other hand if one is too cautious one risks inadvertently being mannered, something that also must be avoided. However, I seem to have played not too badly.

1 March

I worked for four hours and finished the second act, which induced a mood of boisterous cheerfulness. So at tea at the Lamberts I mercilessly teased Dagmar and Polina, Heifetz's pretty young sister.

2 March

Today was Stella's day. We lunched together (I had issued the invitation as we parted last time) and then she spent several hours with me. It was very different from Dagmar – a watercolour rather than a flamboyant oil painting. Stella was dreamy and tender. I had the fire going and cushions spread on the floor. We kissed, and she grew languorous, but did not respond. The strangest of all was how it ended. She said: 'So, what about Dagmar?'

'Dagmar, indeed!' I replied, and sat down at the piano to play Rachmaninoff's Waltz.[2]

She put on her coat, and coming over to me, said 'Adieu'. I went on

---

1   Prelude in E flat, Op. 45 No. 3, and 'Poème ailé', No. 3 of *Quatre Morceaux*, Op. 51.
2   Valse in A, No. 2 of *Sept morceaux de salon*, Op. 10.

playing. Then she placed herself beside me at the keyboard, and spreading out her hands, said: 'I am going now, but if you don't even want to say goodbye to me, then tonight I shall shed tears.'

What came over me I don't know, but without answering or pushing her aside I continued to play the waltz two octaves higher up, where she had left room on the keyboard for me to do so. It flashed into my head that if she were to go now, all that would be left of my meeting with her would be a beautiful dream. Stella moved away from the piano, and I went on playing. By the time I finished she was no longer in the room, but there on the floor lay the broken flower I had presented to her while we were having lunch in the restaurant.

3 March

I worked out the programme for my third recital, which will take place on 30 March, and also played through and practised more pieces for Duo-Art. I can't do the Andante from the Fourth Sonata because I don't have my manuscript, it is too much work to do all the corrections on the proof, and no doubt there will be quite a few inaccuracies. So I shall stick to the 'March' and the 'Gavotte' from Op. 12.

I felt so sorry for dear, gentle Stella, especially when I thought of her perhaps really spending the night in tears, that I went into a shop and anonymously sent her two dozen white roses.

I dined with Kucheryavy, who was in New York for one day. It was a very cordial meeting.

4 March

A visit to the dentist, then to the photographer, and other such chores. From Stella, not a word. I am sorry that it has all come to pieces like this, but perhaps it is all for the best.

Wrote the libretto of Act Three, which I have long been thinking about and making notes for.

5 March

Practised the Op. 12 'Gavotte' and the 'March' to bring them up to scratch for the recording.

In the afternoon I listened to my Prelude. All the wrong notes have already been corrected, but the slightest unevenness in execution stands out in exaggerated relief, and this is horrible to listen to. I expended great efforts in making the necessary adjustments. I have dragged out the final *meno mosso* much too much, but nothing can be done about that now and it's not worth doing it all over again.

When I got home I found a letter from Stella, spring-like, dreamy and ethereal. Stella is a terribly sweet girl and I'm glad there is no complete rupture between us.

Dagmar came before dinner, but not alone, bringing a girl friend with her, a terrifyingly Kikimoresque[1] type who drove me to a frenzy (I had ordered in a box of delicious sweets: Dagmar munched them all one by one, saying 'pfui, pfui'.) Nevertheless, we went to have dinner at the Biltmore afterwards.

6 March

I started work on the third act; it seems to be going well, but I did not compose much.

In the afternoon an interview, then the dentist, then stayed in expecting Rubinstein, who had promised to call but let me down.

Wrote a short, affectionate reply to Stella, which seemed the right tone to adopt.

7 March

Act Three's music declines to move forward; all my firepower seems to have been temporarily exhausted by the end of Act Two. However, I have written the libretto for the first and second scenes.

8 March

Spring is already in the air on the streets, warm and caressing. It made me think of Stella with her vernal dreaminess, and yet I have been plunged in the whirlpool of city vanities. I was glad when Bookman came for me today in her car and we spent all day driving round the suburbs where the grass is already green although the trees are still grey.

Yes, it's awful, this ceaseless maelstrom. The only time I keep for the opera, for myself and for practising the piano, is from 11 o'clock in the morning until 2 o'clock in the afternoon. I do this every day.

---

1 See above, p. 144 n. 3.

9 March

I went to see Stahl and looked at the translation of the first scene. It's phenomenally accurate, but not quite vivid enough in places. I told him in recitative passages he could add or take away as many notes as he likes. As long as the piece is still fresh it is easy for me to make changes. What is vital is for the phrase to correspond to the idea of the musical phrase, not to be needlessly welded to it.

From Stahl I went on to Liebman, where I found Dagmar, Rubinstein, Capablanca and a whole lot of other guests. Rubinstein was very glad to see me and we spent the whole time discussing the programme for his forthcoming recital. Rubinstein left soon after, and I went home. The first part of the evening I was in low spirits, but then I started working on the quartet I had put aside some time ago, and this was so enjoyable I cheered up.

10 March

Today I was visited by Namara,[1] a prima donna from Chicago, a very beautiful and vivacious young woman who travelled here with fifty frocks in sixteen trunks and has enjoyed great success singing for Campanini. She wanted to meet me, and we spent a nice time together.

This evening I stayed at home and wrote a little of the quartet. This quartet may turn out to be one of my best compositions, but I have to be careful to restrict the amount of time I spend on it.

11 March

My working time – eleven till two – remains sacrosanct, and the third act is making some progress. Parallel with the opera I am preparing for my third recital and for the next piano-roll recording for Duo-Art. Life has been somewhat quieter and calmer this week. I read world history in English, sit by the fire with my pipe and dream of Stella.

---

1   Marguerite Namara (*née* Banks, from Cleveland, Ohio) (1888–1974), studied in Milan and initially made a successful career as an opera diva in Chicago (where she took over Mary Garden's role in *Thaïs*) and the New York Metropolitan. Later she crossed over into operetta and musical comedy on Broadway and in London, Franz Lehár writing one operetta as a vehicle especially for her entitled *Alone At Last*. She also had a career in Hollywood, both in silent films (starring in *Silent Moments* opposite Rudolph Valentino in 1920) and with lead singing roles in the early days of the talkies.

12 March

This morning I received simultaneously, or so it seemed, letters from Stella and from the censor returning the telegram I had sent to Mama in the Caucasus. I had been so overjoyed when I heard they had received it at Yessentuki, but it now appears that they made a mistake at the telegraph office. But soon I shall succeed in making contact with Mama, and then I shall have to get her away from where she is.

This afternoon I recorded for Duo-Art my Etude No. 4 and Rachmaninoff's G minor Prelude, which I do bring off very well indeed.

The copyist brought round the copy of the second act, and played me his compositions. I was astounded: a modernist score of extreme complexity, so much so that at first it was hard to tell if it was any good or not. But there is no question that it was very interesting.

13 March

A letter from the artist Larionov in Paris, full of the joys of spring and urging me to come to Paris (in contrast to Bakst, who insists that now is not the time to go there.) It seems that the scenery he designed for *Chout* was made and painted long ago, and this news pleased me greatly, as I have got used to thinking of *Chout* as a kind of mirage and have almost forgotten the music.

Afternoon tea at Polina Heifetz, sister of the violinist. Dagmar and Rubinstein were there.

14 March

Finished Act Three Scene I as far as the point where Chelio offers Truffaldino the magic ribbon. This first scene will soon be finished. The speed of progress is hardly precipitous, even so I'm inching forward.

Although there is no word from Stella and it's already two weeks since I've seen her, today there appeared the first swallow presaging her existence: I had a telephone call from the lady whom Stella had, on her first visit to me, so meekly asked me to listen to, playing Scriabin's and my music. I was indulgent and made an appointment for her to come and play to me on Monday. I sense that it cannot be long before the disappearing princess herself comes back on the scene.

15 March

I visited the Red Cross and such-like institutions in search of a way to make contact with Mama. It seems Vladimir Nikolayevich[1] might be able to act as a conduit to get a little money to her.

While on my way to Rubinstein's second recital this afternoon, I met Stella. I am sure the naughty girl had deliberately chosen that way to walk, knowing I would be going to this concert at 3 o'clock. It's a strange thing, but although I was thinking of her at the time, I did not recognise her. Stella said: 'You see, you have already forgotten me.' I was terribly pleased at the encounter.

After the concert, tea with Liebman; once again Dagmar, Rubinstein and some others were there.

Mme Lewisohn held a great reception. Among others present was the king of tenors Caruso, to whom I was presented as 'the new Russian genius'. I haven't been to the Lewisohns for a month, and was received with exceptional warmth.

In the evening I caught up with my diary.

16 March

Today, at last, another Stella day, although it was preceded by a great tea at Lambert's, where once again there were Dagmar, Rubinstein, Polina and Liebman. But Dagmar and I did not speak, and I decamped smartly as my rendezvous with Stella was at six o'clock. When she appeared, she asked meekly: 'Perhaps you would rather I went away again?' She was soft and gentle, and delighted with the box of sweets I had ordered in for her. She is tall, almost my height, and supple as Polina in *The Gambler*, whose body can be tied in a knot.[2] We had dinner together at the Biltmore and then came back to my place to spend the rest of the evening in front of the fire. This time Stella responded much more warmly to my kisses than the previous time. Evidently the last two weeks had engendered a good deal of reflection and things had moved forward. Once or twice she exclaimed passionately: 'Oh, I am so quick, but I can't resist!' and then said she did not want to be a plaything in my hands. No doubt she would have been even more loving had she been able to trust completely in my sincerity. But the fear of falling in love with someone who would merely dally with her as one among many held her back.

1 Bashkirov.
2 See Dostoyevsky/Prokofiev character portraits in Appendix 1.

17 March

My time with Stella had put me in a wonderful mood, and today I finished the scene.

18 March

I composed the scherzo – the entr'acte between the first and second scenes of Act Three. I had been afraid this entr'acte might hold me up, but in fact it took one day. This was marvellous.

Vladimir Nikolayevich has promised that funds will be provided on the spot through the 'Co-operatives', and afterwards I can repay it here.[1] In about two weeks' time the first steamer is sailing from here for Odessa, and thereafter there will be a direct regular connection with Odessa. It is absolutely essential that Mama comes here. Once links like that are opened up it should not be too difficult.

Vladimir Nikolayevich takes an extraordinary interest in my affair with Stella. When I said Stella looked so virginal, he replied with cold emphasis: 'There is no such thing as a virgin here in America.' The phrase was quite a shock to me, and it set me thinking. I know there probably aren't any virgins here, even so the aura Stella gives off is so dreamy and soft-toned that the impression she creates suggests something entirely different. Anyhow, my thanks to Bashkirov for nudging me towards such reflections: now I shall look at Stella from two different perspectives, and perhaps that will help me to understand her better.

---

1 'Kooperativy' were a feature of the Civil War environment during which the new Bolshevik regime had initially striven unsuccessfully to bring under control the chaos in the supply and distribution both of military matériel and foodstuffs, causing paralysis of the Red Army in its fight against the various White factions, and intolerable famine in the cities – accompanied naturally by a thriving black market. In a precursor of the New Economic Policy experiment in limited market freedom not formally introduced until 1921, Lenin accepted that the virtually barter system almost universal across rural Russia and embodied in a mass of great and small co-operatives should be tolerated at least temporarily: 'The petty bourgeois do know how to run a shop.' Lenin's tactic worked, not only in dramatically improving the supply and distribution of food and industrial production but in gradually bringing the newly sanctioned co-operative organs into the iron grip of the Party, thus achieving the goal of total nationalisation by a more effective albeit subtler route than the head-on confrontation of the War Communism period.

Vladimir Bashkirov, owner before the Revolution of a vast flour and grain business in the Ukraine, would have maintained good connections with powerful figures in the now-acceptable Co-operatives, and the idea was that through them money could be made available to Maria Grigorievna, which Prokofiev could reimburse to Bashkirov in New York.

19 March

The day began well with a telephone call from Urchs,[1] the director of Steinway, a very nice man who had given me good advice over the contract with Campanini. At my request he had sounded out Otto Kahn[2] about *The Gambler*. Today he sent me a telegram saying that he had had a letter from Kahn to the effect that 'Prokoviev and opera – that's an interesting subject', and suggesting a meeting to talk about it. Hello?[3] Might we be on the brink of a breakthrough here?

I played chess with Elman, desperately wanting to beat him. I could not forgive him for having taken a game off me in Chicago. And today I despatched him quickly and easily, winning two games out of two. (Running total +5 −1 of six.)

20 March

Stella came at seven o'clock; I had been waiting impatiently for her. Today she was a little strange and erratic. First she said that could not allow herself to become my plaything, then burst into tears when I played the piano. She was late for getting home, where she should have been because her sister's husband was arriving from Chicago, so she telephoned home and in the course of the call had an impassioned discussion with her girl friend. What they talked about clearly distressed her, and led to sharing a long and detailed explanation with me, which went some way to clarifying our relationship.

Her friend Blanche, the person she had been speaking to on the telephone, who is older than she, is the only person who has much influence over her. Her mother does not live with them, while the attitude of her father and sister is: love whomever you like provided you observe the conventions – that is how we acted. From further talking I understood that not long

---

1 Ernest Urchs, as head of the Concert and Artist Department of Steinway and Sons in New York, was for the great majority of musicians and their managers and concert organisers the public face of Steinway. The firm has always supported leading pianists and cultivated them as officially designated 'Steinway Artists', inviting them to endorse and use their pianos, in return for which the artists are supplied with pianos prepared to their specification for performance, afforded rehearsal facilities on tour, etc.
2 Otto Kahn (1867–1934) was a stupendously wealthy financier, head of the Kuhn, Loeb, & Co. investment bank, who had not only just built on a 443-acre estate in Cold Spring Harbor on Long Island the second-largest house ever constructed in America – the exterior was used by Orson Welles as Citizen Kane's Xanadu – but was one of the most generous patrons of the arts America has ever known ('I must atone for my wealth'). Joining the board of the Metropolitan Opera, he had reorganised it and saved it from bankruptcy. He was at this time serving as the Chairman of the Board.
3 In English.

ago, probably last autumn, Stella had fallen in love with someone but had been unhappy, so that now that she was beginning to show that she was attracted to me, Blanche was taking steps to stop her, fearing that as a spoilt and doubtless depraved artist I was taking advantage of a young girl whom inevitably I would subsequently throw over. I told Stella I was not toying with her, and she was the only woman for whom at the present time I had strong feelings. How deep and permanent these feelings were I did not know, nor would I try to speculate because I did not wish to deceive either her or myself, but she could be quite certain that as long as I was with her there would be no other woman in my life. And then suddenly, half-seriously, there came a fleeting glimpse of the most tantalising revelation: at the end of May Stella would finish her college course and in June would go away to Canada, where perhaps we would be able to spend a whole month *tête à tête*. If that were indeed to come about, what a wonderful time that would be!

21 March

I began Scene Two, but did not accomplish much.

Urchs has been to see Kahn, and we are invited to lunch on Wednesday. Urchs says Kahn is very interested in my opera, but expects us to encounter opposition in the person of General Director Gatti-Casazza,[1] a conservative Italophile the only hope of persuading whom would be an especially interesting subject. If *The Gambler* could go the Metropolitan, wouldn't that be a brilliant victory?!

Mme Bolm read me a serious lecture: play around with ladies to your heart's content, but have nothing to do with unmarried girls. If you do, under current American law you must marry them straight away or they can take you to court, and while 'they usually start by demanding two hundred thousand dollars, eventually they come down to ten thousand'. This warning was delivered with reference to Dagmar, and is complete nonsense – the last thing she needs is a court case, and in any case I could just as well accuse her of being a flirt. And then there is Stella – a delight, but I don't truly know her. Her father[2] is an artist and a Jew, who at some point had emigrated from Russia. It would be stupid for her to try any tricks with me.

---

[1] Giulio Gatti-Casazza (1869–1940), came to the Metropolitan Opera from managing La Scala in Milan in 1908 and stayed there until 1935. The epitome of the Italian operatic manager, during his long reign he was responsible for bringing in Toscanini, Ponselle, Caruso, Galli-Curci, Chaliapin, Flagstad and a host of the greatest names. Although he was above all a lover of Verdi his programming was by no means narrow, as he introduced Musorgsky's *Boris Godunov*, Debussy's *Pelléas*, Strauss's *Salome*, the entire Wagner canon and neglected operas by Gluck and Mozart as well as the later operas of Puccini to Met audiences.

[2] Jacob Adler (1855–1926), 'Nesher Hagodl' – 'The Great Eagle', 'eagle' being 'adler' in German, 'odler' in Yiddish – was born in Odessa and after Yiddish theatre was banned in Russia in 1883

22 March

This afternoon there was a concert by Janacopulos, who sang three of my songs, which I accompanied.

I had lunch with Stella, who was looking very attractive. I fed her wild strawberries, and it was a source of great pride to her that just before the first performance of my songs[1] (!) I should be spending my time with her. But the premiere was a matter of indifference to me, and I was not counting on any great success from them. In fact, however, they did have quite a success, more than when Koshetz sang them in Moscow. Janacopulos sang very well, but not of course to be compared with Koshetz.

23 March

As we had agreed, Stella telephoned me at eight o'clock in the morning and we set off together to go out of town. The past few days have been wonderful spring weather, and spring has always, right back to the days of Max Schmidthof, given me the urge to get away from the city, so I set off with anticipatory feelings of enjoyment, whereas Stella was positively overjoyed. Not having been able to find anyone to advise us where there was beautiful country round about, we boarded a train and forty minutes later got out on the shores of the Hudson River to walk among the hills and woods. It was a cold, but bright, day, the green grass was beginning to come through, and here and there flowers could be seen, but the trees had still not come to life. We walked until three, and then had lunch in an elegant restaurant with a view over the Hudson to New York. When I started to nag a little at Stella, she said that she was seeing a different side of me today, to which I replied that it was better she should know me from several perspectives.

---

came first to London and later to New York. In a famous production by Arthur Hopkins on Broadway in 1903, Adler played Shylock in *The Merchant of Venice*, speaking his lines in Yiddish while the remainder of the cast delivered Shakespeare's original text. The part defined both Adler's supreme acting skills and his racial and artistic credo. Whereas Henry Irving had played Shylock as morally superior to his Christian tormentors, driven to barbarous cruelty only by their even more vicious and corrupt persecution, Adler scorned such justification. In his own words: 'Shylock from the first was governed by pride rather than revenge. He wishes to humble and terrify Antonio for the insult and humiliation he has suffered at his hands. This is why he goes so far as to bring his knife and scales into the court. For Shylock, however, the desired climax was to refuse the pound of flesh with a gesture of divine compassion. When the verdict goes against him, he is crushed because he has been robbed of this opportunity, not because he lusts for Antonio's death. This was my interpretation. This is the Shylock I have tried to show.'

1 *Five Poems of Anna Akhmatova*, Op. 27.

24 March

Play-back and editing of the piano rolls. This is interesting work, but very time-consuming. The main problem with the instrument is that when playing a chord it is impossible to bring out individual notes. Likewise one cannot bring out a theme in an inner voice.

I went to see Bashkirov and told him a little about Stella. When I asked his opinion of Mme Bolm's warning, he shrugged and said: 'If at the end of the day you are sure she loves you, go to Canada with her and God be with you.'

25 March

I wrote a letter to Mama, as I have met an officer who is going to the Caucasus. I want to get her here, but the situation in the Caucasus is obscure and after fierce fighting the Bolsheviks are at the gates of Odessa, the very place from which the liner leaves for New York. All Europe is a seething cauldron. A Soviet republic is in power in Hungary, and the Peace Conference in Paris has no idea how to resolve the situation.

I had an idea for a short story about a beautiful woman and a game of bridge with political overtones. Even though I don't want to write about contemporary themes, I feel that in the way I plan to treat the subject it won't be topical but universal.

26 March

In the morning I walked along Park Avenue and thought about how to present the subject of *The Gambler* to Kahn.

We lunched together at half-past one. Kahn was nice, and very interested in the subject. He said that he very much wanted to present *The Gambler*. He was not in a position to tell Gatti what to do, but would try to influence him and hoped that Gatti would be interested in the idea. He asked me to provide an outline of the plot for Gatti in French, and said that in about three weeks' time, when Gatti would be clear of the present opera season, he would do his best to arrange a play-through of *The Gambler*.

This is a splendid beginning, and I believe the odds are now stacked in favour rather than against.

27 March

I spent the evening with Stahl going through his and Verochka's translation of *Oranges*. They have got the measure of it now and are doing pretty well; I am happy about them adding crotchets, i.e. to put in extra notes because the

French language has more syllables and always needs more notes than Russian. All the same, I am insisting strictly on the text conforming exactly to the musical sense of the phrase.

30 March

My third recital. The hall was packed, but yet again by a rather stiff-necked audience. I was relaxed and played well – by common consent my best yet. The programme was successful throughout. Even *Sarcasms*, which I placed at the end, did not spoil the audience's mood of enjoyment, and my encores, consisting of my popular pieces and Rachmaninoff's G minor Prelude, provoked a hugely enthusiastic send-off. As usual there was a great crowd of people in the Green Room almost pulling my arms off. Stella hung back but I went up to her and introduced Bashkirov to her, in order that he should see what she looks like.

There was tea in my honour at Liebmans' after the concert, a mass of people, beautiful women and artists.

31 March

The reviews today were briefer than before, because there was a clash with a Philharmonic concert and the critics were rushing hither and yon. Half of them praised the concert and the other half damned it.

The concert yielded a loss of $200 (box office takings $350, expenses $550). Not much of an improvement over last time. But many people suppose in their naivety that it has made me a rich man.

2 April

Since the accursed dentist has decreed that I have to have two more teeth removed, I decided, as is my wont, that the sooner the better. But last time the gas had such a depressing effect on me that I decided I would even have them out with cocaine, anything but the gas. However the doctor arranged for gas, so from pride and stubbornness I took myself in hand and agreed to gas for the extractions. I was very reluctant to go at all, but forced myself.

I reasoned thus: what actually is so unpleasant about it? Those four or five seconds when you have a choking sensation. But is it really such torture to be gasping for four or five seconds? It cannot be, surely. What is it, then? Pure animal fear. Well then, all I have to do is persuade the animal that sits inside me that I am not dying but going through a medically beneficial procedure, and then it will all be quite easy. The decision made, I clambered into the chair. And indeed, at the first sign of choking I did not feel that it was at all frightening. Joyfully I hung on to this thought and began mentally repeating to myself: 'Not frightening at all.' At that I fell so soundly asleep that I did not feel the two teeth being pulled out at all. As I started to come to, my first impression was of a new face looking down at me. Two phrases jostled amusingly in my still half-asleep brain: 'Who is this man?' (Clarissa in *Oranges*) and 'Who is this? Is it that Marquis?' (Grandmother in *The Gambler*). The face proved to be that of my dear doctor,[1] who had entered the room from next door. Wonderfully relieved I returned home. At dinner with Stella I could take only liquid food.

5 April

Scarlet fever.

6 April – 6 June

I was just getting ready to go to a small city for a two- or three-concert tour when I fell ill and the concerts had to be cancelled. I thought it was Spanish 'flu and was terribly afraid. With the help of the Bolms a doctor was called, Anna Ingerman. It soon became apparent that it was scarlet fever – even so it was a relief that it was not after all influenza. According to New York by-laws I should have been taken to an isolation hospital outside the city, but Ingerman somehow protected me from this. A notice was pinned up on the door that I was an infectious patent, and a nurse assigned to look after me.

Once the initial crisis passed things got easier, but it was followed by a second crisis bringing rheumatism to the arms and shoulders, and a plague of abscesses (one of which was in the throat and almost suffocated me). At first my mood was not bad; I received a lot of letters which in order not to spread the infection I answered by telephone and by dictating telegrams to the nurse. I tried to carry on with the libretto, hiding it from the doctor under my pillow. But while the crisis was at its height I had to stop working altogether, and that made me very depressed. However the crisis was alleviated by the abscesses bursting and the application of an anti-diphtheria serum, after which my temperature came down from its height of 40 and 40.5 degrees.

There were a lot of flowers, because people thought I was dying. Noteworthy were some roses from Stella, huge ones on long stems. Bashkirov provided money when my funds ran out. Recovery started at the beginning of May. The first time I got out of bed my legs refused to work, and I all but fell. Being allowed to shave for the first time was a great event, but the sight that met my eyes was too awful for words.

---

[1] The dentist, Dr Philip Hussa.

Oranges had been interrupted at the opening of the second scene of Act Three, at the point when the violins skitter about while the Prince and Truffaldino creep towards the oranges. When I was allowed by Ingerman to sit down at the piano for the first time, it came so easily that I wrote almost the whole of the scene with the Cook at a single sitting. But my temperature went up again and the piano was once more forbidden.

Then one wonderful, sunny day I was allowed to leave the house. The first thing I did was send an enormous basket of flowers to the Ingermans. Husband and wife had both been treating me: she as a specialist in general diseases, he in ailments of the nose and throat. She believes that she saved my life, and he that he rescued me from deafness, for one of the directions the scarlet fever took very nearly reached my ears and the eardrum was already starting to become inflamed.

Convalescence in the spring was extraordinarily pleasant, even though not all the shadows cast by my illness left me.

I composed the third scene of Act Three with no difficulty. I learned Musorgsky's *Pictures from an Exhibition*, and somehow the fact that I was getting better and it was springtime combined with one of the *Pictures* – 'Limoges' – to evoke for ever after the memory of this blissful state.

Stella came to take me out walking, and her portrait appeared on my desk, where her beauty aroused universal interest. Anna Ingerman, who had grown very fond of me but had at the same time developed a robust tendency towards motherliness, showed remarkable interest in my romance with Stella. However, she warned me about her family, whom she knew: its members were crazy and unstable, so I should beware. Even so I planned to go to Canada with Stella although I had not actually discussed it with Stella herself.

When I did finally broach the subject, Stella unexpectedly objected that I seemed to be demanding more from her than she was willing to give me. She had to put some distance between us, and the following week would be going away on a theatrical tour with her father's company. Everyone in her family was an actor, including Stella. Disappointed in my plans, I either could not or would not dissuade her from going, but with Stella's departure my springtime mood also came to an end.

7 June

Today is a good day on which to take up my diary again: I finished *Three Oranges*. While I had been in the grip of my maladies I was very afraid that I would die before finishing the music. None the less, when today I did finish it, my mood was not particularly joyful (as it had been, for instance, when I finished Act Two): I was too downcast by the previous day's parting with Stella. I therefore made efforts not to be on my own and went to play bridge with the Samoilenkos and in the evening went with them and the Bolms to the theatre. There is no doubt that many sweet illusions have vanished along with Stella.

8 June

I went out with the Bolms to visit the Ingermans in Larchmont, a region of country villas. Although it was raining it was green and beautiful there. A lot of nice people were in the company, but I could not feel very cheerful. The cause? Stella. I have to fill up artificially the void her disappearance has left.

9 June

In the morning I made a few alterations to the final scene. Capablanca came by in the afternoon, back from Havana after winning his match. In the evening I played Bolm the opening of the opera. He flew at me so much for the 'unperformable' rapidity of the action in the second scene that he even gave me pause for thought: suppose there really is not enough time for it all to take place? But I believe the answer is that when I was playing it to him I chose faster tempi than I should have.

10 June

At eleven o'clock in the morning I set off in high delight to West End, an elegant resort on the shores of the Atlantic about an hour and half's journey from New York. The Lewisohns are spending the summer there, and have assiduously tried to persuade me to follow their example. They always have lots of company, usually interesting people, around them. Among the casualties of Stella's volte-face have been my plans to spend the summer somewhere far away from people; on the contrary I now decided I wanted to be somewhere busy and noisy so as to fill the emptiness Stella had left behind her. After all, my only obligation this summer is to produce six hundred pages of score for *Three Oranges*. I'll do ten pages a day and enjoy myself the rest of the time.

Coming back from West End by boat I saw for the first time as I entered New York harbour the Statue of Liberty face to face. The statue is enormous compared with the ships, but even more colossal are the skyscrapers emerging from the mist beyond her.

11 June

Today once again I had to go to see Lilienthal[1] for a third consultation to decide whether or not I have to be operated on. But the bismuth medication he gave me last time has dried out my abscess so much that it was looking much better, and it seems to be healing. So they decided once more to put off the appointment and see if it would not heal completely by itself. Oh, how marvellous it would be not to have an operation!

In the evening I was at Stahl's. The scenes in the desert and outside Creonta's castle have been translated, and much of the Cook's scene. Very skilfully done. I made quite a number of corrections.

13 June

I got a letter from Stella, sent from Boston, which I had not expected. It was a very nice, affectionate letter, but it ended: '*Au revoir* for the future, but farewell for now.' Then why write? I had begun to get used to Stella not being there, but this letter had the effect of raking up the past again. Although somewhere in the depths of my soul I have a feeling that Stella is herself in a ferment and that one day she will come back to me, perhaps soon.

15 June

My lease is up on the apartment. Tomorrow I leave for the country. It is high time, already the middle of June, and it is many years since I have still found myself rooted in the city so late in the year. But this time I shall have to come into the city three times a week for treatment to my still-infected abscess. I was sad to leave my apartment: it was comfortable and cosy. And even though it had some unpleasant associations – the scarlet fever, and the fact that when I moved into it I was still affected by Mme Schindler's death – all the same, Stella brought many precious moments to my memory of it.

In the afternoon I went to Larchmont, where a lot of Russians go for the summer. Among them is the Grandmother of the Russian Revolution, B. Breshkovskaya,[2] to whom I was introduced today and who welcomed me

---

1   Dr Howard Lilienthal (1861–1946) was an altogether exceptional surgeon who practised at the Mount Sinai Hospital. Author (in 1925) of what is still one of the standard textbooks on thoracic surgery, in 1910 he was the first surgeon to carry out an operation using endotracheal anaesthesia. Prokofiev was in good hands.
2   Yekaterina Konstantinovna Breshko-Breshkovskaya (1844–1934), known throughout Russia, and after the October Revolution throughout the Russian émigré community, as 'Babushka Russkoy Revolyutsii' – 'Grandmother of the Russian Revolution' was the only Russian individual of active revolutionary instincts to live through the entire revolutionary period from the early 1860s until the post-Revolutionary Civil War and the embryonic years of the Soviet regime. A

with exceptional warmth, kissing me at length and expressing her pride that the talent nurtured in the soil of Russia was not extinct. She embarked on a somewhat complicated discussion with me about whether it was incumbent on people of talent to establish a school of disciples, and if they did so, would it have an adverse effect on their own creativity? This last, of course, once they have evolved to extreme old age. At that point the very act of summing-up the work of a lifetime, essential for the foundation of a school, would naturally in itself damage and might altogether kill off the person's own creative work.

16 June

The morning was devoted to the doctor and packing up my things. At four o'clock I left for West End, where I have decided to spend the first half of the summer. I think it will be amusing to be with the Lewisohns and their wide circle of friends. 'Fun' – I'm not actually looking for that kind of fun this summer, but in my present state of nerves and without Stella, it's the best I can think of. During the day, and especially in the mornings, I'll do my scoring, having a break after each page with a walk to the ocean, and in the evening I'll socialise.

I put up at the large and almost empty 'Hollywood' Hotel. That evening I walked down to the ocean shore and went early to bed.

This ocean is the real thing, it doesn't have bays or coves. If you were to take a line straight out, the next land you would get to is Portugal.

17 June

I started scoring *Oranges*, but was put off by children practising scales on the piano in the hotel lounge beneath me. Out on the street I met a Frenchman, the owner of the other big hotel in the town, who turned out to know something of my work. He told me he would be delighted to have me in his hotel

---

saintly figure, utterly regardless of her own interests or safety she devoted her entire life to the struggle, by education initiatives and political agitation, to alleviate the injustices suffered by the Russian peasantry. As one of the founders of the Socialist Revolutionary Party (the SRs) she was naturally a target for police harassment and spent more than twenty-five years in Siberian hard-labour camps and exile (she was the first woman in Russia to be sentenced to hard labour). Released immediately after the February Revolution, on her arrival at the railway station in Petrograd Kerensky's welcoming address announced: 'Comrades, the Grandmother of the Russian Revolution has returned at last to a free country.' (When she occupied temporary living quarters in the Winter Palace malicious gossipers dubbed her Kerensky's nanny.) In December 1918, as dismayed by Bolshevik repression as she had formerly been by Tsarist oppression, she followed a similar route to Prokofiev's across Siberia to Japan and thence to the United States. She did not, however, stay there long, moving to Czechoslovakia in 1924 to take up the cause of the Carpathian Russians against the regime in Prague, which she continued until her death in 1934.

and offered me at half-price a small but nice room with a balcony in a quiet annexe of the hotel itself, overlooking the ocean. I moved there today; it is almost next door to the Lewisohns. He provided me with a large table that does not wobble, a convenient lamp, an armchair, and generally looked after my creature comforts very well.

18 June

I went into town to see the doctor, Duo-Art, and to do some shopping. When I got back to West End I orchestrated three pages. It is really time to get down to some serious work.

The Chicago Opera has at last made a concrete proposal to Anisfeld to design the settings for *Oranges*. The production is beginning to take on the character I had been hoping for. Soon I must read the whole libretto through to Anisfeld.

The first steamer has arrived from Russia (Novorossiisk). I am hoping for letters from Mama, although I'm not too optimistic that there will be any.

Just before leaving the Lewisohns, I bumped into Cornelia. She was looking very smart and a trifle loud. She said: 'Je suis très heureuse de vous voir.' I was very pleased. I had guessed that she might be here this summer, but having been at Lewisohns three times in a row and not seeing her, concluded regretfully that I had guessed wrong. She came on her own, driving a car so that she could go for a drive with the Lewisohns' young son.

19 June

I completed a lot of scoring – seven pages – and enjoyed doing it until I grew tired. This is not really much; I should be doing at least ten pages. But clearly I am out of practice, or maybe the scarlet fever has left me weaker than I was before.

I walked along the shore of the Atlantic Ocean. West End is still quiet; the crowds don't come here until July. I'm sometimes bothered by my scar – it is a bit painful, but otherwise my morale is good.

20 June

Capablanca came to see me, we had lunch with the Lewisohns, and then went for a drive in the car. He was nice but didn't have much to say.

I managed less than seven pages today. When I count up what I have to do, I worry that I shall not meet the deadline. There are one hundred days to do more than five hundred pages.

The scar is getting more painful.

21 June

Went to town to read the libretto to Anisfeld and to see the doctor. The scar is swollen – this may be no more than a superficial irritation, in which case there is nothing to worry about. But if a new abscess develops on the site of the old one, that would be bad, and there would have to be an operation. This had a dampening effect on my mood.

Four days have produced twenty-four pages – not much. I might just do it in time if I work without a break.

I laid out some hands of patience.

22 June

I have finished the Prologue and started on the first scene. It's going a bit more quickly now – the orchestration is simpler.

Lunched with the Lewisohns, where there were a lot of high-class guests. But for some reason I adopted a superior tone and didn't condescend to talk to the young people. Very silly of me.

I was in a horrible mood in the evening because my scar was hurting and I am afraid I will have to undergo an operation. Ever since recovering from scarlet fever I have been conscious that I nearly died, and now I fear any form of anaesthetic. Sometimes, going to sleep (less so now, it was worse about a month ago) I even start up in a fright, thinking I am on the point of falling into non-existence.

23 June

Went into town to see the doctor. I make the trip into New York by boat, and that makes it a pleasant journey.

24 June

I went with Dr Ingerman for a consultation with Lilienthal. He found after all that I will need to have an operation. I told him I was afraid of the anaesthetic – ether or chloroform. He said it could be done with gas. This made me very happy: gas I have already come to terms with because of my experiences with having teeth out. It will mean one to two weeks in hospital, and then a further three weeks of having to come in regularly to have the dressings changed. But within three days after the operation I would probably be able to work from my bed, so my orchestration work will not have to suffer so much interruption. Altogether I have been in a terrible state of fear over the operation, but now it has come to a head I can regard it quite calmly.

Today the tally is forty-eight pages in eight days, that is to say five-and-a-half pages per day. Again not much. But bearing in mind my trips into the city it's not negligible as an average figure.

30 June

In theory my operation should be happening now, the room in the hospital is ready, but Lilienthal is going on holiday for a few days, therefore the 'carving of the joint' has been put off for a week. Incidentally, the scar is now looking so good that perhaps it will heal by itself after all.

After each page of scoring I play patience. A pity I know only two games; it's a bit boring. Relations with the Lewisohns have not blossomed, but rather withered.

3 July

The time in West End passes quietly, I'm concentrating on my work of orchestrating. Sometimes I get bored. I thought there would be plenty of people I know at the Lewisohns, but even they pall. Partly I'm bored with the state of my nerves, not quite knowing whether my health is good or bad, whether I am going to go under the knife or not. All in all it is a rather aimless summer, but my joy and my consolation lie in the score.

I think of Stella and am sad she is not with me.

4 July

In New York I bought the newspapers from Philadelphia, the last town on Stella's tour before she returns to New York. I decided to keep my word and go to meet her there. How she will react I don't know, but having promised I will greet her return.

Up till now there has not been a word about her company in the press.

5 July

Anisfeld has finally signed a contract for the designs for *Oranges*. Bolm is also about to do so. I played both of them three acts today, and they were extravagantly pleased with them. This is all extremely pleasant. All the characters that had existed in my imagination are becoming real. But performing three acts just about killed me with exhaustion.

6 July

I spent all yesterday evening and all day today at Larchmont, where there are a great number of Russians, very cultured people: Ingermans, Yakhontovs,[1] Bolm, Kapustin, and others. I found two days constantly being with people very tiring. However, I took my score with me and somehow managed six pages.

7 July

On my return Lilienthal looked at my scar and announced: 'It's looking very good.'

'Well, what do you think then?' I asked.

Lilienthal answered: 'I've already told you that the operation is not urgent; you could be lucky and it will clear up.'

'What is your opinion?'

'I don't think it will clear up.'

'Well then, let's get on with it.'

And indeed the time has come, otherwise it will never be over. There will be a room available in the hospital in a day or two, and they will let me know by telegram. Stella will soon be back, and I'll still be crippled. But everything has a silver lining, and if on the 15th (by which time I'll still be bed-bound) I write to her from hospital, her tender heart will falter and she will be nice to me.

However, since I did not know whether she had given up her apartment or kept it on, and since I wanted to ascertain the answer in good time, I decided to telephone the commissionaire and ask to be put through to the Adlers' apartment. I was quite sure I would hear the Negro telling me the apartment was empty or that they had moved out altogether, but had no time to collect my wits when I heard a voice exactly like Stella's. It must be either her sister, or herself. Hearing no one on the line, the person on the other end quickly replaced the receiver, and I did the same. Surely Stella could not already be in the city? More likely it was her sister. I returned to West End my thoughts full of Stella, and happy that I might be seeing her again soon. All the more reason for getting the operation over, which had now been hanging over me for two months.

---

[1] Yakhontov, a chess-playing friend from St Petersburg who had witnessed some of Prokofiev's triumphs against famous players, was the husband of Boris Bashkirov's younger sister Tatyana. See *Diaries*, vol. 1, pp. 674, 682.

8 July

I worked hard: a hundred-and-fifty pages in twenty-two days, or five-and-a-quarter a day. The daily average has slipped a little, but that was only to be expected with the difficult second scene. I'll have to do some catching up, otherwise the operation will get in the way.

10 July

Taking my score, a French novel and cards to play patience, I set off for the hospital. I did not take my Diary, so it will have a two-week gap and I will later give a brief résumé of what happens.

My mood was on the whole not too bad; the operation had appeared more frightening from a distance. Dr Ingerman came to sit with me during the evening, also some of the doctors from the hospital who had been to my concerts and were interested to talk to me.

11–22 July

The operation took place at half-past eight in the morning. At eight o'clock Ingerman came in to wish me good morning and relax my mood. Then they injected me with morphine and atropin and wheeled me in to the operating theatre. Despite a little anxiety I felt generally good and felt no dread of the operation. The gas-mask was applied. Semi-conscious, I felt some pain, but could not identify what it was or where it was coming from. Then I began gradually to drift off to sleep, that is to say although I could feel something hurting it had no power over me, and in a way I could meet it halfway. Just as I was becoming aware of this, I went off to sleep completely.

Afterwards Dr Ingerman explained that the operation had lasted all of twenty-five minutes, of which fifteen minutes had been spent in preliminary examination and ten on the actual incision. As twenty-five minutes is too long to stay unconscious under the effect of gas, my unconsciousness was prolonged by ether. The wound gave me very little trouble except when I shifted about. I could even have done some work on the score that day, but my head hurt too much. They offered me a night nurse, but I did not need one.

I then had to stay in bed for ten days with a further three days of semi-ambulant rest. I started on the score the day after the operation, and this saved me from the boredom of lying in bed brooding about the waste of time. Between the 12th and the 24th, that is to say thirteen days, I completed sixty-six pages, five pages a day, hardly slower than my normal rate. In between I played patience.

I was visited by the Ingermans, Capablanca and the Samoilenkos. The doctors who knew me from my concerts came in and we had conversations about medicine. The hospital was a Jewish one with Jewish doctors, who took a fancy to me, expressing regret that I was not Jewish. The window of my room looked out on Fifth Avenue so I could watch the people passing by.

From time to time it came into my mind that the amount of time I was confined to bed, first with scarlet fever and now after my operation, ought to be deepening my view of life. And indeed questions of life and death did become clearer and simpler, although I was not able to formulate any definite answers. I came to realise that in the future it will be up to me to find a path and a solution, by means of reading and study and talking with wise and good people. For the time being I find myself pulled in several different directions: the various attitudes of my Petersburg friends, Kantian transcendentalism, Schopenhauer's Will with its rejection of individuality, and the purely materialistic American view of life with its total lack of belief, coming from nothing and leading to nothing. This last approach was somehow bound up with the environment in which I presently found myself, and the experience of having been put to sleep which had clearly been the most powerful impression of my period of illness.

Altogether, then, my time in hospital passed quickly and not too onerously, while the Prince's sick-room, which I was then orchestrating, probably even came out better there than it would have anywhere else (it is not by chance that the nurse pours iodine everywhere).

Two days before I left hospital I wrote to Stella. This was on 21 July; she must have returned from her tour some time ago and had probably already gone to the country somewhere. The letter had long been written in my mind; it was straightforward, neither too loving nor too facetious. I felt that the key would lie not in the tone of the letter but in Stella herself.

23 July

I was allowed to go for a walk in the park, where the recent rain had made everything green, moist and aromatic. Yes, this summer had been a crazy, confused time, in fact I have not really had a summer at all. Once again I dreamed of spending all spring in the country, from the last snows until the first heat. But it must be in a country with a real spring, irresistible in its power and splendour. Where would I find this?

24 July

My last day in hospital. The morning brought a letter from Stella. I was not particularly excited because I was expecting it to be negative. As usual it was so illegibly written that I had great trouble making out what it said, but when I succeeded Stella was enchantingly nice and suggested that we meet at six o'clock this evening at the Savoy. I glowed inwardly.

The final event in the hospital was an appendicitis operation which one of the doctors invited me to witness. We sat in the balcony of the magnificent, white operating theatre while down below on the table, wrapped in flannel, lay the patient. The only part open to view was a small area of the abdomen where the incision was to be made, thickly smeared with iodine. The surgeon stood to one side, his assistant on the other, compressing the veins when they began to spurt blood. Two more people stood alongside, passing scalpels, tampons, sutures. A fifth man, the anaesthetist, cradled the patient's head, holding a finger on his wrist to sense the pulsing artery and giving him ether to breathe. The sick man breathed rapidly with a dull sort of sound, amplified by the continuously inflating and deflating bag into which he was breathing. The rapidity of the breathing made the stomach rise and fall, which seemed to me to get seriously in the way of the procedure.

The operation proceeded in silence, the movements quick and decisive. Sometimes the internal pressure of the intestines caused them to jump out of the incision, upon which they were unceremoniously stuffed back in again. The blind gut was found, pulled to one side with thread and then cut open. And not before time. It was in a terrible state and a single day's delay could have caused it to perforate. They began to sew up the patient, and with that I left the theatre, and the hospital. How pleasant it was to go through the streets in a car. Before me were four more weeks of having my wound dressed, but it did not hurt and was not causing me any problems.

At six o'clock I went to the Savoy. I had decided to be very cool with Stella. She appeared at once, slim, tall and very beautiful. She was in lively spirits, glad to see me, and had much more to say than I did. She thought I was in indecently good form for someone who had only just come out of hospital. She should have left town yesterday, but had stayed behind to see me. We had dinner together and I asked her whether, when she was next in the city, I could take her by boat to West End. She replied no, but then it transpired that the next settlement to West End was Asbury Park, where she was due to visit relations and would telephone me from there.

I thus returned contentedly to West End, thinking that all was well: the weight of the operation had been lifted from my shoulders, and Stella was back. Of course my old dream of true intimacy with her had vanished, but she was being nice to me and, seeing that I was controlling myself, was not perpetually drawing back from me. For my part I was terribly glad to be seeing her again.

25 July

West End and furious work on the score, now free of oppression by the prospect of the operation.

At five o'clock I set out to visit Stahl, half an hour away, in order to check the *Oranges* translation. It was very nice to see them.

26 July

I stayed the night with the Stahls and went into town to have my wound dressed and to do some shopping. I am under great strain from all the things I have to accomplish: pieces to be prepared for Schirmer to reprint; the proofs of the piano score, which has been lithographed for the singers; a letter to Mama to be sent with the steamer going back to Novorossiisk and arrangements for her to come to New York on the return voyage; finding out whether it is possible to make a photocopy of the score; the endless chore of checking the French translation; and finally the relentless obligation to score five pages every day. And I want to find some time to spend with Stella.

27 July

Did four pages, not very difficult ones; not enough. I proof-read the lithograph of Act One.

Stella telephoned at five o'clock. She is in Asbury Park, eight miles away from West End, and wanted to see me. I took a car and went over to her. We went for a drive in the countryside, dined in West End and walked by the sea. Stella said she had been sure in her mind we were not going to see one another again, and asked me why I had sought her out. I replied: no particular reason, I simply missed her. When I took her back to Asbury Park late in the evening, matters progressed to a tender kiss. The breach and the coolness both seem to be over.

28 July

Stella telephoned from Asbury in the evening and asked me how many pages I had done. 'Only four,' I said. 'Would you like to come over to Asbury?' she asked. 'Of course I would,' I replied and set off at once.

At Asbury there were, as usual, masses of people, but we got in the car and went deep into the country along the highway. We drove for about three hours and spent the time in tender communion. This time Stella embraced me, holding me very close, and said: 'I am happy today.' I said: 'So am I.'

Stella's behaviour both astonished and overjoyed me.

29 July

I went again to see the Stahls. We did our best to finish off the translation, but again did not quite manage. I am in desperate need of the $1,500 from Chicago. So many bills are piling up, several of them reminders, and they have to be paid. Also, it won't be long before I run out of money for my own expenses.

Stahl and Janacopulos live a blissful and loving life together. But I remembered yesterday and thought: I have Stella.

30 July

Back to the city today, and the doctor. The wound is healing.

Stella fell off a horse while riding, and is all black and blue down one side. 'I would show you if I didn't love you so much,' she said. However I already know her form is Venus-like. She was angry today that I was rushing back to West End to do more pages, and I got angry in turn that she could not seem to understand that however much I love spending time with her I simply cannot default by one iota. In the event I missed the boat and had to rattle back on a soot-smoky train. I did not feel like orchestrating when I got back to West End, so read some proofs instead. This is the first day since my operation I have not done a single page.

31 July

I am beginning to be seriously worried that I am not going to finish the score by the date on the contract, 1 October. I got stuck and could not do more than one page (although to be fair it was a difficult one, the people laughing at the Prince's laughter).

1 August

Five pages today. Still not much, but they took a long time. In the evening I made some corrections to mistakes in the score.

The Omsk Government is clearing out of Omsk and will now become the Irkutsk Government. The victorious Bolsheviks are advancing.[1] What is going on? Why does a strong Russia of the future have to be forged by brutality and rapine?

---

1 During the summer and autumn of 1919 Admiral Kolchak's Omsk Government was falling apart, weakened by a combination of its own venality and incompetence, an increasingly organised and well-supplied Red Army, a desperately overstretched supply line from the Pacific four thousand miles away linked by a highly problematical railway line, and above all attacks

3 August

Six pages. I worked almost all day until dinner.

4 August

Went to see Stella at Asbury. We quarrelled over some trifle and said harsh things to one another. In the end we made up and kissed. I think she is angry with me because of the Odessa pogroms. Jews are being massacred in Odessa and Stella is taking revenge on a Christian. ('If you're not a cruel man you cannot be a Christian!')

5 August

The translation of *Oranges* is finally done and checked, and to all appearances has come out very well. I sent off the score and await the cheque. I am now down to fifty dollars, with a mass of bills to pay.

8 August

Stella came to West End and dined with me. As I always dine alone and pay no attention to anyone around me, all eyes goggled at us today. After dinner Stella came up to my room. At ten o'clock the hotel proprietor, a French-speaking Jew, appeared and asked me to step outside into the corridor. Wide-eyed, he asked me in French: 'Ecoutez, mais vous avez une femme?'[2] Naturally he had no wish to interfere in my affairs, but people were talking downstairs, there were mothers with daughters, and so on.

Stella was extremely embarrassed and said that it was normal for Christians to be swines, but when a Jew behaved like a swine he would be the swine of all swines. I took her back to Asbury by car.

---

and sabotage by countless partisan groups of hostile peasantry. Omsk itself did not in fact fall to the Red Army until November, but Kolchak was already preparing to retreat with the remnants of his forces and administration (not forgetting the Tsarist gold Prokofiev's acquaintance the music-loving V. I. Lebedev had brought to Omsk from Kazan, see above p. 358), eastwards to Irkutsk. He never got there, at least not as leader, having by that time acknowledged defeat and passed command to the warlord Semyonov. In Irkutsk his formerly loyal Czech Legion handed him over to the Bolsheviks, who put him on trial as an enemy of the people and executed him on 7 February 1920. See O. Figes, op. cit., pp. 653–9.

2 'Listen, have you got a woman in there with you?'

9 August

I had a frosty exchange with the hotel proprietor. I feared that it was going to end up costing me money, because he would no longer give me the discount he promised. But in his office he was extremely polite. I decided to declare war on the residents of the hotel, so I told him the children yell and scream as if they are in the market place and give me no peace.

Began scoring Act Three. I don't believe I shall be able to finish by 1 October. My eyes get tired. As it is I hardly ever take a day off. The only hope is that the second half of Act Three will be easier and won't take so long. And another thing: maybe the whole opera isn't five hundred and fifty pages, as I have been calculating, but will work out at less, perhaps five hundred. In that case I might just manage it.

11 August

A cheque for $1,500 from Chicago. Very nice and prompt, not like the first time, and I'm back in the black. Only nominally, however: if I aggregate all my debts ($1,200 to Bashkirov, $500 to the Russian consulate, $450 to Vyshnegradsky, $160 in fines, $100 to Lilienthal, a lot – I don't know exactly how much – to the Ingermans, $100 to Minster), the temperature is still well below zero on the scale.

Regarding the piano score, I did brilliantly sending it a month before the deadline. Will I get the score done on time? Between it and the operation the whole summer has been taken up. Of course I should not really complain: here I am living comfortably, by the lovely Atlantic Ocean; even so the summer seems to have passed me by.

12 August

I am much occupied with obtaining permission for Mama to come here. When the *Vladimir* sails to Novorossiisk, which she is shortly to do, I can send with the ship a ticket for Mama for the return voyage, but the visa situation is still far from clear. There is no American Consul in the Caucasus. Perhaps I can obtain the visa here?

19 August

I have started to play the piano again, not having touched it since 1 April. However, the fingers seem to be in good shape. I would even say there has been a step forward as far as flexibility of touch is concerned; there must have been some momentum from all the practising I did in the spring. I believe this can happen, and have more than once had occasion to test the theory.

I am going to learn the Fifth French Suite of Bach, three Beethoven Contredanses (which I played with Glière when I was twelve) and the F sharp minor Sonata of Schumann, which I played when I graduated from the Conservatoire. As far as I personally am concerned learning these pieces is a waste of time, but I have to make some concessions to American taste, which always wants 'something we know'.

The first recital will be on 12 October. It's rather soon, but that is all right with me (any later and all the Sundays in the halls will have gone).

21 August

Stella tells me that she is probably going with her father for a two month tour to London.[1] I responded: 'Fine, then I'll look for someone else.' This alarmed her: surely I didn't place so little value on our relations that I could contemplate replacing her with 'any old person'? We had dinner together somewhere in the country and spent the time very voluptuously.

22 August

A very nice letter from the Secretary at our Embassy: Mama will get her visa and it will all be easier than has hitherto appeared. Because there is no Consul in the Caucasus, authority for the visa will be telegraphed to the Consulate and instructions sent to Novorossiisk to allow Mama on to the boat.[2] The Secretary sent me the letter with Baron Wolf, an official representative who is travelling to the Caucasus. This visa has given me great joy.

24 August

I finished the Cook, and with her the second scene of Act Three. When composing it I had in mind a different orchestration for the repeat of the entr'acte scherzo, but the first-time scoring feels so firmly anchored I can't at the moment think of alternatives. I therefore left some pages blank and will give the score as it stands to the copyist; meanwhile I shall get straight on with the third scene.

---

1   The tour did take place, Stella Adler was a member of the company, playing the part of Naomi in performances of *Elisa Ben Avia* for a full year in the Pavilion Theatre on the Whitechapel Road, the 'Drury Lane of the East', splendid home of Yiddish Theatre in London between 1906 and 1934.
2   Presumably the American Consulate in Petrograd or, more likely, Moscow. From there the relevant authorisation would be telegraphed to an official agent in Novorossiisk.

25 August

I was in town. The copyist, scoundrel that he is, having copied 200 pages of score now refuses to do more on the grounds of ill health and tired eyes. It's true he was cheap, at 25 cents a page. He said that when he recovers he will be able to resume, but at 60 cents a page. I said that I would be happy to pay 80, but not to him. Still, it is not a good situation: I have to deliver it by 1 September and there are 50 pages still to do. I telephoned Altschuler to see if he could suggest another copyist, but Altschuler has not paid his telephone bill and I could not get through to his number.

Stella and I went out of town for dinner. She is leaving on 15 September and since we have become reconciled to this she has been nicer and more loving.

26 August

Monteux came back from Paris; he is now the conductor of the Boston Symphony Orchestra. He brought with him from Switzerland Mme Bolm's fifteen-year-old daughter (she is not Bolm's though) where she has been studying.

Scarcely had I got back from New York to West End, and was about to sit down to work, when I was summoned back to the city: Monteux wanted to get to know the *Scythian Suite*. I played it through to him, badly and inaccurately as usual, but he understood something of it and promised to perform it. I don't doubt that he will, but he should also have invited me to appear as soloist with the orchestra.

27 August

The third scene glides smoothly onwards; it is less complicated than Act Two. Hopes rise that I may finish on time.

28 August

Three hundred and forty-five pages. There must be, I suppose, a hundred and fifty to go. I think I will manage it.

29 August

A letter from Sklyarevsky in Java. I am mildly envious of him being in such a wonderful place. But I will get there myself one day. He writes that my works were performed in Batavia. I was boasting about this at lunch to the maître d'hôtel, who is always extremely interested in my music, when he asked: 'Java – is that in New York?' and my aim somewhat missed the target.

September

It has now transpired that Stella will be leaving on 18 September, and apparently not for two months but for much longer. Her father is going on tour to London, and with him his wife, Stella's elder sister and Stella herself, all of whom will appear in the production with him.

As it is very awkward for us to meet in the city – we have the choice either of the park or a car – and coming to West End is too difficult for her, Stella has persuaded me to move back to New York. The beginning of the autumn was a glorious time in West End, but Stella's days in New York were numbered and so I moved back there. I took two rooms, a bedroom and a sitting-room, in the Laurenton, a pleasant hotel. Stella came on my first evening there.

I asked her not to go to England, but she said she had to look after her family. She wanted my faithful promise that I would come to see her off on the boat, but I replied that since she was leaving me to go to London, I was going away a few days before her departure, on a car trip to Niagara with friends. Samoilenko, who had a little car, had actually suggested such a trip, but in the end it never took place.

The last evening, when I took Stella home, she said many loving things to me, told me how much she admired me, and declared that whatever our relationship was, whether one of love or not, she would always have the fondest memories of it.

All the same, I did not go to see her off. Why should I? To be a foolish face in the crowd? But after she left, on the 18th, I found I was missing her very much and tried not to stay at home alone.

The orchestration of *Oranges* was proceeding, but the more complicated Fourth Act presented more problems than the Third. However I drove it doggedly forward and finished it on time, by 1 October. I spent some time with the Samoilenkos, playing bridge with them and going out with them in their car. We went to see some motor racing. This produced a great impression on me, thirteen automobiles covering a hundred-mile course round a huge (mile-and-a-half long) circuit. Would they all get to the end? One car's axles caught fire when it was going at tremendous speed, followed by various other parts overheating. It was a spectacular scene, the driver and the mechanic had to stand on the backs of their seats trying to apply the brakes and steer the car. As soon as the speed had reduced enough they jumped clear, and came to not much harm.

Because all the rooms in my hotel including mine had been taken for the whole of the winter, but I only had a short-term booking for two weeks, I soon had to face the problem of finding somewhere to live. For the time being I moved in with Vladimir Bashkirov, who had a relatively large and empty apartment, and there continued my work on the scoring.

Going away, Stella had entrusted to my care her friend Blanche Gang (actually Wolfgang, but her parents had dropped the first syllable when they emigrated to America). A week after Stella's departure I rang up Blanche and invited her to dinner, not knowing her at all well at that time. She reminded me very strongly of Stella. Blanche told me that when she had come home after our last meeting, Stella had cried the whole evening. As the gigantic liner *Aquitania* on which she was sailing moved away from the shore on a gloriously sunny day, she asked Blanche to tell me how lovely it looked.

I remembered that during the summer, trying to improve my command of English, I used to write every day a few new English words that I would then learn by heart. One day Stella caught sight of the piece of paper on which I was doing this, and I asked her to note down some words I would not understand. Stella wrote down: 'Love, comprehension, Stella.' When I told Blanche this, she exclaimed: 'It is just Stella!'[1]

1 October

Today is the contractual deadline for the score of *Three Oranges*, and I finished the last page at exactly two o'clock in the afternoon. 'Terribly chic,' as Max Schmidthof would have said. Quite true; it was calculated to a nicety.

2–11 October

Early October went in preparations for my concert, and life was easier once I had finished the *Oranges* score. Generally, though, October passed in a fairly uneventful and uninspiring manner. The void left by Stella's departure and the end of work on the score meant that I could not find much interest in the people surrounding me. One person who did appear over the horizon was the cellist Iosif Chernyavsky, my fervent supporter from the performances of the *Scythian Suite* in St Petersburg, in which as a cellist in the orchestra he had defended me against the attacks of his fellow musicians.[2] Every now and again I had dinner with Blanche, and once she came to my apartment where I played to her, although the talk was, of course, all of Stella. At the time I was living entirely alone in a huge, rather vulgarly furnished apartment, thanks to Vladimir Bashkirov, one of whose business

---

1 These phrases are written in English.
2 See above, pp. 69–71.

partners[1] had rented the apartment and then gone away, leaving it unoccupied.

Blanche and I went together to visit an artist, who had painted a portrait in oils of Stella. The artist was a rather pathetic young man, quite poor although possibly not untalented. Stella had told me about this portrait; it was flattering to her vanity that she should be painted by a real artist (as she thought him). On one of our last evenings together, sitting with me until eleven o'clock at night, she had even left to dash off to his studio so that he could (at night!) put the finishing touches to the portrait, expressing surprise that I was prepared to let her go. In short I was a little jealous, not of the artist himself, he was too pathetic a specimen, but of the whole business with the portrait, and felt inclined to be critical. The picture was terribly yellow.

Good news came that my mother was now in possession of her visa to come to America. Now what I had to do was arrange from this side to pay her passage, and to make it possible for her to board a boat on the Black Sea and come directly to New York. There were not many Russian boats doing this. My conduit was Bashkirov, but he could sometimes be inexcusably slipshod, which eventually led to us even quarrelling, despite our friendship and the trouble he had gone to over the apartments I was living in.

12 October

My first recital. A little early on in the season, but we had wanted a Sunday, and all the later ones had been taken. I was a little nervous of the Bach, but the performance passed off without incident. The Beethoven Contredanses were very good, also the Schumann Sonata. But the greatest success was reserved for the five shorter pieces of mine with which I concluded the programme, ending up with *Suggestion Diabolique*. This had an extraordinary success, reminiscent of the good old days in Petrograd. I gave six encores. They were calling for the *Toccata*, but I was not up to playing it, I could not remember it, not having played it for a long time, so instead I repeated *Suggestion Diabolique*. The hall looked full, but again quite a number of people had been invited – a 'papered house', as the Americans call it. A lot of people came to the Green Room afterwards; they seized me by the hand, gripped my shoulders and practically pulled me to pieces in their enthusiasm. The reception had been less demonstrative after the concerts in the spring, but on the other hand Stella and Dagmar had been there then, which perhaps had added a little zest.

After the concert the Stahls took me out to Staten Island, where they live, and where the air is fresh and the ocean most beautiful (although not as sparkling as it is near Petrograd).

---

1 A 'Kooperator', a term that could refer to a partner in a Kooperativ – see above, p. 400 n. 1.

A telegram from Coates in London, asking for the score and parts of the *Scythian Suite*. Splendid! Clever old Coates! This suggests the possibility of an English tour in the spring and a London production of *Three Oranges*.

13 October

A good crop of reviews, and although they are not particularly ecstatic, they are all favourable. The classics are dragging me up by the ears from the mire that engulfed me after the spring concerts. All the same the critics are fools: I played five movements not seven in the Bach, and I cut nearly half of the finale of the Schumann. Not one of them noticed.

14 October

Chernyavsky and Bellison showed me some Jewish melodies; some of them were not of much interest, but others were absolutely lovely. I took the material home and immediately decided to write an *Overture on Hebrew Themes* for piano, string quartet and clarinet, that is for their ensemble.[1] I worked on it all day and by the end got the whole *Overture* in the bag. Of course, there are many details as yet unsettled, but the bones of it are there. If I could tidy it up in two days and settle the instrumentation, it would all be done very quickly.

15 October

Began scoring the *Overture*, but clearly it is going to take more than two days, please God not more than a week, though. I thought I would be able to have a rest after the recital, but all of a sudden there was the *Overture*, I have to prepare the Chicago recital, and in a week's time I have to go to Chicago (so far, for a week).

16 October

A postcard from Mama, after eighteen months' silence. She complains of her health, badly affected by all she has gone through, of her failing sight, and of

---

1 This was the Zimro Ensemble, formed by the clarinettist Simeon Bellison (1881–1953) in Petrograd in 1918 specifically to tour Jewish and Jewish-influenced music to Palestine via America under the auspices of the Russian Zionist Organisation. Bellison's unusual gifts as a clarinettist were, however, spotted as soon as the ensemble debuted in New York, and he was invited to become the New York Philharmonic's principal clarinettist, a position he occupied for the next twenty-eight years, thus curtailing (although not completely abandoning) the ensemble's touring plans and altering their eventual destination from Palestine to New York.

her depressed state of mind. This last affected me very much. After half a year of struggling I still have not succeeded in getting her here. All my energies must now be devoted to this. I even had thoughts of going to fetch her myself, if I could raise the money, but it would do no good. I would miss the opera and the season, consequently if I did bring her here neither of us would have anything to eat. I went to see Stahl on Staten Island. He said that Soskice was travelling direct to the Caucasus in a few days on a diplomatic passport, and he would sort everything out. Soskice is certainly someone to rely on. I felt a little easier in my mind.

17 October

Talked to Bashkirov about the best way to send for Mama. Letters and telegrams don't get through, so the only route is through people who are going there. But Bashkirov said that Soskice might after all not be going, and was generally so ineffectual and indifferent that I became furious and almost quarrelled with him. Stahl reassured me that in fact Soskice probably was going.

A telegram about Petrograd having been captured by the 'Anti-Reds'. Could this be true? What joy! Tomorrow the residents of the capital will be able to eat for the first time in two years! Will I really be able in a month or two to make contact with my friends? Perhaps by the spring there will be a direct route open to the city.

18 October

I am getting on with the score of the *Overture* and will have it finished by the time I go to Chicago.

Went with a large group, including Ingermans and Yakhontovs, to the Stahls, where it was very nice and sunny. I flirted with my new admirer, Linette, who in spite of her youth – she is twenty – is quite demure. Stahl says, however, that this is only a façade, and indeed she agreed to sing in front of everyone provided that I accompanied her.[1]

And Stella – well, it is now a month since she left, and I have not heard a word from her. About ten days ago I sent her a box of chocolates but I didn't write either, although I have thought of her a lot.

---

1 Carolina Codina, who used her mother's maiden name of Llubera as a stage name, was in New York to study singing when she first encountered Prokofiev backstage after his performance of the First Piano Concerto and the 'Classical' Symphony at Altschuler's concert on 27 November/ 10 December the previous year. Half Spanish, a quarter French and a quarter Russian, the twenty-one-year-old girl was at first too shy to come into the green room, but as years later she told the writer Harvey Sachs: 'Slowly I opened the door, slipped my head in and looked. I saw

19 October

Stayed the night with the Stahls and then went to be photographed: a group picture for *Three Oranges* consisting of Miss Janacopulos, Ansermet, Bolm and me. At the last moment Ansermet suddenly announced, giving no reason, that he did not want to be photographed. I tried to persuade him but he dug his toes in like a ram. At that I lost my temper and was rude to him.

Rachmaninoff's concert, the first this season. He played a Beethoven sonata magnificently, Chopin not so well, and after that Mendelssohn's *Rondo Capriccioso* and three waltzes, by Chopin, himself, and from Gounod's *Faust*. If he had played a programme like that in Russia they would have thrown a dead cat at him. Of his own things only one *Etude Tableau*, very good indeed. Rachmaninoff preserves an Olympian detachment; some things he plays wonderfully, others like a block of wood, but his programmes sell audiences short. In me he arouses a strange mixture of feelings: sometimes he absolutely transports me, at others exasperates me dreadfully. I went backstage after the concert, not so much to see him as to see other people I know. We exchanged a few words, but fairly coolly.

20 October

I continued composing the *Overture* and practised the programme for Chicago (the same as for my recital in the spring). Dined with Blanche, who was remarkably nice to me, showering me with compliments and asking if I wasn't missing Stella. She came back to my apartment after dinner and I played her my Chicago programme. Blanche is a dear girl, prone to a kind of misty pessimism. In much of what she says and the way she looks at life I see something of Stella. Or rather, the other way about: Stella absorbed them from Blanche.

21 October

Petrograd has not been taken, but there is fighting all around it: in Krasnoye Selo, Tsarskoye and Tosno. My lovely dacha in Sablino, where I spent such a wonderful summer, may have been burnt to the ground and destroyed, although Yudenich's right wing is bogged down in Tosno, and I have not

---

them talking to him, and he saw me over their shoulders and smiled at me and laughed because I looked so funny. Then I laughed too, and my friends said: "Oh, there she is," and they drew me in, and I could not run away because it was too late. And I felt a sort of attraction – he was tall, thin, with blond, slightly reddish hair.' (From transcript of an interview with Harvey Sachs preserved in the Serge Prokofiev Archive, Goldsmiths College, London.)

heard of his crossing the eastern Nikolayevsky railway. The Bolsheviks have mobilised all the young people for the defence of the city.[1]

What a terrible situation for all my friends: Boris Verin, Asafyev, Suvchinsky, Myaskovsky! The only hope for them and all those who live for art is that they will be protected by Lunacharsky. Also, I have no news of the fate of my apartment at No. 1 Rota. Before I left Russia Suvchinsky sent in a dependable man, his building superintendent. I'm not concerned about my goods and chattels, and don't even mind much about my prize piano. But there were letters from several previous years in the drawer of the desk, and a thick notebook containing my diary – one of the later years, I don't remember which. I should be very sad to lose that notebook.

22 October

Spent almost the whole day scoring the *Overture*, also practised for Chicago.

23 October

I've spent all the past days composing and scoring the *Overture*, and finished it today. It has turned out to be a more interesting piece than I expected, and I suppose it deserves to be given an opus number.[2] Chernyavsky came in the evening. I played it to him; he was thrilled and accepted it for performance.

24 October

Soskice's travel to Russia has been delayed, moreover I have discovered that although it is not possible to send a telegram to Novorossiisk directly, one can do so via the agent of the Volunteer Fleet in Constantinople.[3] I therefore

---

[1] Prokofiev refers to the desperate gamble of General Yudenich's German-backed North Western Army (motto: 'Against the Bolsheviks Without Politics') to capture Petrograd while the Red Army was looking the other way. It could have stood some chance of success if Yudenich had been willing to enlist the support of Finland, there for the asking, but the unreconstructedly absolutist general would not contemplate guaranteeing independence (which *de facto* they already more or less had) to Finland, so went it alone with predictable results. By 20 October Yudenich was at the Pulkovo Heights, within sight of Petrograd, but Trotsky swiftly brought up crack army reserves and mobilised the city's terrified population to drive the North West Army back into Estonia, chillingly dismissed by Trotsky as 'the kennel for the guard-dogs of the counter-revolution', where it disbanded, and that was the end of that. (See O. Figes, op. cit., and p. 186 n. 1 above.)

[2] *Overture on Hebrew Themes* for clarinet, two violins, viola, cello and piano in C minor, Op. 34. Prokofiev later (1934) made a version for small orchestra, which is Op. 34a.

[3] The Russian Volunteer Fleet was originally formed during the Russo-Turkish War of 1877 to provide fast, armed freight and commerce-raiding ships more manoeuvrable than the Navy's powerful but clumsy battle cruisers. After the war the Volunteer Fleet, having proved its usefulness, was placed under the aegis of the Navy Ministry and in wartime (e.g. the Russo-Japanese

took $400 to Shestakovsky (the Volunteer Fleet's local representative here) as a deposit for Mama's ticket from Novorossiisk to New York, and he will let her (and the office in Novorossiisk) know about this by telegram.

After leaving his office I almost missed the Twentieth Century[1] but at 2.45 pm left New York for my concert in Chicago. I said goodbye to my enormous apartment, albeit without much regret. Its vulgarity was positively painful.

My travelling companion on the train was a doctor from Winnipeg, who wanted to invite me to perform in his city. His thirteen-year-old daughter was with him, a rosy-cheeked little American girl.

25 October

Arriving in Chicago in the morning I was met at the station by N. T. Kucheryavy, who drove me to his home in his new car.

In the afternoon I called on Newman, my Chicago manager, and then practised on the piano in the horrible Kimball Hall, where I am due to play my recital. Chicago doesn't have a better hall if one excepts the huge one seating several thousand.

26 October

At half-past three, I played the first of my two recitals. The programme was the same as last February in New York: the Fourth Sonata, three Scriabin pieces, ten *Vision Fugitives*, Musorgky and the *Toccata*. The little hall was full. As for the Fourth Sonata, I worried that it would be too much for the audience, but it was fine, the finale warmed them up. The rest of the programme went equally well. I was told that it was a select audience, serious and musical, as is right and proper for Chicago where of course they understand more than they do in New York. I played three encores.

After the concert there were greetings and congratulations in the small, cramped Green Room, although less extravagantly than in New York. One young lady showed me a list of all the keys of V*isions Fugitives* and embarrassed me by asking what key No. 3 was written in. I could not tell her (tonalities are not something I ever think about). After the concert I had dinner with Kucheryavy at Volkov's, the very nice Russian Consul. Volkov told me that the delay last January over the opera contract had been because of a

---

War of 1904, the First World War) functioned as a parallel navy to the Imperial Navy, while in peacetime it instituted commercial freight and passenger services from Odessa to Vladivostok and later to New York. After Russia signed the Brest-Litovsk Treaty ceasing hostilities against Germany, most of the Volunteer Fleet ships came under Allied control for the duration.

1   The Twentieth Century Limited express train from New York to Chicago.

dastardly plot to replace my opera with a ballet by Carpenter.[1] Only when Volkov brought pressure to bear on Campanini by insisting that 'the word given by the latter in the present of the Russian Consul was more valuable than gold' did Campanini yield to the compromise of staging both works.

27 October

Called on Campanini, who is ill in bed and looks far from well. The maestro enquired about my success yesterday, and was generally very civil. We allocated parts to the singers (not knowing any of them, I sketched the main features of the characters, and he would say 'ecco!' and give the name of the singer).

The conductor, Marinuzzi, said to be a new star from Buenos Aires, is still on his way here by sea.[2] Most of the singers have also not yet gathered here, and work on learning the opera cannot begin earlier than 15 November, so for the time being there is nothing for me to do here. Not wishing to fatigue the sick maestro, I soon took my leave.

Kahn, whom in February I had written down as a scoundrel and treated appropriately, and whose attitude to me had been one of hostility all autumn, evidently now considers it more politic to be civil and invited me to lunch. I decided that although he was not in a position to do me any great harm, he could still play the odd little dirty trick, so likewise assumed my politest demeanour, and the appearance of harmony was restored.

The reviews were good. I have made much more of an impression here than in New York.

28 October

In the morning I practised the programme for this evening's recital (the same as I gave two weeks ago in New York), after which Kucheryavy took me

---

[1] John Alden Carpenter (1876–1951), composer who had studied with Elgar and, like Charles Ives, combined composition with a day job as a business executive. Interested in incorporating into his music elements of popular culture, he was one of the first American composers to use material derived from jazz and Tin Pan Alley. His best-known work, the ballet *Skyscrapers*, written in 1923, had had its origins in a hoped-for commission from Diaghilev, but the provisional contract expired without a production and allowed Carpenter to offer it to the Metropolitan Opera, where it was produced to great acclaim in 1926 and helped to make Carpenter a household name in America. See p. 516 below.

[2] Gino Marinuzzi (1882–1945) came from Palermo in Sicily where he began his conducting career at the Teatro Massimo. His career was mainly in Italy, conducting for example the premiere of Puccini's *La Rondine* in 1917, with latter appointments at the Rome Opera and La Scala. In 1919 and 1920, however, he held a brief appointment at the Chicago Opera, and it was during this period that his son, Gino Marinuzzi Jr, was born, who was to become one of the most prominent and successful composers of the Italian film industry.

round Chicago in his car. We covered about thirty miles along the parks and boulevards that ring the city. The town itself is divided into a grid of regular squares built with small houses, not nearly as impressive as the great buildings of New York. Only the city centre – Michigan Avenue – is splendid.

This evening I played the second of my recitals, for which the hall was only two-thirds full, which considerably dampened my fire. I played the classical part of the programme with little temperament but rather nervously (I don't know why), in a word it was not as good as in New York. However the Schumann Sonata had a great success, and I was called back to the stage four times. I played my own pieces well, and was rewarded with three encores. There were not many people in the Green Room this time, and none of them were at all interesting. I felt terribly tired.

29 October

I was afraid the newspapers would take me apart, but this was far from the case – I was praised as never before. A certain Mr Faust interviewed me for the pro-Bolshevik paper *New Republic*[1] and flattered me with such extravagant verbal bouquets (especially for the 'Procession of the Sun' from the *Scythian Suite*, which he had heard the previous year) that even I felt quite uncomfortable.

I sent a registered letter to Stella, the first time I have written to her. There has been no word at all from her either to me, or to her friend, or to her sister. In the letter I tried to be nice, as nice as Stella herself.

30 October

Today I was taken to see an exhibition of paintings by the artist Vitkovich, who insists that originally he was meant to get the commission for the settings for *Three Oranges*, but it was later given to Anisfeld. I looked at about sixty pictures, of which the majority were no good but a few were successful, although as soon as there was a substantial subject it would all fall apart.

The Bolsheviks have brought up reinforcements and have repulsed the assault on Petrograd. Again and again one has to give credit to their weaponry. But the joy of feeling that I might someday be reunited with friends has

---

1 'Pro-Bolshevik' may be a slight exaggeration, but it is certainly true that the general tendency of the *New Republic*, founded in 1906 with financial backing from Willard Straight and his wife Dorothy Payne Whitney Straight (later to become the wife of Leonard Elmhirst, the philanthropist who created the educational, artistic and socially experimental community that was and is Dartington Hall in Devon) was one of sympathy to the Communist experiment, and this broadly prevailed until the end of the Second World War, after which the magazine moved more towards its present mainstream liberal standpoint.

dimmed and receded. I am even afraid that in days like these there will be some whose very survival may not be guaranteed. Hunger, typhoid, search-warrants, denunciations...

Was Demchinsky right to say, just before I left, that having 'fled from history', when I return to a tortured and exhausted Russia she will not accept me because she will be a country that thinks and feels quite differently? But no, he cannot be right, not when thinking of such as Bashkirov, Asafyev, Myaskovsky. They are fine, their judgement goes deep, and they love me too much.

I took the Broadway Limited Express and went back to New York. On the way I caught up with my Diary, watched the autumn countryside flash by, disfigured by an excrescence of factories, and went to sleep early.

1 November

When I arrived in New York the following morning, a letter from London was waiting for me, proposing a production of *Three Oranges* at Covent Garden in June. Now this is an event of truly enormous importance! A year ago I entered into correspondence with Bakst trying to get *Three Oranges* produced in the autumn season in Europe, but it came to nothing because Bakst was relying on Diaghilev, and I already knew that there would be no resurrection (at least in the operatic sense) for Diaghilev in that season. But now Coates, the clever fellow, has had the excellent sense to take up the idea. If it works, then hurrah! in six months I shall have a quick and brilliant *entrée* into Europe.

In the afternoon I attended Janacopulos's concert, some of which she sang very well, and some passably. In the evening I went with the Stahls to the country.

In between times I managed to find myself an apartment for November, something which is for some inscrutable reason extraordinarily difficult to find in New York just now. This apartment is furnished in rather lacklustre style, but it has a lot of space in it and it gets the sun. The main thing is I found it right away, and have it until December, when I have to leave to go to Chicago for the opera. One reaction to hearing my new address was to exclaim: 'Have you lost your mind? Nobody lives there but tarts!' I found this a bit embarrassing, but there were others who said: 'All the jollier for you.' So I don't give a damn.

2 November

A warm and sunny day. I had guests, among them Linette, and we mowed the grass in the garden, altogether we had a very nice time. In the evening I took Linette back to her home, and in a dark corner of the platform I kissed her. This appears to have given both of us pleasure.

3 November

All in all my apartment is very nice. I'm waiting for a piano to be delivered, so that I can start work on *Carnaval*, for which I am developing a great love.

Smallens[1] from the Chicago Opera came to see me; it will be his job to coach the singers. I played the whole opera to him, and he was very impressed, but then clutched his head and complained about how difficult it was going to be to teach the singers their parts.

5 November

The piano has arrived and I set to work on the programme. Essentially there are only seventeen days to the concert.

8 November

Had a good morning's piano practice and then with much pleasant anticipation accompanied the Stahls to the country. I thought that Linette might be there too, but tomorrow the Stahls are going to a concert in the afternoon so there won't be any guests.

9 November

A delicious autumn day, and I went for a long walk in the beautiful autumnal scenery. Linette herself had the idea of telephoning, and while Stahl was starting to explain that they were going off to a concert, I managed to interject an invitation to come to their place. In this way we contrived to spend a few very pleasant hours with the hosts not there. Linette is completely in love with me.

10 November

Piano practice, as well as a long letter to Kling in London setting out my conditions for *Three Oranges*.

Tried to work out a way of transferring money to Mama without that rogue Shestakovsky getting to hear of it.

Mlle Blanche says that Stella and all her family and company are in trouble in London as their season has not done well at all. The work has been very

---

1 Alexander Smallens (1889–1972), conductor, had been born in St Petersburg but his family had migrated to the USA when he was a child, and he therefore trained there and at the Paris Conservatoire. He later rose to prominence as the conductor of the premiere in 1935 of Gershwin's *Porgy and Bess*, a work with which he remained associated in its successful Broadway revivals and world tour. He would later work on the eventual Chicago Opera production of *Love for Three Oranges* and conduct the second performance on 5 January 1922.

hard, but the success only moderate. They do nine performances and eight rehearsals a week, and Stella has become ill with fatigue. She asked Blanche to pass on to me that she hoped I would not forget her. I'm sorry for Stella, but she could at least have sent me a line.

11 November

The dentist's brutal infliction of root-canal fillings has utterly ruined my life.

In the evening I visited Samoilenko, whom I have not seen for six weeks since they went to the country. I played them my programme for 22 November (*Carnaval*, etc.) Their reaction: at last you have a decent programme.

Apparently I shall be able to transfer money through the kind co-operation of the Russian and English Consulates via the English Military Mission in the Caucasus. This question is causing me a great deal of worry.

Dr Winkelstein sent me a book by Freud; he is much read here. I thought it would be philosophy, but it is much more concerned with medicine. The book promises to be very interesting and instructive.

12 November

Learned my recital programme and read Freud. In the evening I went to the cinema with Linette and kissed her all the way home. But for some unknown reason she obstinately refused to come home with me.

Blanche came to see me yesterday and I played her the programme for the forthcoming recital. She was as usual very nice, very complimentary, and predicted a brilliant success. Stella has written to her several times. The affairs of her theatre company have taken a turn for the better, as has Stella's mood.

14 November

The man who is going to conduct my opera, maestro Marinuzzi, is still on his way from Buenos Aires. I hear also that the arrival of the French singers has been held up because of a strike of steamship employees. It looks inevitable that the opera production is going to be delayed.

15 November

It was a great joy in the morning to go off to spend the weekend with the Stahls. The days I spend with them are the most pleasant of all. Linette and some other guests also came. Miss Janacopulos sang with the Boston

Orchestra in Cambridge and in Boston and had a colossal success, as a result of which the domestic atmosphere was particularly sunny. Stahl was full of praise for my performance of *Carnaval*, and especially of the Russian pieces.

16 November

We spent the morning frantically raking up leaves in the garden and got so hungry we could hardly wait for lunch. In the afternoon Stahl and Janacopulos left to go to a concert in New York, leaving Linette and me alone. We made good use of the time. When our hosts returned in the evening, we discussed their trip to Brazil. Later Linette and I went out to look at the stars.

18 November

Next morning I played *Carnaval* to Samoilenko on a very stiff piano and damaged the first finger on my left hand. I've been nursing it for a month now, putting collodion on it and wrapping it in cottonwool, but today it is inflamed and swollen and looked so angry that I dashed to consult Ingerman. He said that an abscess on the finger was coming to a head, and lanced it. He said it would be all right by Saturday, the day of the concert.

Dined with Linette and afterwards went to the cinema with her, since the beastly girl will not come home with me. I did not try very hard to persuade her today because she had a headache, and took her back home early.

19 November

The finger seems to be a little better, but of course I still can't play the piano with it, so I practised just with my right hand only. If the left hand stumbles in the concert, I'll just have to use the right one to get out of trouble.

I handed a nice fat sterling cheque to our Consul, which he will forward with a covering letter to the British Military Mission in the south of Russia. God grant it gets there, but it gives me no peace.

In Russia the political web is drawing ever tighter, for the Bolsheviks are winning, but surely it cannot be that theirs will be the final victory? If not, all the towns they are now capturing are being taken in vain. But in the meantime what slaughter, what looting, what rape, what typhoid and syphilis their inhabitants will endure!

20 November

I think the finger is getting worse, but Ingerman says no, it is better. Whatever the case it is painful to the touch and there can be no question of playing with it in such a state. I rang up Haensel and asked whether he thought I should cancel the recital. He said the $500 budget has all been spent, and that if I cancel now I shall be saying goodbye to the lot. His advice was therefore to wait until Saturday and see whether the finger improved, not touching the piano in the meantime but practising mentally. I followed his advice and it certainly was very helpful, but dreadfully fatiguing to the brain.

I dined with Linette and again invited her to my apartment, since it is very boring always to have recourse to the cinema. At first she hesitated, but then said: 'No, no, not today! Put me on the subway and I'll go home.' This made me angry, and after taking her to the subway, I said goodbye. An hour later she telephoned, called me a bear with a sore head, and peace was restored.

21 November

A letter from Mama via the Russian Embassy in Rome, with the same date as the postcard I received a month ago. Poor Mama, what she has had to endure! I am relieved that my cheque has at least been sent, and I think by a reliable route. The whole question of Mama troubles me greatly, but it is quite impossible for me to go there at just the time when I am beginning to establish myself in America. In any case I simply do not have the money for the journey.

My finger is better, and tomorrow I shall be able to play, although at no more than 75 per cent of my capabilities. Spoke to Linette on the telephone. When I asked her if she would spend the evening before my concert with me, she said she was busy today. I said: 'Well, I expect I'll manage to find someone else who would be more inclined than you are to spend the evening with me.' Her response was: 'Vous êtes méchant.'

In the evening I played bridge with Samoilenko. He roasted his leg (that is to say, a whole leg of lamb) superbly.

22 November

Linette telephoned and enquired how my evening had been, and whom I had spent it with. I declined to tell her. She offered to visit me this afternoon, but later called to say that she would be going to the piano recital by Hofmann. She then called again to ask me not to be angry with her.

All afternoon I was bored and nervous. My finger was better, but it still hurt and I did not practise, so as not to irritate it. The concert was at half-past eight; the hall was full, and I was warmly received. The first item was Schuman's *Carnaval*. I played it all right, but not as well as I had before I hurt my finger when I played it for Stahl and Deryuzhinsky,[1] for instance. The finger was bandaged with a thick layer of cottonwool and collodion, and kept catching the black notes, which was very distracting. But in the end it was not a bad performance of *Carnaval*, although not everything was completely clean and I did not play all the numbers with inspiration. I was in considerable pain during the 'March of the Davidsbündler' and felt that I was making a bit of a dog's breakfast of it. However the Russian pieces were well played and I got six curtain calls. I played my Sonata No. 3 not terribly well but the *Toccata* with great brio. There were four encores. There were a lot of people and congratulations in the Green Room. Ingerman and Stahl came and bandaged my finger, which was bleeding, and Stahl then took me to his house. The Samoilenkos were also there, and it was all very cheerful and nice; we had supper and drank wine. Since I have had my root canals cleaned out the neuralgia has disappeared and not even wine makes it come back.

23 November

Today, as usual on Sundays, it was lovely, sunny weather. But there were a mass of visitors to see me, so there was a real scrum and poor Linette was the victim of a concerted assault behind my back – she was almost reduced to tears by all the teasing she was subjected to on my account. Even Soskice, to whose pretty wife I was mildly paying court in order to turn attention away from Linette and me, could think of nothing more intelligent than to tease Linette by telling her how I was running after his wife.

I'm keeping my finger in an alcohol compress. I can only hope it heals by Friday, for Washington.

24 November

There were not many reviews of the concert, and they were cursory and indifferent. The loss amounted to $250 (takings of $300 against expenses of

---

1   Gleb Deryuzhinsky (1888–1975), sculptor and member of the Peredvizhnik school of late nineteenth-century realist artists. Deryuzhinsky, who had been strongly influenced by Rodin during a period of study in Paris, attracted notice in Petrograd as a portrait sculptor and was commissioned to make a bust of Kerensky immediately after the February Revolution. He made his escape from Russia at the beginning of 1919 by the original tactic of signing on as a midshipman on the steamship *Vladimir* bound from Novorossiisk to New York, where along with Boris Anisfeld he was one of the first émigré Russian artists to arrive in the USA. His figurative work is to be seen in many major American collections and museums.

$550), much more than I expected. I had thought that with a programme like that, and after the success I had in October, it would be a real sensation. But then Hofmann came up with his afternoon concert, to which everyone had gone and so were tired by the evening, not to mention another concert by Russian so-called folk singers, actually tavern songs by Tarasova, to which all the Russian East Side had swarmed.[1] In consequence quite a number of my admirers held back from coming.

However that evening Linette came to my apartment. I imagine it was the first time in her life she had been alone with a bachelor in his apartment, so she was trembling with such anxiety that I had to go to great lengths to reassure her. All the same the time passed very enjoyably, lovingly and quickly.

26 November

There was an afternoon concert by a not very good singer, Dora de Philippe,[2] whose programme included my *Akhmatova Songs* translated by her into English. She sang nicely enough, but she has not much of a voice, and the hall was empty. The songs were successful, and had to be encored.

I am a free man this week (something that has not happened for a long time). I cannot play the piano because of my finger, although it is getting better. I have been thinking: suppose I were to give another concert in a couple of months, what should I play? I don't yet have the answer to this. But if I could extract a little suite from *Three Oranges*, that might be interesting.

I hear Rachmaninoff is also not in 'battle formation': in the middle of his seventy thousandth tour he felt unwell and had to abandon it in the middle to return to New York.

27 November

Since the Chicago Opera is definitely and extremely objectionably postponing the production of my opera (because of the delayed arrival of Marinuzzi and of many of the French singers), and I even hear rumours that 'some' of the scheduled operas may be put off altogether until next season, I looked out my contract and consulted with Stahl. Stahl's view is that Chicago is under a perfectly clear obligation to present *Three Oranges* this season, and

---

1   Nina Tarasova had learnt a large repertoire of Russian folk songs from her old nurse when growing up as a child in the Crimea, and put them over with an earthy brio that charmed audiences in Petersburg, and later in America, where she met and married a prominent and wealthy sportsman Stuart Fitzhugh Voss and lived in some style on Long Island.
2   Dora de Philippe was a soprano whose main career was in the early days of radio opera.

if it is not performed this will constitute a breach of contract, that is to say they will forfeit the right to present it next season. Since, according to Anisfeld, they have already spent $50,000 on the sets, they will not be too pleased about this. (So why not make a bit of an effort and produce it this season?) Moreover I would be entitled to claim consequential compensation for the money I have lost through their not presenting *Three Oranges*: reduced popularity, fewer concert invitations, the loss of a London production (assuming such does not take place), and so on.

This advice cheered me, and I resolved to press them to produce it as energetically as is in my power, if it is really true that they are having second thoughts.

28 November

At midnight yesterday I boarded the train and at seven o'clock this morning arrived in Washington after a wonderful night's sleep. I took very much indeed to Washington, it is one of the best cities in America: spaciously laid out, peaceful, and green. I walked round the town for two hours, then called in to see my manager, played the piano for a while, then had lunch and went to our Embassy in order to thank Karpovich for the trouble he had gone to over Mama's visa.

I then went to the National Theatre to give my recital, which began at half-past four. The hall is quite big, and was nearly full. My finger is much better, and although it had a plaster on it did not trouble me. I played *Carnaval* better, and to greater acclaim, than I had done in New York. The second part, the Russian repertoire, and the third – my own works – were less well received than in New York, but still well enough.

After the Russian pieces (ending with Rachmaninoff's G minor Prelude) I was called back five times. I gave only one encore at the end of the recital: a Beethoven Contredanse. The audience in the orchestra stalls was somewhat cool, but those higher up in the balcony were warmer. There was no post-concert reception, but afterwards, as I was sitting in the prima donna's dressing-room surrounded by powder and rouge and wigs, some wonderful ladies came in. One of them said:

'You played the *Toccata* wonderfully well, but I don't like the music.'

'You will,' I replied, 'once you have heard it five times.'

The manager tugged at my sleeve and whispered: 'Quiet, that's our principal music critic.'

In the evening I was entertained by the local *beau monde*, and at midnight went back to New York.

29 November

Finding nothing particularly important waiting for me on my return to New York except the usual bills for publicity, I changed and set off, as previously arranged, for the Stahls. Linette arrived soon after and we had a pleasantly restful day, except for the evening when Linette and I went out to look at the stars and kissed anything but restfully.

As I'm still waiting for an answer from Chicago, I don't know when I should go there.

30 November

Today passed in the same peaceful rural bliss as yesterday. Janacopulos sang her forthcoming programme, and we went through it all with a fine-tooth comb. It is such a shame that they are soon going to Brazil (to collect an inheritance) and our Sundays will come to an end.

It is some time since I have had any Russian books in my hands, but Samoilenko has just given me one, and it is very good: Bryusov's *The Fiery Angel*, which Boris Verin mentioned to me about two years ago. The reader is plunged immediately and irretrievably into the heart of sixteenth-century superstitions. The hero of the story is a man of reason who tries, with the understanding of his times, to shake them off.

1 December

Returning to the city I had all sorts of business to attend to, and in the evening went to Lhévinne's concert. He possesses fabulous fingers and nothing whatsoever in his head. Linette was also in the box, and we drank chocolate afterwards. She has promised to come to me tomorrow.

2 December

I'm reading *Fiery Angel* with the greatest interest. Linette came in the evening. Even though she suffers agonies of terror lest anyone should see her coming to see me, she is still prepared to come.

3 December

Samoilenko tells me that Volkov has sent a telegram to Bashkirov urging him to get me over to Chicago as soon as possible, since Campanini is near death and there is a move to postpone the opera. As I am not speaking to Bashkirov since he behaved so foolishly in response to my appeals for help with

Mama, I telephoned his secretary. Bashkirov, however, wanted to read the telegram to me himself over the telephone, for which I thanked him coldly. Indeed it did request my immediate departure for Chicago. I thereupon telephoned Volkov in Chicago (seven dollars fifty cents) and heard his voice with perfect clarity over a distance of a thousand miles. Volkov said that Campanini was a little better, but it was true that they wanted to put off my opera until next season on the grounds that the singers had been delayed arriving from France and the entire programme for the season was in disarray. I said that I would lay everything out clearly in a letter to Volkov, and asked him to let me know by telegram in three days' time whether or not I should travel there. I had not the slightest desire to go: if the singers had not made a start on learning their parts the production must in any case be some way off, and nothing would be decided while Campanini was ill. Meanwhile, Linette was here!

In the evening I saw Fokine.[1] He has recently arrived in America and was excellent company. When I got home I wrote a long letter to Volkov laying out clearly the central point: if they did not produce the opera this season they would forfeit all rights to it for the following one.

4 December

Saw Haensel, who had been in Chicago. He was in buoyant mood, saying that everyone there was very interested in my opera and it was a great pity there was a hitch. According to him Bolm was recommending me not to go: I would only get angry and make a bad situation worse by upsetting everybody. This advice was the precise opposite of what I had received yesterday. Haensel was very surprised to learn that my New York recital had cost me $250 and said I need be in no hurry to repay him his expenses, on the contrary he would extend me credit to arrange another concert.

Linette came in the evening.

---

[1] Mikhail Fokine (1880–1942), the choreographer whose insistence on naturalism and symbolism had unlocked the aesthetics of dance from 'the currant smiles of the ballerinas ... and the vegetable obedience of the *corps de ballet*' (Osip Mandel'shtam, *The Egyptian Stamp*, translated by Clarence Brown, in *The Prose of Osip Mandel'shtam* (Princeton University Press, 1965), quoted in L. Garafola, *Diaghilev's Ballets Russes* (Da Capo Press, New York, 1998). Among Fokine's imperishable creations were *The Dying Swan*, a solo vehicle for Anna Pavlova, *Chopiniana/Les Sylphides*, and for the Ballets Russes *The Firebird*, *Petrushka*, *Le Spectre de la Rose* and *Schéhérezade*. Since 1912, except for a brief and uneasy return for Diaghilev's last pre-war season in 1914, he had parted from the Ballets Russes, displaced by Diaghilev's unconcealed idolisation of Fokine's new rival Nijinsky.

6 December

Went to a morning rehearsal of Stravinsky's *Pribaoutki*, which Janacopulos was rehearsing with an orchestra of eight players for its New York premiere. I remember Stravinsky playing it from his manuscript score in Milan in 1915 and liking it very much then. Now I listened to the rehearsal with great interest, and did as much as I could to help the orchestra players make sense of their parts. Much of it sounds marvellous.

On my return home I found two telegrams, one from Bolm stating that Johnson has announced the cancellation of my opera, and signing off with the irritable exclamation (in English): 'I am disgusted.' The other, rather more restrained, was from Volkov, saying that he was using all possible efforts to talk to the financial directors. Since I have given him all the pertinent information, I have some confidence in this discussion.

By evening my mood was rather sombre, and Linette took me off to the cinema in order to divert me.

7 December

Janacopulos has gone to Boston where she is appearing. Stahl was left on his own in Staten Island suffering from a cough. I spent a very nice day with him in casual conversation and walks around the island. I made a piano transcription of the scherzo from *Three Oranges* as one movement of the suite I plan to make from the opera; later perhaps I shall also make an orchestral version.

8 December

Came back to town, where I found a bulging packet of letters, each one more disagreeable than the other. Johnson and Kahn are announcing that the opera has to be postponed until next season. Having spoken to Haensel, who is more distressed than I about what has happened (my mood is one of anger and aggression), I questioned whether Johnson's decision to postpone until next season had taken sufficiently into consideration a careful reading of the contract. Haensel's opinion is that I should exert as much pressure on them as I possibly can, even retaining a lawyer, but not to go as far as court action, since it would not be an easy matter to determine the extent of my losses.

I wanted to see Linette this evening, but she was busy. So was Samoilenko. Because I was upset and could not settle to anything useful, I went to the cinema.

9 December

Wrote a long letter to Mama via Constantinople. I also finally got my score of *Three Oranges* back from the copyist. I read through it with love, but alas, surely it is not being put off until next season? It has been the fate of all my stage works to be cut down before the rise of the curtain (*Maddelena*, *The Gambler*, *Chout*, *Oranges*), and such also seems to be the fate of all my spring romances.

Linette came in the evening. It is a long time since anyone loved me as this dear girl seems to do.

10 December

Vera Janacopulos's concert this afternoon. She sang Stravinsky's *Pribaoutki*. I was deeply interested in the performance and also quite exercised: how would the work sound, and how would the public react to it? The first number sounded so peculiar that in the box where I was sitting with Stahl and Fokine, although we had all resolved in advance to clap and cheer, we looked at one another and no one applauded. The audience, however, got the measure of it before we did: the clapping soon began, mixed with laughter, and success was immediately assured. I applauded for all I was worth and called for encores, shouting so loudly that people turned to look at me.

In the Green Room afterwards everyone was asking me what about the opera, and when was I going to Chicago, and I did not know what to say to them.

After the concert I drank chocolate with Linette and then went home and wrote to Stravinsky.[1] I thought of Nina Meshcherskaya: she would be twenty-three now, but where was she? In Petrograd? Alive or dead? I have always thought that we would meet again, but she is far away from me.

11 December

A letter from Volkov. He had been to talk to Harold McCormick (not my McCormick but his brother, the Chicago Opera's main financial backer).[2] He did not seem to have made any use of the facts I laid out for him. Volkov's

---

1 'She treated [the songs] affectionately, and sang them excellently, except, perhaps, "Kornila" ("Uncle Armand") which is too low for her voice.' (From Prokofiev's letter to Stravinsky, 10 December 1919, quoted in S. Walsh, op. cit.) 'Kornila' is the first song in the set of four.
2 Harold Fowler McCormick (1872–1941) was the youngest son of Cyrus McCormick, the founder of the giant International Harvester Company and brother of Cyrus McCormick Jr, eldest son of Cyrus Sr and the man whom Prokofiev had met in Petrograd. Harold and his wife Edith Rockefeller were indeed the principal backers of the Chicago Opera.

letter said that 'they have decided to stage the opera next season'. What the devil is this 'decided'? They have forfeited all rights and the most they can do is propose; any decision will be made by me. McCormick said that concerning the financial question they will be 'very generous', and that sounds promising, but I take leave to doubt that they will remember their generous intentions when I ask them for $15,000.

Linette came this evening, and was very nice and uncomplicated.

12 December

Had a telephone conversation with Linette. She has a headache, but is generally in good spirits. We cannot meet today; she has to stay at home as her mother is starting to worry where she gets to all the time.

The collapse of *Three Oranges* has set me thinking about composing a new opera on *Fiery Angel*. I have read it through once again and am thinking about it. It could be a fascinating and powerful opera: it must express high drama and terror but avoid bringing any devils or apparitions on to the stage, otherwise it risks toppling over and collapsing into pure theatrical sham. Another difficulty is that the entire opera is centred around two main characters, and if they are never off stage all evening we will never find anyone prepared to undertake the roles. The scenario demands a great deal of very careful thinking.

13 December

Pondered the scenario of *Fiery Angel*, even though I am very far from deciding to embark on writing this opera. Linette again cannot come to me today, but tomorrow we shall go together to the Stahls.

This afternoon I worked on the Suite from *Three Oranges*. This section is the Conspiracy.

Spoke on the telephone to Blanche, whom I do not see very often, but it is always nice when I do. She says she has not heard from Stella for a whole month, and bearing in mind that a letter from London takes a month, that means at least two months must have passed since she last wrote. I have got used to the idea that Stella has not written a single word to me, and have come to the conclusion that this is a tactic of some kind.

14 December

Although it was raining, I met Linette on the pier at ten o'clock and we set off for the Stahls. And right on cue the weather soon improved, the sun came out and we had a marvellous day in the country. Stahl said: 'Look, with your

Fiery Angel you are going to create a scandal with the Church in Catholic countries.' I objected that *Fiery Angel* contains nothing impious, either in the concept or in the actions that will be seen on stage. I gave him the book to read so that he could study it in detail, and then give me his opinion.

In the evening I played through with Janacopulos around thirty of Rimsky-Korsakov's songs, each one feebler than the last. I cannot understand how the composer of *Sheherezade* and *Kitezh* could perpetrate such things!

Denikin has abandoned Kharkov and Poltava. For some reason I have not been following his activities, and today, when I learned this, I began to worry for Mama: suppose in a month or two the Bolshevik wave overwhelms even the Caucasus?

Will she have time to get away? The cheque was sent via London three weeks ago. She should get it within another month. All these thoughts kept me awake.

15 December

On my return I found a letter from Johnson, unacceptable in one way but in another acceptable. The unacceptable part was that it is out of the question for the opera to be produced this season. More acceptable was that he made no mention of their rights to produce it next season; on the contrary the entire letter consisted of an attempt to justify the opera company's position at the present time. I take this as an intimation that they will consider paying me compensation as a means to acquire the right to stage it next season.

16 December

My mood is middling. I cannot say that I am particularly crushed by the cancellation of *Three Oranges*, on the other hand it has to be admitted that my whole season has collapsed in ruins and gone to the devil. I am now in effect rudderless and have to wait for further negotiations with Chicago in order to have at least some financial resources to see me through next year. If I should fail in this, the net result of my eighteen months' striving in America will be nothing but debts.

My state of mind is much eased by the presence of dear Linette.

Linette is what I have long been seeking but up till now have not found. So I try to tell myself the following: you may not have the opera, but you do have Linette – take joy in her. Fretting over the opera will not bring it any nearer, but it will diminish your joy in Linette. She was with me for two hours today and was very loving.

17 December

On the advice of Stahl and Haensel I consulted a lawyer, Mr Purrington. Purrington mumbled and drivelled interminably, telling me exactly what I did not want to hear. His opinion was that if I institute a court action it was far from certain that I would win it. On the other hand, if the matter did come to court, the Chicago Opera would likewise have to calculate that they might lose. Since legal action could last up to two years, it would be in both sides' interest to come to an amicable settlement, i.e. to extend the agreement in return for financial compensation. He advised me to lay the most emphatic stress on the opera company's breach of contract and in consequence that they had forfeited their contractual rights, but to state my case calmly and to avoid at all costs falling out with them or going so far as actually to institute legal proceedings.

In the afternoon I pasted reviews into my scrapbook and jotted down some themes I have in mind for *Fiery Angel*.

In the evening I went to the cinema, which in my present volatile mood affords me the best relaxation.

18 December

Another meeting with the lawyer. He had drafted a long letter for me to send to Johnson, which I tore to shreds and completely rewrote from start to finish. This made the lawyer look at me with new respect, and when the letter had been retyped, he took me to lunch at the advocates' club.

The letter lays out the grounds of my claim for compensation. Clarification of all the circumstances will follow in a vital face-to-face conversation that will take place when I go to Chicago on 29 December for my recital.

19 December

My finger has still not completely cleared up and is beginning to hurt if I play too much, so I am trying not to overdo the playing. Little by little I am composing themes for various elements in *Fiery Angel*.

Had dinner with Linette.

20 December

A letter from Mama, eight pages, written on 27 September and filled with both love and despair. Mama is now almost blind. I am grievously distressed. All hopes now rest on her soon receiving my cheque for £100 and coming to America. I shall send her a telegram via the Russian Consulate in Constantinople. Maybe it will reach her.

In the afternoon I went to the Stahls. Today is Vera's birthday, but I was nervous and downcast.

21 December

Passed the day peacefully and quietly in the country. Vera – Stahl, Linette – me.

Campanini has died. This is a great loss to the Chicago Opera and also to me, because it is not clear which way the wind will now blow in that organisation. But I am more concerned with the question of Mama.

This evening Stahl and I discussed *Fiery Angel*. He proffered several fruitful thoughts, and we successfully planned out the opera in seven short acts. The concept of the opera is becoming more definite and tangible.

22 December

Sent Mama a telegram via the Consul. Ilyashenko[1] is going the day after tomorrow straight to Rostov, where Mama currently is. I must send some money with him for her. Although it will take him five weeks to get there, there may be a delay in the £100 cheque reaching her, and the Bolsheviks may get really close to Rostov, in which case somehow or other she will have to get away to Constantinople.

23 December

Scraped together my last remaining money (there's not much left) and bought a cheque for £40 for Constantinople (cheques for Russia are unobtainable). Ilyashenko came to see me in the evening; he loves my music very much. I played to him until I dropped, so that he would take the greatest care of my letter and cheque.

Bought a ticket to go to Chicago and took $100 for expenses. After paying for the apartment there are $80 remaining in the bank account. Not much. If the Chicago concert doesn't produce any profit, I'll have to borrow from Kucheryavy.

24 December

Practised the piano for Chicago. Lunched with Blanche, who, not having heard from Stella for over a month, is very annoyed with her. Some reports say that the theatre company is in trouble and will be coming back to America in January, but others say that everything is going very well for

---

1 Andrey Ilyashenko (1884–1954), a composer from St Petersburg of choral and liturgical music for the Russian Orthodox Church, known for his harmonisations of *znamenny* chant.

them and Stella is 'happy as a butterfly'. Well, so she may be. Although I always think of her with happiness, might I not be better concentrating more intently on Linette's gentle devotion? And when, that evening, Linette and I took the boat on our way to the Stahls to celebrate Christmas Eve and Christmas Day, my heart somehow felt more loving towards Linette knowing that over there Stella was 'as happy as a butterfly'. Linette has a new squirrel coat, in which she looks most becoming.

Where can Demchinsky be now? I spent three Christmas Eves with him.

25 December

Christmas. But the immediate news is not good: Denikin continues to retreat before the Bolsheviks. Will the money get to Mama before they get to Rostov? And will she ever manage to get away from Russia? Counting on my fingers, I believe the money will be with her within two weeks from today. If so, I should be all right, because the Bolsheviks are not likely to be able to capture Rostov before February. All morning I was in a state of anxiety, calmed only by walks with Linette around the island in the bright sunshine and white snow. The Stahls said goodbye to us early in the day, as they need to pack before going to Brazil. Linette and I went to the top of the Woolworth Building, where despite the hellish cold we had a beautiful view of the whole of New York. Linette then came home with me.

In the evening I went to the Ingermans, where a man who had recently been undercover in Petrograd told us what he had seen there. Petrograd is quiet, deserted, all the shop signs have been torn down. There are no cars, and very few horses. There are Chinese traders selling meat, some say human flesh. There is no sign of any of the intelligentsia: they have either dispersed or have perished. For those that are left all hope has fled, and no one can think of anything except food. The houses are ferociously guarded by building committees, who are on duty night and day. I do not regret the loss of my apartment, the only thing I mourn is the one thick notebook containing my Diary, which I left in the drawer of my desk.

And where are my friends? I asked our informant about B. Verin, as I knew that Bashkirov had charged him with finding out what he could about his family, but he had not managed to find out anything.

26 December

In the morning I collected together my things and left my apartment at 340 West 57th Street to start my journey to Chicago. I had lunch at the Pennsylvania Hotel with Linette, who was playing truant from her work. In her new grey fur coat she looks so nice, and I cannot think anyone has ever looked more loving. She saw me off on the 2.55 Broadway Limited to

Chicago. I looked out of the window at the grey and white winter scenery and thought about my forthcoming meeting with Johnson. I must avoid becoming irritated, must not be stubborn, must not get heated, must not pack the lot of them off to the devil, but coldly play my hand, probing their psychology while not letting them see mine.

My mood is reasonably equable, my chief solace being Linette and my chief source of worry Mama.

27 December

In Chicago N. T. Kucheryavy met me at the station with his car and took me to his home, where he is putting me up for as long as I have to stay in Chicago. This may be for several days or even as much as two weeks, depending on the negotiations with the Opera. The day passed uneventfully. Kucheryavy gave me something to eat and generally looked after me. In the evening he drove me to Kimball Hall so that I could practise on the piano I will be using tomorrow.

28 December

The concert was at half-past three. The little Kimball Hall was not full, but at least no complimentary tickets had been given away. My finger was still bandaged, but did not get in the way. I played *Carnaval* really well, also the Russian pieces and my Third Sonata. The success was very great, as in New York. I played four encores. In the Green Room were mostly compatriots: the Kucheryavys, the Volkovs, the Bolms, a lady who asked me if we did not perhaps have mutual Prokofiev relations. I told her I did not have any Prokofiev relations. Dinner at the Volkovs, attended also by Kahn. He said it was all to the good that my opera was not going to be produced. Since the moment I finally determined to my own satisfaction that he is a scoundrel, he has become in fact rather good company and amusing. Volkov whispered in my ear that he would try to arrange for me to meet H. MacCormick, who is a great gentleman and whose money is the main reason for the Chicago Opera's existence.

29 December

Today I had my meeting and talk with Johnson, who greeted me most courteously and said how sorry he was that the opera had had to be postponed until the following season. Bolm was also there when I arrived, but talked mainly about his own affairs. Once he had gone, Johnson went straight to the matter in hand: he had received my letter in which I raised the question of compensation, and asked me to put a figure on it. I answered as follows:

I had proposals for the opera to be produced at Covent Garden and at the Metropolitan, there was a promise from Bakst (which I inflated virtually to a production), in short if my opera were now to be produced with the success that all these people were predicting, we would probably now already be talking about a new opera rather than this one. However, if *Three Oranges* were not now to be produced, these offers would doubtless lapse, since no one would have any idea what the opera consists of.

From another point of view, I had lost all the concert engagements to the end of the season and for next season that could have been expected to flow from a highly successful production of the opera. If we were to put a figure of four opera contracts at no more than $10,000 and a year's concert activity at a further $10,000 (Johnson's eyelids did not flicker), this could be considered no more than a modest estimate. Needless to say, I was not claiming the whole of this sum in compensation, but I believed that I had every right to half of it, that is to say to $10,000. Further, were compensation of $10,000 thus to be agreed on this basis, I would be prepared to sign a new two-year contract for $5,000.

At this point Johnson swivelled round in his chair and his face grew dark, then red, and he said sharply: 'No, that is too much. It is most unlikely we shall be able to produce your opera under such conditions.' However he immediately collected himself, no doubt recalling that they had already spent $50,000 on the opera. I said that nevertheless these figures should not surprise him, since $5,000 for the contract was a sum they already knew about, while $5,000 for a year's lost concert activity was a modest estimate and if they tried to cut it down they would not only be diminishing the significance of their own production but my reputation as a pianist. Finally, $5,000 for four lost opera agreements, or if they wished so to argue three, or even two, was still only half or a quarter what they themselves were paying me under contract.

Finally, I could justify my figure of $15,000 from another direction: as things stand with the opera postponed for a year, I find myself in the position of having worked for the Chicago Opera for nothing. While there was nothing they could do to assuage the moral damage I had suffered, they were certainly in a position, indeed under obligation, to provide me with the wherewithal for a year's work as a composer. After paying $3,000 of debts I owed for publicity and medical bills, of the $15,000 I would have left $1,000 a month, $200 of which would go on publicity in order that America should not entirely forget about me, and $200 sent to my mother. The remaining $600 a month was the trifling sum we were discussing.

Johnson replied that he was not himself in a position to make the decision, but he would discuss the matter with Pam[1] and others, and let me

---

1 Max Pam, at the time Financial Director of the Chicago Opera.

know. As I took my leave I asked him to impress upon the directors that it was not my intention to extort money from them, merely to secure for myself the opportunity to work peacefully for a year.

I did not try to sum up for myself the result of the conversation, but I did take note of the significance of Johnson's not once having attempted to challenge my contention that they were in breach of the agreement.

The concert reviews were not lengthy, but they were all positive.

In the evening I went to the Bolms' recently staged ballet to music by the American composer Carpenter. It made me feel angry that pieces with music resembling yesterday's leftovers can get produced, while my opera, a truly contemporary work, is left on the shelf and the composer has to expend all his energy and resources on squeezing out a crust of bread (even if spread with a bit of butter).

30 December

At three o'clock Volkov and I went to see Harold McCormick, who received us in his office. Harold is one of the richest men in America. He is fifty years old, energetic, healthy, almost good-looking, well dressed and very courteous. He said he was very pleased to make my acquaintance, and that he was extremely interested in my opera. After a few minutes' general conversation he asked me if I had any particular questions for him. Since Volkov and I had agreed beforehand that our main tactic would be to make a good impression, arousing his interest and only hinting at our concerns, stopping short of any specific matters of business, I said that Johnson had told me the opera was to be postponed until next season, as a result of which I had asked Johnson for help in surviving for this year and thus being able to continue working. Since Johnson was not in a position to make a decision on his own authority but must account to him, McCormick, I was now taking the opportunity to ask him not to give Johnson too hard a time.

McCormick replied that everything would be done 'what is fair and square and just', and of course the opera was only being postponed, not cancelled altogether, and therefore I should not be demanding as much money as I would have received had it been produced. Expressing this in financial terms, I should not be asking for as much as the $2,500 due to me for the present season. Thus does the multi-millionaire McCormick, unaware of the arrow I have in my quiver in the shape of my injunction for the following season, make a great parade of offering me exactly one-sixth of what I want. Next, I described to him Anisfeld's settings, telling him America has never before seen anything like them, and as a parting shot said I hoped he would laugh a lot during the performance of my opera. 'Oh, is it a comic opera?' he asked. 'Yes, very much so,' I replied.

One interesting detail fleetingly appeared during our conversation: it seems that before my arrival in America Cyrus McCormick had mentioned to Campanini the existence of my opera *The Gambler*, and Campanini had without any discussion simply invited me sign a contract. So that Harold, as chairman of the board, had been left no option but to confirm the fact of an agreement with me.

In the evening I went to hear three new operas by Puccini.[1] The music is pretty empty, sometimes pleasant, sometimes bad, but the way he uses the stage is masterly, although not irreproachably so. However this may be, there were things to enjoy in the evening, unlike yesterday's ballet.

31 December

Apparently I can expect an answer from Johnson in about three days. I spent the day quietly at home, composing themes for *Fiery Angel* and playing some Scriabin pieces I found at the Volkovs.

We did not properly see in the New Year: at around eleven I went with Kuchyeravy to some terrible show or other, where at midnight the Americans set up a deafening whistling racket, which rather pleased me. Then we went home, clinked glasses of port, and went to bed.

---

[1] *Il Trittico*: *Gianni Schicchi*; *Suor Angelica*; *Tabarro*, the premiere of which had taken place in Rome in January 1919.

1920

1 January

The first day of the New Year brought no better news from Russia than had the first day of Christmas: Rostov is being evacuated because of the escalating Bolshevik assault on the city. What of Mama? Is she in Rostov? Or has she already found her way to Novorossiisk? I am sure she will not yet have received the cheque for £100; it is most probably still *en route* between London and Russia. But at least she has a visa, and 29,000 roubles as well. Surely she will decide to get to Constantinople and contact me from there? I was seized with anxiety all day long, and cabled the Russian Embassy in Constantinople asking them to let her know that the cheque had already been sent to her there.

In the evening was again at *Pelléas*, and once again fell under its spell. The most astonishing work! The music, elusive as it is, catches you as if in a web.

2 January

The Bolsheviks are taking town after town and forcing their way south. Rostov will fall in a matter of a day or two, but I have a feeling Mama is already in Novorossiisk. My state of mind is terrible. I started another read-through of *Fiery Angel*, thinking out the first act, and managed to lose myself a little in it, worked until fatigue set in and all but finished the libretto for the whole of the first act. Now I need to go through it again line by line and fill in a few blanks.

In between I play Scriabin, some albums Mme Volkova gave me. The F sharp minor Prelude from Op. 74 fits my mood at the moment.

3 January

Today being the sixth day since I last heard from Johnson, I rang him up. He told me that they had not yet come to a decision, but he would try to get everything clarified by Monday, when he would ask me to come back for further discussions. Kucheryavy's view is that they have refined a sophisticated delaying system designed to wear me down so that I lose heart, and the delay could go on not for days but for months.

In the evening played bridge with Volkov and Baklanov,[1] and enjoyed it.

4 January

Another day of quiet and calm. I thought out and made some notes for the libretto of Act Two, and made a start on composing themes. Am learning Scriabin.

As the Bolsheviks get nearer to the Black Sea ports they have opened negotiations with the Italians for trade relations. A representative of the Soviet Government has already set up shop in Italy. If I conclude my business with the Chicago Opera and discover that Mama has not succeeded in getting away from the Bolsheviks, perhaps I should go to Italy and try to get in touch with her from there, and most importantly of all, get some money to her.

5 January

Rang Johnson repeatedly all day and could not get hold of him. Kucheryavy repeated his theory of the delaying tactic. In the evening I went to the premiere of Ravel's *L'heure espagnole* and ran Johnson to earth in his office. He asked me to come to see him tomorrow at three o'clock.

L'heure espagnole is typical Ravel: diffuse, liquescent, elegant, wonderful-sounding, often very witty. The subject is frivolous, insipid, and in choosing it as a subject Ravel sometimes miscalculates: in places he is too slow and lags behind the jokes; and elsewhere, when he pastiches banality, he can produce, if you like, too elegant a banality, and this one should not do.

But in general Ravel's music is beautiful, and of course on second hearing I was able appreciate much that had slipped past unnoticed the first time.

6 January

My meeting with Johnson took place at three o'clock. Volkov was also present, as he had been to see Johnson earlier and Johnson had asked him to stay. Our discussion was conducted in a friendly and low-key manner. Johnson again complained that I was asking more than they could afford to pay, while for my part I again enumerated my demands, laying stress on their modesty.

Johnson then proceeded to counter my points one by one. He said he could not understand why I was asking $5,000 for a new contract; after all I

---

1 Georgy Baklanov (1880–1938), a baritone at the Chicago Opera. He would become a close friend of Prokofiev when *The Love for Three Oranges* was eventually produced the following year. See below, p. 583 n. 1.

had already been paid $4,000 for the opera commission, and the second year of the original contract would have yielded only another $1,000. Therefore, he argued, a new two-year contract should be paid at the rate of $1,000 for each year. I replied that when Campanini had commissioned the opera he had agreed that I would receive $5,000 for ten performances, that is to say $2,500 a year, but as $2,500 would not be sufficient to live on for a whole year I would receive $4,000 in the first year and $1,000 in the second.

Johnson then switched his attack to the second $5,000, the sum I was demanding for the loss of the opera agreements in Europe. He said: all right, you are asking for $5,000, but these engagements may in the meantime very well come to pass. I said that yes, they might, but there can be no doubt that the financial compensation offered would be three times less than if I was in a position to negotiate them after a successful production of *Three Oranges*.

Next, Johnson opposed the third $5,000 that I was claiming in respect of the lost income from a concert season: how could I justify this amount? I answered that it was true I might not be able to produce specific figures to support the claim, and I accepted that the six engagements offered to my manager and then withdrawn because I was unable to offer a classical programme were outside the equation. However, to cite the example of Novaes,[1] I knew that her earnings from fees amount to $18,000 a year. Popular artist though she undoubtedly is, I considered that by comparison $5,000 is extremely modest, less than $1,000 a month over the season.

Thus rebuffed on all three points, Johnson sat for a long time in thought, covering his eyes with his hand. He made no counter-proposals, however, and said that since any decision would have to be ratified by Max Pam, who would be returning on Friday, it would better to postpone further discussion until then, when we could have a three-way negotiation. I asked if he thought at that time we would be able to come to a final resolution one way or another? He said: 'Oh yes, without question.'

On that note we parted, with reasonable expectation on my side that there would be a satisfactory outcome.

7 January

Today and tomorrow are again going to be days of leisurely inactivity, and I would relax were it not for thoughts of Mama constantly on my mind. I finally received a letter from Linette, simple and loving. I very much want to

---

1 Guiomar Novaes (1886–1979), legendary Brazilian pianist with a particular reputation in Schumann, Chopin and Debussy. In 1899 at the age of thirteen, before a panel consisting of Fauré, Debussy and Moszkowski, she had taken first place in a field of 388 pianists auditioning for acceptance to the Paris Conservatoire. She made her American debut in New York's Aeolian Hall in 1913 and toured the United States almost every season for the next fifty-seven years.

see her, but it would be wrong to hurry unduly the business with the Chicago Opera: it is the point of departure for the whole of 1920.

8 January

Composed some themes, played the piano, wrote my diary, stayed at home.

9 January

Johnson informed me that Pam had been delayed and would be arriving back tomorrow, not today. More delay. I had calculated that if we met today we would be able to sign the contract tomorrow, and the day after, Sunday, I would be able to leave to be by Monday in the arms of Linette. But now, obviously, it is going to drag on until next week.

In the evening Gottlieb, a very nice young man who dances attendance on me all the time, took me to the Cosmopolitan Club at Chicago University, which had arranged a reception in my honour. The Club has tiny premises of three small rooms, and its members are a mixture of male and female students and professors, about a hundred altogether. I was at one end of the room, flanked on my right by the President, a delightful Mexican, and on my left by Madame President, a young blonde. All present then paraded past, being presented to me by the President, then shaking my hand and bidding me welcome. It was the most fantastic parade I have ever witnessed, consisting of people of all ages, sizes, nationalities and colours – yellow, brown, pink, pale-white, Chinese, Filipinos, Panamanians, Spaniards, Jews, Armenians, Finns, and many others. Some of them proffered handshakes as stiff as a board, others squeezed my fingers in a vice-like grip, the Japanese bowed several times and tittered obligingly. I enjoyed it all immensely and responded with pleasure to the greetings in all forty languages.

Then, of course I had to play, my performance being met with deafening applause, and then someone sang, and a professor made a short speech in honour of me and of Russian art. In the ensuing general conversation I tried to flirt with a pretty Armenian girl, but so many people were besieging me on all sides that I soon lost track of her. Gottlieb then drove me home.

10 January

Spent the whole day by the telephone waiting for news about the meeting with Pam. I myself rang several times, but Johnson had disappeared as if under water. By evening my patience had run out, so I went to the theatre to find him. On the way I reminded myself not to get angry and recalled the lawyer's advice: 'Whatever happens, keep your temper; let the others lose theirs.' I found Johnson and spoke to him politely enough. Shortly thereafter Pam himself appeared: he had genuinely come back only that evening. Pam (a small man with a little beard and a paunch) looked me over with angry eyes, doubtless on account of the $15,000. We set a meeting for the day after tomorrow at noon.

11 January

Another quiet, long-drawn-out day. I worked on the libretto for Act Two. In the evening Professor Novakovsky[1] talked about how the Bolshevik invasion of the Caucasus had been greatly exaggerated. Although I do not have any particular faith in the truth of what he says, it is comforting to lull oneself with the thought that Mama may be spared some of the horrors awaiting her. Perhaps the Bolsheviks will not be able to spread over the whole of the Caucasus?

12 January

Noon was the appointed hour for the final confrontation about *Three Oranges*. As I was half an hour early, I went for a walk along Michigan Avenue, where in a shop window I spotted a marvellous suitcase in a special kind of leather, with which I decided to celebrate the new contract and the receipt of my 'annual pension', assuming such was the result.

When on the dot of noon I presented myself at the office, I had to wait as Pam was still engaged in a preliminary discussion with Johnson. At half-past twelve I was invited into his office, and our tripartite meeting lasted two-and-a-half hours.

It began with a long peroration from Pam. He gave me the works: the educational importance of the Chicago Opera, the losses they were sustaining, the wonderful possibilities opening up before me, their unstinting efforts to present my opera in the best possible way, the risk they were taking in accepting an unknown work, the fact that whereas they could in theory have included it in the present season they would not have been able to do so to a satisfactory standard. But that was just what they would do in the future, hence their wisdom in deciding to postpone the production had been greatly to my advantage. To sum up, although they would be within their rights presenting five performances next season at a fee of $200 a performance, in the circumstances they are willing to offer eight performances at $250.

I listened patiently, nodding my head meekly as if to indicate how grateful

---

[1] S. J. Novakovsky was a distinguished economic geographer with a special interest in Siberian fisheries.

and appreciative I was at their attitude, until finally we arrived at their miserable proposition, presented with all the portentous solemnity he could muster. At this point I could contain myself no longer and the corners of my mouth twitched with barely suppressed laughter. Pam, who had become convinced during his twenty-minute disquisition that he had persuaded me to his point of view, suddenly realised that he was entirely mistaken and dried up like a clam. I proceeded to outline my objection to each of his points, concentrating my fire on precisely those reasons why, and how, they should have produced the opera in the present season (arguments Pam and Johnson did not accept), and wound up by saying that of course there was no question of accepting their proposal, that as I had already explained to Johnson and would once again go through with them, I had suffered substantial losses and demanded compensation in the order of $10,000.

Pam lost his temper, red patches appeared on his face, and from that moment on behaved unreasonably and discourteously. Johnson, by contrast, said very little and retired into the background. Throughout the two-and-a-half hours of the talks I preserved an impeccably polite demeanour.

'If you decline the two thousand we are offering you, then you shall not have it,' said Pam, jabbing the table with his finger. 'You shall not have it. We will produce the opera without your consent and pay you the one thousand as per the contract.'

I objected that from the moment they had failed to fulfil the contract in the one particular that was of prime importance to me, the agreement was null and void.

'Our inability to fulfil the contract was the result of circumstances beyond our control, and American law takes that into consideration,' retorted Pam.

I said that despite this, I was sure that the law would allow me the right to prevent the opera being performed.

'It will be performed,' raged Pam, 'and you will not receive so much as one cent of your ten thousand!'

From this point the conversation, which lasted another hour and a half, entered into the realms of complete pointlessness because, as Johnson at one point cautiously observed, we were not speaking the same language. 'All your arguments lead to the same point,' Pam exploded. 'Shall I show you what that point is?' And he snatched up a piece of paper, wrote on it $10,000, and broke the pencil in half. 'Nobody had any idea you were going to write music like that!' he shouted.

I replied that they were perfectly well aware of what sort of music I composed, since Campanini had attended a performance of the *Scythian Suite*, which is far more complicated than *Three Oranges*, and as for the complexity of the stage action, that is down to Gozzi, whose play they themselves had chosen as the subject for the opera they had commissioned from me.

Eventually it became clear that there was no purpose in prolonging the discussion. I said goodbye politely to Johnson, but added to Pam that I regretted his rudeness to me.

Victory or defeat? Defeat. All evening I was heartsick, as the denouement was not the one I had expected. But in the final analysis, how much does it matter? Not very much, because even if this production does not happen I have still composed a good opera.

13 January

My mood is more fighting than cowed. In the near future I still have two or three weeks of concerts that will bring me in $1,200, which will be enough to live on for three months provided I do not have to pay off my outstanding debts. Kucheryavy is convinced that yesterday's conversation was no more than a bluff intended to throw dust in my eyes, and that it will not be long before some roundabout way will be found for the Chicago Opera to make me a fresh proposal. I also cannot see why they should wish to kick against the pricks, since both the lawyer and Stahl are in agreement that I do have the right to block the production next season if I choose.

At 12.40 p.m., accompanied to the station by the Consul and Nikolay Titovich, I left for New York on the Broadway Limited.

14 January

Arrived next morning in New York, which despite the hideous cold appeared very pleasant compared to Chicago. Had lunch with Linette, and when her work was over for the day she came to my place and spent all evening there. This was our first proper evening of love.

In the afternoon I went to Kreisler's concert. This season his success has eclipsed that of all other violinists. He played well, including in among the dross some good music. That's a great artist for you! For shame!

Bolm says that there is a powerful group working hard to sow a few mines in Max Pam's path. I'm not sure how much I believe this, but it is nice to hear.

15 January

Was at Duo Art. They have agreed that instead of waiting until 1921 I can record five new rolls for them now. This will net me $1,250, which means I will have altogether $2,500, and then something can get moving.

Spent the evening with Samoilenko. Fatma Hanum is distraught because her father has died in Moscow. Not long ago she had good news of him, but it now transpires that he died three months ago. I told her about my Mama, and we shared our grief at the events. Boris Nikolayevich[1] says that many of Denikin's troops with their generals have gone over the Bolsheviks, and that generally all the best Russian generals are now fighting on the Bolshevik side. Things are happening of which we know nothing here.

16 January

Had lunch with Linette and asked her to come back with me, but she has not yet recovered enough to do that. In the evening Sklyarevsky came to see me. He has just arrived in New York after a long tour of China, the Philippines and Java. He saw many fascinating sights, had some success and amassed some money, not a huge amount but several thousand dollars. He is now going to try his luck here.

17 January

Finished the libretto of Act Two. I went to *Blue Bird*, an opera by the undistinguished French composer Wolff.[2] I did my best not to listen to the music in order not to spoil my impression of Anisfeld's scenery, which was fabulous, with gorgeously rich colours and not without a touch of the grotesque in the design.

That evening I discussed with Samoilenko an outline for *Fiery Angel*. We came to an important conclusion: the sixth scene (with Count Wellen in the castle) is superfluous. I decided to eliminate it, leaving an opera of six scenes rather than seven.

In Paris they have decided on a partial lifting of the blockade of Russia. Events are assuming a new direction.

18 January

I took part in a kind of afternoon concert at the Manhattan Theater,[3] for which I was paid $250. It was not until after I had performed that I learned the concert had been organised by local Bolsheviks. I laughed and said that I would probably be arrested the next day and deported to Russia. My First Sonata and some pieces by other composers were a success.

1 Samoilenko. Fatma Hanum was his Azerbaijani wife.
2 Albert Wolff (1884–1970) was actually Dutch, although born in Paris, and for most of his career was identified with French music and French institutions including the Opéra Comique (whose Music Director he eventually became), the Théâtre des Champs-Elysées and the Orchestre Lamoureux. The exception was the 1919–20 and 1920–21 seasons at the Metropolitan Opera in New York, where he was brought in to replace Pierre Monteux as head of the French repertoire. His opera *The Blue Bird*, based on the play by Maeterlinck with designs by Boris Anisfeld, was premiered on 27 December 1919 and subsequently performed seven more times.
3 Presumably the Manhattan Opera House on 34th Street owned by Oscar Hammerstein I.

I dined at Linette's, to be precise at her mother's, as Linette likes me to put in an appearance there from time to time. After dinner I took Linette to the cinema, at least that is what we said we were going to do, but in fact she came home with me. She was very loving with me, but still inclined to be terribly touchy.

19 January

I went to see the Russian Consul about a visa for Canada, where I have to go to give concerts, and also to find out if there was any news of the money I have sent to Mama. He said he had no news of this, but commercial links have now been established between the Allies and the Bolsheviks. This is a significant development, and even if Mama is in a Bolshevik-controlled zone, I should probably soon be able to make contact with her.

20 January

Began composing *Fiery Angel* and wrote a page of the scene between Rupprecht and the Landlady. A rough outline of the scene had been in my head since Chicago.

Haensel has got me an engagement to appear with the Philharmonic Orchestra. Since they did not want my Concerto at any price, I chose Rimsky-Korsakov's, which is completely unknown here. The concert is in three weeks' time, so I must get down to practising in order to learn it.

In the evening I played bridge, a serious session that went on late. I won $16.

21 January

Continued *Fiery Angel* and learned the Rimsky-Korsakov Concerto. Evening with Linette.

22 January

A letter from Otto Kahn in response to mine. He would be happy for my opera to be at the Metropolitan Opera. Unfortunately he is leaving for Europe, but he has had a talk with Gatti and Gatti would like to see the libretto of *Fiery Angel*. It is the kind of letter that is too strong to be merely the form of politesse for which Kahn is famous. Naturally, if it were left to Gatti to take a decision independently my opera would no doubt be strangled at birth, but if before he leaves Kahn were to tell them to put it on, it would be in the bag. For all that at the present time I am resisting the temptation to build too many seductive castles in the air, it is still a pleasant feeling.

A little baron, recently arrived from Palestine, passes on greetings from Stella, whom he saw when passing through London. That produced a nice feeling too. Blanche is hoping that she will be coming back to America in January. But I am not telephoning Blanche.

23 January

The influenza has again been building up quite a head of steam: yesterday there were a thousand cases in New York. Of course, I am frightened. To live in a city in the grip of an epidemic is like waiting to be shot in the back. But the epidemic this year is not as virulent as last year, and the mortality rate is lower.

A letter from Coates in London. He is now a huge star in England, but his letter is quite enchanting. He is very interested in *Three Oranges*, and even though he cannot guarantee that it can be produced in London this June he regards it as a certainty for next season. Yes, I must definitely go to London in April.

Dined with Linette, after which she came to the station to see me off. She was very loving, and sad that I was leaving her for five days. At 7.45 I got on the train and left for Montreal.

24 January

Early-morning Montreal, frost, sun and blinding snow, so deep that it got into my shoes when I crossed the street. I stayed with the Fortiers, very nice people whom I had met through Stahl. They have a lot of music by Scriabin and Medtner which I much enjoyed playing through. The shops are selling Belyayev editions printed in Leipzig, but the price of the Rimsky-Korsakov Concerto, instead of the one rouble it used to be, is five dollars because there is a 400 per cent customs tariff on imports from Germany.

The influenza epidemic in New York is growing: there are already 1,400 cases. The epidemic has not reached Montreal, and the air is so pure one would think it never could. Should I stay here until New York comes back to health? There is no sense in going to an infected city unless one has to. But I want to see Linette. Also, while the iron is hot, I should start talking to Gatti.

25 January

The Fortiers put boots on my feet, a warm hat on my head, wrapped a muffler round my throat, and drove me to the concert hall. The trams scudding along the streets have posters on the front of them saying: 'His Majesty – Prokofieff'. His Majesty's is the name of the theatre where I am to play.

The theatre is quite large, and a pleasant environment, but there was not a very big audience, less than half full. The piano was excellent and the audience listened attentively. This time I played without a bandage on my finger. It was a great success and I was called back three or four times after each group of pieces, but I played only one encore at the end. I had expected Scriabin to go down better in Montreal than anywhere else, but it was not as much liked as Rachmaninoff, Musorgsky and my own works. There was a reception after the concert at the Fortiers: congregated in their drawing-room were the artistically progressive elite, many of whom greeted me with adulation. There were a few interesting men but no attractive single women.

26 January

The critics, in both English and French, varied between positive and very good. In the morning I learned the Korsakov, and at five o'clock was seen off by the Fortiers to Quebec, five hours away. They introduced me to some French Canadians in my carriage, who stood me dinner and criticised the cultural environment in America (the United States, that is), which they stigmatised as mechanical and empty. I immediately had the feeling that I had landed in an entirely different environment and atmosphere. Quebec has sleighs with furry coverings overhead, hung with little bells and pulled by mettlesome horses. It is three years since I had seen a proper sleigh and the sight gladdened my eyes. The town has steeply rising streets, old buildings and the language is French – Quebec is the oldest and most French of all Canadian cities. The hotel was excellent, it looked from the outside like a castle and had a marvellous view of the river. My manager here and his *associé*, cheerful characters who are evidently fond of a drink, took me off for a whisky, after which I walked round the sleeping town and went to bed.

27 January

Next morning I tried the piano and in the afternoon took advantage of the sunshine to go for a drive round the town in a sleigh, well wrapped up in a fur rug. In the evening I played my concert in the Columbus Hall, a modest-sized auditorium seating some seven hundred. It was not full, but there were enough people. The programme was the same as in Montreal, and the success comparable, or perhaps a little warmer. I played four encores, some of them within the programme, which I do not usually like to do at all, but on this occasion acceded to the requests of my manager.

Influenza cases in New York have risen to 3,000; there is a slow but steady rate of increase, not really all that slow in fact. Clearly I should stay on here in Quebec for a day or two longer, until I see what is happening with the epidemic. In any case I like the city very much. Linette will be disappointed at my delayed return, and my desire to see her is no less, but it will only be a matter of a few days.

28 January

The reviews are not just good, they are naively ecstatic. The manager brought me $500 instead of $600 telling me I would have to take a cut in fee because he had lost money on me in Montreal. There did not seem much future in discussing the point, as he also told me he had no more money in any case. Let Haensel fight with him for the other $100.

In the afternoon one of my travelling companions from the train took me to a session of the local parliament, where the proceedings were conducted in a decorously peaceful, even somnolent fashion. I was presented to the President, M. Francœur, who entertained me to whisky, and I played some pieces for the benefit of a few Members of Parliament. In the evening the Viceroy's[1] ADC asked if he might bring some ladies and gentlemen into my room to listen to me play. So many came that all the tables and chairs and even the bed had to be commandeered for them to sit on. Among those present was a slim, elegant woman who, as I was later informed had the rare distinction of having danced several times with the Prince of Wales, heir to the throne of England, during his visit here last autumn. He had been so taken with her that he invited her to accompany him to Montreal and other cities for more dancing and flirtatious exchanges. Unintentionally my style seems to have surpassed that of the Prince: he had to make arrangements for her to travel to other towns to see him, whereas here she was sitting on my bed and I hardly even noticed her.

29 January

Learned the Rimsky-Korsakov Concerto. Thought out Renata's lamentation scene while Rupprecht sleeps. In the afternoon I was taken out to tea somewhere and in the evening Major Peltier (the Viceroy's ADC) invited me to a ball that was taking place in my hotel. I did not dance, as I don't know any American dances, but girls kept running up to me and asking for my autograph. I failed to recognise the 'Canadian Princess' (as my fair lady of yesterday is known locally) but she smiled and nodded to me first. Evidently, however, she charges a lot for her smiles, because when I approached her to atone for my social gaffe, she disappeared. Elegant she certainly is, but not particularly beautiful, and she has a disagreeable voice. Perhaps she managed to make it sound charming to the Prince's ears.

---

1 The Canadian Governor General at the time was the Duke of Devonshire.

The influenza in New York has risen to 5,000 cases, which is as high as the level it reached last year, although the proportion of mortalities is considerably lower. Yesterday, when we were visiting the President of the Parliament, he emerged from the next room where he had been speaking on the telephone, to say: 'I have just been given some bad news: there are five hundred cases of influenza in Montreal.' But today's papers report nothing of the kind, and it seems that the President was merely making a pleasantry to keep me longer in Quebec.

30 January

Since I have now spent long enough in Quebec and the Fortiers were ringing up from Montreal to ask me to go back to them, I took a convenient train and arrived there at six o'clock in the evening, to a cordial welcome from the hospitable Fortiers.

31 January

It is horribly cold, 28° Celsius below freezing. Practised the Rimsky-Korsakov Concerto and went through some Scriabin pieces. Guests came for the evening, some very nice and cultivated Canadians.

Tomorrow I must go back to New York, because on Monday I have to record for Duo Art, and in the evening the Bohemian Club is organising a reception for the first performance of my *Overture on Hebrew Themes*. The afternoon is reserved for Linette, and in the evening, after the reception, I leave infected New York for Buffalo for my concert there. Coincidentally, some cases of 'flu have occurred in Montreal.

1 February

A concert by Cortot in the afternoon, the King of French pianists as he is announced here. He played the *Twelve Préludes* of Debussy. Many of them are beautiful and elegant, but many are also watery, oh so watery! At eight o'clock in the evening, accompanied by Mr and Mrs Fortier, who have quite fallen in love with me, I departed for New York, quite convinced that I was leaving pure air for a bacterial stew. However, I comforted myself with the following calculation: every day slightly more than two hundred people die, that is one-thirty-thousandth of the population. Therefore if I spend one day there (and that is all I am going to do), I have a one-in-thirty-thousand chance of dying from being munched by microbes. Which seems a low probability ratio.

2 February

Arrived in New York at nine o'clock next morning, the city as usual wearing an air of vibrant and comfortable prosperity. And very warm by comparison with Montreal. I hardly had time to get myself sorted out before I had to go to the Aeolian Hall for a noon recital for Duo Art, designed to showcase their instrument and the artist performing on it. I played a few pieces and then the Rachmaninoff Prelude on a concert grand piano equipped with the Duo Art mechanism. When the audience, which had greeted me very warmly, applauded, instead of an encore I turned on the device on to which had already been loaded the same Prelude, in the performance I had recorded the previous spring, and the piano played the piece while I sat at the keyboard with my arms folded. Not bad at all, really pretty good, although of course it is not the same thing. The audience was delighted, and I had no objection to receiving $250. God knows it is not a fortune, but it is money all the same.

Linette came at five o'clock, and we had a joyous and tenderly loving reunion. But it had to be cut short at seven o'clock for dinner, farewells, packing, dressing up in tails, before being taken by one Fonaryov to the Bohemian Club, the musicians' society that was giving the reception for the first performance of the *Overture on Hebrew Themes*. It was a members-only event, not open to the public, and there were about eighty people present, who gave me an ovation when I entered.

Our Zimro Ensemble then played the Brahms Clarinet Quintet, serious and boring music, a set of Variations by Gnessin, ditto, and my *Overture*. This sounded most attractive, occasionally a little strident (for the information of future performers, the clarinet should not force the tone and the piano should not be too percussive) that as an antidote to the inertness of the preceding corpses its freshness and vigour brought the audience back to life and provoked thunderous applause. The *Overture* had to be repeated, and I followed it with a performance of the Third Sonata.

It was on this occasion that I met the pianist Moiseiwitsch,[1] who has performed many times and with great success in England. He told me that I already have a big reputation in England, and advised me to go there soon. I do indeed plan to do that, and it was a pleasant observation to hear, as it were *en passant*. At half-past eleven, still in my tails, I boarded the train for Buffalo.

---

1 Benno Moiseiwitsch (1890–1963), Odessa-born pianist, had studied with Leschetitsky in Vienna. He was especially admired by Rachmaninoff, who referred to him as his 'spiritual heir'. Moiseiwitsch eventually settled in London and took British citizenship in 1937.

3 February

Buffalo, eponymous city of the animal, at 11 a.m. A large, dirty and boring-looking city.

It was warm, the grey snow already melting. The hotel was very good, but there is not a single announcement in any of the papers of today's concert. As I did not know the name of the hall in which I was due to play and could not find the local manager's name anywhere in the telephone directory, I found myself in an idiotic situation. Putting off until tomorrow a trip to Niagara, which is about an hour away by train or tram, I walked up and down the streets in the hope of seeing a poster about myself. Instead, I happened on a music shop selling tickets for my concert, and in that way solved the problem.

The concert took place in the evening in a huge hall seating four thousand, and was reasonably well filled, but the manager had distributed piles of cheap tickets around the colleges and schools so the audience consisted almost entirely of young people who were hearing an unknown pianist playing unfamiliar music that they clearly did not, for the most part, understand, and consequently did not know what to do, whether to applaud or not. I had the impression that they were a very reserved audience, although at the end of the recital there was quite a warm response, and after Rachmaninoff's Prelude and my *Suggestion Diabolique* I had to play encores.

I was also exercised as to whether I was going to get my fee or not, since Haensel had warned me that the manager was in the habit of not paying the full amount, and therefore I should not go on to the platform until I had got my $300 in my hand. However, just before the start, he brought me $200 and at the end a further $25 (in silver!) and promised to give me the balance tomorrow.

A dozen or so schoolgirls piled into the Green Room afterwards, almost every one of them wearing spectacles, and I had to sign my name on their programmes.

4 February

Spent the morning thinking out the libretto for the third act and wrote some of it out.

The concert manager brought another $25 and an IOU for the remaining $50, which he will give me tomorrow or send. Apparently the total receipts were no more than $230, but the reviews, comparing me with the French pianist Cortot, who was appearing simultaneously in another hall, awarded the palm to me.

As the number of influenza victims, which had dropped to less than 3,000, had now soared again, I decided to take a day off and go to Niagara. I took my suitcase and went there by tram. Spurning the services of the guides, who I was sure would bore on relentlessly about the volume of falling water expressed in cubic feet, I decided to view the Falls independently and as a first step bought a map of the locality. But it was windy and very cold, so I took a saloon car and spent two hours touring round all the main sights. When we approached the Falls from the side, a fantastic picture opened up before my eyes, and for a while I could not orientate myself at all, because Niagara was encased in massive snowdrifts, entire mountains of frozen spray and fields of broken, lumpy ice extending right to the Falls and beyond. In the midst of this icy kingdom the water seethed and boiled, now disappearing into the frozen abyss, now bursting out from underneath the ice. We circled round both Falls, the American and Canadian sides, then I descended to the bottom. The scenery was interesting, sometimes majestic and sometimes merely picturesque. Smoking factory chimneys blacken the sky, but the industrial area is all squeezed up together off to one side. The most exciting thing to do, apparently, is to go behind the waterfall, but this is impossible in winter because of the ice: on either side the water is simply arrested in mid-descent, frozen into gigantic icicles like the iced-up moustaches of an *izvozchik*[1] driver.

Chilled to the marrow, I returned home. I tried to carry on with the libretto of Act Three, but it would not flow. I was in a rather agitated frame of mind, thinking of Mama, disturbed by the influenza, annoyed by the Chicago Opera. I decided to kill time in the evening by going to the cinema – good therapy for the nerves.

5 February

A better mood, and the weather is warmer. I walked round Niagara on foot, looking at it from every viewpoint. After that I went a long way out on the tram line that has been especially extended along the river bank below the Falls.

Worked on the Act Three libretto. In the evening I went back to New York.

6 February

Because of unusually heavy snow falls, the train was twelve hours late getting to New York. Instead of eight o'clock in the morning it was eight o'clock at night by the time we got there. The morning was a wash-out because until noon we were without a restaurant car on the train and had to sit there famished. Later on I worked on the libretto and achieved a lot: finished Act Three, and tidied up and wrote out some of Act One.

---

1 Horse-drawn cab.

In New York I found a telegram from Constantinople: Mama's visa has arrived and been forwarded to her by the British Consul. But this does not get me any further forward: what I need to know is, has she received the cheque and where is she, in Rostov, with the Bolsheviks, or in Novorossiisk, safely away from them?

7 February

I have an appointment with Gatti-Casazza on Monday at five o'clock. It will be very interesting to see what comes of it.

Lunched with Ingerman, who applied ointment to my throat infection. Schindler showed me the programme for a recital the Spanish pianist Viñes[1] had given two years ago in Madrid, which included my *Sarcasms*. The programme book included four pages of commentary about me and about *Sarcasms*, stating among other things that he had previously played them in Paris, where they had created a sensation. I was very interested and pleased by this: I did not know that my music had been played in those two capitals.

Linette came at four o'clock and stayed until nine. Today she was somewhat agitated and ill at ease, but later cheered up and did not want to go home.

8 February

Learnt the Rimsky-Korsakov Concerto, which is beginning to go well, but I am having trouble with my finger (another one), which I have managed to cut, an classic achievement for a pianist just before a concert.

Arthur Rubinstein, after spending some time in Europe, has returned to America for a concert consisting exclusively of new music, including Szymanowski's Second Sonata. There are interesting moments in the Sonata's Variations, but as a whole the words of Rimsky-Korsakov (junior) came irresistibly to mind: 'an adjective, rather than a noun substantive'.[2]

After the concert there was a big tea-party at Liebman's. There I made the acquaintance of Hofmann,[3] an exceptionally nice and gentle man whose

---

1. Ricardo Viñes (1875–1943), Spanish pianist. Viñes, a man of exceptionally wide culture, was a close friend and fellow student of Ravel and a significant influence on him especially in the provision of literary inspirations. He gave the first performances of *Jeux d'eaux*, *Miroirs* (*Oiseaux tristes* is dedicated to him, according to Ravel because it amused him to dedicate to such a good pianist a piece that was not all pianistic), and of *Gaspard de la nuit*.
2. See above, p. 109. The jibe was actually Julia Weisberg's, with a gloss added by A. Rimsky-Korsakov.
3. Josef Hofmann (1876–1957), Polish pianist who studied with Moszkowski and Anton Rubinstein, and along with Rachmaninoff and Godowsky was one of the most celebrated virtuoso pianists of the early twentieth century. Asked by a Green Room admirer how, with hands as small as his, he could possibly have acquired keyboard control of such consummate power,

Russian is extremely good. Played bridge with Bodanzky,[1] one of the most important conductors in New York today. He used to detest my music, but for some reason was very friendly today, complimenting me on the way I play bridge and telling me he was very interested to learn that I had written an opera on a Dostoyevsky subject because he worships Dostoyevsky. Some people who had been at the Bohemian Club performance came up to me full of apologies, saying that they had not previously liked my compositions, but now that they had heard such an excellent overture performed in their club, they could see that I was not at all the person I had been painted to be. How often in my life I have had to meet people who are genuinely shocked by the music I write, and do everything in their power to block my career, only later, having done me all kinds of harm, to discover that after all I am a good composer. They come up to me, look me straight in the eye, and ingenuously apologise for having formerly tried to shoot me dead!

9 February

Felt depressed and not very well, even though my temperature is normal.

Dined with Rubinstein. He says artistic life is going at full tilt in London and Paris: they are people of a quite different stamp, with different views. Of course one cannot make as much money there as here, but he would still like to get away from America as fast as possible. Yes, in the middle of April I will go to London.

Yesterday Linette came with me to the Liebmans', and enjoyed much success while I was playing bridge, becoming the centre of attraction from all sides, up to and including Bodanzky and Hofmann.

Gatti-Casazza received me at five o'clock and asked me what it was I wanted to see him about. I replied that I had three operas that might be of interest to him. Gatti said that it would be inappropriate to talk about *Three Oranges*, since this was already linked to the Chicago Opera, while regarding *Fiery Angel*, as a rule he did not accept a work he knew nothing about, moreover one for which the music had not yet been composed. A libretto on its own was not sufficient. 'I am reluctant to believe it,' he added, 'but I hear that

---

poetry and passion, he is said to have replied: 'Madam, what makes you think that I play with my hands?' Hofmann was also a gifted engineer and inventor, responsible among other things for the pneumatic shock absorber for cars, the patent for which made him exceedingly rich.

1 Artur Bodanzky (1877–1939), Austrian-born conductor, had studied composition with Zemlinsky and become assistant conductor to Mahler in his native Vienna before moving to America in 1915 to become head of German repertory at the Metropolitan Opera, a job he held (with a brief and notably unsuccessful interregnum by Joseph Rosenstock in 1928) until his death. He also regularly conducted the New York Philharmonic. His Wagner performances gained him an especial reputation, particularly in the early years of his tenure.

when the Chicago Opera accepted a work before you had written it, you provided them with something they are quite unable to perform.'

My response to this was: 'Perhaps if I were to acquaint you with *Three Oranges*, and then with the subject of *Fiery Angel*, do you think you would then be able to form an opinion as to the kind of music I would compose for such a subject?' Gatti agreed readily to this suggestion, and said he would grant me a longer interview after the 19th, when they would have disposed of *Parsifal*.[1]

10 February

Had lunch with Moiseiwitsch, who introduced me to his English manager Ibbs.[2] Ibbs undertook to get in touch with the London orchestral institutions (of which there are two, one associated with Coates and the other with Wood),[3] regarding my visit in May.

Linette came in the evening.

11 February

Still feeling out of sorts, although my temperature is normal.

Learned Medtner's *Fairy Tale*, Op. 8, which I got to know and love many years ago in Petrograd. Now I set about learning it by heart, and rather to my surprise found it easy to memorise the whole work. Of course I did know it before, all the same my musical memory, currently in a well-trained state from all the concerts I have been doing, has definitely developed.

In the evening I took part in a Carnegie Hall concert by the Philharmonic Orchestra, for which although it was a public event I received no fee. The work I played was Rimsky-Korsakov's Piano Concerto, a work that has hardly ever been heard in New York. To my amazement Stransky,[4] who had only

---

1 'The stiffness of his large burly body, of his voice, of his Risorgimento mustachio, reaffirmed that touch of the military that had been so evident in his written summons.' (*Time Magazine*, 2 November 1925, reporting on Gatti-Casazza's annual no-nonsense press conference announcing the forthcoming season.)
2 Robert Leigh Ibbs, who with John Tillett had founded the London music agency Ibbs & Tillett in 1906.
3 Respectively, the London Symphony Orchestra, founded in 1904 as a musicians' co-operative by fifty players who left Sir Henry Wood's Queen's Hall Orchestra in protest at his banning the practice of deputies, and the New Queen's Hall Orchestra (the 'New' having been added in 1915, the twentieth anniversary of Sir Henry Wood's first Promenade concerts in the Queen's Hall). Albert Coates was Principal Conductor of the LSO from 1919 until 1922.
4 Josef Stransky (1872–1936), Czech conductor and composer, had become the Music Director of the New York Philharmonic in succession to Mahler in 1911, remaining in that post until 1922 when the baton passed to Willem Mengelberg.

had one brief rehearsal, and I, who had got the work up in a mere two weeks, were splendid together and the Concerto had a great success: I was called back to the platform five times, but it is not appropriate to play an encore in a symphony concert.

12 February

Rang up Blanche, whom I have not spoken to since December, undoubtedly swinish behaviour on my part as she is an extremely nice girl, but she was not at home.

Composed some of *Fiery Angel* and played the Medtner, trying not to go out as I was still feeling not very well and a bit depressed. In the evening, however, I did go out to play bridge, and ended up being relieved of $32.

13 February

With enormous difficulty I succeeded in worming out of Schirmer Myaskovsky's Second Sonata, the work I have been trying to get hold of for two years now. I was extraordinarily happy about this, it was almost as good as seeing Myaskunchik himself. I shall learn it immediately and play it here or in London.

When I got home I found a note telling me that Miss Adler had telephoned. Stella? Can she have returned? Stella, from whom not a word for six months, back and ringing me up? My feelings were in a whirl, and I was very worried that her reappearance might upset the relations with Linette I already held so dear. I must be very sensible here, must take great care to have regard to Linette and her feelings, but what Stella is up to, and what her feelings towards me may be, remain a mystery.

14 February

Myaskovsky's Sonata is a complicated and extraordinarily difficult work, and although I decided I would learn it straightaway by heart, flushed as I was with my success with the Medtner *Fairy Tale*, it proved a far from easy task.

At twelve o'clock Stella telephoned, and it was wonderful to hear her voice. My tone was friendly, but reserved: I have no idea what she has been doing these six months or why she did not write a single word to me. And then I cannot get Linette out of my mind. At half-past one Stella and I met. I brought her roses and this seemed to give her the greatest pleasure of all. We spent two hours together, both probably experiencing similar feelings of joy and wariness. What had we been doing during these six months? I was a little less outgoing than Stella. I found her much the same as before, and she did not think I had changed much either. She said she had heard so much about me in London, and she wanted to take piano lessons with me. I asked her to come at half-past two on Monday for a lesson, then I took her home and she promised to bring me some Bach.

An hour later I was with Linette. She was so uncomplicated and so in love that the shadow of Stella soon left me and our evening together passed in a serene tenderness.

15 February

Carried on with *Fiery Angel*: Renata's hysterical scene. I expected this to be very difficult, but it developed with ease and clarity, and today I got as far as Rupprecht's Latin prayer, where I had to stop as I do not know where the stresses fall in Latin.

16 February

Sent a telegram with prepaid reply to Ilyashenko in Constantinople asking about Mama. Perhaps this telegram will spur him into some activity. Novorossiisk has still not fallen to the Bolsheviks, and my hope is that Mama is there at this moment waiting for a Volunteer Fleet steamer with money to pay for a cabin.

Stella telephoned to say that she could not have a lesson with me because she had done no preparation for it; she was going today to Philadelphia for a week to appear with her father's theatre company, but would definitely come in to see me before she went. As a result, instead of coming at three she appeared at eight. After looking at my reviews, photographs and my operas, she took down her hair and was very nice. So was I, but still keeping my distance. Curiously, it even seemed to make me happy that I am now able to feel remote from her. However, when I noticed a simple platinum ring on her finger, so slim it was hardly more than wire, my mood turned very black indeed.

We had dinner at the Hotel Savoy, as we had done many times before, and I took her home. Tomorrow morning she goes to Philadelphia for a week.

17 February

Am composing Renata's account of her story and am deeply absorbed in it, especially my lyrical 'Pacific Ocean' theme.[1]

---

1   See above, p. 296.

18 February

Renata's story.
Learning the Myaskovsky Sonata. Its constantly shifting chromaticisms are terribly hard to remember.

20 February

Janacopulos and Stahl are not coming back to America as they planned, but going straight to Europe. Therefore the concert on 27 March, when she was supposed to sing *The Ugly Duckling*, cannot take place. This is a great shame, I love both of them very much, and the intention was for them to be here for a month before going to Paris. Linette had thought of joining up with them to go to Paris where ostensibly she would study singing, but in reality to spend the summer with me.

21 February

Stella telephoned in the morning. She should have stayed another half-week in Philadelphia, but the performances did not take place as planned and she had come back early. She will come for her lesson tomorrow. For some unknown reason this made me terribly happy and I walked about the streets with a smile on my face.

22 February

Did a lot of work on *Fiery Angel* and moved Renata's story forward to the very end, turning down lunch with Ingerman so as not to interrupt the flow of work. But from Gatti there is not a word, although I think by now I really should have heard something.
Stella arrived at three o'clock for her 'first lesson'. But she had done no preparation at all, having failed to find a copy of the Bach I had set her. She demonstrated her technique to me; needless to say, it is in a sorry state of disrepair. I explained some exercises I wanted her to do. The lesson lasted a quarter of an hour, after which Stella stayed a further two hours with me. I read her the first act of *Fiery Angel*, translating it into English, and I think the libretto impressed her.
Stella then said that her time in London had shown her a great deal and changed her in many ways. And certainly she was not the same person she had been in the spring. She believes she is entering on a 'transitional' period of her life. We treated one another with restrained warmth, and I do not think I am mistaken in imagining that we both harboured vague expecta-

tions, hopes at least, of something stronger developing. Whether it will flare up or die down is for the moment an unknown. But when we parted I was left with a feeling of something between discontent and actual annoyance.

23 February

Finished Renata's story. It is very good.

In the afternoon I sat for Deryuzhinsky, who is making a bust of me. It was astonishing how quickly it began to take shape. Then I dined with the Wiborgs, rich Americans.

This afternoon saw the premiere of a new ballet[1] by Carpenter, an American composer of modest gifts, followed by a dinner in his honour. How pleasant to reflect that while the untalented is honoured and his ballet staged, my opera remains unperformed on the shelf. The dinner was quite enjoyable, an ebullient and fashionable occasion that was, nevertheless, completely alien to me. I therefore made my escape as soon as I could and went to play bridge with Samoilenko.

Apparently there has been a brief mention in the newspapers of Rostov having been recaptured by Denikin's forces.[2] It raises hopes of Mama managing to get away to Constantinople, but I don't know whether to believe it or not. There has been no answer to the telegram I sent to Ilyashenko a week ago.

1 The ballet was the jazz-pantomime *Krazy Kat*, based on the magnificent comic strip created by George Herriman and syndicated in the Hearst newspapers between 1912 and 1944. An essay by e.e. cummings on the surreal world of Herriman's Krazy Kat perfectly encapsulates the timeless triangle of the subject Carpenter chose to set: 'What concerns me fundamentally is a meteoric burlesk melodrama, born of the immemorial adage love will find a way. This frank frenzy (encouraged by a strictly irrational landscape [Coconino County] in perpetual metamorphosis) generates three protagonists and a plot. Two of the protagonists are easily recognized as a cynical brick-throwing mouse [Ignatz Mouse] and a sentimental policeman-dog [Offissa Pupp]. The third protagonist – whose ambiguous gender doesn't disguise the good news that here comes our heroine – may be described as a humbly poetic, gently clownlike, supremely innocent, and illimitably affectionate creature (slightly resembling a child's drawing of a cat, but gifted with the secret grace and obvious clumsiness of a penguin on terra firma) who is never so happy as when egoist-mouse, thwarting altruist-dog, hits her in the head with a brick. Dog hates mouse and worships "cat", mouse despises "cat" and hates dog, "cat" hates no one and loves mouse.' (Introduction to *Krazy Kat* (Henry Holt & Co., New York, 1946).)
2 The recapture of the bitterly fought-over – because strategically crucial – Rostov-on-Don (it changed hands six times between 1918 and 1920) on 8 February 1920 by Denikin's disintegrating Volunteer Army was to be the last White success of the Civil War. Not long afterwards, fatally weakened by the defection of the Kuban Cossacks, the Volunteer Army was routed by Budyonny's Konarmiya Red Cavalry, and both Rostov and Yekaterinodar had to be abandoned. Novorossiisk was inundated by a flood of desperate refugees, the fortunate among whom (including Prokofiev's mother) were taken by the few remaining ships of the Black Sea Fleet along with British, Italian and French warships to the Princes Islands, while Denikin himself fled to Constantinople.

24 February

Worked on the Landlady.

Sat for Deryuzhinsky. The bust is turning out wonderfully well, and is almost finished. Deryuzhinsky pronounced on the subject of American women: they are more sexually aroused by rich men than by any others. Malicious, and almost true.

Rostov has again been captured by the Bolsheviks. I am in despair over Mama being in a town that passes from one set of hands into another. Deryuzhinsky's mother is in Kherson,[1] and Anisfeld's in Odessa: all three cities are under siege by the Bolshevik host. And we three artists sit here, at one in our total helplessness and in the terrible pictures that come unbidden into our minds when we wake in the night.

25 February

Deryuzhinsky has finished my head and considers it his most successful work of recent times.

Anisfeld came in to listen to what I have composed so far of *Fiery Angel*. While he was still there Stella appeared, as apparently we had a date for today which I had mixed up. She at once made a dead set at Anisfeld, in whom she had long been interested, but Anisfeld's English is not good and he made the mistake of praising her sister, whom he had seen on stage. Stella bit her tongue and suppressed her ire, while Mme Anisfeld hurried her husband out of the door and away home. After they had gone I teased Stella that she battens on famous men so passionately that their wives have to drag them away from her clutches.

26 February

Finished the Landlady.

Decided to call a halt to my Violin Sonata, the sketches for which date back to when I was in Japan. One theme from it I took for *Fiery Angel*.

27 February

Mme Liebman invited Linette and me to her box at the Philharmonic concert where Rachmaninoff was to play the Liszt Concerto. On this occasion Rachmaninoff played magnificently; not a single nail did I hear him hammer in. After the concert, at tea at Stransky's, I had a very relaxed and friendly talk

---

1 Black Sea port at the mouth of the Dnieper river.

with Rachmaninoff. He was wearing his usual exhausted look and cannot wait for the season to end. I said: 'Sergey Vasilievich, you really ought to be getting on with your Fourth Symphony.' He agreed, but said that it would be impossible this summer: he had to prepare a new concert programme for the following winter. He has got to earn money, but in a year's time he would be able to sit back and have some time to himself.

After tea Liebman dragged me off to the cinema where there was a film in which Dagmar[1] appeared as a fallen woman. It was highly diverting to see on the screen someone I knew so well. She showed herself to be not at all a bad actress, and the film itself – according to Liebman – bore a remarkable resemblance to a scandalous real-life story the protagonist of which was, needless to say, none other than the wondrous Dagmar.

28 February

Lunched with the Izvolskys, a young couple whom I recently met. He is the son of our former Foreign Affairs Minister,[2] and she is a native of Havana. They are nice, handsome, and rich.

At lunch also was Mrs Joe Thomas, a young woman who asked me if there was any reason why I should not play another recital right away, this spring. I said it was because there was no hall available in which to do so. She said: 'If that is the case, then the hall in my house is at your disposal. It cannot accommodate more than a hundred and fifty people, but we will be able to sell tickets at $10 and that will make you a good profit.' At this the ladies announced that they would take charge of all the arrangements for the concert, and all that was left for me to do was thank them. This is very kind of them, and fits in well with my plans for the summer.

The evening with Linette proceeded in so incandescent a manner that at night, after I had taken her home, I had the most terrible migraine.

---

1   The irrepressible Dagmar Godowsky not only had a short-lived but action-packed career as a Hollywood vamp, but also a spell at running her own nightclub. On one occasion Leopold Godowsky was heard to observe ruefully: 'My daughter is planning to go to work again. I only hope it won't cost me too much.'
2   Alexander Izvolsky (1856–1919) was Tsarist Foreign Minister between 1906 and 1910 and devoted much of his energies to the negotiation of a vitally important agreement with Austria to guarantee Russia's free passage through the Dardanelles and the Bosphorus in order to gain access for the Black Sea Fleet to the Mediterranean. The quid pro quo was Russia's acquiescence to Austria's annexation of Bosnia-Herzegovina, which made Izvolsky an object of revilement to pan-Slavists who considered this a betrayal of Serbia, especially when Austria insouciantly annexed it anyhow. The iron entered Izvolsky's soul and he resigned to accept the post of Russian Ambassador to Paris, where he remained after the February and October Revolutions. His elegantly written but sadly unfinished *Mémoires d'Alexandre Iswolsky* (Payol, Paris, 1923) actually appeared first in an English translation by his friend Charles Louis Seeger (*The Memoirs of Alexander Iswolsky* (Hutchinson, London, 1920)).

29 February

Composed a great deal.

1 March

Obtained a new passport from the Embassy in exchange for the one the Bolsheviks had provided me with, as I believe it will help me encounter fewer obstacles when moving from one country to another. I booked a transatlantic passage for 17 April, but there are no berths left on the *Mauretania*.

Rubinstein called. I played him the Myaskovsky Sonata, which he liked, but not excessively. My *Tales of an Old Grandmother*, however, pleased him enormously. 'They are so simple!' he said. I said I thought I had called a halt to progress in the sense of searching for new paths. Rubinstein was delighted, and exclaimed: 'That is splendid! Believe me, whenever I see a composer deciding it is time to stop innovating, that is precisely the time he embarks on his new path.' I then played him Renata's hysterical scene, which sent him into ecstasy.

I dined with Stella, who told me that she could not continue with her music because they did not allow her to practise at home. Among the general matters we talked about she let slip that she had had a romance in London, bordering on love.[1] This had the effect of piercing and assuaging me when I thought about Linette.

2 March

Life flows on evenly, troubled only by my deep nagging worry about Mama. In the mornings I compose the opera and in the afternoons check the Duo Art recordings. Evenings are spent with the loving but perpetually distracted Linette, who is afraid that she will not get everything arranged so as to be able to go to Europe in the summer. 'I don't know what I shall do if I have to stay here alone,' she said. 'I will fall ill . . .'

As the time during which it was reasonable to expect Gatti to call me back has now long passed, I took the initiative and telephoned his secretary. He apologised and explained that the Director was overburdened with work and would receive me next week, when he would have more time.

---

1 Stella Adler's daughter Ellen, now resident in New York, confirms that during her mother's stay in London performing at the Pavilion Theatre she had met the man who was to become her first husband and the father of her daughter.

3 March

A registered letter from Johnson with a prepaid reply, advising me of the inclusion of the opera in the repertoire for next season. It was what I had been expecting, except that I thought it would be accompanied by a cheque for $1,000 intended to beguile me into agreement, and that another month would elapse before I got it. But I had happened to run into Kahn when I was at the Consulate getting my passport to go to England, so I suppose that was what had prompted them to hurry matters along. My response will be firm and resolute.

4 March

Composed the 'rape scene'.

Rubinstein was supposed to come by in the afternoon, but as usual let me down, for which I resolved not to pardon him. In his stead Stella unexpectedly appeared, but today she was in a strange mood, no doubt a prey to memories of her London attachment. More than ever I felt remote from her.

5 March

Collaborated with Haensel to write my reply to Johnson, polite but firm. As a last resort, if I absolutely need to promote my name in America, I could do this: allow them to give one performance and then immediately have an injunction put on further ones. That would make plain to them in no uncertain terms why they must compensate me for their breach of the original contract.

In the afternoon I called on Mrs Joe Thomas, the lady who had offered to arrange my concert at her house. She has applied herself to the matter, and has chosen the date: 28 March. The only pity is that they have knocked the ticket price down from $10 to $5, meaning that the take will be $700 rather than $1,500. But that too is good, especially if Gatti lets me down.

6 March

Had a bit of a headache, and therefore did not compose much. Then Linette came, and her presence made my headache go away. We went out together to the outskirts of the city to see some people called Trusov, where we had been told we would meet someone who was going to Constantinople and, if he found it was still possible, on from there to Rostov. I asked him to take Mama a money order in the amount of £30 sterling, and to give her news of me. From the Trusovs I went to Deryuzhinsky, who had invited people to view the clay model of my head.

A letter has arrived from Ilyashenko in Constantinople that he had been unsuccessful in finding any of the people he had been asked to make contact with (and there was a huge number of such requests) with the exception of Prokofiev's mother, who was expected to arrive in Constantinople in a few days' time. This news transported me with incredible joy: of course Mama has not yet reached safe harbour, and will not have done so until she actually reaches Constantinople, nevertheless this is news that I had almost forgotten even to hope for. An as yet unpronounced verdict had been hanging over my head: was I a man who had rescued both himself and his mother from the maelstrom of Russia, or was I someone who had looked after himself but abandoned his mother to the mercy of events?

7 March

Woke up in the most wonderful mood, as if a stone had been lifted from my heart, a stone that had been weighing on me for almost three months now. From the moment we heard that the Bolsheviks were advancing on Rostov, Mama's fate had cast a shadow over my every joy.

Composed a great deal. Renata sleeps, and Rupprecht alongside her. The 'knocks' begin to be heard.

In the evening Linette and I were at the Bolms for a big fancy-dress evening. I met one young Russian woman, I cannot remember her name, I think she was Jewish. She came from an artistic milieu, and without the slightest notion that she was doing so, echoed those circles' gestures and attitudes with such fabulous verisimilitude that I derived much more pleasure from watching her than I did the professional entertainer who had been paid to mimic the guests.

8 March

Again a marvellous mood. I did very little composing, as I was busy with things I had to do: a money transfer to Mama, which I still want to send, and an English visa for myself. I thought the visa would be an easy and straightforward matter, but it appears to be a long-drawn-out procedure involving permission having to be sought from London.

A telegram from Ilyashenko has come via our Embassy in Washington. In it he repeats that Mama is expected in Constantinople. At first I was overjoyed, but then it dawned on me that he must have sent the telegram several weeks after his letter, and if Mama had still not arrived this was a bad sign. But these days telegrams sometimes take two weeks, and if someone had perhaps taken the letter to Paris it might have got here almost as quickly.

9 March

Composed the 'knocks'. The pace of composition seems to be slackening. Either I should take a break for a while, or something must happen to energise me, for example a meeting with Gatti, but the liar has still not been in touch to ask me to see him.

I left the afternoon free to go to see Stella, who was today making her debut in a major role with the Jewish Theatre with her father. Learning her part and preparing for the production had been such an anxious time for her over the past few days that she had not wanted to see me. But I had mixed up the date: she is performing tomorrow.

In the evening I went with the Ingermans to the Russian Theatre, a tiny, poorly equipped place. But they did Gogol's *The Wedding* with love and although by no means everything was perfect, there was much to enjoy.

10 March

Met Blanche at two o'clock, who was taking me to the Jewish Theatre. Despite the weekday timing, it was a packed house – Adler is adored by the Jewish community. Blanche was extraordinarily nice, desperately concerned both for Stella and for me, that I should not have a bad impression of the audience or the play. But she need not have worried: the impression was first class even though the Jewish argot is not especially beautiful and I could understand only a few German words in it. Stella's father is very good, his acting economical to the point of schematic. Her sister Julia is a most affecting mime. Stella herself projects well on stage but her acting sometimes lacks sincerity. I divided my attention between feasting my eyes on her and sulking about something, I don't know what. Blanche passed on an invitation to have supper with Stella, her father and sister afterwards, and I was very flattered, but could not even stay until the end of the play as I had a rendez-vous with Linette at half-past five. Once again the jolting dislocation of moving from one world into another, and once again a loving, shy and then passionate Linette.

11 March

Composed, but not much.

I thought about yesterday's play. I am sure Stella was offended that I did not stay to the end of her debut appearance and did not come to dinner with her and her father. In fact I was quite pleased about it: her London adventure still sits like a worm inside me, setting me against her.

Spent the afternoon making corrections to the recordings, going to the dentist, and played bridge in the evening.

12 March

Worried away at my income tax. I had to show all my earnings, in return for which I did not spare them a single one of my professional expenses. The outcome was that I owe $140. I thought it would be more, but at the end I was in pieces from exhaustion.

Mme Samoilenko has had a telegram from Paris to say that Mama has arrived in Constantinople with no money and a certain Yakovlev has sent her a thousand francs. Hurrah, everything is now all right! Even the lack of money is, I suspect, a misunderstanding, as Ilyashenko knows she is coming and is holding the money order for her.

In the evening I went to see Stella to try to smooth over my failure to turn up after the performance. It was the first time I had been to her house. In the spring she had asked me to come many times, but I had always declined. Today I found her alone, looking lovely; the rest of the family was all at the theatre. But I was still terribly tired after my exertions with the income tax, and on top of that she upset me by telling me that she was probably going to Europe in the summer, to London, Paris and Vienna, and was very excited about the prospect. I shrivelled up inside, and withdrew into myself. Stella tried to be nice, but soon exhausted her reserves of indulgence. After an hour I left an obviously puzzled and no doubt offended Stella. Altogether it had been a stupid evening and our relations seemed to have descended into a rut of idiotic misunderstanding. Walking home I racked my brains trying to work out my true feelings and what this might all be leading to. It would be a real pity to lose Stella.

But is she perhaps already lost?

13 March

Slept not very well, and woke up with a headache, as a result of which I did not compose. At four o'clock Linette came, and all yesterday's caprices vanished over the horizon. I revolve between Stella and Linette as the earth spins between the moon and the sun. At seven o'clock I parted from Linette and went to a grand dinner organised by Liebman exclusively for gentlemen. It proved to be a fascinating occasion. Quite a number of celebrities were present, there were manuscripts by Wagner, Liszt, Goethe and Heine to look at that had been illicitly spirited out of Germany, there was wine, and serious bridge.

There was also a competition to see who could come up with the most inspired nonsense phrase. We had fifteen minutes to think, write the phrase, and put it into a printed envelope with a number rather than a signature. For this competition there were three prizes: an elegant gold matchbox-stand, a marvellous suitcase, and for some reason an ivory-handled umbrella. I was dying to win the suitcase, but having drunk wine and with all the noise and hubbub going on around me, in fifteen minutes I could not think of anything. However, little by little I made myself concentrate and began to get the glimmerings of an idea. I scribbled out something in Russian and then wrote in French: 'Un esprit brillant et clair reflété dans une sottise ressemble à un beau diamant que l'eau noir des égouts reflète comme un précieux diamant noir.'[1] Written out, it seemed pretty good to me, and I began to entertain hopes of a prize.

And so it happened, and when my number was called out I felt extremely proud and clever. But disappointment followed: I only won third prize and was accordingly presented with the umbrella, God knows what use it will be. The first two prizes were awarded for mildly indecent rubbish, and in fact this was just, because what had been asked for was foolishness expressed through wit, whereas what I had attempted to express was something intelligent about foolishness.

14 March

Amusing. I woke up in an excellent temper remembering my prize from yesterday. After all, Hofmann, Bauer, Bodanzky and Bolm had all had a go, and none of them had won anything.

Went on composing, but in the morning I encountered a block and could make no progress. By evening, however, my muse had returned and I could even sense the end of the act looming up in the distance.

15 March

Did not compose. Went to the bank and transferred a thousand francs to Paris. Had lunch with Linette.

16 March

Got on well today and almost finished the first act, all but a few bars. I played it through from beginning to end – thirty-five minutes! – and only now did

---

[1] 'A clear and brilliant mind is reflected in a preposterous absurdity as the reflection from the black water of the gutter resembles a beautiful and precious black diamond.'

I realise why it had taken me so long to compose this act: it is equivalent to very nearly two acts of *Three Oranges*.

17 March

A letter from Sonya Brichant, my second cousin,[1] who has recently emigrated with her husband, a Belgian, from south Russia to Brussels. She had seen Mama two months ago and says she looked not at all well. This concerns me very much, although Mama was walking with a stick when I left her, and I already knew about her poor eyesight from her September letter. My cousin Andrey Rayevsky[2] has fallen ill with spotted typhoid. This is dreadful.

Finished Act I. The final twenty bars are very good.

Linette came in the afternoon, and then we went together to a performance by Bolm's Ballet Intime company.[3]

18 March

Was all set to start on Act Two, but there was no manuscript paper. I went out to buy some and then worked on the Myaskovsky Sonata and other piano pieces, putting aside for the time being composition work on Act Two.

Sent a cable to Sonya, asking her to try to get permission for Mama to come to Brussels.

Linette returned at six o'clock and we went out again, this time to Sklyarevsky's concert. He played conscientiously but unremarkably, which was what I had been expecting. Afterwards we went to Deryuzhinsky's studio, where the artist did not talk about himself as obsessively as usual, was good company and flirted with Linette.

---

[1] As the grandchild of a sibling of one of Prokofiev's grandparents (it is not known which) Mme Brichant was not a close relation.

[2] Prokofiev's first cousin Andrey (Andryusha) Rayevsky, the son of his mother's sister Yekaterina (Aunt Katya) Rayevskaya and her husband Alexander Rayevsky. The Rayevskys were the Prokofievs' closest family connections in St Petersburg. Tatyana (Tanya) Rayevskaya was Andrey's wife. See *Diaries*, vol. 1, p. 9n and *passim*.

[3] After Adolph Bolm had been injured while performing in the second of the Ballets Russes tours of America in 1916 (apparently as the result of negligence by Nijinsky, who was officially managing the company in tandem with Bolm in the absence of the impresario himself, too frightened to make a second wartime crossing of the Atlantic) he had decided to stay in America and pursue an independent career as dancer, choreographer and impresario. The first fruit of this was the Ballet Intime company Bolm established in 1917 with a stellar group of international dancers, including his former student Ruth Page.

19 March

A letter from Nina Koshetz in Batum, passionate and distracted. She is in despair, utterly exhausted, and desperately wants to come to America. I was much moved by her letter and immediately went to see Haensel to ask him to help arrange for her to come here. It is strange; I had been imagining that when we met again there would not be a great deal of warmth between us, but all it took was this letter to infect me with the turbulence of her emotions. The energy discharged by the person of Koshetz is so great that even on paper it can still be felt at a distance of tens of thousands of versts. Nevertheless, my relationship with Koshetz as a woman will go no further than it had in Moscow.

In the evening I stayed at home and wrote letters. Sklyarevsky called in, very agitated and asking for my advice. He is still determined to give another recital.

I got my visa for France easily, in five minutes, through the recommendation of the Russian Consul. But from the English Consulate there has been neither response nor acknowledgement.

20 March

The other people whose equilibrium will have been disturbed by Nina Koshetz's letter are Rachmaninoff and his wife.

I had a bad head today and so did not compose, although I did play the piano quite a lot. Went for a walk in the park. The snow is melting there, but there is still no grass to be seen.

21 March

The newspapers are heralding the first day of spring. And so it is: the spring equinox has brought with it warmth and sunshine, and one could even detect a faint scent of spring through the petrol fumes of New York. I rang up Linette, who was thrilled at the prospect of going out of town, and we gaily set off for Hastings on Hudson. Afterwards Linette came back with me and it was eleven o'clock by the time I took her home.

I had managed to do some work in the morning, before our trip. I made a start on the second act, up to the entrance of the Merchant.[1] The dreamy, mystical atmosphere with which the act begins is hardly in tune with today's smiling weather.

---

1   The bookseller, Jakob Glock.

22 March

The scene with the Merchant.

The Bohemians have begun to show a great interest in me and my *Overture on Hebrew Themes*; they are going to perform it again at a big dinner in the Biltmore Hotel. I am glad about this, as there will be a lot of musicians present. Thank God the lousy rotten Bohemians have at last had the wit to place some trust in me.

In the evening I attended a rehearsal of a Spanish choir. It was very interesting. Perhaps I should write a sonata for wordless choir? Especially if it has a lot of staccato and if I succeed in getting an instrumental colour into the vocal sonorities. The choir director suggested that he could send a telegram to Madrid asking for me to be invited there in May for a series of concerts. I should love to go to Spain, where I have heard there is a burgeoning musical life. The musicians I have spoken to who have been there are in love with it.

23 March

The entrance of the Students.[1] Something after the manner of a German folk song, although it does not necessarily have to be German, since in Bryusov some of the students are Italian and some are from the south.

From Gatti, the swine, not a word, not so much as a syllable. I foresee the matter ending like this: he will drag it out for another three weeks, and then say he is so sorry, the repertoire has now been settled.

In the evening I visited Natasha Voynova, Medtner's niece, who melted when I played her uncle's *Fairy Tale*, but did not scruple to make very critical comments whenever my interpretation differed from his.

24 March

Composed the quarrel with the Students.

Succeeded for the first time in playing the Myaskovsky Sonata right through by heart.

Lunch with Linette.

---

1 In the first draft of the libretto for *Fiery Angel* Prokofiev incorporated from Bryusov's novel two 'disciples' of the necromancer Agrippa von Nettesheim, Aurelius and Hans, who make an entrance just after the bookseller Jakob Glock has brought magic treatises to Renata and Rupprecht and promises to take them to meet Agrippa. By 1927, when Prokofiev completed the version of the opera seen in present-day productions, they have been excluded, nor do they appear in the revised scenario he worked out for a possible Metropolitan Opera production in 1930.

25 March

Dined with Mrs J. Thomas, the lady who wants to organise my concert. This is now set for 8 April. I am pleased: if I can take away $600 to $700, that will put bread on the table very nicely. My funds are running low and I cannot count on earning much during the summer, nor from Gatti, while Mama will soon arrive and I am going to Europe.

26 March

Finished Rupprecht's quarrel with the Students.

Linette came, and we went together to the concert by Fuleihan,[1] a young Syrian pianist and composer. There is no question that he has talent, but he thrashes the keys so hard it is impossible to hear anything. There are clear evocations of the East in his music, mixed in with all sorts of modernist ballast from yesteryear. After the concert Linette and I went to Deryuzhinsky's studio, where he was very nice and proposed that he and I use the intimate 'ty' form of address to one another.

A letter from Vera and Stahl – twelve pages – from Rio. They are both falling over themselves with excitement over the glories of the country, and will go back there after their trip to Paris. They suggest I join them there at the same time; while there are no guarantees of concert engagements there are any amount of chances for success and money. Invitations of this sort are always tremendously attractive, but I would probably have to make it next summer rather than this, since my immediate plans are to go to Europe, Mama is coming there also, and Linette may very well go too.

27 March

Composition today did not go well and my mood was generally apathetic. However, just before evening I succeeded in harmonising two Russian songs for some anthology or other, and they turned out so well I cheered up greatly.

---

[1] Anis Fuleihan (1900–1970) was a prolific American composer and pianist of Cypriot (not Syrian) origin. His oeuvre includes symphonic, chamber and vocal works, and a number of concertos for piano, violin, cello, two pianos, plus one for Thereminvox, the electronic invention of Léon Theremin that produces a pitched sound by means of a player moving (without touching) his hands and arms around two antennae connected to heterodyne oscillators.

28 March

This Sunday, like last, was sunny and warm. Linette and I went out of town, to Staten Island, but the other side from where the Stahls live. We walked along the sea shore; it was warm but still 'nature through sleep greets the morning of the year'.[1] Linette came back home with me and the day ended with the most loving endearments.

29 March

At last, a telephone call from Gatti's secretary asking me to attend a meeting on Thursday. This is very good, and I am glad it did not fall to me to have to remind him of our arrangement. I imagine in fact this meeting will be little more than a formality, as any question of whether or not to mount a production will already have been decided. If Kahn said to Gatti: 'Please listen to Prokofiev's opera and see whether you like it or not,' of course he will not like it, but if Kahn has said: 'Please listen to Prokofiev's opera, I would like you to stage it,' then whatever he thinks of it, staged it will be.

30 March

Composed some of *Fiery Angel* and went through *Three Oranges* in anticipation of playing it to Gatti. The scene I picked was 'The bedroom of the hypochondriac Prince'.

1 April

In the morning I played through my operas, including *The Gambler*. This definitely needs major revision: the vocal parts have too many unnecessarily rough and awkward passages. I then packed into my suitcase *The Gambler*, *Fiery Angel* and *Three Oranges* (full score and vocal score). Impressive, I thought, for a composer to need a whole suitcase for his scores.

Gatti had set up a full-scale audition consisting of himself and six conductors, but essentially this was just for show: the decision would be made by Gatti and Bodanzky and the others would sit quietly by minding their own business. After giving them a preliminary outline of the action I played the scene with the Prince, followed by some excerpts from the first act of *Fiery Angel*. So far as I could judge the effect created was not very favourable. Gatti found all the music very difficult, with not enough for the voice to get

---

1 Pushkin, *Eugene Onegin*, Chapter 7 Stanza 1: 'Nature with her serene smile/Greets through her sleep the morning of the year.'

hold of. Had it been a one-act opera they might have taken the risk, but five acts . . .

Summing up, Gatti said I would naturally understand that they could not give an immediate answer to such a significant proposition. This is tantamount to a rejection. I find it upsetting, both on my account and for the Metropolitan, that a fine institution cannot put on a real opera, opting instead to suffocate under an agglomeration of rubbish. For me it represented the height of unpleasantness, not to mention a distinct financial crisis, which made my winning of $61 at bridge in the evening all the happier a circumstance. Later, I was told that the French conductor Albert Wolff had spoken up for me, prompting Gatti to call him an anarchist.

2 April

In the morning I continued with the composition of *Fiery Angel* – Agrippina. Even if it has not been accepted, that is no reason for abandoning work on a good opera.

My mood is so-so. But outside the sun is shining and it is spring!

3 April

Dinner at the Biltmore with the Bohemians in honour of Bauer, a grand occasion. Linette – whom I had invited as my partner – and I were seated at the top table, which at first made her very uneasy.

My *Overture* and *Bassoon Scherzo* sounded less than robust because of the size of the hall and the dreadful acoustic. They were well received, however, and I bowed my acknowledgement although I had expected much more enthusiasm than in fact they were accorded. Chernyavsky told me they had played the *Overture* on 22 March in Chicago and it had been an exceptional success.

4 April

Easter Day in America, Palm Sunday for us in Russia, but the weather was overcast and rainy so there was no trip out of town for Linette and me as there had been on the two previous Sundays. I worked, continuing to compose, and went to eat *paskha*[1] with the Voynovs.

---

1   The pyramid-shaped cream-cheese dessert traditionally eaten in Russia at Easter.

5 April

Ilyashenko has arrived back from Constantinople and I had dinner with him. He did not see Mama as he left before she got there, but he had spoken to our Embassy about me and left a money order for £40 there in her name. He also discovered that they were holding another cheque for her, but had not discovered whether this was a duplicate of the same draft as he had given them, or whether it might be the famous £100 draft sent via the British Military Mission.

He had some terrible tales to tell, but to my mind the most terrible was the spotted typhoid fever, which lurks unseen in the background, gives no sign, and is merciless.

6 April

An unexpected manifestation during the afternoon: as I was sitting at home working on Act Two, Blanche and Stella suddenly appeared at the door. They did not stay long, and Stella looked wonderful. I mentioned in passing that I had telephoned several times, being told that the whole family was away in Buffalo. We talked idly about this and that; the conversation flowed easily, even poetically. Then I took them to their train, and later sent some roses to Stella with instructions that they should be given to her tomorrow morning. It was a great joy to see her, but memories of Linette held me at arm's length.

7 April

A letter from Mama – or rather a letter dictated by her, from Princes Islands, where she now is with Tanya Rayevskaya and her son. Andryusha has died from the typhoid, as I had feared when I read Sonya Brichant's letter.

I am full of joy that Mama has at last escaped from the calamity, but full of sadness that she is in such a bad state, weak and almost blind.

9 April

Sorted out contracts and explanatory covering letters for Koshetz. Sklyarevsky is leaving for France today and will send them on to her from there to Constantinople. I sent Mama a telegram to let her know that I am coming to France and Italy. My plan is to get an Italian visa for her and for myself, and to meet her in Brindisi, which by direct steamer from Constantinople is three days' voyage.

Sent the ladies – Mme Izvolskaya and Mrs Thomas – large bouquets of red roses as a gesture of thanks for their efforts on behalf of my concert.

Bolm says that the Chicago Opera has so drastically overspent this season that they will certainly have to draw in their horns for the next few seasons. This is already in the wind, and I should bear it in mind.

10 April

Today Liebmans organised bridge on a grand scale, beginning at four in the afternoon and finishing at two in the morning. It was very enjoyable; Linette came for the dinner recess, also Deryuzhinsky, whom I was introducing to the house for the first time. Also at dinner were Rachmaninoff, Hofmann and many other such luminaries. Rachmaninoff was aloof to begin with, but later on we had a very pleasant talk. I tentatively raised the subject of Koshetz, and even got so far as discussing with him what we could do for her in America.

Today is Easter Saturday, and Deryuzhinsky went to the Russian Church at eleven o'clock. I should have liked to go as well, but everyone said there would be a fearful crush there and it would be impossible to see or hear anything. A great pity, as this is a service I love.

11 April

A warm, sunny day, so Linette and I went into New Jersey, crossing the Hudson river, where we walked for five hours. Linette said: 'My dear, today is your birthday,' and gave me a cigarette case. I replied that she had robbed my life of thirteen days, as I had been born on 11 April according to the old calendar, and still could not feel in the slightest that I was twenty-nine.

In the evening there was a dinner in honour of Auer, attended by all the New York celebrities and a mass of pretty women, but I was placed next to Mme Rachmaninoff, which spoilt the whole dinner. She asked if it was true that Koshetz was coming. It certainly is.

Auer has aged, and sort of crumpled into a little ball. He was very civil to me and asked how my affairs were going.

12 April

Another letter from Sonya Brichant: she received both my telegram and Mama's letter from Princes Islands, and is doing everything in her power to get Mama to Brussels. This is wonderful and greatly reassuring news. Had dinner with Linette and then accompanied her to the cinema.

13 April

Played the piano and went through all of my works that I envisage playing in London. I have put *Fiery Angel* to one side, as is only to be expected after the rejection by the Metropolitan, but I hope it is only a temporary interruption and that after a few days I will be motivated to press on with it.

In the afternoon Mme Izvolskaya took me to tea with Mrs Otto Kahn,[1] whose house is a quite remarkable edifice, something like an Italian palazzo. I had hoped to raise the question of the opera, since she is said to have an even greater influence than her husband, but the occasion was a reception with a large number of guests, so conversation was confined to courtesies and salutations. However, a French singer from the Metropolitan Opera, not knowing who I was, did tell me that recently some Russian composer or other ... Proko ... Proko ... she could not quite remember his quite unpronounceable name, had played Gatti his opera, which had been completely crazy Futurist nonsense. All the same she still hoped that it might be produced, because at least it would do her some good if she got a part in it.

14 April

Played Myaskovsky's Sonata, which is beginning to hang together quite well, and also my Second Sonata, which I have not touched for a year and a half. I think I shall play it much better now, as since coming to America I have made great strides as a pianist.

There is no news from the English about my visa, and I have been asking our Consul to investigate. He telephoned the British Consulate but reported back that the rule there is to preserve an impenetrable wall of rigid correctness, vouchsafing no more than that they have written to London and a reply is awaited. Meanwhile, I have essentially done everything I needed to in America, and am ready to go.

15 April

Linette cannot decide whether or not she is going to Europe, and of course the poor girl is torn between the abysses of 'yes' and 'no'. At lunch today we even had a slight tiff on the subject. Taking advantage of the coolness I rang up Stella, who was delighted to hear from me. She had rung me twice to thank me for the flowers, but had not caught me in, and they had not passed on the message. She agreed to come and see me tomorrow.

---

1 Mrs Kahn was born Addie Wolff, daughter of another prominent partner of the Kuhn-Loeb bank.

16 April

I went to the British Embassy myself – there is still no word from London. If by Tuesday I still do not have an answer I shall be forced to cancel the cabin I have reserved for the 24th and instead go to France and from there to London.

When I got back home at five o'clock Stella was already waiting for me, looking very nice and attractive. She was thrilled that I had sent her flowers, and was now bringing her favourite forget-me-nots. It was a long time since anyone had given her flowers, as currently she has no admirers, at least none whom she liked, and this was a deprivation as she so loved flowers. I accompanied her to the theatre where she was performing, and was exactly an hour late for dinner with Zimbalist.

17 April

The Chicago Opera has written saying that in view of the fact that they have spent $100,000 on my opera they would be grateful if I would start court proceedings as soon as possible, should such be my intention. I consulted Purrington on my answer. As before, Purrington drivelled on humming and ha-ing. He had very little advice of substance, but corrected and edited the reply I had drafted.

At five o'clock I went to Bolm's to meet Marinuzzi, who is now the Music Director of the Chicago Opera and thus will conduct *Three Oranges*. He had told Bolm that he had been aware for some time of the continuing friction between me and the opera company, but having no involvement with the financial side of things he would very much like me to demonstrate *Three Oranges* to him so that he could get to know it. I agreed that this would be a good idea, and this is why we were meeting on neutral territory at Bolm's house, where I played the whole opera through to him.

Marinuzzi is a very good musician and a first-class conductor. It was apparent that he had a good understanding of *Three Oranges* and that much of it appealed to him, but, as he said, the work proved to be considerably more difficult than he had imagined. To my great surprise he found two places where in his opinion cuts could be made: the Prince's farewell to the King in Act Two, and Chelio's dialogue with the Prince and Truffaldino in Act Three. I said that if he truly found that these passages suffered from *longueurs*, then by all means they could be cut. Not a word was said of my disagreement with the directors of the Opera.

18 April

In the morning, despite its being a Sunday, I met Purrington to finalise a letter to Chicago with fresh proposals. Now that the campaign with the Metropolitan Opera has run into the sand, it is imperative to achieve at least one performance of *Three Oranges* in Chicago before imposing a veto.

Linette and I went out of the city in the afternoon, where the weather was sunny and there was a lot of green coming through – but surprisingly, no flowers. We had a lovely long walk.

19 April

The morning went on a multitude of pre-departure chores after which I rang up Stella, having kept the evening free for her. But Stella was busy and said that she would not be able to see me. This made me angry, and when she asked when she could ring me, I replied that I did not want her to, but that I would ring her myself in a few days' time. It is most upsetting that it should all have turned out like this: it was such a lovely, sunny spring evening . . .

Wrote letters and called on Deryuzhinsky, who was in the dumps and delighted to see me.

20 April

Haensel, whom I had presented with my photograph inscribed 'To the nice and phlegmatic man'[1] said that he had two engagements for me in the autumn at $500 and $400 respectively, but was not sure whether he could get any orchestral engagements as although he was getting some interest the only offer he had was $300 for a double booking, which was below the threshold of acceptability. I told him that I would be going to Europe with no more than $800–900, to which he responded by saying that if this turned out not to be enough I could telegraph him and he would transfer more to me, as he has faith in my future.

The English Consul has informed me that I still have no visa, and this is the date by which I must release my cabin reservation for the 24th. However, Thomas Cook undertook to change the reservation to the 27th or 30th, on a wretched little vessel sailing to France. I put up with this because so great is the demand for transatlantic passages that people sometimes wait months for them, and I could spend a few enjoyable days with Linette and would also be able to hear my *Overture* in Carnegie Hall.

1 In English.

21 April

The £100 cheque I had sent to Mama in Novorossiisk via the British Military Mission was safely returned today because the English had not managed to trace Mama in order to give it to her (probably they did not try very hard). I had placed such hopes in this draft, and it had all come to nothing. I must send a telegram to Sonya and transfer francs to her.

Linette was due to come in the evening, but she was not feeling well and so I went to see Anisfeld. I get on extremely well with him, and he is incensed at the Metropolitan's black-balling of *Fiery Angel*.

22 April

Mme Izvolskaya gave me a packet of letters of introduction to various French aristocrats in view of my probable sojourn in Paris. They are all society ladies much interested in new artistic directions, who will be delighted that I am coming to Paris.

Composed a little of *Fiery Angel*.

Linette came in the evening and we had a very passionate time.

23 April

When I went into Cook's today to find out if they had transferred my reservation they informed me that they had resold it without obtaining a replacement booking for me, and were now doubtful of being able to do so. In other words they had swindled me in the most despicable way. I raised hell with them and demanded to see the manager, but he backed up his sales staff, doubtless sharing the resultant bribe with them.

I was now in a most unenviable position, because the tickets were return tickets valid only until July and hundreds of people were waiting for reservations for the return voyage. The ocean had turned into a wall between me and Europe. Instead of being able to earn money in France and England in what was now the height of the season, I was condemned to kick my heels and eke out my remaining resources in America. I was distraught, and determined to exploit all my connections to try to secure a passage.

24 April

Went down town in the morning to settle the money orders and other business matters. I was told that a reservation might turn up at the last moment, just before sailing, so I should be ready to pack up and leave at a few hours' notice.

Rehearsed *Sarcasms*, but found I had well and truly forgotten them, and to boot someone had run off with the music. My American repertoire had perforce consisted of my most accessible compositions, but I hoped that in Paris there would be a demand for newer work, and therefore I must work on preparing it.

Linette and I dined with Liebman and Deryuzhinsky. Afterwards I suddenly remembered that yesterday I had passed my twenty-ninth birthday, at which Liebman kissed me and made Linette follow suit. What a dreadful thought – my thirtieth year of existence!

After dinner we went to Carnegie Hall to hear the Zimro concert at which my *Hebrew Overture* was to be played. The concert was long and not terribly interesting, the *Overture* was the last number on the programme. It had a tremendous success and twice I had to stand up in the box and take a bow. I like taking a bow from a box: everyone in the audience turns round and fidgets about in their seats.

I rang up Stella, who was coquettish on the phone and seemed pleased about the difficulties I was experiencing over my departure. She is busy today and tomorrow, with a matinee and an evening performance on both days, but I am to ring her again on Monday and can have some time with her then.

25 April

As it was Sunday, sunny and spring-like, Linette and I went out of the city. Linette chose our destination, which was called Orange, and had three parts: East, West and North Orange, i.e. Three Oranges. It was an attractive place and we had an enjoyable walk, although again we were surprised by the lack of flowers. All we could see were occasional glimpses of trees covered in white blossom, like Honolulu. Linette later spent the evening with me.

26 April

Liebman, whose help I have been asking for three days in getting a passage on a liner, telephoned in the morning to say that I could get one for tomorrow on a small ship called the *New York*, bound for England via France. I immediately dashed to the office and did indeed obtain the reservation.

There then ensued a frightful, panic-stricken rush to get ready to leave. Linette came at six, not expecting me to be going away so soon. I pleaded with her to come to Europe and left her $150 for the voyage 'as advance payment for her translation into English of *Three Oranges* for the Covent Garden production'. She vacillated between a desire to come and fear of doing so. It took until midnight to get my apartment shipshape with all the things I needed to take sorted out, although not yet packed. I collapsed into bed, virtually asleep on my feet.

27 April

I asked to be woken up at seven, and by nine had everything packed. Linette had told me how much she would be missing me, and how sad she would be at not being telephoned at eleven o'clock – something I did every day – so I ordered red roses to be delivered to her tomorrow at eleven. I also sent a bunch of forget-me-nots to Stella. Then my trunk and two small suitcases were loaded into a taxi and at ten o'clock I arrived at the pier. Formalities were light: my documents were checked and stamped, I had my trunk put in the hold right through to Paris, and then went on board. It was not a very big boat, nor was it particularly clean, and the three-berth cabin was very cramped, hardly bigger than a sleeping compartment on a Russian train. But any grumbles were outweighed by the joy of having a reservation at all.

Not having had time to say goodbye to anyone in New York I then wrote a fistful of letters to Liebman, Ingerman, Anisfeld, Yasyuk,[1] Linette and Stella, including to the last-named some endearments and my regrets to be leaving in such unexpected haste. As there was still time left before sailing, which was in any case delayed for an hour, I went ashore and rang up Linette: a few parting words, she asked me to write, I asked her again to come to Paris, and then we said goodbye. I went back on board and from that moment basically lost interest in America.

The weather was grey and rainy, and I was much more interested in when we would be given something to eat, as I had had nothing since seven o'clock and was starving. Hardly had we cast off when we were summoned to table, and by the time the meal was over the skyscrapers and the Statue of Liberty were well astern. It was no longer a novelty to see them: I had anyhow gazed my fill on them going on the Staten Island ferry to see the Stahls in the autumn; it is indeed a spectacular view, but not on such a grey day as this. After dinner the scramble for deckchairs commenced: there were 250 first-class passengers and only 160 chairs. The passengers all clamoured round the deckchair superintendent, and only after two hours of pushing and shoving was I allocated a place on the wrong side (the port side, facing north), after which I went for a walk to assuage my aching head. Nothing much happened after that: I was hailed by a passing New York acquaintance, then accosted by an Englishman, and retired to bed early to find that my neighbour did not want to turn off his electric light, which stopped me going to sleep.

---

1 Probably short for Yasyukovich. The Yasyukoviches were a powerful factory-owning dynasty from the Ukraine. Ignat Yasyukovich launched his company on the New York Stock Exchange in 1917, and may have been one of the contacts whose help Prokofiev was enlisting to get funds to his mother and secure her passage out of Russia.

28 April

Wind, cold, rain and the ship rolling. In the morning I felt all right, but the Englishman took me into the smoking-room to play chess and after that I began to feel a little queasy, so spent the remainder of the day on deck in my chair wrapped up in a rug, my hat and a warm scarf. More prudent passengers had equipped themselves with long travelling fur coats. I did not feel like going below to dinner, but as this wretched old tub has no deck service I went into the dining-room, helped myself to food on a plate and took it back up to eat on deck in my chair.

29 April

The weather has cleared up and the rolling subsided. The dark blue ocean glistens silver in the sun, but the blue is not as deep as the Pacific. I played six chess games with the Englishman and won all six. I caught up on my diary and tomorrow may do some work on the *Fiery Angel* libretto.

My table in the dining room has been invaded by a family from California, who had kept to their cabin all the time the ship was rolling. They turned out to be admirers of mine and are thrilled beyond words to be in my presence. I asked them not to spread the word too much, as the passengers will start badgering me to play.

30 April

The sea is not as lovely as yesterday, but still not bad. I take my meals in the dining-room, but have put *Fiery Angel* aside for now as I cannot find a quiet corner to work in: the cabin is awful and it is very draughty on deck.

My neighbour persists in keeping his light on until one o'clock at night. I approached him to ask him not to, but the cunning old boy feigned deafness. He wears an English army uniform, and judging by his age I took him for a general, but he is only a captain and a South African at that, a colonial.

1 May

The ship has been rolling quite a bit, and there have been times when the waves came right over the bow, but the passengers, myself included, have got used to it. Nevertheless, at times my stomach felt distinctly queasy and I preferred to stay put in my deckchair, declining invitations to play bridge.

In the evening my neighbour the captain switched on his light and settled down to read in his bunk. Because the plug happened to be near me, I turned it off without saying a word. The captain did not at first realise what had happened, but when he did he was enraged and demanded I switched it back on. Now it was my turn to pretend to be deaf. But the captain leapt from his bunk and took hold of my arm, insisting that I turn on the light (it had to be me, you see, he would not simply do it himself). To tell the truth I had not expected such a belligerent reaction, and was rather embarrassed, because naturally I did not want to fight with an elderly sixty-year-old. Therefore I asked him three times what he wanted, and finally pretending to understand, turned the light back on. The captain climbed back into his upper bunk while I gave him a little talking-to about not disturbing other people's peace. The captain stubbornly persisted for a while, but before long extinguished the light and peace reigned once more.

2 May

The idea of a chess tournament had been canvassed for three days, and finally took place with six people taking part. I had already acquired the reputation of a champion, and as a result there was invariably a little knot of spectators clustered round whichever table I was playing at. I concentrated hard and won four games in a row. The tournament and the breaks between play effectively took up all day.

The sea was calm, the weather warm and sunny. My captain had turned off his light by the time I turned in, so there was no incident today. A gentleman with whom I had been conversing all the time in French or in English turned out to be a Russian Baron, whose name I believe was Shelking. 'I suppose you are an officer?' he asked. I contented myself with answering in the negative.

3 May

The sea is almost flat calm, and the slight rolling is not affecting any of the passengers. The day's main event continued to be the chess tournament, to which I devoted all my intellectual efforts, and won another four games, enough to assure me the first prize. Baron Shelking presented me to his Baroness, recommending me as the chess champion, and during the conversation enquired whether I might not be the son of the famous composer. When I told him he was speaking to the man himself he was thrilled and declared himself a great admirer, possessed my works and had been on the point of playing them himself at a charity concert during a voyage from Japan.

A charity concert was similarly arranged on our boat today, and the organising ladies went around asking all the passengers if there was any capacity in which they could perform – all the passengers that is except for the two genuine performers among them, myself and a Danish reciter who had spoken to me on the first day of our voyage. We were of course indescribably happy not to have been approached. The passengers all put on evening dress and went to the concert (a truly appalling event) while I, the Baron, a Frenchman and an American played bridge until one o'clock. When I returned to my cabin, my captain neighbour, evidently a sufferer from senile insomnia, was still reading, but behaved decently and turned off his light almost as soon as I had undressed and got into bed.

4 May

The two final chess matches: having won all ten of my games I took the first prize. The second prize was won by Ferraris, an Austrian who won eight games (those taking part all put in $3, the first prize taking 75 per cent of the prize money and the runner-up 25 per cent). If the tournament had taken place on a Russian boat nobody would have paid any attention, but the English and the Americans are sportsmen and there was always a little group of people looking at and discussing the tabulated results pinned up on the wall, so that I frequently heard behind my back people saying, 'There goes the chess champion.'

The rest of the time I played bridge with the same little group, all of whom are very good players. It was impossible to do any work on this boat, there was no such thing as quiet corner in which to do so, and in any case I was not in the mood. Apparently we shall be docking at Cherbourg tomorrow afternoon. The weather has turned colder, as we have left the Gulf Stream.

5 May

A strong southerly wind, but no rolling. It is amazing how often there seems to be no connection between the state of the wind and the ship rolling.

We were playing bridge from quite early in the morning, and when I went out on deck at noon I could see some schooners under sail and in the distance, away to the north, a hilly coastline: this was the south-western extremity of England, the Isles of Scilly. The islands soon disappeared to be replaced by the coast of England herself, a narrow, grey strip just visible on the horizon. This was a surprise, as I thought that France would come into view first, but we were entering the Channel from the north.

The day passed peacefully at the bridge table, my companions contriving to relieve me of all the winnings I had laboriously accumulated during the preceding days. The liner made way slowly, as there was no point in hurrying to arrive at Cherbourg during the night. At around eleven o'clock in the evening some lighthouses and then the French coast hove into view. It was a strange feeling to be approaching France from the west, not the east. Tomorrow I shall be in Paris and will have completed my circumnavigation of the globe.

6 May

After only two hours' sleep I was up and about. The liner was at anchor and a wonderful sight met my eyes: the sea, the shore and a squadron at anchor in the harbour all shimmering in the bluish light that presages the dawn, from which gradually emerged the bright green forms of the hills behind. The air smelt fresh and fragrant, especially grateful when nearing land after a long time at sea. A French tender was already hove to near our liner, and the authorities had begun checking passports. 'Why does it say in your passport that you are travelling to Russia?' I was asked. I said it was merely a formality, and that I was not going there. The official made a note of everything in the passport, took down my Paris address, and let me go in peace. Nobody bothered us in Customs, and we were soon on the train. However, the train was not due to leave for another two hours, so I walked round the town relishing the old buildings, the French I heard spoken all around, the polite way people address one another, a practice of which there is not the faintest trace in America, and generally the difference in people and customs. America has two advantages: the population is healthier, and everything is much cleaner. But how much pleasanter and more poetic everything is here!

The comfortable but shabby train bore us swiftly through France, which appeared as green and flowery as a garden. After the boring, flat fields of America it was hard to tear one's eyes from the burgeoning landscape of smiling France. At eight o'clock in the evening there loomed up in the distance the outline of the Eiffel Tower, which I had at one time saluted in one of my short stories, and soon we disembarked at the Gare St Lazare.

All the hotels, both large and small, near the station were full to bursting, and since all establishments would shut at ten o'clock, there was a risk of being stranded on the pavement. I and one of my travelling companions, a Jew, dragging our luggage after us, managed to find a horrible set of furnished rooms for eight francs (that is to say, half a dollar in American money) and decided to spend the night there. I telephoned Samoilenko and Stahl, but no one was in. Then I went for a walk down the Champs-Elysées to find that Paris is economising on electricity and was completely dark. But how fine are the buildings and how spacious the squares! Beside the Elysées, New York and its Fifth Avenue are little more than long, narrow canals! Couples were embracing on every corner, taking advantage of the darkness. I went back to the furnished room and, exhausted by the day, fell asleep.

Diaghilev is in Paris, and the first night of his season is tomorrow. I did not know about this and was overjoyed to find him not only here but flourishing. Next morning I set off to try to find the Stahls: they were still away, but were to my great satisfaction expected back from Rio today or tomorrow. I then tracked down Samoilenko, with whom I had an affectionate reunion and a delicious lunch in a gourmet restaurant. After America, French cuisine is truly magnificent. After lunch I went to the Grand Opéra to find out where Diaghilev was staying, and ten minutes later found the man himself at the Hôtel Scribe. 'Seryozha Prokofiev has come!' screamed Diaghilev, and we kissed, also Massine,[1] who was with him. Neither of them seemed to have changed much. Diaghilev said he had cabled me in response to the letter I had sent him a year and a half ago and had asked me to come to London, but had had no reply. He is ready to present my ballet[2] the moment the score is ready, but on condition that I am present. The sets and costumes had long ago been produced by Larionov and are splendid. We met at eight o'clock for dinner, and Stravinsky was also there: we kissed affectionately and altogether had the warmest of reunions. All kinds of rumours had been circulating about Stravinsky in America, that he was ill and virtually reduced to beggary, but now he appeared to have regained his strength, and was full of vigour and consuming quantities of alcohol with evident enjoyment. He told me I was the only living Russian composer he loved, and recommended me to have my works published by Chester in London. I was enchanted to be once again in the company of Diaghilev and Stravinsky, although this did not prevent an acerbic difference of opinion whenever they expressed contempt for all Russian music except the most blatantly nationalistic, dismissed Scriabin as a composer and utterly wrote off opera as a genre.

8 May

In the morning I went for a walk with the Samoilenkos in the Bois de Boulogne and had lunch there in a delightful restaurant. But the prices were shocking: lunch for four cost 200 francs. However, at the current rate of exchange this is only $12. Fatma Hanum had heard back from Mama in response to the letter she had sent her: Mama is feeling more cheerful but is still in Princes Islands. I wrote to Sonya in Brussels and, depending on her response, will decide what action to take. At two o'clock I had an incredibly happy reunion with the Stahls, both of whom had just arrived from Rio and were looking radiant. They will be here for about five weeks and will then go back. They want me to join them there if not now, then in September. Stahl guarantees my success there and even offers to subsidise my voyage. An idea! Perhaps I should go in September?

In the evening I joined Stravinsky, Mme Edwards[3] and others in

---

1 Léonide Massine, having replaced Vaclav Nijinsky as Diaghilev's *premier danseur* and choreographer, was now effectively leading the Ballets Russes, as (except for a three-year Bronislava Nijinska interregnum from 1921 brought about by Diaghilev's fury at Massine's marriage to Vera Savina) he continued to do until the impresario's death, and thereafter in the company's reincarnation as the Ballet Russe de Monte Carlo. See *Diaries*, vol. 1, pp. 705, 757, and above p. 21 n. 1.
2 *Chout*.
3 Misia Edwards, née Godebska (1872–1950), a good pianist and musician, hostess of a glittering

Diaghilev's box for the opening performance of the Ballets Russes. After the lamentable efforts New York has been making to ape the Ballets Russes with poor scenery and inadequate dancers, it was such a joy to see the real thing, albeit in a less extravagantly luxurious form than six or seven years ago. *The Good-humoured Ladies* to Scarlatti's music[1] is highly entertaining and imaginatively staged by Massine, while the *Petrushka* was in a wholly different league to the New York production.[2] After the performance I dined with Diaghilev, who was in a state bordering on rapture, dispensing champagne as if it were water, told a stream of stories and was magnificently in his element. Stravinsky got tipsy and made scabrous remarks, but was also a delight. A marvellous evening.

9 May

Spent the morning with Stahls, who talked much of Brazil and again urged me to go there. Stahl may have stars in his eyes, but he is observant and has a penetrating understanding. All right, I might well go! But first I have to see what happens with Mama and Linette.

In the afternoon I took my letters of recommendation to the two Princesses, one of whom was not at home (I left the letter and my card) and the other away from Paris.[3]

---

salon and muse to an extraordinary collection of great artists, including Proust (she is the model for Princess Yourbeletieff in *La Prisonnière*, but also less generously for some aspects of the culturally pretentious social climber Mme Verdurin),Renoir, Vuillard, Lautrec, Bonnard, Ravel, Debussy, Poulenc, Stravinsky, Cocteau, Verlaine, Mallarmé, and above all Diaghilev – the list of leading figures in the Parisian arts world whom she befriended, loved, supported and quarrelled with is almost endless. 'For most of her life she was too rich to be a true bohemian, and too passionate about art to be a true representative of high society. Instead, she was, for her time, the incarnation of that special energy released when talent and privilege meet.' (Clive James, reviewing in the *London Review of Books* in 1980 the biography of Misia Sert by A. Gold and R. Fizdale, *Misia* (Macmillan, London).)

1 Orchestrated by Vincenzo Tommassini.
2 In December 1918 at the Metropolitan Opera, conducted by Pierre Monteux with choreography by Adolph Bolm. Stravinsky, who did not see the production, was nevertheless vicious in condemnation: 'I don't go on about the décors and costumes which I discovered in *Vogue*, and whose Judeo-boche taste cannot be denied to be contrary to my intentions. I suppose the rest of the show, including the dances (M. Bolm is a Jew) displays the same influences.' (I. Stravinsky, letter to an American acquaintance, quoted in S. Walsh, *Stravinsky: A Creative Spring* (Jonathan Cape, London, 2000).)
3 One Princess was no doubt the Princesse de Polignac (née Winaretta Singer, the sewing-machine heiress), and the other may have been the Comtesse Greffuhle: both were prominent among the many aristocratic patrons of the Paris musical and artistic milieu, and in particular supporters of Diaghilev and his circle.

10 May

In the morning I called on Stravinsky, who promised to arrange for me to have a piano. As he and I and a Swiss writer[1] were walking along the Rue de la paix we met a young woman, not very tall, whose form reminded me of Nina Meshcherskaya. I looked closely at her and from the way her eyebrows joined together was almost certain I recognised her. Noticing the keenness of my gaze she turned her head, but by this time we were abreast of one another and I also averted my gaze, virtually certain that it was indeed Nina Meshcherskaya. It was not impossible, because some time ago I had heard that her father was in the south of Russia and at the time that was the direct route to Paris.[2] The meeting did not disturb me, although I did find it interesting. I am very far from Nina now, even though I remember both her venom and her affection.

Stravinsky took me to a rehearsal of an old Italian opera being directed by Diaghilev with extraordinary verve and mastery, drilling the singers in every note and every word.[3] Stravinsky then asked me to do a second proofreading of the overture to his new ballet *Pulcinella*, boasting that it was completely error-free. I did so, and unearthed two. The ballet is written in antique style, and it is an extraordinary coincidence that three years ago I had composed my 'Classical' Symphony and now Stravinsky, knowing nothing about this, had written a classical ballet.

Stravinsky and I left where he was staying to go to Mme Edwards, where we found Diaghilev as well. Here I was made to play *Visions Fugitives* and *Tales of an Old Grandmother*. I did not play them very well, having forgotten them and not having touched a piano for three weeks. Diaghilev and Stravinsky liked best the third of the *Grandmother's Tales* and the fifteenth *Vision*, but obviously still retained the strongest impression of the Second Piano Concerto, which Diaghilev now begged me to remember and play, but

---

1 Possibly C. F. Ramuz, the librettist of *The Soldier's Tale*, with whom discussions (not very fruitful) were taking place around this time about the idea of making a ballet from the theatre piece.
2 This was possible, as Nina's memoirs explain that her initial escape route had been in December 1919 by sea across the Gulf to Finland, where in February 1920 she obtained a visa for France and took 'the usual emgirant's route' via Stockholm, Copenhagen and London to Paris. So she could have been in Paris in May 1920, although the memoirs go on to relate that until June 1924, when she married her second husband and settled for the duration in Paris, she lived a peripatetic life moving frequently between Belgrade, Paris, Constantinople, Berlin and Nice. The memoirs also state that her father, who had been arrested in April 1918 and imprisoned in the Butyrka and Lubyanka prisons but had been released as a result of the successful intervention of the woman who was to be his second wife, Yelena Grevs, had earlier used the Finland escape route, meeting up eventually with his daughter in Paris, so the information that he had been in south Russia seems not to be correct. (N. Krivosheina, op. cit.)
3 Cimarosa's opera-ballet *Le Astuzie Femminili* (*Women's Wiles*) orchestrated by Respighi according to a contract that, in contrast to Stravinsky's Pergolesi, obliged him to 'create all the recitatives in conformity with the themes of the composer and totally change the orchestration, adding the dances agreed upon with Diaghilev'.

which I neither could nor would. When I played them Medtner's *Fairy Tale*, Op. 8, and then wanted to go on to Scriabin, they chorused their disapproval, at which I told them they suffered from a blinkered, émigré perspective. Diaghilev retorted that a cannon firing along a narrow line is still a cannon.

When I had finished playing there entered a small man with a tanned face and hair streaked with grey. Stravinsky reacted excitedly and introduced us: Prokofiev – Ravel. I was fascinated to meet the famous composer, but we had hardly any time to talk. On parting I said to him: 'Au revoir, maître', it being the custom in Russia, and in Italy as well, to refer to any composer as 'maestro', but Ravel reacted as though I had kissed his hand. He replied: 'Oh, non, non! Confrère alors . . .' After all these encounters I went for a walk in the Bois de Boulogne and then, tired out, went to bed.

11 May

A letter from Sonya Brichant, but she knows no more of Mama than I do. I therefore appealed to Samoilenko to bring me in contact with the Russian Embassy so that I could start the process of applying for a French visa for Mama. Samoilenko told me that the Minsters had just arrived from Constantinople and would have news of Mama.

Froska-san and Japan! That is something to think about, here in Paris! Both had spent some time in India and Turkey, were as brown as berries, and although they had not actually seen Mama, they had seen Tanya Rayevskaya. According to what they told us, the refugees were living reasonably well; also there were good steamer connections between Marseilles and Constantinople, a voyage of about seven days. I shall try to get Mama a visa, send her some money, and then she must get herself a passage on a steamer and I will meet her in Marseilles.

In the evening I was in Diaghilev's box for the second performance by the Ballets Russes (they perform three times a week) and saw the *Chant du rossignol*, the ballet fashioned by Stravinsky from *The Nightingale*.[1] I listened with tremendous interest, especially to the orchestration; as for the music there is much that is interesting, but also much that is redundant scratching. I must hear it again. *The Rite of Spring*, when Stravinsky and I played it four-hands in Milan, produced a far stronger effect on me than this ballet. Massine's staging is very effective and imaginative; he is a gifted choreographer. Picasso's designs[2] are interesting in places, but are sometimes inept. Picasso himself was in the box, but in the general mêlée we were not introduced and it was only afterwards that I heard it was he. Stravinsky was dis-

---

1 Based on the first two acts of the opera, the parts Stravinsky had composed in 1913–14, with choreography by Massine and designs by Matisse.
2 Prokofiev is mistaken: scenery and costumes for the original Paris production were by Matisse.

tracted and in a bad temper, as he claimed the orchestra played badly and had not properly learnt the score.

The Stravinsky was followed by *Schéhérezade*, which had resplendent sets and costumes by Bakst and was sheer pleasure.

I have been in Paris for five days now and am beginning to draw some conclusions. In my opinion there is not much I can accomplish here: I must settle the passport business both for Mama and for myself, and get myself to London. As far as I can see Paris is no longer a fruitful source of money either from concerts or from wealthy households; anything one can get would be no more than kopecks. And I think I can sense a feeling in the wind that Paris, before the war the hub of the artistic universe, is losing its pre-eminent status and influence. There is no real point in working here 'for the glory of it'. I have to think carefully about money now: I am no longer alone but shall be responsible for Mama. I'll hang on here another week or two and then go to London.

12 May

Janacopulos gives her first Paris concert on 2 June and is spending 7,000 francs on good publicity for it. I do not envisage presenting myself in recital in Paris: expense, fuss and bother – and all for no particular end that I can see.

Samoilenko has spoken to Prince Lvov[1] about arranging a French visa for Mama and an English visa for me, and Lvov has agreed to receive me the day after tomorrow.

In the evening the Stahls, the Samoilenkos, the Minsters and I all had dinner in Montmartre. The company was excellent, although Stahl and Samoilenko sparred acrimoniously with one another. After dinner Stahl took me to a sort of nightclub where they sing a requiem mass over you, put you in a coffin and then by means of mirrors spots start appearing all over your body which then turns into a skeleton. It's an old trick, very entertaining but of course not at all frightening.

I keep thinking of Linette and how nice it would be if she were here.

---

1   Prince Georgy Lvov, Kerensky's predecessor as Prime Minister of the Provisional Government, was arrested and imprisoned after the October Revolution, but escaped to Siberia, whence he made his way via Japan and the United States to Paris, becoming head of a White Russian organisation calling itself the Russian Political Conference (Russkoye Politicheskoye Soveshchaniye). The Conference, claiming to be the only authentically constituted Government of Russia, put itself forward formally to represent Russia at the 1919 Paris Peace Conference that resulted in the Treaty of Versailles, but was rejected, as was the Bolshevik Government of the RSFSR. The leaders of the Conference continued, however, to base themselves in Paris and to represent the interests of Russian émigré individuals and organisations. France recognised General Wrangel's short-lived government in the Crimea in August 1920, but did not formally recognise the Soviet Union until October 1928.

13 May

With Janacopulos met Yovanovich, the same who twelve years ago was supposed to be the first pianist to play my works in public and with whom on this matter I had a serious falling-out.[1] Later we made it up, and now he has heard more of my compositions he describes them as the best among contemporary works. He told me he had heard of the death of poor, dear Nikolay Vasilievich Andreyev from spotted typhoid, and that his wife together with Boris Verin had made their way to the Crimea. I am overjoyed that Boris Verin has managed to extricate himself from Petrograd and suspect that it was Anna Grigorievna who got him away, but even so, of course, the Crimea is not necessarily salvation from the dreadful epidemic. As for dear Nikolay Vasilieivich, I am very, very sorry for this person with his radiant smile and uniquely gentle character. And how many are still unaccounted for. Yes! A black cross must be placed over all those friends still in Russia who are dear to me, and I shall count as resurrected from the dead any who miraculously appear from behind its shadow . . .

On the street today, in the same place as before, I think I again saw Nina Meshcherskaya. This time she seemed tiny, looking the same as ever, wearing a light brown dress with a big black hat, very attractive and looking straight at me. If it was indeed her then our relations are undoubtedly severed once and for all, as I did not bow to her. But it could very easily not have been her at all, since Nina always had a French look about her and I have never been good at recognising people, so I may have mistaken someone else for her.

At half-past ten that evening I was due to meet Heifetz, who had also come over from America, at the Grand Hôtel, and we were planning to visit a few nightclubs together, but in Paris the hotels all close their doors at ten o'clock and so we were not able to make contact.

After American women, French women are charming, elegant and have such friendly manners.

14 May

B. N. Samoilenko has set up a meeting for me today either with Prince Lvov or with Vyrubov[2] with the object of getting their help to obtain visas, French for Mama and English for me. Which of them actually received me I am not sure, but from his outward appearance I believe it was Lvov: a gentle, portly

---

1 See *Diaries*, vol. 1, pp. 85–6, 279.
2 The name resonates because of Anna Vyrubova, the confidante of the Tsarina and notoriously her go-between with Rasputin. Anna had married Alexander Vyrubov, a naval officer, but they soon divorced. This man may be her former husband or a connection of his.

individual who could do nothing to help me since, as he said, extra-stringent conditions and obstacles had recently been introduced in the path of Russians wishing entry into France. He said Mama should start off her application in Constantinople, from where enquiries would be made in Paris, and it would be my job to support those enquiries here. Minster's advice is that Mama should try to get a visa for Belgium, which is easier to obtain, and once she had that the French would not raise any difficulty in granting a transit visa.

I lunched with the Princesse de Polignac.[1] The Princess is an elderly woman, very musical, who commissions works from all composers – Stravinsky, Ravel, Falla – and pays good money. She has a magnificent house and maintains what amounts to strict etiquette. After lunch I played several of the *Visions Fugitives*. She was already acquainted with my compositions.

15 May

Went to the Russian Embassy, to the Russian Consulate and to the Préfecture, all in pursuit of my English visa. The Consulate's hours for reception were running late, and the Préfecture takes bribes. There was a notice on the wall announcing 'the offering of money is strictly forbidden'. You can't help wondering what lies behind a notice like that. I achieved very little and returned home in a foul mood: things are not working out but it is absolutely essential that I get these visas and also some money, otherwise I shall not have enough to last until the autumn. I sent a telegram to Mama telling her to apply in the first instance for a Belgian visa and then a transit visa for France.

In the evening I attended the premiere of Stravinsky's new ballet *Pulcinella*, based on music by Pergolesi that Diaghilev had dug up from somewhere or other.[2] It is very interesting, although Stravinsky has sometimes rather overdone the antique style. The keening after Pierrot's murder is wonderful.

I was not in a good temper and hardly spoke to anyone in the box. Diaghilev was distracted and failed, so it seemed to me, to show sufficient

---

1 Born Winnaretta Singer (1865–1943), eighteenth of twenty children of the sewing-machine magnate, Princesse Edmond de Polignac was the wealthiest, most influential and most imaginative patron and salon hostess of the Parisian artistic milieu of the early twentieth century. Among the composers and writers who benefited from her support were Ravel, Debussy, Poulenc, Cocteau, Satie, Ethel Smyth, de Falla, Proust, Stravinsky, Colette and Nadia Boulanger.
2 Diaghilev and Massine had found in the Naples Conservatory some unpublished instrumental pieces by Pergolesi, and it had been Diaghilev's idea, encouraged by the success of the Tommasini–Scarlatti *Good-humoured Ladies*, that Massine should create a *commedia dell-arte* ballet based around the Pulcinella character. As Stephen Walsh points out, Diaghilev had almost certainly envisaged a conventional orchestral arrangement like Tommasini's or Respighi's, very far from the idiosyncratic transformation wrought by Stravinsky (S. Walsh, op. cit.).

interest in my compositions, while Mme Edwards did not pay me much attention at all. I repaid her with a double dose of indifference.

16 May

Wrote to Sonya asking her to apply for a visa for Mama. Called on Stravinsky to talk to him about yesterday's performance of the ballet, because I had not said anything to him and felt uncomfortable about it. Stravinsky was very nice. When I told him how depressed I was about my failure to get a visa for Mama, he said that was undoubtedly a very difficult problem, but Mme Edwards could do anything and I should speak to her. Thank God, Stravinsky rates my music highly and regards me as the only Russian composer worth speaking of (after himself, naturally), but while I appreciate the relevance of the exclusively nationalistic perspective from which he views me, I do not share it to the same extent.

17 May

Went again to the English Consulate, where I was expecting to be met with more procrastination and difficulties, but untypically for English officialdom the Consul was friendly and told me that as soon as I could get my passport stamped by the Paris Préfecture he would grant me a visa immediately. The Préfecture is no obstacle at all, so I should be able to leave at any time. This is good news, but where is the logic in it? In New York after seven weeks they still had not given me a visa, but here in Paris I can get it without difficulty.

Stravinsky said that he had seen Mme Edwards and she had promised to arrange Mama's visa. He played me his *Ragtime*, a rhythmically fascinating piece, but I am not sure I would be able to play it in America as I am afraid it would be hopelessly beyond their understanding.[1] I played all twenty *Visions Fugitives* for Stravinsky, five of which he found very good, and the rest rather inconsequential. I can never predict what Stravinsky will like and what he will not like.

Called on Wiborg, who has just come from London, and met with her Larionov and Goncharova, who both flung their arms round me. Larionov has all manner of hopes and schemes to collaborate with me on projects,

---

1   It is not clear whether this was the piano version of the ensemble piece *Ragtime* or the *Piano Rag Music* Stravinsky wrote for Arthur Rubinstein in June 1919, but probably the latter. Whichever it was, Prokofiev's strictures on the understanding of the American public seem to have been justified, as the critic Olin Downes was to savage *Ragtime* in the *New York Times* in January 1925: 'Evidently to many it was funny. Others found it merely poor ragtime, often vulgar and farcically obvious, now and again malicious, but without the saving grace of humanity, laughter and invention, which redeem malice and make it the fitting sauce of comedy.' (Quoted in S. Walsh, op. cit.)

bypassing Diaghilev. Of course I believe that Diaghilev does things a thousand times better than any of those who have broken away from him and tried to compete with him, but whenever one has dealings with Diaghilev it is always helpful to have some ammunition in one's pocket, and therefore I replied to Larionov that I was very interested in his plans. Besides Larionov, who was charmingly disorganised, Wiborg also had with her another gentleman whom I at first took for an Englishman, then for a Russian, and was about to say something disrespectful to him, but he turned out to be the Grand Duke Dmitry Pavlovich.[1]

In the evening I again attended *Pulcinella* which this time I followed with the score, a model of neatness and clarity that gave me great pleasure. After the performance there was supper at Mme Edwards, where Stravinsky and Diaghilev very nearly came to blows. Stravinsky complained that at the end of *Pulcinella* the curtain had come down too slowly, to which Diaghilev retorted: 'C'est parce que tu as raté la fin.'[2] Stravinsky went for him then, declaring that *Pulcinella* was a work of genius and that Diaghilev had no understanding of music. Diaghilev objected that the composers he worked with had all been saying that for twenty years, and all his designers that he knows nothing about painting, but thank God it has all been successful, while *Pulcinella* had been through three phases of composition: (1) Pergolesi – Stravinsky; (2) Stravinsky – Pergolesi; and (3) Stravinsky *à la* Pergolesi. Eventually they were pulled apart, and five minutes later were drinking champagne peaceably together.

18 May

I visited Mme Edwards, who confirmed that she would be glad to arrange a visa for Mama at short notice, and also one for me to come back into France from England.

Janacopulos is giving her first concert on 2 June and her second on the 10th, and is suggesting I join forces with her for the second one. In a way sharing the platform with a singer instead of appearing in his own concert would be a rather unimpressive way for a composer to make his debut; on the other hand I have no plans to appear solo and perhaps it would be better to have half a concert than none at all. But in the last analysis it makes little difference, since Paris today is not a place to give concerts.

Yesterday I had a second letter from Linette, one more loving than the other, but saying nothing about coming to Europe. I believe this is temporary, and in two or three weeks she will miss me and will have to reopen the subject.

---

1 The Grand Duke Dmitry Pavlovich Romanov (1891–1942), grandson of Tsar Alexander II, was one of the conspirators in the murder of Rasputin. Despatched to Persia, after the Revolution he joined the British Army, and after his discharge settled first in London and then in Paris.
2 'Because you messed up the ending.'

19 May

Last evening at the performance Stravinsky handed me a document signed by an important functionary at the Ministry of Foreign Affairs giving me the right to leave and re-enter France, and Mama's visa has already been despatched. This is all the work of Mme Edwards, and I could do no more than offer her my grateful thanks. She had achieved it quickly and well, and I had written her off as simply vulgar! Of course, one characteristic does not necessarily contradict the other.

After the performance Stravinsky took me to the home of the Princess Murat, who was holding a grand reception in honour of the Ballets Russes: Diaghilev, Stravinsky, Larionov, the Grand Duke Dmitry Pavlovich, Picasso and several young French composers, one of them a decorative young female, and a host of other guests. The amount of talk and noise and leaping about was tremendous; at three o'clock in the morning Stravinsky was underneath the piano with his enemy Cocteau, a gramophone was screeching away on top of the piano while someone was thrashing the keys and Diaghilev seemed to be dancing a Lancers with our hostess. I alone preserved a dignified composure.

20 May

After a very late night I had to get up early because at ten o'clock I had arranged to read three scenes from *Fiery Angel* through to Stahl and consult with him on the rest. Stahl has an incisive intelligence and an excellent feeling for the stage. I would trust Demchinsky even more, but Stahl too gave me unexpected and very interesting advice. I am not clear in my mind about the psychology of Renata in the fourth scene,[1] about which Bryusov says little, nor about the conclusion of the inn scene with Mephistopheles. I also wanted to see what Stahl would have to say about the liberties I was taking with Bryusov in the last act. Our discussion was extremely interesting, only it was a pity it could not be longer, because the Diva[2] was rushing to go out somewhere and was all the time interrupting and disturbing us. I was very angry, and said to her that discussion of the outline of an opera was once for all time, but a petticoat could be purchased any day of the week.

In the afternoon I went to see Larionov to see his sketches for *Chout*, which he had made five years ago. They are, to my mind, quite brilliant and even in the light of the opulence of Anisfeld overwhelmingly effective, with a wealth of fantasy and inventiveness. They produced in me an intense desire to have *Chout* staged soon, but I must be firm in my negotiations with

---

1 Act Three Scene One in the completed opera, during which Renata incites Rupprecht to seek out and kill Heinrich/Madiel.
2 Vera Janacopulos, Stahl's wife.

Diaghilev and insist on additional payment for the score. To write a huge work now and not be paid anything for it is impossible.

21 May

I played through a ballet by Carpenter, whose wife is in Paris and wants me to arrange for her to meet Diaghilev. I will do so, but doubt whether Diaghilev will want to produce this ballet: a procession from the banal to the ephemeral, often easy on the ear but always nugatory.[1] As we rode together in a large and comfortable automobile I reflected how strange it was that there existed people who possess large cars and who do not have to worry about what the morrow will bring! As if in answer to my thoughts Mme Carpenter let out a great sigh: 'Oh, what would John not give to have Diaghilev accept his ballet!' Everyone wants what he does not have.

22 May

I arranged for the Diva (although I am still cross with her) to meet Stravinsky so that he could give her a lesson on the singing of *Pribaoutki*. He also played his new songs,[2] from a proof copy. They are very interesting; I did not expect them to be so good. Very Russian, and in places he plumbs the depths I so admire in *The Rite of Spring*, which I do not find in many of his things.

In the evening I went to *The Firebird*, which I enjoyed. The sets by Golovin, who should have designed *The Gambler*,[3] are also very nice. After the performance I played bridge with Gunsbourg,[4] winning 120 francs.

---

1 The ballet was *Skyscrapers*, which Diaghilev eventually failed to take on and which was produced by Carpenter himself at the New York Metropolitan in 1926. Described by the composer as a portrait of 'the many rhythmic movements and sounds of modern American life', it is a large, exuberant score blending Whitemanesque jazz, Tin-Pan-Alley tunes and spirituals with modernist signatures such as bitonalism.
2 *Four Russian Folk Songs*, to folk-song words with a translation into French by C. F. Ramuz.
3 See above, p. 167 and *passim*.
4 Raoul Gunsbourg (1859–1955), half French and half Romanian, was, along with Gabriel Astruc and Diaghilev himself, one of the key figures in the world of international opera and ballet presentations. As Lynn Garafola has made clear in her book *Diaghilev's Ballets Russes* (OUP, New York, 1989, and Da Capo Press), all three circled continually round one another competing for prestige, money, venues, product and artists, not always in the most gentlemanly fashion although the exigencies of this most precarious trade often made co-operation essential. Gunsbourg, Director of the Monte Carlo Opéra, had for instance first bought and then sold back to him all the sets and costumes of Diaghilev's 1909 Paris season, including *Pskovityanka*, the original Ballets Russes *Gesamtkunstwerk Le Pavillon d'Armide*, and the *Polovetsian Dances* from *Prince Igor*. Since 1911 the Ballets Russes had regarded Gunsbourg's Théâtre de Monte Carlo as its regular rehearsal and try-out venue for the major presentations in Paris and London. Rather like Sir Thomas Beecham, Gunsbourg was, at various times and in various circumstances, Diaghilev's partner and his rival.

23 May

Mmes Carpenter and Wiborg took me to lunch outside Paris, and then to the races, where there were many fashionable people and a mass of Russians. I was not much interested in the races themselves as I did not know the horses and had no favourites to back. Afterwards I paid a farewell visit to Mme Edwards, where Mme Noble and her very pretty daughter invited me to visit them when I am in London.

24 May

Had intended to finish off all my pre-departure commitments, but it was a holiday and everything was closed. It was therefore a wasted day for me, except for the bicycle races Gunsbourg made me come to with him. They were fun at first, but boring after a while. Car racing is much more entertaining. But it was a lovely day, and the company was agreeable.

In the evening I played bridge again and lost 440 francs. Very disappointing indeed.

25 May

The day was spent in clearing up things I had to do before going to London. They gave me my English visa promptly and even offered me one which would be valid for a year, which I declined (stupidly) as I grudged the 56 francs it would cost. I then changed money, alas at 13.20 francs to the dollar instead of the 17 francs I had been quoted in New York.

In the afternoon I looked in on a rehearsal of *Cimarosa*, an opera being presented by Diaghilev with a sprinkling of ballet.[1] The designs by Sert[2] are worthy but uninspired, although Diaghilev and Stravinsky praise them. To my mind they are going against their conscience because Sert is 'one of us', but in fact the designs are warmed-up yesterday's fare. My farewells with Stravinsky were affectionate, and with Diaghilev cordial. But I think Stravinsky must have passed on to him my intention to argue for more money for *Chout*, which is why Diaghilev is keeping himself slightly at arm's length and girding up for the struggle.

Spent the evening with Samoilenko and the morning with Stahl, and

---

1 An opera-ballet adaptation of Cimarosa's opera buffa *Le Astuzie femminili*, for which Diaghilev had commissioned new orchestration from Respighi, with choreography by Massine. The first two scenes were straight opera, the third a moonlit fête in which the guests watch a ballet. This final scene was subsequently presented just as a ballet under the title *Cimarosiana*. See above, p. 508.
2 Jose-Maria Sert (1876–1945), Spanish painter, mural artist and scenic designer. He was now married to Misia Edwards (her third husband and the one she loved most deeply). See *Diaries*, vol. 1, p. 706; also Gold and Fizdale, op. cit.

agreed that I would telegraph him on 10 July to let him know whether or not I was coming to Brazil in September, and if I was then he would send me money.

26 May

The train was due to leave at ten so I rose at seven. As I did not have much to pack, I had time to go and collect any letters from Linette. She wrote that she very much wanted to come, but could not get a ticket as there are none available until August. Of course there are not, but if one really wants to, one can always manage it somehow. Nevertheless, I think she will come, and then it will be wonderful.

At ten o'clock I was on the train and remembering how seven years ago I was on the same train with dear N. V. Andreyev on my way to London for the first time. This time we were late arriving at Dieppe, but there were not many formalities and we were soon on board the ferry, a tiny little thing after the ocean-going liners. The view as we left Dieppe was rather fine: the steep coastline and a soft light, but soon the rain poured down and I went down into the saloon to write to Linette a letter of a mildly hortatory nature.

Then English Customs, where I was detained for a short time for questions about where and why I was going, but after they saw my newspaper cuttings they were satisfied and I got on the train. I was in London by nine o'clock in the evening, where I displayed uncommon resourcefulness, carrying my bags myself, hailing a taxi and being driven to a hotel whose name I had been given by someone on the boat. London was bursting at the seams and it was not easy to find a room, and it was only at the third attempt that I succeeded, albeit expensively and badly: ten shillings for a measly casemate with a bed, a washbasin and a chair, but no table or wardrobe. The food was also poor after the wonderful Paris cuisine.

I found Coates's telephone number and spoke to him, to be greeted by exclamations of joy, in the course of which Coates demonstrated that he had not forgotten a single word of his Russian. He asked me if I had brought my compositions with me, and said that I should come to him in Covent Garden the next day at one o'clock.

27 May

I found myself a room in a quiet hotel, not chic but quite spacious and comfortable, with windows overlooking a garden and breakfast, for two-and-a-half guineas a week, that is to say $1.40 a day, and moved there. The problem of where to stay had been settled satisfactorily.

At one I presented myself at Covent Garden – a theatre with a large stage and astonishingly capacious stalls seats, disposed in a way that clearly pays no regard whatever to economy. Coates evidently sees himself as England's number one conductor, shouting at the chorus and generally imposing his authority, although in a genial manner. We had lunch together after the rehearsal. Coates kept saying how glad he was to see me; the composer whose works he was mainly performing all through the current season was Scriabin, but next season would concentrate on me. There were some buts: he has not yet played the *Scythian Suite*, as the parts arrived only after the programmes had been made up; nothing was said about the opera (apparently there is some friction between him and the Covent Garden director Beecham, a millionaire and indifferent conductor who is jealous of Coates.) Whether or not he would have a symphony concert in the near future in which to include me was not certain; there might be one on 11 June, in which case I would definitely be invited, but as yet this concert was not a firm fixture. To sum up: there were many excellent prospects for the future (and I do trust Coates) but for the present there was nothing concrete in view, so I shall have to wait until the various possibilities assume a more definite character.

From Coates I went to see Kling (junior),[1] the director of the music publishers Chesters. He was as nice as it is possible to be, but is not offering anything at the present time, not even a studio with a piano to work in, as his papa had done six years ago.

28 May

The opening of Yakovlev's (Sasha-Yasha's) exhibition, attended by a large number of Russians, some of whom had recently arrived from Petrograd. I could not find anything out about Myaskovsky, Asafyev, Suvchinsky or Boris Verin. Benois and Ziloti are in Finland. Medtner, Borovsky and Koussevitzky are safely in Moscow. Karatygin and Glazunov are still in Petrograd, and when last seen were not looking at all good. The death of N. V. Andreyev is, alas, confirmed but I did not hear of any others who had died. When I asked my interlocutor if the two-and-a-half years he had lived in such terrible conditions had left him morally maimed, he answered that towards the end of his time in Petrograd he had begun to feel, to his horror, that he was completely losing his grip on life and with it any sense of being human, but as soon as he left Russia a renewal of proper perspective came remarkably quickly.

The exhibition itself consisted exclusively of Oriental portraits, mostly Chinese, which admirably caught the features of the East, notably in the

---

[1] Otto Kling's son Henry was gradually assuming a greater role in the management of the music publishers J. & W. Chester as his father began to suffer ill health (he died in 1924). Henry's reputation was a good deal more abrasive than his father's. See *Diaries*, vol. 1, pp. 704–5.

eyes, some of which looked unseeing straight to the front, some gazed superciliously at Europeans, and some were slyly lowered to the work their owners were engaged on.

The exhibition had made me tired, and when I left it I boarded a bus and went out to relax in Greenwich Park to 'visit the meridian'. Having travelled right around the globe I thought it only right to pay my respects to the meridian from which the earth's surface takes its measurements. At the top of the hill the Observatory towers up, a forbidding-looking, grey building, but all around the park is green and welcoming.

29 May

Coates has been busy yesterday and today with his stage rehearsals. The Covent Garden season is in full swing at the moment and therefore they are playing all kinds of Italian rubbish or, as Coates puts it, not having forgotten any of the Russian expressions that have long vacated my head – 'all kinds of shit'. In consequence we have only seen one another fleetingly, but tomorrow he has asked me to go with him for a drive out of the city. I am looking forward to this, especially as we have much to talk about and I am in need of his advice.

I spoke to Adams, my former manager in America, who has now opened an office in England. He says that the cost of putting on a recital is £90, but of course it would be better if I could first appear with orchestra. I knew this without him having to tell me.

I went to Roerich's exhibition, having seen him yesterday at Yakovlev's. Roerich's canvases are full of fairy-tale imagery and wild northern landscapes, with huge expanses of sky and wide-open spaces, which he loves and feels strongly. I visited him in the afternoon and we drank tea. Roerich is a dear man, he plans to go to India and is deeply absorbed in spiritualism. He and his wife are dedicated mediums, and say that at their séances they experience astounding visitations and manifestations, even ancient coins and a little wooden cross entering into their consciousness. Sometimes they hear very interesting chords played on the piano, and they promised at their next séance to ask permission for me to be present as well in order that I should write down the harmonies. After two years of prosaic American materialism their conversation had a different and very seductive aroma. If one hears such things from people one does not know they are apt to go in one ear and out of the other, but when a man like Roerich speaks with such simplicity and seriousness, and in such detail, one is impelled to listen more attentively.

30 May

Spent the whole day with Coates and his family driving out of London in their car. We went to Windsor, and even further afield; it was a splendid excursion, enjoyable and interesting, and it was midnight by the time we returned.

I played him the March and Entr'acte from *Three Oranges*, at which Coates went into paroxysms of delight: he said that next season he would engage me for two appearances with the orchestra. He did not think it was a good idea to appear in recital now: it would be a waste of money in view of the fact that I would be appearing with him in the autumn.

31 May

Went with Sasha-Yasha to the British Museum in the morning and looked at Egyptian antiquities. In the evening we went to a Turkish bath, where we were reduced to a state of stupefaction before having our torsos subjected to an unmerciful massaging and pummelling.

It is a little dull here, as I have so much time on my hands. I have little inclination to compose and have no piano on which to practise, as it is very difficult to get hold of one here. I am all the time conscious of having come to London with the aim of achieving something, but I must understand that this 'something' consists of discussions, plans and negotiations about my future, and such things do not happen overnight.

1 June

Today at last I got fixed up with a piano: Steinways gave me a room for two hours and tomorrow will send a piano to my hotel room. I must begin little by little to learn my programme for the autumn.

I walked about London and looked at the shops, which are good, and the goods in them display much more taste and care in their manufacture. But I must restrain myself from buying anything at the moment; I have to save my money.

2 June

Fatma Hanum has forwarded two letters that came for me from America. One is from Linette, the other from Haensel. Linette writes that although she wants to come she cannot, as all reservations are booked out until August. This made me extremely angry. Haensel's letter presented me with a dilemma: there are two attractive concert engagements, at $500 and $400, and he has fixed the date of 7 October for them. If I go to Brazil I cannot be in New

York any earlier than November, so I must choose between these concerts and Brazil. Coates's advice was to spit on the concerts and go to Brazil.

To Mrs. Peto in the afternoon with a letter of recommendation, and there I met Lady Cunard,[1] who plays a vitally important role in the affairs of Covent Garden (and incidentally detests Coates as she lives with Beecham, who also conducts there but enjoys less success than Coates). Lady Cunard said: 'I am most interested to meet you, please come to lunch with me.' Coates advised me to go and to be charming, but to keep quiet about our friendship.

In the evening I sent a telegram to Linette pointing out ways to obtain a transatlantic passage.

3 June

Another letter from Haensel, this time with unexpectedly pleasant reading: a contract for a tour of California with four concerts for two-and-a-half thousand dollars. Well, that is a horse of a different colour! At last I am beginning to be offered real money, and about time, for I was really losing heart and had already started the miserable practice of counting every penny. Obviously I shall have to 'spit on' Brazil and get myself back to the United States at the beginning of October, otherwise I shall not be able to return here again in time. If I am to appear with Coates in London then it should be no later than January, because by February and March the London concert season has begun dying on its feet in order to resurrect itself by late spring. Accordingly, I can stay in America only until the New Year, bearing in mind that I cannot accept too many concerts in November and December so as to devote enough time to fighting the Chicago Opera. Hence the only time for a three-week tour of California would be in late October or early November. The year's schedule is beginning to look like a school timetable.

I lunched with the Nobles, very nice people with a pretty daughter. They turn out to be inordinately rich and among the most generous benefactors of Covent Garden, although they do not play as energetically interventionist a part in its management as Lady Cunard does. Later I was also at her house,

---

1 Lady Cunard, née Maud Alice Burke of Manhattan, had married Sir Bache Cunard, grandson of the founder of the shipping line, on the partial rebound from a long-lasting affair with the Irish novelist, memoirist and art critic George Moore, whom she later abandoned (as in effect she already had abandoned her husband) for Sir Thomas Beecham. For the best part of fifty years this formidable American ruled over the world of the London salon, as the society columnist Elsa Maxwell revealed: 'Shortly before the turn of the century [she] brought London society to its collective knee and kept it there for close to fifty years. Lady Cunard loved to gather her lions together, lash them with the whip of her tongue, and watch them fight to the blood. By pitting them one against another she sought to make her guests more interesting to herself, to each other, and, not at all incidentally, to exploit her own acid wit.' (E. Maxwell, *How To Do It or The Lively Art of Entertaining* (Little, Brown & Co., New York, 1957).)

but nothing much happened because there were other guests present, except that as I was leaving she gave me two tickets in the stalls for tomorrow and a box for the day after, saying that she would like me to get to know their theatre.

That evening I played *Three Oranges* through to Coates, who followed it with the score. And what a pleasure it was to play to someone who understands you! A sour taste still lingers in my mouth from the time I played it to Bodanzky and Gatti. Coates liked the opera enormously, laughed liked a child and said that whereas, of course, Covent Garden itself would not have the money to spend on the production as it should be done, there ought to be possibilities of obtaining it by other means. He advised me to make friends with Lady Cunard and concluded by saying that while it would not be easy to get the opera staged at Covent Garden, it was by no means impossible.

4 June

Practised the piano a lot and learned some short pieces by Schumann and Beethoven as well as going through the Myaskovsky Sonata. My mood has improved thanks to the Californian contract and the relative financial security it offers. In the evening I went to the semi-serious opera that is Puccini's *Tosca* which, it must be admitted, contains some very expertly done things. The singers were not bad, the settings mundane, and the orchestra good. I looked for Lady Cunard but could not find her. Bored, I left after the second act.

5 June

A lovely letter from Linette: she has 'unexpectedly' – of course – got a berth for 10 June, but now there is another potential obstacle: her mother is not very well and is now waiting for the results of an X-ray examination. If it proves to be something serious Linette will have to stay with her, but if not, then – so Linette thinks – there would be positive benefits in their being away from each other for three months.

In the afternoon I meant to take possession of the box Lady Cunard had given me for *Pelléas*, but the performance was cancelled.

6 June

Joined a two-car excursion with Coates and some people I did not know, and did not much care for, to drive out into the country. Although I found the somewhat boorish company tedious, I decided to suppress my feelings as the weather was glorious and the cars very comfortable.

On Coates's instructions wrote a letter to Lady Cunard thanking her for the Covent Garden tickets and expressing my desire to play *Three Oranges* to her. I would never normally bow and scrape like this, but Coates is clear that Lady Cunard is a subterranean reef on which any enterprise may founder.

7 June

Called on Lady Lavery,[1] an American-born friend of Mrs Carpenter. In the evening she took me into her box for *Louise* (complete trash).[2] I saw Lady Cunard again, who invited me with an imperious air to play my opera to her on Friday. It is a shame that all this is taking so long, because if Linette arrives on the 18th, I must be in Paris then, otherwise the poor girl will feel quite alone and bereft. But Coates counsels that there is nothing to be done about it; Lady Cunard is the conduit through which things have to be done, even though he has on his own account written to Beecham about *Three Oranges*.

8 June

Today and tomorrow are essentially wasted days from the point of view of advancing the prospects for my opera. When Coates and I came into Covent Garden we met Diaghilev there, just arrived from Paris. I found it utterly absorbing to watch these two great pioneers of Russian art, Diaghilev and Coates, talking to one another. Diaghilev was extraordinarily nice to me, and such is the irresistible charm of this man that although I had been spoiling for a fight with him over *Chout*, the only thing I wanted now was to smooth over our differences. Diaghilev looked as if he had not had a haircut for two months, and I said to him: 'Sergey Pavlovich, you must get your hair cut . . .' Diaghilev replied in a tone of some irritation: 'Fifteen people before you have already told me that.' His ballet season opens on Thursday and he will give me the score of *Chout* then so that I can read it through and then play it to him. It will be very pleasant to renew my acquaintance with Mr Buffoon: I can hardly remember him at all, apart from five or six themes, but I do remember that it is a very successful composition. It will be interesting to hear something new written by oneself.

---

1 Née Hazel Martyn of Chicago, Lady Lavery (1880–1935) was the wife of the well-known Irish artist Sir John Lavery. Sir John painted over four hundred portraits of his beautiful wife, one of them appearing on Irish Republic banknotes after the Anglo-Irish Treaty of 1921 gave Eire its independence, and remaining there in the shape of a watermark until the introduction of the Euro in 1998. The Laverys held court in a palatial mansion in Cromwell Place, South Kensington.
2 Opera (1900) by Gustave Charpentier.

9 June

While I was in Paris Stravinsky had suggested to me, in relation to my repertoire for America, that I should get hold of some Schubert waltzes, which he loves. 'Some of them are pure Glinka!' exclaimed Stravinsky. Today I bought a volume of Schubert containing a ton of waltzes and played some of them, marking with a pencil those I liked. It is a long time since I have seen all in one place such a vast quantity of nonsense as these waltzes, the only thing one could compare them with is a collection of Rimsky-Korsakov songs. Nevertheless, every now and again one turns up that is truly enchanting. I think I could put together a suite that would make a really good concert number.

Walked a good deal, going right through Regent's Park to the north and then some other parks, eventually breaching the limits of the city map.

10 June

Continued playing through the Schubert waltzes and chose about fifteen or twenty from the hundred and fifty in the volume. Now all I have to do is arrange them in a pleasing sequence, and then I think it will turn out very nicely.

Lunched with Lady Lavery and some other ladies. I played them a lot of my music, which excited them wildly, and sparked among them a real interest in producing *Three Oranges* at Covent Garden. We discussed ways and means of bringing pressure to bear on Lady Cunard.

I went in the evening to the opening night of the Diaghilev ballet, which compared to Paris was a tremendous success,[1] on which I congratulated Diaghilev. I heard *Pulcinella* with the greatest pleasure and excitement.

No letter from Linette, which I have been anxiously awaiting because today is the day when, if nothing has happened to prevent her, she should be leaving for Europe. I am consumed by longing for her to come.

11 June

I took the full score and piano score of *Oranges* and went to Lady Cunard's to play it to her. At first I felt very uncomfortable, as she had gathered a whole group of people for the audition, about six people, but most of them proved to be the same ladies as yesterday who had come in order to exert their influence on Lady Cunard. I felt that my main hope of success lay in the

---

[1] This was Diaghilev's only post-war season at Covent Garden, presented by the impresario in partnership with Sir Thomas Beecham: an 'International Grand Opera Season' with 'ballet programmes organized by M. Serge de Diaghilew'. It was not, to put it mildly, a financial success, resulting in the liquidation of the Sir Thomas Beecham Opera Company and severe losses for Diaghilev.

subject of the opera, so outlined the plot in some detail. I then played the second act, but I am not sure they all fully got the measure of it. Then some of the ladies shrewdly asked me to play one or two of my piano pieces, and certainly my ingratiatingly gentle performance of *Visions Fugitives*, preludes and scherzos went down very well with Lady Cunard. Towards the end Beecham appeared, the Artistic Director of Covent Garden and its presiding genius, a very nice gentleman, a conductor who evidently knows something about music. He looked at the score and told me that Coates had already been singing its praises to him. Because it was getting late he asked me to leave the score with him so that he could study it more closely.

Everything seems to be going well.

12 June

I thought I would get a letter from Linette, as the liner must already have sailed from America, but nothing came. This is a worrying symptom and may mean that her planned departure has not taken place because of her mother's illness, and she simply does not know what or how to tell me.

In the afternoon I went to Covent Garden, where Diaghilev was extremely affable, but he still has not retrieved the score from the bottom of his trunk, which is apparently crammed full of pictures. I said I might be staying another week or so in London, but it might also be that I would have to leave in a few days if I get a telegram from Mama in Constantinople. This worried Diaghilev, who promised to dig out the score from his trunk by Monday.

When I relayed to Coates the details of my rendezvous with Lady Cunard, his considered judgement was that the omens appeared favourable. He hopes to be able to arrange a meeting between the three of us (Beecham, himself and me) in the next few days to talk business. That would be excellent. It's time for brass tacks.

13 June – 30 July

At this point the Diary breaks off daily entries because of the frenzied activity of the period.

Diaghilev finally handed me my ballet with the words: 'Here is your treasure'. This happened at Covent Garden during the interval. I was so excited at seeing my 'new ballet' that I surreptitiously crept out of Lady Cunard's box, where I was sitting, and sneaked out to look at it in the foyer, deserted at the time because of the performance in progress. Some of the ballet pleased me, it was good, but I had retained almost no trace of it in my memory. Some of it, by contrast, struck me as coarse and in need of revision. Some things I did not like at first glance, but came round to after a few days. By and large, however, I was delighted by my 'new acquaintance', and returned to the box with a smile on my face.

The following day I studied the score in detail so as to be able to play it to Diaghilev, which I did in the presence also of Massine and Ansermet. Ansermet was loud in his praises, while Diaghilev and Massine seemed to grasp some idea of it but combined to voice their 'emigré' point of view, which was that there were many beautiful things, pure Russian themes, in the ballet.

The next day the whole group descended on me to hear the ballet, after which Diaghilev embarked, cautiously at first, as if fearing that I might fly at him, on a peroration. The gist of what he said was that the ballet in its present form followed too closely the events of the action on stage. At one time this had been seen as a desirable objective to pursue, for example when *Petrushka* was being composed, but nowadays attitudes had moved on and it was generally accepted that the effect achieved was much greater when the music maintains a broader sweep, with full symphonic sections corresponding to complete scenes of the ballet without resorting to too much detail *en route*. In this situation not only does the music benefit by gaining in fluency and symphonic coherence, but the plastique of the choreography on stage is also enhanced by being allowed to grow in independence and unity. If, however, individual movements are reproduced illustratively in detail, as in my ballet score, no section of the music has a unified form: it has to all be chopped into fragments and its shape distorted, while the dance in turn must slavishly conform to the musical phrase and risk descending to simple pantomime.

Therefore, if I were to agree to revise my ballet in such a way as to eliminate purely illustrational passages and in their place develop melodic ideas, as I would do in a symphonic work, the ballet would benefit as a musical entity, and so would the dance, enabled thus to free itself from the shackles of being bound to each and every phrase.

Diaghilev had obviously prepared himself to weather a comprehensive counter-attack from me, but I considered that his comments were eminently reasonable, and the prospect of revising *Chout* with the object of making it a more cogent symphonic production appealed to me very much. In this way the matter was very soon resolved, and our next three meetings, which took place on a daily basis, and sometimes twice in a day, were spent by Diaghilev and me looking in detail at the score, marking which passages needed to be developed and which excised.

Diaghilev said that he had another objection to *Chout*, in that each scene should be distinct, with its own individual physiognomy, and he did not find this characteristic in my ballet. He cited *Petrushka* as an example. But I objected that *Petrushka* could not in fact be other than it was, seeing that the very scenario of the ballet dictated a complete contrast between the intimate surroundings of the two inner scenes and the streets and crowds of the two outer scenes. In *Chout*, however, the buffoons appear in every scene, albeit in different contexts, and therefore even if it were possible to make each short three- or four-minute scene contrast with the others, six such dislocations in the space of a half-hour ballet would result in such a kaleidoscope that the overall 'buffoonery' of the piece would be diluted. In any case, at this stage it was really too late to attempt such a radical make-over.

Following our artistic discussions, the financial side was equally amicably settled. Diaghilev began by stating that he would be happy to pay for the work involved in recasting the ballet, but not the creation of the full score since he considered he had already paid for the complete ballet. (This was true: he had in fact paid me 3,500 roubles rather than 3,000, in addition to which my return visit to Italy ought to have come out of this sum, but I had never made it.) But I presented the situation in a different light: I was now going to have to spend the whole summer rewriting the ballet, and I must have some money to live on during this period. For this reason he might be a thousand times right, but if I had no money with which to support myself I would not be able to work on the ballet, but would be reduced to taking up Stahl's invitation to go to Brazil purely so as to have somewhere to park myself.

If he wanted me to recast the ballet and orchestrate it during the summer (the autumn and winter were completely out of the question from the time point of view) he would have to provide me with something of the order of 3,000 francs a month for the four months until the autumn. 'Not four, three,' put in Diaghilev. I settled for three, and Diaghilev agreed to a retainer of 3,000 francs a month. From one perspective this seemed quite a generous sum, but when translated into pounds sterling, which was the currency Diaghilev had available at the time, it came to a modest £60 a month. Considering that Diaghilev was himself paying £11 a day for his hotel room, this did not seem over-generous. 'Mind you make a good job of it, now,' said Diaghilev, agreeing the deal. I replied to this sally with a quotation from *The Snow Maiden*: 'Giving treasure, you must know what it is for.' 'It is for this,' rejoined Diaghilev, 'that the fickle French are now accusing me of having no more discoveries to make after Stravinsky.' I drew the conclusion that Diaghilev was genuinely reposing great hopes on my ballet.

I said I should like to conduct it myself, as I did not have total confidence in Ansermet. 'Fine,' replied Diaghilev, 'by all means conduct if you are able to.' I said: 'You have no idea how I can conduct.'

We thus parted on the best of terms and within a week I received the first cheque for 3,000 francs. The ballet will be presented in Paris next May and in London on 7 June. The season's other novelty is to be Stravinsky's *Les Noces*.[1]

1 *The Wedding*; in Russian *Svadebka*.

Once the question of my conducting was decided, Diaghilev smiled and said: 'We seem to have ended up by your becoming one of the Ballets Russes conductors.' I said that conducting as such did not interest me for the present, but I would very much enjoy conducting my own ballet.

My meeting with Beecham took place on 17 June, the first day he was free to do so, being until then fully occupied with his estates and his pills. Coates took charge, while I responded to the questions Beecham asked me. Discussions centred on the cost of producing the opera, and naturally Covent Garden could not think of matching even half the $100,000 squandered on it by the Chicago Opera. When we came to talk about a designer who could produce settings for the opera, I suggested Goncharova, who had told me in Paris that she would take much pleasure in it and do the work cheaply, and she was someone whose work I very much like. Beecham said he would like her to provide a rough estimate of costs and if they were not too high he had no objection to producing *Oranges*, although in the summer season, not during the winter, that is to say May–June.

Coates said: 'Now, what will the boy get?'[1] Beecham replied that he could not remember the terms he had agreed for Puccini and for Strauss, but he would offer the same to me. I asked if he could guarantee ten performances over two years and advance half the amount on signature of the contract. Beecham agreed half, or a little less than half. We parted with my promising to see Goncharova in Paris and then to pass along her estimate of costs.

When we emerged from the meeting with Beecham, Coates said that when he had been having lunch with Diaghilev prior to our meeting, Diaghilev had asked him if it was true that Covent Garden was going to put on *Three Oranges*, to which Coates had replied he was 99-per-cent certain they would. Now he put the chances at 99.5 per cent.

Regarding my orchestral appearances, I shall appear on 7 January at the Philharmonia,[2] and before that Coates will give two performances of the *Scythian Suite* and the 'Classical' Symphony.

And with that I left London, as I had received a telegram from Mama that she had left Constantinople for Marseilles. I had been waiting for this moment for so long that the telegram came as a shock. On the evening of 18 June I left London, and after a night on a hideously overcrowded ferry woke up at Le Havre. On disembarking I went to find out when the *Touraine* was

---

1   In English.
2   Meaning presumably the London Symphony Orchestra season of concerts in the Queens Hall with Albert Coates; Prokofiev must be using the term 'Philharmonia' in the continental European sense of a concert promoting organization. This engagement did not materialize, the whole London situation from Prokofiev's point of view having been thrown into disarray by the collapse of the Sir Thomas Beecham Opera Company after this Diaghilev season at Covent Garden. Coates did, however, perform the *Scythian Suite* with the LSO in the Queen's Hall on 1 November 1920, and the London premiere of the Third Piano Concerto with Prokofiev as soloist on 24 April 1922.

expected, although I did not know whether Linette was on board or not. I was told the *Touraine* would be coming into port in about two days; I was going to leave a letter for Linette, but then calculated that I could probably just get to Marseilles and back in time to get back to Paris by the time she arrives there.

I was in Paris by noon, and by two o'clock already *en route* to Marseilles. Even though, thanks to my 'salary' from Diaghilev, I felt reasonably secure financially, especially with the 99.5-per-cent probability of *Three Oranges*, the money for this journey seemed to be pouring away at a rate suggesting coins rather than banknotes. All day we travelled through beautiful, lush France, then after a very short and sleepless night, at four o'clock in the morning I was standing at the open carriage window feasting my eyes on the southern landscape, bathed in the light of the rising sun.

Coming into Marseilles we skirted the bay and had our first glimpse of the matchless deep blue of the Mediterranean. After a wash and brush-up at the station I made my way to the pier to find out when the *Souirah* from Constantinople would be coming into port, and after some persistent enquiries learned that she should be docking at about ten o'clock, and in an hour and a half's time she should be coming into view from the top of the bell-tower. While waiting I walked around Marseilles, and indeed at ten, there was the *Souirah*. It was a glorious, sunny, southern day, and I felt wonderful although a prey to nagging unease about the state Mama was likely to be in. As the *Souirah* came alongside the pier I searched for Mama among the mass of people milling about on deck, but could not see her. I waited another hour and a half, staying right up close to the vessel, until as soon as the medical inspection was over the passengers started to disembark.

I went on board but after searching all over the ship could find no one until I suddenly heard a voice behind me saying: 'I'll just go and say goodbye to Mme Prokofieva before I go ashore.' I spun round and asked what Mme Prokofieva she was talking about. 'Oh,' cried the woman, 'are you the composer Prokofiev?! Delighted to meet you . . .' and dragged me with her all over the ship. The people turned out to be the Schloezers, husband and wife; Scriabin's wife was Mr Schloezer's sister, and he had the reputation of being one of those who had inspired Scriabin's path of spiritual development.[1]

---

1   Boris Schloetser (1881–1969), philosopher and writer on music who in France became known as Boris de Schloezer, was to become one of the most influential music critics in Paris, writing in French as the music critic of the *Nouvelle Revue Française* and also contributing to the *Revue musicale*, and in Russian for Milyukov's paper *Poslednye Novosti* (*Latest News*). Schloezer's sister Tatyana was married to Scriabin, and Schloezer made a lifetime's study of the composer, writing a biography entitled *Scriabin: Artist and Mystic*, translated by Nicolas Slonimsky (Oxford University Press, 1987), concentrating on Scriabin's transformation of eroticism and the occult into music. Schloezer also wrote a monograph on Stravinsky, *Igor Stravinsky* (Editions Claude Aveline, Paris, 1929) and prolific translations of Tolstoy and Gogol, as well

Mama was not in first class as I had expected but in a frightful sort of seamen's bunkroom, having been unable to secure better accommodation and not wanting to wait any longer. When I entered the big cabin for eighteen people she was looking the other way and did not see me come in, so I was not able to tell whether she was completely blind or whether she could see a little. She was as brown as parchment from the sun, was wearing dark-blue spectacles and was terribly thin. But our reunion was jubilant and we wasted no time in getting happily down to our plans. Her luggage consisted of two quite decent-looking medium-sized suitcases and a quite appalling-looking 'refugee's' package, the contents of which included some of my papers: the manuscripts of *Seven, They Are Seven* (not the score, but full sketches for it), the full score of the Violin Concerto and the piano score of the Second Piano Concerto. There were also three notebooks of my Diaries and three of my short stories. This was a great joy: I had been afraid that it would all have perished in raids in Russia, or would have been confiscated by Customs on the journey.

Arm in arm, Mama and I went ashore and to a hotel: there were no tickets for the night train, and we decided to wait until the morning to leave for Paris. The day passed in talking (so much had happened in two years!) and Mama's descriptions of the privations she had suffered in Russia and during her flight from there (eighteen days in the hold of the ship from Novorossiisk to Constantinople). Now she could hardly believe it was all over. The next day was all taken up by the train journey, but by evening we were in Paris and installed in the Hôtel Quai Voltaire on the banks of the Seine.

Next morning I went to the Samoilenkos, where – hurrah! – they handed me a cable from Linette. The *Touraine* had come in, Linette was here and in accordance with the telegram I had sent her on board from Marseilles was letting me know of her arrival. I immediately went to her hotel, which quite by chance was two steps from mine, but she was out. I left her a note and when I returned to her hotel two hours later there was Linette, who took me off to another nearby hotel she had moved to. But she said it would not be proper to go upstairs to her room and so we wandered round Paris. It all seemed very strange to us, so closely was our relationship bound up with New York. Linette seemed rather nervous, but just as lovely and dear as ever. We went to visit the Stahls, but they had left for Brazil two days before. In the evening we went to the Bois de Boulogne and there in the bosky groves we kissed tenderly, although Linette was still shy of too much physical contact.

Thus, in the space of three or four days, all my uncertainties had been resolved: Mama, Linette and Diaghilev. The summer stretched out before us

---

as the works of the philosopher and literary critic Lev Shestov, who first became known in the West as a result of Schloezer's advocacy.

as invitingly as one could imagine, and Brazil could be 'spat on'. Goncharova was thrilled with the chance to do the sets for *Three Oranges* and dashed about Paris checking on prices for the estimate of costs, while I set about finding a dacha for us. This proved to be quite difficult, as most had already been taken, and it took me a week, more than twenty letters, a pile of rejected applications and a trawl round five outlying towns, before I found a very nice house on the banks of the Seine at Mantes-sur-Seine, an hour from Paris. True, it was not the depths of the countryside I would ideally have wanted, because just behind it lay the town itself, and at 4,000 francs until the end of September the price was a little steep, but the house itself was spacious, very comfortable, even elegant, the area was delightful and the river was just at the end of the garden. A bonus was that a splendid cook came with the rent (incredibly cheaply compared to America), and I found an upright piano in Mantes itself. I found the dacha on 2 July and we moved there on the 6th.

In the meantime I had also found a good singing teacher for Linette, and she buckled down with a will to her daily lessons. I presented her to Mama as an 'American' who was going to translate *Three Oranges* into English for the Covent Garden production; they immediately took to one another, while Sonya Brichant, who had come from Brussels to see Mama, found her remarkably attractive. Goncharova and Larionov also became good friends with her. Linette, however, did not want to move straight away to Mantes, so as not to alarm Mama, but said she would visit. Another thing was that in view of the regular singing lessons she was having, it would be too tiring to commute every day into the city. Since this was purely a way of getting things started I agreed, but later became angry with Linette for coming out only on Saturdays and Sundays.

Once I had settled in at Mantes I got down to *Chout* and quite quickly and pleasurably revised the first four scenes, inserting two new dances in major keys (Diaghilev had complained that the whole ballet was in the minor): the 'Dance of the Buffoons' Wives' in the second scene (just before the fugue); and the 'Dance of the Buffoons' Daughters' before the 'Entry of the Bridegroom'. I then proceeded to revise the first entr'acte and on 21 June progressed to the score, which proceeded without difficulty, albeit not very quickly: three to five pages a day. I practised the piano for one or two hours a day working up my programme for America and paying particular attention to making my technique as accurate as possible with the aim of ensuring that I did not play a single note carelessly or without thinking deeply about it. I cannot deny that it was listening to Rachmaninoff that gave me the impulse for this degree of precision, and I see it as the way forward for my future development of keyboard mastery. For anyone who does not have a natural predisposition to keyboard technique this can be a dangerous path to choose, as it can lead to dryness, but I do not think I have anything to fear in this respect.

Living in the dacha has done wonders for Mama's health and her vision has improved so much that she can walk unaided in the garden. I, as usual, go on quite long rambles round the surrounding country and am enchanted by the beauty of the French countryside. We take a Russian language newspaper published in Paris, and like true provincials read it aloud from cover to cover. Politically these are such interesting times: on the one hand the Bolsheviks are stronger than they ever been and are routing the Poles to their heart's content, but on the other Wrangel[1] is extending ever more widely the area of his domination in the south, and the 'Allies' vacillate wildly, unable to decide whom to back – the Bolsheviks or Wrangel.

The dacha is on three storeys: a drawing-room and dining-room on the ground floor, Mama's bedroom and a guest room on the first floor, and my room (a delightful room with a large sofa and a balcony overlooking the Seine) on the top floor, with another small guest room next door. This is where I installed Linette, at which Mama, evidently having decided not to interfere in my affairs, did not bat an eyelid, so Linette and I were very happy up at the top of the house. I am tremendously looking forward to her moving to Mantes permanently.

Fatma Hanum's sister gave a dinner party in Paris on 29 July; among the guests were Alexey Tolstoy, Kuprin and Bunin.[2] I had met Tolstoy in Moscow at Koshetz's, but was meeting Kuprin and Bunin for the first time. Kuprin

1   Baron Pyotr Wrangel (1878–1928) had assumed command of the White forces after the defeat of Denikin's army at the beginning of 1920, restoring morale and command organisation to the demoralised White forces. While the Red Army was still heavily engaged with the Polish incursion into the Ukraine Wrangel was successful, and was making headway with the general population as a result of his proposals for land reform, but when, following the armistice agreed with Poland in October 1920, the Red Army was able to turn its full attention to Wrangel he was driven into smaller and smaller pockets of the Crimea and eventually at the beginning of November 1920 with his forces and attendant civilians, a total of 150,000 people, was evacuated to Constantinople by 126 ships of the British and French Navy. In his memoirs, Wrangel wrote: 'Three years of determined struggle, of fighting and suffering, of heroism, victory and defeat, followed by fresh victory, then came to an end. We left the last strip of land of our fathers.' The Civil War thus came to an end. (*The Memoirs of General Wrangel*, trans. Sophie Goulston (Williams & Norgate Ltd, London, 1929).
2   Count Alexey Tolstoy (1883–1945), historical novelist, emigrated to Germany and France in 1917 but returned to the Soviet Union in 1923 to become one of the most committed and celebrated of Soviet writers. At the time of this meeting he would have been engaged on the first and most successful volume of *The Road to Calvary*, his long and sweeping examination of Russian life during the First World War, Revolution and Civil War. Alexander Kuprin (1870–1938), hailed by (Lev) Tolstoy as the true successor to Chekhov, also emigrated after the Revolution and later returned to Soviet Russia, but not until much later, the year before his death. Kuprin wrote almost nothing during his time abroad, and the best of his pre-Revolutionary work, often in the short-story genre, deals with adventure, action and sensation, somewhat after the style of Jack London. Ivan Bunin (1870–1953) was from the literary point of view by

interested me the most of the three. A gentle, ingratiating personality, he had an unprepossessing, provincial air about him. Bunin was the image of a retired civil servant. I played the piano a good deal and the writers were all deeply impressed, going so far as to kiss me. Someone said: 'These are sounds that have been cleansed by the ether.' Tolstoy said: 'Up until now my impression of modern composers has been that they are like flies dashing themselves against glass in their search for the new, but your music has simply opened the window, it is so new and understandable.' Even the morose Bunin said to me: 'You are very good company.' When the writers had gone everyone congratulated me on an extraordinary success and Fatma Hanum, alone with me on the balcony, astonished me by coquettishly laying her head on my shoulder.

31 July

Up to today (from the 21st) I have completed thirty pages of score, that is less than three pages a day: it is not a quick rate of progress, although a ballet, especially one that is fairly densely composed, will never speed ahead like an opera.

Nothing has been heard about Covent Garden, and I am beginning to think that things must have gone wrong there. Diaghilev has not sent any further instalments of my salary. Mama is also feeling down as the doctor is not pleased with her eyes. But there is one pleasant development: at six o'clock today Linette will move into the dacha. I am terribly happy about this.

August

The month of August passed happily and peacefully in Mantes. Linette finally moved in, only going into Paris three times a week for her singing lessons. Our relations were warm and loving, and if we bickered occasionally it was over trifles and we soon made it up. Once in a while she would seem to be visited by melancholy, but not deeply, and it soon passed. I worked away at the ballet, completing eighty-seven pages in the month, and also composing the second and third entr'actes. I also made progress with my recital programmes: I now had repertoire for two programmes firmly grounded. I practised only in the evenings, an hour or two, not more.

Diaghilev was a cause for concern: he sent money neither on the first nor

---

some way the most considerable of the three guests and the only one who neither returned to Russia nor wavered in his detestation of Bolshevism. *The Village* is a naturalistic study of the squalor of rural life following the decay of the landowning gentry, while his masterpiece, *The Gentleman from San Francisco*, is a Tolstoy-like study of the irony of death, all the more powerful for its understated economy of language.

on the tenth of the month, and I should have received an instalment on the twentieth of the preceding month, which also did not arrive. Since I had to pay for the rent of the house, my general financial situation began to look less than rosy. I went into Paris and there learned that Diaghilev had returned from London but spent a mere two days in Paris without letting me know he was there before going to Venice. His London season had ended in an argument with Beecham and a financial collapse, as Beecham had paid only a quarter of what Diaghilev should have had from him.[1] Some of the artists in the company had not been paid anything, Diaghilev was instituting court proceedings and had gone to Paris with barely enough money for his own needs. This placed me in a stupid position: I had rented a house, 'spat on' Brazil and based my entire well-being on a bankrupt Diaghilev! Boris Samoilenko, that true friend and gentleman, at once came to my assistance and gave me 3,000 francs until things should improve.

I sent Diaghilev a telegram describing my position (with some exaggeration) as critical and soon, to my utter amazement, received 3,000 francs from him. This was not only an enormous financial relief, but also very flattering, since Diaghilev always deals meticulously with people he needs, but rarely so with those who matter less to him. The fact that, in the critical circumstances in which he finds himself, he continues to find money for me, means I must stand high in his estimation.

N. P Ruzsky[2] has come here from Russia. He has fled from the Bolsheviks, but his family, accused of 'White' propaganda, has been imprisoned. He says that Zakharov is still teaching at the Conservatoire and 'making a very good impression'. I am so glad for him and would very much like to see him. Balmont has also come, given permission to leave with honour by the Bolsheviks. I immediately went to welcome him and found him still in bed not fully awake, as rubicund as ever and wearing his hair in ringlets. He had brought with him his daughter and two wives. 'Russia is in chaos, everyone is rushing about in a ferment, but out of this chaos art will be born,' he said, 'while France is carrion; there is no hope of anything being created here.'

They had heard unconfirmed rumours that Boris Verin was in the

1 Beecham and Diaghilev had been personally at odds even before their joint season began. 'The consequences of the season, however, far transcended personal rivalry. In 1913 the Ballets Russes had been the rock on which the theatrical empire of Gabriel Astruc foundered. [See *Diaries*, vol. 1, p. 426 n. 2.] In 1920 the "heavy losses sustained during the ... grand season of foreign opera and Russian ballet" drove the Sir Thomas Beecham Opera Company out of business. No matter how deep the rancor he bore his former "angel", surely Diaghilev must have realised the implications of Beecham's failure: in Europe the old system of private operatic enterprise was dead.' (Lynn Garafola, *Diaghilev's Ballets Russes* (Oxford University Press, New York, 1989). See also *The Times*, 2 July 1921.)
2 Nikolay Ruzsky, a close and generous friend from Petrograd for whom Prokofiev had written the *Ballade*, Op. 15. See *Diaries*, vol. 1, p. 77 and *passim*.

Crimea, but nothing definite. Koussevitzky had left Russia together with Balmont, but I did not manage to see him as he had left for Aix-les-Bains almost as soon as he got to Paris. From a letter he wrote to me I had some pleasant news: my trunk is undamaged and in a safe place.[1] Asafyev and Myaskovsky are alive. The Russian Music Editions will soon resume their activities. He asked me to go to see him in Aix to talk about everything, but I had to watch my expenditure and in any case was reluctant to leave Mantes.

Kokhánski also put in a fleeting appearance in Paris, bringing with him the superb solo part for my Violin Concerto he had made himself. I hope he will play it in London.[2] Kokhánski told me that Suvchinsky was in Sofia, and I at once wrote to him there. I heard from Eleonora's uncle[3] who was, as I had read in the newspapers, in Copenhagen, that she was still in Petrograd, while Boris Borisovich is in Constantinople. And finally, another familiar face appearing over the horizon was that of Mlle Jung, Vera Miller's friend. Having learned that her father was teaching at the recently opened Conservatoire in Riga, I wrote to her on the off-chance and to my great surprise received a reply very quickly. Miller is alive, in Petrograd, but has lost her father and her mother and almost perished herself from pneumonia. Now recovered, she is hoping to come to Riga to be with Jung. According to Jung they are in contact by letter – and we had thought there was no postal nor other communication with Bolshevik Russia, it was like another planet. Miller had been a few times to my apartment, which had been broken into and robbed, and all the papers burnt.

This is very bad news indeed, it means that the score of the Second Piano Concerto is lost (thank heavens Mama brought the piano score with her), and it is a tragedy for me that one of the volumes of my diary has gone for ever, the one covering the period from September 1916 until February 1917. This was the time of *The Gambler* rehearsals with the singers and with the orchestra (Acts One and Two), my concerts in Kiev, Saratov and Moscow (at which Rachmaninoff, Medtner and Balmont were all present), the Petrograd concerts of my chamber works, my appearance together with Gorky at which I got to know him, the adventure with Polina, my trip to Kharkov to see her, the letters I had from Wanda Ossolinskaya, Natasha, Boris Verin, probably the episodes with Eleonora – all consigned to the flames. Also destroyed will have been my correspondence for one or two years, and much

---

1 See p. 225.
2 The hope was unfulfilled. The first performance of the Violin Concerto was given in Paris by Marcel Darrieux, the leader of Koussevitzky's orchestra, on 18 October 1923.
3 Eleonora Damskaya's uncle was Boris Gershun (1870–1954), a prominent lawyer who emigrated after the Revolution and finally settled in Berlin, where he became president of the émigré Association of Russian Advocates. In 1933 he moved to Paris, where he occupied a similar position. Boris Borisovich was his adopted son, the poet Boris Bozhnev (see p. 189 n. 2).

else besides, if my friends did not manage to save it. It also gives me little comfort to think that the diary and the letters may have fallen into the wrong hands!¹

Life in Mantes thus continued on its even and contented way, its calm disturbed only by the occasional pebbles cast into it from the frenzied whirlwind that was Russia. One event was the appearance of Herbert Johnson, now Executive Director and in full charge, albeit not particularly dynamically so, of the Chicago Opera.² He had come to Europe to select singers and asked me to come to Paris for a talk. The talk, when it happened, was friendly and I adopted a flexible attitude, giving him to understand that I would be prepared to settle for $6,000. Johnson found this proposal 'quite satisfactory',³ and said that as soon as he returned to America he would put it to the directors and cable me. Afterwards I was afraid I had given in too easily, but then decided that on the contrary this was a good outcome: it was desirable for them to be inveigled as deeply as possible into the production, making it all the more difficult for them subsequently to back out – especially as they will have only two new works in the repertoire, *Three Oranges* and Marinuzzi's modest opera *Jacquerie*,⁴ so they would not want to lose *Oranges*. I cannot deny that I was greatly excited by the prospect of a production I had long ago resigned myself to seeing abandoned, and was seized by a strong desire to go to America for its rehearsals.

September

The month began with something of a misunderstanding. My plan had been to leave for America on the 18th, and I had a passage booked for the 22nd from Liverpool because the first of the Chicago concerts was scheduled for 7 October. Then I suddenly received a letter from my manager, making a passing reference to a Chicago concert on 7 December. I immediately cabled asking if this was a mistake, and received the reply that it was not, the concerts were in December. There was now no need for haste, and I postponed my departure. To tell the truth it was very pleasant to be able to stay longer in Mantes, and Mama in particular was pleased because the doctor wanted her to have an operation on her eyes at the beginning of October, and it would be a great relief that this could now be done while I was there.

---

1 But see below, p. 693 n. 3.
2 Campanini had been General Director of the Chicago Opera, but on his death his responsibilities were divided between the newly created positions of Artistic Director (Marinuzzi) and Executive Director (Johnson).
3 In English.
4 The best-known of Gino Marinuzzi's three operas, dealing with a fourteenth-century peasants' revolt; it was first produced in Buenos Aires in 1918.

There remained the question of finances: my budget had been carefully calculated up to 7 October, on the grounds that on the 7th and 8th I would receive $900. This sum would now not be in my hands until two months later, and the problem was how to fill the resultant gap. My first thought was of Koussevitzky and his mention of the revival of Russian Music Editions, so I wrote to him in Aix asking if he would publish my piano pieces Opp. 31 and 32,[1] explaining why I needed the money. I thought that if the worst came to the worst I would be able to rely on Vyshnedgradsky advancing me some money on the strength of my American contracts. In addition, Diaghilev still owed me 3,000 francs, although I did not have much hope of this since Beecham had not only not paid Diaghilev but had also had a financial crash himself, being forced to abandon Covent Garden. A Covent Garden production of *Three Oranges* had therefore also vanished over the horizon, as seems to be the inevitable pattern when there is a possibility of any of my operas being produced. All the more reason to tread carefully with the Chicago production. Haensel sent $400 as a loan for my passage.

I decided not to get too worked up about the financial situation and life at Mantes continued pleasantly and peaceably as before. Relations between Linette and me were affectionate, even more so than in August. Linette worked with Mama on her English and they were getting on very well with each other. Sonya[2] and her son came to visit for a whole week, an incursion that initially filled me with horror, but both Sonya and her nineteen-year-old son Andryusha turned out to be very nice and their sojourn was quite bearable. It had in any case been quite impossible not to invite them, as Mama was proposing to spend the winter under their roof. I got through a lot of work: I composed the three remaining entr'actes, revised the fifth and sixth scenes and completely recomposed the final dance. I also scored as much of the ballet as I had done the previous month – eighty-seven pages – and got as far as the beginning of Scene Five, after which I stopped work on the orchestration for the whole month of October.

In this way September merged into October, and neither Linette nor I had any desire to leave our quiet, cosy Mantes. Although the weather often shrouded us in thick mists, the days were lovely, sunny, and the trees richly coloured with the glorious tints of autumn. On 30 September we held a family meeting, Mama, Linette and I, to take stock. We decided regretfully that we should move back to Paris. Mama was awaiting her operation, I had to do something about getting hold of some money, not to mention my visa and to book a passage, and Linette was anxious to resume her singing lessons, which had been in abeyance during September. The summer had been an idyllic interlude. Now it was time to plunge back into the maelstrom.

---

[1] Respectively the *Tales of an Old Grandmother* and the *Four Pieces for Piano*, composed in 1918.
[2] Brichant.

October

We moved back to Paris on 2 October, and Mama went straight into hospital where they carried out the operations, first on one eye and then on the other. They were not too serious: they involved making incisions in the whites of the eyes in order to reduce their size, and Mama endured them courageously. We were not expecting a dramatic improvement from the operations, but it was necessary for her to have them as otherwise blindness threatened.

Remembering that my operation in New York had cost $100, I was not anticipating having to have pay more than 1,000 francs for Mama's, but the final bill was 4,000, which had the effect of increasing still further my financial difficulties without any immediate prospect of resolving them. Koussevitzky returned to Paris and we had a joyful reunion. But speaking of the publishing house he explained that there was still a hold-up due to Struve sitting in Copenhagen unable to get a visa to come to Paris. Struve has great experience of all the ins and outs of the business, and as soon as he gets to Paris the publishing activities will start up again.

I took rooms in the Hôtel Quai de Voltaire, and although Linette really thought she should be in a different hotel in order to avoid whispers about a compromising situation, it so happened that the Voltaire had available an excellent and quite inexpensive room, so we all settled in there although on different floors. Linette went off to Litvinne,[1] who professed herself enchanted with her voice: 'Nous en ferons un petit bijou',[2] and took her on as a student. Linette blossomed and the spleen that sometimes visited her dissipated.

I met Stravinsky in Paris and he played me his new Quartet,[3] very interesting but as usual with too much scratching in it. I played him *Chout*, which he liked very much. I appealed to him to point out places where the orchestration could be improved, but he confined himself to correcting a few slurs in the woodwind to make them stand out in greater relief.

Not long after this Diaghilev himself appeared, on his way from Venice to London. As ever he had risen once again from the ashes, obtained money and secured engagements. He listened again to *Chout* and praised the changes I had made, paid me my 3,000, asked me to make a Phonola reproducing piano version for rehearsals, and generally was in splendid form. I must

---

1 Felia Litvinne (1861–1936), St Petersburg-born dramatic soprano who had studied with Pauline Viardot. As a singer Litvinne had a truly international reputation, having taken principal roles in St Petersburg, Moscow, Milan, New York, Paris and Brussels, with several Wagner premieres to her credit (Isolde and Brunnhilde in Paris and Brussels and La Scala under Toscanini, Kundry in Brussels). Among her many students had been Nina Koshetz.
2 'We will make a little gem of her.'
3 The four-minute single-movement *Concertino* for String Quartet.

admit that the compliments Stravinsky and Diaghilev paid me filled me with pride and were a great encouragement to me. There was one disappointment: it seems that there will be no Diaghilev spring season in Paris or London because in May he is planning a tour of South America. When *Chout* will now be produced is not at all clear.

But at least I had 3,000 francs from an unexpected source, since of all my prospects I had thought Diaghilev was the least likely. But it was still not very much. I turned to Vyshnegradsky asking for 5,000 francs against the $7,000 total of my American contracts, but was turned down.

I worried ceaselessly, went the rounds with my begging bowl, and finally leaned on Koussevitzky, who came up with 3,000 francs. In this way ends were eventually just about made to meet and I was able to leave both Mama and Linette with some money although I could not pay the doctor's bill in full, having to promise to pay the balance in December. I allocated to myself least of all, because this mattered least, and left on my travels on 16 October. It was time to head for Chicago, where I would either play my part in assisting with the production, or meet the directors of the opera company in court.

16–24 October

I rose at six and packed my things, which did not take long as by this time the seasoned traveller's every last toothbrush knew its allotted place in the suitcase, ran in to kiss goodbye to Linette, and was on the train as it pulled out at nine o'clock. I caught a glimpse of Mantes through the mist as we passed through, and at two o'clock we were in Le Havre. The formalities were not so onerous, even though there were five separate controls to pass through. The *Savoie* was not a particularly big liner, about the size of the *New York* on which I had come from America, but a more elegant and comfortable ship. I shared a stateroom with a bearded Frenchman, a genial father of nine children whom, thank God, he had left behind in France.

I left my two suitcases, the yellow one and the black one, in the cabin and went into the saloon to write letters. When I came back the black one was where I had left it but the yellow one had vanished. I informed the purser, who took a written statement from me and said that the case had no doubt been taken by mistake to another cabin, and would be found by tomorrow. It must still be somewhere on the ship, because the only connection to the shore was a single gangplank which was supervised to make sure nothing was taken out that should not be. The suitcase contained my suit, my dinner suit, linen and shoes, and most importantly drawings by Larionov: portraits of me in various poses; a caricature of the (imagined) first performance of

Chout with me, Diaghilev, Stravinsky, Goncharova, Massine and Linette; also Goncharova's pencil sketch of my head.

It was a less than propitious start to the voyage, and it continued in the same vein. On the second day out the ship began to roll, and this went on almost until we arrived in New York. For the first two days I was confined to my deckchair, feeling slightly seasick but not to the extent that I was forced to feed the fishes. Most of the passengers lay in their bunks, and the barometer was set to 'stormy'. By the third day, however, I was used to the rolling, took to walking round the deck and going below to the dining-room, after which I started work on making a piano version of the ballet for Diaghilev. However, the weather remained windy, cold and generally unfriendly, while the stateroom was hot and stuffy. My companion developed a cold, coughing and snuffling the whole night long. In another cabin a passenger died from a carbuncle; his body was embalmed and placed in the hold. Later on a ten-year-old boy in third class died. A search was conducted for my missing case, and the purser and I went over the whole ship going through every one of a hundred and fifty cabins, but without result.

Fellow passengers on board included Morin,[1] formerly one of Diaghilev's conductors who has now been engaged by Chicago, and Bellini, Marinuzzi's repetiteur. Gradually the realisation that I was some kind of pianist and composer seeped into the consciousness of the company on board, causing the passengers to treat me with respect, but for the most part they did not importune me, and if anyone tried to do so I was quick to brush them off. Only on the last day of the voyage did the general depressing atmosphere lift: after a wonderful sunrise we had a calm sea and cloudless skies that lasted all day.

25 October

We came into a fog-bound New York harbour on a calm sea. I felt exhausted after seven days of the ship pitching and tossing, and was upset by the loss of my suitcase, but overall my spirits were high and I even flirted a little with Clarette Verrier, a delightful blonde coming to America to marry some man or other. As we approached New York I took up the question of my lost case with one of the directors of the shipping company, but it seemed the chances of either recovering it or getting compensation for it were low. Once ashore, Morin and his wife and I went to the Brevoort Hotel,[2] where I had once rendezvoused with Stella. That afternoon I went to see Haensel, who had not

---

1 The French conductor Henri Morin.
2 The Brevoort Hotel was the first hotel to be built on Fifth Avenue, in 1854. John Dos Passos, in *42nd Parallel*, wrote that 'all the artists and radicals and really interesting people used to stay

secured any more engagements for me and advised me that my best course of action was to come to terms with the Chicago Opera. He said he thought they might add perhaps another $1,000 to their offer.

Koshetz is due to arrive tomorrow. I went to call on the Bolms, who have a new baby, and to Roerich, a recent arrival in New York who, like me, finds the view of Manhattan as one approaches by sea inspiring. I called on Deryuzhinsky but he was not in. During the summer he had won first prize in a competition to create a memorial bust of Roosevelt.[1] At dinner in a restaurant with Morin, I came face to face with Vladimir Bashkirov, and he gave me such a charming smile that I went up to him, and I am very glad that I did so, because he straightaway told me that Boris Verin had not long ago made his escape from Petrograd into Finland, had been sent money and a visa, and might very soon be in America. I rejoiced exceedingly at this news: Boris Verin is my closest friend and the one of whom I have not had news for the longest time.

26 October

In the morning I continued clothing my ballet in its new dress, and in the afternoon Mr Parmelee, Haensel's press agent, and I went down to the harbour to meet Koshetz. When we arrived at the pier we enquired where the first-class passengers were, to be told that on this ship there was only second class. Disembarkation began soon afterwards, and a steady stream of Greeks, Spaniards, Italians filed down the gangplank, bedraggled, grimy specimens of humanity laden with parcels done up with string – in a word, a deeply dispiriting spectacle. And all of a sudden, there was Koshetz in her furs and diamonds flanked on one side by a clearly besotted Captain and on the other by his First Officer, behind them her husband, her daughter,[2] her cousin, her secretary, an enormous doll, stewards staggering under the weight of her trunks – the press representative and I could only stare at one another with

---

there and it was very French'. Among its habituees were Eugene O'Neill, Isadora Duncan, Edna St Vincent Millay and Lincoln Steffans. Nathanael West lived there in 1935–36. Banquets were held in it for Margaret Sanger, indicted for distributing birth-control information, and for Emma Goldman on the eve of her 1919 deportation to the Soviet Union. The American Labor Party was founded there in 1936. The hotel's barber is credited with inventing the 'bob' (for dancer Irene Castle). The hotel's owner, Raymond Orteig, put up $25,000 for the first person to fly across the Atlantic, and Charles Lindbergh collected the money at a breakfast there on 17 June 1927. The hotel was demolished in 1948 because it could no longer be brought up to prevailing standards.

1 Theodore Roosevelt died in January 1919.
2 The daughter thus making her first bow in the limelight was Marina, then six years old but later to become well known equally as an opera singer and a Hollywood actress in roles requiring a good singing voice (*On the Riviera* with Danny Kaye, *The Singing Nun*, and most famously *The Great Caruso*).

a wild surmise at this triumphal procession. The only thing I could possibly compare it with was the arrival of Babulenka in *The Gambler*. Koshetz, who had by the way become even lovelier than before, threw herself into my arms and called me the saviour of her and all her family.

We went to the Brevoort, where I had reserved a two-room suite for her, and I told her of the truly intriguing correspondence that had occurred between Haensel and Rachmaninoff. Haensel had, in the most courteous terms imaginable, let Rachmaninoff know that the singer Koshetz was coming to America, and as she was not well known here might he, Rachmaninoff, find it possible to be of assistance to his compatriot by introducing her to the Boston Symphony? Rachmaninoff replied by enquiring what sort of a manager Haensel could be, not to be aware that orchestral engagements were all settled in April, not October. (He must have forgotten that he himself had arrived in November and had immediately been offered engagements with all the symphony orchestras.) Haensel in turn responded that he had not expected a 'rude answer' to his 'polite letter'. If he had ventured to make an approach to Rachmaninoff, it was purely as one gentleman to another. He regretted that in this he had been mistaken.

This information produced on Koshetz an effect like a thunderclap: as she said, when she had parted with Rachmaninoff three years ago he had promised that whenever or wherever they met in future he would always do anything he could for her.

In the evening we toured New York from the top deck of an omnibus, which made a colossal impression on all the party. When I was in Paris New York had seemed so narrow and cramped. Yes, here every square inch is jealously exploited, but how imposing it is in its massive piling-up!

Koshetz had brought two interesting letters to give to me: from Tcherepnin, now the Director of the Tiflis Conservatoire but straining every nerve to get abroad, and from Suvchinsky, to whom I had written twice but with no result. The latter of these was extremely full and interesting. His former building superintendent[1] had stayed for a time in my apartment in Petrograd but had eventually been forced to move out. What remained in the apartment he could not say, but he hoped that Asafyev was taking care of it.

Koshetz herself was preoccupied with the letter she had decided she must write to Rachmaninoff, not to mention that she had in her possession several letters from other people she had been asked to pass on to him. I did not think much of her first draft, and recommended that she recast it according to my suggestions. Having established that Haensel's approach to Rachmaninoff had been without Koshetz's knowledge, my version ended thus: 'As I never asked you for anything in the past, still less would it now have entered

---

1 See above, p. 52.

my head to ask you for anything.' Koshetz was enraptured and called it a stroke of genius to end the letter in this way.

I went to dinner with Bolm and played through on their piano the piano transcription of *Chout* I had made on the voyage across the Atlantic, to see how it sounded. Some of it could not be bettered (although I had done it without access to a piano) but there were places that did not sound very good. The question is, is it possible to improve them or not?

28 October

I brought about the meeting between Koshetz and Haensel by taking her to see him. Koshetz immediately and grandiloquently launched into her prima-donna role, while Haensel sprawled on the sofa. It took me all my time and effort to steer the conversation into a more sensible direction. Koshetz could not understand what the man was doing if he was not prepared immediately to spend a fortune on publicity to launch her career. Haensel is not yet convinced of Koshetz's true stature, and is feeling his way cautiously. When Morin heard her he could hardly believe his ears, and indeed she does sing wonderfully. She did 'Memory of the Sun'[1] with such simplicity and perfection of finish that beside her my dear Vera[2] is a student.

Koshetz is smothering me with praise and endearments. A fortune-teller has told her she will be Prokofiev's lover. 'Why don't we leave this lot behind and go off together to another town!' she said. 'All right,' I replied, half jokingly, 'come with me to California.'

That evening Strock, my manager in Japan, surfaced. He has made money and wants to offer Koshetz engagements there. He impressed all of us as being a crook.

29 October

Booked tickets to go to Chicago because Johnson and Marinuzzi will both be there from tomorrow. Even though Koshetz is in despair that without me she will be a lost babe in the wood, I must go and look after my affairs. Strock was slobbering over Koshetz again today and it looks as though Haensel may be stupid enough to give her up to him. She has not yet sent the letter to Rachmaninoff, and to my great disappointment is vacillating whether to or not. When I asked her about Litvinne, who used to be her teacher and about whom she is crazy, Koshetz with extraordinary perception cried out: 'Look at him, he's got himself some little singer in Paris and now wants to look after her!'

1 No. 3 of Prokofiev's *Five Poems of Anna Akhmatova*, Op. 27.
2 Janacopulos.

30 October

Koshetz's husband Schubert, an artist, has drawn my portrait and although I sat patiently for him for two hours I do not think it is a particularly good likeness. I played Nina the first act of *Fiery Angel*, it made a tremendous impression on her and I may say on me too, not having set eyes on it for many months.

I had lunch with Vladimir Nikolayevich. He was full of praise for Boris and said he would be glad to see him in America. And so would I, very much so! He will have changed a great deal, but in which way I do not know. I shall read him my stories when he comes; I have not read them to anyone at all, except a few passages to Linette.

At five o'clock Nina and I kissed our tender farewells and I went off to Chicago. Train journeys have become much more expensive than they were, and I have so little money that I took a slow train, twenty-eight hours instead of twenty.

31 October

Travelled all day. The train limped along and was two hours late. The scenery between Pittsburgh and Chicago is boring. I caught up on my Diary. Arrived in Chicago at eleven o'clock to be met by Kucheryavy in his car.

1 November

Wrote to Johnson that I am in Chicago to establish my rights, but my desire is to settle matters amicably and therefore I should like to see him.

Called on Mrs Carpenter. She and her husband are very influential in Chicago society and in opera circles particularly. Ever since in Paris I had been fortuitously instrumental in helping her to see Diaghilev and show him her husband's ballet, she has been extremely warmly disposed to me. They are very nice people.

2 November

A letter from Johnson. I thought it would be to suggest an appointment to meet, but it was something very different: two weeks ago they had sent a telegram to me in France informing me that *Oranges* was to be cancelled altogether, and they wished to let me know of their decision so that I would not waste their time with a pointless lawsuit. I confess that this was an earth-shattering revelation, so much so that as I read the letter everything went dark before my eyes. Next, I thought it must be a bluff to propel me into their waiting arms, because how could they possibly tear up $80,000 and throw it out of the window because of a dispute over $2,000? To do that one would have to be either inconceivably rich or inconceivably stupid. It was a development I had not remotely foreseen, and only now did I realise how important it was from the external point of view, and how greatly it was cherished internally, that my opera should be produced and seen.

I replied to Johnson in diplomatic terms: the decision is a preferable outcome to insisting on producing the opera against the wishes of the composer, but I regretted that it should have been taken so precipitately at the very time when I was prepared to negotiate my position (I said this in order to probe the extent to which they might be bluffing). I asked for permission to come in and see him tomorrow to retrieve my music.

That night I slept badly. I felt angry and bereft without my opera.

3 November

Saw Johnson, correct behaviour and polite smiles on both sides. However, I repeated that I was ready to agree a lower figure of $4,000, and said what a pity it was that distance had placed obstacles in the way of our coming to an agreement. Johnson said yes, it was one of those unfortunate occasions when things had not worked out. I asked whether it was their intention to make use of any of the scenery for another production. Johnson said: 'No,' and then added, with a wave of his hand, 'except perhaps for one scene, the funeral.'

So it is not a bluff. This is horrible. No doubt their psychology is as follows: better tear up $80,000 than allow ourselves to be browbeaten by the demands of this young whipper-snapper whom we were trying to help. Whatever the reason, my strategy, so stoutly endorsed by Kucheryavy, has suddenly been turned on its head.

Now there are no bright prospects on the horizon, and I have three dollars in my pocket. I shall stay with Kucheryavy until 7 December and insist on paying a quarter of the expenses for food and accommodation.

That night I again slept very badly.

4 November

I went to see Volkov and related to him the débâcle with the opera. He said he would go himself, as Consul, to test the lie of the land with Johnson and express his dismay at the removal of a Russian opera from the repertoire. He advised me to see Cyrus McCormick, who was presently in Chicago, purely to apprise him of the situation.

Gottlieb, the nice young Jewish man who is a passionate admirer of my music, is in despair at the cancellation of *Oranges*. Although he has no money himself he has contacts with a number of rich and influential Jews in the city, who are interested in my music. His strategy is to get an enormous scandal whipped up about the cancellation, and then, who knows, it might after all be put on this year.

5 November

Volkov has been to see Johnson who told him there is nothing to be done, the decision is irreversible. Volkov then telephoned McCormick's secretary, and she said that he was going away on Monday and was terribly busy in the meantime (as always). But then she posed an interesting question: 'When is Mr Prokofiev's opera going to be performed? Mr McCormick is so interested in it . . .' Volkov replied that the opera production had been cancelled, and he would write a long letter explaining the circumstances in detail. Here was a ray of light: the people who finance the opera company had no idea that $80,000 had been thrown away.

In the evening I went to see Volkov again, and he showed me his letter so that I could make any changes I considered necessary. The letter was calm, reasonable and diplomatically expressed.

I got a letter from Miller in Petrograd (!), the first such communication I had had from that city for three years. I was so happy to have this letter; to all appearances Vera loved me as she had done in the past, devotedly and almost hopelessly. She confirmed that the apartment had been broken into and robbed and the papers destroyed, except for those I had given to Asafyev before I left. What were they? Had I really given some papers to him? Diaries? Letters? I don't remember doing so at all, but if I had, it would have been a very intelligent thing to do.

6 November

Called at the Consulate in the morning, where Volkov showed me the letter, tidied up and incorporating the changes I had suggested, which he then signed and sent to Cyrus.

In the afternoon I played the piano. The opera has gone down the drain, so I must concentrate on the piano and use it as the route out of my present difficulties. In the evening Gottlieb took me to the theatre and to see Lob, a rich Jew who had invited me.

7 November

A busy day. Gottlieb had arranged for me to be asked to lunch by Mme Rosenwald, whose husband is worth 5 million. From her we went on to her brother, who is worth 75 million and is one of the backers of the Chicago Opera. There we met Rosenthal, one of the most prominent lawyers of the city and a good friend of McCormick. I gave my account of the incident, in a tone of high-minded reproach at the waste of money. They listened attentively, and were clearly indignant. Rosenthal promised to speak to Harold.[1]

Leaving the Jewish domain, I moved over to the Christian one.

Dined with the Carpenters. Told the story. Tone – high-minded reproach. Carpenter got on the telephone and made a series of calls. Harold arrives in Chicago tomorrow and Carpenter will speak with him. This is splendid, everyone preparing to have a go at him. Carpenter said that for the present the best tactic would be to do some clandestine spy work, to find out who and why. But if this undercover approach fails to discover what we need to know, then we will have to break cover and agitate openly for an official enquiry as to how such things can have been allowed to happen and money wasted in this way. In a word, in a quite unexpected manner I have successfully set in motion a powerful conspiracy.

8 November

Sat quietly at home. The plot we instigated yesterday is developing by its own momentum without intervention from me. I sent Diaghilev the piano transcription of four scenes of *Chout*, and also wrote to Mama and to Linette. I got a second letter from Linette. I played the piano a good deal: the programme is going very well, with a precision and accuracy Rachmaninoff would be proud of. My mood is reasonably buoyant, and I want very much to believe in the success of our conspiracy, when . . . oh, then! But on the whole it is better to be philosophical. If the answer is no, it is no. Whatever happens, I have composed a good opera.

9 November

Gottlieb took me to the University in the morning, where we met several professors, some of whom had heard me at the reception in the Cosmopolitan Club and were now delighted that I was present in their University. One of them, Levitt, has good connections with opera circles, and said he would be asking questions about why my opera had been cancelled. This is excellent, an attack from a third flank. Gottlieb is trying to arrange for me to play a recital at the University. There is a strong movement for this to happen, and the question is how it should be organised practically.

In the afternoon I saw Carpenter. He is making strenuous efforts on behalf of my opera and said he would unleash an avalanche of powerful

---

1 Harold McCormick, Cyrus McCormick's younger brother and the chairman of the board of directors of the Chicago Opera.

people on Harold, who had arrived the evening before. He thought it would be better if he were not directly involved, since he and his wife had not long ago set up a similar trap for Pam and they were beginning to be seen as 'troublemakers'.[1] Based on another talk he had had with Johnson, he had formed the conclusion that the reason the Opera had acted as it had was the 'narrow understanding they had of the opera company's pride', along the lines of: 'Oh, he is digging in his heels, so we won't give him anything, and that will teach him a lesson.'

Johnson is now claiming that in any case it is physically impossible to produce the opera this year, but Carpenter does not believe this: until 30 October the company was on tour and this week they are rehearsing Marinuzzi's new opera. Carpenter also recommended that Haensel should write formally to Johnson stating that I accepted their terms. Johnson would thus have the last defensive weapon in his armoury shot from under him, and Carpenter could then launch his propaganda offensive.

10 November

A letter from Koshetz, who is bouncing about all over New York and finding all sorts of causes for furious indignation, much as I did two years ago when I first came to the city.

Nothing much happened today; I tried to get down to the orchestration of Scene Five, but it would not flow. I played the piano instead.

Gottlieb telephoned to say that Mme Julius Rosenwald (she of the 75 million) is very concerned by what has occurred and is working very hard to get my opera produced. Not only that, but she wants to invite me to give a recital at her house, and that means money.

I thought of Linette and of Miller, and generally felt sad and lonely.

11 November

With Gottlieb I visited Mr Rosenthal, who once again questioned me about the opera situation and said he would speak to Harold McCormick. He asked me to play at his house at a soirée on the 23rd. I thought this would mean $500, but he gave me to understand that several professors had given lectures at his house on similar occasions, and had been paid $50. I said I would play gratis.

Lunched with the Carpenters, but they had no more news to report. Carpenter has asked two of his friends to speak to Dawes, who in a few days' time is going to be appointed to the position formerly held by Pam, that is

---

1   In English.

to say vice-president of the finance committee of the board of directors.[1] Carpenter thinks that it will be more productive to lean on Dawes than on Harold, as he provides money without involving himself in the direction of the company.

Gottlieb rang up in the evening: the recital in the University is all arranged and the date fixed for the 22nd. He thinks the fee will be not less than $600. It will be a pleasure to play in front of such an audience.

12 November

A quiet day in terms of external activities. I played the piano and tried to get down to scoring the ballet, but again it would not flow. However, I did have one achievement: I had another look at the 'Dance' from Op. 32, which has obstinately defied my attempts to compose it and has been lying in a half-finished state for two years now. Today an idea came to me and I finished the piece, spending almost the whole day on it. Now I must finish the 'Waltz' and Op. 32 will be ready.[2]

13 November

Worked for quite a long time on the 'Waltz', and finished it. In the evening I went to the symphony concert, and when I went into the artists' room to see Zimbalist, who was the soloist, instead of him I found there Stock and Rachmaninoff. Since despite his promises Stock had not invited me since I appeared in Chicago with the *Scythian Suite*, I did not relish the thought of a long conversation with him, and therefore made a bee-line for Rachmaninoff. For some reason he was in a genial and welcoming mood, asked me what I was doing, what I was composing, and said that he himself was composing nothing. When I asked him if it was true what the newspapers were saying, that he was writing an operetta, he replied: 'There's not a word of truth in it!' I said I would be coming to his concert the following day, and afterwards would like to come and shake his hand in the artists' room, to which he responded with unusual promptness: 'Please do come, I shall be very glad to see you.' I could not quite understand what had suddenly made

---

1 Charles Gates Dawes (1865–1851), banker, Nobel Peace Prize laureate (for the ultimately unworkable Dawes Plan for post-war German reparations), future Vice-President of the United States to Calvin Coolidge's Presidency, US Ambassador to the United Kingdom, self-taught pianist and composer of 'Melody in A major', the basis of the hit pop standard 'It's All In The Game' as covered by the Four Tops, Van Morrison, Cliff Richard, Elton John, Barry Manilow, Keith Jarrett, etc., etc. This colourful character was an early ally of Harold McCormick in the formation of a resident opera company for Chicago and became its first vice-president. He continued to serve in this capacity well into the Civic Opera reign of Samuel Insull.
2 *Four Pieces for Piano*, Op. 32.

him so friendly. No doubt the arrival of Koshetz has something to do with it.

Rachmaninoff did have one very sad piece of news: Struve, whose arrival in Paris Stravinsky and I had been so eagerly awaiting, had indeed come to revive the operations of the Russian Music Editions, but had been killed in an accident with an elevator on the staircase of Koussevitzky's building. It is a tragedy for Struve, and for Russian Music Editions, and now, of course, no one can say when anything will be published.

14 November

I attended Rachmaninoff's concert, at which he played well to a huge audience. When I went into the artists' room to see him he waved his hand from afar to indicate his pleasure at my presence. He never used to do anything like that. At the same time Marinuzzi, with Smallens and Bellini, his two assistants, came rushing up to me full of regrets that *Oranges* was not to be produced. He said they had all been astonished by the decision, as they had been working hard at preparing it – and to prove it, sang a couple of excerpts from it. Marinuzzi invited me to come tomorrow to see a rehearsal of his opera and also to have a talk, as he could not understand at all why my opera had been cancelled. This raised my hopes somewhat.

The Green Room then began to empty until the only people left were Rachmaninoff, Fokine and I. Rachmaninoff was extremely nice and friendly, and wanted to know what had happened with *Oranges*. He asked me to have dinner with him, but I could not as I had already committed myself to some Jewish plutocrats. 'My advice to you', he said on parting, 'is to stick close to Marinuzzi.'

15 November

Wrote letters and played the piano.

In the evening Gottlieb came round with Dina Saknovska, a young and far from unattractive Jewish girl who is going to sing at my concert in the University. Quite why she is singing I do not know, but apparently she is a protégée of Gottlieb's. Let her sing by all means, I won't interfere. She was nice and very modest.

In the afternoon at Marinuzzi's invitation I attended the rehearsal of *Jacquerie*. It was better than I had expected, and although if one regards it purely as music it does not have any great merit, from the operatic point of view it is expertly done and often effective, and vulgarity is kept to a minimum. Morin said that Marinuzzi had had nothing to do with the cancellation of my opera, and that like Morin he had been very surprised when Johnson told him about it. Many of the French singers came up to me and said that they had spent several months learning their parts, knew them well, and all this had gone to waste.

Although the reason Marinuzzi had given for inviting me today was to talk about *Oranges*, evidently in all the commotion and preoccupations of his rehearsal he seemed to have forgotten all about it, so nothing was said. I took it that when he had raised the matter yesterday it was not to any specific end, but out of politeness.

16 November

I was expecting a reply from Rosenthal today as by now he should have spoken to Harold McCormick. But although Gottlieb made five telephone calls to him he could not reach him as Rosenthal was in court all day. Life carries on in its quiet and slightly tedious way. I have no particular desire to show my face anywhere because of the opera situation, as expressions both of sympathy and indignation have begun to grate on me. Also, I have in my pocket precisely two dollars, and Kucheryavy is cleaned out as well. There is nothing for it but to wait until the 22nd.

17 November

More news: Haensel has written that he has spent so much money on Koshetz the time has come for me to pay him the money I owe him for my concerts. I did not expect this from Haensel. What has Koshetz to do with me? The percentages from her earnings will go to him, not me. In any case, I had hoped Haensel would hold off making any financial demands on me until I was in a position to pay him. However, along with this letter was another, more pleasant one: an offer from New Orleans.

In the afternoon I stayed at home and played the piano. Carpenter rang to invite me to dinner tomorrow and to the opera. I said I would accept with pleasure, except that I still did not have my new evening trousers to replace those that had been stolen, whereupon the invitation was extended to dinner and trousers, as he has two pairs and is the same size as me.

Linette sent the reviews of the *Scythian Suite* which Coates had performed in the first concert of the London Symphony's season on 1 November.[1] Evidently the *Suite* has made a good impression.

---

1 In *The Times*, 3 November 1920.

18 November

Nikolay Titovich has been in Indianapolis to try to sell his lace, the same as he tried unsuccessfully to sell two years ago, but nobody bought it this time either. As any money he has earned has all gone on payments for his car, we decided to pawn our 'valuables' and drove to the pawnbroker. I took the diamond brooch from Eleonora and the gold watch from Koshetz, and Kucheryavy two pairs of gold cuff-links. For all of this we got $20. Pretty good? We bought some patent-leather shoes for me with eleven of the dollars, and split the remainder between us.

In the afternoon I visited Professor Cheville, who had brought together some of his professorial colleagues with their wives, and I played to them. I think this the first time in the two years I have been in America that I have been in the society of genuinely cultured people. Then 'dinner with trousers' at the Carpenters, followed by the opera, *The Jewels of the Madonna* (trash).[1]

Carpenter has had his conversation with Dawes about *Three Oranges*, but apparently it was not very long and not very conclusive. Dawes said that in principle his responsibilities were financial and not concerned with practicalities. In what way is $80,000 not a financial matter?

19 November

When I called at the Carpenters' to return the trousers, they were as charming as ever, but they are leaving tomorrow to go to New York for a week, and I shall thus lose my main ally. Mme Carpenter said that a granddaughter of the famous General Grant had come to Chicago, a Princess who was a childhood friend of both McCormick brothers. They want to invite both me and the Princess to lunch tomorrow, in the belief that the Princess could prove useful to me.

I am getting enthusiastic letters from California and hope that my appearance there will create a stir. It's about time it happened somewhere. California seems to be the brightest star in my American firmament.

20 November

Mrs Carpenter rang to say that, after all, it would be better if I did not come to lunch so that they could talk to the Princess without me being present, and please would I ring after lunch? I did so, and the Princess will receive me tomorrow at noon. Rosenthal has still not managed to arrange a meeting

---

1 Opera (1911) by Ermanno Wolf-Ferrari.

with Harold McCormick. I think I shall be playing for him for nothing, as he is not going to do anything for me.

21 November

I went to see the Princess, who although she does speak some Russian does so in such a fractured way that we immediately changed to English. I told her the whole story, to which she listened very attentively and with great interest. She said that although Pam had been unseated from his presidential position, he still wielded a great deal of influence in the affairs of the Chicago Opera and in all probability the abolition of the *Oranges* project was the work of his hands. She asked me to put in writing what I had told her, and to make two copies which I should give her tomorrow. The following day she would be having dinner with both McCormicks, and would have a serious talk with them. 'I think', she said, 'that I shall be able to do more for you than anyone else. The McCormicks are very generous and honourable people, and I shall do my best to defend your creation as a Russian work of art. I feel myself to be a Russian, and am proud of it. I also hope that the incident with your opera will prove to be the final blow[1] that puts paid to Pam.

This meeting revived serious hopes in me, and as soon as I got home I applied myself to the memorandum, excusing myself on that account from spending the evening with the Volkovs.

22 November

From eleven o'clock until three I was in the Consulate finalising my memorandum with the help of the Embassy stenographer. At four o'clock I took it to the Princess, and then went to try the piano that I was to play that evening at the University, not getting home until six with a splitting headache. I took some pyramidon, and the headache went away.

At eight p.m. in the Kucheryavy automobile we went to the concert. The hall was very fine, but there were not many people, which surprised me as Gottlieb had been telling me they would have to put seats on the stage. I very much enjoyed performing a programme on which I had worked so thoroughly. For the first time I played the Schubert waltzes and also, not counting the charity concert in Kislovodsk before I left Russia, Chopin. It was a tremendous success, but I played only three encores, not wanting to give any more. Dina sang her numbers in the middle of the programme; she wore a gorgeous gown and looked quite pretty, but her singing was no more than average. After the concert we had tea at Professor Cheville's. Gottlieb was upset that there had not been more people at the concert.

1 In English.

25 November

A letter from Koshetz, as volcanic as ever. She had finally sent my version of her letter to Rachmaninoff and had received a terse and sarcastic reply. Her career is slowly getting under way. She asked me to write some songs without words for her to sing at her concert on 12 January. She was thus repeating a request she had earlier made in New York, and I find the idea attractive.

I began to compose again today, and became so absorbed that I missed the time I was supposed to ring the Princess, at twelve o'clock. When I remembered I did ring, but she had gone out. Most annoying. I rang again at seven. The Princess was very nice, she had handed my memorandum to H. McCormick attaching a handwritten note from herself, and had taken care to deprecate Pam to McCormick. She hopes that some good will come of this. We shall see!

1 December

In the morning through the window there was snow and the mountains of the Sierra Nevada, although we had gone through the pass during the night. But an hour later we were in a different world: warmth, sun, green and palm trees – all trace of December had vanished! I sat on the open platform of the observation car at the rear of the train, breathing in the spring-like air and rejoicing that I was in California. When two years ago I had been in San Francisco in August there had been such a cold wind blowing that I had hardly expected such a pleasant surprise in December. At half-past one in the afternoon I arrived in San Francisco, where I put up in the Saint Francis, the city's best hotel, extremely stylish and hideously expensive, but one must keep up appearances. Jessica,[1] my manager, proved to be an ebullient lady, quite young, with incredibly long teeth bared in a perpetual smile. I have four concerts in one week and then after a three-week gap another concert in Los Angeles, but I resolved to try to squeeze out of her one more engagement, so agreed to wait on condition she could add one more concert. She replied that she was not in a position to confirm this at the moment, but if my appearance in San Francisco was a success she would arrange another concert. Accordingly we agreed to wait until the San Francisco concert had happened, and postponed further discussion until after the 19th.

14 December

Thanks to letters of recommendation I had with me from Chicago I was soon provided with quite a number of acquaintances, perfectly pleasant

---

[1] Colbert.

people although none of them remarkable. The Russian Consul, on whom I called, was also a very nice man.

Jessica and her friend, a singer called Gentle, called for me in the evening with a splendid car, and we took the ferry over to Oakland for the first of my Californian recitals. There was much joshing and teasing and we had a jolly time of it on the journey. I made a great effort to play well, in order to impress Jessica, and I think I managed it although it was hard to concentrate because the audience was so pitifully small. All the same the recital was very warmly received, and Jessica gave me her congratulations and a beaming smile.

The building in which I played (The Auditorium) was most interesting. The hall looked like a hall, and the stage looked like a stage. But all of a sudden a door opened at the back of the stage and one could see into another hall, and what a hall! Ten thousand seats. My jaw dropped.[1]

16 December

At four o'clock we set off for San José, an hour and a half's drive away. The concert was at half-past eight, and the programme was the same as for Oakland. I played well and with great enjoyment, except for the Op. 12 'Scherzo', which I never seem to be able to bring off technically (to the standard I set myself) and the Rimsky-Korsakov *Novelettes*, pieces for which I have always found it hard to develop a satisfactory interpretation in performance. This time there was a large audience and a very enthusiastic reception, which is why I played so well. If I do the same in San Francisco on Sunday, that will be just the ticket.

The stage on which I was playing had scenery on it, consisting of a wall with a large window in it through which could be seen, some distance away from it, another piece of scenery depicting the night sky with stars. Before the concert began I asked for the window to be covered over because of the howling draught coming through it, and what should happen in the break before the last section of the programme but the appearance of a poetical American lady pleading with me to have the window opened again so that the stars could be seen. I explained that if the window was opened a cold draught came through it. 'Oh, but please, at least just for the last number!' 'Perhaps at my next concert.' When I went out to play my Prelude I suddenly remembered the stars and could hardly prevent myself from bursting out laughing. I had to bite my lips hard to get through the Prelude to the end without collapsing.

---

1   On the shores of Lake Merritt, the Oakland Civic Auditorium, described as 'a California million-dollar recreation and amusement palace', opened its doors in 1914.

Among the numerous and enthusiastic post-concert visitors to the Green Room was an extraordinarily pretty seventeen-year-old girl from the South whom nobody seemed to want to introduce to me. She hung about until everyone else had left, and then stammeringly started to tell me how much she liked my music. As I very much liked the look of her I decided to be sly and say to her that I would send her my *Visions Fugitives* if she would write to me in San Francisco and let me have her name and address. What, I thought, could be simpler than for her to tell me her name and address there and then, but the clever girl immediately cottoned on to the trap and said she would certainly write to me as I suggested. In the meantime an impatient voice was calling for her outside the door, presumably her Mama (it must have been her Mama), indignant that she was spending so much time with me alone, but not daring actually to enter the artists' room. Eventually I said goodbye to the ardent young lady and an elderly spinster, Miss Ives, the local manager, came in and took me off to eat ice-cream.

I was delighted with my stay in San José.

17 December

Next morning I went back to San Francisco smiling in recollection of my young friend from yesterday.

In the afternoon I went to a symphony concert. Hertz, the conductor,[1] a heavy man with a limp, still manages to direct impressively. After the concert I had dinner with him and then played chess with the leader of the orchestra, a passionate chess-player, while several people looked on reverentially. The game ended in a draw, but I was concentrating so hard I got a bad headache.

18 December

Spent the morning composing a song in B minor for Koshetz and also played through the programme for tomorrow even though it is the same as for Oakland and San José. I got a letter from my unknown San José friend, somewhat incoherent but very touching and respectful. Her name is Leona Spitzer and she is intending to come to my concert. This is a pleasant

---

1 Alfred Hertz (1872–1942) was a fine conductor of the old school. Born and trained in Germany, and crippled by a childhood attack of infantile paralysis that caused him to walk with a stick, he had come to America to head the Metropolitan Opera's German opera department, which he did until 1915 when he accepted the post of Music Director of the then four-year-old San Francisco Symphony Orchestra, a post he held for the next fifteen years. A noted Wagnerian, he conducted the American premieres of *Parsifal* and Richard Strauss's *Salome*, and as early as 1913 recorded the Orchestral Suite from *Parsifal* with the Berlin Philharmonic.

thought, and I hope we shall be able to talk for a little longer this time.

Hertz took me to his club to play bridge. I won $20.

19 December

Today is the main concert of my Californian tour, because San Francisco is unquestionably the capital city of the West Coast. I therefore practised seriously in the morning, longing though I was to get on with my B minor song. The concert started at three o'clock. There was an audience of about five hundred, which is not really such an insignificant number but in a theatre seating two thousand looks very empty, and for that reason I started the concert not in my best form. On top of that, I have never yet succeeded in feeling completely on top of the Beethoven Sonata.[1] Also, the appearance of Leona in the front row, although alluring, did little to add to my composure. But by the end of the programme I warmed up and the success was very great. A dozen or so admirers came into the Green Room afterwards, but no Leona. I waited a while for her, but she did not come. I went home rather disappointed.

In the evening I was at Steinhardt's playing bridge with the crocodiles.

20 December

Jessica said that she was very happy with my artistic success and hoped to have me next year for a longer series of concerts, but there had not been enough public for her to risk an extra performance. She advised me strongly to wait for the Los Angeles concert on the 13th, first because there was always the hope that something might come up in the meantime, and secondly it would save her from making a loss on the whole tour. As a tour next season might bring me in four or five thousand I decided to put a good face on it and accepted. Since there is nothing more for me to do in San Francisco, I went south this evening, to San Diego.

21 December

I arrived in the morning in Los Angeles, a famously balmy spot. As recently as three or four years ago hardly anyone knew of it, but now Los Angeles has overtaken San Francisco in terms of population. Adolph Tandler, a dreamy Viennese conductor of a bankrupt orchestra[2] and my local manager, met me

---

1 Sonata in A, Op. 101.
2 The bankrupt orchestra was the Los Angeles Symphony, which had been established in 1898 and performed in the 1,500-seat Trinity Auditorium under the baton of the Viennese-born

with outstretched arms and immediately plunged me into a round of interviews and so forth. He is a fanatical admirer of my music and was the first person in America to insist that he wanted my concert to consist exclusively of my works.

Not long after there appeared Professor Kal,[1] the same who had fallen desperately in love with Ariadna Nikolskaya and had followed her to America. Kal was overjoyed to see me; he was beginning to establish himself in America and was giving a course of lectures on Russian music, concluding with a lecture on me. He treated me to lunch in celebration of my presence in Los Angeles, and then revealed that Ariadna herself was here and was turning into a very talented composer – 'you know, self-taught, just like Borodin or Rimsky-Korsakov' – and very much wanted to see me, so I must not be too patronising about her compositions.

Dagmar Godowsky is also here; in short these three weeks that I am going to spend here among the palms, the sunshine and beautiful women are going to be a carnival. It was a seductive prospect after gloomy Chicago and the concentrated hard work of my concert tour. My bitterness at the collapse of *Oranges* evaporated completely, so that if the Chicago company had suddenly appeared with new proposals, I would probably have played very hard to get.

At three o'clock I took a train and went even further south, to San Diego, almost on the Mexican border. 'While you are there, go on to Tijuana, into Mexico itself,' urged Kal as we parted, 'you don't need a passport. But be careful not to lose too much money at roulette.' I arrived in San Diego in the evening, found out how to get to Tijuana, and as there were still twenty-four hours before the concert decided I would go to Mexico the next day.

22 December

Next morning in a businesslike manner I set about going to Mexico. There were a lot of cars parked outside the hotel, and for 65 cents they would take you to Tijuana and back, as soon as a carload was full up. The journey took about an hour and went through rather beautiful country. I was a little nervous about entering Mexico, the sort of nerves one always has at a border

---

Adolph Tandler. When in 1918 the multi-millionaire amateur musician William Andrews Clark, Jr announced that he wished to endow a new symphony orchestra, Tandler offered to merge his organisation into the new one, but was rebuffed. A year later the LA Symphony went into liquidation, many of Tandler's best players joined Clark's Los Angeles Philharmonic, which took over Trinity Auditorium, and Tandler was out of a job. But not for long, because this gifted and imaginative musician became one of the leading composers of scores for Hollywood, not least his compatriot Erich von Stroheim's epic but troubled *Queen Kelly* with Gloria Swanson, and Howard Hawk's Al Capone movie *Scarface, the Shame of a Nation*.

1 Alexey Kal, critic and former Professor of Music History at St Petersburg/Petrograd University. See *Diaries*, vol. 1, pp. 553, 624.

with another country, a barrier beyond which one's local customs, laws and language suddenly lose their force and become alien. Not only that, but I had no passport with me and was afraid of being detained at the frontier, which would not matter on my way out but most certainly would on the way back. However, everything was fine, I was given a permit in the little Customs hut to get back into the country and then we went over to another small building on the Mexican side. Here a gentleman with a pointed beard and a wide Mexican hat, without asking us any questions but with the elegant gestures of a Spanish grandee, motioned us through and three minutes later we were in Tijuana.

Here a disappointment awaited me: a racetrack with spectator stands, a long row of stables, a depressed-looking building decked out with flags that was the casino – and that was all. Inside the casino American tourists greedily supped alcohol. Because it was still early in the day the racetrack was as dead as a doornail and the roulette tables were closed altogether on account of a law passed by the new Government of Mexico. Humble thanks for that. However, I decided not to be too downcast but to see what I could see of Mexico. The countryside struck me as unusual but not especially beautiful: all around were low hills covered in yellow grass and bright in the blazing hot sunshine. In the distance could be seen a village, approached by a long bridge over a dried-up river. I bent my steps in that direction and found a collection of little cottages, none too clean, and heard occasional snatches of Spanish. But the main thing was the bars, all of them jam-packed with American tourists escaping from their 'prohibition'. There were a few clubs where one could dance, and I saw about five cheap-looking heavily made-up girls. I sent a dozen or so postcards with Mexican stamps on them and then returned to San Diego.

My performance that evening was rather an uncommitted one, and I warmed up only towards the end. It was not a very important concert, the hall was only half full, and playing the same programme for the fourth time in a week had begun to pall. However, the success was the greatest I had had on the tour, I was called back repeatedly to the stage and played six encores.

23 December

I returned to Los Angeles and booked into the Hotel Clark. I rang Kal, who immediately asked me to come over. He lives in a detached two-room house which he never locks. There is a piano, a mass of Russian music, a box of cigars, the walls are covered with portraits of famous conductors – and, in the place of honour, Ariadna Nikolskaya. Hardly was I through the door when he suddenly cried out: 'Sit down at this table and write: zhuk zhuzhzhit!'[1] This was an amusing and original way to welcome a guest.

'Hurry up, this is of the greatest possible importance!' screeched Kal. I sat at the table and wrote out the phrase in my best hand. Kal came and watched me in uncontainable excitement, then let out a shriek: 'That's it! Incredible! Incredible!' and rushed to the telephone. The first number he dialled was the wrong one, but then he got through to the person he wanted. 'Radochka, is that you? . . . You can't imagine, it's absolutely true, here is your "ж" on the page, as large as life! Incredible.'

Dimly I began to divine what this was all about. It was the anonymous letters Max and I had sent to Ariadna about eight years ago, in which we had not troubled to disguise our handwriting. The missives themselves must have disappeared long ago, but the characteristic way the letter 'ж' was written had lodged itself in Ariadna's memory, and she must have relied on it as evidence with which to convince Kal of the veracity of her story. Of course, the similarity of this one letter could hardly demonstrate the authorship of the whole text of the letters, all the same it was annoying to have been caught out. If I had written this 'ж' in the normal way, Kal would never have been able to puzzle it out.

At this point Kal handed me the telephone receiver, so I pasted a smile on my face and talked politely, keeping a little on my dignity. Ariadna said how pleased she was to be speaking to me, as 'really and truly we were never acquainted', and added that tomorrow she would definitely come to my hotel and see me. This was very handsome, I thought. Kal and I then went to see a desperately feeble American woman composer of some sort, and then on to Levin, a Russian who has completely forgotten how to speak the language, but who plied us with whisky and gin. Dagmar Godowsky is here in Los Angeles acting in films, and is as usual embroiled in some kind of scandalous love affair. She also should have been at Levin's today but was not able to come, and on learning that I was due there had insisted that I telephone her. I was put on the line to her, and we had a raucous conversation.

24 December

My head ached all day as a result of yesterday's drunkenness. There was another very jolly telephone conversation with Dagmar, and she invited me to go to their house for Christmas Eve this evening, but unfortunately I could not as I had already committed myself to Tandler, where it was all rather decorous and boring.

---

[1] The meaning is: 'the bug is buzzing', and the point, as becomes clear, is that the phrase features the Russian letter ж, the seventh letter of the Cyrillic alphabet: жук жужжит. 'ж' is normally transliterated as 'zh'.

25 December

Christmas Day, sunny, green and warm. Spent all morning reading Kuprin's stories. I did not know his stories were so marvellous, and done with such superb technical finesse. Oh, why did I give up writing mine! But one day I will go back to them. On my word of honour, I deeply love writing, but composition has swallowed it up.

Kal appeared at noon, with Ilya Tolstoy,[1] the son of the writer, and Nyushel, a wealthy and charming Russian Jew. We got on a bus and went to Nyushel's for lunch, staying until seven o'clock in the evening. After the letter 'ж' incident Kal said not a word about Ariadna, and she herself did not appear yesterday either, although she had said she would. But when I played *Tales of an Old Grandmother* Kal, deeply moved, came to me and unobtrusively kissed my hand.

26 December

Because of the holiday the piano has not been delivered to my hotel room, so I went to work at Kal's, who let me in and then went out so as not to disturb me. I got on with the B minor song, part of which I had already composed in San Francisco and another part on the journey to San José, but which still had gaps in the piano part. But before long Nyushel turned up in his car, and collecting the Tolstoys on the way we went for a drive round the environs of Los Angeles. These are very beautiful, but they have been so much talked about that I had somehow expected more.

27 December

In the morning I busied myself sending money to Mama and Linette. I did quite well, francs are relatively cheap to buy, almost seventeen to the dollar.

Tandler came for me in the afternoon with his car and drove me to the ocean, which at sunset shimmered with the most beautiful colours.

28 December

---

1 Count Ilya Lvovich Tolstoy (1866–1933) was Lev Tolstoy's third child and second son. 'Ilya, the third, has never been ill in his life; broad-boned, white and pink, radiant, bad at lessons. Is always thinking about what he is told not to think about. Invents his own games. Hot-tempered and violent, wants to fight at once; but is also tender-hearted and very sensitive. Sensuous; fond of eating and lying still doing nothing.' (From Tolstoy's letter to his great aunt Alexandra in 1872, when Ilya was six years old, quoted in I. Tolstoy, *Reminiscences of Tolstoy*, trans. George Calderon (The Century Co., New York, 1914).)

Rang up Kal, of whom nothing has been heard for two days. He said I could go to work at his place, and I went there to finish the song. As I entered, Kal said, not looking at me, that the Rumanovs[1] wanted to invite me tomorrow evening, and that Rumanov himself was on his way to make my acquaintance and extend the invitation. Not long after this he did indeed come, and his appearance somewhat disappointed me: small, pale and puffy. Surely the superb Ariadna could have chosen better?[2] He passed on his wife's invitation, then he and Kal left, while I stayed to work and soon finished my song, the fifth of the set.

In the afternoon I took a tram and went to the ocean where I enjoyed a go on the roller-coaster. It was splendid – really high.

29 December

In the morning I telegraphed 3,000 francs to Samoilenko to repay the sum he had loaned me in the summer. In the afternoon I wrote a whole pile of letters.

In the evening I paid my visit to the Rumanovs. This was no ordinary social call, it was a major event. How 'frightfully chic' Max would have called it had he known that eight years after we had sent her our teasing letters, Ariadna would be entertaining me at Christmas amongst the green palm trees somewhere in California! The Rumanovs live modestly. Ariadna herself opened the door to me with a smile of welcome. 'Would you have recognised me?' she asked. 'After all, we were never really properly introduced!' Certainly she has changed a good deal, and not altogether for the better; somehow those brilliant tints which she employed to such dazzling effect when she was fifteen, have lost some of their bloom. The three of us talked easily and amiably for a few minutes, her husband showing himself to be a very cultivated person, and then a new face appeared, Baranovskaya, a former student of Meyerhold, a beautiful young woman who suffered not at all by comparison with Ariadna, and finally Kal.

We drank tea, and then at Kal's request Ariadna played her compositions. Her songs – one of which, 'The Letter Zh'[3] was in imitation of my style – are fairly sugary although a listener prepared to be indulgent might from time to time hear some not uninteresting turns of phrase. The songs were followed by a symphonic poem with a fully written-out score. This was hideously inept, and yet in amongst the ineptitude one would suddenly

---

1 Ariadna *née* Nikolskaya's married name was Rumanova.
2 But see *Diaries*, vol. 1, p. 717, where in July 1914 Ariadna's new husband is described as 'a tall, strapping officer'. Perhaps Rumanov was her second husband.
3 'Ж'.

come across a real invention, often incoherent but a real invention nonetheless. Initially I was not inclined to have any time at all for her music, but these attempts to say something new did win me over. On top of that, the score was beautifully written, with never a missing accidental.

I said I would be happy to share with her a few principles that might help her find the right path in orchestration. Ariadna exclaimed: 'I shall die of happiness!' and said that if I could see her she would like to come tomorrow. I asked her to telephone beforehand, as tomorrow was the day they had promised to deliver the piano but if it did not come it would be better to wait until it did.

The evening passed easily and enjoyably, and I talked a lot of my experiences. Overall, Ariadna made less of an impression on me than I had expected, but the impression she did make was of a good and kind person rather than a fiery, tempestuous one. Baranovskaya I very much took to.

30 December

I had a bit of a headache and the day passed rather slackly. They did not bring the piano. Instead of ringing, Ariadna came in person, on her own, and I ran into her in the lobby of the hotel. She had brought her music, but when she learned that there was still no piano agreed that we would have to put off our session for a few days. Her demeanour was modest; she behaved as she used to do all those years ago, when she was a student of Glazunov. In the meantime I gave her Widor's book on orchestration[1] to read.

Spent the evening at Kal's. I related my biography and played some of my compositions for a big article he is writing for Paris.

31 December

Wrote out a fair copy of the song for Koshetz and gave it to Kal. He is going to New York in a few days and will pass it on to her there. I went to lunch at a big women's club where ladies of a certain age discussed politics, not sparing what they viewed as Russia's oppression of Poland. In the evening I donned tails and went to collect Kal, who had planned an extensive evening of visits to bring in the New Year.

Our first port of call, at ten o'clock, was the home of one Becker. We were there as the result of a conspiracy by the Rumanovs and above all Baranovskaya: Kal, without telling me anything about it, had promised I would be there. There were quite a number of fashionable women, elaborate *couverts*

---

1 Charles-Marie Widor, trans. E. F. E. Suddard, *The Technique of the Modern Orchestra: A Manual of Practical Instrumentation* (J. Williams Ltd, London, 1906).)

at table, and a determined attempt to jolly everyone along by making the gentlemen move round one seat to their right at the sound of a bell, each time having to declaim verses in various languages. Rumanova and Baranovskaya, glamorous and *décolletées*, were looking extremely beautiful and did their best to stay near me.

According, however, to our prearranged timetable, Kal and I bade them all farewell and went on to the Nyushels. The fog was as thick as milk, and on the way we very nearly ran the car straight into a lamp-post. The atmosphere at the Nyushels was more democratic, considerably livelier and less artificial. There was much noise and laughter, posters had been stuck on the wall and over the lavatory hung a sign saying 'Many years of health to you'. Someone had procured wine from somewhere, so people were getting tipsy and making comic speeches.

It was a good place to spend an hour and a half and see in the New Year, but I wanted to go to the Godowskys, having promised Dagmar I would be there by eleven, and it was now after one. A half-drunk Dunayev, who fancies himself as a poet, drove me there in his car, talking non-stop about how famous he was. By now the fog had more or less cleared, and seizing his chance he cranked his car up to 75 versts an hour, and whenever he reached a particularly emotional part of his diatribe he would take both his hands from the wheel, wave his arms about and trust the car to go wherever the will of God might determine. In his drunken state he lost his way, mixed up the streets, and we spent an eternity careering round the deserted city until at length we pulled up outside the small detached house where the Godowskys lived.

A figure resembling a murdered corpse was sprawled out in a chaise-longue on the terrace in front of the house, obviously having drunk himself into a state of oblivion. I ran into the house, happy to get away from the automobile chase I had just endured, and immediately found myself in the midst of a bacchanalian orgy. About fifty people were crammed into four small rooms, almost all of them in fancy dress, the majority of the men dressed as women and vice versa. The wailing of a saxophone and the beat of a drum accompanied a wild dance that was snaking chaotically across the floor. The whole scene resembled the last part of *Petrushka*, at the point where the composer has made a note in the score: 'the Shrovetide Fair reaches its apogee'.

I somehow forced my way through two rooms and attained a wall against which I could lean to survey the scene. It was impossible to recognise anyone behind the painted faces and absurd wigs, and in any case I knew no one there except Dagmar. Most of the guests were film stars, because for more than a year now Dagmar had been acting in movies in Los Angeles, which is the centre of the cinematographic world. Most of the women were staggeringly good-looking, some already a little brittle in their beauty, but others just the opposite, abandoning themselves without a trace of inhibition to the merry-making. I felt I really ought to have come at eleven; now at two o'clock they had all got to know one another, couples had paired up, and I felt like a visitor from another planet. And indeed everywhere there was a dark corner people were embracing, sitting on one another's knee, and so on.

A woman came up to me and said: 'Ich bin Frau Godowsky,' to which I replied 'Und ich bin Herr Prokofiev.'[1] We introduced ourselves and she went to try to find Dagmar, but without success. After about twenty minutes, however, Dagmar herself appeared and clung to me in a way I had hardly expected. She dragged me off to meet a whole series of people, including Nazimova,[2] who in Russia had a moderate career as an actress but here is such a great movie star that she is known all over America. Soon Rumanova and Baranovskaya made an unexpected appearance, and we formed a stylish little nexus of our own, pleased with one another's company.

By this time the atmosphere was fairly steamy, but more from the dancing, the generally erotic ambiance and the wailing of the saxophone, as no wine was served and anyone who was drunk had either become so before arriving or had discovered a source outside. I wanted to dance myself, and although I had never danced in America and did not know any of the American dances, I asked Baranovskaya to teach me, which she did very willingly and very successfully.

'Is that all I have to do?' I asked, having easily mastered the steps. 'Yes, but you need to be a bit more immoral,' she said. 'You have to press your legs right up against your partner, as high and as hard as you can.'

Dagmar flitted in and out of my orbit, gay and affectionate each time we met. But when we sat together in a corner, she cried: 'Do be careful, Frank is dreadfully jealous.' Frank Mayo[3] is a Californian actor and celebrity with whom she has been living for a year. He is currently divorcing his wife and

---

1 'I am Mrs Godowsky'; 'I am Mr Prokofiev.'
2 Alla Nazimova, or as she liked to be known simply Nazimova, the stage name of Yalta-born Miriam Edez Adelaida Leventon (1875–1945), had since her arrival in America in 1905 undoubtedly become a very big star indeed both on Broadway and in silent films. She was regarded as one of the leading interpreters of Ibsen and Chekhov, and such was the esteem in which she was held, not to mention the wealth she had amassed, that she screenwrote, produced and starred in her own movie adaptations of the classics, an enterprise which lost her most of her money even more quickly than she had made it. In true Hollywood-legend style her private life was notorious, as much for its sexual ambiguity as its variety.
3 Frank Mayo (1886–1963), was one of the leading male stars of the silent-picture era, but his career gradually dwindled as the talkies came in. During the 1930s and 1940s it was hard to find a Hollywood movie that did not have Frank Mayo in a bit part as a waiter or a sheriff or some other bystander. He did eventually marry Dagmar Godowsky, but the marriage was annulled in 1928. Photographs in movie magazines of the 1920s show him to have had more than his fair share of rugged, masculine good looks.

wants to marry Dagmar. At first she had been crazy about him but her passion was now cooling, while his was becoming more and more inflamed, his jealousy fuelled by what I must confess was ample cause provided by Dagmar. I heard all this not only from Dagmar's own lips, but from general gossip. At one time I had my arm round Dagmar's waist, at which Ariadna rushed up and pulled me away. 'For heavens' sake what are you doing?' she said. 'He'll kill you or at least will create a scandal. Just look at him watching us.' And certainly Mayo did look rather bloodcurdling, dressed in his convict's costume, although he is very tall and handsome.

I danced with Dagmar's elder sister, Vanita, a plump girl but clearly even more amorous than Dagmar. Towards the end of the party the lights were put out in one of the rooms and people danced in there in the dark. It was five o'clock in the morning by the time we decided it was time to go home, and when Ariadna and Baranovskaya went upstairs to get their coats, they were alarmed to find a Pierrot fast asleep underneath the pile of furs and coats on the bed. Then the Rumanovs drove me home.

1921

1 January

After yesterday's bacchanalia I slept until twelve and woke up rested and in the best of spirits. I rang up Kal, who said: 'I must congratulate you on still being alive after being driven by Dunayev. He came back without his car and still has no idea where he left it.' Kal then revealed that after I had left the Nyushels a furious argument had broken out when Kal declared that Prokofiev was a more important composer than Glazunov or Rachmaninoff. Everyone fell on him and abused him roundly.

Nevertheless, when after a walk in the glorious sunshine that afternoon I called at Kal's, I found all the same company assembled as yesterday, still continuing their New Year celebrations. Kal and I dined with the Rumanovs, and I gave in to Baranovskaya's request to play. Her cheeks burned, and she was clearly very much affected by my playing. She is twenty-eight, but looks younger, comes from a good family and has had several husbands. For some time she lived in Paris, and then came to study with Meyerhold. The combination of these experiences has given her the stamp of refinement. The Baranovskys and the Rumanovs had met in San Francisco and had become friends, whereupon the gentlemen swapped partners, Rumanov and Baranovskaya going to New York while Ariadna and her man – I am not sure whether it was Baranovsky or by this time someone else – stayed by the Pacific. Baranovsky has in any case disappeared into the blue yonder, and the remaining trio live together in perfect harmony and friendship. Whether Rumanov divides his attentions between the two women or whether there is some other combination I do not know, but he is easy to get along with, cultivated and obliging.

2 January

Kal left for New York this morning. I saw him off and then installed myself in his tiny little house with its two modest rooms, quite separate from other buildings. At three o'clock the Rumanovs came to collect me with Baranovskaya and a Mme Brunswick, a millionairess, to take me to the Philharmonic concert. We were supposed to go on afterwards to call on the young pianist who was the soloist at the concert, but he played so badly that I said I was not inclined to waste my time on such a nonentity. Only after the entreaties of all the ladies not to break up the party did I consent to go with them. There was a great crowd of people, glamorous women and movie celebrities, and Dagmar, who enquired jealously why Mrs Rumanova was paying me so much attention. I said that apart from her, Dagmar, I did not love anyone.

3 January

I slept wonderfully in my new abode, although it was cold at night in the flimsily built wooden house. Lunched with Dagmar, who told me all about Mayo and about her own life, and was amazingly loving to me. All the same, when the violinist Mark Rosen appeared, a very good-looking youth, this did not prevent her being amazingly loving to him too.

In the afternoon Ariadna came to see me and brought her score. Our meeting was very workmanlike, I conscientiously tried to eliminate the infelicities in her score while preserving the good ideas it contained. Our session went on for nearly two hours and was strictly confined to the matter in hand.

In the evening I was visited by a violinist from San Diego for whom I had not managed to find time before. He had come on behalf of the Director – a woman – of the San Diego Conservatory of Music to sound me out about the possibility of my becoming a professor there for a term of ten weeks. I asked him to outline the conditions. This could be an idea! If the money is good, why not spend a couple of months next winter in sunny San Diego?

4 January

In the morning I despatched a cheque to Polack, the final payment for Mama's eye operation, and in the afternoon went to Mme Brunswick's extremely elegant drawing-room to hear Baranovskaya give a lecture, in impeccable French, on Molière. Then I hurried home, as the Director of the San Diego Conservatory, having been told that I was interested in the proposal, had postponed her departure from Los Angeles in order to see me today to negotiate the details. She proved to be an exceptionally nice woman, and told me what a great impression my appearance in San Diego had aroused. What she proposed was as follows: a guaranteed fifteen students at $10 for a half-hour lesson twice a week, adding up to $300 a week for two-and-a-half hours of daily work. This was not bad at all, but I decided I would try to improve on the deal and said that I would be prepared to come for eight weeks, September and October, for a guarantee of twenty students at $15 a lesson, that is $600 a week. This would be splendid and would net me almost $5,000, even though the prospect of killing four hours of each day on untalented students was not exactly one to fill me with joy.

The Director countered with a proposal of either $12 and fifteen students or $10 and twenty students, making $400 a week, and said she would make enquiries to find out whether students would in fact be willing to pay such a sum ($15 being in her opinion rather steep for half an hour). If so she would draw up a contract before I left for Europe. Good, very good indeed! It may be that once I start the teaching I shall find it exhausting and curse myself, but for now I take pleasure in knowing that I have been offered a salary of $1,600 a month, which will mean a worry-free summer for me with an assured future.

In the evening Ariadna and Baranovskaya called for me and took me to Levin's, where I had been with Kal on my first evening in Los Angeles, to eat duck killed on a recent duck-shoot. I stuffed myself and then retired to the corner of a sofa to savour the San Diego offer (how unexpectedly had my stay in Los Angeles resulted in this splendid outcome!). Ariadna and Baranovskaya took it in turn to come and sit by me, Ariadna happily recalling the spoof communications I had sent her, and relating not without wit her reaction to them, in particular the blank sheet of paper with the attached imaginary formula the implementation of which would allegedly enable her to read what had been written on it – needless to say with no result as there was nothing there.[1] I explained that Max Schmidthof had been very smitten with her and had invented all sorts of tricks to play on her, in which I had assisted him. This was disingenuous of me, since in fact we had dreamed them up together. To my surprise she did not remember Max at all, but she had adopted the unconventional way of writing the letter 'ж' and had incorporated it in her handwriting ever since!

Baranovskaya was rather more reflective than Ariadna and we talked about art and life, danced a little, in which art she declared I had made progress, and on the way home in the car rested her head on my shoulder.

5 January

I read and wrote letters, and gave an interview. Rumanova came again with her score. The evening before she had been thrilled when I invited her a second time, and that was the reason for her coming so soon. She is meticulously altering her score according to my suggestions, and it is beginning to assume a more 'educated' appearance. Her application and love of composition is truly astonishing. Some pages needed so many changes it would have been easier to write them out afresh. Our relationship was easy but businesslike, as it had been the time before.

In the evening I caught up on my Diary.

---

1 See *Diaries*, vol. 1, p. 326.

6 January

Received a letter from Linette, which made me very happy. The distractions of California have not made me forget Paris.

Today there was a costumed evening at Nazimova's (actually at her girl friend's house) to which all the guests were invited to come dressed as apaches. Rumanova and Baranovskaya made it their business to dress me up, and got from somewhere or other a perfectly appalling white suit with short trousers and bedroom slippers, while Ariadna with great skill made my face up, contriving to elevate one of my eyebrows so that I seemed to have frozen into a permanent expression of astonishment at the wretched fate of the apache. Baranovskaya appeared as a cheap little circus bareback rider, and Ariadna as a youthful gigolo out at the knees. Rumanov was a stout matron with rounded shoulders bared to the world, and was so convincing that on arrival he was shown to the ladies' powder room. Dagmar was clothed in dreadful-looking rags, and was almost naked. Mark Rosen, from the moment he clapped eyes on Ariadna, drank her in as thirstily as if he were draining a goblet of wine. I danced with Baranovskaya and tried to get together with Dagmar, but mad Mayo was circling round us like a demon and she pushed me away. There was quite lot of wine and some people became very merry. Rosen went home at midnight as he has a concert tomorrow. I went into the library and looked at some rather interesting books about the creation of the world and the history of mankind. Eventually the guests began to disperse, and our little group went out on to the street to wait for a car. Soon one was provided, and we set off for home. As I was still dressed in my rags we first called in at the Rumanovs, where I was persuaded to stay the night.

7 January

At ten the next morning the four of us gathered in a café for breakfast. Rumanov's eyes were puffy and dull as he had not recovered from the previous evening's imbibing. Baranovskaya had a headache, and only Ariadna and I were feeling on top of the world. After talking over and laughing at the events of yesterday we separated, and on my way home I rang up Dagmar. She said she would be at the Hotel Clark at one o'clock to have lunch with me. At home I had scarcely sat down at the piano when Dagmar rang. 'Forgive me,' she said, 'but I couldn't talk to you then. Mayo was standing right next to me. But I can't have lunch with you today. I'll come by for you in the car about four o'clock.' This annoyed me, and I said: 'Don't come too late, otherwise I will be with Mme Baranovskaya.' 'You like her?!' shrieked Dagmar. 'Very much,' I replied.[1] 'Very well, I'll be there at two.'

---

1   This exchange in English.

However, I waited at two, and at three, but there was no sign of Dagmar. Obviously she was angry about Baranovskaya, who also telephoned to say that she would not be coming either as she was in bed with a headache (she had meant to come to look at *Three Oranges*, which interested her as a student of Meyerhold). In short, the day turned out to be much less interesting than it had promised to be in the morning. By the evening Baranovskaya felt better and we went as a quartet to the theatre. Baranovskaya was delighted to have been the cause of Dagmar's punishing me.

8 January

I placed an order for a typewriting machine for Mama. Rumanov and I went together to the seaside to ride on the roller-coaster (it was magnificent). In the evening all four of us went to the Philharmonic concert; Dagmar, very beautiful, sat in a box with Mayo but I trained my eyes away from looking in her direction. Afterwards Ariadna and Baranovskaya went home, but Rumanov and I went to see some Americans who had invited us to drink real beer, very delicious. The first two glasses were wonderful, but then I was persuaded to drink seven, which was disgusting and gave me a headache. The Rumanovs asked me to stay with them again, but I decided it was time I spent a bit of time on my own at home.

9 January

In the morning I went back to the Rumanovs, where they told me that Dagmar had just been on the telephone asking for me. Levin then took us by bus to Altadena, to some people he knows, which took about an hour. The weather was glorious, the colours bright and our mood perfection. We arrived at a very beautiful house belonging to a boring man, and after vain attempts to get people to come for a walk, I set out on my own. I took the funicular railway to the top of Mount Echo, from where there was a magnificent view.[1] As dusk approached, the city of Altadena could be seen far below, thousands of lights shining like an upturned bowl of the sky at night. When I came down from the mountain at seven o'clock it was quite dark, and I could not find the house. Stupidly I could remember neither the

---

1 The funicular up the Great Incline was part of the Mount Lowe Railway, an extraordinary feat of engineering and tourist attraction, the only scenic mountain electric railroad ever to be built in the United States. Echo Mountain was so called because a loud enough shout from the 'sweet spot' could generate as many as nine reverberations from the canyons below. Sadly, over time a series of natural disasters destroyed the hotel, the observatory, the menagerie, a Swiss-style chalet 'Ye Alpine Tavern', a searchlight capable of projecting its beam thirty-five miles (later prohibited as a public nuisance) and other attractions on the mountain top. Finally in 1938 floods washed away the railway itself.

address of the house nor the name of its owner, and I wandered for over an hour along the unlit suburban avenues, growing extremely cold as I was wearing only a jacket, and in the darkness of the unfamiliar terrain stumbling painfully over obstacles. At last I joyfully spotted the lights of a tramcar and boarded it. As I did so I was visited by a flash of inspiration and remembered the name of our host: Petersen.

I leapt off the tram, found a chemist's shop, and telephoned him. The Rumanovs and Baranovskaya, much perturbed at my absence, had already returned to town. I took another tram and within an hour was back at the Rumanovs' in Los Angeles. Here I was smothered in embraces; they thought I must have been murdered and were just about to inform the police. The evening passed in stories and reminiscences, Ariadna working on correcting her score and plying me with questions. I sat *à deux* with Baranovskaya, and this time she showed herself to have more depths than I had previously realised. A terrible disease, kidney tuberculosis, had befallen her a year or two ago, and yet her whole attitude to the illness and her serene indifference to its outcome had the effect both of astonishing me and increasing the tenderness of my regard for her. I again stayed the night with them, this time because it would have too cold for me to go out without the overcoat I had left behind at Petersen's.

10 January

Mrs Mason, the millionairess President of Honour of the local Symphony, of which Tandler had been the conductor until it collapsed, organised a great reception today in my honour. She had invited over four hundred people, of which about three hundred actually came, all the beau monde and cream of Los Angeles society. The newspapers had been trumpeting this reception for about ten days. I stood beside the hostess at the door into the drawing-room and was introduced in turn to each lady (because it was in the afternoon the majority of guests were ladies) as she entered. A smile, a few words and on to the next one. This went on for approximately two hours (from half-past four until half-past six) and I was almost dead on my feet from exhaustion. I dined in town with Rumanov and then spent the evening and then the night at their house. Baranovskaya, who was tormenting herself in the throes of preparing a lecture on *commedia dell'arte*, was in bed feeling very low and unwell: one of her kidneys is tubercular.

11 January

I was almost dressed when Baranovskaya came and knocked on my door. She was not only not better, but worse, and went straight back to bed, where she stayed all day. I sat by her bedside and marvelled again at the composure with which she faced her illness. Ariadna settled again to the changes she was making in her score according to the indications I continually gave her, and then I went home to play the piano and to write letters. I came back to the Rumanovs for dinner, but Baranovskaya was no better, still in bed, and I had to feed her with a spoon. She knows Kerensky well, he had been married to one of her cousins and during his time in power had divorced his wife in order to marry another cousin. Her family, wealthy monarchists to a man, were very hostile to him, but Baranovskaya herself was a friend and told me many interesting things about his daily family life. She said he was a hysteric, and this, in her opinion, was the source of both his strength and his weakness.

12 January

Next morning Baranovskaya announced that her kidney crisis had passed and she was feeling better. We all congratulated her on her recovery, and on the fact that it was her birthday, she having attained the age of twenty-seven or perhaps twenty-eight. I then went home, and not long after Baranovskaya arrived to look at *Three Oranges*. Some of the text of the libretto I read to her, for some of it I explained the context, and played the music. As someone familiar with *commedia dell'arte* and the ideas of Gozzi and of Meyerhold, Baranovskaya identified strongly with the opera and was terribly excited by it. Her eyes sparkled and her cheeks flushed.

She was reluctant to leave, but was obliged to as I was due to go to Tandler's office where I collected a long letter from Koshetz and some gloves from Linette. When I wrote to her I had mentioned that I had lost my good Paris gloves, and in Chicago I had no money to buy new ones, so the dear girl had sent me a new pair wrapped up in a newspaper, and I still cannot understand why nobody stole them. Koshetz's success is growing all the time; she received my songs and found to her surprise that she could not understand my harmonies. I hardly expected this of her, but in time she will work them out. The aura leaping out from Koshetz's letter, was, as usual, one of seething, bubbling life. She is singing two of the songs in New York today, as it happens.

Glushakova appeared at my door at six o'clock. She shyly asked me to play something for her, but I cannot understand what makes her come to see me. Soon I had to excuse myself and leave to go to some dinner or other, after which at nine o'clock I telephoned the Rumanovs to see if they had plans for the evening, and if not whether they would come to a small cinema to see a film in which Dagmar was acting. But Rumanov was not in a good mood, Ariadna was working on revising her score. After a family debate it was decided that if I liked to take Baranovskaya she would come on her own, but we could come back and all meet for tea afterwards.

Baranovskaya was extremely animated, and still under the spell of *Three Oranges*. When we arrived at the cinema the picture had already started and the box office was closed, so we were let in free. We saw Dagmar in the role of a wild woman; in places she was very good indeed, but by no means all the time. Her lover Frank Mayo was excellent.[1] After the cinema we bought a birthday cake for Baranovskaya and went back for tea at the Rumanovs'.

13 January

This evening was the date of my concert, therefore I spent the day quietly at home concentrating on playing through my programme. Ariadna and Baranovskaya telephoned several times anxiously asking how I was and whether I needed anything, and saying they were very concerned for me.

The concert took place at half-past eight in the evening in a far-from-full hall, but as the hall seated three thousand the number of people attending was actually quite large. I played well and avoided disasters. It was also a good success, but less so than in San Diego. I played several encores and was presented with a bouquet of flowers done up in a Russian bow (from the Rumanovs and Baranovskaya), but I was left with the feeling that it had been a struggle to get the audience really engaged. The Green Room afterwards was literally heaving with admirers: the Rumanovs, Baranovskaya, Nazimova, Ilya Tolstoy, Glushakova, Neishin[2] and so on. As planned beforehand, Nazimova invited us to her house for the Russian New Year, and indeed shepherded us out so insistently that I had no time to cool down properly after playing or even to shake hands with all the well-wishers. Nazimova's house is beautiful, and the company small and select, mostly movie actors plus the four of us.

The evening, or rather night, passed very pleasantly, everyone getting merry with drink, and I danced with Baranovskaya. At midnight all the lights were doused, we shouted 'hurrah' and someone sang 'God Save the Tsar' and then immediately the Marseillaise. We agreed on 'Slavsya!' from *A Life for the Tsar*, which I predicted would be the future Russian National Anthem, and which Ariadna and I there and then played on the piano four-hands.[3] At five

---

1 Dagmar Godowsky and Frank Mayo made several films together but the one that seems to fit the chronology is *The Peddler of Lies*, directed by William C. Dowlan for Universal, in which Dagmar played a character called Patricia Melton and Frank Mayo the male lead, Clamp, an amateur detective masquerading as a travelling peddler.
2 Possibly a misspelling of Nyushel.
3 The final chorus, 'Glory!' from Glinka's opera. An arrangement had been made by Tchaikovsky for the coronation celebrations of Tsar Alexander III in Moscow's Red Square in May 1883, specifically designed to segue into 'God Save The Tsar'. Tchaikovsky's arrangement is for

o'clock in the morning, before going home, we all went into the garden, to savour the warmth and fragrant freshness of the Californian winter.

14 January

Called on Tandler in his office. He professed himself delighted with my visit to Los Angeles and invited me back next season to play with the orchestra and for a recital. The reviews were good. In the afternoon I called on Mrs Mason to thank her for the reception, and then dined with the Neishins, who with gentle sarcasm noted that in the two weeks since I had fallen into the clutches of the Rumanovs and Baranovskaya they had heard and seen nothing of me. They were, all the same, very nice. At nine o'clock I went to the Rumanovs, where Baranovskaya insisted that I give a recital in Santa Barbara. She was sure it would be a success, and she had lined up a patroness who would take care of the organisation of an event to take place in three or four days' time. She and Ariadna excitedly discussed the details of the plan, which partly owed its inception to Baranovskaya's reluctance to see me leave for New York so soon, and to Ariadna's desire to complete the transformation of her score. In the course of my frequent visits to their house I invariably sat with Ariadna over her score for half an hour or so. She had completely recomposed it according to my suggestions and in the process had revealed both an unusual facility and a love for orchestration. So eager was she to pursue it that she would sit over her revision for five or six hours a day.

15 January

Baranovskaya telephoned Mrs Murphy, a very important lady on whose support Tandler depends, and Mrs Murphy's view was that a concert in Santa Barbara should definitely be arranged; she would immediately take the appropriate steps, and summoned Tandler to discuss what should be done.

Levin took us for a drive in the afternoon, and while on the surface everything appeared amicable, inside I was aware of a tension between the three of us. I was on edge, because on the one hand nothing had been settled about the Santa Barbara concert, and on the other I felt more and more that it was time for me to go back to Chicago. Incidentally, there is extremely interesting news from that quarter: Johnson has been eased out of his Managing Director position and the new Director is Mary Garden.[1] Hurrah! That is the

---

massed choirs and orchestra, and was sung on a specially built platform to accommodate the 10,640 performers.
1 Mary Garden (1874–1967) was born in Aberdeen and died there, but was mainly heard in France, where she made her debut in 1900, and America. Debussy, enchanted by her voice, chose her as his Mélisande for the Opéra-Comique premiere of *Pelléas* in 1902, and also

way forward. I should not be surprised if *Three Oranges* was not one of the rocks over which Johnson tripped and broke his neck.

We had dinner at the Levins'; Ariadna had cooked some soup and served it to us, for which I grandly tipped her a quarter.

16 January

Next morning Baranovskaya revealed with a sheepish smile that she had just spoken on the telephone to Mrs Murphy and the concert cannot take place, because the hall is booked for the next two weeks. It is all the more annoying as there was a financial guarantee for the box office. However, Murphy is ready to do everything she can to guarantee me a minimum of five concerts next season in Los Angeles and environs. I have put off my departure from today until tomorrow, because the train leaves at eleven and I would have had no time to pack and get ready.

Baranovskaya came to see me in the afternoon and I played and narrated to her the third and fourth acts of *Three Oranges*, as well as some excerpts from *Fiery Angel*. This sent her once again into ecstasies, as did my photograph, which I presented to her with some verses. 'These verses will stay with me until my dying day,' she said. We all spent the evening together. I suggested to Ariadna that rather than immersing herself too deeply in her beloved score and concentrating exclusively on problems of orchestration she should compose a symphony during the summer. She jumped at the idea and said the symphony would be dedicated to me, her first teacher, 'from Matryosha'.

Baranovskaya and I sat together and talked quietly, just the two of us. 'I have to get away from here,' she said, 'either to New York or to Europe. If I go to Kerensky, he is bound to drag me into work for the Party, and I don't want that.[1] If only I could get to Russia, I am sure I would find work there.' 'I had the idea of going to Petrograd this summer,' I said. 'If I do, I am certain they will allow me in to the country and to leave again.' Baranovskaya exclaimed: 'Oh, please take me with you! I should so like to go with you!'

We then talked again of her husband and of the school she had had to go

---

accompanied her in recital and made recordings with her. Her association with the Chicago Opera began in 1910, again as Mélisande, and continued for twenty years. A formidable, often headstrong manager and self-publicist, despite her reputation as a canny Scottish negotiator her reign as Director of the Chicago Opera was financially disastrous and her programming brought the company to the brink of collapse. As she wrote in her autobiography, 'I believed in myself and I never permitted anything or anybody to destroy that belief . . . I wanted liberty and I went my own way.' (Mary Garden, *Mary Garden's Story* (Arno Press, New York, 1951).)

1 Having narrowly escaped the Bolshevik manhunt for him, Kerensky arrived in Paris, where he lived until the German Occupation in 1940, when he moved once again to the United States. He lived there until his death in 1970.

through. When we parted, she pointed out that I do not know how to kiss hands properly. 'Would you teach me?' I asked. Baranovskaya was embarrassed and left the room.

17 January

In the morning I packed my case and at eleven o'clock was supposed to meet everyone at the station. But Baranovskaya telephoned and said: 'You must excuse me, I probably should not come to the station. I have been crying all morning, I have had some bad news.' At first I was not certain who was speaking, whether it was Ariadna or Baranovskaya, so I said I was sorry and she immediately hung up. However, the first person I met at the station was Baranovskaya. 'I had another telephone call, a much better one,' she said, 'and everything is much better now.' Then the Rumanovs arrived and the train pulled out to the extravagant waving of Ariadna's hat.

I left Los Angeles with many thoughts still firmly anchored there. But it was time to go. Events were moving in Chicago with the opera, in New York there was Koshetz, and I had a rendezvous arranged with Linette in London.

18 January

I did not go straight to Chicago, but made a detour to the Grand Canyon. This gigantic crack in the earth's surface descends to a depth of one or two versts, and is said to be one of the most spectacular sights in all America. But I was fated not to see it. The train was three hours late so I missed the connection and instead of reaching the Grand Canyon at eight o'clock in the morning we did not get there until five o'clock in the afternoon, and as at this time of year the sun goes down at five it was not worth going. I therefore continued my journey straight to Chicago.

For this disappointment I have to blame Frou-frou.[1] If I had not stayed an extra twenty-four hours on account of the Santa Barbara castle in the air I would have made it to the Grand Canyon. But I should not really complain: as a result of this very Santa Barbara chimera I can look forward to five concerts in Los Angeles next season.

19 January

The journey continues peacefully and enjoyably. I wrote yesterday to Baranovskaya, and today to Ariadna, and caught up on my Diary. I am returning to Chicago enormously refreshed by comparison with how I was

---

1 Maria Baranovskaya's nickname.

when I left. There are excellent prospects for a new contract for *Three Oranges*. It is strange, though, how detached I have become from the concept of the production; I find myself thinking of the contract purely in terms of the financial advance of one or two thousand dollars, money I badly need for Europe. At least I have something in my pocket, $1,200, but this is not enough, and to make matters worse the exchange rate is deteriorating.

20 January

Arrived in Chicago at two o'clock, Gottlieb met me at the station. During the course of the day I met Volkov, Kucheryavy and Morin, most of my information coming from the last named. The whole affair had blown up over the extent of Italian music which from the proclivities of Marinuzzi and Johnson had virtually driven everything else out of the repertoire this year. This had provoked counter-attacks from various quarters, and Marinuzzi, who was in any case tired and upset by the sniping, had over-reacted and tendered his resignation as Artistic Director. He calculated that he would be asked to reconsider and that this would strengthen his position, but instead Mary Garden, who had been conducting a vigorous campaign on her own account, had been appointed Director with unrestricted powers. Johnson was simply asked to make himself scarce, which he did, albeit with great reluctance. At the present time Garden is in a very strong position, an empress determined to implement all kinds of reforms in the Opera, while all the artists are fearful for their positions and vying to get her ear, all of which makes her the more powerful. Asked by a reporter about my opera, Mary replied: 'I do not know it, but if I like it, it will be produced.' The entire company is moving to New York in two days' time for a tour there, and Morin intends to ask the new Director if she will decide the question of *Three Oranges*, one way or the other, before the composer leaves for Europe.[1]

1 There was another reason for the departure of Music Director Marinuzzi and Executive Director Johnson. Harold McCormick's estrangement from his wife, the former Edith Rockefeller, and infatuation with Ganna Walska, a Polish chansonnière with a dubious past – prime gossip-fodder for Chicago society during most of the time Prokofiev was battling with the management of the Chicago Opera to get *Love for Three Oranges* produced, and indeed later while it was in rehearsal – had just erupted in satisfyingly lurid particulars. In his irresistibly freewheeling study *Makers and Breakers of Chicago* (Academy, Chicago, 1985) Jay Robert Nash tells the story of McCormick's insistence that his inamorata take the title role of Leoncavallo's *Zazà* (an appropriate piece of casting, at least from the dramatic if not the musical point of view, one might think) in December 1920. After one conductor and two directors had either given up in despair or been summarily dismissed by the diva, Walska stormed off the stage and into the opera company's office, finding the unfortunate Marinuzzi and Johnson in anguished discussion of their predicament, whereupon she is reported to have announced: 'Gentlemen, I am packing my bags. At the end of this season you will be packing yours.' *Zazà* was cancelled; Johnson and Marinuzzi subsequently left the company, their departure no

21 January

Yesterday's conversation with Morin essentially wrapped up all that I have to do in Chicago. The *Oranges* question clearly has to wait until New York. I went to see Carpenter, but he was unwell and in an enfeebled state, and had no more to add either about Garden or about the changes in the management of the Opera. The only new twist I gleaned was that it would be better to raise the matter of *Oranges* with Mary Garden through Baklanov[1] than through Morin, as she is very attached to Baklanov while having had some differences of opinion with Morin.[2] As Mary is at the moment relishing her power and autocratically scattering bombshells to left and right, it would be advisable to approach her with circumspection. I therefore made shift to find Baklanov, but he had gone off somewhere so I had to put off contacting him until New York. I went to a symphony concert and saw Stock, who asked me not to forget my new symphony for his next season. I said that next season there would be a new piano concerto.

22 January

Back in the train today, all day. As I had left Chicago in the evening, even by the express I would not get to New York before nightfall, so I took a slow train which would take two nights and deposit me in New York at seven in the morning. That way I saved $10 on the ticket plus a night in a hotel, which was useful in view of the uncertainty of my finances and the disastrous fluctuation in the dollar–franc exchange rate. At New Year a dollar would have bought 17 francs, before I left Los Angeles 16, and in Chicago only 15. It is always the way when you have to buy.

---

    doubt tinged with relief. Asked by a newspaper reporter if he was glad to be leaving, Johnson replied: 'If you were here half an hour, you'd be glad to get out too.' Nash makes a compelling case for arguing that this incident, as well as the frequent other occasions on which McCormick hired theatres, singing coaches, publicity agents, etc., by the cart load, was the basis for Orson Welles's operatic adventure in *Citizen Kane*, although the primary model for the newspaper tycoon was, of course, William Randolph Hearst.

1 Georgy Baklanov (1880–1938), baritone. Physically and artistically a very powerful presence (six feet three inches and two hundred pounds), Baklanov had sung in the premieres of Rachmaninoff's *The Miserly Knight* and *Francesca da Rimini* under the composer's baton during his tenure as Music Director of the Bolshoy Theatre in Moscow, as well as leading roles in the Mariinsky, before appearing in Western Europe and, later, America. He sang many leading roles at the Chicago Opera between 1917 and 1928.

2 During rehearsals of Erlanger's opera *Aphrodite* conducted by Morin, in which Mary Garden sang the role of the courtesan Chrysis on New Year's Eve 1920 with mesmerising eroticism, she had apparently stalked over to Morin in full view of the cast and orchestra, wrenched the baton from his hand and castigated him for having not an ounce of musical understanding in him.

23 January – 3 February

I spent no more than eleven days in New York, from 23 January until 3 February, staying at the Brevoort Hotel. The day I arrived was a Sunday, and so all the business part of my stay had to wait until the next day to begin. I rang up Koshetz, but she was away on a concert tour in Cleveland, returning tomorrow. After her initial enormous success in New York she had sung again on 12 January and suffered a reverse, since she had not sung well and had been savaged by the critics. Haensel, who had already begun to demand $1,000 for an appearance by her, was mortified, and seems to have blamed me for the fact that she did not sing well. Nevertheless, he was very civil to me and did not repeat his demands for his commission either for last year or for this.

My business in New York was as follows: I had to try to get to meet Mary Garden and try to persuade her to accept *Three Oranges*. Then I had to cajole Duo-Art into letting me cut at least four rolls and be paid $1,000. As I had already recorded and been paid for a year in advance, I could foresee some objections to this. And finally I was due to play a concert in Elmira, a town not far away from New York, but it soon became clear that this engagement had collapsed as a result of the recession that was generally affecting the American economy this winter. For the same reason there was much pursing of the lips at Duo-Art, and all I could get from them was an advance of $500 on condition that I refrained from pestering them again until the following season.

Anyway,[1] the $500 and Haensel's waiving of his percentages just about brought my finances into balance, and I would have a little, not much but a little, for Europe, as long as the franc stayed at 17 to the dollar, but it was already below 14.

There remained my meeting with Mary Garden. I did not know how to gain access to her, nor what attitude she was likely to take when we did meet. I asked Morin to inform her that I was about to leave for Europe and would like to speak to her about *Oranges* before I left. And then by chance I met Kokhánski, who had just arrived in America, and his wife has a friend, Miss Draper, who was Garden's secretary and a great admirer of my music. In this way a meeting was arranged at a day's notice and on Saturday the 29th I was received by the Director.

The omens were very good, since Draper had told me on the telephone that Miss Garden was very interested in *Oranges*. However, when I called on her at the Ritz Hotel neither she, nor Draper, nor anyone else, was there. I waited for a while, then became irritated and went away. But as in fact I had

---

1 In English.

no other destination in mind, after walking along Fifth Avenue for an hour I made a telephone call thinking that the appointment might have been for half-past three and not half-past two. Both ladies were now in, and full of contrition asked me if I could come immediately. I bit my lip and walked back.

I had heard that Mary Garden was forty-two years of age, but she looked a good deal older than that. She welcomed me most cordially, and sitting on the sofa began to question me about what kind of opera it was, and first of all what nationality. I replied that it was written in French on an Italian subject by a Russian composer for an American theatre. Mary laughed, and the conversation continued in similar vein. In a few words I outlined the history of the commission and its subsequent decommission, describing *Three Oranges* as a child of Campanini that after his death had been persecuted by Pam and Johnson and was now awaiting rehabilitation by Mary Garden. As she worshipped Campanini and detested Pam, she did not wait to learn anything more about the opera but immediately vowed that it would be produced with as many rehearsals as required, with whatever singers I deemed necessary and under my personal control and supervision.

The effect on me was extraordinary: up till now I had had to deal with low-grade accountants and salespeople; now, suddenly, I was talking to a real artist. I narrated the subject to her, which made her eyes shine with pleasure, and played one piece of music, the March, to illustrate the story. 'Oh, how cute,'[1] she cried. We touched only briefly and in passing on the financial side: I said I would like a guarantee of eight performances at a fee of $500, to which she replied: 'Oh, of course.' I had the impression that, had I asked for $8,000 instead of $4,000, she would have equally happy to reply 'oh, of course'. But in fact I asked for precisely what I was due, because my calculations had relied on the original agreement with Campanini, and Mary did all that Campanini would have done.

She then asked if there were any new singers I would like to suggest for my opera, and I said that while for the present I did not feel able to make specific recommendations, the best Russian soprano, Koshetz, was currently in New York. Draper immediately backed me up, saying she had heard a lot about her. Garden said: 'That's fine, please bring her to see me the day after tomorrow', and our meeting ended with many expressions of mutual regard and gratitude.

Koshetz was ecstatic both at my success and her invitation, was beside herself with nerves, and two days later accompanied me to see Garden. She sang wonderfully, enchanted Garden and was immediately engaged for the role of Fata Morgana, and probably for other roles besides. Two miracles were thus achieved in the space of three days.

---

1   In English.

This time when I was with her in New York, Koshetz heaped on me incredible protestations of love and admiration, more even than she had in Moscow: I was the only man in the world, her only ray of sunshine, the only possible saviour of her art. At first this was very flattering, but when later the talk turned to suicide, tears and hopelessness, it became very difficult. She sang my songs to me only once, and then *mezzo-voce*, but they sounded good, perhaps better than I had imagined.

The actual contract with the Opera's business manager Mr Spangler[1] was concluded on the eve of my departure and took from ten o'clock until four, with a break for one hour. Their side had two lawyers sitting alongside Spangler, while I defended my rights unaided, and I think not too badly. Garden put in no more than a brief appearance, shook my hand and said she would be glad to see me in the summer at Monte Carlo. For their part, the three devils squeezed the last drop possible out of the $4,000 she had so airily agreed. For all that, I took away an advance of $1,000 with a second $1,000 tranche to follow on 1 July, and this will satisfactorily assure my summer independently of the fluctuations of the franc. I paid $400 to Haensel, $1,000 to my dentist and $140 to the newspapers, bought my transatlantic liner passage (on the *Aquitania*, no less!) and still had $2,000 clear to take to Europe. This will be enough until July, and then we shall see, moreover by then Koussevitzky should be getting going again with his publishing house.

I wanted to attend a spiritualist séance at Roerich's, who by the way has had a very successful debut exhibition in New York, and who is very well disposed towards me. But when he asked the spirits if I might attend, the answer came: 'No outsiders.' I felt genuinely aggrieved. People at Roerich's séances are always asking questions about dollars and worldly success, but if someone serious wants to attend the answer is 'no outsiders'.

I had lovely letters from Los Angeles. If Baranovskaya's first bordered on the flirtatious, her next two were frankly love letters. Ariadna also wrote very affectionately and amusingly, but naturally without Baranovskaya's refinement of style.

I had lunch with Vladimir Bashkirov. Borenka[2] is in Helsingfors[3] and his mother is *en route* there: she has already managed to escape from Russia but the Finns are holding her in quarantine. As soon as she gets to Helsingfors, Vladimir would like them both to come to New York. I explored the

---

1   George M. Spangler, formerly Convention Manager of the Chicago Association of Commerce, had recently been appointed Business Manager of the Chicago Opera, 'as the man', according to the board's official statement, 'who by American business methods is best fitted to wipe out the annual deficit of the company, amounting last season to $350,000'. He did not survive long under the withering crossfire of Mary Garden's genius for spending money.
2   Boris Bashkirov (Verin).
3   The Russian name for Helsinki.

prospects for Boris coming to France for the summer, but Vladimir stubbornly protested against the separation of the family, insisting that at times like this they need to stay together, and in any case there was not the money to spare. I nevertheless cabled Borenka to say that I would be going for six months to France and received a reply to the effect that he had no money, and please could I send him some. I very much wanted to invite him to stay for the full six months with me in the country (in the south of France, as I had planned) and to tell him that I would send him money for the journey, but I was afraid of complications with Linette, who was aware, because I had told her so, that he was an inveterate gossip. I therefore decided to hold my response until I got to London when I would be seeing Linette, and in the meantime, so that he would not be mortally offended at my silence after he had asked for money, sent him another cable as from Haensel, saying that 'Prokofiev has left for London and your telegram has been forwarded to him there'.

On 3 February I set off on my voyage, in excellent spirits thanks to my new contract.

3 February

At 9.30 in the morning I was already at the pier ready to board the *Aquitania*, the enormous, white, four-funnelled vessel lying at anchor beside the dock. After some fussing with the luggage and minimal passport formalities, I went on board. Seeing me off were Schubert (Nina, just as she had been when I left Moscow to start my journey to America) had a cold and was in bed, the Kucheryavys, themselves about to leave for Riga in two weeks' time, and Kal, who rushed up to say goodbye at the very last moment. At noon we made our farewells, as the ship's siren had begun to sound its signal for departure, although we did not actually cast off for another two hours, and then so smoothly I did not even notice. The *Aquitania* – 'tout ce qu'il y a de plus chic'[1] – is unbelievably spacious, with a vast quantity of rooms, decks, promenades, a huge Louis XVI dining-room, a wonderful dark smoking-room with deep armchairs, sombre walls and a fireplace. If there is no rolling (although February, so they say, is prime rolling weather) it will be very pleasant indeed to spend six days in the luxury of this floating castle.

I unpacked the Corona typewriter I had brought with me for Mama and started to type. The idea was to make it look as though it had been used and thus avoid import duty. I began by typing out my old story 'A Bad Dog' and got so absorbed I worked at it for four hours. I did not see the sea at all that day, as by the time I went on deck it was already dark. But the ocean was so

---

1 'The last word in chic.'

calm and the ship so huge that it was impossible tell whether we were in motion or at anchor. For dinner I put on my dinner-suit, as did most of the passengers, and as the splendour of the dining-room seemed to demand. After dinner I did a bit more typing and then went to bed. Mme Otto Kahn is also among the passengers, but I have forgotten what she looks like.

4 February

People are afraid of rough seas in February, but it was quite calm and the weather was sunny. I tapped away with a will at the typewriter, sitting for hours transcribing 'The Poodle'. In the evening, the dinner-jacket again and a formal dinner. My neighbours are excruciatingly boring, and I made no friends. I am longing for London and Linette.

5 February

There is a slight roll to the ship, but not enough to stop me working. I finished typing out 'Poodle' and decided to make a start on a piano transcription of the orchestra part of my Violin Concerto, since even Kokhánski refuses to learn it from the full score. I must really buckle down to it, and if I do I should be able to finish it by the time we arrive in London. The only annoying thing is that there seem to be draughts everywhere, and I think I have already caught a cold, at least I am sneezing mightily today.

In the evening I started typing out another of my stories, 'The Wandering Tower'. I must not forget I have some letters to write, to Miller, Capablanca and, perhaps, Baranovskaya.

8 February

Finished the transcription of the Violin Concerto.

9–21 February

On the evening of the 9th, after a calm and pleasant voyage, we docked at Cherbourg, where a stream of passengers disembarked along with tons of luggage, and next morning, the 10th, dropped anchor at Southampton.

By noon I was in London where I made my way to the National Hotel, the rendezvous Linette and I had agreed upon. But I still did not know whether or not she was coming, as I had never had positive confirmation from her. Perhaps she was already in London? Or might there be a letter from her? There was neither. Since trains from Paris arrive between six o'clock and eight o'clock in the evening, I sat and waited in the hotel lobby to see if she would appear. But instead of Linette there was a telegram: she was coming tomorrow. At least she is coming! Until that moment I had not been sure.

The next day I met her at Victoria, looking very pretty in her grey fur coat, and we went to the National. This is a large but rather strange hotel, with small rooms all very similar. They do have larger ones, so-called double rooms, but these are terribly expensive. We decided not to share a room (in America we would have been ejected with no argument about it) and accordingly Linette took a double room and I a small single just opposite, in which I never once spent the night but carefully rumpled the bedclothes each morning for the sake of appearances.

We spent a lot of time in London getting a French visa for me. I cabled Stravinsky about it, and he replied that he would make all the arrangements. Even so it took ten days to get my passport visaed, but the time with Linette passed very happily. True, we ran through $500, that is a quarter of my worldly wealth, but I bought clothes, and Linette bought clothes – this will be the end of purchases for another six months.

I had counted on seeing Coates, who was in New York at Christmas time; he had had a tremendous success there and had already been invited back for next season. I wanted to arrange a New York performance with him of the Third Piano Concerto. In London I had little to hope for: Covent Garden was still closed after last summer's crash. It is quite scandalous to think that the greatest city in the world has no opera! But Coates was not in London; he was away with the orchestra on tour in the provinces. Very annoying.

Koussevitzky, however, was in London. He said he was ready to publish my compositions, and in a large *tirage*, but was not able to pay any fees. On the other hand he offered royalties of 50 per cent of the sale price. He also said that I should remit the 3,000 francs I owed him directly to the publishers in Berlin, and with that money they would immediately start engraving my Opp. 31 and 32. The result was that instead of the earnings of 13,000 francs or thereabouts for my works I had been counting on, I was going to have to pay out 3,000. Nevertheless, 50 per cent is a very large royalty, and it is urgent to get my works into print quickly. I therefore agreed, and he took *Tales of an Old Grandmother* and Op. 32.[1]

On 21 February I finally got my French visa (Linette, being a Spanish citizen had had hers for some time), and that same evening we left for Paris. We spent the night on the ferry, waking up in Le Havre on French soil.

---

1 *Four Pieces for Piano*, Op. 32.

22 February – 20 March

I did not plan to stay long in Paris. It was the first time for many years that spring had not seen me bound hand and foot to the city, and I wanted to take advantage of this to spend the spring in the country, something I had long dreamed of. The task now was to decide where exactly to rent our country house: if it was in northern France it would be too cold for the next two months, but if it were to be in the south, it would be too hot in July. As well, Linette wanted to be by the sea. This meant either the Mediterranean or the Atlantic. After exhaustive and detailed researches about the Mediterranean coast it seemed clear that it would be too hot in July and August. We therefore decided to migrate to the Bay of Biscay, and after yet more lengthy searching, debating and study of the map, I went down early in March to the area round Nantes. Two days of frantic looking brought me to a large stone house in Plage des Rochelets, not a particularly beautiful house and very simply furnished, but perfectly comfortable, free of intrusive neighbours, and right beside the ocean. It lacked the elegance of last summer's house, but was well away from any crowds. Not only that, but the cost was 3,000 francs until 1 October, and as the money was disappearing at a rapid rate of knots, and the dollar rate of exchange showed no signs of improving, I took it without a great pause for reflection. There would be plenty of room for Boris Verin, and for the Stahls if they decided to come in the summer.

I returned to Paris, where there seemed little to detain us: Mama's eyes no longer needed the doctor's care, and her health was generally good (although she still had poor vision), but at this point a new problem arose: the doctor diagnosed Linette as suffering from appendicitis, and in quite an inflamed condition. He prescribed an insanely problematical diet and recommended an operation as soon as possible in order to deal with the problem once and for all. We discussed it and decided that life would be impossible if the operation was not carried out, and the sooner the better. Linette went to the best surgeon, and a week later he operated on her. The poor girl suffered this unexpected situation bravely, and the only time she cried out was when they came for her with the stretcher to take her into the operating theatre. The operation itself went extremely well and after three days Linette was already well on the way to recovery.

In Paris I found Diaghilev, but he was in a distraught state as Massine had left him, exchanging him, just as Nijinsky had done before him, for a real woman.[1] As Massine had at the same time left the ballet company,

---

1   Vera Savina was originally Vera Clark, rechristened by Diaghilev with the obligatory Russian name. She was the only Diaghilev ballerina of British origin to dance the principal role in *Les Sylphides*, and seemed set fair for a successful career in the Ballets Russes, but Diaghilev, upset at her burgeoning love affair with Massine, instigated what would nowadays be seen as 'con-

Diaghilev's contract with South America had collapsed. The company was supposed to be touring there in the spring, and Massine was the star. Diaghilev accordingly decided on a Paris season, but naturally some new productions were needed for Paris, and that meant *Chout* and Stravinsky's *Les Noces*. Of course I was delighted by this turn of events, but it was not long before it turned sour: Diaghilev initially planned to present the season in the Grand Opéra and to invite the old-timers Fokine and Bolm, so *Chout* was taken out of the repertoire. When the Grand Opéra project in turn miscarried, because Fokine arrived determined to be obstructive, Diaghilev was forced to migrate to the Théâtre des Champs-Elysées,[1] and to include some new productions in order to spike Fokine's guns – so enter once again, *Chout* and *Les Noces*.

In place of Massine, Diaghilev promoted two of his *premiers danseurs*, and gave Larionov *Chout* to produce. It was the first time an artist rather than a ballet-master had been asked to choreograph a ballet, but Larionov is a cunning and talented little devil and in accepting the job must have had some idea in mind. In any case his designs are superb. And thus, after I had lost all hope of ever seeing *Chout* produced on stage, all of a sudden within the space of three days it was given the green light. Diaghilev's attitude to me was one of extreme affection, but said not a word of thanks for my having dedicated *Chout* to him (which I did when I wrote to him in November). Common decency dictates that it should be gratefully acknowledged. I think I shall remove the dedication.[2]

I had not scored half of the fifth scene, the fifth entr'acte and the whole of the sixth scene. I had to get a move on, because on top of all this, there was the matter of making the orchestral parts. Accordingly, as soon as Linette was clearly on the mend (she still had to stay in bed another eight to ten days), I rounded up Mama and we set off for the country. This was on 20 March.

To my great joy I received from Boris Verin, to whom I had sent a telegram inviting him to stay for the whole of the spring, an acceptance and expressions of gratitude. There remained the questions of money and his visa (I had sent him 3,000 Finnish marks), but I think I managed to settle these matters before leaving Paris.

In Paris the people I saw most of, besides Larionov and Goncharova, were the Stahls and Samoilenko. They are all very close friends. Among the musicians I saw a good deal of Schloezer, who is working on an article about me,

---

structive dismissal' by abruptly cancelling both dancers' principal roles, resulting in the couple's resignation from the company at the beginning of February 1921 and their departure for South America. At a stroke Diaghilev had lost his star *danseur* and faced unwelcome competition in his touring plans. Massine and Savina married in London at Fulham Registry Office on 16 April 1922.
1   Eventually the season was presented at the Gaîté Lyrique. See p. 601 below.
2   The dedication was not removed.

and Prunières,[1] a very cultivated Frenchman and publisher of the excellent music journal *La Revue musicale*. I heard music by Poulenc and Milhaud (members of 'Les Six') in which the occasional interesting idea disappears into an abyss of bad taste.

Linette and I stayed in different places, but saw each other every day. There was one contretemps: she accused me of putting her in a compromising position by maintaining an illicit liaison with her, and was concerned that this was beginning to be noticed. Although I reacted angrily, in my heart I was very sorry for her, but I could see no solution. Get married? From her perspective it was so easy and clear to see that this was what we should do. But to me marriage was like a heavy stone attached to my foot.

20–29 March

On 20 March at half-past two in the afternoon Mama and I boarded the train and at eleven o'clock that evening arrived in St Nazaire, where we had to spend the night. Next morning I went in search of a piano and a copyist. I soon tracked down a piano, although not a very good one, but the copyist was quite another matter. Then we and all our luggage boarded a little steamer to cross the Loire (where it flows into the ocean), and finally a tiny, toy train into Rochelets, eight kilometres the other side of the river. Here we were met by our landlord and we entered into possession of our house. It was a glorious day, the sun was shining and the fresh breeze from the ocean mingled with the scent of the pines and a mass of flowering bushes, but the cold at night was hellish and the fire we tried to light produced more smoke than heat.

I got down to the score, and in a week's time Scene Five was ready. I succeeded in finding a copyist in Nantes, although it took a whole day to get there and back. Altogether it is a most disagreeable burden, this copying of the parts, wished on to my shoulders by Diaghilev! But he is with the company in Madrid, and of course it would be hard for him to take care of getting parts copied there. Also in Madrid is Larionov, who has already begun rehearsing the choreography of *Chout*.

All in all, if only it had not been so cold (I already have a sore throat, and the soles of Mama's feet hurt), life in the dacha would be splendid. But the prospect of imminent sun, the arrival of Linette and after her of Boris Nikolayevich – all this is cause for rejoicing that I took the house for six months and not a shorter period.

---

[1] Henry Prunières (1886–1942), musicologist and avid proponent of contemporary art in all its forms but especially music, had founded the *Revue musicale* the previous year and already established it as the leading forum for intelligent and in-depth consideration of new music. Boris de Schloezer wrote on music for the magazine. Prunières continued as the magazine's editor until 1939.

30 March

On 30 March in the evening I arrived in Paris to collect Linette and went straight to the Stahls, where Stahl was today celebrating his birthday and where Linette had been staying for the last two days since she came out of hospital. She was still a little weak, but able to move reasonably freely, and was touchingly pleased to see me. After the birthday festivities and a night with the Stahls we moved the following day to a hotel, and after one more day which I spent tidying up some odds and ends, not least finding additional copyists for the ballet, Linette and I left for the country on 1 April.

1–30 April

On 1 April in the evening Linette and I arrived in St Nazaire, stayed the night in the Grand Hotel and on the morning of the 2nd installed ourselves in Les Rochelets. I gave it out to our neighbours that Linette was my wife, acceding to Linette's desire to avoid needless discussion and sidelong glances. She loved being there, but her convalescence was a slow process, she complained of the pain, was a prey to anxiety and easily burst into tears.

It was wonderful to be in the country, even though it was still pretty cold, especially at night. Going to bed in the evening we would ask each other: 'How do you feel about a swim in the Arctic Ocean?' before shiveringly burrowing into the icy cold sheets. There was a mass of flowers, the predominant colour being yellow, a sea of *genêt*[1] bushes.

We waited for news of Boris Nikolayevich, but he stayed mute in his Helsingfors. I sent him a telegram asking what was happening and got a reply that he was still waiting for a visa. But Mme Sert had told me as long ago as 17 March that this would be arranged. I wrote to Nouvel in Paris asking him to find out the position from Mme Sert, but the only response was that she did not think it would be so easy to arrange. How do you like that! While I was in Paris she was promising me it would be done, but now I am immured in the country, 'I don't think it will be so easy.' Meanwhile B.N. sits and waits. At this, exploiting Diaghilev's presence in Paris and the good graces I was in for having completed the piano score of *Chout* and sent it to him for the rehearsals in Madrid, I explained the present state of affairs to him and appealed for his help over Bashkirov. A few days later Diaghilev sent me a telegram about various matters connected with the ballet, with an added postscript that he would speak to the Minister about Bashkirov. I was delighted by this and sent him another cable thanking him.

In the meantime I worked intensively on orchestrating *Chout*. The

---

[1] Prokofiev wrote 'jeunets', a word that does not exist, at least not in this context, in French, but is a pardonable homonym for 'genêt', the yellow-flowering broom bush.

beginning of Scene Six went very smoothly, but I got well and truly stuck on the final dance, and despite torturing myself with unremitting efforts I could hardly get it to move. But at last, on 20 April, the work was done and I could breathe freely again. However, another torture was the copyists. It is true that their demands are one-third of their colleagues in America, but my God, what a horrific picture met my eyes with the first scene as sent to me by the copyist in Nantes, rejoicing in the poetic surname of Tristan. The pages seethed with errors like an anthill. As I set about correcting them, I devised a way of venting my spleen by putting a mark on a separate sheet of paper every time I found a mistake, in order to have a record of how many there were. I abandoned the attempt when the number of my marks reached four figures.

At the same time as I was struggling to finish the score, an avalanche of telegrams began descending on Rochelets: Diaghilev, Koussevitzky, Schloezer, Nouvel. Koussevitzky is to perform the *Scythian Suite* in Paris on the 29th and wants my presence at the rehearsals. Diaghilev, on learning that Koussevitzky had plans to present the *Suite* two weeks before the ballet, exploded in wrath and began firing two-page telegrams at me to explain in detail the dire consequences of this premature exposure, and to state his view that if Koussevitzky did indeed play the *Suite* in advance of *Chout* I would perish, and he would perish, and the entire world would come to an end. I, however, was interested in the chance to hear the *Suite* as a listener, since at all performances I had been at hitherto I had conducted it myself. But now was of course not the time to fall out with Diaghilev, especially as he had promised to help with Bashkirov.

Finally on the 21st I got a cable from Diaghilev on another subject: could I come immediately to Monte Carlo for rehearsals of *Chout*, travel and other expenses paid? While the company had been performing in Madrid Larionov had taken a number of *Chout* rehearsals, and now they were in Monte Carlo Diaghilev, who was already there, wanted me to come and supervise them. For a long time I had myself wanted to be present at these rehearsals, and also to see the Côte d'Azur, but Diaghilev had maintained so dogged a silence on the subject I concluded he must grudge the money my presence would cost. And now, suddenly, please, be my guest. Delighted, I said goodbye to Mama and Linette and set off for Paris on the 22nd.

My first port of call was Nouvel, who said that naturally Diaghilev was most unhappy about the Koussevitzky performance of the *Scythian Suite*, but agreed that it was now too late to do anything about it. I next went to see Koussevitzky, who roared that the question was not worth discussing, the *Suite* was the *pièce de résistance* of the whole concert, and as far as Diaghilev was concerned I should simply put all the blame on him, Koussevitzky. I was only too pleased by all of this and instead of protesting went through the whole *Suite* with Koussevitzky before leaving at six o'clock for Monte Carlo.

One other encounter I had in Paris was with Boris Gershun.[1] After staying for some time in Sofia, where he had spent time with Suvchinsky, he had eventually fetched up in Paris, where he had no occupation and no money either. I was very glad to see him, but he wore the expression of a disturbed and unhappy man and before long had borrowed 200 francs from me. He came with me to the station at six o'clock. My train was a splendid *de luxe* express, as recommended by Nouvel, on the grounds that Diaghilev wanted me there as soon as possible and this was the quickest train.

By the time I awoke we had already passed Marseilles and were heading east along the coast of the Mediterranean, whose dark-blue waters could be glimpsed behind the forests and the hillsides, a series of beautiful views in the hot sunshine of the red earth and the lush southern vegetation. To cap it all, I was in the sunniest of moods. We flashed through St-Raphael, Cannes, Nice, and finally arrived in Monte Carlo through a succession of increasingly elegant villas and manicured gardens, the only jarring note for me being the red-tiled roofs. The '*couleur locale*' it may be, but how much more attractive another colour would be. In Monte Carlo I expected someone would be there to meet me, as I had sent a telegram announcing my arrival time, but nobody was at the station. I made my way to the Hôtel de Paris where Diaghilev was staying, a tremendously fashionable and luxurious hotel, but he had gone off somewhere. In time his secretary, Kochno,[2] a good-looking youth with very polished manners who had taken Massine's place, appeared and explained that Larionov had been supposed to meet me but had mistaken the time of the train. Lunch followed not long afterwards: Diaghilev, Matisse, the youth, a contrite Larionov and I. We had something to drink and were merry. It was a Sunday, so there were no rehearsals.

---

1   See above, p. 189 n. 2. Boris Gershun's life in emigration was one of almost unrelieved poverty, lack of recognition and suffering. At the beginning of the Second World War he and his wife left Paris for Marseilles, where matters only became worse, the constant threat of internment and deportation in occupied Vichy France causing the Gershuns to live in a succession of hiding places in cellars and attics, and for one horrendous week in an open trench in a field. Only comparatively recently, with the publication of a two-volume collection of his verse in Berkeley, California, in 1987, is his distinctive and classically inspired poetic voice beginning to be recognised.

2   Boris Kochno (1904–1990). He is, perhaps unfairly, as famous for his string of glamorous lovers as for his very real contributions to literature and dance: in approximate, and partial, chronological order the former included Szymanowski (in Kiev, when Kochno would have been a mere fifteen years old), Diaghilev, Cole Porter and the designer Christian Bérard ('Bébé'). Kochno had deliberately made a dead set at Diaghilev a month or so before this meeting and, profiting from the defection of Massine, had been taken on as Diaghilev's secretary, a position he occupied with ever-growing influence and involvement until the impresario's death in 1929. His baptism of fire had been the Madrid season from which the company had just returned. Kochno, eventually creator and instigator of many librettos, including Stravinsky's *Mavra*, tried his best in collaboration with Serge Lifar to hold the Ballets Russes together after Diaghilev's death, later entered into collaborations with George Balanchine and Roland Petit. (See S. Walsh, op. cit.)

Monte Carlo is not a very interesting place, the town on its small hill on first impression appearing to consist of nothing but hotels clustered round the casino, which also houses the theatre. The sea is a deep blue unlike anywhere else, the mountains are delightful, as is the climate, but ultimately, what use was it to us? We, that is to say the company, were up to our necks in the ballet, and the remainder of the population never seemed to emerge from the gaming hall.

Larionov immediately set about getting me a ticket to visit the gambling rooms, which consist of an extensive suite of large rooms, furnished with tables set a decent distance from one another, each one surrounded by a larger or smaller crowd of spectators. The actual play proceeds at a more leisurely pace than I had imagined: it takes a long time for the bets to be placed and the winnings and losses to be calculated. In my *Gambler* the pace is much hotter, but this is how it needs to be depicted on stage: people who gamble in real life get so absorbed in the play that they lose all sense of time. In order to convey an impression of feverishness it was essential for me to speed up the action.

I decided not to play, unwilling to risk losing any money, and some instinct told me I was unlikely to be a winner at roulette, my mind was too focused on the ballet and on the other aspects of my visit. Watching the play was interesting. Just as I was there a Swede was having a run of luck; I was told he had already passed the 600,000 mark. I studied his face. It was exhausted and the eyes were clouded over. People were sketching his portrait; all the talk was only of him. I saw the same Swede on another evening. That morning he had won more than a million, which he proceeded serially to lose, following which he again began winning. He was handed packets of 1,000-franc chips, and his pockets bulged with them. Several times I saw him give the croupiers tips of 2,000 francs.

At seven o'clock in the evening he went off to have dinner, for which he put on evening dress, a touch which pleased me very much. At this time his face bore the marks of terrible fatigue. He was playing two tables at the same time, moving from one to the other and giving instructions to the croupiers, and he was followed by a crowd of people including several beautiful women. Apparently they were customarily deployed to accompany anyone with a winning streak, in order to make sure he came back. Three times in my presence he staked the maximum on '31', his chips completely surrounding this number, and it came up three times in a row. I heard that he went on playing and by the time he finally left he had won 10 million.

Rehearsals started on Monday the 25th. Larionov told me he had already staged three scenes, but they were in such a dreadful condition that he might just as well have not choreographed them at all. The music was being provided by a pianist called Zemskaya, and it became clear that it was here, in the musical accompaniment, that the main problem lay. The lady had simply been given the music and told to work it out as best she could, and then to play it for the rehearsals. She had not the slightest notion of either the music or the tempi, nor of the rhythm nor, most importantly, of the orchestration, so that for example she would play a solo for three bassoons *forte*, and an orchestral *tutti* softly, while the choreography Larionov had devised for the three solo bassoons was an energetic crowd dance and for the orchestral *tutti* a solo for a single dancer. I found it incredible that the approach to the musical aspect of a serious artistic enterprise such as Diaghilev's should be distinguished by such cavalier ineptitude. I did hear that in Madrid Stravinsky had made a few suggestions, but as he had done so off the cuff and casually, he had succeeded only in making matters worse (for example in one place he had apparently identified a waltz fragment, whereas in my score there was no such thing anywhere).

The ballet was being staged by Larionov, who certainly had a profound knowledge of the dances of many different ages, and whose concept of how the work should be choreographed was in places perfectly good. He came to rehearsals with a thick notebook filled with sketches of poses and ensembles for *Chout*, and no doubt, had he been able to work with Massine it would have turned out well. But in Massine's absence the young Slavinsky[1] was singled out for promotion, a good dancer but with nothing whatsoever in his head. It was quite out of the question to expect him to invent anything, although he was well equipped to grasp quickly what Larionov said and transmit it to the dancers. To crown it all, neither Larionov nor Slavinsky understood anything about music, and as a result the entire burden of musical authority was gathered into the hands of the pianist Zemskaya, who was incapable of grasping even the haziest conception, musically speaking, of *Chout*.

This, then, was the condition in which I found the staging of the ballet. And I thank God that they had invited me. Everything had to be purged and started again from the beginning, and the first thing that had to be done was to train Zemskaya, with whom I had a series of private sessions that reduced her on more than one occasion to tears. Nevertheless, eventually she learned to play the score quite decently. She was a young Jewish woman from Poland who, once she had dried her tears, began to flirt openly with me.

Next, a tacit alliance was struck with Larionov. He did everything I asked

---

1 Tadeusz Sławinski (1901–1945), Polish-born dancer. He was gifted and fluent in character roles and apparently was Diaghilev's third choice to choreograph *Chout*, or rather, as Boris Kochno expressed it – because in fact Sławinski had no experience of choreography and not much knowledge of music – 'to be the interpreter of Larionov's theatrical ideas . . . he was to translate these ideas into a dance idiom and act as intermediary between Larionov and the dancers.' (B. Kochno, *Diaghilev and the Ballets Russes*, trans. Adrienne Foulke (Harper & Row, New York, 1970), quoted in Stephen D. Press, *Prokofiev's Ballets for Diaghilev* (Ashgate, Aldershot, 2006).) Lydia Sokolova, who danced the Buffoon's Wife, was not impressed: 'The wretched . . . Slavinsky had no more idea of inventing a ballet than flying over the moon, and what ballet there was must certainly have been the work of Larionov.' (L. Sokolova, ed. R. Buckle, *Dancing for Diaghilev* (John Murray, London, 1960).

him to, and in turn I trusted his enormous store of inventiveness and good taste. Only one hurdle was left to overcome: his lack of technical ballet experience. To some extent this was achieved, but looking forward to the eventual outcome, the staging of *Chout* ran into many problems. We did our best to take Slavinsky in hand. Diaghilev frequently put in an appearance at rehearsals, and these were the best moments, as he invariably gave excellent advice.

In short, every day there were two three-hour rehearsals, and on top of those, I rehearsed twice a day with Zemskaya, whose fingers began swelling up from eight hours a day at the keyboard. From early in the morning until late at night we did nothing else but rehearse, and I saw nothing of Monte Carlo but the rehearsal studio, and was dead on my feet with tiredness.

I had one day out, when I went to Nice to see Matisse, who at Diaghilev's request was making a drawing of my head[1] for the Paris programme. Diaghilev was thrilled with Matisse's drawing, but I did not like it. Nice has a wonderful corniche and the sea is glorious, but I should not like to live in such a busy place and am amazed that Matisse chooses every year to spend four months there in the summer.

Larionov and I made three short late-night visits, about eleven o'clock, to the casino's gaming rooms. I had not a *sou* to spend, as I had brought very little money with me, having relied on Diaghilev providing for me as he had promised, but he gave me no money. In the end Larionov persuaded me to gamble and lent me some money against my cheque. I had no sense of the play, and the result was as one would expect. We staked parsimoniously, a little at a time on dozens.[2] Hardly any of my bets won and I soon lost 200 francs. The next evening I had even less desire to go, but Larionov again persuaded me and again lent money. This time it all came out well and I won 100 francs by putting down small stakes, but the roulette closed because of the lateness of the hour. Thus ended my career as a gambler.

After three days I was ready to go. Diaghilev, realising that the reason I was leaving was to be present at Koussevitzky's rehearsal of the *Scythian Suite*, flew into a huge rage and created a scandal. He sent Koussevitzky an abusive telegram, and to cut a long story short I stayed another two days and missed all the *Scythian Suite* rehearsals, arriving just in time for the concert. Actually staying was the right thing to do, because although during my short time in Monte Carlo I inflicted torture both on the dancers and on myself, we did more or less put the ballet production on its feet. I myself played no small part in the production, and it was at my insistence that the dance of

---

1 The drawing was, apparently, left in a hotel room or on a train and has been lost.
2 There are three 'dozens' in a standard European roulette wheel consisting of 36 numbers plus 0: 1–12, 13–24 and 25–36. The odds are 2.167 to 1 against winning, and the payout is twice the stake. Betting on a 'dozen' is therefore a relatively low-risk strategy.

washing the floor was included right at the beginning of the ballet, something that had stayed in my memory since 1915 when we were discussing the ballet and Massine happened to demonstrate this movement. In short, during those five days everything except the last scene was firmly planned out, and on the 28th, in the company of Diaghilev and Kochno, I went back to Paris.

There was an incident over money just before I left, arising from the fact that Diaghilev, who of course had not given me any money, had bought my ticket to Paris on the *de-luxe* train and was waiting for me at the station. But I had nothing with which to pay the hotel, and turned up at the station without my luggage, since I had been unable to take them out of the hotel without settling my bill. On hearing my explanation, Diaghilev grandly flourished his wallet and said: 'But of course, of course, how much do you need?' Once I had the money in my hand, I said: 'Thank you, but this should have been done earlier.'

As the hotel was very near the station I still just managed to catch the train, and when we were all safely aboard (in different compartments) Diaghilev said: 'Now then, my dear Mr Petushkov, let's go and have lunch!' Over lunch Diaghilev really let himself go, told stories and drank a great deal of wine. Regarding the visa for Bashkirov, he said that the promise to help had been made by Nouvel without his knowledge, and so when he got my telegram in gratitude he could not at first work out what it was I was thanking him for. But as things stood he would try as soon as we were in Paris to arrange for me to meet M. Péan, the chief official in charge of visas, and, if I wished, would accompany me. And indeed, on arrival we did go together to see M. Péan, the *ministre plénipotentiaire*, who with a courteous smile arranged the accursed visa in one minute flat. I immediately sent a rapturous telegram to Helsingfors. Diaghilev can sometimes turn up trumps.

I found Linette at the Stahls, where she had come to stay the previous evening so as to attend the performance of the *Scythian Suite*. Her information from America was that Koshetz had renewed her association with Rachmaninoff, and certainly Koshetz had stopped writing to me since February. Linette never lost her jealousy of Koshetz, and could never be persuaded that there was never anything between us.

In the evening we went with the Stahls to the concert. I was given a box, which unfortunately was too near the orchestra, not to mention that the Salle Gaveau is too small for such a huge orchestra. The audience packed out the hall, there were people standing everywhere and it was only with some difficulty that I was able to elbow my way to the box. The first work on the programme was Rachmaninoff's *Isle of the Dead*, which Koussevitzky did magnificently. It had a good success, but I would not put it higher than that.

Next came *Scythian Suite*. I was passionately interested to hear it – my first time from the body of the hall. Pretty good! In the first movement the first half sounded a trifle garish, resplendent all the same, and the second half was excellent. Koussevitzky dragged out the tempo rather too much, and the movement seemed over long, also he ended it 'with temperament' so the audience was not emboldened to applaud. The second movement had plenty of life, but alongside those sonorities that were successful were some that were insufficiently subtle, giving rise to a few places that sounded vulgar. There was much enthusiastic applause at the end of the second movement; Koussevitzky motioned towards my box, and I took several bows.

The third movement, 'Night', lacked temperament, and some effects did not sound; I must look again at the way I have scored them. The audience's reaction to this movement was muted. In the fourth movement there are a few holes that will need filling, but all was triumphantly redeemed by the 'Procession of the Sun', which truly sounded overwhelming, especially the place that caused Glazunov to get up and walk out of the hall (the penultimate page).

The end of *Scythian Suite* provoked a tremendous ovation and a mass of congratulations. Stravinsky came into the box after the second movement and did not cease to extol the work's virtues. Linette bridled at his patronising tone. There were many Russian poets and artists in the audience, and a number of Frenchmen as well, among them Florent Schmitt.[1] There was supper afterwards: the Stahls, Koussevitzky, Linette and I. The next day, Linette and I went back to our country retreat.

1–31 May

We arrived back at Rochelets on 1 May, as we had done on the same day of the previous month. We were there only a week, as on the 7th I had to be back in Paris for the final rehearsals of *Chout*. It was wonderful to be in Rochelets, where the country everywhere was bursting out in flower, but I was overburdened with work, not least with the problems of the orchestral parts. The copies had a million errors, and I could never relax into the certainty that they would all be ready in time. In the meantime I dry-conducted from the score in order to be on top form when I stepped on to the podium in Paris.

On the 7th Mama, Linette and I left for Paris, Mama having insisted on being present at the production. Despite the extreme importance of this event in my life, the first time a scenic work of mine would be seen on the stage, I was reluctant to leave Rochelets where life was so good and so peaceful. In Paris Mama stayed at her eye clinic, and Linette and I went to the

---

1 Florent Schmitt (1870–1958), composer and critic, member of the 'Apaches' group of composers.

Hôtel Vauban, opposite the theatre. We occupied separate rooms, not for the same reason we had done so in London but in order that I could have time to myself to rest and sleep; it was going to be a busy and demanding time.

And indeed I plunged immediately into an unending maelstrom of rehearsals, first with the ballet company and later with the orchestra. But even before that there were terrible complications with the late-delivering copyists. It was a mercy that the hotel was so near the theatre. This theatre, the Théâtre de la Gaîté-Lyrique, is not so large, and is quite old. Hitherto Diaghilev had always presented his seasons in top-flight theatres, but this season had been arranged in a hurry and all the good venues were already taken.

For me, the most important event was the start of the orchestral rehearsals. Unfortunately, these were taking place not in the auditorium but in a small foyer, with the result that the sound differed greatly from how it would be in the theatre. The orchestra was no better than indifferent. From the point of view of conducting I knew the score inside out, and although God only knows how long it was since I had stood behind the conductor's desk it took me no time at all to get back into my stride. The only problem was that I tired quickly, and after an hour's rehearsal I would pass the baton to Ansermet, who was rehearsing other repertoire.

I found it difficult to assess precisely whether it sounded good, indeed whether the sonorities were those I had intended. But Ansermet and Diaghilev were both deeply impressed, as were the critics who from time to time came into rehearsals. Diaghilev alternated between being very nice and very distant, the latter especially when I needed money to pay the copyists, whose tardiness in delivering the work brought me to the brink of apoplexy. I complained bitterly to Diaghilev. Larionov was also not quite up to speed with his choreography, and many places were done hastily or not at all. Naturally, it would have been better if the first night could have been on the 27th rather than the 17th. As for me, I had four rehearsals every day, going straight from the orchestra rehearsal to the choreography rehearsal, and I became so tired that at times I suffered 'lapses', forgetting what I was about to say. Linette and I tried to have lunch and dinner together, and these were the only times we saw one another.

At long last there came a telegram from Boris Nikolayevich, with the surprising but pleasant news that he was already in London, having decided to go there without waiting for the French visa. As soon as this had arrived in Helsingfors it was telegraphed to him in London, and he was now cabling to say that he would come to Paris immediately. He arrived on the evening of 13 May, but made no contact with anyone at that time as he was, according to his own words, exhausted with his travels, unshaven and not fit to be seen. On the 14th he appeared at Mama's clinic (the only address he had for any of us).

I got to hear of his arrival only at six o'clock in the evening when I returned from rehearsals, and was somewhat put out that he had been in Paris for twenty-four hours without seeing me. I was just in the process of ringing up the Hôtel Select, where he was staying with his mother, who had come with him, and where his sister Varvara[1] had been for some time, when he appeared in my hotel just outside the telephone booth. He had changed very little: his face a little coarsened, and a few lines appearing round the side of his mouth. Our joy at meeting again was unconfined on both sides, questions seemed inappropriate. After an hour the three of us (with Linette) went to have dinner and drank a bottle of champagne to celebrate our reunion. B.N. declared that it was the fulfilment of an impossible dream that had sustained him through three dreadful years in Petrograd. Looking at the stars, he had associated me for some reason with Deneb,[2] as if I, like Deneb, existed in some other, inaccessible, world. After dinner I had to go immediately back to rehearse, since the production of *Chout* could not be deflected on account of the arrival of a friend, whoever that friend might be. B.N. kept himself a little aloof from Linette, finding her presence something of an inhibition on our being together.

On the eve of the first performance there were two dress rehearsals with orchestra, in the morning and the afternoon, to which I invited my friends. There were quite a few spectators, including a number of critics and, for some reason, a clutch of American conductors: Damrosch, Hertz, Smallens and later on Monteux. Most of the scenery, costumes and the action on stage passed me by, so concentrated was I on the orchestra. The costumes were attractive, clownish, but very uncomfortable for the dancers, and Larionov had to defend himself against their protests. I thought the rehearsal went pretty badly, but Diaghilev considered it better than the dress rehearsals of many other ballets he had produced. The orchestra was poor. French musicians are members of a union, and according to the rules of their union players have the right, in case of need, to substitute other players as deputies. They constantly exploit this concession, so that for example in the course of all the rehearsals I saw a whole succession of different leaders, who made a complete hash of the long solo in the final dance.

After the final dress rehearsal on the morning of the 17th, instead of resting in the afternoon they decided to add another training session with the corps de ballet. The result was that they were all dead on their feet by the time of the performance. Tickets cost 100 francs for the best seats, and the audience was a model of glittering exclusivity. All the streets round about were filled with expensive automobiles, and because the Gaîté, a compara-

---

1   Princess Magalova. See *Diaries*, vol. 1, pp. 38, 769–70; pp. 136–8 above and *passim*.
2   The most luminous star in the Cygnus constellation.

tively modest establishment, had never previously presented anything of so elevated a status, people streamed out of the surrounding homes to gawp at the fashionable public. I did not have a box, but three seats had been reserved for Mama, Linette and B.N.

The first item on the programme was *Firebird* (could this have been on purpose – Stravinsky's first ballet followed by my first?). I then went out to conduct. I was not especially nervous, any discomfiture I suffered being on account of the three buttons the correct pressing of which I had to master: the first to signal the rise of the theatre's house curtains, the second to take out Larionov's front curtain, and the third to lower it again. Since the Larionov curtain was raised and lowered six times, and the knob had to be pushed twice on each occasion, first as a warning and then for the actual raising or lowering, and as this procedure had been explained to me only at the last rehearsal, the whole business added an unwelcome extra complication to my responsibilities as a conductor.

My appearance on the rostrum was greeted warmly, there was applause which I acknowledged. When all was quiet I pushed the first button. The house curtains rose to reveal Larionov's incredible, absurd, colourful curtain, which provoked an outburst of movement and laughter in the auditorium. When this quietened down once more I pushed the second knob (the warning signal) and launched into the music. After six bars I pushed it again and the Larionov curtain began its ascent, but on its way up it got caught and continued on the skew. However, it was soon righted, and this was the only untoward incident; everything went smoothly after this. Needless to say, I could see very little of what was happening on stage. As for the orchestra, it had pulled itself together for the first performance and played, one might almost say well. The end of the work received an enthusiastic reception.

I went up on stage to acknowledge the applause, but by the time I got there the dancers had already taken several bows. My appearance was greeted by audibly redoubled applause accompanied, however, by some booing and catcalling. The dancers were very nice, shaking my hand and also applauding. Everyone was happy. Backstage afterwards there was a flood of congratulations, following which Larionov, Goncharova, Linette, B.N. and I resolved to get momentously drunk. My heart was light, the burden was lifted from my shoulders, it had all gone wonderfully well.

We went to a fashionable Montmartre nightclub, a brightly illuminated room with wall-to-wall red carpet, a lot of foreigners, wine, flowers, people throwing paper balloons at one another, alarmingly décolletées *cocottes* clinging to the men, and a generally convivial atmosphere. We commandeered a convenient table in the corner, and with a rapidity born of unprecedented thirst despatched in quick succession five bottles of champagne and a large glass of liqueur each. We were extraordinarily merry. B.N. held up best. I was drunk, but in control and happy; Larionov, *vin-triste*, was drunk and maudlin; Goncharova likewise became progressively more lachrymose as she drank more and confided to Linette that no one loved her. Linette bore up well until the champagne was replaced by a large glass of liqueur, upon which she suddenly became very drunk, which frightened her and her courage immediately evaporated. At this point we decided it was time to go home. Someone stole Linette's watch, probably in the foyer when we were putting on our coats. We got back to the hotel in a conspicuously inebriated state, and I put Linette to bed in her room.

Next day the group reassembled, pleased with our previous evening's drinking bout. *Chout* was given three more times, the orchestra playing worse and worse on each occasion, and in the final performance I heard someone deliberately accompanying the Merchant's theme in thirds. At the end of the performance I confronted the orchestra manager in a fury. He made enquiries among the musicians but they were adamant that no one had done this, and the orchestra manager declared himself satisfied that he was not being lied to. But none of this caused me to alter my opinion.

The reviews were good, some of them long and excellent. The piece was an exceptional success among musicians. Ravel described it as a work of genius, Stravinsky as the single modern work he could listen to with pleasure. 'Les six'[1] spluttered with delight, although the appearance of *Chout* was a blow to them, representing as it did something they ought to have done themselves but had not been able to. Larionov wittily and cruelly punned on the six-of-one-and-half-a-dozen-of-the-other nature of 'Les six'.[2]

On the 20th Vera Janacopulos included *The Ugly Duckling* in her concert, in the French translation she had recently made of the text, also the *Akhmatova Songs* and two of the *Five Songs Without Words*. Unfortunately I could not attend, as I was conducting the third performance of *Chout*, and we could get together only afterwards, at supper. That morning, when I had been going through my songs with Yovanovich, who was accompanying Vera, he suddenly let fall that 'the day before yesterday, in the evening, I met Nina Meshcherskaya. She said she would definitely be coming this evening.' Where would she be coming? To *Ugly Duckling*, or to *Chout*, seeing that they were both taking place at the same time? Probably to *Duckling*, although as I concentrated on conducting that evening, it several times came into my mind that she might be in the auditorium.[3]

---

1 The group of French composers comprising Darius Milhaud, Artur Honegger, Francis Poulenc, Georges Auric, Germaine Taillefer and Louis Durey.
2 Like most puns, this will not translate. It depends on the dual meaning in Russian of 'dyuzhinnyi', the adjective formed from 'dyuzhina', meaning both 'dozen' and 'commonplace'. 'Nedyuzhinnyi' is, by extension, the opposite, 'outstanding'.
3 *The Ugly Duckling* was a more likely choice for Nina Meshcherskaya to attend, seeing that she had been responsible for the work's text and it was dedicated to her. See *Diaries*, vol. 1, p. 740.

The last performance in the Ballets Russes's short season was on the 23rd, and was devoted entirely to Stravinsky's ballets. It was the first time I had seen *Le Sacre* on the stage,[1] and it made a colossal impression on me: I was truly awestruck, and embraced Stravinsky with unaffected emotion. What with the success of *Chout*, and its favourable comparison to the now somewhat faded *Firebird*, and hearing on all sides that Stravinsky had been unhorsed by *Chout* and was grinding his teeth in frustrated rage, I had been misled into underestimating Stravinsky. Today he again reared up before my eyes in all his full stature.

After this performance everyone prepared to leave Paris, as the company was in a hurry to get to London. Earlier I had hoped very much that Diaghilev would ask me to go too so that I could conduct the premiere of *Chout*, but now I felt so desperately tired that all I wanted was go to Rochelets as soon as possible. Diaghilev, however, confined his discussions with me to cuts he wanted to make in the ballet, in particular the desirability of running the fifth and sixth scenes together, and did not say a word about London. B.N. also fervently wanted to be in the country, as he considered that in Paris we were not seeing nearly enough of one another. But when it came to the point he was not ready to leave: he had to see the doctor, he had to get money from someone or other – in short, Mama and I left on the 26th and Linette the following day, while B.N. lingered another week.

A major event has occurred in Linette's life: until now she has been studying singing with Litvinne, an enchanting woman but not a strict enough teacher. Linette is now moving to another teacher, Calvé,[2] one of the most famous French singers. While we were in the country in April Linette had sung a good deal, I had also been working with her, and during this period her voice had seen remarkable growth. Calvé wants her to go to study with her in her château, and the result is that I shall have to part with Linette for three or four weeks in June. This is sad, but it is important that Linette cements her relationship with Calvé, who takes incredible pains with her students and can virtually create careers for them. It is very important for me that Linette should be self-sufficient and enabled to forge an independent career.

Neither did Linette relish the prospect of parting, fretting over her impending departure as soon as we arrived in Rochelets, but it made her exceptionally nice and loving. It was warm in the country, almost hot, and the flowers had mostly disappeared, to be replaced on the bushes of yellow broom by a species of caterpillar that left a slimy trail over whole areas of the bushes. I took a short break from work, but soon got down to the Third Piano Concerto and finished the variations.

1   In the production by Massine.
2   Emma Calvé (1858–1942), one of the most celebrated French singers of the belle époque, an admired Carmen both in Europe and in America.

1–30 June

At the beginning of the month we relished the calm of the countryside and the tenderness of our relationship, born of the fact that Linette was soon going to have to go away for several weeks' study with Calvé. I worked on the variations and soon finished the first draft. B.N. was still held up in Paris with his various affairs. Suddenly I received a telegram from Diaghilev asking me to go to London to conduct the premiere of *Chout* on 8 June, travel and expenses paid. Exactly, in fact, what I had earlier hoped for, but now I was so ensconced in the country that I felt most disinclined to move. Nevertheless, Linette would in any case be leaving on the 5th, I could go up with her to Paris, and then come back again immediately after the 8th. It would be interesting to conduct in London. In a word, having discussed the proposal I cabled Diaghilev accepting and prepared to leave. Right on cue, the day before I left B.N. appeared, terribly disappointed to find that I was going away. He liked our house more than I expected, and immediately donned an open-necked shirt and rope sandals, assuming a summery air. The next day Linette and I departed.

I spent no more than a few hours in Paris, seeing Schloezer and Larionov. The latter had not been summoned by Diaghilev to London, and he was anxious to know from me how things stood there. Saying goodbye to Linette, I left that evening for London, dozing the night away amidst the rolling of the ship and my seasick companions.

Diaghilev was uncommonly friendly, and had intended to come and meet me off the ten o'clock train, but in fact I arrived at eight. He invited me to stay with him in the Savoy Hotel, but I had already made my own arrangements in the rather more modest Imperial Hotel. I immediately went to the rehearsal of the ballet to settle the cuts that were to be made as a result of our discussion in Paris before the company left. The main cut consisted of making a transition directly from the fifth scene into the sixth, that is to say immediately after the matchmakers have entered in answer to the Merchant's call for help. The Buffoon comes on straight away with his seven soldiers, and the blackmail scene demanding the return of his sister takes place in the bedroom. When the Merchant is released, the stage goes to black for a moment and the final dance takes place in the setting for the sixth scene.

I raised no objection to the cut, even though I was sorry to lose the final section of the fifth scene, the shaking to death of the goat. By contrast, I was quite happy to lose the opening of the sixth scene, and although I love the fifth entr'acte very much, it is almost never listened to properly because of the audience talking.

We therefore rehearsed the cut, and I was very glad to see our ballet troupe, a delightful and amusing group of people. We then went to lunch at the Savoy, and then back to rehearse with the orchestra. Ansermet had already done some preliminary rehearsals with the orchestra before I arrived in London, moreover the orchestra was greatly superior to the Frenchmen. Not only that, but there was a completely different atmosphere. These are serious and attentive musicians, not Parisian hirelings. As well as *Chout* I rehearsed the 'Classical' Symphony, because in London Diaghilev interpolated between ballets a musical offering of contemporary works, in which he included my 'Classical' Symphony. I was very happy to renew my acquaintance with it, but when I asked Ansermet how he had enjoyed it, he said it was a feeble piece and as much as he had loved *Chout*, so much had he thought the Symphony a failure. Ansermet is generally a good musician, but he has no opinions of his own, and as the creature of Stravinsky swallows all the latter's opinions whole. In accordance with these he has decided the Symphony lacks Russian-nationalist elements and any new discoveries, and therefore it is no good. How astonished he was when Stravinsky came to the second rehearsal and praised it to the skies! Stravinsky found it very well done and full of inventive modulations. After this Ansermet had the grace to feel awkward and treated me to lunch.

The *Chout* first night was postponed from the 8th until the 9th, and a general rehearsal held on the 8th to which a public audience and critics were invited – all the leading figures in artistic London. It was the first time that Diaghilev had undertaken a rehearsal of this sort in London. The rehearsal started well (although I was still not *au fait* with those accursed knobs, which were arranged in a different order here from those in Paris). However, in the middle of the first scene the orchestra went astray, so I stopped them, put matters right and then continued. Diaghilev flew to my side in a panic and whispered in my ear: 'You have just shat all over London, don't you dare stop again, even if not a single instrument is together, this is just the same as a performance!'

The actual first night was on the 9th. As I came out to conduct I was greeted by a great ovation and bowed twice. Why was this? Was I already that well known in London? Surely Diaghilev could not have organised it? To do so would have meant handing out free tickets to a claque, and all the tickets had long ago been sold. More likely it was Russians applauding, as there were a lot of them in the audience. The show went well, and I was only nervous when we got to the cut we had instituted. The orchestra played far better than the one in Paris. At the conclusion there was a tremendous response, greater even than after the first night in Paris. From Diaghilev came a huge laurel wreath embellished with red and white ribbons. Afterwards we sat in the Savoy with Diaghilev, his young man[1] and his very nice secretary

---

1   Boris Kochno.

Barocchi,[1] drinking champagne. The mood was a little subdued at first, but later on Diaghilev embarked on reminiscences and talked about Russian tsars, which was interesting.

Two days later, on the 11th, *Chout* was on again, but this time I asked Ansermet to conduct while I sat in the house like a lord, listening. Before *Chout* I conducted a performance of the 'Classical' Symphony, which was well but not sensationally received, and then sat in the box with Stravinsky listening to *Chout*. Our box was in a rather prominent position, so the whole audience was goggling at us.

Hearing *Chout* from a box in the auditorium was an experience ten times more pleasant than from the conductor's rostrum. Everything sounded much more beautiful – literally more beautiful. Also, it was the first time I had heard the trumpets and trombones play loudly enough, that is to say at the volume I intended. From where the conductor stands, for example, I had never heard, or more precisely could barely hear, the trombone theme among the general tumult of the final dance. Perhaps there was too much *cantabile* in the first violins? But I love this *cantabile*. Another thing was that I saw for the first time what was happening on stage; when conducting, I could cast only the occasional worried glance at it. As a spectacle I found it interesting, with many marvellous ideas, but also much that had not been fully worked out, and places where the movements did not correspond with the music. A bit of remedial work wouldn't hurt, if only for next season.

At the end of the performance I was called out to take a bow, and then had an affectionate farewell with Diaghilev before leaving next morning to return to Paris. Diaghilev said that in August and September he would be taking time off in Venice and hoped I would be able to join him there then so that we could have a quiet time to discuss a new ballet.

Before I went I had the opportunity to hear the first performance of Stravinsky's *Symphonies for Wind Instruments* conducted by Koussevitzky. I did not grasp it all, especially the passages of two-part polyphony. I must hear it again. But the monkish notion of writing just for winds does appeal to me.

I arrived back in Paris on the evening of the 12th. Larionov met me at the station and we went together to the hotel, where he asked me to show him the reviews for *Chout*. He was very interested in them, especially the ones with illustrations, and asked me to translate as he speaks not a word of

---

1 Randolfo Barocchi. Barocchi was in fact Diaghilev's company manager and had been married to the ballerina Lydia Lopokova. Before joining Diaghilev's company he had been assistant to Henry Russell, the Metropolitan Opera's European agent, and played a prominent role in the negotiations between the Metropolitan Opera and the Ballets Russes for their first American tour in 1915–16. After Lopokova and Barocchi divorced, Lopokova married the economist John Maynard Keynes.

English. Taking advantage of the concentration with which I was translating, he secreted the cuttings in his pocket. At one point I spotted him doing so, and asked: 'What are you hiding in your pocket?' But he answered: 'Just my notebook.' After he went away I realised I was missing a number of interesting reviews and programmes of the first performance. I was furious and wrote him a sharp letter.[1]

That evening in Paris I spent at Tamara Hanum's, where were also her sister Fatma, Fatma's friend Sar Khan, a beautiful Persian woman who had recently arrived from Moscow, Svirsky, and Sasha Yasha. Samoilenko[2] had not yet returned from London where we had, incidentally, seen one another. 'What's this I hear?' screamed Tamara Hanum. 'Diaghilev treating you to champagne? What's wrong with me that he doesn't do that for me?' This was properly regarded as a call for champagne, which duly appeared and was well and truly imbibed. Tamara Hanum said: 'This is the last of my substance I'm drinking to you: my money's at an end, I only got forty thousand for my necklace.' And indeed, the necklace had gone. I walked home unsteadily and extremely merry. But the next morning I woke up with a terrible headache. I went as agreed to Fatma Hanum's for lunch, where I found the same company as yesterday, but could eat nothing and by two o'clock was already on the train bound for Rochelets.

At home were Mama and B.N., who has really taken to Rochelets. He has even started bathing naked because the beach is absolutely deserted, but someone saw him and he was told that if he did not wear a bathing costume he would be sent to prison. B.N. could not sleep all night and the next day rushed into St Brévin to buy one.

Life fell into a daily routine that suited us and to which we kept precisely. In the morning I worked on composing the finale of the Concerto, making use of themes I had written in Japan and during the voyage from Japan to America (the two first 'white' melodic ideas were originally destined for the 'white' quartet.[3] All this thematic material is, incidentally, from 1918, since the material for the first two movements was composed in 1917–18. Lunch

---

1 They will not have made very comforting reading for Larionov, or Prokofiev for that matter. The London press was almost universally uncomplimentary: in a letter to Eleonora Damskaya of 15 July Prokofiev writes: 'Diaghilev presented it [*Chout*] with extreme pomp in Paris and London, with me conducting it. It had an extraordinary success; the French modernists went especially crazy over it. In London 114 reviews have appeared, but 113 of them are abusive.' (*Selected Letters of Sergei Prokofiev*, ed. and trans. Harlow Robinson (Northeastern University Press, Boston, 1998).) A pained Cyril Beaumont particularly disliked the subject: 'The book of the ballet, adapted from a Russian legend, was one of those examples of tortuous Russian humour which strike no responsive chord in our breasts.' (Cyril W. Beaumont, *The Diaghilev Ballet in London* (Putnam, London, 1940).)
2 Boris Samoilenko was the husband of Fatma Hanum.
3 See p. 296.

was at half-past twelve, and then a game of chess, not more than one game a day because we were playing a match, the first to win ten points. The result for the month of June was: 5 to me, 3 to B.N., 4 drawn.

Chess was followed by bathing, during which B.N. taught me to swim with my arms below my stomach. After bathing, tea with gooseberry jelly and the newspapers, for this was the time of the most important event of the day – the arrival of the postman, bringing three newspapers and always several letters. From six to half-past seven I did some more work, then dinner, after which the 'privat-docent'[1] would give a lecture. What this meant was that while Mama and B.N. went to get the milk, I would read a chapter of H. G. Wells's *Outline of History* and then solemnly reproduce it in Russian.[2] The audience listened with great interest and subjected what they had heard to analysis. At about ten o'clock Mama went to bed, B.N. retired to his room to read and I wrote letters or continued working until eleven. At this time we went out for a walk, looked at the stars or strolled down to the sea, then ate some *tvorog*[3] with milk and went to bed. We were in bed by eleven thirty or twelve. This would not have suited Linette!

Thus life went on from the 14th until the 26th of the month, but then I had to bestir myself and go to Paris. The reason was that Balmont had for some time been in very straitened financial circumstances, and his friends the Tsetlins had conceived the idea of organising a combined benefit performance in their spacious apartment in which he and I would both appear. At about the same time Koussevitzky invited me, most insistently, to perform at a *Mir Isskustva*[4] exhibition in Paris, part of which was to consist of two performances in his residence, one devoted to Stravinsky and the other to me. I therefore decided I could make both appearances, one straight after the other, and proposed the 27th for the Balmont performance and the 28th for the *Mir Isskustva*. I had very little desire to perform in the context of an exhibition, but recalling how glad I had been to perform at the closing event of this exhibition in Petrograd five years ago,[5] I decided I would do so. They promised that in addition to my appearance all my songs would be performed, and my *Scherzo for Four Bassoons*, and Koussevitzky said my travelling expenses would be paid.

As for Balmont, information from another source was that his situation was not so bad, and that he and B.N. had been enthusiastically knocking back the port at 200 francs a time, for which Balmont had insisted on pay-

1 A privat-docent was a University lecturer without tenure.
2 H. G. Wells's *The Outline of History, Being a Plain History of Life and Mankind*, was originally published in two volumes by Garden City Publishing Co. Inc. in New York in 1920.
3 *Tvorog* is curds, or cottage cheese.
4 *World of Art*.
5 See p. 111.

ing the whole bill. B.N. and I therefore amicably agreed that I should go and play, as a way of reimbursing Kostya[1] for the wine, and on the 26th I left for Paris. The following evening in the Tsetlins' apartment all went splendidly: I played my Second Sonata and Balmont read his 'White Country' (rather a long piece to read to an audience).[2] After his reading I played again, a series of small works – *Visions Fugitives*, *Tales of an Old Grandmother* and some earlier pieces. Unfortunately – and I say this in all sincerity – my success was much greater than Balmont's: he had exhausted everyone's patience with the length of 'White Country'. But he was happy, because many more tickets had been sold than he had expected. In conclusion Balmont ceremoniously read the sonnet he dedicated to me, 'Thou richly blessed child of the sun',[3] everyone clapped and there was satisfaction all round.

But the evening of the 27th turned out to be a horrible occasion. The only good thing about it was the beautiful hall, the walls covered with canvases by our artists. In the first place, instead of there being two singers to sing my complete voice and piano oeuvre there was only one, Davydova, from the Musical Drama Theatre, who performed, badly, three *Akhmatki*.[4] The bassoonists did the *Scherzo* rather well (it was encored), and everything else was left to me to play. The audience reaction was moderate, verging on cool. At the end I was presented with a drawing by Grigoriev,[5] but not one of his best, and there was no mention of the 370 francs the journey had cost me.

The Samoilenkos wanted to take me to a nightclub somewhere, but I was already engaged elsewhere, namely to Lucy Khodzhayeva, the elder of two sisters with whose family I had become friendly in Kislovodsk.[6] When I was in America I had many times remembered with great pleasure our times together, and had even sent them postcards which, to my great surprise, actually arrived at their destination. Soon after I left Russia, according to Lucy's account, 'a fairly rich young man called Davydov turned up and I decided to marry him'. Subsequently they fled to Constantinople and thence to Paris, where they were virtually destitute. He had joined Baliyev's troupe,[7]

1 Konstantin (Balmont).
2 'White Country' is in fact the title of one poem in a major collection Balmont published as *Buildings on Fire* (*Goryashchiye Zdaniya*) in 1900. If Prokofiev is referring to the whole of *Buildings on Fire*, it would indeed have made a long evening, consisting as it does of over a hundred and twenty poems of varying lengths. 'White Country' is one of the shortest, at twelve lines.
3 Written as an ecstatic response to a private play-through of the Third Piano Concerto.
4 That is, three of the *Five Poems of Anna Akhmatova*, Op. 27.
5 Boris Grigoriev (1886–1939), an artist associated with *Mir Isskusstva* and also, as illustrator, with Prokofiev's favourite arts and literary journal, *Satyricon*. He made a number of fine portraits of musicians and figures in the arts world, including Rachmaninoff, Chaliapin, Gorky, Yesenin and Meyerhold. He had left Russia with his family in 1919 and settled in France.
6 See p. 248.
7 Nikita Baliyev, a former actor with the Moscow Arts Theatre, had started a cabaret in Moscow which after the Revolution he transplanted to Paris, calling it the 'Théâtre de la Chauve-Souris'

and she was getting a few parts in films. The first time I met her in Paris was at a performance of *Chout*, where to my shame I did not recognise her. This evening, after the concert, we repaired to a café and talked until one in the morning, while our coffee got cold.

The next morning I was all for going home, but the Stahls, who had recently acquired a car, persuaded me to accompany them to Fontainebleau. They had been planning to come to stay with us in June, but the Diva had been suffering from an attack of angina and now their plans had changed. Our Rochelets regime had settled into such a pleasant routine that I did not insist. We made a wonderful excursion to Fontainebleau, and then at six o'clock I returned to Paris and went to dine with the Koussevitzkys, with whom I have become great friends. Koussevitzky said that next season, probably in the spring, I would perform with him the Third Piano Concerto in Paris and London (splendid!) and Mme Koussevitzky told me the name of the hotel in which Mary Garden was staying. I knew she was in Paris somewhere and had very much wanted to make contact with her, particularly as I had also heard that she was looking for me, but despite all my efforts had not succeeded in finding her address. Having now ascertained this from Mme Koussevitzky, I hastened to go to the hotel, but was told that Mary Garden was no longer in Paris but that I could write to her if I wished. I did so, but later discovered that her absence was a fiction; she was in Paris but did not want anyone to know, in order to avoid being pestered.

I spent the evening with Lucy strolling up the Avenue des Bois and sitting in a café in the woods. As we parted, she kissed me, and I responded by kissing her several times. Next morning, at seven o'clock, I was on the train going home. This was the fourth time in a row that I would be coming back to Rochelets from Paris precisely on the first day of the month.

At home there were Mama and B.N., but still no word from Linette as to when she would be coming back, and it was really time she did. B.N. was recovering from a mild fever that had been pulling him down and making him depressed.

21 October[1]

We were woken at seven as the *Aquitania* was already in New York harbour being met by an entire squadron of minesweepers in honour of Admiral

---

('Theatre of the Bat'). A little piece of old Russia, and a significant employer of émigré talent, its sketches, songs and dance routines pressed all the sentimental, gently ironic and allusive buttons to appeal to Russians nursing a nostalgic ache for their lost homeland.
1   There are no entries in the original manuscript from 30 June until 20 October. During this period Prokofiev was mainly based in Les Rochelets, working on the Piano Concerto No. 3 and on a set of songs, *Five Poems of Konstantin Balmont*, Op. 36, for Lina Codina ('Linette'), his future wife. Balmont and his wife were staying in a nearby house, and the expatriates saw a

Beatty, who was also on board. I did not see Mary Garden again. It was two o'clock by the time we were disembarked, and I went in celebration to the Pennsylvania Hotel, where I obtained a good room for $5. New York looked gay, lively and prosperous, and bathed in sunshine. I was happy to be coming back to the city.

Haensel received me, as is his wont, less than cordially, that is to say courteously but preoccupied with other matters, so that we hardly discussed anything. All the same, I shall have to get $200 from him tomorrow.

I did not really have much to do in New York, but at the same time there was no point hurrying to Chicago either. Essentially I had come a week earlier than I needed to. I decided I would try to look up Stella and rang her number several times, but could get no answer. Evidently there was no one living in her apartment. A bad sign.

At nine o'clock the desire to sleep overwhelmed me and I went to bed.

22 October

Before getting dressed I set to work on conducting *Three Oranges*. Then I took a bath and went down to have coffee. Haensel advanced me $200 until my first concert, and today was very charming. He restated his opinion that I should definitely give two, or three, or five concerts in New York. I restated my opinion that this would cost a great deal of money.

I resumed my attempts to telephone Stella, but there was still silence from her apartment. I then tried Blanche, who was clearly delighted to hear from me and deluged me with endearments. Stella had moved, and did not have a new telephone number. For some reason Blanche had not seen her for three weeks, and it was possible that today and tomorrow – Saturday and Sunday – she would have gone out of town. I immediately sent her a letter special delivery, and working on conducting the score in my room after lunch, waited for her to call. But Blanche was probably right: Stella would have gone to the country for the weekend. A great pity. There was no one else I had any great desire to see, and actually no one knew that I was in New York. I enjoyed the sensation of teasing Koshetz and Boris Nikolayevich[1] in this way.

---

good deal of one another. David Nice suggests that one motive for the *Balmont Songs* for Lina may have been to counteract suspicions about the relationship with Nina Koshetz, for whom the *Akhmatova Songs* and the *Songs Without Words*, Op. 35, had been composed. (See D. Nice, *Prokofiev from Russia to the West 1891–1935* (Yale University Press, New Haven and London, 2003).) In August Mary Garden asked Prokofiev to conduct the premiere of *Love for Three Oranges*, an undertaking, as he wrote to Natalya Koussevitzkaya, 'I had not bargained for when I wrote something so terribly difficult; now I lament the fact many times over.' The Diary resumes as the *Aquitania*, on which Prokofiev sailed to America in October in company with Mary Garden, docked in New York.

1 Bashkirov had in the meantime returned to New York and was staying with his brother.

At nine o'clock I was again overcome by the desire to sleep. This must be because in Paris it is two o'clock in the morning, and the organism has grown accustomed to that hour.

23 October

As yesterday, I worked on conducting in the morning and then had my bath.

There was no word from Stella, but I will wait another day. In the afternoon I went to Damrosch's concert, to which I had been given a ticket by Saminsky,[1] whom I met by chance on the street. I heard an appalling piece by an American composer called Gruenberg,[2] who has just won a prize worth $1,000. I then went to visit the Kokhánskis, who are passionate admirers of my compositions. Koshetz is in New York and is singing somewhere this evening. I asked the Kokhánskis not to tell her that they had seen me, but they themselves regard her as an impossible hysteric and try to keep their distance. My bed again began to call me to it around nine o'clock.

On learning that I did not want to see Koshetz, Mme Kokhánskaya's interest was piqued to know what kind of women I do like: 'Vyshnedgradsky said he would point out to me a young lady (?) you were once in love with,' she said, 'but we left before he could do so.' Who could this have been? Of course, Nina Meshcherskaya. This means that Nina is going round Paris, and the legend of my love affair with her is also going the rounds, doubtless not to my advantage.

24 October

Worked on my conducting and then went to see Kokhánski again, to show him the proofs of the *Hebrew Overture* and consult with him on bowings. He was, as always, perceptive and remarkably resourceful in coming up with solutions, and made some suggestions, although not many seemed to be needed. In the afternoon I stayed at home making the necessary corrections to the score and parts, so that I could send the corrected proofs back.

---

1   Lazar Saminsky, conductor. See *Diaries*, vol. 1, p. 4 and *passim*.
2   Louis Gruenberg (1884–1964). Gruenberg, originally from Brest-Litovsk but based in America from infancy, studied the piano with Busoni (who thought he was so talented he apparently tried hard to dissuade him from transferring his allegiance to composition) and was a prolific and versatile composer of symphonic music, opera (best known for *The Emperor Jones*, a one-act opera based on the play by Eugene O'Neill) and jazz- and Broadway-influenced operetta. Along with Carl Ruggles, Edgard Varèse and Leo Ornstein a leading member of the International Composers' Guild, he conducted the American premiere of Schoenberg's *Pierrot Lunaire*. He also wrote a great many successful movie scores for Hollywood, three of which won Academy Awards. The award of the $1,000 Flagler Prize for *The Hill of Dreams* in 1919 established his reputation as an important American composer; this was no doubt the piece heard and so disliked by Prokofiev in the concert by the New York Symphony Orchestra under Walter Damrosch.

I went to see the Ingermans, with the covert intention of finding out whether Baranovskaya was in New York, as she had written to me in France she might be. I hit the bull's-eye at the first attempt: just two days ago she had come to see Ingerman with a sore throat. I immediately rang her up at the Biltmore, but she was not in. So much did I want to see Frou-frou that after dinner with the Ingermans I went to the Biltmore, but she was still not there. I left her a note: 'Frou-frou, witch of my heart, I long to see you,' and returned to my hotel to find another note – from Stella. She would ring me at noon the next day. Stella and Frou-frou – quite a combination! Very interesting. What a pity I have to go to Chicago. But I must keep in mind that the opera is my first priority; I have been waiting three years for it.

25 October

Did more conducting practice, but not very assiduously, waiting for telephone calls from Stella and Frou-frou. Frou was the first to call and expressed herself with her customary sparkle. Next was Stella, who rejoiced at our reconnection, as did I. She said she would come to see me at four o'clock and asked whether it would be appropriate for her to come straight to my room. I said yes, with delight, wondering whether the hotel would let her in. But when four o'clock came and Stella arrived, she was intercepted in the corridor on her way to my room and I was rung up with the announcement that there was a woman wishing to see me. I emerged into the corridor, and we had a happy reunion, somewhat inhibited by the presence of the female floor superintendent (oh idiotic America!). There was nothing for it but to go downstairs to have tea. Stella was a little more dressy and wore more make-up than previously, but her eyes seemed even bigger. We had many memories to recall. I said that I had intended to go to Chicago tomorrow, but would delay my departure for a couple of days. We sat for two hours and then I took her home, only just managing to get to the Biltmore for my seven o'clock rendezvous with Frou-frou to take her to dinner.

Frou-frou had altered, had put on twelve pounds and was definitely plumper than she had been, pinker and in some ways a little coarser on the outside, although inside of course she was still the sensitive and vital person she always had been. We had dinner and then went to see Nazimova in her new picture (excellent). Being with Frou-frou was the greatest possible pleasure for me, and she also revelled in our meeting, 'like being resurrected'.

26 October

Next morning, instead of practising conducting, I went in search of another hotel, and had the inspiration of going to the Clint, the apartment building

I had lived in eighteen months ago and which, although it normally let apartments only by the month, allowed me as a former resident to take one for two days. Stella telephoned, and at half-past two she was already at my hotel with her father's car to transfer me to the Clint. I thus appeared there with all my suitcases and Stella, but that is not the sort of thing the Clint bothers about. Stella stayed with me for a while, looking through the programmes from the Paris ballet season and various photographs. She was different, exactly in what way I could not say, but there was no question that she was even more beautiful. At one point she had to make a telephone call, to someone she was due to meet this evening, but the person in question called the meeting off.

When Stella returned from her telephone call she was irate that someone she liked had dared to refuse to do her bidding, and I was immediately transformed into the scapegoat. She emphasised how much she had grown apart from me, and when I asked her if perhaps she would grow more used to me again tomorrow, she replied that she would not come again to see me in my apartment but would accompany me to the concert by the Philharmonic. She might also come to Chicago for the premiere of *Three Oranges*. I said that if she did she would encounter there her brothers – the Empty-heads – and declined the suggestion of going to the Philharmonic. Then, talking of this and that, we went back to her house. 'Until Chicago?' she asked, as we said goodbye. I answered: 'I will be a sportsman,[1] and will bring the opera to you. Until January.'

27 October

Worked on conducting and wrote out a fair copy of 'Pillars'.[2] Yesterday evening Frou-frou came to see me and went into ecstasies over the lyric of this song. I called on Haensel, who teased me about keeping my address a secret because, no doubt, I was embroiled in a passionate love affair. Koshetz and B.N. had both been to see him, but he had in perfectly good conscience been unable to tell them where I was. They both left their telephone numbers with impassioned demands for me to ring them, but I begged him to forget that I had been there today and to hide all the telephones in his office.

I went to the Philharmonic concert with Frou-frou, and sat in a corner so that if Stella should happen to be there too she would not be likely to see me. I much enjoyed hearing Beethoven's Fifth Symphony. No harmonic novelties at all, but what an utter delight!

---

1   In English.
2   No. 5 of *Five Poems of Konstantin Balmont*, Op. 36.

28 October

Went in to Breitkopf's to talk about copyright. The situation with Russian music is that, to put it simply, nothing will be paid for existing material, and one has to engage in all kinds of artful contrivances to ensure that future compositions are protected. Nothing can now be done about Opp. 31 and 32.[1] Anyone who wants to can freely reprint them.

At six o'clock in the evening I left for Chicago, accompanied to the station by Frou-frou and Voynov. Frou-frou sparkled and made witty remarks, and like Stella, said she would like to come to the premiere. As she is a real expert on *commedia dell'arte* this would be a real event for her, and I should not be surprised if she really did come.

29 October

The whole day on the train. I could have taken another one and been in Chicago during the afternoon, but it would not have made a great deal of difference and this one was cheaper. While there is no inflow of cash, and the obligations are mounting up, there is no occasion to splash out. All the same, by the end of the American season, I calculate that my assets should be in a reasonably healthy state. My achievements during my travel day amounted to five letters written and several days of my Diary brought up to date.

The faithful Gottlieb met me when I got to Chicago, regretting that I had elected to arrive in the evening, as otherwise he would have had me met by newspaper reporters. Hardly had we got inside the Auditorium Hotel, where I had asked him to reserve a room for me, and which was connected to the theatre,[2] when Smallens came to greet me, the repetiteur for *Three Oranges*. My room was a large one with a huge window looking out over Lake Michigan. Gottlieb and Smallens both piled into the room after me. Smallens has already taken five orchestra rehearsals for *Oranges*, which did not please me at all since I wanted to do them all myself, but Smallens seems to think that he will be conducting the performances himself. Obviously my first task is going to be to engage in some theatre politics, but I refrained from mentioning to him directly that I would be conducting, as I did not want to dampen his enthusiasm for the work.

And so, welcome to Chicago. How different are my present circumstances from those in which I was here last year!

---

1 Respectively *Tales of an Old Grandmother* and *Four Piano Pieces* – the works Prokofiev composed for American publishers soon after he arrived in 1918.
2 The Auditorium building also included a hotel and some offices, intended to produce revenue to support the operations of the theatre.

30 October

Gottlieb assumed control from early morning, bringing two reporters to see me, and then took me to lunch with the Rosenwalds, wealthy and extremely cultivated Jews whom I had visited last year.

At three o'clock I had my first meeting with Polacco,[1] setting the tone for our relationship as one in which we mutually exchanged *politesses*. It was decided that tomorrow I should make the acquaintance of the chorus director and the producer, with the object of starting work with both of them, while Smallens would introduce the soloists to me as and when they had learnt their parts. Polacco recommended starting orchestral rehearsals a week before the singers were ready to begin working with the orchestra. This seems sensible. After Polacco I worked with Smallens, going through the tempi with him. When we finished, Smallens asked me directly if I had 'ambitions' to conduct myself. I replied that Garden had invited me to conduct the first performance and I had seen no reason to decline. That evening we continued our work together. During the summer I had promised Linette that Princess Violetta, whose name I had simply picked out of a hat, would be renamed Princess Linette, and today, when we reached her in the score, I informed Smallens of the change of name. 'What made you do that?' he asked. 'That's how it is in Gozzi,' I replied.

31 October

Today I was introduced to the producer, Coini,[2] and the chorusmaster, Nipoti. The impression the former produced on me was less than favourable (I may have been prejudiced, since Koshetz had written to me that he had not been in favour of producing *Oranges*) and that of the latter frankly negative when he informed me that my presence at chorus rehearsals would not be needed for another week, and it would be another four days before he divided the chorus into its various ensembles.[3] But the chorus has the most

---

1 Giorgio Polacco (1873–1960), Italian conductor. After successful stints at the Teatro Municipal in Rio de Janeiro and the Teatro Colón in Buenos Aires, and La Scala, Polacco returned to Italy to become Principal Conductor at La Scala before coming to New York in 1912 at Gatti-Casazza's invitation to take over the Italian repertoire of the Metropolitan Opera. Poached by Chicago in 1918 to replace the now ailing Campanini, when Mary Garden took over the reins she appointed him Music Director, in which position he remained until 1930, finishing his tenure with a final performance of Mary Garden's crowning achievement as Mélisande.

2 Jacques Coini was another of Mary Garden's new appointments. He had previously been resident producer for Oscar Hammerstein I in the days of the Manhattan Opera Theater.

3 In *The Love for Three Oranges* the chorus is divided into eight groups who separately and in combination interact with one another and with the principal characters: Cranks (*Chudaki*), Tragicals (*Tragiki*), Comicals (*Komiki*), Lyricals (*Liriki*), Empty-heads (*Pustogoloviye*), Little Devils (*Chortenyata*), Physicians (*Mediki*) and Courtiers (*Pridvorniye*). There are also non-singing roles for Monsters, Drunkards and Gluttons.

important and the most difficult part in the opera. So concerned was I by this that I went to take the matter up with Polacco, who promised to take charge of it personally. Coini and I started work on the *mise-en-scène* and today got through almost all the first act. Coini is a hard worker and is conscientious, but so far as I could see lacks the vital spark. All he did was undertake to carry out my proposals. Well, I suppose that is not the worst approach.

I went to call on Volkov at the Consulate. He was friendly, but asked me if I did not feel it might be better for Smallens to conduct.

Garden arrived back in Chicago yesterday and immediately took to her bed as she felt unwell. I hope it won't be too long before she crawls out of her burrow again.

Needless to say, Gottlieb was circling round all day and brought two new female reporters to interview me. One of them had already written an article, some of which was amusing, the remainder the most fearful nonsense.

1 November

Coming out of the hotel restaurant downstairs after coffee I ran into Koshetz, fresh off the train from New York. We kissed. She is also staying in the hotel, on the floor below mine. She passed on a verbal message from B.N., rather incoherent, but the gist of it was that he was in a state of complete collapse and I must rescue him. Koshetz's gloss on this was that he had been sincerely distraught at my having been in New York without saying a word to him, he was ruing the day he left France and now felt himself the unhappiest man in the world to be living with his brother, with whom he had nothing in common, and who doled out to him dollar by dollar a pitifully inadequate allowance. Accompanying this sad story were a series of hilarious tales, for example the pimple which had erupted on his lip, striking the fear of death into him to such an extent that he had to take to his bed for several days until it cleared up.

After meeting Koshetz I carried on working with Coini, who today actually thought of something all by himself: when Leander, Clarissa and Smeraldina summon up Fata Morgana at the end of Act One, they should turn and face all four sides in turn, as if not knowing from which direction Fata Morgana might appear. The most depressing aspect is the hold-up with the chorus, and also that there is no sign of Mary. The singers are working with might and main.

I was lunching with Gottlieb, when Koshetz wandered up. When I got back to my room, it was a pleasant surprise to find a piano there. I got to work straight away. In the evening Koshetz came and sat with me, and told me that her physical passion for me had subsided, but this would not prevent her from throwing herself at me occasionally and kissing me. I showed her our summer photographs with Balmont, and to tease her, with Linette.

2 November

In the morning, another session with Coini, during which we finished Act Two and went through almost all of Act Three. Gottlieb took me to lunch with Dr Schmidt, a rich German. In the afternoon I practised the piano, learning the Third Piano Concerto and going through the programme for my concert on the 12th in Cleveland. An amusing thing with the Piano Concerto: in my haste to finish the score in France, I did not trouble to write out the whole of the piano part in the finale, and when I packed my trunk I left all the sketches and working material for the Concerto with Mama, so that in case the trunk should go missing, at least they would remain intact. I now realise that the middle section of the finale has no piano part, and I can hardly remember this passage. I will be able to restore it, but it will take time and that is something I don't have much of.

Koshetz and I dined together. During the summer she had chanced to be staying near where Rachmaninoff was living, but they only met once and ... did not greet one another. She told me a great deal about him, and it was most interesting.

In the evening I was told that there would be an orchestra rehearsal for *Three Oranges* tomorrow. This put me in a funk, and I sat down to study the score. Tomorrow is a big day: I shall be hearing *Oranges* for the first time.

3 November

The orchestra is first class, and the sound in the auditorium is wonderful. Not only that, but Smallens, whatever else he did, had five three-hour rehearsals in October, and as a result everything went smoothly and pleasantly. It all sounded good, sometimes very good, and original, especially Scene Two, the Infernal scene. But what delighted me more than anything was the bassoon trill when Leander says: 'You've been eavesdropping on state secrets!' I had completely forgotten about this trill, and it sounds marvellous, particularly as the bassoons are sitting right under my nose. During the afternoon I sat in the library and made corrections to some of the parts. Polacco was complimentary about my conducting and especially for not wasting time in rehearsal.

Koshetz played and sang for me her new songs, written not by her but by her 'teacher': they had come to her by a spiritual path, dictated by tabletapping. Two of them were very good indeed and original, they really made me stretch my eyes and ears. They were totally unlike what she had played to me four years ago in Moscow. What is going on? I must listen to them again.

This evening I developed a torticollis – a stiff neck, probably from being in a draught after the rehearsal. Koshetz massaged the back of my head. A liberty.

4 November

In the morning I studied the score for the next rehearsal, and played the piano, trying to remember the missing part of the Concerto's finale.

At two o'clock there was another orchestral rehearsal. I began by repeating the scene with the Physicians, which had not gone right before, and then continued with Act One Scene Two and beyond. The rehearsal, as yesterday's, went splendidly, the orchestra first class and very attentive. Fata Morgana's curse came off very well, as did Chelio's summons of Farfarello, and the intermezzo was not at all bad. In sum, I am as happy as can be. Smallens, who came in to listen to the rehearsal and jealously to survey my conducting technique, gave me a few hints on little things I could have done better.

I am not feeling particularly well: my stiff neck has extended itself upwards and downwards, so that not only the back of my head but my spine and the whole of my head hurt. I took some aspirin and massaged my neck, without the assistance of Koshetz.

5 November

I thought I was going to have a free morning, but Polacco telephoned at nine to say that there was to be another orchestra rehearsal at ten o'clock. My neck is better. We went through Act Three, and I quickened the tempo in the scene where the Prince and Truffaldino creep towards the kitchen. It is all going well and Polacco is full of praise. I spent the afternoon in the library again, correcting the parts, and when I emerged I went into the hall where the orchestra was rehearsing *Salome*. Richard Strauss was present, having just arrived in Chicago, and Mary Garden as well. Garden hung on to my arm and asked me how *Oranges* were. '*Oranges* are growing,' I told her, but Garden was already talking to someone else.

I asked her to introduce me to Strauss, which she willingly did, recommending me as 'the famous Russian composer'. Strauss (we conversed in French, as I had forgotten my German) was absent-mindedly charming and said that when he returned to Chicago in the middle of December he would come to a performance of *Oranges*. He has a pleasant face, with none of the vulgarity one sometimes finds in his music.

Before dinner I restored more of the missing part of the Concerto I had left behind in Paris. I think I shall be able to finish the job without too much trouble, except for the expenditure of several hours.

Koshetz, with whom I have dined every night, said that since a certain event had occurred in the summer (the end of a great love, was it with Rachmaninoff or with Prokofiev?) all passion had finally died in her and she is now totally impotent. Not true. She is playing a game.

In the evening I went to the Chicago Symphony to hear Kokhánski, but before that I was bored out of my life by Mahler's Seventh Symphony. Who needs this music? Nevertheless, there are some musicians like Mengelberg who adore it. It is like kissing a still-born child.

6 November

There are no rehearsals today, and so I had a good piano practice this morning. My sore head has gone, but I have been struck down by a cold.

After lunch with Koshetz I watched a parade in honour of Foch,[1] who was paying a visit to America. The parade, as if on purpose, took place immediately in front of the hotel. At three o'clock we went to Strauss's concert: on our left a demonstration in honour of the French; on our right, a celebration of a German. It is a wonder no one thought to position a limbless torso in between the two, a heroic victim of the conflict!

Strauss's concert consisted of his songs, for which he himself played the piano. His accompaniments were a delight, a touch on the dry side. The first songs were simple and good, but later on there crept in such a convoluted mish-mash of bad taste that halfway through I left. Vulgarity in a low tavern I can understand. When an orchestra plays in the park I simply don't hear it. But when vulgarity is presented with all the trimmings of first-class technique, all the marks of high-minded seriousness and international celebrity, it becomes disgraceful, there is no other word for it.

Gottlieb took me to dine with the Rosenthals. It was very dull.

I wrote an olive-branch letter to Bashkirov. I very much do not wish to quarrel with him, and my uncommunicative passage through New York is already punishment enough for his behaviour.

7 November

I went to see Spangler, the managing director of the opera company, about my conducting contract. I should have done this a week ago, but I had been hoping that Mary herself would do as she had promised and inform Spangler of the situation. Also, I wanted the discussion to follow the first orchestral rehearsals so that there could be no doubt of my ability as a conductor. Spangler said that Mary had gone away again for a couple of days

---

[1] Maréchal Ferdinand Foch (1851–1929), Supreme Commander of the Allied Armies at the end of the First World War.

and asked me to come back and see him in four days' time, a delay I perhaps should have foreseen. Never mind, I have $40 in my pocket, and I can manage with that. For some reason I felt rather inhibited talking to Spangler, but he behaved impeccably, calmly and with great courtesy. In fact, courtesy seems to be the watchword of everyone's attitude to me in the theatre. Evidently Mary has given a good report of me.

In the afternoon there was another rehearsal (the fourth) with the orchestra, with such a frightful draught to the back of my head that I resorted to wrapping a scarf round my neck and wearing a hat, thus working up a tremendous sweat while I was conducting. I got right through the whole opera, and the final pages sounded so marvellous (which I had not expected) that I realised the orchestra must have strained every last nerve for the final bars. The orchestra gave me an ovation which I acknowledged, removing my hat to do so.

In the evening Koshetz and Gottlieb dragged me to the cinema, which was a most irritating waste of an evening. I would have done much better to stay and play the piano.

Yesterday, during the orchestra rehearsal, the scarf successfully protected my head and neck from the draught, but it was still blowing on my waist muscles, which today are painful. Granted, sore waist muscles are neither here nor there, but this would absolutely not be the time to catch pleurisy. Not that there is ever a good time for that.

The fifth rehearsal with orchestra started at eleven in the morning, or rather the fifth half-rehearsal, as for the time being I have asked not to be allotted full three-hour rehearsals; I would not be able to stay the course for so long. We began the opera from the beginning. It went extremely well, although Smallens later criticised me for failing to achieve some effects of detail (which he, needless to say, would have achieved). My back hurt even more at the end of the rehearsal. Koshetz appeared and scolded me for not taking aspirin and hot tea with lemon. Nevertheless I felt not too bad and had a good session at the piano.

In the evening I wrote to Linette (my third letter). I am afraid my letters cannot be bringing her much joy, more likely disappointment, as they consist more of a record of events than lyrical effusions. But what can I do? Lyrical effusions would only lead to an even more complicated situation than presently exists.

Outside there are storms and pouring rain. But I hardly go out at all: my entire world has shrunk to the hotel and the theatre. In the evening I took aspirin, rubbed iodine on my back and drank tea with lemon, following Koshetz's prescription.

9 November

As a result of my sudorific remedies I did not sleep well, but my state of health is better. Thank God there is no rehearsal this morning, so I was able to play the piano and write letters, and then went into the theatre for the chorus practice. The chorus director and I finally agreed on how the chorus is to be divided, and they went through the first act for me, singing very well but terribly ponderously, since when the rapid chatter of the ten Eccentrics is being roared out by a chorus of forty-five people, it comes out like an elephant dancing on *pointe*. I also heard Pantalone rehearsing with Smallens. Pantalone is talented and very funny. It is a great pity that Smallens has so far refused to let me vet any of the singers. I suspect that he wants them to learn the whole opera with him.

In the afternoon I corrected some orchestral parts. In the evening Coini and I should have finished Act Four, but he was not free, so I sat and read some of Lazarevsky's[1] stories about provincial high-school love. I really rather enjoyed them.

Downstairs, talking to Baklanov and Smallens, I met Johnson, the former Director of the Opera (office-boy, as I used to call him). Of course to say hello to him, and Smallens, the idiot, saw fit to congratulate me on the absurdity of *Oranges*, at which Johnson smiled a crooked smile. I was inwardly enraged and silently vowed not to forgive Smallens for this, but later decided not to brood over it, what did he matter anyhow? In general, nothing matters except that *Oranges* should be well performed.

10 November

Smallens took a rehearsal of the first scene with all the singers. It was very interesting and, I thought, successful. People have been insisting to me for so long that I do not write well for voices that it was a pleasant surprise to listen to a scene like this and see how admirably it turned out. After the ensemble, the Mexican Mojica[2] sang the Prince, and it was absolutely marvellous: he is

---

1 Boris Lazarevsky (1871–1936), a popular and entertaining writer of short stories and feuilletons rather in the manner of the early Chekhov, whom he knew personally and by whom he was strongly influenced. His subject matter was drawn from rural life and provincial cities, and there is a racy, not to say mildly erotic, tone to much of it. Some of his stories are written in Ukrainian. Lazarevsky left Russia in 1921, first for Berlin, then Prague, and finally for Paris, where he remained until his death.

2 José Mojica (1895–1974), tenor and film actor, later Catholic priest. Mojica, startlingly handsome in a Rudolf Valentino way, rocketed to fame after Caruso recommended him to Mary Garden as Pelléas to her Mélisande. In his 1958 autobiography *Yo Pecador* (translated as *I, A Sinner* (Franciscan Herald Press, 1963) Mojica recounts how the aftermath of an affair in Chicago with a married Canadian soprano had put his whole career at risk (the soprano was

musical and committed, and trotted out the most difficult passages as if they were child's play. Everything is going so well.

In the afternoon I practised, corrected parts, and went to dinner with Professor Mead,[1] whose family are very fond of me and where there always seem to be a whole bevy of beautiful nieces.

I had a letter from Zakharov in reply to the one I had sent him from Paris congratulating him on his exodus from Bolshevizia. Zakharov was exceptionally loving and affectionate in his letter, and I shall be very happy if our relationship, which for so long has been ridiculously strained, can be restored to its old harmony.

11 November

Each morning at seven o'clock the sun rising beyond the lake wakes me up, but today the weather was so overcast that not a single ray penetrated my room and I overslept so as almost to miss my sixth half-rehearsal. This began at ten o'clock and during it I got through Acts Three and Four. In the afternoon I had another meeting with Spangler, who confirmed my engagement to conduct the first performances in Chicago and New York, at a fee of $500 for each appearance. I asked who would be conducting the other performances, and Spangler said that in any case it would not be Smallens.[2]

Five hundred dollars a performance is splendid, but had not Mary in her letter invited me to conduct all the performances? I expressed my thanks to Spangler and left, forgetting to ask him if they could pay me the $1,000 due to me for the production of the opera this season, on 15 November rather than 15 December. This was silly of me, very silly, as I must send some money to Mama and some to Linette, and repay Haensel the $200 I owe him. The $400 I am going to get for Cleveland and the $300 for Pittsburgh will not be enough to see me through until the premiere.

---

dismissed, but the chastened Mojica survived). Hollywood later embraced his fine voice and dark good looks and he starred in a number of movies between 1928 and 1938. The death of his mother in 1940 impelled him to spend a year in a Franciscan monastery in Peru, and he took holy orders in 1947.

1 George Herbert Mead (1863–1931) was one of the most influential figures in American philosophy and one of the founders of Pragmatism, along with John Dewey and probably its best-known exponent, William James, whose children's tutor he was. Mead's theory of the emergence of mind and self out of the social process of significant communication became the foundation of the symbolic interactionist school of sociology and social psychology. In addition to his social philosophy, Mead's thought includes significant contributions to the philosophy of nature, the philosophy of science, philosophical anthropology, the philosophy of history, and 'process philosophy', by which is understood the theory that an individual's psychology and self-consciousness within the field of his or her experience is intelligible only in terms of social processes.

2 But it was. See below, p. 661.

I learned the Concerto and filled in the missing place in the finale, and at eleven o'clock that night, accompanied by Gottlieb, left by train for Cleveland. Just before leaving I received a cloyingly grateful letter from B.N., who was clearly overjoyed at the resumption of peaceful relations between us. Attached to the letter were some quite respectable verses.

12 November

Early morning in Cleveland, powdered with snow which, however, was gone by noon. Cleveland is a typical good, solid sort of American city. The hall – the Masonic Hall – was excellent and so was the piano. There were, all the same, a few less attractive aspects: I had to get the fee from the manager before the concert, as he is known not always to pay up afterwards, and the programme was shared with Titta Ruffo,[1] a famous baritone, who was dishing up such awful rubbish that it made one feel quite queasy just to look at the programme. Naturally, his name was top of the bill, rightly I must accept, since I am not widely known in Cleveland. In any case, this is all trivial: I came here to earn $400 I badly need, I will play well, and at eleven o'clock this evening I shall get back to Chicago just as quickly as I can.

The concert was at half-past eight. I played well, although I dozed off in the Medtner and forgot to play the piece's middle section. My success was moderate to begin with, but by the end was very big, just as big as Titta's who, as it happened, was not in particularly good voice. Encores were demanded, and I had forgotten to prepare any. However, I still played four. By eleven I was already on the train and on my way back to Chicago.

[1] Titta Ruffo (1877–1953), stage name of Ruffo Cafiero Titta, was one of the most famous, if not the most famous, baritones of his generation. Possessed of a huge, burnished voice – 'voce del leone' – and fabulous good looks, he had not, in 1921, as yet appeared at the New York Met, but when he did the following year he sang another forty-six performances there, covering most of the great roles in Italian and French opera, as well as making a huge number of recordings for Victor, both acoustic and electric. Melba: 'I'm not singing with him. He's too young to be my father.' Ruffo: 'I'm not singing with her. She's too old to be my Gilda.' Some idea of his gifts may be derived from the critic of the *Gramophone* when Nimbus not long ago brought out a remastered CD collection of some of these recordings: 'The world is running out of folk who heard Titta Ruffo in the flesh, so it is a rare experience now to hear at first hand the tales of wonder, to see the eyes grow wide with the marvel of it, to catch that moment's silence while the mind searches for words that might possibly do justice to the miracle.' One of the most attractive features of Titta Ruffo seems to have been his self-awareness, not necessarily a universally encountered characteristic of Italian opera stars universally to be found. Explaining his reluctance to teach (like Caruso, he had had very little formal training), he said: 'I never knew how to sing; that is why my voice went by the time I was fifty. I have no right to capitalise on my former name and reputation and try to teach youngsters something I never knew how to do myself.' By an odd coincidence, when Ruffo's autobiography *La mia parabola* appeared in a Russian translation (*Parabola moyey zhizni: vospominaniya* (Muzyka, Leningrad, 1966) the author of the introductory essay was Prokofiev's former devoted admirer Alexandra Bushen.

13 November

Back in Chicago I remembered the last missing bit of the finale of the Concerto and wrote nearly all of it out. Koshetz was moaning and groaning about all her troubles. Certainly, when one has debts of $11,000 one may be forgiven for waking up in the middle of the night with a cold sweat on the brow. After dinner with the Consul we played bridge: the Consul, Baklanov, Smallens and I. I finished down $9. Not helpful at all. Once I have sent money to Europe I shall have barely enough to live on and pay for my travel to Pittsburgh.

14 November

In the morning I chased round the banks sending 1,000 francs to Mama and 500 francs to Linette, as well as 3,000 marks to Miller. I wanted to cheer her up a bit; this will be quite an event in her life.

At noon there took place the first complete rehearsal of Act One, without the chorus, which needless to say was not ready and no one can tell me when it will be. Smallens accompanied and I conducted. It went well and the singers deserved all praise. The least good is Leander, who has a fine voice but is no use as an actor. He does not understand that Leander must look from the outside like a noble figure but inside is a scoundrel. Clarissa acts well but her voice is too high: she is a mezzo, and the part needs a contralto. I went in search of Coini to see whether there could be another Leander and Clarissa, but today is the first night of the season and Coini is in a state of complete hysteria.

After the rehearsal Koshetz and Gottlieb suggested we go and have lunch together, but my nerves were frayed and I was tired, so I snapped: 'I'm bored with the lot of you!' Koshetz took mortal offence and flew at me in a rage. But it was true, they were all boring me unbearably.

Letters from Linette, Boris Nikolayevich and Balmont, all of which had in their various ways something to upset me. Balmont's situation is quite unendurable, and he does not know where to turn for money. He is extravagantly affectionate. As soon as I have any money, after 15 December, I will send him some, even if it is no more than $100. B.N. is repining with his brother and moaning about it. Linette's letter was cool. This is, however, the proper way forward for our relationship. Otherwise I cannot see what is to become of it.

15 November

Yesterday evening Koshetz telephoned to make peace, but I said I did not feel like it and needed a break from her. Her emotionalism is terribly tiring.

There is no rehearsal today, and I hardly know what to do with myself. I played and put the finishing touches to a Buxtehude fugue, a thing of wonder that I had often played to Balmont during the summer and that excites me every time. Ten years ago, at the suggestion of Taneyev, I had played a fugue by Buxtehude at the Conservatoire, which in my youth earned me among the other students the nickname of The Buddha. This is not the same, but one in an adjacent tonality, D minor. Transcribing it from the organ to the piano and shortening it turned out not to be difficult and was very enjoyable to do.

Reviews from Cleveland. My performance attracted more praise than Ruffo's and my success is an established fact. Tremendous! For Medtner to vanquish 'Toreador' in the American provinces is quite something!

At midnight, when I was just falling asleep, I got a telephone call from Volkov, who was with Koshetz. They had been to the opera together and were now having tea, so thought it would be a good idea to call me. I said: 'I am already sleeping, so wait for a while and I will ring you at half-past four in the morning.' Volkov was upset by this and said: 'Well, in that case we don't have anything to talk about.' With that the conversation ended, I went back to bed regretting that I had offended a blameless wolf.[1]

16 November

Wrote to Volkov so that he should not be angry with me, because it was a storm in a teacup.

Cancelled a singers' rehearsal of Act One. They are prepared now, and could start stage rehearsals, but Coini is dead on his feet from the opening week of the season and it is clear that *Three Oranges* will not have much attention paid to it this week.

I'm no longer on speaking terms with Nipoti, because when I ask him how the chorus rehearsals are going and should I not perhaps come to them, he answers through gritted teeth that there is no need for me to be present and that he is extremely busy with other rehearsals. Smallens's explanation is that composers are always the most dreaded people in the theatre because they can never see beyond their own opera and as far as they are concerned the other thirty-five works in the repertory can go to hell. But one of the choristers, a Russian, told me that the chorus has already gone through the

---

1 The Russian word 'volk', as in Volkov, means 'wolf'.

whole opera, although they do not yet know it by heart. I console myself with the thought that at least things are moving forward.

17 November

Rehearsed Act Two with the Prince and Truffaldino, the first time I had heard the latter. He is a good actor, but I fear has a weak little voice.

In the afternoon, learned the Concerto. Will I manage it in time, or not? I have to believe I will. At eight o'clock that evening, seen off by Gottlieb, I left for Pittsburgh. I sat in the club car and read Gorky.

18 November

Had a not very good night in the sleeping-car. In the morning, Pittsburgh, city of smoke and soot, as it is usually described, although this morning it was a lovely, sunny and remarkably warm day, with only a slight admixture of smoke. Went for a walk in the afternoon, wrote letters and tried the piano. The concert was in the evening.

19 November

By ten in the morning I was back in Chicago, where I was annoyed at Smallens, who has decided that we must make a cut in the second scene of Act Three, just at the point where the Prince and Truffaldino have seen the sign signalling that they are about to encounter the Cook. This would mean losing the whole of Truffaldino's breathless exchange with the Prince against a background of scurrying strings as he creeps towards the kitchen. I took particular pains with this passage, because it ought to be very effective on the stage, and the music is not bad either. Smallens, however, insists that the music is no good and the action is dramatically uninteresting, to which I retort that it was merely difficult to learn and he was too lazy to make the effort.

There had been no rehearsals while I was away, and it is obvious that *Oranges* has been in hibernation for a week. Nevertheless, I decided to maintain a policy of silence on the subject: it makes little difference whether it opens on 1 or 10 December, just so long as it is not on the 17th when it would clash with the Third Piano Concerto. Incidentally, Spangler has gone (why?) and has been replaced, according to some, by Shaw, and according to others, by Johnson. It would be interesting, if it was Johnson!

Went to the Symphony concert in the evening and became very nervous thinking that in three weeks' time I shall be the soloist, and the Concerto is not yet in my fingers.

20 November

Buckled down to serious efforts to learn the Concerto; it is really time to concentrate the mind, particularly as the opera has got stuck.

Read *Latest News*.[1] I thought I would find in it interesting information about theatrical events, but instead there emanated from its pages such a breath of horror from Russia and Constantinople[2] that it seemed shameful that while such misery was being endured there, life here should be concerned with something as unimportant as the *Oranges* production. But how could anything I do be of help? There may be a tinge of justification (formal! purely formal!) in that a consequence of the products of my brain may give cause to celebrate the name of Russia and Russian art. But such a justification is a purely political concept, all humanitarian considerations have been swept out with the tide.

In the afternoon I went to Rachmaninoff's concert, a second-rate programme which he played simply magnificently. I went back to see him afterwards, he seemed younger and more sanguine, joked and wanted me to stay near him. He asked how the production was going. We did not actually have much chance to talk as people kept coming up to him and interrupting us. ('Please don't go away, we must go on talking', he smiled. 'Maybe that will put them off and they won't bother me.') I should send him *Tales of an Old Grandmother*, perhaps they will mean something to him and he will have a better opinion of my compositions than he has done up to now.

In the evening I went with Koshetz and Gottlieb to the Rosenthals', where there was a colourful guest list and a film show for entertainment. I sat on a little sofa with the Princess Linette,[3] who flirted openly with me. Peace has broken out between Koshetz and me. She was in the box next to mine, together with Rachmaninoff's wife, and inevitably they were immediately 'introduced' to one another. Mme Rachmaninoff flushed bright red and displayed such agitation that Koshetz asked me: 'What was that all about?'

21 November

Practised the Concerto. Went into Smallens's rehearsal with Truffaldino. Smallens was in a bad temper: I thought he had gone no further than raise

---

[1] *Latest News* (*Posledniye Novosti*) was the Russian émigré newspaper edited between 1920 and 1940 in Paris by Pavel Milyukov, the former leader of the Constitutional Democrats (Kadets), friend and political associate of Prokofiev's friend Gessen, who edited the sister organ *Rul'* (*The Helm*) in Berlin.

[2] Wrangel's army and the thousands of Russians fleeing the Bolsheviks were finally evacuated from Sevastopol on 14 March 1921, in the first instance to arrive as refugees in Constantinople.

[3] That is, the singer taking the role of Princess Linetta in *The Love for Three Oranges*.

the possibility of the cut, but apparently he has already excised it from the piano score. I said that so long as it was just a joke it was acceptable, but if he was actually proposing that the passage be omitted I formally forbade it.

Coini, who up till now has been so busy it has not been possible to speak to him, informed me that *Oranges* was now scheduled for the evening of 17 December, with a general rehearsal on the afternoon of the 16th. It would be hard to conceive anything more awkward, since at both these times I shall be involved in the first performance of my Third Piano Concerto with the Chicago Symphony and conducting the 'Classical' Symphony. Coini said that in that case it would be possible to postpone the first night for three days. Furthermore, he said that there would be no time in the present week to begin stage rehearsals. It is now essential that I see Garden, otherwise *Oranges* is going to collapse altogether.

In the evening Koshetz and I were honoured guests at some kind of women's club dinner, at which the majority of other guests were old ladies.

22 November

Practised the Concerto. Not bad, it is beginning to come together. If I really concentrate all my efforts I shall be able to learn it in time.

Koshetz has a rendezvous with Garden at eleven o'clock. I wanted to take advantage of it to see Garden as well, but she did not appear in the theatre at all.

In the afternoon one of last night's ladies appeared, a pianist who has given recitals in a number of provincial cities playing an extremely modern programme, including my *Sarcasms*. Today she wanted to take advantage of my presence to play it to me and get from me any suggestions I might have. She was not bad at all, really quite good.

23 November

Lunch with Carpenter. He played me his new small ballet. Of course it is not first class, and the taste is not always irreproachable, but it is an entertaining and accomplished piece of work.

Coini said that stage rehearsals were not likely to start next week either, which made me determined to speak to Garden at all costs, otherwise *Oranges* will not get to the stage before January. But how is this to be achieved? No doubt on purpose in order to avoid being pestered she has no secretary and no regular hours for receiving visitors. Finally someone told me that the only way to get access to her was through Pater,[1] so I told him of

---

1 Presumably one of the Chicago Opera administrators.

my wish to see the Director. His response was that this was one of the most difficult things of all to achieve. But I insisted, saying: 'However that may be, I absolutely must see her.' Pater promised that he would see her tomorrow and find out when Mary could grant me an interview.

24 November

Practised the concerto. Had a headache. Went for a walk.

A grand evening at Rosenthal's, along the lines of the previous year except that this year Koshetz sang. I also played a couple of pieces. There was a heterogeneous guest list, and it was not too boring an occasion. Koshetz sang one of her songs, and I marvelled anew how it could be so fresh and so beautiful. She is obviously telling the truth and the song truly did manifest itself through the tapping of the table (if she is fibbing, then there is no way of explaining the difference between this and what she produced in Moscow, they are chalk and cheese). If she herself was knocking the table it would be impossible randomly to produce beautiful music.

But if the music really is being dictated from 'out there', how is it that her instructor has been given the ability to create beautiful music? This was the question I asked Koshetz on our way home. Her answer was that she had been told on one occasion that her teacher had in a previous incarnation been Schumann, but she was not sure whether or not to believe it, since in the course of any séance many false statements are always included among those that are true. This is an interesting explanation, but if it really was Schumann, why have her songs turned out so Russian? This would be plausible if the creative flow were emanating from 'out there' and being incarnated through Nina's music-making, but Koshetz apparently does nothing except literally take down dictation.

25 November

Went to see Pater to find out when my rendezvous with Mary was to happen. He said: 'She is on stage right now, rehearsing *Carmen*, and this would be the best time to fix it up with her.' I said I would have thought it was actually the very last moment to interrupt her, but he insisted: 'I assure you, now is the time. Go and speak to her.' Reluctantly I did so, and Mary immediately came rushing up to me with every sign of pleasure, and enquired: 'How are our *Oranges*?' My response was to pull a bit of a long face and to ask when I might have a chance to see her and talk about it. Mary said: 'Not just now, come to my house on Sunday.' 'What time?' At this point Mary leapt back on to the stage shouting: 'You see, I don't have a notebook!'

This annoyed me, and I decided I would have to put my request in writing, but then I thought better of it and waited for her to come back. This she did, and asked: 'Do you need me for long?' 'Five minutes.' 'Well, come on Sunday at noon. Hold on, I'll write down my address for you.'

While she was writing, I said: 'I'll make sure I have my watch with me when I come.' She frowned. 'Who?' 'My watch.' 'Oh, that's all right then.'

I kissed her hand and we parted.

At Carpenter's invitation I delivered a lecture on *Three Oranges* in English to a fashionable, predominantly female audience at five o'clock in a club of which Mme McCormick was President. Note: in English! Last year Marinuzzi had spoken on the subject of his opera, and hardly anyone had understood a word he said. I was nervous, as it was the first time I had spoken in public in English, but all went well.

I began by saying that I divided the women of Chicago into two groups: those in the first group know that I am a crazy Futurist and that was why I had given my opera its ridiculous title, and those in the second assume my reason for doing so was to parody another opera performed here last year, *L'amore dei tre re*.[1] Neither group is right, for the title *Love for Three Oranges* is considerably older than either Futurism or the *Three Kings* opera, in fact it is older than Chicago itself since it existed as a folk tale in Italy as long ago as the sixteenth, or even fifteenth century. I then told them the story of the tale itself, something about Gozzi, and finally my own libretto. The lecture lasted an hour, and when it was finished I got a respectable amount of applause. The room was not big enough for everyone who wanted to get in.

26 November

Practised the Concerto. Embarked on writing down a few little melodic ideas. While *Oranges* is fresh in my mind I must make a concert suite from it, or at least draw up a plan for one.

In the evening, bridge at Baklanov's: twenty-four rubbers from eight in the evening until half-past two in the morning. I was down on the evening, and was cleaned out of $18.

---

1 Opera (1913) by Italo Montemezzi to a pastiche-archaic libretto by the playwright Sein Benelli. Now a rarity, in the years after its premiere at La Scala it was extremely popular, especially in America following its introduction to New York audiences by Toscanini the year after its Italian premiere. Mary Garden and Rosa Ponselle were among those who were drawn to its heady d'Annunzio-inspired atmosphere of erotic decadence and Montemezzi's lush, Wagnerian score. The heroine Fiora was the only role Mary Garden ever sang in Italian.

27 November

Rose later than usual after last night's bridge. At noon I went to Mary's home, which is a delightful apartment on the lake shore with a stylish footman. Mary was not in when I arrived, but I was welcomed by her sister (not the one with whom I had corresponded during the summer, who had always been very civil to me). Mrs Walsh (this sister) told me that Mary was a keen bridge-player and that some time later in the week we should have a session. Mary then appeared and asked me to stay for lunch. Regarding *Oranges* she declared that it was the most important event of the season and that its first night would be no later than 23 December, which was an excellent date for a first night, and that all Chicago would be there.

My business with her I formulated thus: the chorus's learning of their part had to be completed quickly and there needed to be at least two rehearsals a week on stage, otherwise there was no hope of mounting the production in time, or at least doing so only superficially, and the result would be a muddle. Frowning, Mary said that everything necessary would be put in hand at once. I departed, in thrall to her personality.

Received a letter from B.N., very affectionate and happy at my recent expression of the strength of our friendship.

28 November

Going down to breakfast and thinking about what letters might have arrived for me, I felt sure that there would not be any, or at least not interesting ones. But waiting for me was a letter from Vera Miller, and what a letter! It had a quite earth-shattering effect on me, which lasted more or less all day. I determined to wait a few days before replying, so as not to make a fool of myself.

Yesterday's meeting with Garden has already borne fruit: Coini met me with a beaming smile and spent an hour and a half working with me on the scenario of the last act, which we have not done before. Tomorrow I have an orchestra rehearsal scheduled, which I do not particularly need but which has no doubt been arranged to shut my mouth.

Stage rehearsals will not start until the 12th, that is to say ten days before the first night! It is good news that Mary has invited me to dinner on Thursday, we shall be able to have another talk.

29 November

In the morning I studied the score in preparation for the rehearsal, which was from one o'clock until three. We played through three acts with relatively few stops. It sounds very well. Afterwards I was half dead from fatigue and lay down in my room, drinking tea. I played the piano very little today, although I really have to keep it up.

In the evening Garden's sister (I believe she is engaged to Baklanov) invited me to her box to hear *Monna Vanna*,[1] but seemed rather put out when I criticised the music of the opera and professed myself astonished that singers as good as Garden, Baklanov and Muratore[2] would waste their efforts on such rubbish. Incidentally, also in the cast were my royal characters, the Prince and the King. The Prince looks like an oil painting but in the large theatre auditorium neither voice sounded as good as they had seemed to me in the rehearsal room.

Yesterday my portrait appeared in the *Daily News* with the caption 'the best-dressed man in Chicago'. On the strength of it I went about with a real swagger.

30 November

A free day, so that I could really get down to practising the Concerto. At two o'clock I played it to Stock, for him to get an idea of the tempi. Stock was very enthusiastic about the Concerto and plans to play it through with the orchestra in five days' time. He asked me if I could somehow or other manage to play the piano part then as well. That is quite a tall order, especially as I am nowhere near ready yet!

This afternoon, when I went to have tea with Koshetz, she started talking about spiritualism and read me the Credo that had been dictated to her during one of the séances. I drew attention to the fact that all the words contained the letter 's', and sometimes the letter 'sh',[3] which lent a rustling, sibilant sort of sound to the whole phrase, an aspect of versifying much exploited by Balmont. Koshetz then became very interested in who my 'protector' might be, and without further ado sat down at her spiritualist table. To do this she sat on the floor stretching out her legs in front of her and leaning her back against the bed placed both palms on a light, low table resting on her knees. After a few seconds the table started to rock. I sat sprawling out on the sofa opposite, not wishing to alter my pose. Koshetz began to read the

---

1 Opera (1909), described as a *drame lyrique*, by Henri Février to Maeterlinck's eponymous play. The action takes place in besieged fifteenth-century Pisa, where the defending commander Guido learns from his father that the foe will end the siege and even turn the battle against his own forces if Guido's wife Monna Vanna will come to the besiegers' tent alone that night, clad only in a mantle. In 1908 Rachmaninoff completed in vocal score one act of a projected three-act opera to a libretto by his friend Mikhail Slonov, but had to abandon the project when Maeterlinck withheld permission for his text to be used, his publishers, Heugel, having assigned international opera rights exclusively to Février. No disrespect to the French composer, but what a loss to Russian opera.

2 Lucien Muratore (1878–1954) had started his stage career as an actor with matinee-idol looks, playing leading roles in Sarah Bernhardt's company, but for several years between 1913 and 1922 was Chicago's, and Mary Garden's, favourite tenor, an outstanding Faust and Samson and in the French repertoire generally, until an acrimonious disagreement over what Muratore considered his exclusive preserve of Samson ended the relationship early in 1922, one more casualty of Mary Garden's autocratic style of management.

3 In the Russian alphabet this is one, independent, letter.

alphabet. The table lifted and tilted towards her and then at a given letter fell slowly back into position. It would have been possible to induce it to do this deliberately, but I was quite ready to accept that the table was moving independently of Koshetz's will.

The first word it began to spell out was 'napara . . .' and I was sure it was going to be 'naprasno', but it eventually turned out to be 'napravo'.[1] Koshetz, as if reading my thoughts, exclaimed: 'I thought it was going to be "naprasno".' When the whole phrase was completed it read: 'To your right is standing Uchshikay' (Koshetz's protector, who lived under this name in the fifth century AD. After a few questions of a preliminary nature, Koshetz asked who my protector was. The answer was: Uchshikay. Koshetz was wild with excitement at learning that, in the first place, we had the same protector, and in the second that mine should be such a wonderful person. She added: 'You see, in one of his incarnations he was Schumann.'

At this I asked (addressing my question not to the table but to Koshetz) why so evidently enlightened an individual as Ushchikay should have later been incarnated in the body of so manifestly unenlightened a person as Schumann? Koshetz passed on this question to the table, and the answer was as follows: Uchshikay was not enlightened. This led me to contemplate a further question: if Uchshikay was no more an enlightened person than Schumann was, how could he be regarded as a protector and teacher? But before I could formulate this enquiry in words, the table rocked vigorously three times. Koshetz said: 'It is asking for the alphabet', and began reading the letters. The resulting sentence was to the effect that before posing questions of this sort, first I should better acquaint myself with the theosophical literature. So I was being put in my place: don't engage in debates on subjects about which you know nothing.

This rebuke was followed by another phrase, this time directed at me: 'If you wish to hear me, you must clear your mind of clutter by means of faith and reading theosophy.' I said: 'But I do not wish to hear you, because the world I see before my eyes is clear and bright enough for me not to risk throwing myself into the abyss of doubt that is spiritualism.' This elicited an astounding response: 'Sergey, you do not yet feel me, but I say to you, in the words of your poet: "Remember me!"'[2] With that the séance ended, and I

---

[1] 'Naprasno' in Russian means 'in vain', pointless. 'Napravo' means 'on the right'.
[2] A reference to Pushkin's famous ballad 'The Lay of Oleg's Prophecy' ('Pesn' o veshchem Olege'), which retells the legend of the ninth-century Prince Oleg of Novgorod and Kiev, whose death at the hands of his beloved horse is foretold by a soothsayer. To forestall the prophecy Oleg sends his beloved stallion away, bidding him a tearful farewell with the words: 'Adieu, my comrade, my faithful servant,/The time has come when we must part;/Rest now, no longer shall my foot enter thy gilded stirrup,/Farewell! Grieve not – but remember me!' Years later Oleg learns that the honoured animal has died, and asks to see his remains. As his boot touches the horse's bleached skull a venomous snake emerges and bites him, causing Oleg's death.

went home deeply stirred, mainly on account of this last utterance. Everything that preceded it could be discounted, but the beauty of this phrase stays with me, an incontestable treasure!

1 December

A damp, rainy day with dark, lowering clouds. My head ached and the work proceeded slowly and laboriously. In the afternoon Smallens was rehearsing all the Act Two ensembles, but as this was the first time the singers will have sung them together I am not being asked to attend until tomorrow. Baklanov passed on to me the information that the dinner with Garden is cancelled. The arrangements for both the dinner and the bridge game afterwards were being made by Garden's sister, and since I had been churlish enough the day before yesterday in her box to criticise the opera she had invited me to attend, I expect this is the reason the bridge was aborted as well. In one way it is good news, as I have a bad headache, but in another it is to be regretted because it would have been a good opportunity to remind Mary about the rehearsals.

The opera company's office was very willing to advance me $500 from the $1,000 I am due to receive on the 15th.

2 December

I sent Koussevitzky the £75 I owe him. I wanted to send Mama 2,000 francs, but the franc has just leapt up in value so I postponed the purchase until Monday. Gottlieb borrowed $50 from me. The $500 is disappearing fast. We rehearsed the ensembles: those in Act One went well. Koshetz came to the rehearsal and also thought the singers knew their parts well. When I wanted to practise the Concerto (I must concentrate on it for the rehearsal on Monday) they asked me not to play as there was a sick woman in the next-door room. In the evening I practised in Koshetz's room, while Koshetz sat at her spiritualist table writing down a song – inasmuch as she was doing any of the writing, rather taking down dictation independently of her own self. All the same I found it surprising that she imagined she could do it at all, seeing that someone was playing completely different music in the same room. And indeed, on this occasion the table did not produce a single note.

Koshetz was very enthusiastic about the Concerto, and later, when I had finished practising, she told me that as she had been concentrating hard to receive dictation for her song, Uchshikay suddenly vouchsafed, via the table: 'I like the Concerto too.' This is unbelievable! However, I am quite certain that Koshetz is not telling lies and that if she told me this was said, the table must have genuinely tapped it out to her.

3 December

I went to have my photograph taken by the opera company's photographer, and then took the orchestral material of the Concerto to the Symphony's office. At eleven o'clock there was a singers' rehearsal of Acts One and Two. I conducted, and Smallens accompanied. Relations between Smallens and me are now on a more civil, and correct, footing, because at one point earlier he was insolent to me and I checked him sharply. The singers know their parts well. But when, oh God, when, will we have any stage rehearsals? I am advised that I should have another word with Garden, but I do not want to importune her.

Koshetz and I went to see Chaliapin, who arrived in Chicago yesterday; Koshetz rang him up and he invited both of us to come together. Chaliapin is as superb as ever, greying slightly round the temples and a little depressed because since getting to America he has been plagued by a cold. In New York he was not in very good voice and to date has already cancelled seven concerts. And now with a concert coming up tomorrow, right on cue starts another cold.

I asked about Meyerhold, Asafyev, Myaskovsky. About the last-named he had not heard anything, Asafyev now has a prominent position with the Mariinsky Theatre, Meyerhold is ill with, alas, consumption. And I so badly want him to produce *Oranges* some day. We went out together with Chaliapin; he is such a magnificent figure of a man that everywhere we went people turned to look at him.

In the afternoon I worked long and hard at the Concerto, and played bridge in the evening: twenty-four rubbers, and a catastrophe: a loss of $38! Koshetz says she has heard all sorts of gossip about *Three Oranges* flying round the theatre: one rumour has it that the production will be postponed once again, another that the composer is an impossible character, while in fact, exceptionally, I am being irreproachably courteous in all my dealings with the singers and the orchestra.

4 December

Rehearsal at eleven o'clock, again Acts One and Two which the singers have learnt. Next came some good news: Coini announced that the first stage rehearsal would take place the day after tomorrow, and as the chorus now knew its part rehearsals would henceforward always take place on the stage except when it was needed for current repertoire rehearsals. At last! Obviously, my conversation with Garden has helped.

A congratulatory telegram from Linette for the first performance (I had earlier written that it was to be on the 5th). Probably she has only just received my 1,500 francs. The telegram left an unexpected feeling of bitterness. It is so long since Linette wrote that she has become very remote from me. I cannot marry Linette as she wants me to do, but to continue our relationship is to go on hearing, or at least sensing, her complaints that I am ruining her reputation. But the telegram served as a reminder that she, at least, wishes the relationship to continue.

In the afternoon and evening I practised the Concerto, declining a dinner invitation from the Volkovs.

5 December

Rehearsal with Stock. Wisely, he has decided to go through the work with the orchestra well in advance. He wanted me to play the solo piano part, but in the first place the piano had no pedals as the lyre had been broken off when the piano was brought on to the stage, and in the second I do not yet thoroughly know the piece. Some passages are fine, but in others I go wrong when I am together with the orchestra. But Stock was not asking for a note-perfect performance, and I spent more time beside him on the podium looking at the score. The accompaniment sounded soft and pleasant. Stock was very complimentary, and the orchestra clapped me at the end. In general the Concerto has turned out much better than I thought it was going to do when I was composing it during the summer.

At one o'clock I got some good news: I was asked in to listen to the chorus, which was now said to be completely ready and in three days' time would have their music off by heart. Hurrah, the production has advanced a step forward to the first night. Nipoti has been meticulously making them learn every individual note of the passage where Koshetz curses the Prince, and was most disgruntled when I asked them merely to swoop up and down, confining accuracy to the top and bottom notes but nothing in between.

In the afternoon and evening I practised the Concerto with the score, taking careful note of the orchestra's material so that next time I would not make mistakes. I don't wish to emulate a well-brought-up provincial young lady who has been slaving away at her solo part without having an inkling of what the orchestra does.

6 December

Today is a big day – my first stage rehearsal. We worked intensively from ten until one, and got through almost all Act One. Anisfeld's throne has been placed in its position on the stage, Smallens accompanied on the piano, I conducted, the prompter – a very nice Frenchman – by my side, and Coini darting out now and then from behind his producer's desk. Things went with a swing from the word go, as the singers by now know the music well and in addition are having their chance to demonstrate their excellence as performers. When we rehearsed the scene with the King, the Prince and Truffaldino, everyone burst out laughing. Coini is not as bad as I thought, at least from the technical point of view, and even came up with a really amusing sort of hopping jump when Pantalone hurls himself at Leander with cries of 'Traitor!' Altogether I was extremely well satisfied.

In the afternoon there was a music rehearsal of Act Three. The Princesses are endearing creatures. Ninetta (Dusseau)[1] has a gloriously pure voice. Linette would just suit this part! Smallens has after all carefully coached Pantalone and Truffaldino in the passage he wanted to cut, so I am happy about that.

I came across a copy of the libretto they have printed in French and English, evidently from two years ago. Oh horrors! They have laid the text out as if it were poetry, starting each sentence on a new line. How dared they do this without consulting me?!

During the break I practised the piano for two hours.

7 December

The second stage rehearsal. For some reason they also called the people needed for Acts Two and Three, but after an hour and a half on the third scene of Act One let everyone go. Coini had several good ideas, but often failed to grasp what is really needed and sometimes lapses into vulgarity. But at least he always listened when I took him off to a corner to explain what should be done. He took me to task for having written too much music between the point when Leander catches sight of Smeraldina and the moment when she begins to sing. I explained that this was a confrontation between them: Smeraldina is trying to creep away like a mouse while Leander is standing over her like a large predator. Once I had explained it, this is how it was done.

People are still insisting that the first night is not going to be on the 23rd, but the 30th. Oh well, it can't be helped!

I played the Concerto right through quite acceptably, and for the first time felt it could be a success.

8 December

Rehearsed with the chorus, which is doing fine, my misgivings were unfounded. In the afternoon I went through Act Three with the singers,

---

1 Jeanne Dusseau, born Ruth Thom in Glasgow in 1893, but brought up and trained in Canada.

who now know it by heart. I hear rumours that the Prince's spitting in the bedroom scene will be banned, as Americans, hypocrites that they are, would be shocked to see this on stage. I was very agitated: how dare they decide this without me!

Practised the piano for two or three hours, but felt rather tired. What will I be like in ten days' time, though?

A letter from Mama, in which she described the success the *Scythian Suite* had under Koussevitzky in the Grand Opéra in Paris on 24 November. Ravel sat next to Mama and exclaimed 'Vive la Russie', to which she replied 'Vive la France.' Linette and Boris Bashkirov were there with her. This mention of Linette once more made me feel uncomfortable. It is an illusion that our relationship has drifted apart and will not arrive at a fulfilment of some kind. But how can I marry if I am convinced it will not bring me happiness?

9 December

Today's stage rehearsal, the third, began with a conflict between me and Coini. Without discussing it with me he flatly told the Prince that instead of spitting he was to sneeze. I said tersely that I would not permit this change. The fight then began in earnest, during which all the singers fell silent. Coini attempted to bring the full weight of his authority to bear, screaming was he or was he not in charge of the stage?! I replied that when I was dead he would be free to mangle my opera as he wished, but the reason for my presence just now was to prevent this happening.[1] This escalated to: 'In that case the opera will not be produced at all!' and my riposte that 'this should have been thought of when the contract was agreed.'

Realising that the heavy artillery was not going to lead to victory, Coini calmed down and said that such a trifling matter was not worth all this discussion, and that sneezing was no less effective than spitting, it was simply more acceptable behaviour. I in turn, seeing that he was moderating his tone, also softened and said that in situations of this kind changes should first be discussed with the composer, and only then instructions given to the singers. Coini conceded yet another moral point by explaining that the idea had only come to him late yesterday evening, and his action in proposing it directly to the Prince had been governed purely by a desire to save time. The end result was that after a twenty-minute stand-off I agreed to the sneezing, and to give Coini his due, the way he staged it was very amusing.

After this the rehearsal proceeded very productively with no more

---

[1] In the 1941 *Short Autobiography* Prokofiev quotes (possibly with the benefit of hindsight) a more cutting riposte to Coini's infuriated demand to know who was the boss on stage: 'You are – to carry out my wishes.' (*Kratkaya Avtobiografiya*, in Shlifshteyn, op. cit.)

contretemps, Coini even mining an unexpected vein of inventiveness, and if I took issue with any of his suggestions he was quite willing to revise it according to my wishes. The rehearsal lasted from eleven o'clock until four, five hours with a forty-minute break for lunch. Then I had a rest, and in the evening went to *Carmen*, in which I did not especially care for Garden in the title role.

I played the piano very little today, about an hour, but there are no rehearsals tomorrow so I shall practise all day.

10 December

A free day from rehearsals, which I used for detailed work on the Concerto. I practised for three hours, the most I can do. Koshetz and I were honoured guests at a dinner in some women's club; I played the 'Gavotte' after the meal and then fled to Baklanov's to play bridge. After we had played sixteen rubbers I got embroiled in an argument: St Leger, an extremely nice Englishman who is one of the repetiteurs and an excellent bridge-player, made a whole series of egregious mistakes which I made no bones about pointing out to him. An excessively proud man, he thereupon announced that he would play no more, and began totting up his score. Deaf to all entreaties, he stopped playing. At this I got up from the table, said goodbye to all present except St Leger, and left. The result: early on I was up $14, but later – oh dear! – down the same amount.

11 December

Got up late, as yesterday's bridge had kept me up until 2 a.m. Practised the Concerto and played it through with the score so as to fix firmly in my memory what the orchestra was doing. I have not made a two-piano reduction, so cannot play it through with anyone. At three o'clock there was another *Oranges* rehearsal, this time not on stage, with the singers in Acts Two and Three. Although it was a Sunday, we carried on working until almost six o'clock. A stage rehearsal had been scheduled for eight o'clock, but Coini was ill and had lost his voice, and it was cancelled. During the rehearsal that did take place the singers were often convulsed with laughter. Pantalone, Truffaldino and the Cook are all splendid comedians and throw themselves into the play with abandon.

St Leger sent me a note of apology, and we met again as friends.

The first crop of reviews of the *Scythian Suite* has arrived from Paris. It seems the work had met not only with applause but also protests from some quarters in the audience, people even demonstratively walking out, reminiscent of the good old days of Glazunov. After the unanimous success of the

April performance, this surprised me. But that is just the point: in April the audience was largely composed of Russians, while now it was French. Russians are already educated to Prokofiev, while the French have not yet reached this level.

12 December

I was woken at seven thirty, and by nine was already at the rehearsal for the Concerto. This time the piano had pedals, but it was still not a concert grand and its action was unbearably stiff. Stock was serious and attentive, and his tempi were moderate, which suited me very well as it was easier to play the notes. We worked until almost one o'clock. I tried not to listen to the orchestra (and found it interesting to concentrate solely on the piano part). Generally speaking, things were beginning to come together and there are only a few passages, perhaps five, that continue to defeat me. After two rehearsals it is going, if one cannot exactly say well, then at least respectably. All the same, I do not yet have an overall view of the Concerto because I am still too preoccupied with the technical hurdles of performing it. After the Concerto I went through the 'Classical' Symphony, which was splendidly played. Altogether, one could not wish for a better orchestra!

From this rehearsal I almost had to run to the next, in the theatre, and arrived on stage just as it was beginning. The stage was crowded to overflowing, as they had brought on the full chorus and even the ballet for the Little Devils. The ballet dancers were a sight for sore eyes, as they were all aged about sixteen or seventeen and looked a picture in their light dance slips. But even more interesting was the fact that today, for the first time, they had fitted up the scenery for Act One, and the towers. The settings are original and marvellously done, and Anisfeld's colours simply leap out at you even without proper theatre lighting.

Coini was busy getting the Tragicals and the Comicals into groups and handing out umbrellas, spades, palm branches. He had almost completely lost his voice and spoke through a megaphone, spraying his throat continually. We began the rehearsal with the Prologue. The chorus knew their parts perfectly and got everything right. Coini dealt with them efficiently, but needless to say it was beyond his powers of imagination to devise appropriate gestures for each group. Thank God he listened to everything I said to him, even though he tried to teach me my business when he insisted that these were choristers, not soloists. Nevertheless, all in all the rehearsal, which lasted from eleven until four with a break for lunch, was a spirited and invigorating occasion, frequently interrupted by gales of laughter from those taking part.

I was thoroughly immersed in the production, did not feel in the least tired, and derived the keenest satisfaction from it.

Afterwards I slept, and then spent the evening working out a simplified version for the passages in the Concerto that I had not been able to manage today, because there is obviously no hope of mastering them by Friday as they stand.

13 December

It is now settled that *Oranges* will be presented on the 30th, but now that rehearsals are under way with such *élan* I do not particularly care whether the performance is a week earlier or later. Today there was another large-scale rehearsal on stage with the chorus and the ballet – Act Two and almost all of Act Three. Working out the 'divertissements' in Act Two took up a seemingly interminable amount of time.[1] I had three furious rows with Coini: once because he found first that there was not enough, and then that there was too much music for the entrance of the Empty-Heads; next over the way the Cook discovers Truffaldino (in both of these conflicts I got my way after putting my foot down); and finally a tragic-comic incident occasioned by the little trolleys on which the three Oranges make their entrance squeaking so loudly that the Prince could not be heard when he started to sing. Coini's only solution was to ask me to write more music to cover the noise, to which I replied that I was not going to write good music merely to drown out a noise, and that those useless trucks for the Oranges would have to be remade. Coini said: 'Je m'en fiche des oranges.' I replied: 'Vous vous en foutez de votre business.'[2] We compromised on the curtain going up eight bars earlier, which provided more music, and Coini will put the Oranges' trucks in to the workshop for modifications. As we left, he said: 'Eh bien, sans rancune!'[3]

14 December

Third rehearsal of the Concerto. It is all going smoothly (for the orchestra) but I am still hitting wrong notes and twice completely lost the place, although I am getting to grips with the work and beginning to master it. The Symphony is fine. When I got home I lay down, tired out.

There is a whole saga going on about the costumes for the opera: instead of thirty women and fifteen men Courtiers, they have done them the other way round, and the tone of voice in which they informed me of this fact was as much as to say that I was to blame. Thank God, Anisfeld arrives on the 23rd.

---

1 The entertainments Truffaldino has dreamed up to try to make the Prince laugh in the great courtyard of the Royal Palace.
2 'I don't give two hoots about the oranges.' 'You don't give a damn about your job, either.'
3 'Well, no hard feelings!'

In the afternoon there was supposed to have been a rehearsal with the ballet dancers, but as some of them have been called for a rehearsal of *Salome*, ours could not take place. I saw the end of *Salome*, and although I know the story well I still found it terrifying. The music does seem to heighten the effect, but I need to listen to the whole of the opera. I have the impression it is too long.

15 December

Continued rehearsing the Oranges from the point where they come on. Coini's solution to them making so much noise is that they should not move at all. The Princesses sang well. While Ninetta was singing I remembered the letter Linette had sent me and thought how happy she would be to be singing this role in Chicago. Happy is hardly the word. It would have been lovely, but so far I do not have enough influence in the Chicago Opera, and what will happen in future years remains to be seen. Not only that, but I am not absolutely sure just what voice Linette has, and they tend to pick singers with smaller voices from here in America, to save the bother of importing them from overseas.

At one o'clock I had to leave the rehearsal and pass the baton to a delighted Smallens, in order to go to the general rehearsal of the Concerto. It gets better each time we rehearse it, but it is still not good enough. The Symphony is excellent. When I finished that rehearsal I came home, changed, rubbed myself down with eau de Cologne and went back on stage, where after the lunch break they were still working around the Oranges. Coini wants to dispense with the final dashing around in the last scene. I can see that the narrow wings of the theatre make it impossible to do what I had envisaged, so I gave Coini carte blanche to do what he thought best, demanding only that everyone in the chorus should run around like mad. Coini muttered irritably into his beard and complained that it would ruin the entire production, and that there was too much music, but as I proved unshakeable he eventually rehearsed them like this and even ran around with them.

In the evening, despite my tiredness, I worried away at a passage in the Concerto. During dinner (with Koshetz, and Roerich, who had come in from New York) I mentioned Balmont, from whom I had just received a delicious letter. Koshetz interjected the phrase: 'Well, we know poets who are better than Balmont', and this made me see red. I realised that Koshetz was referring to Uchshikay. Uchshikay does indeed have a beautiful turn of phrase, but this does not give her the right to speak thus of Balmont. Not only that, but the inference of her whole expression was 'people like us, initiates'. I am perfectly willing to believe that Koshetz has access to a well-spring of knowledge denied to me, but neither does that confer on her the right to use such a tone.

Nevertheless, I held myself in check out of respect for Roerich, but when he had gone and Koshetz was also getting ready to leave, she suddenly stopped and wanted to know why I was so morose. 'I didn't like the way you were speaking of Balmont,' I said. Koshetz said she was only joking. I said: 'There are jokes, and there are jokes. And now please go away.' This was enough to set her off on a ten-minute tirade, the result of which was an idiotic argument in which I was harsh enough to conclude every point by asking her to 'go now, please, I am asking you to go away'. After a frenzied shouting match she did eventually withdraw in a violent rage, leaving me in much the same state.

Back in my room I thought for a long time about what had caused me to lose my temper so violently, and eventually came to the conclusion that Koshetz was in the wrong: it is all very well to venerate Uchshikay to one's heart's content, but this is no reason to disparage Balmont, the very Balmont whom Uchshikay himself cites with approval. I even went so far as to contemplate ringing up Koshetz to explain this to her properly, but at that very moment an idea for a story came to me and I spent the next two hours working at it.[1] Oh, my lovely stories, so long have I forsaken you! By then it was already half-past twelve, and too late to ring.

16 December

The concert was at half-past two. I decided I must play with total concentration, not hurrying, making sure I play everything perfectly, and most importantly paying no attention to the orchestra. Making this resolution dispelled all my nerves, and the first movement went very well. The hall was full (the Friday afternoon orchestral concerts are always full) and the audience applauded quite heartily, considering most of them were white-gloved ladies.[2] In the second and third movements I made a few slips, but in the end it was all quite satisfactory and was met with, not overwhelming success, but good all the same: I was called out three times. The reception for the Symphony was warmer.

I then went home, followed by Gottlieb and Smallens, both very enthusiastic. I changed my clothes and rested before the first general rehearsal of the music of *Oranges* with the full complement of orchestra, chorus and soloists but seated rather than with the action on stage. It went extremely well and gave me great pleasure, although I was utterly exhausted afterwards. I had the impression that the chorus and soloists were barely audible behind the orchestra, but it always seems like that from the conductor's podium, and contrary to what I had thought the singers came up to me to thank me

---

1 'Death of the Watchmaker'.
2 In English.

for not drowning them. Present at the rehearsal was Milyukov,[1] who has been in Chicago for a few days and is leaving today. He sat and listened with the vocal score I had given him, and liked the opera very much. He was apparently particularly impressed by the passion and conviction with which the principals sang their parts. In two weeks' time he will be on his way back to Paris, where he will pass on his impressions.

17 December

The reviews hardly reflected the success the concert had been. They all praised the Symphony but among the dolts there was not one who valued the Concerto for what it was. One or two, not more, attempted some sort of analysis of the Concerto, but they were way off target. The truth is that America has excellent symphony orchestras and their programme booklets contain well-informed commentaries, but criticism is an entirely hit-or-miss affair and the pity is that so many people pay attention to it.

I was so tired after yesterday that I had two sleeps between lunch and dinner, and in between practised the difficult passages and wrote to Mama and to Linette. In the evening the concert was repeated, and this time my performance would have near enough got me a five.[2] The applause was greater than the day before's, as is only to be expected since in the evening a higher proportion of the audience is men, who clap louder. Secondly, the audience had by then read the reviews and thereby been told whether the work merited applause or not, and could thus avoid getting it wrong and looking foolish. The Symphony again was the more successful piece, a real success, I could even say a resounding success, as I took seven curtain calls. Home again, I again played host to Gottlieb and Smallens, and after reading Gippius's[3] delightful story 'Suor Maria', went contentedly to bed.

Koshetz, whom I have not seen since our *contretemps*, told Gottlieb that I am an excellent composer but that I have no heart. Roerich, although he never ceases to speak of the 'cosmic nature' of my art and once even floated

---

1 Pavel Milyukov (1859–1943). See above, p. 84 n. 1 and *passim*.
2 The Russian grading system for exams goes from one (bad) to five (good), with half-points, stars for merit and so on.
3 Zinaida Hippius (in Russian Gippius) (1869–1945), a leading Symbolist poet and the central figure in an influential coterie of Silver Age writers dedicated to overturning convention, both literary and social. Prokofiev set one of her poems, 'The Grey Dress' as one of his Op. 23 in 1915. Although married to the poet and critic Dmitry Merezhkovsky she had overt lesbian inclinations, some of which found sublimated expression in her short stories, regarded by some as superior to her verse. 'Suor Maria' is the sequel, written in 1904, to the earlier 'Miss May', and opposes the earth-mother Katya, all womanly warm, solid flesh and physical, to the idealised purity of abstract femininity represented by Maria May, who in this second of the two linked stories has become a nun. Gippius and her husband emigrated to Paris after the Revolution and became passionate opponents of the Bolshevik regime.

the idea of my writing a ballet with a cast of characters composed of spirits,[1] elected to trade cosmic art for a bowl of soup by going to dinner with Volkov and failing to get to the concert at all, claiming that he not been able to get a car. Baklanov did rather better, confining his excuse for non-attendance by saying 'I couldn't resist', throwing away his tickets and going to play bridge.

18 December

How nice! No more Concerto weighing on me and no more need to sit at the piano and slave away at difficult passages. I could write letters, read, and not have to worry about running out of time. People know about the success of yesterday's concert, and offer me their congratulations. I said to Baklanov: 'Well, I hope at least you won yesterday?' but apparently he lost.

In the morning there was supposed to be a 'measurement' rehearsal at which the cast would come to have any necessary alterations made to their costumes, but it was cancelled. By 8 p.m. the stage rehearsal to piano accompaniment, which had been going on since half-past twelve, was still a complete mess (especially the Eccentrics), even though the next rehearsal will be with orchestra. Coini, whose brains have not yet concocted anything to make sense of the frantic dashing around in the final scene, asked me again to cut it altogether. I refused. 'You are very stubborn,' he said, and the running about commenced. I fell out with Smallens's playing of the piano accompaniment at the rehearsal, because he would rush the tempos and not look at my baton. Koshetz came to me and said that for yesterday's concert she would forgive me everything. I found this extremely irritating: nothing is more redundant than unsolicited forgiveness!

Roerich, whom I berated for the discordance between his words and his actions, is now trying to keep away from me, causing Koshetz to confide pathetically in Gottlieb: 'Look, he's driving away all his friends!'

19 December

Went to the bank and cabled 1,500 francs to Balmont. But the franc has again risen against the dollar, while I also need to send some to Linette, to the Stahls and to Mama. However, people I know at the bank say that in a week or so it will fall again.

The Art Club has an exhibition of Anisfeld's sketches for *Three Oranges*, and at the opening there was a small but evidently discerning crowd. As the composer of the opera I was introduced to a mass of people, and I even found this agreeable: the way I have been working recently has virtually turned me into a reclusive wild man of the woods.

---

[1] Presumably Remizov's *Alaley and Leila*. See pp. 144–5, 185 above.

20 December

Taking advantage of the fact that there is no rehearsal today and my leisure is continuing, I made plans for an orchestral suite from *Three Oranges* and thought out the whole work. The first number, 'Eccentrics', I cut and pasted from fragments, and I shall do the same for the 'Conspiracy', 'The Prince' and 'The Princess'. The other three numbers can be lifted more or less straight from the opera. The amount of work entailed is not great, all I need is the will to do it and a clear head, and then I'll have to find a copyist and get him to transcribe the movements.

When not working on this I have been reading books from the library. All month I have been reading, rather to my surprise, about twenty works of Russian fiction. I am not sure how this came about, but it was mainly for relaxation between and after rehearsals.

21 December

A very important rehearsal: the first time on stage with the orchestra. The pleasure of my expectations were tempered with some apprehension, but in the event all went much more smoothly than I anticipated. The only weaknesses are still some of the chorus scenes: the Prologue is not snappy enough, and the rushing about in the last scene is still much too aimless.

There was only one flare-up with Coini. In his view there was no music to accompany the bringing down of the curtain at the end of Act Two, and he demanded that I write a few extra bars. I said this could easily be solved by starting to bring in the curtain slightly earlier. We argued about this, and then rehearsed it again, with my making a small fermata after Pantalone's final words. We agreed on this solution. The rehearsal lasted for five hours with small breaks, and the best thing of all was to be able when it was over to change my clothes, rub myself with eau de Cologne and lie down to drink tea and smoke cigarettes. In the evening I played a short session of bridge, winning $3.

22 December

A similar rehearsal to yesterday's. It went very well, except for the same chorus scenes as yesterday. After this one the next rehearsal will be the General Rehearsal in a week's time. In the meantime there will be 'refresher' rehearsals with piano, during which Coini promises to liven up the chorus.

I had hardly returned to my room after the rehearsal when there was a telephone call from Baranovskaya, who had just this morning arrived in Chicago. I almost jumped down her throat, why had she not rung me straight away, I so badly wanted her to see what Coini was doing! She is, after all, a reflection of the spirit of Meyerhold. The next person to appear was Anisfeld, just in from New York and too late for the rehearsal. This was similarly disappointing, but I was so glad that Anisfeld was here at last: I know that we shall work together hand in glove, and together it will be much easier to control Coini ('the flea', truly he is just like a flea). Anisfeld and I spent the whole evening together.

A letter from Linette, deeply reproachful at my leaving her alone and not caring about her life or her career as a singer. I understand why she is despondent, and it only makes it the more heartsick to read. But until now I have had no chance to recommend her as a singer. How this may change when *Oranges* has been a success I cannot say, perhaps I shall be able to arrange for her to sing Ninetta next season, but I still do not know how good her voice really is and whether I shall be able to push her in.

23 December

Visited the wardrobe with Anisfeld and rifled through the costumes, which are not yet in a perfect state. Anisfeld insisted that I go with him as he speaks very little English or French. Frou-frou came to lunch with me, and from the start we were deep in conversation. Later in the day our baritones were very curious to know who this remarkably attractive woman was. In the evening I had dinner with her, or to be precise with the rich Americans with whom she is staying. But I felt a headache coming on and left early to go home.

24 December

Anisfeld came with me to a rehearsal of the Monsters' fight in Act Two. Their cudgels proved to be so heavy the dancers could hardly lift them, and as a result the fight was turgid and not very amusing, not to mention that they could not get hold of the rhythm at all. I explained and demonstrated the movements they should employ. Anisfeld and I then went into the wings to discuss the lighting. He is upset that they have not given him the green lanterns he stipulated.

Lunched with Frou-frou, who was as attractive, refined and witty as usual, but complaining that her kidneys were once again giving trouble. In the afternoon I caught up on correspondence, which (particularly business letters) has been piling up disproportionately. Koshetz sent me a Christmas present cum peace offering of a black ribbon for my watch with a gold clasp, hoping, as she wrote on the accompanying card, that 'this ribbon will finally bind us together in a bow of friendship'. To which I replied, also in writing, that friendship is better bound not in black knots but in the brightness of good relations.

In the evening I dropped in at a symphony concert to hear Carpenter's

Krazy Kat.[1] Carpenter is one of the liveliest (the others are still-born) composers in America. He is technically proficient and he knows how to orchestrate, but sadly often strays too close to bad taste for comfort.

Later, bridge at Baklanov's until half-past two. Result, up a measly $2.50.

25 December

Despite the holiday, there was a costume-measuring session, and as is inevitable on such occasions the singers all in turn raised howls of protest: one's costume is too tight, another's has no room for her bust, someone else's hat is too heavy, while yet another's train is too long. Koshetz was no exception, and clashed with Anisfeld in true prima-donna style.

At half-past four there was a 'dry rehearsal', a technical run-through for the stage management and lighting. Although Anisfeld had finally been given his green lanterns, from the very first scene there were confrontations with the electricians, with Coini, and with everyone else. I thought it would all end badly, but eventually everyone calmed down and the work went on for seven hours without a break, until eleven thirty at night, covering all the scene changes, lighting and other effects through to the end of the show. From time to time I helped Anisfeld explain what he wanted to the technical and stage staff, and even on occasion offered suggestions, but for the most part I tried not to interfere, sitting with Frou-frou in the auditorium, enjoying the stage decorations.

26 December

A relatively free day. Baranovskaya was again unwell with her kidney and stayed in bed. I read, went for a walk and planned the Prince's and Princess's numbers for the Suite from *Oranges*. Koshetz rang up to tell me that Anisfeld had put everyone's backs up at the Opera and this had reached the ears of Garden; he is the object of universal opprobrium and since she knows I back him up in everything it would be best if I kept out of the way. It was kind of Koshetz to let me know this, but in the first place it was not very pleasant to hear all this malicious gossip, and secondly Anisfeld had been absolutely right to leave Coini, the property-master and the electricians in no doubt of his dissatisfaction at the slipshod way in which things had been done. If they chose to be upset at this intrusion into their quiet, comfy little nest, to hell with them. Anisfeld is a true artist, and they are just hired hands.

In the evening, bridge at Baklanov's with Smallens, both of them playing like old boots and losing. I won $10.

---

1 See above, p. 479 n. 1.

27 December

Today a 'refresher' stage rehearsal with piano had been planned, as a run-up to the General Rehearsal. But Coini judged that no refreshing was necessary, any that was could be done to piano in a rehearsal studio, not on stage, so he called only the chorus for the Prologue and the running around in the final scene. I intervened actively, demonstrating gestures for the Tragicals and the Comicals. Generally speaking the chorus has pulled itself together quite a bit. It was a short rehearsal and it took place on stage behind the iron curtain, so that Frou-frou and Gottlieb, who had come to watch (Frou-frou was as nervous as a little girl beforehand) did not actually see anything.

Koshetz could think of no better a time and place than the rehearsal to start interrogating me with a mulishly insistent series of questions about why I had so changed towards her. Was it because of Baranovskaya? Koshetz is beginning to act on me like a spark on gunpowder. I answered: 'Get out, for God's sake!'

At four o'clock we had a seated 'refresher' rehearsal with piano, which proceeded rather sleepily since everyone now knows everything they need to know and are getting tired of rehearsing it. Koshetz did not appear, pleading trouble with her heart.

Afterwards I sat in my room and read a very interesting essay by Merezhkovsky on Lermontov. In the evening, bridge with Baklanov: lost $13.50.

28 December

A quiet day, no rehearsals. Anisfeld put finishing touches to the costumes. I went for a walk in the afternoon, read, and played the piano. Prince Arabelov called on me, a nice young man, Koshetz's friend, commissioned by her to sound me out on why I have turned against her. Spent the evening with Baranovskaya, but her American ladies kept hanging round us and it was dull.

29 December

At eleven o'clock, the General Rehearsal. Coini has a cold and is below par. The orchestra manager informed me that the extra instruments, the piccolo clarinet, the fifth and sixth horns and the extra percussionist, who have so far been at only one rehearsal, would not be coming. This immediately put me in a bad temper: what the devil is the point of having fifteen orchestral rehearsals if five of the musicians turn up only for the performance and wreck the whole thing! After some fairly dramatic exchanges on this topic, the rehearsal eventually started. I went through the Prologue no more and no less than four times, making Coini beside himself with rage. But the choruses either came in too early, or not vigorously enough, or kept beating the first beat of the bar with their arms. I was sure things would go more smoothly later on.

I also repeated the second scene. At the end of the first act Garden summoned me to her office to tell me how very much she liked it, after which I reviewed with Baranovskaya any imperfections. Act Two went well, except that there were no fountains and the offstage March sounded weak. When the Prince finally laughs, the whole audience laughed too. In the interval I drank coffee with Frou-frou. Among other highly perceptive comments on the staging, Frou-frou mentioned that during Koshetz's [Fata Morgana's] curse, the bass drum was too loud. I had in fact noticed this myself but had forgotten. At this moment, up came Koshetz to complain that the chorus of Little Devils was drowning her (she was wrong about this). I said: 'The chorus is fine, but Baranovskaya reminded me about the bass drum, and I will quieten him down.' Koshetz then flew at Baranovskaya, that nobody paid any attention to her, Koshetz, but as soon as Baranovskaya, this nobody, appears, all of a sudden to suit her the bass drum needs attention.

Act Three went smoothly, and at Coini's urging I made a repeat in the Intermezzo so that the scene change could be done with less of a scramble. During the Cook's scene, loud laughter could be heard coming from Mary, who was sitting in the auditorium. In the last scenes with the entire cast on stage, there were a few problems, and I stopped and went over some passages several times, but Coini was in a hurry as the rehearsal had to be finished by three o'clock. 'We'll go though it again tomorrow with piano,' he called from the stage.[1]

After the rehearsal I immediately went home, as I was wet through as a frog. I rang Garden to ask her what impression she had. She heaped praise on the opera and said she was proud to have been instrumental in presenting it. I replied that I was happy that my opera was being given under the auspices of such a director. Baranovskaya sent me flowers. She has completely lost her head over *Three Oranges*, and I do not believe she is completely rational about me either. We went out together in the evening, and she told me that tomorrow morning she would have to leave to go back to New York. It was on the tip of my tongue to ask her to stay for the performance and for the New Year.

---

1   The writer Ben Hecht was in the audience for the General Rehearsal, and it is impossible to resist quoting his account of it, both for its richly comic but sympathetic description of the activities on and off stage, and for the light it throws on some of the main participants. It is reprinted, by kind permission of Snickersnee Press, as Appendix 6.

30 December

And so, the day of the premiere. However, it started very ordinarily, I slept well and spent the morning drifting about in a leisurely fashion. Anisfeld and I went together to the barber's to have our hair cut for the evening. My mood was a little anxious, made considerably more so by an endless succession of telephone calls. The first of these came at eight o'clock: a young lady of fashion whom I had met at Anisfeld's exhibition wanted a ticket for d'Indy,[1] who had just arrived in Chicago. I yelled at her that it was an intolerable intrusion to waken a composer and conductor at the crack of dawn on the day of a premiere. Later, a whole scandal ensued on this subject.

At twenty past seven, forty minutes before curtain up, Anisfeld and I, in our tails, were already on stage where Anisfeld fussed over the costumes and the make-up and I over the offstage March, the signals for raising and lowering the curtain, and so on. We hardly noticed the forty minutes flying past, when Coini announced that it was eight o'clock, and time to begin. The auditorium did not look absolutely full. The management had done almost no newspaper advertising of *Oranges*, either Mary had been over-confident that all Chicago was already talking about the production, or the conservative *bel-canto* faction had succeeded in discrediting it. However, the seats soon filled up until the only empty places were a few of the boxes and perhaps about a hundred seats in the stalls. Not many complimentary tickets had been distributed.

Finally, I went out to conduct. The orchestra and the audience greeted me with applause, I bowed, and began. As the first bars of music sounded the house curtains rose and the Tragicals made their entrance. How the chorus performed their actions in the Prologue I do not remember, so preoccupied (even though I was not particularly nervous) was I with conducting, but the singing was good. I do know that the Eccentrics, when they appeared, were not very impressive. The Herald had such stage fright that he sang everything a tone sharp and could not stop himself beating time with his hand. After this everything went smoothly and there were no untoward incidents until the third scene, when Leander came in with 'I will feed him a diet' a bar early. But I kept my head and kept going, and the prompter soon got him back on track. For the first time I realised what an ally the prompter can be!

The act came to an end and I left the podium to applause. By the time Anisfeld and I met in the wings the singers had taken several bows. We went out together and the applause redoubled. The bright row of footlights, and

---

1 Vincent d'Indy (1851–1931), French composer and teacher, himself a devoted student of and mainly influenced by César Franck. Apart from a couple of orchestral works he is mainly remembered today for his activities as an exceptionally knowledgeable teacher for three decades at the Paris Conservatoire and the Schola Cantorum.

beyond them, as if in a fog, the cheering and clapping audience. I had the impression that the applause was not particularly rousing, but this auditorium is so huge that no amount of applause in it sounds very great, as I discovered for myself a couple of days later when I went to Chaliapin's concert. We took several more bows together with the singers, but Anisfeld point-blank refused to invite Coini to come out with us. Baklanov came running up to say: 'It's a real triumph!' I went up to Coini, but he was obviously offended that he had not been asked to take a bow.

Act Two began, and the audience burst out laughing at the Prince's sneezing. Everything went splendidly. As the curtain rose on the second scene there was applause for the March, or more likely for the scenery. There was laughter in the audience when the Prince laughed, followed by a wave of clapping, and there were also applause and cheers for Koshetz casting her spell.

The act ended in a tremendous glow of success. I went out to bow with the singers, who took Coini along with them. I also beckoned him out; after all he had worked hard, even if not particularly successfully. But Anisfeld, noticing that Coini was part of the company going out to bow, turned sharply on his heel and left the group, not wishing to be seen associated with him. We went on stage without Anisfeld, and then both I and the principals took several more curtain calls. Koshetz congratulated me, and I, not wishing to spoil the triumph, congratulated her on her success, at which she blossomed and wanted to kiss me. I shrank away, dissembling behind a reluctance to disarrange her make-up. An apoplectic Coini was screaming, how could Anisfeld dare to make such a public exhibition of himself? I went to Coini and said: 'As he obviously does not want to come out with us, the best thing would be if at the end of Act Three he takes a bow on his own, which is in any case quite justified as his scenery is having the greatest success of all.'

Act Three, and all went well. Much laughter in the audience at the Cook's scene, and a round of applause for the scenery of the third scene (with the Oranges). During Linetta's scene I thought of Linette. But overall the act did not have the success of Act Two. When Baklanov came backstage he said merely that he thought there should be some cuts.

In Act Four Chelio came in a bar late and half of his quarrel with Fata went awry. In the second scene St Leger did not start the March on time.[1] The guards' firing of their weapons was late. The final rushing about still seemed aimless; I took an insanely fast tempo. I do not remember going out to bow at the conclusion of the opera, but at the start of Act Four, when I went to take my place on the conductor's stand, I received a prolonged ovation, initiated by the orchestra. There was a crush of people in the Green Room:

---

1   St Leger was conducting the offstage band for the March.

Mary was in a state bordering on ecstasy, and just behind her Harold McCormick. Then the Rosenwalds, the Rosenthals, the Carpenters, the Consul and his wife, Baranovskaya, Gottlieb and all the rest.

When the flood of well-wishers had departed, we decided to go to Froufrou's, or rather to the Nelsons, with whom she was staying, to drink wine. Wine in America is something of a rarity, but after a successful performance we really did need a drink. The party consisted of Carpenter, the Anisfelds, Gottlieb and myself, plus some Americans. As for Koshetz, I said it would be better if she did not come with us, but soft-hearted Baranovskaya felt sorry for her and on the way there talked me into allowing her to be invited. I immediately downed three cocktails and got pleasantly tipsy. Altogether it was a very merry occasion, although never touching the bacchanalian heights we reached after *Chout*.

Koshetz came after an hour with Prince Arabelov; many people, on hearing that he was a prince, jumped to the conclusion that he had played the part of the Prince and congratulated him on his success. By general demand I played the March several times, and Koshetz sang. She was wonderful, and I said to her: 'If only you would stick to singing and stop all that rubbish you keep spouting!' She and Baranovskaya sat near me, Koshetz whispering something into Baranovskaya's ear; later it transpired that it was about how much she loved me. Baranovskaya got up and tactfully moved to the other end of the table in order not to annoy Koshetz. It was after two by the time we called it a day and went home, all of us more or less drunk, I most of all and feeling serenely happy. In the car Koshetz, sitting next to me (the Prince and Gottlieb opposite us) several times snuggled up to kiss me.

31 December

Woke up in a wonderful mood, albeit with a sick headache, and I think I may still have been slightly under the influence. Out on the street I greedily gulped down the air and sat in a little restaurant drinking tea with lemon and reading the reviews. These, I felt, once again failed to reflect the success of the performance, although at least they did acknowledge it. Not one of them had anything serious to say.[1] Returning home I went back to bed and

---

[1] 'The music, I fear, is too much for this generation. After intense study and close observation at rehearsal and performance, I detected the beginning of two tunes . . . For the rest of it Mr. Prokofieff might well have loaded up a shotgun with several thousand notes of varying lengths and discharged them against the side of a blank wall.' (Edward Moore, *Tribune*, 31 December 1921.) On the other hand: 'Prokofieff's score is a masterpiece of modern descriptive music . . . It is true that there is nothing in the entire score which one may whistle as one goes out. It is only an ingrate who would demand sweet melodies; with Mr. Prokofieff's crackling, shimmering miracle in the air, melody seems no more indispensable than a pretty, stupid woman of the eighteen-nineties.' (*New Republic*, 31 December 1921.) (Both reviews quoted in Ronald L. Davis, *Opera in Chicago* (Appelton-Century, New York, 1966).)

slept, not answering the telephone, solitary in my triumph. I even delayed opening a letter from Miller, although I did so later, when I felt more normal. However, it was not a reply to my reply but an acknowledgement of the last amount of money I had sent her. In this way I spent the day seeing hardly anyone, but by evening I had returned to my usual self and went off to Frou-frou with the aim of finding somewhere we could see in the New Year together. Some time ago she had arranged to be with friends at this time, and on the grounds that it would be the nicest way to celebrate it I went along too. It was yet another rich American home, with champagne despite prohibition, and as the hero of yesterday's premiere I was greeted as the guest of honour.

As soon as the midnight hour had struck I took Frou-frou off to the Volkovs. It was my idea, for several reasons: first, I had been invited, and it would have been terribly insulting not to put in an appearance at all (in fact they were offended that I was late, and still more so that I had not included them in the previous evening's carouse). Secondly, Koshetz was going to be there, and I knew that the appearance of Prokofiev with Baranovskaya at one o'clock in the morning would be a dagger to the heart. So turn up we did at the Volkovs at one o'clock, to be leapt on by Smallens and St Leger dancing and yelling and playing the March from *Three Oranges* on toy Christmas whistles. The Consul and his wife were a little cool to me, despite the bottle of champagne (a real rarity) Baranovskaya had brought along. I sat beside her and Koshetz. It was all a little dull, and at half-past two the party began to break up. I took Frou-frou home.

So ended the year. It has been a good one, getting off to a fine, happy start in California, followed by the agreement with Mary Garden, the production of *Chout*, a magical summer in St Brévin and finally the production of *Oranges*. What could be better? A phenomenal year.

1921-22 Grand Opera Season

MARY GARDEN, General Director

WORLD'S PREMIERE—SPECIAL PERFORMANCE
FRIDAY EVENING, DECEMBER 30, AT 8.

The Love for Three Oranges

A Fantastic Opera in Four Acts and Ten Scenes,
with a Prologue.
Words and Music by Serge Prokofieff, after the Fairy Tale
by Carlo Cozzi.

The King of Trifle, king of an imaginary kingdom..Edouard Cotreuil
The Prince, his son.................................Jose Mojica
The Princess Clarice, niece of the King............Irene Pavloska
Leandre, Prime Minister.............................William Beck
Trouffaldino ....Octave Dua
Pantalon ....Desire Defrere
The Magician Tchelio..........................Hector Dufranne
Fata Morgana, a witch......................Nina Koshetz (debut)
The Devil Farfarello................................James Wolf
Smeraldine ....Jeanne Schneider
The Creonte..................................Constantin Nicolay
The Master of Ceremonies.....................Lodovico Oliviero
Linetta   ⎧ Frances Paperte
Violetta   } the Princesses...................⎨ Philine Falco
Nicoletta   ⎩ Jeanne Dusseau
The Herald ....Jerome Uhl

Ridicules, Comiques, Lyriques, Tragiques, Empty Heads. Devils.
Incidental Dances by Corps de Ballet.
Orchestra Under the Direction of the Composer, Serge Prokofieff.
Mise-en-Scene Established and Staged by Jacques Coini.
Scenery, costumes and properties especially designed and executed
for this production by Boris Anisfeld.

Mason & Hamlin Piano Used Exclusively.
In the interest of the art, encores are not permitted.

1922

1 January

The first day of the New Year was marked by a reception in honour of Mary Garden organised by some people called Chalmers, to which the Nelsons dragged Frou-frou and me. A number of the opera company's sponsors were at the reception, and for the first time I fully appreciated that my opera had truly been a resounding success: it is a very long time since I heard so many lavish compliments both from people I knew and people I did not know. I failed to recognise Muriel McCormick, Harold's daughter, because on the occasion when Coini had introduced us we were in the darkness of the wings of the theatre, but she was exceptionally charming to me, and Baranovskaya, in whose company I spent most of the time at the reception (she was by some way the most striking woman present) observed that Muriel's eyes were constantly straying in our direction. I saw Garden for only a moment, when we exchanged the usual gush of compliments and *politesses.*

In the evening I went with Baranovskaya to Chaliapin's concert, where he was received like a prophet. But he traduced his prophethood by singing too much unworthy trash, and although the voice is a magnificent instrument it was not always in perfect order.

2–15 January

At noon on the 2nd Frou-frou left for New York, Koshetz having departed the previous day to the same destination. Life in the Auditorium became quieter. I did not show myself much in public, staying in to read, to work on the Suite from *Three Oranges* and to rest from the noisy activities of the previous week. The second performance of *Oranges* took place on the 5th, conducted by Smallens. I sat with Gottlieb in the back row of the stalls, from where one can see and hear very well. But from my seat (and for all I know from most seats in the hall) the orchestra, and especially the strings, sounded extremely weak. The result was a very particular effect, probably not unlike that at Bayreuth, where the orchestra is deliberately distanced. But the singers were ideal: every note and every word clearly audible, in contrast to passages where the orchestra should dominate, which sounded feeble, for example the Infernal scene came across as less menacing than I would have wished, and the strings could not be heard at the end of the March.

At the beginning of the performance I was apprehensive at what I knew to be tricky passages, but then I decided to wash my hands of it: let Smallens sort it out and I would just listen. The chorus's acting was hopeless in the Prologue (devil take that Coini). The first act was received with cautious approval, but the second, with the March, the Prince's laughter and the Curse of Koshetz, elicited great applause, bringing me to the stage several times to acknowledge it. I listened to the third scene of Act Three specifically to judge whether or not it really was too long, and eventually concluded that it was not: only to those who do not understand the music does it sound long. In the second scene of Act Four the rushing about and disappearance of the Empty-heads was the usual undirected chaos. Coini is useless. The performance was greeted less warmly than the premiere, all the same the applause was solid and the theatre was full, with hardly any complimentary tickets having been distributed. Smallens conducted well.

After this I settled down to prepare for my recital at the University, and performed it on the 10th to great acclaim. On the 13th I appeared again, this time with Koshetz in aid of famine victims in Russia. However, this event had been organised by Bolsheviks, and in the middle of it the opportunity was unfortunately taken for a political harangue. It was most disagreeable for politics to be brought in at all, and particularly so at the Bolsheviks' instigation, and I was afraid there might be trouble, but in the first place $2,000 was collected for the starving, and in the second, we were each paid $400. I played Musorgsky and some of my own compositions; Koshetz was not in good voice and sang three of my songs no more brilliantly than she did the rest of her programme. The audience was mainly working class, and the concert was successful, with curtain calls and encores.

My third and final appearance was on the 15th, a benefit occasion for the children of Chicago. This time I was not paid a fee but it was one invitation I could not refuse, as in the first place the Carpenters had asked me to take part, and in the second Chicago had been so good to me that I wanted to give the city something back by performing for it. However, the event itself was a frightfully pompous affair in the Auditorium Theatre with one of the stars from the Opera. There was an interesting manifestation during my performance: when I embarked on the March from *Three Oranges* as an encore, the audience immediately signalled its pleasure and began applauding during the opening bars. So the March is already gaining the kind of popularity that threatens to make it as 'unpleasantly fashionable' as Rachmaninoff's Prelude.

An unusually active part was played in the organisation of this concert by Muriel. In this connection she made several telephone calls to me, came to see me in the hotel, and while discussing the programme in the lobby flirted outrageously with me, first in her conversation but before long graduating to squeezing my fingers. Muriel is the only daughter of Harold McCormick, is some twenty years of age and not at all bad-looking. She wants to take up acting and is madly in love with everything to do with the theatre, which no doubt explains the uncommon degree of interest she takes in me.

Her father, incidentally, has ceased to be the president of the finance board of directors of the Chicago Opera, having been replaced by one Insull, unknown to me. The management echelons of the Opera are awash with infighting, intrigues and confusion. Mary has apparently squandered so much money this season that the guarantors are clutching their heads in horror. Nevertheless, she has survived as Director for the coming season, but it seems that her autocratic ways have sharply alienated many of those who hold the purse-strings of her operation.[1] Formerly I thought that, if *Oranges* was a success, *Fiery Angel* would almost automatically be brought into the repertoire for next season, but it is beginning to look as though such will not be the case.

11 January

Spent the morning packing, and took the 12.40 Twentieth Century train to New York. I leave with good feelings: everything has been accomplished in Chicago, and in New York I have much to look forward to: the concert with Coates, the New York premiere of *Oranges*, time with Bashkirov and with Frou-frou, after which I shall be going to Europe. Before leaving I had another letter from Linette, an affectionate one with no mention of the future. I cabled her 2,000 francs. I also had a letter from Balmont, ravishingly

---

1 Mary Garden resigned as General Director in April 1922: 'I am an artist, and I have decided that my place is with the artists, not over them.' Samuel Insull (1859–1938) was probably not unknown to the majority of opera-lovers in Chicago: as 'The Prince of Electricity' he was one of the most powerful tycoons in a city of tycoons. A rags-to-riches businessman, he had at one time been Thomas Edison's private secretary and had then become head of the Edison Company in Chicago, a position from which he went on to build a utilities empire reputed to be worth $3 billion. At the Chicago Opera Insull's achievements would be first to steer the company into relatively safe fiscal harbour after the ending of the era of private funding (chiefly McCormick money) that had hitherto kept the company afloat, and secondly to provide for the future by his vision of a new, self-financing opera house to replace the Auditorium, already threatened with demolition (although in fact it survives to this day as part of Roosevelt University). Insull commissioned and raised the money for a forty-five-storey skyscraper, the first six floors of which were to accommodate the new Civic Opera House while rents from the thirty-nine floors above it would secure the financial operations of what had by now become the Civic Opera Company in succession to McCormick's Chicago Opera. The new enterprise opened its doors on 4 November 1929, six days after the Wall Street crash that triggered the Depression. The Civic Opera, Insull and his empire survived for a time, but eventually the Depression put paid to them all: on 30 January 1932 the Civic Opera finally ran out of funds and closed its doors, and three months later Insull's business empire was forced into bankruptcy and he himself was indicted for fraud and embezzlement (he was eventually acquitted, but ruined). Over the next two decades a succession of enterprises under various names struggled to fill the operatic void until the establishment in 1954 of Lyric Opera of Chicago brought a fully fledged opera company back to 'Insull's Throne' on Wacker Drive, since when it has thrived to become the internationally recognised major international house it is today. Insull's legacy did not die with him.

phrased. I attempted to get some money for him by means of a begging letter to Mrs Kohnwald, but so far the omens are not looking good. I shall renew the search in New York, and must enlist Baranovskaya's aid in this endeavour.

17 January – 25 February

In New York I installed myself on the corner of 7th Avenue and 55th Street, next door to the Wellington, where I lived three years ago. I have two rooms at $14 a month – a little expensive, but in view of the opera premiere I have to keep up appearances.

I met Boris Nikolayevich[1] the same day and we talked for nine hours, which cost me a severe headache the next day. B.N. said that seeing me is life-saving for him; his brother depresses him terminally, and he leapt at my suggestion that he spend the spring and summer with me somewhere in the country near Munich. Yes, Germany is a wonderful country, yes, Munich is a lovely old city, yes, the countryside round about is miraculously beautiful – an outpouring of joyful exclamations. From that moment on Munich was our main topic of conversation, the house we were going to rent and move to. B.N. was counting the days until we were able to set off, but the actual date could not be settled before the opera had been presented and it became clear whether there was any need for me to stay longer in New York or if I could leave with a clear conscience.

The Chicago Opera's New York tour opened on 23 January, but *Oranges* would not enter the repertoire earlier than the second or third week, and as a result I did not have anything particular to do for the first few days I spent in New York. Baranovskaya was not well: her tubercular kidney which had protested at the amount she had drunk in Chicago and was now so bad that on the day I arrived Frou-frou was obliged to check herself into a private hospital. She planned to stay there a week, and we had already made plans for our joint re-appearance back into society, but her health, instead of improving, grew worse and at the beginning of February poor Frou-frou was taken back to California and the sunshine. When B.N. made her acquaintance he completely lost his head, declaring Baranovskaya was the most interesting woman he had ever met in the whole of his life.

Frou-frou's conversations gradually took an increasingly candid and specific direction. Our intercourse was conducted urbanely, with taste and a surface veneer of half-joking irony, but the underlying meaning was undoubtedly serious. Her idea was that I should marry her. Apparently the husband from whom she had separated two years ago had died in Mexico,

---

1 Bashkirov.

and she had the documents to prove it. 'I am good-looking, quite presentable, why should I not be your wife?' And certainly, if one was looking for one it would be a hard task to find a better wife than Baranovskaya, but those very qualities of refinement and delicacy and aesthetic discrimination I so valued seemed to have suppressed the woman in her. As such she aroused no feelings in me whatsoever (and by the way, B.N. felt exactly the same).

Just as I was pondering this conundrum I ran unexpectedly into Stella at the Metropolitan Opera where I went to the first night of *The Snow Maiden*,[1] designed by Anisfeld. The encounter provided an immediate answer to all of the delicate traceries of Frou-frou's refined mind. The instant I saw Stella I felt such a powerful attraction to her, Baranovskaya was erased from my mind. The conversation was not a long one, but it was pungent, spiced equally with compliments and point-scoring on both sides. She had been hearing a continual buzz about the *Three Oranges* performances and this had clearly impressed her, while from my side I was stunned by how much more beautiful she was even than before. The next day she invented some business or other she needed to see me about, came and stayed and talked the whole evening.

The day after that we met again for lunch, quarrelled, and parted. A few days later she went to Florida with her sick father. Altogether, my relations with Stella are ridiculous, they make no sense at all, but each time I see her she has a tremendous effect on me, and nothing could have given me a clearer illustration of how remote marriage to Baranovskaya was from what I desired. Accordingly, I imparted to Frou-frou in the bantering tone we habitually adopted just how misconceived such a step would prove to be, and the subject was not raised again even though I continued to see her every day.

On the 26th and 27th I played the Third Piano Concerto with Coates. Of course, performing with him was unalloyed pleasure. The quality of the performances and the warmth of their reception were comparable to Chicago, but the reviews were even more superficial, not to say downright careless. Haensel was happy with the success of the concerts (but not the reviews) and insisted that I ought to give one or two recitals. According to his calculations they could not lose more than two to three hundred dollars, and they could be a very helpful investment for next season. He even agreed to waive his fee. I agreed, and the concerts were scheduled for 14 and 17 February. This meant I had to settle down to bring the programmes up to the necessary level, while the performances of *Oranges* kept being put back, and there were even rumours that it might not be presented at all. Mary, of course, remained invisible.

In the meantime Ziloti, Szymanowski and the Kokhánskis had all put up

---

1   Opera (1882) by Rimsky-Korsakov.

at the Wellington, next door to me, and we met continually for lunch and dinner. We became the greatest of friends, and I went on plotting in pursuance of my efforts to get hold of some money for Balmont.

Oranges was originally in the schedule for 6 February, but the influenza then raging in the city, although not as serious as two years ago when the infection rate had been 5,000 a day (it was now 1,000), laid low Truffaldino and the Prince. Instead of *Three Oranges* a somewhat startled audience was treated to *La Traviata*, the substitution having been decided upon only hours before the show. *Oranges* was postponed until the 14th which was, as luck would have it, the date of my recital, in fact the recital was in the afternoon, and the opera in the evening. I decided to put a brave face on it, fearing only that I might catch the 'flu that very day. B.N. was already in bed with a temperature of 39.5° Celsius, and even missed my concert with Coates.

However, in the event all was well. The recital programme was not onerous and consisted of well-known works, and afterwards I followed Capablanca's advice and took a hot bath, drank some hot milk, and lay down for two hours. I then put on my tails and went to conduct the opera. There was no orchestral rehearsal for New York, but the orchestra was in such good form that there were no disasters from that quarter. The theatre was full, but I was told a lot of complimentary tickets had been issued: sales had been excellent for the 6th, but after *Traviata* was presented in place of *Oranges* ticket sales failed to pick up again. There was absolutely no advertising: either undue reliance had been placed on people already knowing about *Three Oranges*, or someone in the management was digging a hole for me. The performance was good, avoiding embarrassing moments, although of course the acting performance of the chorus left much to be desired. The audience reaction was similar to that at the Chicago premiere, that is to say a great success; I was presented with a wreath (from Liebman), and all that was missing was the sustained ovation I had been granted in Chicago at the beginning of Act Four.

Afterwards we went to Bookman's to drink wine, and next day I opened the newspapers. I felt as though I was being savaged by wild animals.[1] Enormously long articles were devoted to the opera, but only in two of them (the *Globe* and the German-language paper) was there any praise for it. I

---

[1] Robert Aldrich, delivering himself of one of the most virulent attacks in the *New York Times*, wrote: 'The audience was large, and after the first shock of surprise, evinced considerable amusement at the proceedings onstage...There are a few, but only a very few, passages that bear recognizable kinship with what has hitherto been recognized as music... What, in fine, is the underlying purpose of this work? Is it satire? Is it burlesque? Whose withers are wrung? If it is a joke it may be a good one, but it is a long and painful one.' Twenty years later Prokofiev remembers in the *Short Autobiography*: 'It was as though a pack of dogs had scrambled out from underneath the gate and hurled themselves on me, tearing my trousers to shreds.' (*Kratkaya Avtobiografiya*, in Shlifshteyn, op. cit.)

read all the reviews very carefully, and was thoroughly perplexed. What was wrong with these people? Why were they so lacking in understanding? Haensel was positively distraught. On top of this it appeared that there would be no more performances of the opera, as the season had only one more week to run and the repertoire had long ago been settled for it. It seemed that the malicious press attacks had reduced to naught all the success *Three Oranges* had enjoyed.

The second recital, on the 17th, began less than promisingly. I had a bad headache in the afternoon which I succeeded in overcoming with the help of powders only an hour before the concert. I started with a Beethoven Sonata I was nervous about, and fluffed part of the second movement, barely managing to recover myself, but I did so and finished the sonata in good order. The second and third parts of the programme, however, I played well, gave six encores and altogether scored a resounding success. But the loss on the two concerts was $375. It was another occasion for Haensel to be surprised and disappointed, and he said: 'I have such faith in you, I don't understand why you have these problems!'

After this recital it was abundantly clear that my American business was over for this season. I could have expected the opera performances and the recitals to yield some fresh engagements, but none was offered and so there was no reason not to leave. I myself wanted to go to Europe, and B.N. was positively straining at the leash, but there was not a great deal of money, less indeed than last year. Nevertheless, the fall in value of the German currency would make it possible to live comfortably until the autumn.

It was not at all clear whether the Chicago Opera would revive *Three Oranges* next season, since the company was undergoing many changes and nobody seemed to know much about future plans.

Our departure was fixed for 25 February. My last week was filled with matters I had to attend to: tickets, passports, changing money, the dentist, Duo-Art, a few sessions of bridge and some farewell calls.

On the 23rd Capablanca, who has become a close friend and who, incidentally, has just got married, played a simultaneous match at the Manhattan Club against forty opponents, B.N. and me among them. It was a great event. Sitting watching us were Liebman, Deryuzhinsky and several others. I developed a furious attack and thought I was going to topple his eminence. To this day I do not understand how he managed to extricate himself and launch a counter-attack. Even so, I held out longer than anyone, and Capablanca, once he had despatched all the others, sat down opposite me with the words: 'Maintenant je vais jouer avec mon ami.'[1] A crowd of forty or fifty people gathered round us. I was confident I could force a draw,

---

1 'Now I am going to play with my friend.'

but after heroically resisting for twenty moves eventually had to lay down my arms. In the meantime B.N., not without my help, had drawn his game – a genuine draw, which made him very proud and happy. Altogether, the evening was a truly exceptional occasion.

The following evening, while I was immersed in packing my suitcases, a lady telephoned me saying that she needed to see me urgently in connection with *Oranges*. On the assumption that this would be yet another interview, I categorically declined to see her, but she insisted that her business was more important than any interview. I gave in and let her come at eight o'clock in the evening, and what she told me was the following: they (she and another lady) had come to the conclusion that *Three Oranges* was one of the most brilliant productions they had ever seen, and in their judgement could be performed nightly. They therefore proposed to rent a large theatre in which to present the opera right through the following winter. They needed my agreement in principle, whereupon they would set about negotiating with the Chicago Opera, with the theatrical venture they had chosen, and with the singers. If it proved to be a great success in America they would subsequently tour it to Europe and to Australia.

This was a proposition I could never have imagined! Were it to come about I would at one bound become a rich man and famous across the world. But I was not sure I believed them: something was not quite right about it. After seriously talking through every aspect of the proposal we parted with an agreement that by the time I arrived in Paris they would be clear how matters stood, and in the meantime they would clarify the situation with the Chicago Opera because it would be necessary to secure from them the rights for the following season and to hire the scenery. From my point of view, even if the project fell through I could still regard it as an interesting proposition. It was a good final note on which to leave America, and B.N. and I set off in high spirits next morning in a car piled to the roof with luggage.

25 February – 23 November

On 25 February our Dutch liner the *Noordam*, a 12,000-ton steamer, not in her first youth but still good, left New York bound for Europe.[1] There were not many passengers, and we both had a cabin to ourselves. For the first two days out the weather was calm and sunny, but then things got more exciting and a first-class storm blew up that buffeted us mercilessly for eight days. Although it did not interrupt my work on making a two-piano reduction of

---

1 The S/S *Noordam*, operated by the Holland–America Line, was launched from the Harland and Wolff shipyard in Belfast in September 1901.

the Third Piano Concerto (I seem to be fated to make piano scores on steamer crossings) there were times when the storm exceeded anything I had experienced before. B.N. was terrified and ran to ask the cook if the ship was going down, and once the captain did genuinely turn the ship to head into the wind in order to lessen the effect of the waves, saying that we had run into a hurricane.

Ten days out we dropped anchor in Boulogne and I parted from B.N., who was travelling through Holland straight to Munich. I was going to Paris, where I could stay only a few days as I had only a transit visa 'sans arrêt'. In any case, I had no particularly urgent business in Paris: I needed to see Mama, Koussevitzky and Diaghilev, and once I had done that I could go on to Berlin and thence to Munich to look for a house where we would all be able to live in the country. Koussevitzky told me I would be playing with him at the Grand Opéra on 20 April, and that it was essential to publish all my works. Diaghilev was glad to see me, cordial, but vague. He had been badly burned in London with his extravagant production of *The Sleeping Beauty* and was now without money.[1]

In Berlin I had arranged to meet Miller: I had to establish finally what manner of a person she was. I also wanted to taste what Berlin musical life had to offer, to see Suvchinsky, and to call on my publishers. Then I would travel on to Munich and find a dacha.

It was certainly very interesting to see Germany in its post-war state, torn between remnants of menacing militancy and acquiescence in the obligation to pay the reparations demanded of it, but always maintaining the trappings of a well-ordered society. Everything is amazingly cheap owing to the collapse in value of the German mark, but I have very little money this year and it is thanks only to this rate of exchange that we shall be able to get by. For this reason, at first I had no sense of what was expensive and what was cheap, and what I could and could not afford.

With Suvchinsky I had a most warm and friendly reunion. We have much

---

1   Everything had gone wrong with this hugely expensive re-staging of the Tchaikovsky–Petipa ballet, renamed *The Sleeping Princess* but usually referred to by Diaghilev as simply *Belle*, at Sir Oswald Stoll's Alhambra Theatre, which had also invested heavily in the production on the understanding that it would run for six months, like a successful musical. Diaghilev had taken sweeping liberties with the original libretto, interpolating numbers (e.g. the 'Dance of the Sugar Plum Fairy') from other Tchaikovsky ballets and commissioning additional orchestrations by Stravinsky. At one stage, according to Cyril Beaumont, he even had a (probably fortunately) unrealised plan to invite George Bernard Shaw to write a spoken commentary to introduce each scene. With sumptuous designs by Bakst, the massively overspent production opened on 2 November 1921 and ran until 4 February, by which time such was the financial catastrophe that Stoll impounded the sets and costumes, as a result of which Diaghilev could not include it in the forthcoming Paris season. (See Walsh, op. cit., p. 347, and Beaumont, op. cit. pp. 191–215.)

in common in our general approach, and in particular our views on the present situation in Russia and Europe.

Miller arrived a few days after I did and appeared with that familiar questioning expression on her face. She seemed much the same as I expected: emotionally insecure, devoted, naive, a simple person despite her knowledge of four languages. I spent about a week with her and then left for Munich.

I also saw Glazunov, who had come from Russia to conduct a concert of his works. He was polite to me, but not more, evidently still regarding me as a harmful element. Medtner (whom I approached very discreetly after he had been told that I was playing his compositions in America) was extremely friendly and invited me to dinner, something quite new in view of the aphorism he came up with in Moscow that 'either Prokofiev's music is not music, or I am no musician'. In recent years in Moscow, with Scriabin dead, Rachmaninoff and me absent and the later works of Stravinsky not played, Medtner has assumed a dominant position. He has now come to Berlin in hopes that the Germanic cast of his music will be very much to people's taste here, but he was deceived: no one is paying him any attention, he therefore feels *déraciné* and this is the reason for his mellowness. I had dinner with him, gave him some insights into America where Rachmaninoff is trying to arrange for him to go, and played him *Tales of an Old Grandmother*, but the only one he understood was the second. 'Such a pity,' he later confided to Zakharov. 'Prokofiev is such a nice person, but the things he writes I simply cannot understand.'

I enjoyed seeing Zakharov and Cecilia again, although our encounter was not a long one. He gave me a whole-hearted welcome, and stressed how fond he had always been of me. Cecilia had a tremendous success in Berlin, and did indeed play magnificently. She tried to get to grips with my Violin Concerto, but could make little of it. 'She is pure *chair-à-violon*',[1] exclaimed an infuriated Suvchinsky. I also saw Remizov and got to know Andrey Bely,[2] who greatly interested me.

I arrived in Munich on 25 March and despite the early hour was met at

1 'A violin made flesh', i.e. without many intellectual resources.
2 Andrey Bely (pseudonym of Boris Bugayev, 1880–1934), one of the main theoretical and spiritual creators of Russian Symbolism as an aesthetic movement. Influenced by the mystic poet–philosopher Vladimir Solovyov, Bely described his first published work, the prose poem *Second Symphony: Dramatic*, as a poetic symphony, in which the use of Joycean techniques of rhythm and structure derived from musical composition symbolises an attempt to synthesise mathematics, philosophy, music, aesthetics and mysticism into the principle of the Divine Feminine, or Sofia, the only source according to Bely from which ultimate reality may be revealed to the poet. Bely's long autobiographical poem *First Encounter*, which was soon to have such a profound effect on Prokofiev, was published in 1921, the year of his emigration. Thought by many to be Bely's greatest work, it describes the effect of his friendship with the Solovyov family when he was a young man in Moscow at the turn of the century, and constitutes a requiem for the vanished intellectual, artistic and spiritual life of Silver Age Russia.

the station by B.N. He had already succeeded in losing some of the money I had given him, but was nevertheless staying in one of the best hotels, where he had not paid the bill, and instead of doing something about looking for a house to rent had spent his time wandering about the shores of the lake. He was ecstatic about Munich and said he was very happy there. Obviously I was going to have to take matters into my own hands, so I bought a map and began a systematic search of the environs. The first place we went to was Berchtesgaden, a wonderful place, but two days there yielded nothing to suit our purpose.

The second expedition was to Garmisch, whence we were directed on to Ettal,[1] a quiet little place near a large monastery, in a valley hemmed in by mountains, and four kilometres from Oberammergau, famous for the Passion Play performed there every ten years, a representation of the biblical story commemorating the village's deliverance from the plague around the time of the *Decameron*. We came into Ettal at seven o'clock in the evening, by which time it was already dark and the snow was piled up thickly on the ground (after all, Ettal is 900 metres above sea level). The first thing that struck me in the house we were taken to was a Futurist painting. After that everything turned out to be wonderful: the house was spacious, elegantly furnished and comfortable, with magnificent stoves, a library, portraits of Schopenhauer and astronomical maps. We were under the spell of the house when we were offered it for an annual rent of 40,000 marks (approximately the price we had notionally fixed on in New York), although there is no doubt that the owners could have asked for 80,000 or even 120,000 marks. The landlady was a German woman married to a Frenchman, and co-owned the property with her brother Keil, the painter of the canvas we had admired. Keil's wife was a beautiful Jewish woman, and the family were highly sensitive and cultivated people. To sum up, we had resolved our quest in a far better way than we could have imagined, and returned to Munich with the intention of installing ourselves in our palace three days later.

Miller came to Munich after a few days and put up at a different hotel. Although she had a visa for only two weeks, in Bavaria she succeeded in getting permission to stay for an unspecified period, and was delighted since she had no desire to go back to Riga. But Miller's presence did not make me forget Linette; indeed I soon came to realise how far superior to her Linette was in terms of perception and refinement.

On 1 April B.N. and I moved into our house. The owner behaved with

---

1   Lina Prokofieva recalled that Ettal had previously been recommended by Valery Bryusov, whom Prokofiev had also met in Berlin during his recent stay there, as being a setting reminiscent of *Fiery Angel*, the novel Prokofiev had found in a second-hand bookshop in New York in 1919 and was already pondering as a subject for his next opera. (See Simon Morrison, *Russian Opera and the Symbolist Movement* (University of California Press, Berkeley and Los Angeles, 2002).)

extreme delicacy, unobtrusively finishing everything she had to do before moving out, and left altogether after a few days. The house was miraculous, we could not contain our delight at its tranquillity, spacious proportions, its 'aesthetic qualities'. Alas, it did not have a tennis court, nor anywhere to bathe in the summer. It was also hard to know where I could get hold of an instrument, either in Munich or locally. I was finishing the piano reduction of the Concerto, and in the absence of a piano to practise on for my forthcoming Paris and London appearances went to a shopkeeper's neighbouring house.

A great event was the appearance of a contract from Miss Beirne, the woman who had come to see me on the eve of my departure from New York about producing *Oranges*.[1] She had promised to cable me while I was still in Paris, but had not kept her word. But now here was a formal contract, lengthy and complicated, and to crown it all, signed. I spent several days studying it and came to the conclusion that it could make me a rich man. There were just a few points that needed to be amended, and I would need an advance. I wrote to her along these lines and also sent her a telegram, for the time being putting the contract signed by her but not yet by me away in my desk.

On the 15th I went to Paris to perform the Third Piano Concerto with Koussevitzky. The concert took place in the Grand Opéra, a very grand occasion. It was important, so it seemed to me, that my performing debut in Paris should take place in such illustrious surroundings. There was supper after the concert: Koussevitzky (who drank to our friendship and the intimate *tutoiement* form of address), the Stahls, and Frou-frou, whose appearance was very striking. She had recently arrived from California. I saw Diaghilev the following day, and he told me that for next season he had

---

1   Miss Beirne was Deborah Beirne of the New York National Irish Theatre Company, whose correspondence subsequent to her meeting with the composer in New York is in the Serge Prokofiev Archive at Goldsmiths College in London. Miss Beirne, no shrinking violet, had ideas of her own on how to make the opera palatable to a mass audience: 'To meet the needs of New York, the music of the Ballet must be as sensuous in color and rhythm as possible, the more so the better. As it will be given during the sleep of the Prince as in the nature of a dream, this will be a logical interpolation in the Opera. And the duett between the Prince and the Princess in the last Act must be sentimental, and please make the aria for Fata Morgana as lyrical as possible. These additions will give greater possibilities for a financial success and they will not in any way destroy the artistic beauty of the Opera. I would not want to present it at all if the Opera should lose any of its exquisite charm.' (Letter of 21 March 1922.) Prokofiev, no doubt biting his tongue, drew the line at Fata's aria in an addendum (in English) to the contract he signed on 20 April: 'No aria for Fata Morgana. She is an angry, turbulent witch. How can she sing a lyric aria?! Other aria than a declamatory one won't fit for character, but such an aria cannot aim the hearts of the crowd. And again: the only possible place for Fata's aria is the third scene of the third act – the longest scene of the longest act. But we already added to this scene a ballet, and if now comes an aria the scene will be interminable. I will compose it should you insist, but my scenic feeling is strongly against.' No further word coming from Miss Beirne, the signed contract seems to have stayed in Prokofiev's desk and the project died a natural death.

agreed the rent of a Paris theatre for nine months and was minded to commission from me an opera based on Lermontov's 'The Tambov Treasurer's Wife'.[1] I then crossed the Channel and went to London, where I was likewise due to make my debut as a pianist, with Coates. Between rehearsals in London I rested from all the heady activity of Paris, since in comparison I don't have many friends in London. The Third Piano Concerto had an even greater success than in Paris, something I had not expected from the cool English. I was called back six or seven times and Coates, against his practice, even made me play an encore.[2]

The next evening I was back in Paris, where I had some good news from Diaghilev: *Chout* was to be revived this spring – which means money. But Mama was giving me cause for concern: we went together to see our celebrated Dr Manukhin, and he detected a swelling which he could not be certain was benign. He told us it was a good thing we were going to Munich, as there she would be able to have radium treatment and x-rays that would arrest any disease in its embryonic stage.

Next day we left for Munich, where Mama consulted Dr Stubenrauch and was admitted to the Red Cross for a week's treatment of radium and x-rays, while I returned to Ettal. How good it was to be in the country! The Ettal spring had compassionately refrained from galloping ahead during my two-week absence. But from 1 May the burgeoning began in earnest: 'La nature tombe en ivresse',[3] in the words of our landlord Dr Keil. Ettal's elevated altitude means that spring begins later here. Two weeks ago from the windows of my railway carriage I was looking at cherry blossom and apple trees in bloom all the way from Munich to the Channel, and now here it was all happening again before my eyes.

Miller was living in Murnau, where I had suggested she move to from Munich, a small town about an hour away from Ettal, and I visited her every three or four days. As a start she translated into German the texts of my songs, and even *Three Oranges*, and pasted my reviews into a book, as they had accumulated to a great pile.

In the meantime I settled down to the piano score of *Three Oranges*. It would be good to have it published because of the American contract, besides the publishers say that if I can let them have the manuscript quickly they will get it ready for July. The lithographed vocal score for Chicago was

---

1   Mikhail Lermontov's satirical and rather heartless, if lightly penned, Pushkinesque narrative poem written in 1837, about a love affair between a young officer and the wife of a rich burgher, who loses his wife to the officer in a card game.
2   'Music entered the room with Mr. Prokofiev... We must honestly confess we never understood Mr. Prokofiev's music until he played it himself. As he plays it, the orchestra is like a vast resonator applied to the piano... The thing must look very weird on paper, and is certainly amazingly difficult to play, but it was all put before us with complete clarity and proportion.' (*The Times*, 26 April 1922.)
3   'Nature swoons in intoxication.'

made from my original sketches, and was therefore highly inconvenient to play from. I now had to redo the piano score completely from scratch, writing in the Russian and French texts. I thought the work would take me a month, and indeed this was approximately the case (six weeks), but I had not bargained for its being such a laborious job – six or seven hours a day almost every day. Meanwhile, America was silent!

In the evenings B.N. and I played chess. I won two matches, the first, a serious one, +5 −2 =2, and the other consisting of speed games +100 −40.

Our other competition had something of a medieval flavour – a contest of sonnets. In New York B.N. had discovered a slim volume of elaborate, formally strict sonnets by Heredia,[1] and had translated about ten of them. He was inordinately proud of this achievement, boasting that many poets had come to grief trying to make versions of Heredia. I looked at them, and thought this was nonsense! Of course it was possible to translate a sonnet. I challenged my friend to a match: each to produce ten versions of Heredia sonnets and have them adjudicated to see whose were best. Naturally the translations must adhere strictly to the rules of sonnet form, preserving the same metre as the original. We each nominated a judge: mine was Balmont, B.N.'s Severyanin, and we agreed to send them the sonnets typed on a typewriter so that they would not know which of us had produced which version. They would ascribe marks to each sonnet, and we would collate the results. The one who obtained the highest number of points would win the contest.

The competition was devised in April, and by May three sonnets had been despatched for the judges' deliberations. First to reply was Severyanin, with a mass of stimulating comments. Our excitement was intense. I won by a margin of several points. This was followed by a sonnet of welcome from Balmont, receipt of which invested our tournament with considerable pomp. Finally Balmont's marks themselves arrived, sadly without a commentary similar to that provided by Severyanin, but nevertheless to my advantage. The grand total for the three sonnets was as follows: 57 to me, 49 to B.N. B.N., a poet born and bred, was shocked by the affront and even tried to abandon the competition or at least introduce new rules, but I declared that in this case I would compile a report on his defection, type it out and distribute it with a record of the scores among all our friends. B.N. was indignant, thought about it – and the contest continued.

So passed the month of June. Mama, after her week in Munich, now joined us, reassured that Stubenrauch had not found anything malignant.

---

[1] José Maria de Heredia y Giraud (1842–1905), Cuban-born poet who lived in France and wrote in French. One of a group of poets centred around Leconte de Lisle styling themselves the 'Parnassiens', his interest lay in the perfection of form rather than emotional content, and the collection of sonnets published in 1893 under the title *Les Trophées* are still considered exemplars of the form comparable to those of Petrarch. Confusingly, there is another José Maria Heredia, also a poet (1803–1839): this was his cousin, who remained in Cuba and wrote in Spanish.

My correspondence with Linette continued, and at the beginning of June she wrote that her singing studies were proceeding splendidly and she hoped to be making her debut in October. In July, perhaps, she would come to Ettal 'for a week or two, for a rest'. I was delighted. I was missing her in Ettal, and she would love it here. On 12 June, to my great joy and relief, I completed the piano score, but it was soon followed by proofs that needed correcting.

I received no word from Haensel or from Beirne and therefore had resigned myself to the absence of an American season next winter. Nevertheless, having taken Christophorus[1] for a year, the $1,000 I possessed would, at the current rate of exchange, provide for our needs for quite a long time.

The proofs of the *Oranges* piano score tormented me for a large part of June. They were really pressing ahead with the printing, and so there were frequent deliveries of packages containing thirty pages of proofs, and since I did my proofreading conscientiously and with meticulous care, it consumed a great deal of time. The job was not finished until the middle of July. However, the point of all this work grew gradually fainter as the silence from Beirne continued, she did not return my contract nor give me any information, while Haensel, who was in Europe this summer and dropped in for an hour to see me in Ettal, told me that while plans had definitely been cooking at one time, nothing had come of them.

As soon as I had dealt with the proofs, on 6 July I got down to the third act of *Fiery Angel*, my plan being to finish the opera this summer. It had been in abeyance for two years, and after all, the music was not bad! Act Three made brisk progress and I was deeply absorbed in composition.

At the end of the month Kleiber,[2] the conductor of the Mannheim Opera, appeared at my door. He had heard from somewhere or other about *Three Oranges*, and as he was passing, wanted to acquaint himself with it. He liked the opera very much and undertook to accept it for production the following season; the theatre's Intendant, he said, would write to me on the subject. The impression Kleiber made on me was of a young and not entirely reliable partner, and indeed in the event nothing came of the proposal, although there was some correspondence with the Intendant and I even met him in

---

1 The name of the villa in Ettal.
2 Erich Kleiber (1890–1956), the Austrian-born conductor, was at this point on the brink of a truly international career: the following year, after an exceptional performance of Beethoven's *Fidelio* at the Berlin Staatsoper he became its Music Director. Two years later in Berlin he directed the premiere of Berg's *Wozzeck*, but resigned when the Nazi Party condemned Berg's unfinished *Lulu* as *entartete Musik*. A man of the highest principles, Kleiber, who was not Jewish, also declined to conduct at La Scala when Jews were banned from appearing there. Instead he went to the Teatro Colón in Buenos Aires and in 1938 took Argentinian citizenship. After the war he refused an invitation to return to the Staatsoper, then in the Soviet sector, in protest against totalitarian regimes generally, and continued his career as a guest conductor with no permanent appointment.

Munich. Kleiber did, however, arrange a piano for me, which was quickly brought out from Munich, as the only instrument I had found to hire up till then was so terrible it was almost unplayable.

The summer was cold and rainy. Apparently this was so all over Europe, and even in America, but this did not stop us cursing Ettal for its climate. Nevertheless, there were a mass of strawberries, redcurrants and blackcurrants, gooseberries, and the like. Mama and B.N. made jam and fruit liqueurs.

This summer we had to do without bathing, as the nearest lake for swimming was near Murnau (where Miller was living) and to get there and back took the whole day. Miller was kind and devoted, making careful translations into German of my songs and even operas, but her part in my life was not a significant one.

Halfway through June B.N. and I started playing tennis, because the boys at the school attached to the monastery (a privileged and generously equipped institution) left for the holidays and the premises became free. The school had a tennis court and the Director gave us permission to play there. We did so with enormous enjoyment but not much skill, although eventually we did improve a little. B.N. usually won, which gave him great satisfaction. He could give me fifteen and still win, but with thirty he lost.[1]

Our chess match, however – of simple games – ended once again in a commanding victory for me. We continued it all through July and August, the winner being the first to reach a hundred. By my hundredth win B.N. had won thirty-four. Since there were constant bad-tempered altercations and mutual recriminations about the length of thinking time we took, we sent for a control clock and I devised a marvellous rule: either player exceeding by more than five minutes his opponent's thinking time for a given move would lose the game, or rather the game would continue with his opponent being awarded one penalty point. This is an ingenious rule because, while it does not actually curtail the time for play, the quick-thinking and -moving player thereby imposes a time limit on his opponent. The score in the sonnet competition continued to favour me, and Igor Severyanin sent more wonderfully perceptive comments. But B.N. dragged his feet, too lazy to translate his sonnets, so the competition lost momentum. Altogether, his limitless capacity for lying prone and contemplating the ceiling often caused me to lose patience and explode in wrath at his indolence.

Frou-frou turned up at one of the German spa resorts and made a fleeting appearance in Ettal, but I was waiting for Ptashka,[2] who had still not succeeded in getting a visa. It was not until 7 August that she arrived, from

---

1 The scoring of points in a tennis game is: fifteen, thirty, forty, game (= win), unless the scores at forty are level, in which case deuce is called and the winner must win two points in succession, otherwise the score reverts to deuce.
2 Prokofiev's nick-name for Lina Codina ('Linette').

Milan via Switzerland. I went to meet her in Munich. She had grown much more beautiful, and was altogether much better than I had expected. I was extraordinarily happy that she came, and Christophorus came to life. As a trio with B.N. we went on excursions, climbed up mountains, saw the Oberammergau Passion Plays (the performance lasted eight hours, but still produced a strong impression). B.N., despite the eight-hour span, meant to go again, but sloth prevailed and he did not.

At the end of September Ptashka and I joined up with the Stahls for a motor tour in their car from Stuttgart through the Black Forest and the Rhine valley to Alsace. We went through the Vosges, dazzlingly beautiful in their autumn dress, and down into the valleys of France. The trip was a tremendously enjoyable experience; the Stahls are wonderful companions and I love them very much.

During September I composed the fourth act of *Fiery Angel* and pondered a Suite to be drawn from *Chout*. I had made a rough plan for it while I was in London in the spring, and now it was a matter of composing closing passages for the various numbers and stitching together the separate sections. The Suite turned out to be very long, more than thirty minutes altogether. But I would rather not waste any of the good material in the ballet, and if a conductor finds it is too long he can make a selection and not play the whole work. I shall even make a note to this effect on the first page of the score.

September also marked my growing admiration for Andrey Bely, specifically his *First Encounter*. I had sent for the book and liked much of it when I first received it, but I also found it so obscure it was difficult to understand. A month later I took the book up again, and now discovered one sublimity after another. I summoned B.N., he started to penetrate the essence of the poem, the spark ignited in him as well, and a day later we were in love. *First Encounter* was never far from the table, and we quoted endlessly from it. Even Ptashka knew the first page by heart. After a month B.N. knew the whole poem by heart.

On 4 October I completed Act Four, taking particular pleasure in the scene between Mephistopheles and Faust. *Angel* then faltered, as I needed to devote much thought to the libretto, and indeed the whole structure, of Act Five – a difficult and pivotally crucial matter. This was not work one could simply undertake by sitting down to it with a clear head: it demanded long cogitation and the patience to wait for the moment when inspiration might in its own good time suddenly strike.

Ptashka went back to Milan on 7 October. Her voice has developed and acquired real schooling; now she must work and practise, and try to get engagements for the stage. But this time has brought us together, and Ptashka herself has developed, become more beautiful, and in every respect moved forward in the right direction.

The day after Ptashka left, B.N. went to Berlin. After five years of somewhat listless effort he has managed to put together a book of verses. Igor Severyanin, with whom B.N. is on very friendly terms, happens to be in Berlin at this time, and B.N. is hoping that with his connections – since of course Severyanin knows all the publishers – he will be able to get his book into print.

Mama and I remained on our own. Her health has taken a knock this year: she has had instances of heart attacks. The doctors say there is nothing to be done, the machine is breaking down, repairs are not possible, and all that remains is for her to be cherished and looked after.

In September I began receiving letters from a certain Salter[1] in Berlin. Enquiries revealed him to be a powerful theatrical entrepreneur, energetic and of questionable probity. His proposition was that I enter into an agreement whereby I would assign to him the rights to present *Three Oranges*, in return for which he would guarantee to produce *Oranges* on six(!) stages, taking 20 per cent of the receipts from German venues and 30 per cent of others. We had some correspondence and then arranged a meeting with Salter's son and partner in his business, following which I signed a contract assigning the rights excluding America, France, the Diaghilev companies and non-Soviet Russia. Of course, were Salter's project to be successful it would be splendid to have *Oranges* revived, but if not, neither he nor I had anything to lose. Personally I did not believe he would achieve as many as six(!) venues, the task of introducing such a problematical opera into so many theatres, especially in Germany's presently straitened circumstances, appearing to me to lie beyond the bounds of probability. But the project might well end up with one or two theatres next July and then, although thereafter our agreement would expire, there was no reason why it could not be extended on a partnership basis. After all, even two theatres would be better than nothing!

In the second half of October I went to Paris to perform the Third Piano Concerto with Koussevitzky, a re-engagement after the successful April premiere. It was again a great success: in Paris I am loved. However, the March and Scherzo from *Three Oranges*, which Koussevitzky also included in the

---

1 Norbert Salter was one of the most powerful theatre and concert impresarios in Germany. Starting as a cellist in the Hamburg Orchestra at the time when the young Mahler was its Music Director, he gave up playing to become the orchestra's manager. By the time of this encounter Salter's business had expanded to encompass representation of a remarkable range of the greatest musicians and theatrical talents of the time, as well as producing opera. The son mentioned by Prokofiev as assisting in the business may have been Georg (George) Salter, who was later, on emigrating to the United States as a result of the Nazis' increasingly punitive racial laws, to become probably the most celebrated book designer and typeface designer in America, but as Georg was already by that time well established as a stage designer at the Volksoper it was more likely to have been his brother Julius.

programme for this concert (and which, when he played them in London in the spring had been encored) did not make much impact in this context. Even I did not much care for the March – but how splendid it had sounded in Chicago as part of the opera! Two days later, on the 26th, I gave a recital with the Diva,[1] with a Musorgsky–Prokofiev programme devised by Stahl. The Stahls and I are true friends; I stayed with them and they call me 'notre fils adoptif' (the Diva is a year younger than me). She is an first-rate singer and gave a very good performance of the '*Akhmatki*'.[2]

I played Musorgsky's *Pictures from an Exhibition* and some of my smaller pieces, ending up with the *Toccata*. The recital was a tremendous success and the hall (not a large one) was full. A mass of people, many of them celebrities, filled the Green Room to offer their congratulations: Balmont, Bakst, Larionov, Goncharova, Milyukov. Among them were Harold McCormick and his new wife Ganna Walska, a famous beauty.[3] B.N. had come across her ten years before, in Petersburg and in Kiev, when she was little more than a nightclub or *café chantant* singer. She had gradually worked her way up the marriage tree with ever richer husbands, and eventually crowned the cycle with Harold McCormick. She has a small voice, but is consumed with ambition to become an opera singer (she did make some appearances in America, but without much success). She sat with McCormick in the front row, clapping wildly, and in the Green Room afterwards invited me to visit them tomorrow. On her, or rather on her ambition yoked to the millions at her command, repose the hopes of dozens of musicians and entrepreneurs (Diaghilev among them). The next day I called on her, and we chatted amiably for half an hour or so, but there was no reference to any business matters.

From Paris I decided to go home, making a brief detour to Berlin where Koussevitzky, Diaghilev and Stravinsky were all going to be. I planned also to take the opportunity of meeting Salter personally, and of seeing Suvchinsky. Diaghilev raised with me the idea of a short, plotless ballet, that is to say a 'dance symphony' lasting about twelve minutes, to which choreography would be created once the music had been composed. The idea interested me.

The few days I spent in Berlin were very interesting ones. First of all, I was delighted to see Suvchinsky, whom I met every day. I introduced him to Diaghilev, who was impressed by his opinions and perceptions. Diaghilev was charm itself, inviting us to supper every evening, and also present were Stravinsky, Mayakovsky and Chelishchev (a young artist).[4]

1   Vera Janacopulos.
2   *Five Poems of Anna Akhmatova*, Op. 27.
3   Not everyone agreed about the beauty. See above, p. 582 n. 1.
4   Pavel Tchelitchew (1898–1957), painter and stage designer. Having left Russia in 1920, he lived for two years in Berlin before moving to Paris, where he was associated with the French

In Paris, Diaghilev had asked me to play through to him *The Gambler* and *Three Oranges*, which provoked yet another attack on me for wasting time composing operas. Stravinsky chimed in to back him up, saying he also thought I was on the wrong path. A noisy altercation ensued, accompanied by much bad-tempered shrieking. I told Stravinsky that I was always ready to listen to his comments on orchestration, in which field I regard him as a master, but that he was in no position to lay down a general artistic direction, since he is himself not immune to error. Stravinsky, a man profoundly certain that he alone has discovered the true path of art and that all others are false, became incandescent with rage and shouted at the top of his voice, hopping up and down like a sparrow. The gist of what he said was that orchestration could not be isolated from the rest of music: either he was a master in everything he did as a musician, or I did not understand him.

With the object of inflaming him to lose complete control of himself (his tirade interested me chiefly as a theatrical spectacle) I screamed at him: 'How can you possibly presume to show me the way when I am nine years younger than you, and therefore nine years ahead of you! My path forward is the true one, and yours is the path of the past generation!' The effect of this sally exceeds my powers to describe: we almost came to blows and were separated only with difficulty. None of this prevented us from going out together arm in arm, and meeting again in Berlin, where he arrived two days after I did.[1]

One especially interesting encounter I had in Berlin was with Mayakovsky. Mayakovsky, who is a fearful apache (I always wonder: is he going to hit me, not for any particular reason, just because?), is very well disposed towards Diaghilev, and they spent every evening together for the most part feverishly disputing the merits of contemporary artists. Mayakovsky, who needless to say has no time for anyone but his own group of Futurist artists, had just come from Russia with the intention of informing a waiting world that the present and future of art lay in the hands of artists in Moscow. An exhibition of their work was just then opening in Berlin. But in Diaghilev he was up against a formidable opponent, for Diaghilev had spent his life involved with new artistic directions and was well aware of up-to-the-minute developments abroad, while Mayakovsky had not stirred outside Moscow for some time, and none of his bluster was able to cut much ice against Diaghilev's solidly grounded propositions. In the end Diaghilev was

---

Surrealist movement, moving finally to New York in 1934. At heart a Surrealist, he also experimented successfully in other genres, notably neo-romantic canvases, drawings of circus performers and innovative stage designs.

1 'When they yell, sometimes for two hours at a time, I understand nothing, I snap back, so as to add fuel to the fire, I take delight in the scene from the point of view of its picturesqueness, but within my head is aching – what sort of spring is unwinding inside them, why is there so much energy in this spring, and where is this spring aiming?' (Prokofiev's letter to Suvchinsky of 1 December 1922, quoted in Nice, op. cit.)

reduced to pounding his fist on the table to press home his points to Mayakovsky. Observing these battles was highly instructive and diverting.

My own demeanour towards Mayakovsky was reserved, although he obviously liked me and therefore *a priori* disliked Stravinsky. His attempts to prove to Diaghilev that I was a real composer while Stravinsky was worthless were no more persuasive than his other theses, because here too Mayakovsky was short of real ammunition. However, where he was on truly unassailable ground was in his poetry, which he declaimed *à la* Mayakovsky, gratingly, with a cigarette between his teeth. His recitations sent Stravinsky, Suvchinsky and Diaghilev into ecstasy, and I liked them too, very much.

The whole group joined frequent common cause mainly in order to attack me in chorus for setting the poetry of Balmont and Bryusov. To tease Mayakovsky I added meekly that I had also written some songs to poetry by Akhmatova, to which Mayakovsky retorted that he could see there might sometimes be a certain attraction in boasting that, see, they all tell me one thing, and I deliberately go and do just the opposite! But the poets I like are relatively so uncontroversial that there is nothing to boast about. Diaghilev was loud in support of Mayakovsky.

Suvchinsky came with me to visit Bely (I wanted to see him to tell him how much I admired *First Encounter*). Bely was touched, and full of complaints about Berlin ('They'd like to bury me under a ton of concrete here').[1] His face lit up when I invited him to come and visit us in Ettal; he said he would come in two weeks' time, but did not keep his word.

I saw Salter only fleetingly, at Koussevitzky's. He told me that Smallens never tired of playing him *Three Oranges*, but was silent about how his plans to present it were developing. The general impression I took away of him was of a devious and not altogether reliable person. Koussevitzky was of the same opinion: 'I wouldn't stick your fingers in Salter's mouth – he'll bite them off!'

1   It would take a book to explain why Bely was in such distress in Berlin. This is not the place to elaborate, especially since Prokofiev was not at this time, when first working on the composition of *Fiery Angel* – because he did not learn the autobiographical background until 1926 – aware that Bryusov's occult, demonic novel was in fact a *roman à clef* dealing with real events and personalities, the three protagonists being Andrey Bely (Count Heinrich/Madiel), Valery Bryusov (Rupprecht) and the woman they both loved obsessively, Nina Petrovskaya (Renata). To such an extent were the overwrought relations in the triangle a factor in Petrovskaya's self-identification with the novel's heroine that she committed suicide in 1928 in order to prove to herself, to her former lovers and to the world that she was indeed the demonically possessed Renata. The Modernist poet and critic Vladislav Khodasevich (1886–1939), who was intellectually and personally very close to all three individuals, explains that one of Bely's main reasons for having left Russia in 1921 was to reconnect with the anthroposophy community in Dornach of Rudolf Steiner, where for five years he had been Steiner's disciple but was now being ignored. Rebuffed, Bely sank into a life of despairing and often extreme dissolution, not helped by the reappearance of the by now half-insane Nina Petrovskaya. Such was the background to Bely's complaints of being 'buried alive'. Bely returned to Russia in 1923, still adhering to the tenets of anthroposophy.

Koussevitzky conducted a concert in Berlin including the March and the Scherzo from *Three Oranges*. I thought it was an ill-advised idea to debut in Berlin with such small pieces, but Koussevitzky had already settled his programme and there was no room to squeeze in the *Scythian Suite*. I sat in a box with Mme Koussevitzky, Diaghilev and Lourié. To the last-named I turned my back, not so much on account of his being a Bolshevik Commissar, but because he is a rotten composer trying to get his foot in the door.[1] The excerpts from my music passed without attracting much notice. Downstairs, outside the cloakroom where Diaghilev, Suvchinsky and I congregated before going to have supper, I caught sight of Nina Meshcherskaya a few paces away from me, also putting on her coat. Our group was rather stylishly got up in dinner-jackets (people do not necessarily dress up in Berlin). Nina was with two other women, looking a little dowdy. We did recognise one another but gave no sign of recognition, although I noticed myself talking more loudly than usual.

The encounter with Nina was not without its effect on me, but supper brought other news. For some reason or other I mentioned that Borovsky was going on a concert tour of South America. Suvchinsky said: 'Yes, yes, he's getting married and going to Argentina.' I was surprised, and said: 'Who to?' 'Someone called Baranovskaya.' 'Which Baranovskaya?!' 'Maria Viktorovna, a most attractive and interesting woman.'

I was stunned. At the concert, Borovsky had mentioned to me that Frou-frou was in a sanatorium near Berlin, and had suggested that he and I go together the next day to visit her. Leaving the restaurant with Suvchinsky in a state of some agitation, I said to him that this was incredible, that I knew Maria Viktorovna very well, and that it was quite inconceivable that she should contemplate marrying a sweating lump like Borovsky. In reply Suvchinsky said: 'I am very much afraid that tomorrow you will go and rescue her from her fate, and marry her yourself.'

I reassured him on this point, and the next day accompanied Borovsky to see Frou-frou. Borovsky was respectful, the soul of courtesy, and would not let me pay for my ticket. As soon as we were together with Frou-frou he immediately absented himself on some pretext or other. Frou-frou was in seventh heaven that I had come to see her, because being unaware of the

---

1 After the October Revolution Lourié had been appointed Commissar of Music in Lunacharsky's Commissariat of Popular Enlightenment ('Narkompros'). Disillusioned with the Bolshevik regime, however, he defected to the West following an official visit to Berlin in 1921, and was therefore no longer a Commissar, or even a shadow of one. By the end of 1922 he had moved to Paris, where because of his earlier friendship with Sergey and Vera Sudeykin he joined the Stravinsky entourage, writing a series of articles about the intellectual and aesthetic origins of his music although, as Stephen Walsh points out, 'much of this shows Lourié as an intellectual opportunist (not to say a profoundly inaccurate historian and highly tendentious reasoner)'. (S. Walsh, op. cit, pp. 458–62).

situation with Linette she had not understood my lack of enthusiasm for her to come to Ettal. Then she asked: 'Well, Prokosha, have you still no plans to marry?' I answered: 'Not at the moment.'

She then somewhat mistily explained that, for the sake of variety, she had decided she might marry Borovsky. I found it very hard to say yes or no to the idea, to approve it or condemn it. Of course, had I shown any sign of going along the path that had so alarmed Suvchinsky yesterday, Frou-frou would have been mine in two words. But as nothing could have been farther from my thoughts, what place was it of mine to dissuade her? After all, there she was, lying quite alone with her tubercular kidney. It was not impossible that she might soon die. Borovsky, meanwhile, was head over heels in love with her, and a better carer could not be imagined. And when all was said and done Borovsky, despite his comic appearance and occasional tendency to lapse into vulgarity, was a very famous musician both here and in South America, and his circle of acquaintants was an interesting one. 'He is like wax in my fingers,' said Frou-frou, 'I can mould him as I please.' This in answer to my mention of his clumsiness.

'Does it not worry you at all to be marrying a Jew?' I asked. She replied that Jewish men were more considerate to women then Slavs; Slav men were all sadists. Frou-frou then touched me by adding: 'And since Prokosha is not going to be around, at least by marrying Borovsky I shall always be able to hear Prokosha's music.' I kissed her. Borovsky then came back, the talk turned to other matters, and he took me back to the station.

These three or four days in Berlin left me with so many impressions I fear I shall never get to the end of describing them. Suvchinsky read me the scenario of his opera *The Great Movement*, conceived in the latest, *ne-plus-ultra* of contemporary style. It was extremely interesting, but would have meant a colossal amount of work. And I had still not finished *Angel*.

Finally, on 5 (I think) November I returned to Ettal and was happy to be in tranquillity again and away from the crowds. I could get back to work, deal with the mountain of letters that had accumulated, dust off the chess-board. The sonnet competition reached its seventh stage invariably with higher scores to me from both Balmont and from Igor.[1] By this time I was so far ahead on points that Boris Verin saw it would be impossible for him to gain the palm. For a long time he hung back from proceeding to the next stage, and then announced that he was conceding the match. To defeat a poet – not bad! If I had not been a composer, I would probably have become a writer or a poet. One thing of which I can be certain: I write better poetry than Tchaikovsky did.

Thoughts of Linette. I am drawing ever closer to her. Her last visit played

---

1 Severyanin.

a big part in my feelings. The thought of marriage has by no means crystallised in my mind, but it is stronger than it was.

24 November

Act Five obstinately refuses to move today: I cannot work out the Grand Inquisitor's entrance, nor do I have a clear vision of the tone of his address. As result I am in a bad mood. I proof-read the piano score of the Third Piano Concerto and then went for a walk. The snow is up to one's knees, the sun is shining, and everywhere around is incredibly beautiful. Stillness. Perhaps even too much. Since B.N. took himself off to Berlin for four days there has not been a cheep out of him, a nice way to behave! Ptashka also has not written. In the evening I read Gorky's *The Old Man*.[1] Very talented. How dare all those politicians of the right, whose own strategies have failed so miserably, gnash their teeth at Gorky, a man of the profoundest gifts and humanity?

25 November

Pressing on with Act Five. Decided to leave out for the time being the passages that are sticking, and move forward. A postcard from Ptashka, very tender. I am beginning to think far too much about Ptashka.

26 November

Recast the Inquisitor and moved on to the knocks. Sometimes it seems to me that the whole of the beginning of Act Five is good, but at other times it seems boring. Still no news of B.N., and Mama is beginning to worry about him. In the extreme tranquillity of our life at present, the arrival of the post is the main event of the day. Zederbaum[2] tells me of an invitation to appear

---

1 One of Gorky's later, lesser-known and generally disregarded plays, written in 1919. The subject is sin and retribution, in the shape of the unwelcome appearance of the Old Man, a figure from factory-owner Mastakov's chequered past, to disturb his successful, comfortable life in the early years of the twentieth century. Gradually it becomes clear that this is less a simple case of blackmail as the avenging sword of fate. *The Old Man* has recently (May 2007) been made into a powerful film by Boris Blank, under the title *Grekh* (*Sin*).

2 Vladimir Zederbaum was Koussevitzky's secretary and assistant at his publishing company. In Nicolas Slominsky's irresistible autobiography there appears the following touching account of Zederbaum's relationship to the Koussevitzky household, at least as it had developed by 1925: 'I was to replace Koussevitzky's former secretary, a Russian journalist and physician named Vladimir Zederbaum. Although Zederbaum's medical degree was not operative in the United States, he prescribed a whole battery of pills and liquids for Koussevitzky's periodical ailments, including one for his recurring fainting spells. Mrs Koussevitzky, the real power behind the throne, remonstrated with Zederbaum for his excessive ministrations. Tensions grew between them, until Mrs Koussevitzky finally told him to pack and leave. For further emphasis, she

with the Pasdeloup orchestra.[1] Paris has a more generous attitude to me than any other city. They do not pay much – 1,500 francs is not something one would look at in America – but with the cost of living in Germany as it is, it represents a significant something. Am reading *Goha le Simple* by Adès.[2] Very nice. I also read a story by Ehrenburg, which was not good at all. But his *The Face of War*[3] is better.

27 November

A letter from Eberg,[4] once again demonstrating how unwise I had been to have become entangled in the agreement with Salter. I went over the agreement again, thinking about it, and became angry and upset, because contracts are in a sense my *point d'honneur* and I hate making mistakes over them. More or less the whole day went in brooding over this letter, although I did to go Oberammergau to change some money.

Composed some of the start of the knocking section in Act Five. Had a long letter from Suvchinsky with his impressions of Stravinsky. Regarding Stravinsky's attacks on me and his conviction that I am taking the wrong

---

ordered that Zederbaum's suitcases and other belongings be put out on the porch of their house. Poor Zederbaum, who had a heart condition, had to be hospitalized, and eventually returned to Paris. Still rankling over the manner in which he was dispatched, he bombarded Koussevitzky with letters and telegrams full of abject apologies and assertions of his undying loyalty. He was finally offered, and gladly accepted, a public relations position for Koussevitzky's European affairs.' (N. Slominsky, *Perfect Pitch* (Oxford University Press, 1988).)

1 One of the oldest orchestral societies in the world, the Pasdeloup Orchestra of France, established in 1861 by the conductor Jules Pasdeloup, has never been a permanent contract orchestra but a long-standing group of independent musicians.
2 *Le Livre de Goha le simple*, by Albert Adès and Albert Josipivici, published by Calmann-Lévy in Paris in 1919, is a charming collection of stories drawn from the Arabic oral tradition about the archetypal simpleton whose crazy, child-like logic defeats the sophisticated reasoning of conventionally 'clever' people. In Turkey, for example, the consonants in his name are reversed – Hoga, or Hoja – to illustrate the deeper truth of unreason over rational argument. All Russian children know Hodja Nasreddin the legendary medieval Persian Sufi master. Goha/Hoga has many Western counterparts: King Lear's Fool, Jaroslav Hašek's Švejk, Chesterton's Father Brown, Voltaire's Candide, Joseph Heller's Yossarian, Winston Groom's Forrest Gump, Afanasiev/Prokofiev's own Buffoon, not to mention Socrates. As Touchstone observes in *As You Like It*: 'The fool doth think he is wise, but the wise man knows himself to be a fool.'
3 Novel published by Ilya Ehrenburg (1891–1967) in 1920, based on his experiences as a war correspondent during the First World War. Between 1921 and 1924, when he settled in Paris and lived until his final return to the Soviet Union in 1940 – a trajectory that has some correspondences with Prokofiev's own life – Ehrenburg lived a peripatetic life in Europe, so Prokofiev would have regarded him, rightly, as one of the many artists and writers who were pursuing their calling outside Russia, rather than the committed Soviet writer we tend to classify him as today.
4 Ernest Eberg (d. 1925), Estonian managing director of Koussevitzky's Russian Music Editions and Editions Gutheil, who had been appointed to the post in 1921 following the accidental death of Nikolay Struve the previous year.

path, I am very interested in Suvchinsky's views, so to speak from the sidelines. I have great faith in the keenness of his insights.[1]

28 November

A telegram from B.N. I thought it would be to say he was on his way back, but it turned out to be quite different: 'Prière télégraphier 50,000, situation très compliquèe.'[2] Before he left, he had extracted from me, almost by force, 50,000 marks, and when I asked him why he needed so much, he replied: 'For reassurance.' I suppose 50,000 marks is not such a huge amount of money, but what a way to behave – to keep silent for ten days and then, when the spirit moves him, to ask for more money without giving any reason! I replied: 'Vous envoie 1,000 mark, revenez immédiatement 4⁻ᵉ classe.'[3] Even without this diversion my head was aching, probably because of yesterday's letter-writing. I really should keep a log of my headaches and the powders I take to relieve them.

Did a little work on the Sonata No. 5.[4]

29 November

One would have thought that my telegram to Boris Nikolayevich was an arrestingly effective move, the sort that in a chess-game notation would be followed by an exclamation mark (!). But the reply it elicited merited two exclamation marks: 'Viendrai dimanche avec ma fiancée',[5] accompanied by a further request to send 50,000. 'Avec ma fiancée!' indeed – how about that! After five years of monastic chastity!

The effect on me was a complex amalgam of feelings. There was regret that the old B.N. seemed to have vanished without trace. Mixed in with it was the same blend of amusement and sadness I felt when I thought of the tragicomic figure of Borovsky. Would we all be able to live together in one house? Would I have to marry Linette and organise the wedding in a day?!

I replied: 'Vous êtes fou. Télégraphiez explication. Envoie argent.'[6] And sent the money.

1 Following Prokofiev's visit to Berlin, Suvchinsky and he engaged in an extensive and revealing correspondence about the true meaning and value of modernism, in which the attitude of Stravinsky and Diaghilev figured prominently, their rejection of his operas having clearly bitten deep into Prokofiev's soul. (See *Pyotr Suvchinsky i yego vremya* (*Pyotr Suvchinsky and His Times*), ed. Alla Bretanitskaya (Kompozitor, Moscow, 1999).)
2 'Please telegraph 50,000. Situation very complicated.'
3 'Sending you 1,000 marks, come back immediately 4ᵗʰ class.'
4 Piano Sonata No. 5 in C, Op. 38.
5 'Arriving Sunday with my fiancée.'
6 'You are mad. Telegraph explanation. Sending money.'

30 November

No explanation was forthcoming from B.N. Mama observed: 'Don't hold your breath for a telegram, now he's got the money.' Alas, she was obviously right. If I had cabled, 'Expliquez-vous. Enverrai argent,'[1] no doubt I would have an explanation today, but I did not feel I could gamble with 100 francs when the poet was experiencing his moment of crisis! But I am not very impressed by his behaviour.

Began composing the Inquisitor's exorcism.

Finished reading *Goha* – a most aromatic book.

Ptashka has not written.

1 December

Went to Murnau in beautiful weather, returning at half-past four expecting to find a telegram from B.N. Nothing of the sort. Mama is right in her materialistic analysis: when money is needed there is a flurry of telegrams; once the money has been received – silence.

A letter from Suvchinsky, roundly condemning Myaskovsky's Songs, Op. 20,[2] which I had sent him. There is justice in much of what he says, but the problem lies not so much in the songs' lack of vital sap as in the doubtful taste of many passages in them.

2 December

The day passed quietly. I made progress with the 'exorcism', and did some proof-reading. B.N.'s behaviour had made me angry and I prepared a real beware-of-the-bull reception for him. I was also annoyed that Ptashka had not written. Thinking about her I could not decide: clearly there is a process of some kind maturing inside me. A definite 'no' has metamorphosed into a vacillating 'maybe this way, maybe that'.

3 December

A telegram from B.N.: he is coming today 'alone'. I did not go to meet him and decided that instead of screaming at him a more effective tactic would be to stage a silent protest. Half an hour before he was due to arrive I strolled over to Oberammergau and went for a two-hour walk. When I returned home he was sitting in his room upstairs and did not appear. On my desk lay

---

[1] 'Explain yourself. I will send money.'
[2] *Six Poems of Alexander Blok for Voice and Piano*, Op. 20 (1921).

a note to the effect that he was in a dreadful state, momentous things were happening in his life, he apologised unreservedly for his actions, etc., etc. I went up to him; he did indeed look very agitated and had lost weight, endlessly repeated how sorry he was and all but fell on his knees in front of me as I sat in his armchair. His bride to be? Irina Odoyevtseva, a young poetess from Petersburg.[1] I was quite upset, but suppressed my feelings – after all, I do not yet know 'Irène' and perhaps since B.N. is so infatuated, there may really be something very interesting there.

This was followed by an account of the affair, his falling desperately in love, his declaration of the same, his subsequent doubts and retreat to Ettal following my 'you've gone mad' telegram. I had not realised my telegram would be such a douche of cold water! Now the questions were, should he send for her to come to Ettal, would I admit her if she came, should he break with her, should they get married? He was completely losing his head. I told him the first thing he should do was spend three days in Ettal rather than send any more telegrams in the heat of the moment. On this we agreed, he cheered up and we spent the evening playing chess.

4 December

B.N. was still asleep when a telegram arrived from Irène. In fact, he slept until one o'clock, love having deprived him of rest or appetite the whole time he was in Berlin. The telegram announced that she would be arriving in Munich today.

Energetic work! I said that this was a Muzio gambit,[2] involving the sacrifice of a knight. B.N. was all for going straight to Munich, but I advised

[1] Irina Odoyevtseva (1895–1990), born Iraida Geinike in Riga, had early in her life come under the influence of Nikolay Gumilyov, becoming a member of his and Gorodetsky's *Tsekh Poetov* (Guild of Poets), where she met her husband, the poet Georgy Ivanov whom she married and with whom she emigrated in 1921. Clearly the episode with Boris Verin was a passing inclination, and it is not clear from the *Diaries* whether or not Prokofiev was aware of the fact that she had a husband in tow. Eventually, husband and wife both enjoyed considerable success in Paris émigré circles, Odoyevtseva's lament 'The Ballad of Gumilyov' for the murder of her mentor by the Cheka in August 1921 shortly before she left Russia, achieving almost talismanic status. Today Odoyevtseva is best remembered for two books of memoirs *On the Banks of the Neva* (*Na beregakh Nevy*, 1967) and *On the Banks of the Seine* (*Na beregakh Seny*, 1978), marvellously personal reflections of literary life and luminaries respectively in pre-Revolutionary Petrograd and émigré Paris. Ivanov also wrote his memoirs (*Petersburg Winters*; *Peterburgskie Zimy*) and between them they became more or less self-appointed arbiters of émigré literature, the true surviving representatives of the Silver Age, in which arena they quarrelled combatively but ingloriously with Vladimir Nabokov. Ivanov died in 1958, but Odoyevtseva lived on and in 1988, two years before her death, returned to Russia, to become something of a living memorial to an age whose time was, in a sense, about to come again.

[2] The Muzio gambit is a chess opening sacrificing a knight to prepare the way for an aggressive attack.

waiting until tomorrow to bring her to Ettal, sending a telegram today. We were sitting playing chess, and I was making facetious remarks about the Muzio gambit, when suddenly there was a ring at the door – and there was Irène. B.N., embarrassed, rushed her upstairs and then brought me up to be introduced to her. I did not particularly take to her: she talked in a loud voice and the lower half of her face was unattractive, the upper half being hidden by her hat. Nevertheless, she made an impression of elegance and resourcefulness. In the evening, I liked her better.

A letter finally arrived from Ptashka, tender in tone but after a three-week silence I thought it could have been more demonstrative. I was tempted to torment her by similarly waiting three weeks to answer, but in three weeks' time it would be Christmas, and I thought that if I wrote back right away she might come for Christmas.

5 December

A letter from Haensel: he has only one engagement for me, for 19 January in Indianapolis, for a fee of $400. Of course I shall not go, but there is a small 'but'. I have to cut four rolls for Duo-Art in accordance with my old contract with the firm. It is possible they might agree, as we have discussed many times, to let me do this in London, but supposing they do not? Then it would be better to go and play them in New York. But no, it would really be humiliating to go all that way for a single engagement, and if the London idea for recording the rolls does not work out, I could play them in New York next autumn as long as, God willing, we manage to struggle on with the money until then.

Irène is passable, but I would not put it any higher. B.N. whispered in my ear that he is already beginning to find her conversation tedious, and probably nothing will come of the affair. I am not much enamoured of her poetry.

Finished reading the first proofs of the Third Piano Concerto.

6 December

Fiery Angel is under way again. Outside there is a tremendous blizzard, the snow is lying an arshin deep.[1] I wrote to Ptashka, chiding her severely for her long silence, telling her of B.N.'s romance and asking her to come for Christmas. Oh, oh! What if this visit were to end in the manner of the little poem I wrote for Eleonora just before my engagement to Nina Meshcherskaya:

---

1 An arshin is 0.71 of a metre.

> Oh, my dear and loyal friend,
> Gallant wars have long been waged,
> Now weep for me, lament my end:
> Life is over – I'm engaged!

In the evening B.N. read aloud Bely's *First Encounter*, which we all know well. What an overwhelmingly splendid thing it is!

Irène is still with us. Sometimes she is a little too vociferous, but otherwise does not intrude. After midnight, when Mama and I are already asleep, she sits up talking to B.N. until four o'clock. According to B.N. the conversations consist of impassioned critiques of their situation, and she is exhausting him.

7 December

Quite a heavy post. A letter from Derzhanovsky, in which he says that my 'Gavotte'[1] from Op. 32 was played in Moscow, to which the score had somehow trickled through, and people had 'gone crazy' about it. A new bookshop, 'Kniga' has opened on Kuznetsky Bridge and there is a whole window display devoted to me.

Another letter from Igor Severyanin, asking if I could lend him some money.[2] I am not in a position to and declined, diplomatically. B.N. has changed his mind about him, apparently because Igor published his most recent books with a Bolshevik publisher. But Igor is a child, and has not the least idea of adopting a political platform.

11 December

Irène has left. Every night they sat up and talked until five or six or even eight o'clock in the morning. B.N. complained of fatigue, but it is doubtful whether he would ever have been able to expend such energy on his poetry!

I got back from the copyist my Suite from *Chout*, selected and transcribed according to my instructions. I sat and proof-read it. Now I must compose and orchestrate endings for the individual numbers, which I have more or less done but only in my head.

---

1 No. 3 of the *Four Pieces for Piano*, composed in New York in 1918.
2 Severyanin had left Russia immediately after the Revolution and was now settled in Tallinn, Estonia.

12 December

Sorted out the Suite and composed the endings.

B.N. returned from seeing off Irène, with whom he had gone as far as Munich. He said that in their final hours together she had said some things that had succeeded in fanning the flames once again. No plans for a wedding. 'What about an Indian marriage?' I asked, ironically. For the present he awaits telegrams or letters.

15 December

B.N. has rushed back to Berlin, anxious that I approve his trip. I did not. He has really made me angry. Since April he has written no more than a handful of mediocre poems, the rest of the time lying in a chair with a flagon of beer, belly up, gazing at the ceiling. And now, all he can think of to do is to go to Berlin and dance attendance on a girl. It staggers me that a man who in certain respects really does desire to improve himself can be so apparently oblivious to his own parasitic accidie! If during this time he had written thirty sonnets he would perhaps have had some justification to go chasing off to Berlin.

16 December

A letter from Eleonora that deeply disturbed me. She confirmed what I already thought I knew but still could not be sure of because in Berlin Suvchinsky and Lourié had told me otherwise: that Asafyev had not salvaged my manuscripts and papers from the apartment on Pervaya Rota Street, and that they had perished. Among the things now known to be lost are: the score of the Second Piano Concerto (this does not matter greatly, because Mama brought the piano score with her from Kislovodsk, in addition to which I wanted in any case to revise and re-orchestrate it, the only problem being that this will now take much longer); the compositions from my childhood and youth – the operas *On Desert Islands* (aged nine) and *A Feast in Time of Plague* (aged twelve); my Symphony in G major (aged eleven); almost certainly a thick oil-cloth-bound notebook containing my piano pieces (more than seventy of them, written between the ages of thirteen and seventeen, among them the theme of the March from Op. 12); the notebook containing my Diary between September 1916 and February 1917 (because I have its predecessor and successor); one or two years of my correspondence carefully arranged for binding as was my practice for other years; possibly my letters to my father between the ages of fifteen and seventeen; the stories and plays I wrote as a child; a little book with rebuses of my own devising and my project to calculate the military coefficient of battle cruisers (aged thirteen, the time of my absorption in the Japanese War); chess games from the tournaments I had taken part in at the St Petersburg Chess Society and my games in the simultaneous matches when I won against Capablanca and drew with Lasker – my two most famous successes. No doubt there is much else that I have forgotten, some of which I shall remember in time and some which is now forgotten for ever. My photographs have also gone: of my parents, of myself in childhood and adolescence, of Max Schmidthof, Zakharov, Tonya Rudavskaya.[1]

But most of all I mourn the loss of the Diary, followed by the correspondence, then the Capablanca and Lasker games. All the music of the Second Piano Concerto still exists, the childhood compositions do not mean so much to me because I was not then the person I am now, and the main thematic material I remember and can note down 'for my biography'. But the loss of the Diary is a tragedy, as there was so much of interest in it: it was my last winter in Petrograd which saw the production of *The Gambler* and a general flowering of my talent. The autumn of 1916 suffered from the delay caused by the slow copying of the parts for *The Gambler*. Since this was under the direct control of Malko it was clear that he had taken offence at not being asked to conduct the opera and had held up the copying, which led to a series of furious rows with him. Eventually the piano rehearsals began, and Dranishnikov, then a repetiteur and now, so I hear, a conductor at the Mariinsky,[2] really got down to it with the singers. I listened to some of the rehearsals but mainly stayed out in the smoking-room and played chess with the singers. Generally, for a young composer whose recently composed opera was in rehearsal there, to be admitted through the portals of the Imperial Theatre was in itself a source of joy. There were only two or three orchestral rehearsals, of the first two acts: I was terribly interested to hear how my orchestration sounded. I don't remember if there was a play-through of Act Three; Act Four did not yet exist.

Then there were my concerts in Kiev and Saratov, and the return journey from Saratov in the depths of winter, through blizzards and snowdrifts, during one of the wartime 'provisions weeks' which had the happy consequence of my luxuriating in a first-class carriage coupled to a provisions train. The journey dragged on for several days, during which my travelling companion was the delightful A. I. Skvortsov, since shot by the Bolsheviks.[3] Immediately after Saratov came my concert in Moscow (arranged by Suvchinsky's *Musical*

---

1 See *Diaries*, vol. 1, p. 131 and *passim*.
2 Vladimir Dranishnikov had been conducting performances at the Mariinsky Theatre since 1918, and served as its Music Director and Principal Conductor from 1925 to 1936. See *Diaries*, ibid., p. 272 and *passim*.
3 See p. 169.

Contemporary magazine. This was a most prestigious concert, with all musical Moscow in attendance: Koussevitzky, Rachmaninoff, Medtner, Balmont. Rachmaninoff sat like an idol carved from stone; Medtner produced his famous judgement: 'Either this is not music, or I am not a musician.' After the concert there was supper at T. N's.,¹ sister of B. N, with whom I was staying, with Balmont, Suvchinsky and Asafyev. I said to Balmont (whom I did not know at all well at the time) that I wanted to compose music to *Seven, They Are Seven*, to which Balmont replied: 'You are a brave man.'

This winter also saw the premiere in Ziloti's concert season of *Autumnal*, also the tremendously successful repeat of the *Scythian Suite*, outdoing that of the preceding work in the programme, Rachmaninoff's performance of his own Second Piano Concerto. Rachmaninoff heard the *Suite* standing in the gangway of the Mariinsky Theatre, and said (as it was reported to me): 'I do not understand this music, but I sense that it is talented.' During this winter there was also the first complete concert devoted to my works, a chamber music concert in Ziloti's season, and the scandal of Sabaneyev, who so disastrously gave himself away over the *Scythian Suite*.²

In the sphere of romance, there was the saga with Polina Podolskaya, whom both Max and I had fruitlessly lusted after four years previously when she was a delightfully chubby fourteen-year-old. In autumn 1916 she wrote to me out the blue, our relationship blossomed, and when I performed in Kiev she ordered flowers from Kharkov which were presented to me at the concert. This produced such an effect on me that instead of returning to Petrograd I charged off for two days to Kharkov, to the great bemusement of Glière. There followed contact with Polina by correspondence, and she came to stay with me in Petrograd at Shrovetide.³

At this point the next diary notebook takes over, which I have with me here in Ettal. But my correspondence for the first half of 1917 is also missing, including the copy of the letter I wrote to Polina when she decided not to join me in my madcap plan to travel to Honolulu. Some passages of this furious letter have lodged in my memory: 'And so, Polina, you have weighed and calculated everything with an accuracy that would do credit not merely

---

1   Tatyana Nikolayevna, Boris Bashkirov's sister. See above pp. 131 and 170.
2   See above, p. 172.
3   In fact, as is clear from the Diaries for 1916 and 1917 included in this volume, the notebook whose loss Prokofiev so much regrets was preserved. It must have been in the trunk full of papers he left in Koussevitzky's safekeeping in August 1917 (see above. pp. 225 and 536) that had subsequently been passed to Myaskovsky. At considerable personal risk Myaskovsky had kept all the potentially compromising papers and was able to give them to Prokofiev, to the latter's great joy, when they met on the occasion of his first visit to the Soviet Union in 1927. This Prokofiev tells us in his Diaries for the period (22 January 1927), but although after a gap of almost five years the two friends resumed correspondence in January 1923, it was naturally not a subject to be put in writing, hence it would be another four years before the fate of the contents of the trunk could be established.

to a medical student but to a fully-fledged pharmacist's wife, and you, solid and prosaic female that you are, have elected to go to the bright "new" land that is the town of Taganrog! And when you look out of your window at the pigs rooting in the mud of the Taganrog streets and fall to contemplating the sweeping vistas before your eyes, be aware that at that very moment I shall be able to hear you!' and so on, I do not recall the whole letter, but it was written not with ink but with the venom of my spittle.

Now that I have been for a time immersed in these recollections I am a little calmer, but when I first read the letter I had received from Eleonora I was in a rage: at Asafyev, for not having rescued and preserved the papers in time; at that scoundrel Lourié for not giving him permission to do so when he, Lourié, had the power; and at Suvchinsky, who installed his 'loyal building supervisor' in my apartment, a man who then disappeared without trace and abandoned my apartment to the four winds.[1]

Now, however, I have calmed down, and my fury is assuaged: there is no point in being angry any more, the ashes from my burnt manuscripts have long ago been scattered by the wind! It would be a more profitable focus for my energies to establish for sure whether the manuscript of my score of *The Gambler* is intact (I believed it had been destroyed at Tyulin's and only a copy still existed, as Eleonora writes) and if so whether I could somehow spirit it and get it here so that I could revise it and turn *The Gambler* into a tidier piece of work than it currently is.

17 December

I have remembered something else that perished in Pervaya Rota: the 'Sacred Yellow Book' to which Max and I confided our amorous yearnings, very childish and innocent.[2] The Diary will have notes on my readings of Schopenhauer with B.N., beginning with *Aphorisms on the Wisdom of Life*[3] and continuing with *The World as Will and Representation*. That winter I spent a good deal of time at B.N.'s house, and we spent whole evenings reading Schopenhauer. This reading profoundly interested me and served to deepen my understanding. It gave rise to the summer of 1917 that I passed in solitude, and *Seven, They Are Seven* was the fruit.

A tenderly affectionate letter from Ptashka. It tormented her that I had let

---

1 'The score of my Second Concerto [the whereabouts of which Myaskovsky had been cautiously enquiring about] perished in the looting of my Petersburg apartment, because that swine whom you so courteously refer to as Artur Sergeyevich [Lourié] would not, at the time he had the power to do so, provide Asafyev with the official documents he needed to remove my manuscripts from the apartment and keep them safe.' (Letter from Prokofiev to Myaskovsky, 6 February 1923)
2 See *Diaries*, vol. 1, p. 244 and *passim*, also above p. 95, 95n.
3 One of the essays in Schopenhauer's last major work, *Parerga und Paralipomena* (1851).

her go away from Ettal without saying anything. I wrote back that I loved her very much, that I awaited her coming for Christmas, that henceforward we must not be so often apart, but that I was still fearful that marriage might dim the brightness of love.

18 December

Worked intensively composing endings for the sections of the Suite from *Chout*, and checking the copyist's work. Wrote to Derzhanovsky. My mood is good. In the evenings Mama and I read Ehrenburg's *Julia Jurenito*.[1] There is much wit in it, but too much of it is overlaid with a scum of the disorderly belligerence that afflicts our world today.

19 December

Continued the work I was doing yesterday: I want to finish the Suite and put it behind me as quickly as possible. I waited for B.N. to reappear, but in his usual manner he failed to keep his word. He neither came nor cabled. I am already anticipating with pleasure the feeble excuses he will produce when he does come.

A letter from Zederbaum, who is currently with Koussevitzky in Barcelona. It seems I shall have a concert there. This is very pleasant news: Spain is a highly musical country and the peseta enjoys a favourable rate of exchange. On top of that, if I am successful in Spain it is always possible to get a lot of concert engagements.

20 December

Sat for six hours and finished the Suite from *Chout*. The copyist produced a total of 195 small pages of manuscript, and like all copyists sometimes deviated into the realms of fantasy. I got very bored with it, and the notes started swimming before my eyes.

A telegram from B.N.: 'Viendrai dans quelques jours.'[2] He wants to demonstrate his independence! For a month, with endless seductive protestations of 'How indispensable a friend you are to me!' he managed to

---

1 *The Extraordinary Adventures of Julia Jurenito and his Disciples* was Ehrenburg's first novel, written in 1922, and one of the most interesting of his oeuvre. A parody of the Gospels, its main protagonist is a cynical Mexican Antichrist figure, examining Candide-like the foibles of capitalist, communist and religious, etc., societies through the eyes of his seven stereotyped disciples. Real-life individuals such as Picasso, Diego Rivera, Mayakovsky and Charlie Chaplin make cameo appearances.

2 'Shall come in a few days.'

wheedle 400 francs (200,000 marks) out of me. I would rather have sent Mayakovsky a parcel with a new suit in it!

It has to be finally admitted, B.N. is not a poet. The well-spring is dry! But he is not bad as a translator, and might this not be a better path for him to take? Has Bunin ever done anything better than his translation of *The Song of Hiawatha*?[1] Perhaps I should try to persuade B.N. of this.

21 December

Myaskovsky has sent me a manuscript of his four of his piano *Caprices*.[2] Two of them are very good indeed, and if Barcelona comes off I will play them there.

Now that I have finished the Suite from *Chout*, I got back to *Fiery Angel* and got bogged down in the mayhem,[3] which is even more difficult to conceive than it is to compose. It will mean a lot of work: a schematic plan (as I did for *Seven, They Are Seven*), and filling out the text, which involved much rooting around in Bryusov.

I read the second volume of Blok. It is better than the first, which is often unreadable. I very much liked 'When you stand on my path' and 'The Song of Faina'. Could this be because these poems are the least like Blok?

24 December

Christmas Eve promised to be just an ordinary day: Mama and I were sitting on our own, with no word from B.N., and not even a letter from Ptashka. But suddenly at seven o'clock in the evening B.N. appeared, the telegram he sent had not arrived, and at nine o'clock – Ptashka. This was a real surprise! She had also telegraphed, but the cable's journey had taken longer than her own. The poor girl had had to trudge up the hill in the snow and the dark for a whole hour while the stationmaster's son carried her suitcase. I could not believe she had actually come. Champagne was produced, and then there was no holding back the festivities.

Christmas altogether was the gayest of times. We went sledging down the Ettal mountains.

---

1 Narrative poem written in 1855 by H. W. Longfellow, based on American Indian stories and legends.
2 This opus would eventually be *Prichudy* [*Caprices*]: *6 Sketches for piano*, Op. 27 (1922–7).
3 In the last act of *Fiery Angel*, to the horror of the Abbess and the Grand Inquisitor – and in a good production to the delight of the audience – Renata infects the nuns with her demonic possession, leading to a general display of wildly erotic nudity and satanic degeneracy.

1923

5 January

Set some chess problems for Ptashka; B.N. solved them, but they are too hard for her.

> With molars thirty-six to bite
> Hussa's fixed him up all right.[1]

13 January

Composed the whole of the final scene between Mephistopheles and Rupprecht, thus completing *Fiery Angel*. Of course, many places are so far not properly integrated, and the joins in Act Five are as yet plain for all to see, but it is important that I have got to the end of the work and, as B.N. put it, 'the battleship has been launched upon the waves'.

The second significant event of the day was the first performance in Brussels, indeed in Belgium, of any of my works, at least of a major work: the *Scythian Suite*. And finally, a third great achievement: Mama finished knitting a scarf she plans to send to Aunt Katya in Penza, a task on which she has been engaged for half a year. In short, we decided we had cause enough to celebrate the Old Russian New Year, which we did with great glee, polishing off a bottle of champagne to the sound of the midnight bells from the monastery tower.

14 January

Had a headache from the New Year toasts. Ptashka is getting her things together as it is high time she went back to Italy to continue her studies. She might get an engagement there as well, and make a start on a career as a singer, but here in Ettal it could all just slip past her.

At six o'clock we set off for Munich in snow and frost.

---

1 Dr Philip Hussa was Prokofiev's dentist in New York. See above, p. 385.

15 January

All day Ptashka and I ran around Munich dealing with visas and tickets, and also because of the xylophone. We went into four music shops ostensibly to find out the price of xylophones, and also into three bookshops again ostensibly looking to buy an Italian dictionary, but we had no success in finding out whether there exists in Italy such a thing as a silofono, or as it is universally styled, xylophone. In one of the shops they showed me an instrument and told me that as it was a German invention, the only correct name for it was 'xylophone'.

At half-past eleven at night Ptashka left for Milan, and we parted with mutual endearments.

16 January

My train hardly managed to struggle out of Munich, as a snowstorm was raging and we had to stop several times. From Oberammergau to Ettal I went on foot, getting completely bogged down in the snowdrifts and almost drowning in the blizzard. All was well at home, only quieter without Ptashka. Seven letters were waiting for me: Borovsky wrote to say that he had been playing my compositions in Barcelona with tremendous success.

Revised the end of Act Four. In the evening played a lot of chess with B.N., with the result: 7–2. The Diva wrote from Brussels to tell me that the *Scythian Suite* had been extremely well received.

17 January

Revised and filled in some gaps in Act Five, and made a plan for the conclusion of Act Two, which so far does not exist. Wrote letters. Outside, the blizzard continues unabated.

18 January

Did some cleaning up of *Fiery Angel* and patched here and there.

23 January

Two letters from America: the *Musical Courier* and Haensel would both like to know when I am going to be in a position to pay their bills. The fact is, I still have debts in America amounting to $2,500, and it is extremely disagreeable to be reminded of them.

Walked to Oberammergau and changed $5, for which I received 95,000 marks. Something to think about: here I have $5, and over there I owe $2,500!

Miller came to Oberammergau to say goodbye. She is going back to Riga.

24 January

Today I received from Barcelona an invitation for two chamber music evenings with a cellist (something I am already used to from America!), with very convenient dates between 15 and 20 February, that is immediately before I go to Paris. The fee is 2,500 francs plus my train ticket (second class!), a pathetically small amount, but in my present impoverished state it will put a bit of bread in our mouths. I thought about it, and wrote a lengthy reply.

A thought occurred to me: I might be able to get there via Milan, and then I could see Ptashka! But would the Italians let me have a transit visa? Then in the evening I had another thought: if the Italians would not give me a visa I could go via Strasbourg – Lyon – Tarascon. Ptashka is not far away from these last two places, and we could have a couple of days together while I was *en route*. The idea brought on a wonderful mood.

Today's result from our chess games was 4–1, but recently B.N. has been getting stronger and the results were even.

25 January

Zederbaum writes that Koussevitzky may engage a chorus in the spring, and therefore it may be possible to perform *Seven, They Are Seven*. If this is the case, I shall need to prepare a piano score, and since I am taking a break from *Angel* (I have been doing a lot over the last few days and have had enough of it for the time being) now is the time to get on with it. I started work on it.

Wrote letters. I got a letter from Daniel offering me a series of ten concerts next autumn in Spain at a fee of 500 pesetas a concert. Not a great fee, but the prospect of a tour in Spain is enticing!

26 January

My good spirits on account of an invitation to go to Brussels and meeting up with Ptashka continue. I visited the monastery and looked through the guidebooks they have there. To get to Brussels seems a remarkably complicated journey! And it is not very easy for Ptashka to get to Lyon either.

Wrote letters, but was troubled by my persistent headache. Composed a little of the finale of the Fifth Sonata. A letter from Myaskovsky, a lovely one although slightly polite and reserved, somewhat reminiscent of the terms in which Tchaikovsky wrote to Nápravnik.[1] I love Myaskovsky very much, and am glad we are in contact again.

27 January

Began the task of making a piano transcription of *Seven, They Are Seven*. I thought at first it was going to be an impossible task, but after all it seems that something can be done.

30 January

They write from Barcelona that strenuous efforts are being made to obtain my Spanish visa, so I dropped everything and went to Munich. Evidently my compositional activities will be put on hold for a period while I return to the vagabond life of a concert performer.

31 January

To my astonishment, the Spanish Consul in Munich gave me a visa immediately 'as a musician'. I then went to the Austrian Consulate, where the same thing happened. Now all I need is an Italian visa, and then I shall be able to go via Milan! The rate of exchange is currently 45,000 marks to the dollar, so everything is very cheap: I bought myself an opera hat, pyjamas and some gloves. In the evening I went to Passau, a small town situated at the confluence of the Danube and Inn rivers near the Austrian border, where we have been strongly recommended to look for a house. Our lease of Ettal will come to an end in April and we are looking for somewhere else to move to, since despite all its comforts Ettal is cold, there is not much sun, nowhere to bathe, and – the most important thing – it seems to be bad for Mama's health.

As I was informed that all hotels in Passau were full, I stayed in a wretched little apology for a town called Plattering, where I got a room above a greasy-spoon restaurant for 200 marks, i.e. half of one cent.

1 February

Got up at eight, still dark and raining. The train timetables are in a complete shambles because owing to the French occupation of the Ruhr and diffi-

---

[1] Eduard Nápravnik (1839–1916), Czech conductor and composer, for many years Chief Conductor and Music Director of the Mariinsky Theatre. He conducted the premieres of many of Tchaikovsky's operas and also, nine days after the composer's death, the performance of the 'Pathétique' Symphony that incontrovertibly established it as one of the composer's greatest masterpieces.

culties with the supply of coal, rail traffic has been sharply reduced.[1]

After some time looking in Passau and Degendorf I still had not found a villa to rent, but three agents to whom I spoke and offered commission percentages promised to let me have proposals in a few days' time. Exhausted, I returned to Munich late in the evening.

2 February

Eventually managed to get my Italian visa, and as my business was now concluded I was free to go back to Ettal where today, in contrast to how it has been recently, the sun is shining and the first hints of long-delayed spring are beginning to show themselves. B.N. says that although I have done all that is humanly possible to find another house, he does not believe the agents will find anything. This is a device to ensure that we stay on in Ettal.

A huge pile of letters, many of which demand urgent replies. Only in the evenings do we have time to read together, otherwise the whole day is taken up with answering letters, not to mention the fact that I have to practise for my concerts.

We are reading the Wells *Outline of History* and Tolstoy's *Circle of Reading*.[2] There is much wisdom in it, but also much that is sanctimonious and often provincial.

7 February

My cases were already packed, and in the morning, accompanied by Boris Nikolayevich, I embarked on my long-distance travels. Having almost missed the train, I had a long wait in Garmisch for visa checking and financial transactions, followed by the border crossing at Mittenwald, borders being

---

[1] On 11 January in protest against the Weimar Republic's failure to keep up its crippling reparations payments, French troops occupied the Ruhr industrial heartland of coal-mining, iron and steel production. Unrest, sabotage and strikes continued until September 1923, although passive resistance continued long after that and the last French troops did not withdraw until August 1925.

[2] Tolstoy's last major work, translated into English as *A Calendar of Wisdom* (Leo Tolstoy, *A Calendar of Wisdom*, trans. Peter Sekirin (Simon & Schuster, New York, 1997), is an extraordinary attempt, in the author's words in his Preface, to 'present for a wide reading audience an easily accessible, everyday circle of reading which will arouse their best thoughts and feelings'. The outcome was a commonplace book designed to evangelise the ideals he struggled to put into practice in his later years. Tolstoy believed that a daily reading from the world's great literature was essential for both his own spiritual edification and that of his readers, so he set himself the task of gathering examples of a huge range of wisdom for every day of the year. He himself translated, and in many cases paraphrased, excerpts from sources including the New Testament, the Koran, the Greek philosophers, Lao-Tzu, Buddhist thought, and the poetry, novels, and essays of ancient and contemporary writers.

milestones that I invariably approach with a certain respect: leaving one state to enter another with different laws, different destinies, different clothes, different money. The journey from Mittenwald to Innsbruck is extraordinarily beautiful and interesting. The line goes up quite high, clinging to the side of the mountain; on one side the traveller's view is of the shapely outline of the peaks standing out against the rays of the sun, and on the other a precipice, and far below the valley along the bottom of which winds the River Inn. Innsbruck itself was less attractive than I had imagined, but as I did not want to spend the night on the train I stayed in the town. The prices are in five figures, much more expensive than in Germany. Even so, it is a lot cheaper than Spain, but those five figures are alarming, for example 28,000 crowns for a room. I walked round the town, felt tired and went early to bed, pleased with life.

8 February

It was still dark when I got up and at seven o'clock in the morning continued my journey. The way was still beautiful, especially in the slanting rays of the sunrise. Before long we had crossed Austria (at the border the Italians picked on me, going through my luggage looking for Bolshevik propaganda and in the process soiling my starched shirts) and then we were in land recently annexed from Austria by Italy. This was interesting, as it is not often one has the opportunity of being in 'conquered' territory. It soon grew warmer with the southern sun, and I dozed off with the rocking of the train and my early start. At seven o'clock in the evening we drew into Milan and there was Ptashka at the station. She had told her pensione she would be away for a few days, and we installed ourselves in the Como Hotel directly opposite the station. Not long before she had auditioned for the theatre, and it was possible she would be making her debut in *Rigoletto* right here in Milan.[1] Splendid! We had dinner in the city centre and drank Asti.

9 February

Milan was foggy, damp and not particularly attractive. We visited the cathedral, where we wanted to go up to the roof, but the drizzling rain put us off. There is no performance at La Scala today.

11 February

The morning was devoted to writing letters I had not managed to finish in Ettal. At eight o'clock we left for Genoa, arriving there later that evening in the rain. A slight tiff was soon resolved and harmony restored. Genoa promises to be interesting with its steep, narrow streets and ancient palazzos.

---

1   Lina Codina does not seem to have appeared in a public performance of *Rigoletto*.

12 February

We looked round Genoa and spent all day going up and down the steep streets. Milan is an international, German city, while Genoa is much more of an Italian one. We went to the famous cemetery, a marble bacchanalia of the dead, and a pretty park in the middle of the town near the embankment illuminated by a magnificent sunset, where there was a house with an incredible colonnade which local informants told us the owner had lost gambling at Monte Carlo. We ended the day tired, but very happy.

13 February

After an emotional farewell with Ptashka I journeyed on from Genoa to Marseilles. This promised to be in interesting trip, along the Italian and French Rivieras. The sun was shining and the line ran all the way along the shore of the bright blue sea.

The Riviera was full of life, with people dressed in their holiday best for Shrovetide. Menton and Monte Carlo are too chocolate-boxy for my taste, amusing places to stay but not for long. Also, I found the preponderance of idlers quite insufferable: in this respect I have quite 'socialist' views! Nevertheless, overall I very much enjoyed the trip. In the evening, coming into Marseilles, I had a conversation with a Frenchman with a fractured skull, a thorough-going bantam-cock who sitting in his tank had faced head on an entire German battery. This was a man who knew to the precise millimetre the distance between one bullet and another fired from a machine-gun, how many seconds it would take for a shell to reach an aeroplane at a height of three versts (two and a quarter), and so on. He was thirsting to have another crack at the enemy and break their heads. At eleven o'clock we reached Marseilles, where I spent the night before continuing on the following morning.

14 February

Left Marseilles at eight o'clock, by an express train with very few people on board. I read the French newspapers with great interest: after the German press I was curious to know how the French regarded the Ruhr. In my opinion now the French had clamped their bulldog jaws around it they were not about to let go.

After a fairly brisk sprint we stopped for a while at a little border town and then entered Spain at seven o'clock. I have a great partiality for Spain, but had been warned that they can be very awkward at their borders. My train did not have a connection, so there was plenty of time to get things sorted out. This proved to be just as well: my visa failed in some unknown respect to be satisfactory and a telegram had to be sent to Barcelona, and I would have to wait for the reply. At first I was annoyed, but then I reflected that since the advent of the Bolsheviks such is frequently the distressing fate of Russian travellers, and in their time Koussevitzky, Janacopulos and Larionov had all been aggravated in just this place and just this way. Accordingly I decided to pay no attention but to wait patiently for the telegram from Barcelona, which was promised for noon the next day.

The officials were very pleasant and themselves indignant at the inconvenience to which I was being put; no doubt had I spoken better Spanish and been able to plead my case more eloquently they might have let me through. But as things were, knowing no more than one and a half words of Spanish, I babbled something in a mixture of Italian and French, and at nine o'clock found a hotel where I could go to bed.

15 February

The good side of my detention was that I had a wonderful sleep, from nine o'clock until nine o'clock. If they had let me go straight away I would have had to leave at four in the morning and lose a whole night's sleep. The officials had asked me to return at noon, so I spent the morning wandering round the little town in the sunshine and looking at the dark blue waters of the bay carved out of the Mediterranean. It was a peculiar idea that I was not allowed to go to Barcelona, but at the same time could go wherever else in Spain I liked. It followed that my guards must regard me as a trustworthy person – but then, what were they detaining me for? If they had had any suspicions of me they would hardly have given me my freedom to go wherever I pleased without a passport. It seemed illogical.

At noon I presented myself again to the officials, but there was still no answer from Barcelona. At this my mood distinctly took a turn for the worse. I came back at half-past three. Still no telegram. I suggested that they retain my passport and allow me to go to Barcelona without it, giving my word that I would return to the same place on my way back. Sympathetic smiles, mutual consultations, much thumbing through my passport and exclamations of 'stupido'. Finally, they entrusted my person to another official (or he may have been a detective) and proposed that I get on the Barcelona express that had just pulled in, and take it as far as the next station, where there was a police commissar.

Hastily gathering up my things, I threw myself on to the splendid express along with the official, who most of the time discreetly absented himself, and went to Figueras. There, he and I walked together through the little town to the police station, where I was asked to wait while they took my passport away. After some time they returned saying 'passo', meaning 'it passed the test', accompanied me back to the railway station, wished me well, and I took the next mail train to Barcelona, happy indeed to be finally rid of these throwbacks to Bolshevik culture. It was late in the evening by the time I got to Barcelona, I was dog-tired and immediately went to bed.

16 February

Rested, washed, spruced and dressed up, I wandered round Barcelona. I had heard so much about this city (Beloúsov[1] was telling me about it as much as ten years ago) that I was expecting something magnificently out of the ordinary, but this I did not find. However, the sun was warm on my back, the boulevards were filled with luxuriant flowers and lined with whole aviaries of canaries, humming-birds and parrots for sale, which made a fearful racket. Clausells, the secretary of the music society for whom I was playing, was distressed to hear of my detention at the border, and said that they had written and telegraphed the Ministry in Madrid, who had promised to take care of it, but that is the attractive way things are in Spain. I practised in the afternoon and went for another stroll, then read the French and German newspapers. German reaction to the occupation of the Ruhr is to yelp like a cur, while the French hiss and spit like a cat. How pleasant it is to look at Spain and know that it has kept itself apart from the murderous aggression of the rest of the world!

17 February

From Ettal they forwarded a cable from Daniel inviting me to perform in Valencia, but it was not clear when. Pleased, I cabled him back and looked up the location of Valencia on the map. Then I practised, and went out to walk. The way of life here is peaceful, even a little boring. My first concert was at ten o'clock that evening (life is generally two hours later here); it was a short concert, because the first two parts were given over to the cellist Alexanian.[2] In the third section, which was mine, I played six of the *Pictures from an Exhibition* and my Third Sonata. The audience was noisy and coughed continually, and were more inclined to applaud lyrical playing than virtuosity. They were polite about *Pictures*, but responded very warmly to the Sonata. The piano was stiff and dull, and I quite often had to force the

1 Yevsey Beloúsov, cellist who in January 1914 had given with the composer the first performance of Prokofiev's *Ballade*, Op. 15. See above, p. 75 n. 7.
2 Diran Alexanian (1881–1954), one of the most gifted cellists and teachers of his generation. Born in Constantinople, as a student in Leipzig he had played trios with Brahms and Joachim; later Casals made him his assistant at the Ecole normale de musique in Paris. Among his own students were Janigro, Fournier, Piatigorsky and Feuermann. Today Alexanian is remembered not only for his place in the pantheon of great cello pedagogues, but for his masterly edition of Bach's Cello Suites, published in 1929.

sound. Afterwards some of the members of the Society took Alexanian and me to supper.

18 February

Either because of the Spanish beer I drank last night, or because I have the beginnings of a cold, I had a headache all day. Had lunch with Mompou,[1] a young composer from these parts, who played me some of his rather nice compositions and then he took me to see the environs of the city, including a superb avenue which is just now in the process of construction. I have now realised what is good about Barcelona: its narrow streets, brilliantly illuminated at six or seven o'clock in the evening and thronged with gaily animated crowds.

19 February

The cellist and I were taken up the funicular railway to Tibidabo,[2] a nearby peak from which there is a view over the city, the sea and the mountains. Very beautiful, but there was a strong wind blowing and I have the most horrible cold nicely brewing up.

The second concert took place that evening. I played even less than in the first: six of my short pieces. It was a good success, and there was much noisy appreciation after *Suggestion Diabolique*, so I played two encores. The management was happy and even went so far as to give Alexanian and me each a 'tip' of 100 pesetas because the franc, the currency in which the contract had been drawn up, had lost so much of its value. Afterwards they again took us out to supper.

20 February

I thought I would take the ten o'clock train to Paris, but it transpired that it would be possible for me to obtain a re-entry visa into Spain, and this is

---

1 Federico Mompou (1893–1987), Catalan composer who studied in Paris. A private and reserved miniaturist whose brief experience of working in a bell foundry in Barcelona had a great influence on his musical thought, he was perhaps the complete opposite of Prokofiev in acknowledging that his music was not destined to create an impact on the wider world. In a late memoir, discussing his collections of short piano pieces *Musica Callada* (*Quiet Music*) he wrote: 'My music has a weak heart beat. You cannot ask it to reach more than a few inches into space, but its mission is to reach the profound depths of our soul and the secret regions of our spirit's spirit. This music is quiet (*callada*) because one listens to it within.'
2 Tibi dabo, from the Latin of the Vulgate Bible: 'tibi dabo potestatem hanc universam et gloriam illorum . . .' 'All this power will I give thee, and the glory of them', as the devil tempted Jesus from the top of the mountain when he showed him all the kingdoms of the earth.

important, so I decided to stay an extra day. Daniel believes I could with advantage make a longer tour, and suggested concerts in Valencia and Madrid. I proposed that he arrange three concerts for me in April or May.

I now have a streaming cold, and consigned my pile of unanswered letters to perdition.

21 February

At ten o'clock Alexanian and I, accompanied by several members of the Society, left for Paris. At the border I was met very kindly by my former captors, and when I showed my return permission from the Barcelona police, they smiled and wished me a pleasant journey.

My usual travelling methodology is to be on the move until the evening, then sleep in a hotel and continue the next morning. Alexanian, however, persuaded me not to maintain this 'stupidity' and so we went straight on, spending the night, five of us, in a second-class compartment. I slept on a sort of half-bench stretching my legs out over suitcases placed between the benches. It turned out in the end not to be too bad, and when we arrived in Paris at nine the next morning I felt in good form.

1 March

Spent the morning packing and then, having said goodbye to the Stahls, left for Antwerp at noon. It was a fast train, there were no delays at the frontier, and at seven o'clock I was met at Antwerp station by Van Camp, the very nice secretary of the Society for whom I am playing. He fixed me up with a discounted price in a good hotel. In the evening I walked round the town, which looks a good, solid sort of place, as far as one could tell in the evening. I was tired from the journey and went to bed early.

2 March

The first rehearsal of the Piano Concerto No. 3 was a long one, with two-and-a-half hours devoted to it. That's how they work in the provinces!! The conductor was young but very committed. His tastes lean to the conservative, but when he went to Brussels to hear the performance of the *Scythian Suite* he had come back wildly enthused, so he is now making great efforts.

The directors are exceptionally friendly and courteous. One of them had been in command of a fortress at the time the Germans captured the town, and told me many interesting things about the siege and the battle. I still remember the excitement with which in Petrograd we followed the newspaper accounts of the battle for Antwerp, and for that reason to hear about it from the lips of one of the commanders at the time was not only piquant but downright absorbing. B.N. always recalls with emotion the firepower the Germans unleashed against Antwerp.

3 March

Practised in the morning, because while I have been on the road both the Third Concerto and my programme for the Brussels recital have been neglected. In the morning one of the Society's directors took me to see the Plantin House Museum, which had belonged to one of the founders of the printing business in the sixteenth century.[1] This is a real living museum of old books, manuscripts and drawings, all housed in an environment created at exactly the time when Rupprecht[2] lived, and since on account of Renata he spent so much time rummaging through books this house is a perfect illustration of the ambiance in which the story of *Fiery Angel* unfolds. When someone comes to stage my opera, I recommend him to pay a visit to this house. It has been meticulously preserved from the sixteenth century, and almost certainly it would have been in such a setting that Faust and Agrippa of Nettesheim worked.

14 May[3]

The concert with Balmont.[4] The receipts amounted to 4,000 francs; Balmont had previously suggested that we divide the takings fifty–fifty but when the concert was over gave me nothing. A thousand had been spent on organising the event, a further thousand on renting the apartment, then Balmont had spent eight hundred on a new suit, and if the remainder were to be divided there would be practically nothing left. Although I am short of money, it is less this aspect that upsets me than Balmont not keeping his word.

1   Christoffel Plantin (1520–1589) established his printing house 'De Gulden Passer' ('The Golden Compasses') in 1555. The firm's most famous achievement was the publication of the *Biblia Polyglotta*, a typographical masterpiece in five languages, between 1568 and 1773, but it was also a great centre of humanist learning and scholarship. The firm continued in business until 1876, when the house, the printing and works and the fabulous library and archive were taken over by the city and turned into the Plantin-Moretus Museum.
2   The knight Rupprecht is the main male protagonist of Bryusov's and Prokofiev's *The Fiery Angel*. Renata is the heroine, or anti-heroine. Faust and Agrippa are other characters in the novel and the opera.
3   The Diary is scanty between early March and September 1923, perhaps because of the domestic contentment of what was effectively married life in Ettal. Prokofiev performed with triumphant success in Antwerp and Brussels and partnered Lina Codina in recital in Milan. At home he continued recasting the Second Piano Concerto and started work on the Fifth Piano Sonata.
4   This concert took place in Paris.

1 September

I begin my Diary again from the first of the month simply to have a point of reference. Ettal is like a beautiful woman who has reached the age of fifty: still fresh and on the surface young, but the moment there is a touch of influenza, when she rises again from her bed she is an old woman. This is how it is with us; the summer has been like a real summer, but when the rain comes it is suddenly like October.

I am revising the finale of the Second Concerto. But I cannot work very energetically: my heart begins to race and then the pain comes.

Life is becoming significantly more expensive, and there is talk of civil disturbances. Should we find another country to move to?

2 September

Eberg writes that there has to be a temporary interruption in the publication of my compositions as prices have leapt up twenty times even when calculated on gold. Therefore the engraving of the 'Classical' Symphony, the Schubert Waltzes and other works has been put on hold indefinitely. He asks me to make haste with proof-reading the Suite from *Chout*, so I got down to it straight away.

Colonel Ewald and his wife came to stay. We are not too fond of having guests, but these ones we can support tolerably well.

3 September

I am making use of the Colonels' stay – that is, the Colonel and his lady – to press on with proofing the *Chout* Suite. In the evening I showed off to him the high standard of chess play in these parts by playing the fourth game in my current match against B.N. I won, much to B.N.'s exasperation. Since my heart has recovered its strength and we resumed our former pattern of play I have become truly invincible: of the last eight games I did not lose a single one, winning five and drawing three.

The Colonel says there will not be any social revolution in Bavaria. If the unrest worsens in Berlin, Bavaria will immediately secede. He is advising us to stay in Bavaria and rent a villa belonging to Count Manteuffel, which he says is very good indeed. I wrote to the Count, just in case.

4 September

Went for a walk with the Colonel and obtained some confidential information on how best to arrange my marriage to Ptashka. In America this could be done very easily, it would take about seven minutes, but in Deutschland there are so many formalities and delays that even seven weeks would not be enough to get the job done. The Colonel was uncommonly kind and promised to lean on his contacts in Munich to expedite the process.[1]

A letter from Zederbaum to say that Koussevitzky would perform my Violin Concerto in Paris on 18 October (at long last, seven years after it was composed, albeit with a poor violinist),[2] and the Second Piano Concerto with myself as soloist on the 25th. Although he has engaged a chorus on 8 November he is not going to do *Seven, They Are Seven* at all. I am disconsolate at this news: *Seven* is the most important work I want to be played! Also, I am not at all sure I shall manage to learn the solo part of the Concerto by the 25th; my heart is still not strong enough to work myself into a lather over it, which is what I would have to do.[3]

5 September

The Colonels have left us. In the end, it was nice having them.

8 September

Very relieved that I do not have to thrash the Second Concerto into shape for October. All the same, I must keep going on it, because if I don't finish it this autumn it will drag on until the spring. I worked on the Intermezzo.

Wrote to Tokugawa and Otaguro because of the earthquake in Japan. Are they alive?[4]

---

1 Towards the end of the summer it emerged that Lina Codina was pregnant, and the couple married in a simple civil ceremony in Ettal on 29 September.
2 The concert took place in the Paris Opéra with Koussevitzky conducting the Paris Opéra Orchestra, the leader of which, Marcel Darrieux, was the soloist in the Violin Concerto, more celebrated virtuosi having apparently turned it down. At least Josef Szigeti, among other luminaries, was in the audience to hear it, and gave the work its first performance in Russia in the newly renamed city of Leningrad the following year before making it one of his principal repertoire pieces in almost every major city of Europe and America (not, however, before Nathan Milstein and Vladimir Horowitz had played it in a violin-and-piano version in Moscow only three days after the Paris premiere). At this same Paris concert Stravinsky conducted the orchestra's principal wind-players in the premiere of his Octet.
3 Prokofiev did not have to: the premiere of the revised Second Piano Concerto was postponed until May 1924, partly in consequence of the colossal row that erupted over Koussevitzky's reluctance to pay the enormous cost of a large choir and tenor soloist for a 7-minute work, leading to the cancellation of the November premiere of *Seven, They are Seven*.
4 On 1 September 1923 the Great Kanto Earthquake, one of the worst earthquakes in history, struck the area around Tokyo and Yokohama, causing 100,000 deaths in those cities.

9 September

Ptashka and I went to mass in the monastery, during which there took place the ceremonial tonsure of three monks. Not only that, but the office was performed by a cardinal from Munich, so a great show was put on and millions of people were there. The Cardinal was a tall, strapping man with regular features similar to the recently deceased President Harding, but with a voluptuous curve to the lips. He was dressed in gold with a red cap, and down his back ran a white band with two black crosses that made him look exactly like the two of clubs. The whole service was very interesting.

On our return I got into an argument with B.N. when he announced that henceforward he would be going to bed in the morning and getting up at five o'clock in the evening, as he was 'moving to a nocturnal regime'. We were all up in arms at his claimed motivation that he would be able to work better at night. I told him he should stop trying to deceive us in this way: the truth was precisely the opposite, aimed at avoiding the need to do any work at all with no one to observe his indolence. It ended with me losing my temper and saying that in no circumstances would this be tolerated, and for the rest of the day he went around with a headache.

APPENDIX 1

Prokofiev's Notes on Characters in *The Gambler*, based on the descriptions in Dostoyevsky's eponymous novella

These notes appear in three languages (Russian, French and German) in the printed edition of the piano score of *The Gambler* prepared by the composer for Koussevitzky's Editions Russes de Musique, Berlin, 1929. This English translation is by Anthony Phillips.

THE GENERAL

Fifty-five years of age, overall an imposing and presentable figure, almost tall, with dyed side-whiskers and moustaches (formerly a cavalry officer) and distinguished if now somewhat flabby facial features. Impeccable manners, wears a frock-coat as to the manner born; the sort of man with whom it would be not merely acceptable but one might even say a recommendation to stroll along the boulevard.

THE BABULENKA (GRANDMA)

A wealthy and intimidating seventy-five-year-old, Antonida Vasilievna Tarasevicha is a Moscow *grande dame* and landowner with a large country estate. Having lost the use of her legs she has been confined for the past five years to a wheelchair, without losing any of her accustomed qualities of energy, pugnacity and wilfulness. Sitting bolt upright, she issues to all and sundry a stream of censorious, peremptory demands at the top of her voice. Grandma stems from a caste accustomed to exercising power, and although she does not rise from her chair one senses, looking at her, that she is an extremely tall woman. Never for a moment slumping in her chair, she holds her back as rigid as a board. Her large, grey-haired head, with its strong, even harsh features, is held up high, and as she looks around her with a haughty, imperious air it is perfectly clear that such is her normal, instinctive demeanour. Despite her seventy-five years, her complexion is reasonably fresh and even her teeth are sound. She is dressed in a black silk gown and a white bonnet. From the moment Grandma's chair is wheeled in, her imperious manner is the principal source of her ability to dominate the scene.

POLINA

The General's step-daughter. To see her, especially when she sits alone deep in thought, is to realise that she is marked out for an ill-fated, accursed destiny! But she is pretty, a really lovely girl, tall and slender, although delicate-looking. I imagine her capable of being entirely tied in a knot, or bent in two. Her hair has a reddish tinge. Her eyes are truly feline, but how proudly and disdainfully she can use them!

ALEXEY

Twenty-five years old, a university graduate from a well-born family. Irreproachably dressed, even dandified, as befits a young man belonging to the most elevated stratum of society.

THE MARQUIS

Unquestionably a member of polite society, his general attitude is arrogant and aloof. It is true that the previous year the Marquis came to the aid of the General by providing him with 30,000 roubles he lacked to discharge his financial obligations; he holds the General's IOU for this amount, as a result of which there is no question but that the General is in his clutches. Affable and friendly when it suits him, intolerably surly when there is no longer a need to be pleasant, he makes no effort to conceal his contempt for Alexey. He has a small goatee beard. I know a man here who swears he has encountered the Marquis somewhere under another name.

BLANCHE

Mlle Blanche is a very beautiful woman. But although I cannot precisely explain why, she has one of those faces which can frighten one. At any rate, I have always been wary of such women. She is probably about twenty-five years old. A tall, strapping figure with broad, rounded shoulders, she boasts a voluptuous neck and bosom; her complexion is swarthy-sallow and her abundant hair, of which she has enough to suffice for two coiffures, is black as ink. Her black eyes with their slightly yellow whites have a brazen look to them. Her teeth are dazzlingly white between her invariably rouged lips; the scent of musk always hangs about her. She dresses expensively and for effect, but with *chic* and good taste. Her feet and hands are amazing, her voice a husky contralto. From time to time she laughs out loud, and when she does she exposes all her teeth, but usually she observes the scene silently and slyly. I envisage her life hitherto to have been not without incident. If one is to be strictly honest, it is entirely possible that she is actually no relation to the Marquis, and her mother is not her mother.

ASTLEY

He fixes me with his penetrating, steely gaze, his jaws firmly clamped together. It is impossible to detect the slightest sign of concern or confusion in his face. Never in my life have I met anyone of such reserve as Astley. I believe he is hopelessly in love with Polina. Mr Astley is colossally rich. Mr Astley is the nephew of a lord, and the lord is also somewhere around.

PRINCE NILSKY

Insignificant, unprepossessing, wears spectacles.

POTAPYCH

Attired in white tie and frock-coat, but with a peaked cap. The majordomo of Grandma's establishment; an old, grey-haired man with a pink bald spot.

THE BARON

Tall and desiccated, with lopsided features honeycombed with a thousand wrinkles. Wears spectacles, about forty-five years of age. His legs come up almost to his chest, an irrefutable mark of his breeding. Vain as a peacock. His clothes hang baggily on him. He is inclined to mistake the sheep-like expression on his face as evidence of intellectual profundity.

THE BARONESS

Dressed in a light-grey robe of inconceivable vastness with flounces and a train over a crinoline. Short, squat, and extremely stout, with a gross and pendulous double chin that entirely obscures her neck. Purple complexion, with small, malicious and crafty eyes. As she passes by, it is as though she confers honour by her presence.

MARFA

Grandma's forty-year-old chambermaid, a spinster already going grey. White bonnet, cotton dress and kid-skin boots that squeak.

PALE LADY

Excessively modest and neatly dressed woman, rising thirty. Her pale, ill, exhausted-looking face still, however, bears traces of great former beauty.

APPENDIX 2

Description of 'The Seven'

I

Destructive storms and evil winds are they,
A storm of evil, presaging the baneful storm,
A storm of evil, forerunner of the baneful storm.
Mighty children, mighty sons are they,
Messengers of Namtar are they,
Throne-bearers of Ereshkigal.
The flood driving through the land are they.
Seven gods of the wide heavens,
Seven gods of the broad earth,
Seven robber-gods are they.
Seven gods of universal sway,
Seven evil gods,
Seven evil demons,
Seven evil and violent demons,
Seven in heaven, seven on earth.

II

Neither male nor female are they.
Destructive whirlwinds they,
Having neither wife nor offspring.
Compassion and mercy they do not know.
Prayer and supplication they do not hear.
Horses reared in the mountains, hostile to Ea.
Throne-bearers of the gods are they.
Standing on the highway, befouling the street.
Evil are they, evil are they,
Seven they are, seven they are,
Twice seven they are.

III

The high enclosures, the broad enclosures like a flood
　　they pass through.
From house to house they dash along.
No door can shut them out,
No bolt can turn them back.

> Through the door, like a snake, they glide,
> Through the hinge, like the wind, they storm.
> Tearing the wife from the embrace of the man,
> Snatching the child from the knees of a man,
> Driving the freedman from his family home.

(Translation by R. C. Thompson in *The Devils and Evil Spirits of Babylonia*, vols 1 and 2, Luzac & Co., London, 1903–4)

Lines added by Prokofiev:

> They make the sky and the earth shrink
> They confine whole countries as if behind doors
> They grind nations as nations grind corn.

APPENDIX 3

The Russian Composer Prokofiev in Japan
by Eleonora Sablina[1]

The Japanese Centre for Modern Music (Nihon Kindai Ongakukan) is in a narrow lane in Tokyo, directly opposite the Russian Embassy. Inspired by the Diaries of Sergey Prokofiev, I visited the Centre in the hope of discovering more information about his two-month stay in Japan during the summer of 1918.

The Archive of Contemporary Japanese Music was opened in October 1987. Preliminary work had begun in 1984 with the establishment of the Society for the Creation of a Modern Music Archive, to which four hundred people actively working in the field of Japanese culture contributed under the direction of the well-known composer Akutagawa Yasushi (1925–1989), son of the celebrated Akutagawa Ryunosuke.

The Archive contains materials on Western music in Japan from the time of the Emperor Meiji (1868–1912).[2] The collection includes scores, books, journals and recordings (on records, tapes and CDs) of works by the founder of the Japanese compositional school Yamada Kosaku (1886–1965), such well-known composers as Hashimoto Kunihiko (1904–1949), Ikebe Sinitiro (b. 1943), and others. The basis of the collection consists of composers' autographs preserved on microfilm, but there are also a large number of concert programmes. The archive contains works of musical scholarship by such well-known musicologists and critics as Otaguro Motoo (1893–1979), Nakamura Rihei (1932–1994), and Toyama Kazayuki (b. 1922). There is a dedicated information centre with a computer database of the history of Western music in Japan, beginning with the earliest newspaper publications from the end of the Tokugawa Shogunate (1603–1867) and the early Meiji period. The Centre itself forms part of the International Association of Music Information Centers (IAMIC) and thus offers the opportunity of obtaining news of the latest developments in musical culture around the world.

And thus, on 2 July 1918, Sergey Prokofiev wrote in his Diary:

> I dined in a Japanese restaurant with a Japanese journalist, a meeting that had been set up by the Director of the Imperial Theatre with the object of generating some publicity. Otaguro's book about music contains several

---

1 Translated from the Russian by Anthony Phillips, with kind permission, from the Annual *Yaponiya 2004–2005* (AIRO–XXI, Moscow, 2005).
2 All materials preserved in the archive are accessible for study. A reader's pass costs 500 yen for one year; photocopies are 50–60 yen per page, depending on size. (Note by E.S.)

references to me. When the book first appeared it created a great impression in the press; Otaguro himself, who is also the director of the publishing house, is extremely well informed about Russian music and we spent the whole dinner, served Japanese-style with us squatting on our haunches, talking (in English). It was a place where geishas danced, so opposite each diner sat two young, attractively dressed Japanese girls. Very nice.

The Otaguro referred to in the Diary was the above-mentioned music critic and scholar Otaguro Motoo. It is interesting to note that his father, Otaguro Jugoro (1866–1944), graduated from the Russian Department of the Tokyo School of Foreign Languages (today the Tokyo State University of Foreign Languages, Tokyo Gaikokugo Daigaku), where his fellow student and friend was [the writer] Futabatei Shimei (1864–1909). After Futabatei's death, Otaguro Jugoro wrote his reminiscences of the writer to honour his friend's memory, and published his complete works. In parallel with the School of Foreign Languages Otaguro Jugoro also graduated from the Tokyo School of Trade and Industry (today Hitotsubashi University), went to work at the Mitsui Group and became one of the founders of the Shibaura factory (now the world-renowned Toshiba Corporation).[3] Otaguro Motoo himself as a child had studied music with his mother Raku, and later graduated from the Tokyo Music School (today Tokyo Ongaku Daigaku). From 1912 until 1914 he continued his musical education in London alongside the study of economics, until interrupted by the onset of the First World War. Motoo returned to Tokyo and settled in Omori, a small town between Tokyo and Yokohama, which during the reign of the Emperor Taishō (1912–1925) hosted a community of prominent writers and artists. He organised a series of 'Piano Soirées' at his home and at the first of these ('An Evening of Debussy') himself performed works by the composer never before heard in Japan. Also in Omori, in partnership with a group of friends, Otaguro Motoo established a musical-literary publishing house and commenced publication of the journal *Ongaku to Bungaku*, on the back cover of which appeared a column 'News from Omori'. *Ongaku to Bungaku* appeared from March 1916 until August 1919.

Early in August 1918 Otaguro Motoo published in his magazine (vol. 3, no. 8, pp. 2–13) his interview with Sergey Prokofiev, who was at the time on a visit to Japan. This interview has never been republished in Japan, nor has it been translated into other languages, and thus now appears for the first time in Russian. For this reason it is here presented in full.

---

3   After the Second World War various components of the Mitsui Group separated to form independent companies, among them Shibaura/Toshiba, Toyota and Suntory. (English translator's note.)

CONVERSATION WITH PROKOFIEV

'I never dreamed of meeting such a person as you in Japan,' – such were my first words on meeting Prokofiev. When he heard this, he smiled, and I noticed some slight perspiration at the end of his nose and the corners of his mouth. Our meeting was taking place on a warm evening at the height of the rainy season.

Prokofiev is quite a slim young man, but gives the impression of being in rude health. His physical appearance is that of a normal student, with a friendly and communicative disposition. On both sides our conversation was carried on in halting English, and although this naturally affected our complete understanding, we both took the greatest pleasure in our talk.

First of all, I asked: 'What is the state of Russian music today?'

'Better than one might imagine. I even managed to give a concert this April. And there are still plenty of orchestras.'

The conversation began to flow. 'Who is the best conductor in Russia today?'

'Who? In first place, I should say, Koussevitzky. And Ziloti is very well known.'

'I heard Ziloti play the piano in London.'

'Yes, he was a student of Liszt. For a pianist, of course, he is already getting on in years. That is why he has turned to conducting. However, I would not describe him as a good conductor. But he is a master at organising concerts, and therefore is very successful. There is also an Englishman, Albert Coates, and he is an excellent conductor.'

'Who are your favourites among contemporary Russian composers?'

'I love Scriabin. Also Stravinsky and Myaskovsky.'

'How is Scriabin's music regarded in Russia?'

'I would say that today he is beginning to be better understood.'

'Is that so? I also heard Scriabin in London, but his music is quite difficult. I heard his *Prometheus*.'

'*Prometheus*? That's very good. I was myself in London in June 1914. That must have been at the same time as you were there.'

'Which of Scriabin's sonatas do you like best? For instance, I have not heard the Tenth, but I heard the Ninth performed by him.'

'I would not say that I especially like the Ninth, but the Fifth and the Sixth are good. And the Tenth is good as well, although short.'

'What a pity Scriabin is no longer with us. In the past few years a number of famous personalities have left us.'

'Yes, Max Reger has died, and Debussy. Reger I always preferred to Strauss. The death of Granados is a great loss.'

'I agree with you. But Debussy is the greatest loss of all.'

'Of course. I have not met Ravel, but I was fortunate to meet Debussy.'
'When was that?'
'Shortly before the outbreak of war. Debussy came to Petrograd to conduct one of Koussevitzky's concerts. They played *La Mer* and *Nocturnes*.
'I should have liked to continue discussing Debussy, but at that moment several *maiko* entered the room,[4] and the subject naturally changed. I indicated their beautiful kimonos.
'How do you like the kimonos. Aren't they lovely?'
'Yes, they are very beautiful.'
'By the way, when did you come to Japan?'
'I arrived in Tokyo on the 1 June, and then spent ten days in Nara and Kyoto.'
'Both Nara and Kyoto are beautiful, are they not?'
'Yes, peaceful and beautiful places. In Nara I started work on a violin sonata. But here there are so many things to wonder at that since I arrived in Japan I have not been in the right state of mind to compose. I cannot build up enough inner concentration.'
'But I am sure that eventually, just as Charpentier did with his *Impressions d'Italie*, you will write music about Japan. And I am sure that when you do the result will be very interesting.'
'Well, I will try. My plan now is to go to America, and I am already savouring the prospect of composing music inspired by my voyage across the Pacific.'
'That will be a "Pacific Ocean Suite", I suppose? Or perhaps a "Sunrise" or "Sunset", or even maybe a "Hurricane"? I think "Hurricane" would be the most suitable for you.'
'Oh no, surely not. In any case, the thought of twenty days at sea is giving me enormous pleasure, as it will be my first voyage of such a length.'
'How long do you plan to be in America?
'Probably a month or two, but I will see how things develop. I want to see Niagara Falls, and I want to experience what a great city like New York is like. In short, I intend to be a regular tourist. Incidentally, one American magazine in a feature article about me described me as a Futurist composer. As applied to me, this is an absolutely incorrect description. But if one is talking about Russian Futurists it is quite right to say that they are far in advance of American Futurists.'
'Do you know any American composers?'
'No, none at all. Although, yes, I do know one called Kurt Schindler. He came to visit me in Petrograd. He knows a great deal about Russian music.'
'I also know his music, only his songs though. They are widely performed.'

---

4 An apprentice *geisha*, undergoing a period of training (up to a year) to become a full *geisha*. (English translator's note.)

'Yes. He presented me with his songs and in return I gave him some of my compositions.'

While we were thus deep in conversation, a tray of refreshments appeared before us, and Prokofiev exclaimed in astonishment at the tiny cups. I explained that in Japan we drink *sake* from them, and we proceeded to do just that. But his response was: 'Oh, it's very strong.' Then he was brought a glass of beer, but he hardly drank any of it. After some clumsy attempts to master the chopsticks he turned to me and resumed the conversation. I wanted to pursue some details about orchestras in Russia, and it was in that direction that our talk continued.

'You studied with Tcherepnin, didn't you?'

'Yes. He is a good composer and an excellent orchestrator, but lacking in originality.'

'Is Cui still alive?'

'No. Cui, sadly, is no longer with us. We all used to refer to him as "the old General" – after all, he was the armed forces' oldest and most respected General. But Cui could not bear my music.'

'Imagine that! In that case, is Glazunov also of the "old guard"?'

'Very much so. Glazunov could not stand my music either. On one occasion, when I was performing my *Scythian Suite*, he came to listen but walked out before the end.'

'Surely not? Lyadov did not care much for you either, did he?'

'Certainly not. Although he was my teacher he behaved more like a committed opponent.'

'And what do you hear of Rachmaninoff?'

'I believe he is in Sweden at the present time. He is a very vulnerable individual and the war affected him terribly. I have heard that he is planning to come to America soon to conduct.'

'His own works?'

'I suppose so. And he will also appear as a pianist.'

'Rachmaninoff is a superlative pianist, is he not? I heard him in London and was quite bowled over. He is staggeringly good, you must agree.'

'Yes, indeed. In Russia he is Number One. As for his compositions, some people like them and some do not, but everyone agrees about his supremacy as a pianist. He is at his best in his performance of his First Piano Concerto. My route to America is through Siberia and Japan, Rachmaninoff's through Sweden and the northern countries. It will be interesting when we meet there and can shake one another by the hand.'

'What about Vasilenko and Akimenko?'

'I suppose they are in Petrograd. But they are both composers of the second or third rank.'

'Are they, indeed? I thought Vasilenko was quite well known.'

'What an idea! Medtner is far superior to them.'

'Medtner . . . there is something German about him.'

'Whether there is nor not, he is an excellent composer. But I prefer Myaskovsky to Medtner.'

'I have never had the opportunity to hear any of Myaskovsky's music. You cannot find any of his works here, and it is impossible to order them. To tell you the truth, I first heard of you in Montagu's book,[5] and this was where I first read about Myaskovsky as well. Yes, I remember: the book includes a statement by you to the effect that Myaskovsky's sonatas are complex.'

'What are you saying? Certainly, Myaskovsky's sonatas are very complicated works. Myaskovsky was wounded during the war, then came back and wrote five symphonies.'

'Five? That is a lot! How would you specifically characterise his music?'

'His music is sombre, to put it briefly. He is a very shy man and tends to put everything he writes away in a drawer, consequently very few of his works have been published.'

'It would be interesting to know where is Stravinsky at the moment?'

'That I do not know for certain. He lives mainly either in France or in Switzerland, but he is hardly known at all in his native land. I met him four years ago in Milan, where I happened to have gone at the invitation of the Futurist Marinetti.'

'I very much like Stravinsky's music. Scriabin was a genius. If I had to name a genius after Scriabin, it would be Stravinsky.'

'Yes, he is a rare genius. In the matter of orchestration he has no peer. Whatever else can be said of him, his music is truly, colourfully, pictorial even if it is perhaps not especially profound.'

'Have you heard *Les Noces*?'

'You mean his latest work? That time in Milan he played part of it on the piano, but no more. Have you heard *Le Rossignol*?'

'Yes. I was absolutely stunned by it.'

'I do not particularly care for *Rossignol*. I consider *Petrushka* and *Le Sacre du printemps* far better.'

---

5 Montagu Montagu-Nathan (1877–1958) published a number of books and articles on Russian music, musicians and critics, the most widely read of which was his comprehensive survey, originally published in 1914, *A History of Russian Music – Being An Account Of The Rise And Progress Of The Russian School Of Composers, With A Survey Of Their Lives And A Description Of Their Works*. This ground-breaking account begins with the pre-Nationalists such as Bortnyansky, continues through Glinka and Dargomyzshky to the Nationalists and the Mighty Handful, followed by 'The Decline of Nationalism' (Tchaikovsky, Glazunov, Arensky, Taneyev) and ends with 'The Present Movement' (Rachmaninoff, Scriabin, Stravinsky, Steinberg, Medtner, etc.) In the first edition Prokofiev and Myaskovsky are confined to an appendix. (English translator's note.)

'Yes. *Petrushka* is a wonderful work. He uses a number of folk songs in it, does he not?'

'Yes, a great many. And also dares to bring in musical phrases that sound truly awful to some people's ears.'

'Do you mean like this one?' – saying this, I started to sing the Nurses' Dance.[6] He immediately took it up, whistling and laughing, and then continued: 'You know, I understand Petrushka very well, but *Le Sacre* is really hard to grasp. On my first hearing I understood nothing of it whatsoever. In any event, when I got to know Stravinsky in Milan and listened to *Le Sacre* in a version for piano four-hands, only then did I feel I was able to understand the work. Whatever one says, it is an outstanding composition.'

'Do you write music for the ballet?'

'I have done so. In fact the *Scythian Suite*, for example, is one such composition. I wrote it in response to a commission from the famous Diaghilev. It is a ballet-tragedy on the theme of the life of people at the dawn of humanity, living on the ancient land of Russia before the appearance there of the Slav people. The hero and heroine are called Ala and Lolli. But during the course of composing the ballet the music took the form of a symphonic work, and it seemed to me that the music would be better in this symphonic form than as a ballet.'

'What became of the ballet?'

'I wrote different music for it. There are plans to present it in Paris once the war is over.'

'Is Diaghilev in America just now?'

'No, he is in Madrid.'

'And Nijinsky?'

'Nijinsky was wandering about Austria when war broke out, and was arrested there. I hear that he dances every night on the stage of the Imperial Opera in Vienna.'

'Imagine! I never heard that. By the way, how did it come about that you were not sent to the front?'

'Because I am an only son, and only sons are not conscripted into the army. Not only that, but at the present time they try to protect musicians, and so I never became a soldier.'

'You were fortunate. And now you can compose, and travel.'

'Yes. Not so long ago I was in the Caucasus, composing, but then all the unrest began and I was unable to return to Petrograd. So I had no help for it but to stay there and go on composing, and while I was there I wrote the Third and Fourth Sonatas and a Violin Concerto.'

---

6   The folk song 'Vdol' po Peterskoy' ('Along Peter's Street'), heard at the beginning of Part IV, the Shrovetide Fair. (English translator's note.)

'*Visions fugitives* and *Fantasia*, which you are to perform at your concert in the Imperial Theatre, are new works?'

'Yes. *Visions fugitives* is a very short composition. I finished proofreading it just before leaving Petrograd, and it is already in print. *Fantasia* is in fact the concluding movement of my Fourth Sonata, but I am not going to play the whole sonata because it is too long. I'm just going to play the last movement.'

'Although you have written a Sinfonietta, you have not yet composed a symphony?'

'No, that is not correct. I have written a Classical Symphony, and to all intents and purposes the *Sinfonietta* is a symphony. And one of my very latest works is a "Vocal Symphony".'

'What is its title?'

And at this point Prokofiev had to pause for thought, because he did not know what to call his symphony in English. He did give me the French title, but unfortunately at the time I did not understand, as I do not speak French at all. As a result we did not succeed in clarifying the name of this composition, but I did understand that Prokofiev had set to music an Assyrian religious poem in a version by Balmont. Prokofiev explained: 'In any case, it is a work for chorus accompanied by wind and string instruments, with the role of the priest sung by a solo tenor. The work calls for a large number of performers, so it is extremely demanding to perform in full.'[7]

'I believe Balmont was in Japan last year?'

'Yes, and to this day is in thrall to Japan.'

'Did he really like it so much here?'

'Very much so.'

'But it is so terribly hot at the moment. It would have been marvellous if you could have been here two months ago.'

'Well, hot weather is hot weather. It makes it difficult to sit down at the piano during the heat of the day.'

'Yes, it must be very hard. And your concerts are just after one o'clock in the afternoon.'

'But then I am going to America, and by the time I return it will probably be easier. It must be very nice here in Japan in the autumn.'

'Yes, October–November is the best time of year for us.'

At this point the sound of a *shamisen*[8] was heard, and two of the *maiko* began to dance. We refilled our cups with *sake* and watched them. The name of the dance was the *Matsusima*, but as I did not know its subject I was not

---

7 Prokofiev is referring to the cantata *Seven, They Are Seven*. (Note by E.S.)
8 A traditional Japanese instrument, approximately the size of a guitar but with a fretless fingerboard, having three strings stretched over a rounded rectangular body made usually of cat or dog skin. (English translator's note.)

able to explain it to Prokofiev. We therefore reverted to the subject of our conversation.

'Will you play some Chopin in your recital?'

'Yes, I plan to. As a matter of fact, up till now I have performed only my own works. But as my forthcoming concert in Japan will be my debut here I decided it would be inappropriate to programme nothing but unknown and inaccessible music, so I will add some Chopin on the grounds that everybody will understand him here. But I have not practised for two and a half months, and am worried that my fingers will not be as agile as they should be.'

'Surely you are not going to perform without rehearsing?'

'Of course not. I tried to practise a bit today, at my friend's house in Yokohama.'

'Ah, you went to the Grand Hotel?'

'Yes.'

'In that case, as I live halfway between Yokohama and Tokyo, you must come to my house. It's in a place called Omori.'

'Ah, Omori? I remember there is a station with that name. After my performance in the Imperial Theatre I shall definitely call on you.'

'Yes, yes, please do. And although my piano is nothing special, it is at your disposal. Perhaps you would play me some of the *Scythian Suite*? I should love to hear it on the piano.'

'The *Scythian Suite*? By all means. I was thinking that I might have to conduct it in America, so I have the score with me. I'll show it to you.'

'Would you? That would be splendid.'

I looked at my watch, and saw that it was nine o'clock. A photographer I had engaged earlier came into the room where we were talking, and we went out with him into the garden. Standing side by side with Prokofiev I noticed that he was a good 10 centimetres taller than me, which means he must stand around 1.79 metres. The white linen jacket he was wearing was rather short, exposing several centimetres of red-and-white-striped shirt, to which he seemed to pay no attention. Having arranged his appearance he turned to the camera and stood there, smiling. There was a brilliant flash, blinding us, and the session was over.

'Please excuse me for leaving you at this point. We shall meet again at the Imperial Theatre,' I said as we shook hands. In reply he silently pressed my hand. I set off immediately for Simbasi station, and as I jolted my way in the car to the station I could not help smiling as I recalled our conversation.

5 JULY

This conversation took place on the eve of the concerts in the Imperial Theatre. A few days before, in the 'News from Omori' column of his journal

(*Ongaku to Bungaku* 1918, vol. 3, no. 7), Otaguro Motoo had announced: 'The composer Prokofiev has arrived among us. We are delighted to inform you that a veritable wonder is about to take place, when this composer innovator performs his own composition for us in Japan. It will be interesting to see what further celebrities come to visit us.'

Indeed, a good many celebrities did visit Japan. The fact is that, paradoxically, the First World War had a particular, and beneficial, effect on cultural life in Japan. In contrast to the ruins in which Europe lay, the Far East offered excellent opportunities for musical and theatrical activity, the result of revolution and civil war in Russia. Many artists desirous of reaching America left Russia via Siberia to stop over in Japan's rapidly developing musical environment, where they invariably paid tribute to the welcome accorded to their artistry when they performed on the stage of the Imperial Art Theatre (Teikoku Gekije).

The Imperial Theatre opened its doors to the public in 1911, and as to stage and backstage facilities was entirely constructed according to European models. It represented a striking symbol of the of the Taishō era, which in sharp contrast to the preceding Meiji period was a time when, culturally speaking, 'Western civilisation reached into a second generation and European culture began to lose that taint of the alien by which it had formerly been distinguished.'[9] It was here in 1918 and 1919 that, before audiences of Japanese art lovers, Prokofiev's Conservatoire colleagues the piano and violin duo Alfred Meyerovich and Michel Piastro appeared. In his Diary entry for 4 June 1918 Prokofiev wrote: 'In the evening I went to the recital by Meyerovich and Piastro, and took away a very favourable impression. The audience was European, well turned out, and the programme consisted of serious music pretty well played. Meyerovich is not bad, although I would not call him a truly outstanding pianist. Piastro, though, is an excellent violinist. It gave me an idea: to compose a violin sonata!'

Major events in the Teigeku were appearances by famous violinists: in 1921 Mischa Elman (1891–1967), son of Russian émigrés to America; in 1922 Efrem Zimbalist (1889–1935), who had moved to the USA as long ago as 1911; Leopold Auer (1845–1930), outstanding musician and teacher at the St Petersburg Conservatoire who left Russia for America in 1918; and finally the King of Violinists – as he was styled – Jascha Heifetz (1901–1987). Ticket prices for these concerts were no less sensational: 15 yen for a seat in a box, 10 yen in the stalls, and the cheapest seats in the house from 2 to 4 yen (by comparison, the starting [annual] salary for a secondary school teacher amounted to no more than 40 yen. Substantial discounts were, however, available to music students and musicians in military orchestras.

---

9 Mine Takashi, *Teikoku Gekije Kaimaku* (*Curtain Up at the Imperial Theatre*), Tokyo, 1996, p. 226.

And so it was here, in Tokyo's Imperial Theatre, that Prokofiev made his appearances in 1918. The posters announced: 'Pianoforte Recital of his own Compositions by Sergey Prokofiev, world-famous Russian Composer and Virtuoso Pianist. Saturday 6 and Sunday 7 July at 1.15 p.m.'

The programme for the recital on 6 July was: Sonata No. 1, Op. 1; Prelude, Op. 12 No. 7; Etude in C minor, Op. 2 No. 4; Gavotte, Op. 12 No. 2; Toccata, Op. 11; Sonata No. 3, Op. 28; 'Reproach' (1907); 'Fairy Tale', Op. 3 No. 1; 'Despair', Op. 4 No. 3; 'Suggestion diabolique', Op. 4 No. 4; Chopin's Ballade No. 3, and three Etudes.

For 7 July the programme was: Sonata No. 2; 'Daydream'; 'Why?'; 'Novelette';[10] March, Op. 12 No. 1; Scherzo, Op. 12 No. 10; *Visions fugitives*, Op. 22; the *Fantasia* finale from Sonata No. 4; a Chopin group including a Nocturne, a Mazurka, a Waltz and an Etude. There was a special note in the printed programme indicating that the recital was to be played on a Yamaha piano.

Prokofiev's impressions recorded in his Diary were that although the concerts were poorly attended because of the heat and the time of day, the audience listened 'extremely attentively. The greatest success was reserved for technically difficult pieces.' But let us hear the judgement of a music critic, Otaguro Motoo, in *Ongaku to Bungaku* 1918, vol. 3 no. 8:

> Prokofiev's music seems to have been born of a mixture of revolutionary ideas, striving towards a new freedom of expression, and a genuinely pure love of the beautiful. And this sincere love of the beautiful lends his compositions an especial delicacy, resulting in an unusually lyrical melodic gift. Prokofiev's spiritual essence is manifest in his music. The listener can sometimes be astonished by his musical idiom, and find it shocking, but at the same time he cannot mistake the truth of the composer's inner exaltation. Various leading composers have influenced his art, and of these the most significant are Musorgsky, Scriabin and Stravinsky; this arises from his tremendous love and sympathy for these geniuses. But at the same time his music is distinguished by an incomparable originality, most vividly to be felt in his latest works.

Prokofiev and Otaguro Motoo met several times after his concerts in the Teigeku, and the composer played Otaguro the works they had discussed during the interview. Otaguro came to Yokohama to bid farewell to Prokofiev when he left the country for America, and made a prophetic

---

10 No pieces, even juvenilia, with these titles appear among Prokofiev's known works, so presumably he decided to include some Schumann genre pieces, *Träumerei*, *Warum?* and one of the *Noveletten*, Op. 21. (English translator's note.)

prediction that in America the composer would learn much and become a world-renowned figure.

Meanwhile, there are unquestionably treasures without number still hidden in Japan's Musical Archive.

APPENDIX 4

September 28, 1918 MUSICAL AMERICA 9

REPORTS FINE ARTS FLOURISHING IN "RED RUSSIA"

Serge Prokofieff, Much-Discussed Ultra-Modern Russian Composer, Now in New York, Tells of Conditions Under Bolsheviki — Latter Paying Big Salaries to Noted Artists, Bringing Out New Musical and Dramatic Works in Sumptuous Style, and Regard Artists with Favor

Contemporary German Music Still Barred—Rachmaninoff's Estate Burned and Plundered by Those in Power—Music Paper as Valuable as Paper Currency — Mr. Prokofieff's Standing, Works and Plans

By FREDERICK H. MARTENS

OUT of the topsyturvydom of the Bolshevist Russia, from Petrograd by way of Siberia, Japan and San Francisco, there has just arrived in New York one of the leading figures in ultra-modern Russian composition, Serge Prokofieff. A pupil of Glière, Rimsky-Korsakoff and Liadoff in composition, he has already blazed new musical creative trails on his own account, and in his own land is hailed as the peer of Stravinsky, Rachmaninoff, Medtner and others of the little group which represents the last word in Russian music.

He is not known only in Russia. Montagu-Nathan, who, in 1913, accorded him only brief mention in his "History of Russian Music," devoted an extended, enthusiastic article to him in the London *Musical Times* the year following, speaking of him as "young Prokofieff, who has tweaked the ear of the pedagogue and warmed the cockles of the progressive musician's heart." And Montagu-Nathan found amusement in the thought that this "Rubinstein prize winner (Petrograd Conservatory), triumphant virtuoso, composer and performer of fine piano concertos and ambitious sonatas, this symphonist, the trump card of Siloti, Diaghileff's latest find [Prokofieff had just completed a new ballet for the 1915 Russian season in Paris and London; a season which was one of the earlier victims of the war], whose 'Scythian Suite' drove Glazounoff from the hall in which it was being performed, this 'futurist,' 'barbarian,' *enfant terrible* [echo seems to answer "Ornstein"!] was introduced to a London promenade audience as the composer—of an inoffensive *Scherzo* for four bassoons!"

If Serge Prokofieff be an *enfant terrible*, he is at least a most engaging one. Of the blond Slav—not Turko-Slav—type, tall, slender, distinguished, with honest grey eyes and a forceful, spontaneous manner, there is something prepossessingly direct and genuine about this composer in his twenties. When the writer made his acquaintance at the home of Adolf Bolm—who knew everyone worth knowing in the pre-revolutionary Petrograd world of art and music, and to whom temporary exiles from what might now be called "Unholy Russia" naturally gravitate when they reach New York—he found no difficulty in inducing Mr. Prokofieff to talk of present-day musical conditions in his native land.

Serge Prokofieff, Russian Composer, with His Friend, the Japanese Author, M. Ohtaguro, Who Has Written a Book on the Russian Ballet, and Mme. Ohtaguro. Right: Mr. Prokofieff

"I reached San Francisco a few weeks ago on my way from Japan where, though it was out of the season, I had been giving a series of piano recitals in Tokio and Yokohama. Yes, there is a real, genuine interest in occidental music in Japan, and I had large and appreciative audiences at my recitals. I was even asked to undertake, with excellent guarantees, a concert-tour of the eastern coast of Asia." Mr. Prokofieff laughed and added: "Do not let the phrase call up a vision of a piano and pianist wandering per camel-back among barbarian tribes to give them 'cacophony without a lucid interval,' as some of my earlier compositions have been called. Not at all; the concerts were to be given in Shanghai, Hong-Kong, Manila—places in which there are large English and American colonies—in Batavia and Surabaya. These Javanese cities are especially music-loving, and I know of two Russian artists who gave a splendidly successful series of sixty recitals in Java during the season preceding my arrival in Japan.

Eager to Know Our Music

"I did not see my way clear to undertake the proposed Asiatic concert-tour," continued Mr. Prokofieff. "I am a natural-born traveller, and though I enjoyed immensely my two months in Japan, and met a number of interesting people, I wanted to see the United States, listen with an open ear and mind to American music, and meet American musicians. You see, we know American literature—Poe, Mark Twain, Holmes, Bret Harte, et al.—they have all been translated—better than we do American music in Petrograd. So I have absolutely new impressions and experiences to which I may look forward. Fortunately I have a very good friend in this country, Kurt Schindler, whose acquaintance I made in Petrograd in 1914, and who will no doubt make it easy for me to learn as much of American music as I can during my stay here.

"Will I remain long in this country? Not more than a few months; but long enough, if possible, to introduce some of my own compositions—symphonic and for the piano—to American audiences. I *have* to write when the spirit moves. In Kislovotsk ('Sour Water'), in the Caucasus, a famous health-resort where Safonoff was conducting an orchestra at the time of his death from an attack of asthma, it was practically impossible to get music-paper, but I could still jot down themes too precious to lose in my pocket note-book" (he showed it to me), "and I did the same on the steamer. A theme is an elusive thing—it comes, it goes, and sometimes it never returns. Some of my critics might say, no doubt" (his eyes twinkled), "that the more themes of mine which never returned the better!"

Musical Criticism in Russia

"Music criticism—serious, valid critical study and analysis of new compositions—is really on a high level in Russia. Our critics in Petrograd and Moscow are scholars, *savants*, men of distinguished literary and scientific attainment who have specialized in music, such as V. G. Karatygin, professor of history at the *ci-devant* Imperial Academy of Music in Petrograd, Igor Gleboff, Victor Belaieff. They lay stress on the musical, not the personal equation, in their critiques. And even now we have some splendid music magazines—the Petrograd *Melos* and *Musica*, though they, as well as such music as is still published, are printed on paper of very poor quality, all that is available, and appear at irregular intervals. In fact, only songs and piano pieces are published now by Jurgenson and 'The Russian Musical Edition,' though they are accepting symphonic works for publication 'after the war.'

"Russia is a land of paradoxes. While the state of affairs in general grows darker and darker, and the whole social and economic equilibrium of the country has been overturned, one might think that the present government, which I am convinced cannot endure, and which is part and parcel of the existing chaos, would be the last to give time and money to the arts. And there we have one of the paradoxes in question. It is the Bolshevist government, under which a clean collar has become a symbol of imperialism and the hall-mark of a *bourgeois*, and under which I found it necessary to wear a red shirt in Petrograd to show that my heart was not black—from its point of view—that is providing liberally for Russian art and artists.

"The Bolshevist government keeps all the ex-Imperial theaters running in Petrograd and Moscow, and pays the artists and musicians well. The former 'Court Orchestra' plays on Sundays in what used to be the Imperial Chapel as before, under the name of the 'State Orchestra,' Kousswitsky directing; though the Imperial Intendant, General-Count Stachelberg, has disappeared. While I was in Petrograd last year during the season, there were sometimes as many as three important concerts given *in the same hall the same day*, and I had to wait a month for a hall in which to give a piano recital.

"Yes, these same Bolsheviki who seem to regard cleanliness and the little decencies of life as the sinister stigmata of reaction, are paying distinguished artists big salaries, 10,000 to 25,000 roubles; are paying for the production in sumptuous style of new operas, ballets, dramas; have made the famous painter Benoit an unofficial Minister of Fine Arts—for they say that artists work hard and are a genuine source of national wealth and glory. Their political principles and the application they make of them I can only condemn, but with their views regarding the fine arts I am heartily in accord. Of course, this active musical and theatrical life is more or less intermittent; and there were months when during party struggles for supremacy, all theaters and concert halls closed at nine, and the entire absence of police control exposed anyone who ventured to use the streets much after that hour to robbery and assassination. It is a pleasure for me to think that the very valuable library of old music, much of it in ms., at the Petrograd Conservatory, has been safely removed to various central towns, where it is preserved.

"Of course, at the beginning of the war no German music whatever was played in Russia. We have now so far relaxed this rule as to perform the works of dead German composers—Wagner, Beethoven, Mozart, et al.—but those of the living are still strictly barred, and will continue to be by patriotic Russian opinion. In general Russian manufacturers and business men refuse to deal with Germany, and the Germans themselves are not keen to accept Russian paper money. The way we Russian artists feel may be gathered from the following incident. The conductor of a Berlin symphony orchestra—I cannot recall his name—who had been taken prisoner in 1915, was preparing to go back to Germany under the treaty conditions—the Germans do not mind their artists coming back, though they discourage the return of the common soldiers, whom they suspect of being infected with Bolshevism—and thought he'd like to take along some new Russian symphonic works for production in Berlin. He asked me for something and of course I refused. And when he had made the rounds of all the composers of standing in Petrograd, it turned out that not one would give a Russian work to an enemy for production in an enemy land. He may, of course, have picked up something in the shops, but this we could not control.

Shadows on Musical Life

"But the war has cast shadows on Russian musical life that no Bolshevist foot-lights can dispel. Rachmaninoff's beautiful estate in the government of Tomboff, into whose improvement he had put all that his music had brought him, was burned and plundered by the Bolsheviki. When, heart-sick and depressed, he went to Sweden, German intrigue prevented the success of his concert tour. He has produced but little that is new of late, though he has rewritten his first piano concerto in a more complex form. Maskovsky, for three years at the front as an officer, has only recently begun to compose again, and Glière seems to have disappeared in the German occupation of Kiev. Tscherepnine, however, is still at the Petrograd Conservatory, and has written his fourth Ballet, a sinfonietta and songs set to the poems of Balmont, the greatest Russian poet of the day, whose Russian translation of Poe is a masterpiece. But many of our musicians have suffered and lost, some in one way, some in another, and the end is not yet.

"The singers' salaries I mentioned before sound better than they really are, for music-paper is almost, if not more, valuable than paper currency. You may get an idea of some of our complications

[Continued on page 10]

THE CALL TO FREEDOM

A Patriotic Ode for Mixed Voices

By VICTOR HERBERT

Price, 43 cents, postage extra

Quotation on 100 or more mailed on request

Orchestra Parts: Grand $8.00 per month; full $5.00 per month

The attention of singing societies, schools and patriotic meetings is directed to this notable short choral work from the pen of one of our most uniquely gifted and popular composers.

"Is far above the average patriotic composition. * * * This ode is the product of a composer of immense experience, backed by the best of training and founded on an unusually fine natural talent for music. Rich in harmony, broad in style, vigorous, effective alike for voices and instruments, **The Call to Freedom** will add to the composer's reputation as a sterling musician, if it is possible to add anything more to the esteem in which Victor Herbert is already held throughout the entire United States." —*Musical Courier.*

Teachers! Singers! Players!

Be sure to visit the Free Bureau of Musical Service conducted by Henrietta Straus at our New York office from 9 A. M. to 1 P. M. daily.

OLIVER DITSON COMPANY, 178-179 Tremont Street, Boston

CHAS. H. DITSON & CO., 8-10-12 East 34th Street, New York

Order of your local dealer

REPORTS FINE ARTS FLOURISHING IN RUSSIA

[Continued from page 9]

when I tell you that any number of provincial towns and cities have established their own mints and issue money guaranteed by the town. Press is really the word, not mint, for all gold and silver money went promptly into hiding at the beginning of the war. So urgent was the need of currency, and so hard was it to get skilled workmen, that the municipal authorities sent to Siberia for counterfeiters, who were set to work making good money under armed guards. Sounds like *opera comique*, does it not? Another amusing paradox is that the peasants in general prefer the bank-notes of the ex-Imperial currency to those issued by the present *de facto* government; and the repudiated money of the dead and gone *regime* circulates at a premium!

"My own compositions? I cannot well praise them myself, but I can tell you what they are. And I think you will have an opportunity to judge some of them when I give my orchestra concert and recitals here. I have written piano sonatas, violin sonatas, two concertos for piano and one for violin, songs, piano pieces, among them my collection of 'Sarcasmes' and the twenty miniatures, 'Moments Fugitifs.' Then there are two symphonic poems, 'Dreams' and 'Autumn'; my 'Scythian Suite,' which was received in Petrograd in the same way Stravinsky's 'Sacre' was in Paris (I'll be curious to know how it will be received here); several operas, the latest, 'The Gambler' after Dostoevski, in four acts, accepted for the Imperial Theaters of Moscow and Petrograd; a ballet, 'Harlequin's Story,' for the Russian ballet-season in Paris of 1915—unfortunately both the Russian season of that year and the 'Imperial' theaters came to be non-existent—and my last work, 'The Conjuration of the Seven,' for chorus, solos and orchestra, set to Balmont's poetic version of an ancient Assyrian cuneiform hymn, dealing with the conspiracy of the seven evil spirits of the fall and winter months, against the five good spirits of the others—a wonderful text!

"That is an outline of my work as a composer—you can fill it in with criticism when you hear some of my things played." And that this music will be worth hearing may be inferred by the dictum of the eminent Russian critic Karatygin, who says: "It is from Serge Prokofieff, more than from any other, that we must expect to hear a new language in musical art, one more deep, comprehensive and individual!"

"Tales of Hoffmann" Admirably Given by Brookfield School

Offenbach Work Is Second Opera Presented During Warm Months by Summer School's Students

BROOKFIELD CENTER, CONN., Sept. 1.—The Brookfield Summer School of Singing presented the second opera of the season, Offenbach's "Tales of Hoffmann," on Aug. 27. The large cast called for by that opera gave opportunity to many students to perform, and it was one of the most successful presentations that the school has ever attempted. The light character of the music and the frequent chances for byplay and cleverness in action were taken advantage of. The audience manifested marked enthusiasm.

Among the students having prominent parts and deserving special mention were Ellen Carrier Hart of the Hart Conservatory of Music, Enid, Okla., who sang the rôle of *Olympea*; Miriam Gilbert of the Winthrop College vocal teaching staff, as *Giulietta*; Ruth Groeneveld of Philadelphia, in the part of *Antonia*, and Frank Tatham Johnson of the University of Illinois, who sang the difficult rôle of *Hoffmann*. Two character rôles were treated with much cleverness, that of the servant, taken by Mary Frances Scott of New York City, and *Dr. Miracle*, sung by Marjorie Wilson of Philadelphia.

The summer school, under the direction of Herbert Wilber Greene, has been the largest in numbers in many years.

Scenes from "Tales of Hoffmann"; Ruth Groeneveld as Antonia; Frank Tatham Johnson as Hoffmann

Alice McDowell and Elizabeth Gutman Give Concerts in Camps Near Boston

BOSTON, Sept. 14.—Alice McDowell, pianist, appeared with Elizabeth Gutman, soprano, last week in a series of entertainments given by the Y. M. C. A. for the soldiers and sailors in the vicinity of New London. Performances were given on four successive evenings at a submarine base, Fort Trumbull, the State Pier, and Fort Terry. The soldiers are reported as not caring for piano solos, so Miss McDowell did not go with the expectation of playing any. But after Miss Gutman's songs had been received with great enthusiasm, the other performers insisted that Miss McDowell play something alone. She tried some "short things with pep," as she described them, which were not only well received, but encored.

C. R.

Oct. 17th at 3:15

A début recital in Æolian Hall by an American pianist named AURORE LA CROIX

They fight with their whole souls

You are reading every day of our boys over there—of Pershing's divisions charging into the blasting fire of the Boche trenches; of small detachments smashing their way from house to house through ruined villages; of single-handed deeds of sacrifice and valor.

One thought, one impulse only fills their souls—to *fight and keep on fighting*, until the war is won.

They know that all America is back of them; they know that they can count on us at home to send them all the guns and supplies they need to win.

There is only one way we can do it. All of us must work and save and buy Liberty Bonds, with our whole souls, the way our men are fighting over there!

No less will win. There is no other way to provide the money the Government must have. No other standard can make the Fourth Liberty Loan a Success.

Lend the way they fight— Buy Bonds to your utmost

This space contributed to winning the war by
MUSICAL AMERICA

The Witherspoon Studios

are now at

44 West 86th St

New York City

Mr. Witherspoon Resumes His Teaching on Monday, September the Thirtieth

Witherspoon Studios
44 West 86th Street
New York

Miss Minnie Liplich, Secretary

Telephone: Schuyler 5888

The New Witherspoon Studios

APPENDIX 5

Interview in *Vechernye Birzhevye Novosti*, 12 May 1916

In the Petrograd newspaper *Stock Exchange Evening News* (*Vechernye Birzhevye Novosti*) on 12 May 1916 there appeared an account of an interview Prokofiev had given to a reporter the previous day in the Mariinsky Theatre office of Baron Kuzov, the Deputy Director of the Imperial Theatres, in which the composer outlined his approach to opera in general and the matter of setting to music Dostoyevsky's prose in particular. The following is an excerpt from the interview, translated by Anthony Phillips.

In my new work I have been paying particular attention to the scenographic plasticity of opera, because in recent times the interest of composers in this aspect appears to have declined markedly. As a result operas have become static, full of boring conventions, and this has led some prominent musicians, among them Diaghilev and Stravinsky, to predict the imminent degeneration of the form.

I have long been attracted to Dostoyevsky's *The Gambler* as a subject for an opera, precisely because this novella, in addition to its compelling story, consists almost entirely of dialogue. This gave me the opportunity of shaping the libretto according to Dostoyevsky's prose style. Mainly concerned as I was with the dramatic aspects of the opera, I have tried as far as possible to relieve the singers of all unnecessary conventions, in order to give them the freedom to develop the dramatic representation of their roles.

To the same end the orchestration will be transparent, in order that every word should be heard, a matter of great importance when one considers how incomparable is Dostoyevsky's text. I am of the opinion that the convention of writing operas to metric texts is quite absurd. In the present case Dostoyevsky's prose is more vivid, more colourful and more compelling than any verse could be.

And will there be nothing extravagant or overstated, in your Gambler?

Nothing whatsoever. My whole aim is to make it as simple as possible.

APPENDIX 6

Fantastic Lollypops
by Ben Hecht

In 1921 the young writer Ben Hecht (1894–1964), later to become a prolific novelist, playwright and Hollywood scriptwriter, was working as a reporter on the *Chicago Daily News*, for which he wrote a total of 424 daily columns on life in the city, many of which were subsequently collected and published under the title *1001 Afternoons in Chicago* by Covici-McGee (Chicago, 1922).[1] Hecht later put his experience of the newspaper world to good use in one of his most famous plays, *The Front Page*. This piece, describing the characteristically far from smooth-running final dress rehearsal for the world premiere of a new opera, appeared in the *Chicago Daily News* on New Year's Eve.

They will never start. No, they will never start. In another two minutes Mr Prokofieff will go mad. They should have started at eleven. It is now ten minutes after eleven. And they have not yet started. Ah, Mr Prokofieff has gone mad.

But Mr Prokofieff is a modernist; so nobody pays much attention. Musicians are all mad. And a modernist musician, du lieber Gott! A Russian modernist musician!

The medieval face of Mr Boris Anisfeld pops over the rows of empty seats. It is very likely that Mr Anisfeld will also go mad. For Mr Anisfeld is, in a way, a collaborator of Mr Prokofieff. It is the full dress rehearsal of *The Love for Three Oranges*. Mr Prokofieff wrote the words and music. Mr Anisfeld painted the scenery.

'Mees Garden weel be hear in a meenute,' the medieval face of Boris whispers into the Muscovite ears of Serge.

Eleven-fifteen, and Miss Garden has arrived. She is armed, having brought along her heaviest shillalah. Mr Prokofieff is on his feet. He takes off his coat. The medieval face of Mr Anisfeld vanishes. Tap, tap, on the conductor's stand. 'Lights out.' A fanfare from the orchestra's right.

Last rehearsal for the world premier of a modernist opera! One winter morning years ago the music critics of Paris sat and laughed themselves green in the face over the incomprehensible banalities of an impossible modernist opera called *Tannhäuser*. And who will say that critics have lost

---

1 Information from the Snickersnee Press (www.snickersneepress.com), which is attempting the almost impossible task of collating and making available the entirety of Ben Hecht's writings in all its various genres, is gratefully acknowledged, as is permission to reproduce the article here.

their sense of humor. There will unquestionably be laughter before this morning is over.

Music like this has never come from the orchestra pit of the Auditorium. Strange combinations of sounds that seem to come from street pianos, New Year's Eve horns, harmonicas and old-fashioned musical beer steins that play when you lift them up. Mr Prokofieff waves his shirt-sleeved arms and the sounds increase.

There is nothing difficult about this music – that is, unless you are unfortunate enough to be a music critic. But to the untutored ear there is a charming capriciousness about the sounds from the orchestra. Cadenzas pirouette in the treble. Largos toboggan in the bass. It sounds like the picture of a crazy Christmas tree drawn by a happy child. Which is a most peculiar way for music to sound.

But, attention! The curtain is up. Bottle greens and fantastic reds. Here is a scene as if the music Mr Prokofieff were waving out of the orchestra had come to life. Lines that look like the music sounds. Colors that embrace one another in tender dissonances. Yes, like that.

And here, galubcheck (I think it's galubcheck), are the actors. What is it all about? Ah, Mr Prokofieff knows and Boris knows and maybe the actors know. But all it is necessary for us to know is that music and color and a quaint, almost gargoylian, caprice are tumbling around in front of our eyes and ears.

And there is M. Jacques Coini. He will not participate in the world premier. Except in spirit. Now M. Coini is present in the flesh. He wears a business suit, spats of tan and a gray fedora. M. Coini is the stage director. He instructs the actors how to act. He tells the choruses where to chorus and what to do with their hands, masks, feet, voices, eyes and noses.

The hobgoblin extravaganza Mr Prokofieff wrote unfolds itself with rapidity. Theater habitués eavesdropping on the rehearsal mumble in the half-dark that there was never anything like this seen on earth or in heaven. Mr Anisfeld's scenery explodes like a succession of medieval skyrockets. A phantasmagoria of sound, color and action crowds the startled proscenium. For there is no question but that the proscenium, with the names of Verdi, Bach, Haydn and Beethoven chiseled on it, is considerably startled.

Through this business of skyrockets and crescendos and hobgoblins M. Coini stands out like a lighthouse in a Cubist storm. However bewildering the plot, however humpty-dumpty the music, M. Coini is intelligible drama. His brisk little figure in its pressed pants, spats and fedora, bounces around amid the apoplectic disturbances like some busybody Alice in an operatic Wonderland.

The Opus mounts. The music mounts. Singers attired as singers were never attired before crawl on, bounce on, tumble on. And M. Coini, as undisturbed as a traffic cop or a Loop pigeon, commands his stage. He tells the singers where to stand while they sing, and when they don't sing to suit him he sings himself. He leads the chorus on and tells it where to dance, and when they don't dance to suit him he dances himself. He moves the scenery himself. He fights with Mr Prokofieff while the music splashes and roars around him. He fights with Boris. He fights with electricians and wigmakers.

It is admirable. M. Coini, in his tan spats and gray fedora, is more fantastic than the entire cast of devils and Christmas trees and lollypops, who seem to be the leading actors in the play. Mr Prokofieff and Miss Garden have made a mistake. They should have let M. Coini play *The Love for Three Oranges* all by himself. They should have let him be the dream towers and the weird chorus, the enchantress and the melancholy prince. M. Coini is the greatest opera I have ever seen. All he needed was M. Prokofieff's music and the superbly childish visions of the medieval Boris for a background.

The music leaps into a gaudy balloon and sails away in marvelous zigzags, way over the heads of the hobgoblins on the stage and the music critics off the stage. Miss Garden beckons with her shillalah. Mr Prokofieff arrives panting at her side. He bows, kisses the back of her hand and stands at attention. Also the medieval face of Mr Anisfeld drifts gently through the gloom and joins the two.

The first act of *The Oranges* is over. Two critics exchanging opinions glower at Mr Prokofieff. One says: 'What a shame! What a shame! Nobody will understand it.' The other agrees. But perhaps they only mean that music critics will fail to understand it and that untutored ones like ourselves will find in the hurdy-gurdy rhythms and contortions of Mr Prokofieff and Mr Anisfeld a strange delight. As if some one had given us a musical lollypop to suck and rub in our hair.

I have an interview with Mr Prokofieff to add. The interview came first and doesn't sit well at the end of these notes. Because Mr Prokofieff, sighing a bit nervously in expectation of the world premier, said: 'I am a classicist. I derive from the classical composers.'

This may be true, but the critics will question it. Instead of quoting Mr Prokofieff at this time, it may be more apropos merely to say that I would rather see and listen to his opera than to the entire repertoire of the company put together. This is not criticism, but a prejudice in favor of fantastic lollypops.

Bibliography

Acton, E., V. I. Cherniaev and W. G. Rosenberg (eds.), *Critical Companion To The Russian Revolution 1914–1921*, Indiana University Press, Bloomington, 1997

Adler, Jacob P., tr. Lulla Adler Rosenfeld, *A Life on the Stage: A Memoir*, Knopf, New York, 1999

Akhmatova, Anna, *Stikhotvoreniya i Poemy* (*Verse and Poems*), Sovietskii Pisatel', Leningrad, 1976

Apetyan, Z. A. (ed.), *Vospominaniya o Rakhmaninove*, 2 vols., Izdatel'stvo 'Muzyka', Moscow, 1988

Bal'mont, Konstantin, *Stikhotvoreniya* (*Poetry*), Novaya Biblioteka Poeta, St Petersburg, 2003

Barber, Charles, *Lost in the Stars*, Scarecrow Press, Lanham, 2003

Beaumont, Cyril W., *The Diaghilev Ballet in London*, Putnam, London, 1940

Bely, Andrey, *Sochineniya* (*Works*), 2 vols., Khudozhestvennaya Literatura, Moscow, 1990

Benn, Anna, and Rosamund Bartlett, *Literary Russia: A Guide*, Picador, London, 1997

Bertenson, Sergei, and Jay Leyda, *Sergei Rachmaninoff: A Lifetime in Music*, Indiana University Press, Bloomington, 2004

Bolshoy Theatre, Moscow, ed. T. Bielova, programme booklet for S. Prokofiev's *Fiery Angel*, GABT (Gosudarstvennyi Akademicheskii Bol'shoy Teatr Rossii), Moscow, 2004

Buckle, Richard, *Diaghilev*, Weidenfeld and Nicolson, London, 1979

Chamberlain, Lesley, *The Philosophy Steamer: Lenin and the Exile of the Intelligentsia*, Atlantic Books, London, 2006

Chasins, Abram, *Speaking of Pianists*, Alfred Knopf, New York, 1957

Cropsey, Eugene H., 'Prokofiev's *Three Oranges*: A Chicago World Premiere', *Opera Quarterly*, 2000, vol. 16, pp. 52–67

Davis, Ronald L., *Opera in Chicago*, Appleton-Century, New York, 1966

Dostoyevskii, Fyodor, *Sobranie sochinenii v 15ti tomax*, vol. 4, 'Igrok' ('The Gambler'), Nauka, Leningrad, 1989

Duke, Vernon, *Passport to Paris*, Little, Brown & Co., Boston, 1955

Ehrenburg, Ilya, *Neobychayniye pokhozhdeniya Khulio Khurenito i yego uchenikov* (*The Extraordinary Adventures of Julio Jurenito and his Disciples*) Helicon, Moscow and Berlin, 1922

Figes, Orlando, *A People's Tragedy: The Russian Revolution 1891–1924*, Pimlico, London, 1997

– *Peasant Russia, Civil War: The Volga Countryside in Revolution 1917–1921*, Phoenix Press, London, 2001

Filippov, Boris, *Aktyory bez grima* (*Actors Without Make-up*), Sovietskaya Rossiya, Moscow, 1971

Garafola, Lynn, *Diaghilev's Ballets Russes*, Da Capo Press, New York, 1998

BIBLIOGRAPHY

Garcia-Marquez, Vicente, *Massine: A Biography*, Alfred A. Knopf, New York, 1995
Garden, Mary, *Mary Garden's Story*, Arno Press, New York, 1951
Godowsky, Dagmar, *First Person Plural: The Lives of Dagmar Godowsky by Herself*, Viking Press, New York, 1958
Gold, Arthur, and Robert Fizdale, *Misia: The Life of Misia Sert*, Knopf, New York, 1980
Gray, Camilla, rev. edn by Marian Burleigh-Motley, *The Russian Experiment in Art 1863–1922*, Thames & Hudson Ltd, London, 1986
Gutman, David, *Prokofiev*, Omnibus Press, London, 1990
Harkins, W. E., *Dictionary of Russian Literature*, George Allen and Unwin, London, 1857
Ivanov, Gyorgii, *Peterburgskiye Zimy (Petersburg Winters)* Rodnik, Paris, 1928
Izvolsky, Alexander, *Mémoires d'Alexandre Iswolsky*, Payot, Paris, 1923; tr. and ed. C. L. Seeger, *Memoirs of Alexander Iswolsky*, Hutchinson, London, 1920
Jacobs, Arthur, *Henry J. Wood, Maker of the Proms*, Methuen, London, 1994
Jaffe, Daniel, *Prokofiev*, Phaidon, London, 1998
Kamenskii, Vasilii, *Zhizn' s Mayakovskim (Living with Mayakovsky)*, Moscow, 1940
Kennan, George F., *Soviet-American Relations 1917–1920*, vol. 1: *Russia Leaves the War*, Princeton University Press, 1958
– *Soviet-American Relations 1917–1920*, vol. 2: *The Decision to Intervene*, Princeton University Press, 1989
Knyazeva, V. P., *Kratkaya Khronika deyatel'nosti 'Mira Isskusstva' 1897–1927 (A Short History of the Activities of 'World of Art' 1897–1927)*, www.roerich-museum.org/PRS/book4/20-Knjazeva.pdf
Kochno, Boris, *Diaghilev and the Ballets Russes*, Harper and Row, New York, 1970
Krivosheina, N. A., *Chetyre Treti Nashei Zhizni (Four Thirds of Our Life)*, Russkii Put', Moscow, 1999
Lermontov, Mikhail, *Tambovskaya Kaznacheysha (The Tambov Treasurer's Wife)*, Polnoye Sobranie Stikhotvorenii, 2 vols., Sovetskii Pisatel', Leningrad, 1989
Lockhart, R. H. Bruce, *Memoirs of a British Agent*, Pan Books, London, 2002
Magarshack, David, *Dostoevsky: A Life*, Secker & Warburg, London, 1962
Makarov, Yu. V., *Moya sluzhba v staroy gvardii 1905–1917, mirnoye vremya i voyna*, Buenos Aires, 1951
Marsh, Robert C., and Norman Pellegrini, *150 Years of Opera in Chicago*, Northern Illinois University Press, DeKalb, 2006
Martyn, Barrie, *Nicolas Medtner: His Life and Music*, Scolar Press, UK, 1995
– *Rachmaninoff, Composer, Pianist, Conductor*, Ashgate, Aldershot, 1990
Massine, Léonide, ed. Phyllis Hartnoll and Robert Rubens, *My Life in Ballet*, Macmillan, London, 1968
Maxwell, Elsa, *How to Do It or The Lively Art of Entertaining*, Little Brown, New York, 1957
Minturn, Neil, *The Music of Sergei Prokofiev*, Yale University Press, New Haven, 1997
Mirsky, D. S., ed. F. J. Whitfield, *A History of Russian Literature*, Routledge & Kegan Paul, London, 1949
Mojica, José, *Yo, Pecador (I, A Sinner)*, Franciscan Herald Press, Chicago, 1963
Morrison, Simon, *Russian Opera and the Symbolist Movement*, University of California Press, Berkeley, 2002
Nabokov, Nicolas, *Old Friends and New Music*, Little Brown, Boston, 1951
– *Bagazh: Memoirs of a Russian Cosmopolitan*, Atheneum, New York, 1975
Nash, Jay Robert, *Makers and Breakers of Chicago*, Academy Press, Chicago, 1885

Nest'ev, Israel, tr. Rose Prokofieva, *Sergei Prokofiev: His Musical Life*, Knopf, New York, 1946

Nice, David, *Prokofiev From Russia to the West 1891–1935*, Yale University Press, New Haven and London, 2003

Norris, Geoffrey, *Rakhmaninov*, J. M. Dent & Sons, London, 1978

Odoyevtseva, Irina, *Na beregakh Nevy* (*On the Banks of the Neva*), Khudozhestvennaya Literatura, Moscow, 1988

Paléologue, Maurice, tr. F. A. Holt, *An Ambassador's Memoirs*, George H. Doran, New York, 1924

Pipes, Richard, *The Russian Revolution 1899–1919*, Fontana Press, London, 1992

– *Russia Under the Bolshevik Regime 1919–1924* Harvill (Harper Collins), London, 1992

Pozharskaya, M. N. (ed.), *Russkiye Sezony v Parizhe: Eskizy Dekoratsii i Kostyumov 1908–1929* (*The Russian Seasons in Paris: Sketches of the Scenery and Costumes 1908–1929*) Izdatel'stvo 'Isskustvo', Moscow, 1988

Press, Stephen D., *Prokofiev's Ballets for Diaghilev*, Ashgate, Aldershot, 2006

Prokofiev, Sergey, ed. Svyatoslav Prokofiev, *Dnevnik* (*Diary*) *1907–1933*, 3 vols., sprkfv, Paris, 2002

Prokofiev, Sergey, tr. and annotated Anthony Phillips, *Prodigious Youth: Diaries 1907–1914* (vol. 1 of *Diaries 1907–1933*), Faber and Faber, London, 2006

Prokofiev, Sergei, ed. and tr. Oleg Prokofiev and Christopher Palmer, *Soviet Diary 1927 and Other Writings* (some stories also tr. David McDuff), Faber and Faber, London, 1991

Prokofiev, Sergey, ed. M. G. Kozlova, *Avtobiografiya* (*Autobiography*) Sovietskii Kompozitor, Moscow, 1973; 2nd edn, Sovietskii Kompozitor, Moscow, 1982

Prokofiev, Sergei, tr. Guy Daniels, abridged and ed. Francis King, *Prokofiev by Prokofiev*, Macdonald General Books, London, 1979

Prokofiev, Sergey, ed. V. Blok, *Materialy, Stat'i, Intervvyui* (*Materials, Articles, Interviews*) Progress Publishers, Moscow, 1976; English translation, 1978

Prokofiev, Sergey, eds. I. Nest'ev and G. Edel'man, *Stat'i i Materialy* (*Articles and Materials*) Muzyka, Moscow, 1965

Prokofiev, Sergei, ed. and tr. Harlow Robinson, *Selected Letters*, Northeastern University Press, Boston, 1998

Prokofiev, S. S., ed Semyon I. Shlifshteyn, *Materialy, Dokumenty, Vospomoniniya* (*Materials, Documents, Reminiscences*) Gosudarstvennoye Muzykal'noye Izdatel'stvo, Moscow, 1956

Prokofiev, Sergei, ed. M. P. Rakhmanova, *Vospominaniya, Pis'ma, Stat'i* (*Reminiscences, Letters, Articles*) Gosudarstvenny Tsentral'nyi Muzyey Muzykal'noy Kul'tury imeni M. I. Glinki/Izdatel'stvo 'Deka-BC', Moscow, 2004

Prokofiev, S. S., eds. M. G. Kozlova and M. G. Yashchenko, *S. S. Prokofiev i N. Ya. Myaskovsky: Perepiska* (*S. S. Prokofiev and N. Ya. Myaskovsky: Correspondence*) Sovietskii Kompozitor, Moscow, 1977

Prokofiev, S. S., ed. Alla Bretanitskaya, *Rasskazy* (*Stories*), Izdatel'skii Dom 'Kompozitor', Moscow, 2003

Proust, Marcel, *A la recherche du temps perdu*, 3 vols., Bibliothèque de la Pléiade, Paris, 1954

Proust, Marcel, tr. C. K. Scott Moncrieff and T. Kilmartin, *Remembrance of Things Past*, 3 vols., Random House, New York, 1981

Rachmaninoff, Sergey, ed. Z. A. Apetyan, *Literaturnoye Naslediye*, 3 vols., Sovetskii Kompozitor, Moscow, 1978
Robinson, Harlow, *Sergei Prokofiev, a biography*, Northeastern University Press, Boston, 2002
Rosenthal, Harold, *Two Centuries of Opera at Covent Garden*, Putnam, London, 1958
Rubinstein, Arthur, *My Many Years*, Jonathan Cape, London, 1980
Ruffo, Titta (Ruffo Cafiera Titta), tr. A. Bushen, *Parabola moyei zhizni Muzyka* (*Parabola of my Life*), Leningrad, 1966
Sabaneyev, Leonid, *Vospominaniya o Srkyabinye* (*Reminiscences of Scriabin*) Klassika-XXI, Moscow, 2000
Schipperges, Thomas, tr. J. M. Q. Davies, *Prokofiev*, Haus Publishing, London, 2003
Schmidt, Paul, ed. C. Douglas, *The King of Time, Poems, Fictions, Visions of the Future by Velimir Khlebnikov*, Harvard University Press, 1985
Schonberg, Harold C., *The Great Pianists*, Simon & Schuster, New York, 1963
Schopenhauer, Arthur, tr. Yuli Aikhenwald, *Sobranie sochinenii v shesti tomakh* (*Collected Works in six volumes*), Terra-Knizhnyi Klub, Respublica, Moscow, 2001
Schwartz, Boris, *Music and Musical Life in Soviet Russia 1917–70*, Barrie & Jenkins, London, 1972
Seroff, Victor, *Sergei Prokofiev – A Soviet Tragedy*, Leslie Frewin, London, 1969
Slonimsky, Nicolas, *Perfect Pitch: A Life Story*, Oxford University Press, Oxford and New York, 1988
Sokolova, Lydia, ed. Richard Buckle, *Dancing for Diaghilev: The Memoirs of Lydia Sokolova*, John Murray, London, 1960
Stravinsky, Igor, ed. Robert Craft, *Selected Correspondence*, 3 vols., Faber and Faber, London, 1982, 1984, 1985
Stravinsky, Vera, and Robert Craft, *Stravinsky in Pictures and Documents*, Simon and Schuster, New York, 1978
Suvchinsky, Pyotr (Pierre Souvtchinsky), ed. A. Bretanitskaya, *Pyotr Suvchinsky i yego vremya* (*Pyotr Suvchinsky and His Times*), Kompozitor, Moscow, 1999
Taruskin, Richard, *Stravinsky and the Russian Tradition: A Biography of the Works Through Mavra*, 2 vols., Oxford University Press, 1996
Tolstoy, Ilya L'vovich, tr. G. Calderon, *Reminiscences of Tolstoy*, Century, New York, 1914
Tolstoy, Lev, ed. and tr. R. F. Christian, *Tolstoy's Diaries*, 2 vols., Athlone Press, London, 1985
Tolstoy, Lev, *Krug Chteniya* (*Circle of Reading*), Kushnerev & Co., Moscow, 1909–10
Tolstoy, Lev, tr. Peter Sekirin, *A Calendar of Wisdom*, Simon & Schuster, New York, 1997
Three Oranges, ed. Noëlle Mann, 13 vols., Serge Prokofiev Association, London, 2001–7
Vishnevskaya, Galina, tr. Guy Daniels, *Galina: A Russian Story*, Hodder & Stoughton, London, 1984
Walsh, Stephen, *Igor Stravinsky: A Creative Spring, Russia and France 1882–1934*, Jonathan Cape, London, 2000
Wells, H. G., *The Outline of History, Being a Plain History of Man and Mankind*, Garden City Publishing Co., New York, 1920
White, Eric Walter, *Stravinsky: The Composer and His Works*, Faber and Faber, London, 1966
Wrangel, Baron Pyotr, tr. Sophie Goulston, *Memoirs*, Williams & Norgate, London, 1929

Yershova-Krivosheina, Ksenya, *Russkaya Ruletka* (*Russian Roulette*) Logos, St Petersburg, 2004
Young, Julian, *Schopenhauer*, Routledge, London and New York, 2005
Zavgorodnyaya, Galina, *Aleksey Remizov: Stil' Skazochnoy Prozy* (*Aleksey Remizov: Prose Style in Fable*),Yaroslavl, 2004
Zil'bershteyn, I. S., and V. A. Samkov (eds.), *Sergey Dyagilev i russkoye isskustvo* (*Sergey Diaghilev and Russian Art*), 2 vols., Moscow, 1982

Index

Adams, impresario in Honolulu 296, 313–14
Adams, A.F.: SP's first manager in New York, 330; also Rachmaninoff's manager, 352; advice to include accessible works by other composers, 349; and on London recital, 520; agreeable to ending business relationship, 380, 381; coaches platform demeanour, 355, 365; discussion of future plans, 358; lack of future engagements, 368; lackadaisical about organising solo recital, 346, 349, 353
Adès, Albert: *Le livre de Goha le simple* 685, 685n, 687
Adler, Jacob, actor-manager, father of Stella 402, 402n, 424, 435–6, 449–50, 477, 485, 665, 685, 685n
Adler, Julia, sister of Stella 480, 485
Adler, Stella xv, 393, 393n, 394–5, 396, 397, 398, 399–400, 401–2, 403, 405, 406, 408, 409, 410, 413, 414, 416–17, 418–19, 420, 422, 423, 424, 425–6, 428, 429, 433, 449–50, 465, 466, 477, 478, 479, 480, 482, 482n, 483, 486, 494, 496, 498, 500, 501, 613, 614, 615, 616, 617, 665; contrasted with Lina Codina, 485, 486; performs at New York Jewish Theatre, 485, 497; plans month's absence in Canada, 402; but declines to let SP accompany her, 407
Aeolian Hall, New York 348–9, 348n, 355, 470
Afanasiev, Alexander Nikolayevich: *Russian Folk Tales* (*Russkiye Narodnye Skazki*) 26–7, 26n
Agnitsev, Nikolay, poet: 'The Wizard' 154, 154n
Aix-les-Bains 536
Akhmatova (Gorenko), Anna Andreyevna, poet 89n, 122n, 148n, 681; Suvchinsky proposes poems for setting, 148; 'Poem Without a Hero', 89n, 148n
Akhron, Iosif Yulievich, violinist 55
Akhvlediani, Elli Kornelievna 158, 169, 177
Akimenko, Fyodor Stepanovich, composer 87, 87n
Ala and Lolli, see Sergey Prokofiev, *Scythian Suite*
Albéniz, Isaac, composer 304, 391; *Pepita Jimenez*, opera, 115, 115n
Alchevsky, Ivan Alexeyevich, tenor 66, 66n, 75, 78, 82, 98, 103, 109, 124; cast as Alexey in *The Gambler*, 112, 125, 141; engaged for Ziloti chamber concert, 124, 149, 154; interest in SP's songs, 88, 101; opinion of SP's works, 101; rehearses and performs *The Ugly Duckling*, 146; also mentioned 109

Aldrich, Richard, *New York Times* critic 357n
Alekhine, Alexander Alexandrovich, chess grandmaster 192
Alenitsyn, Alexander, champion tennis player 136, 136n
Alexanian, Diran, cellist 707, 707n, 708, 709
Alexeyev, Alexey Ivanovich, Russian Consul in Rome 7, 8, 9, 11, 12, 14–16, 18–20
Alsace 677
Altadena 575; Mount Echo, 575–6, 575n
Altschuler, Modest Isaakovich, cellist and conductor 322, 322n, 333, 423; New York concert, 364–6; press reviews, 366; proposal to include *Scythian Suite* barred by Rachmaninoff, 373; orchestration of Scriabin's 9th Sonata and *Poème satanique*, 335–6
Alya P, short-lived romance 88
Amanaus glacier, Caucasus 232
America; appendicitis operation witnessed by SP 417; attitude to Russians, 266, 267, 289; distinction drawn between Russians and Bolsheviks, 312, 322; fear of German spies, 316; and of Bolsheviks, 316; first thoughts of going to, 241; girls sampled, 380, 383; idea takes root, 245; immigration procedures, 316–21; impresarios, 247; overview of initial sucess or failure, 378; plans to set out from Kislovodsk, 250, 253; but postponed, 254; prohibition on issuing visas to Russians, 264; SP sceptical of public's musical understanding, 292; various travel plans contemplated, 248, 249, 252, 256, 257, 258, 260, 264, 299
Ampico, mechanical reproducing piano company 391
Anapa 51, 51n
Anarchists 237, 260, 262
Andreyev family 37, 52, 55
Andreyev, Nikolay Vasilievich, tenor 5, 5n, 39, 115; attempts to smooth over rift, 105; bridge with, 196; cast as the Marquis in *The Gambler*, 112, 125; death of, 511, 518, 519; disappointment at being passed over to perform songs, 124; visits Bashkirov dacha at Kuokkale, 136; also mentioned, 120
Andronnikov, Prince Mikhail 136, 136n, 137
Angara river 279, 280
Anichkov, chess-playing acquaintance 187–8
Anisfeld, Boris Izrailovich, artist 337, 358, 412, 441, 480, 499, 501, 515; appeals for money to fund solo recital, 348; designs for *Love for*

INDEX

Three Oranges, 411, 413, 639, 643, 644, 648, 650, 651, 652, 654, 655; exhibition at Brooklyn Museum, 348; scenery for *The Blue Bird*, 464
Ann Arbor 366–7, 366n
Ansermet, Ernest, conductor 429, 527, 528, 601, 607, 608
Antonelli, Countess, acquaintance in Rome 23
Antwerp: battle for, 709–10; Plantin House Museum, 710; SP's concert in, 709–10
Apollon magazine 28, 104, 104n
Apukhtin, Alexey, poet: 'The Boat Cast Off', 78, 110, 154
Aquitania, transatlantic liner 586, 587, 612–13, 612n
'Ara' laxative pills 93
Arabelov, Prince, friend of Nina Koshetz 656
Aragvi river 135
Argentina 267; Buenos Aires, 271, 274, 281; Pampas, 281
Arkhara 281
Armavir, city near Krasnodar 255, 255n
Artemyova-Leontevskaya, Zinaida, soprano 122n, 171, 171n
Asafyev, Boris Vladimirovich, composer and critic 75, 75n, 259, 265, 269, 273, 274, 297, 352, 430, 434, 519, 536; adulation of Nina Koshetz, 169; appointed to Mariinsky Theatre, 638; hears play-through of *The Gambler*; and comments 100–101; ineffectual guardian of SP's Petrograd apartment, xiv, 543, 547, 691, 694; notion that Russian music lacks true joyfulness, 207–8; proposes *The Gambler* to Musical Drama Theatre, 206; reviews *Autumnal*, 143; rift with A. Rimsky-Korsakov over new music, 174, 174n; SP's letter to, confirming intention to return to Russia in the autumn, 278; starts new magazine with Suvchinsky and Belyayev, 174, 174n; also mentioned, 109, 111, 170–11, 171, 217, 265
Asbury Park, New Jersey 417, 418, 420
Aslanov, Alexander Petrovich, conductor 48–9, 48n, 55–6, 75; engages SP for concerts, 114–15; hears Myaskovky's Third Symphony, 120; joins SP on trip down Volga, 199–200, 201; rehearses *Le Prophète*, 145; rivalry with Fitelberg, 55–6, 114–15; understudies Coates as conductor of *The Gambler*, 116–17, 138, 143, 168
Astoria Hotel, Petrograd 36
Astrakhan 133–4, 138, 200, 200n
Athens 17–18; Acropolis, 17–18
Atlantic Ocean 337, 410, 411, 421
Auer, Leopold Semyonovich, violinist and teacher 289, 289n, 327, 495
Augusteo Orchestra 20–22
Austria: reported seeking peace terms, 344; territory annexed by Italy, 704
Avanova, Sonya, admirer of Nina Koshetz, 216, 217, 275
Averchenko, Arkady, writer 4, 4n

Babastro, fellow traveller to Italy 9, 11–15, 18, 20; Babastro family, 9, 10, 12, 14–16
Bach, Johann Sebastian, composer 476; French Suite No. 5, 422, 427; organ fugues, 130, 158
Baikal, Lake 279, 280
Bakhmetiev, Boris, Russian (not Soviet) Ambassador in New York 341, 341n; possible source of financial support, 339–40, 344, 421
Baklanov, Georgy Andreyevich, baritone 458, 458n, 583, 583n, 624, 627, 642, 648, 651, 652, 655
Bakst, Léon (Lev Rosenberg), artist and designer 4n; designs for *Schéhérezade*, 510, 679; unsuccessful recommendation of *Love for Three Oranges* to Metropolitan Opera and to Diaghilev, 434, 452
Baku 386–7; reported captured by the English, 315
Bakuriani 134, 134n
Baliyev, Nikita, actor and cabaret owner 611, 611n
Balkan Wars 15n
Balla, Giacomo, Futurist composer 27n, 28; *Printing-Machine Ballet*, 27n
Ballets Russes 507, 509, 515; 1921 European spring season cancelled because of proposed South American tour, 540; reinstated, 591; London season, 525, 525n; performing in Madrid, 592, 593; South American tour, 1921 540; cancelled, 591
Balmont, Konstantin Dmitrievich, poet and translator 82, 82n, 214, 256, 275, 635, 645, 663–4, 679, 681; acts as judge in sonnet competition, 675, 683; dedicates verses to Nina Koshetz, 263; despised by Mayakovsky, 187; emigrates to France, 535–6; hears SP play settings of his poems, 83; imagines programme for *Sarcasms*, 146; impoverished in emigration, 610, 627, 648, 664, 666; benefit concerts for, 610, 710–11, 710n; inscribes book to SP 'magician of sounds', 149; knowledgeable in astronomy, 223; Moscow dinner honouring, 363; new orthography, views on, 219–20, 220n; observes 'walking stomachs' in Kislovodsk, 222–3; proposes poems as song lyrics, 147; reads Malay incantation, 222; reasons for not planning to leave Russia, 263; summer in France with, 620; views on North and South America, 224; 'A-oo', 148n; *Buildings on Fire* (*Goryashchiye Zdaniya*), 611n; 'Dmitri The Fair' ('Smert' Dmitriya Krasnogo'), 115, 115n; 'I do not know the wisdom' ('Ye ne znayu mudrosti'), xiii; 'In my Garden' 154, 154n; *Seven, They Are Seven*; account of Koussevitsky's reaction to SP's play-through, 263n; gives reading of, 222; 'one of the most fearsome things ever written', 222, 222n; SP proposes setting, 171, 171n, 219, 693; and plays through to, 262–3; 'White Country' 611, 611n; also mentioned, 223, 268

Balmont, Mirra, Balmont's daughter 219, 219n, 220, 221, 535
Balmont (née Tsvetkovskaya) Yelena Konstantinovna, Balmont's third wife 171, 219, 220–21, 535
Baltimore 246, 664–5
Baranovskaya, Maria Viktorovna ('Frou-frou') 563–4, 565, 566–7, 571, 572, 573, 574, 575, 576, 577, 578–81, 586, 588, 615, 616, 617, 649, 650, 651, 652, 653, 656, 657, 661, 663, 664, 672, 675; engaged to Borovsky, 682–3; proposal of marriage rejected by SP, 664, 665
Baranovsky, former husband of Baranovskaya 571, 580
Barcelona 700, 707–9; recitals in, 695, 696, 701, 702, 703–9; Tibidabo, 708, 708n
Bari 19
Barkova, Lidia, *see* Karneyeva, Lidia
Barocchi, Randolfo, Ballets Russes company manager 608, 608n
Baron and Baroness Shelking, shipboard acquaintances 503
Bashkirov, Boris Nikolayevich (Boris Verin, 'the prince', B.N., Borya, Borenka, Boryusya) 3n, 16, 38, 41, 46, 50–51, 52, 58, 58n, 63, 69, 73, 73n, 76, 78–9, 82, 88, 92–3, 99, 126, 274, 297, 430, 434, 450, 519, 536, 545, 677; and SP: accompanies on trip down Volga, 120–30, 132–4; adoraton of his music, 85; arranges birthday roulette session, 272; arrives in Europe, 601–3, 605, 606; chess matches and tournaments with, 90, 93, 94, 101, 105–6, 108, 115, 166, 610, 676, 688, 689, 700, 701, 711; contemplates travelling to America with, 267–8; dines with, 209, 230; distressed at not meeting in New York, 616, 619; existence of short stories concealed from, 268; gifts exchanged, 114, 115, 120–1, 128; 'house-sits' Petrograd apartment, 230; invited to France, 586–7, 591, 592, 593; and to spend summer in Germany, 664, 667; invites SP to his clubs, 206, 210, 213; and to family dacha in Kuokkale, 129; joyous reunion in Petrograd (1918), 265; lends money, 86–8; persuades SP to hear Lotin, 102–3; and to play chess with his cousin, 93; plans for 1916 summer, 124; and to repeat Volga expedition, 191; plays tennis with, 131; presents inscribed lyre ,155; recommends Bryusov's *Fiery Angel*, 442; reconciliation, 622, 626, 634; rift over leaving chess tournament, 145; Schopenhauer, readings of, 140, 175, 191, 694; sonnet competition, 674, 676, 683; SP misses his company, 350, 663; SP's letters to, 278–9, 280, 288; supports SP in quarrel with Prince Magalov, 138–9; trip down the Volga river with, 132–4; but fears atrocities by marauding gangs, 199; urges more focus on pianism, 139–40; visited by, 73, 116, 155–6; Berlin, trip to in search of publisher for poems, 678, 684; and in pursuit of Odoyevtseva, 691; returns, 696; boastful tendencies, 7; condemns Severyanin for publication by Bolshevik press, 690; efforts to obtain French visa, 593; embarrassed by attentions of Anna Zherebtsova-Andreyeva, 100; encounter with Ganna Walska, 679; enthusiasm for Munich, 664, 670–71; escapes from Petrograd to Finland, 542, 587; flees Petrograd for Crimea, 511, 535–6; indolence of, 671, 675, 676, 677, 691, 713; interest in the occult, 62, 73, 77; introduced to Balmont, 221; and gives reading of his poems, 223; love affairs: Baranovskaya, impressed by but not physically attracted to, 664, 665; with Kira Nikolayevna, 260; with Odoyevtseva, 686–91; with Suroshnikova, 132–3; consents to *mariage blanc* with Lyudmila Kurlina, 165, 198, 199n; makes debut as poetry reciter, 79; medically examined for call-up, 105; 'Monday Evenings' At Home, 142, 265, 268; mother, 586, 602; mud treatment at Yessentuki, 138; name-day party, 129; news of possible arrival in New York, 345; nude bathing, 609; offered large sum of money by brother, 79; plans to escape German invasion by motor-boat, 188; rents dacha in Yessentuki, 214, 219; returns to New York, 613, 616; but worsening relationship with brother, 627, 664; suffers from neuralgia, 86, 92, 93, 138; talent for translation rather than poetry, 696; 26th birthday banquet, 187; whereabouts of Sablino dacha concealed from, 194; also mentioned, 3, 4, 44, 64, 74, 95, 98, 107, 116, 119, 140, 149, 155, 157, 165, 174, 189, 197, 213, 223, 230, 268, 612, 641, 666, 703
Bashkirov, Vladimir Nikolayevich, brother of Boris 87, 130, 345, 354, 370, 371, 372, 377, 378, 381, 383, 392, 407, 442–3, 450, 542, 545, 586, 613n, 619; conduit for Maria Grigoriyevna's exit route from Novorossiisk, 426, 428; financial link possible through Cooperatives, 399, 400, 400n; contemplates return to Russia via Nice and Vienna, 349; emigrates to New York, 331; finds New York apartment for SP, 425–6; lends SP money, 344, 421; meets SP in New York, 341, 342, 343; SP moves in with, 425; SP's residual resentment over Boris's wedding, 331–2, 333; suggests SP marry Yevgenia Kurlina, 155–6, 165; and that Boris marry Lyudmila Kurlina, 165; uneasy relationship with brother in New York, 627, 664; views on SP's relationship with Stella Adler, 400, 404, 405
Bashkirova, Tatyana Nikolayevna, Boris Bashkirov's sister 131, 136, 138, 170–71, 173, 191, 414, 428, 693
Batalpashinsk, Cossack *stanitsa* 232, 232n
Batavia 423–4

746 INDEX

Batum 489; reports of English landing at, 249
Bauer, Harold, pianist 343, 487, 493
Bavaria 671; could secede in the event of unrest in Germany, 711
Bayreuth 661
Bazavov, Sergey (Serge), cousin of Meshcherskaya sisters 39
Beatty, Admiral 612–13
Becker, Los Angeles acquaintance 564–5
Beecham, Sir Thomas, conductor 516n, 519, 522, 524, 526, 535, 535n; Beecham Opera Company, collapse of, 535, 535n, 538, 589; *Love for Three Oranges* at Covent Garden, 526, 529
Beethoven, Ludwig van, composer 429; Contredanses, 422, 426, 441; Piano Concerto No. 4 in G, Op. 58, 107; Piano Sonata No. 8 in C minor, Op. 13 (Pathétique), 203; Piano Sonata No. 23 in F minor Op. 57 ('Appassionata'), 187–8; Piano Sonata No. 28 in A, Op. 101, 558; Symphony No. 5 in C minor, Op. 67, 616
Beirne, Deborah, would-be impresario for *Oranges* 667, 673–4, 675; sends contract, 672, 672n
Bellini, Marinuzzi's repetiteur ar Chicago Opera 541
Bellison, Simeon, clarinettist, founder of Zimro Ensemble 427, 427n
Beloóstrov, border town between Russia and Finland 91, 91n
Beloúsov, Yevsey Yakovlevich, cellist 75, 75n, 707
Bely, Andrey (Boris Nikolayevich Bugayev) 670, 670n, 681, 681n; *First Encounter*, 677, 681, 690; 'To Her', 148n
Belyayev, Mitrofan Petrovich, example of disinterested Russian publisher 335, 335n; Editions Beliaeff, 466
Belyayev, Viktor Mikhailovich, musicologist and critic 174, 174n
Belyayev, Yury, playwright and theatre critic 89, 89n; *Psyche* 89, 89n
Benois, Alexander Nikolayevich, artist and designer 4, 44, 73, 81, 83, 90, 92, 100, 268, 274, 519; admiration for 'Classical' Symphony Gavotte, 206; contacted by Diaghilev about season of performances, 266, 266n; enlists Gorky's aid to spare SP conscription, 204; hears play-through of *The Gambler*, 126; and advises on designs for the production, 167; installed in Winter Palace, 266; introduces SP to Lunacharsky entourage, 269–70, 271; sketches SP, 273; SP sees in New Year with, 159; SP's letter to, 290; suspected of trying to seize power in post-Revolution Ministry of Culture, 188; 'Thursdays' At Home, 72–3, 100; also mentioned, 131, 186
Benois (Braslavksya-Benois), Yelena Alexandrovna (Lyolya), painter and sculptor,
daughter of Alexander Benois 159
Berchtesgaden, Bavaria 671
Berdyayev, Valerian, conductor 215, 215n, 222
Bering Straits 316
Berlin 669–70, 679–83
Berlioz, Hector, composer: *La damnation de Faust*, 108
Berlitz Language Institute 39
Besanzoni, Gabriella, mezzo-soprano 391
Beshtau, mountain in Caucasus 231, 231n
Bessel, Vasily Vasilievich, music publisher 31, 31n
Bizet, Georges: *Carmen*, 632, 642
Black Hundreds 136n
Black Sea 233, 249
Blagoveshchensk 279, 279n, 281
bliny 259, 259n, 263
Bloch, Ernest, composer 353, 353n
Blok, Alexander Alexandrovich, poet 122n; 'In My Garden at Night', 148n; *The Rose and the Crown*, 144n; 'The Song of Faina', 696; 'When You Stand on my Path', 696
Blumenfeld, Felix Mikhailovich, composer, conductor and teacher 109, 109n
Boccaccio, Giovanni: *The Decameron* 671
Bodanzky, Artur, conductor 474, 474n, 487, 492, 523
Bogolyubov, Nikolay Nikolayevich, Mariinsky Theatre opera producer 149, 159, 163, 167–8, 215
Bohemian Club of New York 378, 469, 470, 474, 490, 493
Bolakhovsky, French consul in Kiev 151–2
Bolm, Adolph, dancer and choreographer 330–31, 330n, 332, 334, 335, 339, 352, 354, 356, 365, 368, 370–71, 406, 408, 414, 429, 444, 451, 453, 463, 484, 485, 495, 497, 542, 544, 591; attempts to raise money for solo recital, 348; Ballet Intime, 488, 488n; dances to *Visions fugitives* at Anisfeld exhibition in Brooklyn Museum, 348; engaged for Chicago Opera production of *Love for Three Oranges*, 413; hosts 'punch party' for SP to meet critics, 335, 336, 336n; production of *Petrushka*, 507
Bolm, Beatrice (Beate), wife of Adolph Bolm 335, 345, 352, 402, 542; birth of baby, 542
Bolshevik regime 200, 203, 253, 253n; Bolshevik Military Organisation, 209; attempts overthrow of Provisional Government, 209–10, 210n; culture of, 705, 707; murder of Imperial family, 332; propaganda, 704; rumours of universal military conscription, 256
Bolsheviks 184n, 200, 203, 210, 211, 220n, 227n, 234n, 237n, 238–9, 240–41, 245, 245n, 248, 249, 250n, 253, 253n, 260n, 261n, 272n, 278n, 283, 285, 291, 296, 299, 300n, 312, 313, 316, 319, 320, 330, 331, 332, 337, 338, 341n, 347, 353, 358, 369, 383, 387, 400n, 404, 410n, 419, 420n, 430, 430n, 433, 433n, 437, 447, 449, 450, 457, 458,

461, 465, 473, 477, 480, 482, 484, 510n, 533, 535, 536, 580n, 630n, 647n, 662, 682, 682n, 690, 692, 704, 706, 707; concerts organised in New York, 464; and in Chicago, 662
Bolshoy Theatre, Moscow 259; possible production of *The Gambler*, 172–3
Bookman, female acquaintance in New York 396, 666
Borodin, Alexander Porfirievich, composer 22
Borovsky, Alexander Kirillovich, pianist 64–5, 68, 83–4, 98, 519, 700; engaged to Baranovskaya, 682–3; performs Sonata No. 2 and Scherzo, Op. 12 No. 10, 150; plays anniversary recital of Scriabin works, 121; but disappoints SP, 190; SP's admiration for as pianist, 84–5; SP's regular lunches with, 86, 150; also mentioned, 171
Borzhom 134
Borzhomi, *see* Borzhom
Bossé, Gwalter, bass: cast as the General in *The Gambler* 125, 145
Boston 246, 437
Boston Symphony Orchestra 423, 437, 543
Bozhnev, Boris, *see* Gershun, Boris
Brahms, Johannes: Clarinet Quintet in B minor, Op. 115, 470; Piano Concerto, 392
Brazil 437, 450, 531–2
Breitkopf and Härtel, music publishers 617
Breshko-Breshkovskaya, Yekaterina Konstantinovna, 'Grandmother of the Russian Revolution' 409–10, 409n
Brest-Litovsk, Treaty of 284n, 331
Brewer, repetiteur at the Mariinsky Theatre 140
Brichant, Sonya, SP's second cousin 488, 494, 495, 499, 506, 509, 513, 532, 538
Brindisi 18, 19, 32, 494
British Military Mission 274, 279, 436, 437, 494, 499
Broadway Limited Express 434, 450–51
Bronstein, Lev Davidovich, *see* Trotsky, Léon
Brooklyn Museum: recital of Russian music to concide with Anisfeld exhibition 348
'Bruderschaft' ritual 234, 234n
Brunswick, Mrs, Los Angeles socialite 571, 572
Brussels 488, 495, 701; premiere of *Scythian Suite*, 699, 700, 709
Bryskin, Arkady Borisovich, conductor 35, 35n
Bryusov, Valery Yakovlevich, Symbolist poet and novelist 681; finds Villa Christophorus appropriate setting for *Fiery Angel*, 671n; *The Fiery Angel*, 442, 681n, 696; 'The Pied Piper', 148n
Bucharest 11, 13
Buffalo 470–71, 494
Bugayev, Boris, *see* Bely, Andrey
Bulgaria: capitulation of, 340; difficulties of travel through, 20; hostility to Russians, 12, 32; possible war with Romania and Serbia, 8, 30
Bunin, Ivan Alexeyevich, poet and novelist 533, 533n, 534; *Hiawatha*, translation of, 696
Burlyuk, David Davidovich, artist: poet and Futurist, 187, 187n; present at Moscow Poets Café event, 262
Bushen, Alexandra Dmitrievich (Shurik), former Conservatoire fellow student 85, 85n
Butomo-Nazvanova, Olga Nikolayevna, mezzo-soprano 86, 86n, 122n; sings *The Ugly Duckling*, 85, 90; takes part in Moscow recital 171

Calendar, change from Julian to Gregorian 256
California 321–2, 323, 370, 544, 555, 664; concert engagements in, 522, 523, 553
Calvé, Emma, singer and teacher 605, 605n
Cambridge, Mass. 437
Campanini, Cleofonte, music director of the Chicago Opera 387, 432, 537n, 585; agrees to present *The Gambler*, 339, 361, 453, 462; contemplates *Love for Three Oranges* as alternative, 362, 363; contract negotiations with, 363–4, 367–8, 378, 380, 381, 383, 432; impressed by *Scythian Suite*, 363, 397; preliminary casting for *Love for Three Oranges*, 432; illness and death, 432, 442–3, 449
Canada 321, 324, 326; Viceroy Duke of Devonshire, 468; Peltier, ADC to Viceroy, 468
Canadian Pacific Express 325
Cannes 595
Capablanca, José Raúl, chess grandmaster 357, 393, 397, 408, 411, 416, 588, 666, 692; SP's simultaneous match with, 667–8; and Boris Bashkirov's, 668
Capri, Island of 26
Carpenter, John Alden, composer 432, 432n, 548, 549, 550, 552, 553, 583, 631, 633, 656, 662; Princess deployed as ally in conflict with Chicago Opera, 553, 554, 555; *Krazy Kat*, ballet, 479, 479n, 650–51; *Skyscrapers*, ballet, 432, 432n, 453, 515
Carpenter, Mrs 515, 517, 524, 549, 656, 662
Caruso, Enrico, tenor 356, 399; raises money for American Loan, 346; as Samson in *Samson et Dalila*, 352
Caspian Sea 133–4
Caucasus: possibility of being overrun by Bolsheviks, 447, 461; possibility of German occupation, 307; scene of fierce Civil War fighting, 404
Caucasus mountains 232–3
Chaliapin, Fyodor Ivanovich, bass-baritone 130–31, 130n, 256, 638, 655, 661; expresses interest in *The Gambler*, 273; in Kislovodsk, 214, 219
Chalmers, organisers of reception in Chicago 661
Charpentier, Gustave, composer: *Louise*, opera 524, 524n

Chauve-Souris, Théâtre de la, Paris 611n
Cheka (Chrezvychainaya Kommissiya) 271, 271n
Chelishchev, Pavel, *see* Tchelitchew, Pavel
Cherbourg 504, 505, 588
Cherdynya 201
Cherkasskaya-Palechek, Marianna Borisovna, soprano: cast as Polina in *The Gambler*, 112, 112n, 125
Chernyavsky, Iosif, cellist, member of Zimro Ensemble 70–71, 70n, 74, 147, 425, 430
Chesnokov, Pavel Grigorievich, composer and choral conductor 115, 115n; *Sappho*, opera, 115
Cheville, Professor in Chicago 553, 554
Chicago 87, 241, 246, 321, 326–7, 359, 365, 366, 367, 493; Auditorium Hotel, 617, 617n; Auditorium Theatre, 360–61, 361n, 617, 617n, 662; acoustic in, 661; Chicago Opera: New York tour 383, 387; *Love for Three Oranges*, 368, 378, 381, 383, 386; considered unperformable, 474, 475; financial concerns, 495; negotiations, xvi-xvii, 363–4, 367–8, 431–2; *Oranges* preferred to *The Gambler*, 359, 362; production cancelled, 444, 471, 522; Chicago Symphony: 358, 359, 360–61, 362–4, 583, 620, 629–40, 642–6; Congress Hotel, 359–60; Conservatory of Music, 327; *Daily News*, 635; Japanese Consul, 364; Kimball Hall, 431; Lake Michigan, 360; Michigan Avenue, 433; University of Chicago, 548, 550, 554; Cosmopolitan Club, 460, 548; SP's recitals for, 555, 662
China 267, 464
chiromancy 246
Chita 278, 278n, 280
Chkheidze, Nikolay Semyonovich, Georgian Social Democrat and Menshevik 184–5, 194n
Chopin, Fryderyk, composer 63, 554; Ballades, 251; Etude in A minor ('Winter Wind'), Op. 10 No. 2, 63; Etude in E, Op. 10 No. 3, 275, 275n; Etudes, 251; Mazurkas, 251; Nocturnes, 251; Nocturne in F sharp, Op. 15 No. 2, 251; Sonata No. 2 in B flat minor, Op. 35, 251, 251n; Waltzes, 251, 429
Christophorus Villa, *see* Villa Christophorus
Cimarosa, Domenico, composer: *Cimarosiana*, ballet, 517; (orch. Respighi) *Le Astuzie Femminili* (*Women's Wiles*), 508, 508n, 517
Civil War: Admiral Kolchak and the Omsk Government, 249, 249n; Bolshevik advance on Pyatigorsk, 249; Bolsheviks reported at the gates of Odessa, 404; conflict in Baku, 386–7; Czech Legion, 278n, 291, 291n, 296, 298; disrupts telegraphic communications, 291; Denikin retreats from Poltava and Kharkov, 447, 450; disruption on railways, 252; famine, terror and lawlessness post-Revolution, 337, 362, 372, 378, 434, 437, 450, 519, 630; fighting: at Armavir, 255, 255n; at Krasnoye Selo, 429; at the Nikolayevsky railway line, 430; at Tikhoretsk, 257, 257n; at Tosno, 429; at Tsarskoye Selo, 429; on the Don, 240–41, 245, 250, 250n; round Petrograd, 430; General Wrangel's control of Southern Russia, 533; Grigory Semyonov, Cossack warlord, 278, 278n, 280, 280n; North Western Army, 300n, 423, 429, 430, 430n, 433; Omsk Government, 249, 249n, 278n, 358, 419, 419n
Clausells, secretary of Barcelona Music Society 707
Cleveland 584, 626; Masonic Hall, 626
Coates, Albert, composer and conductor 61, 61n, 67–8, 73, 75, 80, 82–3, 139, 475, 475n, 518, 519, 520, 522, 523, 524, 552, 663, 665; SP: introduces to A. S. Taneyev, 158–9; loving reunion in Petrograd (1918), 265; offers orchestral engagements in London, 521, 529, 529n; offers orchestral engagements in Petrograd to SP, 101, 108; praises conducting, 143; SP's desire to collaborate with, 101; Third Piano Concerto in New York, 589; *The Gambler*: as conductor, 138, 168; hears play-through, 93–4, 101, 103–4, 111–12, 129, 140, 141; indisposed for rehearsals, 145, 149, 150; interest in, 61, 91; present at Mariinsky Theatre audition, 116–19; proposes cast, 112; proposes Lambin as designer, 94, 111; regrets impossibility of rehearsing Acts Three and Four, 190–91; *Love for Three Oranges*: auditions, 523; proposes for Covent Garden, 427, 434, 466, 518, 526, 529; conducts *Tsar Saltan*, 140; socially more polished than Malko, 101; *Assurbanipal*, opera, 82–3, 82n, 94, 140; also mentioned, 73, 167, 174
Cocteau, Jean, poet, dramatist and designer 515
Codina, Carolina (Linette, Lina, 'Ptashka') 428n, 548, 599, 600, 604, 612, 671n; first encounter with SP, 428; Boris Bashkirov, reservations about, 587; chess problems, 699; compared to Miller, 671; and to Stella Adler, 485, 486; desire for marriage, 592, 593, 650, 663; SP's qualms about, 592, 623, 627, 638, 641; and growing acceptance of, 683–4, 686, 687, 694–5; early birthday gift to SP, 495; London rendezvous with, 581, 586, 588–9; meets Maria Grigorievna, 532; CC's mother, 465, 523, 526, 574; moves in to Prokofiev home in Mantes-sur-Seine, 534; operation for appendicitis, 590, 591; presented as translator of *Love for Three Oranges* into English, 500, 532; qualities as a singer, 645, 650; relationship develops with 84, 434, 435, 436, 437, 438, 439, 440, 442, 443, 444, 445, 446, 447, 448, 449, 450–51, 458–60, 463, 464, 465, 466, 467–8, 469, 470, 473, 474, 476, 477, 478, 481, 483, 485, 487, 488, 489, 490, 491, 492, 493, 494, 495, 496, 498, 499, 500; returns unexpectedly from Milan, 696;

Rigoletto in Milan, auditions for, 704, 704n; sends present of gloves, 577; singing lessons, 532, 538, 539, 540, 541; with Félia Litvinne, 539, 539n; with Emma Calvé in Milan, 605, 606, 675, 677, 699–700; SP meets in Milan, 701, 704–5; SP urges to come to Europe, 500, 501, 507, 510, 514, 518, 521, 522, 525, 526; makes plans to come, 523, 529–30; and arrives in France, 531, 532; Villa Christophorus, arrival at, 676–7; marriage, xv, 711–12, 712n; also mentioned, 562, 592, 594, 600, 601, 603, 625, 627, 648, 655, 657

Coini, Jacques, stage director, producer of *Love for Three Oranges* 618, 618n, 619, 620, 624, 627, 628, 631, 634, 638, 639–40, 641–2, 643, 644, 645, 648, 649, 651, 652–3, 654, 655, 662

Colbert, Jessica, SP's manager in California 555, 555n, 556, 558

Collini, Lina 232, 234, 238, 245, 253–4, 257, 297; abandons plan to go to America in favour of Romania, 257, 258; departure from Kislovodsk postponed because of fighting, 255–6; originator of idea of going to America, 241, 250; psychology, 258

commedia dell'arte 141n, 576, 577

Commissariat of the former Imperial Court Ministry 206; SP appointed to Committee for the Arts, 206, 207

Compagnie Internationale des Wagons-Lits, *see* International Company

Constantinople 4, 16, 250, 449, 457, 473, 630; Maria Grigorievna's arrival in, 526, 529, 530–31; reports of occupation by English, 249; disproved, 249; Russian Embassy or Consulate in, 448, 457; steamer connections with Brindisi, 494; and with Marseilles, 509

Constitutional Democrats (Kadets), political party 84n, 85

'Contemporaries', *see* Evenings of Contemporary Music

Continental Telegraphen Compagnie of Berlin, *see* Wolff Agency

Cook, Thomas, travel agency 308, 313, 498, 499

Cooper, Emil Albertovich, conductor, music director of Bolshoy Theatre 157–8, 157n, 171–3

Cooperatives 400, 400n, 426, 4426n

Copenhagen 536

Coppicus, F. C., head of Metropolitan Music Bureau: wishes to represent SP, 356

copyright convention, non-existence between America and Russia 329, 617

Corfu 19

Corinthian Canal 18

Cornelia, acquaintance in New York 411

Cortot, Alfred, pianist 469, 471

Cossack *stanitsa* 232, 232n, 253

Court Orchestra, *see* Petrograd, Court Orchestra

Covent Garden 520, 522–3, 526; Beecham Opera Company, collapse of, 535, 535n, 538, 589; *Love for Three Oranges*, 427, 434, 452, 518, 521, 524, 525, 526, 529, 534

Crimea 511

Cui, César Antonovich, composer 115; *The Mandarin's Son*, opera, 97, 97n

Cunard, Lady Emerald 522, 522n, 523–4; listens to *Love for Three Oranges*, 524, 525–6

Czech Legion 278n, 291, 291n, 296, 298; disrupts telegraphic communications, 291, 307

Damrosch, Walter, conductor, Music Director of the New York Symphony Orchestra 330, 330n, 614; auditions 'Classical' Symphony and 1st Piano Concerto 332, 334

Damskaya, Eleonora Alexandrovna, harpist and pianist 3, 3n, 4–5, 8, 12, 39, 41, 44, 46, 52, 61, 62, 81–2, 100, 113, 142, 224, 268, 274, 297, 536, 689–90; commissioned to provide Wooden Book, 95; competes in Conservatoire piano competition, 126, 126n; death of cousin Vovka, 139; and of wealthy suitor Sergey Vladimirovich, 139, 139n; first person to hear short stories, 225; friendship with Kerensky, 3n, 225; exploits to secure SP's release from conscription, 204, 205, 211–12; help sought for Katya Schmidthof, 93; intercedes with Lunacharsky for SP's exit visa, 260–61; letter informing SP of looting of Petrograd apartment, xiv, 691–4; performs as harpist, 89–90; present of brooch, 314; pawned, 553; pursued by Zakharov, 128; says goodbye to SP as he finally leaves Petrograd, 275; SP buys gift for, 114, 115–16; successfully exports diamonds to Switzerland, 265; supplies SP with creature comforts in Sablino, 225; and in Petrograd (1918), 265, 274; whereabouts of Sablino dacha concealed from, 57, 194; also mentioned, 32, 35, 55, 73, 75, 92, 120, 140, 152, 155, 189, 213, 230, 267, 272

Damskaya, Vera Alexandrovna, Eleonora's sister 55, 73, 92, 140, 155

Daniel, impresario in Spain 701, 707, 708

Danilov, A., bridge and chess partner 98, 98n, 347, 347n, 352

Danish Mission 279

Danube river 12, 702

Dardanelles, opening of 348

Dargomyzhsky, Alexander Sergeyevich, composer 22; *Rusalka*, 34, 34n; *The Stone Guest*, 120–21, 121, 167

Darial Gorge 135, 135n

Darrieux, Marcel, violinist 536n; premiere of First Violin Concerto, 712, 712n

Davydov, husband of Lucy Khodzhayeva 611

Davydova, singer at *Mir Isskustva* recital 611

Dawes, Charles Gates, banker and statesman,

financial director of Chicago Opera 550, 553, 549, 549n
De Lamarter, Eric, conductor, critic, choirmaster and composer 360–61, 361n, 362, 363
Debussy, Claude 31, 304, 391; *Douze Préludes*, 469; *Feux d'artifice*, 293; *Pelléas et Mélisande*, opera, 387, 394, 457
Degendorf 703
Demchinskaya, V, F., wife of Boris Demchinsky 75, 120, 140
Demchinsky, Boris Nikolayevich 63, 63n, 75, 110, 116, 140–41, 269, 351; and SP: chess games with, 73, 88, 123, 145; chosen to inaugurate Wooden Book, 95–6, 99, 99n; eulogises musical progress exemplifed by *Visions Fugitives*, 189; SP regularly spends Christmas Eve with, 159, 450; disapproval of frivolous *Oranges* anticipated, 359; distrust of Lotin, 99, 102; expounds on Altaic legends, 185; friendship with Tcherepnin, 187; indifferent to chess tournaments, 159, 166; irritation with Boris Bashkirov, 90, 99, 121, 159; as literary adviser, 515; advises on *Gambler* libretto, 64, 123–5, 127; discourages choice of *Alaley and Leila* as opera subject, 185; tells SP by leaving Russia he is 'running away from history', 362, 434; also mentioned, 103, 114, 120, 121, 155, 267, 267n
Denikin, General Anton Ivanovich, C-in-C White Armies 447, 450; battle for Rostov-on-Don, 480, 480n; troops deserting to Reds, 463
Deryuzhinsky, Gleb Vladimirovich, sculptor 479, 480, 483, 488, 489, 491, 495, 498, 542, 667
Derzhanovsky, Vladimir Vladimirovich, writer: critic and musical entrepreneur, 34, 34n, 155, 157, 690, 695; revives *Muzyka* magazine, 157
Diaghilev, Sergey (Serge) Pavlovich 4n, 42, 43, 506, 507, 508, 509, 512, 513–14, 515–16, 524, 529, 531, 541, 548, 592, 601, 602, 607–8, 609; and SP: criticises his music, xvii, xviii–xix; insists on 'Russian' rather than 'international' music, 22–3, 196, 506, 509, 527; invites SP to Rome, 7, 20–23; opposes Paris performance of *Scythian Suite*, 593–4, 598; proposal to commission opera based on Lermontov's 'The Tambov Treasurer's Wife', 672–3, 673n; and plotless symphonic ballet, 679; rejects *Ala and Lolli*, 22–4; SP declines suggested return to Europe, 45, 51, 57–8; with SP in Milan, 27–9; used as bargaining chip in SP's negotiations with Mariinsky Theatre, 118–19; and in Berlin, 679–82; and *Chout*: advances money, 87, 91, 108–9, 110, 111, 137; for full score, 534, 535, 540, 538, 539; approves revisions, 539; ballet dedicated to, 590, 591, 591n; commissions ballet, 33; conceives ballet with SP and Massine, 27; invites SP to Monte Carlo for rehearsals, 594–9; makes detailed recommendations for revision, 527, 605, 606; negotiates fee, 30–32; for revised score, 515–16, 517, 524, 528; plans for 1922 revival, 673; ready to present ballet, 506, 515–16, 524, 526; received score in America but did not understand it, 331; to be produced in Paris, May (1921), 528; SP invited to conduct, 528–9; admiration for French music, 80; approached by Bakst to present *Oranges*, 434; attitude to Futurism, 27–8; Ballets Russes Company, 4n, 21n, 33n, 34n, 57, 81, 330, 330n, 29.30; possible US tour, 39; takes place, 87, 108; fear of water, 25n; financial collapse of London season, 535, 535n; and of *The Sleeping Princess*, 669, 669n; help obtaining Bashkirov's visa, 593, 599; rejects opera as valid contemporary art form, 23, 680, 680n, 685–6, 686n
Diederichs, Andrey, piano manufacturer (Diederichs Gebrüder) and concert promoter 56, 224, 234, 271
Diederichs, Leonid 56
Dieppe 518
d'Indy, Vincent 654, 654n
Diva, The *see* Janacopulos, Vera
Dmitry Pavlovich, Grand Duke 514, 514n, 515
Dobychina, Nadezhda Yevseyevna, gallery owner 41, 41n; performances at gallery, 173; SP contemplates taking refuge with during street unrest, 180; urges SP to compose National Anthem, 186; also mentioned, 189, 204
'Donon' restaurant 103–4, 103n; dinner after Finnish Exhibition, 197
Dostoyevskaya, Anna Grigorievna, née Snitkova, Dostoyevsky's widow 163–5, 164n
Dostoyevsky, Fyodor Mikhailovich, novelist 215, 474; *The Brothers Karamazov*, 167; 'The Gambler', 61n, 62, 64n, 74
Dranishnikov, Vladimir Alexandrovich, conductor 34, 34n, 692, 692n; conducts rehearsals of *The Gambler*, 145; SP praises musicianship, 85; appointed to Mariinsky Theatre, 692, 692n
Draper, Miss, Mary Garden's secretary 584–5
Driesen von Osten, Baron Nikolay, Tsarist literary censor and theatre historian 81, 81n; Antique Theatre Project, 81, 83–4
Dubrovin, Alexander, leader of the Black Hundreds 136n
Duke, Vernon, *see* Dukelsky, Vladimir
Dukelsky, Vladimir Alexandrovich (Vernon Duke) 152n, 282, 282n
Dukes, Paul (Sir Paul Dukes), Mariinsky Theatre repetiteur and Secret Service agent 94, 140
Duma, *see* State Duma
Dunayev, Los Angeles acquaintance 565, 571
Duo-Art mechanical reproducing piano company 339–40, 391, 392, 394–6, 397, 404, 411, 463, 469, 470, 482, 485, 584, 689

Dusseau, Jeanne (Ruth Thom), soprano 640, 640n
Dvinsky, journalist 122
Dzbanovsky, Alexander Tikhonovich, critic 65, 74
Dzerzhinsky, Felix Edmundovich, head of the Cheka 136n
Dzhunkovsky brothers, acquaintances in Yessentuki 2232–3

Eberg, Ernest, director of Russian Music Editions 685, 685n, 711
Editions Russes de Musique, *see* Russian Music Editions
Edwards (Sert) (née Godebska), Mme Misia 507, 507n, 508, 512, 514, 515, 517; help obtaining visa for Maria Grigorievna, 513, 514, 515; and for Bashkirov, 593
Ehrenburg, Ilya Grigorievich, writer: *The Extraordinary Adventures of Jurenito and his Disciples*, 695, 695n; *The Face of War*, 685, 685n
Eksuzovich, Ivan Vasilievich, post-Revolution Director of Petrograd State Theatres 273–4, 273n
Elman, Mikhail Saulovich (Mischa), violinist 289, 289n, 338n; chess matches with SP, 338–9, 401
England 500; distinction drawn between Bolsheviks and Russians generally, 347
English Channel 337
English Military Mission, *see* British Military Mission
Erasmus, Artur Andreyevich, friend of SP's second cousin 88, 88n
Esche, Sofia Nikolayevna (Sonya) 23, 57
Esel Island, Baltic Sea 188
Ettal, Bavaria 671, 671n, 673, 673–6, 675, 676, 681, 683, 688, 689, 693, 695, 696, 699, 700, 702, 703, 704, 707, 710n, 711, 712; monastery, 676, 713
Evenings of Contemporary Music, *see* Musical *Contemporary* magazine
Ewald, Colonel 711, 712

Fatma Hanum, *see* Samoilenko, Fatma Hanum
February Revolution: first intimations of, 175; call for a new National Anthem, 185–6; establishment of Provisional Government, 184; formation of Temporary Committee, 181, 181n; Order No. 1, Proclamation of the Petrograd Soviet, 183, 183; SP's personal experience of, 175–84; feelings reflected in 19th *Vision Fugitive*, 184, 184n
Ferraris, shipboard chess-playing aquaintance 504
Février, Henri: *Monna Vanna*, opera, 635, 635n
Figueras 706
Finland 519, 542

Finnish Exhibition 186–7, 186n; SP as member of Committee of Honour, 187
First World War: 15n; threat of German advances into Russia, 1917, 188, 223, 224–5, 255, 256
Fischer, Carl, music publishers 333; Walter Fischer: interest in publishing *Tales of an Old Grandmother*, 342, 344; and in *Four Pieces for Piano*, 343
Fischer, Kuno: *Kant's Life and the Basis of his Teaching* (*Kants Leben und die Grundlagen seiner Lehre*), 210, 210n, 215, 229
Fitelberg, Grzegorz, conductor 35, 48, 55–6, 156, 213; rivalry with Aslanov, 55–6, 114–15
Flannery, Mrs, New York socialite 351
Florida 367, 370, 665
Foch, Maréchal Ferdinand 622, 622n
Foggia 20
Fokine, Mikhail Mikhailovich, dancer and choreographer 443, 443n, 591
Foll, Karl: *Experiences in the Comparative Study of Paintings*, 315, 315n
Fonaryov, Bohemian Club acquaintance 470
Fontainebleau 612
Fortiers, SP's host family in Montreal 466–7, 469
France 497, 500, 504, 505
Freud, Sigmund, psychoanalyst 436
Friebus, Alexander Ivanovich ('Diminished Fifth'), librarian of the Petrograd Conservatoire 177, 177n
Fuleihan, Anis, composer and pianist 491, 491n
Futurists 27–8, 187, 260, 633, 680; 1st May placards 274; Manifesto: *A Slap in the Face of Public Taste*, 187n; SP plays 1st Piano Sonata to, 263, 263n; SP's attitude to, 260, 262, 263; reactions to 'Man', 263, 263n; Vladivostok Futurists, 283
'Fyaka', nickname for Meshcherskaya, Nina

Gang (Wolfgang), Blanche, friend of Stella Adler 401–2, 425–6, 429, 435–6, 447, 449, 466, 476, 485, 494, 613
Garden, Mary, soprano 387n; as Carmen, 632, 642; 'Directa' of Chicago Opera, 579, 579n, 582–3, 584, 585, 586, 612, 613, 619, 621, 622, 623, 625, 631–3, 634, 638, 653, 654, 656, 661, 663, 665; resigns, 663, 663n
Garmisch 671, 703
Gatti-Casazza, Giulio, general director of the Metropolitan Opera 402, 404, 473, 474, 475, 475n, 482, 483, 490, 491, 492–3, 496, 523
geishas: in Vladivostok, 280; and Japan, 294, 299, 302
General Staff of the Russian Army: gives SP pass to reside anywhere in Russia, 212; but queries exemption, 224
Genoa 13, 704, 705
Georgian Military Road 134–5, 134n, 233, 233n

Germany: peace finally declared, 351; reported to be seeking peace terms, 342; surprising speed of military collapse, 347–8
Gershun, Boris, lawyer, president of Association of Russian Advocates, uncle of Eleonora Damskaya 536, 536n
Gershun (Bozhnev), Boris Borisovich, poet, adopted son of Boris Gershun 189, 189n, 536, 536n, 595, 595n
Gertrude, female admirer in New York 390, 390n; introduces SP to Stella Adler, 393
Gessen, Iosif Vladimirovich, journalist and Kadet political activist 44, 74, 74n; declines to predict new form of government, 183; gives advice on Dostoyevsky copyright issue, 163; presents wreath, 155; publishes *Rul'* in Berlin, 300, 300n; SP appeals for help over Polina Podolskaya, 156; SP's visits, 76, 80–81; and gives private play-through of *the Gambler*, 126
Gippius, Zinaida Nikolayevna, poet, critic and memoirist 101n; 'Suor Maria', 647, 647n; 'The Grey Dress' ('Seroye Platye'), 101, 101n
Glazunov, Alexander Konstantinovich 62, 62n, 65, 85, 109, 120, 170, 519, 571, 670; attempts composition of new National Anthem, 185; declines to serve on committee of Society of Workers in the Arts if SP is elected, 186; examines SP in organ, 130; handwriting, 335; walks out of performance of *Scythian Suite*, 75, 600, 642; and other hostile comments, 388; *Masquerade*, incidental music, 174n; Piano Concerto, 241; Piano Sonata No. 2, 86; Symphonies, 49; also mentioned, 144n
Glebov, Igor (pen name), *see* Boris Asafyev
Glebova, Tamara Andreyevna (Tamochka) 111, 111n, 269
Glebova-Sudeikina, Olga, actor 89n
Glière, Reinhold Moritsevich, composer 33, 33n, 35, 49, 207; as director of Kiev Conservatoire, 150–51; criticised for allowing SP's music to be performed to students, 169–70
Glinka Capella, *see* Petrograd, Pevchesky Chapel
Glinka, Mikhail Ivanovich 25; *A Life for the Tsar*, opera, 185, 185n; 'Slavsya!' ('Glory!') chorus, 578; *Ruslan and Lyudmila*, opera, 49
Glushakova, Los Angeles acquaintance 577, 578
Gnessin, Mikhail Fabianovich, composer and teacher 66, 66n; Theme and Variations for cello and piano, Op. 67, 470
Godowskaya, Dagmar Leopoldovna, *see* Godowsky, Dagmar
Godowsky, Dagmar xv, 389, 389n, 390, 391, 392, 393, 394, 396, 397, 399, 402, 559, 561, 565–7, 572, 574–5; as film actor, 481, 481n, 578, 578n
Godowsky, Leopold, pianist and composer 389, 389n

Godowsky, Mme, mother of Dagmar 566
Godowsky, Vanita, sister of Dagmar 567
Goethe, Johann Wolfgang von, writer: manuscripts of, 486
Gogol, Nikolay Vasilievich, writer: 'The Tale of How Ivan Ivanovich Quarrelled With Ivan Nikiforovich', 88; *The Wedding*, play, 485
Golitsyn, Princes 106, 106n, 110, 191
Golovin, Alexander Yakovlevich, artist and theatre designer: as designer of *The Gambler*, 94, 112, 167–8, 271, 515; designs *Masquerade*, 174n; enthusiasm for *Alaley and Leila*, 185; and for *The Gambler*, 185; keeps low profile after February Revolution, 196
Golovin, Fyodor Alexandrovich, President of the Second State Duma, commissar of Imperial Theatres, 188–9, 188n
Golubovskaya, Nadezhda Iosifovna, pianist 65, 65n
Goncharova, Natalya Sergeyevna, artist and designer 34, 34n, 513, 541, 591, 603, 604, 679; proposed as designer of Covent Garden *Love for Three Oranges* production, 529, 532; sketch of SP's head, 540–41
Gorky, Maxim (Alexey Maximovich Peshkov), writer 536, 629; accused of being pro-German, 211; appeals to Kerensky to spare SP conscription, 204, 206, 212; founder and editor of *New Life* magazine, containing his regular column 'Untimely Thoughts', 208, 211, 245n; makes speech at Finnish Exhibition, 187; praises *Sarcasms* and Bassoon Scherzos, 173, 204; suspected of attempting to seize power in Ministry of Culture, 188; *The Old Man*, play, 684, 684n; also mentioned, 186
Gorodetsky, Sergey Mitrofanovich, poet 5, 5n, 81
Goryansky, Vyacheslav, poet 101, 101n; 'Under the Roof' ('Pod krishey'), 101, 101n
Gottlieb, Ephraim, admirer of SP in Chicago 460, 546, 547–8, 548, 549, 550, 551, 552, 554, 582, 617, 618, 619, 620, 622, 623, 626, 627, 629, 630, 637, 646, 647, 653, 656, 661
Gounod, Charles, composer: *Faust*, opera, 429
Goya, Francisco 357
Gozzi, Carlo, playwright 271n, 462, 577, 633; *The Love For Three Oranges*, play, 141n, 618
Granados, Enrique, composer 304; piano roll recordings for Duo-Art, 340, 340n
Granat, Tatyana (Tanyusha) 46, 49, 53, 132, 137, 209
Grand Canyon 581
Grand Duke Dmitry Pavlovich, *see* Dmitry Pavlovich, Grand Duke
Grand Duke Konstantin Konstantinovich ('KR'), *see* Konstantin Konstantinovich, Grand Duke
Graves, *see* Grevs
Great Kanto Earthquake 712, 712n

Grechaninov, Alexander Tikhonovich, composer: publishes new National Anthem, 185
Grevs, Zora (Zorya) 50, 55
Grieg, Edvard, composer 63; Piano Concerto in A minor, 71
Grigoriev, Boris Dmitrievich, artist 611
Grigoriev, Sergey Leonidovich (Serge), Diaghilev's ballet-master 58
Grotius, Dutch steamer sailing from Java to San Francisco 309–16
Gruenberg, Louis, composer 614n; *The Hill of Dreams*, 614, 614n
Gubenko, composer: *Valisneria*, 80
Gulf Stream 504
Gunsbourg, Raoul 516n, 517; bridge with, 516, 517
Gutheil, music publishing house 143, 153; acquired by Koussevitzky, 112–13; pays fees for *Visions fugitives* and songs, 192
Gutman, former Petrogad Conservatoire student 134

Haensel, Fizhugh W., SP's second New York manager 43, 382, 384, 443, 444, 465, 468, 471, 483, 498, 521, 522, 541–2, 549, 584, 586, 587, 613, 616, 625, 665, 667, 675, 689; correspondence with Rachmaninoff about Koshetz, 543–4; payment owed to, 700; SP introduces Koshetz, 489, 544, 552
Halévy, Fromental, composer: *La Juive*, 217, 217n
Handschin, Jacques, organist and teacher 77, 77n, 78; insists on SP graduating, 158; SP's studies with, 77–8, 86, 90, 99, 105, 124, 130
Hansen, Cecilia, violinist, married to Boris Zakharov: joint recital with Zakharov, 100; also mentioned, 109, 132, 155
Hansen, Cecilia, violinist, wife of Boris Zakharov 3n, 51, 91, 107, 136, 670
Hansen, Elfrieda (Frieda), pianist, sister of Cecilia 91
Hanum, Fatma, *see* Samoilenko, Fatma Hanum
Hanum, Tamara, Fatma Hanum's sister 533, 609
Harbin 279
Harding, Warren G., President of United States 713
Hartmann, Foma (Thomas de), composer, official of Petrograd IRMS 241, 241n
Hastings-on-Hudson 489
Hawai, *see* Sandwich Islands
Heifetz, Jascha, violinist 289n, 394, 511
Heifetz, Polina, sister of Jascha 394, 398, 399
Heine, Heinrich, poet; manuscripts of 486
Helsingfors 121–2, 121n
Helsinki, *see* Helsingfors
Heredia y Giraud, Jose Marie de, Cuban-born poet 674, 674n
Hertz, Alfred, conductor 557–8, 557n

Hippius, Zinaida, *see* Gippius, Zinaida
Hofmann, Josef, pianist 438, 440, 474, 474n, 487, 495
Holland 669
Homer, Louise, soprano: as Dalila in *Samson et Dalila*, 352
Horowitz, Vladimir, pianist: accompanies Nathan Milstein in SP's First Violin Concerto in Moscow, 712n
Hosan-Maru, steamer from Vladivostok to Yokohama 284–6, 285n
Hudson River 327
Hungary 404
Hussa, Dr Philip, New York dentist 385–6, 395, 396, 405–6, 586, 699
Hylaea Futuro-Cubist Group, *see* Futurism

Iasi, Romania 10, 10n
Ibbs, Robert Leigh, London artist manager 475, 475n
Ignatiev, E. I., writer on astronomy: *The World of the Heavens* (*Nebesny Mir*), 145, 145n
Igumnov, Konstantin Nikolayevich, pianist and teacher 171, 171n, 236n
Ilyashenko, Andrey, composer 449, 449n, 477, 478, 484, 486, 494
Imperial Russian Musical Society (IRMS) 7, 67–8; SP engaged as solo pianist by, 7n, 33, 165
India 17, 520
Ingerman, Dr Anna, SP's doctor in New York 406–7, 408, 412, 414, 415, 416, 428, 485; counsels against unreliability of Stella Adler's family, 407, 421, 501, 615
Ingerman, Dr Sergius, ENT specialist in New York 406–7, 408, 414, 416, 421, 428, 437, 438, 439, 450, 473, 485, 501, 615
Inn River 702, 704
Insull, Samuel 663, 663n
International Company 8, 8n, 225, 230, 256, 274, 275
Intervention, by Western Powers in Russia 207, 207n, 274, 279, 284n, 286, 304, 329, 533; *see also* Western Powers intervention
Ionin, Petersburg acquaintance: secures letter of credit from British Military Mission for SP, 274, 279, 282
Irkutsk 267, 279, 280
Isaakian, Averik, poet 148n
Ivanov, Gyorgy Vladimirovich, poet and memoirist 688n
Ivanov, Vyacheslav Ivanovich, Symbolist poet 263–4, 263n
Ivari monastery 135n
Izhevsky, doctor treating Boris Bashkirov 92
Izmailovsky Regiment 181
Izvolsky, Alexander, Tsarist Foreign Minister 381n
Izvolskys, New York acquaintances, son and

daughter-in-law of Alexander Izvolsky 481, 494, 496, 499

Janacopulos, Vera, soprano, Brazilian wife of Alexey Stahl 330n, 331, 331n, 371–2, 403, 429, 434–6, 437, 442, 444, 445, 449, 478, 510, 511, 514, 515, 544, 604, 612, 700, 706; joint recital with SP, 679
Japan 267–8, 345; SP's stay in, 286–309; Argentinian Consulate, 287; attraction of geishas, 294, 299, 302; cable connections with America broken, 304; and repaired, 307; charm of landscape, 285–6, 293–4, 298, 305; difficulty of getting down to work, 295; interest in intervention, 284n, 286; preferences of Japanese audiences, 296, 301; rumours of alliance with Germany, 260; water deity, 290, 290n; women sampled, 290
Java 288, 423, 464
Johnson, Herbert, business comptroller of Chicago Opera 322, 322n, 444, 585, 624, 629; appointed Executive Director, 537; and dismissed, 579, 582, 582n; cancels *Oranges* production altogether, 545–6, 547, 549; negotiations over cancellations of *Oranges*, 451–3, 458–60, 461–3, 483, 537, 545, 551
Josipivici, Albert 685n
Jung, Adelina Avgustovna, Petrograd friend of Vera Miller 268, 268n, 536
Jurgenson, Boris Petrovich, music publisher 31–2, 31n, 33–4, 33n, 55, 66, 72, 75; declines to offer advance on royalties, 74; SP reluctant to offer more works, 92
Jurgenson, Grigory Petrovich, music publisher, brother of Boris 33, 33n

Kadets, *see* Constitutional Democrats
Kahn (née Wolff), Mrs Otto 496, 588
Kahn, Otto, Chairman of Metropolitan Opera, New York 401, 402, 404, 465, 492
Kahn, secretary to Campanini 367, 383, 387, 432, 444, 451, 483
Kal, Professor Alexey Fyodorovich, teacher and music critic 79, 79n, 559, 559n, 560–2, 563–5, 571, 572, 573, 587
Kaledin, General Alexey Maximovich, Ataman of the Don Cossacks 250, 250n
Kalinnikov, Vasily Sergeyevich, composer 207, 358; Symphonies No. 1 in G minor and No. 2 in A, 207n
Kama river 100n, 200–201
Kamenka, legal expert 163
Kamensky, Vasily Vasilievich 262, 262n: description of SP at Poets Café, 262n
Kant, Immanuel 210, 215, 229, 231, 237, 240; *Critique of Pure Reason*, 205, 205n
Kapustin, acquaintance in New York 414
Karakash, M.N., baritone 120, 120n, 141, 143, 147, 154

Karatygin, Vyacheslav Gavrilovich, critic 44, 44n, 142, 519; dines with French Ambassador, 96; gives advice on Dostoyevsky copyright issue, 163; hears play-through of *The Gambler*, 126; invites SP to review concert, 90; SP rejects proposal of *Akhmatova Poems* for *Musical Contemporary* recital, 174–5; SP translates his articles, 315–16, 316n, 326
Karenin, Lev, chess-playing acquaintance 145
Karneyev family 209
Karneyev, Lev (Lyova) 46, 46n, 49; chess matches with, 137
Karneyeva, Lidia 46, 46n, 49, 52–3, 55–6, 92, 137, 159, 268
Karneyeva, Zoya 46, 46n, 49, 52–3, 55–6, 92, 137, 268
Karnovich, composer 132; *Variations for Orchestra*, 132n
Karpovich, official at Russian Embassy in Washington 441
Karuizawa, Japan 305
Kastalsky, Alexander Dmitrievich, composer 207
Kavos sisters 111, 111n, 122
Kazan 199–200, 201; Kazan gold, carried off for Omsk Government, 358
Kedrov, Nikolay Nikolayevich, baritone, founder of Kedrov Vocal Quartet 68
Keil, Dr, co-owner of Villa Christophorus 671, 672
Kellomyaki 46, 46n
Kerensky, Alexander Fyodorovich, Minister for War, later Prime Minister of Provisional Government 580n; connection with Baranovskaya, 577, 580; connection with Eleonora Damskaya, 3n, 204, 211–12, 225; as Minister for War: gives verbal order for SP to be exempted from conscription, 206, 211–12; confirms and signs the order, 212, 224; orders all medical personnel to the front, 202; SP delivers letter from Gorky, 204–5; as Prime Minister: is deceived as to Kornilov's intentions, 227n; leaves Petrograd at the Bolshevik uprising, 237, 238; also mentioned 330
Khabarovsk 280, 281, 282
Khan, Sar, friend of Fatma Hanum 609
Khantsin, Isabella, former Conservatoire fellow student 35, 35n, 37
Kharkov 152–3, 536; premature May Day celebrations, 190, 190n; visit to Polina Podolskaya, 152–3, 190, 693
Kherson 480, 480n
Khlebnikov, Velimir (Viktor Vladimirovich), Futurist poet 187n; present at Moscow Poets Café event, 262, 262n
Khmelnitskaya, Asya, *see* Lesnaya, Asya
Khodasevich, Vladislav Felitsianovich, poet and critic 681n
Khodzhayev family, acquaintances in

Kislovodsk 248, 255, 256; Khodzhayeva, Liza (daughter), 255; Khodzhayeva, Lucy (daughter), 255, 612, 612n
Khvoshchinskaya, Ruzhina, wife of Vasily 21, 26, 29
Khvoshchinsky, Vasily, Russian Embassy Secretary in Rome 21, 36
Kiev 35; Conservatoire, 150–51; SP's visits to, 9, 33, 145, 150–53, 169–70, 536, 692
Kikimora, mythological house spirit 144, 144n
Kind, Anna, painter, wife of Alexander Benois 72n
Kira Nikolayevna, inamorata of Balmont 220–21, 223, 234; Bashkirov falls for, 230; provides French title for *Mimolyotnosti*, 221, 221n
Kishinskaya, Varvara, friend of Nina Meshcherskaya 68
Kishinyov 10
Kislovodsk 51, 134, 199, 215, 227, 237, 267, 269, 282, 326, 387, 555, 611; appears immune from unrest elsewhere in Russia, 240; danger arising from Bolshevik battles with Cossacks on the Don, 240; earthquake in, 254; Grand Hotel, 233–4, 237, 239, 240; police search of, 249; SP's recital in, 255; Hill of the Cross, 236, 236n; Kursaal: Operetta performances, 237; SP's recitals in, 235, 236, 255; Narzan Galleries: notion of spending winter in, 223; performance of 1st piano concerto, 222; plans to leave for America on 15th February 1918 (OS), 250; but postponed, 254; 'Rock of Perfidy and Love', 220, 220n; rumours of impending massacre of bourgeoisie, 248; Soviet of Workers' Deputies, provides SP with travel permissions, 255, 256, 257, 264; SP finally leaves, 256–7, 283; but quickly returns because of disorders and disruption to travel ,238–9
Kleiber, Erich, conductor: music director of Mannheim Opera, 675, 675n; proposes to produce *Oranges*, 675
Kling, Henry, director of Chesters music publishers 435, 519, 519n
Kling, Otto, father of Henry 519n
Klukhor Pass, Caucasus mountains 233, 233n
Klyuyev, Nikolay Alexeyevich, poet 122n
Kobe, Japan 290
Kochno, Boris 595, 595n, 599, 607
Koh-I-Noor crayons 119, 119n
Kohnwald, Mrs, potential benefactor of Balmont, 664
Kokhánskaya, Mme 614, 665–6
Kokhánski, Pawe?, violinist 33, 33n, 536, 588, 614, 621, 665–6; advises on bowings for *Overture on Hebrew Themes*, 614; checks parts of Violin Concerto, 230; possible Far East tour with, 292
Kokovtsov, Count Vladimir Nikolayevich, former Tsarist Prime Minister 254, 254n
Kolchak, Admiral Alexander Vasilievich, Commander-in-Chief, Black Sea Fleet, later Supreme Ruler of the anti-Bolshevik Omsk Government 249, 249n, 278n, 419n
Kolpino, village near Sablino 226
Komarovo, *see* Kellomyaki
Konshin, Alexey Vladimirovich, banker 302
Konstantin Konstantinovich, Grand Duke 48, 48n
Kooperativy, *see* Cooperatives
Koposova-Derzhanovskaya, Yekaterina Vasilievna, soprano 34, 34n
Korevo, M., and Mme, acquaintances in Sofia 13
Kornilov, General Lavr Georgevich, Commander-in-Chief of the Russian Army under Provisional Government 206n; Kornilov's 'rebellion', 226–7, 227n
Korzukhin, acquaintance of Rachmaninoff 388
Kosato, acquaintance in Yokohama 308
Koshetz, Nina Pavlovna, soprano xv, 148n, 149n, 265, 549, 552, 564, 584; arrival in America, 542–4; in Chicago for *Oranges*, 619, 620–21, 622, 623, 627, 628, 631, 638, 642, 645, 648, 651, 652, 653, 654, 661, 662; engaged to sing Fata Morgana in *Oranges*, 585; *Fiery Angel* played to, 545; in *La Juive*, 217; performs songs by Medtner, 168; relations with Rachmaninoff, 217–18, 219, 261, 335, 543–4, 599, 620, 622, 630; performs his songs, 148; and with SP, 261, 263, 264, 280, 489, 544, 545, 577, 581, 586, 599, 612n, 613, 614, 616, 619, 620, 622, 628, 645–6, 647, 648, 652, 653, 656, 657; SP develops partiality for, 168–9; after initial hostility to, 148, 169; *Bruderschaft* ritual, 275; introduced to Haensel, 489; intuition about Lina Codina, 544; invites SP to tour with her, 218; and to stay in Moscow, 259, 275; letters from SP to Koshetz, 276; and to Asafyev, 278; performs *Akhmatova Songs* in Moscow, 259; possible Far East tour with, 289, 290, 292, 296, 297; present of gold watch, later pawned, 553; and of black ribbon and gold clasp, 650; request for songs without words, 555; sings version of Chopin Etude Op. 10 No. 3, 275, 275n; spiritualism, interest in, 620, 632, 635–7, 637, 645–6, 647; Suvchinsky's adulation of, 149, 169; and Asafyev's, 169; as Tatyana in *Yevgeny Onegin*, 259–60; wishes to come to America, 489, 494; in Yessentuki, 214, 216–18; also mentioned, 171, 223, 533
Kouro-Sivo current 285, 285n
Koussevitzkaya (née Ushkova), Natalya Konstantinovna, wife of Koussevitzky 682, 684n; assistance with obtaining dollars, 268
Koussevitzky, Sergey (Serge) Alexandrovich, conductor 29, 256, 261, 262, 519, 536, 540, 586, 589, 608, 610, 672, 678, 679, 681, 682, 684n, 695, 706; and SP: advances money for America, 263; advice on American fees, 263;

dines with, 103–4; gives premiere of First Violin Concerto, 712; impressed by *The Ugly Duckling*, 90; lends money, 540, 637; offers engagements for Third Piano Concerto in London and Paris, 612; performs *Scythian Suite* in Paris, 594, 599, 600; as potential publisher, 87, 112; agrees to publish SP's works with Gutheil, 143; and Russian Music Editions, 589, 669; praises conducting, 143; proposes Moscow performance of *Scythian Suite*, 109; and later cancels, 143; reaction to *Seven, They Are Seven*, 261, 262, 263n; plans to perform in Paris, 701; then cancels, 712, 712n; SP's papers and manuscripts deposited in Moscow vault, xiii–xiv, 225; and preserved, 536; suggests SP remain in Russia, 264; appointed Director of the Court Orchestra, 224, 224n; as conductor and concert organiser, 107, 109; as double-bass player, 104; example of disinterested Russian music publisher, 335, 335n; gives financial support to Petrograd IRMS, 165; provides SP with introduction to Altschuler, 333; also mentioned, 171, 693
Kozlovskaya, glamorous friend of Boris Bashkirov 187
Krasilnikov, acquaintance in Kislovodsk 255
'Krasnaya Shapochka' ('Little Red Hiding Hood'), *see* Lesnaya, Asya
Krasnoyarsk 278
Krasnoye Selo 429
Kreisler, Fritz, violinist 463
Kreisler, former Conservatoire conducting student 34, 34n
Kronstadt Garrison 210, 210n
Kropotkin, Prince Pyotr Alexeyevich, Anarchist thinker 237, 237n
Kruchonykh, Alexey Yeliseyevich, Futurist poet, co-inventor of 'zaumny' language 187n
Krylov, Ivan Andreyevich, fairy-tale writer 97n
Kucheryavy, Nikolay Titovich, engineer and dilettante artist manager 3, 315, 321, 323, 324, 327, 328, 336, 337, 364, 395, 431, 432–3, 449, 451, 453, 457, 458, 463, 545, 546, 552, 553, 554, 582, 587; moves to Indianopolis, 341
Kuchinsky, cousin of the Meshcherskaya sisters 37, 37n, 50
Kuokkale 129n; Bashkirov dacha at, 129, 131–2, 136–9
Kuprin, Alexander Ivanovich, writer 533–4, 533n, 562
Kurlina, Lyudmila (Lyunechka), proposed bride of Boris Bashkirov 165–6, 191
Kurlina, Yevgenia (Zhenechka), proposed bride of SP 155–6, 165–6
Kurlyandsky, official in the Petrograd Red Cross 199, 203–4
Kurov, Nikolay, critic 260, 261
Kurzner, Pavel Yakovlevich, bass 129, 129n

Kusov, Baron, vice-director of the Imperial Theatres 129, 130
Kuzmin, Mikhail Alexeyevich, poet 122n
Kyoto: SP's visit to, 293–4, 297; tea-house, 294

Ladoga, Lake 127
Lamberts, New York hosts 394, 399
Lambin, Pyotr Borisovich; house designer at the Mariinsky Theatre, 94, 94n; proposed as designer of *The Gambler*, 94, 97, 111, 139; but fails to inspire confidence, 167
Lanier, Harriet Bishop, financial backer of the Society of Friends of Music of New York 343, 343n, 353
Larchmont, near New York 408, 409, 414
Larionov, Mikhail Fyodorovich, artist and designer 34, 34n, 398, 513–14, 532, 591, 679, 706; caricature of imaginary first night of *Chout*, 541; as choreographer of *Chout*, 592, 595, 596, 596–8, 601; as designer of *Chout*, 398, 506, 515, 602, 603, 604, 606, 608, 609; lost portraits of SP, 540–41; takes SP to Monte Carlo Casino, 596, 598
Lasker, Emanuel, world chess champion and grandmaster 692
Lavery, Lady 524, 524n, 525
Lavrov, Nikolay Stepanovich, pianist and teacher 85
Lazarevsky, Boris Alexandrovich, writer 624, 624n
Le Havre 529, 540, 589
Lebedev, V. I., former Navy Minister in the Provisional Government 358
Lenin (Ulyanov), Vladimir Ilyich; death reported, and SP's assessment of historical significance, 325; and contradicted 326; reported assassination, 248; and as having fled counter-revolutionary forces, 313
Leoncavallo, Ruggero, composer: *Zazà*, opera, 582n
Lermontov, Mikhail Yurevich, poet and novelist 652; *Masquerade*: production by Meyerhold at the Alexandrinsky Theatre, 174, 174n; 'The Tambov Treasurer's Wife', 673, 673n
Les Six 604, 604n
Leschetitsky, Theodor (Fyodor) Osipovich, pianist and teacher 96n
Lesnaya (Khmelmitskaya), Asya, drama student of Meyerhold 236, 236n, 237, 240
Levin, chess player in Petrograd 89
Levin, Los Angeles acquaintance 561, 573, 575, 579.580
Levitsky, Nikolay Ivanovich, Nina Meshcherskaya's first husband 236, 236n, 265
Lewisohn, Mrs Adolph 372–3, 372n, 382, 399, 408, 410–13
Lhévinne, Josef, pianist 442
Liebmans, hospitable New York household 389n, 391, 397, 398, 405, 474, 480, 481, 500, 501,

666; nonsense competition, 486–7; obtains transatlantic liner reservation, 500
Lilienthal, Dr Howard, New York surgeon 409, 409n, 410, 411, 412, 413, 414, 421
Lipinskaya, former Conservatoire student 35, 35n
Liszt, Franz (Ferenc); manuscripts of 486; Piano Concerto, 480; *Tasso*, 134
Littauer, Lt Vladimir (Volodya), friend of the Meshchersky family 39
Little Russia 88, 88n
'Little Sunshine', *see* Solnyshko
Litvinne, Félia 539, 539n, 544
Liverpool 537
Llubera, Lina, *see* Codina, Carolina
Loire river 592
London 237, 474, 475, 476, 486, 496, 510, 513, 517; Greenwich Meridian and Observatory, 520; Imperial Hotel, 606; National Hotel, 588, 589; Regent's Park, 525; Savoy Hotel, 606; Turkish Baths, 521; Victoria Station, 589
London Symphony Orchestra 475n, 529, 529n, 552
Los Angeles 558, 559–81; Hotel Clark, 560, 574; Philharmonic, 571; Symphony, 558n, 576
Lotarev, Igor, *see* Severyanin, Igor
Lotin, mesmerist and preacher 77, 109; attacks SP while preaching, 102–3; criticises SP, 82
Lourié, Artur (Arthur) Sergeyevich, composer and commissar 89n, 682, 682n, 691, 694
Luna Park 337, 337n
Lunacharsky, Anatoly Vasilievich, Bolshevik Commissar of Enlightenment (Narkompros) 260n; appealed to for foreign passport, 260, 267, 270, 272; attends rehearsal of 'Classical' Symphony, 270, 271, 272; possible Diaghilev season, 266
Lvov, Prince Gyorgy Yevgenievich, former Prime Minister of Provisional Government, head of Russian Political Conference in Paris 510, 510n, 511, 512
Lyadov, Anatoly Konstantinovich, composer 120n; Myaskovksy's distaste for his music, 120; *Alaley and Leila*, ballet (abandoned), 144; *Kikimora*, 144n
Lyapunov, Sergey Mikhailovich, composer, pianist and teacher 115, 115n
Lykiardopoulos, Michael, journalist, critic, theatre administrator 80, 80n
Lyon 701
Lyuban, town near Petrograd 53

McCormick, Cyrus Jr., American agricultural machinery tycoon 319, 327, 329, 454, 546, 547, 548; financial backer of Chicago Opera, 367, 378, 554; given scores of *Scythian Suite* and *The Gambler*, 207; and works by Myaskovsky, 207, 360, 364; letter of recommendation, 292; considered excellent reference, 304; raises money for the American Loan, 346
McCormick, Harold Fowler, younger brother of Cyrus Jr 445, 445n, 548, 548n, 549, 552, 656; compensation for cancellation of *Love for Three Oranges*, 451, 453, 661, 662–3, 679; principal financial backer and board chairman of Chicago Opera, 451, 454, 554, 555; resigns as chairman of the Chicago Opera board, 663, 663n; takes up with Ganna Walska, 582n
McCormick, Muriel, daughter of Harold 661, 662–3
Madrid 592, 708
Maeterlinck, Maurice, poet and dramatist 464n, 635n
Magalov, Prince 136, 137; SP quarrels with, 138–9
Magalova, Princess Varvara Nikolayevna (Varya), Boris Bashkirov's sister 131–2, 131n, 136, 138, 602
Mahler, Gustav, composer; Symphony No. 7 621
Malko, Nikolay Andreyevich, conductor 35, 35n, 46, 68, 73; conducts First Piano Concerto, 165; proposes to become SP's impresario 68; and *The Gambler*: at Mariinsky Theatre, 109–10, 116–19; quarrel over copying of vocal scores, 137–41, 165, 692; also mentioned, 75
Malozemova, Sofia, pianist and teacher 64
Malyutin, Boris Yevgenievich, President of the Petrograd Chess Society 89n
Mandelshtam, Osip Emilievich, poet 122n
Manhattan Theater, *see* New York, Manhattan Opera House
Mannheim Opera 675–6
Mantes-sur-Seine 532, 533, 534, 536, 537, 538
Manteuffel, Count 711
Manukhin, Dr Ivan Ivanovich, specialist immunobiologist in Paris 673
Mariinsky Theatre 74, 77; Asafyev appointed to, 638; Dranishnikov appointed to, 692, 692n; proposed production of *The Gambler*, 89, 94, 115; stage set-up for orchestral concerts, 147, 147n; Ziloti appointed Intendant, 197, 212, *see also The Gambler*
Marinetti, Filippo Tommaso 27–8, 27n, 54; *The Founding and Manifesto of Futurism*, 27n
Marinuzzi, Gino, conductor 432, 432n, 436, 551, 633; appointed Artistic Director of Chicago Opera, 537; resigns, 582, 582n; auditions *Love for Three Oranges* and suggests cuts, 497; *Jacquerie*, opera, 537, 537n, 549, 551–2, 633
Marseilles 529–30, 595, 705; steamer connections with Constantinople, 509
Martens, Frederick H., writer and critic 332–3, 333n, 335; SP dictates article about Russian sonatas to 343
Mason, Mrs, President of Los Angeles Symphony 576

Massine, Léonide, dancer and choreographer 21, 21n, 23, 25–6, 28, 506, 506n, 509, 517, 527, 541, 595, 597; contributes to libretto and invents floor-washing dance for *Chout*, 27, 599; marriage to Vera Savina, 590, 590n
Matisse, Henri, artist 509n, 595; portrait of SP, 598, 598n
Mauretania, transatlantic liner 482
Maximalists, *see* Bolsheviks
Mayakovsky, Vladimir Vladimirovich, poet 141n, 260, 696; attends SP's Moscow recital, 171, 171n; present at Moscow Poets Café event, 262; SP hears read, 195; SP meets at Finnish Exhibition dinner, 187; and in Berlin, 679, 680–1; 'Man' 263, 263n; *Misteria-Bouffe* 141n
Mayevsky, Pyotr, botanist and writer: *Flora sredney Rossii* (*Flora of Central Russia*), 207n
Mayo, Frank, film actor 566–7, 566n, 572, 575, 578, 578n
Mead, Professor George Herbert 625, 625n
Mediterranean Sea 530, 595, 706
Medtner, Nikolay Karlovich, composer 65, 303, 306, 466, 519, 536, 626, 670; and SP: dislike of *Dreams*, 98; opposed to SP's publication by Russian Music Edition, 96, 143, 392; psychology, 96; SP's affection for his music, 168; and gaffe about domestic performance of sonatas, 168; music disliked by Diaghilev and Stravinsky, 509; violent antipathy to modernism of SP's Moscow recital, 171, 670, 693; as pianist, 96, 107; songs performed by Koshetz, 168; tries but fails to appreciate *Tales of an Old Grandmother*, 670; cadenzas to Beethoven's Piano Concerto No. 4, 107; *Fairy Tales* (*Skazki*), Op. 8, 96, 475, 476, 490; Sonata No. 7 in E minor ('Night Wind'), Op. 25/2, 96, 168; Sonata No. 8 in F sharp minor (Sonata-Ballade) Op. 27, 96; Sonata No. 9 in A minor, Op. 30, 96; also mentioned, 169
Melos, short-lived successor to *Musical Contemporary* magazine 174n
Mendelssohn-Bartholdy, Felix: Rondo Capriccioso, Op. 14, 429
Mengelberg, Willem 621
Menton 705
Merezhkovsky, Dmitry Sergeyevich, Symbolist writer and religious thinker, husband of Zinaida Gippius 652
Meshcherskaya, Natalya Alexeyevna (Talya) 36, 43, 56, 80, 235–6
Meshcherskaya, Nina Alexeyevna 3, 10, 32, 36–8, 74, 79–80, 159, 165, 235–6, 240, 246, 331, 445, 508, 511, 604, 604n, 614, 682, 689–90; SP's strength of feeling for, xv 3, 5, 6, 7, 36, 38, 98–9, 98n; considers marrying, 3, 6, 23–4, 30, 36–7; failed elopement, 39–43, 45–6; terminates relationship, 47, 50, 52, 53, 54, 72–3; SP hears of marriage, 236, 236n, 265

Meshcherskaya, Vera Nikolayevna, Nina's mother 5, 36, 41–3, 47, 56, 80, 235–6; encounters SP's mother in Kislovodsk, 235–6
Meshchersky, Alexey Pavlovich, Nina's father 39–43, 508
Meshchersky family 3, 37, 39, 52, 56; impoverished after Revolution, 265; SP's visits to, 3, 6, 36–7
Metropolitan Opera 330–31, 330n, 344, 352, 382, 452, 507, 665
Mexico 559–60
Meyer, potential New York manager 381
Meyerbeer, Giacomo, composer 160; *Le Prophète*, opera, 145, 149, 391
Meyerhold, Vsevolod Emilievich, theatre director 141n, 289, 563, 571, 575, 577, 638; *The Gambler*, 141, 167, 185, 268, 271, 272; directs *Masquerade*, 174, 174n; enthusiasm for *Alaley and Leila*, 185; keeps low profile after February Revolution, 196; suggests *Love for Three Oranges* as opera subject and gives SP copy to read, 271, 271n, 273; also mentioned, 188
Meyerovich, Alfred Berngardovich, pianist, touring Japan 287–8, 287n, 289; SP accompanies to Kyoto and Osaka, 292–3; and to Nara, 295–7; SP attends recital with Piastro, 289; ticket prices, 296; SP considers good, but not first class, artist; suggests concert in Honolulu, 294
Mikhailovsky Palace, *see* Petrograd, Engineer's Palace
Mikhelson, Irina Sergeyevna (Irinochka), pianist 104, 140, 140n
Miklashevskaya, Irina, *see* Mikhelson, Irina
Milan 701, 702, 704; Carolina Codina's audition for *Rigoletto* in, 704, 704n; Como Hotel, 704; meeting Carolina Codina in, 701, 704–5; SP's visit to, 27–9, 509
Miller, Vera: Petrograd friend 268, 268n, 536, 547, 588, 634, 657, 669–70, 671, 673, 675; returns to Riga, 701; translates song texts into German, 274; and *The Gambler* libretto into French and German, 274, 277, 673
Milstein, Nathan, violinist: performs SP's First Violin Concerto with Horowitz in Moscow 712n
Milyukov, Pavel Nikolayevich, historian, political figure, founder of Constitutional Democrats 84–5, 84n, 647, 679; converted to SP's music, 84–5; hears play-through of *The Gambler*, 100; Paris newspaper, 530n; speech at Finnish Exhibition, 187
Mineralnye Vody 218, 232, 238, 239, 257
Minster, Aron Pavlovich, acquaintance in Japan 305, 308–9, 509, 510, 511; lends SP money and gold pieces, 309, 314, 327, 421
Minster, Mme ('Froska-San') 305, 307, 308–9, 310, 509, 510

Mir Isskustva: members of, 4n; exhibitions, 180, 610, 611; SP attends exhibition, 100; and performs at, 111, 610, 611
Mittenwald 703, 704
Miyanoshita, mountain resort in Japan 307
Modern Music Society of New York 379; SP's tenth anniversary as performer, 379, 379n
Moiseiwitsch, Benno, pianist 470, 470n, 475
Mojica, José, tenor and priest 624–5, 624n
Molière (Jean-Baptiste Pocquelin) 572
Molinari, Bernardino, conductor 20–2, 21n
Mompou, Federico 708, 708n
Montagu-Nathan, Montagu, critic 145n
Monte Carlo 594–9, 705; Casino, 596, 598; Hôtel de Paris, 595
Montemezzi, Italo: *L'amore dei tre re*, opera, 633, 633n
Monteux, Pierre, conductor 351, 423; auditions *Scythian Suite*, 423
Montreal 469, 470; His Majesty's Theatre, 466
Montreux 20
Morin, Henri: conductor engaged by Chicago Opera. 541, 541n, 542, 544, 551, 582, 583; differences of opinion with Mary Garden. 583, 583n
Morolyov, Vasily Mitrofanovich, childhood friend and music-loving vet 53n; SP's letter to, 325
Moscow 25, 256; becomes capital of Russia, 274; 'Kniga' bookshop opened, 690; Kuznetsky Most, 263, 263n, 690; Metropole Hotel, 259; Poets Café: Futurist celebration of SP, 261–2, 262n; 'Praga' restaurant, 153; SP's visits to, 153; and emotions on revisiting, 259, 263; Zamoskvorechye, 259, 259n
Moscow Art Theatre 141n; production of *The Brothers Karamazov*, 167
Moscow Conservatoire 65
Moskovsky Railway Station, *see* Petrograd, Nikolayevsky Station
Mount Kazbek 135
Mtkari River 135n
Mtskheta 135, 135n
Mukhomor, *see* mushrooms, fly-agaric
Munich 664, 669, 670–1, 674, 675, 699, 700, 702, 703, 712; Austrian Consulate, 702; Italian Consulate, 703; Spanish Consulate, 702
Murat, Princess 515
Muratore, Lucien, tenor 635, 635n
Murnau, Bavaria 673, 675, 687
Murphy, Mrs, potential concert organiser in Santa Barbara 579–80
mushrooms, fly-agaric 229, 229n
Musical Contemporary (*Muzykal'nyi Sovremennik*) magazine 87n; as concert promoter, 33, 66, 67, 68, 76, 84, 96, 149, 379–80; presents SP's Petrograd recital, 33, 84; and Moscow recital, 114, 169–72, 536, 692–3
Musical Courier; payment owed to 700

Musical Times 145n
Musina-Ozorovskaya, harp professor 105, 105n
Musorgsky, Modest Petrovich, composer 22; *Boris Godunov*, 129, 306; *Pictures from an Exhibition*, 144n, 405, 407, 431, 662, 679, 707
Muzio gambit (chess) 688, 688n
Muzyka, music journal 38
Myasin, Leonid, *see* Massine, Léonide
Myaskovsky, Nikolay Yakovlevich, composer 75, 75n, 119, 119n, 430, 434, 519, 536, 638, 701–2; admiration for *Sarcasms*, 120; and for *Visions fugitives*, 269; distaste for Lyadov's music, 120; plays four-hand version of his Third Symphony, 120; restores SP's lost papers to him, xiv; scores presented to Cyrus McCormick, 207; SP's article for Myaskovsky, 306; SP's letters to, 281; suffers nervous breakdown, 267; *Caprices* (*Prichudy*): *Six Sketches for piano*, 696, 696n; Piano Sonata No. 2 in F sharp minor, 48, 87, 476, 478, 482, 488, 490, 496, 523; *Six Poems of Alexander Blok*, Op. 20 (1921), 687, 687n; Symphony No. 3 in A minor, Op. 15, 120; Symphony No. 4 in E minor, Op. 17, 267; Symphony No. 5 in D, Op. 18, 267; also mentioned, 155

Namara, Marguerite, soprano 397, 397n
Naples 20, 24–6; National Museum, 25; Vesuvius, 25
Nápravnik, Eduard, conductor and composer 702
Nara, Japan 295, 296–7
Nazimova, Alla (Miriam Edez Adelaida Leventon), film actor 566, 566n, 574, 578, 615
Neishin, *see* Nyushel
Nelsons, Chicago hosts of Baranovskaya 656, 661
Nemirovich-Danchenko, Vladimir Ivanovich, theatre director 141n
Nevinnomyssky, Caucasus 232
New Orleans 552
New Queens Hall orchestra 475n
New Republic 433, 433n
New Times, newspaper and publishing house 89
New York 241, 250, 292, 298, 301, 321, 322, 507, 521; arrival in, 327–8; efforts to establish himself, 332; Biltmore Hotel, 378, 396, 493, 615; Brevoort Hotel, 541, 541n, 543, 584; British Consul in, 436, 489, 497, 498, 513; Bronx Park, 357; Carnegie Hall, 345–6, 349, 365, 498, 500; Clint, The, 615–16; Coney Island, 337, 337n; Crystal Room, 391; Fifth Avenue, 505; Laurenton Hotel, 424; Lexington Theatre, 387; Manhattan Chess Club, 667; Manhattan Opera House, 464; Metropolitan Museum of Art, 357; parade in the belief that the war was ended, 350–51; and the real thing, 352; Pennsylvania Hotel, 450, 613; Philharmonic

Orchestra, 616; Ritz Hotel, 584–5; Russian concert in aid of the American Loan; SP's participation, 345–6; Russian Consul, 465, 496; Russian Embassy, 339, 436; Savoy Hotel, 477; SP finds apartment in, 434; Staten Island, 426, 434, 435, 450, 492; Staten Island ferry, 501; Statue of Liberty, 408, 501; Wellington Hotel, 346, 386, 664, 666; Woolworth Building, 450
New York, transatlantic liner 500–505, 540; annoying cabin companion, 502–4; chess tournament, 502–4
Newman, SP's manager in Chicago 431
Niagara Falls 327, 424, 471, 472
Nice, France 595, 598
Nietzsche, Friedrich; *Also sprach Zarathustra* 191
Nijinsky, Vaclav Fomich, dancer and choreographer 27
Nikolayev, Leonid Vladimirovich, pianist and teacher 322
Nikolayeva, Lyubov Alexandrovna, contralto 112
Nikolayevsky railway line (Petrograd–Moscow) 53, 53n
Nikolayevsky Station, Petrograd 41
Nikolskys, Kislovodsk acquaintances, hosts of Maria Grigorievna 253
Nikopol 325
Nipoti, chorusmaster of Chicago Opera 618, 628, 639
Niš, Serbia 9, 9n, 14–15
Nizhni Novgorod 199
Noble, Mrs, London hostess 517, 522
Noordam, transatlantic liner 668–9, 668n
Norddeutsche Lloyd 37, 37n
Nouvel, Walter Fyodorovich, critic and writer, 45, 45n, 75, 75n, 160, 593, 594, 595; also mentioned, 189
Nouvelle revue française (NRF) 530n
Novaes, Guiomar, pianist 459, 459n
Novakovsky, Professor S. J. 461
Novorossiisk 139, 223, 411, 473, 477, 531; possible exit route for Maria Grigorievna, 421, 422, 426, 431, 457
Nurok, Alfred Pavlovich, critic and writer 45, 45n, 73, 75, 75n; also mentioned, 73, 189
Nyushel, Los Angeles acquaintance 562, 565, 571, 578, 579

Oakland 556; Civic Auditorium 556, 556n
Oberammergau 671, 677, 685, 687, 700, 701; Passion Play, 671, 677
Obolsky, acquaintance in Japan offering help with US visa 292, 304, 334–5, 345, 346, 349, 350–51
Obukhov, Nikolay, composer 76, 76n, 103, 104, 121, 156; discussion about harmony, 109
Ochs, Russian-American acquaintance 358

October Revolution: first intimations of, 237; Bolshevik siege of Moscow Kremlin, 331; effect on currency exchange market, 273; growing unrest aborts SP's Moscow recital, 238–9; and continues to spread, 240
Odessa 400, 480; pogroms, 420
Odoyevtseva, Irina Vladimirovna (Iraida Geinike), poet and memoirist 688–90, 688n
Okhotsk, Sea of 285
Olenin, Pyotr Sergeyevich, baritone and opera producer 172
Olga Borisovna, Class Inspector at the Petrograd Conservatoire 158, 158n
Omori, town with artistic community between Tokyo and Yokohama 305, 306, 307, 311; earthquake, 308
Omsk 277, 345; Omsk Government, 249, 249n, 278n, 358, 419, 419n
Ongaku to bungaku, music magazine published by Motoo Otaguro 299n
Orange, township near New York 500
Oregon, State of 324
Orlov, chess-playing acquaintance in Petrograd 187
Orlov, Nikolay Andreyevich, pianist in Moscow 236, 236n
Ormandy, Eugene, conductor 337n
Osaka 293
Ose, Aiko, Japanese newspaper publisher 291
Osman-pasha 13, 13n
Ossetian Military Road 233, 233n
Ossolinskaya, Wanda 156, 536
Ossovskaya, Varvara Alexandrovna, pianist and teacher 44n, 92
Ossovsky, Alexander Vycheslavovich, musicologist and critic 44, 44n; intercedes on SP's behalf with Russian Music Editions, 74, 78, 87, 92, 112
Otaguro, Motoo, writer on music and publisher and tea-ceremony practitioner 299, 299n, 306, 712; interview with, 299, 299n

Pacific Ocean 279, 287, 288, 291, 298, 309
Palechek, Osip Osipovich (Josef), singer (bass) and opera director 82
Paléologue, Maurice, French Ambassador to Russia 92, 92n; SP dines with, 97, 131, 219; *Le Crépuscule des Tsars* (*An Ambassador's Memoirs*), 92n, 136n
Palermo 20
Palmyra of the North 135n
Pam, Max, financial director of Chicago Opera 454, 459, 460–64, 549, 555, 585; anti-Pam faction in Chicago, 463
Panina (Panafutina), Antonida, mezzo-soprano; considered but rejected for Babulenka in *The Gambler* 125, 127
Paris 475, 478, 486, 487, 491, 499, 500, 505, 530, 590, 708, 709; Allied decision to lift blockade

of Russia, 464; Bois de Boulogne, 506, 509, 531; Champs Elysées, 505; Eiffel Tower, 505; English Consulate in, 513; Gare St Lazare, 505; Grand Hôtel, 511; Grand Opéra, 505, 591, 672; Hôtel Quai Voltaire, 531, 539; Hotel Scribe, 506; Hôtel Select, 602; Hôtel Vauban, 601; Montmartre, 510, 603; Préfecture de police, 512, 513; Russian Embassy in, 509, 510n; Salle Gaveau, 599; Théâtre de la Gaîté-Lyrique, 591n, 601–3; Théâtre des Champs Elysées, 591; no longer leading centre for a musician, 510, 514

Paris Peace Conference 404; Princes Island meeting between Council of Five and Russian belligerents, 383–4, 384n

Parmelee, publicity representative of Haensel & Jones 542

Parvus, Alexander 136n

Pasdeloup Orchestra 685, 685n

paskha, Russian Easter confection 493, 493n

Passau 702, 703

Pater, administrator at Chicago Opera 631–2

Patras 18

Pavlova, Maria Nikolayevna (Marusya, Marinochka), former Conservatoire singing student 57, 107–8, 121–2, 124, 125–9, 135, 147, 196; engaged by Musical Drama Theatre, 198; expedition to Schlüsselberg, 127, 127n; SP suggests repertoire, 110; SP suggests trip to Norway with, 109, 125, 127–8, 129; SP takes to 'Kontan' restaurant, 198; Zakharov's jealousy of SP, 125

Pavlovsk 35, 44, 51, 54, 54n; SP's performances in, 54–6, 132, 137–8, 199; strategic position in Kornilov 'rebellion', 226; also mentioned, 35, 44, 51, 54, 54n, 122–3

People's Conservatoire (*Narodnaya Konservatoriya*) 107, 107n

People's House 106, 106n

Pergolesi, Giovanni Battista, composer; (adapted Stravinsky) *Pulcinella* 508, 512

Perm 200, 201

Peshkov, Alexey Maximovich, *see* Gorky, Maxim

Petersen, Altadena acquaintance 575–6

Peto, Mrs, London hostess 522

Petrauskas, Kipras, *see* Piotrovsky, Kipras

Petrograd: Admiralty; Kerensky's base as Minster for War, 204–5; Alexandrinsky Theatre, 117; Astoria Hotel, 86; 'Bear' restaurant, 173, 224; 'Bronze Horseman', arts and literary club, 80, 81, 84, 97, 104, 110, 122; SP meets Larissa Reisner, 113–14; SP writes article for, 84; Chess Club, 76; tournaments participated in, 692; Yuli Sosnitsky, Pyotr Saburov and Boris Malyutin as 'three pillars', 89n; Court Orchestra (Pridvorny Orkestr), 25, 35, 35n; Engineer's Palace, 179; *Evening Times*, 65, 74; famine, terror and lawlessness after the Revolution, 337, 362, 372, 378, 434, 437, 450, 519; fashionable restaurants, 198n; fighting round, 430; Gostiny Dvor, 182; Kirochnaya Street, Meshchersky family home, 39, 111; 'Kontan' restaurant, 198, 198n, 209, 230; Mikhailovsky Theatre: SP nominated as representative of music to Society of Workers in the Arts, 186; Music Studio, 25, 25n, 111, 111n; Musical Drama Theatre, 55, 107, 198, 611; *The Gambler* proposed for production, 206; Nikolayevsky Station, 210, 214; Peretz restaurant, 178; Pevchesky Chapel, 38, 38n; recitals planned by SP (1918), 266; city reported occupied by White Guard peasants, 332; and by Yudenich's North Western Army, 428; but incorrectly 429, 430, 430n, 433; reports of Allied occupation, 372; rumours of German occupation, 255, 256; St Isaac's Cathedral, 173; Sennaya (Hay) Square, 71; Smolny Institute, Bolshevik Party HQ, 272, 272n; Soviet of Workers' and Soldiers' Deputies ,188, 237; 'Stray Dog' café and cabaret, 89n; threat of 1917 German advance, 188, 223, 224–5; does not materialise, 261; Tsarskoye Selo station, 54; unrest over opening of Constituent Assembly, 223, 225; Winter Palace: seat of the Provisional Government, 189, 207, 237

Petrograd Conservatoire 39; Easter Prime Service, 120, 120n, 185; Graduation Concerts, 44, 196; Malozemova Piano Competition, 64, 66

Petrov, Alexey Alexeyevich, musicologist 130

Petrov-Vodkin, Kuzma Sergeyevich, artist 100, 100n, 111

Petrovsk 134

Petrovskaya, Nina 681n

Philadelphia 246, 477

Philippe, Dora de, soprano 440, 440n

Philippines 464

Piastro, Mikhail (Misha), violinist touring Japan 287–8; SP accompanies to Kyoto and Osaka, 292, 294; SP attends recital with Meyerovich, 289; SP considers good, but not first class, artist, 290

Picasso, Pablo, artist 509, 509n, 515

Piotrovsky (Petrauskas), Kipras, tenor 112, 112n

Piraeus 17

Pittsburgh 629

Plague, 'The Dreaded Empress' 247, 247n

Plattering 702

Plevna 12–13, 13n

Podolskaya, Polina 152–3, 152n, 185, 214, 313, 536, 693; desire to study at Petrograd Women's Medical Institute, 153, 156, 173; equivocates about going to Sandwich Islands, 190, 191; sends telegram declining, 192; sends flowers to SP in Kiev, 152, 152n, 693; SP's letters to, 258, 279, 284, 693–4

Pokhitonov, Daniil Ilyich, conductor and teacher 117, 117n

Polacco, Giorgio, conductor, music director of Chicago Opera 618, 619, 620, 621
Polack, eye surgeon in Paris 572
Polignac, Princess de 507n, 512, 512n
Polish incursion into the Ukraine 533
Polotskaya-Yemtsova (Sara), Sofia Semyonovna, pianist 90, 90n
Pomerantsev, Yury Nikolayevich, composer and conductor 49
Pompeii 25–6
'Poodle', *see* Sergey Prokofiev, Literary Works, 'A Bad Dog'
Popova, Yelena, soprano 75, 75n, 78, 112, 112n, 147; cast as Polina in *The Gambler*, 120, 125, 141, 143, 145, 149; engaged for Ziloti chamber concert, 124, 149, 154
population census 332
Portugal 410
Poslednye Novosti (*Latest News*), Milyukov's newspaper in Paris 530n, 630
Postnikov, Alexander: connoisseur and collector 259, 259n, 260, 334; estimates cost of establishing oneself in America, 261; relationship discouraged by Koussevitzky, 261
Preobrazhensky Regiment 101
President of Planet Earth, *see* Khlebnikov, Velimir
Prince of Wales 468
Princes Islands, Turkey 297, 297n; Russian émigrés held in, 494, 495, 506, 509
Prokofiev, Sergey Alexeyevich, SP's father 207; correspondence with lost, 691

Prokofiev, Sergey Sergeyevich
apartment in Pervaya Rota Street, Petrograd: xiv, 150, 159, 159n; and looted, 62, 536, 547, 691–5; 'house-sat' by Boris Bashkirov, 230; still intact in March 1918, 264; Suvchinsky's representative installed, 430, 543, 691, 694; archeology and ancient history, interest in, 388; astronomy, passion for, 145, 149, 174, 194, 200–201, 211, 214, 218, 223, 223n, 240, 298, 309, 311, 312, 334, 602; Fraunhofer telescope, 194–5, 194n, 195–6, 198, 213, 223; belief in his value as an artist, 362, 630; cards as gambling activity, attitude to 213, 213n; Committee for the Arts; SP appointed to, 206
composition, approach to; comic opera, operetta and musicals, interest in, xvii, 98, 237–8, 342; operetta proposals rekindles interest in *Love for Three Oranges*, 342; difficulty of getting down to work in Japan, 295; harmony, satirical lecture on, 67; nationalism in music, attitude to, 44, 51; opera librettos, strong views on, xv; piano, composing without the use of, 194, 248; stage works, 368–9
as conductor: *Chout* in Paris, 600–604; and in London, 606–8; 'Classical' Symphony with Court Orchestra, 269; and with Chicago Symphony, 631, 643, 645, 646; and for Diaghilev in London, 607, 608; *Oranges* in Chicago, 620–21, 623, 627, 634, 638, 639–40, 641–2, 643, 645, 648, 649–50, 652–5; and in New York, 666; *Sinfonietta* in Pavlovsk, 114, 137–8; Ziloti Concert Series: *Autumnal*, 143; *Scythian Suite*, 65–76, 146–8
critic, interest in becoming, 90; *Diaries*, extreme importance of, xiii–xiv, 225, 430, 450, 531, 536, 692; February Revolution, personal experience of, xvii, 175–84; financial difficulties: in Europe, 535, 536, 538, 539, 540, 700, 701; in Chicago, 546, 552, 553; in New York, 328, 329, 336, 341, 344, 354, 421; foreign language studies: English, 90, 110; Esperanto, 306; Italian, 201; Spanish, 277, 278, 279, 281, 283, 306, 307; grand piano, sale of, 91;
health: damaged finger, 437, 438–9, 440, 441, 448, 451, 473; dentistry, 385–6, 405–6, 436, 485; gymnastics, interest in, 229; Miller exercises, 229, 229n, 231, 287; Sokol (Falcon) club, 39, 39n, 69, 78, 88, 90, 99, 104; headaches, aches and pains, 93, 99, 104, 106, 108, 110–11, 114, 116, 248, 249, 251, 259, 310–11, 316, 359, 483, 486, 489, 564, 588, 592, 623, 632, 637, 650, 656, 664, 667, 686, 699, 701; heart pains, 711, 712; scarlet fever, xvii, 406–7; operation for abscess, 409, 412–17; throat infection, 473; toothache, 382; hypochondria: cancer, 365; Spanish 'flu, 345, 346; typhoid, 156–8
income tax, 486; memory, attempts to develop, 260; military conscription, prospect of, 30, 43, 45–6, 51, 52–3, 58, 124, 158–9, 202, 211–13; as foreign national in America, 312, 322; secures exemption and permission to reside anywhere in Russia, 212; name-day celebrations, 140; organ studies, 77–8, 86, 90, 99, 105, 124, 125, 130, 140
pastimes: bridge, 3, 4, 37, 39, 64, 65, 78, 98, 99, 115, 122, 137, 177, 196, 213, 288, 304, 308, 377, 389, 390, 458, 474, 476, 479, 485, 486, 493, 495, 504, 558, 627, 633, 638, 642, 651, 652; chemin-de-fer, 192, 197, 213; chess, 63, 69, 73, 88, 93, 98, 101, 106, 108, 115, 251, 311, 312, 338, 339, 502, 503–4, 557, 676, 688, 689; Blitz chess, 94, 94n; organises 'Pervaya Rota' chess tournaments, 145, 159, 166, 187–8; records of matches with Lasker and Capablanca lost, xiv; speed games, 676; Macao, 71, 71n, 78, 87, 99; 'Ninth Wave', 177, 177n; sea-bathing, 610; 'sixty-six', 137, 137n, 138; sonnet competition, 674, 676; tennis, 131, 136–7, 675; vint, 124, 124; walks, 174, 198; philosophy, interest in, 416; Kant, reading of, 210, 215, 229, 231, 237, 240, 416; Schopenhauer, reading of, 140, 175, 191, 194, 198, 201–2, 205–6, 208, 230, 240, 253, 416
as pianist; accompanying *The Ugly Duckling*, 6–7, 154; accompanying Vera Janacopulos, 403; Altschuler concert in New

York, 365; Bashkirov urges to focus attention on pianism, 139–40; on board ship, 18, 202–3; Bronze Horseman, 104; Brooklyn Museum recital, 348; Buffalo recital, 469, 470, 471; press reviews, 471; California recitals, 555, 556–7, 558, 560, 578; Chicago recitals, 427, 429, 431, 432–3, 451, 537, 662; estimated cost of, 368; press reviews, 432, 433, 453, 579; Chicago Symphony concerts, 363–4; Chicago University recitals, 555, 662; Chopin pieces, learning, 63; for American repertoire, 251, 252, 253; Cleveland recital, 602, 626; press reviews, 628; Court Orchestra 2nd piano concerto, 35, 38; development of memory, 475; Diederich's plans for autumn 1917 recitals in Petrograd and Moscow, 230, 238; Dobychina Gallery, 173; for IRMS 1st piano concerto, 165–6; for IRMS, 2nd piano concerto, 7, 7n, 33; Kiev, 1st and 2nd piano concertos, 145, 151–2, 692; and recital, 151, 536; Kislovodsk, 1st piano concerto; Kislovodsk recitals, 235, 236, 255, 268; Manhattan Opera House appearance, 464; Montreal recital, 466–7; press reviews, 467; *Musical Contemporary* Petersburg recital, 33, 84; and Moscow recital, 114, 169, 171–2, 536, 693; Musical Drama Theatre with Fitelbert, 1st piano concerto, 213; New York Philharmonic concert, 465, 475–6; New York performance of 3rd piano concerto with Coates, 665; New York recitals, 348, 350, 353, 354–6, 389–90, 405, 422, 426, 435, 436, 437, 438–9, 666, 667; Adams lackadaisical about organising, 346, 349, 353; Aeolian Hall, 348–9, 348n, 355; losses on, 391, 405, 439, 668; mental preparations for, 354–5, 389–90; press reviews, 356, 390, 405, 427, 439; unresponsive piano, 354–5; overhauling keyboard technique, 532–3; Pavlovsk: first piano concerto, 199; first piano concerto with Fitelberg, 55; second piano concerto, 114, 132; second sonata, 56–8; Petrograd recitals (1918), 268–9; Pittsburgh recital, 625, 627, 629; Quebec recital, 467–8; press reviews, 468; recitals in Barcelona, 707, 708; Rome, second piano concerto, 20–22; Saratov recital, 156, 169–70, 536, 692; Sestroretsk, 2nd piano concerto, 46–7; Sosnitsky's house, 89; Tenishev Hall, for Music Studio, 111; and for war-wounded, 122; Washington recital, 441; Stravinsky *Rite of Spring* four-hands, 29; Ziloti Chamber Music series, 5, 154

political attitudes: general neutrality of, xv–xvi, 184, 184n, 226–7; welcome for and optimism about Provisional Government, 184; praise, applause and criticism, reaction to, xvii, xviii–xix, 36, 84, 145, 185–6, 253, 363, 365, 366, 390; skeleton, decides to donate to a museum, 208–9; Society of Workers in the Arts, elected committee member of, 186, 188–9; stock exchange investments, 137, 137n; strongbox of MS and papers, deposits in Koussevitzky's vault, 225, 225n

travel: attempts to obtain passport to travel abroad, 188; love of, 106; mental preparation for, 252, 283; Russia, reasons for leaving, xiii; 26th birthday celebration, 189; writing, love of and attitude to, xvii, xviii, 215, 225, 253, 266, 297, 562, 646; Severyanin's opinion of SP's poetry, 266; stories read by American immigration censors, 315, 323

WORKS
JUVENILIA
A Feast in Time of Plague, opera (1903), 691; 'doggies' ('sobachki'), 53, 691; 'little songs' ('pesenki'), 691; *On Desert Islands*, opera (1901), 691; Suite for Strings, 191, 191n; Symphony in E minor (1908), 191, 191n; Symphony in G (1902), 691

MATURE WORKS
Op. 1 Sonata No. 1 in F minor (1909), 28, 55, 151, 170, 335, 405, 464
Op. 2 *Four Etudes for Piano* (1909), 170, 355; No. 4, 38; recorded for Duo-Art, 398
Op. 3 *Four Pieces for Piano* (1911), 170; No. 1 'Fairy Tale', 38
Op. 4 *Four Pieces for Piano*, 170; No. 4 'Suggestion Diabolique', 151, 170, 171, 269, 301, 355, 426, 471, 708
Op. 5 *Sinfonietta* (1909, rev. 1914), 39, 52, 65, 78, 81, 137–8
Op. 6 *Dreams* (*Sni*) (1910), 47, 55, 78, 98
Op. 7 *Two Poems for female chorus and orchestra* (1909–10): 'The Wave' ('Volna'), 83; 'The White Swan' ('Belaya Lebed'), 83
Op. 8 *Autumnal* (*Osenneye*) (1910, rev. 1915), 51, 75, 78, 141, 142, 143, 693; reviewed in *Musical Contemporary*, 143
Op. 9 *Two Poems for Voice and Piano* (1910–11): 'The Boat Cast Off', 78, 110, 154; 'There Are Other Planets', 78, 83; submitted to RME, 172
Op. 10 Piano Concerto No. 1 in D flat major (1911–12), 43, 46, 48, 62, 90, 101, 199; auditioned by Damrosch, 332, 334; performance for Altschuler in New York, 365; performance in Chicago, 358, 361, 363–4; performance in Kiev, 145; performance in Kislovodsk, 222; performance in Musical Drama Theatre, 213; performance in Pavlovsk, 55; performance for Petrograd IRMS, 165, 165n; score believed lost in Petrograd apartment, xiv
Op. 11 *Toccata*, 29, 151–2, 154, 348, 405, 431, 439, 441, 679
Op. 12 *Ten Pieces for Piano* (1912–14), 111, 170; No. 1 'March', 691; No. 2 'Gavotte', 4, 65, 170, 206, 221, 306, 355, 405; No. 3 'Rigaudon', 7;

No. 6 *Legenda*, 170, 170; No. 7 'Prelude', 89, 106, 348, 355, 394; No. 10 'Scherzo', 65, 84–5, 98, 106, 113, 355, 556; No. 1 'March', No. 2 'Gavotte', No. 7 'Prelude' recorded for Duo-Art, 394–5

Op. 12a 'Humoresque' Scherzo for four bassoons, 145, 145n, 154, 365, 493, 610; English press reports of, 145, 145n

Op. 13 *Maddalena*, opera in one act and four scenes (1911–13), 78

Op. 14 Sonata No. 2 in D minor (1912), 29, 33, 56–7, 58, 104, 170, 355, 379, 496; appreciated in Moscow, 150; as basis for 'astronomical dance', 99; performed by Borovsky, 150; Scherzo, 348

Op. 15 *Ballade* for cello and piano (1912), 43, 43n, 154;

Op. 16 Piano Concerto No. 2 in G minor (1913), 3, 5, 29, 48, 65, 78, 132, 508, 509; finale revised, 711; full score lost, 536; Paris performance of revised score with Koussevitzky postponed, 712, 712n; performance with Court Orchestra, 35, 38; performance in Kiev, 145, 151–2; performance in Rome, 21–3, 38; performance in Sestroretsk, 46–7; piano reduction, 86, 531; revised orchestration, 47; Stravinsky's suggestion for cadenza, 35, 35n

Op. 17 *Sarcasms* (1912–14), 44–5, 45n, 66, 78, 82, 97, 104, 132, 221, 500, 631; admired by Alchevsky, 101; and by Balmont, 146; and by Koussevitzky, 104–5; hidden programme of, 146, 146n; inscribes copy to Balmont, 149; Obukhov's opinion, 109; performance in Kiev, 151; performance in New York, 405; performance in Saratov, 170; played in Paris, 473

Op. 18 *The Ugly Duckling* (*Gadky Utyonok*), fairy tale for voice and piano (1914), 6, 78, 478, 604; admired by Alchevsky, 101, 146, 154; and performed by, 146, 154; first performance, 6; anniversary of, 247; submitted to RME, 172; success in Moscow, 103, 171

Sans op. abandoned *Ala and Lolli*, ballet, 22–4, 52

Op. 19 Violin Concerto No. 1 in D (1917), 536n; desire to compose, 157; first movement development, full score of, 531; not appreciated by Cecilia Hansen, 670; orchestration: away from piano, 194, 196, 201; of finale, 208, 210; of scherzo, 206; piano score, 588; premiere in Paris, 712, 712n; premiere scheduled by Ziloti, 238; and postponed, 238; revives first movement exposition, 174; sketches: of finale, 174; of scherzo, 174; solo part, 536; works on during February Revolution, 177

Op. 20 *Scythian Suite*, 52, 78, 79–80, 425, 462, 519, 682; anniversary of first performance, 247; attacked by Lotin, 102–3; auditioned by Monteux, 423; Belgian premiere, 699, 700, 709; copy of score made for Cyrus McCormick, 207; Koussevitzky's interest in publishing, 103–4; performances by Koussevitzky in Paris, 599, 600, 641; press reviews, 642–3; performances in Chicago, 360, 363–4; rehearsals, 361, 362; performances in Ziloti concert series, 64–6, 69–75, 147–8; rehearsals, 145, 146; timpani head split, 74; performed by Coates and LSO, 552; 'Procession of the Sun' seen by Asafyev as example of unbridled exultation, 208; proposal to include in New York concert barred by Rachmaninoff, 373; proposed Moscow performance in Koussevitzky season, 109, 113, 143; 'reviewed' by Sabaneyev, 693; score and parts requested by Coates, 427; SP writes own review, 74; also mentioned, 152, 191

Op. 21 *Chout*, ballet, 27, 43–4, 78, 118, 612, 657; auditioned by Stravinsky, 539; Ballets Russes performances in London, 606–8; press reviews, 608–9, 609n; Ballets Russes production in Paris 1921, 600–604; praised by Ravel, Stravinsky and Les Six, 604; Ballets Russes rehearsals in Monte Carlo, 595–9, and press reviews, 604; continuing composition of, 45, 45n, 46, 48, 51; copying of orchestral parts, 591, 592, 593, 594, 600, 601; Diaghilev receives score in America, 331; Diaghilev returns score in London, 524, 526–7; further advance received from Diaghilev, 86–7; negotiations for commission fee from Diaghilev, 30–32; and with publisher, 34; orchestration, 532, 534, 538, 591, 592, 593–4; piano score of, 541, 544; Phonola recording requested, 539; receives advances from Diaghilev, 86–7, 91, 108–9, 110, 111, 137; revisions of, 532, 538, 539, 605, 606; scenery designed by Larionov, 398, 506; SP proposed to conduct, 528–9; SP temporarily stops work on, 52; suite from, 677, 690–91, 695, 711

Op. 22 *Visions fugitives* (*Mimolyotnosti*), 53, 165, 191, 199, 213, 261, 266, 335, 508, 514, 526, 557, 611; experience of February Revolution reflected in No. 19, 184, 184n; first performance in Kislovodsk, 235; first performance in Petrograd, 268; looks out 'doggies' for, 174; performance at Brooklyn Museum with Bolm dancing, 348; performance in Chicago, 431; performance in New York, 390, 431; played to friends, 189; title taken from Balmont, 221, 221n; tonality of No. 3, 431

Op. 23 *Five Poems for Voice and Piano* (1915), 101n; No. 1 'Under the Roof' ('Pod krishey'), 101; No. 2 'The Grey Dress' ('Seroye platye'), 101; No. 3 'Trust Me', 110, 110n; No. 4 'In My Garden', 154, 154n; No. 5 'The Wizard', 154, 154n

Op. 24 *The Gambler* (*Igrok*), opera in 4 Acts, 61–2, 61n, 78, 88, 110, 110n, 399, 406, 474, 515, 543; Aslanov as second conductor, 116–17, 138;

auditions: by Coates, 93–4, 101, 103–4, 111–12, 129; by Malko, 100; by Mariinsky directorate, 116–19; Chicago Opera: Campanini undertakes to produce in Chicago, 339, 454; preparing for audition by Campanini, 359, 361–2; composition: difficulty in finishing, 128, 130; final scene, 123, 124, 125, 128, 130; general progress of composition, 1, 61, 61n, 64, 76, 77–8, 80, 81, 83, 85, 91, 92, 98, 99, 100, 101, 103, 106, 108; Hoppe & Co., 64, 64n, 89, 91; libretto, 105, 106, 110–11; roulette scene, 113, 114, 115, 120, 123–4, 130, 596; copyright claim by Dostoyevsky's widow, 159–60, 163–5, 167, 173; February Revolution will cause production delay and possible cancellation, 184–5, 197, 224; *L'Illustration* as source of ideas for setting, 160; Mariinsky Theatre: auditioned by directorate, 116–19; casting, 112, 125, 127, 141, 143, 145; delay in copying vocal parts, 137–41, 143, 157, 692; included in 1919 repertoire plans, 269, 272; Meyerhold and Golovin engaged as producer and designer, 173; new contract demanded, 224, 271, 272, 273; and third party power of attorney suggested, 273–4; Popova invited to sing Polina, 120; possibility of full score still preserved at, 694; production proposed to, 89, 94, 109, 111, 115; score submitted to library for copying, 128, 130; SP insists theatre has breached contract, 244; Metropolitan Opera: suggested for audition, 401, 402, 492; orchestration, 131–2, 136, 138, 139, 142, 191; Act Four begun, 140; Act Two completed, 138; entr'acte, 157; final scene, 157; lovers' embrace, 166; opera completed, 166–7; Polina's hysterical scene, 159; roulette scene, 140, 141, 143; piano score given to Cyrus McCormick, 207; possibility of Moscow production, 173; press reports on forthcoming production, 122, 130–31, 130n; private playthrough at Gessen's, 126; proposed to Musical Drama Theatre, 206, 213; rehearsals, 143, 145, 536, 692; chaos of Revolution precludes orchestral rehearsals of Acts Three and Four, 190–91; with orchestra, 167; roulette scene, 158; SP misses through illness, 157; SP temporarily stops work on, 86; also mentioned, 122–3, 123n

Op. 25 Symphony No. 1 in D ('Classical') (1916–17), 508; auditioned by Damrosch, 332; who compares it to Kalinnikov's symphonies, 334; composed away from piano, 194; composition proceeds at Sablino, 206, 208, 210; desire to compose, 157; expects criticism for distorting classicism, 196; Gavotte, 642; admired by Benois, 206; performed in New York, 405; piano roll made by SP, 340; transcribed for piano, 306; and played to Balmont, 221; orchestration, 218–19, 225, 227; original finale abandoned, 207–8; parts copied by Ziloti, 230; performance for Diaghilev season in London, 607, 608; performance in New York, 364–5; performance with State Orchestra (former Court Orchestra), 269, 269n, 270–71; performances with Chicago Symphony, 631, 643, 645, 646; press reviews, 647; premiere scheduled by Ziloti, 238; and postponed, 238; publication schedule delayed, 711

Op. 26 Piano Concerto No. 3 in C (1917–21), 138, 583; celebratory sonnet by Balmont, 611, 611n; desire to compose, 144, 157; first movement conceived away from piano, 248; London performance with Coates, 673; press reviews, 673n; New York performances with Coates, 665; press reviews, 665; Paris performances with Koussevitzky, 672, 675; performance in Antwerp, 709–10; performance with Chicago Symphony, 620, 629, 630, 631, 632, 633, 635, 637, 638, 639–40, 642, 643, 644, 645, 646; press reviews, 647; piano reduction of, 668–9, 672, 684, 689; preliminary work on, 241, 247; progress of composition, 249, 250, 605, 606, 609, 610, 612n; solo piano part of finale left behind, 620, 621, 626, 627; work temporarily set aside, 252, 253

Op. 27 *Five Poems of Anna Akhmatova*, 148–9, 440, 604, 610; composed after hearing Nina Koshetz sing, 218; invitation to perform in Evenings of *Musical Contemporary* recital rejected, 174–5; original suggestion by Suvchinsky, 148; performed by Vera Janacopulos, 403, 679; premiered in Moscow, 171; published by Gutheil, 260; sung by Nina Koshetz, 259, 403; their intimate lyricism, 149

Op. 28 Sonata No. 3 in A minor, 261, 266, 269; first performance in Kislovodsk, 235; first performance in Petrograd, 268; learning, 231; New York performances, 365, 439; performance in Barcelona, 707; performance for Bohemian Club, 470; performance in Chicago, 451; played to friends, 189, 191; practising, 251; recast from juvenile Sonata in A minor, 174, 174n; score believed lost in Petrograd apartment, xiv

Op. 29 Sonata No. 4 in C minor, 266, 379; composed from juvenile Suite for Strings, 191, 191n; Andante added from juvenile Symphony in E minor, 191, 191n, 235, 237, 266, 395; completed, 240; first performance in Petrograd, 269; learning, 251; performance in Chicago, 431; performance in New York, 390; publication fee received, 260; score believed lost in Petrograd apartment, xiv

Op. 30 *Seven, They Are Seven*, cantata for tenor, chorus and orchestra: composition and structure, 227–9; detailed sketches begun, 240; and finished, 241; fruit of solitude in Sablino, 694; lays plans to compose, 191; manuscript of, 531; more detailed composition, 231, 235; Paris performance with Koussevitzky planned then cancelled, 712, 712n; piano score, 701, 702; score completed, 246; SP suggests setting to Balmont, 171, 171n

Op. 31 *Tales of an Old Grandmother* (*Skaski staroy babushki*) (1918), 336, 338–9, 341, 344, 358, 482, 508, 562, 611, 617, 630; admired by Stahl, 343; first performance, 379; offered to Carl Fischer, 342; performed in New York, 405; publication by Russian Music Editions, 538, 589

Op. 32 *Four Pieces for Piano* (1918), 343, 345, 617; No. 1 'Dance', 345n, 550; No. 2 'Minuet', 343, 345n; No. 3 'Gavotte', 345, 345n, 405, 690; No. 4 'Waltz', 343, 344, 345n, 550; publication by Russian Music Editions, 36, 538, 589

Sans op. Suite arranged from Schubert Waltzes (1920), 525, 554, 711

Sans op. Orchestration of Rimsky-Korsakov's 'The Rose and the Nightingale' (1918), 371–2, 381

Sans op. Buxtehude Organ Fugue in D minor arr. for piano (1921), 628

Op. 33 *The Love For Three Oranges* (*Lyubov k tryom apel'sinam*), 406, 429, 551–2, 575, 577, 580, 657, 681; Act Two copied, 398; Benois provides Italian version of Gozzi's play, 294, 294n; Chicago Opera: Anisfeld engaged to design sets, 411; cancels *Oranges* production altogether, 545–50, 551–2, 553–5; conducting preparation for, 613, 614, 615, 620; considered unperformable, 474, 475; delay in production, 436, 440, 441, 443; cancelled, 444–6, 447; postponed, 446, 483; general rehearsal, 652–3, 653n; libretto printed as poetry, 640; negotiations over contractual position and potential legal action, 440–41, 448, 451–3, 458–60, 461–3, 497, 522, 531, 538, 545, 545–6, 547, 549, 551, 552, 553, 554, 555, 559; new contract negotiations, 585, 586; New York performance, 663, 664, 665, 666; press reviews, 666–7, 666n; *Oranges* might be preferred to *Gambler*, 359, 362; possible revival following season, 667; premiere (Chicago), 654–6; press reviews, 656, 656n; rehearsals, 617–25, 627–9, 630–31, 632, 634, 638–45, 648–53; SP invited to conduct, 612n, 617, 618, 625; SP lectures in English, 633; composition: completed, 407–8; continues, 370, 371–2, 381, 382, 383, 384, 386, 388, 391, 394, 396, 397, 398, 400, 407; March, 384; Prologue completed, 369; starts, 368; Covent Garden, 427, 452, 466, 518, 529, 530, 534, 538; disapproval of frivolity anticipated, 359, 369–70; genesis, 141n; March, 653, 655, 655n, 656, 657, 662, 678–9, 682; Metropolitan Opera: audition, 492–3; Meyerhold's impetus, 271, 273; orchestration, 408, 410–16, 418, 419, 420, 421, 422, 423, 424, 425; completed on time, 425; played to Diaghilev and Stravinsky, 680; Scherzo, 678–9, 682; score copied, 423, 445; SP recasts ending of Gozzi's play, 342; and subject generally, 359, 359n, 366, 369; suite from, 440, 444, 446, 633, 649, 661; vocal score, 392, 418, 421, 673–4, 675; proofs 675; work on libretto, 364, 366, 368, 372, 382, 395, 406

Op. 34 *Overture on Hebrew Themes* (1919), 427, 428, 429, 430, 430n, 469, 470, 493, 498, 500, 614

Op. 35 *Five Songs Without Words* (1920), 555, 557, 558, 562, 564, 577, 604

Op. 36 *Five Poems of Konstantin Balmont*, 612, 612n; No. 5 'Pillars', 616

Op. 37 *The Fiery Angel*, opera, 580, 683; Chicago Opera production hoped for, 663; composition, 454, 460, 465, 476, 478, 479, 480, 484, 485, 487, 488, 489, 490, 490n, 491, 492, 493, 494, 499, 675, 677; of Act Five, 684, 685, 687, 689, 696n; blocked, 684, 696; completed, 699; interrupted after Metropolitan Opera rejection, 496; and by tour to Spain, 701; conception, 446, 448; Act Five mayhem, 696, 696n; Renata's lamentation scene, 468, 482; Metropolitan Opera: auditioned, 465–6, 473, 474, 475, 492–3; rejected, 493, 496, 498, 499; revision, 700; scenario advice from Stahl, 449; work on libretto, 457, 461, 471, 472, 502, 515, 677, 696

Op. 38 Sonata No. 5 in C (1923), 686, 701

Op. 40 Symphony No. 2 in D minor (1923), 381n

Works planned but abandoned or not immediately realised: concerto for two pianos and orchestra, 347; Fairy Tale for orchestra, 380–82, Variation theme later used for 2nd Symphony, 381n; opera based on simultaneous action in cross-section of a house, 197; opera *The Anarchist*, 238; orchestration of Scriabin's 5th Sonata, 336; small-scale 'Russian' symphony to parallel 'Classical', 196; violin sonata: encounters block, 292; first movement abandoned, 302; ideas for, 289, 290, 291, 315, 332; work abandoned, 480; 'white quartet', 296, 296n, 315, 343, 397, 609; wordless chorus, 490

LITERARY WORKS

'A Bad Dog', aka 'Poodle', 215, 215n, 225, 246, 295n, 587, 588; 'An Incident With A Leg', lost or abandoned short story, 215, 215n, 295n; *Autobiography*, 284n; 'Death of the Watchmaker', 295n, 646, 646n; *Diaries*, notebooks of, 225, 430, 450, 531, 691; 'Do you know when the boat for Africa sails?', unfinished short story, 295n; 'Guilty Passion', aka 'The White Friend', unfinished short story, 277, 277n, 291, 292, 294, 295, 295n, 305, 306,

311; 'Mirror of the Soul', lost short story, 268, 295, 295n; 'Misunderstandings Sometimes Occur', 284, 295, 295n; *Short Autobiography*, 61n, 184n, 641n; 'The Smoking-Room', 295n; 'The Tale of the Poisonous Mushroom', 229, 229n, 231, 295n; 'The Toads', 295n, 298, 300, 301, 302, 311; 'The Two Marquises', 295n, 346; 'The Wandering Tower', 277, 277n, 278, 281, 295n, 306, 307, 310–11, 588; 'Ultra-Violet Freedom', aka 'Rameses-Yankee', 268, 268n, 277, 277n, 295n, 354, 388; unidentified short stories, 247, 247n, 382, 404, 531; 'You, with DM', poem, 266
Prokofieva, Maria Grigorievn, SP's mother 11, 12, 32, 34, 41, 47, 62, 69, 73, 90, 206, 231, 306–7, 328, 371, 491, 507, 687, 699; arrival from Constantinople, 526, 529–32; assists SP financially, 87, 239, 256; attempts to obtain French visa for, 509, 510, 512, 513, 514, 515; or for Belgium, 512, 513; attitude to SP marrying, 6, 54; concerned for SP's safety during February Revolution events, 181; SP's efforts to transfer money to, 399, 400, 431, 435, 436, 437, 438, 449, 450, 457, 472, 483, 484, 487, 494, 499; escape from Russia, plans for, 426, 428, 431, 479, 483, 484, 486, 494; experiences during, 531; financial transactions, 248; health, 488, 494; deteriorating generally, 678; eyesight, 448, 488, 494, 534, 537, 538, 539, 572, 590, 601; improves in France, 533; not helped by Ettal, 702; hears play-through of *The Gambler* with Albert Coates, 93–4, 141; learns English, 250; lets Petrograd apartment to Boris Bashkirov, 230; looks at Revolutionary Petrograd, 182–3; meets Vera Nikolayevna Meshcherskaya in Kislovodsk, 235–6; no news of, 387; opening of Dardanelles offers possibility of communication with, 348; postcard received from, 427–8; and letters, 438, 448; reports on *Scythian Suite* in Paris, 641; room searched in Kislovodsk, 253; shocked by Balmont's tolerance of Rasputin, 222; SP buys typewriter for, 575, 587; SP writes to, 445; SP's concern for her safety, xvi, xvii, 225, 253, 306, 447, 451, 459, 461, 463, 472, 482, 484; and difficulty of communicating with, 328, 348, 371, 373, 382, 398, 399, 404, 477; possibility of channel opening up through Italy, 458; or through lifting of Allied trade blockade, 464–5; suspected of possible cancer, given radium treatment, 4, 673; travels to and from Caucasus, 53, 54, 138, 188, 191, 211; US visa, efforts to obtain, 421, 422, 422n, 426, 457, 472; also mentioned, 75, 159, 173, 214, 538, 548, 562, 591, 592, 594, 603, 605, 609, 612, 620, 637, 647, 648, 669, 690, 695
Prunières, Henry 592, 592n
Prut, river 10, 10n
Pskov; falls to Germans 256

Puccini, Giacomo, composer: *Il Trittico*, 454, 454n; *Madama Butterfly*: Coates believes phrase in *The Gambler* borrowed from, 112, 128; *Tosca*, 523
Purrington, New York lawyer 448, 463, 497, 498
Pushkin, Alexander Sergeyevich: 'The Lay of Oleg's Prophecy', 636–7, 636n; *The Stone Guest (Kamenny Gost')*, 122; *Yevgeny Onegin*, 189, 189n, 492, 492n
Putilov workers 210
Pyatigorsk 247, 248, 254; Bolsheviks advancing on 249; criminals escape from jail, 251, 251n
Pythagoras 142

Quebec 467–9; Columbus Hall, 468; Francoeur, President, 468
Quebec Parliament 468

Rachmaninoff, Irina Sergeyevna, Rachmaninoff's daughter 352
Rachmaninoff (née Satina), Natalya Alexandrovna, Rachmaninoff's wife 261, 261n, 352, 489, 495, 630
Rachmaninoff, Sergey Vasilievich, composer 87, 168, 170, 236, 356, 365, 365–6, 378–9, 392, 429, 440, 466, 480–81, 532–3, 536, 550–51, 571, 630, 635n, 670, 693; advises how to perform with damaged finger, 353; approves decision to concentrate on composing opera, 370; arrives in New York, 351–2; Bohemian Club dinner for, 378; correspondence with Haensel about Koshetz, 543–4; decides also to launch with solo recital, 357; programme, 369; defends *Scythian Suite* against attacks of Glazunov, 388; fundamental contempt for American audiences, 369, 379; lack of success and difficult circumstances in Scandinavia, 262; leaves Russia, 261, 261n; meets and approves of Vladimir Bashkirov, 370; opinions on publication of SP's works by Russian Music Editions and Gutheil, 143, 148; playing of Scriabin criticised by SP, 352, 392; reaction to *Scythian Suite*, 147–8, 693; and other music by SP, 352; relationship with Nina Koshetz, 216, 217, 218, 261, 261n, 489, 551; support sought for Koshetz in America, 495; sits 'immobile as a Buddha' at SP's Moscow recital, 171–2, 380, 693; success in America contrasted with SP's, 373–4; 'would need a nanny for America', 335; Etude-Tableau, 429; *Isle of the Dead*, 599; Piano Concerto No. 1 in F sharp minor, Op. 1 (rev. 1917), 353, 384; Piano Concerto No. 2 in C minor, Op. 18, 147, 380, 693; Piano Concerto No. 3 in D minor, Op. 30, 41; Polka, 369, 379, 379n; Prelude in C sharp minor, Op. 3/2, 373, 373n, 662; Prelude in G minor, Op. 23/5, 373, 373n, 405, 441, 470, 471; recorded by SP for Duo-Art, 398; *Sept morceaux de salon*, Op. 10 No. 3

'Valse in A', 394; *Six Songs for Voice and Piano*, Op. 38, 148, 148n, 169, 218; Symphony No. 2 in E minor, Op. 27, 365, 373; Three Preludes, 349, 350, 354, 355; also mentioned, 548
Rachmaninoff, Tatyana Sergeyevna, Rachmaninoff's daughter 352
Raikh, Zinaida, actor, wife of Vsevolod Meyerhold 141n
Ramuz, C. F., writer and librettist 26n, 508
Rasputin, Grigory Yefimovich 136n, 157; Balmont's tolerance of, 222; murder of, 157
Rausch, *see* Traubenberg, Baron Rausch von
Ravel, Maurice, composer 31, 303, 509, 641; meets SP, 509; praises *Chout*, 604; *L'heure espagnole*, 458; *Rapsodie Espagnole*, 80
Rayevksaya, Yekaterina Grigorievna, (Aunt Katya) 141, 155, 215, 215n, 699
Rayevskaya, Tatyana, Andrey Rayevsky's wife 488n, 494, 509
Rayevskaya, Yekaterina Alexandrovna (cousin Katya, Katechka) 141, 155, 215, 215n
Rayevsky, Andrey Alexandrovich (Andryusha), SP's cousin, 488n; ill with typhoid, 488; death of, 494
Rayevsky family, SP's relations in Petrograd 36, 36n
Razin, Stenka (Stepan), suggested as possible opera subject by Chaliapin 131
Rech, newspaper edited by Iosif Gessen 183, 300, 300n
Red Cross 399, 673; HQ personnel wrongly believed to be exempt from being sent to the front, 202, 203–4; SP's obligations to, 192–3, 199; SP's secondment to, 192, 192n, 212
Reger, Max, composer 303
Reisner, Larissa, poet and revolutionary 113–14, 113n, 195
Rembrandt van Rijn 357
Remizov, Alexey Mikhailovich, writer and fabulist 144, 144n; *Alaley and Leila*: considered as possible subject for ballet or opera, 144–5, 144n, 185, 648, 648n; subsequently abandoned, 197
Repino, *see* Kuokkale
Respighi, Ottorino, composer: *Cimarosiana*, ballet, 517; *Le Astuzie Femminili*, 508, 508n, 517; *The Pines of Rome*, 21n
Revel 75, 119, 119n; falls to Germans, 256
Revue musicale, La 592, 592n
Reznikov, proprietor of Kislovodsk Grand Hotel 234
Rhine Valley 677
Riga 536, 587, 671; reported in German hands, 224–5, 227
Rimsky-Korsakov, Andrey Nikolayevich, critic, editor and writer, son of Nikolay Rimsky-Korsakov 87n, 109, 473n; *see also Musical Contemporary*
Rimsky-Korsakov, Nikolay Andreyevich, composer: difference of opinion with Suvchinsky and Asafyev over new music, 174–5; *Legend of the Invisible City of Kitezh*, opera, 112n, 217; *Novelettes*, 556; Piano Concerto, 72, 465, 466, 467, 468, 469, 473, 475–6; *Sadko*, 19, 19n; *Schéhérezade*, 510; Songs, 525; *Tale of Tsar Saltan*, 37, 37n; *The Golden Cockerel*, opera, 382; 'The Rose and the Nightingale', 371–2, 381; *The Snow-Maiden*, opera, 528, 665; *The Tsar's Bride (Tsarskaya Nevesta)*, opera, 82, 85; LITERARY WORKS: *Principles of Orchestration*, 72
Rio de Janeiro 505
Rochelets, Plage des 590, 592, 593–4, 600, 605, 609–10, 612, 612n
Rocky Mountains 325
Rodichev, Fyodor Izmailovich, member of State Duma, prominent Kadet, Governor-General of Finland during the Provisional Government, 163, 187
Roerich, Nikolay Konstantinovich (Nicholas), artist and designer 81, 81n, 83, 144n, 645–6, 647–8; arrival in America, 542; London exhibition, 520; séances, interest in, 520, 586, 645
Roger-Ducasse, Jean, composer 303, 303n
Romania: cholera in, 10; concludes separate peace with Germany, 257; possible war with Bulgaria, 8
Romanovsky, Gavriil Ivanovich, pianist 55, 68, 85
Rome 20–23, 26–7, 30–32, 37; Appian Way, 23; Russian Embassy in, 32, 36, 438; SP sightseeing in, 20
Roosevelt, President Theodore 542, 542n
Rosen, Mark, violinist 572, 574
Rosenthals, financial backers of Chicago Opera 548, 549, 552, 622, 630, 631, 656
Rosenwalds, financial backers of Chicago Opera 547, 549, 618, 656
Rostov-on-Don 223, 252, 252n, 257, 449, 450, 473, 483; evacuation in anticipation of Bolshevik occupation, 457
Rostovsky, chess-playing acquaintance 159, 166
Rozhdestvensky, Admiral Zinovy 284n
Rubinstein, Arthur, pianist 330n, 386, 386n, 387, 391, 392, 396, 397, 398, 473, 474, 482; advises touring South America to make money, 391
Rudavskaya, Antonina Alexandrovna (Tonya), adolescent romance with 692
Rudin, chess-playing acquaintance 145, 166
Ruffman, English acquaintance in Yessentuki 232–3
Ruffo, Titta (Ruffo Cafiera Titta), baritone 626, 626n, 628
Ruhr, occupation by France of 702–3, 703n, 705, 707
Rul', Berlin newspaper published by Gessen 300n
Rumanov, husband of Ariadna Rumanova 563,

567, 571, 574, 575, 576, 577, 578, 581, 597
Rumanova (née Nikolskaya), Ariadna Nikolayevna, pianist and would-be composer 291, 291n, 292, 306, 559, 560–61, 563–7, 571–81, 586
Rushchuk 12, 12n
Russia: between the February and October Revolutions; Constituent Assembly; elections, 240, 245, 245n; unrest on account of, 223, 245, 245n; difficulties with essential supplies to the cities, 197; funding reduced for theatre productions, 197, 224; July Days, 209–10; SP's personal experience of, 209–10; release of political prisoners, 203; rumours of marauding soldiers and deserters, 199; severe strain on the railway system, 190, 191, 203; vulnerability and instability of Petrograd, 191, 223; conduct of the First World War after the February Revolution; June Offensive, 206, 206n
Russian Music Editions, Koussevitzky's publishing house 153, 260, 536, 537, 539, 586, 589; interruptions to publishing schedule, 711; SP's ambitions to be published by, 74, 78, 86–7, 103–4, 112, 143; strongbox of MS and papers deposited in Moscow vault, 225; and preserved, 536
Russian Orthodox Church, Easter Prime Service: in Moscow, 275; in Petrograd Conservatoire, 120, 120n, 185; Easter Prime Service in New York, 495; marriage ceremony, 98–9, 98n
Russische Musikverlag, *see* Russian Music Editions
Russo-Japanese War: Battle of Tsushima Straits, 284, 284n; boyhood grief over loss of Russian ships, 384n; calculation of military coefficiency of cruisers, 692
Russo-Turkish War 13n
Russolo, Luigi, composer, 'noise machines' (*intonarumori*) 28n
Ruzskaya, Irina Niolayevna, daughter of N. P. Ruzsky 61n; working as nurse in Kiev, 120
Ruzskaya, Olga Petrovna, wife of Nikolay 61n
Ruzskaya, Tatyana Nikolayevna (Tanya), daughter of N. P. Ruzsky 61n, 71, 82; working as nurse in Kiev, 120
Ruzsky family 61, 61n, 76, 535; silver wedding celebration, 68
Ruzsky, General Nikolay Vladimirovich 234–5, 234n; murder of, 387
Ruzsky, Nikolay Nikolayevich (Kolya), son of N. P. Ruzsky 61n; also mentioned, 120
Ruzsky, Nikolay Pavlovich, businessman and amateur cellist 44, 535; also mentioned, 120
Ryazan 281
Rybinsk: danger from gangs exaggerated, 199

Saaremaa, *see* Esel Island
Sabaneyev, Leonid Leonidovich, critic and biographer: 'review' of cancelled performance of *Scythian Suite*, 172, 172n, 693; snubbed by SP, 261
Sablino, town near Petrograd, SP rents dacha in 53–5, 57, 58, 193–4, 198–9, 205, 206, 207, 210–11, 225–30, 370, 694
Saburov, Pyotr Petrovich, Vice-President of the Petrograd Chess Society 89n
Safonov family 234; puzzlement at SP's interpretation of Chopin, 251
Safonov, Vasily Ilyich, pianist: conductor, director of Moscow Conservatoire, 234, 234n, 236; death of, 254; funeral, 255
St Brévin, *see* Rochelets, les Plages de
St Leger, repetiteur at Chicago Opera 642, 654, 657, 657n
St Nazaire 592
Saint Nikolay, patron saint of sailors 19n
Saint Petersburg, *see* Petrograd
St Raphael 595
Saint-Saëns, Camille, composer: Piano Concerto No. 2, 140; *Samson et Dalila*, opera, 352
Saknovska, Dina, singer 551, 554
Salonika 15–17, 29, 32
Salter, Georg, designer 678n
Salter, Julius, son of Norbert 678n, 6878
Salter, Norbert, impresario 678, 681, 685
Samara 130, 155
Saminsky, Lazar, composer and conductor 613, 613n
Samoilenko, Boris Nikolayevich 377, 377n, 382, 389, 416, 424, 436, 437, 439, 505, 506, 510, 517, 531, 591, 611; advises elimination of sixth scene of *Fiery Angel*, 464; arranges interview with Prince Lvov, 509, 510, 511; bridge with, 377, 389, 390, 408, 424, 438, 463, 478; gives SP Bryusov's *Fiery Angel* to read, 442; lends money, 435, 563; watches motor racing with, 424
Samoilenko, Fatma Hanum 377n, 386–7, 416, 439, 486, 521, 533, 534, 609, 611; correspondence with Maria Grigorievna Prokofieva, 506; death of father in Moscow, 463
'samosud' (Revolutionary lynch-law) 182–3
San Diego 558, 559, 560, 578; Conservatory of Music, 572–3
San Francisco 246, 286, 313, 316, 323, 555, 562; Alcatraz Island, 317; Angel Island, 317–21, 329; arrival in, 316–21; Italian Consul in, 321, 336; Plaza Hotel, 321; Russian Consul in, 321; Saint Francis Hotel, 555
San José 556–7
San Martino, Count 21, 23
Sandwich Islands 190, 190n, 191–2, 193, 267, 298, 316; arrival in, 312–13; Honolulu, 296, 299, 301, 304, 308, 311, 312, 323, 330, 500; Aquarium, 315; Waikiki Beach, 314; SP advised to continue voyage to San Francisco, 313–14

Santa Barbara, 579–80, 581
Sarapul: SP encounters music student from 202–3
Saratov: Conservatoire, 65, 169, 169n; recital in, 156, 169–70, 170n, 171, 536, 692
Sarovich, Romanian casino owner, acquaintance in Kislovodsk, believed lover of Lina Collini 249, 255, 256; proposes to organise concerts for SP on Riviera, 249; urges immediate departure for America, 249–50
Satyricon, literary magazine 4, 67
Savina (Clark), Vera, ballerina 590, 590n
Savoie, transatlantic liner 540; loss of suitcase on board, 540, 541
Sazonov, Sergey Dmitrievich, Tsarist Foreign Minister 81
Scarlatti, Domenico, composer (orch. Tommassini): *The Good-humoured Ladies*, 507
Schindler, Kurt, composer, conductor and publisher's reader 329, 329n, 332, 338, 358, 365–6, 473; advances SP money from fund for 'politicals', 338, 341; arranges 'smotriny' of SP for local New York musicians, 343, 343n; attempts to raise money for solo recital, 348, 370
Schindler, Mme: announces arrival of Rachmaninoff, 351; death of, 384–5, 386, 409
Schirmer, music publishers in New York 329, 329n, 418, 476; Ernest Charles Schirmer, 329n, 336; promises to find SP a piano, 334, 336, 338; recommends A. F. Adams as manager, 330
Schloetser, Boris, *see* Schloezer, Boris de
Schloezer, Boris de 530, 530n, 591, 606
Schloezer, Mme 530
Schlotburg 127n
Schlüsselberg 127, 127n
Schmidt, Dr, acquaintance in Chicago 620
Schmidthof, Maximilian Anatolievich 8, 8n, 88, 272, 291, 403, 425, 561, 563, 573, 692, 693; Fourth Sonata dedicated to, 282; influenced by Schopenhauer, 201; SP's dream about, 281–2; third anniversary of death, 127
Schmidthof-Lavrova, Yekaterina Alexandrovna (Katya Schmidthof) 32, 32n, 46
Schmitt, Florent, composer 600, 600n
Schoenberg, Arnold, composer 76
Schopenhauer, Arthur 671; biography found in New York Public Library, 347; influence on SP, 140, 175, 191, 194, 198, 204, 208, 215; insights into nature of happiness, 201–2, 230; *Aphorisms on the Wisdom of Life*, 140, 140n, 198; *Parerga and Paralipomena*, 140n, 198, 201–2; *The Fourfold Root of the Principle of Sufficient Reason*, 205–6, 205n, 208; *The World as Will and Representation*, 205, 240, 296–7, 303
Schubert, Alexander von, artist, husband of Nina Koshetz 259, 261, 276, 587; portrait of SP, 545

Schubert, Franz, composer: Waltzes, 525
Schumann, Robert, composer 523; *Carnaval*, Op. 9, 435, 436, 437, 439, 441, 451; Piano Sonata No. 1 in F sharp minor, 422, 426, 427, 433
Schuré, Edouard, poet, playwright and theosophist 133n; *The Great Initiates* (*Les grands initiés*), 133, 133n
Scilly Isles 504
Scriabin, Alexander Nikolayevich, composer 392, 454, 457, 466, 469, 519, 530, 530n, 670; handwriting, 335; music dismissed by Stravinsky and Diaghilev, 506, 509; recital on anniversary of death, 121; *Désir*, Op. 57/1, 380, 390, 431; *Deux Etudes*, 355; Etude in D sharp minor, Op. 12/12, 390, 431; *Feuillet d'album*, Op. 45/1, 355; Piano Concerto, 46; 'Poème ailé', Op. 51/3, recorded by SP for Duo-Art, 394; *Poème satanique*, 335–6, 339, 405; Prelude in E flat, Op. 45/3, recorded by SP for Duo-Art, 394; Prelude in F sharp minor, Op. 74, 457; *Prélude*, Op. 59/2, 380, 390, 431; Preludes, 189–90; Sonata No. 4 in F sharp major, Op. 30, 68, 85; Sonata No. 6, Op. 62, 121; Sonata No. 7, Op. 64 ('White Mass'), 190; Sonata No. 9, Op. 68 ('Black Mass'), 190, 335–6
Seattle 324
Sebryakov, Sergey Alexeyevich, SP's second cousin 88n, 140
Semechkina, head of lithographic copying department at Mariinsky Theatre 137, 139, 141
Semyonov, Grigory Mikhailovich, Cossack warlord 278, 278n
Semyonov, Imperial Court Privy Councillor, occultist 62, 73
Serbia 14–16; Serbian passport, efforts to obtain, 248, 250; typhoid prevalent in, 14–16, 32
Sert, José-Maria, husband of Misia 517, 517n; designs for *Cimarosa*, 517
Sert, Misia, *see* Edwards, Mme Misia
Sestroretsk 35, 46, 129n, 139
Severyanin, Igor (Igor Vasilievich Lotarev), poet 148n, 678; acts as judge in sonnet competition, 674, 676, 683; criticised by Boris Bashkirov for publication by Bolshevik press, 690; opinion of SP's poetry, 266; requests loan, 690; SP hears read, 195, 195n; 'Daisies', 148n
Shaginian, Marietta Sergeyevna 148n
Shanghai 287, 288, 292
Shchuchye Lake, beauty spot near Kellomyaki 91, 91n
Shestakovsky, New York representative of Volunteer Fleet 431, 435
Shestov (Schwarzmann), Lev Isaakovich, philosopher 532n

INDEX

Shkafer, Vasily Petrovich, tenor and opera producer 172
Shreder grand piano 3n
Shteiman, Mikhail Osipovich, conductor 73, 73n
Siberia, Japan's interest in annexing 286, 304, 329
Sierra Nevada 555
Siloti, Alexander, *see* Ziloti, Alexander
Simferopol 13
Sinaia, fashionable resort in the Carpathians 249
Singer, Winaretta, *see* Polignac, Princesse de
Sklyarevsky, Alexander Fyodorovich, pianist and teacher 65, 315, 315n, 325, 423, 464, 488, 489, 494
Skobolev, Mikhail Dmitrievich, general 13, 13n
Skopje, *see* Üsküb
Skvortsov, Alexandr Ivanovich, lawyer 169–70, 173; shot by Bolsheviks, 692
Slavina, Maria Alexandrovna (Baroness Medem), mezzo-soprano 143n; cast as Babulenka in *The Gambler*, 143, 145
S?avinsky, Tadeusz, dancer 597, 597n, 598
Slonimsky, Nicolas 684n
Smallens, Alexander, conductor 435, 435n, 617, 618, 619, 620, 621, 622, 623, 624, 625, 625n, 627, 628, 629, 630–1, 637, 638, 639–40, 645, 646, 647, 648, 651, 657, 681; conducts second performances of *Oranges*, 661, 662
Society of Friends of Music of New York, concert promoting organisation: proposes to arrange concert of SP's works 333, 343, 353
Society of Workers in the Arts: Glazunov declines to serve if SP elected, 186; protest against creation of Ministry of Culture, 188–9; SP member of delegation to see Fyodor Golovin, State Duma Deputy, 188; SP nominated as committee member, 186
Sofia, capital of Bulgaria 12–15, 18, 536, 595
Sokol (Falcon), gymnastics club 39, 39n, 69, 78, 88, 90, 99, 104
'Solnyshko' ('Little Sunshine'), chess-playing cousin of Boris Bashkirov 93, 95, 129
Sologub, Fyodor Kuzmich (Fyodor Teternikov), poet 122n, 149; heads delegation of Society of Workers in the Arts, 189; *Dreams*, 148n
Solovyov, Nikolay Feopemptovich, composer 115, 115n
sonnet competition, xviii
Sorrento 25
Soskice, New York acquaintance in the diplomatic service 428
Sosnitsky, Yuli, vice-president of Petrograd Chess Club 89, 89n
Souirah, steamer between Contantinople and Marseilles 530–31
South America 259, 266, 288
Southampton 588

Spain 490, 695, 704, 707; SP's visa problems in, 705–7
Spangler, George M., business manager of Chicago Opera 586, 586n, 622, 623, 625, 629
Spanish 'flu 341, 344, 392, 407, 466, 467, 469, 471, 472, 666; death of Mme Schindler, 384–5, 386; severity of, 347; SP fears catching, 345; but avoids infection, 345
Sretensk 280
Stahl, Alexey Fyodorovich, lawyer, formerly Public Prosecutor of the Provisional Government 330, 330n, 337, 387, 463, 466, 517–18; agrees that the Bolsheviks are in league with Germany, 337; falls ill with influenza, 344, 345; foresees scandal with *Fiery Angel* in Catholic countries, 446–7; offers advice on *Fiery Angel* scenario, 449, 515
Stahls (Alexey Stahl and Vera Janacopulos) 333, 341, 418, 419, 426, 428–9, 434, 435, 436–7, 439, 442, 446, 449, 450, 492, 501, 505, 507, 510, 531, 593, 599, 600, 612, 672, 679, 709; French translation of *Love for Three Oranges*, 388, 397, 404–5, 409, 418, 419, 478; motor tour through Black Forest, 67; urge SP to accompany them to Brazil, 491, 506, 518, 521, 522
State Duma, representative assembly established by Tsar Nicholas II with limited legislative powers 86
Stavrovich, friend of Boris Bashkirov 116, 120, 140, 155, 265
Steinberg, Maximilian Oseyevich, composer, teacher, son-in-law of Rimsky Korsakov 73, 73n; Overture *La princesse Maleine*, 80
Steiner, Rudolf 681n
Steinway & Sons: offer SP piano, 338
Steinway, Frederick T., head of Steinway & Sons New York 322, 322n
Stepanova, Yelena Andreyevna, soprano, wife of Nikolay Malko 68, 68n, 76
Sternberg, Paul, Lunacharsky's deputy for higher education 270, 270n, 271
Stock Exchange Evening News (*Vechernye Birzhevye Novosti*) 122
Stock, Frederick, music director of Chicago Symphony 550, 583, 635, 639; auditions SP, 336
Stokowski, Leopold, conductor 337–8, 337n, 363, 367; issues invitation to conduct *Scythian Suite* in Philadelphia, 343
Stransky, Josef, conductor 475–6, 475n, 480
Strasbourg 701
Strauss, Richard 109, 621, 622; *Josephslegende*, 30; *Salome*, 621, 645; Songs, 622
Stravinsky, Igor Fyodorovich 20, 22–5, 29, 31, 66, 506, 507, 508, 509, 510, 514, 515, 517, 528, 530, 530n, 539, 589, 597, 600, 605, 670, 679–80, 681; admiration for SP's music, 29; considers orchestration inseparable from the rest of composition, 680, 680n; criticism of SP's

music, xvii; endorses idea of *Chout*, 29; Futurism, attitude to, 28; illness and money worries, 331, 331n; insists on 'Russianness' in music, 506, 509; listens to *Chout*, 539; meets SP in Milan, 27–9; *Mir Isskusstva* concert for, 610; praises *Chout* 604; recommends Chesters as publishers, 506; rejects opera as valid contemporary art form, 680, 680n, 685–6, 696n; second wife Vera Sudeikina, 89n; SP's relations with, 28; studies with Akimenko, 87n; suggestion of Schubert Waltzes, 525; *Le chant du rossignol*, 509; *The Nightingale (Le Rossignol)*, 94, 94n, 509; *Les Noces*, 528, 528n, 591; *The Rite of Spring*, 29, 509, 515, 605, 605n; four-hand version played with composer, 29, 509; *Concertino* for string quartet, 539, 539n; *Four Russian Songs*, 515; Octet, 712n; *Petrushka*, 26, 30, 507, 527–8; *Piano Rag Music*, 513n; *Pribaoutki*, 26n, 29, 29n, 444, 445, 445n, 515; *Pulcinella*, 508, 512, 514, 525; *Ragtime*, 513, 513n; *The Firebird*, 28, 30, 515, 603, 605; Symphonies for Wind Instruments (1920), 608; Symphony in E flat, Op. 1, 47–8; also mentioned, 118, 122n, 151
Strock, impresario in Japan and the Far East 287–8, 289; contacts Honolulu impresario, 296; organisation of Tokyo concerts, 292, 297, 300–301; and in Yokoyama, Kobe and Osaka, 301; proposes concerts and tours, 288; throughout Far East and India with Koshetz, 289, 290; wishes to represent Koshetz, 544
Struve, Lidia Ivanovna, former attachment of SP 35, 35n
Struve, Nikolay Gustavovich, composer, director of Russian Music Editions 147, 147n, 153, 539; death of, 551
Stubenrauch, Dr, oncologist in Munich 673, 674
Subbotin, Igor Mikhailovich, brother of Oleg Subbotin 134–5
Subbotin, Oleg Mikhailovich, friend of the Meshchersky family 98–9, 98n
Subbotkina, Mme, acquaintance in Sofia 13
Sudeikin, Sergey Yuryevich, artist and designer 89n
Sukhum 232; Sukhum Military Road, 232–3, 233n
Sumarokov-Elston, Count Felix, *see* Yusupov, Prince Felix
Suroshnikova, Vera 132–3
Suvchinsky, Pyotr Petrovich (Pierre Souvtchinsky), writer, editor and philanthropist 77–8, 77n, 84, 96, 98, 104, 269, 271, 274, 277, 278, 297, 352, 430, 519, 669–70, 679, 680n, 681, 682, 683; and SP: correspondence about Stravinsky and modernism, 685–6, 686n; expresses admiration for, 101; given power of attorney for *Gambler* contract, 274; installs building supervisor in apartment, 430, 543;

694; invites to his estate near Kiev, 185; proposes recital in Moscow, 114; reunion in Petrograd (1918), 265–6; SP's letter to, 293; suggests poems by Anna Akhmatova for setting, 148–9; with Asafyev and Belyayev co-founds music journal to rival *Musical Contemporary*, 174, 174n; condemnation of Myaskovsky's Songs, Op. 20, 687; founder and editor of *Musical Contemporary* journal, 87n, 114, 169–72, 692–3; and of short-lived *Melos* journal, 174, 174n; hosts reception, 109; moves to Sofia, 536, 595; post-Revolution circumstances, 265; Rachmaninoff's conversation with, 265; rift with A. Rimsky-Korsakov over new music, 174, 174n; welcomes formation of new government, 181; *The Great Movement*, opera scenario, 683; also mentioned, 103, 109, 155, 171, 217, 267
Svanetia, Georgia 158, 158n
Svetlov (Ivchenko), Valerian Yakovlevich, ballet critic 57
Svirsky, pianist in Japan 306, 308, 609
Svyatlovsky, Professor V. V., anthropologist and ethnographer 97
Szigeti, Josef, violinist: gives Russian premiere of First Violin Concerto, 712n
Szymanowski, Karol, composer 33, 33n, 665–6; Piano Sonata No. 2 in A, Op. 21, 473; SP's critique of his music, 109

Taganrog 153, 214, 284, 258, 279
Taine, Hippolyte, French critic and historian 310, 310n, 312
Talashkino 144n
Tallinn, *see* Revel
Tandler, Adolph, conductor and concert organiser 558, 558n, 561–2, 576, 577, 579
Taneyev, Alexander Sergeyevich, composer, Oberhofmeister at the Imperial Court 77, 77n, 115; intercedes over SP's possible conscription, 158–9, 163; *The Snowstorm*, opera, 77, 77n, 158
Taneyev, Sergey Ivanovich, composer, death of 49–50, 107n; Minuet, 276
Tarascon 701
Tarasova, Nina, folk singer 440, 440n
Tartakov, Joachim Viktorovich, baritone, director of productions at Mariinsky Theatre 117, 117n, 120, 121, 122; and *The Gambler*: casting proposals, 125; present at audition, 117–19; reassures about production, 150
Tbilisi, *see* Tiflis
Tchaikovsky, Pyotr Ilyich, composer 25, 683, 702; first person to conduct in Carnegie Hall, 351; Sonata No. 3 in G ('Grand Sonata'), Op. 37, 380, 382, 390; Symphony No. 1, Op. 13 ('Winter Daydreams'), 67; Symphony No. 2 ('Little Russian'), 88n; *Yevgeny Onegin*, opera, 91; student production rehearsal, 177

Tchaikowsky, André, pianist and composer 209n
Tchelitchew, Pavel, painter and stage designer 679 679n
Tcherepnin, Alexander Nikolayevich (Sasha), composer, son of Nikolay Tcherepnin 91–2, 92n; SP hears early compositions, 91–2; also mentioned, 104
Tcherepnin, Nikolay Nikolayevich, composer and conductor 4n, 31, 65, 68, 71–2, 85; detects 'Diaghilevshchina' and 'Stravinshchina' in SP's music, 72; director of Tiflis Conservatoire, 543; friendship with Demchinsky, 187; invites SP to dine, 91; conntributes to Wooden Book, 271; *Alphabet*, 5; *Narcisse*, 30; *Red Mask* (*La Masque de la mort rouge*), ballet, 65, 69–70; *The Tale of the Fisherman and the Fish*, 5; also mentioned, 4, 118, 189
Tcherepnina (née Benois), Maria Albertovna, wife of Nikolay Tcherepnin 91
Teberda, Caucasus 232–3
Telyakovsky, Vladimir Arkadyevich, Director of Imperial Theatres 89, 89n, 173n; *The Gambler*: auditions, 89, 116–19; considers producing, 94, 109, 111, 115, 121, 122; delay in signing contract, 123–4, 128, 129; recommends Golovin to design settings for *The Gambler*, 167; also mentioned, 125, 144n, 167
Tenishev Hall 111, 111n; charity concert in aid of war-wounded, 122, 122n
Tenisheva, Princess Maria Klavdievna 144n
tennis 131, 136–7, 306, 676, 676n
teplushka, heated railway goods van 254
Tereshchenko, Mikhail, Provisional Government Minister, philanthropist, cultural entrepreneur and publisher 144n
Tereshchenko, N. S, chess-playing acquaintance in Petrograd 55
Terioki 44, 47, 49–50, 52, 54, 90–91, 132, 137, 209
Teternikov, Fyodor, *see* Sologub, Fyodor
Thomas, Mrs Joe, New York socialite 481, 483, 491, 494
Tiflis 134; Conservatoire, 543
Tijuana 559–60
Tikhoretsk, civil war-torn city near Krasnodar 257
Togo, Admiral 284n
Tokugawa, Marquis Yoshichika 303, 303n, 712; intention to commission a work, 304, 305, 306, 307, 308–9
Tokyo: American Embassy in, 304, 307; authorises US visa, 308, 345; concerts organised by Strock, 288, 292, 297, 299, 300–301; Imperial Theatre, 293; Number Nine, brothel, 289–90; press reports on SP, 290; prospect of concerts in, 288; Russian Embassy, 292; Baron Behr, Secretary, 292, 304, 305, 306, 307, 308; Station Hotel, 286, 298; The Ginza ('Silver Mint'), shopping and entertainment area, 289

Tolstoy, Count Alexey Nikolayevich, novelist 533, 533n, 534
Tolstoy, Count Ilya Lvovich, son of Tolstoy 562, 562n, 578
Tolstoy, Lev Nikolayevich: *A Calendar of Wisdom* (*Circle of Reading*), 703, 703n
Tommassini, Vincenzo, composer: *The Goodhumoured Ladies*, 507, 507n
Tosna River, near Sablino 226, 226n
Tosno 429; Yudenich's army in, 703n, 430, 703
Touraine, transatlantic liner 529–30
Trans-Siberian Railway 267, 272, 280, 280n, 291n, 296; Trans-Siberian Express: cheap ticket provided by Ionin, 275; SP's journey from Moscow to Irkutsk, 274–9; SP's train the last to get through, 291n, 296
Trapezund (Trabzon), Turkey 247
Traubenberg, Baron Rausch von, artist and chess player 76, 76n, 95, 159
Tristan et Iseut 310
Tropic of Cancer 312–13
Trotsky, Léon 313
Trusov, New York acquaintance travelling to Constantinople 483
Tsarigrad 14
Tsaritsyn 252, 252n, 254, 257
Tsaritsyno 132–3
Tsarskoye Selo 55; Nina Meshcherskaya's sojourn in, 37–40; Petrograd railway station, 54; strategic point in Kornilov 'rebellion', 226
Tsetlins, friends of Balmont in Paris 610, 611
Tsintinator, chemist's shop in Kislovodsk 246, 246n
Tsurugi, Japan 285–6, 285n
Tsushima Straits, Battle of 284, 284n; boyhood grief over loss of Russian ships, 284n
Turkey: reported seeking peace terms 344
Tver 199
'Twentieth Century Limited', New York–Chicago train 364, 431, 663
typhoid 156–8; spotted typhoid, 488, 494, 511
Tyuflev (possibly Tyufyayev), official of Mariinsky Theatre 130, 163, 167
Tyulin, Yury Nikolayevich (Yuli), musicologist and chess player 69, 69n; chess matches and tournaments with, 95, 145, 166, 187; *Gambler* score possibly left with, 694; *Scythian Suite* and *Sinfonietta* four-hand versions proposed, 72
Tyumen 277
Tyurisyavi, Gulf of Finland holiday resort 91, 91n

Uchshikay, believed by Nina Koshetz to be her spiritualist protector and inspiration 620, 632, 635–6, 637
Umnova, Lidia Ivanovna ('Umnenkaya') 65, 73
Ungheni 10, 32–3
'Untimely Thoughts', column by Gorky in *New Life* 208

Urchs, Ernest, head of Concert and Artist Department of Steinway & Sons 401, 401n, 402
Urusov, Prince, Kislovodsk acquaintance 241, 252
Ushki, town near Petrograd 53
Üsküb 15–16

Valencia 707
Valparaiso 286, 288
Van Camp, secretary of Antwerp Music Society 709
Vancouver 321, 323, 324
Vater invective, see The Gambler, Hoppe & Co.
Velikhov, L. A., member of State Duma and editor of Municipal Affairs magazine 89
Verdi, Giuseppe: La Traviata, 666; Rigoletto, 704
Verkhovsky, director of Women's Medical Institute 156
Verne, Jules, novelist 98; Hector Servadac, 19, 19n; La fantaisie du docteur Ox, 98, 98n
Vernettas, Italian co-internees on arrival in San Francisco 318–19, 323, 324, 336
Verrier, Clarette, shipboard flirtation with 541
Vienna 486
Vilkreiskaya, pianist 106, 113
Villa Christophorus, Ettal, 671–2, 675; lease ends, 702
Vindavo–Rybinsk railway line 8
Viñes, Ricardo, pianist 473, 473n
Vishera River 201
Vitkovich, artist claiming original commission to design Love for Three Oranges 433
Vladikavkaz 134–5
Vladivostok 17, 250, 256, 278, 279, 280, 281, 282–5; Japanese Consul, 283
Volga River 169; SP's trips down, 132–4, 192, 199–203; possible danger, 199; steamers on 133–4
Volkov, A., Russian Consul in Chicago 360, 364, 378, 380, 381, 431, 442–3, 444, 445–6, 451, 454, 457, 458, 463, 546, 547, 582, 619, 627, 628, 628n, 639, 648, 656, 657
Volunteer Fleet, Russian 431–2, 431n, 477
Vosges Mountains 677
Voynov, husband of Voynova 493, 617
Voynova, Natalya (Natasha), Medtner's niece 490, 493
Vyatka, city west of Ural Mountains 277, 277n
Vyrubov, official of Russian Political Conference in Paris 511
Vyshnegradsky, Alexander, former head of Petrograd International Bank 421, 538, 540, 614; ready to underwrite New York solo recital, 348, 350; and later orchestral concerto, 349; suggests possible route for SP's mother to come from Odessa to Italy, 359
Vysotsky, acquaintance in Yokohama 289, 290

Wagner, Richard, composer: manuscripts of, 486; Parsifal, opera, 474
Wahrlich, Hugo 35, 35n
Walsh, Mrs, sister of Mary Garden 634, 635, 637
Walska, Ganna 582n, 679, 679n
Walter, Viktor Grigorievich, violinist and critic 73, 73n
Washington, DC 441; National Theatre, 441; Russian Embassy in, 441; SP's recital in, 441
Weisberg, Yulia Lazerevna, composer 87, 109, 174, 473n; also mentioned, 122n
Wells, H. G.: Outline of History 610, 610n, 703
West End, New Jersey 408, 409–15; Hollywood Hotel, 410
Western Powers intervention: American Mission, 207n; British Military Mission, 274, 279; Danish Mission, 279; Japan, interests in Siberia, 284n, 286, 304, 329; rumours of Russia declaring war on Western Powers, 311–12, 312n
white ticket-holders (belobiletniki) 105, 105n; also in America, 332
Wiborg, Mme, female acquaintance in Paris 513–14, 517
Widor, Charles-Marie, composer: The Technique of the Modern Orchestra, 564, 564n
Wieniawski, Adam Tadeusz, composer 97n; Megaye, opera, 97n, 125, 127
Wihtol, Joseph (Jazeps Vitol), composer and teacher 130, 130n
Winckler, Hugo, archeologist: Babylonian Culture 276, 307, 312
Winkler, Alexander Adolfovich, SP's piano teacher at the Conservatoire 96n
Winkler, Mme, piano sales agent 91, 99
Wolf, Baron, Russian consular official in New York 422
Wolf-Ferrari, Ermanno, composer: The Jewels of the Madonna, opera, 553, 553n
Wolf-Israel, Yevgeny Vladimirovich, principal cello of the Mariinsky Orchestra 149, 154
Wolff Agency 175
Wolff, Albert, composer and conductor 464, 464n, 493; The Blue Bird, opera, 464, 464n
Wood, Sir Henry 475, 475n
Wooden Book: inaugurated by Demchinsky 99, 99n; concept and physical appearance, 95; contribution by Nina Koshetz, 217; contribution by Tcherepnin, 271; other contributors, 100, 165; sonnet written by Balmont, 221
Wrangel, Baron Pyotr Nikolayevich 533, 533n

xylophone, sought in Munich 700

Yablonskaya, Mme, friend of SP's mother 175
Yakhontov, chess-playing acquaintance and husband of Tatyana Bashkirova 414, 428
Yakhontova, Tatyana Nikolayevna, see Bashkirova, Tatyana Nkolayevna

Yakovlev, Alexander Yevgenievich ('Sasha-Yasha'), artist 81, 100, 290, 519–20, 609
Yamada, Kosaku, composer 383, 383n
Yasyukovich, Ignat (Yasyuk) 501, 501n
Yavorsky, Boleslav Leopoldovich, musicologist and teacher 107n
Yekaterinodar 224
'Yellow Book' 95, 95n, 694, 694n
Yershov, Ivan Vasilievich, tenor 85; cast as Alexey in *The Gambler*, 125, 143, 145, 149; replaces Palechek as opera director at Conservatoire, 82
Yesipova, Anna Nikolayevna, SP's piano teacher at the Conservatoire 96, 96n
Yessentuki 53, 53n, 191, 193, 211, 213, 214–23, 231, 234, 253; SP suspected of being a deserter, 216–17
Yokohama 285, 287, 305; American Consulate in, 304; issues US visa, 308; Grand Hotel, 288, 298, 300; SP's concert in, 288, 301–2
Young, Eleanor, former lover of Capablanca 357
Yovanovich, Mladlen Emanuilovich, pianist 511, 511n, 604
Yudenich, General Nikolay 300n, 430, 430n, 433
Yusupov, Prince Felix Felixovich, murderer of Rasputin 157, 157n; *Lost Splendor*, 157n

Zaitsev, Kirill 55, 57; as suitor of Nina Meshcherskaya, 3
Zakharov, Boris Stepanovich, pianist 3, 3n, 4, 35, 35n, 48, 51, 58, 58n, 71–2, 78, 109, 111, 535, 625, 670; affair with Maria Pavlova, 107, 125; betrothed to Cecilia Hansen, 100; conceals pursuit of Damskaya while accompanying, 126; friendship with Grand Duke Konstantin Konstantinovich, 48; invites SP to Terioki, 44, 46, 49, 98–9, 135–6, 209; joint recital with Cecilia Hansen, 100; lack of sympathy with new music, 87; takes Communion because of impending marriage, 120; also mentioned, 37, 39, 47, 132, 137, 140, 177, 197, 692
Zakharov family 132, 135–6; SP depressed by tedium of family life, 209
'Zaumny'('trans-sense') language 187n
Zederbaum, Vladimir, Koussevitzky's secretary 684–5, 684n, 695, 712
Zelenogorsk, *see* Terioki

Zelikman, A. V., pianist 322
Zemskaya, pianist for *Chout* rehearsals 598, 596–7
Zet, *see* Sablino
Zheleznovodsk 132, 132n
Zhenechka, *see* 'Solnyshko'
Zherebtsova-Andreyeva, Anna Grigorievna, mezzo-soprano 5, 5n, 38, 56, 78, 80, 109, 115, 142, 145, 511; makes eyes at Boris Bashkirov, 100
Ziloti, Alexander Ilyich, conductor and pianist 35–6, 35n, 68, 71, 79, 141, 519, 665–6; and SP: Concert Series plans for 1917 autumn, 238; discusses SP with Koussevitzky, 104–5; expresses admiration for SP, 101; fails to respond to Altschuler's requests for scores, 333; has *Scythian Suite* parts copied, 64–7; includes *Autumnal* in concert series, 141–3, 693; insists on presence at rehearsals, 69; invites to call without ceremony, 76; offers to programme *Scythian Suite* in Concert Series, 35–6, 52; in addition to *Sinfonietta*, 39; followed in autumn 1917 by 'Classical' Symphony, Violin Concerto and *Seven, They Are Seven*, 224; organises concert of SP's chamber works, 75, 78, 88, 124, 154–5, 693; promises to premiere *Akhmatova Songs*, Sonatas Nos. 3 and 4, and *Visions Fugitives* in chamber music series, 175, 224; *Scythian Suite*; rehearsals and performance, 65–76, 146–8, 693; wants to donate split timpani skin as souvenir, 74; supports appeal for deferment of military service, 212; *The Gambler*: hears play-through, 116; sees possibility of Mariinsky production, 89; wants to premiere all SP's orchestral works, 45, 73, 112; appointed Intendant of Mariinsky Theatre, 197, 212; post-concert dinners, 75, 147–8; also mentioned, 62, 98, 115, 131, 155, 169, 192
Ziloti, Vera Pavlovna (née Tretyakova) 76, 665–6
Zimbalist, Efrem, violinist and teacher 289, 289n, 497, 550
Zimro Ensemble 427, 427n, 430, 470, 500
Zlobin, Hofmeister, acquaintance of Boris Bashkirov 116, 116n, 142
Zmiyev, anarchist 237–8, 240
Zvyagintseva, Yelena (Lyola) 34, 34n, 172

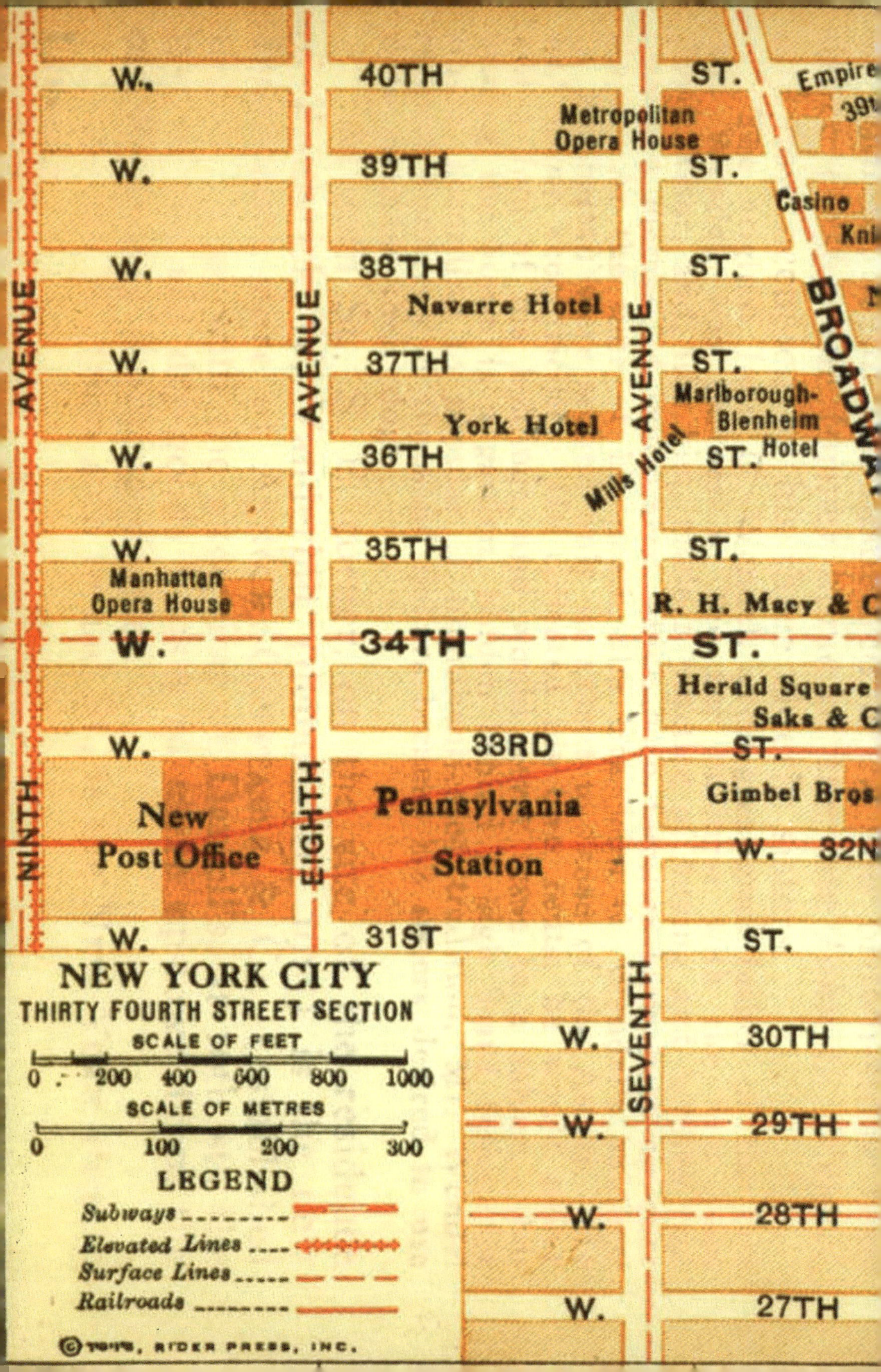

NEW YORK CITY
THIRTY FOURTH STREET SECTION

SCALE OF FEET
0   200   400   600   800   1000

SCALE OF METRES
0   100   200   300

LEGEND
- Subways
- Elevated Lines
- Surface Lines
- Railroads

© 1915, RIDER PRESS, INC.

Streets (north to south): W. 40TH ST., W. 39TH ST., W. 38TH ST., W. 37TH ST., W. 36TH ST., W. 35TH ST., W. 34TH ST., W. 33RD ST., W. 32ND ST., W. 31ST ST., W. 30TH ST., W. 29TH ST., W. 28TH ST., W. 27TH ST.

Avenues: NINTH AVENUE, EIGHTH AVENUE, SEVENTH AVENUE, BROADWAY

Landmarks:
- Metropolitan Opera House
- Empire (39th)
- Casino
- Knickerbocker
- Navarre Hotel
- York Hotel
- Mills Hotel
- Marlborough-Blenheim Hotel
- Manhattan Opera House
- R. H. Macy & Co.
- Herald Square
- Saks & Co.
- New Post Office
- Pennsylvania Station
- Gimbel Bros.